# THE OXFORD ANTHOLOGY OF
# ROMAN LITERATURE

# THE OXFORD ANTHOLOGY OF
# ROMAN LITERATURE

*Edited by*

PETER E. KNOX

and

J. C. McKEOWN

OXFORD
UNIVERSITY PRESS

# OXFORD
## UNIVERSITY PRESS

Oxford University Press is a department of the University of Oxford.
It furthers the University's objective of excellence in research, scholarship,
and education by publishing worldwide.

Oxford    New York
Auckland    Cape Town    Dar es Salaam    Hong Kong    Karachi
Kuala Lumpur    Madrid    Melbourne    Mexico City    Nairobi
New Delhi    Shanghai    Taipei    Toronto

With offices in
Argentina    Austria    Brazil    Chile    Czech Republic    France    Greece
Guatemala    Hungary    Italy    Japan    Poland    Portugal    Singapore
South Korea    Switzerland    Thailand    Turkey    Ukraine    Vietnam

Oxford is a registered trademark of Oxford University Press
in the UK and certain other countries.

Published in the United States of America by
Oxford University Press
198 Madison Avenue, New York, NY 10016

Library of Congress Cataloging-in-Publication Data
The Oxford Anthology of Roman Literature / edited by Peter E. Knox and J. C. McKeown.
    pages. cm.
Includes index.
ISBN 978–0–19–539516–7 (pbk. : alk. paper)—ISBN 978–0–19–539515–0 (hardcover : alk. paper)
    1.    Latin literature—Translations into English.   2.    Latin literature—History and criticism.
I.  Knox, Peter E.  II.   McKeown, J. C.
PA6163.O95 2013
870.8'001—dc23
2012036950

1  3  5  7  9  8  6  4  2
Printed in the United States of America
on acid-free paper

# CONTENTS

# PREFACE

THE AIM OF THIS ANTHOLOGY IS TO PROVIDE A GENERAL INTRODUCTION TO THE literature of the Roman world at its zenith, between the second century B.C. and the second century A.D. Two features of this extraordinarily fertile period in literary achievement will be immediately and repeatedly clear: how similar the Romans' view of the world was to our own and, perhaps even more obviously, how different it was.

On the one hand, we can easily trace the direct link between, for example, Plautus's *Brothers Menaechmus* and Shakespeare's *Comedy of Errors,* written in close imitation of it nearly two millennia later. The novels of Petronius and Apuleius stand at the beginning of a tradition still thriving today. The emotional vicissitudes of lovers, as described by Catullus, Propertius, and Ovid, are still recognizable—perhaps disconcertingly so. Even atomic theory, a subject on which the modern age might expect to have a particular claim, was many centuries old before Lucretius expounded it in his great poem.

On the other hand, whereas modern Western legal codes are largely based on the Roman judicial system, no trial lawyer nowadays would be allowed to indulge in the sort of vehement, and largely irrelevant, personal attack that Cicero directs against Clodia in his speech on behalf of Caelius. Pliny the Elder was the greatest source of scientific wisdom to survive in the West from antiquity, but his knowledge is often defective and his beliefs often incredible: strange beasts, such as the basilisk, the hippocentaur, and the manticore, and strange peoples, such as the Baltic tribe with ears so big that they wrap themselves in them instead of wearing clothes, or the mouthless people of India who live on air and the scent of fruits and roots, are unlikely to appear in a modern scientific text.

We might well expect such differences to be vast and fundamental, given how alien so many aspects of Roman life in general were from those of modern times. Perhaps one-third of the population of Italy at the end of the first century B.C. were slaves. Women, regardless of the social status of their family, had few legal rights and no political power. Exposure of unwanted children was legal. Fanatical interest was shown by all levels of society in gladiatorial combat, which was first introduced in the third century B.C., apparently as a ritualized form of human sacrifice. Superstition and fear of dark powers were rife. Punishments were violent and very public, as when the remnants of the army of slaves who had revolted with Spartacus were captured and six thousand of them were crucified along the road between Capua and Rome as a warning to others.

Roman literature was wonderfully creative and diverse, and the texts in this volume are chosen from a broad range of genres: drama, epic, philosophy, satire, lyric poetry, love poetry, the novel, and so on. There is, however, no corresponding diversity in the range of writers represented. Nearly all the authors are wealthy, and all, without exception, are men. Ninety percent of skeletons datable to Roman times show signs of chronic malnutrition; for most people, life at any period before the advent of technology was a daily struggle for survival. Literature was a privilege accessible only to the affluent, a much smaller section of the population than in our own society. Almost all those who created the literature of the Roman empire belonged to the higher echelons of society, and their views and interests are consequently those of the elite. We hear very little about the aspirations, ideals, and daily life of the great majority, the poor and the enslaved, and practically nothing is conveyed to us in their own personal voice. Even more conspicuous by their absence are female writers. Roman women, while not so actively oppressed as their Greek counterparts, were nevertheless expected to lead quiet lives at home. Few engaged in literary activities, and just about everything we are told about Roman women is recorded by men.

The passing of the centuries has also conspired to make this anthology less representative of Roman literature as a whole than we might wish. Until the invention of the printing press in the fifteenth century, every copy of every text had to be written out by hand, and manuscripts were always vulnerable to many perils, such as fire, insects, mice, mildew, ignorance, and deliberate suppression. It is therefore hardly surprising that the survival of literary works has been haphazard at best. Some have been lost almost entirely: for example, the epic poetry of Ennius, the love poetry of Cornelius Gallus, the antiquarian studies of Terentius Varro. Others are dependent on a single manuscript, the most celebrated example being the poems of Catullus, which were found in a manuscript in his hometown of Verona and copied before being lost again. Others survive only in part: for example, the histories of Livy and Tacitus and *The Satyricon* of Petronius.

This is not a literary history. There are several excellent surveys of Roman and Greek literature of this period, some of which are listed in the suggestions for further reading. Texts are arranged in a roughly chronological order and are presented for the most part either in full or in substantial unbroken passages, rather than in unconnected extracts. The introduction to each work is intended to set it in its context, while the afterword gives a brief overview of its later influence. Nearly all the texts are taken from the Oxford World's Classics series. It is our fervent hope that this small selection will persuade readers to look further at the individual authors and works introduced here.

The literature of a distant time and a different place does not always make for easy reading, but for the most part, the texts in this volume should be allowed to speak for themselves, because they can. We have therefore eschewed that happy device, adored by scholars and ignored by students, the footnote. Instead, each selection is prefaced by a headnote intended to provide the minimum context necessary for understanding the passage. The glossary at the end of the volume can be consulted for basic information about names and places, with further assistance provided in the accompanying maps and chronological table. But the important thing is to read, and our goal has been to stand behind the curtain as much as possible.

We have incurred many debts in the course of bringing this volume to print, chief among them to Stefan Vranka, Sarah Pirovitz, and Judith Luna at Oxford University Press. We have also received much sage counsel from the Press's four not so anonymous readers. We would like to say that any errors or infelicities that remain in this anthology are owed to them, but in fact they are entirely ours.

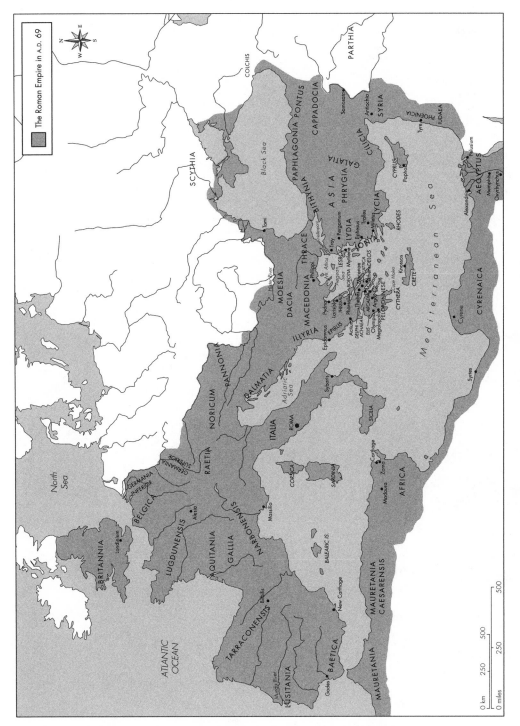

**Map 1**
The Roman Empire in A.D 69.

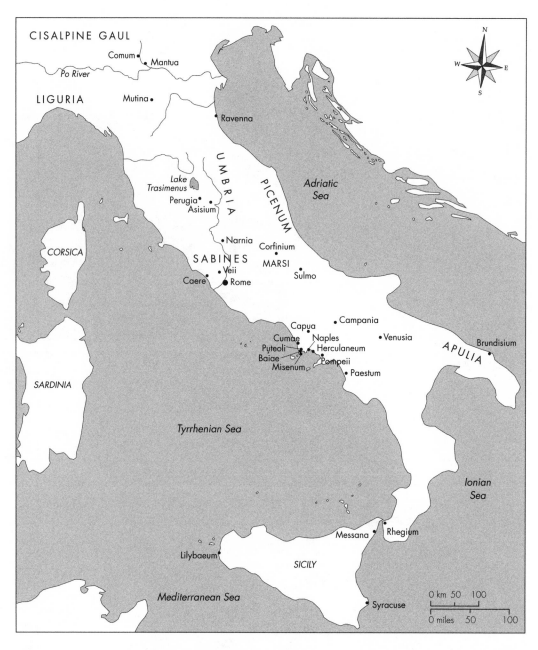

**Map 2**
Italy

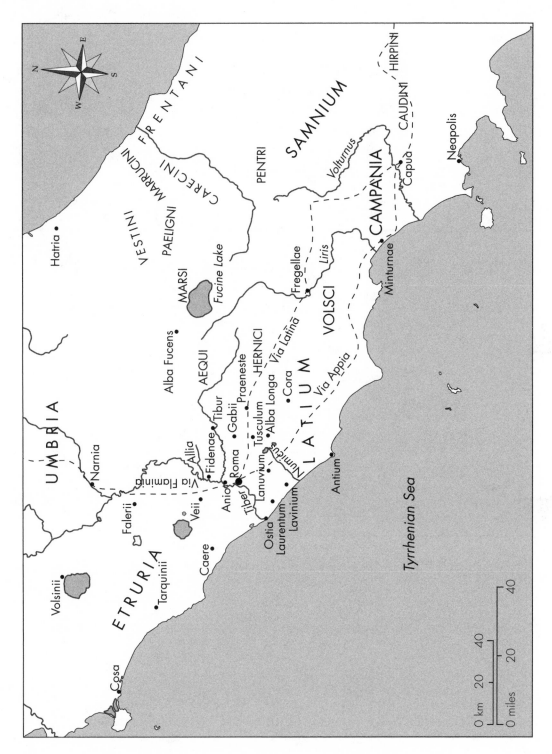

**Map 3**
Latium and Surrounding Regions

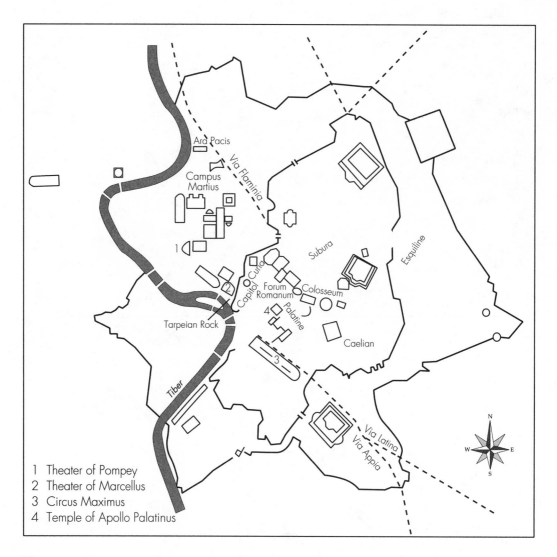

Ara Pacis

Via Flaminia

Campus
Martius

1

2

Capitol

Tarpeian Rock

Tiber

Curia

Forum
Romanum

Subura

Colosseum

4

Palatine

3

Esquiline

Caelian

Via Latina

Via Appia

N
W        E
S

1   Theater of Pompey
2   Theater of Marcellus
3   Circus Maximus
4   Temple of Apollo Palatinus

**Map 4**
The City of Rome

# THE OXFORD ANTHOLOGY OF
# ROMAN LITERATURE

# THE ROMAN WORLD OF BOOKS

By the middle of the second century a.d., the "Empire of Rome," as the historian Edward Gibbon famously put it, "comprehended the fairest part of the earth, and the most civilized portion of mankind." One may legitimately take issue with the Eurocentric perspective of the author of *The Decline and Fall of the Roman Empire*, but the phenomenon that he described—a political entity that controlled most of western Europe, northern Africa, and a large swath of western Asia—is nonetheless imposing. Gibbon is in fact only echoing the Romans' own words in describing their world. Already by the late Republic Sallust writes of Rome's empire that extends "from the rising to the setting sun" (*Catiline's Conspiracy* 36.4), a phrase that would be repeated throughout the literature of the period. The Romans certainly were aware of cultures beyond their borders that might rival their own: in the dossier of his achievements, the emperor Augustus records his reception of ambassadors from India (*The Deeds of the God Augustus* 31.1), and the Romans had trade contacts with China. But distance relegated these exotic foreign places to the realm of fantasy, and for inhabitants of the Roman world, theirs was the whole world.

When Ovid wrote that "I am the most widely read author in the entire world" (*Sorrows of an Exile* 4.10.128), he was thus not engaging in hyperbole. Neither was Horace, when he declared at the end of his second book of *Odes* (2.20.17–20):

> The Colchian will know me, and the Dacian who pretends
> not to fear a cohort of Marsians, the Geloni
>     at the ends of the earth, learned Iberian,
>         the Rhone-swigger.

Horace claims a readership across the Roman world, from the boundaries of the empire with the Colchians to the east, the Dacians and the Thracian Geloni to the north, the Iberians in the west, and Gauls beside the river Rhone. A century later, the poet Martial covers the same terrain when he complains, tongue-in-cheek, that he makes no money from his books (*Epigrams* 11.3.1–6):

> It's not just the lazy city-folk who enjoy my Muse,
>     nor do I offer my work only to idle ears;
> No, in the snows of Thrace beside the standards of War
>     my book is thumbed by a frozen centurion,
> And it's said that my verses are recited even in Britain.
>     So what? My wallet knows nothing of that.

At nearly the same time as Martial was writing this poem, at the Roman fort of Vindolanda, on the northern frontier of Britain where Hadrian would build his wall, someone, a frozen centurion perhaps, or more likely his son, was reading Virgil. Among the documents recovered from the outpost's trash heaps by excavators is a scrap of writing material made from birchbark with one line of the *Aeneid* carefully copied out. At the opposite end of the empire the Roman army briefly held an outpost on the upper Nile during the 20s B.C. at a place now known as Qaṣr Ibrîm. It was probably an officer who carried with him a papyrus roll of the poetry of Cornelius Gallus, a fragment of which was uncovered in excavations there. The Roman world of books was indeed coextensive with the Roman Empire, and it included more than literature written in Latin. With the development of the empire into a politically and economically integrated entity around the Mediterranean, there was increasing interpenetration of its many distinct cultural communities. As Greek intellectuals took up residence in Italy and the West, their writings took shape against the background of a world that was now Roman. In addition, there were flourishing outposts of the Jewish Diaspora not only in the eastern Mediterranean but in Rome and throughout Italy, in North Africa and southern Gaul, and above all in Alexandria in Egypt. The language of this community was Greek, and the surviving works of Roman Jews writing in Greek to interpret the Hebrew scriptures and Jewish history are further testimony to the diversity of the Roman literary world.

## ROMAN WRITERS

The Romans traced the beginnings of literature in their own language to an appropriately multicultural event: at the celebration of the Roman Games in August 240 B.C., Livius Andronicus, a native of the Greek city of Tarentum who had come to Rome as a prisoner of war, staged plays of his own composition in Latin. These were translations or adaptations of Greek scripts, drawing on the classic tragedies of the Athenian stage and the currently popular Greek New Comedy, practiced by poets like Menander. In noting this landmark date, Cicero (*Brutus* 18.72) connects it with the birth in the following year of Quintus Ennius, Rome's first great national poet, whose cultural background is also significant. Born in Rudiae (near modern Lecce in southern Italy), he allegedly proclaimed that he had three hearts because he knew how to speak in Oscan, his native, south Italian tongue, Greek, the language of learning, and the Latin of his adopted city. A generation or two later the poet Porcius Licinus summed up the origins of Latin literature thus:

> In the Second Punic War, the Muse, with winged pace,
> Insinuated herself into Romulus's warlike race.

Porcius Licinus was not a great poet, and much later Horace made the same point more elegantly when he wrote in his *Epistle to Augustus* (156) that "captured Greece captured its fierce victor and brought the arts to rustic Latium." As far as the Romans were concerned, Latin literature began when Roman writers like Livius Andronicus and Ennius began absorbing Greek forms.

Greek influences, largely mediated through the Greek states of southern Italy (known as "Greater Greece") and Sicily, had exercised a powerful influence at Rome for centuries. This is evident in early Roman material culture and visual arts, in trade contacts, and in myth. It is even evident in the Roman alphabet, which was derived from the Greek by a somewhat circuitous route. But although there is evidence that writing had reached Rome well before the beginning of the Republic, which the Romans dated to 510 B.C., almost three hundred years were to pass before a literary culture began to develop, and that, apparently, only under the direct impetus of Greek or Greek-inspired immigrants. There had been writing, to be sure—the records of priests and magistrates, official documents, laws and treaties. Songs were sung, too, and heroic tales told, but whatever the conditions under which they were composed and performed—about which we know next to nothing—they were not handed down in books. Only traces survive of this primitive literature, and the old forms did not long survive the new fashion of poetry composed in imported Greek rhythms. There was no tradition of literature in prose either from this earliest period: no histories, speeches, letters, or treatises. Ironically, the earliest attested such text was a speech inveighing against a Greek invader. In the year 280 B.C., when Pyrrhus, king of the Greek state of Epirus, sent his ambassador to treat with the Roman Senate over peace, the great statesman Appius Claudius Caecus spoke against making a settlement. The speech that he gave was famous in its effect, and it was still available for Cicero to read two centuries later. Appius might well have deserved to be enshrined as Rome's first writer, but so deeply imbued were the Romans with Greek conceptions of literature that he is never mentioned in this regard.

The year 146 B.C. represents one of those fortuitous juxtapositions of events that take on special meaning from the rearview perspective of history. In geopolitical terms the destruction of Carthage, Rome's once-powerful rival for hegemony in the Mediterranean basin, appeared the more significant event, but the capture of the Greek city of Corinth in the same year was in many respects just as noteworthy. In response to an uprising in Greece, the consul of that year, Lucius Memmius, marched to the Isthmus and sacked the ancient city. In the aftermath the Senate decreed that Corinth should be razed and everything in it of any value shipped off to Rome. The booty in art and other valuables was immense, but it also had symbolic value. Roman political hegemony over Greece was now complete, and henceforth a crucial plot line in the story of Roman culture is its increasing integration of Greek art and letters. Books were included in the booty acquired from Roman territorial expansion around the world, but it was only Greek books that the Romans were after. Following the sack of Carthage in the same year, its libraries were so lightly regarded that the Romans gave them to allied chiefs in Africa, with the exception only of the twenty-eight-book agricultural treatise of the Carthaginian general Mago, which they then had translated into Latin (Pliny, *Natural History* 18.22).

Earlier, at the end of the Third Macedonian War in 168 B.C., the victorious Aemilius Paullus had brought to Rome the books of the royal library of the king of Macedon, Perseus, which must have constituted an enormous increase in the works available to the literate elite back in Italy. This was accompanied by the first of several waves of Greek intellectuals who came to the imperial city, whether as hostages, slaves, or opportunists. Included in their number was a Greek aristocrat, Polybius (ca. 200–118 B.C.), who eventually made his way in Roman society and wrote a history of Rome in his native Greek. Only the first five books of his *Histories* survive intact out of the original forty, intended to explain the rise of Rome to world dominion. Polybius's place in Roman society as a friend to the powerful Scipio Aemilianus, as well as his contribution to Roman historiography (he was an important source for Livy a century later), illustrate the degree to which integration and absorption had supplanted pilfering as the hallmark of Roman engagement with Greek culture.

The flow of intellectual property from east to west was steady throughout the remainder of the Republic, culminating in the last, most spectacular acquisition, the capture of Egypt and its riches by Octavian in 30 B.C. There were other notable events in this period. Sulla seized the library of Apellicon of Teos in Athens, which contained little-known works of Aristotle and Theophrastus; Pompey took the medical library that had belonged to Mithridates, the king of Pontus; and, most notably, Lucullus's booty from the wars against Mithridates included an enormous haul of books. The library that Lucullus outfitted in his villa at Tusculum became famous as a resource for scholars. In the next generation, we find the younger Cato reading Stoic philosophy in the shade of its porticoes. During the same period as Greek literary culture was being absorbed in Rome, the Romans themselves headed eastward to acquire more. A stint in the rhetorical schools of Athens or Rhodes became a standard component in the education of the aspiring youth of the aristocratic elite, who then took their tastes with them on military and administrative service throughout the empire.

As Roman influence expanded westward and to the north this increasingly became the means by which Hellenic culture was mediated to other parts of the ancient world.

The growth of a culture of books in Roman society was accompanied by an increasing number of aspiring authors. By the first century B.C., literature, not only its consumption, but its production too, was an important part of an educated Roman's life. Much of the evidence comes from the letters of Cicero, a unique witness to the social history of the Roman world. We hear of his younger brother Quintus on assignment with Caesar in Gaul, whiling away the tedious hours in camp by writing four tragedies in sixteen days; the elder brother's response was to suggest lightheartedly that perhaps a bit of plagiarism might have helped him along (*Letters to His Brother* 3.5.7). As a pastime this was apparently not unique: as a young man Julius Caesar wrote an *Oedipus* and his adopted son Octavian wrote an *Ajax*. When the future emperor Augustus was asked what had happened to that play, he joked that his *Ajax* had fallen on its sponge, an allusion to the famous suicide of the Greek hero and the everyday tool for erasing a sheet of papyrus. For every successful author known there were dozens of dilettantes who have faded from view.

There was also a flourishing world of literary activity largely lost to us. Senators wrote political pamphlets and published speeches. There were less refined forms of literature like the mime, a popular entertainment that might combine elements of "serious" comedy with somewhat lower genres, for example, striptease. The growing popularity of this and other forms of literary entertainment increasingly attracted official attention, not all of it favorable. The most successful writer of mimes in the late Republic was a Roman knight, Laberius, who used to make fun of Julius Caesar in his scripts. By way of revenge, when Caesar became dictator, he made Laberius act out his own mimes, a harbinger perhaps of more serious acts of repression to come.

## ROMAN READERS

We have no way of knowing just how many people in the city of Rome or across the empire indulged in the habit of reading for pleasure. The Romans did not keep track of literacy statistics—the very idea would have struck them as odd—nor do we have sales figures for best-selling books. What we know or can guess about the audience for literature has to be gleaned from other sources and from the anecdotal evidence of what the Romans wrote about themselves. We would like to know a good deal more about the intended audience for literature, not so much for what that might reveal about the texts themselves but so that we might approach these works by imaginatively recreating the experiences of those readers. It is also worth questioning some of our preconceptions about the first readers of the works in this volume: the community of readers for the first edition of Ennius's *Annals* in the city of Rome was different in important ways from the readership of Livy in the province of Gaul in the first century A.D., or a Greek-speaking Roman of the second century who took her copy of Lucian's *True History* down from a shelf in her villa's library. While the period covering our earliest Roman texts to the end of the second century A.D. was marked by considerable continuity, there were also great changes, even though we cannot gauge their exact extent: in the size and makeup of the audience for literature, in the financial and social circumstances of writers, in the distribution of books and the reading public's access to them. One of the most important constants throughout this period, however, is the technology of the book.

A recreation of the experience of reading in the Roman world can at best be a composite of scattered references to individual experiences that were recorded in works that have survived. Some contours can be added, too, by the evidence of archaeology and ancient art. In the largely Greek-speaking eastern portion of the empire, book culture continued the evolution that had been progressing for centuries. The technology of book production must have been imported into Rome by the late third century B.C., when works of literature began to be composed there in the Latin

**Figure 1: Writing tablet with implements**
A writing tablet, a box of book-rolls, and a money bag in a wall-painting from Pompeii. Learning to write in wax on such a small tablet will have required a lot of practice.

language. The organization of Ennius's *Annals* into eighteen books presupposes dissemination in papyrus rolls in the manner that had become widespread in Alexandria and the Greek world.

For a Roman living during the period covered by this anthology, the basic act of reading a book involved holding a papyrus roll in two hands, unrolling it with the right hand while rolling up the finished portion with the left. The text was set out horizontally to the long edge of the roll, in columns typically about two to four inches wide. The writing itself was continuous, without separation of individual words—for reasons that we can only guess at, the Romans had abandoned their early practice of word division. And texts were not punctuated, although ancient readers would sometimes add marks for their own reference. For the most part, only one side of the papyrus sheet was written on, although it was not uncommon for the back side of a papyrus roll to be used for secondary purposes, presumably after its owner had decided that this particular book was of less value. Many other materials were used for keeping records, writing first drafts, doing school lessons, composing letters, or drafting legal documents. These included wooden tablets, folded sheets made from bark that were sometimes strung together, or parchment from animal hides. Works of literature will also have circulated in these less formal media. But the definitive format for the finished literary production was the papyrus roll, and its physical characteristics are reflected in the texture of Roman literature, for the limitations on the size of a papyrus roll compelled authors to structure their works in ways that could be accommodated to it. For its earliest readers Livy's vast history of Rome in 142 "books" was a box or a shelf loaded with 142 papyrus rolls: it is no wonder, then, that abridged versions were being produced soon after its completion.

If the level of literacy in the city of Rome during Augustus's reign was about 10 percent, as is often assumed by scholars, with a population then of roughly a million, that would have meant about one hundred thousand people who might in theory pick up a copy of Sallust, for example. In reality that number was probably much smaller, but the spread of literature, both horizontally across the western regions of the empire and vertically to levels of society below the aristocratic elite, is a constant theme throughout this period. Romans provided themselves with books for their private enjoyment in libraries that soon became symbols of status. Cicero had libraries in his house on the Palatine, Rome's prime residential neighborhood before it was entirely occupied by the imperial palace, as well as at his villas in Antium, Cumae, and Tusculum. He employed the services of a Greek intellectual who had been brought to Rome as a prisoner by Lucullus, Theophrastus of Amisus, nicknamed

"Tyrannio," to help him set up his library at his seaside estate at Antium. As he writes to his friend Atticus (*Letters to Atticus* 4.8.2) in the mid-50s B.C., it is "the quietest, coolest, pleasantest place in the world…And now that Tyrannio has put my books straight, my house seems to have woken to life." Pliny the Younger describes in some detail the layout of his villa at Laurentum, on the coast south of the mouth of the Tiber, including a room for seaside reading (*Letters* 2.17.7–8): "Interposed between this room and the dining room is enclosed a nook which holds and intensifies the heat of the wholly unclouded sun. This serves as both a winter retreat and a gymnasium for my staff, for all the winds subside there except those which bring in the rain-clouds, and dispel the day's brightness before depriving this area of its use. Adjoining this nook is a room which bends round like the arc of a circle, and which from all its windows follows round the circuit of the sun. Into its wall is fitted a cupboard which acts as a sort of library, containing books that are not merely read but repeatedly read." In so situating his library, Pliny was following the advice of Vitruvius, who, in his treatise on architecture published during the reign of Augustus, had advised that "libraries should face east, for the morning light makes them serviceable, and furthermore, the books will not rot. For in libraries that face south and west, the books are spoiled by worms and moisture" (6.4.1). When we contemplate all the literature of the ancient world that has been lost, it is worth considering that more damage may have been done by worms, "the worst enemies of the Muses," as one Greek poet put it (*Palatine Anthology* 9.251), than by all the emperors and religious zealots combined.

Most Romans divided their collections into separate sections for literature in Greek and in Latin, a circumstance that accounts for the discoveries at the best-known private library from the Roman world, the so-called Villa of the Papyri at Herculaneum. Once the home of Julius Caesar's father-in-law, Lucius Calpurnius Piso Caesoninus, the villa attracted an intellectual crowd, including the Greek Epicurean philosopher and poet Philodemus. Excavations at the site began in 1752 with the goal of recovering works of art, plenty of which were found. But arguably the most precious discovery was the large number of Greek books, mostly of Epicurean philosophy, from what must have been the Greek library of the villa. That there was also a Latin library is suggested by the few fragments of texts in Latin that have also surfaced, including Lucretius and Ennius, and it is a tantalizing possibility that more could be found. The practice of maintaining two libraries in one's home was so well established in the early empire that Petronius's social-climbing and utterly crass freedman Trimalchio could boast of having "three libraries, one Latin and one Greek."

A well-to-do Roman would have his own specially trained staff to copy the texts that he required, but there was also a developing industry in bookselling. Catullus writes of the bookstalls where one could find some of the worst poets in Rome. In Horace's day the most famous booksellers were the Brothers Sosius, and Martial mentions a well-known book dealer named Tryphon (*Epigrams* 4.72.2). Book shops were concentrated in the street known as the Argiletum, which connected the Roman Forum with the somewhat seamy district known as the Subura, but there were also booksellers in the nearby street known as the Vicus Sandaliarius (so named because it had once had a concentration of shoemakers). When Mark Antony tried to murder Publius Clodius during a political brawl in the Forum in 53 B.C., Clodius managed to escape by diving into a nearby book shop. Nor was the market for books limited to Rome: we know that there were Greek books for sale at Brundisium, and there were also booksellers in Gaul and Britain. The younger Pliny was surprised to learn that there were booksellers in Lyons, and delighted to hear that his books were for sale there (*Letters* 9.11.2). Book shops were good places to browse and chance upon literary conversation. Aulus Gellius recounts how, as a young man, he was looking around the booksellers in the Vicus Sandaliarius when he ran into a well-known professor of literature, Apollinaris Sulpicius, and listened as he put another customer in his place, an aficionado of Sallust who thought he knew everything there was to know about his *Histories*.

The other great resource for literature in Rome was the public library. The Romans had not pilfered all the great libraries of the East during the period of conquest. The great royal library at

Pergamum, which held 200,000 rolls, was left untouched, and the greatest of them all, the library at Alexandria with more than half a million rolls, was intact until it was damaged by fire, perhaps severely, in the siege of Alexandria in 49 B.C. But there was nothing at Rome in those days to rival these great institutions. Julius Caesar had planned to endow Rome with a library and to employ the greatest scholar of the day, Varro of Reate, to organize the collection, but he did not live to execute his design. The first public library at Rome was actually inaugurated later, after 39 B.C., by one of Caesar's lieutenants, Asinius Pollio, who was himself a historian of note. It was located in an ancient monument, the Atrium Libertatis, the headquarters of the censors, dedicated to the personified deity "Freedom." Pollio decorated it with busts of Greek and Latin writers of the past, but among living writers, in a gesture to Caesar's plan, only Varro was included. The place of literature in Roman public life was cemented a decade later, when Octavian, who was now consolidating his position as sole ruler, completed a sumptuous temple to Apollo on the Palatine, adjacent to his home, and included in the complex a library with separate sections for Greek and Latin literature. Patronage of literature was increasingly becoming primarily the emperor's preserve, so that nothing so definitively signaled an author's rejection as exclusion from the Palatine Library, a fate that Ovid later laments for his *Art of Love*. Future emperors followed Augustus's example, and we know of libraries in Rome founded by Vespasian, Caracalla, and Diocletian. A third-century A.D. inventory reports twenty-eight public libraries in Rome, but none equaled the spectacular library built by Trajan in his new Forum early in the second century. It adjoined the Fora of Caesar and Augustus and encroached on the site of Rome's oldest library in the Atrium Libertatis. Its two reading rooms each covered 5,000 square feet: such splendid amenities for scholarship surely provided a boost to the resurgence of interest in early Roman authors in the decades that followed its opening.

Rome served as a model for cities across the empire. Within the capital city such patronage was the exclusive prerogative of the emperor, but throughout the Roman world local dignitaries erected public libraries for the betterment of their communities and to the greater glory of their names. In A.D. 97, Pliny the Younger donated a million sestertii for the foundation of a library in his native town of Comum (mod. Como) and a further 100,000 sestertii for its upkeep: in exchange, his fellow townspeople had only to endure his speech at the opening ceremony. In the eastern portion of the empire there were new public libraries founded in Ephesus and Athens. The emperor Claudius's private physician, Gaius Stertinius Xenophon, returned to his native island of Cos and endowed a public library there. An officer on Trajan's staff, Lucius Flavius Aemilianus, contributed 170,000 sestertii for the foundation of a library at Dyrrhachium (Durrës in mod. Albania). There is less evidence for the spread of libraries in the western provinces, but we know of public libraries in the north African cities of Carthage and Timgad. By the early empire, it would seem that if one knew how to read and wanted a book, getting hold of a copy was a soluble problem.

Certainly not every Roman who enjoyed reading immersed himself in philosophy, tragedy, or epic poetry. In addition to a flourishing literature on technical subjects, such as agriculture, astronomy, grammar, or medicine, there were also works of a more popular kind. In the early first century B.C., Lucius Cornelius Sisenna translated the sexy "Milesian Tales" by the Greek writer Aristides of Miletus. Literary mimes, like the lost works of Laberius from the late Republic, or the surviving collection of fables by Phaedrus, composed in the early years of the empire, may well have had a broader circulation than merely as an occasional diversion for the more serious-minded among the elite. Our best evidence for the everyday life of Romans outside the upper aristocracy is in the excavated ruins of the cities of Campania destroyed in the eruption of Vesuvius in A.D. 79. The homes of the merchant class citizenry of Pompeii, many of them quite humble, are decorated with scenes from mythology made famous in literature. One of them, near the amphitheater at the east end of town, belonged to Decius Octavius Quartio, who was evidently a great fan of Ovid's *Metamorphoses*, since he had his garden dining area decorated with scenes from two of the more celebrated tales in

**Figure 2: A Pompeian couple**
The baker Terentius Neo and his wife pose proudly but rather awkwardly in this Pompeian fresco. Her hairstyle is fashionable, but contrasts with the undoubted verism of his rather plain facial features. Their eagerness to display their literacy is endearing.

the poem—Narcissus and the suicide of Thisbe—signed by the artist, Lucius. Other homes are decorated with portraits of the owners holding papyrus rolls or other writing implements, illustrating the prestige that attached to a knowledge of literature. In one home, the so-called House of Menander, archaeologists are confident that they have identified a room for a private library.

The most lively testament to the literary pursuits of the people of Pompeii is to be found in the wealth of graffiti that covered the streets and public buildings of the city. Scraps of poetry were scrawled all over town, including bits of Ennius, Homer, Lucretius, Ovid, Propertius, Seneca the Younger, and Tibullus. But by far the most quoted author on the walls of Pompeii was Virgil, who appears almost fifty times. One of his admirers started to write the first line of Book 2 of the *Aeneid* on the wall of a brothel but never got past the first word, presumably because he was distracted by other business. On the facade of a house that belonged to the launderer Marcus Fabius Ululutremulus, someone wrote a parody of the opening verse of the *Aeneid,* "I sing of launderers and an owl, not of arms and a man," punning on the word for "owl" (*ulula*) and the proprietor's name. But more indicative of the penetration of literary culture outside the elite, perhaps, are the original poetic compositions found among the graffiti of Pompeii, many of them love poems. Someone named Tiburtinus was so proud of his skills that he put his name to a series of verses on the wall of the Covered Theater. Many more anonymous compositions appear around town. On a tomb outside the Nucerian gate, someone took a motif from Ovid (*Amores* 2.15), added a dash of Virgil, and inscribed a couplet to a girl by the name of Primigenia of Nuceria: "I could have wished to be your signet ring for one hour, no longer, so that I might implant kisses on you while you affix your seal." The same lines, without the heading, were later found on a wall in the house of Marcus Fabius Rufus, which apparently had been used as a guest house, since it carries the poetic efforts of other residents in abundance. The habit of writing poetry in public was so widespread that we find the following graffito repeated several times around town: "I am amazed, wall, that you have not collapsed from having to carry the tedious scribblings of so many writers."

One of those scribblings is particularly evocative. In 1887 excavators found on the door of a home known as the "Doctor's House" a poem composed in a jumble of hexameter lines and couplets. Unfortunately, the writing was almost immediately washed away in a rainstorm, but a transcript had already been made, so the text survives:

> O that I might entwine my arms about your neck
> and with tender lips give you kisses!
> Go now, little girl, and trust your hopes to the winds;
> little girl, trust me, fickle are the ways of men.
> Oft at the midnight hour, as I poor girl lay awake,
> musing thus with myself: many whom Fortune has exalted,
> these she now suddenly rejects and casts headlong down.
> So after Love has suddenly joined the bodies of lovers,
> dawn separates them and a wall. O what am I to do?

The literary tradition includes a great many poems about lovers locked out from the house of their beloved. Here is an actual example of such a poem, affixed to the door of the house and written, apparently, by a woman or at least in a woman's persona. If Pompeii is at all representative of a prosperous but otherwise ordinary community, then literature was a part of its life, even for the many people who might never read a "serious" book.

## READING LIKE A ROMAN

In an oral culture the poet sings to his audience, or rather the Muse sings through him, a song that he has heard from an older poet, and this song is in turn heard, learned, and performed by the next generation. By the third century B.C., when Appius Claudius's speeches were written down and Livius Andronicus began composing plays, Rome's was no longer primarily an oral culture. The literature produced from this point on was intended for preservation in books, and so the expectations of the experience of a reading audience were integral to the aesthetics of composition. But Roman literature, like those genres of Greek literature that influenced writing in Latin and were incorporated into the literary life of the Roman world, retained a distinctly aural dimension. When Virgil opens his epic *Aeneid* with the word *cano*, "I sing," this is not a sterile gesture to the oral epic tradition represented by Homer but a reflection of the importance attached to the effect of his great national poem upon the ear. Cicero's speeches were crafted for live delivery, with verbal effects that might be recovered in a postperformance reading. The Greek novels were probably always read privately, but in language and technique they draw as much on rhetorical effects as the display oratory of Dio Chrysostom. Just how these effects were experienced by Virgil's first readers, or by the first-century A.D. student of Cicero, or the casual reader of Apuleius is a question susceptible of as many responses as there were readers.

It used to be taken as a given that all, or almost all, reading in antiquity was done aloud, but there was never much evidence for that view. There is indeed considerable evidence that many people often did read aloud to themselves or were read to by a professional reader (*lector*) among the household slaves. The younger Pliny's friend Spurinna liked to spend his afternoons before dinner listening to someone read "a work of a more relaxing and pleasurable kind" (*Letters* 3.1.8). One thinks, perhaps, of *The Satyricon* or some Catullus. Pliny's uncle, the elder Pliny, also enjoyed the services of a reader but not when he was studying late into the night; rather, being the consummate workaholic that he was, he would listen to a reader during moments of relaxation in the summer sun or over dinner. Anyone in search of a modern parallel for this practice might think of a commuter listening to an audiobook so as not to waste time. Private study, however, and silent reading were at least as common as reading aloud: that is what the younger Pliny was doing on the night of August 24, A.D. 79, while Vesuvius erupted in the distance: the book he chose was one by Livy (*Letters* 6.20.5). Reading is what Cicero liked to do in the morning hours after his first meetings with clients. Cato the Younger used to bring a book with him to occupy himself at meetings of the Senate while his colleagues were finding their places. Reading was an activity for anywhere and anytime.

Literature was also a form of entertainment both in the home and in public venues. Cicero's friend Atticus was particularly fond of regaling his guests at dinner parties with literary readings: he kept a specially trained reader on his domestic staff for just this purpose, and it was the only form of entertainment he indulged in, "so that his guests might feel pleasure in their souls as well as in their bellies" (Nepos, *Life of Atticus* 14.1). The younger Pliny sometimes had readings at his dinner parties, but they were only one among many forms of diversion. If your dinner guests included a poet, of course, you might well arrange a recitation, especially if you were the emperor and your guest was Virgil. It was presumably in some such private setting that Virgil recited parts of his *Aeneid* to the imperial family, causing the emperor's sister Octavia to faint away when he reached the lines about the death of her son Marcellus (*Aeneid* 6.884). Public recitations became common in the late Republic, and Ovid recalls hearing many of Rome's greatest poets, including Propertius and Horace, although he only got to see Virgil, not hear him recite. By the early empire complaints about the ubiquity of poetry readings become a staple in the satires of Persius and Juvenal. Readings of prose works, especially history and oratory, were also common: we do not know what the elder Pliny liked to hear when he was read to, but we can imagine that it was something practical and prosaic.

The modern reader who wants to recover something of the experience of reading Roman literature in antiquity need not make an enormous imaginative leap. But there is an aesthetic reward in at least occasionally contemplating the moment of that initial experience: to situate oneself, preferably in a comfortable villa, with the first roll of Livy's histories, to unroll to the opening columns and begin reading from a text consisting of a string of letters without division between words and with no punctuation marks or any typographical devices to indicate pause or effect. Part of the translator's task is to elide the remaining differences, to substitute comparable rhythmic and verbal effects in English for the metrical schemes of Latin and Greek poetry; to endow the prose with cadences that reflect something of the impact on its first readers. What distinguishes the Roman world among the great cultures of antiquity is not only its political power or monumental architecture, or its great artistic or religious heritage; it is that we hear its variegated voices in writings of enduring value and, not least of all, delight.

# I

# THE EARLY REPUBLIC

IN 54 B.C., CICERO COMPLAINED TO HIS BROTHER QUINTUS ABOUT THE DIFFICULTY of acquiring the Latin texts that Quintus had requested for his library, because of the poor quality of the copying by booksellers (*Letters to His Brother* 3.5.6). Given what we know of Cicero's tastes in literature—he was not a fan of the modern—he was probably talking about earlier works from the formative period of Latin literature. For us the situation is much worse. Of the two most prominent poets of the late third century B.C., Livius Andronicus and Gnaeus Naevius, we have only fragments. Livius's adaptation of Homer's *Odyssey* was still being read in Cicero's day, but most Romans who wanted to know Homer would now be reading him in Greek. Of his tragedies—we know the titles of eight—and his comedies virtually nothing survives. His slightly younger contemporary Naevius, a Roman citizen from Campania, also wrote tragedies and comedies, which likewise have been lost. Naevius's most famous work was Rome's first national epic, *The Punic War,* a poem that must have been several thousand verses long, beginning with the story of Aeneas but focusing primarily on the First Punic War with Carthage. From what little survives of the poem, we can see many of the quintessential characteristics of Latin literature taking shape. Naevius would have been very familiar with Greek culture from his native Campania, and it suffuses his retelling of Roman traditions, even as he composed in the native meter of the Latin language, known as the Saturnian. Naevius's preeminence did not last long in this field, as he was soon superseded by the greatest writer of the period, who also represents our greatest loss, Quintus Ennius.

Ennius was an extraordinarily prolific author in many genres. He wrote tragedies, which were still popular in Cicero's day, comedies (not his forte), and a variety of minor works, including didactic poetry and satire. But the work that made his name endure was his historical epic, the *Annals,* in eighteen books, which recounts the story of Rome from Aeneas's arrival in Italy up to the time of the poet's own death in 169 B.C. Fragments of about six hundred verses, many of them quite incomplete, survive to give a sense of the excitement that would attend the discovery of more. A scorched papyrus roll recovered from Herculaneum that was once an entire book of the *Annals* unfortunately yielded only a few lines of what many Romans considered the most important poem in their language until the *Aeneid.* But even from these fragmentary remains it is possible to get a sense of the role played by Ennius's poem as an inspiration for Virgil.

If any extensive portion of the *Annals* had survived, it would have pride of place in any anthology of Roman literature, but as it is, the only works in Latin to have survived intact from this earliest period are the comedies of Plautus and Terence. There were other comic playwrights in the period, some of them, such as Caecilius, ranked quite highly by ancient readers who knew their works. An important text in the emerging picture of a literary world formed of works in Latin composed under the influence of the Greeks is the history of Rome by Polybius, himself a Greek writing in his native language for the benefit primarily of his fellow countrymen in the latter part of the second century B.C. But his place in Roman society, in which he moved among the upper echelons, is indicative of the ways in which Rome's political dominance in the Mediterranean created new avenues for a common culture. Unfortunately, our knowledge of literature in Latin written in the period after Ennius is less clear because so little of it survives. The most significant gap was caused by the disappearance of Gaius Lucilius's (180–102 B.C.) thirty books of satire, a genre that the Romans claimed as entirely their own invention. Horace acknowledged him as a predecessor, and fragments of roughly 1,400 lines survive. But we know these fragments largely because they were quoted, usually without any indication of context, by later grammarians who were interested in some peculiarity of vocabulary or grammar, so it is hazardous to try to speculate about the content of his works—so hazardous, in fact, that the celebrated Latin scholar and poet A. E. Housman famously (and maliciously) remarked of one editor who attempted the task that "none has such cause to wish that the earth may lie heavy on Herculaneum and that no roll of Lucilius may ever emerge into the light of day." In the wreckage of so many texts, however, the complete comedies of Plautus and Terence are no small treasure, and so from the modern perspective, Latin literature begins with laughter.

# PLAUTUS

(Titus Maccius Plautus, ca. 245–ca. 180 B.C.)

Very little is known about Plautus's life. We are told that he was born sometime after 250 B.C. in Umbria, a region to the north of Rome. Considering the importance of Greek literary models for his work, this comes as something of a surprise, since he would have had much less exposure there to Greek culture than in the south of Italy, and this bit of information might have been made up. Even his name, Titus Maccius Plautus, is unlikely to be genuine, for few people other than those at the top of the social scale during this period had a forename (*praenomen*), family name (*nomen*), and supplementary name (*cognomen*). It is probably a comically portentous stage name. Maccius is almost identical with the name of the clown in Atellan farces, a popular form of stage entertainment. Plautus means "flat-footed" and is synonymous with Planipes, the name of a stock character in mime. Titus is a standard forename, but it is also a slang term for "penis." Plautus's plays have very little of the vigorous sexual obscenity that is so characteristic of Greek Old Comedy, and of many Italian genres of comedy, but it is quite likely that his characters sometimes wore oversized phalluses, such as were worn in mime and other lowbrow performances. And so Plautus's very name evoked the comic stage.

Although comedy had great popular appeal, Plautus is one of only two comic dramatists whose works have survived. The other is Terence (Publius Terentius Afer), who was born, perhaps as a slave, in North Africa, in about 195 B.C. Between 166 and 160, six of his plays were produced, but he died soon after, apparently while returning from a trip to Greece to collect material for further comedies. His comic style is quite different from that of Plautus, with less ebullient visual humor and a more subdued use of language. Considerations of space are the sole reason for his exclusion from this anthology.

There is a lingering prejudice against Roman comedy, fostered by the Romans themselves, who have given us plenty of reasons why we might dismiss it as unsuccessful. Not only did the Romans suffer from a general sense of intellectual inferiority to the Greeks, but comedy is especially vulnerable to this unfavorable judgment. No other genre loses out more heavily in comparison to its Greek equivalent than does comedy. Writing almost three centuries after Plautus, in his review of Greek and Roman literature, Quintilian says, "We limp particularly in comedy...We can scarcely produce a faint shadow of Greek comedy. It is as if the Latin language were incapable of the charm granted to the Athenians alone" (*The Education of the Orator* 10.1.99). In the century after Quintilian, Aulus Gellius is less dogmatic but just as damning (*Attic Nights* 2.23):

Comedies translated and adapted from Greek originals are quite enjoyable, in fact they seem to be written with such wit and elegance that one couldn't imagine how they could be

**Figure 3:  Mimes**
Such scenes from Greek comedies are popular subjects for mosaics and paintings.

improved upon. But, if one compares them to their Greek originals, carefully reading the two versions of individual passages one after the other, the Latin version starts to seem dull and clumsy, eclipsed by the wit and brilliance of the Greek one, which it cannot rival.

It contributes to the impression that the Romans were not connoisseurs of drama in their own language that there was no permanent theater at Rome until 55 B.C., when Pompey dedicated a temple to Venus Victrix (Conquering Venus), to mark his triumphant campaigns in the East. The marble steps that led up to the temple were unusually wide, forming a vast semicircle, just like the seats in a theater. They *were,* in fact, the seats in a theater. By incorporating it within the sanctity of a temple, Pompey had craftily circumvented the prohibition against building a permanent theater. His trick was a necessary subterfuge because, as Tacitus reports, there was still some suspicion of the theater in conservative Roman circles (*Annals* 14.20):

> It is said that Pompey was criticized by some of the older people for building a permanent theater. Up till then, plays had been performed on a stage put up for the occasion, with temporary seating for the audience, and, if one looks back to even earlier times, the spectators had to stand, for fear that, if they sat down in the theater, they would pass whole days in idleness.

In the previous century, in 150 B.C., the Senate had ordered the demolition of a theater as being "useless and likely to harm public morality," even though it had been authorized by the censors, the two magistrates responsible for safeguarding morality (Livy, *Epitome* of Book 48). It is important, however, to note that resistance to theater-building signified neither a lack of appreciation of drama nor objections to any possibly subversive content of the plays themselves; rather, the government feared that it would encourage idleness. Cato the Elder, who was censor in 184 B.C. (the year in which Plautus is said to have died), had advocated paving even the

Forum with sharp stones, to make it uncomfortable to loiter there (Pliny, *Natural History* 19.24). Attitudes toward idleness in the theater changed as time went on: by the third century A.D., there were one hundred days of theatrical performances in Rome every year, to say nothing of other entertainments, designed to distract and control the vast and largely underemployed population.

Before the erection of Pompey's theater, plays were staged in temporary structures, which were dismantled after the performance but were by no means cheap and insubstantial. In 58 B.C., Aemilius Scaurus sought to gain favor with the electorate by erecting a temporary theater on a magnificent scale with shocking splendor and scandalous extravagance, capable of seating 80,000 spectators. (By way of comparison, the Colosseum had a capacity of only 50,000.) In the late 50s B.C., Scribonius Curio built two theaters back to back, with the audience in the one facing away from the audience in the other. Pliny the Elder reports that he put on plays in both of them in the morning; suddenly, the theaters revolved, forming an amphitheater, in which he staged gladiatorial contests in the afternoon (*Natural History* 36.117).

Theaters were not the venue for plays alone, and some of these other spectacles were distinctly less elevated, and perhaps detract from the theater's reputation as a center for Roman intellectual life. When he learned that a striptease performance was scheduled, the younger Cato, known for his strict morality, left the theater so that the populace could enjoy the spectacle without being embarrassed by his austere presence (Valerius Maximus, *Memorable Deeds and Sayings* 2.10.8). Augustus put on boxing matches (a very bloody spectacle) in the theater (Suetonius, *Life of Augustus* 44) and marked the inauguration of the Theater of Marcellus by displaying the first tiger ever seen in Rome (Pliny, *Natural History* 8.65). At a festival in honor of his mother, Nero had an elephant with its rider descend a tightrope from the top of a theater (Cassius Dio, *Roman History* 62.17). Terence's *Mother-in-Law* was a failure on the first two occasions it was put on. At the first performance, the audience preferred to watch a boxing match and were expecting to see tightrope artists; at the second, the play was disrupted by a surge of new spectators who jostled for seats, thinking they were going to see a gladiatorial contest. Horace sneers that, even when plays are actually in progress, the "pathetic plebeians" clamor for boxing or bear fights instead (*Epistles* 2.1.186).

Since the prejudice against Roman comedy is so entrenched, and since accepting it not only condemns Roman comedy as second-rate but also has the much broader consequence of endorsing the view that the Romans were culturally inferior to the Greeks, it is fortunate that even a brief consideration shows that the prejudice is, by and large, ill-founded and quite unfair, or at least in need of considerable qualification.

Athens may have been the origin of drama, both tragic and comic, but were the Greeks really so different from the Romans? Even Athens might have continued without a permanent theater throughout the heyday of Attic drama, if the wooden benches on which spectators were sitting had not collapsed in 499 B.C. (the year in which Aeschylus first competed). It is hard to imagine striptease artists or tightrope-walking elephants performing in the Theater of Dionysus at Athens, but cockfights were held there on one day every year in commemoration of the defeat of the Persians in the early fifth century B.C. Late in the first century A.D., Dio Chrysostom berated the Athenians for allowing gladiator shows in the Theater of Dionysus, with fighters sometimes being slaughtered right where the priests sat; by contrast, the (notoriously decadent) Corinthians held such spectacles outside the city walls, in a sordid spot, not suitable to be even a burial ground for freeborn people (*Oration* 31.121). Somewhere in Greece there was a pig-imitating contest held in a theater, at which the pig mimic Parmeno defeated a real pig hidden under a rival's arm, and the consolatory comment "Nicely done, but nothing compared to Parmeno's sow" became proverbial (Plutarch, *Table-Talk* 674c; he remarks casually in the same passage that people enjoy listening to imitators of hens cackling and crows cawing). Perhaps the oddest theatrical performance in Greece was given by shaven-headed professionals who entertained crowds at festivals by having boiling pitch poured over their heads or by having their heads butted by rams trained to charge at them from a distance (Synesius, *In Praise of Baldness* 13).

Quintilian's notoriously low opinion of Roman comedy is colored by his extremely high opinion of Menander, universally regarded as the best writer of Greek New Comedy, the comedy produced in Athens in the late fourth and third centuries B.C., but that opinion is based not on literary merit so much as on the practical value of his plays to the aspiring orator (Quintilian, *The Education of the Orator* 10.1.69):

> I believe that the careful study of Menander alone would be enough to assure the development of the qualities I am trying to teach: he is so good at representing real life, he has such an abundant power of invention and eloquence, and he adapts himself so well to every different situation, character, and emotion.

A blinkered or limited assessment of comedy is evident also in Plutarch's *Comparison between Aristophanes and Menander*. Most people nowadays regard Aristophanes, the greatest exponent of Greek Old Comedy, the comedy produced in Athens in the late fifth and early fourth centuries B.C., as a comic genius of the highest order, but Plutarch dismisses his work as "sickening nonsense…which captivates ignorant common folk but irritates educated people," and asks, "What other reason would an educated man really have for going to the theater than to see a play by Menander?" Even if it is true that Menander makes a stronger appeal to the educated classes, need that be the main criterion for assessing a comedian's merits? We shall return to this question later.

It is probable that all or nearly all twenty-one of Plautus's surviving comedies are based on Greek models (as is certainly the case with all six of Terence's plays). Such plays were known as *comedia palliata,* "comedy in a [Greek] cloak," in contrast to *comedia togata,* "comedy in a [Roman] toga." It is natural, therefore, that modern scholarship on Roman comedy tends to be dominated by a comparison with Greek comedy. This is especially understandable given the huge advances made in the last century or so in our direct knowledge of Greek New Comedy, particularly Menander, who was the model for at least four of Plautus's plays (and probably for many more), as well as four by Terence. Until the late nineteenth century, Menander was known only from short quotations in later authors, the longest of which was sixteen lines. The fact that there are almost a thousand such quotations attests to his great popularity, even though they gave us no opportunity to assess his plays as drama. But papyri found in Egypt, sometimes used as wrappings on mummies, have brought to light one almost complete play, the *Dyscolus* (*The Angry Man*), and substantial sections of six more. One of these papyri, found in the 1960s, preserves just over one hundred lines of Menander's *Dis Exapaton* (*The Double Deceiver*), which Plautus reworks at *Bacchides* 494–562. It is by far the longest passage of Menander that can be compared directly with a Roman adaptation. Plautus adheres very closely to some parts of Menander's dialogue, but he notably omits two scenes. These scenes, which are discussions between a father and his son, typify the ethical element in Menander's comedies but are all but devoid of humor and must have seemed to Plautus to offer little potential for a comedic reworking.

Plautus would be severely frustrated and disappointed to be assessed only as an imitator of Greek plays. The crucial point to bear in mind is his intended audience. Most Roman literature was written for the educated elite, but not comedy, and particularly not the plays of Plautus. Several of Plautus's prologues acknowledge his debt to his Greek models in an ironically self-deprecatory manner. For example, in the prologue to his *Trinummus,* Plautus claims to have taken a Greek play by Philemon and "turned it into barbarian." If taken at face value, this would suggest that Plautus is admitting his inferiority, but his audience obviously did not come to see what clever things he did with a Greek model that would have been quite unknown to most of them; to the majority of Plautus's audience, the Greek original was just unfamiliar raw material that he adapted to the far more familiar Italian tradition, and to contemporary Roman tastes.

It is difficult to assess in detail the various types of comic drama that constituted the Italian tradition. The reason for this is quite simple: they were mostly performed without a formal script, and therefore none of these plays have survived. They included the following:

*Atellan farces,* named after Atella, a city in Campania, consisted of low-life rustic scenes mostly improvised in verse by stock characters, most notably Bucco the fool, Dossennus the glutton, Maccus the clown, and Pappus the old man. Atellan farces were composed on a literary level in the century after Plautus, but even of these only sparse fragments survive.

*Fescennine verses* were abusive banter in improvised verse, named after the south Etruscan village of Fescennia.

*Phlyaces,* farcical scenes from everyday life or mythology, originating in the Greek settlements in southern Italy.

*Mime,* originally a Greek genre, seems to have been much like the *phlyaces,* improvised dialogues on a limited range of themes, in which sexual innuendo was prominent. (Modern-day mime, involving gestures without speech, was known in antiquity as pantomime.)

When Horace is discussing the origins of comedy, he links the *comedia togata* with Menander but goes on immediately to link Plautus with Epicharmus, a Sicilian writing comedy in the early fifth century B.C. (*Epistles* 2.1.57f.). The precise implications of this are disputed, but it is yet another strand of influence on Plautus that is distinct from Attic comedy. From these various genres, Plautus inherited such features as music, dancing, fast-paced plot, and subliterary buffoonery. He may not have had the fantastic stage settings characteristic of many Greek Old Comedies (Aristophanes's *Birds* is a splendid example), but his plays must have been wonderful entertainment on Roman holidays.

Plautus derives his stock characters from Greek New Comedy, among them the young lover, the miserly father, the beautiful courtesan, the crafty slave, the parasite, and the pimp. With the exception of *The Rope,* which is set on the desert shore of North Africa, all of Plautus's plays are set either in Athens or in some other Greek city. Even so, he makes frequent allusions to Roman legal, political, religious, and social institutions, while making very few references to contemporary events and avoiding, in particular, any political comment of the sort that had been a feature of Aristophanic comedy, but is not found in Greek New Comedy. It is possible that Plautus did occasionally make fun of specific living individuals and that such jokes came to be omitted in later productions when they were no longer current and had therefore lost their point. Given that one of Plautus's recent predecessors had been imprisoned for criticizing prominent political figures, however, such mockery is unlikely to have been frequent. Plautus instead confines his mockery to, for example, figures like an old man who dotes on a young courtesan, a character who is a far cry from the severe Roman ideal of the *paterfamilias,* the "father of the family," who, at least in theory, had the power of life and death over all members of his family.

One of the defining features of Menander's plays was his clever manipulation of very intricate plots. According to Plutarch, "when the Dionysiac festival was drawing near, one of Menander's friends asked him if he had written his play yet, and Menander replied that he had, for the plot was all worked out, and he had just to add the lines" (*On the Glory of the Athenians* 347f). Plot was not of primary importance to Plautus, but the occasional weaknesses and improbabilities in the working out of his stories will have been well disguised by the high degree of fast-paced comic action taking place onstage. Not only did Plautus add substantially to the material he found in his Greek originals, but he also chose not to follow certain formal restrictions to which Greek New Comedy was subject. Ignoring these conventions gave Roman comedy greater freedom. Whereas, for example, Menander and his Greek contemporaries observed the three-actor rule, which allowed no more

than three characters (whether with speaking roles or not) to be on the stage at any one time, Plautus
has six characters on stage at one point in *The Brothers Menaechmus* (351ff.). Greek New Comedy
has four choral interludes, producing five acts, a convention that must have slowed down the development of the action. Plautus's plays, in contrast, had no act divisions. As it happens, *The Brothers
Menaechmus* comes closest of all Plautus's plays to a five-act structure, with fairly even divisions in the
development of the plot usually marked by entrances by Menaechmus II.

Plautine comedy is not particularly complex literature and arguably requires little scholarly analysis (though the great late-Republican scholar Terentius Varro devoted a three-volume study to his
plays). Plautus wrote to entertain and can be enjoyed in that spirit. A prologue added to his *Pseudolus*
for a later performance gets it exactly right. Omitting any long explanation of the plot or of Plautus's
ideals as a playwright, it says simply: "It's a good idea to stand up and have a stretch, for a long Plautine
play is about to come on stage."

## THE BROTHERS MENAECHMUS

*This is Plautus's only comedy of errors. The story revolves
around a pair of twins from Syracuse, Menaechmus and
Sosicles, who were separated as infants when their father
took them with him on a trip to Tarentum. Menaechmus
was taken off to Epidamnus by a merchant who raised
him there. The unhappy father died soon after his return
to Syracuse with the remaining twin, who was renamed
Menaechmus in honor of his lost brother. Upon becoming an adult, that Menaechmus arrived in Epidamnus in
search of his lost brother, thus setting in motion a series of
mistakes in identity until recognition is achieved at the end.*

## DRAMATIS PERSONAE

PENICULUS, a parasite
MENAECHMUS I
MENAECHMUS II, his twin brother (born
Sosicles)
MESSENIO, slave to Menaechmus II
EROTIUM, a lady of pleasure
CYLINDRUS, a cook in Erotium's employ
MAID, also in Erotium's employ
WIFE of Menaechmus I
OLD MAN, father-in-law of Menaechmus I
DOCTOR

*The scene is a street in Epidamnus. There are two houses. On
the right (from the audience's view) is MENAECHMUS's
house; on the left, EROTIUM's house. The forum is offstage to the audience's right. The harbor is offstage to the
audience's left.*

*Enter the CHIEF ACTOR to speak the prologue*

Now first and foremost, folks, I've this apostrophe:
May fortune favor all of you—and all of me.
I bring you Plautus. [*Pause*] Not in person, just
    his play.
So listen please, be friendly with your ears today.
Now here's the plot. Please listen with your whole
    attention span;
I'll tell it in the very fewest words I can.
[*A digression*] Now comic poets do this thing in
    every play:
'It all takes place in Athens, folks,' is what they say.
So that way everything will seem more Greek to you.
But I reveal the real locations when I speak to you.    10
This story's Greekish, but to be exact,
It's not Athenish, it's Sicilyish, in fact.
[*Smiles*] That was a prelude to the prologue of
    the plot.
I now intend to pour a lot of plot for you.
Not just a cupful, fuller up, more like a pot.
Such is our storehouse, brimming full of plot!
[*Finally, to business*] There was at Syracuse a merchant
    old and worn
To whom a pair of baby boys—two twins—
    were born.
The babies' looks were so alike their nurse
    confessed
She couldn't tell to which of them she gave which
    breast.    20
Nor even could their own real mother tell
    between them.

I've learned about all this from someone who has
    seen them.
I haven't seen the boys, in case you want to know.
Their father, 'round the time the boys were
    seven or so,
Packed on a mighty ship much merchandise to sell—
The father also packed one of the twins as well.
They went to Tarentum to market, with each other,
And left the other brother back at home with mother.
A festival chanced to be on there when they
    docked there,
And piles of people for the festival had flocked
30    there.
The little boy, lost in the crowd, wandered away.
An Epidamnian merchant, also there that day,
Made off with him to Epidamnus—there to stay.
The father, learning that he'd lost the lad,
Became depressed, in fact he grew so very sad
A few days later he was dead. It was that bad.
    When back to Syracuse this news was all dispatched,
The grandpa of the boys learned one was snatched,
And word of father's death at Tarentum then came.
The grandpa took the other twin and changed his
40    name.
He so adored the other twin, who had been snatched,
He gave the brother still at home a name that matched:
Menaechmus. That had been the other brother's
    name.
It was the grandpa's name as well, the very same.
In fact, it's not a name you quickly can forget,
Especially if you're one to whom he owes a debt.
I warn you now, so later you won't be confused:
[*Emphatically*] for both of the twin brothers one same
    name is used.
                    [*Starts to cross the stage*]
Meter by meter to Epidamnus now I must wend,
50  So I can chart this map unto its perfect end.
If any of you wants some business handled there,
Speak up, be brave, and tell me of the whole affair.
But let him give me cash, so I can take good care.
If you don't offer cash, then you're a fool, forget it.
You do—[*smiles*] then you're a bigger fool, and you'll
    regret it.
I'll go back whence I came—still standing on
    this floor—
And finish up the story I began before:
    That Epidamnian who snatched the little lad,
He had no children; lots of cash was all he had.
60  So he adopted him he snatched, became his dad.

And gave his son a dowried female for his bride.
And then—so he could make the boy his
    heir—he died.
By chance, out in the country in a rain severe,
He tried to cross a rapid stream—not far from here.
The rapid river rapt the kidnapper, who fell,
Caught in the current, heading hurriedly to hell.
The most fantastic riches thus came rolling in
To him who lives right in the house—the kidnapped
    twin.                              70
    But *now,* from Syracuse where he had always
        been,
Today in Epidamnus will arrive the other twin,
With trusty slave, in search of long-lost brother-twin.
    This town is Epidamnus, while the play is on.
But when we play another play, its name will change
Just like the actors living here, whose roles can range
From pimp to papa, or to lover pale and wan,
To pauper, parasite, to king or prophet, on and on.

**Enter the parasite PENICULUS. *He speaks directly to
the audience***

PENICULUS. By local boys I'm called Peniculus the
    sponge,
For at the table, I can wipe all platters clean.
[*A philosophical discourse*] The kind of men who bind
    their prisoners with chains,
Or clap the shackles on a slave that's run away,    80
Are acting very foolishly—in my own view.
If you compound the wretchedness of some poor
    wretch,
Why, all the more he'll long to flee and do some
    wrong.
For one way or another, he'll get off those chains.
The shackled men will wear the ring down with a file,
Or smash the lock. This kind of measure is a joke.
But if you wish to guard him so he won't run off,
You ought to chain the man with lots of food and
    drink.
Just bind the fellow's beak right to a well-stocked
    table,
Provide the guy with eatables and drinkables,    90
Whatever he would like to stuff himself with every
    day.
He'll never flee, though wanted for a murder charge.
You'll guard with ease by using chains that he
    can chew.
The nicest thing about these chains of nourishment—

The more you loosen them, the more they bind more
        tightly.
[*End of discourse*] I'm heading for Menaechmus; he's
        the man to whom
I've had myself condemned. I'm hoping that he'll
        chain me.
He doesn't merely feed men, he can breed men and
Indeed men are reborn through him. No doctor's
        better.
100    This is the sort of guy he is: the greatest eater,
His feasts are festivals. He piles the table so,
And plants so many platters in the neatest piles
To reach the top, you have to stand up on your couch.
And yet we've had an intermission for some days
And tabled at my table, I've expended it.
I never eat or drink—except expensively.
But now my army of desserts has been deserting me.
I've got to have a talk with him. But wait—the door!
Behold, I see Menaechmus himself now coming out.

Enter MENAECHMUS, *still facing indoors, berating*
*someone. We will soon see that he is hiding a lady's*
*dress under his usual garments*

MENAECHMUS [*singing, in anger at his wife in the*
        *house*]. If you weren't such
a shrew, so uncontrolled, ungrateful too,
Whatever thing your husband hated, you'd find hateful
110    too.
And if you act up once again, the way you've acted
        up today,
I'll have you packed up—back to Daddy as a divorcee.
However often I try to go out you detain me, delay
        me, demand such details as
Where I'm going, what I'm doing, what's my
        business all about,
Deals I'm making, undertaking, what I did when
        I was out.
I don't have a wife, I have a customs office
        bureaucrat,
For I must declare the things I've done, I'm doing, and
        all that!
All the luxuries you've got have spoiled you rotten.
        I want to live for what I give:
120            Maids and aides, a pantry full,
            Purple clothing, gold and wool:
            You lack for nothing money buys.
            So watch for trouble if you're wise;
            A husband hates a wife who spies.

But so you won't have watched in vain, for all your
        diligence and care,
I'll tell you: 'Wench to lunch today, lovely dinner off
        somewhere.'
PENICULUS. The man now thinks he hurts his wife;
        it's me he hurts:
By eating dinner somewhere else, he won't give me my
        just desserts!
MENAECHMUS [*looks into house, satisfied, then turns to*
        *audience with a big grin*]. My word barrage has put
        the wife in full retreat. It's victory!
Now where are all the married 'lovers'? Pin your med-
        als right on me.
Come honor me *en masse*. Look how I've battled with
        such guts,
And look, this dress I stole inside—it soon will be my
        little slut's.                                    130
I've shown the way: to fool a guard both hard and
        shrewd takes aptitude.
Oh, what a shining piece of work! What brilliance,
        glitter, glow and gloss!
I've robbed a rat—but lose at that, for my own gain is
        my own loss!
[*Indicates the dress*] Well, here's the booty—there's my
        foes, and to my ally—
now it goes.
PENICULUS. Hey, young man! Does any of that stolen
        booty go to me?
MENAECHMUS. Lost—I'm lost—and caught
        in crime!
PENICULUS. Oh, no, you're found—and found in
        time.
MENAECHMUS. Who is that?
PENICULUS.            It's me.
MENAECHMUS.                    Oh, *you*—my Lucky
        Charm, my Nick-of-Time!
            Greetings. [*Rushes to him; they shake hands*
            *vigorously*]
PENICULUS. Greetings.
MENAECHMUS.            Whatcha doing?
PENICULUS.            Shaking hands with my good-luck
        charm.
MENAECHMUS. Say—you couldn't come more
        rightly right on time than
        you've just come.
PENICULUS. That's my style: I know exactly how to
        pick the nick of time.                            140
MENAECHMUS. Want to see a brilliant piece of
        work?

PENICULUS.                What cook concocted it?
Show me just a tidbit and I'll know if someone
    bungled it.
MENAECHMUS. Tell me, have you ever seen those
    frescos painted on the wall—
Ganymede snatched by the eagle, Venus…likewise…
    with Adonis?
PENICULUS. Yes, but what do those damn pictures
    have to do with me?
MENAECHMUS. Just look.
        [*He strikes a pose, showing off his dress*]
    Notice something similar?
PENICULUS.            What kind of crazy dress is that?
MENAECHMUS [*very fey*]. Tell me that I'm so
    attractive.
PENICULUS.            Tell me when we're going to eat.
MENAECHMUS. First you tell me—
PENICULUS.            Fine, I'll tell you: you're attrac-
    tive. So attractive.
MENAECHMUS. Don't you care to add a comment?
PENICULUS [*a breath*].        Also witty. Very witty.
MENAECHMUS. More!
PENICULUS.            No more, by Hercules, until I know
150    what's in it for me.
Since you're warring with your wife, I must be wary
    and beware.
MENAECHMUS. Hidden from my wife we'll live it up
    and burn this day to ashes.
PENICULUS. Now you're really talking sense. How
    soon do I ignite the pyre?
Look—the day's half dead already, right to near its
    belly button.
MENAECHMUS. You delay me by interrupting—
PENICULUS.            Knock my eyeball through
    my ankle,
Mangle me, Menaechmus, if I fail to heed a single word.
MENAECHMUS. Move—we're much too near
    my house.
        [*Tiptoes to center stage, motions to*
            PENICULUS]
PENICULUS. [*follows* MENAECHMUS].        Okay.
MENAECHMUS [*moves more, motions*]. We're still
    too near.
PENICULUS [*follows*].        How's this?
MENAECHUS. Bolder, let's go further from the bloody
    mountain lion's cave.
PENICULUS. Pollux! You'd be perfect racing chari-
160    ots—the way you act.

MENAECHMUS. Why?
PENICULUS.        You're glancing back to see if she's
    there, riding after you.
MENAECHMUS. All right, speak your piece.
PENICULUS.        *My* piece? Whatever piece you say
    is fine.
MENAECHMUS. How are you at smells? Can you
    conjecture from a simple sniff?
PENICULUS.            Sir, my nose knows more than all
    the city prophets.
MENAECHMUS. Here now, sniff this dress I hold.
    What do you smell? You shrink?
PENICULUS. When it comes to women's garments,
    prudence bids us smell the top.
Way down there, the nose recoils at certain odors
    quite unwashable.
MENAECHMUS. All right, smell up here, you're such
    a fussy one.
PENICULUS. All right, I sniff.
MENAECHMUS. Well? What do you smell? Well—
PENICULUS [*quickly*]. Grabbing, grubbing, rub-a-dub
    dubbing                                                      170
Hope I'm right.
MENAECHMUS.        I hope so too…
Now I'll take this dress to my beloved wench, Erotium,
With the order to prepare a banquet for us both.
PENICULUS.            Oh, good!
MENAECHMUS. Then we'll drink, we'll toast until
    tomorrow's morning star appears.
PENICULUS. Good, a perfect plan! May I proceed to
    pound the portals?
MENAECHMUS. Pound.
No, no—wait!
PENICULUS. Why wait? The flowing bowl's more than
    a mile away!
MENAECHMUS. Pound politely.
PENICULUS. Why? You think the door is made of
    pottery?
MENAECHMUS. Wait wait wait, by Hercules. She's
    coming out. Oh, see the sun!                                180
How the sun's eclipsed by all the blazing beauty from
    her body.

*Grand entrance of EROTIUM from her house*

EROTIUM [*to* MENAECHMUS]. Greetings, O my
    only soul!

PENICULUS.                              And me?

EROTIUM [*to* PENICULUS]. Not on my list at all.

PENICULUS. Such is life for us unlisted men—in
    every kind of war.

MENAECHMUS [*to* EROTIUM]. Darling, at your
    house today, prepare
        a little battleground.

EROTIUM. So I will.

MENAECHMUS.          We'll hold a little drinking duel,
    [*indicating* PENICULUS]
        the two of us.

Then the one who proves the better fighter with the
    flowing bowl.

He's the one who'll get to join your company for night
    maneuvers.

    [*Getting more enthusiastic*] Oh, my joy! My wife, my
        wife! When I see you—how I hate her!

EROTIUM [*sarcastically*]. Meanwhile, since you hate
190     your wife, you wear her clothing, is that it?

What have you got on?

MENAECHMUS.      It's just a dress addressed to you,
    sweet rose.

EROTIUM. You're on top, you out-top all the other
    men who try for me.

PENICULUS [*aside*]. Sluts can talk so sweet, while
    they see something they can snatch from you.

[*to* EROTIUM]. If you really loved him, you'd have
    smooched his nose right off his face.

MENAECHMUS. Hold this now, Peniculus; religion
    bids me make redress.

PENICULUS. Fine, but while you've got a skirt on,
    why not pirouette a bit?

MENAECHMUS. Pirouette? By Hercules, you've lost
    your mind!

PENICULUS.         Not more than you.

Take it off—if you won't dance.

MENAECHMUS [*to* EROTIUM].
                        What risks I ran in stealing this!

Hercules in labor number nine was not as brave as I,

200 When he stole the girdle from that Amazon
        Hippolyta.

Take it, darling, since you do your duties with such
    diligence.

EROTIUM. That's the spirit. Lovers ought to learn
    from you the way to love.

PENICULUS [*to the audience*]. Sure, that way to love's
    the perfect short cut to a bankruptcy.

MENAECHMUS. Just last year I bought my wife this
    dress. It cost two hundred drachmae.

PENICULUS [*to the audience*]. Well, there goes two
    hundred drachmae down the drain, by my accounts.

MENAECHMUS [*to* EROTIUM]. Want to know what
    I would like prepared?

EROTIUM.          I know, and I'll prepare it.

MENAECHMUS. Please arrange a feast at your house;
    have it cooked for three of us.

Also have some very special party foods bought in
    the forum:

Glandiose, whole-hog and a descendant of the lardly
    ham.                                                     210

Or perhaps some pork chopettes, or anything along
    those lines.

Let whatever's served be *stewed*, to make me hungry
    as a hawk.

Also hurry up.

EROTIUM.                              I will.

MENAECHMUS.              Now we'll be heading
    to the forum.

We'll return at once and, while the dinner's cooking,
    we'll be drinking.

EROTIUM. When you feel like it, come. It will be all
    prepared.

MENAECHMUS.          And quickly too. [*to*
    PENICULUS]
    Follow me—

PENICULUS.          By Hercules, I'll follow you in
    every way.

No, I'd lose the gods' own gold before I lose your
    track today.

        [MENAECHMUS and PENICULUS *exit toward
            the forum*]

EROTIUM. Someone call inside and tell my cook
    Cylindrus to come out.

**CYLINDRUS** *enters from* **EROTIUM**'s *house*

Take a basket and some money. Here are several coins
    for you.

CYLINDRUS. Got 'em.

EROTIUM.                          Do your shopping. See
    that there's enough for three of us,                    220

Not a surplus or a deficit.

CYLINDRUS.          What sort of guests, madam?

EROTIUM. I, Menaechmus, and his parasite.

CYLINDRUS.              That means I cook for ten:

By himself that parasite can eat for eight with greatest ease.

EROTIUM. That's the list. The rest is up to you.

CYLINDRUS.          Consider it as cooked already.

Set yourself at table.

EROTIUM.        Come back quickly.

CYLINDRUS [*starting to trot off*].        I'm as good
    as back.

                     [He exits]

*From the exit nearer the harbor enters the boy from
Syracuse—MENAECHMUS II—accompanied by
his slave MESSENIO. As chance [i.e., the playwright]
would have it, the twin is also wearing the exact same
outfit as his long-lost brother. Several sailor types carry
their luggage*

MENAECHMUS II. Oh, joy, no greater joy, my dear
    Messenio,

Than for a sailor when he's on the deep to see

Dry land.

MESSENIO. It's greater still, if I may speak my mind,

To see and then arrive at some dry land that's *home*.

But tell me, please—why have we come to

230    Epidamnus?

Why have we circled every island like the sea?

MENAECHMUS II [*pointedly, melodramatically*]. We
    are in search of my beloved long-lost twin.

MESSENIO. But will there ever be a limit to this
    searching?

It's six entire years since we began this job.

Through Istria, Iberia, Illyria,

The Adriatic, up and down, exotic Greece,

And all Italian towns. Wherever sea went, we went!

I frankly think if you were searching for a needle,

You would have found it long ago, if it existed.

We seek and search among the living for a dead

240    man.

We would have found him long ago if he were living.

MENAECHMUS II. But therefore I search on till I can
    prove the fact;

If someone says he knows for sure my
    brother's dead,

I'll stop my search and never try an instant further.

But otherwise, I'll never quit while I'm alive,

For I alone can feel how much he means to me.

MESSENIO. You seek a pin in haystacks. Let's
    go home—

Unless we're doing this to write a travel book.

MENAECHMUS II [*losing his temper*]. Obey your
    orders, eat

what's served you, keep from mischief!

And don't annoy me. Do things *my* way.

250  MESSENIO.        Yessir, yessir.

I get the word. The word is simple: I'm a slave.

Concise communication, couldn't be much clearer.

[*A chastened pause, then back to harping at his master*]

But still and all, I just can't keep from saying this:

Menaechmus, when I inspect our purse, it seems

We're traveling for summer—very, very light.

By Hercules, unless you go home right away,

While you search on still finding no kin…you'll be
    'bro-kin'.

Now here's the race of men you'll find in Epidamnus:

The greatest libertines, the greatest drinkers too,

The most bamboozlers and charming flatterers        260

Live in this city. And as for wanton women, well—

Nowhere in the world, I'm told, are they more
    dazzling.

Because of this, they call the city Epidamnus,

For no one leaves unscathed, 'undamaged', as it were.

MENAECHMUS II. Oh, I'll have to watch for that. Give
    me the purse.

MESSENIO. What for?

MENAECHMUS II.        Because your words make
    me afraid of you.

MESSENIO. Of me?

MENAECHMUS II.        That you might cause…
    Epidamnation for me.

You love the ladies quite a lot, Messenio.

And I'm a temperamental man, extremely wild.

If I can hold the cash, it's best for both of us.        270

Then you can do no wrong, and I can't yell at you.

MESSENIO [*giving the purse*]. Take it, sir, and guard it;
    you'll be doing me a favor.

*Re-enter cook CYLINDRUS, his basket full of goodies*

CYLINDRUS. I've shopped quite well, and just the sort
    of things I like.

I know I'll serve a lovely dinner to the diners.

But look—I see Menaechmus. Now my back is dead!

The dinner guests are strolling right outside our door

Before I even finish shopping. Well, I'll speak.

              [*Going up to MENAECHMUS II*]

Menaechmus, sir…

MENAECHMUS II. God love you—God knows who
    you are.

CYLINDRUS [*thinks it's a joke*]. Who am I? Did you
    really say you don't know me?

MENAECHMUS II. By Hercules, I don't.

CYLINDRUS.        Where are the other guests?        280

MENAECHMUS II. What kind of other guests?

CYLINDRUS.        Your parasite, that is.

MENAECHMUS II. My parasite? [*to* MESSENIO] The
    man is simply raving mad.
MESSENIO. I *told* you there were great bamboozlers
    in this town.
MENAECHMUS II [*to* CYLINDRUS, *playing it
    cool*]. Which parasite of mine do you intend,
    young man?
CYLINDRUS. The Sponge.
MENAECHMUS II [*jocular, points to luggage*]. Indeed,
    my sponge is here inside my bag.
CYLINDRUS. Menaechmus, you've arrived too early
    for the dinner.
Look, I've just returned from shopping.
MENAECHMUS II.          Please, young man,
What kind of prices do you pay for sacred pigs,
The sacrificial kind?
CYLINDRUS.            Not much.
290 MENAECHMUS II.          Then take this coin,
And sacrifice to purify your mind at my expense.
Because I'm quite convinced you're absolutely raving
    mad
To bother me, an unknown man who doesn't know
    you.
CYLINDRUS. You don't recall my name? Cylindrus,
    sir, Cylindrus!
MENAECHMUS II. Cylindrical or Cubical, just
    go away.
Not only don't I know you, I don't *want* to know you.
CYLINDRUS. Your name's Menaechmus, sir, correct?
MENAECHMUS II.          As far as I know.
You're sane enough to call me by my rightful name.
But tell me how you know me.
CYLINDRUS.          How I know you? ... Sir—
[*discreetly, but pointedly*] You have a mistress ... she
300    owns me ... Erotium?
MENAECHMUS II. By Hercules, I haven't—and
    I don't know you.
CYLINDRUS. You don't know me, a man who many
    countless times
Refilled your bowl when you were at our house?
MESSENIO.                Bad luck!
I haven't got a single thing to break the fellow's
    skull with.
[*to* CYLINDRUS] Refilled the bowl? The bowl of one
    who till this day
Had never been in Epidamnus?
CYLINDRUS [*to* MENAECHMUS II]. You deny it?
MENAECHMUS II. By Hercules, I do.

CYLINDRUS [*points across stage*]. And I suppose
    that house
Is not your house?
MENAECHMUS II.          God damn the people living
    there!
CYLINDRUS [*to audience*]. Why, *he's* the raving
    lunatic—he cursed himself!          310
Menaechmus—
MENAECHMUS II. Yes, what is it?
CYLINDRUS.    Do take my advice,
And use that coin you promised me a while ago,
And since, by Hercules, you're certainly not sane,
I mean, Menaechmus, since you just now cursed
    yourself—
Go sacrifice that sacred pig to cure yourself.
MENAECHMUS II. By Hercules, you talk a lot—and
    you annoy me.
CYLINDRUS [*embarrassed, to audience*]. He acts this
    way a lot with me—he jokes around.
He can be very funny if his wife is gone.
[*To* MENAECHMUS]          But now, what do you say?
MENAECHMUS II.                To what?
CYLINDRUS [*showing basket*].          Is this enough?
I think I've shopped for three of you. Do I need more
For you, your parasite, your girl?          320
MENAECHMUS II.          What girls? What girls?
What parasites are you discussing?
MESSENIO [*to* CYLINDRUS].          And what madness
Has caused you to be such a nuisance?
CYLINDRUS [*to* MESSENIO].          What do *you* want
    now?
I don't know you. I'm chatting with a man I know.
MESSENIO [*to* CYLINDRUS]. By Pollux, it's for sure
    you're not exactly sane.
CYLINDRUS [*abandons the discussion*]. Well then,
    I guess I'll stew these up. No more delay.
Now don't you wander off too far from here.
[*bowing to* MENAECHMUS II] Your humble servant.
MENAECHMUS [*half aside*]. If you were, I'd
    crucify you!
CYLINDRUS. Oh, take a cross yourself—cross over
    and come in—
Whilst I apply Vulcanic arts to all the party's parts.          340
I'll go inside and tell Erotium you're here.
Then she'll convince you you'll be comfier inside.
    [*Exit*]
MENAECHMUS II [*stage whisper to* MESSENIO].
    Well—has he gone?
MESSENIO. He has.

MENAECHMUS II.      Those weren't lies you told.

There's truth in every word of yours.

MESSENIO [*his shrewd conclusion*]. Here's what I
     think:

I think the woman living here's some sort of slut.

That's what I gathered from that maniac who left.

MENAECHMUS II. And yet I wonder how that fellow
     knew my name.

MESSENIO. Well, I don't wonder. Wanton women
     have this way:

They send their servants or their maids to port

To see if some new foreign ship's arrived in port.

To ask around, 'Where are they from? What are their
     names?'

Right afterward, they fasten on you hard and fast.

They tease you, then they squeeze you dry and send
     you home.

Right now, I'd say a pirate ship is in this port

And I would say we'd better both beware of it.

MENAECHMUS II. By Hercules, you warn me well.

MESSENIO.               I'll know I have

If you stay well aware and show I've warned you well.

MENAECHMUS II. Be quiet for a minute now; the
     door just creaked.

Let's see who comes out now.

MESSENIO.           I'll put the luggage down.

[*To the sailors*]. Me hearties, if you please, please guard
350      this stuff for us.

### EROTIUM *appears, in a romantic mood, singing*

EROTIUM.

    Open my doors, let my welcome be wide,

      Then hurry and scurry—get ready inside.

See that the incense is burning, the couches have
     covers.

     Alluring decor is exciting for lovers.

Lovers love loveliness, we don't complain; their loss is
     our gain.

But the cook says someone was out here—[*looks*]
     I see!

It's that man of great worth—who's worth so much
     to me.

I ought to greet him richly—as he well deserves
     to be.

360   Now I'll go near, and let him know I'm here.

     [*To* MENAECHMUS] My darling—darling, it's a mite
     amazing

To see you standing out-of-doors by open doors.

You know full well how very much my house
     is yours.

All you ordered we're supplied with,

All your wishes are complied with.

So why stay here, why delay here? Come inside
     with . . . me.

Since dinner's ready, come and dine,

As soon as suits you, come . . . recline.

[*To say the very least, Menaechmus II is stunned.*
     *After a slight pause, he regains his powers of*
     *speech*]

MENAECHMUS II [*to* MESSENIO]. Who's this woman
     talking to?

EROTIUM. To you.

MENAECHMUS II. To me?

What have we—?

EROTIUM. By Pollux, you're the only one of all my
     lovers          370

Venus wants me to arouse to greatness. You deserve
     it, too.

For, by Castor, thanks to all your gifts, I've flourished
     like a flower.

MENAECHMUS II [*aside to* MESSENIO]. She is surely
     very mad or very drunk, Messenio.

Speaking to a total stranger like myself so . . . sociably.

MESSENIO. Didn't I predict all this? Why, these are
     only falling leaves.

Wait three days and I predict the trees themselves will
     drop on you.

Wanton women are this way, whenever they can sniff
     some silver.

Anyway, I'll speak to her. [*To* EROTIUM] Hey, woman
     there.

EROTIUM [*with hauteur*]. Yes, can I help you?

MESSENIO. Tell me where you know this man
     from.

EROTIUM.            Where? Where he knows me
     for years.

Epidamnus.

MESSENIO.          Epidamnus, where he's never set a
     foot,          380

Never been until today?

EROTIUM [*laughing*]. Aha—you're making jokes
     with me.

Dear Menaechmus, come inside, you'll see that
     things . . . will pick up right.

MENAECHMUS II [to MESSENIO]. Pollux, look, the
creature called me by my rightful name as well.
How I wonder what it's all about.
MESSENIO.                The perfume from your
purse.
That's the answer.
MENAECHMUS II.                And, by Pollux, you
did warn me rightfully.
              [Gives purse back to MESSENIO]
Take it then. I'll find out if she loves my person or
my purse.
EROTIUM. Let's go in, let's dine.
MENAECHMUS II [declining]. That's very nice of you.
Thanks just the same.
EROTIUM. Why on earth did you command a dinner
just a while ago?
MENAECHMUS II. I commanded dinner?
EROTIUM.        Yes. For you, and for your parasite.
MENAECHMUS II. What the devil parasite? [Aside]
390    This woman's certainly insane.
EROTIUM. Your old sponge, Peniculus.
MENAECHMUS II.          A sponge—to clean your
shoes, perhaps?
EROTIUM. No, of course—the one that came along
with you a while ago.
When you brought the dress you'd stolen from your
wife to give to me.
MENAECHMUS II. Are you sane? I gave a dress I'd
stolen from my wife to you?
[To MESSENIO]. Like some kind of horse this wom-
an's fast asleep still standing up.
EROTIUM. Do you get some pleasure making fun of
me, denying things,
Things completely true?
MENAECHMUS II.          What do you claim I've
done that I deny?
EROTIUM. Robbed your wife and gave the
dress to me.
MENAECHMUS II.              That I'll deny again!
Never have I had or do I have a wife, and never have I
Ever set a single foot inside that door, since I was born.
400    I had dinner on my ship, then disembarked and
              met you—
EROTIUM.                        Oooh!
Pity me—what shall I do? What ship is this?
MENAECHMUS II.                A wooden one,
Much repaired, re-sailed, re-beamed, re-hammered and
re-nailed and such.
Never did a navy have so numerous a nail supply.

EROTIUM. Please, my sweet, let's stop the jokes and
go inside together ... mmmm?
MENAECHMUS II. Woman, you want someone else.
I mean ... I'm sure you don't want me.
EROTIUM. Don't I know you well, Menaechmus,
know your father's name was Moschus?
You were born, or so they say, in Syracuse, in Sicily,
Where Agathocles was king, and then in turn, King
Phintia,
Thirdly, King Liparo, after whom King Hiero got the
crown.
Now it's still King Hiero.
MENAECHMUS II [to MESSENIO]. Say, that's not
inaccurate.
MESSENIO.                        By Jove—
If she's not from Syracuse, how does she know the
facts so well?
MENAECHMUS II [getting excited]. Hercules,
I shouldn't keep refusing her.
MESSENIO.        Oh, don't you dare!
Go inside that door and you're a goner, sir.
MENAECHMUS II.          Now you shut up!
Things are going well. Whatever she suggests—I'll just
agree.
Why not get a little ... hospitality? [to EROTIUM] Dear
lady, please—
I was impolite a while ago. I was a bit afraid that    420
[indicating MESSENIO] he might go and tell my
wife ... about the dress...
about the dinner.
Now, when you would like, we'll go inside.
EROTIUM.                    But where's the parasite?
MENAECHMUS II. I don't give a damn. Why should
we wait for him? Now if he comes,
Don't let him inside at all.
EROTIUM.        By Castor, I'll be happy not to.
Yet [playfully] there's something I would like
from you.
MENAECHMUS II.    Your wish is my command.
EROTIUM. Bring the dress you gave me to the
Phrygian embroiderer.
Have him redesign it, add some other frills I'd like
him to.
MENAECHMUS II. Hercules, a good idea. Because of
all the decoration,
When my wife observes you in the street, she won't
know what you're wearing.
EROTIUM. Therefore take it with you when
you leave.

MENAECHMUS II.     Of course, of course, of course.

430  EROTIUM. Let's go in.

MENAECHMUS II.     I'll follow you. [*Indicates*
     MESSENIO]

          I want a little chat with him.
                    [*Exit* EROTIUM]

Hey, Messenio, come here!

MESSENIO.     What's up?

MENAECHMUS II.     Just hop to my command.

MESSENIO. Can I help?

MENAECHMUS II.     You can. [*Apologetically*]
     I know you'll criticize—

MESSENIO. Then all the worse.

MENAECHMUS II. Booty's in my hands. A fine
     beginning. You continue, fast—

Take these fellows [*indicating sailors*] back to our
     lodging tavern, quicker than a wink,

Then be sure you come to pick me up before the sun
     goes down.

MESSENIO [*protesting*]. Master, you don't know about
     these sluts—

MENAECHMUS II. Be quiet! Just obey.

If I do a stupid thing, then I'll be hurting, not
     yourself.

Here's a woman stupid and unwitting, from what I've

440     just seen.

Here's some booty we can keep.

MESSENIO. I'm lost. [*Looks*] Oh, has he gone?
     He's lost!

Now a mighty pirate ship is towing off a shipwrecked skiff.

I'm the fool as well. I tried to argue down the man
     who owns me.

But he bought me only as a sounding board, not to
     sound off.

Follow me, you men [*to the sailors*], so I can come on
     time—as I've been ordered.
                    [*They exit*]

*Stage empty for a moment [musical interlude?].*

### Enter PENICULUS—*all upset*

PENICULUS. More than thirty years I'm on this earth
     and during all that time

Never till today have I done such a damned and
     dopey deed!

Here I had immersed my whole attention in a public
     meeting.

While I stood there gaping, that Menaechmus simply
     stole away,

Went off to his mistress, I suppose, and didn't want me
     there.                                                     450

Curse the man who was the first to manufacture pub-
     lic meetings,

All designed to busy men already busy with their
     business.

They should choose the men who have no occupation
     for these things,

Who, if absent when they're called, would face fantas-
     tic fines—and fast.

Why, there's simply gobs of men who only eat just
     once a day,

Who have nothing else to do; they don't invite, they're
     not invited.

Make these people spend their time at public meet-
     ings and assemblies.

If this were the case today, I'd not have lost my lovely
     feast.                                                     460

Sure as I'm alive, that man had really wished to feed
     me well.

Anyhow, I'll go. The thought of scraps left over lights
     my soul.

But—what's this? Menaechmus with a garland, com-
     ing from the house?

Party's over, I'm arriving just in time to be too late!

First, I'll spy how he behaves and then I'll go accost
     the man.

### MENAECHMUS II *wobbles happily out of* EROTIUM's *house, wearing a garland, and carrying the dress earlier delivered by his brother*

MENAECHMUS II [*to* EROTIUM]. Now, now, relax,
     you'll get this dress today for sure,

Returned on time, with lovely new embroidery.

I'll make the old dress vanish—it just won't be seen.

PENICULUS [*indignant, to the audience*]. He'll deco-
     rate the dress now that the
          dinner's done,

The wine's been drunk, the parasite left in the cold.      470

No, Hercules, I'm not myself, if not revenged,

If I don't curse him out in style. Just watch me now.

MENAECHMUS II [*drunk with joy—and a few other
     things*]. By all the gods,
          what man in just a single day

Received more pleasures, though expecting none
     at all:

I've wined, I've dined, I've concubined, and robbed
     her blind—

No one but me will own this dress after today!

PENICULUS. I just can't bear to hide and hear him
    prate like this.

Smug and satisfied, he prates about my party.

MENAECHMUS II. She says I gave her this—and tells
480    me that I stole it.

I stole it from my *wife*! [*Confidentially*] I knew the girl
    was wrong,

Yet I pretended there was some affair between us two.

Whatever she proposed, I simply said, 'Yes, yes,

Exactly, what you say.' What need of many words?

I've never had more fun at less expense to me.

PENICULUS. Now I'll accost the man, and make an
    awful fuss.

MENAECHMUS II. Now who's this fellow coming
    toward me?

PENICULUS [*in a fury*].            Well, speak up!

You lighter than a feather, dirty, rotten person,

You evil man, you tricky, worthless individual!

490 What did I ever do to you that you'd destroy me?

You stole away from me, when we were in the forum;

You dealt a death blow to the dinner in my absence!

How could you dare? Why, I deserved an equal part!

MENAECHMUS II. Young man, please indicate pre-
    cisely what you want from me.

And why you're cursing someone you don't know at all.

Your dressing-down of me deserves a beating-up!

PENICULUS. By Pollux, you're the one who beat me
    out, just now.

MENAECHMUS II. Now please, young man, do intro-
    duce yourself at least.

PENICULUS. And now insult to injury! You don't
    know me?

MENAECHMUS II. By Pollux, no, I don't, as far as I
500    can tell.

I've never seen you, never met you. Whoever you are—

At least behave, and don't be such a nuisance to me.

PENICULUS. Wake up, Menaechmus!

MENAECHMUS II.        I'm awake—it seems to me.

PENICULUS. And you don't recognize me?

MENAECHMUS II.        Why should I deny it?

PENICULUS. Don't recognize your parasite?

MENAECHMUS II.        My dear young man,

It seems to me your brain is not so very sane.

PENICULUS. Just answer this: did you not steal that
    dress today?

It was your wife's. You gave it to Erotium.

MENAECHMUS II. By Hercules, I have no wife.
    Erotium?

I gave her nothing, didn't steal this dress. You're mad.

PENICULUS [*to audience*]. Total disaster! [*to     510
    MENAECHMUS II*] But I saw
        you wear that dress

And, wearing it, I saw you leave your house.

MENAECHMUS II.            Drop dead!

You think all men are *fags* because you are!

You claim I actually put on a woman's dress!

PENICULUS. By Hercules, I do.

MENAECHMUS II.            Oh, go where you
    belong!

Get purified or something, raving lunatic!

PENICULUS. By Pollux, all the begging in the world
    won't keep me

From telling every single detail to your wife.

Then all these present insults will rebound on
    you.                                                    520

You've gobbled up my dinner—and I'll be revenged!
        [*He storms into
            MENAECHMUS's house*]

MENAECHMUS II. What's going on? Everyone
    I run across

Makes fun of me...but why? Oh, wait, the door just
    creaked.

*Enter* EROTIUM's MAID, *a sexy little thing. She
carries a bracelet*

MAID. Menaechmus, your Erotium would love
    a favor—

Please, while you're at it, take this to the goldsmith
    for her

And have him add about an extra...ounce...of gold,

So that the bracelet is remodeled, shining new.

MENAECHMUS II [*ironically*]. I'm happy to take care
    of both these things for her,

And any other thing that she'd like taken care of.

MAID. You recognize the bracelet?

MENAECHMUS II.    Uh—I know it's gold.     530

MAID. This very bracelet long ago was once your
    wife's,

And secretly you snatched it from her jewel box.

MENAECHMUS II. By Hercules, I never did.

MAID. You don't recall?

Return the bracelet, if you don't remember.

MENAECHMUS II. Wait!

I'm starting to remember. Why, of course I gave it.

Now where are those two armlets that I gave as well?

MAID. You never did.

MENAECHMUS II.          Of course, by Pollux—this
    was all.
MAID. Will you take care of things?
MENAECHMUS II [*ironically*].          I said I'd take
    good care.
I'll see that dress and bracelet are both carried back
540    together.
    MAID [*the total coquette*]. And, dear Menaechmus,
        how about a gift for me?
Let's say four drachmae's worth of jingly earrings?
Then when you visit us, I'll really welcome you.
MENAECHMUS II. Of course. Give me the gold, I'll
    pay the labor costs.
MAID. Advance it for me, afterwards I'll pay you back.
MENAECHMUS II. No, you advance it, afterwards I'll
    double it.
MAID. I haven't got it.
MENAECHMUS II.          If you ever get it—give it.
MAID [*frustrated, she bows*]. I'm at your service.
                                                [*Exit*]

MENAECHMUS II. I'll take care of all of this
As soon as possible, at any cost—I'll sell them.
Now has she gone? She's gone and closed the door
550    behind her.
The gods have fully fostered me and favored me
    unfailingly!
But why do I delay? Now is the perfect chance,
The perfect time to flee this prostitutish place.
Now rush, Menaechmus, lift your foot and lift the pace!
I'll take this garland off, and toss it to the left,
So anyone who follows me will think I'm thataway.
I'll go at once and find my slave, if possible,
And tell him everything the gods have given me today.
                                                [*Exit*]


*From* **MENAECHMUS**'s *house enter* **PENICULUS**
*and* **MENAECHMUS**'s **WIFE**

WIFE [*melodramatic, a big sufferer*]. Must I keep suffer-
    ing this mischief in my marriage?
Where husband sneaks and steals whatever's in the
560    house
And takes it to his mistress?
    PENICULUS.          Can't you quiet down?
You'll catch him in the act, if you just follow me.
He's drunk and garlanded—at the embroiderer's,
Conveying that same dress he stole from you today.
Look—there's the garland. Do I tell you lies or truth?
He's gone in that direction; you can follow clues.

But wait—what perfect luck—he's come back right
    now!
Without the dress.
WIFE.          What should I do? How should I act
    with him?
PENICULUS. The very same as always: make him
    miserable.
But let's step over here—and spread a net for him.          570


*Enter* **MENAECHMUS I**


MENAECHMUS [*singing*]. We have this tradition, we
    have this tradition,
An irksome tradition, and yet it's the best
Who love this tradition much more than the rest.
They want lots of clients, all want lots of clients.
Who cares if they're honest or not—are they rich?
Who cares if they're honest, we'll take them with zest—
    If they're rich.

If he's poor but he's honest—who cares for him?
He's dishonest but rich? Then we all say our prayers
    for him.
So it happens that lawless, corrupting destroyers          580
Have overworked lawyers.
Denying what's done and delivered, this grasping and
    fraudulent sort
Though their fortunes arise from exorbitant lies
They're all anxious to step into court.
When the day comes, it's hell for their lawyer as well,
For we have to defend things unjust and unpretty
To jury, to judge, or judicial committee.

So I just was delayed, forced to give legal aid, no evad-
    ing this client of
        mine who had found me.
I wanted to do you know what—and with whom—
    but he bound me and
        tied ropes around me.
Facing the judges just now, I had countless despicable
    deeds to defend.                                          590
Twisting torts with contortions of massive
    proportions,
I pleaded and pleaded right down to the end.
But just when an out-of-court settlement seemed to
    be sealed—*my client appealed!*
I never had seen someone more clearly caught in
    the act:
For each of his crimes there were three who could
    speak to the fact!

By all the heavens, cursed be he
Who just destroyed this day for me.
And curse me too, a fool today,
For ever heading forum's way.
The greatest day of all—destroyed.
The feast prepared, but not enjoyed.
The wench was waiting too, indeed.
The very moment I was freed
I left the forum with great speed.
600    She's angry now, I'm sure of it.
The dress I gave will help a bit,

Taken from my wife today…a token for Erotium.

[*A pause.* MENAECHMUS *catches his breath, still not noticing his* WIFE *or the* PARASITE, *who now speaks*]

PENICULUS. Well, what say you to that?
WIFE.                    That I've married a rat.
PENICULUS. Have you heard quite enough to
    complain to him?
WIFE. Quite enough.
MENAECHMUS.    Now I'll go where the pleasures
    will flow.
PENICULUS. No, remain. Let's be flowing some pain
    to him.
WIFE. You'll be paying off at quite a rate for this!
PENICULUS [*to wife*].       Good, good attack!
WIFE. Do you have the nerve to think you'd get away
    with secret smuggling?
MENAECHMUS. What's the matter. Wife?
WIFE.                    You're asking me?
MENAECHMUS [*indicating* PENICULUS]. Should
    I ask him instead?
WIFE. Don't turn on the charm.
PENICULUS.       That's it!
MENAECHMUS.    But tell me what I've done to you.
Why are you so angry?
WIFE.       You should know.
PENICULUS.              He knows—and can't
    disguise it.
MENAECHMUS. What's the matter?
WIFE.                    Just a dress.
MENAECHMUS.              A dress?
WIFE.                    A dress.
PENICULUS [*to* MENAECHMUS].    Aha, you're
    scared.
MENAECHMUS. What could I be scared of?

PENICULUS.              Of a dress—and of a
    dressing-down.                              610
You'll be sorry for that secret feast. [*To wife*] Go on,
    attack again!
MENAECHMUS. You be quiet.
PENICULUS. No, I won't. He's nodding to me not
    to speak.
MENAECHMUS. Hercules, I've never nodded to you,
    never winked at you!
PENICULUS. Nothing could be bolder: he denies it
    while he's doing it!
MENAECHMUS. By Jove and all the gods I swear—is
    that enough for you, dear Wife?—
Never did I nod to him.
PENICULUS [*sarcastically*]. Oh, she believes you. Now
    go back!
MENAECHMUS. Go back to what?
PENICULUS. Go back to the embroiderer's—and get
    the dress!
MENAECHMUS. Get what dress?
PENICULUS. I won't explain, since he forgets his
    own…affairs.
WIFE. What a woeful wife I am.
MENAECHMUS [*playing very naïve*]. Woeful wife? Do
    tell me why?
Has a servant misbehaved, or has a maid talked back
    to you?                                    620
Tell me, dear, we'll punish misbehavers.
WIFE.                    Oh, is *that* a joke!
MENAECHMUS. You're so angry. I don't like to see
    you angry.
WIFE.                    *That's* a joke!
MENAECHMUS. Someone from the household staff
    has angered you.
WIFE. Another joke!
MENAECHMUS. Well, of course, it isn't me.
WIFE.       Aha! At last he's stopped the jokes!
MENAECHMUS. Certainly I haven't misbehaved.
WIFE.              He's making jokes again!
MENAECHMUS. Tell me, dear, what's ailing you?
PENICULUS.       He's giving you a lovely line.
MENAECHMUS. Why do you annoy me? Did I talk
    to you?
              [*Throws a punch at* PENICULUS]
WIFE [*to* MENAECHMUS].    Don't raise your hand!
PENICULUS [*to* WIFE]. Let him have it! [*to*
    MENAECHMUS]
Now go eat your little feast while I'm not there.

Go get drunk, put on a garland, stand outside, and
    mock me now!
MENAECHMUS. Pollux! I've not eaten any feast
630    today—or been in there.
PENICULUS. You deny it?
MENAECHMUS.     I deny it all.
PENICULUS.     No man could be more brazen.
Didn't I just see you here, all garlanded, a while ago?
Standing here and shouting that my brain was not
    exactly sane ?
And you didn't know me—you were just a stranger
    here in town!
MENAECHMUS. I've been absolutely absent, since the
    second we set out.
PENICULUS. I know you. You didn't think that I could
    get revenge on you.
All has been recounted to your wife.
MENAECHMUS.     What 'all'?
PENICULUS.     Oh, I don't know.
Ask her for yourself.
MENAECHMUS. Dear wife, what fables has this man
    been telling?
What's the matter? Why are you so silent? Tell me.
WIFE.     You're pretending,
Asking what you know.
MENAECHMUS.     Why do I ask, then?
640 PENICULUS.     What an evil man!
How he fakes. But you can't hide it, now the whole
    affair is out.
Everything's been publicized by me.
MENAECHMUS.   But *what*?
WIFE.     Have you no shame?
Can't you tell the truth yourself? Attend me and
    please pay attention:
I will now inform you what he told, and why I'm angry
    at you.
There's a dress been snatched from me.
MENAECHMUS.     There's a dress been snatched
    from me?
PENICULUS. Not from *you,* from *her.* [*to* WIFE] The
    evil man resorts to every dodge.
[*To* MENAECHMUS] If the dress were snatched from
    you, it really would be lost to us.
MENAECHMUS. You're not anything to me. [*To*
    WIFE] Go on, my dear.
WIFE.     A dress is gone.
MENAECHMUS. Oh—who snatched it?
WIFE.     Pollux; who'd know better than the
man himself?

MENAECHMUS. Who is this?
WIFE.     His name's Menaechmus.
MENAECHMUS.     Pollux, what an evil deed!   650
What Menaechmus could it be?
WIFE.     Yourself.
MENAECHMUS.     Myself?
WIFE.     Yourself.
MENAECHMUS.     Who says?
WIFE. I do.
PENICULUS.     I do, too. And then you gave it to
    Erotium.
MENAECHMUS. *I* did?
WIFE.     You, you, you!
PENICULUS.     Say, would you like an owl
    for a pet—
Just to parrot 'you you you'? The both of us are all
    worn out.
MENAECHMUS. By Jove and all the gods, I swear—is
    that enough for you, dear Wife?—
No, I didn't give it to her.
PENICULUS.     No, we know *we* tell the truth.
MENAECHMUS [*backing down*]. Well…that is to
    say…I didn't give the dress. I loaned it
    to her.
WIFE. Oh, by Castor, do I give your tunics or your
    clothes away—
Even as a loan? A woman can give women's clothes
    away.
Men can give their own. *Now will you get that dress
    back home to me?*   660
MENAECHMUS [*cowed*]. Yes, I'll…get it back.
WIFE.     I'd say you'd better get it back, or else.
Only with that dress in hand will you re-enter your
    own house.
Now I'm going in.
PENICULUS [*to* WIFE].   But what of me—what
    thanks for all my help?
WIFE [*sweetly bitchy*]. I'll be glad to help you out—
    when someone steals a dress from you.
PENICULUS. That'll never happen. I don't own a
    single thing to steal.
Wife and husband—curse you both. I'll hurry to the
    forum now.
I can very clearly see I've been expelled from this
    whole house.
[*He storms off*]
MENAECHMUS. Hah—my wife thinks that she hurts
    me, when she shuts the door on me.
But, as far as entering, I've got another, better place.

[*To* WIFE's *door*] You don't like me. I'll live through it
670    since Erotium here does.

She won't close me out, she'll close me tightly in her
arms, she will.

I'll go beg the wench to give me back the dress I just
now gave,

Promising another, better one. [*Knocks*] Is there a
doorman here?

Open up! And someone ask Erotium to step
outside.

**EROTIUM** *steps outside her house*

EROTIUM. Who has asked for me?

MENAECHMUS.         A man who loves you more
than his own self.

EROTIUM. Dear Menaechmus, why stand here
outside? Come in.

MENAECHMUS. Wait just a minute.

Can you guess what brings me here?

EROTIUM.                     I know—you'd like
some...joy with me.

MENAECHMUS. Well...indeed, by Pollux. But—that
dress I gave to you just now.

Please return it, since my wife's discovered all in full
detail.

I'll replace it with a dress that's twice the price, and as
680    you like it.

EROTIUM.          But I gave it to you for embroidery a
moment back,

With a bracelet you would bring the goldsmith for
remodeling.

MENAECHMUS. What—you gave me dress and
bracelet? No, you'll find that isn't true.

No—I first gave you the dress, then went directly to
the forum.

Now's the very second I've returned.

EROTIUM.                Aha—I see what's up.

Just because I put them in your hands—you're out to
swindle me.

MENAECHMUSS. Swindle you? By Pollux, no! Why,
didn't I just tell you why?

Everything's discovered by my wife!

EROTIUM [*exasperated*].     I didn't ask you for it.

No, you brought it to me of your own free will—and
as a gift.

Now you want the dress right back. Well, have it, take
690    it, wear it!

You can wear it, or your wife—or lock it in your
money box.

But from this day on you'll never set a foot inside
my house.

After all my loyal service, suddenly you find me hateful,

So you'll only have me now by laying cash right on
the line.

Find yourself some other girl to cheat the way you've
cheated me!

MENAECHMUS. Hercules, the woman's angry! Hey—
please wait, please listen to me—
                    [EROTIUM *exits, slamming her door*]

Please come back! Please stay—oh, won't you do this
favor for me?

Well, she's gone—and closed the door. I'm universally
kicked out.

Neither wife nor mistress will believe a single
thing I say.

What to do? I'd better go consult some friends on
what they think.                                                    700
                    [*Exit* MENAECHMUS]

*A slight pause* [*musical interlude?*]. *Then enter*
**MENAECHMUS II** *from the opposite side of the*
*stage. He still carries the dress*

MENAECHMUS II. I was a fool a while ago to give
that purse

With all that cash to someone like Messenio.

I'm sure by now the fellow's boozing in some dive.

**WIFE** *enters from her house*

WIFE. I'll stand on watch to see how soon my
husband comes.

Why, here he is—I'm saved! He's bringing back
the dress.

MENAECHMUS II. I wonder where Messenio has
wandered to....

WIFE. I'll go and greet the man with words that he
deserves.

[*To* MENAECHMUS] Tell me—are you not ashamed
to show your face,

Atrocious man—and with that dress?

MENAECHMUS II.          I beg your pardon,

What seems to be the trouble, madam?

WIFE.          Shame on you!                              710

You dare to mutter, dare to speak a word to me?

MENAECHMUS II. Whatever have I done that would
    forbid my talking?

WIFE. You're asking me? Oh, shameless, brazen,
    wicked man!

MENAECHMUS II [*with quiet sarcasm*]. Madam, do
    you have any notion why the Greeks

Referred to Hecuba as…female dog?

WIFE.              I don't.

MENAECHMUS II. Because she acted just the way
    you're acting now.

She barked and cursed at everyone who came in sight,

And thus the people rightly called her…female dog.

WIFE. I simply can't endure all this disgracefulness—

720  I'd even rather live my life…a divorcée

Than bear the brunt of this disgracefulness of yours.

MENAECHMUS II. What's it to me if you can't stand
    your married life—

Or ask for a divorce? Is it a custom here

To babble to all foreigners who come to town?

WIFE. 'To babble'? I won't stand for that. I won't!
    I won't!

I'll die a divorcée before I'd live with you.

MENAECHMUS II. As far as I'm concerned you can
    divorce yourself,

And stay a divorcée till Jupiter resigns his throne.

WIFE. Look—you denied you stole that dress a
    while ago,

730  And now you wave it at me. Aren't you ashamed?

MENAECHMUS II. By Hercules, you are a wild and
    wicked woman!

You dare to claim this dress I hold was stolen
    from you?

Another woman gave it to me for…repairs.

WIFE. By Castor—no, I'd better have my father come,

So I can tell him all of your disgracefulness.

[*Calls in to one of her slaves*] Oh, Decio—go find my
    father, bring him here.

And tell my father the entire situation.

[*To* MENAECHMUS II.] I'll now expose all your
    disgracefulness.

MENAECHMUS II. You're sick!

All what disgracefulness?

WIFE.         A dress—and golden bracelet.

740  You rob your legal wife at home and then you go

Bestow it on your mistress. Do I 'babble' truth?

MENAECHMUS II. Dear Madam, can you tell me
    please what I might drink

To make your bitchy boorishness more bearable?

I've not the slightest notion who you think I am.

I know you like I know the father-in-law of Hercules!

WIFE. You may mock me, by Pollux, but you can't
    mock him.

My father's coming. [*To* MENAECHMUS II] Look who's
    coming, look who's coming;

You do know *him*.

MENAECHMUS II [*ironically*]. Of course, a friend of
    Agamemnon.

I first met him the day I first met you—*today*.

WIFE. You claim that you don't know me, or my
    father?                     750

MENAECHMUS II. And how about your grandpa—I
    don't know him either.

WIFE. By Castor, you just never change, you *never
    change*!

    [*Enter the* OLD MAN, MENAECHMUS's *father-in-
    -law, groaning and wheezing*]

OLD MAN [*to the audience, in halting song*].

Oh, my old age, my old age, I lack what I need,

I'm stepping unlively, unfast is my speed,

But it isn't so easy, I tell you, not easy indeed.

For I've lost all my quickness, old age is a sickness.

My body's a big heavy trunk, I've no strength.

Oh oh, old age is bad—no more vigor remains.

Oh, when old age arrives, it brings plenty of pains.

I could mention them all but I won't talk at length.   760

But deep in my heart is this worry:

My daughter has sent for me now in a hurry.

She won't say what it is,

What it is I've not heard.

She just asked me to come, not explaining a word.

And yet I've a pretty good notion at that:

That her husband and she are involved in a spat.

Well, that's how it is always with big-dowry wives,

They're fierce to their husbands, they order their lives.

But then sometimes the man is…let's say…not so
    pure.

There's limits to what a good wife can endure.

And, by Pollux, a daughter won't send for her dad.   770

Unless there's some cause, and her husband's
    been bad.

Well, anyway I can find out since my daughter is here.

Her husband looks angry. Just what I suspected,
    it's clear.

           [*The song ends. A brief pause*]

I'll address her.

WIFE.                    I'll go meet him. Many greetings,
   Father dear.
OLD MAN. Same to you. I only hope I've come when
   all is fine and dandy.
Why are you so gloomy, why does he stand off there,
   looking angry?
Has there been some little skirmishing between the
   two of you?
Tell me who's at fault, be brief. No lengthy arguments
   at length.
WIFE. *I've* done nothing wrong, dear Father, you can
780   be assured of that.
But I simply can't go on and live with him in any way.
Consequently—take me home.
OLD MAN.          What's wrong?
WIFE.                         I'm made a total fool of.
OLD MAN. How and who?
WIFE.               By him, the man you signed and
   sealed to me as husband.
OLD MAN. Oh, I see, disputing, eh? And yet I've told
   you countless times
Both of you beware, don't either one approach me
   with complaints.
WIFE. How can I beware, when he's as bad as this?
OLD MAN.          You're asking me?
WIFE. Tell me.
OLD MAN.               Oh, the countless times I've
   preached on duty to your husband:
Don't check what he's doing, where he's going, what
   his business is.
WIFE. But he loves a fancy woman right next door.
790 OLD MAN. He's very wise!
Thanks to all your diligence, I promise you, he'll love
   her more.
WIFE. But he also boozes there.
OLD MAN.          You think you'll make him booze
   the less,
If he wants to, anywhere he wants? Why must you be
   so rash?
Might as well go veto his inviting visitors to dine,
Say he can't have guests at home. What do you women
   want from husbands?
*Servitude?* Why, next you'll want him to do chores
   around the house!
Next you'll order him to sit down with the maids and
   card the wool!
WIFE. Father dear, I called you to support my cause,
   not help my husband.
You're a lawyer prosecuting your own client.

OLD MAN.                    If *he's* wrong,
I'll attack him ten times harder than I'm now attacking
   you.                                                      800
Look, you're quite well dressed, well jeweled and well
   supplied with food and maids.
Being well off, woman, why, be wise, leave well
   enough alone.
WIFE. But he filches all the jewels and all the dresses
   from the house.
Stealing on the sly, he then bestows the stuff on
   fancy women.
OLD MAN. Oh, he's wrong if he does that, but if he
   doesn't, then you're wrong,
Blaming blameless men.
WIFE.               He has a dress this very moment,
   Father,
And a bracelet he's brought from her because I've
   found him out.
OLD MAN. Well, I'll get the facts, I'll go accost the
   man, and speak to him.
                    [*He puffs over to* MENAECHMUS II]
Say, Menaechmus, tell me why you're muttering. I'll
   understand.
Why are you so gloomy? Why is she so angry over
   there?                                                    810
MENAECHMUS II. Whatever your name is, old man,
   and whoever you are,
   I swear by Jove supreme,
Calling all the gods to witness—
OLD MAN.          Witness for what, about what in
   the world?
MENAECHMUS II. Never ever did I hurt this woman
   now accusing me of
Having sneaked into her house and filched this dress.
WIFE. He's telling lies!
MENAECHMUS II. If I've ever set a single foot inside
   that house of hers,
Anxiously I long to be the very saddest man
   on earth.
OLD MAN. No, you can't be sane too long for that, to
   claim you've not set foot
In the house you live in. Why, you're the very *maddest*
   man on earth!
MENAECHMUS II. What was that, old man? You
   claim I live right here and
in this house?                                               820
OLD MAN. You deny it?
MENAECHMUS II.               I deny it.
OLD MAN.                         Your denial isn't true.

That's unless you moved away last night. Daughter,
  come over here.
  [*Father and daughter walk aside;*
    OLD MAN *whispers confidentially*]
Tell me—did you move away from here last night?
WIFE.                    Where to? What for?
OLD MAN. *I* don't know, by Pollux.
WIFE.            He's just mocking you—or don't you
  get it?
OLD MAN. That's enough, Menaechmus, no more jok-
  ing, now let's tend to business.
MENAECHMUS II. Tell me, sir, what business do you
  have with me? Just who *are* you?
What have I to do with you or—[*points to* WIFE] that
  one, who is such a bother?
WIFE. Look—his eyes are getting green, a greenish
  color's now appearing
From his temples and his forehead. Look, his eyes are
830  flickering!
MENAECHMUS II [*aside, to the audience*]. Nothing
  could be better. Since
they both declare that I'm raving mad
I'll pretend I am insane, and scare them both away
  from me.
            [MENAECHMUS II *begins to 'go berserk'*]
WIFE. What a gaping mouth, wide open. Tell me what
  to do, dear Father.
OLD MAN. Over here, dear Daughter, get as far as pos-
  sible from him.
MENAECHMUS II [*caught up in his own act, 'hearing'
  divine words*]. Bacchus!
  Yo-ho, Bacchus, in what forest do you bid me hunt?
Yes, I hear you, but I can't escape from where I am
  just now:
On my left I'm guarded by a very rabid female dog.
Right behind her is a goat who reeks of garlic, and this
  goat has
Countless times accused a blameless citizen with perjury.
OLD MAN [*enraged*]. You you you, I'll—
MENAECHMUS II [*'hearing'*]. What, Apollo? Now
840  your oracle commands me:
Take some hotly blazing torches, set this woman's eyes
  on fire.
WIFE. Father, Father—what a threat! He wants to set
  my eyes on fire!
MENAECHMUS II [*aside, to audience*]. They both say
  I'm crazy; I know
they're the really crazy ones!

OLD MAN. Daughter—
WIFE          Yes?
OLD MAN.      Suppose I go, and send some servants
  here at once.
Let them come and take him off, and tie him up with
  ropes at home.
Now—before he makes a bigger hurricane!
MENAECHMUS II.                I'm caught!
I'll be taken off unless I find myself a plan right now.
['*Hearing oracle,*' aloud] Yes, Apollo, 'Do not spare thy
  fists in punching in her face?
That's unless she hurries out of sight and quickly goes
  to hell!'
Yes, Apollo, I'll obey you.
OLD MAN. Run, dear Daughter—quickly
  home!                                                    850
Otherwise, he'll pound you.
WIFE.      While I run, please keep an eye on him.
See he doesn't get away. [*A final groan*] What wifely
  woe to hear such things!
  [*Exit*]
MENAECHMUS II. Hah, not bad, I got her off. And
  now I'll get *this*—poisoned person,
White-beard, palsied wreck. Tithonus was a youth
  compared to him.
[*to 'Apollo'*] What's my orders? Beat the fellow limb
  from limb and bone from bone?
Use the very stick he carries for the job?
OLD MAN.                    I'll punish you—
If you try to touch me, if you try to get much closer
  to me!
MENAECHMUS II [*to 'Apollo'*]. Yes, I'll do thy bidding: take a double axe and this old fogey,
Chop his innards into little pieces, till I reach
  the bone?
OLD MAN [*panicked*]. Goodness, now's the time for
  me to be on guard and very wary.                        860
I'm afraid he'll carry out his threats and cause some
  harm to me.
MENAECHMUS II [*to 'Apollo' again*]. Dear Apollo, you
  command so much. I now
must hitch up horses,
Wild, ferocious horses, and then mount up in my
  chariot,
Then to trample on this lion-creaking, stinking,
  toothless lion?
Now I'm in the chariot, I've got the reins, I've got
  the whip.

Up up up, ye steeds, now let us see the sound of
  horses' hoofbeats.
Quickly curve your course with splendid speed and
  swifty swoop of steps.
OLD MAN. Threatening me with hitched-up horses?
MENAECHMUS II.        Yea, Apollo, once again,
Now you bid me charge and overwhelm the man
  who's standing here.
[*Fakes Homeric divine intervention*] But what's this?
  Who takes me by the hair
870  and hauls me from the car?
Look, Apollo, someone's changing your command as
  spoke to me!
OLD MAN. By Hercules, he's sick, he's very sick.
  Ye gods!
And just a while ago, the man was very sane,
But suddenly this awful sickness fell on him.
I'll go and get a doctor—fast as possible.
        [*Exit at a senile sprint*]
MENAECHMUS II. Well, have they disappeared from
  sight, the two of them,
Who forced a normal, healthy man to act insane?
I shouldn't wait to reach my ship while things
  are safe.
[*To the audience*] But, everybody, please—if that old
880  man returns,
Don't tell him, please, which street I took to get away.
[*He dashes offstage, toward the harbor*]

**Enter OLD MAN, *tired, annoyed, complaining***

OLD MAN. My limbs just ache from sitting and my eyes
  from looking,
While waiting for that doctor to leave office hours.
At last, unwillingly, he left his patients. What a bore!
He claims he'd set Asclepius's broken leg,
And then Apollo's broken arm. I wonder if
The man I bring's a doctor or a carpenter!
But here he's strutting now. [*Calling off*] Why can't
  you hurry up?

**Enter DOCTOR, *the superprofessional***

DOCTOR [*right to the point*]. What sort of illness does
  he have? Speak up, old man.
890  Is he depressed, or is he frantic? Give the facts.
Or is he in a coma? Has he liquid dropsy?
OLD MAN. But that's precisely why I've brought
  you—to tell me—

And make him well again.
DOCTOR.        Of course. A snap.
He shall be well again. You have my word on that.
OLD MAN. I want him to be cared for with the
  greatest care.
DOCTOR. I'll sigh a thousand sighs, I'll take great
  pains with him.
For you—I'll care for him with all the greatest care.
But here's the man himself: let's see how he behaves.
        [*They step aside to eavesdrop*]

**From the forum side enter MENAECHMUS,
*addressing himself in soliloquy***

MENAECHMUS. Pollux, what a day for me: perverted
  and inverted too.
Everything I plotted to be private's now completely
  public.                                                                  900
My own parasite has filled me full of fearful accusations!
My Ulysses, causing so much trouble for his royal
  patron!
If I live, I'll skin him live. I'll cut off all his livelihood.
What a foolish thing to say. What I call his is really mine.
My own food and fancy living nurtured him. I'll starve
  him now.
And my slut has been disgraceful. Typical of slutitude.
All I did was ask her to return the dress to give my wife.
She pretends she gave it to me. Pollux, I'm in awful
  shape!
OLD MAN [*to DOCTOR*]. Did you hear his words?
DOCTOR [*nods*].        Admits his 'awful shape'.
OLD MAN.                        Go up to him.
DOCTOR [*aloud*]. Greetings, dear Menaechmus. Do
  you realize that your
cloak has slipped?                                                       910
Don't you know how dangerous that sort of thing is
  for your health?
MENAECHMUS. Why not hang yourself?
OLD MAN [*whispers to DOCTOR*]. You notice anything?
DOCTOR.                Of course I do!
This condition couldn't be relieved with tons of
  hellebore.
[*To MENAECHMUS again*]. Tell me now,
  Menaechmus.
MENAECHMUS.                Tell what?
DOCTOR.                Just answer what I ask.
Do you drink white wine or red?
MENAECHMUS. And why don't you go straight
  to hell?

DOCTOR. Hercules, I notice teeny traces of insanity.

MENAECHMUS.                    Why not ask

Do I favor purple bread, or pink or maybe even mauve?

Do I eat the gills of birds, the wings of fishes—?

OLD MAN.                    Oh, good grief!

Listen to his ravings, you can hear the words. Why

920     wait at all?

Give the man some remedy before the madness takes
        him fully.

DOCTOR. Wait—I have more questions.

OLD MAN. But you're killing him with all this blab!

DOCTOR [*to* MENAECHMUS]. Tell me this about
        your eyes: at times do they get

glazed at all?

MENAECHMUS. What? You think you're talking to a
        lobster, do you, rotten man!

DOCTOR [*unfazed*]. Tell me, have you ever noticed
        your intestines making noise?

MENAECHMUS. When I've eaten well, they're silent;
        when I'm hungry, they make noise.

DOCTOR. Pollux, that's a pretty healthy answer he just
        gave to me.

[*To* MENAECHMUS]. Do you sleep right through till
        dawn, sleep easily when
                you're in bed?

MENAECHMUS. I sleep through if all the debts I owe

930     are paid. But listen you, you

Question-asker, you be damned by Jupiter and all
        the gods!

DOCTOR. Now I know the man's insane. Those final
        words are proof.

[*To* OLD MAN] Take care!

OLD MAN. He speaks like a Nestor now, compared to
        just a while ago.

Just a while ago he called his wife a rabid female dog.

MENAECHMUS. *I* said that?

OLD MAN.                    You're mad, I say.

MENAECHMUS.                    I'm mad?

OLD MAN.          And do you know what else? You

Also threatened that you'd trample over me with
        teams of horses!

940  Yes, I saw you do it. Yes, and I insist you did it, too.

MENAECHMUS [*to* OLD MAN] You, of course, have
        snatched the sacred crown of Jove, that's what
        I know.

Afterwards, they tossed you into prison for this
        awful crime.

When they let you out, while you were manacled, they
        beat you up.

Then you killed your father. Then you sold your
        mother as a slave.

Have you heard enough to know I'm sane enough to
        curse you back?

OLD MAN. Doctor, please be quick and do whatever
        must be done for him.

Don't you see the man's insane?

DOCTOR.          I think the wisest thing for you's to

Have the man delivered to my office.

OLD MAN.                    Do you think?

DOCTOR.                              Of course.

There I'll treat him pursuant to diagnosis.

OLD MAN.                    As you say.

DOCTOR [*to* MENAECHMUS]. Yes, I'll have you
        drinking hellebore for twenty

days or so.                                          950

MENAECHMUS. Then I'll have *you* beaten hanging
        upside down for thirty days.

DOCTOR [*to* OLD MAN]. Go and call for men who
        can deliver him.

OLD MAN. How many men?

DOCTOR. From the way he's acting, I'd say four, none
        less could do the job.

OLD MAN [*exiting*]. They'll be here. You watch him,
        Doctor.

DOCTOR [*anxious to retreat*].          No, I think I'd best
        go home.

Preparations are in order for the case. You get the slaves.

Have them carry him to me.

OLD MAN.                    I will.

DOCTOR.                    I'm going now.

OLD MAN.                              Goodbye.

MENAECHMUS. Doctor's gone, father-in-law's gone.
        I'm now alone. By Jupiter!—

What does all this mean? Why do these men insist
        that I'm insane?

Really, I have not been sick a single day since I've
        been born.

Nor am I insane, nor have I punched or fought with
        anyone.                                          960

Healthy, I see healthy people, only talk with folks
        I know.

Maybe those who wrongly say I'm mad are really mad
        themselves.

What should I do now? My wife won't let me home, as
        I would like.

[*Pointing to* EROTIUM's *house*] No one will admit me
        there.

All's well—well out of hand, that is.

Here I'm stuck. At least by night—I think—they'll let
    me in my house.
[MENAECHMUS *sits dejectedly in front of his
house, all wrapped up in his troubles*]

**From the other side of the stage, enter MESSENIO
singing about How to Succeed in Slavery**

MESSENIO. If you should seek the proof of whether
    someone's slave is good,
See, does he guard his master's interest, serve right to
    the letter
When Master is away—the way he should
If Master were at hand—or even better.
For if the slave is worthy, and he's well brought up,
He'll care to keep his shoulders empty—not to fill
970    his cup.
His master will reward him. Let the worthless slave
    be told
The lowly, lazy louts get whips and chains,
And millstones, great starvation, freezing cold.
The price for all their misbehaviors: pains.
I therefore fully fear this fate and very gladly
Remain determined to be good—so I won't turn
    out badly.
I'd so much rather be bawled out than sprawled out on
    a pillory,
I'd so much rather eat what's cooked than have some
    work cooked up for me.
So I follow Master's orders, never argue
980    or protest.
Let the others do it their way; I obey; for me, that's
    best…
But I haven't much to fear; the time is near for
    something nice.
My master will reward his slave for 'thinking with his
    back'—and thinking twice.

**Enter OLD MAN, *leading four burly servants***

OLD MAN. Now, by all the gods and men, I bid you all
990    obey my orders.
Be most careful so you'll follow what I've ordered and
    will order.
Have that man picked up aloft, and carried to the doc-
    tor's office.
That's unless you're not a bit concerned about your
    back and limbs.

Every man beware. Don't pay attention to his threats
    of violence.
But why just stand? Why hesitate? It's time to lift the
    man aloft!
[*Not very brave himself*] And I'll head for the doctor's
    office. I'll be there
    when you arrive.
MENAECHMUS [*notices the charging mob*]. I'm dead!
    What's this? I wonder
why these men are rushing swiftly toward me?
Hey, men, what do you want? What are you after?
    Why surround me now?
            [*They snatch up MENAECHMUS*]
Where are you snatching me and taking me? Won't
    someone help me, please?
O citizens of Epidamnus, rescue me! [*to slaves*] Please
    let me go!                                        1000
MESSENIO. By the immortal gods, what am I seeing
    with my very eyes?
Some unknown men are lifting Master in the air,
    outrageously!
MENAECHMUS. Won't someone dare to help?
MESSENIO. Me, me! I'll dare to help with derring-do!
O citizens of Epidamnus, what a dirty deed to Master!
Do peaceful towns allow a free-born tourist to be
    seized in daylight?
[*To slaves*] You let him go!
MENAECHMUS [*to MESSENIO*]. Whoever you may
    be, please help me out!
Don't allow this awful outrage to be perpetrated on me.
MESSENIO. Why, of course I'll help, and hustle hur-
    riedly to your defense.
Never would I let you down. I'd rather let myself down
    first.                                            1010
[*To MENAECHMUS*] Grab that fellow's eye—the one
    who's got you by the
        shoulder now.
I can plough the other guys and plant a row of fists
    in them.
[*To slaves*] Hercules, you'll lose an awful lot by taking
    him. Let go!
                [*A wild mêlée ensues*]
MENAECHMUS [*while fighting, to MESSENIO*] Hey,
    I've got his eye.
MESSENIO. Then make the socket in his head appear!
Evil people! People snatchers! Bunch of pirates!
SLAVES [*together*]. Woe is us!
Hercules! No—please!

MESSENIO.          Let go!

MENAECHMUS.          What sort of handiwork
is this?
Face a festival of fists.

MESSENIO.          Go on, be gone, and go to hell!
[*Kicking the slowest slave*] You take that as your
reward for being last to get away.
[*They are all gone.* MESSENIO *takes a deep breath of
satisfaction*]
Well, I've really made my mark—on every face I've
faced today.
Pollux, Master, didn't I come just in time to bring you
1020    aid!

MENAECHMUS. Whoever you are, young man, I hope
the gods will always
bring you blessings.
If it hadn't been for you, I'd not have lived to see the
sunset.

MESSENIO. If that's true, by Pollux, then do right by
me and free me, Master.

MENAECHMUS. Free you? I?

MESSENIO.          Of course. Because I saved you,
Master.

MENAECHMUS.               Listen here, you're
Wand'ring from the truth—

MESSENIO.               I wander?

MENAECHMUS.     Yes, I swear by Father Jove
I am not your master.

MESSENIO [*stunned*].          Why proclaim such
things?

MENAECHMUS.               But it's no lie.
Never did a slave of mine serve me as well as you
just did.

MESSENIO. If you're so insistent and deny I'm yours,
then I'll go free.

MENAECHMUS. Hercules, as far as I'm concerned, be
free. Go where you'd like.

MESSENIO.          Am I really authorized?

MENAECHMUS. If I've authority for
1030    you.

MESSENIO [*dialogue with himself*]. 'Greetings,
patron.'— 'Ah, Messenio, the
fact that you're now free
Makes me very glad.'—'Well, I believe that's true.' [*To*
MENAECHMUS]
But, patron dear,
You can have authority no less than when I was a slave.
I'll be glad to live with you, and when you go, go home
with you.

MENAECHMUS [*doesn't want some strange person in his
house*]. Not at all,
no thank you.

MESSENIO [*jubilant*]. Now I'll get our baggage at
the inn—
And, of course, the purse with all our money's sealed
up in the trunk
With our travel cash. I'll bring it to you.

MENAECHMUS [*eyes lighting up at this*]. Yes! Go
quickly, quickly!

MESSENIO. I'll return it just exactly as you gave it to
me. Wait right here.
[MESSENIO *dashes off toward the harbor*]

MENAECHMUS [*soliloquizing*]. What unworldly
wonders have occurred
today in wondrous ways:
People claim I'm not the man I am and keep me from
their houses.                                                                    1040
Then this fellow said he was my slave—and that I set
him free!
Then he says he'll go and bring a wallet full of
money to me.
If he does, I'll tell him he can go quite freely where
he'd like—
That's so when he's sane again he won't demand the
money back.
[*Musing more*] Father-in-law and doctor said I was
insane. How very strange.
All this business seems to me like nothing other than
a dream.
Now I'll go and see this harlot, though she's in a huff
with me.
Maybe I'll convince her to return the dress, which I'll
take home.
                              [*He enters* EROTIUM'*s house*]

**Enter MENAECHMUS II *and* MESSENIO**

MENAECHMUS II [*angry with* MESSENIO]. Effrontery
in front of me! You
dare to claim we've seen each other                                1050
Since I gave you orders that we'd meet back here?

MESSENIO.               But didn't I just
Snatch and rescue you from those four men who carried you aloft
Right before this house? You called on all the gods
and men for aid.
I came running, snatched you from them, though with
fists they fought me back.

For this service, since I saved your life, you made a
    free man of me.
[*Ruefully*] Now just when I said I'd get the cash and
    baggage, you sped up and
Ran ahead to meet me, and deny you've done the
    things you've done.
MENAECHMUS II. Free? I said you could go free?
MESSENIO.       For sure.
MENAECHMUS II.      Now look, for super-sure
I would rather make myself a slave than ever set
    you free.

**MENAECHMUS I** *is pushed by* **EROTIUM** *out of
her house*

MENAECHMUS I. If you would like to swear by your
    two eyes, go right
1060    ahead, but still
You'll never prove that I absconded with your dress
    and bracelet—[*door slams*] hussy!
MESSENIO [*suddenly seeing double*]. By the gods,
    what do I see?
MENAECHMUS II. What do you see?
MESSENIO.      Why—your reflection!
MENAECHMUS II. What?
MESSENIO.      Your very image just as like your-
self as it could be.
MENAECHMUS II. Pollux—he's not unlike
    me...I notice...similarities.
MENAECHMUS I [*to* MESSENIO]. Hey, young man,
    hello! You saved my life—whoever you may be.
MESSENIO. You, young man, if you don't mind, would
    you please tell me your name?
MENAECHMUS I. Nothing you could ask would be
    too much since you have helped me so.
My name is Menaechmus.
MENAECHMUS II.      Oh, by Pollux, so is mine
    as well!
MENAECHMUS I. Syracuse-Sicilian—
MENAECHMUS II.      That's my city, that's my
    country too!
MENAECHMUS I.      What is this I hear?
MENAECHMUS II. Just what is true.
MESSENIO [*to* MENAECHMUS II]. I know you—
1070    *you're* my master!
[*To audience*] I belong to this man though I thought
    that I belonged to that man.
[*To* MENAECHMUS I, *the wrong man*] Please excuse
    me, sir, if I unknowingly spoke foolishly.

For a moment I imagined he was you—and gave him
    trouble.
MENAECHMUS II. Madness, nothing but! [*To*
    MESSENIO] Don't you recall
    that we were both together,
Both of us got off the ship today?
MESSENIO [*thinking, realizing*]. That's right. You're
    very right.
*You're* my master. [*To* MENAECHMUS I] Find another
    slave, farewell. [*To* MENAECMUS II] And
    you, hello!
[*Pointing to* MENAECHMUS II] Him, I say, this man's
    Menaechmus.
MENAECHMUS I.      So am I!
MENAECHMUS II.          What joke is this?
    You're Menaechmus?
MENAECHMUS I.      That I say I am. My father's
    name was Moschus.
MENAECHMUS II.      *You're* the son of my own
    father?
MENAECHMUS I.      No, the son of *my* own father.
I'm not anxious to appropriate your father or to steal
    him from you.    1080
MESSENIO. Gods in heaven, grant me now that hope
    unhoped-for I suspect.
For, unless my mind has failed me, these two men are
    both twin brothers.
Each man claims the selfsame fatherland and father
    for his own.
I'll call Master over. O Menaechmus—
MENAECHMUS I and II [*together*]. Yes?
MESSENIO.          Not both of you.
Which of you two traveled with me on the ship?
MENAECHMUS I.          It wasn't me.
MENAECHMUS II. Me it was.
MESSENIO.      Then you I want. Step over here
    [*motioning*].
MENAECHMUS II [*following* MESSENIO *to a corner*].
    I've stepped. What's up?
MESSENIO. That man there is either one great faker or
    your lost twin brother.
Never have I seen two men more similar than you
    two men:
Water isn't more like water, milk's not more alike
    to milk
Than that man is like to you. And what's more he
    named your father.    1090
And your fatherland. It's best to go and question him
    still further.

MENAECHMUS II. Hercules, you do advise me well.
I'm very grateful to you.
Please work on, by Hercules. I'll make you free if you
discover
That man is my brother.
MESSENIO.           Oh, I hope so.
MENAECHMUS II.               And I hope so too.
MESSENIO [*to* MENAECHMUS I]. Sir, I do believe
you've just asserted that you're named Menaechmus.
MENAECHMUS I. That is so.
MESSENIO.        Well, his name is Menaechmus,
too. You also said
You were born in Sicily at Syracuse. Well, so was he.
Moschus was your father, so you said. That was his
father, too.
Both of you can do yourselves a favor—and help me
as well.
MENAECHMUS I. Anything you ask me I'll comply
1100    with, I'm so grateful to you.
Treat me just as if I were your purchased slave—
although I'm free.
MESSENIO. It's my hope to prove you are each other's
brothers, twins in fact,
Born of the selfsame mother, selfsame father, on the
selfsame day.
MENAECHMUS I. Wonder-laden words. Oh, would
you could make all your
words come true.
        MESSENIO. Well, I can. But, both of you, just
        give replies to what I ask you.
MENAECHMUS I . Ask away. I'll answer. I won't hide a
single thing I know.
MESSENIO. Is your name Menaechmus?
MENAECHMUS I.          Absolutely.
MESSENIO [*to* MENAECHMUS II].       Is it yours as
well?
MENAECHMUS II. Yes.
MESSENIO.       You said your father's name was
Moschus.
MENAECHMUS I.        Yes.
MENAECHMUS II.          The same for me.
MESSENIO. And you're Syracusan?
MENAECHMUS I.           Surely.
MESSENIO [*to* MENAECHMUS I]. You?
MENAECHMUS II. You know I am, of course.
MESSENIO. Well, so far the signs are good. Now turn
1110    your minds to further questions.
    [*To* MENAECHMUS I] What's the final memory you
    carry from your native land?

MENAECHMUS I [*reminiscing*]. With my father…vis-
iting Tarentum for the fair.
Then after that…
Wandering among the people, far from
Father…Being snatched—
MENAECHMUS II [*bursting with joy*]. Jupiter above,
now help me—!
MESSENIO [*officiously*]. What's the shouting? You
shut up.
[*Turning back to* MENAECHMUS I] Snatched from
father and from fatherland,
    about how old were you?
MENAECHMUS I. Seven or so. My baby teeth had
barely started to fall out.
After that, I never saw my father.
MESSENIO.             No? Well, tell me this:
At the time how many children did he have?
MENAECHMUS I.          I think just two.
MESSENIO. Which were you, the older or the
younger?
MENAECHMUS I.         Neither, we were equal.
MESSENIO. Do explain.
MENAECHMUS I.       We were both twins.
MENAECHMUS II [*ecstatic*]. Oh—all the gods are
with me now!                               1120
MESSENIO [*sternly, to* MENAECHMUS II]. Interrupt
and I'll be quiet.
MENAECHMUS II [*obedient*].        I'll be quiet.
MESSENIO [*to* MENAECHMUS I].       Tell me this:
Did you both have just one name?
MENAECHMUS I. Oh, not at all. My name is mine,
As it is today—Menaechmus. Brother's name was
Sosicles.
MENAECHMUS II [*mad with joy*]. Yes, I recognize the
signs. I can't keep from embracing you!
Brother, dear twin brother, greetings! I am he—I'm
Sosicles!
MENAECHMUS I. How is it you afterward received
the name Menaechmus, then?
MENAECHMUS II. When we got the news that you
had wandered off away from Father
And that you were kidnapped by an unknown man,
and Father died,
Grandpa changed my name. The name you used to
have he gave to me.
MENAECHMUS I. Yes, I do believe it's as you say.
    [*Goes to embrace him,
        suddenly stops*] But tell me this.        1130
MENAECHMUS II.        Just ask.

MENAECHMUS I. What was Mother's name?

MENAECHMUS II.            Why, Teuximarcha.

MENAECHMUS I.            That's correct, it fits.

Unexpectedly I greet you, see you after so much time!

MENAECHMUS II. Brother, now I find you after so
   much suffering and toil,

Searching for you, now you're found, and I'm so very,
   very glad.

                        [*They embrace*]

MESSENIO [*to* MENAECHMUS II]. That's the reason
   why the slut could call you
     by your rightful name,

Thinking you were he, I think, when she invited you
   to dinner.

MENAECHMUS I. Yes, by Pollux, I had ordered dinner
   for myself today,

Hidden from my wife—from whom I filched a dress a
   while ago—and

Gave it to her. [*Indicates* EROTIUM's *house*]

MENAECHMUS II. Could you mean this dress I'm
   holding, brother dear?

MENAECHMUS I. That's the one. How did you get it?

1140  MENAECHMUS II.            Well, the slut led me to
   dinner.

There she claimed I gave it to her. Wonderfully have
   I just dined,

Wined as well as concubined, of dress and gold
   I robbed her blind.

MENAECHMUS I. O by Pollux, I rejoice if you had fun
   because of me!

When she asked you in to dinner, she believed that
   you were me.

MESSENIO [*impatient for himself*]. Is there any reason
   to delay the freedom
     that you promised?

MENAECHMUS I. Brother, what he asks is very fair
   and fine. Please do it for me.

MENAECHMUS II [*to* MESSENIO, *the formula*]. 'Be
   thou free.'

MENAECHMUS I. The fact you're free now makes me
   glad, Messenio.

MESSENIO [*broadly hinting for some cash reward*].
   Actually, I need more
     facts, supporting facts to keep me free.    1150

MENAECHMUS II [*ignoring* MESSENIO, *to his
   brother*]. Since our dreams have
          come about exactly as we wished, dear
          brother,

Let us both return to our homeland.

MENAECHMUS I.            Brother, as you wish.

I can hold an auction and sell off whatever I have
   here.

Meanwhile, let's go in.

MENAECHMUS II. That's fine.

MESSENIO [*to* MENAECHMUS I].            May I request
   a favor of you?

MENAECHMUS I. What?

MESSENIO.            Please make me do the
   auctioneering.

MENAECHMUS I.            Done.

MESSENIO.      All right. Then please inform me:
   When should I announce the auction for?

MENAECHMUS I.    Let's say—a week from now.
    [*The brothers go into*
      MENAECHMUS's *house*,
    *leaving* MESSENIO *alone on stage*]

MESSENIO [*announcing*]. In the morning in a week
   from now we'll have Menaechmus's auction.

Slaves and goods, his farm and city house, his everything will go.

Name your prices, if you've got the cash in hand, it all
   will go.

Yes, and if there's any bidder for the thing—his wife
   will go.    1160

Maybe the entire auction will enrich us—who
   can tell?

For the moment, dear spectators, clap with vigor. Fare
   ye well!

## AFTERWORD

It has always been the case that a successful comic formula will be recycled repeatedly, and Plautus's
popularity ensured that his plays would be performed often in the years after his death. One consequence of this history of performance is that the text that we read differs from the original scripts in
ways that cannot always be determined. In the case of the *Casina,* the prologue preserves not only
Plautus's original lines but also some that must have been composed by a director for a performance

around the middle of the second century B.C. Another problem for Plautus's literary reputation was the large number of imitations his work attracted. In around 100 B.C., the scholar Lucius Aelius Stilo certified only 25 plays as authentically by Plautus, but by the middle of the second century A.D., Aulus Gellius reports that there were 130 plays circulating under his name. It is often noted that after Plautus and Terence there were no great comic playwrights in Rome, but the large number of the works that could be mistaken for Plautus implies a lively theatrical culture with writers talented enough to be taken for the master. It was probably the great first-century B.C. scholar Varro who established the corpus of Plautine comedies that we know today when he determined that only 21 of the plays then in circulation were certainly authentic, a number that corresponds—hardly by coincidence—to the plays surviving in the manuscript tradition. Varro did not doubt that there were other Plautine plays making the rounds, but without his imprimatur of authenticity they were eventually lost.

While Plautus's comedies continued to be performed, there was also a growing audience for his works in books. When Cicero ranks Plautus's brand of humor on a par with that not only of Athenian Old Comedy but also of Socratic philosophers, describing it as "elegant, urbane, clever, and witty" (*On Duties* 1.104), he is surely thinking of the experience of *reading* scripts of Plautus, not just viewing his plays in performance. It was at roughly this time in the middle of the first century B.C. that Cicero's slightly older contemporary Varro was working on Plautus and Roman comedy. Varro's high opinion of Plautus might well have secured him a place in the school curriculum, but since Varro's works have been lost, it is difficult to gauge exactly how he rated him. In one fragment in which he appears to be ranking the classic comic poets of the previous century (*Menippean Satires* fr. 399), he writes that "Caecilius claims the palm for plot, Terence for character, and Plautus for dialogue." And Varro is the source for what he vouched to be Plautus's own epitaph in limping iambics:

> Comedy mourned, after Plautus met his death.
> The stage was deserted: then Laughter, Play and Jest,
> And Meters without measure at once and all together wept.

If that was the judgment of the generation of Cicero and Varro, a countervailing view took shape soon after, as represented by Horace, who contradicts this assessment of Plautus in his *Art of Poetry*, faulting Plautus on every count, meter, wit, and style (270–74):

> But your ancestors had praise for Plautine rhythm
> And wit, admiring both too indulgently,
> Not to say stupidly. That is, if you and I know
> How to distinguish between elegant and inelegant wit,
> Or we can detect a proper beat by tapping a finger.

Because Terence was read in the schools, his survival was more or less assured, but, for example, Caecilius, whom Varro and Cicero had also admired, and all the other comic poets were lost. Only Plautus among them retained sufficient popularity to remain in the hands of readers in spite of the strictures of the more severe critics in the first century A.D., like Quintilian, who did not have much time for Roman comedy.

Readers with no particular stylistic axe to grind were still finding pleasure in Plautus, among them the growing number of women readers. Pliny the Younger complimented the epistolary style of a friend's wife, saying that he had thought he was "reading Plautus or Terence in prose" (*Letters* 1.16.6). In the second-century A.D. revival of enthusiasm for earlier Latin literature, moreover, Plautus was, in fact, all the rage. The traits that had kept Plautus from becoming a standard author in the schools—chiefly linguistic features that struck readers as old-fashioned and a comic style that was considered too crude and unrefined—only endeared him to an age in which Fronto, the tutor and correspondent of the emperor Marcus Aurelius, would recommend

Plautus and Ennius first and foremost as required reading. The dilettante Aulus Gellius took a distinct interest in Plautus, citing him repeatedly while ignoring the likes of Horace and Ovid. Gellius calls him "the glory of the Latin language" (*Attic Nights* 19.8.6) and "a man of the first rank when it comes to the Latin language and verbal eloquence" (1.17.4). It was probably about this time, or perhaps in the following century, when an unidentified aficionado had the edition of the twenty-one Varronian plays prepared in codex form (i.e., no longer on papyrus rolls) that became the ancestor of all the surviving manuscripts of Plautus. It was perhaps in this edition that St. Jerome still found Plautus hard to resist (*Letters* 22.30), but not long afterward Plautus's plays dropped out of the hands of readers. In the latter part of the sixth century, an Irish monk at the monastery of Bobbio thought it more useful to have a copy of the *Book of Kings* in the Vulgate version, so he reused a manuscript of Plautus for his new text. It was not until the nineteenth century that this manuscript of the Vulgate was discovered to be a palimpsest, or reused manuscript. The German scholar Wilhelm Studemund sacrificed his sight while laboring to recover the Plautine scripts that lay underneath the later writing.

Most medieval manuscripts contained only eight of the plays, probably as a result of an earlier manuscript having been split in two to facilitate the process of copying. So when Petrarch read Plautus, for example, this was all he had available to inspire his own attempt to write comedy in Latin—ironically enough, the play that he wrote, *Philologia,* is also now lost. In 1429 the humanist Niccolò di Treviri brought to Rome a manuscript containing twelve plays that had been unknown to the Middle Ages, and the Plautine revival began in earnest. The first printed edition appeared in 1472, and soon afterward Plautus's plays were being performed onstage. Under the sponsorship of Pomponio Leto (1425–98) *The Pot of Gold* was seen again in Rome in 1484. During the elaborate wedding celebration of Lucretia Borgia in 1502, five plays of Plautus were performed on five consecutive days, and in the same year Pope Alexander VI, Lucretia's father, was treated to a performance of *The Brothers Menaechmus* in the Vatican.

During the century that followed, hundreds of comedies inspired by Plautus were written throughout Europe not only in Latin but also, increasingly, in the vernacular languages as well. The earliest surviving representative in English is *Ralph Roister Doister* (1552), written by the schoolmaster Nicholas Udall, drawing largely on Plautus's *The Braggart Soldier* as a model. The best-known adaptation of Plautus in English is Shakespeare's *Comedy of Errors* (1594), based on *The Brothers Menaechmus*. In adapting Plautus, Shakespeare goes one, or rather two, better, by introducing a second pair of twins as servants to the twin brothers, thus multiplying the opportunities for comic confusion. Shakespeare had certainly studied both Plautus and Terence in the original language in school, so he was quite familiar with Roman comic conventions, including the practice known by the Romans as *contaminatio,* or the mixing of plots. He introduces a scene from the *Amphitruo* into his adaptation, making one of the brothers endure a lockout by his wife, like the lead character in Plautus's play.

The roster of comic playwrights who were influenced by Plautus is long and distinguished, including Calderón, Corneille, Molière, and Mozart's librettist, Da Ponte. Interest in Plautus declined again in the late nineteenth and early twentieth centuries, only to experience a brilliant revival on the New York stage, with the Broadway opening of *A Funny Thing Happened on the Way to the Forum* in 1962. With music and lyrics by Stephen Sondheim and a script by Burt Shevelove and Larry Gelbart, the play combines elements from a number of Plautus's plays, chiefly *Pseudolus, The Braggart Soldier,* and *The Haunted House,* in a rollicking romp through ancient Rome. The play won several awards for its initial production and has been successfully revived several times since then, both on and off Broadway. In 1966 a film version was produced by Richard Lester, with several members of the original cast. The film, too, was a commercial success, and when it was made available in recorded formats, it became the principal vehicle by which Plautus was reintroduced into the curriculum in college and university courses on ancient comedy.

# POLYBIUS

(ca. 200–118 B.C.)

The Romans conquered Greece in the first half of the second century B.C. By then, the classical age of Greece was long over. The Homeric poems had been written down at least five hundred years before; the Persians had been repulsed at Marathon and Salamis in the early fifth century, the century that saw Athens reach the height of its political power and intellectual creativity, with the building of the Parthenon and the heyday of Athenian tragedy; between 336 and 323 B.C., when he died in Babylon at the age of thirty-three, Alexander the Great of Macedonia conquered his vast eastern empire; his successors divided the empire among themselves, with the centers of power shifting far from the Greek mainland to Pergamum, Antioch, and, above all, to the Ptolemaic capital at Alexandria in Egypt. The once dominant city states in Greece—Sparta, Athens, Thebes—were in eclipse, and federations of smaller states had arisen, the Aetolian League in central and western Greece, and the Achaean League in the central and northern Peloponnese. It was these federations, along with the still powerful kingdom of Macedon, that faced the Romans, who turned their attention to Greece after their victory in the Second Punic War (218–202 B.C.).

Much of what we know about the Second Punic War and the Roman conquest of Greece is derived, either directly or through other writers, from one historian, Polybius, who is the first Greek writer to tell us anything substantial about Rome. Writing in Greek from the vantage point of Rome, he represents an important stage in the development of the multicultural world of Roman literature. Apart from a few slight and sporadic references in third-century B.C. texts, Rome might as well not have existed as far as earlier Greek writers are concerned. Polybius is not only the first Greek to tell us about Rome but also predates all surviving historical texts written by Romans. This special prominence is enhanced by his excellence as a historian: he may not be on quite the same level as Thucydides or Tacitus, but he writes with authority, objectivity, and intelligence, qualities that he himself repeatedly complains are conspicuously absent in most historians.

Polybius was born sometime between 208 and 200 B.C., at Megalopolis, in the center of the Peloponnese and one of the most prominent states in the Achaean League. His father, Lycortas, had several times been the annually elected leader of the league, and Polybius himself seemed set to follow such a career. He was given the honor of carrying the ashes of Philopoemen, the founder of the league, at his funeral in 182; he was appointed to a diplomatic mission to Ptolemy V of Egypt in 180; most significantly, he was elected deputy leader of the league in 170/169. In 168, however, the Romans conclusively defeated King Perseus of Macedonia at the Battle of Pydna. Polybius's father had played a leading role in keeping the Achaean League out of that conflict. When, therefore, the Romans took a thousand hostages from the league, partly as punishment for its neutrality, and partly to ensure against further wars in Greece, it was hardly surprising that Polybius was among those transported to Italy. Nearly all the hostages were detained in towns throughout Italy, where they stayed until 151, when those who were still alive, fewer than three hundred, were permitted to return to Greece.

Polybius himself, however, was sent to Rome, where, as a well-educated Greek aristocrat, he easily found a niche in the higher echelons of Roman society. Aemilius Paullus, the victor at Pydna, appointed him tutor to his two sons, with the younger of whom he formed a lifelong friendship. This friendship is very significant, for that Roman, Publius Cornelius Scipio Aemilianus Africanus Numantinus, was not only the son of the conqueror of Greece but also the adopted son of the eldest son of Scipio Africanus, who had defeated Hannibal, and he himself would destroy Carthage in 146 B.C. and establish Roman rule in Spain in the decade that followed. Polybius was with Scipio in the ruins of Carthage and probably also in Spain, at the capture of Numantia, the final stronghold of Spanish resistance, in 133. He was therefore ideally placed to record the momentous Roman conquests of this period.

Since the Roman Empire reached its greatest extent in the second century A.D., and since the first centuries B.C. and A.D. are so much more richly documented than is the second century B.C., there is a tendency nowadays to understate the importance of this earlier period, but Polybius was by no means alone in his view of the importance of the events in his lifetime. Scipio and Lucius Mummius Achaicus, the generals who destroyed Carthage and Corinth, respectively, in 146 B.C., thus establishing Rome's unchallenged control over the Mediterranean, were appointed censors together in 142, to review the Roman state. Scipio is said to have altered the wording of the census's concluding prayer (a very surprising step, given the highly conservative nature of Roman rituals): instead of praying that the gods should improve and extend the prosperity of the Roman people, he observed that Rome's rule was extensive enough, and prayed that the gods should keep Rome safe forever (Valerius Maximus, *Memorable Deeds and Sayings* 4.1.10).

In the early 140s B.C., for obscure reasons, the Achaean League took on Rome in a war it could not hope to win. In 146, therefore, the year Carthage fell, the Romans also destroyed Corinth, the most prosperous city in Greece, and finally took over all of Greece. In the aftermath of this unusually bloody event, Polybius was appointed by the Roman Senate to oversee the settlement of a pro-Roman administration in the various Greek cities. Several communities are known to have erected statues in his honor, so we may infer that he succeeded in ensuring that Roman rule was not imposed too harshly. He is unlikely to have been a mere puppet in the hands of the Romans, but his long and intimate experience of Roman political and military power will have convinced him that Greek freedom was a thing of the past, and that Greece must adapt to its future within the Roman Empire. The positive view of Polybius as an active politician is clearly expressed by Pausanias in commenting on a memorial to him still standing in his hometown of Megalopolis three hundred years later (*Guide to Greece* 8.30):

> On the memorial are verses stating that he wandered over every land and sea, and that he became an ally of the Romans, and restrained their anger against the Greek people…Whenever the Romans followed Polybius's advice, things went well for them, but it is said that, when they did not follow his advice, they made errors.

Few details are known of Polybius's later years. He is said to have died falling from his horse at the age of eighty-two, sometime around 120 B.C.

Apart from his *Histories*, Polybius at various times wrote several other, now lost, works: a biography of the Achaean statesman and soldier Philopoemen, which was used by Plutarch in his biography nearly three hundred years later; a monograph on Greek and Roman military tactics, a subject to which Polybius pays particularly close attention in the *Histories*; a report on the equatorial regions (he sailed down the west coast of Africa); and, finally, an account of the Romans' war in Spain in the 130s. Polybius's reputation depends, however, on his *Histories,* of which perhaps less than a quarter survives. Books 1 through 5 are the only ones still complete, most of the other books being known only through epitomes and excerpts of widely varying scale. (Books 17 and 40 are entirely lost.) Polybius is undoubtedly a fine historian, but he was not always fully appreciated in antiquity. Dionysius of Halicarnassus, who, like Polybius, was a Greek subject of the empire who greatly admired the Romans, nevertheless admitted that his style was unattractive, making it uncongenial to read right through the whole work (*On the Composition of Words* 4.110). This lack of favor and the growing tendency to read lengthy texts in excerpted form (Polybius's *Histories* will have been about five times as long as that of Thucydides, his most important model) are the main causes of the loss of so much of the work.

Polybius originally intended to give an account of the events of the years 220 to 168 B.C., chronicling the Romans' defeat of the Carthaginians in the Second Punic War (218–202 B.C.) through to their conquest of Greece, culminating in the Battle of Pydna in 168 (1.1):

> Is there anyone on earth who is so narrow-minded or uninquisitive that he could fail to want to know how, and thanks to what kind of political system, almost the entire known world was conquered and brought under a single empire, the empire of the Romans, in less than fifty-three years—an unprecedented event? Or again, is there anyone who is so passionately attached to some other marvel or matter that he could consider it more important than knowing about this?

Subsequently, however, he broadened the scope of the work, to begin with the First Punic War (264–241 B.C.), and to continue on to 146, the epoch-making year that saw the destruction of Carthage and Corinth. Whereas, however, this extension is natural enough per se, it is readily apparent that Polybius does not introduce it in terms of military conquest, but rather of political adjustments, in which he himself had a major role to play (3.4):

> As far as this period is concerned, the scale and the extraordinariness of the events that took place then, and most importantly the fact that I myself witnessed very many of them, mean that I had no choice but to write about it as if I were making a fresh start. In fact, I was not only an eyewitness, but a participant in some of these events and responsible for others.

Since he is giving an account of the rise of Rome to dominance over the whole Mediterranean world, Polybius is able to claim that he is writing universal history, not simply, as earlier historians had done, recounting events in one particular region.

The first two books are introductory, setting the scene with an account of the First Punic War (264–241 B.C.), Carthage's appallingly gruesome wars with its mercenaries (not to be read by the squeamish!), early Roman incursions into Greek affairs, and the Celtic invasions of northern Italy. Thereafter, Polybius frames his history in accordance with the Greek system, to start at the 140th Olympiad (220–216 B.C.), drawing together events within that period from each region of the Mediterranean, usually progressing from west to east.

The Second Punic War, otherwise known as the Hannibalic War, is perhaps the most famous of all Rome's wars, an uncompromising struggle with Rome's greatest and most dangerous rival. It began with Hannibal's epic trek from Spain, mostly through hostile territory, across the Pyrenees, the Rhone, and then, of course, the Alps. The Carthaginians won several rapid and sensational victories, at the river Trebia late in 218, at Lake Trasimene in 217, and, most devastatingly, at Cannae in 216. Roman losses at Cannae are not precisely known, but it was probably the most devastating massacre ever suffered by a Western army in a single day. The armies of

**Figure 4: J. M. W. Turner,** *Hannibal Crossing the Alps*
For Turner, who first exhibited this painting in 1812, Hannibal's crossing of the Alps had resonances with contemporary events and the wars with Napoleon. He concentrates not on the figure of the general, but on the awesome force of nature over which he must triumph.

both consuls were all but wiped out, and Rome was at Hannibal's mercy. If he had marched straight to Rome after the battle, nothing could have stopped him. Fatefully, perhaps not quite able to comprehend the scale and significance of his victory, he gave his troops a day to rest and recover. His cavalry commander begged to be allowed to ride ahead, guaranteeing that within five days Hannibal would be dining on the Capitol; when Hannibal refused to give permission, he retorted, "The gods have not given everything to any single person; you know how to gain the victory, but you don't know how to exploit it" (Livy, *From the Foundation of the City* 22.51). Hannibal was to remain in Italy for thirteen more years, a constant threat to Rome's stability, until a Roman counterinvasion of Africa forced his recall for the final showdown at Zama in 202, where the Romans ended the Carthaginian threat once and for all.

Nearly all Roman writers are indebted, to a greater or lesser degree, to Greek models, and nearly all Greek works surviving from the centuries after the Roman conquest of the Greek world are written with a detailed awareness of Rome. Polybius, however, stands alone in writing as a Greek primarily for Greek readers with relatively little understanding of Rome and its institutions, or indeed of the wider, non-Greek, world in general. He feels no need to include background material on the dynasties that ruled the Greek world, the Antigonids of Macedonia, the Seleucids of Syria, and the Ptolemies of Egypt—important figures in his world that we nowadays find comparatively unfamiliar.

On the other hand, as he makes clear at the outset (1.3), he includes information about Rome that later writers, whether Roman or Greek, normally take for granted. Roman readers would not need to be told about, for example, the powers granted to a dictator in Rome to counter a national emergency (3.87), or the layout of Campania, just south of Rome (3.91), or the organization and deployment of the Roman legions (3.107). There is a rather more extensive description of north Italian topography for the benefit of his Greek readers at 2.14–16, and a very lengthy discussion of the Roman political and military institutions occupies almost all the surviving portion of Book 6. But Polybius's focus on explaining Rome to Greeks recurs constantly throughout his work. A typical, but particularly memorable, example occurs in his account of the destruction of New Carthage in Spain in 209 B.C., where he speculates on the motivation for Roman terror tactics (10.15):

> When Scipio decided that enough of his troops were in the city, he unleashed the majority of them against the citizens, according to Roman practice, with orders to kill without mercy anyone they came upon, and not to turn to plundering till the signal was given. The reason for this policy is, I think, to inspire terror. This is why, when the Romans take a city, one sees not only human beings slaughtered, but also dogs cut in half and the limbs of other animals hacked off.

During the First Punic War, Marcus Atilius Regulus was captured and taken to Carthage. Later Roman tradition, most notably Horace *Odes* 3.5, casts Regulus as a hero: sent back to Rome to urge the Senate to grant Carthage peace on favorable terms, he speaks against such a deal and returns to Carthage, to face torture and death as a noble and honorable Roman. Polybius knows, or at least says, nothing about any such gallantry (1.35): "Here was a man who, a little earlier, had refused to pity or pardon people in adversity, and now all of a sudden he was being taken to beg those same people for his life." Even when praising the Romans, Polybius is restrained. He singles out Horatius Cocles for his selfless heroism in defending Rome against hopeless odds. Whereas, however, Livy has the gods bring him safely home, swimming across the Tiber in full armor (*From the Foundation of the City* 2.10), in Polybius he sinks and drowns (6.55).

Likewise, Polybius does not color his narrative with the accounts of Carthaginian cruelty that are typical of Roman versions. In describing Hannibal's ingenious extrication of his forces from almost certain annihilation, Livy says (*From the Foundation of the City* 22.13):

> Hannibal was now in danger of being trapped by the Romans, so, after flaying and crucifying the guide, he tied torches to the horns of 2,000 cows and drove them off into the night. Having tricked the Romans into thinking that this was his army on the move, he led his men to safety in the opposite direction.

In Polybius's version of this episode (3.93), which is Livy's model, the same event is narrated without any mention of Hannibal's cruelty to an incompetent guide.

Later Roman accounts of Cannae begrudged Hannibal credit for the brilliant generalship with which he defeated Roman forces that were numerically so vastly superior to his own. Valerius Maximus, for example, claiming that Hannibal forced the Romans to fight with the sun in their eyes, concluded that "Punic valor consisted of tricks, treachery and deceit! That is very definitely the reason why our bravery was foiled: we were cheated rather than defeated" (*Memorable Deeds and Words* 7.4 *ext.* 2). Polybius had said nothing about any such Carthaginian trickery. His version specifically rules out any devious maneuvering to dazzle the Romans (3.114): "Since the Roman army, as I said, faced south and the Carthaginians north, they were neither of them inconvenienced by the rising sun." He does, however, indulge rather surprisingly in such racial stereotyping when he describes as "a truly Punic trick" Hannibal's perfectly reasonable ploy of adopting a variety of wigs to disguise his appearance and thus prevent assassination by his untrustworthy Celtic allies (3.78).

Impartiality is a quality often claimed by historians, but few aspire to it as earnestly as does Polybius. He declares his aspiration most notably in his criticism of the pro-Carthaginian bias of Philinus of Acragas and the pro-Roman bias of Fabius Pictor, the first Roman to write history, though he wrote in Greek (1.14):

Their lives and characters give me no reason to think that they deliberately falsified their accounts, but I do think that they behaved rather like people who are in love, in the sense that, because of their biases and their overriding loyalties, Philinus always has the Carthaginians acting sensibly, honorably, and courageously, and the Romans doing the opposite, while Fabius does the same the other way round. Now, although there is no reason to dispense with such partiality in other areas of life—for instance, loyalty to friends and country are good qualities, as is having the same enemies and friends as one's friends—when a man takes on the role of historian, he must put all such considerations out of his mind: he often has to speak well of his enemies, and even honor them with words of undiluted praise, when their actions demand it; and he often has to challenge and censure his closest friends unforgivingly, when their errors suggest that this is appropriate. An animal is completely useless if it loses its eyesight, and in the same way history without truth has as little educational value as a yarn. That is why a historian should not hesitate either to condemn his friends or praise his enemies, and should not worry about praising and blaming the same people at different times. After all, it is as impossible for men of action to always get things right as it is unlikely that they will constantly go wrong. We have to stand back from their actions and assign the appropriate judgments and opinions in our works of history.

That he is not impervious to personal prejudice is shown by, for example, his hostile attitude to the decadence and despotism of Philip V of Macedonia and his eulogies of Scipio Aemilianus, as a fine warrior and an upholder of the traditional Roman moral code. Nevertheless, Polybius is by and large true to his aspiration to impartiality. That is not to say that he confined himself to a simple narration of facts. He understood with extraordinary clarity the significance of Rome's meteoric rise to supremacy, and his *Histories* is therefore pervaded by his conviction that he should try to persuade his fellow Greeks of the inevitability of Roman rule and the need to acquiesce in it. It was his success in his public life in working toward this same goal, the smooth integration of Greece into the Roman Empire, that inspired many grateful Greek cities to erect statues in his honor.

# THE HISTORIES

## Book 3

*The book opens with an introduction summarizing the main events to be covered (1–5), before moving on to a discussion of the causes leading up the Second Punic War between Rome and Carthage (6–33). Polybius apportions equal shares in the responsibility for the outbreak of hostilities both to the Carthaginians for violating a treaty with Rome and to the Romans for their seizure of Sardinia. Much of the following narrative (34–56) is taken up with Polybius's account of Hannibal's march to Italy and dramatic crossing of the Alps (47–56). Our selection begins with Hannibal reaching Italy and a brief excursus on the subject of geography (57–59).*

[57] My narrative, the generals of both sides, and the war have now reached Italy, but before the action begins I want to say a few words about the governing principles of my history. The point is that, since I very often mention places in Libya and Iberia, some people may wonder why I have not written more about the strait at the Pillars of Heracles, or about the Outer Sea and its distinctive features, or indeed about the tin-mining industry in the British Isles, or about the mining of silver and gold in Iberia itself. These are all topics to which historians devote long excursuses, in which they take issue with one another.

My reason for avoiding these topics is not because I think such matters are irrelevant to history. But, first, I do not want constantly to interrupt my narrative or distract readers from the underlying political purpose; second, rather than mentioning them in scattered asides, it seemed better to assign each of them its own separate place and time and to give as true an account of them as I could. So if in what follows as well I omit such matters, when we come across any such places, this should not occasion surprise: I do so for the reasons I have just given. Any readers who absolutely insist on hearing detailed descriptions of each place as it occurs may not appreciate that they are behaving rather like gourmands at a dinner-party, who sample every available dish, without truly enjoying any of the food at the time and without deriving from it any future benefit in terms of assimilation or nourishment. Quite the opposite, in fact. And the same goes for those who approach reading in a similar manner: they fail to gain any genuine pleasure from it at the time, or the appropriate educational benefit in the long term.

[58] Now, it is undeniable—the main reasons will emerge from what follows—that this aspect of history writing is particularly in need of a rational approach, and of correction in the light of improved information. Nearly all historians, certainly the majority, have tried to describe the locations and distinctive features of places at the extremities of the world known to us. Since these historians were often wrong, it would be altogether remiss of me to keep quiet, but any points I make against them are best made in a coherent fashion, not in asides or in scattered passages. Also, my remarks should not just be critical or deprecatory. It would be better to give credit where credit is due, and to correct their mistakes, knowing that, if they had the advantages we have nowadays, they too would have corrected and altered many of their statements.

Long ago, research into the extremities of the world was rarely undertaken by Greeks, because the attempt stood no chance of success. There were countless risks to sea-travel in those days, and overland journeys were many times more dangerous even than traveling by sea. And suppose, by accident or design, someone reached the limits of the known world: even so, he could not see the project through, because it was usually far from easy to examine things at first hand, due to the fact that those places were either desolate or overrun by barbarians. And reliable information about anything one saw was even harder to come by because of linguistic differences. Finally, even if someone did manage to make himself acquainted with the facts, the hardest thing of all was for any of these eyewitnesses to avoid exaggeration and scorn talk of marvels and monsters; it was almost impossible for them to prefer the truth for its own sake and to give us the facts without embroidering them.

[59] Since in times past it was not just difficult to attain historical truth, but nearly impossible, for the reasons I have given, we should not criticize these writers for their omissions or errors. We should praise and admire them, rather, for the accurate information they *did* manage to obtain, and for advancing our knowledge of such matters at all, given the conditions under which they were working. In our times, however, almost everywhere can be reached by sea or by land: Asia has been opened up by Alexander's empire and everywhere else by Roman supremacy. At the same time, men who are capable of being effective in the world have been freed of the obligation to devote themselves to warfare and statesmanship, and therefore

have the perfect opportunity to investigate and study these matters. Under these circumstances, better and more reliable information about matters that were formerly obscure ought to be available, and that is what I shall attempt to provide, when I find a suitable place in my work for this topic. It will be my intention to give those who are interested in such matters fuller information. That, in fact, is the main reason why I accepted all the hazards of traveling in Libya, Iberia, and Gaul, and sailing the sea that washes the outer coastlines of these places: I wanted to correct the mistaken notions of my predecessors, and give the Greeks reliable information about these parts of the world too.

*The narrative begins (60–75) with Hannibal's operations in Italy in the valley of the river Po after crossing the Alps late in the year 218 B.C. The first encounter with Roman forces took place at an unidentified location near Ticinum, the site of modern Pavia. It was soon followed by a more devastating Roman defeat by the river Trebia, not far from modern Piacenza. The focus shifts briefly then (76) to actions by a Roman expeditionary force in Spain under the command of Gnaeus Cornelius Scipio. Polybius's account of the disastrous Roman defeat at Lake Trasimene, where our selection resumes, is one of the masterpieces of ancient historical narrative. He describes Hannibal's risky march to the south to the region of Etruria (77–79) in the spring of the following year, 217 B.C., and the even rasher response by the Roman general Flaminius (80–82). Hannibal was able to lure Flaminius's forces into battle, and the resulting defeat (83–84) dealt a devastating blow to the Romans on Italian soil. In the aftermath, the Romans elected a dictator to deal with the crisis, Quintus Fabius Maximus, who adopted delaying tactics that did not appeal to public opinion but probably saved the day for Rome (85–94).*

[77] That was how things stood in Iberia. Early in the spring, Gaius Flaminius marched through Etruria with his army and encamped in front of Arretium, while Gnaeus Servilius took his forces to Ariminum, to guard against an enemy invasion from that quarter. Hannibal, who was wintering in Celtic territory, kept the Roman prisoners from the battle in confinement and gave them barely adequate rations. The allied prisoners, however, he treated with consummate kindness right from the start, and then later he convened them and made a speech in which he said that he had come to make war not on them, but on the Romans, on their behalf. If they were sensible,

then, they should seek his friendship, because his primary objective was to restore freedom to the peoples of Italy, and to help them regain the cities and land that the Romans had stolen from them. After delivering this speech, he let them all return to their homes unransomed, in the hope that this would help him win the inhabitants of Italy over to his cause, drive a wedge between them and the Romans, and stir the anger of those who thought that the importance of their cities or ports had been undermined at all by Roman rule.

[78] While Hannibal was in winter quarters, he also resorted to a truly Punic trick. Knowing the duplicity of the Celts, and bearing in mind that his alliance with them was recent, he was worried about an attempt on his life. He had a number of wigs prepared, made to look suitable in all respects for men of different ages, and he wore them one after another, in a random order, while at the same time changing his clothes to match the wigs. Even those who knew him well found it hard to recognize him when he was in disguise, let alone people who just happened to glance at him.

He could see that the Celts would not take kindly to the war continuing in their own territory, and that their anger at the Romans—or rather, the prospect of booty, which weighed more with them—made them look forward restlessly to fighting on enemy territory. So he decided to take to the field as soon as possible and satisfy his troops' desires. As soon as the weather began to improve, he questioned people who were supposed to be well acquainted with the region, and he found out that, while all other routes into enemy territory were long and would offer no concealment from his opponents, there was a short cut into Etruria through the marshes—not an easy route, but one which Flaminius would not expect him to take. Since he was in a sense always naturally inclined towards surprises, this was the route he decided to take.

When word got around the camp that Hannibal was planning to lead them through marshes, everyone was worried at the prospect of quagmires and bogs.
[79] But Hannibal's careful enquiries had shown that the route involved firm ground and little standing water, and so he set out. He had all his best troops, especially the Libyans and Iberians, take up the front of the column, with the baggage interspersed among them. He wanted his men to have access to plenty of supplies for the time being, but in the long term he was completely unconcerned about the baggage train,

because, once they reached enemy territory, if they were defeated they would not need supplies, and if they gained control of the countryside they would not run short of provisions. Behind this division of the army came the Celts, and then the cavalry brought up the rear of the column. He left his brother Mago in charge of the rear, for a number of reasons, but chiefly as a safeguard against the Celts' lack of resolve and tendency to give up in the face of trouble: if they turned back when the going got difficult, Mago could use the cavalry against them and stop them.

The Iberians and the Libyans got through the marshes without too much trouble, as the ground was still fresh and to a man they were tough and inured to such hardship. The Celts, however, found progress difficult: the marshes had been disturbed and trampled into deep pools, and the effort exhausted them and dampened their ardor; this was, after all, the first time they had experienced such miserable conditions. But the cavalry posted behind them prevented them from turning back. The entire army suffered above all from lack of sleep, since they marched non-stop through water for four days and three nights, but the Celts became far more exhausted and debilitated than the rest. Most of the pack animals collapsed and died in the mud, but they did continue to serve human needs in one respect, even in death: by sitting on the animals and the piled-up baggage, men could keep above the water level and sleep for at least a little of each night. Quite a few of the horses also lost their hoofs as a result of constantly walking through mud. Hannibal just made it on the last surviving elephant, but it cost him dearly, since he was suffering from a severe and agonizing eye infection. Later, in fact, he lost the use of one of his eyes, since he had no chance to rest and was in no position to treat the infection.

[80] Against all the odds, Hannibal had crossed the marshes into Etruria, where he found Flaminius encamped in front of Arretium. For the time being, Hannibal stayed where he was, by the marshes, since his troops needed time to recover, and he wanted information about the enemy and about the terrain he would face. He found out that the land before him was rich in booty, and that Flaminius was the kind of man who courted the favor of the mob, an out-and-out demagogue with no talent for the management of warfare in real life, and with excessive self-confidence as well. He came to the conclusion, then, that if he carried straight on and passed close by the Roman camp,

Flaminius would be too anxious about the scorn of the rank-and-file troops to be able to stand by and watch the land being plundered, and too worried not to hurry after him wherever he went, in his eagerness to be personally responsible for victory without waiting for the arrival of his consular colleague. In short, it seemed to him that Flaminius would give him plenty of opportunities for attacking him.

This was all sound, practical thinking on Hannibal's part. [81] Anyone who claims that any aspect of generalship is more important than knowing the character and temperament of the enemy commander certainly does not know what he is talking about. In a fight between individual soldiers, or between one rank and another, winning depends on seeing how to get through to the target—on spotting an exposed or undefended part of the opponent's body. The same goes for those who lead whole armies, though they are concerned not with physical vulnerability, but any mental weakness that the opposing leader displays. Many commanding officers have lost their own lives and caused the utter ruin of their states as a result of complacency and general inertia; many others are so fond of wine that they cannot even get to sleep without drugging themselves with drink; others are so addicted to sex and its attendant derangement that they have been responsible for homes and cities being razed to the ground, and have brought personal disgrace upon themselves by the manner of their deaths.

Cowardice and sluggishness are contemptible enough in private individuals, but they are disastrous for a state as a whole when they are attributes of one of its leaders. A general of this sort makes his troops ineffective, and often exposes his dependants to extreme danger. Then again, impulsiveness, recklessness, irrational ardor, a false conception of one's abilities, and arrogance are characteristics that make a man vulnerable to his enemies and highly dangerous to his friends; such a man reacts too readily to any plot, ambush, or trick. A general is most likely to prevail, then, if he has the ability to understand others' flaws and can get at his enemies by exploiting their commander's particular weakness. Just as a ship that has lost its helmsman will fall into enemy hands, crew and all, so a general who can outwit or out-think the commander of an army will often capture the entire army.

So, on the occasion in question, Hannibal's plan succeeded because he had worked out and foreseen what Flaminius would do. [82] He left the region of

Faesulae, passed close by the Roman encampment, and encroached upon the nearby land. Flaminius immediately became beside himself with anger at the thought that the enemy were treating him with disrespect. Then, when the farmland began to be destroyed, with smoke everywhere indicating the extent of the devastation, he was furious. He found what was happening so intolerable that he was deaf to anyone who advised him not to go straight out after the enemy and engage them. He was advised to be cautious, especially in view of the size of the enemy's cavalry contingents; he was advised, above all, to wait until the other consul arrived, and to fight only with an army consisting of all the legions combined. But Flaminius could not even bear to hear any of this, and told his advisers to think about what people at home would most likely say if the land was ravaged almost up to Rome itself, while they stayed behind enemy lines in their camp in Etruria.

True to his word, he eventually broke camp and took to the field. He gave no consideration to timing and terrain, and had no plan except to engage the enemy. He treated victory as a foregone conclusion, and he had raised the hopes of the mob to such a pitch that soldiers under arms were outnumbered by non-combatants bearing chains and fetters and so on, who accompanied the army in the hope of booty. Meanwhile, Hannibal was advancing through Etruria in the direction of Rome, with the city of Cortona and its hills on his left, and with lake Trasimene on his right. As he advanced, he burnt and destroyed farmland, deliberately to provoke the enemy's anger. By the time Flaminius had made contact, Hannibal had found a location that suited his purpose and was getting ready for battle.

[83] The road ran through a flat-bottomed valley, which was flanked on both sides by unbroken, high hills. Straight ahead, at one end of the valley, lay an inaccessibly steep ridge; behind, at the other end, was the lake, between which and the flanks of the hills there was room for only a narrow corridor into the valley. Hannibal entered the valley from the lake shore. He secured the ridge straight ahead and set up camp on it with the Iberians and the Libyans; he had his Balearic slingers and spearmen peel off from the vanguard and hide in an extended line behind the hills to the right of the valley; and he likewise had the cavalry and the Celts circle round behind the hills to the left and form an unbroken line there, with the last of them stationed right at the opening to the valley, the entrance between the lake and the flanks of the hills.

These dispositions were made during the night, and after that Hannibal took no further action; the valley was encircled by his troops, waiting to spring the trap. Flaminius was right behind him, eager for the fray. He had set up camp late in the previous evening right by the lake, and at dawn the next day he led his vanguard along the lake shore and into the valley, with the intention of engaging the enemy.

[84] There was a particularly thick mist that day. Hannibal waited for the majority of the Roman column to enter the valley, by which point the vanguard had made contact with his men, and then he gave the signal for battle and passed the word to the troops who were lying in ambush. His men attacked from all sides at once.

The sudden appearance of the enemy took Flaminius completely by surprise. With visibility severely reduced by the conditions, and the enemy charging down and attacking them from higher ground in a number of places at once, the Roman centurions and tribunes could hardly even comprehend what was happening, let alone respond to emergencies. They were under attack simultaneously from the front, the rear, and the sides, and very many of them were cut down while they were still in marching order. They were incapable of defending themselves; it was as if they had been betrayed by their general's poor judgment. Taken by surprise, they were dying while they were still trying to decide what to do.

It was during this phase of the battle that Flaminius too died, in the utmost dejection and despair, in an engagement with some Celts. Close to 15,000 Romans fell in the valley, incapable of either giving in or doing anything, since they were conditioned never to flee or break rank under any circumstances. Others, still on the march, were trapped in the defile between the lake and the flanks of the hills, and died in an appalling and particularly humiliating way. They were forced back into the lake, where some of them desperately tried to swim in their armor and were drowned, while others, the majority, waded as far as they could into the lake and waited there with only their heads above water. At the approach of the cavalry, faced with the certainty of death, they lifted up their hands and begged in the most heart-rending terms to be spared, but in the end they were killed either by the enemy or, in some cases, at their own request by their comrades.

About 6,000 of those in the valley defeated the men they were facing, but failed to help their own men or take the enemy in the rear, because they could not see what was going on, even though they could have made an enormous difference to the outcome. They did nothing but face forward and advance, believing that they were sure to encounter others, until they found themselves off the battlefield and on high ground. From the ridge they could see the extent of the disaster, since the mist had dispersed by then, but it was too late for them to do anything: the battle was already lost and the field was everywhere in enemy hands. So they closed ranks and retreated to a certain Etruscan village. After the battle, Maharbal, dispatched by Hannibal with a force of Iberians and spearmen, surrounded the village. With their problems only compounded, the 6,000 negotiated a truce, laid down their arms, and surrendered, on condition of their lives being spared.

Such was the course and the outcome of the battle between the Romans and Carthaginians in Etruria.

[85] Once all the prisoners had been brought back, including those who had surrendered under a guarantee of safety, Hannibal gathered them all together. There were more than 15,000 of them. He first informed them that Maharbal did not have the authority to guarantee the safety of prisoners under a truce without his permission, and then he launched into an invective against the Romans. Afterwards, he distributed the Roman prisoners among the units of his army, for them to watch over, but he let all the allies return to their homes, free and unransomed. Before letting them go, he repeated his assertion that he had not come to fight the peoples of Italy, but to try to gain them freedom from Rome.

While allowing his men time to rest and recover, he buried the ranking officers among his own dead. There were about thirty of them, out of a total of around 1,500 dead, with the Celts having suffered the worst losses. And then he conferred with his brother and his friends about where they should strike next, and how to go about it, since he was now confident of the final result.

When news of the disaster reached Rome, the authorities could not conceal or downplay it: it was just too great a catastrophe. Since they had no choice, they convened a general assembly in order to tell the people what had happened. The praetor started to address the mob from the *rostra* with the words "We have lost a great battle"—and such a hue and cry immediately broke out that those who had been present on both occasions felt far worse about the defeat then than they had during the actual battle. This was perfectly comprehensible. For many years the Roman people had neither heard about nor experienced the reality of an indisputable defeat, and so they could not react to the disaster with moderation and restraint. The Senate, however, stayed suitably calm as they debated the future, to try to decide what everyone should do and how they should go about it.

[86] At the time of the battle, Gnaeus Servilius, the consul responsible for the Ariminum region, had heard that Hannibal had entered Etruria and had confronted Flaminius. He wanted to bring his entire army and link up with Flaminius, but the heavy infantry made this impracticable, so he sent Gaius Centenius racing ahead with 4,000 cavalry to get there before him, in case the situation was critical. But the battle was over by the time they arrived. When Hannibal heard of these enemy reinforcements, he sent Maharbal out to meet them, with a force consisting of the spearmen and some of the cavalry. In the very first clash, Centenius lost almost half his men, and the next day all the rest, who had been chased onto a hill, were taken prisoner.

The news of this fresh disaster reached Rome two days after they had heard about the main battle, when the city's fever, so to speak, was at its peak, and this time the Senate was thrown into as much turmoil as the common people. They suspended the constitutional system whereby consuls were elected every year and decided to adopt a more drastic approach to the situation. It seemed to them that events and the current crisis demanded the appointment of a single general with full powers.

There was no doubt in Hannibal's mind that he would eventually win, and so he decided to stay away from Rome for the time being. Instead, he set out towards the Adriatic coast, destroying farmland as he went, without meeting any opposition. He passed through Umbria and Picenum and reached the coastline ten days after setting out. On the way, he gained so much booty that his men could not carry it or drive it all off. The slaughter also continued, because, motivated by his long-standing, deep-rooted hatred of the Romans, he had given the order that all adult male Romans who fell into their hands were to be killed, as is the practice when cities are sacked.

[87] He encamped by the Adriatic in a district that was exceptionally rich in all kinds of crops, and made every effort to ensure that his men, and his horses too, recovered their health. They had wintered in the open in Gaul, and as a result of the cold and the lack

of oil-massage, exacerbated by the hardship of their subsequent march through the marshes, almost all the horses and the men were suffering from scurvy and similar ailments. And so, with good land available to him, he built up the strength of his horses, and improved both the physical and the mental condition of his men. He re-equipped his Libyan troops in the Roman fashion, giving them the pick of the huge amount of arms and armor he had captured, and, since this was the first time since invading Italy that he had access to the sea, he also seized the opportunity to send messengers by boat, carrying news of events to Carthage. The report cheered the Carthaginians immensely, and they made every effort to provide for and support the two campaigns, in Italy and Iberia.

The Romans appointed as their dictator Quintus Fabius, an exceptionally intelligent and gifted man. In fact, even today members of his family are called "Maximus," which means "greatest," because of this man's victories and achievements. The differences between a dictator and a consul are that a dictator is attended by twenty-four lictors, while each consul has twelve, and a dictator has plenipotentiary powers, while consuls often cannot see their measures through without the Senate. On the appointment of a dictator, however, all other political officers in Rome stand down, except for the tribunes of the people. But I will analyze these matters in more detail elsewhere. At the same time they appointed Marcus Minucius Rufus as Master of the Horse. The holder of this office is the dictator's second-in-command and is, so to speak, the heir to his command when the dictator is otherwise occupied.

[88] Hannibal gradually moved camp, but stayed by the Adriatic coast. There was plenty of old wine, enough to bathe the horses and cure them of their mange and emaciation, and the wounded also made complete recoveries. As for the rest, he made sure that they were fit and ready for the coming campaign. He invaded successively the territory of the Praetuttii, of Hatria, of the Marrucini, and of the Frentani, and then carried on towards Iapygia, which is divided into three districts, named after the Daunii, Peucetii, and Messapians. He first invaded Daunia, and began by targeting Luceria, a Roman colony there, whose land he destroyed and plundered. Then he made camp near Vibinum, overran the farmland of Argyripa, and plundered all Daunia without meeting any opposition.

Meanwhile, after taking up his appointment, Fabius sacrificed to the gods and then took to the field with his colleague and the four legions that had been raised in response to the crisis. He was reinforced by the army from Ariminum, which he met up with at Narnia. He relieved Servilius of command of the land army and sent him with an escort to Rome, with orders to respond as circumstances demanded to any Carthaginian naval ventures. He and his colleague took over Servilius's forces and encamped at Aecae, about fifty stades away from the Carthaginian position.

[89] When Hannibal heard of Fabius's arrival, he decided to try to overwhelm him straight away. He took to the field and drew his men up in battle order near the Roman camp, but this elicited no response, and after a while he withdrew back to his camp. Fabius had decided to avoid battle and to take no risks, but to make his primary and overriding aim the safety of his men. His adherence to this decision was unwavering. At first, this earned him contempt and made people accuse him of being a battle-shy coward, but as time went by he forced everyone to concede that he had come up with the most sensible and intelligent way of dealing with the current crisis.

Before long, in fact, events themselves bore witness to the soundness of his thinking. This was hardly surprising. The enemy troops had been trained, ever since they first reached military age, by continuous warfare; they had a commander who had shared this upbringing and had been accustomed since childhood to campaigning in the field; they had won many battles in Iberia, and had defeated the Romans and their allies twice in succession. Above all, they had nothing to lose: in victory lay their only hope of survival. The Roman army, however, was in exactly the opposite situation in all these respects. Fabius was therefore reluctant to assent to a decisive battle, because that would inevitably have led to defeat. To his way of thinking, he should fall back on his strengths, make them his focus, and rely on them for his conduct of the war. And the Romans' strengths were an inexhaustible supply of provisions and plenty of men.

[90] Over the following weeks, then, he shadowed the enemy, and used his knowledge of the terrain to occupy strategic positions before they got there. He had more than enough provisions in his rear, so he never let his men go out foraging or leave the camp at all. He kept them all together in close formations, and waited and watched for suitable terrain and opportunities. This

enabled him to capture or kill large numbers of the enemy, who contemptuously strayed from their camp on foraging expeditions. In adopting these tactics, his intention was to whittle away at the enemy's limited numbers, and at the same time gradually, by means of partial successes, to revive and restore his men's confidence, which had been shattered by overwhelming defeats. But he remained reluctant to resolve the situation once and for all by assenting to formal battle. These tactics were not at all to the liking of his colleague Minucius, however, who shared the view of the mob and never missed an opportunity to disparage Fabius. He accused him of conducting the war in an ignoble and indolent manner, and declared himself in favor of risking battle.

After ravaging farmland in Iapygia, Hannibal crossed the Apennines and came down into Samnite territory, fertile land that had long been untroubled by war. The Carthaginians found themselves surrounded by so much bounty that there was plenty left even after they had killed and consumed all the livestock they could. They also overran Beneventum, a Roman colony, and took Venusia, an unwalled town that was well stocked with all kinds of goods. The Romans were constantly on their tail, one or two days' march away, but were never inclined to close and fight.

It was clear that, although Fabius was refusing to give battle, he was also refusing to give up the countryside altogether, and under these circumstances Hannibal made a bold strike into the Capuan plain, or to be precise the Falernan Fields. He expected one of two outcomes. He would either compel the enemy to fight, or he would make everyone recognize that he had the upper hand and that the Romans were ceding the countryside to him—in which case, he hoped, the terrified cities would rush to rebel from Rome. For up until then, despite two Roman defeats, not a single Italian city had left them and gone over to the Carthaginians; they had all remained loyal, even though some of them had suffered a great deal. This is a good indicator of the fear and respect the allies felt for the Roman state.

[91] Anyway, Hannibal had good reasons for thinking as he did. There is no land in Italy more famous for its fertility and beauty than the plain around Capua. Moreover, it is a coastal region, and the ports it commands are called in at by merchants coming to Italy from pretty much everywhere in the known world. The most famous and beautiful cities in Italy are located there. On the coast, there are Sinuessa, Cumae,

Dicaearchia, then Naples, and finally Nuceria. Inland, there are Cales and Teanum to the north, Daunia and Nola to the east and south, and, in the middle, Capua, once the most prosperous city in the world.

The myth that is told about this plain is perfectly plausible: there is nothing more likely to have caused friction among the gods than its beauty and fertility. In addition to the advantages I have already mentioned, the plain appears to be strongly protected and perfectly inaccessible: some of it is bounded by the sea, and most of it by continuous ranges of unremittingly tall mountains. There are only three passes through these mountains from the interior, and they are narrow and forbidding. One comes from Samnium, the second from Latium, and the third from the territory of the Hirpini. So when the Carthaginians established themselves in this plain, their intention was to make it their stage, from which they would intimidate and astonish the world, and on which they would display a battle-shy enemy, while they appeared indisputably in control of the countryside.

[92] With this plan in mind, Hannibal left Samnium via the defile that runs beside the hill called Eribianus, and encamped by the river Athyrnus, which more or less cuts the plain in two. He built his camp on the northern side of the river, and his marauders overran and plundered the plain without meeting any opposition. Fabius was surprised by the audacity of the enemy's tactics, but this only made him more determined to keep to his chosen course. His colleague Minucius, however, and all the tribunes and centurions in the army, thought they had Hannibal well and truly trapped, and expected Fabius to make his way to the plain as quickly as possible and do something about the devastation of this choice piece of land.

Fabius pretended to go along with the impatience and incautiousness of his colleagues, at least to the extent of making his way with all due speed to the plain, but once he was close to the Falernan Fields he kept to high ground. He did not want Rome's allies to think that he had abandoned the countryside, so he continued to shadow the enemy, making sure they knew he was there, but he did not bring his army down into the plain. For, whatever other reasons he had for avoiding battle, he was especially concerned about the enemy's clear and considerable cavalry superiority.

Hannibal had succeeded in provoking the enemy and in ravaging the entire plain. In the process, he had collected an enormous quantity of livestock. He decided, then, to move camp, because, rather than waste the booty, he wanted to keep it in a place where he could also make his winter quarters, so that his army would not only have plenty of provisions for the present, but would never suffer any shortage. Fabius realized that Hannibal intended to take the same route out that he had taken on the way in. He could see that the pass was narrow and the perfect place for launching an attack. He deployed about 4,000 men at the actual pass, with instructions to rise to any opportunity that presented itself and to make use of the natural advantages of the terrain, while he took the bulk of the army and encamped on a ridge in front of the defile and overlooking it.

[93] When the Carthaginians got there, they encamped on level ground at the foot of the slopes. Fabius felt sure that he could easily make off with the livestock, and he thought it likely that his advantageous position might even allow him to bring the whole business to an end. So he began to consider how this might be achieved and to lay his plans—to think about where and how he could exploit the terrain, what troops he should use for the attack, and from where they should launch the initial assault. But while the Romans were making these preparations for the next day, Hannibal guessed what they were up to, and pre-empted and spoiled their plans. He summoned Hasdrubal, the commander of the pioneers, and gave him his orders: he was to get his men to make as many brands as they could, out of dry wood of any kind, as quickly as they could, and they were also to herd together in front of the camp about 2,000 of the plough oxen they had captured, selecting only the strongest. Once his orders had been carried out, Hannibal assembled the pioneers and pointed to a trail up the hills between his camp and the defile through which he was intending to march. When the signal was given, they were to drive the oxen forward towards the trail, vigorously and forcefully, and all the way up to the top. Then he issued a general order that everyone was to get to bed early, after eating their evening meal.

At the end of the third watch of the night, he brought the pioneers out of the camp and had them tie the brands onto the horns of the cattle. There were plenty of men, and this did not take long. Then he ordered them to light all the brands, start driving the oxen, and make for the ridge. He posted the spearmen behind the pioneers, and their orders were to help the

pioneers for a while, but then, as soon as the animals began to move forward, they were to run alongside them and make sure they stayed bunched together. They were to make for the high ground, and occupy the ridge, so that they could respond to emergencies, and take on any enemy they met anywhere on the hill trails. Meanwhile, Hannibal set out for the pass through the defile, with the heavy infantry in the van, then the cavalry, then the livestock they had taken as booty, and finally the Iberians and Celts.

[94] When the Romans who were guarding the defile saw the lights approaching the trails, they assumed that Hannibal had set out in that direction, so they left the gorge and went to defend the ridge. As they drew near to the cattle, the lights puzzled them and made them imagine they were going to encounter something worse and more terrifying than mere oxen. When the Carthaginian spearmen arrived, the two contingents skirmished for a while, but then the cattle burst in on them and they separated. Both sides stayed on the ridge and kept themselves in check while waiting for daybreak, because the situation was too confusing.

Fabius decided to play safe. He chose not to take any risks at all, and lay low in his camp, waiting for daylight. He did this partly because the developments were unusual enough for him to "sense a trap," as Homer put it, and partly because he was still adhering to his original plan. Meanwhile, Hannibal's plan was going well, and he brought his army and the livestock through the defile in perfect safety, because the Roman unit that was guarding the gorge had left the area. At dawn, he saw that on the heights the Romans were confronting his spearmen and sent an Iberian division to deal with the situation. They engaged the Romans, slew about 1,000 of them, and had no difficulty in bringing their light-armed troops back down from the ridge, protected within their formation.

That was how Hannibal broke out of the Falernan Fields. Afterwards, he kept safe in his camp and began to think about where and how he should pass the winter, and to make his plans accordingly. He had succeeded in arousing great fear and considerable uncertainty in the cities and people of Italy. Fabius became very unpopular with the masses, who held that it must have been an act of cowardice to let the enemy escape from such a situation, but he did not waver. A few days later, however, he had to leave for Rome, to perform some sacrifices. He delegated command of the legions to his colleague and repeatedly told him, as he left, not to be so concerned about harming the enemy; he should focus, instead, on making sure that *they* did not come to harm. Minucius paid not the slightest attention to this; even while Fabius was speaking, he was wholly committed to risking a battle.

*The scene now shifts again to Spain in the same year (217), where the Romans fared better, winning a naval battle against the Carthaginian fleet (95–99). In the next six chapters (100–105), Polybius describes the growing tensions on the Roman side between those who, like the dictator Fabius, saw the tactical advantages of tying Hannibal down in a war of attrition and the growing chorus of dissenters who desired swifter action. This was played out in the contest between Fabius and his Master of the Horse, Minucius, who disobeyed his orders and attacked the Carthaginians. Fabius's term as dictator was not extended, and new consuls were elected for the year 216 B.C., while the consuls for the previous year took over command of the army in the field. The final sections of the book (106–17) describe the campaign that led up to the Battle of Cannae, which took place in the southeastern portion of Italy known as Apulia. The figures that Polybius gives for Roman casualties in this defeat have been challenged, and other, Roman, sources give lower numbers, but all agree that this was one of the most devastating defeats in Roman military history.*

[106] The time for the general election in Rome drew near, and the consuls chosen for that year were Lucius Aemilius Paullus and Gaius Terentius Varro. Thereupon the dictators resigned, and the consuls for the previous year, Gnaeus Servilius Geminus and Marcus Atilius Regulus (suffect consul after Flaminius's death), were appointed proconsuls by Aemilius and were authorized to direct military operations in the field subject to the consuls' approval. After consulting the Senate, Aemilius quickly enrolled soldiers to make up the shortage and bring the army up to its full quota, and then sent them off to join their legions. His orders to Servilius were that under no circumstances was he to risk a decisive engagement, but he was to seize every opportunity for small-scale skirmishes and prosecute them vigorously, so as to train the new men and make them mentally ready for full-scale battle. He had no doubt that their earlier defeats had happened largely because the legions had consisted of utterly untrained new recruits.

The praetor Lucius Postumius Albinus was given command of an army and sent to Gaul, to give the Celts who were serving with Hannibal something to think about. Arrangements were also made for the return of the fleet that was wintering in Lilybaeum, and for the generals in Iberia to receive all the supplies they had requisitioned. While these and all other measures were assiduously being taken in hand, Servilius received his orders from the Senate and set about only the kind of small-scale operations that had been approved by them. I shall not bother to describe these operations, which achieved nothing decisive or remarkable. His orders and his circumstances combined to ensure that only a great many skirmishes and minor engagements took place. The Roman commanders gave good account of themselves in these fights and seemed to be handling everything in a courageous and sensible fashion.

[107] The two armies stayed encamped opposite each other all winter and spring. Once it was possible to supply his army from that year's crops, Hannibal moved his army from the camp at Gereonium. He had become convinced that it was in his interests to find some way to force the enemy to meet him in battle, and to that end he seized the acropolis of a town called Cannae, where the Romans had stored grain and other provisions harvested from around Canusium.

They had been transporting supplies from there to the army whenever the need arose. The town itself had already been razed to the ground, but the capture of the acropolis and the stores sent ripples of alarm through the Roman army. The fall of the town was a bad blow for them not just because they lost their stores, but also because the town commanded the surrounding region. The generals sent message after message to Rome, asking for instructions. They argued that it would be impossible for them to avoid battle if they came near the enemy, since the countryside was being stripped and all the allies there were restless.

The Senate's decision was that they should meet the enemy in battle, but they told Servilius to wait and sent the consuls to the front. Everyone looked to Aemilius and thought that their best chances of success lay with him. It was not just that throughout his life he had shown himself to be an exemplary character, but also that in his handling of the Illyrian War a few years previously he had shown himself to be a man of courage and one with Rome's interests at heart.

The Senate took an unprecedented step and decided to field eight legions for the battle, with each legion consisting of about 5,000 men—Romans, that is, not allies. As I explained earlier, the Romans usually mobilize four legions, with each legion consisting of about 4,000 foot and 200 horse. But when the stakes are more critical, they raise the number of infantrymen in each legion to 5,000 and the number of cavalrymen to 300. The numbers of allied infantrymen correspond exactly with those of the Roman legions, but as a rule there are three times as many allied cavalrymen as Roman. When they send the consuls out into the field, they give each of them half of the allies and his two legions. Most battles are decided by one consul, with two legions and the usual number of allies, but from time to time they employ all their forces at the same time, for a single battle. On the occasion in question, however, they were so alarmed and terrified that they decided to send not just four, but eight Roman legions into battle at once.

[108] Before sending Aemilius on his way, then, they impressed upon him how critical the battle was in terms of its possible outcomes, one way or the other. He was instructed to decide the issue, when the time came, with courage and as Rome would expect of him. When Aemilius reached the army, he convened a general assembly, at which he informed the men of the will of the Senate, and also, speaking in his own person, addressed them in suitably encouraging terms. Most of the speech was given over to explaining their recent reverses, since the men had become disheartened as a result of these setbacks and needed reassurance on that score. So he tried to get them to understand that there were several reasons why the outcome of those battles had been defeat, but that, leaving the past aside, under current circumstances there was no reason why they should not be victorious, if they were men of courage.

In the earlier battles, he said, the two generals never combined their forces and fought together, and the men at their disposal were untrained new recruits, unfamiliar with the horrors of war. But the most important factor was that previously the troops had been so ignorant of the enemy that it was almost as if they had never even seen who they were up against before forming ranks and meeting them in decisive battles. "The men who were defeated at the Trebia river," he said, "arrived from Sicily, and at dawn of the very next day they formed up for battle. As for those who fought in Etruria, not only had they not seen their foes before, but they were not granted a glimpse of them even during the battle, because of the unfortunate weather conditions.

"But," he went on, "things are quite different for us now. [109] First, we consuls are both here, and we are not only going to fight alongside you in the battle ourselves, but we have also got last year's consuls to stay, and they are ready to play their part too. Then again, you yourselves have not only seen the enemy's weaponry, tactics, and numbers, but you have spent the past two years fighting them almost every day. Since in every particular our situation is quite different from that of the earlier battles, it is likely that the outcome of the present battle will be quite different too. It is hard, if not impossible, to imagine that, after meeting the enemy on equal terms in minor skirmishes and usually winning, we shall lose a full-scale battle when we outnumber the enemy by more than two to one.

"In short, men, there is nothing to stop you winning. All that is needed is your grit and determination, and as far as these are concerned further encouragement from me would, I think, be inappropriate. When men have been hired for military service, or are about to face danger on behalf of others in fulfilment of the terms of an alliance, the battle itself is what they fear most and they are more or less indifferent about the consequences. In their case, encouragement is essential. But when men have become involved in danger for personal reasons, as you have—when they are not fighting for anyone else, but for their own lives, homeland, wives, and children, and the consequences are many times more important than the immediate danger—they do not need to be encouraged to do their duty, but only to be reminded of it. Is there anyone in such circumstances who would not choose, above all, to fight and win? Or if that proved impossible, to die fighting, rather than live to see all that he holds dear violated and destroyed?

"So you have no need of my words, men. Imagine for yourselves the difference between the consequences of winning and the consequences of losing, and present yourselves for battle as though Rome were now risking her very existence, not just her legions. For Rome has exhausted all her resources: if this battle does not turn out well, she has nothing left with which to prevail over her enemies. She has vested in you all her desires and all her power; all her hopes of survival depend on you. Do not cheat her of these hopes. Repay in full the debt of gratitude you owe her. Show the world that the earlier defeats happened not because Romans are less courageous than

Carthaginians, but because of the inexperience of the troops on those occasions and because of circumstances beyond their control." After addressing the troops like this, Aemilius dismissed them.

[110] In the morning, the consuls broke camp and led the army towards where they had heard the enemy encampment was to be found. They made contact with them on the second day and encamped about fifty stades away. Aemilius argued against a battle, since the surrounding area was flat and treeless, and the enemy had cavalry superiority; he preferred to entice them and draw them on to terrain where the infantry legions were more likely to be critical to the battle. Speaking from inexperience, Varro maintained the opposite point of view. The two consuls quarreled and there was bad feeling between them, which is the most dangerous thing that can happen.

As was customary, the consuls were each in command on alternate days. The next day it was Varro's turn, and he broke camp and set out, with the intention of advancing on the enemy, despite Aemilius's protests and opposition. Hannibal came out to meet them with his light-armed troops and cavalry, and caught them while they were still on the march. The unexpected attack caused considerable disruption in the Roman column, but they absorbed the first assault by having some of the heavy infantry form a protective screen, and then sent the skirmishers and the cavalry forward. The Romans had the advantage all over the field, because the Carthaginians had no reserves to speak of, and because the Romans had some of their maniples join the skirmishers and fight alongside them.

The two sides separated as night drew in, with the Carthaginians disappointed in the outcome of their attack. The next day Aemilius not only judged it inadvisable to fight, but it was no longer possible for him to withdraw safely, so he halted by the river Aufidus. He himself made camp with two divisions of the army on one bank, while the third division encamped on the other side, to the east of the ford, about ten stades away from his own camp and somewhat further away from the enemy position. The troops in this second camp were to protect foragers from the first camp across the river, and attack foragers from the Carthaginian camp.

[111] Meanwhile, since it was inevitable now that the two sides would clash and a battle would be fought, Hannibal thought he should take the opportunity to address his troops. He was also concerned that the defeat might have demoralized them. He convened a general assembly, and once they had all gathered, he told them to look around at the surrounding countryside. He asked them to imagine that they had the right to ask the gods for anything: given the circumstances, what else would they have asked for than that the decisive battle should be fought on this kind of terrain when they had cavalry superiority over the enemy? Everyone applauded this vivid way of putting it, and then he went on:

"First, then, you should thank the gods for having led the enemy onto this kind of terrain, which has played a part in ensuring your victory. In the second place, however, you have me to thank. I have left the enemy no choice except battle. They cannot possibly continue to avoid it, and the battle will take place in conditions that favor us.

"I don't think I need say much now by way of encouraging you to be confident and resolute in the coming battle. That was needed when you had no experience of fighting the Romans, and so I used to give you examples of the way they fight in my speeches. But now that you have indisputably defeated them in three successive major battles, what morale-boosting speech could I give that would serve better than the facts themselves? I gave you my word that you would gain control of the countryside and all its blessings, and none of my promises has failed to come true: those three battles have enabled you to do just that. What we are going to fight for now is control of the cities and all *their* blessings. In short order, victory will bring us mastery of all Italy, an end to our current troubles, and possession of Rome's entire fortune. This battle will make you lords and masters of the world. Enough words, then; now is the time for action. If the gods will it, I am as certain as I can be that the promises I have just made to you will come true."

These words of his—and there were more to the same effect—were greeted with rapturous applause from his troops. He praised them and thanked them for their enthusiasm. After dismissing the assembly, he turned immediately to the task of strengthening his position by making a palisaded camp on the same side of the river as the larger of the two Roman camps.

[112] Next day, he ordered all his men to attend to their equipment and to themselves, and the day after that he formed them up beside the river and let the enemy know that he was ready to give battle. But Aemilius lay low, apart from making sure that the camps were well protected; he was unhappy about the terrain, and he

could see that the Carthaginians would soon be compelled to move camp in order to ensure a supply of provisions. Hannibal waited a while, but there was no response to his challenge, so he had most of the men return to camp, except for the Numidians, whom he sent out to interrupt the supply of water to the smaller of the two Roman camps. The Numidians rode right up to the palisade of the camp and stopped anyone coming out to fetch water, which made Varro even more furious. The rank-and-file troops were also eager for battle and impatient with all the delays. After all, there is nothing more difficult to endure than a period of suspense. Once a decision has been taken, however, we are prepared to endure anything, however apparently terrible.

Tension and terror gripped Rome at the news that the two armies were encamped close to each other and that clashes between the outposts were happening on a daily basis. Given that they had so often been defeated before, their prospects seemed grim, and people looked ahead and imagined what would happen in the event of a decisive defeat. Every oracle they had ever collected became a topic of conversation, every sanctuary and every household received endless omens and portents, and the city was filled with prayers, sacrifices, supplications, and entreaties. For at times of crisis the Romans take extraordinary pains to propitiate both gods and men, and at such times there is no aspect of any relevant rite that they regard as unseemly or demeaning. [113] The next day it was Varro's turn to hold overall command and he began to move his forces out of both camps just after sunrise. He had the men from the larger camp cross the river and drew them up in battle order straight away, and he had the men from the other camp join them and form up so that they all made a continuous line, facing south. He posted the Roman cavalry on the right wing, directly by the river, next to the infantry and in a straight line. He reduced the gaps between the maniples more than usual, and increased the number of ranks within the maniples until their depth was several times greater than their length. He deployed the allied cavalry on the left wing, and posted the light-armed troops in front of the entire army and some way ahead. Including the allies, there were about 80,000 foot and a little more than 6,000 horse.

Meanwhile, Hannibal sent his Balearic slingers and his spearmen across the river to take up a forward position. Then he led the rest of his men out of the camp and across the river at two places, and had them take up their positions for battle. On the left wing, by the river, he posted the Iberian and Celtic cavalry, facing their Roman counterparts. Next to them he placed half of the Libyan heavy infantry, then the Iberian and Celtic infantry, then the remaining half of the Libyan infantry, and then on his right wing he deployed the Numidian cavalry. So far the entire army formed a single, straight line, but next he led forward the Iberian and Celtic infantry units in the center, and had the others link up with them in a staggered line, until he had formed a crescent-shaped bulge, which entailed thinning the ranks in the formation. His intention was to keep the Libyans in reserve, with the Iberians and Celts bearing the brunt of the fighting.

[114] The arms and armor of the Libyans were Roman, since Hannibal had equipped the entire contingent with the pick of the battlefield spoils taken in the previous battle. As for the Iberians and Celts, their shields were very similar in design, but their swords were quite different. The tip of the Iberian sword was just as dangerous as its cutting edge, whereas the Gallic sword was good only for cutting, when standing at some distance from one's opponent. Since they were drawn up in alternate companies, with the Celts naked and the Iberians dressed in their traditional short linen tunics bordered with purple, they presented a weird and terrifying appearance. The Carthaginian horse numbered about 10,000 in all, and there were somewhat more than 40,000 foot, including the Celts. The Roman right wing was under the command of Aemilius, while Varro held the left, and Atilius and Servilius, the previous year's consuls, were in charge of the center. Hasdrubal and Hanno were in command of the Carthaginian left and right wings respectively, while Hannibal himself was responsible for the center, along with his brother Mago. Since, as I have already said, the Roman lines were facing south and the Carthaginians faced north, neither side was inconvenienced by the rising sun.

[115] The battle began with a clash between the advance guards. At first, when just the light-armed contingents were fighting, it was an even match, but then the Iberian and Celtic cavalry from the left wing came up to their Roman counterparts, and battle was well and truly joined. But the barbarian contingents dictated the tactics. There was none of the wheeling and turning that cavalry engagements usually involve; as soon as they met, they dismounted and fought man to man. Eventually, the Iberians and Celts won. All the Romans fought with determination and courage, and so most

of them died fighting. The survivors were driven back along the river bank, slaughtered and harried mercilessly by their opponents.

At that point, the light-armed divisions withdrew and battle was joined between the heavy infantry contingents from both sides. For a while, the Iberians and Celts held their formation and struggled valiantly against the Romans, but then they gave way under the weight of the legions and began to fall back, destroying the crescent formation in the process and with the Roman maniples in hot pursuit. The Celtic line was thin, and the Romans easily broke through, especially since their line had become thicker in the center, where the fighting was taking place, than on the wings. This had happened because the wings and the center did not all become engaged simultaneously; the fighting started in the center, because the Celts' crescent formation pushed them a long way forward of the wings, since the bulge of the crescent protruded in the direction of the enemy lines.

In pursuing the retreating Celts, however, the Romans converged on the center, now vacated by the enemy, and they got so far forward that their flanks on both sides became exposed to the heavy Libyan infantry. The situation itself showed the Libyans what they had to do: those on the right wing faced left, dressed ranks from the right, and threatened the Romans' flank, while those on the left wing faced right and dressed ranks from the left. This was exactly the result Hannibal had planned for: in rushing after the Celts, the Romans were caught in the Libyans' trap. The Roman phalanx broke up as men turned and fought singly or in maniples against those who were attacking their flanks.

[116] Aemilius had started on the right wing, and although he had taken part in the cavalry battle, he was still alive at this point. But he wanted to be involved in the action, as he had promised in his address to the troops. It was clear to him that the battle would be decided largely by the infantry legions, so he rode over to the center of the whole line, where he entered into the mêlée and played his part, while at the same time calling out advice and encouragement to his men. Hannibal did much the same; he had been in command of these divisions of his army from the beginning.

Meanwhile, the Numidian cavalry on Hannibal's right wing attacked the cavalry facing them on the Roman left. Due to the peculiar nature of their tactics, they neither inflicted nor sustained serious losses, but they did distract their opponents and prevent them from

playing an effective part by harassing them from all directions. By now Hasdrubal's men had killed all but a very few of the enemy by the river, so they came over from the left wing to support the Numidians. Faced with their imminent assault, the Roman allies turned and fled.

Hasdrubal's response to this seems very practical and intelligent. In view of the fact that there were a great many Numidians, and that they were most effective and dangerous once they had the enemy on the run, he left the retreating Roman allies to them, while he took his men over to where the infantry was engaged, to help the Libyans. Again and again, he attacked the Roman legions in the rear, at many points at once, which served both to boost the spirits of the Libyans and to demoralize and terrify the Romans. This was the point at which Aemilius succumbed to the terrible wounds he had received, and died on the field of battle. The loyal service he gave Rome all his life was unequalled by any other man, and he did his duty to the very end.

The Roman legions held on as long as they could turn and present a front to the enemy who now surrounded them. But the constant attrition of the outer ranks meant that the survivors gradually closed in on one another, and in the end they all died where they stood. Among the dead were Atilius and Servilius, the previous year's consuls, men who had demonstrated their courage in the battle and had proved themselves true Romans. While the infantry engagement was turning into a massacre, the Numidians were following the fleeing cavalrymen, most of whom were either killed or unseated. Among the few who escaped to Venusia was the Roman consul Varro, a man of no redeeming qualities, who did his country great disservice as consul.

[117] This was the course and the outcome of the battle of Cannae, fought between the Romans and the Carthaginians. It was a battle in which both the winners and the losers displayed great courage. The facts themselves demonstrate this. Of the 6,000 Roman cavalry, only 70 escaped with Varro to Venusia, and about 300 of the allied cavalry sought refuge in various places here and there. Of the infantry, about 10,000 were captured fighting (off the battlefield, however), and only perhaps 3,000 escaped from the battle and found refuge in nearby towns. All the rest, about 70,000 men, died bravely. Not for the first time, it was the cavalry numbers that contributed most towards the Carthaginian victory. The battle taught later generations that in wartime it is better to have half as many infantry as the enemy, and

overwhelming cavalry superiority, than to have exactly the same numbers as the enemy in all respects. The losses on Hannibal's side were, in round numbers, 4,000 Celts, 1,500 Iberians and Libyans, and 200 cavalrymen.

The reason why the Romans who were taken prisoner were off the battlefield was that Aemilius left 10,000 soldiers in his own camp. Their job was to rush over to Hannibal's camp during the battle, if he had fielded all his men and left the camp untended, and capture the enemy's baggage; on the other hand, if he took precautions and left an adequate garrison, the Romans would have fewer men to fight in the decisive battle. Anyway, they came to be captured as follows. As the battle started, the Romans carried out their orders. They assaulted the enemy camp, in which Hannibal had left an adequate garrison, and attacked those who had been left there. At first, the Carthaginian garrison held out, but soon they found themselves in trouble. By then, however, the battle had been decided in Hannibal's favor in every part of the field. He came to the assistance of the beleaguered garrison, routed the Romans, and pinned them inside their own camp. Two thousand of them were killed, and all the rest were captured alive. Likewise, the Numidians assaulted the strongholds in the countryside where Romans had taken refuge and brought in about 2,000 of the cavalrymen who had turned to flight.

[118] The result of the battle meant that the war reached exactly the critical point that both sides had expected. Their achievement brought the Carthaginians immediate mastery of almost all the rest of the coastline. Tarentum surrendered straight away, Argyripa and some Campanian towns approached Hannibal, and all the other cities inclined from then on towards the Carthaginian side. The Carthaginians even found themselves in a position to anticipate capturing Rome itself in short order. And for the Romans the defeat meant that they immediately gave up any hope of retaining supremacy in Italy, and brought them to the point where they were at serious risk of losing their lives and the very soil of their homeland, and where they fearfully expected to do so, since they anticipated Hannibal's arrival at any moment.

It seemed, in fact, as though Fortune were using events to dole out an extra portion of bad luck and pile on the agony, because a few days later, with the city already gripped by fear, the general they had sent to Gaul was ambushed by the Celts and he and his army were annihilated. Nevertheless, the Senate continued to do their best: they tried to alleviate the general gloom, they secured the city, and they did not let fear get the better of them as they debated the crisis. And subsequent events showed that they were right. For although at that point the Romans had undoubtedly been defeated, and although their military supremacy had passed into other hands, the peculiar virtues of their constitution and their sound deliberation not only enabled them to regain dominion over Italy and then to beat the Carthaginians, but within a few years they had made themselves masters of the entire known world.

Here I end my third book, having covered the events of the 140th Olympiad in Iberia and Italy. Once I have described what happened in the same Olympiad in Greece, I shall interrupt the narrative with a separate essay on the Roman constitution. I think that such a description is not only formally appropriate for my history, but will also be very instructive for students of history, and very helpful for statesmen wanting to form or reform constitutions.

*At this critical juncture, Polybius breaks off his narrative of the war in Italy to deal in the following two books, 4 and 5, with contemporaneous events in the eastern Mediterranean. Before he returns to the war against Hannibal in Book 7, he devotes an entire book to an account of the Roman political system, in part to supply an explanation for how Rome was able to recover from the devastating defeats inflicted by Hannibal and eventually prevail in the war.*

## AFTERWORD

The weather was oppressive in central Greece on August 8, 48 B.C., the day before the Battle of Pharsalus, the epic clash between two great armies, one led by Pompey the Great, commanding the forces of the Roman Senate, and the other led by Julius Caesar, at the head of his veteran legions, with whom he had conquered all of Gaul. In Pompey's camp men were resting up for the coming battle or anxiously contemplating its outcome, polishing their weapons, or revising their wills. But not Marcus Brutus, the conscience of the Senate, who, according to Plutarch, spent the day writing an epitome of Polybius's *Histories*. There were many others who shared Brutus's evident regard for the *Histories*. Cicero regarded him as "a particularly good author" (*On Duties* 3.113), and Livy used him as a source of information on the period following the start of the Second Punic War, referring to him as "an authority who should by no means be ignored." Later writers such as Pliny the Elder and Plutarch used Polybius extensively as a source, but he did not achieve the widespread recognition accorded to the classic writers of Greek historiography, Herodotus and Thucydides.

Plutarch's anecdote about Brutus is a telling omen for the later history of Polybius's works. For, like many lengthy and well-regarded histories, such as Livy's, Polybius's work was often abridged and circulated in excerpts. Only the first five books of the *Histories* survive complete, because they were copied in manuscripts during the Middle Ages. For the other thirty-five books we have only bits and pieces culled from excerpts, some made in antiquity, and a large number of extracts that were included in a compilation of quotations from ancient historians made in the Greek East during the reign of the Byzantine emperor Constantine VII in the tenth century A.D. It is likely that the compilers of that work did not have a complete text to work from, and much of their knowledge of Polybius may have come from earlier anthologies of the same sort.

Perhaps the last author to have access to something like a complete text of the *Histories* was Zosimus, who was active in the Greek East in the early sixth century A.D. Zosimus relied upon Polybius, who made the rise of Rome his theme, as a counterpoint to his own narrative of the empire's decline. The *Histories* were not reintroduced to a Western audience until 1419, when the humanist Leonardo Bruni published a monograph on the First Punic War, for which he used Polybius as a source. Bruni, it appears, had acquired a copy of Polybius's first five books. Later in the same century Pope Nicholas V decided to commission a translation of these books into Latin. The man from whom he commissioned this work was Niccolò Perotti (1429–80), a distinguished humanist and scholar, who once hired an assassin to do away with a rival scholar—Poggio Bracciolini (the attempt failed). Perotti eventually became archbishop of Siponto, and although he wrote important treatises on Martial and Pliny the Elder, he is best remembered for this translation, the first modern translation into any language, which served as the basis of Polybius's reputation for generations. It, and not the Greek original, was used for the first English translation of Polybius to appear in print, a rendering of Book 1 by Christopher Watson (ca. 1545–80).

By far the most influential part of Polybius's work was his theory of a mixed constitution, which he expounds in Book 6 of the *Histories,* weaving it into his narrative as part of his explanation for the success of the Roman state. Polybius provides a detailed analysis of the theory, which had been sketched out by Plato and then Aristotle, that the best government is a balanced blend of monarchy, oligarchy, and democracy. In his view, the Roman government best exemplified this kind of system during the great war with Hannibal, which is why he breaks off his chronological narrative at that point to describe the Roman constitution for a Greek audience (*Histories* 6.11):

> There were three fundamental building blocks of the Roman constitution—that is, all three of the systems I mentioned above. Each of them was used so equitably and appropriately in the ordering and arrangement of everything that even native Romans were hard put to say for sure whether their constitution was essentially aristocratic, democratic, or monarchic. This is not surprising: the constitution would have appeared monarchic (or a kingship), aristocratic, or democratic, depending on whether one focused attention on the powers of the consuls, the powers of the Senate, or the powers of the common people.

In Polybius's view, the success of Rome was in no small measure due to the interaction of the three main organs of government (*Histories* 6.18), "because none of them is self-sufficient, as I have just been explaining, and the designs of each of them can be effectively counteracted and hampered by the others. Everything remains in its assigned place, then, either because its impetus is checked, or because right from the start it is afraid of being curbed by the others."

The crucial sixth book, which survived only in excerpts, was not included in Perotti's translation, so it is not known in what form Machiavelli (1469–1527) read it, but his familiarity with the text is clear from his posthumous monograph, *Discourses on the First Ten Books of Livy* (1531). The first printed edition of Polybius's Greek text did not appear until 1530, and it contained only the first five books. It was only in subsequent years that what we have of the *Histories* from later books was reassembled, thanks to the labors of scholars such as Isaac Casaubon (1559–1614), who published an edition in 1609, and especially Johann Schweighäuser (1742–1830), whose eight-volume edition remains indispensable.

It was in part due to the influence of Polybius on Montesquieu's *Spirit of the Laws* (1748) that Polybius came to the attention of the Founding Fathers of the United States. Thomas Jefferson once thought the *Histories* important enough that he sent a copy to James Madison at the Constitutional Convention in 1787, although his attitude toward Polybius probably shifted as his own views inclined more in the direction of a strongly based democratic form of government. The most ardent admirer of Polybius's theory of the mixed constitution was John Adams. In the year following the drafting of the US Constitution, while in London, he published *A Defence of the Constitutions of Government of the United States of America,* in which he strongly argued in support of the classical theory of a mixed government. The work consists of fifty-five letters on a variety of subjects relating to this theory, two of which (30 and 31) are devoted to Polybius. He argued that in fact it was possible to improve on Polybius's ideal state by dividing the legislative branch in two and segregating the more powerful elements of society:

> The only remedy is to throw the rich and the proud into one group, in a separate assembly, and there tie their hands; if you give them scope with the people at large, or their representatives, they will destroy *all equality and liberty, with the consent and acclamations of the people themselves.* They will have much more power, mixed with the representatives, than separated from them. In the first case, if they unite, they will give the law, and govern all; if they differ, they will divide the state, and go to a decision by force. But placing them alone by themselves, the society avails itself of all their abilities and virtues; they become a solid check to the representatives themselves, as well as to the executive power, and you disarm them entirely of the power to do mischief.

Although Polybius's name is rarely invoked in contemporary discussions of the US Senate, some might reflect upon Adams's wisdom in departing in this way from the Polybian model.

# II

# THE LATE REPUBLIC

From our perspective, after the death of Terence in 159 B.C., literature in Latin is a mosaic with many pieces missing. A decade later came the death of Marcus Porcius Cato, known to Roman posterity as "The Censor" because of the moral rigor of his performance of that office in 184. In spite of his celebrated denunciation of foreign influences and the decline of traditional Roman values, he embraced the new literary culture of the age and was its most prolific and important representative in prose. Cicero still knew of more than 150 speeches by Cato, but all but a few fragments have disappeared, along with his historical work in seven books, *Origins.* The latter in particular is a great loss, as it was the first such work in the Latin language: the other histories written by Romans during this time were composed in Greek. Only Cato's short treatise *On Agriculture* survives to provide a glimpse of the first stages in the development of literary prose in Latin.

In the decades that followed there were still dramas being produced for the stage, chiefly in tragedy, where the names of Pacuvius (220–ca. 130 B.C.) and Accius (170–ca. 90 B.C.) loomed large in the pantheon for Romans, although they are little more than names to us, since their plays, too, survive only in quotations by later authors. After Cato, we know of many who turned their hand to writing history in Latin, but all of these works—some of which, like the seventy-five books of Valerius Antias's *Annals,* were quite extensive—have been lost. What emerges from the inadequate remains of the literature of the century between Terence and our next surviving texts is an image, fuzzy in its details but sharp in its broader contours, of an expanding literary society negotiating a sometimes uneasy interaction with Greek culture.

The material at our disposal becomes much more tangible when we reach the 60s and the 50s B.C. While much of the work by some of the leading figures of this period has survived, this represents only the leading edge of a vibrant literary community. As the ancient reader unrolled the poems of Catullus, two names in particular mentioned in his poems would have leapt off the columns of writing: Helvius Cinna and Licinius Calvus, much admired by their contemporaries and the next generation of poets. Alas, all but a few lines of their poetry have disappeared. There were others who practiced the new style of poetry that they represented, the last of whom, Cornelius Gallus, set the standard for poetry in the elegiac meter in Latin. The near-total loss of this great poet, to whom Virgil paid tribute in two of his *Eclogues,* has long proved galling to classical scholars. The overwhelming achievement of Cicero in oratory, fifty-eight of whose speeches have come down to us, tends to obscure somewhat the picture of the age that we might have formed if, for example, the speeches of his great rival Hortensius (114–50 B.C.) had survived. That is to say nothing of the orations of some of the other great figures of the period, known to have been available to readers at least into the early empire, such as Caesar, Brutus, and Mark Antony. Nor should we forget Varro's *Antiquities*, forty-one books on Roman religious and secular institutions by the man widely regarded by contemporaries as the greatest scholar of the age; the few fragments that survive are mostly from the last sixteen books, which were dedicated to Caesar in his capacity as Pontifex Maximus. But even though we have lost these and many other works, what we do have from this period, salvaged—sometimes literally—from the sands of time, is enough to give us an appreciation of this turbulent, intense, and exciting period of Roman literature.

# LUCRETIUS

(Titus Lucretius Carus, ca. 94–ca. 53 B.C.)

WE DO NOT KNOW EXACTLY WHEN LUCRETIUS WAS BORN OR DIED, NOR HOW AND where he lived. Even his full name—Titus Lucretius Carus, which appears only in later manuscripts of his work—is in some doubt. *On the Nature of the Universe* is his only known poem, and it reveals very little about his life. Suetonius wrote a biography of Lucretius nearly two centuries after his death, but it is entirely lost. In his biography of Virgil, the only one of his *Lives of the Poets* to survive intact, Suetonius informs us that Lucretius died in 55 B.C. on the same day as Virgil assumed the toga of manhood. According to St. Jerome (who will have read Suetonius's biography), Lucretius was driven insane by a love potion, writing his poem in lucid intervals before finally committing suicide (*Chronicle* for 94/93 B.C.).

*On the Nature of the Universe* expounds the teachings of Epicurus, who founded his philosophical sect in Athens at the end of the fourth century B.C. It is clearly arranged into three sections of two books each, with a logical progression from discussion of the smallest units in the universe to the largest: Books 1 and 2 introduce the basics of atomic theory and phenomena explained through the behavior of atoms; Books 3 and 4 deal most consistently and directly with humanity, the soul, sensations, and mortality; and Books 5 and 6 discuss the mortality of the wider universe and cosmic phenomena.

In 93 B.C., the Roman proconsul Lucius Gellius made a fool of himself by calling a meeting of the various philosophical sects in Athens and offering to act as a mediator, so that they would not have to waste their lives wrangling among themselves (Cicero, *On the Laws* 1.53). Whether or not this anecdote is actually true, it reflects a view of themselves commonly held by the Romans as a practical-minded and deeply unphilosophical people. They were not alone in this opinion. Galen, the influential Greek doctor, sneered at the Romans' view that philosophy was about as useful as drilling holes in millet seeds, and Lucian considered that "a philosopher in a rich Roman's household is a mere status symbol; he will not be required to expound philosophy, but only to look after the sick and pregnant lap-dog of his patron's wife" (*On Salaried Positions* 34). Cicero records the protests and pleas of the Epicurean community in Athens when a rich Roman, one Gaius Memmius, wished to demolish Epicurus's house, which stood in the way of his building plans (*Letters to His Friends* 13.1). Cicero's letter was written in the summer of 51 B.C., probably very soon after the publication of Lucretius's *On the Nature of the Universe*. The Memmius to whom Lucretius dedicated his Epicurean masterpiece, one of the finest philosophical poems ever written, is almost certainly the very same man.

ΓΝѠΘΙ·ϹΑΥΤΟΝ

**Figure 5: Mosaic**
The Greek aphorism *Gnothi sauton* "Know Yourself" on a mosaic found near the Via Appia south of Rome. We should never forget that all that is mortal is destined to perish. The commonest Latin equivalent as an exhortation to enjoy life while we may is MEMENTO MORI "Remember to Die". Note the skeleton's pose, reminiscent of a diner on a banqueting couch.

It is, of course, an oversimplistic generalization to present the Romans as hardheaded pragmatists with no intellectual interests. By the late Republic, philosophy and rhetoric were standard components in the education of the sons of wealthy and powerful Roman families, and other Romans besides Lucretius—most notably Cicero, the younger Seneca, and the emperor Marcus Aurelius (whose *Meditations* are written in Greek)—have made important contributions to our understanding of ancient thought. We are told by several ancient biographers that Virgil studied Epicurean philosophy in Naples, and this has been confirmed by the excavations in Herculaneum, destroyed in the eruption of Vesuvius in A.D. 79; fragmentary transcripts of lectures by the great Epicurean Philodemus, addressed to Virgil and several other members of his literary circle, have been discovered there, in the ruins of the Villa of the Papyri (*Pap. Herc. Paris* 2.21–23, *Pap. Herc.* 253 *fragment* 12). Perhaps it is reasonable to assume that Lucretius had also studied there, though his poem seems curiously detached from Philodemus's own philosophical writings. Even so, *On the Nature of the Universe* stands in splendid isolation as a magnificent work of art, combining deep philosophical engagement with unique literary merit.

Just as the expression "Platonic love" is used today of nonsexual attraction, whereas Plato's own ideal love is so intense that it transcends mortality, so "Epicureanism" is used in two related but contradictory senses. Epicurus taught that pleasure is the supreme good, that the gods do not concern themselves with human affairs, and that things happen through the random clash of atoms. The other sense of "epicureanism" (lowercase), referring only to the search for pleasure, is largely restricted to gourmet eating. This completely ignores the fact that Epicurus himself actually taught that pleasure could only be attained through tranquility, not through the pursuit of fleeting enjoyment, and requires great effort: "I rejoice in the pleasure I derive from my poor body, through water and bread, and I spit on the pleasures of luxury, not for their own sake, but because of the difficulties which they involve" (Epicurus, *fragment* 181). This latter interpretation of pleasure as the chief goal of Epicureanism, negative and much simpler, goes back to the feuding between the various philosophical sects—the feuding that Gellius wanted to stop. Horace cheerfully acquiesces in the blinkered view of Epicureanism as mere gluttony, when he describes himself as "a fat and sleek pig from Epicurus's sty" (*Epistles* 1.4.15–16).

In antiquity, Epicurus was said to have been the most prolific of all philosophers, but very little of his work has survived, so little in fact that it is impossible for us to know the precise extent of Lucretius's own contribution to the Epicurean doctrines he presents. It was extremely slight, if we take his generous praise of Epicurus literally. For all that Epicurus was supposed by Cicero to regard poetry as mere childish entertainment with no solid value (*On the Ends of Good and Evil* 1.72), Lucretius regards his own poetic enterprise as drawing directly on Epicurus and himself as an orthodox Epicurean, as the opening of his third book makes clear (3.1–6):

> You, who from such great darkness could uplift
> So clear a light, lighting the joys of life,
> You, glory of the Greeks, I follow you
> And in your footprints plant my footsteps firm,
> Not in desire of rivalry, but love
> Drives me to yearn to copy you.

In expounding the teachings of Epicurus through the medium of poetry, Lucretius is following in a long tradition, one that stretches back to the earliest period of recorded Greek literature. Hesiod's *Works and Days* and *Theogony*, providing instruction, respectively, on farming and on the genealogy of the gods, may have been composed as early as the late eighth century B.C. Didactic (literally "teaching") poetry did not develop into a distinct and independent genre in the sense that epic, tragedy, or lyric poetry did, but, with the founding of centers of learning in Alexandria, Antioch, Athens, and elsewhere from the late fourth century on, it offered scholarly poets a way to show their virtuosity in meeting the challenge of versifying often rather abstruse subject matter. The most celebrated of such poems are the *Phaenomena* of Aratus, a versification of a treatise on the constellations by the mathematician Eudoxus, and two works by Nicander, the *Theriaca* and the *Alexipharmaca,* on poisonous creatures and antidotes to poisons.

Didactic poetry flourished in Rome also, in such works as Virgil's *Georgics* (modeled on Hesiod's *Works and Days*); Horace's *Art of Poetry*; Ovid's *Art of Love, Cures for Love,* and *Cosmetics for Women*; Grattius's *Cynegetica* (on hunting, especially with dogs); and Manilius's *Astronomica* (on astrology). Writing from exile (*Sorrows of an Exile* 2.471ff.), Ovid reels off a list of subjects treated in didactic poems, all now lost but little lamented: dice playing, board and ball games, swimming, hoop rolling, cosmetics, etiquette, clay modeling, and wine storage.

What sets Lucretius apart from the majority of didactic poets is his gift of presenting serious teaching in a highly poetic form. Other such poems are either on self-evidently trivial subjects, or their achievement lies in the versification of intractable subject matter, with little concern for actually conveying accurate teaching. For example, the *Phaenomena* was acclaimed as soon as it was published, and enjoyed great popularity, and Nicander's poems were required reading for toxicologists for more than a millennium, yet both poets' lack of expertise in the subjects they dealt with was openly acknowledged. Cicero, who is one of several distinguished intellectuals to translate the *Phaenomena* into Latin, remarks quite casually that "Aratus wrote about the sky and the stars in the most resplendent and excellent verses despite his ignorance of astronomy, while Nicander, although he is so very far removed from the countryside, wrote outstandingly about country affairs through his skill as a poet, not as a farmer" (*On the Orator* 1.69).

Lucretius's concern for the accurate exposition of his subject matter links him with the versified teachings of the earlier Greek tradition, not Hesiod himself but rather the philosophers of the sixth and fifth centuries: Xenophanes, Parmenides, and, above all, Empedocles. It would be unfair to judge these early philosophers by the dislocated and mostly very small fragments of their verse that survive, but it would seem that they did not produce high poetry. Aristotle, who had a far fuller view of the evidence than we do, remarks (*Poetics* 1):

> If someone publishes a work in verse on medicine or natural science, it is customary to call the author a poet; and yet Homer and Empedocles have nothing in common except their meter, so that it would be fair to call Homer a poet, but Empedocles a scientist rather than a poet.

Lucretius himself complains more than once about the difficulty of expounding Greek philosophy in Latin, acknowledging "the poverty of our tongue" (1.136) when it comes to philosophical vocabulary. It might therefore seem reasonable to ask why he made his task even more difficult by writing in verse. Little serious teaching is expounded nowadays through poetry, but there was not the same inclination in antiquity to regard versification as merely ornamental: speaking of instructions on the compounding of drugs, Galen says, "I have often said that works in verse are more useful than those in prose not just because they help us to remember details, but also because they ensure accuracy in the mixing of the ingredients" (13.820).

Nevertheless, many passages of *On the Nature of the Universe* stand out as "sublime," a quality that later critics recognized in Lucretius. Many other very extensive passages, however, are austere and hard to follow, though this is perhaps inevitable, given Lucretius's commitment to the intricacies of Epicurean doctrines. He is aware of the difficulties of his subject matter, and in a long passage in Book 1, repeated almost verbatim at the beginning of Book 4, he famously explains how he will try to make his teaching more palatable (1.933–44):

> Of things so dark in verse so clear
> I write, and touch all things with the Muses' charm.
> In this no lack of purpose may be seen.
> For as with children, when the doctors try
> To give them loathsome wormwood, first they smear
> Sweet yellow honey on the goblet's rim,
> That childhood all unheeding may be deceived
> At the lip's edge, and so drink up the juice
> Of bitter medicine, tricked but not betrayed,
> And by such means gain health and strength again,
> So now do I: for oft my doctrine seems
> Distasteful to those that have not sampled it
> And most shrink back from it.

Horace criticizes poets who attach spectacular set-piece passages to enliven their poetry, like purple patches sewn on drab cloth (*Art of Poetry* 15–16). On first reading, it is easy to regard Lucretius as committing the stylistic fault of indulging in "purple patches." We should, however, take seriously his claim to "touch *all things* with the Muses' charm." The more familiar we become with this great poem, the more this claim is borne out.

# ON THE NATURE OF THE UNIVERSE

## Book 1, 1–145: The Proem

*The poem begins with a powerful and moving invocation of the goddess Venus, to whom the Romans traced the foundation of their race through her son, Aeneas, and his descendant, Romulus. This is followed, in lines 50–61, by an address to Memmius, Lucretius's patron, to whom he dedicates the poem. In the next section (62–79), Lucretius praises Epicurus, whom he does not name here, but identifies in line 67 as "a man of Greece." He then briefly touches on a key issue in his philosophical system, the evils done in the name of religion (80–101), taking from mythology the example of Iphianassa, daughter of Agamemnon, who was sacrificed by the Greeks at Aulis on the eve of the Trojan War. Finally, he outlines the reasons for accepting Epicurean doctrine (102–135), even as he concedes the difficulty of expounding Greek philosophy in Latin verse (136–145).*

O mother of the Roman race, delight
Of men and gods, Venus most bountiful,
You who beneath the gliding signs of heaven
Fill with yourself the sea bedecked with ships
And earth great crop-bearer since by your power
Creatures of every kind are brought to birth
5 And rising up behold the light of sun;
From you, sweet goddess, you, and at your coming
The winds and clouds of heaven flee all away;
For you the earth well skilled puts forth sweet
    flowers;
For you the seas' horizons smile, and sky,
All peaceful now, shines clear with light outpoured.
10 For soon as spring days show their lovely face,
And west wind blows creative, fresh, and free
From winter's grip, first birds of the air proclaim you,
Goddess divine, and herald your approach,
Pierced to the heart by your almighty power.
Next creatures of the wild and flocks and herds
Bound across joyful pastures, swim swift streams,
15 So captured by your charms they follow you,
Their hearts' desire, wherever you lead on.
And then through seas and mountains and
    tearing rivers
And leafy homes of birds and verdant plains,
Striking sweet love into the breasts of all
You make each in their hearts' desire beget

After their kind their breed and progeny.
Since you and only you are nature's guide     20
And nothing to the glorious shores of light
Rises without you, nor grows sweet and lovely,
You I desire as partner in my verses
Which I try to fashion on the Nature of Things,     25
For Memmius, my friend, whom you have willed
At all times to excel in every grace.
For his sake all the more endow my words,
Goddess divine, with everlasting charm.
    Make in the meantime brutal acts of war
In every land and sea be lulled to sleep.     30
For only you can succour humankind
With tranquil peace, since warfare's savage works
Are Mars' dominion, mighty lord of arms,
Who vanquished by the eternal wound of love
Throws himself oft upon your holy bosom
And pillowing his shapely neck, looks up     35
And, gazing at you, feeds his hungry eyes,
Goddess, with love and lolling back his breath
Hangs on your lips. As he lies resting there
Upon your sacred body, come, embrace him
And from your lips pour out sweet blandishments,
Great lady; and for your Romans crave the calm
    of peace.     40
Since neither I, in our country's time of trouble,
Can bring a mind untroubled to my task,
Nor in such straits can Memmius' famous line
Be found to fail our country in its need.
For perfect peace gods by their very nature
Must of necessity enjoy, and immortal life,     45
Far separate, far removed from our affairs.
For free from every sorrow, every danger,
Strong in their own powers, needing naught from us,
They are not won by gifts nor touched by anger.     50
    And now, good Memmius, receptive ears
And keen intelligence detached from cares
I pray you bring to true philosophy;
Lest you should scorn and disregard my gifts
Set out for you with faithful diligence
Before their meaning has been understood.
The most high order of heaven and of the gods
I shall begin to explain to you, and disclose     55
The primal elements of things from which
Nature creates, increases, nourishes
All things that are, and into which again
Nature dissolves them when their time has come.
These in the language of philosophy
It is our custom to describe as matter

Or generative bodies, or seeds of things,
60 Or call them primal atoms, since from them,
Those first beginnings, everything is formed.
　　When human life lay foul for all to see
Upon the earth, crushed by the burden of religion,
Religion which from heaven's firmament
Displayed its face, its ghastly countenance,
65 Lowering above mankind, the first who dared
Raise mortal eyes against it, first to take
His stand against it, was a man of Greece.
He was not cowed by fables of the gods
Or thunderbolts or heaven's threatening roar,
70 But they the more spurred on his ardent soul
Yearning to be the first to break apart
The bolts of nature's gates and throw them open.
Therefore his lively intellect prevailed
And forth he marched, advancing onwards far
Beyond the flaming ramparts of the world,
And voyaged in mind throughout infinity
75 Whence he victorious back in triumph brings
Report of what can be and what cannot
And in what manner each thing has a power
That's limited, and deep-set boundary stone.
Wherefore religion in its turn is cast
Beneath the feet of men and trampled down,
And us his victory has made peers of heaven.
80 One thing I fear now is that you may think
There's something impious in philosophy
And that you are entering on a path of sin.
Not so. More often has religion itself
Given birth to deeds both impious and criminal:
As once at Aulis the leaders of the Greeks,
Lords of the host, patterns of chivalry,
85 The altar of the virgin goddess stained
Most foully with the blood of Iphianassa.
The braiding band around her maiden locks
Dropped down in equal lengths on either cheek;
She saw her father by the altar stand
90 In sorrow, the priests beside him hiding knives,
And all the people weeping when they saw her;
Then dumb with fear she sank down on her knees.
Nor could it help, poor girl, at such a time
That she first gave the king the name of father.
95 For men's hands lifted her and led her on
Pale, trembling, to the altar, not indeed
That in fulfilment of the ancient rite
The brilliant wedding hymns should be her escort,
But that a stainless victim foully stained,
At the very age of wedlock, sorrowing,

She should be slaughtered by a father's blade,
So that a fleet might gain a favoring wind.        100
So great the power religion had for evil.
　　You yourself overcome at times by words
Of terror from the priests, will seek to abandon us.
How many dreams indeed they even now
Invent, to upset the principles of life        105
And all your happiness confound with fear.
And rightly so. For if men could but see
A sure end to their woes, somehow they'd find
　　the strength
To defy the priests and all their dark religion.
But as it is, men have no way, no power        110
To stand against them, since they needs must fear
In death a never-ending punishment.
They do not know the nature of the soul,
Whether it is born, or on the contrary
Makes its way into us at birth, and whether
It perishes with us, when death dissolves it,
Or goes to Hades' glooms and desolate chasms,        115
Or into other creatures finds its way
By power divine, as our own Ennius sang,
Who first brought down from lovely Helicon
A garland evergreen destined to win
Renown among the nations of Italy.
Though none the less in his immortal verse        120
He has expounded that there does exist
A realm of Acheron, in which endure
Not souls of ours and bodies, but some kind
Of wraiths or phantoms, marvelously pale.
And thence the form of Homer, ever deathless,
Came forth, he tells, and pouring out salt tears        125
Began to unfold the nature of the world.
　　Therefore we must lay down right principles
Concerning things celestial, what makes
The motions of the sun and moon, what force
Governs affairs on earth, and most of all
By keenest reasoning perceive whence comes        130
The spirit and the nature of the mind.
And we must ask ourselves what thing it is
That terrifies our minds, confronting us
When we are awake but sickened with disease,
Or buried in sleep, so that we seem to see
And hear in their very presence men who are dead,
Whose bones lie in the cold embrace of earth.        135
　　Nor do I fail to see how hard it is
To bring to light in Latin verse the dark
Discoveries of the Greeks, especially
Because of the poverty of our native tongue,

And the novelty of the subjects of my theme.
140  But still your merit, and as I hope, the joy
Of our sweet friendship, urge me to any toil
And lead me on to watch through nights serene
In my long quest for words, for poetry,
By which to shine clear light before your mind
145  To let you see into the heart of hidden things.

## Book 1, 146–634: Introduction to Atomic Theory

*Lucretius sets out five principles of Epicurus's atomic theory: (1) Matter is eternal; it can neither be created nor destroyed (146–328). (2) There exists a void within which matter moves (329–417). (3) The universe consists of matter and void (418–448). (4) The quality of a substance is determined by the essential properties of matter and void, or by accidents, which are by nature transient (449–482). (5) Atoms are solid, indestructible, and indivisible (483–634).*

Therefore this terror and darkness of the mind
Not by the sun's rays, nor the bright shafts of day,
Must be dispersed, as is most necessary,
But by the face of nature and her laws.
We start then from her first great principle
That nothing ever by divine power comes from nothing.
150  For sure fear holds so much the minds of men
Because they see many things happen in earth and sky
Of which they can by no means see the causes,
And think them to be done by power divine.
So when we have seen that nothing can be created
From nothing, we shall at once discern more
155    clearly
The object of our search, both the source from which
each thing
Can be created, and the manner in which
Things come into being without the aid of gods.
For if things came out of nothing, all kinds
of things
Could be produced from all things. Nothing would
160    need a seed.
Men could arise from the sea, and scaly fish
From earth, and birds hatch in the sky.
Cattle and farm animals and wild beasts of every kind
Would fill alike farmlands and wilderness,
Breed all mixed up, all origins confused.
165  Nor could the fruits stay constant on the trees,

But all would change, all could bear everything.
For lacking its own generative bodies
How could a thing have a mother, fixed and sure?
But as it is, since each thing is created
From fixed specific seeds, the source from which
It is born and comes forth into the shores of light
Is its material and its primal atoms.                     170
That is why all things cannot be born of all things,
Because in each dwells its distinctive power.
And why do roses flourish in the spring
And corn in summer's heat, and grapes in autumn,
Unless because each thing that is created              175
Displays itself when at their own due time
Fixed seeds of things have flowed together, and
the seasons
Attend, and safe and sound the quickened earth
Brings tender growth up to the shores of light?
But if they came from nothing, they'd spring up       180
Quite suddenly, at uncertain intervals,
And wrong times of the year, since primal atoms
Would not be there for an unfavorable season
To restrain from generative union.
Nor would time be needed for the growth of things,
For seeds to collect, if they could grow from
nothing.                                                185
For little babes would suddenly be young men
And in a trice a tree shoot up from earth.
None of this happens, it is plain, because
All things grow slowly, as is natural,
From a fixed seed, and growing keep their character.
So you may know that each thing gets its growth      190
And nourishment from its own material.
And add to this that without the year's fixed rains
The earth cannot put forth its gladdening fruits,
Nor deprived of food can any animal
Beget its kind and keep its life intact.
So you may sooner think that many bodies             195
Are common to many things, like letters in words,
Than that anything can exist without first beginnings.
Again, why could not nature fashion men
so huge
That they could walk through the sea as
across a ford                                           200
And tear apart great mountains with their hands,
And outlive many living generations
If not because each thing needs for its birth
A fixed material that governs what can arise?
So we must admit that nothing can come
from nothing,                                           205

For seed is needed, from which all things created
Can spring, and burgeon into air's soft breezes.
      Lastly, since we see tilled land is better
Than untilled, and the work of hands yields
    better fruits,
210 It is plain to see that in the ground there lie
First elements of things, which when we turn
The fertile clods with ploughshare and break up
The earth's good soil, we start to life and growth.
But if they were not there, then without our labor
You'd see things grow much better by themselves.
      The next great principle is this: that
215       nature
Resolves all things back into their elements
And never reduces anything to nothing.
If anything were mortal in all its parts,
Anything might suddenly perish, snatched from sight.
For no force would be needed to effect
220 Disruptions of its parts and loose its bonds.
But as it is since all things are composed
Of everlasting seeds, until some force
Has met it, able to shatter it with a blow,
Or penetrate its voids and break it up,
Nature forbids that anything should perish.
      And all those things which time through
225       age removes,
If utterly by its consuming power
All the material of them is destroyed,
Whence then does Venus into the light of life
Bring back the race of animals, each after its kind,
Or, when brought back, whence has the
    well-skilled earth
The power to nourish them and make them grow,
Providing food for each after its kind?
230 Whence come the rivers flowing from afar
That feed it? Whence does ether feed the stars?
For all things mortal must have been consumed
By time illimitable and ages past.
But if through that length of time, those ages past,
Things have existed from which this world of ours
235 Consists and is replenished, then certainly
They must be endowed with nature imperishable.
Therefore things cannot ever return to nothing.
      Again, all things alike would be destroyed
By the same force and cause, were they not held fast
By matter everlasting, fastened together
240 More or less tightly in its framing bonds.
A touch would be enough to cause destruction,
Since there would be no eternal elements

Needing a special force to break them up.
But as it is, since the bonds which bind the elements
Are various and their matter is everlasting          245
They stay intact, until they meet a force
Found strong enough to break their textures down.
Therefore no single thing returns to nothing
But at its dissolution everything
Returns to matter's primal particles.
      Lastly, showers perish when father ether          250
Has cast them into the lap of mother earth.
But bright crops rise, and branches in the trees
Grow green, trees grow and ripe fruit burdens them.
Hence food comes for our kind and for wild beasts,
Hence we see happy cities flower with children,          255
And leafy woods all singing with young birds,
Hence cattle wearied by their swollen weight
Lie down across rich pastures, and the white
    milky stream
Flows from their udders. Hence the young progeny
Frisk with weak limbs on the soft grass, their
    youthful minds          260
Intoxicated by the strong fresh milk.
Therefore all things we see do not utterly perish
Since nature makes good one thing from another,
And does not suffer anything to be born
Unless it is aided by another's death.
      Well now, since I have taught that things
    cannot be created          265
From nothing, nor, once born, be summoned
    back to nothing,
Lest you begin perchance to doubt my words,
Because our eyes can't see first elements,
Learn now of things you must yourself admit
Exist, and yet remain invisible.          270
      The wind, its might aroused, lashes the sea
And sinks great ships and tears the clouds apart.
With whirling tempest sweeping across the plains
It strews them with great trees, the mountain tops
It rocks amain with forest-felling blasts,
So fierce the howling fury of the gale,          275
So wild and menacing the wind's deep roar.
Therefore for sure there are unseen bodies of wind
Which sweep the seas, the lands, the clouds of heaven,
With sudden whirlwinds tossing, ravaging.
They stream and spread their havoc just as water          280
So soft by nature suddenly bursts out
In spate when heavy rains upon the mountains
With huge cascades have swollen a mighty flood,
Hurling together wreckage from the woods

285 And whole trees too; nor can strong bridges stand
The sudden force of water coming on,
So swirling with great rains the river rushes
With all its mighty strength against the piers.
It roars and wrecks and rolls huge rocks beneath
its waves
And shatters all that stands in front of it.

290 So also must be the motion of the wind
When it blasts onward like a rushing river.
Wherever it goes it drives on all before it,
Sweeps all away with blow on blow, or else
In twisting eddy seizes things, and then
With rapid whirlwind carries them away.

295 Wherefore again and yet again I say
That winds have hidden bodies, since they rival
In character and action mighty rivers
Possessed of bodies plain for all to see.

          Consider this too: we smell different odors
But never see them coming to our nostrils.

300 We can't see scorching heat, nor set our eyes
On cold, nor can we see the sound of voices.
Yet all these things must needs consist of bodies
Since they are able to act upon our senses.
For nothing can be touched or touch except body

          And clothes hung up beside a wave-tossed
305          shore
Grow damp, but spread out in the sun they dry.
But how the moisture first pervaded them
And how it fled the heat, we do not see.
The moisture therefore is split up into tiny parts

310 That eyes cannot perceive in any way.

          Then too, as the sun returns through
                many years,
A ring on a finger wears thin underneath,
And dripping water hollows out a stone,
And in the fields the curving iron ploughshare
Thins imperceptibly, and by men's feet

315 We see the highways' pavements worn away.
Again, bronze statues by the city gates
Show right hands polished thin by frequent touch
Of travelers who have greeted them in passing.
Thus all these things we see grow less by rubbing,

320 But at each time what particles drop off
The grudging nature of our vision stops us seeing.

          Lastly, whatever time and nature add to things
Little by little, causing steady growth,
No eyes however keen or strained can see.

325 Nor again when things grow old and waste away,
Nor when cliffs overhanging the sea are worn

By salt-consuming spray can you discern
What at each moment each of them is losing.
Therefore nature works by means of hidden bodies.

          Yet all things everywhere are not held in
                packed tight
In a mass of body. There is void in things.          330
To grasp this fact will help you in many ways
And stop you wandering in doubt and uncertainty
About the universe, distrusting what I say.
By void I mean intangible empty space.
If there were none, in no way could things move.          335
For matter, whose function is to oppose and obstruct,
Would at all times be present in all things,
So nothing could move forward, because nothing
Could ever make a start by yielding to it.
But in fact through seas and lands and highest
          heaven          340
We see before our eyes that many things
In many different ways do move; which if there were
          no void,
Would not so much wholly lack their restless
          movement,
But rather could never have been produced at all,
Since matter everywhere would have been
          close-packed and still.          345

          And however solid things are thought to be
Here is proof that you can see they are really porous.
In rocky caverns water oozes through,
The whole place weeping with a stream of drops.
Food spreads to every part of an animal's body.          350
Trees grow and in due time put forth their fruits,
Because all over them through trunks and branches
Right from the deepest roots food makes its way.
Sounds pass through walls, and fly into closed
          buildings,
And freezing cold can penetrate to the bones.          355
But if there were no void for bodies to pass through
You would not see this happen in any way.

          Lastly, why do we see some things weigh
                heavier
Than others, though their volume is the same?
For if there is as much matter in a ball of wool          360
As there is in lead, the weight must be the same,
Since it is the function of matter to press downwards.
But void, by contrast, stays forever weightless.
Therefore a thing of equal size but lighter
Declares itself to have more void inside it,          365
But the heavier by contrast makes proclaim
That it has more matter in it and much less of void.

Therefore there is beyond doubt admixed with things
That which we seek with keen-scented reasoning,
That thing to which we give the name of void.
      And here I must forestall what some
370        imagine,
Lest led astray by it you miss the truth.
They say that water yields to scaly fish
Pressing against it, and opens liquid ways,
Because fish as they swim leave space behind them
Into which the yielding waves can flow together;
375  And that likewise other things can move about
And change their place, though every place is filled.
All this is based on reasoning wholly false.
For how, I ask you, shall the fish advance
Unless the water gives way? And how shall the water
Be able to move back when the fish cannot
380    move?
Either then all bodies must be deprived of movement,
Or we must say that void is mixed with things,
So that each can take the initiative in moving.
      My last point is this: if two moving bodies
Collide and then bounce far apart, all the space
385    between them
Must be void until it is occupied by air.
And however quickly air flows in all round,
It cannot at once fill all the vacant space;
It must fill first one place and then the next
Until it gains possession of the whole.
If anyone thinks that when bodies have
390    sprung apart
What happens is that the air becomes compressed,
He's wrong; for in this case a void is made
That was not there before, and likewise
A void is filled which previously existed.
395  Air cannot be compressed in such a way;
Nor if it could, could it, I think, without void
Shrink into itself and draw its parts together.
Wherefore whatever pleas you may advance
To prolong your argument, yet in the end
You must admit that there is void in things.
400      And many another proof I can adduce
To scrape up credit for my arguments.
But to a mind keen-scented these small traces
Suffice: from them you'll grasp the rest yourself.
As mountain-ranging hounds find by their scent
The lair of beast in leafy covert hid
405  Once they have got some traces of its track,
So one thing after another you by yourself
Will find that you can see, in these researches,

And penetrate all unseen hiding places
And draw the truth from them.
But if you are weary and find the going too hard    410
There's one thing, Memmius, I can safely promise you:
Such bounteous draughts from springs
    o'er-flowing drawn
With sweetest tongue my well-stored mind will pour
That first I fear slow-moving age will creep
Over our limbs and loose the bonds of life    415
Before the full store of my arguments
On any single thing has filled your ears.
      But now, to pick up the thread of my discourse,
All nature, as it is in itself, consists
Of two things: there are bodies and there is void    420
In which these bodies are and through which
    they move.
The senses which are common to men declare
That body has a separate existence.
Without faith firmly founded in our senses
There will be no standard to which we can refer
In hidden matters, giving us the power
To establish anything by reasoning.    425
If there were no place and space, which we call void,
Bodies could not be situated anywhere
And they would totally lack the power of movement,
As I explained a little time ago.
      Now here's a further point. Nothing
      exists    430
Which you could say is wholly distinct from body
And separate from void—a third nature of some kind.
For whatever exists must in itself be something;
If touch affects it however light and small
It will increase the amount of matter by much
    or little,    435
Provided it does exist, and swell its sum.
But if it is intangible, and cannot prevent
Anything anywhere from passing through it,
Doubtless it will be what we call empty void.
Besides, whatever exists will either act on things    440
Or else react to other things acting on it,
Or it will be such that things can happen in it.
But without body nothing can act or react
And nothing can give place save emptiness and void.
Therefore apart from void and matter no third
    substance
Can remain to be numbered in the sum
    of things,    445
Neither one that falls within the range of senses
Nor one that mind can grasp by reasoning.

For you will find that all things that can
    be named
Are either properties of these two things
Or else you can see that they are accidents of them.
A property is something that cannot be
450    separated
Or removed from a thing without destroying it.
As weight to rocks, wetness to water, heat to fire,
Touch to all bodies, intangibility to void.
But slavery, by contrast, poverty and riches
455 Freedom, war, peace and all such things
As may come and go but leave things in their essence
Intact, these, as is right, we call accidents.
        Time likewise does not exist by itself
But a sense follows from things themselves
Of what has been done in the past, what now is
460    present,
And what in addition is to follow after.
And no one has a sense of time distinct
From the movement of things or from their quiet rest.
        Moreover, when they say that Helen's rape
And Troy's defeat in war are facts, we must be careful
465 To see that they do not drive us to admit
That these things have an independent existence,
Arguing that those ancient generations
Of whom these great events were accidents
By time irrevocable have all been borne away.
For whatever is done must be an accident
Either of the whole earth or of some
470    place in it.
Moreover, if no matter had existed
Nor room or space for things to operate,
The flame of love would never have been fired
By Helen's beauty deep in Paris' heart
475 Nor kindled blazing battles of savage war.
No wooden horse unmarked by sons of Troy
Spawning the midnight Greeks from out its womb
Had set the towers of Ilium aflame.
So you may see that events never at all
Exist by themselves as matter does, nor can
480 Be said to exist in the same way as void.
But rightly you may call them accidents
Of matter and of place in which things happen.
        Material objects are of two kinds, partly atoms
And partly also compounds formed from atoms.
485 The atoms themselves no force can ever quench,
For by their solidity in the end they win.
Though it is difficult to believe that anything
That is completely solid can exist.

For lightning passes through the walls of houses,
And likewise sound and voices; iron glows
White hot in fire, and boulders burst apart    490
In the fierce blaze of heat; the solidness
Of gold grows soft and melts, the ice of bronze
Is overcome by fire and liquefied;
And warmth and piercing cold both seep through
    silver
As when in solemn rite we hold the cup    495
We feel both when dewy water is poured in.
So nothing in the world seems really solid.
But yet, because true reason and nature itself
Compel, be with me, while I demonstrate
In a few verses that there do exist
Bodies that are both solid and everlasting,    500
Which we teach are seeds or primal atoms of things
From which now all creation has been made.
        First, since we have found that nature is
    twofold,
Consisting of two widely different things—
Matter and the space in which things happen—    505
Each must exist by itself unmixed with the other.
For where there is empty space which we call void,
There matter is not; and where matter takes its stand
There in no way can empty void exist.
Therefore primal atoms are solid and
    without void.    510
        Again, since void exists in things created,
There must be solid matter surrounding it,
Nor could you prove by truthful argument
That anything hides void, and holds it within it,
Unless you accept that that which holds is solid.
And that again can be nothing but an assembly    515
Of matter, able to hold the void inside it.
Matter therefore, which is absolutely solid,
Can last for ever, though all else be dissolved.
        Then further, if there were nothing void
    and empty,    520
The universe would be one solid mass.
On the other hand, unless there were definite bodies
Able to fill the space each occupies,
Then everything would be vacant space and void.
An alternation then of matter and void
Must clearly exist, the two quite separate,
Since the universe is not completely full    525
Nor yet completely empty. So definite bodies
Exist which distinguish empty space from full.
And, as I have just shown, these can neither
    be broken

By blows struck from outside, nor inwardly
Pierced and unraveled; neither can they be
530 Attacked and shaken in any other way.
For without void it is clear that nothing can
Be crushed or broken or split in two by cutting;
Nor can it let in moisture or seeping cold
535 Or penetrating fire, all forces of destruction.
And the more void a thing contains within it
The deeper strike the blows of those assailants.
Therefore if atoms are solid and without void,
As I have shown, they must be everlasting.
540     Besides, had matter not been everlasting,
All things by now would have returned to nothing,
And the things we see would have been born again
    from nothing.
But since I have shown that nothing can be created
From nothing, nor things made return to nothing,
545 The primal atoms must have immortal  substance
Into which at their last hour all things can be
    resolved
And furnish matter to renew the world.
So atoms must be solid single wholes;
Nor can they be in any other way
Preserved intact from endless ages past
550 Throughout eternity to make things new.
    Consider this also: If nature had set
No limit to the breaking of things, the atoms
    of matter
Would have been ground so small as ages past
Fragmented them, that nothing in due time
Could ever have been conceived from them and
    brought
555 Into the full maturity of life.
For we see things can be dissolved more quickly
Than reconstructed. Therefore what past years
And bygone days of all eternity
Had broken up before now, dissolved and shattered,
560 In time remaining could never be made new.
But as it is, a certain end is given
Of breaking, since we see all things renewed,
And fixed times stand for things after their kind
In which they can attain the flower of life.
    And here's another point. Though atoms
565     of matter
Are completely solid, yet we can explain
Soft things—air, water, earth, and fire—
How they are made and what force works in them,
When once we see that void is mixed with things.
570 But on the other hand, if atoms are soft,

No explanation can be given how flints
And iron, hard things, can be produced; for nature
Will utterly lack a base on which to build.
Their pure solidity gives them mighty power,
And when they form a denser combination
Things can be knit together and show great
    strength.                                              575
    Moreover, if no limit has been set
To the breaking-up of bodies, nevertheless
You must admit that after infinite time
Bodies do survive of every kind of thing,
Not yet attacked by any form of danger;                     580
But since by definition they are breakable,
It is inconsistent to say they could have lasted
Through time eternal struck by endless blows.
    Again, since a limit has been set
For the growth of things and for their hold
    on life,                                               585
Each after its kind, and since it stands decreed
What each by nature can do and cannot,
And nothing changes, but all things are constant
So much that every kind of bird displays
Its own specific markings on its body,                      590
They must for sure consist of changeless matter.
For if the primal atoms could suffer change,
Under some strange compulsion, then no more
Would certainty exist of what can be
And what cannot, in a word how everything
Has finite power and deep-set boundary stone;               595
Nor could so oft the race of men repeat
The nature, manners, habits of their parents.
    To proceed with the argument: in every body
There is a point so small that eyes cannot see it.          600
That point is without parts, and is the smallest
Thing that can possibly exist. It has never existed
Separately by itself, nor ever will,
But only as one part of something else;
Then other and other like parts in due order               605
In close formation fill the atom up.
Since these can have no separate existence,
They must needs cling together in one whole
From which they can in no way be detached.
Atoms therefore are solid single wholes
Cohered from smallest parts close packed
    together,                                               610
Not compounds formed by gathering of parts,
But strong in everlasting singleness.
To them nature allows no diminution
Nor severance, but keeps them as seeds for things.

Besides, unless there is some smallest
615          thing,
The tiniest body will consist of infinite parts,
Since these can be halved, and their halves
          halved again,
Forever, with no end to the division.
So then what difference will there be between
The sum of all things and the least of things?
There will be none at all. For though the sum
620     of things
Will be completely infinite, the smallest bodies
Will equally consist of infinite parts.
But since true reasoning protests against this,
And tells us that the mind cannot believe it,
You must admit defeat, and recognize
625 That things exist which have no parts at all,
Themselves being smallest. And since these exist
You must admit that the atoms they compose
Themselves are also solid and everlasting.

          Lastly, if nature, great creatress, forced
All things to resolve into their smallest parts,
She would have no power to rebuild anything
630     from them.
For partless objects must lack the properties
That generative matter needs—the various
Connections, weights, blows, concourses, and
          movements
By which all things are made and operate.

*In the remainder of the book, Lucretius digresses to refute
the theories of three pre-Socratic Greek philosophers—
Heraclitus, Empedocles, and Anaxagoras—before continuing with atomic theory and a proof that the universe
is infinite.*

## Book 3, 830–1094: The Folly of the Fear of Death

*In the second book, Lucretius dealt with the properties of
atomic particles—their movement, shapes, and secondary
qualities. That book ended with a proof that there is an
infinite number of worlds, followed by a refutation of the
principle of divine control of the universe. The third book
then deals with the crucial topic of the nature of the soul;
the importance of the subject is highlighted by a proem
with passionate praise of Epicurus. The bulk of the book
is then devoted to proof that the soul is physical in nature
and thus mortal. From this it follows that there is no reason
to fear death, which is the subject of the next selection and*
*brings this book to a close. Lucretius drives his point home
by denying the existence of the Underworld: there is no
river Acheron, no Tantalus or Tityos or Sisyphus, famous
victims of punishment in the afterlife. As encouragement he
notes that the old Roman king, Ancus, and other famous
men, who were better than any of us, died in earlier times,
as did even the best of them all, Epicurus.*

Therefore death nothing is to us, nothing          830
That matters at all, since mind we know is mortal.
Long years ago, when the Phoenicians
Were coming in upon us from all sides,
When the world shook with the tumult of war
And quaked, and shivered to the heights
          of heaven,                                     835
When all men doubted where by land and sea
The victory would lie, we stood untroubled.
So, when the end shall come, when the close bonds
Of body and spirit that hold us here shall part
And we shall be no more, nothing can harm us    840
Or make us feel, since nothing of us remains,
Though earth be joined with sea and sea with sky.
And if it were true that mind and spirit can still
Have feeling torn from the body, that means to us
Nothing, since the marriage bonds of body
          and spirit                                     845
Weld us together in one single whole.
No more, again, if time should after death
Collect our matter and bring it back, and if
The lights of life were given back to us,
Would that concern us, not one whit, when once  850
Our memory of ourselves has passed away.
And nothing now comes back to us from that self
That was before, nor from it now can fear
Or anguish ever touch us.
          When you review the whole past length of
          time                                           855
Existing measureless, and think how mixed
And various the motions of matter are,
You will easily believe that the same seeds
Of which we now are made, have often before
Been placed in the positions they are now in.
But memory cannot recall it, since in between
A great gulf is fixed, a halt of life, and all     860
The wandering motions have been scattered far
From things we know. If in a future time
A man is to suffer pain and misery,
He must exist, or else he could not feel it.

But death makes this impossible and forbids
865 The man to exist to whom these ills could come.
Therefore we may be certain that in death
There is nothing to fear, that he who does not exist
Cannot feel pain, that it makes no difference
Whether or not a man has been born before,
When death the immortal has taken his mortal life.
870      So when you see a man resent his fate
That after death his body in the tomb
Must rot, or perish in flames or by wild beasts,
You will know that he rings false, that in his heart
Lies deep some hidden sting, though he denies
875 That he believes there's feeling after death.
He does not really accept what he professes,
He does not wholly remove himself from life,
But all unknown to himself he makes something
Of himself to survive and go on living.
For when in life he tells himself his future
880 That after death his body by wild beasts
And birds will be devoured, torn to pieces,
He's pitying himself. For he doesn't separate
Himself from the body lying there, he thinks
It is still himself, and standing by it gives
Some part of his own feeling to it.
Hence he resents that he was born mortal,
885 He does not see that in real death there'll be
No other self that living could bewail
His perished self, or stand by to feel pain
In body torn or burnt. For if in death
It is painful to be mangled by wild beasts,
I do not see how it is not also painful
890 Laid on a pyre to shrivel in hot flames
Or to be packed in honey and stifled, or
To lie stiff with cold upon a marble slab,
893 Or to be crushed under a weight of earth.
912      Men lie at table, goblets in their hands
And garlands on their brows; and in their hearts
They say 'Short is the joy of men,
915 Too soon it is gone and none can e'er recall it.'
As if in death their chief trouble will be
A parching thirst or burning drought, or a desire
918 For something that they crave and cannot get.
894 'No longer now a happy home will greet you
Nor loving wife, nor your sweet children run
To snatch your kisses and to touch your heart
With silent sweet content. Nor shall you prosper
In your life's work, a bulwark to your people.
Unhappy wretch,' they cry, 'one fatal day
Has taken all those sweets of life away.'

But this they do not add, that the desire       900
Of things like these hangs over you no more.
Which if their minds could truly see and words
Follow, why, then from great distress and fear
They'd free themselves. 'You in the sleep of death
Lie now and will forever lie, removed           905
Far from all pain and grief. But we, who saw
You turned to ashes on a dreadful pyre,
Mourned you in tears insatiable. For ever
No day will lift that sorrow from our hearts.'
Then we must ask, what bitterness is this,
If all things end in sleep and quiet, that       910
A man can waste away in ceaseless grief.         911
For no one feels the want of himself and his life 919
When mind and body alike are quiet in sleep.     920
For all we care, that sleep might have no end.
Free from all yearning for ourselves we lie.
And yet, when a man springs up, startled from sleep
And pulls himself together, through our limbs
Those first beginnings are never far away
From the sense-giving motions of the body.        925
Therefore much less to us must death be thought
To be, if anything can be less than what
We see to be nothing. For matter is thrown apart
More widely after death, and no one wakes
When once death's chilling pause has
    halted him.                                    930
         Again, suppose that nature suddenly
Finding a voice upbraided one of us
In words like these: 'What ails you, mortal man,
And makes you wallow in unhealthy grief?
Why do you moan and groan and weep at death?
For if your former life now past has pleased you  935
And if your blessings through a broken jar
Have not run out, all wasted, unenjoyed,
Why don't you, like a man that's wined and dined
Full well on life, bow out, content, and so
Your exit make and rest in peace, you fool?
But if the things you've liked and loved are spent 940
And life's a grievance to you, why then seek
To add more? They will go just like the others,
No joy at all, and all will end in dust.
Better to make an end of life and trouble.
For there is nothing else I can devise
To please you. Always everything's the same       945
And if your body not yet by the years
Is worn and fails, yet everything remains
The same. There is no change, even if you live
Longer than anyone on earth, and even more

If it should be your fate never to die.'

950 What answer can we give to this, except
That nature's charge is just and that this speech
Makes a good case, from which we're not acquitted?
Consider now an old man who complains
Excessively about his death to come.
Nature would justly cry out louder still
And say in bitter words, 'Away, you rogue,
With all these tears and stop this sniveling.
All life's rewards you have reaped and now
955   you're withered,
But since you always want what you have not got
And never are content with that you have,
Your life has been unfulfilled, ungratifying,
And death stands by you unexpectedly
960 Before the feast is finished and you are full.
Come now, remember you're no longer young
And be content to go; thus it must be.'
She would be right, I think, to act like this,
Right to rebuke him and find fault with him.
For the old order always by the new
Thrust out gives way; and one thing must
965   from another
Be made afresh; and no one ever falls
Into the deep pit and black Tartarus.
Matter is needed for the seeds to grow
Of future generations. Yes, but all
When life is done will follow you, and all
Before your time have fallen, and will fall.
970 So one thing from another will always come.
And life none have in freehold, all as tenants.
     Look back upon the ages of time past
Eternal, before we were born, and see
That they have been nothing to us, nothing at all.
975 This is the mirror nature holds for us
To show the face of time to come, when we
At last are dead. Is there in this for us
Anything horrible? Is there anything sad?
Is it not more free from care than any sleep?
     And all those things, for sure, which fables tell
Exist deep down in Acheron, exist
980 For us in this our life. No Tantalus
Unhappy wretch fears the great rock that hangs
In the air above him, frozen with vain terror.
No. It is in this life that the fear of gods
Oppresses mortals without cause: the fall
They fear is that which chance may bring to them.
No Tityos lying in Acheron is torn
By vultures, nor through all eternity

Dig though they may can they find anything        985
In that vast breast; and though his frame be spread
Immense to cover not nine acres only
But the whole globe of earth with limbs outstretched,
Yet not forever will he suffer pain        990
Nor from his body furnish food always.
Our Tityos is here, lying in love,
And torn by winged cares (anxiety
Consumes him) or tortured by some other craving.
Sisyphus also in this life appears        995
Before our eyes. He seeks the people's votes
Athirst to get the Lictor's rods and axes,
And always loses and retires defeated.
For to seek power that's empty and never got
And always vainly toil and sweat for it
This is to strain to push up the steep hill
The rock that always from the very top        1000
Rolls headlong down again to the plain below.
Another simile! The Danaids.
To be always feeding an ungrateful mind
And fill it with good things, and yet never
To satisfy it (as the seasons do        1005
When they come round bringing their fruits and all
Their manifold delights, and yet we are never
Filled full with all the varied fruits of life),
This I believe is what the story means
Of young and lovely girls that must pour water
Into a leaking urn, and all their pains
Can never fill it. Cerberus and the Furies        1010
Dwell in that land where daylight never comes,
They say, and Tartarus flames belching out;
And none of these exist, nor ever can.
But in this life there is fear of punishment
For evil deeds, fear no less terrible
Than the deeds themselves, and expiation
    of crime,        1015
Prison, and the dread hurling from the rock,
Stripes, torturers, dungeons, red-hot plates,
Firebrands, and even if all of these be spared
The guilty conscience filled with wild foreboding
Applies the goad and scorches itself with whips,
Seeing no end to all these miseries,        1020
No final limit to its punishment,
And fears that after death there's worse to come.
So fools make for themselves a Hell on earth.
    Now here is something you might say to
      yourself:
'Even good Ancus lost the sight of day,        1025
A better man than you, you rogue, by far.

And many kings and powers after him
Have fallen, rulers of great states and nations.
And he who laid a highway through the sea
1030 And o'er the deep a road for armies made,
Taught them to walk across the briny lake
And spurned the roaring waves with his cavalry,
He also lost the glorious light of day
And dying poured his spirit from his body.
Great Scipio, the thunderbolt of war,
Terror of Carthage, gave to earth his bones
As though he had been the humblest of
1035    his slaves.
Add men that found out things of science and beauty
Add all the brotherhood of Helicon,
Whose one and only king throughout the ages
Homer lies now in sleep with all the rest.
Democritus, when a mature old age
Warned him his mind and memory were
1040    fading,
Offered his head right willingly to death.
Epicurus himself died when the light of life
Had run its course, he who in genius
Surpassed the race of men, outshone them all
As the sun risen in heaven outshines the stars.
And you, will you doubt and feel aggrieved
1045    to die?
Already, while you live and see, your life
Is all but dead. You waste most of your time
In sleep. You snore while wide awake; and dream
Incessantly; and always in your mind
You're plagued with fear that's meaningless, and often
You can't make out what is wrong with you,
1050    oppressed,
You drunken wretch, by cares on every side,
And drift on shifting tides of fantasy.'
       If they could see, those men who know
            they feel
A burden on their minds that wearies them,
1055 If they could also know the causes of it
And whence so great a pile of woe lies on them,
They'd never live as most of them do now
Each ignorant of what he wants and seeking always
By change of place to lay his burden down.
A man leaves his great house because
1060    he's bored
With life at home, and suddenly returns,
Finding himself no happier abroad.
He rushes off to his villa driving like mad,
You'd think he's going to a house on fire,

And yawns before he's put his foot inside,    1065
Or falls asleep and seeks oblivion,
Or even rushes back to town again.
So each man flies from himself (vain hope, because
It clings to him the more closely against his will)
And hates himself because he is sick in mind
And does not know the cause of his disease.    1070
Which if he clearly saw, at once he would
Leave everything, and study first to know
The nature of the world. For what is in question
Is not of one hour but of eternity,
The state in which all mortals after death
Must needs remain for all remaining time.    1075
       And what is this great and evil lust of life
That drives and tosses us in doubt and peril?
A certain end of life is fixed for men.
There is no escape from death and we must die.
Again, we live and move and have our being
In the same place always, and no new pleasure    1080
By living longer can be hammered out.
But while we can't get what we want, that seems
Of all things most desirable. Once got,
We must have something else. One constant thirst
Of life besets us ever open-mouthed.
And there is doubt what fortunes later years
And chance may bring us and what end awaits.    1085
Nor by prolonging life, one single second
Do we deduct from the long years of death.
Nor have we strength to make in any way
Our time less long once death has come to us.
Live though you may through all ages that
       you wish,    1090
No less that eternal death will still await,
And no less long a time will be no more
He who today from light his exit made
Than he who perished months and years ago.

*In the first part of Book 4, Lucretius describes sensory perceptions in terms of Epicurean physics. Mental images, sight, hearing, taste, and smell can all be explained as physical phenomena. So too sleep and dreams, and sexual desire. This leads to the concluding section of the book, in which Lucretius argues with particular rhetorical force that Venus, or sexual love, is harmful. The final pair of books is devoted to Epicurean cosmology, with Book 5 describing the physical nature of the earth and other heavenly bodies. It ends with a remarkable section on the origins of life and the development of civilization. The sixth book, which many* believe to be unfinished, explains a variety of physical phenomena in terms of atomic theory, including thunder, lightning, earthquakes, volcanoes, and magnets. It concludes, abruptly and unexpectedly, with an explanation of plagues and a description of the great plague at Athens in 430 B.C.

## AFTERWORD

In a letter from Cicero to his younger brother Quintus, sent in February 54 B.C., we learn that the two brothers had been reading *On the Nature of the Universe*: "Lucretius's poetry is as you say—sparkling with natural genius, but plenty of technical skill. But of that more when you come." That would have been an interesting conversation to listen in on, because Cicero never mentions Lucretius again, not even in his philosophical treatises when he is attacking Epicurean philosophy. So it is a bit surprising to learn from St. Jerome that Cicero became Lucretius's literary executor. *On the Nature of the Universe* was studied and admired by succeeding generations of poets. Some of the works that were plainly influenced by him and were considered important by the Romans have been lost, such as the didactic poems of Aemilius Macer on birds and Varro of Atax on the weather, both of which are mentioned by other ancient writers. But Virgil's *Georgics* shows the influence of Lucretius's rhetorical power, and when he writes of "the fortunate man who could know the causes of the universe" (*Georgics* 2.490), he is thinking of Lucretius.

The early Christians were of two minds about *On the Nature of the Universe*. In it they found plenty of ammunition to use against traditional Roman religion, but early Christian writers vehemently opposed Epicureanism's insistence that pleasure is the supreme good, that mankind is mortal, and, in particular, that no deity watches over us. Lactantius (ca. A.D. 250–325) is one example. He was a professor of rhetoric at Nicomedia in Bithynia when he converted to Christianity, and his *Divine Institutes,* written in the aftermath of the Great Persecution of Christians in 303, is one of the landmarks of early Christian literature. Lactantius knew Lucretius well, presumably from his days as a pagan teacher of literature, but Epicureanism was anathema to him after his conversion. He writes of the "stupidity" of Epicurus and the "ravings" of Lucretius (*On the Works of God* 6.1), and of the proem to Book 3 with its praise of Epicurus he says, "I can never read these verses without laughing" (*Divine Institutes* 3.17.28). By the fifth century, however, St. Augustine believed that interest in Epicurus and his teachings had faded to the point where hardly anyone was talking about Epicureanism in the schools (*Letters* 2.118c), and he mentions Lucretius by name only once. Augustine was probably right, for apart from some references in grammarians and lexicographers, there is not much evidence that anyone was reading *On the Nature of the Universe* anymore.

Ovid once said that "the sublime poetry of Lucretius will only perish when time destroys the earth" (*Amores* 1.15.23), but he was very nearly wrong. Three copies of a manuscript of Lucretius were made in the ninth century, when he was being read by a small number of learned scholars, such as the Irishman Dungal or the German Hrabanus Maurus, but there is no evidence that anyone read *On the Nature of the Universe* again until the fifteenth century. In 1417, the humanist Poggio Bracciolini was attending the Council of Constance in what is now southern Germany, when he learned of a manuscript of Lucretius in a "pretty far off place," which he does not name. That manuscript then went underground again (it is now in a library in Leiden), but because Poggio had a copy made, which he sent to Niccolò Niccoli in Florence, texts of *On the Nature of the Universe* began to multiply and Lucretius was being read again.

In Italy during the Renaissance, Lucretius found an enthusiastic reception, especially in Florence under the Medicis. The great scholar and poet Angelo Poliziano (1454–94) studied problems in the text of *On the Nature of the Universe* and imitated passages of Lucretius in his poetry, which he composed in both Latin and Italian. In his tribute to Giuliano de' Medici's victory in a joust, *Le Stanze per la Giostra*, Poliziano evokes the magnificent Hymn to Venus, with which Lucretius began his poem (1.99–101):

A young woman with nonhuman countenance is carried on a conch shell, wafted to shore by playful zephyrs; and it seems that heaven rejoices in her birth. You would call the foam real, the sea real, real the conch shell and real the blowing wind; you would see the lightning in the goddess's eyes, and sky and elements laughing about her . . . and where the strand was imprinted by her sacred and divine step, it had clothed itself in flowers and grass.

This may have been the vehicle by which Poliziano's good friend, the artist Botticelli, came to incorporate elements of Lucretius's Venus in a painting he executed for Lorenzo di Pierfrancesco de' Medici, the famous *Birth of Venus*.

With the advent of the Counter-Reformation, Lucretius fell afoul of the church once again, but he still found readers. One of the most remarkable testimonies to the continuing attraction of *On the Nature of the Universe* is a poem, composed in Latin by a Catholic bishop, Melchior de Polignac (1661–1742). Polignac's *Anti-Lucretius*, published posthumously in 1745, in nine books intended to confute Lucretius, is in fact a close imitation of the Roman poet.

The first English translation of Lucretius was by the Puritan poet Lucy Hutchinson (1620–81), who omitted the attack on sex from Book 4 and later repented of her involvement with Lucretius at all. John Dryden (1631–1700) rendered several portions of *On the Nature of the Universe* into English verse, and other contemporaries, such as John Wilmot, Second Earl of Rochester (1647–80), also set their hand to translating and adapting Lucretius. Lucretius's influence is to be found in poets, philosophers, and scientists as diverse as Pierre de Ronsard, lyric poet of the French Pléiade (1524–85); Michel de Montaigne (1533–92), French philosopher and essayist; Charles Darwin (1809–82), the British naturalist; and Karl Marx (1818–83), who admired his atheism.

There were several admirers of Lucretius among the English Romantics, especially Shelley (1792–1822), who approved of his atheism and in *A Defence of Poetry* called him "the best of the Latin poets." But while Shelley read *On the Nature of the Universe* as an emblem of hope for a more humane world, Lucretius was increasingly being transformed into a gloomy, tragic figure, helped along by contemporary classical scholars. In 1850, the great German philologist Karl Lachmann published his celebrated edition of Lucretius's poem, which not only demonstrated how it had been transmitted from antiquity but also provided an important theoretical model for editing the texts of other ancient authors. In England soon after, in 1864, the Cambridge scholar H. A. J. Munro, inspired in part by Lachmann's work, produced an imposing edition of the poem in three volumes, with text, translation, and explanatory notes. It was this edition that Tennyson perused as he composed his *Lucretius*. For Tennyson, as for Matthew Arnold in his lecture "On the Modern Element in Literature," "depression and ennui" are the hallmarks of the modern, and for them Lucretius was a modern. Tennyson's *Lucretius* takes its starting point from St. Jerome's story about his death from a love potion and thus transforms Lucretius's calmly powerful portrayal of a universe ordered according to Epicurean atomism into a nightmarish vision instead (37–44):

A void was made in Nature; all her bonds
Crack'd; and I saw the flaring atom-streams
And torrents of her myriad universe,
Ruining along the illimitable inane,
Fly on to clash together again, and make
Another and another frame of things
For ever: that was mine, my dream, I knew it
Of and belonging to me.. .

Even Cicero, who thought Epicureanism a bit silly and would have been quite comfortable in Victorian England, might well have been puzzled by this portrayal of the rationalist poet of nature.

# CATULLUS

(Gaius Valerius Catullus, ca. 85–ca. 54 B.C.)

CATULLUS WAS BORN IN VERONA, NORTH OF THE RIVER PO, IN ABOUT 85 B.C. THE TOWN had become a Roman colony just a few years earlier, in the aftermath of the Social War, in which the Italian allies (*socii*) had fought to free themselves from their unequal partnership with Rome. They were defeated after a very bloody struggle but achieved greater representation in the alliance. Until after Catullus's death, the most northerly third of Italy was not integrated into Italy but continued to be designated as a province, Cisalpine Gaul, that is, Gaul on this side of the Alps. It is, however, reasonable to assume that Catullus's family probably belonged to the municipal aristocracy, the local ruling class to whom the Romans typically entrusted responsibility for regional administration.

Like many young men from such a background, Catullus came to Rome to embark on a public career. It seems, however, that he found politics uncongenial. His poems reveal that he strongly detested Gaius Memmius, the governor of Bithynia in 57/56, in whose entourage he served. We know few other firm details about Catullus's short life, and most of those few must be culled from his poetry. He was one of the central figures in the literary world of Rome in his day, a leading member of the circle of poets whom Cicero labels rather dismissively as the "neoterics," or avant-garde. Like many of his contemporaries, he seems to have enjoyed a decadent lifestyle quite out of harmony with traditional Roman values. This is particularly reflected in his poems concerning his turbulent love affairs, most notably with a woman whom he calls Lesbia. We should, however, perhaps be wary of assuming that Catullus's poetry presents a wholly accurate picture of his life; as he himself warns us, "the true poet should be chaste himself, [but] his verses need not be" (16.5–6).

Catullus flatters his mistress by addressing her as "Lesbia," for that pseudonym associates her with Sappho, the great archaic Greek poet from the island of Lesbos. Lesbia was very probably one of the sisters of Publius Clodius Pulcher, who furthered his career as a popularist politician by changing his name from the venerably aristocratic form Claudius and by having himself adopted into a plebeian family (his adoptive father being younger than he was himself). Clodius created a scandal by dressing as a woman in order to attend the festival of the Good Goddess in 62 B.C., allegedly to carry on an affair with Caesar's wife. Since all three of Clodius's sisters were referred to as Clodia, it is not clear precisely which one was Lesbia. It is likely, however, that she is the Clodia denounced by Cicero so memorably in his speech on behalf of Caelius Rufus (see p. 121): among many more serious charges, he criticizes her for buying gardens by the Tiber so that she could leer at young men swimming naked. That speech was delivered in 56 B.C., when Catullus's short poetic career was at its height.

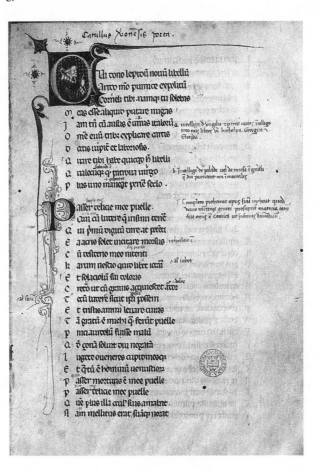

**Figure 6: Catullus ms.**
The first page of a manuscript of Catullus in the Bodleian Library in Oxford. The opening line reads *Cui dono lepidum nouum labellum* (To whom do I give my nice new little book?). Note the use of abbreviations, the addition of marginal comments, and the identification label at the top of the page, written by a later hand: *Catullus Veronensis poeta* (Catullus the poet from Verona).

While the figure of Lesbia has become almost synonymous with Catullus's poetry, fewer than a quarter of his poems, constituting hardly a tenth of his oeuvre, concern her at all, and she is named in a mere thirteen poems. So Ovid can remark (*Sorrows of an Exile* 2.427–30):

> In his saucy strains Catullus often
>     Sang of his lady, Lesbia falsely named,
> And not content with her in many other
>     Passions his own adultery proclaimed.

Catullus names at least three other women as his lovers, and the only time he actually describes himself "tossing on his bed" in frustrated ardor is in poem 32, addressed to a certain Ipsitilla. Two further, male, lovers are also mentioned by Catullus, Juventius (poems 24, 48, 81, and 99) and Camerius (poems 55 and 58*b*), one or the other of whom may be his partner in poem 56.

Catullus lived in the center of a violent world. By the late Republic, bribery, corruption, intimidation, and violence were commonplace in Roman political life. Looking back to the political turmoil at the end of the Republic, the fourth-century historian Ammianus Marcellinus observes that "anyone wishing to know all the different atrocities committed so repeatedly in that period would also be misguided enough to think of investigating the number of grains of sand or the weight of mountains" (14.34). In *A Little Handbook on Running for Office,* attributed to Cicero's brother Quintus, we find the following advice for candidates campaigning for office: "If at all possible, you should arrange for some scandal to be stirred up against your competitors, involving either criminal behavior or sex or bribery, depending on their character."

The trenchant personal attacks in Catullus's poetry reflect his political convictions. Many of his most stinging invectives are directed at adherents of Julius Caesar. Although Caesar felt that his own reputation was irreparably damaged by Catullus's attack on Mamurra (referred to by Catullus in several poems as Mentula ["Prick"]), according to Suetonius he eventually invited Catullus to dinner to heal their differences, just as he also tried to win over Catullus's friend and fellow poet Licinius Calvus. (After Caesar's assassination, another member of Catullus's literary group, Gaius Helvius Cinna, was mistaken by the angry mob for Lucius Cornelius Cinna, one of the assassins, and his head was paraded on a pole through the streets.) Catullus's poem 29, which is addressed to Caesar and concerns Mamurra's profiteering after the invasion of Britain, is typical of such political invective, referring to Mamurra as a "multifucking tool." However surprising such utterly uninhibited and crudely sexual language may seem today, it is typical of the political attacks of its time. When Octavian was besieging Mark Antony's wife and brother in Perugia in 41 B.C., he wrote an epigram preserved by Martial in *Epigrams* 11.20 as an example of the future emperor's ability to express himself with commendable *simplicitas Romana* ("Roman directness"):

> Fulvia has determined that I must fuck her as a punishment because her husband Antony is fucking the eastern queen Glaphyra. What, me fuck Fulvia? Suppose the informer Manius begged me to bugger him? Would I do it? Not while I have any sense. 'Either fuck me or let's fight' says Fulvia. My cock is dearer to me than life itself—sound the charge!

The delightfully appalling abuse of Aemilius in Catullus's poem 97 perhaps shows his gift for personal invective at its most extreme. It takes an unusually robust and earthy cast of mind to devise such imagery as that in lines 5 through 8:

> The mouth has teeth half-a-yard long
> > And gums like an ancient wagon-chassis.
> Moreover when it opens up it's like the cunt
> > Of a pissing mule dehiscent in a heat-wave.

Aemilius would probably be pleased enough that, like that of several other victims of Catullus's invectives, his identity has been otherwise lost to posterity.

It is not known how Catullus himself ordered his poetry, but there is a tendency among scholars nowadays to consider the collection in three rather general sections: the short poems in a variety of meters (1–60), the "long" poems (61–68), and the epigrams (69–116, all written in the same meter, the elegiac couplet). Whole books have been written on the perceived significance of the arrangement, but there is little consensus: each reader sees different things. Perhaps the most attractive feature is the unpredictable ordering of the individual poems. Poem 84 is a pleasantly trivial anecdote ridiculing the pretensions of an upstart:

'Hemoluments' said Arrius, meaning to say
     'Emoluments' and 'hambush' meaning 'ambush',
Hoping that he had spoken most impressively
     When he said 'hambush' with great emphasis.
His mother, her free-born brother and his maternal
     Grandparents, I believe, all spoke like that.
Posted to Syria he gave the ears of all a rest.
     They heard the same words smoothly and gently spoken
And had no fear thenceforward of such aspirates,
     When suddenly there came the frightful news
That after Arrius arrived the Ionian waves,
     Ionian no more, became 'Hionian'.

The poem immediately following, a single elegiac couplet, is much admired for its poignant encapsulation of a lover's tribulations:

I hate and love. Perhaps you're asking why I do that?
     I don't know, but I feel it happening, and am racked.

Similarly, poem 96 is a simple expression of sympathy to his friend Calvus on the premature death of his wife Quintilia:

If anything grateful or welcome, Calvus, can befall
     The silent tomb from grief of ours,
From the longing with which we relive old loves
     And weep for past friendships thrown away,
Quintilia surely feels less grief at untimely death
     Than gladness for your love.

We are wholly unprepared for the radical change in topic and tone in the next poem, the obscenity-filled attack on Aemilius, part of which is quoted above.

Catullus also employs the same kind of dramatic variations within poems. In poem 11, for example, he builds tension with a breathless four-stanza review of the wild and exotic regions of the world, then suddenly dismisses Lesbia in crude terms for her three hundred lovers, "loving none truly but again and again rupturing all's groins"; the poem then concludes with a lovely simile, comparing his love for her to a flower plowed under at the edge of a meadow. Poem 58, a single sentence of five short lines, starts with ecstatic praise for his beloved Lesbia but ends with the gross obscenity that Lesbia "peels great-hearted Remus's grandsons." "Peels" translates the verb *glubit,* which refers literally to stripping the bark from trees; the precise metaphorical sense intended here is debated by scholars, but the wonderfully awful sound of the word and its incongruous juxtaposition to the epic phrase "great-hearted Remus's grandsons" are highly memorable.

Catullus is also a learned poet, steeped in the traditions of Greek and Latin literature, and this learning is often on display. In poem 95, he heralds the publication of his friend Cinna's *Zmyrna,* a short and carefully wrought poem, of which only three brief fragments now survive, preserved by grammarians interested in their linguistic eccentricity:

*Zmyrna,* my Cinna's, brought forth at last, nine harvests
     And nine winters after her inception!
Meanwhile Hortensius five hundred thousand in one...

*Zmyrna* will travel far—to Satrachus's sunken waves,
        Long will the white-haired centuries read *Zmyrna*.
Volusius's *Annals,* though, will die beside the Padua
        And often make loose jackets for mackerel.
Dear to my heart is my comrade's small-scale monument;
        The crowd can admire longwinded Antimachus.

By its close imitation of Callimachus's epigram in praise of Aratus's *Phaenomena,* a versification of a prose treatise on astronomy and a catalog of weather signs, this poem is Catullus's clearest declaration of his allegiance to the poetic principles of Callimachus, the third-century scholar-poet who worked in the Library at Alexandria. Callimachus and his followers advocated short, sophisticated poetry in preference to long, inartistic compositions. It seems probable that interest in Callimacheanism was stimulated by the arrival in Rome of Parthenius of Nicaea, after the capture of his hometown in the late 70s by a relative of Cinna, for he had a reputation as a latter-day Callimachus and became a close friend of Virgil and Cornelius Gallus, the founder of Augustan love elegy. Catullus's own equivalent to Cinna's *Zmyrna* is poem 64, a reworking of the well-known myths of Peleus and Thetis and of Theseus and Ariadne. That *epyllion* (little epic) is his magnum opus, and it is singled out by the minor Augustan elegist Lygdamus when he describes Catullus as *doctus* (learned), an honorific epithet given to him by other poets also.

Sometimes the knowledge needed to unpack Catullus's learned references is hard for us to come by, although the point would have been quite familiar to Catullus's first readers. For example, it was almost two hundred years after the rediscovery of Catullus's poetry before scholars understood the reference in poem 74 to Harpocrates, a chubby little Egyptian god usually portrayed with a finger to his lips enjoining silence:

Gellius had heard that uncle liked to reprimand
        Any who spoke or acted naughtily.
To avoid this for himself he massaged uncle's wife,
        Turned uncle into an Harpocrates,
And thus achieved his aim. For were he now to stuff
        Uncle himself, uncle wouldn't say a word.

By getting his uncle to fellate him, Gellius will prevent him from censuring him for having an affair with his aunt. Sometimes, it must be conceded, scholars expend enormous energy and ingenuity in ways that would have amused Catullus. Since the Renaissance, arguments have raged over the portrayal of Lesbia's pet sparrow in poems 2 and 3: in 2, she plays with it and cuddles it, but in 3 Catullus laments its death and departure to the Underworld. Are we to read the poems literally, or does the sparrow symbolize the poet's penis, once playful but latterly impotent? Perhaps Catullus's contemporaries asked this same question.

Most ancient poets are known to us for their works in a single genre: we have only comedies from Plautus and Terence, only didactic poetry from Lucretius, only satire from Juvenal. When poets write in several genres, there is usually a clear distinction between the various works, as between Virgil's pastoral *Eclogues,* his didactic *Georgics,* and his epic *Aeneid.* Despite the fact that Catullus's poetic corpus is considerably smaller than two books of Lucretius's *On the Nature of the Universe* or three books of Virgil's *Aeneid,* it is truly exceptional in that it ranges over a wide and miscellaneous spectrum that complicates any attempt at generic analysis. Love poems, invective, anecdotes, literary debate, marriage songs, and mythological narratives are all to be found together in a collection that ranges from the trivial and banal to the sublime and profound.

## POEMS 1–60

### 1

*A dedication to Cornelius Nepos, a fellow native of Cisalpine Gaul and author of a lost work called the* Chronica, *which dealt with the history of world in three papyrus rolls.*

Whom do I give a neat new booklet
Polished up lately with dry pumice?
You, Cornelius; for you always
Thought my trivia important,
5  Even when you dared (the one Italian)
Unfold the whole past in three papyri—
Learned, by Jupiter, and laborious!
So take this mere booklet for what it's worth,
Which may my Virgin Patroness
10  Keep fresh for more than one generation.

### 2 and 2b

*A prayer addressed to his girl's pet sparrow, followed by a three-line fragment of another poem, referring to the story of Atalanta.*

Sparrow, my girl's darling,
Whom she plays with, whom she cuddles,
Whom she likes to tempt with finger-
Tip and teases to nip harder
5  When my own bright-eyed desire
Fancies some endearing fun
And a small solace for her pain,
I suppose, so heavy passion then rests:
Would I could play with you as she does
10  And lighten the spirit's gloomy cares!
......
It's welcome to me as they say
To fleet-foot girl was golden apple
That loosed the girdle tied too long.

### 3

*A lament for his girl's dead sparrow, or as some readers have interpreted it since the Renaissance, Catullus's sexual impotence.*

Grieve, O Venuses and Loves
And all the lovelier people there are:
My girl's sparrow is dead,
Sparrow, my girl's darling,

Whom she loved more than her eyes.            5
For honey-sweet he was and knew his
Mistress well as a girl her mother,
Nor would he ever leave her lap
But hopping around, this way, that way,
Kept cheeping to his lady alone.              10
And now he's off on the dark journey
From which they say no one returns.
Shame on you, shameful dark of Orcus,
For gobbling up all the pretty things!
You've robbed me of so pretty a sparrow.      15
O what a shame! O wretched sparrow!
Your fault it is that now my girl's
Eyelids are swollen red with crying.

### 4

*On a boat that used both sail and oars (the "little palms" mentioned twice) to carry the speaker to exotic places in the eastern Mediterranean. Now it is dedicated to the twin gods, Castor and Pollux, the guardians of ancient mariners.*

The sailing-boat you see there, visitors,
Claims to have been the speediest of ships
And not to have been incapable of passing
Any swimming timber if need be
By flying with either little palms or canvas.   5
And he denies the threatening Adriatic
Coast can deny this, the Cycladic islands,
Famous Rhodes, Propontis shivering
In Thracian gales or the grim Pontic gulf
Where he, the future boat, was first of all      10
A long-haired wood; for on Cytorus' top
His hair would often speak in a loud whisper.
Pontic Amastris and box-clad Cytorus,
To you these things were best known and still are,
The boat claims. In his distant origin            15
He says it was your summit that he stood on,
Your sea in which he dipped his little palms,
And from there through so many stormy straits
Carried his master, whether from left or right
The breeze was calling, or a following            20
Jupiter fell upon both feet at once.
Nor were there any vows to the shore Gods
Made for him as he voyaged finally
From the open sea right up to this clear lake.
But that was in the past; now he grows old         25
In quiet retirement and devotes himself
To you, twin Castor, and you, Castor's twin.

5

*The first mention of Lesbia, in a poem of controlled exuberance.*

We should live, my Lesbia, and love
And value all the talk of stricter
Old men at a single penny.
Suns can set and rise again;
5 For us, once our brief light has set,
There's one unending night for sleeping.
Give me a thousand kisses, then a hundred,
Then another thousand, then a second hundred,
Then still another thousand, then a second hundred,
10 Then, when we've made many thousands,
We'll muddle them so as not to know
Or lest some villain overlook us
Knowing the total of our kisses.

6

*Catullus imagines himself poking about his friend Flavius's bedroom and deducing that he has a new love interest that he is keeping a secret.*

Were she not unsmart and unwitty,
Flavius, you'd want to tell Catullus
About your pet and couldn't keep quiet.
In fact you love some fever-ridden
5 Tart and you're ashamed to own it.
That you're not spending deprived nights
Silent in vain the bedroom shouts
Perfumed with flowers and Syrian oils,
The pillow equally this side and that
10 Dented, and the rickety bed's
Yackety perambulation.
It's no good keeping quiet about it.
You'd not present such fucked-out flanks
If you weren't up to something foolish.
15 So tell us what you've got, for good
Or ill. I wish to emparadise
You and your love in witty verse.

7

*A playful reprise of poem 5 with made-up words ("mega-kisses" Lat. basiationes and "silphiophorous" Lat. lasarpiciferis) and allusions to far-off Cyrene, home of the Greek poet Callimachus and burial place of its founder, Battus.*

You ask how many of your mega-kisses
Would more than satisfy me, Lesbia.
Great as the sum of Libyssan sand lying
In silphiophorous Cyrene
From the oracle of torrid Jove        5
To old Battus' Holy Sepulchre,
Or many as the stars, when night is silent,
That watch the stolen loves of humans—
To kiss you just so many kisses
Would more than satisfy mad Catullus;        10
The inquisitive couldn't count them all
Nor evil tongue bring them bad luck.

8

*A dramatic monologue, in which Catullus, like many a young man in Greek New Comedy or Roman Comedy, wrestles with his feelings for an unworthy object.*

Wretched Catullus, you should stop fooling
And what you know you've lost admit losing.
The sun shone brilliantly for you, time was,
When you kept following where a girl led you,
Loved by us as we shall love no one.        5
There when those many amusing things happened
Which you wanted nor did the girl not want
The sun shone brilliantly for you, truly.
Now she's stopped wanting, you must stop, weakling.
Don't chase what runs away nor live wretched        10
But with a mind made up be firm, stand fast.
Goodbye, girl. Catullus now stands fast,
Won't ask or look for you who're not willing.
But you'll be sorry when you're not asked for.
Alas, what life awaits you now, devil?        15
Who'll find you pretty now? What type touch you?
Whom will you love and whose be called henceforth?
Whom will you kiss? and you will bite whose lips?
But you, Catullus, mind made up, stand fast.

9

*A poem of welcome, celebrating the return of his friend, Veranius, perhaps a writer too, from a journey to Spain, probably as part of a magistrate's entourage.*

Veranius, of all my friends
The foremost by three hundred miles,
Have you come home to your household Gods
And like-minded brothers and old mother?
You have? O happy news for me!        5

I'll find you safe, hear you describing
Iberian places, exploits, tribes
In your own fashion. Embracing you
I'll kiss your merry face and eyes.
10    O of all the happier people
Who's happier or more glad than I?


10


*His friend Varus's girlfriend quizzes Catullus about his service on the governor's staff in Bithynia in Asia Minor, about which he has nothing good to say. When he claims, however, to have got himself some slaves to act as litter-bearers, he gets caught in the lie after she asks to borrow them to take her to the temple of the popular Egyptian god Serapis.*


Free in the Forum I was taken
By my Varus to meet his love,
A tartlet, as I thought at first,
By no means unwitty or unattractive.
5    Once arrived there we got talking
On various topics, including
Bithynia—how were things there now
And had it made me any brass?
I answered straight—there was nothing now
10    For praetors themselves or their staff,
Why anyone should come back flusher,
Especially when a shit's your praetor,
Who doesn't give a toss for staff.
'But surely' they said 'you collected
15    What's said to be the local product—
Bearers?' Whereat, to make the girl
Think me one of the luckier ones,
I said, 'Things weren't so bad for me
Despite my drawing a bad province
20    That I could miss eight straight-backed men.'
In fact I'd no one, here or there,
To heave up on his head the broken
Leg of a second-hand camp-bed.
At this she said, like the bitch she was,
25    'Lend them to *me*, please, dear Catullus,
Just for a little. I need taking
To Sérapis.' 'Wait,' I replied,
'What I said just now I had, I
Wasn't thinking. It's my messmate
30    Cinna—Gaius, you know—they're his.
But what's it matter whose they are?
I use them as if they were mine.

But you're damned tactless—a living nuisance
Who won't allow one to speak loosely.'


11


*Two friends of Catullus, Marcus Furius Bibaculus, a poet, and the otherwise unidentified Aurelius, are addressed in this poem, which evokes the far reaches of the Roman world. The reference to Julius Caesar's invasions of Britain in 55 or 54 B.C. provides one of the few dates in Catullus's work.*


Furius and Aurelius, Catullus' comrades,
Whether he'll push on to furthest India
Where the shore is pounded by far-resounding
Eoan rollers,

To Hyrcania or effeminate Arabia,                  5
The Sacians or the arrow-bearing Parthians
Or those levels to which the seven-double
Nilus gives color,

Or make his way across the towering Alps
To visit the memorials of great Caesar,             10
The Gallic Rhine, those horrible woad-painted
And world's-end Britons—

All this, whatever the will of Heaven above
May bring, ready as you are to brave together,
Simply deliver to my girl a brief dis-             15
courteous message:

Farewell and long life with her adulterers,
Three hundred together, whom hugging she holds,
Loving none truly but again and again
Rupturing all's groins;                             20

And let her not as before expect my love,
Which by her fault has fallen like a flower
On the meadow's margin after a passing
Ploughshare has touched it.


12


*Addressed to the brother of Asinius Pollio, historian and poet, who was an important figure in the literary world of the mid-first century B.C. Pinching a napkin at a dinner party was bad form then as now, especially if it was made of linen from Saetabis in Spain.*


Marrucine Asinius, you misuse
Your left hand; while we joke and drink
You lift the napkins of the careless.

You think it clever? You're wrong, you fool.
5   It's a downright dirty and vulgar trick.
You don't believe me? Believe Pollio
Your brother, who would gladly give
A talent to undo your thefts.
For he's a boy full of wit and charm.
10  Return my napkin, then, or expect
Three hundred hendecasyllables.
I'm not concerned about its value,
But it's a memento of my comrade.
For Veranius and Fabullus sent me
15  Saetaban napkins as a gift from Spain.
So I must love them like my dear
Fabullus and Verániolus.

### 13

*A humorous poem inviting Fabullus (perhaps the same person mentioned in the previous poem) to a dinner party where Lesbia will be in attendance.*

You'll dine well, my Fabullus, at mine
One day soon if the Gods are kind to you,
If you will bring with you a dinner
Good and large plus a pretty girl
5   And wine and salt and all the laughs.
If, I repeat, you bring these with you,
Our charmer, you'll dine well; for your
Catullus' purse is full of cobwebs.
But in return you'll get love neat
10  Or something still more choice and fragrant;
For I'll provide the perfume given
My girl by Venuses and Cupids
And when you smell it you'll ask the Gods,
Fabullus, to make you one large nose.

### 14 and 14b

*The poet Calvus, with whom Catullus had much in common, made his reputation as an orator by prosecuting Publius Vatinius. For some inexplicable reason, presumably as a joke, he has sent Catullus an anthology of bad poetry. This is followed by the first three lines of a lost poem.*

Did I not love you more than my eyes,
Calvus you joker, then for that gift
I'd hate you with Vatinian hatred.
What have I done to you or said
5   That you should pip me with all these poets?

May Gods bring curses on the client
Who sent you such profanities.
And if, as I suspect, this choice new
Gift to you is from schoolmaster Sulla,
Then I'm not sorry but delighted          10
That your hard work has not been wasted.
Great Gods, a damned awful little book
For you to send to your Catullus
To kill him outright on that day
Of all days best—the Saturnalia.          15
No, you won't get away with it,
Clever dick. When it's dawn I'll run
To the bookstalls, pick up all the poison—
Suffenus, Caesius and Aquinus—
And pay you back with pains like them.     20
Meanwhile goodbye, be off with you,
Back where you brought your faulty feet from,
Curse of our time, appalling poets!
. . . . .
If maybe any of you there are
Who read my follies and you don't
Shudder to lay your hands on us

### 15

*A spoof on the standard letter of recommendation, threatening Aurelius, to whom he is entrusting his boyfriend, with the punishment reserved for adulterers—a radish or a fish inserted into the anus.*

Recommending to you my love and me,
Aurelius, I ask a modest favor—
That if in your heart you've ever longed
To seek out something pure and unspoiled,
You'll guard the boy for me modestly,      5
Not from the public—I'm not afraid
Of those going to and fro about
The square intent on their own business—
It's you I'm scared of and your penis,
That menace to good boys and bad.          10
Wield it anywhere and—how
Ad lib, given the chance, outside,
With this one, I think, modest exception.
But should ill will or mindless madness
Drive you, villain, to the crime           15
Of treachery against my person,
Ah then you'll rue your wretched fate
With feet trussed up and backdoor open,
Run through with radishes and mullet.

*16*

*An obscene gibe with a literary point. Catullus threatens*
*Aurelius and Furius with anal and oral penetration to*
*demonstrate his manhood, against insinuations that he is*
*effeminate because he writes off-color poetry.*

I'll bugger you and stuff your gobs,
Aurelius Kink and Poofter Furius,
For thinking me, because my verses
Are rather sissy, not quite decent.
5  For the true poet should be chaste
Himself, his verses need not be.
Indeed they've salt and charm then only
When rather sissy and not quite decent
And when they can excite an itch
10  I don't say in boys but in those hairy
Victims of lumbar sclerosis.
Because you've read my x thousand
Kisses you doubt my virility?
I'll bugger you and stuff your gobs.

*17*

*Catullus addresses the Colony of Verona, his native town*
*and site of a celebration of Mars (under the local name of*
*Salisubsalus) on a rickety bridge.*

O Colonia, so keen to
                    celebrate on your long bridge
And all set for dancing there but
                    frightened of the rickety
Legs of the poor old bridge propped up
                    on resurrected timbers
In case it falls flat on its back
                    and settles in the deep bog,
May a good bridge be built for you
5                    exactly to your liking
Where even Salisubsalus
                    in safety can be worshipped,
Provided that you play for me
                    this best of jokes, Colonia,
On a fellow townsman of mine:
                    I'd like him to be thrown down
Slap into the mud from your
                    bridge head over heels
Precisely where in all the lake
10                    and evil-smelling marsh
There is the deepest quagmire and
                    most livid-looking mud.

The creature is a perfect fool
                    with less sense than a child,
A two-year old who's fast asleep
                    rocked in his father's arms.
For though he's married to a girl
                    who's in her greenest flower,
A girl indeed more frivolous
                    than any tender kidling,                    15
Who needs more careful watching than
                    the very blackest grapes,
He lets her fool around at will
                    and doesn't turn a hair
And doesn't rise up for his part
                    but lies there like an alder
That's lying in a ditch hamstrung
                    by a Ligurian hatchet,
As much aware of everything
                    as though she didn't exist.                    20
Yes, this perfect dolt of mine
                    sees nothing and hears nothing,
Not knowing who he really is
                    or if he is at all.
Now, I'd like to throw him down
                    headlong from your bridge
To see if he can suddenly
                    shake off his stupid sloth
And leave behind his spineless
                    spirit in the mire                    25
As a mule leaves her iron
                    shoe in the clinging clay.

*21*

*Three poems inserted after 17 by an early editor of Catullus*
*are not included in modern editions because they were*
*almost certainly not written by him, but editors retain the*
*traditional numbering. In this poem Aurelius is the target*
*again. Here he is depicted as an effete dieter, who hungers*
*only for Catullus's boyfriend.*

Aurelius, father of the hungers,
Not just of these but of all that were
Ere this or will be in other years,
You long to bugger my love, and not
In secret. You're with him, sharing jokes,                    5
Close at his side, trying everything.
It's not good. If you plot against me
I'll get in first and stuff your gob.
I'd keep quiet if you did it well fed;
But it annoys me that the boy                    10

Will learn from you to hunger and thirst.
So stop it while you decently may,
In case you make your end—gob-stuffed.

## 22

*Varus is addressed again (see poem 10) on the subject of
his friend Suffenus, who fancies himself a poet (Catullus
disagrees) and writes out his drafts not on scrap papyrus
but on the most elegant rolls.*

Dear Varus, your not improper intimate Suffenus
Is a charming person, witty and urbane;
Besides, his verse production is enormous—
Ten thousand lines, I calculate, or more
5   He's written out, and not on palimpsest
Like most folk—no, new rolls of royal papyrus,
New bosses, scarlet thongs and parchment covers,
The whole lead-ruled and levelled off with pumice.
But when you read them, that nice urbane man
10   Suffenus now seems a mere clodhopper
Or boob, he's so unlike himself, so changed.
How to explain it? The man who just now seemed
A city wit, or something smoother still,
Even so is clumsier than the clumsy country
15   Whenever he tries poetry—and yet
He's never as happy as when poetizing.
He's so pleased with himself, thinks he's
       so marvelous.
We all, I fancy, have that fault. There's no one
Who's not, you'll find, *suffenous* in some way.
Each person's stuck with his peculiar
20       failing,
But we can't see the sack we're carrying.

## 23

*Catullus enumerates the many blessings possessed by his
friend, the poet Furius Bibaculus, as a reason to decline his
repeated requests for a loan.*

Furius, you've no slave or cash-box,
You've no spider, bug, or fire,
But a father and stepmother
Whose teeth can even chew through flint.
5   A splendid time you have with father
And with father's wooden wife.
No wonder, for you're all in good health,
Digest splendidly, fear nothing,
Not fires or houses falling down,

Crimes of violence, poison plots,                10
Or other dangerous circumstance.
Besides you've bodies drier than horn,
Or whatever's even more dehydrated,
From sun and cold and hungriness.
Why shouldn't you be well and happy?          15
You never sweat, you've no saliva,
No mucus, no nasal catarrh.
That's hygiene. This is more hygienic:
An arsehole clean as a saltcellar;
You shit less than ten times a year            20
And then it's hard as beans and lupins
And if you rubbed it in your hands
You'd never dirty a single finger.
These are rich blessings, Furius;
Don't undervalue or despise them               25
And do stop begging for that hundred
Thousand—you're rich enough already.

## 24

*Addressed to his boyfriend, who comes from a family with
the good, aristocratic name of Juventius. Catullus pokes
fun again at Furius and his alleged poverty.*

O flower of the Juventii,
Not just of these but of all that were
Or will be later in other years,
I'd rather you gave Midas' riches
To that man without slave or cash-box          5
Than let him love you as you do.
'He's a nice man' you'll say. Yes, but
His niceness has no slave or cash-box.
Demur if you must, make light of it,
Still he has neither slave nor cash-box.        10

## 25

*A poem full of precocious language aimed at a man with
a Greek name who has the bad habit of stealing trinkets
from his friends.*

Fairy Thallus, softer than
                         a little furry bunny
Or a goosey's marrow or
                         a teeny-weeny ear-lobe
Or an old man's drooping penis
                         or a spider's dust trap,
But also, Thallus, more rapacious
                         than the wildest whirlwind

Whenever the Goddess of hawks
5              gives notice birds are napping,
Send back to me that cloak of mine
              you've swooped upon and stolen
And the Spanish napkin too
              and those Bithynian face-towels
Which, tasteless idiot, you keep
              exhibiting as heirlooms.
Unglue them pronto from your crooked
              talons and return them,
For fear your flabby little flanks
10              and namby-pamby handies
Are branded in an ugly way
              and scribbled on with lashes,
And there you are—on heat and tossed
              so differently, just like
A baby boat in a big sea
              caught by a roaring storm-wind.

## 26

*Puns make the point in this gibe at Furius. In Latin the
word for "to face" also means "to be mortgaged to."*

Furius, your little countryhouse faces
Not draughts of Auster or Favonius
Or savage Boreas or Apheliotes
But fifteen thousand tenscore sesterces,
5 An overdraft that's not good for your health.

## 27

*A somewhat enigmatic poem, but probably suggesting that
Catullus intends to write still stronger invective in the current climate, where Postumia, wife of a famous jurist and
mistress of Julius Caesar, sets the tone as mistress of the feast.*

Boy server of old Falernian,
Pour me out more pungent cups
As toastmistress Postumia rules,
Who's drunker than the drunken grape.
5 Pure water, find your level elsewhere.
You ruin wine. Shift to the sober.
Here is unmixed Thyonian.

## 28

*Addressed to Veranius and Fabullus, who were last heard
of together in Spain (poem 12). They are serving in a*

*province on the staff of Piso, as Catullus is serving with
Memmius. But neither governor is allowing his staff to
enrich themselves at the expense of the provincials, a circumstance that Catullus laments.*

Piso's lieutenants, needy staff
With baggage packed and portable,
Best Veranius and my Fabullus,
How are you doing? With that creep
You've had your fill of cold and hunger?              5
Do your accounts show any profit,
As mine do costs? In service with
My praetor I enter debt as profit.
O Memmius, you've laid me, good and long—
Stuffed me with all that yard of yours.              10
You two, as far as I can see,
Have fared the same—stuffed by no less
A prick. Find noble friends, they say!
Heaven bring the plagues upon that pair
Of slurs on Romulus and Remus!              15

## 29

*An invective against Mamurra, Julius Caesar's chief engi-
neer on campaigns in Spain, Gaul, and Britain, who had
previously served with Pompey in the East. The last line
makes clear that Caesar and Pompey, who was married to
Caesar's daughter, are Catullus's real targets.*

Who can watch this, who suffer it, unless
He's shameless and a glutton and a gambler—
Mamurra having all the fat that long-haired
Gaul and remotest Britain used to have?
Poof Romulus, you'll watch this and allow it?              5
That supercilious and superfluous figure
Prancing about in everybody's bedroom
Like a white lovey-dovey or Adoneus?
Poof Romulus, you'll watch this and allow it?
You're shameless and a glutton and a gambler.              10
Was it for this, O Generalissimo,
You've been in that far island of the west,
So that your pal, that multifucking tool,
Could eat his way through twenty or thirty million?
Cack-handed generosity—that's what!              15
Surely he's leched and gourmandized enough?
In the first place he blued his patrimony,
Second, the Pontic loot, and third the Spanish,
And for this man shall Gaul and Britain reap?
Why patronize *him*, damn it? What's he good for              20

Except to gobble up fat private fortunes?
Was it for this, you most devoted Romans,
Father- and son-in-law, you've ruined all?

### 30

*Addressed to the otherwise unknown Alfenus, who betrayed Catullus by luring him into love in unspecified circumstances. Alfenus has betrayed Fides, here translated as "Good Faith," for the Romans an important virtue, which was also personified as a goddess.*

Alfenus, forgetful and treacherous to your close
    companions,
Does your hard heart now feel no pity for your 'sweet
    friend'?
Traitor, are you not loath after all to betray and
    deceive me?
The Dwellers in Heaven abhor deceitful men's
    impious deeds.
This you disdain and desert wretched me in
5    my troubles.
Tell me, alas, what can folk do or whom can
    they trust?
Cheat, it was certainly you bade me surrender
    my soul,
Luring me into love, as if all would be safe for me.
Now you back out and allow the winds and the
    airy clouds
To carry away unfulfilled all of your words and
10    deeds.
You may forget, but the Gods remember, Good Faith
    remembers,
And she will later make sure that you wish what you
    did were undone.

### 31

*On his return to Sirmio on Lake Garda, Catullus celebrates the pleasures of home (symbolized by his Lar, or household god) after leaving foreign places to come to this lake, which he calls Lydian because the region was settled by Etruscans (thought to have migrated from Lydia in Asia Minor).*

Of almost islands, Sirmio, and islands
The jewel—of all that either Neptune bears
In clear lake-water or desolate ocean,
How pleased, how happy I am to see you again,

Hardly convinced that I have left Thynia    5
And the Bithynian plains and found you safe.
O what more blissful than to have no worries,
When mind lays down the load and tired of
    foreign
Service we have come to our own Lar
And rest content upon the longed-for bed!    10
This on its own makes up for all the hardship.
Greetings, delightful Sirmio. Enjoy your
Master's joy, and you, the lake's Lydian waves,
Laugh with all the mirth you have at home.

### 32

*A girl named Ipsitilla has inspired Catullus to coin a new noun "fuctions" (Lat. fututiones) from the verb "to fuck" (Lat. futuo).*

Please, my love, sweet Ipsitilla,
My darling, my own clever girl,
Command my presence at siesta
And if you do, help by ensuring
That no one bolts your outer door    5
And that you don't go out on impulse
But stay home and prepare for us
Nine uninterrupted fuctions.
In fact if you're willing command me now.
I lie back after a large lunch    10
Boring holes in tunic and cloak.

### 33

*Public bathing was one of the amenities of Roman life, but the theft of clothing from the baths was a common problem.*

O best of thieves in the public baths,
Father Vibennius, and faggot son,
(Father's right hand is filthier,
Son's arsehole more acquisitive)
Be off to exile and perdition!    5
Why not, when father's larcenies
Are known to all and son can't sell
His hairy buttocks for one penny?

### 34

*A hymn to the goddess Diana, who, according to standard ritual practice, is addressed by her many cult titles.*

In Diana's trust are we,
Girls and boys unblemished.
Of Diana, unblemished boys
And girls, let us sing.

5  O Latona's daughter, great
Progeny of greatest Jove,
Whom their mother bore beside
The Delian olive,

To be mistress of mountains
10  And the greening forests
And unfrequented passes
And strident streams:

Thou art called Lucina Juno
By women in labor pains,
15  Called powerful Three-Ways and Moon
Of borrowed light.

Goddess, by Thy monthly course
Measuring the year's journey
Thou fillest up with good fruits
20  The farmer's barns.

Hallowed be Thou by the name
Of Thy pleasure, and protect
As in days of old from ill
Romulus' race.

### 35

*An invitation to a poet Caecilius to leave Como on the shores of the lake known as Larius (mod. Lake Como) and visit Catullus in Verona. Caecilius is working on a poem on Cybele, the Great Mother goddess from Mt. Dindymus in Asia Minor.*

I'd like you, papyrus, to tell my comrade
Caecilius, the tender poet,
To come to Verona, leaving Novum
Comum's walls and the Larian shore.
5  I want him to consider certain
Thoughts of a friend of his and mine.
So if he's wise he'll eat up the road,
Though a pretty girl should call him back
A thousand times and laying both
10  Hands on his neck should beg him stay.
There's one now, if I'm rightly informed,
Dying of desperate love for him.
For ever since the day she read
His unfinished *Lady of Dindymus*

Fires have been eating the poor thing's marrow.    15
And I don't blame you, girl more learned
Than Sappho's Muse. Caecilius' *Great
Mother* is charmingly unfinished.

### 36

*A humorous address to a historical epic poem, now lost, the* Annals *by a certain Volusius. Catullus's girlfriend had vowed to Venus that she would make the worst poem she could find an offering to Vulcan (the "Hobble-footed God"), in other words, burn it. Venus is then invoked by some of her many cult titles to fulfill this vow.*

Volusius' *Annals,* paper crap,
Redeem a vow in my girl's name.
She vowed to Cupid and St. Venus
That if I were restored to her
And ceased to hurl savage iambics    5
She'd offer the worst poet's choicest
Work to the Hobble-footed God
For frizzling on funereal firewood.
The worst of girls intended this
Vow to the Gods as a witty joke.    10
So, Daughter of the dark-blue Deep,
Who hauntest holy Idalium,
Bleak Urii, Ancona, reedy
Cnidus, Amathus and Golgi
And Hadria's tavern, Dyrrachium,    15
Record the vow as duly paid,
If it's not lacking wit and charm.
But you meanwhile shall fuel the flames,
You load of rural crudities,
Volusius' *Annals,* paper crap.    20

### 37

*The inn of this poem is probably a sarcastic reference to the mansion of Clodia, located in a high-rent district of the Palatine not far from the Temple of Castor and Pollux (the "Brothers with Felt Hats"). The Spaniard Egnatius, who is singled out from his girlfriend's lovers, may also have been a poet (see poem 39).*

Randy Inn and all you 'Inn-attendants',
Ninth pillar from the Brothers with Felt Hats,
D'you reckon you're the only ones with tools,
The only ones allowed to fuck the girls
And that the rest of us are stinking goats?    5

Or, since you clots are sitting in a queue
One or two hundred strong, d'you think I wouldn't
Dare stuff two hundred sitting tenants at once?
Well, think again. For I shall scrawl the Inn's
10   Whole frontage for you with phallic graffiti—
Because a girl who ran from my embrace,
Loved by me as no other will be loved,
For whom a great war has been fought by me,
Has settled here. With her the good and great
15   Are all in love and what's more (shame upon her!)
All the shoddy backstreet adulterers.
You above all, ace of the longhaired mob,
A son of rabbit-ridden Celtiberia,
Egnatius, whom a shady beard upgrades
20   And teeth rubbed down with Iberian urine.

### 38

*Addressed to a poet, Cornificius, author of poems in hen-
decasyllabics and a short epic called* Glaucus, *in other
words, a poet who shared Catullus's tastes.*

It's bad, Cornificius, with your Catullus,
It's bad, by Hercules, hard labor,
And more and more so each day and hour.
But have you (what's least and easiest)
5   Offered him any consolation?
I'm angry with you. So much for my love?
Please, any scrap of consolation
Sadder than tears of Simonides.

### 39

*According to such authorities as Diodorus of Sicily and
Strabo, in Spain the native people really did clean their
teeth with urine. Catullus's lampoon of Egnatius may also
have something to do with his dislike of his poem* On the
Nature of the Universe.

Because Egnatius has white shiny teeth
He's always grinning. In court on the defendant's
Side while Counsel's turning on the tears
He grins. At a devoted son's cremation
5   While stricken mother mourns her only boy
He grins. Whatever's happening, wherever,
However employed, he grins. He has this tic,
Not, in my view, attractive or polite.
So here's a thought for you, my good Egnatius.
10   If you were Roman, Sabine, or Tiburtine
Or stingy Umbrian or obese Etruscan

Or dark Lanuvian with rabbit teeth
Or (not forgetting my own folk) Transpadane
Or anyone who cleans his teeth with water
I'd still not like you to be always grinning.     15
Nothing's more fatuous than a fatuous smile.
But you're Celtiberian and in Celtiberia
Everyone uses his own pee each morning
For rubbing down his teeth and his red gums.
So the more highly polished your teeth are     20
The more the piddle you are proved to have drunk.

### 40

*A jibe directed at a certain Ravidus, in the manner of the ancient
poet Archilochus, who wrote in the iambic meter, which is why
Catullus now calls his hendecasyllabic invective "iambics."*

What bad thinking, wretched Ravidus,
Drives you straight into my iambics?
What God unluckily invoked
Involves you in a stupid feud?
You want to live on vulgar lips,     5
Notorious at any cost?
You shall be, as you've chosen to love
My love and pay the long-term price.

### 41

*An invective aimed at Mamurra, the "bankrupt from
Formiae" (see poem 29) via his girlfriend, who is advised to
check her looks in the mirror (the "brass" in the final line).*

Ameana, female fuck-up,
Has asked me for a cool ten thousand,
That girl with the unattractive nose,
Friend of the bankrupt from Formiae.
Kinsfolk responsible for her,     5
Call friends and doctors to advise.
The girl's not well and will not ask
For brass reflecting her true self.

### 42

*Vigilante justice was not uncommon in the Roman
world: the practice was known as* flagitatio *and consisted
of rounding up your friends and demanding redress from
the person who had wronged you. Here Catullus humorously enlists his hendecasyllabics to retrieve his notebook
from a woman, probably Lesbia, who refuses to return it.*

Come, Hendecasyllables, one and all,
From everywhere, every one and all,
An ugly adulteress thinks I'm a joke
And refuses to give me our notebook back,
5  If you're prepared to stand for that.
Let's chase her and demand it back.
You ask which she is? You see that one
With the ugly walk and the odious actressy
Laugh and the face like a Gallican puppy's?
10  Surround her and demand it back:
'Dirty adulteress, give back the notebook!
Give back the notebook, dirty adulteress!'
She doesn't care tuppence, the filthy trollop
Or whatever's more depraved than that.
15  But let's not think that we've done enough.
If nothing else we ought to be able
To force a blush from that brazen bitch-face.
All shout again *fortissimo*:
'Dirty adulteress, give back the notebook!
20  Give back the notebook, dirty adulteress!'
We're getting nowhere; she's quite unmoved.
You'll need to change your tone and tactics
To find if you're able to get any further:
'Virtuous Lady, the notebook, please!'


43

*The girlfriend of Mamurra, the "bankrupt from Formiae"*
*(see poem 41), is compared unfavorably with Catullus's*
*Lesbia, although the Province, that is, Catullus's own home*
*region of Cisalpine Gaul, disagrees.*

Greetings, girl with no mini-nose
Nor pretty foot nor dark eyes
Nor long fingers nor dry mouth
Nor altogether felicitous tongue,
5  Friend of the bankrupt from Formiae.
And does the Province call you pretty?
Compare our Lesbia to you?
O what tasteless boorish times!


44

*A parody of a poem of thanks, addressed not to a god but*
*to Catullus's country house, where he recovered from the*
*cold he caught while reading a speech by Sestius against*
*Antius. Nothing is known of Antius or his candidacy, but*
*Sestius was a well-known stooge of the conservative faction*

*of the Senate. The Sabine hills and Tibur (mod. Tivoli)*
*were popular country retreats.*

Our Farm, which art or Sabine or Tiburtan
(For whoso have no heart to hurt Catullus
Dub thee Tiburtan, whereas whoso do
Will wager anything that Thou art Sabine),
But whether Sabine or in truth Tiburtan,          5
Right gladly have I been in Thy suburban
Villa and rid my chest of a bad cough
Not undeservedly upon me brought
For coveting rich dinners by my belly.
For while I wanted to be Sestius' guest           10
I read his speech on Antius' candidacy,
Speech packed with poison and with pestilence,
Whereat a feverish cold and chronic cough
Kept shaking me till I fled to Thy bosom
And cured me there with idleness and nettle.      15
Wherefore restored I render Thee great thanks
Because Thou didst not punish my offence,
Nor do I now object, should I accept
Sestius' vile works, if their frigidity
Give Sestius, not me, a cold and cough,           20
Whose invitation means reading bad books.


45

*A conversation between two lovers. Septimius prefers life*
*with his girlfriend Acme to a career of adventure with*
*Caesar in Britain or Crassus in Syria.*

Septimius, his belovèd Acme
In his lap, said 'Acme darling,
If I'm not desperately in love
And set to go on loving you
Forever in utter desperation,                     5
Then lone in Libya or scorched India
I'll face a lion with green eyes.'
At this Love sneezed, first on the right,
Then on the left, approvingly.
But Acme, lightly tilting back                    10
Her head and kissing her sweet boy's
Drunken eyes with that rosy mouth,
Said 'Septimillus, so, my life,
May we always serve this one master
Surely as burns in my soft marrow                 15
A bigger far and fiercer fire.'
At this Love sneezed, first on the right,

Then on the left, approvingly.
Now, setting out from this good omen,
20  With mutual minds they're loved and love.
Poor Septimius prefers his Acme
To all the Syrias and Britains.
Faithful Acme in her Septimius
Finds all desires and delights.
25  Who has seen any happier people?
Who a Venus more starry-eyed?

### 46

*In the spring of 56 B.C., Catullus contemplates some sight-
seeing on his way home from Nicaea, capital of the Roman
province of Phrygia in Asia Minor.*

Now spring brings back unfrozen warmth,
Now the sky's equinoctial fury
Is hushed by Zephyr's welcome airs.
Take leave of Phrygian plains, Catullus,
5  And sweltering Nicaea's lush fields.
Let's fly to Asia's famous cities.
Excited thoughts now long to travel;
Glad feet now tap in expectation.
Farewell, sweet company of comrades,
10  Who leaving distant homes together
Return by different routes apart.

### 47

*Like poem 28, this is aimed at Piso, who is insultingly called
a Priapus, the god whose outstanding characteristic was his
giant penis. His associates might be identified as Gaius Porcius
Cato, an associate of Caesar, and Philodemus (mockingly
called a diminutive Socrates), an Epicurean scholar and poet.*

Socration and Porcius, Piso's pair
Of left-handed men, the world's Itch and Greed,
That docked Priapus prefers you
To my Verániolus and Fabullus?
5  Do you throw smart expensive parties
All day long, while my companions
Tout in the streets for invitations?

### 48

*Like the better-known poems addressed to his girlfriend (5 and
7), this poem plays on multiple kisses of Catullus's boyfriend.*

Your honeyed eyes, Juventius,
If someone let me go on kissing,
I'd kiss three hundred thousand times
Nor never think I'd had enough,
Not if our osculation's crop                     5
Were closer-packed than dried corn-ears.

### 49

*An ironic address to Cicero, the greatest orator of all and
considered by some of his contemporaries (and definitely
by himself ) a great poet.*

Most eloquent of Romulus' grandsons
That are and have been, Marcus Tullius,
And ever will be in other years,
Catullus, the worst poet of all,
Sends you herewith his greatest thanks,           5
As truly the worst poet of all
As you're the best advocate of all.

### 50

*A poem about poetry, addressed to Gaius Licinius Calvus,
whose work Catullus admired.*

At leisure, Licinius, yesterday
We'd much fun with my writing-tablets
As we'd agreed to be frivolous.
Each of us writing light verses
Played now with this meter, now that,             5
Capping each other's jokes and toasts.
Yes, and I left there fired by
Your charm, Licinius, and wit,
So food gave poor me no pleasure
Nor could I rest my eyes in sleep                 10
But wildly excited turned and tossed
Over the bed, longing for daylight
That I might be with you and talk.
But after my tired aching limbs
Were lying on the couch half dead,                15
I made this poem for you, the charmer,
So you could spot my trouble from it.
Now don't be rash, please—don't reject
Our prayers, we implore you, precious,
Lest Nemesis make you pay for it.                 20
She's a drastic Goddess. Don't provoke her.

*51*

*An adaptation of a famous poem by Sappho (fragment 31), the seventh/sixth-century Greek lyric poet, addressed to the woman she loved.*

That man is seen by me as a God's equal
Or (if it may be said) the Gods' superior,
Who sitting opposite again and again
Watches and hears *you*

5   Sweetly laughing—which dispossesses poor me
Of all my senses, for no sooner, Lesbia,
Do I look at you than there's no power left me
<Of speech in my mouth,>

But my tongue's paralysed, invisible flame
Courses down through my limbs, with din of
10     their own
My ears are ringing and twin darkness covers
The light of my eyes.

Leisure, Catullus, does not agree with you.
At leisure you're restless, too excitable.
15  Leisure in the past has ruined rulers and
Prosperous cities.

*52*

*Marcus Nonius Sufenas was a tribune who supported Pompey, Publius Vatinius a tribune and eventually consul who supported Caesar. Their advancement represents for Catullus the degraded state of public affairs.*

What next, Catullus? Why defer decease?
Nonius the tumor sits in curule state;
Vatinius by his consulate's forsworn.
What next, Catullus? Why defer decease?

*53*

*When Vatinius was prosecuted by Calvus in 54 B.C., he is reported to have said to the jury, "Am I to be found guilty because this man is articulate?"*

I laughed at someone in court lately
Who, when my Calvus gave a splendid
Account of all Vatinius' crimes,
With hands raised in surprise announced
5  'Great Gods, the squirt's articulate!'

*54*

*Another jibe against Caesar, the "Generalissimo" (see poem 29), but the poem is entirely obscure.*

Otho's head (it's mighty weak)
And, you hick, his half-washed legs,
Libo's soft and wily fart,
These at least I could wish displeased
You and old warmed-up Fuficius.     5
Once more my innocuous iambics
Will rile you, Generalissimo.

*55*

*Catullus represents himself as looking for his friend Camerius all over Rome, but especially seeking him among its women.*

We beg you, meaning no offence,
To show us where your hide-out is.
We've sought you in the lesser Campus,
In the Circus, in all the bookshops,
In the hallowed shrine of Jove Most High.   5
At the same time in Magnus' Walk
I seized on all the girlies, friend,
Although I saw they looked quite cool.
'Hand him over!' I kept demanding;
'I want Camerius, naughty girls.'     10
'Look,' said one, drawing back her dress,
'He's hiding here—on rosy nipples.'
But enduring you now is a labor of Hercules;
Your absence, friend, is so arrogant.
Tell us where you'll be, speak out     15
Boldly, share it, trust the light.
Are milk-white girls now holding you?
If you shut your mouth and hold your tongue
You'll throw away all the fruits of love.
Venus loves volubility.     20
Or if you like you may seal your lips
Provided I can share your love.

*56*

*Catullus reports to his friend, the poet and critic Valerius Cato, that a funny thing happened when he caught his girlfriend's young slave boy masturbating: invoking the mother of Venus, he turned his own erection on him.*

O a funny thing, Cato, quite absurd,
Worth your hearing and chuckling over.
Laugh as you love Catullus, Cato.
The thing's too funny, quite absurd.
20 I lately caught the girl's boy pet
Wanking, and (so please Dione!)
Banged him in tandem with my hard.

### 57

*Mamurra and Caesar are lampooned again in rather
scabrous terms.*

They're a fine match, the shameless sods,
Those poofters Caesar and Mamurra.
No wonder. Equivalent black marks,
One urban, the other Formian
5 Are stamped indelibly on each.
Diseased alike, both didymous
Two sciolists on one wee couch,
Peers in adultery and greed,
Rival mates among the nymphets,
10 They're a fine match, the shameless sods.

### 58

*Savage and poignant, this short poem is addressed to
Marcus Caelius Rufus, the man who replaced Catullus
as Lesbia's lover, only to be discarded by her in turn. For
Cicero's speech on behalf of Caelius, see below.*

Caelius, our Lesbia, *the* Lesbia,
The Lesbia whom alone Catullus
Loved more than self and all his kin,
At crossroads now and in back alleys
5 Peels great-hearted Remus' grandsons.

### 58b

*A separate poem that was run together with the preceding
lines in the manuscripts. It picks up the theme of poem 55.
Camerius is still missing, and Catullus would be worn out*

looking for him, even if he were the bronze giant Talos who
ran around Crete three times a day, or the famous Spartan
long-distance runner Ladas, or Perseus with his winged
sandals, or if he had Pegasus, the winged horse, or the swift
horses of Rhesus.

Not if I were Crete's fabled guard
Or Ladas or wing-footed Perseus,
Not if I flew on Pegasus
Or Rhesus' swift and snow-white pair;
To these add feather-feet and fliers          5
And ask too for the speed of winds—
Hand me these harnessed, Camerius,
I'd still be worn down to the marrow
And eaten up with lassitude
In the long search for you, my friend.          10

### 59

*The language of this little invective against a woman from
Bononia (mod. Bologna) is reminiscent of ancient Roman
graffiti.*

Bononian Rufa sucks off Rufulus—
Menenius' wife, whom you have often seen
In graveyards grabbing dinner from a pyre,
Chasing a loaf that's rolled down from the flames,
Knocked off meanwhile by the half-shaven
     cremator.          5

### 60

*A short, elegant poem on the theme of betrayal and cruelty,
remaking a cliché as old as Homer that a person can be so
cruel that human parentage is impossible.*

Did lioness among Libystine mountains
Or Scylla barking from groin's lowest part
Produce you with a mind so hard and horrid
That you could spurn in his extremest need
A suppliant's prayer, ah too cruel-hearted?          5

## AFTERWORD

Catullus's impact on poetry in Rome has been called revolutionary, but it is sometimes difficult to
gauge its full extent because so much of the work of his contemporaries has been lost, both those
who shared his approach to literature and those who did not. It is worth contemplating that before

Catullus came upon the scene, Rome's most important poet was none other than Cicero, as Plutarch tells us in his biography (*Life of Cicero* 2.3). Cicero's famous poem *His Own Consulship,* completed in 59 B.C. at around the time of Catullus's earliest writings, was soon to become infamous, with its opening line quoted repeatedly only to poke fun at its inanity and assonance: *O fortunatam natam me consule Romam* (O Rome, fortunate to have been born in my consulship). After Catullus no one would write like that again, but the accident of transmission has made him look even more singular than he was, and it requires an exercise of the imagination to conjure up the literary world of the 50s, when poets like Helvius Cinna and Licinius Calvus were dazzling their contemporaries. After the deaths of Catullus and Calvus, probably both around 53 B.C., Cinna was reckoned Rome's most important living poet, until it was his bad luck to be mistaken by the mob for one of Caesar's assassins in 44. Known not only for his narrative poem *Zmyrna,* which was praised by Catullus, but for poems in a variety of genres, Cinna, not Catullus, was probably on Cicero's mind in 46 B.C. when he grumbled about the "new poets" (*The Orator* 161). His poems are lost, now known only from a few brief references to them, but a generation later they were still being read and studied by, among others, Ovid. We even know of a commentary on Cinna's *Zmyrna* compiled by an Augustan schoolteacher named Crassicius. Catullus's poems can conjure up only a dim vision of the lost riches of the literary life of Rome in that period.

Catullus escaped by the narrowest of margins the oblivion that envelops his contemporaries, even though he was read and admired in the generations that followed. Ovid mentions him in the same breath as Virgil, saying that "Mantua boasts of Virgil, Verona of Catullus" (*Amores* 3.15.7), praise echoed also by Martial (1.61.1–2 and 14.195). Catullus's influence on Virgil is appreciable, especially in the *Aeneid,* improbable though that might seem from a reading only of Catullus's hendecasyllabics. When Virgil writes of Dido's abandonment in the fourth book of the *Aeneid,* it is not hard to detect echoes of Catullus's Ariadne in poem 64. And Virgil even quotes a line from Catullus 66, a translation from Callimachus, when he describes Dido in the Underworld (*Aeneid* 6.460). It is not only Ovid among the elegiac love poets of the Augustan age who acknowledges his importance; Propertius does so explicitly, and echoes of Catullus reverberate throughout the two short books of Tibullus. Catullus continued to be studied and appreciated until at least the second century A.D., but certainly his greatest admirer was Martial, the first-century A.D. writer of epigrams. He acknowledges his debt to Catullus through plentiful allusions to his poetry and adaptation of his themes, especially the obscene ones.

Catullus is mentioned by writers in late antiquity, but not in ways that demonstrate deep knowledge or appreciation; they may only have known him at second hand. He was almost completely unknown in the Middle Ages, and only escaped the fate of Cinna and Calvus because a single manuscript of his works was found around 1300 in his hometown of Verona, reputedly under a sack of wheat. It was recopied just before it too was lost. The first printed edition of his works appeared in Venice in 1472. In Italy of the fifteenth century Catullus was a popular author, and celebrated scholars such as Angelo Poliziano (1454–94) and Antonio Partenio (1456–1506) vied in explaining the obscurities and, especially, the obscenities of his text. At much the same time lyric poets throughout Europe resuscitated Catullus in their imitations; for example, we can hear the echo of Catullus to Lesbia in *The Passionate Shepherd to His Love* by Christopher Marlowe (1564–93):

> Come live with me and be my love,
> And we will all the pleasures prove
> That hills and valleys, dales and fields,
> Woods or steepy mountain yields.

In subsequent periods Catullus was not much favored by readers; the Romantics and the Victorians found little in his poetry to appreciate. His use of obscenities was part of the problem, and since this meant that Catullus was little read in the schools, it was difficult for any but the most specialized scholars to form a just appreciation of his poems. W. B. Yeats, in "The Scholars," wrote how

> Bald heads forgetful of their sins,
> Old, learned, respectable bald heads
> Edit and annotate the lines
> That young men, tossing on their beds,
> Rhymed out in love's despair
> To flatter beauty's ignorant ear.
>
> All shuffle there; all cough in ink;
> All wear the carpet with their shoes;
> All think what other people think;
> All know the man their neighbour knows.
> Lord, what would they say
> Did their Catullus walk that way?

Published in 1915, this poem was a product of its age. Although Latin was Yeats's best subject in his largely undistinguished school career, he is unlikely to have had much exposure to many, or indeed any, of Catullus's more vigorous invectives, or to a poem such as 63, the *Attis,* which describes the self-castration of a devotee of the nature goddess Cybele. The Catullus Yeats imagined was utterly divorced from reality. Yet as recently as 1961 an eminent scholar was obliged by the Oxford University Press to omit from his commentary thirty-two poems on the grounds that they "do not lend themselves to comment in English."

Poets were in the vanguard of scholarship in reviving interest in Catullus's works, especially in the early twentieth century. In Ezra Pound in particular, he found a powerful advocate. Pound regarded him as essential reading; as he once wrote in a letter, "Catullus, Propertius, Horace and Ovid are the people who matter." Pound not only imitated and translated Catullus in his own work but also pitched him to others, including Yeats, with whom he lived for three years (1913–16) during the time when Yeats wrote "The Scholars." As a controversialist, Pound found Catullus an ally in shattering convention, and so did the writers Pound influenced, such as Louis Zukofsky (1904–78), the American Objectivist poet, who "translated" Catullus into phonetically equivalent, semantically unrelated English in 1969, or another modernist poet, Charles Reznikoff (1894–1976), who drew on the poignant conclusion of Catullus's poem 11 when he penned this antiwar protest in *Rhythms* (1918) no. 14:

> How shall we mourn you who are killed and wasted,
> sure that you would not die with your work unended,
> as if the iron scythe in the grass stops for a flower?

Catullus hardly seems controversial anymore; indeed, he ranks as the most popular author in Latin curricula of the twenty-first century.

# CICERO

### (Marcus Tullius Cicero, 106–43 B.C.)

CICERO WAS BORN IN 106 B.C. AND MURDERED IN 43. HE LIVED THROUGH THE turbulent years, plagued by foreign and civil wars, that led to the end of the Republic. His career started off with a splash when, in 80 B.C., in his first notable case, he successfully defended a young man named Roscius from the small town of Ameria on a charge of parricide, in brave defiance of Sulla's powerful freedman, Chrysogonus. In another landmark case in 70 B.C., his relentlessly efficient prosecution of Gaius Verres for corruption and extortion while governor in Sicily resulted in Cicero displacing Quintus Hortensius, Verres's defense counsel, as Rome's leading advocate. The high point of his career came in 63, the year in which he achieved the consulship, when, with little help from the other consul, he put down the conspiracy led by Catiline to overthrow the government. For this service the Senate honored him with the title *pater patriae* (Father of the Fatherland). Cicero was the first to be so honored; other than Julius Caesar in 45 B.C., all later recipients of this illustrious title were emperors.

The most salient features in the rest of Cicero's life are largely negative. He never again attained the prestige that he had won during his consulship, to which he constantly looked back with undiminished pride. (He refers to it several times in his very last surviving speech, the *Fourteenth Philippic*.) Although he remained a significant force in Roman politics as an orator and statesman for the next twenty years, in the years immediately following his consulship his overconfidence allowed his political enemies to outmaneuver him. In 58 B.C., persecuted by Clodius Pulcher, who was probably the brother of Catullus's mistress, Clodia (whom Catullus called Lesbia), Cicero was driven into exile for having executed five of the Catilinarian conspirators without trial. Although he was recalled in the following year, this was a shock from which he never fully recovered. He could not bear prolonged absence from the political scene in Rome, so it was with extreme reluctance that in 51–50 B.C. he served as governor of the province of Cilicia (southern Turkey). Nonetheless, he performed with some distinction, even claiming—but not being awarded—a triumph for his troops' success in suppressing bandits.

Cicero did not distinguish himself during the Senate's armed resistance to Caesar in 49–48, languishing miserably in Pompey's camp. He was one of the first to return to Italy and benefit from Caesar's notorious clemency, but he played little part in politics during Caesar's regime. And yet he could still serve as a potent symbol. Even though he was regarded as too indecisive to be invited to join the conspiracy against Caesar, we know from a fragment of a speech by Mark Antony (quoted by Cicero in his *Second Philippic*) that "Brutus immediately raised his bloody dagger in the air and called out Cicero's name, congratulating him on the restoration of liberty." The sequel brought out the best in him, and he tapped an unexpected vein of courage as he led the opposition to Mark

**Figure 7:  C. Maccari, *Cicero Denouncing Catiline***
Catiline's isolation suggests greater support for Cicero than may have been the case. Cicero is portrayed as a wise elder statesman, but he was actually forty-three years old, two years younger than Catiline.

Antony's usurpation of Caesar's powers. From September 44 B.C. until April of the following year, he attacked Antony with a long series of devastating speeches. At Antony's insistence, he was killed on December 7, 43 B.C., by a man whom he had once defended in court. His head and hands were nailed to the Rostra, the speaker's platform in the Roman Forum, from where he had denounced Antony so often. Cicero's brother and his nephew were also murdered, but his son survived to become consul with Octavian in 30 B.C.

The first member of the Cicero family to be so called was said to have a slight dent at the end of his nose, like the split in a chickpea (in Latin *cicer*). When Cicero himself entered public life, his friends urged him to change this rather droll name. He is said to have replied that he would do his best to make it more distinguished than any of the great names in Rome. When he was dedicating a piece of silver plate to the gods, he had the engraver inscribe the names "Marcus" and "Tullius," and then complete the sequence with a representation of a chickpea (Plutarch, *Life of Cicero* 1). Cicero achieved this ambition to win fame. He was acknowledged as Rome's greatest orator during his lifetime; as such, he not only played a prominent role in politics but also had an unmatched influence on the development of the Latin language. "He was quite justifiably said by his contemporaries to be king of the law-courts, and posterity came to regard *Cicero* as not simply a personal name, but as synonymous with eloquence itself" (Quintilian, *Education of the Orator* 10.1.112). His writings were so prolific and influential that in the Middle Ages it was sometimes assumed that there were two different people named Tullius and Cicero.

Cicero's rise to prominence in politics was remarkable, given the extremely conservative nature of Roman political life, which was dominated by men from patrician families. Two consuls were elected annually. Between 367 B.C., when plebeians were first made eligible, and 46 B.C.,

**Figure 8: Bust of Cicero**
Cicero, perhaps about fifty years old, his age when he defended Caelius.

the consulship seems to have been held only twenty-one times by *novi homines* (new men), the first members of their family to attain important political posts in Rome. These twenty-one consulships were, moreover, shared between probably no more than eleven individuals. Even among the patricians, some families were much more successful than others. The stranglehold on the consulship enjoyed by a few distinguished families is well emphasized in a speech attributed to Quintus Fabius Maximus ("The Greatest") Verrucosus ("Warty") Cunctator ("The Delayer"), the general whose stalling tactics saved Rome from Hannibal after the debacle at Cannae in 216 B.C. (Valerius Maximus, *Memorable Deeds and Sayings* 4.1.5):

> When his son was about to be elected consul with overwhelming support, he observed that the consulship had been held five times by himself, and frequently by his father, his grandfather, his great-grandfather and earlier ancestors. He therefore tried as determinedly as possible to persuade the people in the assembly to give the Fabian family a respite from that honor at long last. It was not that he doubted his son's qualities—for he was a distinguished man—he simply wanted the supreme power not to stay always in one family.

Despite all this prejudice against "new men," Cicero did become consul in 63 B.C. This suggests political abilities of a very high order. Not only was he a *novus homo*, the first to be elected consul for thirty years, but he was also elected "in his own year" (*suo anno*), that is, the first year in which he was eligible to run for the office. What is more, he came first by a wide margin in a ballot of seven candidates.

These were troubled times, however, when political life was not proceeding in the traditional manner, so perhaps it is not so strange that Cicero should have been successful. Seven of the twenty-one consulships won by *novi homines* had been held by Gaius Marius, Caesar's uncle by marriage, the first in 107 B.C., just a year before Cicero's birth. Pompey first held his consulship in 70 B.C., six years before he had reached the normal minimum age and without having held the more junior magistracies; he was therefore so ignorant of political life that he had to ask his friend, the great scholar Marcus Terentius Varro, to write him a manual on procedures in the Senate (Aulus Gellius, *Attic Nights* 14.7). Against all tradition, Pompey was appointed sole consul in 52 B.C. Nor need we suppose that Cicero himself rose to the consulship by merit alone, sweeping aside the corruption of the old ways. In all likelihood he, like every other candidate in this period, engaged in a fair bit of pandering and bribery.

Self-effacing modesty was not a typical Roman quality, but Cicero's drive for recognition was regarded as excessive even among his peers, although even he could, on rare occasions, laugh at his own foibles:

> I thought that people in Rome were talking about nothing else but my administration in Sicily. So I set off for home expecting the Roman people to be eager to heap distinctions on me. I happened to reach Puteoli, intending to journey overland from there, just at the season when that region is thronged with fashionable people. I almost collapsed when someone asked when I had left Rome and whether there was any news. When I replied that I was on my way back from my province, he said, "Why, yes indeed, from Africa, isn't it?" "No," I said coldly, getting upset, "from Sicily." At this juncture, someone who thought he knew it all said "What? Don't you know that this chap has been quaestor in Syracuse?" [Sicily had two administrative centers, at Syracuse and Lilybaeum; Cicero had served at Lilybaeum.] Need I say more? I stopped being disgruntled and mingled with those who had come to take the waters (*In Defense of Plancius* 26).

Plutarch comments that this incident made Cicero realize, at least briefly, the futility of ambition, but he concludes by saying that "the inordinate pleasure he derived from being praised and his pathological desire for glory stayed with him all his life and often clouded his rational judgment" (*Life of Cicero* 6). Cassius Dio gives a more damaging assessment of Cicero's self-importance: "He was extremely boastful, and thought no one as good as he was. In everything he said and did, he sneered at everyone else, and he did not deign to live on equal terms with them. He was tiresome and annoying, and consequently he came to be disliked and hated even by the very people who otherwise agreed with him" (*History of Rome* 38.12).

Such pomposity and self-involvement suggest a rather unpleasant character, so it may be worth adding that, according to Plutarch at least, "Cicero had a jolly, joking disposition, with a calm and smiling expression always on his face" (*Comparison of Demosthenes and Cicero*). And he had a sense of humor; in fact, he was famous for it. Gaius Trebonius, the conspirator who detained Mark Antony outside the Senate on the Ides of March, compiled three books of Cicero's jokes. These books have been lost, but Macrobius preserves several of the jokes. For example: "When Cicero saw his son-in-law, Cornelius Lentulus, a very short man, wearing a sword, he asked 'Who tied my son-in-law to a sword?'" (*Saturnalia* 2.3.3). On the other hand, Quintilian wishes that more effort had gone into selecting, not simply collecting, these witticisms (*Education of the Orator* 6.3.5). In one of his speeches, Cicero made what was quite possibly his most tasteless and gratuitously inappropriate witticism, referring to a Sardinian woman (*Sarda*) who had committed suicide as a "salted sardine" (*sarda salsa*).

We know much more about Cicero than about any other Roman. He features prominently in the accounts of the late Republic by historians such as Sallust, Appian, Cassius Dio, and Plutarch, who also wrote his biography. But Cicero's own writings are by far the richest source of information; nearly three-quarters of all Latin literature now surviving from Cicero's lifetime was written by Cicero himself. Since his works are so wide-ranging and so voluminous, he stands alone in any account of Roman literary life.

Cicero was first and foremost an orator. Over his long career as an advocate and politician, he delivered hundreds of speeches, whether in the law courts or in the Senate or to the citizens in general. The titles of almost ninety speeches are known, and almost sixty still survive complete or nearly so. By contrast, the only substantial speech we still have from all the centuries between Cicero and the late empire is Pliny the Younger's *Panegyric,* a speech of thanks to the emperor Trajan on his appointment to the consulship in A.D. 100. Other than military service, the pursuits thought proper for a high-ranking Roman were politics and the law. Each generation therefore had its leading orators, but we know most of them merely by name, if at all. In this crowded and competitive field, Cicero has totally eclipsed all possible rivals.

The great majority of Cicero's speeches are for the defense, not for the prosecution. Defense had rather more cachet, as Cicero himself says: "Acting for the defense brings more prestige and wins more favor, especially if one is defending someone who seems to be oppressed and persecuted by some wealthy and powerful individual. I have taken on such cases on numerous occasions, notably when I defended Roscius of Ameria during Sulla's dictatorship" (*On Duties* 2.51). Even so, few of his defense speeches are quite so memorable as his great speeches for the prosecution: the six *Verrines,* the four *Catilinarians,* the fourteen *Philippics* (at least three more have been lost). For all his greatness, though, we should not imagine Cicero as an intrepid and unerring advocate of truth and justice. When he was defending Milo, who was charged with the murder of Clodius, the rabble-rousing populist politician, he was thoroughly intimidated by Pompey's soldiers who had ringed the court, and sat down after mumbling ineffectually instead of delivering the speech he had prepared. The extant version of that speech was written later, when he had regained his nerve. It is not known how much it differs from the speech he originally intended to deliver. He sent a copy of it to Milo, when he was living in exile in Massalia (mod. Marseilles); Milo wrote back that he was lucky that Cicero had not delivered that speech, since he would otherwise not be enjoying the excellent Massalian mullets (Cassius Dio, *History of Rome* 40.54).

Nor did he always hold his audience spellbound with his oratorical powers. According to Cassius Dio, "The lower classes were angry with Cicero for his execution of the Catilinarian conspirators. On the last day of his consulship, when he wished to present an account and justification of what he had done, they would not allow him to speak—a great frustration to Cicero, who loved not only to be praised by other people but also to lavish praise on himself" (*History of Rome* 37.38). To us, at an objective distance, this anecdote may conjure up an amusing picture of the incorrigibly pompous Cicero being deprived of a prime opportunity for self-promotion, but it shows how hard he had to struggle in the political turmoil of the period. Feeling against him still ran high enough four years later for him to be forced to go into exile.

Cicero himself encapsulates the rough reality of politics in Rome when he criticizes the naiveté of his ally, Cato the Younger, complaining that Cato gives his opinions as if he were living in Plato's ideal Republic, not down among the dregs of Romulus. Cicero recognized the validity of what Cornelius Celsus, an encyclopedist of the Tiberian period, had to say about the practice of the law: "A lawyer aims only for a semblance of the truth...for a litigant's reward is a favorable ruling, not a good conscience." Cicero had said much the same thing in his last philosophical treatise: "An advocate sometimes has to maintain a semblance of the truth, even if it is not really quite true. I would not dare to say this, especially in a philosophical work, if it were not the opinion of Panaetius, the strictest of the Stoics" (*On Duties* 2.51).

The Roman legal system has had a profound influence on that of many Western countries nowadays. Even so, it differed in many fundamental respects. Most notably, the law was not applied in a fair and even-handed manner. That is, of course, a self-evident principle today, but in a society as sensitive to status as ancient Rome, equality before the law would have seemed a peculiar notion. If a court was biased in favor of the rich, powerful, and aristocratic, that was simply regarded as the natural privilege of rank, not as corruption.

Cicero preached what he practiced. He wrote several treatises on rhetoric, most notably *On the Orator, Brutus,* and *The Orator,* which provide, respectively, a plea for the importance of the place of oratory in education, a history of rhetoric at Rome, and a discussion of the various styles of rhetoric. With their discussion of rhetorical technicalities and short-lived controversies about rhetorical styles, these texts are perhaps not so consistently interesting to the modern reader as are most of Cicero's other works.

Very substantial collections of Cicero's letters have been preserved, correspondence between Cicero and his family, his friends, and many of the most important figures in Roman political life. These letters are a uniquely valuable source of information about the momentous times in which they were written, for Cicero wrote almost all of them with no idea that they might be published. Their style varies from the formal and official to the astonishingly open and candid expression of private opinions, and they are regularly enlivened by references to the most mundane issues of daily life. The largest collection contains more than four hundred letters to Pomponius Atticus, a friend from his schooldays, spanning the last twenty-five years of Cicero's life. A letter written on May 3, 49 B.C., when Caesar was fighting the Senate's armies in Spain, is fairly typical. After quoting verbatim a letter in which Mark Antony tells him that he (Mark Antony) has been appointed by Caesar to see that the ruling classes do not flee from Italy, Cicero goes on to assure Atticus that he intends to disregard Antony's order to stay. Then he adds, "I am very concerned that you are suffering from urine retention. Please have it seen to while it is still in the early stages" (*Letters to Atticus* 10.10).

Cicero also wrote much poetry, almost all of which is lost. It was not highly regarded after his lifetime. Tacitus, for example, says that Caesar and Brutus were luckier than Cicero because fewer people knew about their poetry (*Dialogue about Orators* 21). Not having found anyone else willing to commemorate his quelling of the Catilinarian conspiracy by writing a history of it, Cicero wrote his own version, a three-book poem, *His Own Consulship*, in which he portrays himself as summoned to a council of the gods on Olympus, from where he was dispatched as a guardian for Rome and its citizens. Only one substantial passage (seventy-eight lines) survives; it is the longest quotation from any Latin poem in an ancient text, and—unsurprisingly—it was quoted by none other than Cicero himself. The poem contains the notorious boast *o fortunatam natam me consule Romam!* (O Rome, fortunate in having been born (again) with me as consul!—or in a famous, but less literal, nineteenth-century rendering: O happy fate for the Roman state was the date of my great consulate!). Juvenal quotes that line also, adding, "He could have scorned Antony's swords if he had said everything like that," that is, if his speeches had been as bad as his poetry, he would never have been the victim of a politically motivated assassination.

Cicero wrote many philosophical works, perhaps the most significant being *On the Republic, On the Ends of Good and Evil, The Tusculan Disputations, On the Nature of the Gods, On Divination,* and *On Duties.* Apart from *On the Republic,* which was written between 54 and 52 B.C., all these works were written between February 45 and November 44, an amazingly rapid rate of composition. Plutarch says that Cicero's philosophical endeavors gave him influence over the education of young men from senatorial families, and thus served as some compensation for being marginalized in public life during Caesar's regime (*Life of Cicero* 40). There was no letup, however, in the speed with which he produced philosophical works even when he became increasingly active in politics again after the Ides of March. Cicero had very high aspirations for his philosophical writings (*The Tusculan Disputations* 1.1):

> I decided that I should throw light on philosophy in Latin, not because I thought it could not be learned through Greek writings and Greek teachers, but it has always been my opinion that the Romans are superior to the Greeks, whether in making discoveries for themselves or in refining ideas that they have taken over from the Greeks, as long as they think the studies worth the investment of their effort.

Neither Cicero nor any other Roman made good on such an ambitious claim. Cicero's contribution to the Western philosophical tradition is not, of course, negligible. He gives us a very well-informed assessment of contemporary Greek philosophical schools, an assessment that is none the less valuable for being written in Latin rather than Greek. In the millennium following the disintegration of the empire in the West, during which there was almost total ignorance of Greek, Cicero's philosophical treatises played a very important role in maintaining contact with the traditions of Plato and Aristotle. Moreover, he is still a vital source of information about Greek philosophers who would otherwise be very obscure, since their own teachings are mostly lost.

Like many Romans of his time, Cicero was particularly attracted to Stoicism, but in a qualified form (*On Duties* 1.6):

> In discussing this issue now I will follow especially the Stoics but, as is my usual practice, I will not simply translate them; I will draw on Stoic sources using my own judgment and discretion to the extent and in the manner that seems fitting.

Such an eclectic approach to philosophy contrasts sharply with Lucretius's strict adherence to Epicurean doctrines, but it is not unusual. In Greece, the philosophical sects tended to be aggressively at odds with each other, but eclecticism is a typically Roman attitude. In his *Epistles*, for example, Horace declares that he is "not bound to swear to follow any particular philosophical doctrine," but then he goes on to assert his Epicureanism: "When you want to laugh, you'll visit me, fat and sleek with a well-cared-for hide, a pig from Epicurus's herd." There is therefore nothing implausible about the tradition that Cicero, with his tendency toward Stoicism, was responsible for the publication of Lucretius's Epicurean masterpiece.

## THE FIRST SPEECH AGAINST CATILINE

*Lucius Sergius Catilina belonged to a distinguished, if impoverished, aristocratic family. His great-grandfather had been a hero in the Second Punic War: he was twice captured by Hannibal and kept in chains for twenty months, but twice he escaped; he had a prosthetic right arm made of iron so that he could continue fighting, and twice had his horse killed under him (Pliny, Natural History 7.104–5).*

*Despite having the support of both Caesar and Crassus, Catiline lost to Cicero in the consular election for 63 B.C. This was his third failure to win the consulship, so he then attempted to take control of the state by force, with a motley array of bankrupt aristocrats, veteran soldiers, and displaced farmers. The Catilinarian conspiracy is very substantially documented, especially in a monograph by Sallust and in Cicero's four speeches delivered against Catiline. Even so, many of the details are inevitably obscure, since the conspiracy involved so much intrigue at the highest political level. Some of the worst excesses attributed to Catiline are perhaps not very plausible: he may have had a history of extreme violence, torturing to*

*death the murderer of Lutatius Catulus, consul in 102, over Catulus's grave, but it does not seem likely that he bound his fellow conspirators, including Cicero's fellow consul, Antonius Hybrida, to ratify their oath of loyalty to him by killing a young boy and eating his entrails.*

*Not everyone was convinced of the importance of Cicero's achievement. "Catiline's notoriety is out of all proportion to what he actually did, thanks to the speeches that Cicero delivered against him" (Cassius Dio, History of Rome 37.42). Cicero was endlessly proud of his achievement in suppressing the conspiracy, so he would not have appreciated the following observation by the historian Velleius Paterculus: "The glory of Cicero's consulship was significantly enhanced by the birth in that year, eighty-two years ago, of the Divine Augustus, who was destined, by his own greatness, to put all great men of all nations in the shade" (Histories 2.36.1). In Sallust's monograph on the conspiracy, Cicero plays a much less prominent role in events than his own version of events might have led us to expect.*

*Cicero himself, of course, had a vested interest in making the crisis seem as momentous as possible, and in representing himself as the hero of the hour, the new founder of*

*Rome, who saved the state from a terrible fate. For all that he portrayed himself as the savior of the state, nevertheless, in a letter written a year later, in December 62, he tells a friend, perhaps more in exasperation than in earnest, that the expense of buying a house on the Palatine left him in such debt that he would join any conspiracy that would accept him (Letters to His Friends 5.6). He had bought the house with a loan from Publius Cornelius Sulla, who was implicated with Catiline. When Cicero was exiled for executing five of Catiline's fellow conspirators without a trial (Catiline himself was killed in a battle against the other consul, Hybrida), Clodius Pulcher's gang of thugs demolished the house, and part of it was dedicated as a shrine to Liberty to prevent Cicero reclaiming the site. This personal vendetta will account for much of the vehemence with which Cicero attacks Clodius's sister in his speech delivered in defense of Caelius the year after his return from exile.*

*The first speech against Catiline opens with a brief exordium, or introduction (1–2), followed by a digression (3–6), in which Cicero contrasts the present situation with earlier events in Roman history: the populist movement led by Tiberius Gracchus in 133 B.C., which ended with his murder by the Pontifex Maximus (Highest Priest), Publius Scipio; the assassination of Spurius Maelius by Gaius Servilius Ahala in 439 B.C. because he was suspected of plotting tyranny; the decree of the Senate in 121 B.C. that authorized the consul Lucius Opimius to massacre the supporters of the reformer Gaius Gracchus; and the actions taken by Gaius Marius and Lucius Valerius Flaccus in 100 B.C., authorized by decree of the Senate, against a tribune and a praetor who were flouting the election laws with violence.*

[1] How far, I ask you, Catiline, do you mean to stretch our patience? How much longer will your frenzy continue to frustrate us? At what point will your unrestrained recklessness stop flaunting itself? Have the nightly guards on the Palatine, have the patrols in the streets, have the fears of the people, have the gatherings of all loyal citizens, have these strongly defended premises in which this meeting is being held, have the faces and expressions of the senators here had no effect on you at all? Do you not realize that your plans have been exposed? Do you not see that your conspiracy has been arrested and trapped, now that all these people know about it? Which of us do you think does not know what you were up to yesterday evening, what you were up to last night, where you were, whom you collected

together, and what plan of action you decided upon? [2] What a decadent age we live in! The senate is aware of these things, the consul sees them—yet this man remains alive! Alive, did I say? He is not just alive: he actually enters the senate, he takes part in our public deliberations, and with his eyes he notes and marks down each one of us for assassination. We meanwhile, brave men that we are, think that we have done enough for our country if we merely get out of the way of his frenzy and his weapons.

You, Catiline, ought long ago to have been taken to your death, and on a consul's order. It is on yourself that the destruction which you have long been plotting for all of us ought to be visited. [3] The distinguished chief pontiff, Publius Scipio, as a mere private citizen killed Tiberius Gracchus, when Gracchus was causing a mild disturbance in our country: so are we, as consuls, to put up with Catiline, when he is aiming to devastate the entire world with fire and slaughter? I will pass over precedents that are too old, such as Gaius Servilius Ahala, who killed Spurius Maelius with his own hand when Maelius was contemplating an uprising. Gone, gone is that one-time public virtue which led men of courage to punish a citizen traitor more severely than the deadliest foreign enemy. But in fact we have a decree of the senate against you, Catiline, that is stern and authoritative. So it is not the national deliberations or the resolution of the senate that is wanting: it is we, we the consuls, I tell you, who are failing to act!

[4] The senate once decreed that the consul Lucius Opimius should see to it that the state came to no harm. Not a night intervened. Gaius Gracchus, despite his illustrious father, grandfather, and ancestors, was killed on suspicion of stirring up dissension; and the ex-consul Marcus Fulvius was also killed, together with his children. A similar senatorial decree put the state into the hands of the consuls Gaius Marius and Lucius Valerius—and did even a single day then elapse before death and the state's vengeance overtook the tribune of the plebs Lucius Saturninus and the praetor Gaius Servilius? But we for twenty days now have been allowing the edge of the senate's authority to become blunt. We have a senatorial decree like those earlier ones, but it is filed away, as if hidden in a sheath—but on the strength of that decree, you, Catiline, should have been instantly killed. You remain alive, and yet you live on not to put aside your recklessness, but to increase it. Conscript fathers, my only wish is to be compassionate, my only wish is not to appear remiss in the midst of

a national emergency, but already I find that I am guilty of doing nothing, and doing wrong.

[5] There exists in Italy a military camp, hostile to the Roman people, in the mountain passes of Etruria. Each and every day, the number of the enemy increases. The commander of that camp, and the leader of that enemy, you can see inside the city walls, and even in the senate, plotting some form of ruin for our country each day from within. If I now order your arrest, Catiline, and if I order your execution, I suppose what I shall have to be afraid of is not that every loyal citizen will accuse me of being slow to act, but that someone will say I have been too severe! But as it happens, there is a particular reason why I am still not bringing myself to do what I ought to have done long ago. You will be executed only when no one can be found so criminal, so wicked, and so similar to yourself as to deny the justice of that course of action. [6] As long as there remains a single person who has the temerity to speak up for you, you will remain alive—and live in the way you do now, surrounded by the many strong guards I have posted, and prevented from moving against your country. In addition, the many eyes and ears that you are not aware of will continue, as in the past, to track your every move and keep guard against you.

What is the point, Catiline, in waiting any longer, when night cannot cloak your criminal plots in darkness, when a private house cannot confine conspiratorial voices inside its walls—if everything is exposed to the light of day, everything breaks out into the open? Take my advice: call off your plans, and stop thinking of assassination and arson. Whichever way you turn, you have been thwarted. Your plans are all as clear as day to me. Let me take you through them.

*Cicero now proceeds to the narrative (7–10), describing how he had predicted the uprising of Gaius Manlius, Catiline's fellow conspirator, which was to have been followed by the assassination of leading citizens and the occupation of Praeneste, located in the hills about twenty miles southeast of Rome. He then describes a meeting of the conspirators held in the house of Marcus Laeca on the night of November 6, at which Cicero's assassination was planned.*

[7] Do you remember that I declared in the senate on 21 October that Gaius Manlius, your sidekick and partner in crime, would take up arms on a certain day, and that that day would be 27 October? And was I not correct, Catiline, not just about the rising, so large,

terrible, and extraordinary as it was, but also—and this is much more remarkable—about the actual date? I also informed the senate that you had deferred your massacre of leading senators until 28 October, although by that time many of our national leaders had already abandoned Rome, not so much from a desire to save their lives as because they wanted to thwart your plans. Surely you cannot deny that, when that day arrived, my vigilance, together with the guards I posted, successfully prevented you from taking action against the country? Or that you kept on saying that even though the others had left, you were quite happy with massacring only those of us who remained behind? [8] And when you were confident that you were going to seize Praeneste on 1 November by a night attack, did you have any idea that the town had been fortified on my orders with troops, guards, and watchmen? Nothing that you do, nothing that you attempt, and nothing that you contemplate takes place without me not only hearing about it, but actually seeing it and being fully aware of it.

Now go over with me what happened last night; you will see that I am much more vigilant in defence of the country than you are for its destruction. I declare that yesterday evening you went to the scythe-makers' quarter—I will be absolutely precise—to the house of Marcus Laeca, and that you met there a number of your accomplices in this criminal lunacy in which you are all engaged. Do you dare to deny it? Why do you say nothing? If you deny it, I shall prove it. In fact, I notice that there are here in the senate several of those who were with you. [9] Immortal gods! Where in the world are we? What country do we inhabit? In what city do we live? Here, conscript fathers, here amongst our very number, in this, the most revered and important council in the world, there exist men who are plotting the massacre of all of us and the destruction of this city—and even of the entire world. I, the consul, see them; I ask for their opinion on matters of state; and men who ought by rights to be put to the sword I am not even wounding, as yet, with my words.

So you were at Laeca's house last night, Catiline. You parceled out the regions of Italy. You decided where you wanted each man to go. You selected those you were going to leave behind in Rome and those you were going to take away with you. You designated the parts of the city to be burnt. You confirmed that you were on the point of leaving Rome yourself. But you added that you would nevertheless have to stay just a little longer—because I was still alive. Two Roman equestrians were found to relieve you of that particular concern: they gave their word that they would assassinate me in my bed the very same night, just before dawn. [10] I discovered all this almost as soon as your meeting had broken up. I protected and strengthened my home by increasing the guards, and I denied entry to the men whom you yourself had sent to call on me first thing in the morning—and who did indeed come at that time, as I had meanwhile told numerous prominent people that they would.

*In the argument of the speech (10–27), Cicero calls upon Catiline to leave Rome. He cites the current public interest (11–12) but also brings in Catiline's earlier career and innuendos about his private life, including suggestions that he murdered his first wife and his own son (13–17). Cicero then introduces a personification of Rome herself to appeal to Catiline (18), before directly confronting him (19–27).*

In view of this, Catiline, finish what you have started: leave the city at long last. The gates are open: go. For too long now have Manlius and that camp of yours been waiting for you to assume command of it. And take all your followers with you; or if you cannot take them all, take as many as you can. Purge the city. As for me, you will release me from the great fear I feel, if only there is a wall separating us. At all events, you cannot stay any longer with us: I will not tolerate it, I will not endure it, I will not allow it.

[11] We owe a great debt of gratitude to the immortal gods and especially to this Jupiter Stator, the god who from the earliest times has stood guard over our city, for enabling us time and again to escape this pestilence, so foul, so revolting, and so deadly to our country. But we cannot go on forever allowing the survival of the state to be endangered by a single individual. As long as you, Catiline, set traps for me while I was consul-elect, I used private watchfulness, not public guards, to defend myself. Then at the last consular elections, when you wanted to kill me, the consul, together with your fellow candidates in the Campus Martius, I foiled your abominable plot by the protection and services of my friends, without declaring any public state of emergency. In short, whenever you went for me, I stood up to you on my own—even though I was aware that if anything were to happen to me, it would be a terrible disaster for our country.

[12] But now you are openly attacking the country as a whole. You are calling to destruction and devastation the temples of the immortal gods, the houses of the city, the lives of all Roman citizens, and finally the whole of Italy. Even so, I will not yet venture to carry out my first duty and act as befits my office and the strict traditions of our ancestors: instead, I shall act in a way which is more lenient, but also more conducive to the national security. For if I order your execution, all the other members of the conspiracy will remain within the state; but if you leave Rome, as I have long been urging you to do, the voluminous, pernicious dregs of society—your companions—will be flushed out of the city.

[13] Well, Catiline? Surely you cannot be hesitating to do on my orders what you were already doing anyway of your own free will? The consul orders a public enemy to get out of Rome. Into exile, you enquire? That is not what I am ordering—but if you ask my opinion, it is what I advise.

At Rome, Catiline, what is there, at the present time, that can possibly give you any pleasure? Aside from your degraded fellow conspirators, there is not a single person in this city who does not fear you, not a single person who does not hate you. Is there any mark of disgrace with which your private life has not been branded? Is there any dishonor in your personal affairs that does not besmirch your reputation? From what lust have your eyes, from what crime have your hands, from what outrage has any part of your body ever abstained? Is there any youth that you have ensnared with the enticements of corruption whom you have not then gone on to provide with either a weapon to commit crime or a torch to fire his lusts? [14] Or again, when you recently made your house ready for a new bride by bringing about the death of your previous wife, did you not compound this crime with yet another that is quite incredible? But I will pass over this and let it be veiled in silence, because I do not want such a monstrous crime to appear either to have been committed in our country, or to have been committed and not punished. I will also pass over the financial ruin which you will find hanging over you on the 13th of this month.

I come now to matters which relate not to the shame of your personal immorality, nor to the disgraceful state of your financial affairs, but to the supreme interests of Rome, and the lives and survival of each one of us. [15] Can this light of day, Catiline, or this fresh air afford you any pleasure, when you are aware that nobody here is ignorant of the fact that on 29 December in the consulship of Lepidus and Tullus you stood in the assembly armed with a weapon, that you had formed a body of men to kill the consuls and the leaders of the state, and that it was not any change of mind or failure of nerve on your part that prevented you from carrying out your insane crime, but simply the good luck of the Roman people? But there is no need to go on about that: after all, those crimes are well known, and you have committed a good many others since. But how many times you have attempted to assassinate me as consul-elect, and how many times as consul! How many seemingly inescapable thrusts of yours I have dodged by a slight swerve and, as they say, by sleight of body! You achieve nothing, you accomplish nothing, but that does not deter you from trying and hoping. [16] How many times that dagger of yours has been wrenched from your hands, how many times it has dropped by some lucky chance and fallen to the ground! But you still cannot manage without it. With what special rites you must have consecrated and dedicated it I do not know, for you to plunge it into the body of a consul.

But as for the present, what sort of life are you living? You see, I shall talk to you in a way that will not seem motivated by the hatred I ought to feel for you, but by the pity you certainly do not deserve. A short while ago, you walked into the senate. Who out of that packed gathering of people, and out of so many of your friends and connections, offered you a single word of greeting? If no one else in history has ever been treated like that, do you really wait for the insult to be expressed in words, when you have been crushed by the strongest verdict—that of utter silence? And what about the fact that, when you entered the chamber, these benches suddenly emptied? That all the consulars, men whom you had many times marked down for assassination, left the area of benches near you empty and unoccupied the moment you took your seat? How, I ask you, do you feel about that?

[17] By Hercules, if my slaves were as afraid of me as all your fellow-citizens are of you, I would certainly think I ought to leave my house—so don't you think you ought to leave Rome? And if I saw my fellow-citizens looking at me, even without justification, with such deep hatred and suspicion, I would prefer to remove myself from their sight than remain before the hostile gaze of all of them. But you, knowing the crimes you

have committed and so being aware that the hatred everyone feels towards you is merited and has long been your due, do you hesitate to remove yourself from the sight and presence of those whose minds and feelings you are injuring? If your very own parents feared and hated you, and it was absolutely impossible for you to become reconciled with them, surely, I think, you would withdraw to somewhere where they could not see you. But now your own country, which is the common parent of us all, hates you and is frightened of you, and has long ago come to the conclusion that you are contemplating nothing but her destruction. Will you not then respect her authority, defer to her judgment, or fear her power?

[18] Your country, Catiline, addresses you, and, though silent, somehow speaks to you in these terms: "For years now, no crime has been committed that has not been committed by you, and no crime has been committed without you. You alone have killed many citizens, and have oppressed and plundered our allies, while escaping punishment and remaining free. You have managed not merely to ignore the laws and the courts, but to overturn and shatter them. Your previous crimes, intolerable as they were, I put up with as best I could. But now I am racked with fear solely because of you; whenever there is the slightest sound, it is Catiline that people fear; and it seems inconceivable that any plot can be formed against me without your criminality being the cause of it. That this should be so is unendurable. Therefore depart, and release me from this fear! If my fear is justified, your departure will save me from destruction; but if it is not, it will at long last spare me my alarm." [19] If your country were to address you just as I have done, ought she not to be granted what she asks, even though she could not force you?

But what of the fact that you gave yourself into custody—that, to allay people's suspicions, you said that you were prepared to live at Manius Lepidus' house? When he would not have you, you even had the audacity to come to me and request that I keep an eye on you in my own home! But I gave you the same answer as he did, that I could hardly consider myself safe within the walls of the same house as you, when I was already in considerable danger being within the same city walls. So off you went to the praetor Quintus Metellus. And when he had sent you packing, you made your way to your dear friend, the excellent Marcus Metellus, whom you obviously thought would be very conscientious in guarding you, very quick in suspecting you, and very active in punishing you! But how far away from prison and chains do you think a man ought to be who has already himself come to the conclusion that he needs to be kept under guard?

[20] In this situation, Catiline, if you cannot bring yourself to die, surely you cannot hesitate to flee to some other country, and surrender that life of yours—which you have saved from a whole series of just and well-deserved punishments—to exile and solitude?

"Put the question to the senate," you say. That is what you demand; and if this order should pass a decree saying that it wishes you to go into exile, you undertake to comply. I am not going to put it to the senate: it would not be my practice to do so. All the same, I will allow you to see what view these senators take of you. Get out of Rome, Catiline. Free the country from fear. Go into exile—if that is the term you are waiting to hear. Well then? Don't you hear, don't you notice the senators' silence? They agree, and say nothing. Why then do you hold out for a spoken decision, when you can clearly see their silent preference?

[21] Now if I had spoken to this fine young man here, Publius Sestius, or to the valiant Marcus Marcellus, in the way I have just been speaking to you, the senators would have physically assaulted me, consul though I am, and in this temple too; and they would have been fully justified in doing so. But in your case, Catiline, their inaction denotes approval, their acquiescence a formal decree, and their silence applause. And this does not apply only to the members of the senate, whose opinions you clearly value highly, even if you hold their lives cheap: what I say applies equally to those Roman equestrians, fine and honorable men that they are, and to the rest of the citizens, men of great courage who are surrounding this building, whose numbers you could see, whose feelings you could observe, and whose shouts you could hear only a moment ago. For a long time I have only just managed to keep their hands and weapons away from you; but I am sure I shall have no difficulty persuading them to escort you all the way to the city gates, if you now decide to forsake everything that you have for so long been desperate to destroy.

[22] But why am I saying this? Do I imagine that your resolve could be broken? That you could come to your senses? That you could think of escape? That you could consider exile? How I wish the immortal gods would put that idea into your head! And yet, if my

words did frighten you so much that you were driven to contemplate exile, I can see what a storm of unpopularity would break over me—not necessarily immediately, when the memory of your crimes was still fresh, but at a later date. It would be worth it, however, so long as the consequences only affected me, and did not put the state at risk. But that your character should be reformed, that you should be deterred by the penalties of the law, or that you should put your country before yourself—that is too much to ask. For you are not the man, Catiline, to be turned from disgrace by a sense of decency, or from danger by fear, or from madness by reason.

[23] Therefore go, as I have said often enough now. If I am your enemy, as you say I am, and your aim is to whip up hostility towards me, then go straight into exile. If you do this, it will be hard for me to endure what people will say about me; if you go into exile at the consul's command, it will be hard for me to bear the burden of the odium that will fall on me. If, on the other hand, your aim is to enhance my glory and reputation, then leave with your desperate gang of criminals, take yourself off to Manlius, stir up the bad citizens, separate yourself off from the loyal ones, make war on your country, and revel in banditry and wickedness! If you do that, it will look not as if I have driven you into the arms of strangers, but as if you have been invited to go and join your friends.

[24] Yet why should I be urging you, when I already know that you have sent a force ahead to wait for you under arms at Forum Aurelium, when I know that you have agreed a prearranged day with Manlius, and when I know that you have also sent ahead that silver eagle to which you have dedicated a shrine at your house, and which I trust will bring only ruin and disaster to you and all your followers? How, after all, could you go without the object to which you used to pay homage each time you set out to commit a murder, when you would touch its altar with your sacrilegious right hand before using that same right hand straight afterwards to kill Roman citizens?

[25] You will go, at long last, where your unrestrained, insane ambition has long been driving you; nor will this cause you any regret, but, on the contrary, a sort of indescribable delight. It was for madness such as this that nature created you, your own desire trained you, and fortune preserved you. Not only have you never wanted peace, but you have never wanted war either—unless it was a criminal one. Drawing on the

worst of society, you have scraped together a gang of traitors, men entirely abandoned not just by fortune, but even by hope. [26] What delight you will take in their company, what joy you will experience, what pleasure you will revel in, seeing that from so sizeable a gathering you will be able neither to hear nor to see a single decent man! Those physical powers of yours we hear so much about have set you up for a life of this kind: the ability to lie on the bare ground has prepared you not just for launching sexual assaults but for committing crime, the capacity to stay awake not just for cheating husbands in their sleep but for robbing unsuspecting people of their property. Now you have an opportunity to show off your celebrated capacity to endure hunger, cold, and the lack of every amenity—hardships which you will shortly find out have finished you off! [27] When I prevented you from attaining the consulship, I at least managed to ensure that you would be in a position only to attack the country as an exile, not to devastate it as consul, and that the criminal enterprise you would undertake would only go under the name of banditry, and not war.

*Cicero digresses a second time in this section (27–32), in which he uses the device of personification again, this time to have the nation address an appeal to him for action, which he then turns back to the Senate by calling for the departure of Catiline and his followers.*

Now, conscript fathers, I want to avert and deflect a particular complaint that our country might—almost with reason—make against me. So please pay careful attention to what I am going to say, and store it deep inside your hearts and minds. Imagine that my country, which is much more precious to me than my own life, imagine that all Italy, imagine that the entire nation were to address me like this: "Marcus Tullius, what are you playing at? Are you going to permit the departure of a man whom you have discovered to be a public enemy, who you see will be a leader in war, who you are well aware is awaited in the enemy camp as their commander, a man who is an instigator of crime, the leader of a conspiracy, and the mobilizer of slaves and bad citizens—so that it will look as if you have not driven him out of the city, but let him loose against it? Surely you are going to give orders that he be cast into chains, led away to execution, and made to suffer the ultimate penalty? [28] What on earth is stopping you? The tradition of our ancestors? But in this country it has very often been the case that

even private citizens have punished dangerous citizens with death. Or is it the laws that have been passed relating to the punishment of Roman citizens? But at Rome people who have rebelled against the state have never retained the rights of citizens. Or are you afraid that history will judge you harshly? Although you are known only for what you have done yourself, and do not have distinguished ancestors to recommend you, the Roman people have nevertheless seen fit to raise you, and at so early an age, through all the magisterial offices and elevate you to the supreme power. Fine thanks you will be paying them in return, then, if you neglect the safety of your fellow-citizens through concern for your reputation or fear of any kind of danger! [29] But if you are afraid of being judged harshly, being criticized for showing severity and resolution is no more to be dreaded than being criticized for criminal neglect of duty. Or, when Italy is ravaged by war, her cities destroyed, and her homes on fire, do you imagine that your own reputation will be exempt from the flames of hatred?"

To these most solemn words of our country, and to all individuals who share the feelings she expresses, I will make this brief answer. Had I judged that punishing Catiline with death was the best course of action, conscript fathers, I should not have given that gladiator a single hour of life to enjoy. For if it is the case that our most distinguished and illustrious citizens did not merely not damage their reputations when they killed Saturninus, the Gracchi, Flaccus, and many other figures of the past, but actually enhanced them, then certainly I had no need to fear that killing this murderer of Roman citizens would do any harm in the future to my own reputation. But even if there was considerable danger of its doing me harm, I have always been of the opinion that unpopularity earned by doing what is right is not unpopularity at all, but glory.

[30] And yet there are not a few members of this order who either fail to see what is hanging over us or pretend not to see it. These people have fed Catiline's hopes by their feeble expressions of opinion, and have given strength to the growing conspiracy by their reluctance to believe in its existence. Their authority is such that, had I punished Catiline, many people—not just traitors, but people who do not know any better—would say that I had acted in a cruel and tyrannical manner. But as it is, I know that if he goes to Manlius' camp, as he means to, there will be no one so stupid

as not to see that the conspiracy exists, and no one so wicked as not to acknowledge that it exists.

But if he, and he alone, is killed, I know that this cancer in the state can be repressed only for a short time: it cannot be suppressed permanently. On the other hand, if he removes himself and takes all his followers with him, and brings together in one place all the other castaways he has collected from here and there, we will be able to wipe out and expunge not only this cancer which has grown up in our midst, but also the root and seed of future ills.

[31] We have been living for a long time now, conscript fathers, amid the dangers of a conspiracy and the attempts on our lives, but somehow or other all this criminal activity and this long-standing violence and frenzy has come to a head during my tenure of the consulship. If, out of so many brigands, only this man here is removed, we will perhaps be under the impression, briefly, that we have been freed from our fear and anxiety. But the danger will remain, enclosed deep within the veins and vitals of the state. It is like when people who are seriously ill toss and turn with a burning fever: if they have a drink of cold water, they initially seem to find relief, but are afterwards much more seriously and violently ill than they were before. In the same way, this disease from which our country is suffering will initially seem to abate if this man is punished, but will then break out much more violently, as the other conspirators will still be alive.

[32] Therefore let the traitors depart. Let them detach themselves from the good citizens, gather together in one place, and, as I have said many times now, be separated from us by the city wall. Let them stop attempting to assassinate the consul in his own home, thronging round the tribunal of the city praetor, besieging the senate-house with swords, and preparing fire-arrows and torches to burn the city. Finally, let it be inscribed on the forehead of every citizen what he thinks about his country. I promise you this, conscript fathers, that we the consuls will show such conscientiousness, you will show such authority, the Roman equestrians will show such courage, and all loyal citizens will show such solidarity that, once Catiline has departed, you will see everything revealed, exposed, crushed, and punished.

*The peroration is brief and pointed, closing with an appeal to Jupiter to protect his city.*

[33] With omens such as these, Catiline, and for the sake of the survival of the state, the death and destruction of yourself, and the ruin of those who have linked themselves to you in every type of crime and murder: be off to your sacrilegious and wicked war! And you, Jupiter, who were established by the same auspices as those by which Romulus founded this city, whom we rightly call the "Stayer" of this city and empire, may you drive him and his associates away from your temple and the other temples, away from the buildings and walls of the city, and away from the lives and fortunes of all the citizens! And on these men who are the opponents of decent citizens, the enemies of their country, brigands of Italy, and linked together in an unholy alliance and syndicate of crime, on these, living and dead, may you inflict everlasting punishment!

# IN DEFENSE OF CAELIUS

*Marcus Caelius Rufus, an ambitious young politician, was tried in Rome on April 3–4, 56 B.C., on charges relating to various acts of violence, including murder, attempted murder, and property damage. Caelius spoke in his own defense, with further speeches on his behalf by Crassus and Cicero. Caelius himself was a skillful advocate; in 59, he had successfully prosecuted Cicero's colleague in the consulship of 63 B.C., Antonius Hybrida, even though Cicero spoke for the defense. Crassus was at this time a Triumvir, an ally of Pompey and Caesar, and one of the most influential men in Rome. Cicero was at the height of his powers, freshly back from exile and seething for revenge against Clodius, who had been responsible for his exile and had persecuted his family while he was absent from Italy. One of the charges against Caelius was the attempted poisoning of Clodius's sister, and Cicero will have welcomed the chance to denigrate her. Perhaps not surprisingly, Caelius was acquitted.*

*Relevance to the facts of the case was so much less important in Roman courts than it is nowadays that it is not always easy to deduce from a speech what the precise charges were. Cicero's speech on behalf of Clodius is typical in this respect. He assures the jury (in section 23) that Crassus has disposed of the charges of violence and property damage. Although Cicero makes a claim to relevance for his denunciation of Clodia (in section 31), this is transparently false: the common thread linking most of the charges against Caelius is the political maneuvering to restore Ptolemy the Flute Player to the throne of Egypt. Cicero goes straight on to add that "in talking about this woman, I shall say only what I need to say to rebut the charge." This is not true either; for example, the jury hardly needed to hear his snide insinuations about Clodia buying gardens by the Tiber where all the young people come to swim (36), however much they may have enjoyed such prurient accusations against one of the most glamorous ladies in Roman society. The attack on Clodia is a dodge, intended to stir up the jurors' sympathy for his client, but Cicero relished the opportunity to get at his old rival through his sister and was not going to let this chance slip.*

*The* Pro Caelio *is one of Cicero's most frequently read speeches—deservedly so, for its robust and crafty invective displays his rhetorical skill at its best. Even so, we would doubtless enjoy the speech all the more if we had more precise information about the relationship between the leading characters. Plutarch claims that, when Cicero was consul, his wife suspected Clodia of wanting to steal him from her. Is there any truth to this? Is she the Clodia (Clodius had three sisters, all with that name) whom he attacks in this speech? Is the Clodia of the speech the same sister as was Catullus's mistress? Is the defendant the Caelius and/or the Rufus referred to in several of Catullus's poems? In a letter to Atticus in May 45 (12.38a), Cicero wishes he could buy some gardens belonging to Clodia; is she this Clodia, and are they the gardens he here criticizes her for owning?*

*The trial took place during the festival of the Megalesian Games, when the courts were normally closed, a circumstance that Cicero alludes to in his opening remarks. The speech begins with an exordium (1–2) that was much admired by Quintilian, in which Cicero brushes aside the formal charges against Caelius and identifies the real enemy as Clodia, whom he here alludes to only vaguely as a "prostitute" and "some other person."*

[1] If, members of the jury, there should happen to be present among us here today anyone who is unfamiliar with our laws, courts, and way of doing things, I am sure he would wonder what terrible enormity this case involves, since on a day of festivities and public games, when all other legal business is suspended, this court alone remains in session—and he would have no doubt at all that the defendant must be guilty of a crime so terrible that, unless action were taken, the state could not possibly survive! And if he were then to be informed that there is a law for rebellious and criminal Roman citizens who have besieged the senate-house with arms, used violence against the magistrates, and attacked their country, and that under this law trials may be held on any day of the year without exception, he would not object to the law, but would enquire what charge it is that is before this court. If he were then to be told

that no crime, no enormity, and no act of violence has been brought before the court, but that a brilliantly able, hard-working, and popular young man is being accused by the son of someone he has prosecuted once and is now prosecuting again, and that this attack on him is being financed by a prostitute, he would find no fault with the prosecutor's sense of filial duty, he would consider that a woman's passions should be kept under control, and he would conclude that you yourselves are overworked, since even on a public holiday you are not allowed the day off! [2] In fact, if you are prepared to pay close attention and form an accurate view of the case as a whole, you will realize, gentlemen, that none of the accusers would have taken on this prosecution if they had had any choice, nor, having taken it on, would they have had any hope of winning, were it not for their reliance on the insupportable passion and bitter hatred of some other person. I shall forgive Atratinus, however, a civilized and altogether excellent young man and a friend of mine. He can plead as his excuse either filial duty, or compulsion, or his tender years. If he brought the charge voluntarily, I put it down to his sense of filial duty, if he was acting under orders, I put it down to compulsion, and if he expected to gain something from it, I put it down to his youthful naivety. As for the other accusers, they deserve no such indulgence, and must be vigorously opposed.

*Normally we would expect at this point a narrative of the facts of the case, but instead Cicero launches into a long section (3–50) clearing away the numerous slanders against Caelius's character made by the prosecution. He begins with the insinuation that he mistreated his father, also named Marcus Caelius (3–5).*

[3] I think, gentlemen, that the best way of beginning my defense, in view of the youth of Marcus Caelius, is to reply to those slanders which the prosecutors have come up with in order to discredit him and deprive and despoil him of his good name. His father has been cited against him in various ways, either as not himself living in a manner befitting an equestrian, or as having been treated with insufficient respect by his son. As regards the first of these points, those who know Marcus Caelius and the older ones among us will appreciate that he needs no words of mine to rebut the charge, in silence, himself. Those of us, on the other hand, who are not so well acquainted with him (since his advanced years have long prevented him from mixing

with us much or coming into the forum) may rest assured that whatever distinction a Roman equestrian may possess—and it can undoubtedly be very great—has always been judged as belonging to Marcus Caelius in the fullest measure, and is still so judged today, and not just by his own circle but by all those who may for whatever reason have come into contact with him. [4] In any case, being the son of a Roman equestrian is something that the prosecution should never have used as a smear before these jurors, or before myself as advocate.

As regards your point about my client's respect for his father, we have our own opinion about that, but the verdict surely lies with the parent. Our own opinion you shall hear from witnesses on oath. As for what his parents feel, that is made clear by his mother's tears and her indescribable grief, and by his father's filth and all the sorrow and distress that you see in front of you.

[5] Regarding the further objection that the young man is held in low esteem by his fellow-townsmen, the Praetuttians have never conferred greater honors on anyone in their presence, gentlemen, than they have on Marcus Caelius in his absence. Indeed, they elected him, while he was away, to their senate and granted him, without his asking, certain honors which they refused to the many who did ask for them. They have also sent to this trial a deputation of the most high-ranking men, fellow senators of mine and Roman equestrians too, and these delegates have brought with them an extremely impressive and eloquent testimonial.

I believe I have now laid the foundations of my defense—which will be very secure if based on the verdict of my client's own people. For this young man would hardly come before you with an adequate recommendation if he had incurred the disapproval of a man such as his father is, or of a town so distinguished and so important. [6] Indeed, if I may turn to my own situation, it is from just such a source that I issued forth to make my own reputation, and this forensic labor of mine and my career in general have found a rather wider course to public recognition as a result of the recommendation and approval of my friends.

*In this section (6–9), Cicero dismisses insinuations about Caelius's conduct as a youth, asserting that he himself had taken Caelius under his wing once he put on the toga that signified passage to adulthood.*

Now as for the slur on his sexual morals and the slanderous insults—for they were not proper charges—leveled at him by each of the prosecutors, these will never upset Marcus Caelius enough to make him wish he had been born ugly! For slanders of this kind are commonly directed against any young man of becoming figure and appearance. But slander is one thing, prosecution another. Prosecution requires a basis for a charge, and then to determine the facts, to identify the person responsible, to prove the case by argument, and back it up with evidence. Slander, on the other hand, has no object except to insult. If its character is coarse, it is termed abuse, but if sophisticated, it is termed wit.

[7] Indeed, I was surprised and disappointed that this part of the prosecution was given to Atratinus. For it did not suit him, nor was it appropriate for one so young, nor, as you will have noticed yourselves, did this fine young man's sense of decency allow him to feel at home with language of this sort. I should have preferred it if one of the more hardened prosecutors among you had taken on the task of slandering my client; then I could have contradicted this unfettered slander in rather more free, forcible, and natural terms. But with you, Atratinus, I shall deal more leniently. Your sense of decency leads me to moderate my words, and I ought also to take into account the kindness I have shown towards you and your father.

[8] I should like, however, to give you a word of advice. First, to prevent anyone forming a wrong impression of the sort of person that you are, you must be as strict in avoiding intemperate words as you are in avoiding shameful deeds. Secondly, you should not say against someone else things that you would blush to hear falsely said against yourself. For who is there who cannot go down that road if they choose? Who is there who cannot direct against your youth and grace the coarsest slanders that he pleases? There may be no grounds whatever for the suspicion—but there will be grounds for an accusation! The blame for the part you have played lies, however, with those who wanted you to take it on. Credit, on the other hand, is due to your sense of decency, because we saw how reluctantly you spoke, and also to your talent, because your speech was elegant and polished.

[9] That speech, however, requires only a brief reply. In so far as Marcus Caelius' youth could have given any grounds for suspicion, let me assure you that it was well protected, first by his own sense of decency, and then by the strict upbringing that he received from his father. After that, as soon as his father had given

him the toga of manhood—and here I will say nothing about myself, leaving you to be the judge of that: I shall only say that his father immediately put him in my charge. During this early period of his youth, no one ever saw Marcus Caelius in the company of anyone other than his father or myself, or at the highly respectable home of Marcus Crassus; and all the while he was receiving a principled education.

*The prosecution doubtless figured that it would score points by connecting Caelius with Catiline, but Cicero deals with this head-on in this section (10–16), painting a portrait of the seductive aspects of Catiline's character as an excuse for the young Caelius's attraction to him.*

[10] As for the charge that Caelius was a friend of Catiline, he should by rights be wholly above any suspicion of that kind. You know that he was still very young when Catiline, together with myself, was standing for the consulship. If he ever attached himself to Catiline or detached himself from me—even though there were many patriotic young men who did become supporters of that vile traitor—then let Caelius be reckoned to have been too friendly with Catiline. "But we know that later on he even became a political adherent of his: we could see it with our own eyes." Who is denying it? But at the moment I am only defending that period of youth that is by itself unstable, yet threatened by the passions of others. In that period, when I was praetor, Caelius was constantly by my side, and did not know Catiline, who was serving as praetor in Africa. In the year that followed Catiline was tried for extortion; Caelius stayed with me, and did not even appear in support of Catiline at his trial. The next year was the year in which I stood for the consulship; Catiline also stood alongside me. Caelius never attached himself to him, and never separated himself from me.

[11] So it was only after he had spent many years in the forum without any suspicion or any ill repute that he became a supporter of Catiline, when Catiline was standing for the second time. How long do you think his youth should have gone on being protected? Back in my day a single year sufficed for keeping our arms inside our togas, and for our physical training on the Campus Martius, when we wore our tunics; and if we went straight into the army we served a similar probationary period, in the camp and on campaign. At that age, unless a young man could defend himself by his own strictness, conduct, and purity of morals, coupled with a stern upbringing and a certain inborn virtue, he could not escape a bad reputation (and justified, too), however closely his own people kept guard over him. But a man who preserved those first beginnings of youth pure and undefiled never had aspersions cast on his reputation and morals, once he had finally grown up and become a man among men.

[12] Yes, he did support Catiline, after he had spent a number of years in the forum, Caelius that is—just as many others did from every class and of every age. For Catiline had, as I am sure you remember, a great many indications of the highest qualities—not fully developed, mind you, but sketched in outline. He mixed with numerous individuals of bad character; yet he pretended to be devoted to the best of men. He had the effect of degrading those around him; yet he could also stimulate them to effort and hard work. The fires of passion burned within him; yet he was a keen student of military affairs. For my part I do not think the world has ever seen a creature made up of such contrary, divergent, and mutually incompatible interests and appetites.

[13] Who was more agreeable, at one particular time, to men of high rank, and who more intimate with scoundrels? Who at one time a more patriotic citizen, and who a more loathsome enemy of this country? Who more corrupt in his pleasures, and who more able to endure hard work? Who more avaricious in rapacity, and who more lavish in generosity? That man, gentlemen, had many features that were paradoxical. He had a wide circle of friends, and he looked after them well. What he had, he shared with everyone. He helped all his friends in times of need with money, influence, physical exertion, even, if necessary, with recklessness and crime. He could adapt and control the way he was to suit the occasion, and twist and turn his nature this way and that. He could be stern with the serious, relaxed with the free-and-easy, grave with the old, affable with the young, daring with criminals, and dissolute with the depraved. [14] And so this complex, ever-changing character, even when he had collected all the wicked traitors from far and wide, still held many loyal, brave men in his grasp by a sort of pretended semblance of virtue. Indeed, that dastardly attempt to destroy this empire could never have come into being had not that monstrous concentration of so many vices been rooted in certain qualities of skill and endurance.

Therefore, members of the jury, you should reject the prosecution's argument, and refuse to allow my client's association with Catiline to count against him: this is something he has in common with many other people, including some fine patriots. I, I myself, I tell you, was almost taken in by him on one occasion, when I took him to be a loyal citizen, eager to be on good terms with all the best people, and a dependable and faithful friend. I did not believe his crimes until I came upon them with my eyes, or suspect them until I had laid my hands on them. If Caelius was also among his wide circle of friends, it is better that he should be angry with himself at his own mistake (just as I sometimes am about my own misjudgment of Catiline) than that he should have to fear a charge of having been a friend of his.

[15] So your speech has gone from slanders about my client's sexual morality to using the conspiracy to stir up prejudice against him. For you implied, although in a hesitant and sketchy manner, that because of his friendship with Catiline, he must have been a member of the conspiracy. At this point not only did the charge fail to hang together, but this fluent young man's speech scarcely did so either. So let me ask you, what terrible madness was there that came over Caelius? What terrible wound had he suffered, either psychologically or in his personal circumstances? And when was Caelius' name ever mentioned in connection with the conspiracy? I do not wish to go on for too long discussing matters about which there is not the slightest doubt, but this I will say: if Caelius had been a member of the conspiracy, or even if he had been anything other than implacably opposed to it, he would surely never have used a charge of conspiracy as his preferred means of promoting his youthful abilities.

[16] Apropos of this, I rather think that the question of electoral malpractice and the charges relating to political clubs and the distribution of bribes (since this is the point I have reached) can be disposed of in the same way. For if Caelius had really sullied his reputation with the unstinted bribery that you speak of, he would hardly have been so insane as to prosecute another person for the same crime. Nor would he deliberately cause someone else to be suspected of this crime if he wanted to have the freedom to do it himself in the future. Nor indeed, if he thought that he would run the risk of being prosecuted for bribery once, would he have prosecuted someone else for it a second time. In doing this I admit that he has acted unwisely and without my approval. Yet it is the mark of this type of ambition that it pursues the innocence of

another person instead of betraying any apprehension on its own account.

*Cicero dismisses the allegation that Caelius's extravagances led him into debt and takes this opportunity to give a first hint of what is to come, by quoting a line from a play famous among the Romans, Ennius's* Medea, *to introduce a reference to Clodia, whom he calls the "Medea of the Palatine."*

[17] As for the charge of debt, the complaints of extravagance. the demands for account-books—see how brief is my reply. A man who is under his father's legal authority does not keep accounts. Caelius has never once borrowed money from one creditor to pay off another. It is one particular form of extravagance that he is charged with, his accommodation. This, you say, costs him 30,000 sesterces a year. Ah, now I understand! The block in which my client rents an apartment for, I think, 10,000 a year has been put up for sale by Publius Clodius. You, wishing to do him a favor, have adjusted your lie to suit his purpose.

[18] You have criticized Caelius for moving away from his father's house. But at his age that is scarcely something to be criticized. He had just won a success in a political case which, although unwelcome to me, was a great victory for him, and he was also at an age when he could stand for public office. Moreover, it was not only with his father's permission but with his active encouragement that he moved away from home. For his father lives a long way from the forum, and in order to be able both to visit our houses more easily and to be visited himself by his own people he took an apartment on the Palatine at a moderate rent.

While on this subject I can repeat what the illustrious Marcus Crassus said a little while ago, when he was deploring the arrival of King Ptolemy: "Would that never in Pelion's forest…" And I could go on with the quotation: "for never would a wandering woman" have caused us all this trouble, "Medea, sick at heart, wounded by a wild passion." For you will find out, gentlemen, what I shall show you when I come to that point—that this Medea of the Palatine and the change of residence was the cause of all this young man's difficulties, or rather of all the talk.

*Cicero now dismisses concerns about the testimony that the prosecution claims it will offer by a senator who is not named here. This is Quintus Fufius Calenus, a friend of*

*Clodius and an enemy of Cicero, who would testify that Caelius assaulted him at the pontifical elections. As the text indicates, Cicero omitted much of this section from the published version of his speech. He also impugns the testimony of other unnamed witnesses who would testify that Caelius assaulted their wives after a dinner party.*

[19] So, since I have every confidence in your judgment, gentlemen, I am not in the least afraid of those charges which the prosecution, as I inferred from their speeches, are fabricating to bolster their case. For they gave out that they had a senator who would testify that he had been assaulted by Caelius at the pontifical elections. If this person comes forward, I will ask him first of all why he did not take legal action there and then; and secondly, if he says he preferred to make a complaint rather than go to law, I will ask him why he has been produced by yourselves rather than coming forward on his own initiative, and why he wished to make his complaint so long after the event rather than at the time. If he can supply me with acute and astute answers to these questions, I will then ask, finally, from what source that senator springs. If it emerges that he himself is his own source and origin, I may well be impressed by this, as I generally am. But if it turns out that he is merely a rivulet drawn off and derived from that very fountain-head of your prosecution, I shall be delighted that, although you have such great influence and resources at your disposal, you could nevertheless find only a single senator who was prepared to do your bidding.

[Here followed a section on the witness Fufius which was omitted from the published version of the speech.]

[20] Nor, on the other hand, am I in any way frightened of that other type of witness—those who operate by night. For the prosecution said there would be witnesses who would testify that their wives were assaulted by Caelius when returning from dinner. What impressive witnesses they will be, who will dare to swear this on oath, when they will also have to admit that they never started legal proceedings regarding these terrible wrongs, even to the extent of requesting a meeting and out-of-court settlement!

You are now in a position, gentlemen, to foresee the whole nature of this attack, and when it is launched it will be your duty to beat it back. For the accusers of Marcus Caelius are not the same people as those who are attacking him: the weapons that are hurled at him in public are supplied by an unseen hand. [21] I am not saying this to discredit the prosecutors, who are entitled even to feel proud of what they are doing. They are doing their duty, defending those near to them, acting as men of spirit do. When injured, they feel aggrieved; when angered, they let fly; they fight back when provoked. Men of spirit may indeed have just cause for attacking Marcus Caelius. But you in your wisdom, gentlemen, will appreciate that you should not on this account be guided by other people's grievances rather than by your own sense of honor.

You can see what a mass of people there is in the forum, of how many different classes and occupations, what a variety of humankind. From such a crowd, how many people do you think there are who are used to offering their services, exerting themselves, and promising their evidence, on their own initiative, to powerful, influential, and persuasive individuals, when they believe that there is something those individuals want? [22] If there happen to be some such people who have forced their way into the present trial, then use your wisdom, gentlemen, to put a stop to their greed! In this way you will show that you have taken consideration at one and the same time for the safety of my client, for your own consciences, and for the general public welfare against dangerous and powerful individuals.

For my part, I intend to draw you away from witnesses. I will not allow the facts of the case, which are unalterable, to be made to rely on witnesses' personal inclinations, which can so easily be manipulated, and which can be twisted and distorted with no difficulty at all. Instead, I shall proceed by means of proofs, and shall refute the charges with indications that are clearer than the light of day. Fact will be pitted against fact, reason against reason, argument against argument!

*Cicero brushes away the allegation that Caelius was involved in the assassination of the philosopher Dio, the leader of an embassy from the city of Alexandria to Rome who was killed at the house of Titus Coponius at the instigation of King Ptolemy the Flute Player. Publius Asicius had already been prosecuted for the murder and successfully defended by Cicero.*

[23] I am very pleased, therefore, that Marcus Crassus has dealt so impressively and eloquently with the part of the case that has to do with the civil disturbances at Naples, the assault on the Alexandrians at Puteoli, and the property of Palla. I could wish that he had also

spoken about Dio. But on this last point what can you possibly be expecting to hear, given that the perpetrator of the crime has no fear of punishment, or even admits his responsibility? After all, he is a king! The man, on the other hand, who is said to have been his agent and accomplice, Publius Asicius, has been acquitted of the deed in a criminal trial. So here we have a charge which the guilty party does not deny, whereas the man who did deny it has been acquitted of it. In these circumstances, do you really think my client has any reason to be afraid of the charge when he not only had no involvement in the crime but was not even suspected of being involved in it? And if the help Asicius received from the strength of his case outweighed the harm done to him by the odium of the charge, what harm can your slander possibly do to Caelius, who not only has not been suspected of this particular crime, but has not even been tainted with a bad reputation?

[24] "But Asicius was acquitted as a result of collusion." This point is an extremely easy one to answer, especially for me since I was the defense advocate. But Caelius' view is that however strong Asicius' case is (and he thinks it is very strong indeed), it nevertheless has no bearing on his. Nor is this the view of Caelius alone: it is shared by two highly civilized and cultured young men, possessed of the most virtuous principles and the best literary training, Titus and Gaius Coponius, who were more upset than anyone at Dio's death, and who were attached to him both by their common devotion to culture and civilized values and by the ties of hospitality. Dio, as you have heard, was living at Titus' house, and had known him in Alexandria. What he or his most worthy brother thinks of Marcus Caelius you will discover from themselves, if they are brought forward to testify. [25] So let us put all this to one side, and turn at last to the points on which the case depends.

*Up to this point Cicero has been dealing with the allegations made by Atratinus for the prosecution. He now turns to deal with attacks on Caelius's character made by another member of the prosecution team, Herennius. These he brushes off as irrelevant generalizations about the dissipations of Roman youth who squander their time and money at resorts like Baiae on the Bay of Naples.*

I noticed, members of the jury, that you were listening to my friend Lucius Herennius with close attention. Although it was primarily his ability and his particular manner of speaking that held your attention, I was nevertheless afraid at times that that speech of his, carefully contrived to suggest guilt, might imperceptibly and gently insinuate itself into your minds. For he had a great deal to say about luxurious living, a great deal about self-indulgence, a great deal about the vices of the young, and a great deal about morals. In his life away from the court Herennius is a gentle soul, and elegantly exemplifies the familiar charm and good manners which just about everyone admires nowadays; but in this trial he has shown himself the grimmest type of uncle, moralist, and schoolmaster. He castigated Marcus Caelius as no father ever did his own son; he gave a long lecture on licentiousness and profligacy. In short, gentlemen, I began to excuse your listening so attentively because I myself was shuddering at so grim and so severe a way of talking.

[26] The first part of his speech, however, troubled me less. He claimed that Caelius was on familiar terms with my friend Bestia, that he dined at his house, that he visited him frequently, and that he supported his campaign for the praetorship. These allegations do not trouble me because they are patently false. For the people that Herennius claimed were present at these dinner parties are all people who are either unavailable or else under an obligation to back him up. I am not troubled, either, by his assertion that Caelius is a colleague of his in the Luperci. Clearly the fraternity of the Luperci must be a savage brotherhood, rustic and wild, an association of backwoodsmen formed before the invention of laws and civilization, if its members today not only prosecute one another but even allude to their common membership in the course of their prosecution, apparently afraid in case anyone should be unaware of the connection! [27] But I am going to leave out all of this, and pass on to the points that trouble me more.

Herennius' castigation of pleasures was lengthy; it was also calmly delivered, more like a disputation than a harangue, which is why it was listened to so attentively. As for my friend Publius Clodius, although he threw his weight about very impressively and energetically and gave a fiery speech in the strongest language and at the top of his voice, I found that I thought highly of his oratory without, however, being alarmed by it— for I had seen him in a number of cases on the losing side. No, it is you, Balbus, that I must reply to first, in all humility, if you will allow me, if it is lawful, that is, for me to defend a man who has never refused an invitation to a dinner party, who has visited a pleasure-garden, who has used perfume, and who has set eyes on Baiae!

[28] I have in fact seen and heard of many men in our nation who have not merely taken a sip of this kind of life and touched it with their fingertips, so to speak, but have devoted the whole period of their youth to the pleasures of the flesh, and who even so have eventually risen above it all and turned over a new leaf, going on to become respected and famous citizens. Everyone agrees that the young should be allowed to play around a little, and nature herself has been generous in supplying them with youthful passions; and if these passions should burst out into the open, then so long as they do not upset anyone's life or break up anyone's home they are generally regarded as unproblematic and easy to put up with. [29] But it seemed to me that what you were trying to do was to use the bad reputation of young men in general to stir up prejudice specifically against Caelius. So all that silent attention which was paid to your speech can be put down to the fact that, while there was a single defendant on trial, we were reflecting on the vices of many.

It is easy to attack luxurious living. Daylight would soon fail me if I tried to set forth everything that could be said on the topic: corruption, adultery, wantonness, extravagance—it's a vast subject! Even if you have no defendant to accuse but just the vices in general, the subject in itself offers scope for a full and damning attack. But wise men like yourselves, gentlemen, should not be diverted from the person of the defendant himself. Your own strictness and stern responsibility give you barbs that you can deploy. The prosecutor has aimed these barbs at an abstraction—at vices, at morals, at the age in which we live. You, on the other hand, ought not to deploy them against an individual defendant, when he has been subjected to an unwarranted prejudice not through any fault of his own but because of the failings of many others.

[30] I shall not venture, therefore, to reply to your criticisms as I ought. For I could ask you to make an exception for the young, and beg your pardon. But, as I say, I shall not do this: I shall not take refuge in my client's youth, and I give up the rights to which anyone would be entitled. All I ask is that, whatever general disapproval there may currently be concerning young men's debts, dissipation, and licentious behavior—and I know that on this subject there is considerable disapproval—my client should not be

made to suffer for other people's misdemeanors, or for the vices of youth and of the age in which we live. And yet, although I am making this request, I have no objection to providing the most conscientious answers to those charges which actually relate to my client specifically.

*Cicero now pretends that he is going to deal with the actual charges against Caelius, but it is only a dodge, as he now introduces Clodia, whose character he smears, implying that she commits incest with her brother (32). He conjures up her ancestor, Appius Claudius Caecus (The Blind), famous for the severity of his morals, to lecture her (33–34), and tops this off with an impersonation of her brother, Clodius himself (36).*

There are two charges, one about gold and one about poison; and behind both of them one and the same person is to be found. Gold was taken from Clodia, and poison was sought to be given to Clodia—or so the prosecution claim. All the other accusations are not charges but slanders, more appropriate to an abusive slanging-match than to a public trial. "Adulterer, pervert, dealer in bribes!"—this is the language of slander, not of prosecution. There is no basis for such charges, no foundation; they are insulting remarks thoughtlessly spouted by an angry prosecutor who has no authority for what he says. [31] But as for the two charges, I can see their originator, I can see their source, I can see the specific individual who is their fountain-head. Caelius needed gold: he took it from Clodia, he took it without any witness being present, and he kept it as long as he wanted it. Here I detect the strongest evidence of an extremely close friendship! He wanted to kill Clodia: he sought poison, pestered those he could for it, somehow obtained it, fixed on a place, and conveyed the poison there. Here I detect a bitter hatred, following upon a cruel rupture!

In this trial, members of the jury, everything has to do with Clodia, a woman who is not only of noble birth, but notorious. In talking about this woman, I shall say only what I need to say to rebut the charge. [32] You with your remarkable understanding, Gnaeus Domitius, will appreciate that we are concerned with this woman alone. If she denies that she lent gold to Caelius, if she does not allege that he obtained poison to use against her, then I am behaving outrageously in referring to a respectable lady in terms that are far removed from what is due to a virtuous

Roman matron. But if this woman is eliminated from the case, the prosecution are left with neither charges nor resources with which to attack Marcus Caelius—so surely I as his advocate have no choice but to repel those who are assailing him? Indeed, I would do this more vigorously, were it not for the fact that I am restrained by my personal enmity with this woman's husband, I mean her brother—I'm always making that mistake! I shall treat her gently, then, and go no further than my duty to my client and the demands of the case require. Indeed, I never thought I would be getting involved in quarrels with women, especially with one who is always thought of as every man's friend rather than any man's enemy!

[33] But I should like to ask her first whether she would prefer me to deal with her in a stern, solemn, old-fashioned way or in a relaxed, easy-going, modern way. If she chooses the severe mode of address, then I must call up from the underworld one of those bearded ancients—not with the modern type of goatee beard that she takes such pleasure in, but the rough type such as we see on antique statues and masks—to castigate the woman and speak in my place (for otherwise she might become angry with me!). Let me therefore summon up a member of her own family—and who better than the famous Caecus? He, at any rate, will be the least shocked at her, since he will not be able to see her!

[34] If he appears, this is, I am sure, how he will treat her, this is what he will say: "Woman! What do you think you are doing with Caelius, with a man much younger than yourself, with someone from outside your own family? Why have you been either such a friend to him that you lent him gold or such an enemy that you were afraid of poison? Did you not notice that your father, or hear that your uncle, your grandfather, your great-grandfather, your great-great-grandfather and your great-great-great-grandfather were all consuls? And were you not aware that you were recently the wife of Quintus Metellus, that illustrious and valiant lover of his country, who only had to step out of his front door to surpass virtually every one of his fellow citizens in excellence, fame, and standing? Coming from such a distinguished family yourself, and marrying into one so illustrious, what reason did you have for linking yourself so closely to Caelius? Was he a blood relation, a relation by marriage, a friend of your husband? He was none of these. What, then, was the reason—unless it was some reckless infatuation? And if you were not

influenced by the masks of the men in our family, did my own descendant, the famous Quinta Claudia, not inspire you to rival our family's glory in the splendid achievements of its women? Or were you not inspired by the famous Vestal Virgin Claudia who, at her father's triumph, held him in her arms and so prevented him from being pulled down from his chariot by a hostile tribune of the plebs? Why was it your brother's vices that influenced you, rather than the virtues of your father and ancestors, virtues that have been repeated down the generations from my own time not only in the men but particularly in the women of our family? Did I destroy the peace treaty with Pyrrhus so that you could strike the most disgraceful sexual bargains on a daily basis? Did I bring water to the city for you to foul with your incestuous practices? Did I build a road so that you could parade up and down it in the company of other women's husbands?"

[35] But why, members of the jury, have I brought on this solemn character when there is a danger that Appius might suddenly turn round and start accusing Caelius with that censorial severity of his? But I shall take care of that later on; and I am confident, gentlemen, that I shall be able to defend Marcus Caelius' private life before even the strictest judges. But as for you, woman (I am no longer using a character, but am speaking to you directly), if you intend to justify your actions, your assertions, your charges, your intrigues, your allegations, then you must give a full account and explanation of this familiarity, this intimacy, this entire relationship. The prosecutors go on about orgies, love-affairs, adultery, Baiae, beach parties, dinner parties, carousing, singing, musical entertainments, pleasure-boats—and they imply that they have your approval for everything they say. And since in what appears to be a moment of sheer, unbridled madness you have wanted all this brought up in the forum and in court, you must therefore either explain it away and show it to be untrue or else admit that neither your charge nor your evidence is to be believed.

[36] You may, on the other hand, prefer me to deal with you in a smart, modern way; if so, this is what I shall do. I shall get rid of that harsh and almost rustic old man, and choose instead a different member of your family: your youngest brother. He is the very model of smart, modern manners, and he is exceedingly fond of you. Indeed, when he was a little boy, being, I assume, of a somewhat timid nature and inclined to feel frightened at night for no reason, he always used to sleep with

you, his elder sister! So imagine what he would say to you: "What's all this fuss about, sister? Why have you gone mad? Why do you protest so much, and make so much of nothing? You happened to notice a boy who lives nearby. You were attracted by his pale complexion, his tall figure, his face, his eyes. You wanted to see him more often. You sometimes spent some time with him in the same pleasure-gardens. You are a noble lady and he has a stingy, parsimonious father. You want to keep him tied to you with your money, but you can't: he kicks against the goad, spurns and rejects you, and thinks nothing of your presents. Try somewhere else, then! You own pleasure-gardens on the Tiber carefully sited where all the young men like to come for a swim. You can pick up whatever you fancy there any day you like. So why go on bothering this man who is not interested in you?"

*Cicero now balances the impersonations of Appius Claudius and Clodius with a pair of characters out of comedy, one a stern old father from a play by Caecilius, the other the indulgent father in Terence's comedy* The Brothers. *This leads to some sober reflections on the youth of his day, with Cicero painting a portrait of Caelius as a man who sowed his wild oats, but who has matured into an earnest, hard-working citizen.*

[37] I come to you now, Caelius: it is your turn; and I am going to assume a father's authority and strictness. But I am unsure which particular father I ought to choose—the harsh, overbearing one in Caecilius: "Now at last my mind is ablaze, now my heart is heaped with anger," or perhaps this one: "You wretch, you villain!" Those fathers must be made of iron: "What am I to say? What am I to wish for? By doing such disgraceful deeds, you make all my wishes vain"—intolerable! A father like that would say, "Why did you go to live so near to that prostitute? Why did you not flee the moment you became aware of her allurements? Why have you got to know a woman who is a stranger to us? Scatter and squander for all I care! If you run out of money, it'll be you that suffers; I have enough to see me through the years I have left."

[38] To this blunt and morose old man Caelius would reply that no passion had led him astray nor had he deviated from the straight and narrow. And what evidence did he have? There had been no extravagance, no waste, no borrowing from one creditor to pay off another. But there were rumors. How many of us can

escape such rumors, particularly in a city so full of slanderers? And are you surprised that this woman's neighbor acquired a bad reputation when her own brother was unable to escape unkind gossip?

But to a mild and lenient father—the sort who would say, "He has broken open a door: it can be repaired; he has torn someone's clothes: they can be mended"—Caelius' case is an extremely easy one to make. For what charge could there possibly be that he would not find it easy to defend himself against? I am not at this point saying anything against that woman. But if there were some woman quite unlike her who made herself available to everyone, who always had some man that she had openly designated as her lover; whose pleasure-gardens, house, and place at Baiae were open as of right to every lecher, who even kept men and made up for their fathers' stinginess by paying them herself; if there were a widowed woman living shamelessly, a wayward woman living wantonly, a wealthy woman living extravagantly, and a lustful woman living like a prostitute, then am I really to think of it as criminal if some man should happen to have greeted her a little too freely?

[39] But someone will object: "Is this, then, your way of bringing up the young? Is this how you educate them? Was it this that the boy's father had in mind when he entrusted his son to your care and handed him over to you—for him to devote his youth to lustful pleasures, and for you to defend that kind of life and pursuits?" For my part, members of the jury, if there ever existed a man with so firm a mind and a character of such virtue and self-control as to reject every pleasure and to dedicate the whole course of his life to physical toil and mental exertion, a man who took no pleasure in rest, in relaxation, in the pursuits of his contemporaries, in making love, or in partying, and who considered that nothing in life was worth striving for unless it led to glory and renown—such a man, it seems to me, must have been endowed and distinguished with qualities that are more than human. There have indeed been men like that, or so I believe—men like Camillus, Fabricius, and Curius, and all the others who built Rome's greatness out of nothing.

[40] But virtues of that kind are not much in evidence nowadays: you can scarcely now find them in books. The pages which recorded the ancient austerity have themselves wasted away. And this is true not just of us Romans, who have adopted this approach to life in

practice more than we have in theory, but of the Greeks also, men of considerable learning who, although not up to achieving great deeds, were nevertheless capable of speaking and writing with integrity and brilliance; and now that times have changed for Greece, different moral rules have come to prevail. [41] For there are some who have asserted that the wise man does everything for the sake of pleasure, and learned men have not refrained from talking in this disgraceful way. Then there are others who have supposed that virtue can be combined with pleasure, thus joining by verbal cleverness two things that are entirely incompatible. As for those who have demonstrated that the only direct road to glory consists in hard work, they have now been virtually abandoned in their lecture-rooms.

It is certainly true that nature herself has provided us with many temptations which sometimes cause virtue to slumber and lie still. She has presented the young with many slippery paths on which they can scarcely set foot or walk upon without some accident or fall. She has set out a large assortment of delightful charms to which not only the young but even those of maturer years can sometimes succumb. [42] So if you should happen to come across anyone who shuns the sight of beauty, who is never attracted by any fragrance or touch or taste, who blocks all sweet sounds from his ears, I, perhaps, and some of you might consider him the recipient of the gods' favor, but most people will reckon him the object of their wrath.

So let us abandon this unused and neglected path, now blocked with branches and undergrowth. Let some allowance be made for youth, some freedom given to the young. Let pleasure be not always denied, and true and unbending reason not always prevail. Let desire and pleasure sometimes triumph over reason, provided that in such cases the following rule and limitation be observed. A young man should guard his own reputation, and not attack anyone else's. He should not squander his inheritance nor cripple himself with high-interest loans. He should not assault anyone's home and family. He should not bring shame upon the virtuous, dishonor upon the respectable, or disgrace upon the good. He should threaten no one with violence, have nothing to do with plots, and steer clear of crime. And finally, when he has heeded the call of pleasure and devoted a moderate amount of time to playing around and to the empty desires of youth, he should turn at last to his duties at home, to his work in the courts, and to public life. In this way he will show

that satiety has caused him to reject, and experience to despise, those things which reason, at an earlier time, had not enabled him to disdain.

[43] Indeed, gentlemen, there have been many leading men and illustrious citizens, both in our own times and within the memory of our fathers and ancestors, who, once their youthful desires had simmered down, went on in their maturity to exemplify the very highest virtues. I prefer not to mention any of them by name: you will recall them for yourselves. It is not my intention to associate the great renown of any valiant and distinguished personage with even the slightest misdemeanor. But if I did wish to do this, I could point to many eminent and leading men who were notorious during their youth for their licentious behavior or for their reckless extravagance, the size of their debts, their lavish expenditure, and their wanton passions, but whose vices were later so completely eclipsed by their many virtues that anyone who wished could explain them away on the score of youth.

[44] But in Marcus Caelius—for I shall now speak more boldly about his honorable pursuits, since I also have sufficient trust in your wisdom to make certain other admissions to you—in Marcus Caelius you will discover no extravagance, no lavish expenditure, no debts, and no passion for parties and dens of vice. As for the vice of excessive eating and drinking, that is something which not only does not diminish but actually increases as a man's life goes on. And as for love-affairs and what are called "amours"—which do not generally trouble men of strong character for long (for such passions wither away rapidly and soon)—these have never held him prisoner within their grasp.

[45] You have heard him speaking in his own defense, and you have heard him speaking before as a prosecutor (I say this for his defense, not as a boast): with your customary discernment you have taken note of his oratorical style, his technical ability, and the richness of his thought and expression. And it was not merely his natural talent that you saw shining out in his oratory—something which, even if not backed up by hard work, can nevertheless make its mark on its own by its sheer power; no, his oratory contained (unless my partiality has clouded my judgment) a theoretical foundation based on a sound liberal education and perfected by careful and unremitting toil.

And yet you should realize, gentlemen, that the passions with which Caelius is charged and these pursuits about which I have been speaking cannot easily exist in one and the same person. For it is impossible that a mind given over to passion and hampered by love, desire, greed, often by too much money, but sometimes by too little, can possibly undertake whatever it is that we manage to achieve in speaking, and in the way that we achieve it, and not only as regards the physical exertion, but also in terms of the mental effort needed. [46] Can you think of any other reason why, when public speaking brings such rewards, such personal satisfaction, such renown, such influence, and such honor, there are and always have been so few people willing to undertake this burdensome profession? All pleasures have to be trampled underfoot, enjoyable recreations, amusements, fun, and parties have to be renounced and even conversation with one's friends virtually given up. It is therefore the work required that puts people off public speaking and discourages them from taking it up, not any lack of talent or childhood training.

[47] So if Caelius had really given himself up to the kind of life that is alleged, would he, when still a young man, have brought a prosecution against an ex-consul? If he shied away from hard work, if he were enslaved to pleasure, would he do battle here every day, go in search of personal enmities, bring prosecutions, and run the risk of being prosecuted himself, and would he also maintain for so many months now and in full view of the entire Roman people a struggle for one of two things—his own political survival, or glory?

"So are you honestly saying, then, that that neighborhood gives off no tell-tale scent, that public gossip amounts to nothing, that Baiae itself has no tale to tell?" Certainly, Baiae talks all right, and not only that, it resounds with this report—that the lusts of a single woman have sunk to such depths that she does not merely decline to seek seclusion and darkness with which to veil her immoralities, but openly revels in the most disgusting practices amid crowds of onlookers and in the broadest light of day!

*Cicero now closes this section of his speech by abruptly returning to Clodia: she is a prostitute, so case closed.*

[48] But if there is anyone who believes that young men should not be allowed to have relations even with prostitutes, his view is undoubtedly a strict one (I will not deny that), but also one that deviates both from the permissiveness of the present age and from the custom and allowances of our ancestors. For when was such a thing not common practice, when was it ever criticized, when was it ever forbidden. and when was what is allowed now ever not allowed?

At this point I want to explain what I will be talking about. I shall mention no woman by name: that much I shall leave unclear. [49] But if a woman without a husband throws open her home to every lecher and publicly leads the life of a prostitute, if she is used to attending dinner parties given by men to whom she is completely unconnected, if she carries on like this at Rome, in her pleasure-gardens, and among the crowds at Baiae, and if she conducts herself in such a way that not only her bearing, but also her dress and entourage, not only her blazing eyes and her loose language but also her embraces, her kisses, her beach parties, her boating parties, and her dinner parties all declare her to be not simply a prostitute but a lewd and lascivious prostitute at that—and if some young man should chance to take up with her, then would you, Lucius Herennius, regard that man as an adulterer or as merely a lover, as someone who intended to violate her chastity or merely to satiate his own appetite?

[50] I am forgetting the wrongs you have done me, Clodia. I am putting aside the memory of the pain you have caused me. The cruelties you inflicted on my family when I was away I choose to ignore. So do not think what I said was directed against you. But I do want you to answer me this yourself, since the prosecution declare that you are responsible for the charge, and that you are also their witness to it. If a woman did exist like the one I have just been describing, a woman quite unlike yourself I hasten to add, one with the life and habits of a prostitute, would you consider it so very shocking and disgraceful if a young man should have had some dealings with her? If, then, you are not this woman, as I prefer to believe, what criticism can the prosecution possibly make of Caelius? But if they would have it that you are, then what reason do we have to be afraid of this charge, when you think nothing of it? Show us, therefore, the line we must take in our defense. For either your own fundamental decency will make it clear that Caelius has not acted immorally, or else your utter lack of decency will provide both him and all the rest with an ample means of justifying their behavior.

*Cicero now addresses the two chief allegations against Caelius: first, the charge that Clodia lent Caelius some gold, ostensibly to help him pay for the public games he was producing, but which the prosecution alleges he intended to use to bribe the slaves of Lucius Lucceius, Dio's host in Rome, to murder their master's guest (51–55); second, the claim that Caelius attempted to poison Clodia (56–69). He again takes the opportunity to defame her, ending this portion of the speech abruptly by alluding to a recent scandal involving her and the box that allegedly contained the poison; the details of the scandal are unknown to us but were clearly intended to amuse the jury.*

[51] Since my speech seems now to have got clear of the shallows and avoided the rocks, the rest of what I have to say should all be plain sailing. Two very serious charges are brought against Caelius, both involving the same woman. First there is the gold, which he is alleged to have taken from Clodia. And then there is the poison, which he is charged with having procured to bring about this same Clodia's death.

He took the gold, you say, to give to the slaves of Lucius Lucceius, so that they could murder Dio of Alexandria, who was at that time staying at Lucceius' house. It is certainly a serious charge, to allege that someone plotted to kill envoys or incited slaves to murder their master's guest—a plot full of wickedness, full of criminality! [52] And in reply to such a charge I should first like to ask whether Caelius told Clodia his reason for taking the gold or whether he did not. If he did not, then why did she hand it over? If he did, then she too is implicated in the crime. Did you dare, then, to fetch the gold from out of your chest, to strip of its adornments that Venus of yours, loaded with the spoils from your other lovers, when you knew what a terrible crime this gold was wanted for—to bring about the murder of an envoy, and to cast on Lucius Lucceius, a man with the most scrupulous sense of honor, the everlasting taint of criminality? That welcoming heart of yours should never have consented to so horrific a crime, that open house of yours should never have aided it, that hospitable Venus of yours should never have abetted it. [53] Balbus was aware of this point. That is why he said that Clodia was kept in the dark, and that Caelius gave her the excuse that he needed the gold to pay for some games. But if he was as close a friend of Clodia's as you made out when you were lecturing us on his morals, then he did without question tell her why he wanted the gold; if, on the other hand, he was not so close a friend, then she did not give it to him. So if Caelius told you the truth, you shameless woman, you knowingly gave him gold to commit a crime; and if he did not bring himself to tell you, you never gave it!

Why then, do I need to counter this charge with endless arguments? I could point out that the character of Marcus Caelius is entirely incompatible with such an atrocious and terrible crime, and that it is scarcely credible that such an intelligent and sensible man did not realize how stupid it would be to entrust a criminal act of this magnitude to unknown slaves belonging to another master. I could also put to the prosecution the usual questions regularly asked by myself and other advocates: where did the meeting between Caelius and Lucceius' slaves take place, and how did Caelius make contact with them? If it was in person, how rash of him! If it was through someone else, then through whom? I could talk you through every possible hiding-place where suspicion could lurk, but no motive, no location, no opportunity, no accomplice, no prospect of bringing off the crime or covering it up, no rational scheme, and no trace whatever of such a serious undertaking would come to light.

[54] These are the sort of proofs that orators use, and they could have brought me some benefit (not because of any talent I might have, but simply because of my experience and practice in public speaking): they would give the impression of having been worked up by me on my own and presented in evidence. But to keep matters brief I will forgo all such arguments. For I have instead, members of the jury, a man whom you will readily accept as a partner in the sacred bond of your oath, Lucius Lucceius, a man of complete integrity and a most impressive witness. If so terrible a crime really had been directed against his position and his good name by Marcus Caelius, he could not have failed to hear of it, could not have ignored it, and could not have tolerated it. Or is it conceivable that so civilized a man, with those scholarly interests of his, with all that culture and learning, could have ignored a danger which threatened that very person to whom he was devoted precisely because of those interests that they shared? And would he have failed to protect his own guest against a crime which, even if intended against someone he did not know, he would have viewed with the utmost seriousness? Would he have ignored his own slaves' attempt to commit an act which, even if he discovered that strangers were responsible for it, would have caused him great distress? Would he have taken a relaxed view of a deed undertaken at Rome and in his own house which, even if it had been committed in the

country or in a public place, he would have denounced in the strongest terms? Would he, as an educated man himself, have thought it proper to conceal a plot against a man of learning which, even if it were some rustic who was in danger, he would not have let pass?

[55] But why do I detain you any longer, gentlemen? He himself has sworn a statement on oath. Please take note of its solemnity, and mark carefully every word of his evidence. Read out the evidence of Lucius Lucceius.

[The evidence of Lucius Lucceius is read to the court.]

What more do you want? Or perhaps you are waiting for the case itself, and for truth, to speak out with a voice of their own? No, it is this that is the defense of the innocent, this is the speech of the case itself, this is the sole voice of truth!

The charge itself offers no grounds for suspicion, the facts no proof of guilt. The business that is alleged to have been transacted has left no trace of what was said or where or when. No witness, no accomplice has been named. The entire charge arises out of a malevolent, disreputable, vindictive, crime-ridden, lust-ridden house. The house which is alleged to have attempted this unspeakable crime, on the other hand, is a house of principle, honor, duty, and conscience. From this house you have just heard a statement made under solemn oath. This will leave you in not the slightest doubt about the matter in dispute—whether an impetuous, capricious, and angry woman has fabricated a charge, or whether a serious, scholarly, and temperate gentleman has given his evidence conscientiously.

[56] There remains the charge about poison. But with this I am unable either to discover a beginning or to unravel an end. For what reason could Caelius possibly have had for wanting to poison that woman? So that he would not have to return the gold? But did she ever ask for it back? To avoid being accused? But did anyone ever consider him to be guilty? And would anyone ever have mentioned his name at all if he had not brought a prosecution against somebody himself? Moreover, you heard Lucius Herennius say that he would not have had a single word to say against Caelius were it not for the fact that Caelius has now brought a second prosecution against this friend on the same charge as that on which he has already been acquitted. Is it really credible, then, that so horrific a crime was committed for no reason at all? And can you not see that an extremely serious charge has been fabricated simply in order to provide a motive for the second of the two alleged crimes?

[57] Finally in whom did he confide, whom did he use as his helper, who was his assistant, who was his accomplice, to whom did he entrust so great an undertaking, entrust himself, entrust his own life? The woman's slaves? For that is what has been claimed. But do you think that my client—whom you certainly credit with some intelligence—do you think he was really so stupid as to entrust his entire fate to someone else's slaves? But what type of slaves were they (and this is a very important point): were they slaves whom he knew were treated not as other slaves are, but were permitted to enjoy a free, easy, and intimate relationship with their mistress? For who is not aware, gentlemen, that in a household like this in which the lady of the house behaves like a prostitute, in which nothing that goes on is fit to be made public, in which perverted lusts, extravagant living, and all kinds of outlandish vices and outrages are rife—who does not realize that in such a household the slaves are slaves no longer? In that household every trust is placed in them, everything is left to them, they indulge themselves in the same pleasures as their mistress, they are let into her secrets, and they do quite well for themselves out of the spending and extravagance that goes on on a daily basis. [58] So was Caelius unaware of all this? If he was as intimate with the woman as you make out, then he would of course have been aware that her slaves were intimate with her too. But if his relationship with her was not as close as you would have us believe, then how could he possibly have been on such close terms with the slaves?

Now regarding the actual poison, what theory is made up about that? Where was it sought from, how was it obtained, how, to whom, and where was it handed over? The prosecution claim that Caelius already had it at home, that he tried it out beforehand on some slave that he had bought for the purpose, and that the speedy death of the slave demonstrated the poison's effectiveness. [59] Immortal gods! Why, when people commit the most terrible crimes, do you sometimes overlook what they have done, or else postpone retribution to some future time? For I saw with my own eyes and drank down that bitter grief—the most bitter, perhaps, that I ever experienced—on the day when Quintus Metellus was snatched from the bosom and embrace of his country, when that great man, who considered himself born for the service of our empire, only two days after he had been at the height of his powers in the senate-house, on the rostra, and in our public affairs, when in the prime of his life, in the best of health, and in full bodily vigor, was most shamefully torn from the company of every loyal citizen and the entire nation. At that moment, as he lay dying and his mind in all other respects was already overpowered, he kept back his final thought for his country, and fixing his eyes on me as I wept he signified to me in halting and dying words how terrible a storm was hanging over my head, and how violent a tempest threatened the state. Then, striking again and again the wall which divided his house from the one where Quintus Catulus had lived, he repeatedly called out Catulus' name, and often my own, but most often that of Rome, bewailing not so much the fact that he was dying as that Rome, and I too, would henceforward be robbed of his protection. [60] And had not so great a man been struck down by a sudden, violent crime, just think how he, as a senator of consular rank, would have stood up to his deranged cousin—especially given that, when he was consul and his cousin was only just starting his revolutionary madness and beginning to stir up trouble, he had declared in the senate's very hearing that he would kill him with his own hand! So does that woman, coming from this of all houses, really have the gall to start debating about the celerity of poison? Will she not rather be terrified of that house, in case it should cry out her guilt? Will she not shudder at the walls which know her secret and tremble at the memory of that deadly, mournful night? But I return to the charge. Indeed, the reference I have made to that illustrious and valiant gentleman has caused grief to weaken my voice and sorrow to cloud my mind.

[61] It is not stated, however, where the poison came from, or how it was obtained. The prosecution allege that it was given to Publius Licinius who is here in court, a decent and patriotic young man and a friend of Caelius; that an arrangement was made with the slaves for them to come to the Senian Baths; and that Licinius would join them there and hand over the box of poison to them. At this point I want to ask first, why was it necessary to arrange to meet at the baths? Why did the slaves not simply go to Caelius at his home? If Caelius and Clodia were still seeing so much of each other, and were still on such friendly terms, then surely there could be nothing suspicious about a slave of Clodia's being seen at Caelius' apartment? But if by this time a quarrel had arisen between them, their relationship was over, and they had split up, then "that explains the tears" and there we have the reason for all these crimes and charges.

[62] "On the contrary," he says, "when the slaves reported the plot to their mistress and told her of Caelius' treachery, that intelligent lady instructed them to promise him whatever he asked. But so that Licinius could be caught in the act of handing over the poison, she also ordered that the Senian baths be specified as a meeting-place: she would send some of her friends there to lie in wait and then suddenly, when Licinius had arrived and was handing over the poison, they would jump out from their hiding-places and arrest him."

All this, members of the jury, is extremely easy to refute. For why had she fixed upon the public baths of all places? I cannot see that there would have been any hiding-places there for men in togas! For if they were in the forecourt of the baths, they would not have been hidden from view; but if they were prepared to stow themselves away inside, it would have been rather awkward for them in their shoes and outdoor dress, and they might even have been refused entry—unless of course that influential lady had made friends with the attendant beforehand by means of her usual one-penny transaction!

[63] It was, let me tell you, with an eager sense of anticipation that I kept waiting to discover the identities of those fine fellows who are alleged to have witnessed the interception of the poison; and we have still not been informed of their names. But I have no doubt that they are very responsible characters. For one thing they are intimate friends of this great lady. Then again they willingly took on the job of being packed away inside the baths, something she could never have prevailed on them to do, however influential she might be, had they not been men of the very highest honor and respectability. But why do I need to discuss the respectability of these witnesses? You can judge their character and their diligence for yourselves. "They hid in the baths." What admirable witnesses! "Then they jumped out by mistake." What self-control! For the story you have made up is that when Licinius had arrived on the scene with the box in his hand and was endeavoring to hand it over but had not yet actually done so, then all of a sudden out flew these highly distinguished but anonymous witnesses; at which point Licinius, having already stretched out his arm to hand over the box, drew it back again at this sudden attack and took to his heels.

How great is the power of truth! How easily it can defend itself, unaided, against the ingenuity, craftiness, and cunning of human beings, and against their lies and plots! [64] Take, for instance, this little drama, the work of an experienced poetess with a great many plays to her credit: how devoid it is of plot, how lacking in any proper dénouement! What about all those men (and there must have been more than a few of them if they were to arrest Licinius without difficulty and also provide sufficient eye-witness evidence): why did they let Licinius slip through their hands? Why should it have been more difficult to arrest Licinius after he had drawn back from handing over the box than it would have been if he had actually handed it over? The men were, after all, posted where they were precisely in order to arrest Licinius, to catch Licinius in the act either when he had the poison on his person or after he had handed it over. That was the woman's whole idea, and that was the job of the men she asked to help her. And why you say that they mistakenly jumped out too soon, I simply cannot fathom. They had been asked to do this and had been stationed there specifically for this purpose, to expose the poison, the plot, and the crime that was being committed. [65] Could they in fact have chosen a better moment to jump out than when Licinius had arrived on the scene and was holding the box of poison in his hand? Indeed, if Licinius had already handed it over to the slaves, and the woman's friends had immediately gone out of the baths and arrested him, he would surely then have been imploring their protection and strenuously denying that it was he who had handed over the box. And how would they have proved him wrong? By saying that they had seen him? In the first place, that would only have served to bring down on themselves the suspicion of having committed so terrible a crime. And secondly, they would be claiming to have seen what they could not possibly have seen from the point where they had been stationed. That is why they revealed themselves, instead, at the moment when Licinius had arrived on the scene and was getting out the box, stretching out his arm, and handing over the poison. So here we have the conclusion, not of a proper play, but of a mime—of the sort in which, when no one has managed to devise a satisfactory ending, someone escapes from somebody else's clutches, the clappers sound, and up goes the curtain.

[66] I ask, then, why it was that, when Licinius was hesitating, dithering, retreating, and trying to flee, those woman-led warriors allowed him to slip through their hands? Why did they not arrest him, why did they not use his own confession, the testimony of the many eye-witnesses who were present, and the cry of the deed itself to press home the charge of so terrible a crime? Could they really have been afraid that they would not be able to overcome him, they being numerous and he all on his own, they strong and he weak, they confident and he terrified?

No arguments counting against my client can be found in the facts of the case, nor any grounds for suspicion, nor does the charge itself give rise to any conclusion. In the absence, therefore, of arguments, of inferences, and of those indications which normally shed light on the truth, this case is thrown back entirely upon the witnesses. These witnesses, gentlemen, I now await not just without any trepidation, but even with some expectation of amusement. [67] I am bursting to set eyes on those elegant young men, the friends of a wealthy and noble lady, and on those valiant warriors stationed by their commandress in a fortified ambush at the baths. I intend to ask them how and where they hid themselves, whether it was the famous bath-tub or a Trojan horse that carried and concealed so many invincible heroes waging a woman's war. I shall also make them answer this, why so many big, strong men failed either to arrest this single, defenseless person (whom you see here) when he was standing still or else catch up with him when he was running away. If they do come forward to testify, I do not see how they will ever succeed in extricating themselves. They may be witty and clever at dinner parties, and sometimes even eloquent over a glass of wine. But a dining-room is one thing and the forum another; the couches there and the benches here are altogether different; the sight of revelers and the sight of jurors is not the same; and the light of lamps is quite unlike the light of day. We will therefore shake all their frippery and tomfoolery out of them—if, that is, they come forward. But let them take my advice: let them turn their energies in another direction, let them ingratiate themselves by a different means, let them show off in some other way, let them impress that woman by their elegance, let them outdo all others in their extravagance, let them cleave to her side, lie at her feet, be her slaves—but let them also spare the life and fortunes of an innocent man!

[68] "But these slaves have been given their freedom on the advice of the woman's relations, illustrious men of the very highest rank." At last we have found something that she is supposed to have done on the advice and authority of her valiant relations! But I am curious to know what is behind this act of liberation. It must mean either that a charge had been fabricated against Caelius, or that the prosecution wished to prevent the slaves being interrogated, or that the slaves who were party to so many of her secrets were receiving their well-earned pay-off. "Nevertheless," the prosecution

say, "her relations did approve." And why should they not, since, as you told us yourself, the information that you presented them with was not brought to you by others but was personally discovered by you?

[69] At this point are we even surprised if that fictitious box has given rise to a highly indecent story? With a woman like that, anything is possible. Everyone has heard the story and talked about it. For some time now, gentlemen, you have been aware of what I would like—or rather would prefer not—to say. But even if what I am referring to did take place, then it is quite certain that Caelius, at least, was not responsible for it (for what did it have to do with him?): it was no doubt the work of some young man whose sense of humor was more highly developed than his sense of propriety. But if the tale is an invention, it is of course quite improper—but also quite funny! And certainly people would never have spoken of it and believed it as true were it not for the fact that every story involving a pennyworth of scandal seems to square perfectly with that woman's reputation.

*In the peroration, with the jury still chortling over his story about Clodia, Cicero includes a detailed summary of the life and career of Caelius. The style of this section is more formal and elevated, to impress upon the jury the importance of exonerating this exemplary young man.*

[70] My defense is over, members of the jury, and I have come to the end. You will now be able to appreciate the importance of the decision you have to make and the seriousness of the case before you. You are investigating a charge of violence. The law concerned is one that has to do with the dominion, the sovereignty, the condition of our country and the safety of us all, the law which Quintus Catulus carried at a time of armed civil strife and almost desperate national crisis, and the law which, after those fires which blazed during my consulship had been brought under control, extinguished the smoking embers of the conspiracy. And now it is under this same law that demands are made for the young life of Caelius, not because the national interest requires his punishment, but to gratify the whim of a licentious woman!

[71] In this context the prosecution also cite the conviction of Marcus Camurtius and Gaius Caesernius. How stupid of them! Or should I call it not stupidity but bare-faced cheek? Do you really have the nerve to come from that woman and mention the names of those men? Do you have the nerve to revive the memory of so shocking an outrage—a memory that had not been wholly effaced, I admit, but one that had at least faded with time?

For what was the charge and what the offence for which those men were condemned? Surely it was because they avenged that woman's spite and resentment by committing an unspeakable sexual attack on Vettius? So was the trial of Camurtius and Caesernius brought up again just so that Vettius' name could be mentioned and that veteran tale about the coppers be retold? Although these two men were certainly not liable under the violence law; the crime in which they were implicated was so shocking that, whatever law they were charged under, they could hardly have extricated themselves from its meshes.

[72] But returning to Marcus Caelius, why has he been summoned before this court? No charge appropriate to this court has been brought against him, nor indeed any charge that is outside the scope of the law but nevertheless within the range of your own just censure. His early years were devoted to training, and to those studies which prepare us for work such as this in the courts, for public service, and for honor, glory, and position. He also made friends with older men whose qualities of hard work and self-restraint he was very anxious to imitate, and this, together with the pursuits he shared with his contemporaries, showed him to be following the same course of renown as the best and most high-ranking of our citizens. [73] When he had grown a little older and more mature, he went out to Africa on the staff of the governor Quintus Pompeius, a highly moral man, and a man who performs all his duties with the greatest conscientiousness. Africa was a province in which Caelius' father had business interests and property, and Caelius himself acquired some experience of provincial government there at an age which our ancestors rightly considered suitable. When he left the province he was very highly regarded by Pompeius, as you will hear from Pompeius' own testimony.

It was now Caelius' wish to undertake some spectacular prosecution, so that his hard work should receive its due recognition from the Roman people; and in doing this he was following the long-established custom and precedent set by those young men who afterwards went on to become the most distinguished and illustrious citizens in the state. [74] I should have preferred it, in fact, if his thirst for glory had taken him in some other direction; but it is no use complaining about that now. He prosecuted my colleague Gaius Antonius, whose misfortune it was that the memory of a signal service to our country proved of no avail to him, while speculation about an intended crime did him harm. From that point on, Caelius never yielded to any of his contemporaries in his attendance in the forum, in his dedication to court cases and the defense of his friends, and in the strength of his influence over those with whom he was connected. All the benefits that men are unable to obtain unless they are alert, sober, and hard-working were obtained by Caelius as a result of his industry and application.

[75] At this turning-point in his life (I am going to trust to your sympathy and wisdom, gentlemen, and keep nothing from you), his youthful reputation did briefly come a cropper. This was the result of his recent acquaintance with that woman, the unfortunate proximity of their houses, and his unfamiliarity with those forms of pleasure which, when they have long been bottled up and have been repressed and restrained during one's early years, are sometimes apt to burst out and pour forth all of a sudden. But from this way of life—or rather, I should say, from this chatter (since the reality was nothing like as bad as people said)—anyway, from this, whatever it was, he emerged unscathed and completely broke free and escaped. And today he is so far removed from the disgrace of being associated with that woman that he is actually having to defend himself against her enmity and hatred!

[76] To put a stop to the gossip about idleness and pleasure that had arisen in the meantime—and he did this against my wishes, by Hercules, and against my strong opposition, but still he did it—he prosecuted a friend of mine for electoral malpractice. My friend was acquitted, but Caelius is now returning to the attack and prosecuting him again; he is not listening to any of us, and is showing himself more violent than I could have wished. But I am not considering his wisdom, a quality not to be expected in a man of his age: it is his impetuous spirit, his thirst for success, and his burning desire for glory that I am speaking of. In men of our age, such passions are best kept in their place, but in young men, as in plants, they give an indication of what that virtue will become when it is ripe, and how great the fruits of industry will one day be. It has always been the case that highly talented young men have had to be reined back from glory rather than spurred on towards it; at that age, if their brilliant ability bursts into flower, it is not so much grafting as cutting back that is required. [77] So if anyone feels that Caelius' energy, spirit, and persistence in taking up and pursuing hostilities has gone too far, or if even such trivial details as the shade of purple he wears, the following he attracts, and the brilliance and sparkle he displays have offended anyone, then let me assure you that in due course all these traits will have subsided, and age, experience, and time will have mellowed them all.

I ask you, then, members of the jury, to preserve for our country a citizen of sound education, sound principles, and sound loyalties. I promise you this and I make this pledge to our country that if I myself have served the country adequately, Caelius will never deviate from my own political standpoint. This I feel able to promise partly because of the friendship that exists between the two of us, but also because Caelius has already bound himself personally by the strongest guarantees. [78] For it is impossible that a man who has prosecuted a senator of consular rank, alleging that he had done damage to our country should himself turn out to be an unruly citizen of our country; and it is equally impossible that a man who will not accept the acquittal even of someone already acquitted of bribery should himself go unpunished were he ever to commit that crime. So, gentlemen, our country has received from Marcus Caelius two prosecutions, to serve either as hostages against dangerous behavior or as pledges of his good intentions. This, gentlemen, is a city in which only a few days ago Sextus Cloelius was acquitted—a man whom for two years now you have observed as either a participant in civil discord or else its originator, a man without money, without credit, without hope, without home, and without resources, whose lips, tongue, hands, and entire way of life are defiled, a man who personally set fire to a sacred temple, to the census of the Roman people, and to the public records, who knocked down the monument of Catulus, demolished my own house, and set fire to that of my brother, and who, on the Palatine, in full view of the whole of Rome, incited slaves to commit a massacre and to burn down the city. In this same city I therefore beg and beseech you not to allow Cloelius to be acquitted through a woman's influence while at the same time allowing Marcus Caelius to be sacrificed to her lust, nor to let it be said that this same woman, together with her brother and husband, has succeeded both in rescuing a depraved brigand and in crushing a young man of the very highest sense of honor.

[79] But when you have set the picture of this young man in front of you, place before your eyes also the picture of his old and unhappy father here; he totally depends on this his only son, he places all his hopes on him, and he is afraid for him alone. This old man is a suppliant before your compassion, a slave before your power, and a beggar not so much before your feet as before your instincts and your sensibilities. Recall the memories you have of your parents or the delight you take in your children and raise this man up, so that in assuaging another person's grief you may indulge your own filial duty or else your

own fatherly love. Do not desire, gentlemen, that this old man, who is already in his declining years, should meet his end prematurely from a wound dealt not by his own fate but by yourselves! Do not strike down, as by some sudden storm or tornado, this young man who is now in the first flower of his prime and whose excellent qualities have already taken root! [80] Save the son for the father, the father for the son! Never let it be thought that you have scorned an old man whose hopes are now almost at an end, or that you have not only failed to help but have actually cast down and ruined a young man with the brightest prospects! If you restore Caelius to me, to his family, and to the country, you will have a man who is dedicated, devoted, and bound to you and your children; and from all his exertions and labors, it is you in particular, gentlemen, who shall reap the abundant and lasting fruits.

# AFTERWORD

Cicero's political legacy did not outlast his assassination; first Mark Antony and then Octavian saw to that. It is possible, however, that even Cicero himself would have considered the vast influence of his writings as some small consolation, for no writer of Latin prose exerted as much impact on successive generations or inspired as much controversy on the subject of Latin style. Cicero's importance was not lost even on contemporaries, in spite of the fact that there were many among them, adherents of the terser style of composition known as "Atticism," who were not among his admirers. Within this camp, the great historian and orator Asinius Pollio was a particularly severe critic, and in this he was followed by his son, who wrote a treatise comparing his father's speeches with Cicero's, with the palm going of course to Pollio senior. There is also some irony in the fact that Sallust, the historian who recorded for posterity the details of the Catilinarian conspiracy, was not a devotee of the Ciceronian style. Cicero would probably have been mortified that in composing his monograph Sallust employed the abrupt style and old-fashioned vocabulary that Cicero himself had eschewed. But Cicero's detractors were overwhelmed, at least initially, by his admirers. Already in the immediate aftermath of his death, his speeches were being recommended as models by Livy in a letter to his son, along with those of Demosthenes.

Cicero's works became required reading in the schools very soon after his death. Among the many examples of rhetorical exercises that survive from the Roman world, there are several that take as their themes events from the life of Cicero. Students practiced their craft by making speeches, pretending to be Cicero deliberating on whether to beg Antony for his life. One such exercise, preserved among the works of Sallust, is an invective by Cicero directed against the historian; it was almost certainly the work of a student of rhetoric in the Augustan age. Fragments also survive of a commentary on Cicero's speeches by Quintus Asconius Pedianus, written between A.D. 54 and 57, a sure sign that by then schoolboys were wrestling with Cicero's style and struggling with the topical allusions to events in his orations.

Popular interest in Cicero's life was fed by the labors of his longtime slave, Tiro, who was freed by his master sometime around the year 54 B.C. During his master's and then patron's lifetime, Tiro had served him as secretary and confidant, but he himself was a man of letters. He is credited with having invented a form of shorthand, which certainly stood him in good stead in taking down Cicero's words for eventual publication. He also wrote one of the first biographies of Cicero and played an important role in collecting and disseminating his speeches and the collections of letters. Cicero's death was an especially common topic for historians and rhetoricians, and even became the subject of poetry in an epic written early in the first century A.D. by Cornelius Severus, most of which has been lost, except for this particular scene. By the time Quintilian composed his handbook on rhetoric near the end of the first century A.D., Cicero's place in the curriculum was secure, and Quintilian himself did much to solidify Cicero's status, by establishing him as the standard against which rhetorical eloquence must be measured.

The Catilinarian orations were always the most popular of Cicero's speeches: Virgil may have read them, and in the eighth book of the *Aeneid* he depicts Catiline on Aeneas's shield, representing his torture in the Underworld as an example of what happens to traitors. There are more papyrus fragments of

Cicero's works than of any other Latin author except Virgil, and two of them show that the Catilinarian speeches were, among other purposes, used to teach Latin to native speakers of Greek. In later antiquity Cicero's works caused considerable anxiety for some early Christian readers who admired his style, even as they were troubled by his paganism. St. Jerome, the author of the Vulgate translation of the Bible, dreamed of being flogged by angels for being a Ciceronian, not a Christian. But, in general, Cicero's prestige continued undiminished. The third/fourth-century Christian apologist Lactantius cultivated a Ciceronian style to such an extent that he became a favorite author in the Renaissance and was called "the Christian Cicero." In his *Confessions,* St. Augustine could acknowledge the defining influence of Cicero's philosophical treatises on his intellectual development (3.4), ascribing to Cicero's *Hortensius* (now lost) the inspiration for his own turn to philosophy.

Throughout the Middle Ages the name of Cicero remained important, even as knowledge of his works diminished. It was the philosophical tracts that were best known to medieval readers, but the speeches, with all the difficulties posed by their reference to historical events and persons no longer remembered, were less widely disseminated. Among the speeches it was the *Catilinarians* in particular that were well known, although the *Verrines* and the *Philippics* also continued to circulate. The great rhetorical treatises *On the Orator, Brutus,* and *The Orator* were little appreciated by a readership that preferred the briefer compass of the little treatise *On Invention.* And the letters were largely lost, a circumstance that weighed heavily on Cicero's greatest devotee since Quintilian, the predecessor of the Italian humanists, Petrarch (1304–75). Such was his excitement upon discovering a manuscript containing *Letters to Atticus* in a library at Verona that he immediately penned a letter, in his best Ciceronian Latin, to Cicero himself (*Familiar Letters* 24). Even in antiquity a great part of the appeal of Cicero had consisted in the opportunity to know not only the style but also the man. In the second century Fronto wrote to the emperor Marcus Aurelius that he thought all the letters of Cicero should be read, even in preference to the speeches, for nothing he wrote was "more perfect."

Thanks to the influence of Petrarch and his followers, throughout the Renaissance Cicero's importance remained paramount. The first edition of a classical text to be printed was his treatise *On Duties* in 1465. Much as Quintilian had established Cicero as the essential model for Roman students of rhetoric, the early humanists urged imitation of Cicero as the means for revivifying Latin style, although, ironically, this may have had the opposite effect. A treatise on Latin style by Lorenzo Valla (1406–57) ensured that Cicero's vocabulary and forms of expression would be the basis for educated style, leading to a prolonged debate between "Ciceronians" and scholars who espoused a more eclectic Latin style, such as Angelo Poliziano (1454–94) and, most notably, Desiderius Erasmus. Erasmus stirred up a storm with the publication in 1528 of his satirical *Dialogus Ciceronianus,* which pillories an imaginary devotee of Ciceronian Latinity, Nosoponus (which means both "laboring under a disease" and "made ill by labor"), who is so devoted to Cicero that he has pictures of him throughout his house, sees only him in his dreams, knows his works almost by heart, reads books by no other author, and will only use word forms that occur in Cicero. Nosoponus had once been red-cheeked, chubby, suave, and full of wit, but more than seven years of this Ciceronian compulsion have left him "more like a ghost than a human being."

Now that Cicero no longer claims a position of centrality in our culture, these disputes may seem remote and perhaps even quaint. Nevertheless, he is still a key figure in any study of the history and literature of the closing years of the Roman Republic. Cicero's reputation has largely recovered from the deeply unflattering portrait of him painted by the nineteenth-century historian Theodor Mommsen in his *History of Rome,* which won the Nobel Prize in Literature in 1902. His character is portrayed as somewhat spineless and whining in the television series *Rome* (2005–7), made for HBO—a legacy, perhaps, of Mommsen's view of him as an unprincipled fraud. But in the novels of Robert Harris, *Imperium* (2006) and *Conspirata* (2010, originally published under the title *Lustrum* in 2009), a more complex portrait of the man emerges, a committed adherent of the values of the Roman Republic grappling with political tides he cannot control. Cicero remains the Roman we know best, in his moments of triumph and weakness, and for everything that we think we know about the world of Rome in the momentous decades of the 60s to the 40s B.C., he is at once our surest and our most elusive guide.

# JULIUS CAESAR

(Gaius Iulius Caesar, 100–44 B.C.)

JULIUS CAESAR IS A TOWERING FIGURE. HIS MILITARY SUCCESSES WERE ASTONISHING, often won against stronger opposition, and his political power was unprecedented. His assassination at the age of fifty-six, on the Ides of March 44 B.C., was motivated by fears that he wished to become king: instead, he became a god. When the Julio-Claudian dynasty ended with the suicide of Nero in A.D. 68, subsequent emperors adopted "Caesar" as a title, a practice that extended throughout the Holy Roman Empire, producing the German "Kaiser" and the Russian "tsar." But when the name "Caesar" is used without further definition nowadays, the reference is almost always to Julius Caesar, a reflection of his unrivaled significance.

Whatever his actual accomplishments and his ultimate ambitions may have been, it is fascinating to speculate what Caesar might have achieved if he had heeded the soothsayer's warning not to go to the Senate on the Ides of March. His rule anticipated the introduction of the Principate by his great-nephew and adopted son, the first emperor, Augustus. It seems likely that Caesar would have managed to bring about the almost universal peace and stability that Augustus eventually bestowed on the empire. Many of Augustus's magnificent building projects that transformed the city of Rome were planned already by Caesar. One particular achievement shows Caesar's eagerness to introduce important lasting reforms: by the second half of the first century B.C., the Roman calendar was almost three months out of line with the solar year, a disastrous state of affairs for a society in which most sacred festivals were bound up with the agricultural seasons. As Pontifex Maximus, leader of the priestly college in charge of the calendar of Rome's religious year, Caesar decreed that ten days should be added to every year, with an extra day at the end of February every fourth year. The Julian system came into effect on January 1, 45 B.C., after a year with 445 days had brought the calendar into line with the seasons, and it remained in force until the reforms of Pope Gregory XIII in 1582.

Caesar was not just a brilliant military and political leader; he was also a remarkable man of action. He could ride at a gallop with both hands behind his back (a considerable feat, given that the Romans had no stirrups). As a young man, he was captured by pirates who demanded a ransom of twenty talents for his release. He felt he was worth more and had the demand increased to fifty talents. In the thirty-eight days in which he was kept prisoner, pending the arrival of the ransom, he often told the pirates that he would come back and crucify them. They thought this was a great joke, but he did exactly that, showing mercy by having their throats cut before they were crucified. While fighting in Greece as a junior officer, he was awarded the civic crown, a high honor bestowed on soldiers who saved the life of a comrade in battle. Valerius Maximus records that in an unspecified battle (probably in Gaul), "when a standard-bearer in the Mars legion had already turned to

**Figure 9: Coin of Caesar**
A silver *denarius,* minted by Julius Caesar in 44 B.C., when he was appointed dictator for the fourth time. The curved staff, the *lituus,* symbolized his role as Pontifex Maximus, an office which should have made his person sacrosanct.

flee, Caesar seized him by the throat and dragged him back to face the other way. Stretching out his right hand towards the enemy, he asked him 'Where are you off to? The men we are fighting are over there'. With his hands he stopped a single soldier, but his exhortation was so sharp that it checked the panic in all the legions, teaching them to win when they were ready for defeat" (*Memorable Deeds and Sayings* 3.2.19). After he had routed Pompey at the Battle of Pharsalus in 48 B.C., Caesar was crossing the Hellespont in a small boat when he encountered a flotilla of ten ships commanded by Lucius Cassius Longinus, the brother of the Cassius who was to lead the tyrannicides: rather than try to escape, he boldly demanded Cassius's surrender, and it was duly given.

The *Gallic War* is set against the background of a turbulent period in Roman politics. For more than four hundred years, Rome had been governed by the Senate and a small number of prominent families, whose members contended for the highest political offices, to the exclusion of the vast majority of the citizen body. By the beginning of the first century B.C., power had shifted irrevocably. Rome no longer relied on an army of citizens fighting for the good of the state; the legions were now professional, and their loyalty was to the generals who would provide them with pay, plunder, and pensions. This opened the way for individuals to gain greater power than the Republican system had normally permitted. In 60 B.C., three of Rome's most powerful men—Pompey, Crassus, and Caesar—joined forces with a view to furthering their personal ambitions. This wholly illegal cartel, now known as the First Triumvirate (in contrast to the Second Triumvirate, the alliance formed between Mark Antony, Octavian, and Lepidus to avenge Caesar's murder), was condemned by a contemporary as "the Beast with Three Heads," like Cerberus, the dog that guards the entrance to the Underworld.

All three men had very high aspirations. After some minor victories in Africa, Pompey had been awarded the title *Magnus* (the Great). He played up the associations of this title, styling his hair in the distinctive manner of Alexander the Great, and he was said to have worn Alexander's jeweled cloak in a triumph procession (perhaps the parade that was marred when his elephant-drawn chariot became stuck under an arch). In an inscription commemorating the dedication of spoils in the Temple of Minerva in Rome, Pompey boasted of his achievements: "The commander Gnaeus Pompeius Magnus duly makes this dedication to Minerva, having completed a war of thirty years with the routing, scattering, slaughtering, or capture of 12,183,000 of our foes, and with the sinking or capture of 846 ships, and with the surrender of 1,538 towns and forts, and with the conquering of all the land from the Sea of Azov to the Red Sea" (Pliny, *Natural History* 7.97). His suppression of the pirates was a great achievement: they had infested the eastern Mediterranean in "ships equipped with golden stern-poles, purple canopies, and silver-covered oars" (Plutarch, *Life of Pompey* 24). No doubt Pompey viewed his victories in the East as comparable to those of Alexander, and he was indeed considered a great general, until his ultimate confrontation with Caesar.

Crassus was fabulously wealth, but he grew jealous of the military successes of his colleagues in the Triumvirate. Goaded by Pompey's military glory, and then by Caesar's conquest of Gaul, he also aimed for Alexander-like glory in the East and attempted to conquer the Parthian empire, Rome's powerful eastern rival. In 53 B.C., at Carrhae, in what is now eastern Turkey, his heavily armed infantry legions were unable to engage the Parthian cataphracts (archers on heavily armored horses) at close quarters. Before Crassus himself was killed, his son's severed head was displayed to him on a pike by the Parthians. His own head was taken to the Armenian court, where it was partially filled with molten gold, as a contemptuous response to the acquisitive motivation for his campaign against the Parthians, and used as a stage prop, representing the head of the dismembered Pentheus in a performance of scenes from Euripides's *Bacchae*.

Julius Caesar had long been ambitious. Early in his career, when he was a low-ranking provincial administrator in southern Spain, he saw a statue of Alexander the Great in Cadiz and was dismayed that he himself had done nothing significant yet, whereas Alexander, by the same age, had conquered the world (Suetonius, *Life of Julius Caesar* 7, an anecdote recalling Alexander's frustration that his father, Philip II of Macedon, who had subjugated much of Greece, was leaving him so little to conquer). In the end, it was Caesar, not Pompey, who evoked comparisons with Alexander the Great; in his matching Greek and Roman *Lives,* Plutarch inevitably pairs Caesar with Alexander. Caesar's army was to have set out a few days after the Ides of March to make war on the Parthians, who had slaughtered Crassus and his men. No emperor ever achieved lasting stability in the Eastern regions that Alexander had conquered; perhaps Caesar might have done so.

The First Triumvirate had Caesar appointed consul for 59 B.C. to carry through legislation advantageous to them. Day after day, the other consul, Marcus Calpurnius Bibulus, declared the omens to be unfavorable for senatorial business, but Caesar pushed the legislation through anyway. Since years were usually denoted by the names of the two consuls, 59 B.C. was facetiously known as the consulship of Julius and Caesar. It was customary for consuls to serve as provincial governors after their year in office. The Senate tried to block Caesar's ambitions by giving him proconsular responsibility for "the woods and paths of Italy"; he ignored this ruling and had himself appointed as governor of both Gauls (Gallia Cisalpina and Gallia Transalpina, i.e., Gaul on both sides of the Alps) and of Illyricum, with command of four legions, for five years. Crassus's death left Caesar and Pompey to contend for power. This struggle brought the end of the Republic. "Rome was forced to fight both in her own defense and against herself: even if victorious, she would still be defeated" (Cassius Dio, *History of Rome* 41.57). It was his long years of campaigning in Gaul that gave Caesar the resources, the military experience, and the unswervingly loyal army that ensured his victory.

The Romans were always apprehensive of their fearsome northern neighbors, the Gauls. According to legend, an Etruscan named Arruns had exported wine north of the Alps, so as to entice the Gauls to come south in search of more such unfamiliar luxuries. He hoped that they would attack Clusium, for he was seeking to avenge himself on a nobleman from that Etruscan city who had seduced his wife (Livy, *From the Foundation of the City* 5.33). Whether or not this particular story is true, the Gauls captured Rome around 387 B.C., the most shameful and disastrous event in the city's history. The Gauls agreed to leave Rome on payment of 1,000 pounds of gold; while it was being weighed, the Romans complained that the scales were incorrect. The Gallic leader, Brennus, threw his sword on the other side of the scales, to weigh them down even more, crying *vae victis!* (Woe to the conquered!). The Gallic invasion was long remembered: geese sacred to Juno had given the alarm when the Gauls were about to take the Capitol, whereas the guard dogs that should have alerted the Roman defenders did not do so; nearly 500 years later, in commemoration of this event, dogs were still being crucified annually on a cross of elder wood (Pliny, *Natural History* 29.57), whereas a goose was carried along in a litter in a solemn procession (Aelian, *On Animals* 12.33). In 105 B.C., two Roman armies were massacred by Germanic tribesmen at the Battle of Arausio in southern France. Three years later, an incursion into Italy in overwhelming numbers was only stopped when an estimated 100,000 Germans were killed by Marius's army at the Battle of Aquae Sextiae (Aix-en-Provence); "it was said that the people of Marseilles fenced their vineyards with their bones, and that after the bodies decomposed and the winter rains fell, the ground was so enriched as the putrified matter sank deep into it that it produced bumper crops for many years" (Plutarch, *Life of Marius* 21).

A generation before Caesar, the influential ethnographer and Stoic philosopher Posidonius of Apamea (135–51/50 B.C.) characterized those who lived in the cold northern regions as being brave but lacking in intelligence, and those in hot regions as crafty and disinclined to fight, concluding that those who enjoy a temperate climate, such as the Greeks and the Romans, are superior to all others. Such stereotypes, representing the northern barbarians as awesome but rather stupid, lingered long in the Roman mind. Livy described Gallic warriors as fighting "naked, and the whiteness of their body makes their wounds seem the more horrible. They are not much troubled by gaping wounds. But when an arrow-head or a lead sling-shot buries itself in their body and they cannot remove it, they throw themselves on the ground in rage and shame at such a seemingly insignificant wound" (*From the Foundation of the City* 38.21). As late as the fourth century, the historian Ammianus Marcellinus paints a marvelously satirical picture of the Gauls: "They are almost all very tall and fair-skinned, with reddish hair. Their eyes are intimidatingly fierce, they love quarrelling and are overbearingly arrogant. Indeed, a whole band of foreigners could not match any one of them in a brawl if he should call on his gray-eyed wife to help him, for she is far stronger than he is. She is especially hard to face when she swells her neck, grinds her teeth, swings her massive snow-white forearms, and begins to kick and throw punches like bolts shot from the taut strings of a catapult" (15.12.1).

Caesar's campaigns did much to expand knowledge of northern Europe; he is, significantly, the first writer to distinguish the Gauls from the Germans. Even so, he gives little account of the more sophisticated aspects of Gallic culture and tends to pander to the established stereotypes. But whereas Gaul and Germany seemed outlandish, Britain was almost mythically mysterious to the Greeks and Romans. Some scholars had even expressed doubts about its very existence. More than a generation after Caesar's invasions, the geographer Strabo was still referring to Britain in the same terms as Thule, the unidentified northern island where the air, the sea, and the land are all blended with the consistency of a jellyfish (*Geography* 2.4), and about Ireland, which the Romans never thought worth the trouble of conquering, he adds that he "can say nothing definite about Ierne, except that its inhabitants are wilder than the Britons, for they eat human flesh as well as plants, considering it proper to eat their fathers when they die" (4.5).

Caesar's two short excursions into Britain, in 55 and 54 B.C., had no lasting results. As Tacitus puts it, "The Divine Julius was the first Roman to enter Britain with an army. He was successful in terrorizing the natives in battle, and in gaining possession of the shoreline, but he should be regarded as having shown later generations how to conquer Britain rather than as actually having handed it over to them" (*Agricola* 13). It was almost exactly one hundred years later that the emperor Claudius's legions began the permanent conquest of most of the island. It would seem that Caesar's army expected to find rich plunder in Britain, but this expectation was quickly disappointed. In a letter written in May 54 to a friend serving as an officer in Gaul, Cicero comments, "I hear that there is no gold or silver in Britain. If this is so, I urge you to take one of their war-chariots and rush back to us as quickly as you can" (*Letters to His Friends* 7.7). On October 1 of the same year, Cicero wrote to another friend, "It is now known for certain that there isn't a single ounce of silver in the island, and there's no hope of plunder except in the form of war-captives, and I don't suppose you can expect any of them to be trained in literature or music" (*Letters to Atticus* 4.17).

Brief, inconclusive, and unprofitable as the British raids were, they will have created a sensation in Rome, enhancing Caesar's reputation as a daring military leader. His audacity lay not so much in fighting the Britons as in taking his army out into the mostly uncharted Atlantic. A late third-century oration in praise of the successful campaigning in Britain by the emperor Constantinus Chlorus says that "it had been much easier to conquer the Britons in Caesar's time, when they were used to fighting foes no more formidable than the half-naked Picts and Hibernians [i.e., the Scots and Irish], and Caesar's only real reason to boast was that he had sailed across the Ocean" (*Latin Panegyrics* 8.11). As it was, Caesar's first expedition came close to disaster through the Romans' perhaps surprisingly naive failure to take account of the tides in the English Channel at full moon, far higher than in the Mediterranean. When Claudius's forces invaded Britain in A.D. 43, they took an elephant with them, not only a devastating psychological strategy but also a considerable achievement in transportation by sea (Cassius Dio, *History of Rome* 60.21). The report that Julius Caesar had already taken an armored elephant to Britain (Polyaenus, *Strategems* 8.23) seems rather less plausible; he would presumably have mentioned it in his own *Commentaries*.

Caesar's tireless energy is also apparent in his literary pursuits. When the emperor Marcus Aurelius complained that he could scarcely find time for reading, his tutor reminded him that Julius Caesar wrote a two-book study of Latin grammar during the conquest of Gaul, "discussing the declension of nouns while missiles flew around" (Fronto, *Letters* p. 224 van den Hout). Fronto is referring to the *De Analogia* (On Analogy), which Caesar wrote while returning across the Alps to his army after holding winter assizes in Cisalpine Gaul. This grammatical work was still being cited as authoritative two hundred years later: Aulus Gellius quotes Caesar's opinion that one should "avoid unfamiliar and unusual words just as one would steer clear of a reef in the sea" (*Attic Nights* 1.10.4).

Caesar also wrote a poem called "The Journey" while on a twenty-four-day march from Rome to Further Spain, and the *Anticato*, a two-book attack on his political opponent Marcus Porcius Cato, was written at about the time of the particularly bloody Battle of Munda in 45 B.C. Plutarch records that Caesar was able to dictate letters to two or more scribes while mounted on horseback (*Life of Julius Caesar* 17), but Pliny makes him out to be an even greater dictator, able to keep seven scribes busy at once (*Natural History* 7.91). Three months before his assassination, which Cicero may well have witnessed, Caesar visited him at his villa near Naples. Politically they had little in common, and Cicero was also rather intimidated by the visit; he comments in a letter to his friend Atticus that "Caesar is not the sort of guest to whom one says 'Come back and see me any time you're passing.'" Nevertheless he admits that he rather enjoyed the occasion, for they talked about literature, not politics (*Letters to Atticus* 13.52).

The *Commentaries* on the Gallic war and the civil war are, alas, Caesar's only surviving works, and they hold a unique place in Roman literary history. When Trajan was campaigning in the East early in the second century A.D., the Senate granted him the privilege of celebrating a triumph over as many peoples as he thought fit. They did so because he was constantly sending reports about so many defeated nations that they could not keep track of them or use their names accurately (Cassius Dio, *History of Rome* 68.29). Trajan's reports have not survived, but we can be sure that they were quite different from Caesar's account of his campaigns, whether in Gaul or during the civil war. A crucial difference is that Caesar was not sending dispatches from the front line. His *Commentaries* were written in relative tranquility, when the events described were safely over. They might indeed more appropriately be called *Memoirs*. The closest literary parallel for the *Commentaries* is Xenophon's *Anabasis*, recording the return march of ten thousand Greek mercenaries after a failed attempt to overthrow the king of Persia in 401 B.C. Xenophon played an important part in the march, but, like Caesar, he narrates events in the third person; also like Caesar, he enlivens the narration with directly reported speeches and numerous digressions. With their elegant but simple style, and their military content, the *Anabasis* and *The Gallic War* were the first Greek and Latin texts read by generations of schoolboys being groomed for the officer class in Europe's armies.

In Caesar's case, this simplicity (much praised by Cicero [*Brutus* 262]) is a ploy, intended to portray him as a straightforward, plain-speaking soldier, far removed from the devious sophistry of political life. He needed all the devious sophistry he could muster. The Gallic campaign was little short of genocide. Perhaps as many as a million Gauls were killed. After an unnamed battle in 57 B.C., "the name and fighting strength of the Nervii were almost wiped out … Describing the disaster which had befallen them, the Nervian envoys declared that they had been reduced from 600 senators to three, from 60,000 men capable of active service to a mere 500" (*Gallic War* 2.28). "When Caesar contravened a truce with the Germans and massacred 300,000 of them, everyone thought that a thanksgiving should be celebrated—except for Cato, who kept urging that he should be handed over to those whom he had wronged, so that no pollution should befall Rome" (Plutarch, *Life of Cato the Younger* 51). Cato, Caesar's most implacable political opponent, is playing on the Romans' belief that they only fought just wars, sanctioned by the Senate and the gods, but there was also personal animosity between the two. In the crisis of 63 B.C., when Catiline was plotting against the state, Cato interrupted a speech that he was giving in the Senate in order to challenge Caesar to read aloud a letter that he had just been handed; he suspected that it contained evidence of Caesar's complicity in the conspiracy, but it turned out to be a rather torrid love letter from Cato's half-sister.

## THE INVASIONS OF BRITAIN (GALLIC WAR 4.20–5.23)

*Caesar wrote seven volumes, that is, seven papyrus rolls, of commentaries on his campaigns in Gaul, covering events from 58 to 52 B.C., and he carried on the narrative of his exploits in three volumes of commentaries on the first phase of the civil wars that he fought against Pompey and the Senate, treating events in 49–48 B.C. This left a gap between the conclusion of the story of the Gallic conquest and the onset of the civil wars that was filled by an officer on Caesar's staff, Aulus Hirtius, who added an eighth volume to* The Gallic War. *In the first book, which begins with the phrase recalled by generations of students, "The whole of Gaul is divided into three parts," Caesar recounts the events of 58 B.C., his campaign against the Helvetii, which provided the pretext for his invasion, and operations against Ariovistus and the Germans. The defeat of the Belgic tribes in 57 B.C. occupies the second book, while the third book describes the campaigns of 56 B.C. against the maritime tribes, the Veneti and the Aquitani. An incursion into Gaul by some German tribes in the following year drew Caesar's attention to the region of the Rhine, which he crossed on a punitive expedition. Then he turned to Britain late in the campaign season, the point where this selection begins.*

[20] The campaign season was almost over, and because the whole of Gaul looks northwards, winter comes early in these regions. Despite these facts, Caesar changed his course to set out for Britain, aware as he was that our enemies in almost all our wars with the Gauls had received reinforcements from that quarter. He considered, moreover, that even if the season left no time for a campaign, none the less it would be a great advantage to him simply to land on the island and observe the kind of people who lived there, and the localities, harbors, and approaches. Every one of these points was unknown to almost all the Gauls. No one, except for traders, went there as a matter of course and not even they knew anything beyond the coast line and the areas facing Gaul. Thus, when Caesar summoned traders from every region he was unable to ascertain either the size of the island, the nature and numbers of the peoples living there, their skill in warfare, their established customs, or which harbors were suitable for a fleet of fairly large ships. [21] Before making the landing attempt he needed information on all these matters, and he judged it appropriate to send Gaius Volusenus ahead with a warship. He gave Volusenus instructions to make a thorough reconnoiter and return to him as soon as possible. Then Caesar set out with all his forces

for the territory of the Morini, from where the crossing to Britain was shortest. He gave orders for ships from the surrounding areas, together with the fleet which he had had constructed the previous summer for the campaign against the Veneti, to gather there.

Meanwhile his plan became known, and traders relayed it to the Britons. Then envoys approached him from several of the island's communities: they promised to surrender hostages and to obey the rule of the Roman people. Caesar heard them, and made generous pledges, encouraging them to remain loyal to their avowed intentions. Then he sent them home, and with them Commius, a man whom he had made king over the Atrebates after conquering them. He thought highly of Commius' courage and good sense, and believed him to be loyal to himself; moreover, Commius was thought to possess considerable influence in the area. Caesar ordered Commius to approach what communities he could, urge them to choose loyalty to the Roman people, and declare that Caesar would soon be coming there. Volusenus had spied out the whole area as best he could, considering that he did not dare to disembark and put his safety in barbarian hands. Then he returned to Caesar on the fifth day and reported what he had observed.

[22] While Caesar lingered in this area to make ready his fleet, envoys approached him from the majority of the Morini. They made excuses for their strategy of the previous season, on the grounds that it was because they were barbarians and unaccustomed to our ways that they had made war on the Roman people; and they pledged themselves to carry out whatever Caesar ordered. He considered this circumstance most timely, for he was reluctant to leave an enemy at his back; also, because the season was so advanced, he had no chance of undertaking a campaign against them. He concluded that involvement in such trivial affairs ought not to come before the expedition to Britain. So he demanded from the Morini a large number of hostages, and as soon as these were produced he received them under his protection.

About eighty transport vessels were mustered and collected, a number Caesar considered sufficient to ferry two legions across. Besides this, he divided up the warships in his possession between his quaestor, legates, and prefects. There were also eighteen transport vessels approaching, but a strong wind was holding them back about seven miles off and preventing them from sailing into the same harbor: he assigned these

to the cavalry. He handed over the rest of his army to his legates Quintus Titurius Sabinus and Lucius Aurunculeius Cotta: they were to lead it against the Menapii, and against those districts of the Morini which had sent him no envoys. He ordered his legate Publius Sulpicius Rufus to guard the harbor, with a garrison of a size he considered sufficient.

[23] These matters settled, he took advantage of a spell of good weather for sailing and weighed anchor around the third watch. He ordered the cavalry to advance to the farther port, embark there, and follow him. They were rather late in carrying out the order, but he reached Britain with the first ships at around the fourth hour; there he spied the enemy forces, fully armed and drawn up all along the cliffs. Such was the geography of this place, and so steep the cliffs which bounded the sea, that it was possible for missiles cast from the heights to find their target on the shore. He judged this place wholly unsuitable for disembarkation, so waited at anchor until the rest of the fleet arrived at the ninth hour. Meanwhile he summoned his legates and military tribunes, and set out what he had learned from Volusenus and what he wanted done. He also warned them that military procedure, and especially naval operations (which tend to be subject to instantaneous and irregular changes), required them to carry out all their tasks at a nod and at the right moment. After dismissing them and taking advantage of a favorable wind and tide together, he gave the signal and weighed anchor. He sailed about six and a half miles further on and landed on a flat and open shore.

[24] The barbarians, however, had grasped the Romans' strategy and sent their cavalry on ahead, and their charioteers (it is their usual custom to use chariots in battle). They followed on with the rest of their forces and prevented our men from disembarking. This led to extreme difficulties, because the ships were too large to be beached except in deep water, while the soldiers, ignorant of the land, their hands full, weighed down by the size and weight of their weapons, at one and the same time had to jump down from the ships to find their feet in the surf, and fight the enemy. The Britons, on the other hand, were either on dry ground or in shallow water, their limbs unencumbered, the ground very familiar. They cast missiles boldly and spurred on their horses, which were well used to such work. This led to panic among our men, who were wholly unaccustomed to this style of fighting, and thus

did not display the same eagerness and enthusiasm as they habitually did in infantry engagements.

[25] When Caesar observed this he gave orders for the warships, which were of a type less familiar to the barbarians and more maneuverable at need, to be moved a short distance from the transport vessels, rowed at speed, and halted on the enemy's exposed flank. From there the enemy could be repelled and driven off with slings, arrows, and missiles.

This act was of great assistance to our men. The barbarians were thrown into a panic by the appearance of the ships, the movement of the oars, and the unfamiliar type of missiles used. They halted and then retreated a short distance. Meanwhile our soldiers were hesitating, chiefly because the sea was so deep; then the man who carried the Eagle of the Tenth legion appealed to the gods to see that his action turned out well for the legion, and said: "Jump down, soldiers, unless you want to betray our Eagle to the enemy—I at least shall have done my duty to the Republic and to my commander." He cried these words in a loud voice, then flung himself away from the ship and began to carry the Eagle towards the enemy. Then our men urged each other to prevent such a disgrace and all together jumped down from the ship. When the men who were on the closest nearby ships saw them do this, they followed them and drew close to the enemy.

[26] Both sides fought fiercely. None the less, our men could not keep ranks or get a firm foothold, neither were they able to follow the standards; rather, different men from different ships grouped round whatever standard they ran up against, and they were in great confusion. The enemy, however, knew all the shallows, so when they caught sight from the shore of some of our men disembarking one by one, they spurred their horses on and attacked while our men were still at a disadvantage, their many surrounding our few. Some began throwing weapons against a whole group of our men on their exposed side. When Caesar noticed this he gave orders for the boats of the warships and likewise the spy vessels to be filled with soldiers. Wherever he saw men struggling, there he dispatched assistance. As soon as our men stood on dry ground, closely followed by all their comrades, they charged the enemy and routed them; but they could not pursue them very far, because the cavalry had failed to hold its course and reach the island. This was the one action in which Caesar's previous good fortune was found lacking.

[27] The enemy had been beaten in battle. As soon as they recovered from the rout they at once sent envoys to Caesar to discuss peace terms. They promised to provide hostages and to do whatever he told them. Together with these envoys there came Commius of the Atrebates—I have already described how Caesar sent him on ahead to Britain. When he disembarked and delivered Caesar's demands to them in the role of envoy, they had arrested him and cast him into chains, but when the battle was ended they sent him back. In seeking peace, they blamed the common crowd for what had taken place and begged him to pardon their lack of judgment. Caesar complained that although of their own accord they had sent envoys to the Gallic mainland to seek peace, they had then started a war with no reason; then he declared a pardon for their lack of judgment and demanded hostages. A number of these were surrendered at once, others were summoned from outlying areas and, they claimed, would be handed over in a few days' time. Meanwhile they ordered their men to return to their lands, and their leaders began to assemble from all directions and commit themselves and their states to Caesar.

[28] These acts established the peace. Four days after the arrival in Britain the eighteen ships which had transported the cavalry (and which were mentioned above) set sail with a gentle breeze and left their more distant port. When they were drawing near to Britain and were spied from the camp, suddenly a storm arose which was so fierce that not one of the ships could hold her course. Some were carried back to the place from which they had set out. Others, in terrible danger were swept further down the island's coast, in a westerly direction. They cast anchor but began to fill with seawater, and were thus forced to sail out to sea during a stormy night and make for the Gallic mainland.

[29] As it happened there was a full moon that night. On this day the Ocean tides are usually at their highest—a fact of which our men were unaware. So at one and the same time the tide had flooded the warships by which Caesar had had the army ferried across, and which he had beached, and the storm began to inflict damage on the transport vessels, which were fast at anchor. Nor did our men get any chance to maneuver them or bring them assistance. Several of the ships were wrecked, the rest had lost their ropes, their anchors, and the rest of their rigging, and were unfit to sail. The inevitable result was panic throughout the army. For there were no other ships to transport them back, and they had no materials

of use for naval repairs. Moreover, since it was generally established that they must winter in Gaul, no corn had been provided for wintering in Britain.

[30] Once they learned of this the British leaders who had approached Caesar after the battle held talks among themselves. They realized that the Romans had neither cavalry nor ships nor corn, and understood, from the smallness of the camp, their weakness in manpower—circumstances all the more straitened by reason of the fact that Caesar had brought the legions over without their heavy baggage. Thus they considered it the perfect moment to engineer a renewal of hostilities, to cut our men off from corn and supplies and prolong the action into the winter. They were confident of overcoming our men or cutting off their escape, and so ensuring that no one would ever again cross to Britain to wage war. So they plotted together once more, and began to leave camp, a few at a time, and to call their men back in secret from the fields.

[31] Even though Caesar had not yet learned of their plans, none the less he suspected it would happen, both because of the fate which had befallen his ships and because the Britons had left off the handover of hostages. So he began to prepare safeguards for every eventuality. Every day he gathered corn from the fields into the camp, and he used timber and bronze from the ships which had been most badly damaged to repair the rest. He gave orders for equipment to be ferried over from mainland Gaul for this purpose. The soldiers carried out these tasks with great enthusiasm, and so by the loss of twelve ships Caesar was able to render the rest sufficiently seaworthy.

[32] While this was going on the legion known as the Seventh had been sent out in a body as usual to find corn. As yet no hint of hostilities had occurred, since some of the Britons were still in the fields, while others were even making frequent visits to the Roman camp. Then the men on guard at the gates of the camp reported to Caesar that a dust-cloud, greater than usual, was visible in the place to which the Seventh had marched. Caesar guessed the truth, that the barbarians had started upon some new stratagem. He gave orders for the cohorts which were then on guard to set out with him to the place, and for two cohorts from the remainder to relieve them on guard-duty: the rest were to arm themselves and follow him without delay.

When they had made their way some distance from the camp he caught sight of his men being hard pressed by the enemy and struggling to hold their position.

The legion was crowded together, and missiles were being thrown at it from every quarter. Because all the corn had been cut from the remaining areas, and this place alone was left, the enemy had suspected that our men would come there and had hidden by night in the woods. Then, when our men were scattered and, busy cutting corn, had laid down their weapons, they suddenly attacked, killed a few, cast the remainder into disorder before they could form ranks and surrounded them at once with cavalry and chariots.

[33] Their method of fighting from chariots is as follows. First they drive around in all directions, casting missiles and generally throwing army ranks into confusion through the panic caused by the horses and the noise of the wheels. Then, when they have wormed their way in between the cavalry squadrons, they jump down from the chariots and fight on foot. Meanwhile the charioteers gradually make their way out of the fighting, and station their chariots so that, if they are hard pressed by a host of enemies, they have a speedy retreat to their own side. Thus they provide the flexible mobility of cavalry and the stability of infantry in battle. By means of daily practice and exercises they ensure that even on the steepest of inclines they can hold their horses at full gallop, control and turn them swiftly, run along the beam and stand on the yoke—and from there get quickly back to the chariot.

[34] Because this type of fighting was so unusual, our men were thrown into confusion by such tactics, but in the nick of time Caesar brought them assistance. For the enemy halted at his coming, while our men recovered from their panic. After this he considered that it was an inopportune moment for going on the offensive and engaging in battle, so he stayed where he was, and after a short while led the legions back to camp. During these events all our men were busy, and the rest of the Britons who were in the fields dispersed. Continual storms followed for a number of days, which kept our men in camp and prevented the enemy from fighting. In the meantime the barbarians sent out messengers in all directions who proclaimed to their own people that our troops were few in number, and declared how great was the opportunity of winning booty and of liberating themselves for ever if they drove the Romans from their camp. In this way a huge force of infantry and cavalry was quickly mustered and approached our camp.

[35] Caesar foresaw that the same thing would happen as on previous days, namely, that if they were

repulsed the enemy would use speed to escape the danger. Nevertheless, he had in his possession about thirty cavalrymen whom Commius the Atrebatian (who was mentioned above) had brought across with him, so he stationed his legions in battle formation in front of the camp. Battle was joined. The enemy was unable to withstand the attack of our soldiers for very long, and fled. Our men pursued for as far as their vigor and strength allowed, killed a number of them, then set fire to all the buildings far and wide and returned to camp.

[36] On the same day the enemy sent envoys to Caesar to sue for peace. Caesar doubled the number of hostages which he had previously demanded from them and ordered that they be taken to the Gallic mainland, because the autumnal equinox was at hand and he considered that as his ships were damaged the voyage should not be exposed to winter storms. He took advantage of a period of good weather and set sail a little after midnight. All the ships reached the mainland safely, though two of the transport vessels were unable to make the same ports as the rest and were carried a little further south down the coast.

[37] About 300 soldiers had disembarked from these ships and were marching to the camp, when the Morini, whom Caesar had left pacified when he set out for Britain, were led by the hope of booty to surround them with, at first, a small number of men. They ordered our men to lay down their weapons if they did not wish to be killed. Our men, however, formed a circle and began to defend themselves; then about 6,000 of the Morini massed swiftly on hearing the shout. News of this came to Caesar, who sent the entire cavalry to his men's assistance from the camp. Meanwhile our soldiers withstood the attack of the enemy and fought bravely for more than four hours, receiving only a few wounds and killing several of the enemy. After our cavalry came into sight the enemy threw away their weapons and turned tail; many of them were killed. The following day Caesar sent his legate Titus Labienus, with the legions he had brought back from Britain, against the Morini who had renewed hostilities. The marshes which they had used as a refuge in the previous year were too dry to offer a place of retreat, so almost all surrendered themselves to Labienus' control.

The legates Quintus Titurius and Lucius Cotta, meanwhile, had led their legions into the territory of the Menapii. There they ravaged the fields, cut down the corn, and burned the buildings, because the Menapii had concealed themselves in the depths of the forests. Then they returned to Caesar, who established winter quarters for all the legions among the Belgae. In all, only two of the British peoples sent him hostages there, while the rest failed to do so. Following receipt of a dispatch from Caesar, a thanksgiving of twenty days was decreed by the Senate for these achievements.

## Book 5: 54 B.C.

### The Second British Expedition

[1] During the consulship of Lucius Domitius and Appius Claudius, Caesar left his winter quarters for Italy as he was accustomed to do every year. He ordered the legates whom he had left in charge of the legions to have as many ships as possible built that winter, and the old ones refitted. He specified the form and style of these ships. For speed of loading and beaching he made them a little lower than the vessels we habitually use in the Mediterranean; this was all the more appropriate because he had discovered that the waves there were smaller, because of the frequency of tidal changes. For cargo, and carrying large numbers of pack animals, he made them slightly broader than the sort we use on other seas. For maximum speed, he ordered them all to be constructed with both oars and sails: their low profile helped this aim considerably. He gave instructions for the tackle for arming the ships to be imported from Spain.

Once the assizes in Nearer Gaul were ended he himself set out for Illyricum, because he was receiving reports that the region nearest to the Province was being ravaged by the raids of the Pirustae. On his arrival he levied troops from the peoples there and told them to muster at a particular place. When news of his action came the Pirustae sent envoys to prove that none of these events had happened as a matter of public policy. They showed themselves ready to make reparation by all possible means for any damage done. Caesar heard their speech, then demanded hostages and ordered them to be produced on a given day. If they failed in this, he made it clear that he would pursue a campaign against their nation. The hostages were brought on the appropriate day as he had demanded, and he appointed arbitrators between the peoples to assess the damages and settle penalties.

[2] These affairs thus settled and his assizes at an end, he returned to Nearer Gaul, and from there set out for his army. When he reached it he made the rounds of all the winter quarters, and discovered that thanks to the soldiers' remarkable zeal—and despite a severe

shortage of materials—about 600 ships of the kind
we described above had been constructed, together
with twenty-eight warships. They were almost ready
for launching within a few days. He commended the
men and the officers in charge of the business, then set
out what he wanted to happen and ordered everyone
to assemble at Portus Itius. He had discovered that the
crossing to Britain was easiest from there—a voyage of
only about twenty-seven miles from mainland Gaul.
Leaving behind what seemed an adequate number of
soldiers for the purpose, he took four legions without
heavy kit and 800 cavalry, and set out for the territory
of the Treveri, who were persistently failing to attend
assemblies and obey his commands, and were rumored
to be seeking the support of the Germans living across
the Rhine.

[3] In cavalry the Treveri are by far the strongest
nation in the whole of Gaul. They also have large infantry
forces and, as we mentioned earlier, border the Rhine.
Within their nation two men called Indutiomarus and
Cingetorix were competing for supreme power. As
soon as the arrival of Caesar and his legions became
known, one of the two, Cingetorix, approached Caesar
and promised that he and all his people would be loyal
and not abandon the friendship of the Roman people;
and he revealed what was going on among the Treveri.
Indutiomarus, however, began to make ready for war,
mustering cavalry and infantry, and hiding those who
were not of an age to bear arms in the Ardennes forest. This forest is extremely large and reaches from the
Rhine through the middle of the Treveri's land to the
borders of the Remi.

Some of the leaders of the Treveri were encouraged
by their kinship with Cingetorix, and frightened by
the presence of our army, so they approached Caesar.
They began to consult him in private about their own
affairs, since they could not take measures to protect
their nation. Then Indutiomarus was afraid of being
abandoned by everyone and sent envoys to Caesar. He
claimed that he had been reluctant to leave his own people and approach Caesar, because by staying he would
more easily keep the nation loyal, and the ordinary
people would not fall into ignorant error with all the
aristocracy gone away. In consequence of this the whole
nation was under his control, and if Caesar would permit it he would come to his camp and entrust his own
fortunes and those of the nation to Caesar's good faith.

[4] Caesar was well aware of the reason for
Indutiomarus' words, and of what was deterring him

from the policy with which he had begun. Even so, to
avoid being forced to waste the campaigning season
among the Treveri when everything was ready for the
war in Britain, he ordered Indutiomarus to come to
him with 200 hostages. Once these were produced,
among them his son and all his relations whom Caesar
had summoned by name, he comforted Indutiomarus
and urged him to remain loyal. All the same, he summoned the leaders of the Treveri and one at a time won
them over to Cingetorix. He did this because he realized that Cingetorix, whose good will towards Caesar
himself was evident, deserved this favor; but also
because he considered it a matter of importance for
Cingetorix's authority among his own people to be as
great as possible. Indutiomarus took this restriction of
his own influence among his people badly. Previously
he had been hostile in his intentions towards us, but
now he was even more fiercely ablaze with indignation.

[5] These matters settled, Caesar reached Portus
Itius with his legions. There he learned that sixty ships
built by the Meldi had been unable to hold their course
but were forced back by bad weather. They had returned
to the same place from which they had set sail. All the
rest he found ready to sail and fully equipped. At the
same place all the cavalry of Gaul assembled, about
4,000 in number, and the leaders of all the states. He
had decided to leave a few of them—those whose loyalty was evident—in Gaul. The rest he took with him
in place of hostages, because he feared that Gaul would
revolt during his absence.

[6] Among this majority was Dumnorix the
Aeduan, whom we have mentioned before. Caesar
was particularly anxious to keep this man at his side
because he knew him to be eager for revolution and
eager for power, audacious and influential among the
Gauls. There was also the fact that at an assembly of the
Aedui Dumnorix had claimed that Caesar was offering him dominion over their nation. It was a claim the
Aedui took badly, but they did not dare to send envoys
to Caesar to reject or criticize him for it. Caesar had
learned of this from his own supporters.

At first Dumnorix pleaded all kinds of reasons
why he should be left behind in Gaul. For one thing,
he claimed, he knew nothing of sailing and was afraid
of the sea; for another—or so he alleged—religious
obligations prevented him from going. Once he saw
that his request was obdurately refused, and all hope
of getting what he wanted was snatched away, he
began to stir up the Gallic leaders, to draw them aside

individually and urge them to stay behind on the Gallic mainland. He tried to frighten them—not without reason, he asserted, was Gaul being stripped of all her aristocracy: Caesar was afraid to kill them in sight of Gaul, but planned instead to take them all to Britain and there put them to death. He pledged his word to the rest, and demanded an oath that they should carry out whatever they saw was to Gaul's advantage. A number of informers reported this to Caesar.

[7] Caesar had a high opinion of the status and position of the Aedui, so on hearing this he decided that Dumnorix must be checked and deterred by every means possible. He saw Dumnorix's madness spreading abroad, and so it was his duty to watch out that neither he nor the Republic suffered harm. So when he was detained in the area for about twenty-five days (because the north-west wind, which is the prevailing wind in that vicinity, prevented his sailing) he took steps to keep Dumnorix to his allegiance, but just the same he gathered information about all his plans.

At last Caesar had good sailing weather, and ordered his soldiers and cavalry to embark. But while everyone's minds were preoccupied, Dumnorix and the Aeduan cavalry began to leave the camp and go home, without Caesar's knowledge. When he did learn of it Caesar stopped the expedition and, postponing everything else, sent a large section of the cavalry to pursue Dumnorix and gave orders for him to be dragged back. If he offered armed resistance and would not obey, he told them to kill him: for he judged that a man who had disregarded Caesar's command when Caesar was actually present would certainly not behave like a sensible man in Caesar's absence. As might be expected, when he was summoned to return, Dumnorix began his resistance, defending himself by force and begging his supporters' assistance: he continually cried that he was a free man and a citizen of a free state. Caesar's men surrounded and killed him, as ordered. All the Aeduan cavalry, however, returned to Caesar.

[8] After these events Labienus was left on the mainland with three legions and 2,000 cavalry to watch over the harbors, see to the corn supply, find out what was happening in Gaul, and make his plans according to circumstances and events. Caesar set out with five legions and the same number of cavalry as he had left on the mainland. He weighed anchor at sunset. A gentle south-westerly breeze carried him out, but around midnight it dropped and he could no longer maintain his course. He was then carried too far by the flood-tide, and at dawn saw Britain being left behind to port. Then he followed the ebb-tide back and rowed hard to reach that part of the island where he had found the best landing-places the previous summer. In this the courage of the soldiers was most commendable, for even in the heavily laden transport vessels they managed—by undertaking to row without a break—to keep pace with the course of the warships.

The whole fleet reached Britain at around midday, but there was no enemy visible in the area. Later, however, Caesar learned from prisoners that, although a large host of them had arrived, they had panicked at the size of the fleet, which, including last year's ships and the private vessels which certain individuals had had built for their convenience, was seen to number more than 800 at once. So they had left the shore and hidden themselves away on higher ground.

[9] The army landed and a suitable site for the camp was found. When Caesar learned from prisoners where the enemy forces were stationed he left ten cohorts and 300 cavalry on the shore to guard the fleet, and during the third watch set out against the enemy. He was the less concerned for the fleet because he was leaving it anchored along a sandy, low-lying coast. He put Quintus Atrius in charge of this garrison. During the night he advanced about eleven miles before catching sight of the enemy forces. They brought their cavalry and chariots forward from higher ground to a river and began to block the way of our men and to engage in fighting. They were forced back by our cavalry and hid in the forest, where they occupied a place which was strong in both natural and man-made defences. It was apparent that they had previously made this ready to serve in their domestic warfare, for every one of the entrances was blocked off by the felling of a large number of trees. They came out from the forest to fight in small detachments, and prevented our men from coming within the fortifications. But the men of the Seventh Legion formed up into a "tortoise," piled up a ramp against the fortifications, seized control of the stronghold, and drove the enemy from the forest. They themselves suffered few casualties. Caesar, however, forbade them to pursue the fugitives very far, both because he was not familiar with the terrain and because the day was already far spent, and he wanted there to be enough time left for fortifying the camp.

[10] The following morning he sent the soldiers and cavalry out in three divisions on a foray to pursue

fugitives. After they had marched a considerable distance they caught sight of the enemy rearguard. Just then riders came to Caesar from Quintus Atrius and reported that a terrible storm had blown up the night before, and almost all the ships were damaged and cast up on the shore—for the anchors and ropes had failed, and so the sailors and helmsmen could not withstand the force of the storm. As a result, the ships had been dashed one against the other, and serious damage had resulted.

[11] On learning this, Caesar ordered the legions and cavalry to be recalled and to maintain their resistance on the march. He himself returned to the ships. Then he saw everything for himself, almost exactly as he had heard it described by the messengers and dispatch. Yet although about forty ships were lost, it was apparent that with considerable labor the rest could be rebuilt. So he selected workmen from the legions and ordered more to be summoned from mainland Gaul. He wrote to Labienus to have as many ships as possible built by those legions presently under his command. Then, despite the considerable difficulty and effort involved, Caesar decided the most convenient solution was to beach all the ships and join them with the camp by a single line of fortification. The work lasted for ten days: the soldiers had no break from their efforts even at night. Once the ships were beached and the camp strongly fortified, he left the same forces as before to guard the fleet and returned to the place he had left earlier.

By the time of his arrival even larger British forces had mustered there. By common agreement they had entrusted the supreme command of their campaign to Cassivellaunus, whose lands were separated from the coastal states by a river called the Thames, which is about seventy-three miles from the sea. Between Cassivellaunus and the other states there had previously been continual warfare, but our arrival frightened the Britons into putting him in charge of the entire war effort.

[12] The inland regions of Britain are inhabited by people whom the Britons themselves claim, according to oral tradition, are indigenous. The coastal areas belong to people who once crossed from Belgium in search of booty and war: almost all of these inhabitants are called by the same national names as those of the states they originally came from. After waging war they remained in Britain and began to farm the land. Population density is high, and their dwellings are extremely numerous and very like those of the Gauls. They have large herds of cattle. They use either bronze or gold coinage or, instead of currency, iron rods of

a fixed weight. Tin is found in the midland regions, iron along the coast but only in small quantities. Their bronze is imported. Timber of all kinds is found as in Gaul, except for beech and silver fir. They consider it wrong to eat hare, chicken, or goose, but still they look after them for pleasure and amusement. The climate is more temperate than in Gaul, and the winters milder.

[13] The island is triangular in shape. One side faces Gaul, and one corner of this side, in Kent, is where almost all ships from Gaul put in to harbor. This corner looks east, the other south: the side stretches for about 460 miles. The second side looks towards Spain and the west: in this direction lies Ireland, which is thought to be half the size of Britain. The crossing from Britain to Ireland is the same as that from Gaul to Britain. Midway lies an island called Mona. There are thought to be several smaller islands besides lying nearby, and several writers have recorded that over the winter solstice there is continual darkness there for thirty days. We were unable to find out the truth of this by inquiries, except that by accurate measurements with a water-clock we observed that the nights were shorter than in mainland Gaul. According to the belief of the Britons, this side is some 640 miles long. The third side looks north, and faces no other land: but it is mainly angled towards Germany. It is thought to be about 730 miles long. Thus the whole island is nearly 2,000 miles in circumference.

[14] Of all the island's inhabitants, by far the most civilized are those who live in Kent, a region which is entirely coastal. Their way of life is much the same as that of the Gauls. Inland, the people for the most part do not plant corn-crops, but live on milk and meat and clothe themselves in animal skins. All the Britons paint themselves with woad, which produces a dark blue color: by this means they appear more frightening in battle. They have long hair and shave their bodies, all except for the head and upper lip. Groups of ten or twelve men share their wives in common, particularly between brothers or father and son. Any offspring they have are held to be the children of him to whom the maiden was brought first.

[15] The enemy cavalry and charioteers clashed fiercely in combat with our cavalry on the march, though the outcome showed that our men were superior in every respect and drove them into the woods and hills. Despite killing a number of the enemy, they pursued too eagerly and lost a number of their own side. After a short time, when our men were off guard and busy fortifying the camp, the Britons suddenly rushed out of the woods

and attacked the guards stationed in front of the camp. A fierce fight ensued. Caesar sent two cohorts to their assistance—the primary cohorts of their respective legions—and they positioned themselves with only a very small gap to separate them. Because our men were frightened by the unfamiliar tactics, the enemy boldly broke through their midst and retreated without casualties. On that day the military tribune Quintus Laberius Durus was killed. The Britons were driven back after more cohorts were sent in support.

[16] Throughout this unusual combat, when the fighting took place in sight of all and in front of the camp, it was evident that because of their heavy weaponry our men were ill equipped for such an enemy. For they could not pursue when the enemy ran, and dared not abandon their close formation. The cavalry fought at great risk too, because the enemy frequently drove away from the fighting on purpose, so when our horsemen had gone some little distance from the legions they could jump down from their chariots and fight on foot with an unfair advantage. In fact, their strategy for cavalry battle brought us into equal danger whether in retreat or pursuit. There was also the fact that they never fought in close formation, but rather in small groups with large spaces between: they had squadrons posted at intervals and each group took over from another in turn, so that fresh troops could take the place of those who were tired out.

[17] The following day the enemy took up a position on high ground far from camp. They began to appear in small detachments and attack our cavalry, though less eagerly than the day before. At midday, though, when Caesar had sent three legions and all the cavalry with his legate Gaius Trebonius to forage for food, the enemy suddenly swept down upon the foragers from all directions with such force that they did not stop before coming up with the standards and the legions. Our legionaries attacked fiercely and drove them back; they did not halt the pursuit until the cavalry saw the legions behind them and had the confidence in their support to drive the enemy headlong. They cut down a large number, and allowed them no opportunity to rally or make a stand or jump down from their chariots. Directly after this battle the enemy reinforcements which had mustered all dispersed. Thereafter the Britons were never at full strength when they engaged with our forces.

[18] Caesar learned of their plans and led his army to the River Thames in the territory of Cassivellaunus. This river can only be crossed at a single spot, on foot, and then with difficulty. When he arrived, he observed the large enemy forces drawn up on the opposite bank, the surface of which was protected by a covering of sharpened stakes. Fixed beneath the water, similar stakes were concealed by the river. On learning these facts from prisoners and deserters, Caesar sent the cavalry on ahead and ordered the legions to follow up at once. The soldiers moved with such speed and vigor that—although they had only their heads above water—the enemy could not withstand the assault of the legions and cavalry, abandoned the river-bank, and took to their heels.

[19] As we explained above, Cassivellaunus had given up all hope of a confrontation and dismissed the greater part of his forces, so that about 4,000 charioteers remained. He kept watch on our marches, withdrawing a short distance from the road and keeping himself hidden in difficult wooded terrain. Wherever he knew we would be marching, he forced men and livestock to leave the fields for the forest. Whenever our cavalry rushed into the fields, ranging too freely in search of plunder and devastation, he sent his charioteers by every path and track out of the woods: the clash between them brought our cavalry into great danger. Thus fear prevented them from ranging more widely. All that remained for Caesar was to forbid anyone straying too far from the column of legions, and to inflict as much harm upon the enemy—by ravaging the fields and starting fires—as the legionary soldiers could manage despite the exertion of the march.

[20] Meanwhile the Trinobantes (one of the most powerful states in those parts) sent envoys to Caesar and promised to surrender to him and to obey his commands. A young man of that people, called Mandubracius, had approached Caesar on the Gallic mainland looking for his support: for his father, who had won the kingship in that state, had been killed by Cassivellaunus, while he himself had fled to escape death. The Trinobantes asked Caesar to defend Mandubracius from harm at Cassivellaunus' hands, and to send him to their state to take command and rule over it. Caesar demanded forty hostages from them, and corn for his army, and sent Mandubracius to them. They quickly carried out his commands, and sent the required number of hostages and the corn. [21] Thus the Trinobantes were made secure, and protected from any harm at the soldiers' hands.

Then the Cenimagni, Segontiaci, Ancalites, Bibroci, and Cassi sent embassies and put themselves under Caesar's protection. He learned from them that Cassivellaunus' stronghold, which was protected by woods and marshes, was not far from his present location: he had gathered quite a large number of men and cattle there. The Britons, however, apply the word "stronghold" to a dense wood which they have fortified with a rampart and ditch, and where they always assemble to avoid enemy attack. Caesar made his way there with the legions, and found it a place with admirable natural and man-made defenses. None the less, he exerted himself to attack it on two sides. The enemy lingered a short while, but did not withstand the assault of our soldiers, and burst out from another part of the stronghold. Large numbers of cattle were found there, and many of the enemy were caught as they fled and put to death.

[22] While all this was taking place in that area Cassivellaunus sent messengers to Kent (which, as we explained above, is by the sea). This was a region ruled over by four kings—Cingetorix, Carvilius, Taximagulus, and Segovax. He ordered them to muster all their forces, strike at the Roman fleet's camp without warning, and launch an assault. When they reached the camp, however, our men made a sortie. They killed a large number of the enemy, captured their aristocratic leader Lugotorix, and returned without casualties. News of this battle reached Cassivellaunus. He had suffered many defeats and his lands were ruined: he was particularly disturbed by the defection of allied states, so finally he sent envoys to Caesar through Commius the Atrebatian to surrender. Caesar had decided to winter on the mainland for fear of sudden Gallic uprisings. He realized that not much of the summer remained, and that hostilities could easily drag on, so he demanded hostages and settled the annual tribute which Britain must pay to the Roman people. He ordered Cassivellaunus in strong terms to do no harm to Mandubracius or the Trinobantes.

[23] Once he had received the hostages, Caesar led his army back to the coast, where he found the ships repaired. He had a large number of prisoners, while several of the ships had been destroyed in the storm, so

once the ships were launched he decided to transport the army back in two journeys. So it came about that neither this year nor the year before was any ship carrying soldiers lost altogether, despite the large number both of vessels and voyages. Of those ships which were sent back empty from mainland Gaul—both the ones from which the soldiers who crossed first had disembarked and the sixty vessels which Labienus had had built after Caesar sailed—very few reached the rendezvous. Almost all of the rest were forced back. Caesar waited a while for them, but in vain. To avoid being prevented by the season from making the voyage at all (for the autumnal equinox was near), he was forced to pack the soldiers in more tightly than usual; then when a total calm ensued he weighed anchor at the start of the second watch, reached land at dawn, and brought the whole fleet safely to its destination.

*In the following two books, Caesar tells of the completion of the conquest of Gaul, dealing in particular with the suppression of the Belgians through a campaign of devastation. The seventh is the last book that he wrote himself. In it he tells how he suppressed the general revolt in 52 led by Vercingetorix, king of the Averni. Gallic resistance came to an end with the capture of their stronghold at Alesia and the surrender of Vercingetorix. Caesar surrounded the fortress with ten miles of siegeworks designed to keep Vercingetorix and his 80,000 men trapped within and then built another line outside that to keep out the army that came to relieve them. The Romans were simultaneously attacked by Vercingetorix from Alesia and by an army of 250,000 (if Caesar's numbers are to be believed) that came to lift the siege, but after a battle lasting four days, Caesar prevailed. In the end the Gauls were starved into surrender and Vercingetorix was brought back to Rome, but the civil wars delayed the celebration of Caesar's victory. After six years in prison, Vercingetorix was led in chains in Caesar's triumph, before being taken back to his cell and strangled.*

## AFTERWORD

The assassination of Caesar did not put an end to his plans for lasting change in Rome's political system; on the contrary, his adopted son and heir, Gaius Octavius, known to the ages as Augustus, exploited the aura of Caesar to fulfill his own ambitions. In Roman nomenclature it was standard to include the name of one's father, and under ordinary circumstances Caesar's son would have been called "son of Julius." But once Caesar had been accorded divine status, Octavius, now known as Octavian, became instead "son of the God." A temple was erected at the eastern end of the Forum on the spot where Caesar's body had been cremated, and the statue of Caesar that it contained was conspicuous from most quarters of the Forum. The temple was the scene of important state functions, including the funeral orations delivered for members of the imperial family, so that Caesar literally presided over the continuity of the empire. At the games given by Augustus in honor of Caesar's deification a comet appeared in the skies for seven days. It was generally believed to be the soul of Caesar ascending to heaven. Whether Augustus truly believed this or not, one cannot say, but he put the event to good use in state propaganda: a star was set upon the head of Caesar's statue, and the comet appears on the coinage of Augustus's reign.

Caesar the statesman, Caesar the general, and Caesar the god had a long afterlife. So too did Caesar the ruthless dictator, who is a central character in Lucan's epic poem written about a hundred years after the Ides of March. But Caesar the man of letters has enjoyed less fame. His works were little known in the Middle Ages, and the figure of Caesar as he appears in works of art and literature of the period is drawn more from biographies, especially Suetonius's, and from Lucan's *Civil War*. The name inspired myths and legends, like the one told in *The Deeds of the Romans,* a fourteenth-century collection of stories about the Roman past, equipped with moral interpretations for the edification of monks in need of material for sermons. In the chapter on the sin of pride, it tells how Caesar tricked a giant ghost that appeared to him, blocking the crossing of the Rubicon. The ghost would only let him pass if he swore that he came "on behalf of the peace of the Romans." Caesar duly swore that he came "to benefit Rome," crossed the river when the ghost had vanished, and on the other bank took advantage of Latin grammar to add the qualifier "by breaking the peace."

Another such legend concerns a particularly splendid obelisk, which the emperor Caligula brought to Rome from Egypt in A.D. 37. It was then set up in a racetrack erected across the Tiber on the site of the modern Vatican. Among Rome's many obelisks this one had a particularly checkered career, having first been endowed with an inscription in Egypt by the poet Cornelius Gallus, who had served Augustus as the first prefect of the new province. That inscription was replaced by another after Gallus was forced to commit suicide for some unspecified affront to the emperor. Once in Rome it was erected on the *spina* (center island) of the racetrack built by Caligula on the future site of the Basilica of St. Peter. There it stood, adjacent to the basilica, throughout the Middle Ages, the only one of Rome's obelisks to remain untoppled. It was moved to its present location in the center of the piazza in front of the new basilica in 1586 on the order of Pope Sixtus V. Throughout the Middle Ages this monument was known to many as "St. Peter's Needle," because it was believed that the saint had suffered his martyrdom in that circus, but it had another name as well. Medieval guidebooks call it "Caesar's Memorial" because it was believed that his cremated remains were entombed in the large bronze sphere that sat on its top. This belief arose because so grand a monument simply had to be connected with the name of the greatest Roman of antiquity. When the obelisk was moved, the sphere was removed (it is now in the Capitoline Museum), and there was some considerable disappointment when it was found to be empty.

Caesar's writings had elicited great admiration among his contemporaries. Even his fierce political opponent Cicero praised his commentaries for their clear, straightforward style, comparing them to "nude figures, straight and beautiful; stripped of all ornament of style as if they had laid aside a garment" (*Brutus* 262). Caesar's commentaries were read again in the Renaissance: Petrarch used them as a source in his biography of Caesar, and Michel de Montaigne adopted him as a stylistic model. But it was still the man, not the writings, that mesmerized people. Shakespeare's *Julius Caesar* is drawn from the biographies of Caesar, especially from translations of Plutarch, and not from Caesar's own words. In modern France, however, Caesar's *Gallic War* was the inspiration for a popular comic book series, *Asterix,* which uses the conquest of Gaul to tell a story of the first French Resistance.

For generations of students who were made to learn Latin at school, *The Gallic War* became a rite of passage in the classroom, as Caesar became what he had never been in antiquity, a school text. His seemingly easy style made Latin more acceptable, and the subject matter made the work appropriate for molding young minds, especially those of boys. One edition of *The Gallic War,* produced in 1902 by Princeton professor J. H. Westcott for use in the schools, describes its purpose as in part "to present Caesar as the greatest political person of antiquity, and to show his immense significance as the principal founder of modern civilization." Hand in hand with the perceived utility of Caesar's clear and straightforward style for drumming into students' heads the principles of Latin grammar went the idea that there was value in somehow relating the conquest of Gaul to contemporary culture. Writing in 1918, just after the entry of the United States into the First World War, Francis Kelsey explains the timeliness, as he sees it, of his edition of the *The Gallic War*: "Modern armies have clashed on the battlefields of the Gallic War; modern camps are laid out in a way to suggest the manner of the Romans. The strategy of Joffre and of Hindenburg finds its prototype in that of Caesar...In countless ways—even to Caesar's statement, 'Of all these the bravest are the Belgians'—the World War reproduces on a larger scale the campaigns of Caesar." As a result it is no wonder that readers rarely think of Caesar's commentaries as a literary masterpiece. One of the few acknowledgments of Caesar's literary legacy is found in the annals of American literature. In 1884, out of office, out of money, and dying of cancer, former president Ulysses S. Grant devoted the final year of his life to composing his personal memoirs. He completed the manuscript a few days before his death, and the subsequent sales restored his family's fortune. The book received high praise from his friend and publisher, Mark Twain, who called it the best of its kind since Caesar, singling it out in particular for "clarity of statement, directness, simplicity," virtues that it shared with its ancient Roman counterpart.

# SALLUST

## (Gaius Sallustius Crispus, ca. 86–35 B.C.)

LITTLE IS KNOWN ABOUT SALLUST'S EARLY LIFE, AND THE CONSIDERABLE AMOUNT we are told about his later years comes mostly from unsympathetic or hostile sources, and much of it should therefore probably be discounted as typical of the robust but unfounded vilification of opponents that was a standard feature of Roman politics. He was born, probably in 86 B.C., in Amiternum, in the lovely mountains of the Abruzzi, northeast of Rome, and he died in 35 B.C. He lived therefore through the tempestuous period that saw the fall of the Republic and was the subject of most of his writings. His family probably belonged to the local aristocracy. Nothing certain is known of his public life until 52 B.C., when, as a tribune of the people, he acted against Annius Milo, a political gang leader supported by the aristocratic elite, who was being defended by Cicero on a charge of murdering his populist rival, Clodius Pulcher. He was expelled from the Senate in 50, allegedly for immoral behavior, but probably in retaliation for his efforts in the successful campaign to have Milo condemned. Caesar gave him a military command at the outbreak of the civil war in 49 and subsequently appointed him as first governor of the new province of Africa Nova. His political career, being dependent on the patronage of Julius Caesar, was brought to an end on the Ides of March 44. He was charged with malpractice in his governorship and might have been expelled from the Senate for a second time had he not anticipated condemnation and retired from public life.

He devoted the first period of his retirement to composing his two monographs, *The Conspiracy of Catiline* in 42–41 B.C. and *The War with Jugurtha* immediately after, his account of the war with Numidia in the late second century, in which he showed up the incompetence and corruption of the ruling class. He followed these with his *Histories,* dealing with events in Rome from the death of Sulla in 79. Only the *Catiline* and the *Jugurtha* survive complete. There are about five hundred fragments of the *Histories,* but only a few are substantial, and none refers to any time demonstrably later than 67 (so there is no overlap with his handling of the Catilinarian conspiracy of 63). That there are so many fragments is a testimony to the popularity of Sallust's works; Cicero is the only prose writer quoted more often by later authors. It also reflects the idiosyncrasy of his style and diction, which attracted the attention of writers on grammar and language.

The central theme of all Sallust's writings is his denunciation of the immorality of the times. At the beginning of both the *Catiline* and the *Jugurtha,* he claims to have withdrawn from public life in disgust at the corruption rampant in politics, and the fragments from the opening of the *Histories* show that he continued with the same theme in that work also: "Discord, greed, ambition, and all the other vices that prosperity tends to give rise to, increased drastically after the destruction of Carthage. When the Carthaginian threat had been removed, there was a vacuum that was filled by dissension, with very frequent rioting and unrest, and eventually civil wars...." (1.10).

**Figure 10:  Luca Signorelli, *Sallust***
The portrayal of Sallust in this fresco, as of nearly all Romans other than emperors in subsequent periods, is
entirely imaginary.

Since the integrity of Sallust's own personal moral standards is vulnerable to suspicion, his authority to inveigh against corruption is not beyond question. He was denounced as a hypocrite in some
quarters, even in his own time. The great scholar Terentius Varro observes that Sallust may write
his histories in a severe and puritanical style, as if he were carrying out the duties of a censor, but he
goes on to allege that Milo had thrashed him with straps after catching him in bed with his wife, the
daughter of the dictator Sulla, and had not let him go until he had paid him compensation (Aulus
Gellius, *Attic Nights* 17.18). This would certainly give Sallust a personal motive for opposing Milo, but
Varro was a Pompeian, Sallust a Caesarian, so it may all be political mud-slinging. That is obviously
true, at least to some extent, of the reaction by Lenaeus, a loyal freedman of Pompey, when Sallust
insulted his dead patron by describing him as having "an honest face, but an immoral mind." Lenaeus
retaliated, "tearing him to shreds in a most bitterly satirical fashion, calling him a pathic homosexual,
a glutton, a waster, a tavern-crawler, a monster both in his life and in his writings and, what's more, an
appallingly ignorant plagiarist of Cato's archaic vocabulary" (Suetonius, *On Grammarians* 15).

Nor is it clear how we should assess the charge of malpractice in Africa. That might be little more
than political maneuvering against an opponent by the rigorous application of protocols that were
usually ignored. Condemnation for extortion in provincial administration was rare; the plundering of Sicily by Verres had been on an unusually comprehensive and systematic scale, but even his

condemnation in 70 had caused a sensation and was due almost entirely to Cicero's energetic prosecution, not to the justice of the case against him. Cicero himself boasts of his honesty as governor of Cilicia in the late 50s but admits to making a profit of more than 2 million sestertii (twice the wealth qualification for admission to the Senate).

Since Cato the Elder was the archetypal moralist, Sallust's adoption of his style and vocabulary is a clear assertion that he also wishes to be regarded as a defender of traditional Roman morality, but it is only too obvious that he lacks the moral authority to give validity to any such claim. Especially in the introductory moralizing to his works, he writes rather too dogmatically, adopting a stance that is aggressive and imposing, but at times lacking in convincing intellectual argument. It is even arguable that, in modeling his writing on Cato, and thereby rejecting the influential Ciceronian style, Sallust is also by implication rejecting Cicero's perspective on the Catilinarian conspiracy.

It is impossible to read Sallust's account of the conspiracy without comparing it to the version of events given by Cicero, who had been murdered on Antony's orders shortly before Sallust's monograph was published. It is therefore particularly important to understand, as far as it is possible to do so, the relationship between the two writers. Cicero, in *His Own Consulship*, presents himself as being summoned to a Council of the Gods on Olympus and entrusted with the task of saving Rome from Catiline, and the Senate actually did bestow on him the unprecedented title "Father of the Fatherland." In Sallust's version, on the other hand, he plays a much less significant role. This can to some extent be quantified. The *Catiline* has a total of 10,717 words, of which 1,017 and 845 are in the climactically prominent antithetical speeches by Julius Caesar and Cato, respectively. Combined with Sallust's moralizing diatribes, his narration of the actual events, and such passages as his famously intolerant denunciation of Sempronia as a representative of the corruption of the aristocracy, a section that is disproportionately lengthy in comparison to her significance in the sequence of events, this set-piece debate accounts for almost 20 percent of the total; there is little room left to devote to Cicero.

It is often assumed that the relatively insignificant role allotted to Cicero in Sallust's version reflects extreme antipathy between the two men. That such antipathy existed is suggested by two curious tracts, the *Invective against Cicero* and the *Invective against Sallust*, attributed to Sallust and Cicero, respectively, but both certainly spurious and probably written in the Augustan period. We know enough about Cicero to be confident that the *Invective* against him is a tissue of lies, and the same may well be true of that against Sallust also. If Sallust intended the subordinate role attributed to Cicero as an attack on him, it was hardly very vehement. How acrimonious political attacks could be at the period when Sallust was writing is best demonstrated by Cicero's *Philippics*, the speeches he composed against Antony in the short period between Caesar's assassination and his own murder twenty months later. Very little has survived from Antony's speeches and writings in reaction to the *Philippics*, but Cassius Dio, writing more than 250 years later, gives a very extensive version in Greek of an attack on Cicero by Quintus Fufius Calenus, whom Caesar had appointed consul in 47, and who became one of Antony's staunchest supporters. Calenus's speech (Cassius Dio, *History of Rome* 46.1ff.) is an extraordinary outburst, a concatenation of personal vituperation, the more surprising to modern sensibilities because it was delivered in the Senate, and Dio goes on to report (46.29) that Cicero, who always said exactly what he thought but did not like being the target of candid criticism, wasted the whole day in exchanging such abuse. Calenus diminishes Cicero's achievement in securing the verdict against Verres by alleging that he was so frightened when he was speaking that he lost control of his bladder (and he combines this insult with an utterly gratuitous innuendo that Cicero's father was a lowly and menial laundryman—urine was used to launder clothes); he criticizes Cicero for divorcing his wife so that he could marry a rich young girl, while he was carrying on an affair with an older woman; he even claims that Cicero hired his wife out as a prostitute, and that he had an incestuous relationship with his daughter. Perhaps worst of all, Calenus singles out Cicero's consulship for particular condemnation.

In comparison to this sweeping tirade, Sallust's treatment of Cicero's role in the Catilinarian conspiracy seems very mild. It is probably best to disregard political or personal animus as a significant motive in the composition of the *Catiline*. Cicero is not, in fact, the only figure whose role is perhaps somewhat surprising. Although Sallust was a supporter of Caesar, and although Caesar's speech is so prominent in the monograph, it does not seem that Sallust has used his account to affirm Caesar's innocence of any involvement with Catiline—a nebulous suspicion that Caesar himself never quite shook off and that Sallust hints at earlier in the monograph; it is probably Cato, the senatorial representative of traditional Roman virtues, who emerges best from the affair. This fair and balanced treatment would no doubt have been more obvious if we still had access to the aggressive political pamphlets written for and against the younger Cato by Cicero and Caesar, respectively, soon after his suicide in 46. In much the same way, there is a degree of balance and fairness in the *Jugurtha* that might not have been expected of a historian motivated by a desire to promote the views of the Caesarian faction; had that been so, Marius, as Caesar's uncle by marriage, would have been glorified and Sulla would have been correspondingly vilified.

One further aspect of the relationship between Sallust and Cicero may be worth mentioning. Not long before he died, Cicero divorced his first wife, Terentia, with whom he had had an increasingly stormy relationship, but who had stood by him through so many years of personal and public crisis. She lived on until A.D. 4, dying at the age of 103. She was said by St. Jerome (*Against Jovinian* 1.48) to have subsequently married not only Sallust but also Marcus Valerius Messalla Corvinus, one Augustus's most successful military commanders and an important patron of literature, a rival in this respect to Gaius Maecenas, whose wife was also a Terentia; it would have been uniquely valuable to have a record of these two great women's views of the latter half of the first century B.C.

Most Roman history was written by the annalistic method, that is, events were arranged and discussed chronologically, on a year-by-year basis; see p. 291. Sallust's *Catiline* and *Jugurtha* depart from this structure, taking the form of a monograph, with much less regard for chronological ordering and the systematic discussion of all major events in any given year. He emphasizes this departure at the start of the *Catiline*: "I decided to return to the very study from which my failed ambition had diverted me at the beginning: to write out the history of the Roman people, *selecting the parts that seemed worthy of memory*" (4.2). More space is consequently devoted to other themes that are not so bound by chronology; in Sallust's case, such topics as his diatribes on decadence and his characterization of individuals.

The monograph form was adopted in Rome from Greek models by Coelius Antipater in the late second century A.D. for his account of the Second Punic War, now almost entirely lost. Biography was a specialized version of the monograph and can be difficult to distinguish from broader historical monographs. In a notorious letter to the historian Lucius Lucceius (*Letters to His Friends* 5.12), Cicero takes it for granted that the monograph on the Catilinarian conspiracy that he is trying to persuade him to write will be focused on him, even, he playfully but pathetically urges, at the expense of the truth. On the other hand, Tacitus's *Agricola,* though it actually is a biography, being an account of the life and achievements of his father-in-law, Gnaeus Julius Agricola, nevertheless also manages to give a forceful and vivid portrayal of public life in general under a tyrannical regime.

The *Catiline* is not a biography, the *Jugurtha* even less so. In large sections of the works to which they give their name, Catiline and Jugurtha are not even mentioned. Catiline is not so much the subject of the monograph as a representative of the type of selfish and unscrupulous person who might hope to succeed in the vicious and corrupt political climate from which Rome suffered in the aftermath of Sulla's bloody rule. Sallust's real subject, moral decline, is also to some extent a departure from the norms of historiography. Just as history was conventionally considered the grandest subject for prose writing, so it was generally members of the ruling aristocracy who wrote it. Such writers were unlikely to criticize the decadence of the rich and powerful in the way that Sallust does. As an outsider who felt himself roughly handled by the Roman political system, he must have regarded the criticisms he makes in his writings as being at least some consolation for his "failed ambition."

## THE CONSPIRACY OF CATILINE

*In a brief preface (1–4), Sallust offers a justification for writing history, while explaining his choice of this particular topic.*

[1] All human beings who want to be superior to the other animals ought to struggle with every resource not to be like cattle passing silently through life. It is natural for the cattle to hang their heads and obey their stomachs, but all our strength is situated in our mind as well as our body: we use the mind more for control, the body for servitude; the one we have in common with the gods, the other with the beasts. And so I think it more upright to seek glory with our inner resources than with our physical strength and, since life is itself brief, to make the memory of our lives as long as possible. I say this because the glory of wealth and physical beauty is fluid and fragile; but virtue is held brilliant and eternal.

For a long time, however, there was a dispute among mortals as to whether physical force or mental excellence was most responsible for success in military affairs. The reason: you require both a plan before you begin and timely action when you have made a plan. Thus, each element, insufficient in itself, needs the help of the other. [2] And so it was that at the beginning kings—this being the first name for political command on earth—pursued their goals in different ways, some using their intellect, others using physical resources. Besides, at that time humans passed their lives without being covetous; each person was happy enough with what he had. But afterwards, when Cyrus in Asia and the Lacedaemonians and Athenians in Greece began to subjugate cities and nations, when craving for domination began to be considered a justification for war, and the greatest glory was held to consist in the greatest military command, then, finally, it was discovered through danger and trouble that in war the intellect had the most potent power.

But if the mental excellence of kings and commanders were valued as much in peacetime as it is in war, there would be more justice and stability in human affairs; you would not see everything either moving helter-skelter nor changing and confused. For political command is easily retained by the same means that created it in the first place. But when sloth supplants hard work, and in place of restraint and equity lust and pride march in, then fortune changes along with character.

Consequently, command is always being transferred to the best individuals from the less good.

All that men accomplish in farming, sailing, and building is obedient to the law of virtue. But many mortals are devoted to their bellies and to sleep; without learning and without culture they pass through life like tourists. Their bodies are for pleasure, their soul a burden, and I say that is contrary to nature. I consider their life and their death equally meaningless, since no one has anything to say about either. But what is more, that man alone seems to me to live and enjoy the breath of life who is focused on some undertaking and seeks fame for an illustrious deed or for good character.

Still, there is a great diversity in the world, and nature shows different people different paths.

[3] It is a beautiful thing to serve the Republic with good deeds; but to speak well is also not without importance. One can achieve brilliance either in peacetime or in war. And many win the praise of others, both those who act and those who write up their actions. As for me, although the glory that comes to the writer is not equal to the glory that comes to the author of deeds, still it seems especially difficult to write history: First of all, deeds must find an equivalence in words. Then, there are readers: many will think that what you castigate as offences are mentioned because of hatred and envy; but, when you speak of the great virtue and glory of good men, what each one thinks is easy for himself to do, he accepts with equanimity; what goes beyond that he construes like fictions made up for lies.

But in my own case, as a young man I was at first attracted like many others to politics, and in politics I was thwarted by many obstacles. In place of shame, self-restraint, and virtue, arrogance thrived and graft and greed. My mind, unaccustomed to wicked ways, rejected these things. But I was young and did not know how to resist. Caught in the midst of such corruption, I too was seized and corrupted by ambition. I rejected the wicked character of others, but nevertheless was troubled by the same craving for honor, and I fell victim to the same reputation and invidious attacks as the others.

[4] Consequently, when my mind found peace after a multitude of miseries and dangers, I decided to pass what remained of my life far from the public world. But, it was not my plan to waste the benefits of leisure in idleness and indolence, nor to pass my time engaged in the slavish occupations of farming or hunting. Rather, I decided to return to the very study from which my

failed ambition had diverted me at the beginning: to write out the history of the Roman people, selecting the parts that seemed worthy of memory. I was encouraged all the more to do this because my mind was free from political hopes, fears, and partisanship. I will, therefore, give an account of Catiline's conspiracy in a few words and as accurately as I can. I consider this event especially memorable because of the unprecedented nature of the crime and the danger it caused. But, first, before I begin my narrative, a few things must be said about that man's character.

*Before beginning the narrative proper, Sallust provides a brief but memorable portrait of Catiline (5). This does not lead immediately into the story, however, but is followed by a digression (6–13) on the history of Rome and its moral decline.*

[5] L. Catiline was born in an aristocratic family. He was a man of great strength, both mental and physical, but his nature was wicked and perverse. From early adulthood on, he took pleasure in civil wars, murders, plunder, and political discord, and this was where he exercised his youth. His body could endure hunger, cold, sleep deprivation beyond what one would believe; his mind was arrogant, clever, unstable. He could pretend or dissemble whatever he liked. He coveted others' property but was profligate with his own; he burned with passionate desires. He had some eloquence, but little wisdom. His mind was vast, always longing for the extravagant, the unbelievable, the things beyond his reach. After the "Domination of Sulla" he was overcome by an extraordinarily powerful desire to seize control of the state. He did not care at all about how he attained his goal as long as he got a "realm" for himself. Daily he grew more agitated. His family's poverty and his own guilty conscience made his spirit violent, and both of these problems were exacerbated by the practices I have mentioned above. He was further encouraged by the corrupt moral character of the state, which was depraved because of two destructive and internally contradictory evils, extravagance and greed.

Since there has been an occasion to call to mind the moral character of the state, my subject seems of itself to suggest that I should go further back in time and briefly discuss the institutions of our ancestors, both at home and in the military, and to set forth how they governed the Republic, how great a state they left us,

and how it gradually changed from the most lovely and best and became the worst and most depraved.

[6] The city of Rome, as I understand it, was founded and controlled at first by Trojans. They had no fixed home and were wandering about with Aeneas as their leader. They founded the city together with the Aborigines, a wild race of men, without law, without political institutions, free and unrestrained. These peoples, though they were of different races, dissimilar languages, living each in a different way, after they came together within a single city's walls, it is incredible to relate how easily they coalesced: in so short a time did a disparate and wandering crowd because of internal harmony become a state. But after their community increased in citizens, morality, and territory and began to seem quite wealthy and quite powerful, envy was born from their prosperity, as is usually the case among mortals. Therefore, neighboring kings and peoples began to test them in war. Of their friends, only a few came to their aid, the rest were shaken by fear and avoided danger. But the Romans kept their focus at home and in the field: they hurried about, made preparations, urged each other on, went to meet the enemy, and with their weapons protected their freedom, their fatherland, and their parents. Afterwards, when courageous virtue had driven off danger, they brought aid to their allies and friends; they established alliances more by conferring kindnesses than by receiving them. Their political power was based on law; its name was monarchy. Men were chosen to give advice to the state, men whose bodies were weak with age, but whose minds were strong in wisdom. These men were called "Fathers," either because of their age or from the similarity of their care. At first this regal power served to preserve freedom and to increase the commonwealth; but, after it turned into arrogance and domination, the Romans changed their custom and created for themselves annual offices and two executive officers: they thought that restricting political license in this way would prevent men's minds from becoming arrogant.

[7] But that was the time when individuals began to elevate themselves and to display their native ability more readily. The reason is that kings are always more suspicious of good men than wicked men and they fear the virtue they do not have. But once liberty was attained, it is incredible to recount how great the state became in a short time. So strong was the desire for glory that came over them. Now for the first time the young men, as soon as they could endure battle,

entered camps and began to learn the hard work of a military life; they had passionate desires, but those desires were for splendid armor and warhorses, not for prostitutes and parties. And so for men like this no hard labor was unfamiliar, no place was harsh or difficult, no armed enemy brought fear: their manly virtue had dominated everything. But competitions for glory were among them the toughest competitions. Each man was in a hurry to strike the enemy, to climb a wall, to be noticed doing such deeds. They thought that this was true wealth; this meant a good reputation and great nobility. They were greedy for praise, but with money they were generous: they wanted glory that was huge, wealth that was honorable. I could mention the places where the Roman people with a small band routed the enemy's greatest armies, the cities fortified by nature that they seized, were this not to take us too far from our project.

[8] Still, it is my experience that Fortune governs everything; she exalts and obscures according to her pleasure, not according to the truth. Athenian history, in my estimation, was quite grand and magnificent, but still it was a little less grand than people say. It is because writers of great talent flourished there that the deeds of the Athenians are celebrated as if they were the greatest. And so, the virtue of those who acted is held to be as great as has been the ability of brilliant talents to glorify it in words. The Roman people, on the other hand, never had those resources, because their most thoughtful men were most engaged in public business. No one used their intellectual talents independently of their body, and the best men preferred action to words. They preferred that their activities be praised by others rather than that they themselves tell another's story.

[9] And so at home and in the military good moral character was cultivated; maximum harmony, avarice was minimal. Justice and goodness were strong among those men not because of the law more than because of their nature. They engaged in quarrels, disputes, competition with the enemy, but among citizens the contest was over manly virtue. In their offerings to the gods, they were lavish; at home they were sparing; with friends they were trustworthy. They cared for the constitution and themselves in two ways: they were fearless in war, and, when peace arrived, they were fair. I take the following as the greatest proof of what I say: first, in war disciplinary action was more often taken against those who attacked the enemy without orders and against those who withdrew too slowly when recalled

from the battle than against those who abandoned the standards or dared to give ground when beaten back; second, in peacetime they exercised political power more often with kindness than with fear and, when they received an injury, they preferred forgiveness to prosecution.

[10] But, when hard work and just action had increased the Republic, when great kings were defeated in war, uncivilized nations and vast peoples subdued by force, when Carthage, the rival to Roman power, had been eradicated, when all the sea and all the lands were accessible, Fortune began to grow cruel and confuse everything. Men who had easily endured hard work, dangers, uncertainty and adversity found that leisure and wealth, things desirable at other times, were a burden and the cause of misery. And so, at first, greed for money grew, then greed for power. These things were the root, so to speak, of all evils. For avarice undermined trust, goodness, and other noble qualities, and in their place taught pride and cruelty, taught men to neglect the gods and to put a price on everything. Ambition forced many men to become liars, to hide one thing in their heart and have something else ready on their tongue, to value friendship and enmity according to convenience, not substance, and to put up a good face rather than have a good heart. At first, these things grew gradually, they were punished occasionally; afterwards, when this contagion invaded like a plague, the state changed, and political power which had been most just and best became cruel and intolerable.

[11] At first, however, more than avarice it was ambition that worked the souls of men, which, although a vice, is nearer a virtue. For both the good man and the worthless man desire for themselves glory, honor, power. But the former labors on the true path, while the latter, having no honorable abilities, competes using treachery and deception. Avarice entails a zeal for money, which no wise man covets; it is dripping, so to speak, with dangerous poisons and makes the manly body and soul effeminate; it is boundless and insatiable, and is not diminished by wealth or poverty. But after Lucius Sulla took control of the Republic and from good beginnings created a disastrous outcome, everyone began to steal and rob. One man wanted a house, another fields; they did disgusting and cruel things to their fellow citizens. In addition to this, Sulla had let his army, the one he had led in Asia, live contrary to the custom of our ancestors in luxury and excessive license. He did this to make them faithful to

his cause. The charming and voluptuous locales easily softened the ferocious spirits of the soldiers when there was no work to do. There for the first time the army of the Roman people grew accustomed to making love, drinking, admiring statues, painted tables, and embossed vases, stealing public and private possessions, plundering temples, polluting all things sacred and profane. And so those soldiers, after they attained victory, left nothing for the defeated. Success, to be sure, can try the souls of wise men; those of corrupt character were much less able to temper their victory.

[12] After wealth began to be considered an honor, and after glory, political authority, and power followed in its wake, manly virtue began to lose its luster, poverty was considered a disgrace, innocence was taken for malevolence. And so, as a result of our wealth, extravagance and greed with arrogance assaulted our youth: they raped and devoured; they considered their own possessions worthless and desired the possessions of others; decency and chastity, things human and divine alike, they held nothing of value or moderation. When you consider our homes and villas built to the size of cities, it is worthwhile to visit the temples of the gods which our ancestors made. They were very devout men. But they adorned shrines to the gods with their piety, their own homes with glory, and they did not steal from the vanquished anything beyond their freedom to do harm. But today's men, the most worthless of human beings, do the opposite; in the most criminal way they take from our allies everything which the bravest men had left when they were victorious: it is as if the ability to do injustice is what magisterial power really means.

[13] Why should I bother to mention things which no one can believe except those who have seen them: mountains dug up by private men, seas paved over? To these men wealth seems to be a toy: what they could have used honorably, they were quick to abuse shamefully. But that is not all: other excesses advanced as well, a passion for promiscuous sex, for gluttony. Men accepted the woman's role, women put their chastity up for sale, all the land and sea was scoured for the sake of feeding; they slept before the body wanted sleep; without waiting for hunger or thirst, for cold or weariness, they self-indulgently anticipated all these things. These desires incited the young men to criminal actions when the family wealth was gone. A soul imbued with wicked tendencies does not easily do without what it craves. And so they became in every way all the more inordinately addicted to acquisition and expenditure.

*Sallust now begins the narrative of the conspiracy with a description of the associates whom Catiline gathered (14–16) and their first meeting in June 64 B.C. (17), but this line of narrative is then interrupted by a digression on his first attempted conspiracy (18–19). When the conspirators' meeting resumes (20–22), Sallust inserts his version of Catiline's speech on that occasion (20).*

[14] In such a great and corrupt city, Catiline gathered around him, like a bodyguard, crowds of vices and crimes; it was most easy to do. His companions and friends were those who had wrecked their patrimony with their hand, stomach, penis; any who had enkindled an enormous personal debt in order to purchase immunity from his perversions and crimes; in addition, all murderers and infidels anywhere, convicted in court or fearing prosecution for their deeds; furthermore, those who lived by hand and tongue off perjury and the blood of citizens; and, finally, all who were stirred by perversity, poverty, and guilty conscience. If anyone still innocent of guilt fell into friendship with him, daily experience and temptations easily rendered that man equal and similar to the rest. But Catiline especially sought out intimacy with young men: their minds were still malleable and pliable and easily snared by his treachery. As each man's passion burned in accordance with his age, so Catiline responded: to some he offered whores, for others he purchased dogs and horses; in short, he spared neither expense nor his own modesty, provided he could make them dependent on him and faithful to him. I know that there were some people who concluded that the young men who frequented Catiline's home did not handle their chastity very honorably, but people said this more for other reasons than because there was any evidence of it.

[15] Already as a young man Catiline had engaged in much unspeakable debauchery with a virgin from a good family, with a Vestal priestess, and other things of this type which are contrary to divine and natural law. Finally, he fell in love with Aurelia Orestilla. No good man praised anything about her except her figure. She hesitated to marry Catiline, fearing a full-grown stepson. Because of this it is believed to be certain that Catiline made his home ready for his criminal nuptials by killing his son. In fact, this event seems to me to have been the primary reason that he hastened his conspiracy. For his soul, stained with guilt and hated by gods

and men, could not find peace either in waking or in sleeping. Thus, his conscience irritated and devastated his mind. And so his face was pallid, his eyes bloody, his gait now quick, now slow; in short, there was madness in his face and features.

[16] The young men whom—as we said above—he had lured, learned from him many wicked types of criminal behavior. From them he supplied false witnesses and signatories; their credit, wealth, trials were considered insignificant. After he had destroyed their reputation and their moral sense, he made other greater demands. If the present circumstances did not provide any reason for crime, he nevertheless asked them to trap and slaughter the innocent as well as the guilty. One assumes he preferred to be gratuitously wicked and cruel lest their hands or hearts grow listless through inactivity. These were the friends and allies Catiline trusted. Furthermore, debt was rampant throughout the whole world, and most of Sulla's soldiers, having squandered their own property, were thinking about plunder and their former victories and hoping for civil war. And so Catiline formed a plan for overthrowing the government. In Italy there was no army; Gnaeus Pompey was waging war at the ends of the earth. Catiline himself was seeking the consulship and had great hopes. The Senate, clearly, had no pressing business: everything was safe and peaceful. But this was exactly what suited Catiline.

[17] Therefore, about 1 June, when L. Caesar and C. Figulus were consuls, he first summoned certain individuals; he encouraged some, others he sounded out, he pointed to his own resources, the state's lack of preparation, and the great rewards of a conspiracy. When he had gathered the information that he wanted, he called together everyone who suffered from extraordinary need or possessed unusual daring. The senators he convened were: P. Lentulus Sura, P. Autronius, L. Cassius Longinus, C. Cethegus, P. and Ser. Sulla, sons of Servius, L. Vargunteius, Q. Annius, M. Porcius Laeca, L. Bestia, and Q. Curius; and from the equestrian order: M. Fulvius Nobilior, L. Statilius, P. Gabinius Capito, and C. Cornelius; in addition there were many from the colonies and townships who were aristocrats at home. There were also many aristocrats who participated more secretly in his plan; they were encouraged more by hope of power than by poverty or any necessity. But in general it was the young men who favored Catiline's goals, especially the aristocratic youth: they had the resources to live at ease either lavishly or elegantly, but they preferred uncertainty to certainty, war over peace. At the time, there were also those who believed that M. Licinius Crassus was not unaware of Catiline's plans: that, because his enemy Pompey was in charge of a great army, he was willing to let anyone's resources increase in opposition to Pompey's power; and that he firmly believed he would easily become the leader among the conspirators if the conspiracy succeeded.

[18] Earlier, however, a few men likewise conspired against the state and Catiline was among them. I will speak as accurately as I can about this. When L. Tullus and M'. Lepidus were consuls, P. Autronius and P. Sulla, the consuls elect, were arraigned under bribery laws and fined. A little later, Catiline was prevented from seeking the consulship because he was a defendant on charges of extortion and was not able to submit his petition before the legal deadline. At the same time, there was a young aristocrat, Cn. Piso, full of daring, lacking resources, interested in violence, who was moved by poverty and wicked character to attack the government. Piso shared his plan with Catiline and Autronius, who joined him around 5 December. They were prepared to kill the consuls, L. Cotta and L. Torquatus, on the Capitoline Hill on 1 January, to seize the fasces, and to send Piso with an army to take possession of the two Spanish provinces. The plot was discovered and they postponed their murderous plan to 5 February. This time they were plotting the death not only of the consuls but of many senators. And on that day, if Catiline standing in front of the Senate house had not given his allies the signal too soon, the most wicked act since the founding of Rome would have been accomplished. Because armed men had not yet fully assembled, the plan fell apart.

[19] Afterwards, Piso was sent to Nearer Spain as a quaestor with praetorian powers. Crassus helped in this because he knew that Piso was a bitter enemy of Pompey. Nor was the Senate unwilling to give him the province: this was because they wanted this repugnant man as far from the state as possible, and at the same time because many good men were thinking he could provide some protection: even then Pompey's power was a source of fear. But this Piso, as he was marching through the province, was killed by the Spanish cavalry under his command. There are some who claim that the barbarians were unable to endure his unjust, haughty, and cruel exercise of power; others, however, say that those horsemen, old and faithful clients of Pompey,

attacked Piso on Pompey's orders; further, they point out that the Spaniards had never before perpetrated any such crime, but had endured many savage acts of power. We will leave this matter undecided. Enough has been said about the earlier conspiracy.

[20] When Catiline saw gathered together the men I have just mentioned, although he had often discussed many things with them as individuals, still he believed it was important to address them as a group and encourage them. He withdrew to an inner room of the house and there, with all witnesses far removed, he delivered a speech like this:

'If your manly virtue and loyalty were not already known to me, this opportunity would have arrived in vain; our high hopes and political dominance would be frustrated while within our reach. Nor would I rely upon men of weak and fickle character and grasp at uncertainties instead of what is certain. But because I have found you to be brave and faithful to me in many difficult circumstances, therefore my heart dares to attempt a very great and beautiful action, also because I understand that you and I agree about what is good and bad. Indeed, this is unshakable friendship: to want and to reject the same things.

'You have all already heard individually what I have been considering. But, daily my heart grows more passionate as I think about the terms of our future life, if we do not lay claim to freedom. For after the Republic handed over justice and authority to a powerful few, it is to these men that kings and rulers always bring tribute, to them peoples and nations pay taxes. All the rest of us, hard-working good men, aristocrats and plebeians, we are a common crowd, without favor and without prestige. We are dependent upon those who would be afraid of us if the Republic meant anything. And so all influence, power, honor, and wealth lie in their hands or where they want it; we are left with dangers, electoral defeats, litigation, and poverty. How much longer are we still going to put up with this, I ask you, O bravest men? Isn't it better to die with manly courage than to live wretched and dishonored, the playthings of other men's arrogance, and, then, with disgrace to lose our lives?

'But in fact, and I swear by the faith of gods and men, victory really is in our hands. We are young and vigorous, our spirit is valiant; they, on the other hand, are utterly decrepit, the result of money and years. All we need do is start, the outcome will take care of itself. Indeed, what mortal with a manly heart can endure it!

They squander their superior wealth in building upon the seas and leveling the mountains, while we don't even have family possessions sufficient for the necessities. While they connect one home to another or more, we have no place for our family shrine. They buy paintings, statues, reliefs; they destroy what they just bought and build something else; they plunder and waste their money any way they can; still, their extreme desires cannot overcome their wealth. But for us there is poverty at home, debts everywhere; our circumstances are bad, our hopes are worse. What do we have left but our miserable breath?

'So, why don't you wake up? The things you have often hoped for, liberty, and then wealth, honor, and glory are right before your eyes. All these Fortune has made the prizes of victory. The circumstances, the time, the dangers, poverty, the magnificent spoils of war, these offer more encouragement than my words. Use me as your general or as a foot soldier; I will aid you with mind and body. When I am your consul, this is what I hope to help you accomplish—unless my mind is deceived and you are more ready to be slaves than to be rulers.'

[21] The men who listened to Catiline were rich in troubles but had neither resources nor any good hope. Although they thought that the disruption of the status quo was a great reward in itself, still, after they had listened, they demanded that he lay out the terms of the war, what rewards their weapons would be seeking, what resources or hope they could have and where. Then Catiline promised clean slates, proscription of the wealthy, priesthoods, plunder, everything else that war and the caprice of victors can offer. Furthermore, he said that Piso was in Nearer Spain, P. Sittius Nucerinus was with an army in Mauretania, and they were aware of his plans; that C. Antonius, a family friend broken by poverty, was seeking the consulship and he expected him to be his colleague; and that he as consul would set things in motion with Antonius. In addition, he attacked and maligned all good citizens, he named and praised individually his followers, reminding one of his poverty, another of his desires, most of their danger and ignominy, and many of Sulla's victory, which had brought them booty. After he saw that their hearts were eager, he urged them to take care of his election, and he dismissed the gathering.

[22] There were at that time some who said that after his speech, when he wanted to bind those privy to his crime with an oath, he passed around a bowl

that had in it human blood mixed with wine, that then, when all had tasted the blood and sworn a solemn oath, just as is the custom in holy rites, he disclosed his plan, and that he did this to create a common bond that would make them more faithful to each other, each one being conscious of the other's guilt. Some were of the opinion that these and many other things were invented by men who thought that, if they exaggerated the atrocity of the crimes of those whom Cicero punished, they could mitigate the hatred that later rose up against him. Considering its importance, we have too little information.

*The narrative now moves rapidly, covering events in the remainder of the year 64 B.C., including the election of Cicero as consul over Catiline (23–24), the defeat of Catiline in the elections of the following year, and the activities of Manlius and other conspirators in Etruria and in Rome (26–33). This section includes a memorable characterization (25) of Sempronia, the accomplished wife of Decimus Brutus.*

[23] Now one of the members of the conspiracy was Q. Curius. He was not born in obscurity, but he was shrouded in shame and crimes, a man whom the censors had removed from the Senate for his disgraceful actions. This man was as fickle as he was reckless; he did not keep silent about what he heard or conceal his own crimes; he did not care a whit about what he said or what he did. Fulvia, an aristocratic woman, had been his partner in promiscuity for some time, but he was no longer in her favor, because his limited resources had made him less generous. Suddenly he began to swagger and promise oceans and mountains, and to threaten her occasionally with his sword if she did not yield to him. Ultimately, he became much more ferocious than had been his custom. But when Fulvia discovered the cause of Curius' abusiveness, she did not keep secret such a danger to the Republic. Hiding the name of her informant, she told many the details she had heard about Catiline's conspiracy. It was this event that made men particularly eager to entrust the consulship to Cicero. In fact, before this the aristocracy was in general seething with jealousy; they thought that the consulship was polluted if a "new man," regardless of how outstanding, should attain it. But when danger was at hand, jealousy and pride took second place.

[24] Consequently, when the elections were held, M. Tullius and C. Antonius were declared consuls. At first this event shook the confidence of the members of the conspiracy. And yet Catiline's madness did not diminish; rather he grew more agitated daily: arms were placed throughout Italy in strategic places, money was borrowed in his own name or that of his friends and was taken to Faesulae to a certain Manlius, who afterwards was the first to begin fighting. It is said that he enlisted on his side at that time many men of every class, and even some women. These were women who covered their enormous expenses by selling their bodies; afterwards, when age limited their income but not their extravagant desires, they contracted huge debts. Through them Catiline believed that he could bring the urban slaves to his side, set fire to the city, and either get their husbands to join his cause or get them killed.

[25] Now among these women was Sempronia, a woman who had committed many crimes with the arrogance of a man. She was fortunate enough in her birth and her figure, also in her husband and children, learned in Greek and Latin literature, lyre-playing and dancing more pleasingly than a proper woman should. She knew many other things that were the accoutrements of luxury, but there was nothing she liked less than propriety and restraint. You could not tell whether she cared less about her money or her reputation. Her sexual appetite was such that she more often took the initiative with men than they with her. Before this conspiracy, she had often betrayed faith, defaulted on loans, been accessory to murder. Her expenses and her lack of resources headed her toward disaster. Nevertheless, her abilities were not despicable: she could write verses, make a joke, converse modestly, or tenderly, or raucously; she possessed many pleasant characteristics and much charm.

[26] Although Catiline had made his preparations, he still sought the consulship for the following year. He was hoping that, if he was consul designate, he could use Antonius as he wished. In the meantime he was not idle, but laid traps for Cicero in every way possible. But, Cicero had sufficient guile and cunning to avoid them. At the beginning of his consulship, he made many promises through Fulvia to Q. Curius, whom I mentioned above, and got him to betray Catiline's plans to him. In addition, he reached an agreement about provinces with his colleague Antonius and so prevailed upon him not to oppose the Republic. Secretly, he kept around himself a bodyguard of friends and clients. The election day came. Catiline succeeded neither in his campaign nor in the plots that he had laid for the

consuls in the Campus Martius. Then, since his covert attempts had resulted in exasperation and disgrace, he decided to make war and to let nothing stand in his way.

[27] Therefore he sent C. Manlius to Faesulae and the adjacent parts of Etruria, a certain Septimius of Camerinum to the Picene district, C. Julius to Apulia, and others elsewhere, wherever he thought they would be useful to him. Meanwhile in Rome he was working on many things at the same time: he set traps for the consuls, planned arson, posted armed men in strategic places; he himself was armed and ordered others to do likewise, he urged them to be always alert and ready; he had hurried about day and night, he did not rest, and did not weary of sleeplessness or toil. Finally, when his many activities produced no result, he called on M. Porcius Laeca to convene again the leaders of the conspiracy in the dead of night. And there, after he had complained at length about their ineffectiveness, he told them that he had readied a body of men to take up arms and had already sent Manlius ahead to join them, that he had sent others to various strategic places to begin the fighting; and that he himself was eager to get to his army, if he could first do away with Cicero: that man, he said, was a significant obstacle to his plans.

[28] And so, although the others were terrified and hesitant, C. Cornelius, a Roman knight, promised his help. L. Vargunteius, a senator, agreed to go with him. They would go to Cicero's house a little later that night as if to make a ceremonial visit; they would take with them armed men and without warning they would stab him unprepared in his own house. When Curius heard the extent of the danger that hung over the consul, he quickly told Cicero through Fulvia of the treachery that was under way. And so those men were turned away from the door and the great crime they had undertaken was frustrated.

Meanwhile in Etruria Manlius was stirring up a populace that was eager for revolution because of their poverty and the pain of injustice: during the domination of Sulla they had lost all their fields and property. Furthermore, Manlius solicited robbers of any kind. There were a great number in that region; some came from Sulla's colonists, men who had nothing left from all their plunder because of their appetite and extravagance.

[29] When these events were reported to Cicero, he was deeply disturbed by the twofold danger: he was no longer able through private efforts to protect the city from these plots, and he did not have clear information about the size of Manlius' army or his intentions.

He brought the matter, already the subject of excited rumors among the people, before the Senate. And so the Senate passed a decree, the one which is customary in times of deadly peril: Let the consuls prevent any damage to the Republic. This is the greatest power which the Senate by Roman custom grants to a magistrate: power to raise an army, wage war, coerce allies and citizens in any way necessary, to exercise complete authority and jurisdiction at home and in the military. Otherwise, without an order of the people, the consul has no right to any of these actions.

[30] After a few days, L. Saenius, a senator, read in the Senate a letter which he said had been brought to him from Faesulae. The letter said that C. Manlius had taken up arms with a large number of men on 27 October. At the same time, some men announced portents and prodigies—a common occurrence at such times—others told of meetings, the movement of arms, slave insurrections in Capua and Apulia. Consequently, Q. Marcius Rex was sent to Faesulae by senatorial decree, Q. Metellus Creticus to Apulia and neighboring places—both of these men were in command of armies outside the city walls where they had been prevented from celebrating triumphs by the malice of a few men who habitually put everything up for sale whether honorable or dishonorable. The praetors, Q. Pompeius Rufus and Q. Metellus Celer, were sent to Capua and the Picene district respectively, and they were given authority to raise an army according to the circumstances and the danger. In addition to this, a reward was decreed, if anyone had any information about the conspiracy against the state: for a slave, freedom and a hundred sestertii; for a free man, impunity and two hundred sestertii. They also decreed that gladiatorial troops should be distributed throughout Capua and other towns in accordance with the resources of each place; at Rome, watches were to be posted throughout the city and the minor magistrates were to be in charge of them.

[31] These events terrified the citizens and changed the appearance of the city. In place of the great joy and abandon which years of peace had produced, suddenly gloom overcame all. People hurried, trembled, trusted little in any place or person; they were neither waging war nor enjoying peace; each measured the danger in accordance with his own anxiety. In addition, fear of war, unfamiliar to the women because of the greatness of the Republic, overwhelmed them: they beat their breasts, raised their hands to the heavens

in supplication, wailed over their little children; they questioned everything, trembled at every rumor, grabbed everything they could, and setting aside pride and pleasure they despaired of themselves and their country.

Defenses were readied against Catiline. He was arraigned by L. Paullus under the Plautian law. But his cruel spirit was not moved to change his plans. Finally, he came into the Senate, either to dissemble his intentions or to clear his name as if he had been challenged in some private quarrel. At that time M. Tullius the consul, either because he was afraid of Catiline's presence or because he was carried away by anger, delivered a speech that was brilliant and useful to the Republic, a speech which he later wrote down and published. But when he sat down, Catiline, who was prepared to dissemble everything, began to speak with downcast eyes and suppliant voice. He asked the senators not to form any hasty opinions about him: he was born into a very great family and had lived since adolescence in such a way that he had nothing but good prospects. He was a patrician, he said; he himself and his ancestors had performed a great many services for the Roman plebs. They should not think that he needed to destroy the Republic, when M. Tullius, a rental resident citizen of the city of Rome, said he was going to save it. When he tried to add other insults to this, everyone shouted him down; they called him an enemy and a parricide. Then he became enraged and said, "I'm trapped and I'm being pushed over the edge by my enemies: I'll extinguish my inferno with a general demolition."

[32] He then rushed from the Senate chamber and went home. There he thought over many things: his plots against the consul were not making progress and the city was protected from arson by watchmen. He concluded that the best thing to do was to increase his army and to gather many provisions for war before Roman legions could be enlisted, and so he set off with a few men in the dead of night to Manlius' camp. But first, he gave orders to Cethegus and Lentulus and others whose recklessness he knew was prepared for action. He told them to strengthen the resources of their faction in whatever way they could, to implement the plots against the consul, to arrange for slaughter, arson, and other acts of war; as for himself, he said that he would soon be at the city's gates with a large army. While this was going on in Rome, C. Manlius sent some of his men as legates to Marcius Rex with the following request:

[33] "General, we call upon men and gods as our witnesses: we have not taken up arms against our country and we intend no danger to others. Instead, our purpose is to keep our own bodies free from harm. We are humiliated, impoverished by the violence and cruelty of the moneylenders; most of us have lost our fatherland, but all have lost fame and fortune. None of us has been allowed to enjoy legal protections according to ancestral custom, none has retained his personal freedom once he lost his patrimony: such has been the savage indifference of the moneylenders and the urban praetor. Often your ancestors pitied the common people of Rome, and by their decrees made resources available to the resourceless. Most recently, within our own lifetime, good respectable men were willing to let silver be paid in bronze because of the magnitude of the debt. Often the common people themselves, spurred on by the desire to dominate or by the arrogance of the magistrates, took up arms and seceded from the senatorial fathers. But it is not political power or wealth that we seek, things which are the cause of all wars and struggles among mortals; rather, it is freedom, which no respectable man gives up except with his life. We beg you and the Senate, think about the suffering of the citizens, restore the protection of law which the inequity of the praetor has stolen; and do not force us to ask how we can get the greatest vengeance from the loss of our blood."

*The government reacts to Catiline's activities, and a letter of Catiline to Quintus Catulus is read aloud in the Senate (34–35). This leads Sallust to a further digression on the corrupt state of Roman society (36–39), before he outlines the negotiations between Lentulus, acting on behalf of Catiline, with the Gallic tribe known as the Allobroges (39–41). Disturbances are reported in various regions of Italy and Gaul (42), and the conspirators plan to set fires in Rome and carry out executions (43). The Allobroges betray the plot to Cicero, and the conspirators remaining in the city are arrested and interrogated (44–48). Sallust relates the unsuccessful attempt to implicate Caesar in the conspiracy (49). Our selection resumes with the debate that followed in the Senate on what to do about the conspirators now in custody (50–54), including speeches by Caesar urging moderation (51) and Cato calling for more severe measures (52). The conspirators' execution follows (55).*

[50] While this was going on in the Senate, and they were deciding on rewards for the Allobrogian

ambassadors and for Volturcius, since their information had proved true, some of Lentulus' freedmen and a few of his clients were going to different places in the city urging the craftsmen and slaves to rescue him; others were looking for gang-leaders, men who were accustomed to torment the state for a price. Cethegus, however, sent messengers to his slaves and freedmen, men he had selected and trained; he begged them to be bold, to band together and with their weapons break through to him. The consul, when he heard of these plans, deployed armed guards as time and occasion required. He convened the Senate, and formally asked them what to do about the men held in custody. Just a short time earlier the entire Senate had judged that these men were traitors. D. Junius Silanus, the consul designate, was first asked his opinion about those held in custody, and also about L. Cassius, P. Furius, P. Umbrenus, and Quintus Annius, if they should be captured. He said that they must pay the penalty. Later he was moved by C. Caesar's speech and said he would support the proposal of Ti. Nero to hold a referendum after the number of guards had been increased. But when it came to Caesar's turn, he was asked his opinion by the consul and he spoke as follows:

[51] 'All human beings who debate on matters of uncertainty, conscript fathers, ought to be free from hatred, enmity, anger, and pity. The mind cannot easily see the truth when those emotions get in the way, and no one has ever been simultaneously governed by the demands of his desire and by practical considerations. Wherever you apply your intelligence, it prevails; but, if passion takes over, it becomes master and the mind is powerless. I can recount many examples, conscript fathers, of bad decisions made by kings and peoples under the influence of anger or pity. But I prefer to speak of decisions made correctly and orderly by our ancestors when they resisted their hearts' desires. In the Macedonian War which we waged with King Perses, the great and opulent state of Rhodes, which had benefited from Roman wealth, treacherously turned against us. But, after the war was over and we took up the matter of the Rhodians' actions, our ancestors let them go unpunished, lest anyone say that we had started the war more for money than from injury. Likewise in all the Punic Wars, though the Carthaginians had often committed many horrible crimes both in peace and under truces, our ancestors never reciprocated when they had the opportunity: they preferred to ask what was worthy of them, not what they could justifiably do. You,

likewise, must use the same prudential wisdom, conscript fathers. The crime of P. Lentulus and the others should not have more weight with you than your own dignity, and you should not consider your anger more important than your reputation. For, if the penalty can be found that their deeds deserve, I could approve of an unprecedented course. But, if the enormity of their crime exceeds our ingenuity, then I say we must use the penalties already established by law.

'Most of those who have given their opinions before me have lamented with great eloquence and grandeur the misfortunes of the Republic. They have listed the savage acts of war, the afflictions of the conquered: the rape of girls and boys; children torn from the arms of their parents; matrons yielding to whatever the conqueror desired; shrines and homes plundered; slaughter, arson; in short, everything filled with weapons, corpses, blood, and grief. But, by the immortal gods, what is the purpose of those speeches? Is it to make you oppose the conspiracy? Do you suppose that a speech will energize someone who is not moved by the enormity and cruelty of the facts? Not true: no mortal thinks his own injuries are small; for many they seem greater than is fair. But not everyone has the same freedom of action, conscript fathers. If the humble who have a life in obscurity become enraged and commit an offence, few know; their fame and their wealth are the same. But the actions of those who are endowed with great power and who live exalted lives are known by all mankind.

'And so, in the greatest good fortune there is the least licence; neither zealous partiality nor hatred is appropriate, but least of all rage. What is called anger in others, is named arrogance and cruelty in the powerful. And so this is my assessment, conscript fathers: no torture is equal to the crimes they have committed. But generally men remember the most recent events, and even in the case of execrable men, if the punishment is unusually severe, they forget the crimes and talk about the punishment.

'I am quite certain that D. Silanus, a brave and energetic man, said what he said with the state's interests in mind, and that in a matter of such importance he shows neither favor nor malice: I know his character and his composure. But it seems to me his proposal is not so much cruel—what could be cruel against such men?—as it is alien to our Republic. I am sure that either fear or injustice has forced you, Silanus, a consul designate, to propose an unprecedented punishment. As for fear, there is not much to say, especially since we have so many guards under arms thanks to the diligence of our consul, a most distinguished man. But concerning the penalty I can speak to the point: in times of grief and affliction death is not a torture but a release from misery. It puts an end to all mortal woes; and beyond that neither anxiety nor joy has any place. But why, in the name of the immortal gods, didn't you add to your proposal that they should first be whipped? Is it because the Porcian law forbids it? But there are other laws that similarly forbid taking the life of a condemned citizen; they allow exile. Or, is it because flogging is worse than death? But what punishment could be too harsh for men convicted of such a crime? On the other hand, if flogging is less severe than death, why fear the law that forbids the lesser punishment, when you neglect the law that forbids the harsher punishment?

'But, one might say, who will criticize any decree against the assassins of the Republic? I'll tell you: time, events, fortune, whose pleasure governs the world. Whatever happens to those men, they have earned it; but you, conscript fathers, think about the example you are setting for others. Every bad precedent arose from a good case. But when power slips into the hands of those who don't understand it or those less well intentioned, then that new precedent is no longer appropriately applied to those who deserve it but inappropriately to those who don't. The Lacedaemonians, after they conquered the Athenians, imposed the rule of thirty men. At first, they began to put to death without trial all the most wicked and those whom everyone hated. The populace was delighted and they said it was the right thing to do. Afterwards, as their licence to act gradually increased, they began to kill at will good and bad men alike; the rest they frightened and terrified. Thus, the citizen body was reduced to slavery and paid a heavy penalty for their foolish delight.

'In our own memory, when Sulla ordered the strangulation of Damasippus and others like him who flourished to the detriment of the state, who did not praise his actions? People were saying they deserved it, that he killed criminals and insurgents, men who had threatened the government with seditious revolt. But this action was the beginning of a great slaughter. For whenever someone coveted another man's home or villa, or eventually even his dishes or clothes, he would try to get the man proscribed. And soon after those who were delighted at the death of Damasippus were themselves being dragged away and there was no end of carnage until Sulla had glutted all his followers

with riches. Now, I don't fear these consequences from M. Tullius nor do I fear them at this time, but in a great city there are many different temperaments. It is possible that at some other time, when another man is consul and also has an army at his disposal, a lie will be taken for the truth. When this precedent allows the consul by the decree of the Senate to draw his sword, who will stop or restrain him?

'Our ancestors, conscript fathers, were never lacking in intelligence or daring, but neither did their pride prevent them from adopting foreign institutions, provided that they were good institutions. They took our offensive and defensive military weapons from the Samnites; most of the symbols of civil authority from the Etruscans. They were very eager, in short, to adopt at home whatever seemed to work among our allies or our enemies: they would rather copy what was good than envy it. But at the same time they imitated the Greek custom of flogging citizens and executing condemned men. After the Republic reached maturity and, because of its size, factions prevailed, innocent men were convicted, and other similar abuses began to happen. Then, the Porcian law and other laws were passed, laws that allowed exile for the condemned. This, I think, is an especially good reason, conscript fathers, not to adopt a new policy. I am sure that the virtue and wisdom of those men who created such a great empire from small resources was greater than ours, who have difficulty holding on to what was honorably produced.

'And so, is it my opinion that these men should be dismissed and Catiline's army allowed to increase? Not at all. This is my proposal: their money should be confiscated; they should be held in chains in those towns that have the most resources. Thereafter, there should be no consultation about them before the Senate or referendum presented to the people. If anyone tries to change this arrangement, it is the Senate's judgment that he will be acting against the interests of the state and against the safety of all.'

[52] When Caesar finished speaking, the other senators expressed aloud their varied approval of one or another proposal. But when M. Porcius Cato was asked his opinion, he spoke as follows: 'When I consider the facts and the danger we are in, conscript fathers, I'm of a very different mind from when I think of the proposals some have made. They seem to me to be discoursing on the punishment of men who have attempted war against their own fatherland, parents, altars, and hearths; but the facts admonish us to take

precautions for the future against these men rather than debate what to do to them. Other crimes can be prosecuted after they are committed; but, if you do not act to prevent this crime, when it does occur, justice will be something you plead for but don't get. When a city is captured nothing is left for the defeated, by the immortal gods. But I call on you, you who have always valued your homes, villas, statues, and paintings more than the Republic. If you want to keep those possessions, whatever they are that you embrace, if you want to find leisure for your pleasures, then, wake up at last and take control of the state. We are not talking about taxes and the complaints of our allies; your freedom and our life are at risk.

'I have often spoken at length before this body, conscript fathers, often I have complained about the extravagance and greed of our citizens, and for this reason I have made many enemies. I am the kind of man who could never indulge in himself even the intention to do wrong, and so it was not easy for me to condone the appetite and the misconduct of others. But you paid little attention to what I said, and still the Republic was strong; our prosperity supported your dereliction. But now we are not asking whether we should live with or without a moral compass, or about the size or magnificence of the empire of the Roman people, but whether this which is ours, however it seems to you, will remain ours or will belong together with our own persons to the enemy.

'At this point does anyone bring up "compassion" and "mercy"? Long ago we lost the true names for things: squandering the property of another is called "largesse"; daring to do wicked things is called "courage." And so the Republic is at the edge. By all means let them be "liberal" with the wealth of our allies, since that's how our morals are; let them be "compassionate" with thieves who take our treasure; but do not let them be "generous" with our blood and, while they spare a few criminals, destroy all the truly good men.

'A little while ago before this body Caesar spoke eloquently and well about life and death, regarding, I believe, the traditional view of the afterlife as false: that bad people take a path different from that of good people, and that they inhabit places foul, hideous, revolting, and full of fears. And so he proposed that their money be confiscated, that they themselves be held under guard in the townships, fearing, I assume, that, if they were in Rome, members of the conspiracy or some hired mob would

use violence to set them free—as if the wicked and the criminal were only in Rome and not throughout Italy, or as if their recklessness would be less effective where there were fewer resources to oppose it. And so, if Caesar fears the danger those men present, his policy is futile. On the other hand, if he alone is not afraid when everyone else is so very afraid, it is all the more incumbent on me to be afraid for you and for me. And so when you decide about P. Lentulus and the others, know for certain that at the same time you are deciding about Catiline's army and about all the conspirators. The more vigorously you act, the weaker will be their courage; if they see you hesitate only a little, immediately they will be upon us and they will be ferocious.

'Do not believe that our ancestors made a small Republic great with military weapons. If that were the case, we would now be in possession of the most beautiful of all states: we have more allies and citizens than they did, more military weapons and horses. No, other things made them great, things which we do not have at all: disciplined energy at home, a just empire abroad, a mind free in deliberation, limited neither by guilt nor craving. In place of these qualities, we have extravagance and greed, public poverty and private wealth. We praise affluence, we pursue idleness. We make no distinction between good and bad men; ambition usurps all the rewards of virtue. And no wonder: when each man of you takes counsel separately for himself, when at home you are slaves to bodily pleasures and here you are slaves to money and influence, this is why the Republic, abandoned by you, has been attacked.

'But I let these things go. There is a conspiracy, the most noble citizens have conspired to burn down the fatherland; the Gauls have been provoked to war, the Gauls, Rome's most bitter enemy; the enemy leader stands over our head with an army. Do you still hesitate and wonder what you should do with an enemy that has been captured within the city walls? Oh, let's pity them, I say—they have gone astray, young men led by ambition—and let's send them off with their weapons! No, don't let your compassion and mercy turn, if they take arms, into misery. Of course (you say) the situation itself is difficult but you are not afraid of it. Not true; you do fear it and fear it most of all. But it is your inability to act and your effeminate heart that makes you hesitate, everyone waiting for someone else, trusting, of course, in the gods who have often saved this Republic in times of great danger. But it is not with prayers and womanly entreaties that we earn the help of the gods; it is by being watchful, taking action, making good policy, that all things succeed. When you have handed yourself over to apathy and lethargy, it would be an empty gesture to call upon the gods; they are angry and hostile.

'Among our forefathers, during the Gallic War A. Manlius Torquatus ordered his own son killed because he attacked the enemy without orders. That extraordinary young man paid the penalty for unrestrained courage by his death; you are dealing with the most cruel murderers, and yet you hesitate about what you should decide? Of course, their prior life mitigates their crime. Yes, spare Lentulus' eminence, if the man himself ever spared his own sense of decency, if he spared his reputation, if he spared any god or man. Cethegus is a young man; forgive him, if he has not twice made war on his country. Why should I talk of Gabinius, Statilius, and Caeparius? They would not have made these plans for the Republic, if anything were of value to them. Finally, conscript fathers, if there were any room for error, by god I would be happy to let you be chastised by experience itself, since you hold my words in contempt. But we are hemmed in on all sides. Catiline and his army are at our throats; others are within the walls and the enemy is in the heart of Rome. We can neither make any plans nor have any discussion of policy in secret. Therefore, speed is all the more necessary.

'And so this is my opinion: whereas the Republic is in very great danger because of the wicked plans of its most criminal citizens, and whereas they have been convicted by the evidence of T. Volturcius and the Allobrogian legates and have confessed that they have planned slaughter, arson, and other hideous and cruel deeds against their fellow citizens and their country, the punishment for capital crimes that is inflicted upon those caught red-handed must in the manner of our ancestors be inflicted upon those who have confessed.' [53] After Cato sat down, all the ex-consuls and a great number of senators approved his proposal; they praised to the skies his strength of mind, they scolded each other and called one another timid. Cato was considered a brilliant and a great man. The Senate's decree accorded with his recommendation.

But, for my part, as I read and heard about the many things that the Roman people have done, the brilliant deeds they accomplished at home and in the military, on sea and on land, it happened to become my passionate desire to work out what especially supported such accomplishments. I was aware that a small band had often fought against great enemy armies; I knew that despite meager resources they had waged war with opulent kings; in addition I knew that they had often endured the violence of Fortune, that the Greeks were superior in eloquence and the Gauls in military glory. And as I considered many possibilities, it became apparent that everything we accomplished was due to the extraordinary abilities of a few citizens. This was the reason that our ancestors' poverty overcame wealth, that a few overcame many. But after the state had been corrupted by luxury and self-indulgence, the Republic still could support the vices of its generals and magistrates because of its sheer size, and, just as when a woman is worn out by childbirth, for a long time at Rome there was hardly anyone great in manly virtue. Still, in my memory there were two men of extraordinary virtue, but different character, M. Cato and C. Caesar. And since my discussion has brought them forward, it is not my intention to pass them by without saying something to reveal the nature and character of each, to the extent that my talents allow.

[54] And so I turn to them. They were nearly equal in birth, age, and eloquence; their greatness of soul was similar, likewise their glory; but in other respects they were different. Caesar was considered great for his benevolence and generosity; Cato for integrity of life. The former was made famous by his compassion and mercy; intolerance added to the latter's stature. They both attained glory: Caesar by giving, helping, forgiving; Cato by not bribing. In one there was refuge for the wretched, in the other death for the wicked. Caesar's easy disposition was praised, Cato's steadfastness. Finally, Caesar's heartfelt purpose was to work hard, to be vigilant, to neglect his own interests while being devoted to his friends', and to deny nothing that was proper to give; for himself he longed for a great command, an army, a new war in which his excellence could shine. But Cato's drive was for self-restraint, propriety, moral absolutism. He did not compete with the wealthy in wealth or with the partisans in partisanship; he competed with the fervent in virtue, with the restrained in moderation, with the blameless in abstinence; he preferred to be good than to seem good; and so, the less he sought renown, the more it followed him.

[55] After the Senate supported Cato's recommendation, as I mentioned above, the consul thought it best to take precautions for the coming night and to prevent

any new developments during that time. He asked three men to make the necessary preparations for the execution. Guards were deployed and he himself led Lentulus to prison. For the rest, praetors were responsible. In the prison, when you have gone up a little to the left, there is a place called the Tullianum which is a depression of about twelve feet into the ground. Walls protect it on all sides and above there is a dome made with stone arches, but squalor, murk, and stench make it hideous and terrible to behold. After Lentulus was sent down into this place, the executioners strangled him with a rope as ordered. Thus that man, an aristocrat from the glorious family of the Cornelii, a man who had held consular power at Rome, found an end that suited his character and his actions. Cethegus, Statilius, Gabinius, and Caeparius were executed in the same way.

*The narrative moves to a swift conclusion with a description of the decisive battle against Catiline's army north of Rome (56–61), including a final speech by Catiline to his troops (58).*

[56] While this was happening at Rome, Catiline formed two legions from all the forces he himself had brought together and those that Manlius held. He filled out his cohorts according to the number of soldiers he had. At first he had no more than two thousand men. Then, as volunteers or allies came into camp, he distributed them equally, and in a short time he filled the legions with their quota. Only about one quarter of the entire army, however, had military weapons; the rest were armed as chance would have it with hunting-spears and lances, some were carrying sharpened sticks. But after Antonius began to approach with his army, Catiline marched through the mountains, moving his camp now toward Rome, now toward Gaul, and not allowing the enemy any opportunity to fight. He was hoping soon to have a great number of forces, if his allies at Rome could accomplish their tasks. Meanwhile, he refused to enlist the slaves who had at first come to him in great numbers. He relied on the resources of the conspiracy, thinking that it was incompatible with his plans to appear to make common cause between fugitive slaves and citizens.

[57] Things changed when news arrived in the camp that the conspiracy at Rome had been exposed, that Lentulus, Cethegus, and the rest, whom I mentioned above, had paid the penalty. Then most of those who had been enticed to war by the hope of plunder or an interest in revolution slipped away. Catiline led the rest through difficult mountains on forced marches into the area around Pistoria. His plan was to flee unseen down footpaths into Transalpine Gaul.

But Q. Metellus Celer was on watch in the Picene field with three legions; from the difficulty of the situation he guessed that Catiline would do just what we said he did above. And so, when he learned from deserters where they were going, he quickly moved his camp and took a position in the foothills where that man was to descend in haste into Gaul. Furthermore, Antonius was not far away either, since he, with a great army, was following on more level ground the light-armed men in flight. But when Catiline saw that his path was cut off by the mountains and the enemy forces, that things had turned against him in Rome, and that there was no hope either in flight or for assistance, he thought it was best in such circumstances to try the fortunes of war. He decided to engage Antonius first. And so he called an assembly and delivered a speech like this:

[58] 'I know for a fact, soldiers, that words cannot create manly virtue and that a general's speech does not make an indolent army energetic or a frightened army brave. Whatever daring has been put in each man's heart by nature and training, that's what he will show in war. It is futile to exhort a man who is not stirred by glory or danger. Fear in his soul blocks the ears. Still, I have summoned you to remind you of a few things and at the same time to disclose the reason for my strategy.

'I'm quite sure that you know, soldiers, what a disaster Lentulus' lack of courage and his indolence has brought on us and on himself, and how I was not able to set off for Gaul while waiting for reinforcements from Rome. Now, you know as well as I do what difficulties we are in. There are two enemy armies, one from Rome, the other from Gaul, which block our way. Our lack of food and other supplies does not allow us to remain here any longer, even if we really wanted to. Wherever you choose to go, you must open a path with your sword. And so I warn you to have a brave and ready heart, and, when you enter the battle, to remember that in the strength of your right hand you carry your wealth, honor, and glory, and even your freedom and your fatherland. If we win, there will be safety everywhere: resources will abound, towns and colonies will open their doors. But if we are afraid and yield, everything will turn against us. No place or friend will protect the man who doesn't protect himself with his sword.

'And you must keep this in mind as well: the need that presses on us is not the same as what weighs on them. We are fighting for our homeland, for freedom, for our lives; theirs is an inane struggle for the power of a few. And so, it is all the more necessary that you attack with reckless courage, remembering the manly virtue you have displayed before. We could have spent our lives in exile and in utter shame; some of you, having lost your property, could have waited at Rome for the help of strangers. But you have decided to follow this course because to real men those alternatives seem hideous and intolerable. If you want to get free of these things, you will need reckless courage: only the victor gets peace in return for war. To turn the arms which protect your body away from the enemy and hope to find safety in flight, that is utter madness. In battle the danger is always the greatest for those who are most afraid. Reckless courage is like a defensive wall.

'When I think of your abilities, soldiers, and weigh what you have already done, I have great hopes for victory. Your courage, your age, your manly virtue encourage me, as does necessity, which can make even the timid brave. For the enemy is large in numbers, but the narrow passes prevent them from surrounding us. Still, if Fortune is jealous of your manly virtue, do not lose your life without taking vengeance. Do not be captured and slaughtered like cattle; rather, fight like men, and leave for your enemy a victory filled with blood and grief!'

[59] When he said these things, he hesitated briefly, ordered the bugle call, lined up his men in battle order and led them into the plain. He then removed all the horses; in this way, with all the soldiers facing the same danger, their courage would be greater. He was himself on foot and drew up his army to suit the place and his resources. There was a plain between the mountains on the left and the sharp rocks on the right; so he put eight cohorts in front, and stationed the standards of the rest of the army more closely together in reserve. From those in reserve, he moved all the centurions and the recalled veterans, also all the best common soldiers to the front of the formation. He put C. Manlius in charge of the right side, a man from Faesulae in charge of the left. He himself took his position with freedmen and colonists near the eagle that they said C. Marius had kept in his army during the Cimbrian war.

On the other side, C. Antonius, who had a sore foot, had handed his army over to his legate, M. Petreius, because he could not enter the battle. Petreius placed the veteran cohorts that he had enlisted to resist the insurgency in the front, behind them he put the rest of the army in reserve. He himself rode about on horseback, addressing each soldier by name, encouraging him, asking him to remember that he was fighting against unarmed bandits for his homeland, his children, his altars, and his hearth. He had been a military man for more than thirty years as tribune, prefect, legate, or praetor, and had served with great distinction in the army. For this reason he personally knew most of the men and their acts of bravery. He enkindled the soldiers' courage by mentioning these things.

[60] But, when everything was sorted out and with a bugle Petreius gave the signal, he ordered the cohorts to advance slowly. The enemy army did the same. When they were close enough for the light-armed troops to begin the fight, there was a great shout. They clash with hostile standards. They hurl their javelins; they fight with swords. The veterans, remembering their long-established virtue, press on fiercely fighting hand to hand; those who resist are unafraid. With great violence they struggle. Meanwhile Catiline with his light troops is moving around the front line of the battle: giving aid to those in trouble, sending in fresh troops for those wounded, overseeing everything, himself often fighting, often killing the enemy. He was performing at the same time the duties of the energetic soldier and the good general. When Petreius, to his surprise, sees Catiline exerting himself with great force, he leads his praetorian cohort into the middle of the enemy's line; he throws them into confusion and he kills them wherever they resist. Then, he attacks the rest on each flank. Manlius and the Faesulanian are among the first to die fighting. Catiline sees his troops routed, himself left with a few men; then, thinking of his family name and his long-established dignity, he charges into the thick of the enemy and there, fighting, is impaled.

[61] But only when the battle was over could you truly measure the daring and the mental toughness of Catiline's army. For nearly every man's body, now dead, covered the very place where living he had stood fighting. A few from the middle of the line had been scattered by the praetorian cohort and had fallen apart from the rest, but everyone had taken wounds in the chest when they fell. Catiline, in fact, was found far

from his own men amidst the corpses of the enemy. He was still breathing a little and maintained on his face that ferocious courage he had had while living. To summarize: not a single native-born citizen from all his army was captured either in battle or in flight; that is the degree to which no one spared his own life or the life of his enemy.

Still, the army of the Roman people did not attain a joyful or bloodless victory. The most energetic fighters had either been killed in the battle or had returned gravely wounded. Furthermore, many came from the camp to visit the field or to plunder; when they rolled over the enemy corpses they discovered now a friend, now a guest or a relative; likewise, there were those who recognized political opponents. And so through the entire army men were moved in different ways to joy, sorrow, grief, and happiness.

## AFTERWORD

Within the century after his death, Sallust's works came to be considered classics of historiography, forming part of the essential reading of every Roman schoolboy. But before Sallust achieved such status, he endured much criticism in the generation after him. His contemporary Asinius Pollio, the great patron of letters, faulted him for his archaizing vocabulary, and Livy was not an admirer. But in due course the two monographs, *The Conspiracy of Catiline* and *The War with Jugurtha*, came to be staples on every reader's shelves, and his *Histories* were also much studied. Quintilian considered him a greater historian than Livy, although he did not recommend either of them as models of style for an orator, remarking that Sallust's brevity of expression was as ineffective in public speaking as Livy's milky superfluity. Among Greek predecessors in history, he was most often compared with Thucydides, an apt comparison not only in matters of literary style but also in their political thinking. His most important admirer in the imperial period was certainly Tacitus, who described him as "the most eminent writer on Roman history" (*Annals* 3.29). Tacitus not only took him as a model of style but also adopted Sallust's rather austere moralism in chronicling the history of the early empire. Collections of the speeches and letters embedded in Sallust's historical works were anthologized already in antiquity, and copies of that collection survived into the Middle Ages. As a school author, Sallust was bound to attract interest among the Greek-speaking readers of the empire as well. The wide distribution of his works is attested by the number of papyrus fragments, exceeded among Latin authors only by Virgil and Cicero. In the second century A.D., Zenobius, a Greek grammarian working in Rome, produced a translation of Sallust's works into his native language. Sallust continued to be read throughout late antiquity, attracting interest not only from historians such as Ammianus Marcellinus but also from Christian fathers such as St. Augustine.

In the Middle Ages *The Conspiracy of Catiline* and *The War with Jugurtha* remained standard fare in the schools. Their wide distribution across western Europe can be traced from their presence in library catalogs and the survival of more than five hundred manuscripts of the monographs. In the early Renaissance, Sallust was much admired and taken as a model for historiography. Leonardo Bruni (1370–1444), the influential author of *History of the Florentine People*, referred to Sallust and Cicero together as "the two most outstanding writers in the Latin language" (1.7) and his description of the causes of the decline of Rome is replete with reminiscences of Sallustian pessimism (1.38):

> For liberty gave way before the imperial name, and when liberty departed, so did virtue. Before the day of the Caesars, high character was the route to honor, and positions such as consul, dictator, or other high public offices were open to men who had excelled others with their magnanimous spirit, strength of character, and energy. But as soon as the commonwealth fell into the power of one man, high character and magnanimity became suspect in the eyes of rulers.

Only those were acceptable to the emperors who lacked the mental vigor to care about liberty. The imperial court thus opened its gates to the lazy rather than to the strong, to flatterers rather than to the industrious, and as the administration of affairs fell to inferior men, little by little the empire was brought to ruin.

For Bruni, as for Sallust, history was the story of great men of virtue and the deeds they accomplished. For Angelo Poliziano (1454–94) the same held true, and he employed the model of Sallust's *Conspiracy of Catiline* in writing *The Pazzi Conspiracy,* his narrative of the attempted coup directed at his patron Lorenzo the Magnificent and the Medici family.

Sallust's works were translated into French as early as the fourteenth century, and versions in Spanish and in German were published in the next century. But the first English translation was Alexander Barclay's (ca. 1484–1552) *History of the Jugurthine War,* which appeared in 1520. Barclay was best known in his day for his translation and adaption of the work of the German satirist Sebastian Brant, *The Ship of Fools,* which was printed in London in 1509. The earliest translation of *The Conspiracy of Catiline* was by the poet and playwright Thomas Heywood (ca. 1573–1641), published together with *The War with Jugurtha* in 1608, but Heywood worked primarily from the earlier French translation of Louis Meigret. Sallust's *Conspiracy of Catiline* also inspired works of creative literature, including plays by Ben Jonson (1611), Voltaire (1752), and Ibsen (1850). But in the centuries that followed the Renaissance, Sallust was largely overshadowed by his admirer Tacitus, although his works continued to be read in Latin well into the nineteenth century as part of the standard classical curriculum. He was familiar to the Founding Fathers of the United States, and one in particular, James Dickinson, frequently quoted a line from *The War with Jugurtha*: "I shall certainly aim at the freedom handed down from my forebears; whether I am successful or not in doing so is in your control, my fellow countrymen."

# THE AGE OF AUGUSTUS

WITH HIS GREAT VICTORY OVER THE COMBINED FORCES OF MARK ANTONY AND
Cleopatra in the naval battle at Actium off the western coast of Greece on September 2, 31 B.C.,
Caesar's heir Octavian emblazoned his name on an empire and an age. He did not take the name
Augustus until four years later in 27 B.C. as part of a prolonged process of consolidating power in
his own hands while retaining the outward forms of the Roman Republic, but from the vantage
point of history one may justifiably term the entire period from his arrival on the political scene in
44 B.C. to his death in A.D. 14 "Augustan." Of course, it was not always clear that things would turn
out so. It was not until Octavian had defeated Sextus Pompey off the coast of Sicily in 36 B.C. that
he established himself as the dominant power in the Roman world, and even then it was far from
a sure bet that he would prevail in the coming war with Antony. Much of the great literature of the
early years of this period—including Virgil's *Eclogues* and Horace's first book of *Satires* and book of
*Epodes*—was composed under the shadow of civil wars, both those that had already been fought
in the tumultuous decade of the 40s B.C. and those that loomed on the horizon. It would only have
taken a slight twist of fate for this period to have been dubbed "The Age of Antony."

Renewal is the image of the age that has resonated through history, the product of the emperor's
ceaseless application of the theme in governing. In the political sphere that meant that as Augustus
consolidated power within the imperial family the outer forms of republican government—the
Senate, the assemblies of the people, the magistracies—remained in existence and, where they did
not conflict with his authority, still functioned. During this period Roman military power shifted
its focus from the conquests and civil wars of the preceding century to strengthening the borders
of the empire in Germany and pacifying the still unconquered regions of Spain. Across the Roman
world, but especially within the city of Rome itself, great public works projects altered the everyday
lives of millions of inhabitants of the empire. Augustus brought to completion some of the projects
initiated by his adoptive father, Julius Caesar, most notably his new forum adjacent to the ancient
Roman Forum, to which he added his own new public space, the Forum Augustum, said by many
in antiquity to be the most beautiful structure in the world. The Field of Mars was transformed
into an urban pleasure zone with the construction of public baths and gardens, temples, and water
parks. And everywhere was evident the hand of Augustus, the man to whom the city owed these

adornments, and who wished to advertise the reasons why the people were indebted to him. By the side of the Flaminian Road, which still leads straight from the Capitoline Hill to the north, the emperor erected the Altar of the Augustan Peace, a veritable family monument showing himself and members of his family in a religious procession. All Romans knew to whom they owed this peace that had at last come to the Roman world.

But the period did not begin on this note, something we know best from the great writers whose works have also lent their luster to the Augustan Age. The shepherds in Virgil's *Eclogues* live tenuously in a precarious landscape where they might be evicted from their farms, as many actually were during the reallocations of land that took place during the civil wars. Similar notes of dejection and pessimism may be detected in the early poetry of Horace, and in the earliest works of the elegists. Much of the poetry of the elegiac poets Tibullus and Propertius is concerned with the private world of love and literature, but the ravages of the recent past are evident in them too. It is Virgil's great epic poem, the *Aeneid*, that is most closely associated with the new order in the Roman world, but even in antiquity readers recognized it as something more than a simple, straightforward panegyric to Rome's greatness. Its hero suffers heartache and loss, and those closest to him suffer too. Virgil's greatness as a writer is marked by his ability to translate those intensely personal experiences to a broader, public plane.

With the end of the Republic came a decisive change in the nature of public discourse. No collections of speeches to rival Cicero's survive from this period, because there were none. Historiography, too, has its public dimension, and the new political dispensation posed challenges on this front as well. Only portions of Livy's history survive, and we know very little of how he handled contemporary events, except that Augustus teased him with favoring Pompey in his account of the civil wars. But the emperor could do more than just tease, as was demonstrated by the fate of the elegiac poet Cornelius Gallus, who was driven to commit suicide in ca. 27 B.C. (although his fall from the emperor's good graces was probably not due to his literary pursuits). The last great writer of the age was Ovid, whose most enduring works were published long after Virgil, Horace, and Propertius were dead. In many ways his writings may be considered as best exemplifying the spirit of the age after the memories of the civil wars had faded—brilliant, witty, and confident. This was not to last. The final years of Augustus's reign are a dark period, marked by military setbacks on the borders of the empire and domestic disturbances within the imperial household. Deaths within the family left Tiberius, Augustus's stepson, as the only viable candidate to succeed the now aging emperor. First the emperor's daughter Julia had been sent into exile, and then again in A.D. 8 her daughter was relegated to a barren island off the coast of Apulia on a charge of moral turpitude that may well have been a cover for an offense of a political nature. Tiberius was now in effect co-regent, and the climate for art and literature was altered. The changing tide swept up some minor figures, but most ominously it engulfed Ovid, too, the greatest poet of the time, who was sent to spend the last decade of his life at the most remote outpost of the empire on the Black Sea. From now on, the political reality of the empire was something that every writer had to reckon with.

# VIRGIL

## (Publius Vergilius Maro, 70–19 B.C.)

IT IS SAID THAT, AS HE LAY DYING, VIRGIL ORDERED THE *AENEID*, HIS UNFINISHED masterpiece, to be burned, but that the emperor Augustus countermanded the order. If this dramatic intervention actually happened, it was arguably the greatest of all Augustus's achievements. The *Aeneid* is a soaring work, eclipsing all earlier Latin poetry and exercising a profound influence on later literature. Virgil was acknowledged as Rome's supreme poet in his own lifetime, and not just by the intellectual elite (Suetonius, *Life of Virgil* 11): "Virgil was extremely shy. He very rarely came to Rome and, if he was spotted in a public place, he would take refuge in the nearest building to escape from those who were following him and pointing him out." We hear of no other Roman poet being mobbed by the masses in this way. It is a mark of Virgil's greatness that he had such popular appeal and yet wrote poetry of such subtle profundity that it offers peculiarly daunting challenges to scholars. Even before he began work on the *Aeneid*, his reputation was assured through his earlier works, the *Eclogues* and the *Georgics*. The *Eclogues* were published in the early 30s B.C., and brought Virgil to the attention of Maecenas, the close friend and political adviser of Octavian. Virgil had already shown his support for Octavian in the first *Eclogue*, where he thanks him in the most fulsome manner for the restoration of his farm, ignoring the fact that it was Octavian's controversial land confiscations that had deprived him of it in the first place. The *Georgics* appeared about a decade later, dedicated to Maecenas. It is of no consequence that Maecenas himself was the epitome of urbane sophistication, hardly the most obviously appropriate choice as dedicatee of a poem advocating unremitting toil in the countryside. Maecenas and Octavian will have thoroughly approved the underlying message of the *Georgics*, that Rome could only be restored to its former greatness by a return to the traditional values of hard work, frugality, religious observance, and respect for the family. The *Aeneid* continues this message with its unique blend of traditional mythological epic and dynastic encomium centered on the ancestry of one man, Augustus.

Given Virgil's unparalleled importance, we know disappointingly little about his life. That is not to say that ancient and medieval biographers were not avid to collect whatever information they could about him, and what they could not find, they fabricated. Unlike his contemporaries, Horace and the love elegists, Virgil wrote almost nothing that purports to express his own personal opinions. Much of what we are told about him has been inferred from his poetry, such as the restoration of his land, where it seems reasonable to see Virgil himself in the persona of the fortunate shepherd, Tityrus. Sometimes, we are on safer ground if we accept as facts details that are apparently not drawn from his poetry, such as the mass adoration he had to endure when he appeared in public. There is much other information in the surviving *Life of Virgil* derived from Suetonius that seems credible: for example, that he was born to humble parents on October 15, 70 B.C., near Mantua in the Po Valley; that he studied at Milan and then at Rome (which suggests that his parents enjoyed

**Figure 11: Aeneas and Dido at the Banquet**
An illustration from a fifth-century illuminated manuscript in the Vatican Library. Scholars in antiquity debated why no one is ever portrayed eating fish in the Homeric poems.

a certain degree of prosperity); that he was particularly interested in medicine and mathematics; that he gave up a legal career after pleading just one case, since his delivery was slow and seemingly uncouth; that his recitation of poetry, on the other hand, was pleasant and compelling; that he achieved considerable wealth through gifts from his patrons; that he preferred to live in Campania or Sicily rather than in Rome; that he died of a fever at Brundisium on September 21, 19 B.C., while returning from Greece.

In the Suetonian *Life*, we are told that the poplar tree planted near the ditch in which Virgil's mother gave birth to him came to be a focus of worship by local women. As the centuries went by and admiration for his poetry continued undimmed, such hints at extravagant powers associated with his birthplace were gradually transformed into a representation of Virgil himself as a magician and miracle-worker.

One aspect of Virgil's life not specifically mentioned by Suetonius is his abiding interest in philosophy, an interest strongly reflected in his poetry, especially in the *Georgics* and the *Aeneid*. When Suetonius tells us that Virgil preferred to live in Campania, he may be alluding to his adherence to the Epicurean school centered around Philodemus at Herculaneum and Naples. Little was known about Virgil's links with Philodemus until recent years, when several carbonized papyri of Philodemus's philosophical treatises were deciphered, in which he actually addresses Virgil and other Roman literati, perhaps including Horace.

## THE ECLOGUES

The *Eclogues*, sometimes known as the *Bucolics*, were written in imitation of the pastoral *Idylls* of the third-century B.C. Greek poet Theocritus, from Syracuse in Sicily, who spent much of his career at the court of the Ptolemies in Alexandria. Some definitions will be useful. "Pastoral" refers to the grazing of livestock; in literary terms it signifies a work with a rustic setting, portraying the life of herdsmen.

An "idyll" is literally a "little picture," in literary terms a short poem portraying a picturesque scene or incident, usually in the countryside. "Bucolic" refers to herdsmen, specifically cowherds. "Eclogue" means literally "chosen out," like the more specific "anthology," "a choosing of flowers." (An early spelling variant, "aiglogue," encouraged the false etymology "talking about goats," in Greek *aix*.)

We possess thirty poems, and a few fragments of others, attributed to Theocritus. Some were demonstrably not written by him, and only ten can properly be described as pastoral idylls, and these are generally quite distinct in subject matter from the nonpastoral poems. Theocritus's shepherds are interested only in herding, singing, and love affairs, and the real world intrudes into his pastoral setting rather less than it does with Virgil. Perhaps the closest he comes is in his eleventh *Idyll*, one of the most successful, certainly one of the wittiest, of all Hellenistic poems. As in Virgil's second *Eclogue*, which imitates this *Idyll* closely, a shepherd sings of his unrequited love. Whereas, however, Virgil's shepherd is an ordinary herdsman, Theocritus's shepherd is the monstrous cannibal Polyphemus, in love with the sea nymph Galatea. When he has Polyphemus pray for some stranger to come who could teach him to swim, so that he could go down to the depths of the sea with bouquets of flowers for Galatea, Theocritus is playing with our knowledge of the Cyclops episode in *Odyssey* 9, when Odysseus meets Polyphemus but does not give him swimming lessons to help him in his love life. Theocritus appears in the poem in his own person when he describes Polyphemus as "the Cyclops, my fellow-countryman," alluding to the fact that they were both from Sicily. Reality also intrudes in the address to Nicias, a doctor: Theocritus quotes Polyphemus's song to Galatea to assure Nicias that singing is a better cure for love than any medicine that can be smeared or sprinkled on a wound.

*Eclogue* 4 has always been the most admired poem in Virgil's collection, but it is also the least pastoral. Virgil acknowledges in the opening line that this poem is more ambitious than Theocritean pastoral: "Sicilian Muses, let us sing of slightly greater things." More strongly than any of the other *Eclogues*, it reflects the political and military upheaval of the times, with its yearning for the restoration of peace. This restoration is associated with the imminent birth of a child and the predicted return of the Golden Age. Such predictions were by no means new. We may perhaps note in particular that, as Suetonius reports (*Life of Augustus* 94), "on the day on which Augustus was born [in 63 B.C.], the Senate was debating the Catilinarian conspiracy. Octavius [Augustus's father] arrived late for the meeting on account of his wife's labor. Everyone knows that the soothsayer Nigidius Figulus, on learning why Octavius had come late, ascertained the exact time of the birth and declared that the ruler of the world had been born." Cicero must have detested this stealing of his thunder on his big day in the Senate!

## THE GEORGICS

After the publication of the *Eclogues*, Virgil worked throughout the 30s on his *Georgics*, which, as its name implies ("things to do with working on the land"), is devoted to giving instructions about farming. Virgil's most important model is the earliest of all didactic poems, Hesiod's *Works and Days*, probably composed about 700 B.C., that is to say, around the time that the Homeric epics were first written down. Whereas the *Works and Days* is a single book of just over eight hundred lines, the *Georgics* are more ambitious in scale, at almost twenty-two hundred lines in four books. Hesiod deals with farming at little more than a subsistence level, and his influence is particularly prominent in Virgil's first book, which deals with crop growing, and to a lesser extent in the second book, on trees and shrubs. *Georgics* 3 and 4, on livestock and beekeeping, respectively, draw mostly on other models. Of these the most significant is Terentius Varro's *On Farming*, a prose treatise published in 37 B.C., that is, just after Virgil started work on the *Georgics*. Virgil is known to have been influenced by Hellenistic poems such as the *Phaenomena* of Aratus, the *Aetia* of Callimachus, and the *Georgics* and *Bee-Keeping* of Nicander. These last two works are all but entirely lost, but, in describing the procedure for fumigating a barn to drive away snakes at 3.414ff., Virgil elevates to a much higher poetic level a surviving passage of one of Nicander's poems, the *Theriaca* ("About Wild Animals," on bites and stings from poisonous creatures), so we can be fairly certain that he drew on Nicander's other works too. Virgil is also constantly aware of Lucretius's great didactic poem, *On the Nature of the Universe*. Tradition links these two great poets in time as well, for Virgil is said to have put on the toga of manhood in 55 B.C., at the age of fifteen, on the very day that Lucretius died. Like Lucretius, Virgil is an Epicurean, but the *Georgics* have little of the older poet's austerity and dismissive attitude to traditional beliefs; instead, they convey a warm and deep love for nature and the Italian countryside, as they praise with such affection the simple, rustic way of life that many of Virgil's contemporaries lamented as being by then a thing of the past, submerged in the social and political upheavals that had prevailed all but unremittingly throughout the preceding century.

Virgil is not expecting any of his readers, much less the poem's dedicatee, the highly sophisticated Maecenas, to adopt his message literally. By Virgil's day, the life of the hardy peasant farmer who lived simply but well on his own little plot of land was gone beyond recall, if it had ever really existed. Rome would never again have a leader like the fifth-century hero Cincinnatus, who was called away from his plowing to raise an army and save Rome, and who then returned to his farm after fifteen days when the mission had been accomplished. Reality was different. Life for the rural poor was dreadful, whether for free peasants or for slaves (who are conspicuously absent from the *Georgics*). Skeletal remains show that diseases associated with malnutrition were rampant and endemic. Cato's instructions for the running of a fairly substantial estate are brutal (*On Farming* 2): "Sell surplus wine and grain, aging oxen, runt calves, runt sheep, wool, hides, old carts, old iron tools, old slaves, sickly slaves, and anything else you do not need." Recruits for the army should be sought in the countryside because, with little technology, farming was unremittingly laborious: "A man who knows less about life's pleasures fears death less" (Vegetius, *Military Affairs* 1.3). It was said to have been the plight of the small farmers in the second century B.C. that led the brothers Tiberius and Gaius Gracchus to press for social change, and the problem continued unabated; a century after Virgil, the elder Pliny was to lament that large-scale farming on *latifundia*, "broad farms," had ruined Italy, and now the provinces as well—with six men owning half the province of Africa before Nero had them put to death so that he could confiscate their wealth (*Natural History* 18.35).

The tranquil and uncomplicated existence in the countryside that Virgil evokes was a fantasy sentimentally cherished by the ruling classes in Rome, many of whom benefited personally from the submergence of the traditional smallholdings into *latifundia*. Augustus may have required his daughter and granddaughters to spin wool in the old-fashioned manner of virtuous Roman women such as Lucretia (Suetonius, *Life of Augustus* 64), but Virgil does not expect his readers literally to spread manure on the fields or ointment on scabrous sheep. Like Livy, who wrote the much more explicitly moralizing preface to his great history at just this time, Virgil hopes to inspire an end to the decadence that plagues contemporary Rome. He aims to reawaken pride in the *mos maiorum*, the "ways of the ancestors," through the poem's underlying moral message, whether expressed negatively as in the lament for the ravaging of the countryside, the outbreak of civil war, and the assassination of Julius Caesar with which Book 1 ends, or positively in the sprightly mock-epic praise for the well-ordered social life of bees in Book 4. And the message that peace, a prerequisite for successful farming, can be hoped for only through the firm establishment of Octavian's power recurs throughout the poem and foreshadows Virgil's more ambitious and explicit treatment of this theme in a much broader context in the *Aeneid*.


## THE AENEID

The *Aeneid* is structured in two distinct halves, of six books each. The first half tells how Aeneas faces many dangers as he wanders around the Mediterranean, even visiting the Underworld, in his attempt to find a new home after the destruction of Troy. In the second half, he fights in Italy to establish that new home for himself, his family, his followers, and his Trojan gods. Virgil's primary model for the first half is Homer's *Odyssey*, in which Odysseus endures many of the same long and weary perils, including a visit to the Underworld, before reaching home and reclaiming his kingdom. His primary model for the second is the *Iliad*. The Homeric structuring in Books 7 through 12 is rather less close in its details but still very clear in general terms: just as the *Iliad* moves inexorably toward the duel between Hector, the chief defender of Troy, and Achilles, the best of the Greek warriors, so tension builds throughout the second half of the *Aeneid*, as we await the decisive duel between Aeneas and Turnus, the Italian leader and his rival for the hand of Lavinia, marriage with whom will ensure power and prosperity for the victor.

The Homeric epics have always held an unassailable position as the greatest works of all Greek literature, with a status in Greek society not far short of that held by the Bible in Christianity, or by the Koran in Islam. For Virgil to model his poem on not one, but on both, of these poems was astoundingly audacious. It will seem the more daring if we recall that, years before, in the opening lines of the sixth *Eclogue*, he had declared that "when I tried to sing of kings and battles [i.e., to write an epic], Apollo pulled me by the ear and warned me 'Tityrus, a shepherd should feed his sheep fat, but spin a slender song.'" Virgil is there echoing the proem to Callimachus's *Aetia*, which acknowledges the belief that Homer is the literary equivalent of Zeus, and that other poets should aspire only to more modest genres. And yet, even while Virgil was still in the early stages of composing the *Aeneid*, Propertius felt confident to announce, "Make way, you Roman writers, make way, you Greeks! / Something greater than the *Iliad* is being born" (2.34.65–66).

Comparison of the relative literary merits of Homer and Virgil is at best of limited value, and far more often simply a futile and misguided exercise, for their epics are so fundamentally different. The crucial difference is that the Homeric poems were the product of centuries of crafting and refining by generations of oral poets, whereas the *Aeneid* is the work of a single highly literate genius, and Virgil demonstrates his artistry by drawing on many and various poetic predecessors, not just on Homer. Moreover, whereas the primary aim of most oral epic poetry is to entertain and expound the general values of the society in which it is composed, the *Aeneid*, quite apart from its timeless poetic glory, is also a potent and highly successful vehicle for contemporary propaganda, directly aimed at bolstering the Augustan message that Rome's destiny to rule the world is inextricably bound up with the divine authority invested in the Julian dynasty: Venus, the daughter of Jupiter, was the mother of Aeneas, who was the father of Iulus, from whom the Julian clan acquired its name, passing it down through the centuries to Julius Caesar and Augustus himself.

Ovid tells us that no part of the *Aeneid* is read as often as Book 4, "the part of the poem in which love is joined without a legal agreement" (*Sorrows of an Exile* 2.535–36). This book displays with particular clarity not only the complex ways in which Virgil draws on his poetic predecessors but also the subtle and, to some extent, independent manner in which he advocates Augustus's right to rule Rome and its empire.

The story of Dido and Aeneas is so familiar that it is easy to forget that the form in which we know it is to some extent Virgil's own creation. In particular, there must have been a drastically different version given by Terentius Varro, Virgil's contemporary, for he maintained that it was not Dido herself but rather her sister, Anna, who committed suicide on the funeral pyre because of her frustrated love for Aeneas. We do not have much information about the alternative versions of the story and cannot therefore assess Virgil's modifications in detail. On the other hand, we do have sufficient knowledge of his literary predecessors to appreciate his extraordinarily complex portrayal of Dido. The creative way in which these different models for Dido are blended together illustrates particularly well the truth of Macrobius's observation that Virgil "did not gather his harvest from just one single vine, but rather he exploited for his own purpose whatever was worth imitating" (*Saturnalia* 5.74).

Two obvious Homeric models are the beautiful goddesses Circe and Calypso, with whom Odysseus lingers for one year and seven years, respectively, only to leave them to return to his faithful wife, Penelope. In describing Aeneas shipwrecked in a kingdom in which he will recount his adventures at length, there are reminiscences of Odysseus's meeting with the Phaeacian princess Nausicaa. There are even piquant hints at Penelope herself in the portrayal of Dido courted by suitors from neighboring African kingdoms; whereas Penelope remains loyal to her first husband, the dead Sychaeus, Dido has a love affair with Aeneas. When Dido meets Aeneas in the Underworld, she refuses to speak to him and hurries off to rejoin Sychaeus; in that poignant scene, we are not to recall any beautiful heroine but rather the ghost of the mighty warrior Ajax, who refuses to speak to Odysseus in the Underworld because he blames him for driving him to commit suicide, stabbing himself with his sword, just as Dido does. A further powerful literary influence is Medea, as she is portrayed both in Euripides's tragedy of that name and in Apollonius of Rhodes's third-century epic, the *Argonautica*. In Apollonius, Medea assists Jason in winning the Golden Fleece and then sails off with him, deserting her home and family; Euripides's play is set at a later period, when love has turned to hate, and Medea avenges herself on Jason for abandoning her by killing their sons. In the first line of Book 4, there is an allusion to yet another deserted heroine; in describing Dido as "wounded with care" (*saucia cura*), Virgil is echoing Catullus's description (64.250) of Ariadne watching Theseus's ship sail away from Naxos, where he abandons her despite the assistance she had given him in killing the Minotaur.

Important as these legendary models may be, there is, of course, a far more immediate model ever present in Virgil's portrayal of Dido. Cleopatra was a beautiful African queen who posed a great danger to Rome, especially in the way in which she caused Julius Caesar and then Mark Antony to neglect Rome's interests and waste their time in a love affair with her. Aeneas tries to excuse his behavior when he meets Dido's shade in the Underworld with the words "unwillingly, O queen, I left your shore" (6.460). These words echo the flattery addressed to Queen Berenice by a lock of her hair, as expressed at Catullus 66.39, in a translation of an Alexandrian court poem by Callimachus; it conveys its sorrow at being turned into a constellation instead of staying with the queen in the words "unwillingly, O queen, I left your head." Some scholars are puzzled, even distressed, by Virgil's adaptation of that elegant but essentially trivial poem at such a tragic moment in the *Aeneid,* but it is an ingenious way to emphasize the link between Cleopatra and Dido, for Berenice was not only, like Cleopatra, a queen of Egypt but also her direct ancestor. Virgil makes such a verbal link between Dido and Cleopatra more directly when he describes them both as "pale with imminent death" at 4.644 and 8.709, respectively.

There is yet another important strand of literary influence. The Dido episode will have brought the *Aeneid* closest in subject matter to what had been Rome's greatest epic, the *Annals* of Ennius, which had treated of the Second Punic War, that is, Rome's struggle with the Carthaginians under Hannibal, the long and decisive conflict to which Dido alludes in her great curse on Aeneas and his descendants (4.625ff.). The very fragmentary nature of what survives of the *Annals* makes direct comparison difficult. Many of these fragments are preserved in Servius's commentary on the *Aeneid,* and they rarely give us more than random and sporadic glimpses at the way Virgil reworks his great Roman predecessor.

If Virgil draws Dido from so many models, it is hardly surprising that his portrayal of Aeneas is not straightforward either. In his conflict with Turnus, Aeneas is modeled not on Hector, a Trojan and his own cousin, but on the victorious Greek, his former enemy, Achilles, just as, in the first half, his main model was also a Homeric Greek, Odysseus. Overall, as hero of the poem, Aeneas foreshadows Augustus. Just as Aeneas sets sail from Troy "with his allies, his son, his household gods, and the great gods" (3.12), so Augustus leads the Italians against Antony's Oriental hordes at Actium "with the Senate, the people, his household gods, and the great gods" (8.679). But the equation of Aeneas with Augustus is by no means complete. In the final episode of the poem, Aeneas kills Turnus in a fit of rage; anger is the besetting flaw in Achilles's character, but Augustus was keen to promote an image of himself as a merciful victor. In Book 4, Aeneas is reminiscent not of Augustus but of Julius Caesar and Mark Antony; they wasted time in love affairs with Cleopatra, whereas Octavian is said to have refused even to grant her an audience when she was defeated and trapped in Alexandria.

The ambivalence in the portrayal of Dido and Aeneas is one of the great strengths of the *Aeneid.* If Virgil had invited his Roman contemporaries to view her as little more than a simple and direct equivalent to Cleopatra, then they would not have had any great difficulty in judging her suffering and suicide as a just reward for the threat she had posed to the destiny of Rome. Conversely, Aeneas would be admired for suppressing his personal feelings and answering the higher call of duty to the Roman state. A lesser poet might have painted such a picture, but the sympathy that Virgil evokes for Dido, the founder of Carthage, Rome's most deadly enemy, and the reservations we must feel in our assessment of Aeneas as the poem's hero have assured the *Aeneid* a place among the highest of human achievements.

## ECLOGUE 4

*In many respects this is the least typical of Virgil's pastoral poems, dealing as it does with a larger theme, as announced in its opening lines. Theocritus's numerous court-poems honoring contemporary rulers provide a precedent for this change of setting. The addressee of the* Eclogue *is Asinius Pollio, who held the office of consul in 40 B.C., the most likely date for the poem's composition. It celebrates a child whose birth will usher in a return to a golden age. The identity of the child has been contested for centuries, with Christian apologists seeing this as a prophecy of the birth of Christ, but the most likely contemporary reference is to the anticipated birth of a child from the marriage of Mark Antony and Octavia, the sister of Octavian, who were married in this same year. This prospect came to nothing, however, since Octavia's child was a girl.*

Sicilian Muses, let us sing of slightly greater things!
Not everyone takes pleasure in shrubs and lowly
    tamarisks;
If we sing of woods, may woods be worthy of the consul.
The final age of the Cumaean song has passed;
5  The great order of the generations is born again.
Now the virgin goddess returns, and the reign of Saturn,
Now a new race is sent down from high Heaven.
Pure Lucina, look with favor on the boy whose birth
Will mark the end of the Age of Iron, and the rise
10  Of the Age of Gold. For your Apollo rules now.
In your consulship, Pollio, this glorious epoch
Will begin, as the parade of mighty months moves on.
If any traces of our crimes remain, your leadership
Will wipe them out, and free the world from endless
    fear.
15  He will be granted the life of the gods, and see
Heroes consorting with gods, while he himself is seen
    by them.
With his ancestral virtues he will rule a world at peace.
But, for you, child, the untilled earth will pour forth

Its first gifts, ivy wandering everywhere, and
    cyclamens,
And lotus-flowers mixed with smiling acanthus.    20
Of their own accord, the goats will bring back
    home their milk-distended
Udders, and the herds will not fear great lions. Your
    own cradle will pour out flowers to please you.
Snakes will die, and deceitfully poisonous herbs
Will die; Assyrian spice plants will spring up
    everywhere.    25
But as soon as you are able to read of the glorious
    exploits of heroes
And of your father's deeds, and to understand what
    virtue is,
Gradually the plains will grow yellow with swaying
    wheat,
And ripened grapes will hang on wild brambles,
And hard oaks will ooze forth honey dripping
    like dew.    30
But a few traces will linger still of ancient wrongs,
To bid us assail the sea-nymph Thetis with our ships,
And circle towns with walls, and split the earth with
    furrows.
Then there will be another Tiphys and another Argo
    to carry
The chosen heroes; there will also be another war,    35
And great Achilles will be sent again to Troy.
But then, when strengthening years make you a man,
Merchants will leave the sea, and no ship of pine
Will trade for goods; every land will produce
    everything.
The ground will not feel the hoe, nor vines the
    pruning hook,    40
And the sturdy plowman will take the yoke from
    off his bulls;
Wool will not learn to counterfeit a range of colors,
For already, in the meadow, the ram will turn
    his fleece
To lovely purple, or to a crocus shade of saffron.

Even as they graze, the lambs will be clothed
45      in scarlet.
"May such times run on," said the Fates to their spindles,
In harmony with the fixed will of destiny.
Dear child of the gods, great offspring of Jupiter,
Take up your great honors—for the time is at hand.
Look how the cosmos bows to you, with all its
50      arching weight,
And the lands, and the spacious seas, and the depths
of the sky.
Look how all things rejoice at the time that is to come.
If only the last part of my long life might remain
for me,
And inspiration enough to sing of your deeds,
Neither Thracian Orpheus nor Linus could defeat me
55      with their songs,
Not even if his father favored the one, and his mother
the other,
Orpheus Calliopea, Linus the handsome Apollo.
Even Pan, were he to compete with me, with Arcadia
as judge,
Even Pan would say he was beaten, with Arcadia
as judge.
Begin, little boy, to recognize your mother with a smile;
60      Ten months brought long hardships to your mother.
Begin, little boy. Those who do not smile at
their mother
No god thinks worthy of his banquet, no goddess of
her bed.

## GEORGICS

### Book 1

*The poem opens (1–42) with an address to Maecenas,
Virgil's patron, and a prayer addressed first to the appropriate agricultural deities, then to Octavian.*

What tickles the corn to laugh out loud, and by
what star
to steer the plough, and how to train the vine to elms,
good management of flocks and herds, the expertise
bees need
to thrive—my lord, Maecenas, such are the makings
of the song
I take upon myself to sing.
                    Sirs of sky,
grand marshals of the firmament,
O Liber of fertility, and Ceres, our sustaining queen,

by your kind-heartedness Earth traded acorns
of Epirus
for ample ears of corn and laced spring water with
new wine;
and you, O Fauns, presiding lights of farming folk     10
(come dance, O Fauns, and maiden Dryads,
your gifts I celebrate as well); and you, Neptune,
whose trident's
booming tap on rock first fanfared to bring forth a
snorting horse;
and you, patron of shady woods, whose many hundred head of cattle
fatten, pristine, in the chaparral of Ceos;
and you too, Pan, abandoning your native groves and
glades of Lycaeus,
caretaker of the flocks, if Maenalus means anything at
all to you,
come to me, O god of Tegea, a friend and comforter;
and you, Minerva,
who first discovered olives; and that youth, too, creator of the crooked plough;
Sylvanus, too, who carries on his back a sturdy
cypress, ripped up from the roots—     20
a god or goddess each of you, whose care and
concern is
for land, who nurtures crops not grown from seed,
and who dispatches onto plantings heavy showers
from the heavens;
and I address you too, O Caesar, although none knows
the gathering of gods
in which you soon will be accommodated, or whether
you would choose
to oversee the city or be in charge of countryside, nor
knows if the wide world
will come to honor you as begetter of the harvest or as
master of the seasons
(around your brow already a garland of your mother's
myrtle),
or whether you will come as lord of endless sea, and
seafarers will worship you,
your power alone, and the ends of earth bow to you in
homage,     30
and Tethys forfeits all her waves to have you as a
son-in-law,
or whether you will add a new star to the zodiac to
quicken months
where there's a lull between Virgo and Libra which
comes after it
(already ardent Scorpio contracts its claws for you
and allots to you more than your fair share of sky).

Whatever you will be (let not the nether world of
    Tartarus hope to have you
as its king, nor ever such a dread ambition lord over you,
however much Greece knows the wonders of
    Elysian fields
and Proserpina pays her mother little heed although
    she hears her calling her),
grant me an easy course, and bless the boldness of this
40    undertaking—
who shares my sympathy for countrymen whose lives
    are wanderings in the dark—
look forward now, expert already in the ways to
    answer our entreaties.

*In the first section of agricultural lore, Virgil describes the
seasons for plowing, with rich soil in the spring, and poorer
soil in the autumn.*

Come the sweet o' the year, when streams begin to
    melt and tumble down the hoary hills
and clods to crumble underneath the current of
    west winds,
it's time again to put the bull before the deep-pointed
    plough to pull his weight
and have the share glisten, burnished by the
    broken sod.
There's the crop, which twice has felt a touch of snow
    and twice of frosty weather,
that is a beggared farmer's prayer come true.
That's the one to fill his sheds until they're fit to burst.
And yet before we take our implements to unfamiliar
50    territory
we must work to ascertain its changing weather and
    winds' moods,
to learn the ways and habits of that locality—
what's bound to flourish there, and what to fail.
For here you'll find a crop of grain, and there grapes
    growing in thick clusters,
and over yonder young trees thriving and grasses com-
    ing into green all on their own.
        Can't you see how scented saffron comes
        from the uplands of Lydia,
ivory from India, incense from soft-hearted races of
    Arabia;
and we get iron from unclothed inhabitants of Pontus,
    slimy castor from the Black Sea,
and the choice of mares for breeding from a region in
    north Greece?
Right from time's beginning, nature assigned these
60    laws to last for ever,

each in its specific place, fixed such compacts from
    the moment
Deucalion cast onto the world the stones from which
    mankind
originated, a hardy race!
        And so onward!
From the sun's first tender touch, run your mighty teams
through fertile fields, tossing sods about
for baking heat to break them down to dust.
But if you've not got high yielding soil you will do well
to rake it with a shallow sock by the shine of that
    time's brightest star,
to ensure either that weeds won't block the way for
    wholesome crops
or that a bare sandy plot retains whatever moisture's
    there.    70

*Next follow instructions (71–99) on caring for the
soil—leaving it fallow, rotating, burning stubble, and
cross-plowing. Irrigation is then treated in 100–117.*

        Take turns to let the land lie fallow after it's
        been harvested,
let fields left to themselves recuperate and renew
    themselves with firmer footing
or, with a switch of season, set down, say, tawny
    emmer or einkorn,
where once you'd gathered an outpour of pulses
with their rustling pods, or drawn spindly vetch
and bitter lupins' brittle stalks and susurrating stems.
For it's a fact and true, a crop of flax will parch a place,
as will wild oats, as will a sprawl of poppies doused in
    their forgetfulness.
That said, you'll lighten loads of routine by rotation.
Don't spare dry land its fill of dung,    80
don't hesitate to spread a heap of grimy ashes on spent
    fields.
While your land gets a chance to rest by changing crops
don't think that all the while your fallow isn't earning
    a return.
        Frequently there's much to gain by setting
        flame to idle acres
and letting their thin stubble burn—either because
    it helps
engender some weird force and rich feed for the soil
or because the fire scalds all its faults and failings
and sweats out baleful moisture.
Or is it that the heightened heat unclogs the pores and
    opens passages
through which the sap ascends into new shoots    90

or makes clay even firmer by closing yawning
    waterways
so that it isn't blasted by a fall of rain or sun's excessive
    benison
or the bite of freezing winds that batter from
    the north?
        And as for that, great is the good he does a field
            who with a mattock breaks apart
its lumps and clumps, then with a wicker hurdle
    harrows it,
earning a look he likes from Ceres high on her
    Olympian heights,
just as he contributes much who raises flat land
    into ridges
by ploughing one way, then cross-ploughing,
and regularly works his lands and keeps a tight rein on
    his holding.
        The countryman should pray for wet summers
100             and mild winters;
corn delights in hiemal dust. Then the country's in
    good heart—
there's nothing brings out better in places such
    as Mysia,
and Gargarus can be amazed by its own harvests.
        Need I single him for praise who follows
hard on the heels of setting seed by crumbling heaps
    of unreceptive soil
and steering into tracks streams to irrigate the
    plantings?
And when the countryside's aglow and all that grows
    is withering in the heat
see how he conjures water from the brim to spill
    downhill in sloping channels,
a flow that grumbles over gravel, gushing onward
110  to allay the thirst of scorched places.
    Or indeed the one who, to ensure that stalks won't
        lodge beneath
the weight of ears, grazes to the ground the
    tender shoots
that grow in such profusion as soon as they clear the
    furrow's ridge,
or that one who drains swamp-gathers in a soak-pit,
especially in the course of those unsettled months
    when rivers burst
their banks and smear mudspills everywhere on
    everything,
causing steam to rise again from hollows.

*The first digression on the ages of man and the introduc-*
*tion of work into the world (118–46) follows the mention of*
*the threats to the farmer's success. It was Ceres, then, who*
*introduced agriculture (147–59).*

        And don't imagine that, for all the efforts and
            exertions—
man's and beast's—to keep the sod turned over, there's
    not a threat
from plagues of geese, or Strymon cranes, from
    bitter roots of chicory,                                    120
nor hurt or harm in shade of trees. For it was
    Jupiter himself
who willed the ways of husbandry be ones not spared
    of trouble
and it was he who first, through human skill, broke
    open land, at pains
to sharpen wits of men and so prevent his own
    domain being buried
in bone idleness. No settler tamed the plains before
    our Father held his sway
and it was still against the law to stake a claim to part
    of them.
Men worked towards the common good and the earth
    herself,
unbidden, was lavish in all she produced.
And it was he who instilled in snakes their deadly
    poison,
bade wolves to prowl, and seas to surge.                       130
He shook down honey from the leaves and had all
    fires quenched.
He stopped the flow of wine that coursed rampant in
    the rivers
so that by careful thought and deed you'd hone them
    bit by bit,
those skills, to coax from furrows blades of corn
and spark shy flame from veins of flint.

        That was the first time ever hollowed alders
            sailed on water,
and seagoing men began to number, and then name,
    the stars—
the Pleiades, the Hyades, and Lycaon's child, the glit-
    tering Great Bear.
Then men came up with ways to try to trap wild ani-
    mals, by setting snares
of sticky sticks for birds and rounding game in glades
    with packs of hunting hounds.                               140
And by this time someone was dragging rivers
    with a net,
plumbing their depths; another trawled the open sea
    with his soaking mesh.

Then came tempered iron and the saw-blade's
    rasping rhythm
(for earlier man was wont to split his wood with
    wedges).
All this before the knowledge and know-how which
    ensued.
Hard work prevailed, hard work and pressing poverty.
        It was Ceres who first taught to men the use of
            iron ploughs that
time wild strawberries and oak berries were scanty in
    the sacred groves
and Dodona was miserly with her support.
150    Soon growing grain grew into harder work.
    Blight rusted stalks, and thistles mustered into
        view to lord it over
all that you accomplished; crops began to flounder, a
    rough growth to advance—
goosegrass, or 'cleavers', and bristling burrs—while
    wild oats
and dreaded darnel ruled head and shoulder over your
    well-tended plot.
So, unless you're set to spend the whole day hoeing
    weeds,
and making noise to scare off birds, and slashing back
    with hooks
the branches darkening the lands, and all your prayers
    for rain are answered,
alas, my friend, heaps of grain next door will stare you
    in the face
and you'll be raiding oaks for acorns to ease the ache
    of hunger.

*Virgil now describes (160–75) the tools at the farmer's dis-*
*posal—plow, wagon, hoe, and so forth—to resist nature's*
*onslaughts (176–203).*

Now let me tell about the tools and tackle unflagging
160    farmers had to have
in their arsenal, for none has sowed or saved a crop
    without them.
The ploughshare first, and the curved plough's
    solid board,
and Ceres' hefty carts for sheaves,
threshing rakes and sledges, and the heavy-weighted
    mattock.
And then the lighter implements of wickerwork—
    arbutus gates and hurdles,
and Iacchus' marvellous riddle which serves to sort
    the chaff from grain.
So think ahead—stockpile a cache of these in time

if you're to earn the satisfactions of that heavenly
    estate.
        To make the plough's main curve, fashion
            by force
a pliant elm while it's still growing in the ground.     170
Then to its stock fit and fasten an eight-foot pole,
earth-timbers, and a twin-backed beam.
Light lime you will have kept aside to make the yoke,
and for the tiller a length of beech to steer it from
    behind.
Hung in the hearth, smoke will season wood
    components.

I could, if I'd not seen you back away from such
    concerns,
regale you with a store of ancient learning.
To begin: grade the threshing floor with the heavy
    roller,
taking pains to tamp it tight with chalk
so that no growth breaks through and it holds firm
    and doesn't crumble.     180
Let no blights of pests or parasites squat there;
for often, underground, the mouse sets up his house
    and home
and the groping mole excavates a bolt-hole
and you come upon a shrew or fieldmouse in a hollow
and other creatures earth turns out—the beetle scurries
to spoil heaps of wheat, the emmet hurries to safe-
    guard against a want some rainy day.
        And so pay close attention when stands of
            walnut trees
disport themselves with blossoms and their fragrant
    boughs bend down—
if they produce abundant fruit, your corn crop will be
    bountiful,
great heat will follow and guarantee your harvest.     190
But if, instead, a luxury of leaves abounds and throws a
    shadow over everything,
you'll waste a world of time at grinding, end up all
    chaff and little grain.
I've seen with my own eyes plantsmen steeping seeds
before they set them down, drenching them in saltpe-
    ter and the dregs of olive oil,
so that their deceiving pods would grow a
    greater yield,
one that might amount to something over a low
    flame.
        And I have seen long-tried and tested crops
            begin to fail
where no one took the time each year to sort and save

the finest grain, seed by seed. For that's the way it is—
world forces all things to the bad, to founder
200     and to fall,
just as a paddler in his cot struggling to make headway
        up a river,
if he lets up a minute, will find himself
rushed headlong back between the banks.

*In this section on the farmer's calendar, Virgil first describes*
*the proper times for plowing and sowing (204–30). This*
*leads to a description of the zones of the earth, based on the*
*formulation by the Greek scholar Eratosthenes (231–56). It*
*concludes with a brief adaptation of Hesiod, giving advice*
*on work to be done in bad weather, on holy days, and in*
*winter (257–310).*

What's more, you need to keep a weather eye on sky
        formations—
such as Arcturus, the twin kids of the Charioteer, or
        Draco, that bright light,
and stay vigilant as those mariners who, homeward
        bound, ride stormy seas,
yet venture close to Pontus, the Straits of Abydos and
        their oyster beds.
And when September's equinox doles to day as many
        hours as to night
and splits the world in two fair halves, both equal light
        and dark,
then set to work the oxen, men, broadcast barley in
210     the fields,
until midwinter's whelming showers slap you in
        the face.
Then, too, it's time to plant linseed and seeds of
        poppies (loved by Ceres),
time to tie yourself to the plough while the
        still-dry earth
accepts it and the settled weather lingers.
        Set beans in springtime, the time alfalfa hap-
                pens in collapsing furrows,
and millet clamors for its annual attention,
when Taurus, gilt-horned and incandescent, gets the
        new year
up and running, and the Dog succumbs to his
        advance.
But if you've been working towards a strong output
        of wheat
220   or you're heartset on hardy ears of corn,
hold off until one of the Seven Sisters steals away from
        you at dawn

and the Star of Knossos, the shining Northern Crown,
        retires
before you entrust to the ground seed you've pledged
and invest in soil that couldn't keep its promise to
        repay the hopes of a whole year.
Some cropsmen thought that they could not delay till
        May began to wane
and the crops that they were counting on jeered them
        with hollow heads of oats.
        But if you're the kind who's satisfied with sow-
                ing seeds of vetch and tares
and second-rate green beans and don't look down
        even on Egyptian pulses,
you won't mistake in any way the signs a setting
        Bootes transmits—
you might as well get on with it, and carry on your
        sowing until you're up to here in frosts!     230
        This is the very reason the sun god is so
                faithful to his path
between each of the dozen fixed divisions of
        his orbit.
Five spheres make up the heavens, of which one, and
        only one,
is always blushing brightly and always flushed by his
        flaming fire.
And all around, left and right, a cyanic realm stretches
        far as far can be,
hard frosts and ice and gloomy spills.
Between this and the middle sphere a pair of zones
        is given
by godly grace to pitiful man, through both of which a
        way's laid down
and the series of signs takes turns along their
        roundabout way.
And the universe, just as it rises to the lofty slopes of
        the Riphaean ranges,     240
pitches downward in the south, in Africa.
        There's a pole that always looms above us, while
                its counterpart
lies underfoot in Stygian dark and the infernal shades.
Here the sky's enormous serpent slithers in and out,
the image of a river, between the Big and Little
        Dipper,
those constellations that disdain to be touched or
        tainted by Atlantic's waters.
        There, or so they say, either it's the dead of night
                and so still—
a black shadow stretching over everything as if for ever—

or dawn comes back to them on its way back from us,
    daylight's chaperone,
and, when morning first inspires us with its puffing
250    horses,
there the lamps of evening are coming on, and glow.

And so we have the power to anticipate uncertain
    weather—
the day to reap, the day to sow—
and when the time is right to plunge our oars into
untrustworthy seas, when to launch an armed armada,
when's best, even, to fell a pine tree in the forest.
      It's not for nothing we keep an eye on sky
        for signs
that come and go, or on the year's four equal parts.
Say the farmer's grounded by a cold snap's burst
    of rain,
he'll seize the time for odd jobs he'd be rushing when
260    it's fine.
The ploughman points the blunted share with
    hammer blows
or gouges troughs from trees,
or brands the herds, or checks the stocks of grain;
another whittles stakes and twin-pronged forks
and readies sally switches to tie the dangling vine.
And now might be the time to weave fruit baskets out
    of brambly branches
or roast the corn beside the fire before you crush it
    with the quern.
      For it's a fact, on holidays you're actually
        allowed by gods' laws and by men's
to attend to certain labors—so let no scruple
    deflect you
if you would clear a drain, or fill a gap around the
270    cornfield,
set traps for birds or fire to briars,
and dip the whole flock in the flow to stave off scab.
These are the times the farmer weighs the
    little donkey
down with creels of olive oil and fruit he's picked
and comes back later from the town with a grinding
    stone or a supply of pitch.
      The moon herself prescribed days suitable for
        certain work.
Beware the fifth, the day on which grim Death
was born, as were the Furies, the day the Earth
    whelped ghastly giants—
Coeus, Iapetus, and restless Typhoeus—and another
    heinous brood,

the brothers who conspired to bring down the very
    heavens.        280
Three times did they essay to heap Mount Ossa on
    Mount Pelion,
and then—it followed—to impose on Ossa Olympus'
    leafy heights.
And three times he, the Father himself, blasted those
    piled hills with lightning.
      The seventeenth's a lucky day for laying down
        the vine,
for rounding up and breaking in an ox or heifer, for
    setting up the loom.
The ninth day smiles on anyone who runs away, but
    frowns on those who steal.
      It's true, the small small hours are best for many
        things,
or that very moment the sun is fledging and the land's
    still dabbed with dew.
Night's the best for cutting lighter crops, night's best
    for well drained meadows,
for then there is no lack of lingering moisture.    290

There's a certain sort of man who by winter firelight
stays up all night edging iron implements.
And all the while, with soothing songs lightening the
    load of her routine,
his helpmeet runs across her loom her rattling reed,
and in the hearth a flame reduces the sweet-
    scented must,
its bubbles simmering in a pot she skims with
    brush-strokes of broad leaves.
While, on the other hand, in midday's highest heat,
    you're better off
knocking red or ruddy grain or bruising parched pro-
    duce on the threshing floor.
Plough on days you'd strip to the waist; sow the same.
Winter's the time for farmers to unwind. In colder
    months        300
countrymen enjoy themselves, taking turns to
    entertain.
Congenial winter is a treat: it banishes their woes and
    worries,
as if a laden ship just docked in a safe haven
and sailors had begun to decorate its stern with
    garlands.
Still and all, that season has its labors, they file away
    the hours—
the gather-up of acorns, bayberries and olive-berries,
    and the purple berries of the myrtle.

What's more, it's time for you to set out traps for
    herons, cast nets for stags,
to course the long-lugged hare and fell a hind
by hurling your coarse hempen slings the way they do
    in the Balearics,
all this while snow falls from the heavens, and floods
310    advance their loads of ice.

*In this passage (311–50), Virgil bridges to the following
description of weather signs with an account of a storm,
highlighting its suddenness and devastation, balancing the
depiction of political strife at the end of the book.*

What can I tell about the storms of autumn and
    its signs,
or, even, when the days are closing down and summer
    sun's abating,
what then must men beware of? Or, say, when spring
    comes tumbling
down in showers and crops of corn are tall already,
their green stalks standing proud with sap?
How often I have seen, just as the farmer's driven in
    to reap
the flaxen field and top the fragile barley crop,
the clash of squalls and gales in battle mode
as they ripped up from roots the swathes of ripe and
    ready corn
320   and held them up, the way malefic whirlwinds
    toss beardless stalks around the place, hither and yon.
        At other times a rush of water cascades from
        the sky,
clouds spill their mass into the foul darkness of a
    deluge,
as the heavens open and the rainfall wipes the smiles
off the faces of the crop the oxen worked so hard
    to make.
Ditches fill to the brim, rampant channels overflow,
the sea rampaging up each boiling inlet.
        Then Jupiter, squire of the sky, straddling the
        night clouds, dispatches
from his gleaming hand a thunderbolt and makes the
    whole world quake.
330   Wild beasts take off, and everywhere human hearts
are laid low in a panic. He hurls that blazing dart
onto Athos, Rhodope, and the peaks of Ceraunia;
south winds redouble and rains intensify;
now the great groves in the gale, and now the shores,
    burst into tears.
So, in apprehension, keep an eye on each month's
    constellations,

and note where the cold star of Saturn steals away to,
and in which orbits the planet Mercury is
    wandering.
Above all else, venerate the gods and pay your yearly
    offerings
to Ceres, when the grass is in good heart,
at the very end of winter when spring brings on
    clear skies.          340
Then lambs are fit, wine's at its best.
Sleep's pure delight, and on the heights deep
    shadows lie.
Have all your workers be worshippers of that goddess,
and offer milk and honey and mild wine,
and march a victim three times around fresh crops
    for luck
while all the others celebrate, a band of allies in
    support.
Let them implore her loudly to come and rest
    with them,
but stay the hand of anyone who'd lay a sickle to a
    single ear of corn
who has not wreathed his head with oak leaves in
    her honor
and made up dances and sung hymns to her.     350

*In the final section of the book (351–463), Virgil describes
the weather signs, beginning with those that forecast bad
weather (351–92), followed by those for fair weather (393–
423), with a final section reserved for signs given by the
moon (424–63).*

        And so that we might be prepared to read
        unerring clues—
anticipate heatwaves and showers and winds
    precipitating cold—
he himself, the Father, decreed what each moon phase
would mean, the sign by which south winds subside,
what always indicates that farmers keep their teams
    in stalls
and near to hand. The minute winds begin to swell
and seas to surge, a brattling sound
starts up in the mountains, chaotic noises echo
far along the coast, and murmurs in woodlands
    increase.
Then the waves are in no mood to bear a ship     360
and cormorants dash back from sea and bring their
    throaty roars
to the shore; waterhens more used to waterways
play on dry land—a sign for herons to forsake
the marshes and weave their way high in the sky.

And you can readily predict impending gales
by shooting stars that blaze their way through the
   night sky
and leave a white trail printed there.
You'll see airy chaff and fallen leaves afloat on waves,
down and feathers fluttering there.

But then, when from the quarters of the north wind
370   lightning flashes
and from the home place of the east and west winds
   thunder rumbles,
the countryside's awash with the overwhelm of ditches
and seafarers furl their soaking sails.
      A spill of rain should never catch you unawares,
for either you'll have seen soaring cranes seek protection in the bottoms,
a heifer face the sky suspiciously and work its nose to
   sniff the wind,
sweet-singing swallows circle round a lake,
or heard the frogs stuck in the mud and croaking their
   old grumpy sounds.
More often you'll see ants transporting eggs along a
   narrow, well-worn way
from their safest shelter, or a mighty rainbow
380   bending down
to take a drink, or as they evacuate their feeding
   grounds
a cavalcade of squawky rooks.
      Next, a host of seabirds and those contented
         rummaging
in grassland swamps of Asia Minor or pools along the
   river Cayster
mimic each other by splashing spray onto their upper
   bodies,
now plunging head first into waves, now spurting
   underwater,
so that you'd think they're revelling in the ordinary
   routines of washing.
Then a crow, strutting the deserted shore,
proclaims in its mean caw, Rain, rain, and then more rain.
      In truth, even in the dark of night, young
390         women busy carding wool
can foretell a storm's approach: they notice in their
   lighted lamps
a sputtering, and watch spent wicks begin to clot and
   harden.
And it's as easy to predict sunny days and stretches of
   clear weather
in the wake of heavy showers if you're attentive to
   the signs.

For the points of stars won't then appear blunted
nor the moon's own beams rise up as though it borrowed light from her kin
nor clouds like wispy fleeces be borne across the
   heavens.
Along the strand, kingfishers—favorites of the
   sea-nymph, Thetis—
won't extend their wings in the warm sun
nor filthy lazing swine think of tossing with their
   snouts the bedding in their sties.                        400
Instead, the clouds determine to hang heavy on the
   lowlands,
while, at sunfall, night's silent raptor watches from above
and wastes its time hooting charms and hexes.
High in the skies Nisus comes into view, a sparrowhawk,
and Scylla pays the price for that lock of reddish hair
   she stole.
Whenever she goes flying by, splitting the heavens,
there he'll be, her father and her mortal foe, spitting
   screeches
and in hot pursuit; yes, where Nisus takes himself up
   and away
there she'll ever be, slicing heaven with her wings and
   cutting it to pieces.
Then ravens strain their voices to pour forth their one
   pure note, three times or four,                        410
and, perched high on their roosts, croak from their
   green shade
in ways that we don't understand but with better than
   their customary cheer.
How it seems to lift their hearts, when a rain belt's
   hurried overhead,
to turn back to their new-hatched brood and their
   beloved nestlings.
Not that I accept, however hard I try, that they've the
   slightest talent given them by god
nor that fate bestowed on them any shred of
   ancient lore.
And yet—where there are changes in the weather and
   shifts in atmosphere—
Jupiter, the god of sky, with sodden southern winds
   condenses
all that had been airy and rarefies what had been so
   oppressive.
Then they have a change of heart and give themselves
   to different feelings,                                 420
different from when gusts were shaking up the
   clouds—
and that's the cause, across the country, of concord
   among birds,

of livestock lying down in peace and ravens crying out
    their hallelujahs.
        It's true—you keep your eye on the
            fleet-footed sun
and any run of moons, and dawn won't take you by
    surprise,
nor tricks of cloudless night catch you off guard.
For when the moon collects herself in
    brimming fires,
if she is cradling an amorphous shape and sheen you
    have 'earthshine'
and spills of rain are on the way to those who hoe the
    fields and row the waves.
But if she blushes like a maiden there'll be
430    a breeze;
the advent of the wind precipitates a flush on the fresh
    face of the moon.
And if, on her fourth morning (that most reliable
    of all),
she sallies through an open sky, her horns
    unblurred,
all that day long, and all the days that stem from it
until month's end, you needn't fret yourself about
    wind or rain,
and sailors standing safe ashore may count their
    blessings
and give thanks to those sea-deities, Glaucus,
    Panopea, and Ino's son, Melicertes.
        And the sun itself, on its way up or sliding
            down below the waves,
offers signs—none more deserving of our heed than
    those attached to it
as it rises in the morning or as it meets the
440    winking stars.
If he appears at dawn all stained with spots
or hides in clouds the middle of his face
watch out for heavy showers: there'll be a south wind
    pounding from on high
that is no friend to trees or crops or cattle.
But if he comes pushing through thick clouds in all
    directions
like bright spokes of a section of a wheel
or if the goddess of the dawn rises wanly from her
    consort's saffron couch,
beware: there's nothing you can do for them, your ripe
    shoots of vines,
such heavy hail will bounce and clatter on your roof.
This, too, when he's passed through and is retiring to
450    the heavens,

you'll do well to remember, for often we'll observe
    odd colors
stray across his countenance—dark blues declare
that there'll be rains, while tints of fire forecast
    east winds.
But if those hues begin to blend with glowing red
look out for gales and stormy clouds together.
On such a night, spare me the thought that anyone
    would contemplate
that he'd set sail or as much as touch the tie rope of
    his boat.
But if, when he presents the day and then
    retracts it,
his face is just as clear both times, your storm fears
are a thing of nothing, and you'll see trees tilting in a
    gentle northerly.    460

*The book closes with a listing of the signs and portents that
attended the assassination of Julius Caesar and led to civil
war (461–514).*

        In short, whatever evening's bringing on,
            whence winds propel
fair-weather clouds, and what wet southerlies
    portend,
the sun will advance warning signs. Who'd dare to
    question
the sun's word? For it is he, once more, who forestalls
    troubles,
hidden but at hand, of conflicts festering out of sight.
And it was he who felt for Rome that time that
    Caesar fell
and veiled his gleaming head in gloom
so dark the infidels began to fear that night would last
    for ever;
although, in that catastrophe, the earth itself and
    stretches of the sea,
unruly hounds, and bad-natured birds, sounded their
    predictions too.    470
How frequently we've watched eruptions of
    Mount Etna
and the expulsions from her furnaces spill on the
    one-eyed giants' lands
fireballs and molten lava.
The skies of Germany resounded with the din of war,
weird stirrings caused the Alps to tremble.
What's more, in quiet groves a voice was heard by
    many peoples,
a monstrous voice, and pallid specters loomed

through the dead of night and—dare I say it?—
cattle spoke. The rivers ground to a halt, gaping holes
    appeared,
and in the sanctuary carved ivories began to weep the
480     tears of mourning
and bronzes to perspire. The Po, king river, swept away
    in raging rushes
across the open plains whole plantations, cattle and
    their stalls,
swept all away. That was a time
when entrails, carefully scrutinized, showed nothing
    but the worst
and wellsprings spouted blood all day
and hill towns howled all night with wolves.
And never was a time more streaks of lightning split a
    limpid sky—
nor dismal comets flared at such close intervals.
So was it any wonder that Philippi observed for the
    second time
490 the clash of Roman forces in a civil war,
and gods above did not think it a shame that we, with
    our own blood,
would once again enrich wide-spreading Emathia and
    the plains below Haemus.
Nothing surer than the time will come when, in those
    fields,
a farmer ploughing will unearth
rough and rusted javelins and hear his heavy hoe
echo on the sides of empty helmets and stare in
    open-eyed amazement
at the bones of heroes he's just happened on.
        O Romulus, god of our fathers, strength of our
            homes, our mother Vesta,
who watches over our Etruscan Tiber and the palaces
    of Rome,
stand back, don't block the way of this young one who
500     comes to save
a world in ruins. More than enough, and long ago, we
    paid in blood
for the lies Laomedon told at Troy. Long, long ago
    since heaven's royal estate
begrudged you first your place among us, Caesar,
grumbling of your empathies with the cares of men
    and the victories they earn.
For right and wrong are mixed up here, there's so
    much warring everywhere,
evil has so many faces, and there is no regard for
    the labors
of the plough. Bereft of farmers, fields have run to a
    riot of weeds.

Scythes and sickles have been hammered into
    weapons of war.
Look here, the east is up in arms; look there, hostilities
    in Germany.
Neighboring cities renege on what they pledged and
    launch attacks—                                          510
the whole world's at loggerheads, a blasphemous
    battle,
as when, right from the ready, steady, go, chariots
    quicken on a track
until the driver hasn't a hope of holding the reins and
    he's carried away
by a team that pays heed to nothing, wildly away and
    no control.

# AENEID

## Book 4

*After hearing Aeneas's story of his wanderings, Dido is on
fire with love. The next morning she goes to her sister Anna
and confesses her passion, but she is wracked with guilt
over her resolve not to break faith with her dead husband
Sychaeus (1–30). Anna argues that she should not have to
live alone and counsels Dido to keep Aeneas in Carthage
and marry him (31–53). She manages to sway Dido, who
now cannot bear the thought of being without Aeneas. All
work on building her new city of Carthage comes to a halt
(54–89).*

Now though, the queen, long since pierced through by
    her terrible anguish,
Nurtures the wound with her veins. Passion's blind fire
    feeds on the harvest.
Images course through her mind: of his courage, his
    family distinction.
Each word he's spoken is fixed in her heart, each facial
    expression.
Anguish grants no peaceful repose, no respite for
    tired limbs.                                               5

Next day's Dawn had dismissed sky's dew-dank dark,
    and was shining
Earth with Apollo's lantern, when Dido, her sanity
    fading,
Came to what was her soul's other self, in a
    manner: her sister:
'Anna my sister, what sleepless dreams suspend me in
    terror!

Who is this newcomer guest who has set up his
10    quarters in our home?
Oh, what a grand look he has, how brave in his heart
    and in battle!
Gods generated his line; I believe this, not simply on
    blind faith.
Base-born, degenerate souls are exposed by their
    fear. What a beating
Destiny gave him! What wearying wars sang out in
    his story!
Were it not rooted, immovably fixed in my mind,
15    that I'd never
So much as wish to ally myself with another in marriage,
After my first great love deceived me and failed me
    by dying,
Were I not weary of weddings, my thoughts about
    marriage so altered,
I, perhaps, could rest easily with this one point of censure.
Anna, I have to confess: ever since my poor
20    husband Sychaeus
Died and my brother stained our household's shrines
    with his slaughter,
This is the one man who's suppled my senses and
    pummeled my fainting
Mind's resolution. These embers of long-lost fires,
    I recall them.
I'd rather see Earth yawning her bottommost chasms
    before me,
Feel the Omnipotent Father's fire thrust me to the
25    shadows—
Erebus' pale, dank shadows, and Night's sea of
    darkness—than ever
Violate you, my own honor, or loosen the vows that
    I make you:
He, who first coupled me to himself, robbed me
    of my love life.
So, let him keep it and guard it in death's unlovely
    confinement.'
This said, tears welled up in her eyes and dampened
30    her bosom.
Anna responds: 'You are dearer than life's very light to
    your sister.
Will you then squander your youth in your solitude,
    harvesting sorrow,
Not knowing joys Venus offers: delights that she
    yields, and those sweet sons?
Dead souls, urns full of ash set aside, do you think
    they'll be troubled?
Suitors' pleas, in the past, failed to move you, sick in
35    your grieving:

Tyrians earlier, Libyans now. You rejected Iarbas
Scornfully, and other princes that Africa, goldfield for
    triumphs,
Nurtures. Will you still fight off love even when it's
    appealing?
Aren't you concerned about peoples who share these
    lands you have settled?
We are surrounded: Gaetulian cities, invincible
    warriors.    40
Who can control the Numidians, tame wild tidelands
    of Syrtis?
South lies a region of desert and thirst and of savage
    Barcaean
Nomads. I hardly need talk about Tyre's impending
    invasion,
Threats from your brother.
I think the gods gave us excellent omens when Ilian
    vessels    45
Sailed this way on the winds to our land. We have
    Juno's approval.
Joined in a marriage with him, what a city you'll see,
    what a kingdom
Rising in front of your eyes! In alliance with Teucrian
    forces,
Punic Carthage will soar to the summit of glorious
    achievement.
Ask the gods' pardon, that's all you must do, make the
    right kind of offerings.    50
Play lavish hostess, and reef in his hawsers with rea-
    sons for staying:
Winter and rainy Orion, of course, whip seas
    to a fury,
Ships need refitting; the overcast skies prevent safe
    navigation.'
Stirring an already smoldering soul to love's rashness
    of passion,
Anna fed hope to a hesitant mind, severed chastity's
    moorings.    55
Off to the shrines they went first, these two, and from
    altar to altar
Searched out omens of peace; they selected and ritu-
    ally slaughtered
Hoggets for Ceres the lawgiver, Phoebus, and father
    Lyaeus,
And, above all, for the power that controls all
    marriages: Juno.
Loveliest Dido herself, in her own right hand, holds
    the goblet,    60
Pouring the contents between the two horns of a
    gleaming white heifer.

Sometimes she paces, before heaven's eyes, to the rich
smoke of altars,
Starting the day with her offerings, staring intently as
cattle's
Cavernous chests are cut open, consulting their still
living entrails.
This is the insight of seers? Pure ignorance! What use
65    are votive
Offerings or shrines when you're mad? It is she whose
soft tissue the fire eats,
Hers is the chest still alive with a wound that won't
offer responses.
Dido, unfulfilled, burns on and, in raving obsession,
Randomly wanders the town, like a deer pierced
through by an arrow
Hit long range, when off guard, in the Cretan woods,
70    by a shepherd
Armed for the hunt. He has left his steel-tipped shaft
in her body,
Not knowing he's hit his mark. In her flight, she ranges
all Dicte's
Meadows and woods. Barbed deep in her haunch is
the reed that will kill her.
Now Dido's leading Aeneas all over the heart of her
fortress,
Showing him Sidon's resources, explaining her plans
75    for the city,
Starting to tell him her thoughts, stopping short, halfway through a sentence.
Now, day drooping to dusk, she's the same. She
repeats the same banquet:
Crazily pleading to hear once more what the Trojans
have suffered,
Once more hanging in awe on his lips as he tells her
the story.
Later, when others are gone, when the already dim
80    moon, in its turn,
Snuffs out its light, and the stars as they fade persuade
slumber, she lingers
Ghostlike in grief on the couch he's abandoned, the
sole presence haunting
Emptied halls. He's not here, but she hears him; not
there, but she sees him.
Charmed he's his father's image, she'll take in her lap
young Ascanius,
Hoping that she can delude Love's inexpressible
85    passion.
Bastions started no longer rise, youths' military training
Halts. The port's harbor defenses aren't readied for
war. As construction

Ceases, the growth of the daunting and massive walls
is disrupted:
Cranes that reach high to the skies are left dangling in
idle suspension.

*In this interlude with the gods, Juno suggests a truce to
end her quarrelling with Venus and agrees to the marriage of Aeneas and Dido, an arrangement that would
lead to Carthage's supremacy. Venus only pretends to agree
(90–128).*

Jupiter's darling wife, Saturn's daughter, upon
diagnosing                                                        90
What kind of plague gripped Dido, and knowing that
fear of the damage
Rumor might cause wouldn't stifle her madness, said
these words to Venus:
'Marvelously regal glory you've won, war's spoils in
abundance,
You and this young boy of yours—this memorable
might of divine power!
Thanks to a ruse, two gods tally up one woman
defeated.                                                         95
Your false tricks don't hide your genuine fear of
my city,
I knew how much you distrusted the mansions of
powerful Carthage!
Where will you stop, how far will you go in your wild
competition?
Why not, instead, work together, for endless peace
and a marriage
Sealing it? See, you've attained what you spent your
whole intellect planning:                                         100
Dido is burning with passion, love's madness has
seeped to her marrow.
Under matched auspices, then, let us rule their com-
bined populations
Jointly. I grant that she'll serve as the bride of a
Phrygian husband,
And, as her dowry, deliver the Tyrians into your
keeping.'
Venus, who grasped that her words were staged to
disguise her intention—                                          105
Namely, transferral to Libyan shores of Italian kingship—
Counter-attacked in this way: 'One would have to be
mad not to honor
Terms such as these, to prefer fighting you in a
war—that's assuming
Fortune favors and follows the plan your proposals
envisage.

Yet I'm not clear about fate, not sure whether Jupiter
110    wishes
One city shared by the Tyrians and those who have
     sailed from the Troad.
Does he approve such a mixture of peoples, such
     union by treaties?
You, as his conjugal partner, have rights to implore
     him, to fathom
What's on his mind. I'll follow, you lead!' Royal Juno
     responded:
'That will be my special chore. Now let me explain
115    very briefly
How we will manage the task that we face. So please
     pay attention.
Dido, poor woman, lays down with Aeneas the plans
     for a wild game
Hunt in the forests tomorrow when Titan pulls back
     the wide world's
Covers and radiantly blazes the day's first blushes of
     sunrise.
While their wings flurry their flanks, while they're
120    setting up snares around clearings,
I'll set a blackening storm-cloud on them, rain
     mingled with hailstones
Pouring to earth from above, and I'll rumble the
     whole sky with thunder.
All their companions will scatter; they'll vanish,
     disguised by the darkness.
Dido and Troy's chief will come down together inside
     the same cavern.
I'll be there too. And, if I am sure you'll co-operate
125    freely,
I'll designate her as his, join them both in a durable
     marriage.
This is the day they'll be wed.' Cytherea voiced no
     opposition,
Nodded assent, then laughed. She had seen through
     these obvious ruses.

*Dido appears for the hunt resplendent in her attire, while
Aeneas joins her looking like Apollo (129–59). A storm over-
takes the hunting party, with Dido and Aeneas taking shelter
in a cave, where Nature bears witness to their union (160–72).*

Golden Aurora, surging aloft, left the damp bed of Ocean.
Out from the gates, as sun's rays rose, rode a youthful
130    select corps,
Then came a torrent of fine nets, snares, broad
     iron-tipped hunting

Javelins, troops of Massylian horse, and scent-catching
     dog power.
Still in her boudoir, the queen takes time; the elite
     Punic nobles
Crowd at her doorway and wait. And her steed stands
     waiting, but wildly
Champing its froth-covered bit, quite resplendent in
     gold and in purple.                                         135
Finally, she makes her entrance, attended by hosts of
     retainers,
Draped in Sidonian fabric with needlework fringes,
     her shoulders
Armed with a quiver of gold, hair clasped by a
     golden tiara,
Cloaked in a bright purple mantle secured by a
     brooch-pin of pure gold.
Clusters of Phrygian friends come along; the
     delighted Iulus,                                            140
Too. But most lovely of all, outshining the
     others, Aeneas
Joins with the host as an ally and merges his troops
     with their columns.
He's like Apollo, deserting his wintertime home by
     the Lycian
Streams of the Xanthus to visit his mother's homeland
     of Delos,
Where he's the sponsor of ritual dance. Round his
     altars there mingle                                         145
Cretans, tattooed Agathyrsians, Dryopes, all celebrating.
*He* strides the ridges of Cynthus above, and to pin his
     loose tresses,
Twines supple branches to fashion a garland, secures
     them with gold loops.
High on his back, arrows rattle. Aeneas is no less
     impressive,
Riding among, yet surpassing the others and regal in
     splendor.                                                  150
Once they have reached high mountain terrain past
     the end of the footpaths,
Look, wild she-goats, dislodged from the ledges of
     rock at the summit,
Leap down the ridges; and there, racing out from a
     different direction,
Deer run a course down the mountains and then fan
     out into columns
Pounding up dust as they bound in their flight across
     open expanses.                                             155
Down in the heart of the valley, the youthful
     Ascanius passes

This group and that, at a gallop. He's thrilled by his
   horse's quick spirit,
Prays that among these helpless herds of unchalleng-
   ing livestock,
He'll find a wild boar leaving the heights, or a
   tawny-backed lion.
160 Meanwhile the massive rumbling of thunder begins to
   roil turmoil
All through the heavens. Then follows a cloudburst of
   rain mixed with hailstones.
Tyrian troopers and Troy's young warriors, mingling
   at random,
And Venus' Dardan grandson, all hunt in fear for such
   scattered
Shelter as fields offer. Now it is rivers that rush down
   the mountains!
165 Dido and Troy's chief come down together inside the
   same cavern.
Earth gives the sign that the rites have begun, as does
   Juno, the nuptial
Sponsor. The torches are lightning, the shrewd sky's
   brilliance is witness,
Hymns for the wedding are howling moans of the
   nymphs upon high peaks.
That first day caused death, that first day began the
170 disasters.
Dido no longer worries about how it looks or
   what rumor
Says, and no longer thinks of enjoying a secret liaison.
Now she is calling it marriage; she's veiling her sin
   with a title.

*Rumor of the union of Dido and Aeneas runs through
Libya, reaching Iarbas, Dido's former suitor (173–97). He
calls out bitterly to Jupiter, complaining of his rejection
(198–218). Jupiter hears and sends Mercury to Aeneas
to order him to set sail at once (219–37). Mercury obeys
and delivers Jupiter's message to Aeneas, whom he finds
busily helping to build Carthage (238–78). Aeneas is hor-
rified when Mercury appears and worries about Dido's
reaction, but he orders his men to ready the fleet in secret
(279–95).*

Out in a flash through Libya's cities Rumor is blazing.
No other evil is swifter than she. Rumor's being is fuelled
By her mobility, gaining additional strength as she
175 travels.
Not very fearsome at first, she soon puffs large on the
   breezes,

Striding the ground, but thrusting her head up high
   into cloud-caps.
Earth was her mother, they say, bearing this last child
   in her angry
Spite at the gods. Thus Coeus, Enceladus too, got
   a sister
180 Fast on her feet, and provided with wings of astonishing power,
Huge and horrendous, a monster whose body conceals beneath feathers
Just the same number of spying eyes (a remarkable
   feature),
Just the same number of tongues, and of mouths, and
   of ears pricked to eavesdrop.
Flying at night between heaven and earth, she
   screeches through darkness,
185 Nor does she grant any sweetness of sleep to her eyes
   ever searching.
Seated by day, she does sentinel duty aloft on a
   rooftop,
Or, up in some tall tower, ripples terror through powerful cities,
Clinging to fiction and falsehood as often as telling the
   plain truth.
Now, she is flooding the people with many crosscur-
   rents of gossip,
190 Singing of things done, things not done, without any
   distinction:
That some man named Aeneas has come; and his
   bloodline is Trojan.
That lovely Dido is deeming it proper to join herself
   with him;
That they are passing long winter hours in the high life
   together;
Cupid's slaves in a shameless love, their kingdoms
   forgotten.
195 Such is the gossip the foul goddess scatters at
   random on men's tongues.
Quickly, she twisted her devious course to the ruler
   Iarbas,
Kindled his spirit with words, added more words,
   fuelling his anger.
Born of a raped Garamantian wood-nymph and
   fathered by Ammon,
This man erected a hundred enormous temples, a
   hundred
200 Altars in Jupiter's honor, all over his far-reaching
   kingdom,
There dedicating eternal flames, gods' vigilant sentries,

Floors rich with animal blood, doors blooming with
  garlands of all kinds.
Rumor dissolves his aroused love in sourness and
  razes his reason.
He, it's said, falls to his knees, amidst gods at their
  altars, a changed man,
Desperate, hands stretched upward to Jupiter,
205    pleading intently:
'Mightiest Jupiter, you to whom Moors make our first
  dedications
When, as we feast on our tapestried couches, we
  honor the winepress:
Father, do *you* see *this*? Or are *we* quite needlessly
  trembling
Each time you spin off a thunderbolt? Is it just
  unseeing, cloud-borne
Fire that frightens our souls, compounded by
210    meaningless rumbles?
Here is a woman who wandered within our borders,
  and founded,
Cash down, a very small city. We gave her a few coastal
  ploughlands,
Leased on a contract. And then she rejected our offer
  of marriage,
Took in Aeneas, and made him her master and lord of
  her kingdom.
Helped by his eunuch entourage, this latter-day
215    Paris,
Chin kept in place by Maeonian bows, and his hair by
  conditioning
Perfumes, controls what he's raped. We, meanwhile,
  consecrate offerings
Made in your temples, and place our faith in what's
  just idle Rumor.'
    He, with his prayer so phrased, and tenacious
      presence at altars,
Caught the Almighty's ears; Jove's eyes blazed round
220    to the royal
Walls and to lovers blind to their need of more favor-
  able rumors.
Speaking to Mercury, then, he dispatched him with
  some such instructions:
'Get under way, wake the zephyrs, my son, let your
  wings glide you downwards!
Speak to the Dardan leader, who's now lodged in
  Tyrian Carthage,
Wasting time with no thought or respect for the cities
225    that fate's words
Grant him. Deliver my dictates now through the
  swift-flowing breezes:

That's not the kind of behavior that loveliest Venus,
  his mother,
Promised us. God knows, it wasn't for this that she
  saved him from Greek spears
Twice. Wasn't he once supposed to make Italy preg-
  nant with empires,
Seething with wars, to rule her, sire there a new breed
  out of noble                                                    230
Teucer's blood, and to force the entire world under his
  law's yoke?
If, then, the glory of such great deeds doesn't fire up
  his spirit,
Being indifferent himself to the plaudits earned by this
  hard work,
Can he, a father, with envious eye, begrudge Rome to
  Ascanius?
What does he hope he can build by delay in this
  enemy nation,                                                   235
Sparing no thought for Ausonian sons and Lavinian
  ploughlands?
Tell him to sail. That's final. Let this serve him notice
  of our will.'
    So he spoke. And the other prepared to obey
      these parental
Orders. He first straps boots to his feet. They are
  ankle-high, golden,
And, having wings, take him upwards in flight over
  seas, over dry land,                                            240
Swift as a rising current of air. Next he picks up his
  special
Wand, which he uses to call up the pale, wan spirits
  from Orcus,
Or to dispatch others down below earth, into
  Tartarus' grimness.
With it, he gives or takes sleep, makes eyes remain
  open on deathbeds,
And, with its help, he can navigate winds, weather
  turbulent cloudbanks.                                          245
Now, as he swoops, he discerns both the summit and
  steep flanks of rugged
Atlas, who levers aloft, on his peak, all the weight of
  the heavens,
Atlas, whose pine-covered head is eternally banded
  with storm clouds,
Battered by wind and by rain. Round his shoulders is
  strewn a mantle
Thickened with snowfall; and down from the chin of
  this elderly being                                             250
Cataracts plunge, and his beard-bristle freezes to
  icicled stiffness.

Here Mount Cyllene's god, powered in on his glisten-
    ing paired wings,
First touched down. From there, powered out by the
    weight of his body,
Seaward he dived like a tern, who's been circling
    shorelines and cliff pools
Teeming with fish, skimming wave-tops. In turn, one
255    knowingly pictures
How Cyllene's child now descended from his own
    maternal
Grandfather, feathered his flight between heaven and
    earth to the sandy
Coastland of Libya, cleaving his winding way through
    the breezes.
        Then the god, just as his winged feet land in the
        outskirts of Carthage,
Glimpses Aeneas constructing defenses, refurbishing
260    houses,
Wearing a sword with a star-speckled inlay of
    yellow-green jasper,
Shoulders ablaze with a trailing mantle of Tyrian
    purple,
Wealthy Dido's tribute of honor, the work of her
    own hands,
Threaded with highlights of fine-spun gold worked
    into the cross-weave.
Instantly on the attack: 'You, laying foundations for
265    mighty
Carthage!' he said. 'Obsessed with your wife, you're
    now building a lovely
City for her. You've forgotten your own obligations
    and kingdom!
Heaven's own king, who spins both the sky and the
    earth with his power,
Sends me to you himself, directly from gleaming Olympus,
Tells me himself to convey these instructions through
270    swift-moving breezes:
What do you hope you can build, you deserter, in
    Libya's deserts?
If, in fact, glory from such great deeds doesn't fire up
    your spirit,
Being indifferent yourself to the plaudits earned by
    this hard work,
Think of the growing Ascanius, the dreams for Iulus
    to cherish.
He is your heir. Thus Rome's fine earth and Italy's
275    kingship
Stand as his due.' The Cyllenian addressed him in just
    such a manner,

Yet, before all had been said, much less answered, he
    fled mortal vision,
Vanished away in the thinness of air, far distant from
    eyesight.
        Not that Aeneas could have replied. For the
        sight left him speechless,
Senses lost, hair bristling in shock, voice frozen in
    locked jaws.                  280
Still, though, he burns to get out, to escape from the
    lands that delight him,
Stunned by the mighty force of the gods' command-
    ment and warning,
Wondering what he should do, how he'd dare to get
    round the besotted
Ruler with some explanation, or find ways of broach-
    ing the subject.
This way and that, he channeled his swift mind,
    testing his options,               285
Every alternative he could conceive. He approached
    from all angles.
This, as his thoughts vacillated, appeared the most
    forceful decision:
So he calls Mnestheus, Sergestus as well, and the val-
    iant Serestus;
Then, he instructs them to refit the ships, muster
    crews on the seashore,
Ready their weapons. No word must get out. The
    entire re-equipment          290
Must be disguised. In the meantime, since excellent
    Dido knew nothing,
And wouldn't dream that their great love affair was in
    fact being shattered,
He would himself test out some approaches, and find
    the most tactful
Times for a talk, and how best he could frame it.
    Reaction was instant.
Each obeyed orders and followed instructions. They
    all were delighted.            295

*Dido is not deceived, and upon discovering his plans, she
confronts Aeneas, reproaching him for leaving her alone
and without a child (296–330). Aeneas replies to her fee-
bly, saying that he is leaving her reluctantly, but in accordance with the gods' will (331–61). Dido rejects Aeneas's
explanation and is carried off in a faint by her servants
(362–92).*

Still though, the queen detected his ruse. Who could
    fool a lover?

Scared because things seemed safe, she discovered his
plans for departure

First. Rumor, ever unrighteous, informed on him, telling the furious

Ruler the navy was being refitted and readied for
sailing.

300    Mind now out of control, all ablaze, she screams
through the city,

Bacchic in fury, resembling a Thyiad frenzied by
brandished

Thyrsus and loud Bacchic cries when Thebes'
biennial orgies

Madden her soul, when Cithaeron's voice howls shrill
in the night-time.

Finally, she broached the subject, addressing Aeneas
as follows:

'Was it your hope to disguise, you perfidious cheat,
such a monstrous

305    Wrong, to get out, with no word said, from this land
that I govern?

You are not bound by our union of love, by the hand
you once gave me,

Nor does Dido, doomed to a cruel death, now
detain you.

Why so much work on your fleet? Constellations tell
us it's winter,

310    Yet you are rushing to put out to sea, cruel man, while
the north winds

Rule. Why is this? Were you not in pursuit of some
other man's ploughlands,

Unknown homes, and if ancient Troy were still in
existence,

Would Troy, then, be the goal for your fleet on the
water's expanses?

Could you be running from me? Let me urge you,
with tears, by your right hand

315    (Thanks to my pitiful conduct that's all I have left now
to swear by),

Urge you by love we have shared, by the steps we have
taken to marriage:

If I have ever earned your thanks for services
rendered,

Or given you any pleasure, I beg you, if prayer still has
meaning,

Pity this falling house, shrug off your present intention.

320    Libyan tribesmen, nomad sheikhs all loathe me. The
Tyrians

Hate me on your account; and on your account
I have ruined

My sole claim to a stellar distinction: my chastity's
good name,

Once honored, even by Rumor. I'm dying, and yet
you desert me,

Houseguest—the lone name left for the man I called
"partner in marriage".

What should I wait for? My brother Pygmalion's
attack on my city?                                              325

Or till I'm captured and wed by Gaetulia's monarch,
Iarbas?

If I'd at least, before you ran off, conceived from our
closeness

Some child fathered by you, if there just were a
baby Aeneas

Playing inside my halls, whose face might in some way
recall you,

I would not feel so wholly trapped yet wholly deserted.'

That's what she said. He, conscious, however, of         330
Jupiter's warning,

Never once blinked, and he struggled to keep his anxiety stifled

Deep in his heart. Yet he briefly replied: 'That I owe
you, my ruler,

All you could list in your speech I would never deny.
You have earned it.

Memory will never elicit regret for my missing Elissa

While I remember myself, while my spirit rules in         335
this body!

Now, a few words in defense. This escape: slipping out
like a bandit,

That was not what I hoped. Don't twist my words.
And I never

Formally wed you nor did I endorse any contract as
"husband".

If fate's orders allowed me to live out the life of my
choosing,                                                         340

Putting my anguish to rest as I myself would have
wanted,

Troy is the city where I'd be now, looking after my
own folk's

Relics and remnants; the great house of Priam would
still stand in spirit,

My own hands would have rebuilt Pergamum's shrines
for the vanquished.

But, great Italy now is the land that Apollo of Grynia   345
And Lycian oracles tell me to seize, it is Italy's
great land.

This is my love and my homeland. If you, since you are
a Phoenician,

Focus your gaze on the towers of Carthage, your
   Libyan city,
Why does the vision of Teucrians settling the land of
   Ausonia
Evil your eye? We too have the right to seek overseas
350    kingdoms.
Each time night cloaks earth with opaque, dank shad-
   ows of spectral
Darkness, and fire-born stars rise upwards, my father
   Anchises'
Angry face in my dreams chastises me, stalks me with
   terror,
As does my son, Ascanius. The damage I've done his
   dear person!
Cheating him out of his destined Hesperian kingdom
355    and croplands!
Jupiter now has dispatched his divine intercessor, who
   bears me
Personal orders, I swear by them both, through the
   swift-blowing breezes.
I myself, in clear day's light, saw Mercury
   enter
These very walls, and my own ears heard each word he
   was saying.
Stop enraging me, and yourself, with all this
360    complaining.
Going to Italy's not my choice.'
        Such was his tally of words. For a while, she just
        watched him obliquely,
Eyes flashing this way and that as he spoke, scrutiniz-
   ing at random
His whole being with silent looks. Then her anger
   exploded:
'No goddess gave you birth, no Dardanus authored
365    your bloodline!
Caucasus, jagged with flint, fathered you—in
   Hyrcania! Savage
Tigresses stuck their teats in your mouth, you
   perfidious liar!
Why disguise what I feel, hold back, knowing worse is
   to follow?
When I wept, did he groan, did he soften his glance or
   surrender,
Conquered by torrents of tears? Did he pity the
370    woman who loved him?
Which thought shall I express first? It's clear neither
   mightiest Juno
Nor Saturn's son, the great Father, looks fairly at this
   situation.

Nowhere can one treat trust as secure. I found you in
   dire need,
Shipwrecked; and, fool that I was, I gave you a share in
   my kingdom,
Brought back the fleet you'd lost, at the same time sav-   375
   ing your comrades.
Oh, I am burning with fury! Now: enter Apollo
   the Augur;
Lycian oracles next; then, in person, Jupiter sending
Gods' intercessor down, bringing hideous commands
   through the breezes.
Maybe this is a dilemma for powers above, anguish to
   trouble
*Their* deep inertia.
        I won't try to keep you, or craft a rebuttal.    380
Go with the winds! Pursue Italy! Chase across seas for
   your kingdoms!
My hope, if righteous forces prevail, is that, out on
   some mid-sea
Reefs, you'll drink retribution in deep draughts, often
   invoking
Dido's name. When I'm absent, I'll chase you with
   dark fire! When cold death
Snaps away body from soul, evil man, my dank ghost    385
   will haunt you.
My destination is yours. There'll be no impunity.
   You'll pay.
Tireless Rumor will come to my buried remains. I will
   hear her.'
Breaking away before all had been said, she escaped
   from the outside
Breezes. She felt quite sick, as she turned and then fled
   from his vision.
He was left trapped: hesitating through fear to say
   much, and yet so much    390
Wanting to speak. Dido's failing limbs were supported
   by handmaids
Back to her marbled chamber and there set to rest on
   her mattress.

*Aeneas returns to his fleet, which is speedily being prepared
for departure, while Dido contemplates another approach
to him (393–415). She asks her sister Anna to go to Aeneas
to beg for a delay (416–36). But Aeneas is not moved
(437–49). Dido now prays for death and is tormented in
her dreams (450–73).*

Righteous Aeneas, much as he wished he could soften
   her angry

Pain by consoling her grief and find words to rechan-
nel her anguish,

395   Much as he groaned and felt shaken at heart by the
great force of love's power,

Nonetheless followed the gods' commands, and
returned to his navy.

That's when the Teucrians fell to their work, started
hauling the tall ships

Down to the far-stretched beaches, where hulls were
retarred and refloated.

Eager to launch, crews brought in, as timber for oarage
and planking,

400   Leaf-covered branches and unhewn trunks.

Into and out of the city you'd see them, everywhere,
streaming.

Ants getting ready for winter do this: they attack an
enormous

Mountain of grain and they carry it off to provision
their anthill.

Spanning fields, their black formation snakes across
grassland,

Hauling spoils: one long slim track. Some lever
405   and trundle

Monstrous kernels, shoulders strained; some enforce
the formation,

Bullying idlers along, their entire path seething
with labor.

　　　Dido, what did you feel when you noted and
　　　watched this commotion?

Oh, what groans you expressed, looking out from the
citadel's summit:

Seeing the shore set aboil, and the whole expanse of
410   the water

Stretching before your eyes churn choppy and noisy in
uproar!

Ruthless Love! Hearts break, humans die. How far
must you force us?

Dido is forced once again into tears, once again
attempts pleading,

Bending her pride to its knees before love. For she
wants to leave nothing

Unexplored to ensure that her long-doomed death
415   isn't pointless.

'Anna, you see how the shore now seethes as they
hurry departure.

In they come, this way and that; furled canvas keens
for the breezes,

Sailors are happy, festooning the vessels with garlands
of flowers.

Sister, if I've had the personal strength to foresee this
intense pain,

I'll have the strength to endure it. But Anna, I'm miserable, help me!                                                      420

Do me this last honor. You're the sole person his per-
fidy visits,

Trusts with his innermost secrets. This makes you the
sole person expert

As to the when and the how of making him tactful
approaches.

Go, my sister, and speak to our proud-hearted foe as a
suppliant.

I wasn't with the Danaans in Aulis when they vowed
to wrench Troy                                                         425

Up by its roots, and Pergamum wasn't attacked by
my navy;

I didn't dig up the ashes and ghost of his father
Anchises.

Why, then, does he refuse to admit my words to his
harsh ears?

Why the great haste? Let him grant his poor lover this
final concession:

Simply to wait for an easy escape and for winds in his
favor.                                                                    430

It's not our long-gone marriage, which he has betrayed,
that I'm begging,

Nor that he live without lovely Latium or give up his
kingdom.

Time's what I ask, nothing tangible: space for my
frenzy to calm down,

So, now I'm beaten, misfortune can train me to cope
with my anguish.

This is the final extension I beg (please pity your
sister);                                                                   435

If he approves, I'll repay him, with interest, when my
time expires.'

Such her insistent plea; and such lamentations her sister,

Saddest of all, has to act, re-enact. To laments, he
proves passive,

Motionless; and to their voices, the words that he
hears, unresponsive.

Fate blocks, god obstructs what he, as a man, would
hear calmly.                                                            440

So, in the Alps, wild gales from the north gust this way
and that way,

Vying among themselves to uproot some vigorous
oak tree,

Massive with centuries' growth: there's a roar, and the
uppermost foliage

Flies off and carpets the ground as the trunk shudders.
    Yet the old oak tree
Sticks to the crags; and as high as its crest reaches up
445    towards heaven's
Brightness, its roots stretch down just as low into
    Tartarus' darkness.
Such was the pounding of voices, this way and that
    way, the hero
Underwent ceaselessly; he, in his great heart, felt all
    the anguish.
But, in his mind, he remained unmoved; tears flood,
    but are wasted.
Dido, denied fulfilment as doom closes in, bringing
450    terror,
Now begs for death. It is wearying torture to look at
    the arched skies.
And what resolved her to work for this goal and
    escape from the day's light
Was that while setting her gifts upon altars smoky with
    incense,
She saw an omen grim to describe: for the sanctified water
Blackened, the wine poured out transformed into
455    sickening blood-clots.
No one was told of this prodigy. No, not her very own
    sister.
Further, there was in the palace a marble temple that
    honored
Dido's previous husband, which she maintained with
    astounding
Care, decorated with snow-white fleeces and festival
    garlands.
From it, she thought she could hear both the voice
460    and the words of her husband
Calling, when night held earth in the anxious grip of
    its darkness.
High on a rooftop, a lone screech owl keened death in
    repeated
Dirges, and wailed shrill cries drawn out into pulses of
    sobbing.
Many predictions of old-time seers with their hideous
    warnings
Deepened her terror. Aeneas, a ravenous beast in her
465    fevered
Nightmares, hunted her down. Yet she seemed ever
    wandering lonely
Endless paths, left all by herself without any companion,
Looking, alone, for her Tyrian people in desolate
    landscapes.
She was like Pentheus, stripped of his mind, seeing
    armies of Furies,

Seeing the sole sun double, and Thebes in a duplicate
    presence;                                                            470
Like Agamemnon's child, driven mad in a
    drama: Orestes,
Fleeing his mother who's armored with flames and
    with dark hissing serpents,
While, at the door of the palace, avenging Furies sit
    waiting.

*Having decided to kill herself, Dido conceals her inten-*
*tion by pretending that she will perform a magic rite to*
*win Aeneas back. She thus tricks Anna into helping her to*
*prepare a pyre (474–503). When the pyre is ready, she sets*
*Aeneas's sword upon it, along with an image of him, and*
*prays (504–21).*

    She, then, in total surrender to pain, became
        pregnant with madness.
Passing sentence of death, she determines the time
    and the method                                                     475
In her own counsels. Yet she, when addressing her sor-
    rowful sister,
Masks all trace of her plans and presents a facade of
    serene hope.
'I've found a way, dear soulmate (so say "Well done!"
    to your sister).
I'll either get him back, or get rid of the love that he
    causes.
Close by Ocean's edge, near to sunset, lies the remotest
Outpost of Ethiopian rule. It's where Atlas the mighty    480
Spins sky's sphere, all studded with burning stars, on
    his shoulders.
Someone has just let me know of a priestess from
    there, a Massylian,
Once warden of the Hesperides' shrine, in charge
    there of feeding
Food to the dragon, and guarding the tree with the
    magical branches.                                                  485
Using a mixture of honey and sleep-bringing
    opium poppy,
She, with the right spells, claims she can liberate
    minds when she chooses,
But that, in others, her power can induce intractable
    anguish.
Hers is the power to stop rivers, reverse heaven's stars
    in rotation.
She makes dead spirits stalk dark night; you'll see the
    earth rumbling                                                     490
Under your feet; you'll see ash trees striding down
    from the mountains.

Dearest, I swear by the gods and by you, by your sweet
    life, my soulmate,
I didn't want to invite and embrace such practice
    of magic.
Build me, in secret, an open-air pyre in our innermost
    courtyard.
Then place upon it the arms of the man, which that
495    unrighteous villain
Fixed on our bedroom walls, other gear he cast off,
    and the bridal
Bed where I came to my grief. The idea is to kill, says
    the priestess,
All of the odious memories that impious man left to
    haunt me.'
After these words, she fell silent; her cheeks were
    invaded by pallor.
        Anna, for her part, didn't believe that her soul-
500        mate was shrouding
*Her* death with these novel cults. Anna's mind can't
    conceive such obsessive
Madness, and fears nothing worse than occurred at
    the death of Sychaeus.
        She, then, acts as instructed.
Now, though, the queen, once her pyre is complete in
    the innermost sanctum,
Stacked sky-high in the open with logs cut from ilex
505    and pitch-pine,
Strews the location with wreaths, festoons it with
    funeral garlands.
Over it, she sets a bed with the gear he has left, his
    abandoned
Sword, and his person, in effigy—knowing full well
    what will happen.
Altars are built all round. Then a priestess, hair flowing
    freely,
Thunders by name three hundred gods plus Erebus,
510    Chaos,
Hecate's trinity, all three faces of virgin Diana.
Water, symbolic of death and Avernus, is used for
    lustration,
Fresh young herbs are obtained, lactating with juice of
    black venom,
Sickled with curved bronze blades and gathered at
    night in the moonlight.
Also sought is the love-charm torn, at birth, from a
515    colt's head,
Taken before its mother can snatch it.
She, hands righteously cleansed, offers sacred grain at
    the altars,

Wearing her clothes, and one of her sandals, loose and
    unknotted.
Death-doomed, she calls upon gods and the
    fate-telling stars to bear witness,
Prays to a power that is just (if there is one), a power
    that remembers,    520
Whose jurisdiction embraces all lovers with one-sided
    contracts.

*Night falls, and though all the world around her is at rest,*
*Dido cannot sleep. She blames Anna for talking her into giv-*
*ing herself to Aeneas (522–52). Meanwhile, Aeneas dreams*
*of Mercury, who warns him not to delay any longer. He*
*awakes in alarm, and the Trojan fleet sets sail (553–83).*

Night reigned: all through the world tired bodies were
    harvesting tranquil
Slumber. The woods and the savage seas lay calmed
    into stillness,
Stars at this hour were midway along their rolling
    procession.
Each flock in each field is quiet, and all of the
    bright-painted birdlife,    525
Species at large on the liquid lakes or the rough rural
    thickets,
Nestle themselves into sleep beneath night-time's
    blanket of silence.
Fears are now gentled and hearts now lost to the
    memory of struggles.
Not so the unfulfilled of soul, the descendant of
    Phoenix:
Never was she set drifting in sleep; she never did
    welcome    530
Night with her eyes or her heart. Her anguish redou-
    bles and her love,
Rising again, flares wild as she tosses on flood tides
    of anger.
Then this notion took hold in her heart and she span
    thoughts around it:
'What am I doing? Come on! Shall I check out my
    previous suitors?
How they'd laugh! Should I beg on my knees just to
    marry a nomad    535
When I've so often disdained them all as possible
    suitors?
Or, shall I follow the Ilian fleet—and Teucrian
    orders?
That's what's left, is it? They will agree since I aided
    them earlier,

They will be grateful for past good treatment. But will
    they remember?

Who'll let me come, who'll take me aboard their
540    proud sailing vessels?

Hate for me speaks in their eyes. Don't you know, mad
    fool, don't you sense it?

Perjury's quite a tradition among Laomedon's people!

What? Be a runaway woman alone among jubilant
    sailors?

Well then, suppose I'm protected by all my Tyrians,
    full force?

These are the same troops it took all my efforts to root
545    out of Sidon:

Must I again force them onto the seas and command
    them to hoist sail?

Just go and die! You deserve to. Go parry your pain
    with a steel blade!

*You*, sister, *you* gave in to my tears, you burdened
    my raving

Soul with its first load of evil. You served me up to my
    foeman!

Out of the question, you said, that I should, with no
550    scandal, but no mate,

Eke out a bestial life that avoided the hint of such
    anguish.

I then broke every promise I made to Sychaeus' ashes.'

Such was the voice of her grief breaking forth from her
    heart's desolation.

High on his aft-deck, Aeneas, his business duly
    accomplished,

Sure he could now set sail, was reaping a harvest of
555    slumber.

Then, some shape of a god represented itself to his
    dreaming

Mind, coming back, the same look in his eye, again
    seeming to warn him.

Every detail suggested Mercury: yes, the complexion,

Sound of the voice, blond hair, and the limbs so young
    and attractive:

'Son of the goddess, how can you take charge, in this
560    crisis, by sleeping?

Don't you detect, then, the dangers that have you
    completely encircled?

Don't your ears tell you, you madman, that zephyrs,
    that fair winds, are blowing?

She's got some ruse in her heart, she has some atrocity
    brewing;

She's set on dying, she's rousing the changeable tides
    of her anger.

Why aren't you getting out fast while a fast getaway's
    still an option?    565

Soon you'll see timber churn up waves, massed men-
    acing firebrands

Burst into flame, beaches leap with the fires of a blaz-
    ing inferno,

If, that is, dawn's light catches you still hanging round
    in this country!

Hang the delays! What you face is a complex and
    changeable constant:

Woman.' When he'd said this, he mingled himself with
    the dark night.    570

    Terrified now by this sudden upsurge of
        phantoms, Aeneas

Snatches his body from sleep, then awakens and
    haggles his crewmen:

'Wake up and get up, my lads, settle down to your oars
    on the benches,

Set all sail! Make it quick! Yet again a god sent down
    from heaven

Urgently drives us to speed our departure and cut
    through the looping    575

Hawsers. Whoever you are, holy god, we follow
    you gladly

And, yet again, we obey your command with a feeling
    of triumph!

Stay by our side, we implore, treat us kindly, provide
    us auspicious

Stars in the sky.' So he spoke. And he pulled out his
    blade like a sudden

Lightning flash from its sheath and with bared steel
    sheared through the moorings.    580

All feel the same fire instantly, grab their equipment
    and make haste.

Coasts are already astern, sea's surface concealed by
    the navy.

Straining backs and arms churn foam, oars sweep the
    blue waters.

*In the light of dawn, Dido sees the ships at sea and cries
out in passion, calling down a curse on the Trojan race and
invoking the eternal hatred of her people upon them (584–
629). Now in complete distress, Dido mounts the pyre but
pauses to weep at the sight of Aeneas's sword (630–50).
Then she prays once more, hoping that the Trojans will see
the flames of her funeral pyre and be haunted by the sight.
With that she stabs herself, and the city is filled with lamentation (651–71).*

Dawn was by now beginning to stipple the earth with
    new brightness,
Leaving Tithonus' saffron bed. From her watchtower,
585    the ruler
Watched as the early light whitened and noticed the
    fleet under full sail
Standing seaward, well under way, and observed that
    the empty
Coastline displayed not a single oarsman strolling the
    harbors.
        Three times, four times she pounds on her
           beautiful breast, and rips golden
Hair from her head by the roots. 'Oh Jupiter! Shall this
590    intruder
Go on his way,' she exclaims, 'mocking me and the
    power of my kingdom?
Get a force fitted, pursue them with all of our city's
    resources,
Others must haul out our vessels from storage docks.
    Go to it, right now!
Hurry, bring fire, issue weapons, have rowers press
    hard upon oarlocks!
What am I saying? Where am I? What madness is
595    warping my reason?
Unfulfilled Dido, your unrighteous acts come to
    haunt you!
When action was the appropriate course, you were
    giving him *your* power.
        Witness the word and the honor of one, who,
           they say, carries with him,
Gods of ancestral shrines, who once took on his
    shoulders his aged
Father! Could I not have taken him off, torn his body
600    to pieces,
Scattered it over the sea, or murdered his comrades,
    and even
Served up Ascanius himself as a treat for his banquet-
    ing father?
If war'd ensued, though, the outcome was not, and
    could not have been, certain.
Whom did I fear? I was going to die. I'd have torched
    his encampment,
Filled up his holds with my fires, and once I'd
605    extinguished the father,
Child, and the whole of his race, I'd have thrown
    myself onto the bonfire.
Sun: your cleansing flames survey all earthly endeavors!
Juno: you sense, and are my intercessor in, all of my
    anguish!

Hecate: your name is howled by night throughout cit-
    ies, at crossroads!
Demons of vengeance, gods of the dying, forgotten
    Elissa!    610
Take it all in, focus your divine will, as you should, on
    my sufferings.
Hear what I pray. If it must be that this indescribable
    person
Makes it to port, that he floats back to dry land, and if
    this is really
Jupiter's last word on fate and he must reach the goal
    of his journey,
Let him be hammered in war by the armies of valiant
    people,    615
Forced from his borders, torn far away from Iulus'
    embraces.
Let him beg help, let him watch as his men are dis-
    gracefully slaughtered!
When he surrenders himself to an unjust peace and its
    strict terms,
Grant him no joy in his realm or the light he so loves.
    Let him lie dead,
Well before his due day, halfway up a beach and
    unburied.    620
This is my prayer; these final words I express with my
    life-blood:
Tyrians, drive with relentless hate against his stock
    and every
Future brood, and dispatch them as ritual gifts to my ashes.
No love must ever exist between our two peoples, no
    treaties.
Rise from my bones, my avenger—and there will be
    an avenger!—    625
So you can hound these Dardan settlers with hot fire
    and cold steel,
Now, or some day in the future, whenever that
    strength coalesces.
Menace of coast against coast and of waters hurled
    against waters,
Arms against arms, I invoke. Let them fight, they
    themselves and their grandsons!'
        This said, she started to let her thoughts wander
           in every direction,    630
Seeking to douse, just as soon as she could douse, the
    light she detested.
Then she spoke briefly to Barce, who'd once served as
    nurse to Sychaeus—
Her nurse was back in the old homeland where her
    ashes were buried.

'Please bring Anna to me, nurse dear to me, get me
  my sister.

Tell her to hurry and sprinkle her body with
635   fresh-flowing water,

And to bring with her the cattle and placatory gifts
  designated.

Please have her come. You yourself should righteously
  ribbon your temples.

This is for Stygian Jupiter's rites: I intend to
  complete them.

All the first steps I have duly prepared. I will now end
  my anguish

And set flames to the pyre of that cursed Dardanian
640   creature.'

Done. The nurse used any speed old feet still had to
  assist her.

Dido, fearful yet crazed at the ghastly extent of her
  planning,

Frantically glances about her with bloodshot gaze, and
  impending

Death now discolors her quivering cheeks with its
  pallor and blotches.

Bursting through doors to the innermost courtyard in
645   frenzy, she clambers

Up to the top of the pyre, then unsheathes the
  Dardanian swordblade.

This was the special gift she'd requested, but not for
  this purpose.

Here, catching sight of the Ilian clothing and bed so
  familiar,

She, for an instant, delayed deadly purpose in tears
  and reflection,

Fell, ghostlike, on the bed where she uttered a few
650   final phrases:

'Spoils that were so sweet once, while fate and its god
  gave permission,

Take to yourselves this soul. Cut me loose from all of
  this anguish.

Fortune assigned me a course. I have run it. My life is
  accomplished,

And now the image of me that will pass beneath earth
  has its greatness.

I've laid the ground for a famous city; I've seen my
655   own walls rise,

I have avenged my husband and punished my brother,
  my foeman.

So fulfilled, fulfilled to excess if only Dardanian

Vessels had never, oh never, touched in on the shores
  of my country.'

This said, she pressed her face to the covers: 'We'll die
  without vengeance,

But let us die! This is it, this the path that I choose to
  the dead world.                                          660

This is the fire that, far out to sea, the cruel Dardanian's

Eyes must absorb. He must carry with him these
  omens of our death.'

          Such were her words; and while she was
              speaking, attendants observed her

Slumped on the sword, saw the blade foam streaming
  blood from her body,

Saw that her hands were drenched. And their cry
  soared high through the courtyard's                      665

Open roof. Rumor now raged wild through a city left
  bludgeoned.

Homes are a chaos of noises: laments, groans, keening
  of women.

Skies far above re-echo the breast-drumming,
  grief-stricken sobbing,

Rather as if, after enemy forces had breached the
  defenses,

Carthage or ancient Tyre faced final collapse, and the
  raging                                                   670

Flames rolled in over rooftops of mortal men and
  immortals.

*Her sister hears Dido cry out, but it is too late (672–92).*
*Juno takes pity on Dido, sending Iris, the messenger of the*
*gods, to release her spirit (693–705).*

Hearing the uproar in terror, her soul now lost to
  her body,

Panicked, her sister tore through the crowds, nails
  clawing her features,

Fists beating breasts, and she called her by name as
  she lay there, expiring:

'This was your scheme, dear soulmate? Your fraud had
  me as its target?                                        675

That's what this pyre meant for me? That's what altars
  and fires were preparing?

What, now you've left me, should I protest first? Have
  you not spurned your sister's

Friendship in dying like this? If you'd called me to
  share in the same death,

Then the same pain from the sword, the same hour
  would have killed us together.

680    My hands built this pyre, my voice called out to our
       fathers'
       Gods. Did you cruelly arrange that I'd not be attend-
       ing your deathbed?
       You've killed me and yourself, the Sidonian people
       and senate,
       Sister, your city as well. Give me water to cleanse all
       these gashes;
       If any breath should stray from her mouth in its final
       expression,
685    Let me absorb it in mine.' Before ending, she'd
       mounted the towering
       Steps, nestled snug in her lap her now half-animate
       soulmate,
       Groaned as she blotted the blood's dark flow with the
       clothes she was wearing.
       Dido attempted to lift heavy eyes once again, but
       her body
       Failed her. The wounding sword, jammed deep, rasped
       hard on her ribcage.
       Three times she rose up and she propped herself up
690    on her forearm,
       Three times she slumped back on the couch as her
       eyes, in their wandering,
       Searched for the light high up in the sky; then she
       moaned when they found it.

       Juno Almighty pitied her difficult death with
       its painful
       Anguish long drawn out, and dispatched to her, down
       from Olympus,
       Iris, to unmoor her struggling soul from the limbs'
       web of bondage.                                     695
       Dido was dying a death that was neither deserved nor
       predestined,
       But premature: a poor woman, swept up by the quick
       fire of madness.
       So, as Proserpina hadn't yet taken the locks of
       her golden
       Tresses, and thereby consigned her being to
       Stygian Orcus,
       Iris, rosy with dew, skimmed down through the sky
       upon crocus                                          700
       Wings. Her wake, as she passed by the sun, traced col-
       ors in thousands.
       Standing by Dido's head, she spoke: 'I take, as
       instructed,
       Locks consecrated to Dis. I untether your self from
       your body.'
       Then, as her right hand severed the hair, all warmth
       escaped Dido;
       And as it did, life fluttered away from her into the
       breezes.                                             705

## AFTERWORD

Virgil's stature during his lifetime was such that his last work, the *Aeneid*, was eagerly anticipated by Roman readers, and it is likely that at least a select circle had already read or heard parts of the poem before the author's death. Upon publication it was an instant classic, becoming necessary reading for any Roman schoolboy, as well as for anyone in the Roman world aspiring to learn Latin. Papyrus fragments of school exercises copying out lines of the *Aeneid* have survived from disparate regions of the empire, such as Egypt and the British frontier. Verses from his poems have been found in more than sixty places scribbled on the walls of Pompeii, and one clever fellow parodied the opening line of the epic to write on the wall of a laundry owned by a man named Owl, "Launderers and the owl I sing, not arms and the man." Virgil's richly allusive style immediately drew the attention of scholars and critics, who competed in offering explanations for difficulties of language, mythological references, and historical allusion. Within a century of his death, the general outlines of an interpretive tradition had been formed by the work of scholars such as Valerius Probus and Julius Hyginus. But fame attracts its denigrators too, and there was also a rich tradition of hostile criticism practiced by individuals known collectively to later generations as "detractors of Virgil." His much younger contemporary Ovid never competed directly by composing in any of the same genres, but he acknowledged his debt to his great predecessor on multiple occasions and came closest to equaling Virgil's fame by steering clear of him. Nonetheless, in his own autobiographical poem he writes with a certain mixture of awe and regret that, while he had the opportunity to hear Horace and many other great poets of the time, Virgil he "only saw." Writers of the succeeding generations expressed their admiration in other ways. Most notably, the Flavian epic poet Silius Italicus used to celebrate Virgil's birthday with more solemnity than his own, and he venerated Virgil's tomb outside Naples as if it were a temple. Silius imitated Virgil in his own epic poem about Rome's Second Punic War (with rather little success), and several other minor poems survive from this period by anonymous imitators, some of which were subsequently mistaken for Virgil's own.

Virgil remained extraordinarily popular throughout late antiquity, even among Christian readers who always found some means to treat the poet as one of their own. St. Augustine famously laments in his *Confessions* (1.13) that he used to find himself weeping at Dido's fate:

> For what can be more miserable than a wretch that pities not himself; one bemoaning Dido's death, caused by loving of Aeneas, and yet not lamenting his own death, caused by not loving you, O God, light of my soul, bread of the internal mouth of my soul, and firmest knot, marrying my soul and the bosom of my thoughts … But I bemoaned not all this; but dead Dido I bewailed, that killed herself by falling upon the sword.

And yet Augustine cites Virgil constantly throughout his writings, and contemporaries of his, both pagan and Christian, place Virgil at the center of their literary universe. As a result of Virgil's continuing importance in the curriculum, we possess several manuscripts from this period, including two rare examples with illustrations. We can thus have more confidence that the text of modern editions closely resembles the author's original than with any other ancient writer.

One reason why Virgil was able to remain important in the Middle Ages was the propensity of his readers to see a Christian subtext in his works. The focal point of efforts to appropriate Virgil for Christianity was his *Fourth Eclogue,* in which the birth of a child will bring with it a new golden age. As early as the beginning of the fourth century A.D., the Christian apologist Lactantius read the poem as presaging the birth of Christ. This interpretation was then often repeated, for example, by the first Christian emperor Constantine, St. Jerome, and St. Augustine. In the thirteenth century the Dominican encyclopedist Vincent of Beauvais reported that three pagan Romans converted to Christianity when they read lines 5 through 9 of the *Fourth Eclogue.*

So compelling a figure did Virgil become in the Middle Ages that many legends were attached to his name, especially in the region of Naples, and he acquired a reputation as a magician. The same Vincent of Beauvais reports, "Many marvelous deeds are said to have been performed by this Virgil. At the gate of Naples in Campania he is said to have made a brass fly that drove out all the flies from the city. In the same city he is said to have built the meat market in such a way that no meat there would rot. He is said also to have constructed a certain bell tower in such a way that the stone tower itself would move in the same way as the bells when they were struck." On this last miracle, Vincent expresses some doubt, "since the use of bells had not yet been invented," but he cautiously allows that after all "maybe they were used among pagans earlier than among Christians."

No verifiable portrait of Virgil survives from antiquity, although literary sources mention commemorative images that might have derived from contemporary sources. The poet Silius was known to keep a bust of Virgil in his home, and representations of him are found in mosaics from across the empire. A particularly memorable example, dating from the third century A.D., comes from the ancient town of Hadrumentum (mod. Sousse in Tunisia), depicting Virgil seated between two Muses, holding a partially opened scroll on his lap with a line from the opening of the *Aeneid* written on it. Scenes from Virgil's works proved popular with painters and other artists, beginning almost as soon as they were released to the public. Not surprisingly, the most popular episode from Virgil's works among visual artists from antiquity onward has been Aeneas's love affair with Dido. *The Death of Dido* was painted by Peter Paul Rubens (1577–1640) near the end of his life, and other celebrated painters, such as Claude Lorrain (1600–82), Giovanni Battista Tiepolo (1696–1770), and Paul Cézanne (1839–1906), also treated the theme.

Among writers the influence of Virgil continued through succeeding generations. For Chaucer (ca. 1343–1400) the *Aeneid* was an important model for his *House of Fame*, in which the narrator tells of seeing upon a wall a brass plate, on which was written:

> I wol now synge, yif I kan,
> The armes and also the man
> That first cam, thurgh his destinee,
> Fugityf of Troy contree,
> In Itayle, with ful moche pyne
> Unto the strondes of Lavyne.

This not only serves as the setting for Chaucer's retelling of the story of the *Aeneid* but has the distinction of being the earliest translation of any part of the poem into English. Virgil's Dido is also one of the more memorable stories told in the *Legend of Good Women*. But it is Dante (1265–1321) whose name is most closely associated with Virgil in the Middle Ages, for in his masterpiece, *The Divine Comedy*, the great Florentine poet makes Virgil his guide through Hell and Purgatory. In the second part of Dante's epic, when the poet Statius speaks of Virgil's influence on his works, one can almost sense that he is articulating Dante's own view of Virgil's place in literary history (*Purgatorio* 21): "The sparks which warmed me from the divine flame whereby more than a thousand have been kindled were the seeds of my poetic fire: I mean the *Aeneid*, which in poetry was both mother and nurse to me—without it I had achieved little of worth." In the fourteenth century the Italian poet Petrarch composed an epic in Latin hexameters on the Second Punic War against Hannibal, called *Africa*, which closely imitates Virgil in many respects. He also wrote twelve eclogues in Latin and addressed an epistle in Latin to Virgil (*Familiar Letters* 24.11), whom he calls the "Prince of Latin poets."

While Virgil continued to be read in the original Latin throughout the Middle Ages and into the modern period, among readers who had not mastered Latin the story of the Aeneas was well known from vernacular renditions such as the anonymous Norman *Roman d'Eneas* and Benoit de Sainte-Maure's *Le roman de Troie*, both of the twelfth century. A Scots translation by Gavin Douglas (1474–1522) appeared in 1513, and other poets tried their hand at parts of the epic, such as Henry Howard, the Earl of Surrey (ca. 1517–47), who rendered Books 2 and 4 into blank verse. Among the many English translations of the *Aeneid* produced over the centuries, certainly the most influential proved to be John Dryden's of 1697.

Dido's story inspired *The Tragedie of Dido, Queen of Carthage*, by Christopher Marlowe and Thomas Nashe, which was first performed in 1587/88, but there have been few other representations on the stage. However, Dido has figured prominently in musical drama: the earliest opera based on her story was performed in Venice in 1641, followed by Henry Purcell's *Dido and Aeneas*, with libretto by Nahum Tate, in 1689. The libretto of *Didone abbandonata* composed by Pietro Metastasio in 1723 was first set to music by Domenico Sarro in the following year. It enjoyed enormous success, with at least fifty further settings during the following century. The second half of Hector Berlioz's *Les Troyens*, known as *Les Troyens à Carthage*, which represents the love affair of Dido and Aeneas, was performed separately in 1863, and the whole opera is now considered a part of the canon.

In the twentieth century, Virgil has continued to attract the attention of writers. Most notable—or notorious—perhaps is the verdict of T. S. Eliot, who, in his lecture "What Is a Classic?" (1944), pronounced that "whatever the definition we arrive at, it cannot be one that excludes Virgil." Eliot was in large part responding to the indifference to Virgil that characterized many of his contemporaries, most notably Ezra Pound. But Virgil continued to fascinate authors in many genres. The German writer Hermann Broch took the story of Virgil's dying wish to have the manuscript of his *Aeneid* burned as the inspiration for his novel *The Death of Virgil*. In the environment of the prewar United States, the poet Allen Tate used Virgil's works as a vehicle for a meditation on the New World in "Aeneas at Washington" (1933), which ends on a grim note:

I stood in the rain, far from home at nightfall
By the Potomac, the great Dome lit the water,
The city my blood had built I knew no more
While the screech-owl whistled his new delight
Consecutively dark.
     Stuck in the wet mire
Four thousand leagues from the ninth buried city
I thought of Troy, what we had built her for.

In the last decades of the twentieth century, classical scholars wrestled over the essential question of Virgil's vision, whether he saw the history of Rome in an optimistic or pessimistic vein. For most artists since Ovid that question has been easily resolved, as Virgil's works have been read and reinterpreted as expressions of the anxieties and self-doubt that haunt all human endeavors.

# HORACE

## (Quintus Horatius Flaccus, 65–8 B.C.)

WE KNOW RATHER MORE ABOUT HORACE THAN ABOUT ALMOST ANY OTHER ANCIENT poet, not only from his own poetry but also from a short biography by Suetonius and occasional references to him by other writers. He was born in 65 B.C. in Apulia in the far south of Italy, a region deeply imbued with the culture of many long-established Greek settlements. His father had been a slave but was prosperous enough to take Horace to Rome to be educated by the best teachers, and then to send him to the schools of philosophy and rhetoric in Athens, completing his education in the company of the sons of the richest and most powerful families in Rome. In one of his earliest poems, Horace emphasizes the stigma in status-conscious Roman society of being the son of a freedman: "I was born of a freedman father, and everyone gnaws at me for being born of a freedman father" (*Satires* 1.6.46). He goes on, however, to speak with great and patently genuine affection of his father: "As long as I am sane, I'd never be sorry for having such a father" (89). Horace alludes again to his lowly origins in the final poem of his first collection of *Odes,* in boasting of his achievement as Rome's first lyric poet: "From humble beginnings / I was able to be the first to bring Aeolian song / to Italian measures" (*Odes* 3.30.12–14). We should probably not, however, make too much of Horace's rise from obscure origins: many Italians will have been reduced temporarily to slavery in the political upheavals of the first half of the first century B.C., and Horace's father must have been fairly wealthy to provide Horace with such an education.

Horace was in Athens when Brutus arrived in the aftermath of the assassination of Julius Caesar. Brutus was looking to enroll the younger members of Rome's leading families into his army for the struggle against the Caesarians, led by Mark Antony and Octavian. It was almost inevitable that Horace should join up, rallying with youthful enthusiasm to defend the cause of liberty. He was given the rank of military tribune, a post with responsibilities quite inappropriate for someone in his early twenties with no military experience. The Battle of Philippi in 42 B.C. and the final showdown against Antony at Actium eleven years later ensured the establishment of Augustus's Principate, and could hardly have been more significant for the shaping of the Roman world. In a poem written perhaps more than fifteen years after Philippi, Horace reminds a former comrade of their participation in the struggle (*Odes* 2.7.9–14):

> With you I learned all about Philippi and speedy flight,
> and shamefully left my little shield behind
> when virtue snapped and the chins of blusterers
> touched the dirt of the earth.

But swift Mercury came to me in my panic and
carried me in a dense mist through the enemy ranks.

As so often when recounting the momentous events through which he lived, he ignores the wider
context. He gives us nothing more than a brief account of his own undistinguished part in the battle,
and even what little he does say is clearly meant to be seen as a poetic fantasy. Horace may or may not
have taken part in the actual fighting, but the detail of throwing away his shield is a reminiscence of
the same admission by the Greek poet Archilochus in a battle fought not far from Philippi six hundred
years earlier. Nor does Horace expect us to believe that he was actually transported out of the battle
by Mercury: such divine aid is reserved for Homeric heroes.

These literary allusions help Horace to distance himself from an episode he will have wished to
dismiss as a youthful indiscretion, for he was pardoned after Philippi and obtained a government post
in the treasury, and soon came to enjoy the patronage of Maecenas, Augustus's adviser and the most
prominent literary patron of the time. By the time he wrote the *Odes,* he was a committed advocate for
Augustus and had become, with Virgil, the greatest literary apologist for the regime. He had a particularly warm and lasting friendship with Maecenas. When Maecenas died in 8 B.C., he requested in his
will, addressed to Augustus, "Be as mindful of Horatius Flaccus as of me." Horace died two months
later and was buried near Maecenas in his splendid park on the Esquiline hill.

Most readers nowadays think of Horace primarily as a lyric poet, but he composed in an unusually
wide range of genres, and the contrast in tone can be startling. In many of the *Odes,* he attains a sublim-
ity of thought and expression that is starkly different from, for example, his attack on an unnamed aged
lover in *Epode* 8:

You dare to ask me, you decrepit, stinking slut,
        what makes me impotent?
And you with blackened teeth, and so advanced
        in age that wrinkles plough your forehead,
your raw and filthy arsehole gaping like a cow's
        between your wizened buttocks.

Horace's earliest works are the *Epodes* and *Satires,* written between the late 40s and 30 or 29 B.C. The
*Epodes* are a brief collection of seventeen poems, modeled primarily on the invectives of Archilochus
and Hipponax, from the seventh and sixth centuries B.C., respectively. Archilochus directed a personal
attack against Lycambes, who had changed his mind about allowing the poet to marry one of his
daughters; the attack was said to have been so vehement that Lycambes and his daughters committed suicide. Hipponax conducted a similar campaign of abuse against the sculptor Bupalus. Horace's
low social status and his initially rather shaky political position prevented him from indulging in such
criticism, at least against prominent contemporary individuals. We know little or nothing about the
people Horace attacks, and in any case fewer than half of the *Epodes* are invectives, the majority being
on a wide and disparate range of themes. The first *Epode,* for example, which seems to have a dramatic
setting in the buildup to the Actium campaign, compliments Maecenas on his willingness to follow
his friend Octavian regardless of what danger may befall him; the second enthuses about the idyllic
charms of country life, in much the same vein as the *Eclogues* that Horace's friend Virgil was writing
at this time—but Horace ambushes us in the final lines, when we learn that the speaker is a worldly
moneylender; in the third, Horace tells Maecenas that, if he ever again provides a dinner so strongly
flavored with garlic, his mistress should refuse to let him kiss her.

Horace's *Satires* show much the same perspective on contemporary events as do the *Epodes.* We
might expect virulent personal attack in satire (see p. 541), but Horace maintains his carefully distanced posture. *Satires* 1.5, for example, narrates a leisurely journey down through Italy in the company

**Figure 12:   Thomas Couture, *Horace and Lydia***
The French painter Thomas Couture (1815–79) earned fame for his historical pictures, like this one showing
Horace with Lydia, a woman whom he celebrated in his *Odes.*

of good friends, including Maecenas and Virgil. The story is packed with lively details—lazy boat-
men, burned dinners, girls who leave Horace lonesome all night—but there is hardly a hint at the
actual motive for the journey, to attend a summit meeting between Octavian and Antony, being
held to avert further civil war.

It is not known precisely when Horace began to write the *Odes,* but it is reasonable to assume
that the earliest were composed by the late 30s. It is generally agreed that the first three books were
published together in or very soon after 23 B.C. The final genre in which Horace composed was the
poetic epistle, written, like the *Satires,* in hexameters. There are twenty poems in the first book of
*Epistles,* discussing to some extent the same topics as in the *Satires,* ethical philosophy, literature, and
contemporary life. There are two long poems in the second book, the first, addressed to Augustus,
on the purpose of poetry, the second, to a young courtier named Florus, on Horace's views on his
own career as a poet. Conventionally linked with *Epistles* 2, written in the same period and structured as a letter to the sons of Lucius Calpurnius Piso, consul in 15 B.C., is the *Art of Poetry,* a discussion of how poetry should be written. It is strongly influenced by Aristotle, and that might explain its
curious emphasis on the writing of tragedy, a genre not known to have been particularly prominent
in the Augustan period. Horace returned to lyric poetry only to write the *Secular Hymn,* commissioned by Augustus for the Secular Games in 17 B.C., and a fourth book of *Odes.*

Horace ends his first *Ode* by telling Maecenas that "if you enroll me among the lyric bards /
my soaring head will touch the stars." Bards in Homer, singing epic hexameters, accompanied

themselves on a lyre, and Archilochus, though noted especially as an elegiac and iambic poet, was said to have been given a lyre by the Muses in exchange for the cow he was taking to market, and the term "lyric(al)" is often used rather vaguely nowadays to refer to, usually personal, poetry regardless of meter. Horace, however, is here referring specifically to the canon of nine great lyric poets, ranging from the seventh to the fifth centuries B.C., as established by scholars in the Library at Alexandria: Alcaeus, Alcman, Anacreon, Bacchylides, Ibycus, Pindar, Sappho, Simonides, Stesichorus. These poets composed on a wide range of themes, but they were considered to form a group based on their use of distinctive meters, whether in stanzas, such as alcaics and sapphics (which are not restricted to the poets after whom they are named), or systems not composed of repeated units such as stanzas, in particular the dactylo-epitrites of Pindar and Bacchylides.

At *Odes* 3.30.12–14 (quoted above), Horace is able to boast that he has achieved his ambition of being successful as a lyric poet. It is noteworthy that he claims to be the first to write such poetry in Latin. Modern scholars disagree on the definition of lyric as it applies to Catullus's polymetric poems (1–60), but, if nothing else, Horace is certainly ignoring Catullus 51, written in close imitation of a poem by Sappho in the sapphic meter. More than a century later, Quintilian regarded Horace as almost the only Roman lyric poet worth reading, thus passing over not only Catullus but also Statius, who has two lyric poems in his *Silvae*, 4.5 in alcaics, 4.7 in sapphics, both written in markedly Horatian style (*Education of the Orator* 10.1.96).

Although Horace's models are now mostly lost to us, and it is unclear just how familiar these poets were in Augustan Rome, there is some comfort to be drawn from the probability that he seems sometimes, perhaps regularly, to have restricted himself to a straightforward reference to an archaic Greek lyric poem at the start of an ode, only to go his own way thereafter with little or no further reference to that model. Perhaps the clearest example of this is *Odes* 1.12, which begins "What man or hero do you choose, Clio, / to celebrate with lyre or shrill pipe? / What god?" This is a clear reworking of the opening of Pindar's second *Olympian Ode*: "Hymns that rule the lyre, what god, what hero, what man shall we make famous in song?" Not only does Horace's poem have little or nothing in common with the rest of that Pindaric ode, but, given that so much of Pindar's poetry survives, we can be confident that it probably does not make reference to other poems by Pindar. Much later, Horace begins *Odes* 4.2 by declaring that anyone who tries to imitate Pindar is doomed to failure—but the next stanzas are an impressive imitation of Pindar's grand manner, though not of his subject matter.

*Odes* 1.37 is rather more complex than 1.12 in its borrowing from Greek lyric. It begins:

Now we must drink, now we must
beat the earth with unfettered feet, now,
my friends, is the time to load the couches
of the gods with Salian feasts.

Horace is echoing an ode by Alcaeus, of which only the first two lines survive: "Now we must get drunk, and drink mightily, for Myrtilus is dead." However Alcaeus's poem may have developed, it must have had certain close affinities to Horace's ode, for Alcaeus was celebrating the overthrow of the tyrant who ruled his home city of Mytilene on Lesbos, just as Horace celebrates the defeat and death of Cleopatra, who would otherwise have seized control of Rome. The link with Alcaeus is pointed by the close affinity in sound in the respective first half lines, which both mean the same: νῦν χρῆ μεθύσθην (*noon chrei methysthein*) and *nunc est bibendum*.

Horace proclaims that he is "not bound to swear to follow any teacher strictly" (*Epistles* 1.1.14). In other words, like many Romans, he was eclectic in his philosophy. Even so, a little later in the same book, he memorably declares himself to be an Epicurean: "Come and see me, plump and sleek with my hide well cared for, any time you want to laugh at a pig from the herd of Epicurus" (*Epistles* 1.4.15–16).

Certainly, Horace repeatedly presents us with a picture of himself as living a modest life, free from aspirations to wealth and power, a personification of the Epicurean ideal of "live your whole life through unobtrusively." Variations on the sentiment "Life is short and passes quickly, and we should enjoy it while we can, without troubling ourselves with ambition" recur throughout the *Odes*. In 1.4, Horace reminds us that, when we are dead, we will not be able to enjoy wine and love affairs; in 1.6, whereas others may sing of the achievements of Agrippa, the victorious admiral at Actium, he will sing of the wars of lovers; in 1.7, he urges a military friend to relax from his duties occasionally; in 1.9, he points out that youth is the time for love affairs; 1.11, addressed to a young woman, concludes with the words "Even as we speak, envious time / flies past. Harvest the day, and leave as little as possible for tomorrow." "Harvest the day" is a brilliant image: fruit not gathered in and enjoyed will go to waste. The original Latin is *carpe diem,* probably the most famous two words that Horace ever wrote.

One of the most striking features of Horace's *Odes* is the range and variety of their subject matter: politics, religion, philosophy, literature, the symposium, military achievements, love, friendship all recur throughout the collection. This ever-changing content often makes the *Odes* very difficult to assess, and the difficulty is accentuated by their rather nebulous and shifting context, combining reality with literary convention. This combination, which is no doubt more confusing to the modern reader than to some of Horace's contemporaries, can perhaps be illustrated most clearly in the manner in which Horace composes hymns. Hymns are frequent in the *Odes*; in Book 1, note particularly 10 (to Mercury), 21 (to Diana), 30 (to Venus), and 35 (to Fortune), and there are hymnic elements in other poems also. Horace could not simply employ the forms of archaic Greek hymns, for they were outmoded and alien. Nor would he wish to follow actual Roman practice, for the highly conservative nature of Roman religion will have ensured that the language of cult hymns was archaic and clumsy. Quintilian gives us a vivid impression of the distance between Roman hymns and contemporary Latin when he observes that "even the Salian priests themselves have no clear understanding of the hymns they sing, but religious scruples forbid the making of any changes" (*Education of the Orator* 1.6.41). Horace's compromise is to compose hymns that neither reflect cult practice nor use the normal hymnic language: they are literary compositions, quite different from the observances in any Roman temple. Horace's *Odes,* so far as we now know, were written not for performance but for recitation; Ovid recalls that "many-metered Horace captivated my ears, as he sang his sophisticated poems to the accompaniment of his lyre" (*Sorrows of an Exile* 4.10.49–50). There was, of course, at least one exception. The *Secular Hymn* was performed, as is recorded in the fragments of a huge marble slab found on the Campus Martius mostly in 1890, commemorating events during the Secular Games on June 1 through 3, 17 B.C. (*Corpus of Latin Inscriptions* 6.32323.149). It is not generally regarded, however, as one of Horace's greatest or most appealing achievements. It doggedly expounds Augustan propaganda in sapphic stanzas, a rather implausible medium for a Roman hymn.

In *Odes* 4.2 (see above), Horace declines to attempt to rival the magnificence of Pindar (25–32):

Many a breeze lifts the swan of Dirce [i.e., Pindar]
whenever he soars into the tract of cloud;
as for me, to the style and measure
     of the Matine bee,

all round the well-watered woods and river banks
of Tibur I work busily, sipping
the harvest of sweet thyme and shaping
     my laborious poems.

He is using Callimachean imagery to emphasize his commitment to writing small-scale sophisticated poetry. In the prologue to the *Aetia,* Callimachus rejects aspirations to write overblown epic poetry and prays to be the little, winged, sweet-singing cicada rather than a long-eared braying donkey. In the epilogue to his *Hymn to Apollo*, he likewise affirms that short, highly wrought poetry is best (110–12):

> Bees do not carry water to Demeter from every river,
> but only from a little stream, the best and choicest,
> that rises pure and undefiled from a sacred fountain.

It is endearingly appropriate that Horace should present himself as a busy little bee, for he actually was short and fat. In a wonderfully relaxed and intimate letter, preserved in Suetonius's *Life of Horace*, Augustus banters Horace for not writing about him in his poetry: "Onysius brought me your little book, and, small as it may be, I accept it as an apology. You seem to me to be afraid that your little books will be bigger than you are yourself, but it's height you're lacking, not bulk; you could write on a barrel, so that your book would measure as much around as your belly does."

One example from later in the fourth book may suffice to illustrate what Horace means by "laborious poems." Horace invites a girl to join him to celebrate Maecenas's birthday on the Ides, that is, the thirteenth, of April (4.11.13–16):

> So that you may know what joys
> you are called to, you are to celebrate the Ides,
> the day which splits April, the month
> of Venus of the sea.

One of the ways in which the Hellenistic poets displayed their learning was to incorporate into their poetry explanations of obscure words, especially Homeric words that had become obsolete. Roman poets who followed Callimachean poetic principles had two languages with which to etymologize. Here, Horace offers a Latin etymology of the word "April," as being the month in which Nature "opens" in spring, the Latin for "I open" being *aperio*. The epithet for Venus, "of the sea," also hints at the Greek etymology of Aphrodite, as being the goddess who arose from the foam of the sea, the Greek for "foam" being ἀφρός (*aphros*). This is ingenious enough, but Horace manages something special. The origin of the term "Ides" was not known, and several conjectures were current. One proposed that it was derived from an Etruscan verb meaning "divide." This is particularly apposite here, as a learned compliment to Maecenas, who was said to be descended from the ancient Etruscan kings.

# ODES

## Book 1

*It is most likely that the first book of the* Odes *was published together with Books 2 and 3, but within the complex of the three books, it is itself composed as an organic whole. Horace stakes a claim for himself as a lyric poet in the tradition of Alcaeus but shows that his ambitions are larger. The first nine poems, known since the nineteenth century as the "Parade Odes," are each composed in a different meter. With the ninth, composed in alcaic stanzas, begins a sequence in which the gesture to Alcaeus would have been clear to a reader with a copy of the standard ancient edition of the great male poet of Lesbos. Roman poets of this period show a distinct inclination toward a decimal system in arranging their poetry books—ten eclogues in Virgil's pastoral book, ten satires in Horace's first book—but the number 38 in the first book of* Odes *may have been recognized as corresponding to the number of poems in Alcaeus's first book of lyrics.*

## 1

*The first poem in an ancient collection typically establishes a programmatic theme and contains a dedication, in this case to Horace's first patron, Maecenas, to whom both the* Epodes *and the* Satires *were dedicated. It is cast in the form of a "priamel," setting out the diverse pleasures and pursuits rejected by Horace in favor of a life of poetry.*

Maecenas, sprung from an ancient line of kings,
my stronghold, my pride, and my delight,
some like to collect Olympic dust
on their chariots, and if their scorching wheels

graze the turning-post and they win the palm of glory,
they become lords of the earth and rise to the gods;
one man is pleased if the fickle mob of Roman citizens
competes to lift him up to triple honors;

another, if he stores away in his own granary
10 the sweepings from all the threshing-floors of Libya;
the man who enjoys cleaving his ancestral fields
with the mattock, you could never move, not with
  the legacy

of Attalus, to become a frightened sailor
cutting the Myrtoan sea with Cyprian timbers;
the merchant, terrified at the brawl of African gale
with Icarian waves, is all for leisure and the
  countryside

round his own home town, but he is soon rebuilding
his shattered ships—he cannot learn to endure
  poverty;
there is a man who sees no objection to drinking
20 old Massic wine or taking time out of the day,

stretched out sometimes under the green arbutus,
sometimes by a gently welling spring of sacred water;
many enjoy the camp, the sound of the trumpet
  merged
in the bugle, the wars that mothers

abhor; the huntsman stays out under a cold sky,
and forgets his tender wife the moment
his faithful dogs catch sight of a hind
or a Marsian boar bursts his delicate nets.

30 As for me, it is ivy, the reward of learned brows,
that puts me among the gods above. As for me,
the cold grove and the light-footed choruses
  of Nymphs

and Satyrs set me apart from the people

if Euterpe lets me play her pipes, and Polyhymnia
does not withhold the lyre of Lesbos.
But if you enroll me among the lyric bards
my soaring head will touch the stars.

## 2

*This poem evokes the atmosphere after the Battle of Actium. With a gesture to similar themes in the first book of Virgil's* Georgics, *Horace catalogs a list of portents that suggested a recurrence of the Great Flood, when only Pyrrha and her husband, Deucalion, survived. The flooding of the Tiber (there was a major flood in January 27 B.C.) destroys ancient monuments dating back to Numa, Rome's second king. The poem climaxes in extravagant praise of Augustus, as Octavian was now called, who is represented as the god Mercury manifest on earth.*

Father Jupiter has already sent enough fierce hail
and snow, and his red right arm
has struck his holy citadel bringing
   fear to the city

and fear to the nations. The cruel age of Pyrrha
  seemed
to be returning and the strange sights she had to
  bewail—
Proteus driving his herds to visit
   the high mountains,

shoals of fishes sticking in the tops of elms
where once the doves had nested,     10
and frightened deer swimming in seas hurled down
   upon the earth.

We have seen yellow Tiber wrench back his waves
from the Tuscan shore and rush
to throw down king Numa's memorials
   and Vesta's temple,

eager to avenge the shrill grievances
of Ilia his wife. Without the blessing of Jupiter
this doting husband left his course and flooded
   his left bank.     20

Young men will hear that citizen sharpened against
  citizen
swords that should have slain our Persian enemies.
  They will hear—

what few there are, thanks to the sins of their
    fathers—
        of the battles we fought.

What god can the people call upon to shore up
their crumbling empire? What prayer can the Virgins
din into the ears of Vesta who does not listen
to their chanting?

To whom will Jupiter give the task of expiating
30  our crime? Come at long last, we pray,
your white shoulders veiled in cloud,
        augur Apollo;

or you come if you prefer, smiling Venus of Eryx,
with Jest and Cupid hovering round you;
or, if you take thought for the race you founded
        and your neglected descendants,

come, god of war, sated with your long sport,
exulting in the battle cry, in polished helmets,
in the face of the Marsian foot soldier shouting no pity
40       for his bleeding enemy;

or if you, Mercury, winged son of bountiful Maia,
have changed shape and are imitating
a young man on the earth, accepting the name
        of Caesar's avenger,

do not return too soon to the sky. For long years
be pleased to stay with the people of Romulus,
and may no breeze come and snatch you up too soon,
        angered by our sins.

Here rather celebrate your triumphs.
50  Here delight to be hailed as Father and Princeps
and do not allow the Medes to ride unavenged
        while you, Caesar, are our leader.

3

*A poetic version of a familiar rhetorical form, the
"propempticon," or farewell poem. After honoring
Maecenas, his patron, and Augustus, the Princeps, Horace
indirectly addresses this poem to his friend Virgil, who
is sailing to Greece. He invokes Castor and Pollux, the
brothers of Helen who protect sailors, to see him safely
past Acroceraunia, a treacherous promontory on the
northwest coast of Greece. The theme of the dangers of seafaring leads to a condemnation of the daring pursuits of
men, invoking Prometheus, the son of Iapetus who brought
fire to mortals, Daedalus, the master craftsman who challenged the heavens, and Hercules. The hyperbole here suggests that Virgil too is embarking on something bolder
than a vacation in Greece, perhaps a great national epic,
his Aeneid.*

O ship, to whom Virgil has been entrusted
and who has to repay that debt, may the goddess
    who rules over Cyprus, may Helen's brothers,
those shining stars, and the father of the winds,

shutting them all up except the nor'wester Iapyx,
govern your sailing, if only you deliver Virgil safe,
    I pray you, to the boundaries of Attica,
and preserve half of my soul.

Oak and triple bronze
were round the breast of the man who first committed
    a fragile ship to the truculent sea.          10
He was not afraid of the swooping sou'wester

battling it out with the winds of the north,
nor the weeping Hyades, nor the madness of the
    south wind,
    the supreme judge of when to raise
and when to lay the Adriatic sea.

He did not fear the approaching step of death,
but looked with dry eyes on monsters swimming,
    on ocean boiling, and on
the ill-famed Acroceraunian rocks.          20

In vain in his wise foresight did God sever
the lands of the earth by means of the dividing sea,
    if impious ships yet leap
across waters which they should not touch.

Boldly enduring everything,
the human race rushes to forbidden sin.
    Boldly the offspring of Iapetus brought
        down fire
by wicked deceit to the peoples of the earth.

After the theft of fire from its home
in the heavens, wasting disease and a cohort          30
    of new fevers fell upon the earth
and the slow necessity of death, once so remote,

speeded its step.
Daedalus ventured upon the empty air
    with wings not meant for man.
The labor of Hercules burst through Acheron.

For mortals no height is too steep:
in our stupidity we try to scale the very heavens
    and by our wickedness we do not allow
Jupiter to lay down his angry thunderbolts.          40

4

*When Augustus resigned the consulship in 23 B.C., he appointed Lucius Sestius to fill out the position for the year. Sestius had been a devoted supporter of Brutus in 44 B.C., but he was pardoned by Octavian in the aftermath of the civil war and collaborated with the new regime. He is honored with the fourth poem on the coming of spring, an archetypal lyric theme. The closing twist on death as the great equalizer would have had particular point for the ode's recipient, since Sestius and his family were quite wealthy.*

Harsh winter is melting away in the welcome change
    to spring and zephyrs,
        winches are pulling down dry-bottomed
            ships,
the cattle no longer like the steading, the ploughman
    does not hug the fire,
        and meadows are not white with hoar-frost.

Venus of Cythera leads on the dance beneath a
    hanging moon,
        and the lovely Graces, linking arms with
            Nymphs,
shake the ground with alternate feet, while
    burning Vulcan
        visits the grim foundries of the Cyclopes.

Now is the time to oil the hair and bind the head with
    green myrtle
        or flowers born of the earth now freed from
10            frost;
now too is the time to sacrifice to Faunus in shady
    groves
        whether he asks a lamb or prefers a kid.

Pale death kicks with impartial foot at the hovels of
    the poor
        and the towers of kings. O fortunate Sestius,
the brief sum of life does not allow us to start on
    long hopes.
        You will soon be kept close by Night and the
            fabled shades
in Pluto's meager house. When you go there
        you will no longer cast lots to rule the wine,
nor admire tender Lycidas, whom all the young men
        now burn for and for whom the girls will
20            soon be warm.

5

*In one of his most admired odes, Horace assimilates his renunciation of love to sailors rescued from shipwreck who dedicate their drenched clothes to the gods.*

What slim youngster soaked in perfumes
is hugging you now, Pyrrha, on a bed of roses
    deep in your lovely cave? For whom
        are you tying up your blonde hair?

You're so elegant and so simple. Many's the time
he'll weep at your faithlessness and the changing gods,
    and be amazed at seas
        roughened by black winds,

but now in all innocence he enjoys your golden
    beauty
and imagines you always available, always lovable,    10
    not knowing about treacherous breezes—
        I pity poor devils who have no
            experience of you

and are dazzled by your radiance. As for me,
the tablet on the temple wall announces
    that I have dedicated my dripping clothes
        to the god who rules the sea.

6

*Lucius Varius Rufus was one of the great poets of the age, a friend and contemporary of Virgil, who wrote both epic poetry and tragedy, now lost. He is introduced as a foil to Horace in his address to the great general Marcus Vipsanius Agrippa, Augustus's admiral at Actium, graciously declining to compose an epic on his deeds. The tone is at once light and serious, with jocular references to the* Iliad *as a poem about Achilles's bad temper and the* Odyssey *as the story of the voyages of a double-dealer. Horace slyly suggests that he could write an epic, raising the tone with references to Mars, the obscure Iliadic character Meriones, and Diomedes, the son of Tydeus.*

Varius, the eagle of Homeric song, will write
of your valor and your victories, all the feats
of formidable soldiers fighting under your command
    on ship or on horseback.

We do not attempt, Agrippa, to speak of these things,

nor of the bad temper of Peleus' son who did
　　not know
how to yield, nor of the voyages of Ulixes the
　　double-dealer,
　　　　nor of the savage house of Pelops.

We are too slight for these large themes. Modesty
and the Muse who commands the unwarlike lyre
10　　forbid us
to diminish the praise of glorious Caesar and yourself
　　　　by our imperfect talent.

Who could write worthily of Mars girt in
　　adamantine tunic,
or Meriones, black with the dust of Troy,
or the son of Tydeus, who with the help of Pallas
　　Athene
　　　　was the equal of the gods?

What we sing of is drinking parties, of battles fought
by fierce virgins with nails cut sharp to wound
　　young men.
Sometimes we are fancy free, sometimes a
　　little moved,
20　　　　cheerfully, after our fashion.

### 7

*The ode begins with a eulogy of the hill resort of Tibur,*
*about twenty miles east of Rome, which is contrasted*
*favorably with famous destinations in the East. The iden-*
*tity of the addressee is delayed to the fourth stanza. Lucius*
*Munatius Plancus served with Julius Caesar and founded*
*Lugdunum in Gaul (mod. Lyons). In the 30s he sided with*
*Antony but switched to Octavian before Actium, as the his-*
*torian Velleius Paterculus noted, "because treachery was a*
*disease with him." The second half of the poem is an exhor-*
*tation to him to enjoy life in troubled times, using as an*
*example the story of Teucer, who was driven into exile from*
*his home on Salamis by his father, Telamon.*

Others will praise bright Rhodes or Mytilene or
　　Ephesus
　　　　or the walls of Corinth with its two seas,
Thebes famous for Bacchus or Delphi for Apollo
　　　　or Thessalian Tempe;

there are those whose one task is to celebrate the city
　　　　of chaste Pallas in unbroken song,
and to sport on their brows a crown of olive plucked
　　wherever

they find it; in honor of Juno many a one
will speak of wealthy Mycenae and horse-rearing Argos.
　　　　As for me, I am not so struck　　10
by much-enduring Lacedaemon or the fat plain of
　　Larisa,
　　　　as by Albunea's sounding home

and the plunging Anio, by the grove of Tiburnus and
　　its orchards
　　　　watered by swiftly flowing streams.
The bright south wind will often wipe the clouds from
　　the dark sky.
　　　　It is not always pregnant with rain.

So you too, Plancus, would be wise to remember to
　　put a stop
　　　　to sadness and the labors of life
with mellow, undiluted wine, whether you are in
　　camp among
　　　　the gleaming standards or whether
　　　　　　you will be　　20

in the deep shade of your beloved Tibur. When
　　Teucer was on the run
　　　　from Salamis and his father, they say that
　　　　　　nevertheless,
awash with wine, he bound his brow with a crown of
　　poplar leaves
　　　　and spoke these words to his grieving friends:

'Allies and comrades, Fortune is kinder than a father.
　　　　Wherever she takes us, there shall we go. Do
　　　　　　not despair
while Teucer takes the auspices and Teucer is your
　　leader.
　　　　Apollo does not err and he has promised

that in a new land we shall find a second Salamis.
　　　　You are brave men and have often suffered
　　　　　　worse　　30
with me. Drive away your cares with wine. Tomorrow
　　　　we shall set out again upon the broad sea.'

### 8

*Horace gives a Greek veneer to this ode about a young man*
*so consumed by love that he has given up his usual athletic*
*pursuits and hides from others, as Achilles hid on the island*
*of Scyros to keep from going to Troy.*

　　Tell me, Lydia, by all the gods I beg you,

why you are in such a hurry to destroy Sybaris with
    your love.
        And why is he deserting the sunny Campus?
He never used to complain about dust or heat.

        Why is he not on horseback and training
for war with his young friends? Why is he not
    disciplining
        Gallic mouths with jagged bits?
Why is he afraid to put his toe in the yellow Tiber?

        Why does he avoid athletes' oil
like vipers' blood and why are his arms no longer
10    bruised
        with weapons, this champion of the discus,
champion of the javelin, so often throwing beyond
    the mark?

        Why does he hide as the son of Thetis
the sea-goddess hid, so they say, before the tears
    and deaths
        of Troy, in case his man's clothes
should send him off to the killing and the Lycian cohorts?

### 9

*Cold weather, a warm fire, and a bottle of wine form the
setting for this exhortation to leave the future to the gods.
Mount Soracte is located about twenty miles north of
Rome, from where, with a summit at twenty-four hundred
feet, it is visible in clear weather. This is the first ode in
alcaic stanzas, and the influence of Alcaeus now becomes
more prominent.*

You see Soracte standing white and deep
with snow, the woods in trouble, hardly able
      to carry their burden, and the rivers
        halted by sharp ice.

Thaw out the cold. Pile up the logs
on the hearth and be more generous, Thaliarchus,
      as you draw the four-year-old Sabine
        from its two-eared cask.

Leave everything else to the gods. As soon as
10 they still the winds battling it out
      on the boiling sea, the cypresses
        stop waving
        and the old ash trees.

Don't ask what will happen tomorrow.
Whatever day Fortune gives you, enter it

as profit, and don't look down on love
      and dancing while you're still a lad,

while the gloomy grey keeps away from the green.
Now is the time for the Campus and the squares
      and soft sighs at the time arranged
        as darkness falls.      20

Now is the time for the lovely laugh from the
    secret corner
giving away the girl in her hiding-place,
      and for the token snatched from her arm
        or finger feebly resisting.

### 10

*A hymn to Mercury, who was identified with Hermes, the
son of Jupiter and Maia, Atlas's daughter. It is an imitation of the second poem in the ancient editions of Alcaeus,
also a hymn to Hermes, composed, like Horace's, in sapphic stanzas.*

Mercury, eloquent grandson of Atlas,
who cunningly molded the brutish ways of early man
with the gift of speech and the beauty
      of the wrestling school,

of you shall I sing, messenger of mighty Jupiter
and the gods, father of the curved lyre,
ingenious concealer of whatever in your mischief
      you decide to steal.

Once when you were a baby and Apollo was booming
terrifying threats if you did not return the cattle    10
you had stolen, he suddenly missed his quiver
and burst out laughing.

Then you escorted Priam when he left Troy
laden with riches, and the haughty sons of Atreus,
the Thessalian watch-fires, and the camp of Troy's
    enemies
      were all deceived.

You guide the souls of the righteous
to their blessed seats, and with golden staff you herd
the unsubstantial shades, dear to the gods above
      and to the gods below.      20

### 11

*A brief address to a fictitious character with a pretty
Greek name, which suggests a situation like a symposium.*

*The admonition to "harvest the day" (carpe diem) in the last line is in keeping with the generally Epicurean trend of thought in this little poem, but the fact that it is addressed to a woman also suggests a more down-to-earth context.*

Don't you ask, Leuconoe—the gods do not wish it to
    be known—
what end they have given to me or to you, and don't
    meddle with
Babylonian horoscopes. How much better to accept
    whatever comes,
whether Jupiter gives us other winters or whether this
    is our last

now wearying out the Tyrrhenian sea on the
    pumice stones
opposing it. Be wise, strain the wine and cut back
    long hope
into a small space. Even as we speak, envious time
flies past. Harvest the day and leave as little as possible
    for tomorrow.

12

*Ancient readers will have recognized echoes of Pindar in this celebration of the gods and Augustus. The address to Clio, the Muse now associated with history and mother of Orpheus, establishes a Greek setting in the mountains of northern Greece—Helicon, Pindus, and Haemus—associated with the Muses and Orpheus. After vetting the possibility of singing of the Olympian gods, Zeus, Athena (Pallas), Dionysus (Bacchus), or Apollo (Phoebus), or the Greek heroes, Heracles or Castor and Pollux (sons of Leda), Horace deflects to Roman themes: the early kings Romulus, Numa Pompilius, and Tarquin the Proud; Cato who committed suicide after being defeated by Caesar; and then heroes of the Republic, culminating with Marcellus, who bore the same name as Augustus's nephew. All of this is foil to the concluding praise of Augustus.*

What man or hero do you choose, Clio,
to celebrate with lyre or shrill pipe?
What god? Whose name will the playful echo
    sing back

on the shady slopes of Helicon
or on Pindus or chilly Haemus,
from where the willful woods followed
    sweet-voiced Orpheus,

as by his mother's art he held back swift winds
and the rushing flow of rivers,     10
and led the long-eared oaks with the charm
    of his singing lyre?

What can I do but follow custom and praise first
the Father who governs from hour to hour
the affairs of men and gods,
    the land, and sea, and sky?

None of his children is greater than himself.
There is no living thing like him
or second to him, but at his side Pallas has taken
    the place of honor.     20

Nor shall I be silent about you, Bacchus,
bold in battle, nor the virgin goddess,
enemy of wild beasts, nor you, dread Phoebus
    with your unerring arrow.

I shall speak too of Hercules and of the sons
of Leda, famous for their victories, one with horses
the other with fists. As soon as sailors see
    their bright star shining,

the heaving seas stream down from the rocks,
winds fall, and clouds disperse     30
and when they will it, the towering wave
    subsides upon the ocean.

After these I am at a loss whether to speak of Romulus,
or the peaceful reign of Pompilius,
or the proud rods of Tarquin,
    or Cato's noble death.

With the glorious Muse of Italy I shall gratefully sing
of Regulus and the Scauri, of Paullus prodigal
of his mighty spirit in the victory over Carthage,
    and of Fabricius.     40

Sound in battle, like rough-bearded Curius
and like Camillus he was born
of cruel poverty on his father's farm
    with household gods to match.

The fame of Marcellus grows like a tree,
unseen over time; the Julian Star shines
among them all like the moon
    among the lesser fires.

O father and guardian of the human race,
offspring of Saturn, to whom the Fates have given     50
care over great Caesar, may you reign
    with Caesar second to you.

Whether he routs the Parthians who threaten Latium,
or the Chinese and Indians lying close
to the shore of the sunrise, subduing them
    in a just triumph,

as your subordinate he will rule a joyful world in equity;
you will shake Olympus with the weight of your
    chariot,
you will send down your angry lightning
60  on the groves of the impure.

### 13

*A poem like Catullus's adaptation (Poem 51) of Sappho's
famous lyrics on jealousy, in which the girl's praise of a
handsome youth provokes a profound physical response.*

When you praise Telephus'
rosy neck, Lydia, and Telephus'
    waxen arms, Oh how my liver
boils and swells in indigestible bile.

At such a time neither mind nor color
stays in its fixed seat, and moisture trickles furtively
    on to my cheeks making clear how slow
are the fires macerating me through and through.

I burn if drunken brawling
10  sullies your white shoulders,
    or if that young ruffian's teeth
print their tell-tale mark upon your lips.

If only you would listen to me,
you would not imagine that he would be for ever
    barbarously bruising those sweet lips
dipped by Venus in the quintessence of her nectar.

Three times blessed and more than three
are those held in an unbroken bond, whose love
    untorn by scolding or bad temper
20  will not release them till their last day comes.

### 14

*This allegory of the ship as state and the storm as civil war
was cited as a model by Quintilian (Education of the
Orator 8.6.44). It echoes two poems by Alcaeus, which
survive as fragments (6 and 28), and evokes the parlous
times before Octavian's victory at Actium.*

O ship! Will new waves carry you out to sea
again? What are you doing? Make boldly

for the harbor. Don't you see how
    your side is stripped of its oars,

your mast is crippled by the swift sou'wester,
the yards are groaning, and without roping
    the hull has little chance of holding out
        against the mounting tyranny

of the sea? Your sails are unsound and so are the gods
you call upon once again in dire distress.       10
    Though you are a Pontic Pine,
      daughter of a noble forest,

and boast your useless ancestry and name,
the frightened sailor puts no trust
    in painted sterns. Keep a look out,
      unless you mean to give the winds
        some sport.

Not long ago you were a worry and a weariness
    for me,
and now a longing and a deep love.
    So steer clear of the waters that swirl
      between the shining Cyclades.      20

### 15

*A prophecy told to Paris of his doom and the fall of Troy.
The prophecy was a popular theme in Greek poetry, but
it is usually Priam's daughter Cassandra who foretells
Paris's fate. Horace's innovation is to have the sea god
Nereus tell this to Paris while he is sailing home to Troy
with Helen.*

When the shepherd was dragging Helen off across
    the sea
on Idaean ships, a traitor carrying off the wife of
    his host,
Nereus subdued the swift winds and made them idle
    against their will while he sang

his grim prophecies: 'With an ill omen you take home
    a woman
whom Greece will reclaim with a great army,
swearing an alliance to break your marriage
    and the ancient kingdom of Priam.

Alas! Alas! for the sweat of horses and of men
and for all the deaths you bring to the people of
    Dardanus.      10
Pallas is already preparing her helmet and aegis,
    her chariot, and the madness of war.

Proud in the protection of Venus, in vain
will you comb your locks and set lovely songs
for ladies to your unwarlike lyre.
       In vain will you hide in your bedchamber

to avoid the heavy spears and the barbs
of Cretan arrows, the din of battle, and the speed
of Ajax's pursuit. But too late, alas! will you smear
20       your adulterous hair in the dust.

Have you no thought for the son of Laertes, the doom
of your people? For Nestor of Pylos?
Pressing you hard are fearless Teucer of Salamis,
       and Sthenelus, expert in battle

and no sluggard if there is a call to drive a chariot.
Meriones too you will come to know. See there,
raging to find you is the fierce son of Tydeus,
       a better man than his father.

When you see him, like a cowardly stag seeing a wolf
30  on the other side of the hill, you will forget the grass
and run away with your head in the air—
       this is not what you promised your mate.

The anger of Achilles' fleet will postpone
the day of doom for Troy and the women of Phrygia.
After a fixed number of years Achaean fire
       will burn the houses of Ilium.'

## 16

*The imagined impetus for this poem is insulting poetry in
iambic meter that Horace directed at his lover. (Horace did
write iambic poetry earlier in his career, but there is no necessary connection here.) His plea to calm her temper is pitched
as a discourse on anger, worse than the wild inspiration of
Cybele (the goddess of Mt. Dindymus), or Apollo in Delphi,
or Bacchus (Liber), or the priests of Cybele (Corybantes).*

Daughter lovelier than your lovely mother,
put an end to those scurrilous iambics
      however you wish, whether in the fire
        or in the Adriatic sea.

Neither the goddess of Dindymus, nor the dweller
   in Delphi
so shakes the minds of the priests in their shrines,
      neither Liber nor the Corybantes so violently
        twin their shrill bronzes

as does intemperate anger. The sword of Noric steel

does not deter it, nor ship-shattering sea,      10
      nor raging fire, nor Jupiter himself
        rushing down in fearful tumult.

They say Prometheus had to add to the primeval slime
a particle cut from each of the animals,
      and grafted the violence of rabid lions
        on to our stomachs.

Anger laid Thyestes low in a heavy doom
and stands as the final cause by which
      lofty cities were razed to the ground,
        and insolent armies drove the plough      20

down on the walls of their enemies.
Subdue your mind. I too was assailed by the fire
      of passion in my breast in the sweet days
        of youth and driven raging

to swift iambics. I now wish to change
from harshness to gentleness, if only,
      my insults now recanted, you become my
        friend,
        and give me back your heart.

## 17

*Faunus, an Italic god of the countryside identified with Pan
of Mt. Lycaeus in Greece, shows favor to Horace's villa by
Mt. Lucretilis in the Sabine hills. At the poem's midpoint
he turns it into an invitation to a girl in the city, to whom
he gives the Greek name Tyndaris, to share in the simple
pleasures beneath Mt. Ustica, which include poetry in the
strain of Anacreon of Teos.*

Swift Faunus often exchanges Lycaeus
for my lovely Lucretilis and never fails
      to keep the fiery heat and rainy winds
        from my kidlings.

The wives of stinking billy straggle all over
my wood in perfect safety, looking for
      thyme and arbutus, and the kids
        are never frightened

by green snakes nor the wolves of Mars
whenever the valleys and smooth rocks      10
      on the slopes of Ustica ring, O Tyndaris,
        with the sweet pipe of Faunus.

The gods are guarding me. My piety and my Muse
are near to their hearts. Here for you a rich abundance

of the glories of the countryside will pour
from the full horn of plenty.

Here in my sequestered valley you will escape
the heat of the Dogstar, and sing to the Teian lyre
of Penelope and sea-green Circe,
20                both suffering over one man.

Here in the shade you will drink cups
of harmless Lesbian wine. Semele's son, Thyonian
Bacchus,
will not join with Mars to stir up battles
and you will not have to be afraid

of the suspicions of that hot-head Cyrus. He will not
lay a hand on you in passion—a hand too strong to
resist—
or tear the garland plaited in your hair
or the dress that does not deserve such
treatment.

### 18

*Praise of Bacchus, who is also called by his Latin name,*
*Liber, and the Greek titles Euhius and Bassareus, in the*
*form of advice to someone named Varus, who is probably*
*Alfenus Varus, a famous legal scholar, who may have had a*
*villa at Tibur, a town near Rome founded by Catilus.*

Plant no tree, Varus, before the sacred vine
in the kindly soil round Tibur and the walls of Catilus.
For god has put nothing but obstacles in the way of
sober men,
and wine is the only thing that puts biting cares to flight.

After wine who harps on about the harshness of
soldiering or poverty?
Who does not rather speak of father Bacchus and
lovely Venus?
The fatal brawl of Lapiths and Centaurs over unmixed
wine
gives warning that no man should go beyond the rituals

of moderate Liber. Euhius too gives warning, scourge
of Thracians
10  when in their greedy lust they draw too fine a line
between right and wrong. I will not shake you, fair
Bassareus,
against your will, nor will I drag out into the
light of day

what is screened by your various leaves. Keep in check

your Berecyntian horn, your wild drums, and your
retinue
of blind Self-love, Vainglory raising her empty head
absurdly high,
and Trust betrayed, squandering secrets, more transparent than glass.

### 19

*It is not Scythians or Parthians who assail Horace, but*
*Venus and her accomplices who drive him wild with pas-*
*sion for a girl named Glycera, Greek for "sweet," a common*
*name among prostitutes.*

The cruel mother of Desires,
Theban Semele's boy, Bacchus, and amorous License
order me to give my heart
to love, long since ended.

Glycera sets me on fire, the sheen
of her fair skin, flawless as Parian marble,
her delicious naughtiness,
her face so dangerous to look at.

Venus has deserted Cyprus and rushes
upon me with all her force. She will have no talk     10
of Scythians or of Parthian horsemen
aggressive in retreat, or of anything else bar love.

Put here for me, lads, a piece of living turf,
some greenery for a sacrifice, and incense
with a bowl of two-year-old wine.
I'll kill a victim and she will come more gently.

### 20

*An open invitation to Maecenas, the great man, to enjoy*
*the simple pleasures of Horace's Sabine estate: not the fine*
*Caecuban or Formian wine from Latium, nor Calenian*
*and Falernian from Campania, but Horace's house wine, a*
*native concoction in a Greek container, rather like Horace's*
*lyrics.*

You will drink from plain cups an ordinary Sabine wine
I put into a Greek jar and sealed
with my own hands the day you, Maecenas,
knight of great distinction,

were given such applause in the theater
that the banks of the river of your fathers

and the playful echo from the Vatican Mount
        joined in your praises.

You can drink your Caecuban and the grape
10  tamed in the Calenian press:
    no Falernian vines or Formian hills
        soften my wine.


21

*A religious song to Diana and Apollo, born to Latona on
Mt. Cynthus on Delos. It evokes the haunts of Diana on the
mountains Algidus near Rome, Erymanthus in Arcadia,
and Gragus in Lycia. Apollo's haunts are the valley of
Tempe in Thessaly, the island of Delos, or his shrine at
Delphi.*


Sing, tender virgins, of Diana.
Sing, boys, of unshorn Cynthius
        and of Latona, dear to the heart
            of highest Jupiter.

You girls, sing of the goddess who delights in rivers
and in all the foliage of trees standing out
        on chilly Algidus or in the dark woods of
            Erymanthus
            or green Mount Gragus.

You boys, raise Tempe no less often with your praises,
10  and Delos, birthplace of Apollo,
    whose shoulder gleams with his quiver
        and his brother's lyre.

He will drive war with its tears, and famine and
        pestilence
with their misery, far from the people and from Caesar
        the Princeps, to the Persians and Britons,
            moved by your prayer.


22

*Addressing his friend Aristius Fuscus, Horace tells of an
encounter with a wolf alone in the woods near his villa,
greater than the beasts of Daunia in southern Italy or
Juba's kingdom in Mauretania. His girl's name is Lalage,
from the Greek "to chatter."*


The man who is pure of heart and innocent of evil
needs no Moorish spears, Fuscus,
    nor bow nor quiver heavy
        with poison arrows

whether he is setting out across
the sultry Syrtes or inhospitable
Caucasus or lands licked
        by the fabled Hydaspes.

As I wandered far from my farm
in Sabine forest singing of my Lalage                    10
without a care to burden me, a wolf ran away from me,
        unarmed as I was—

such a monster as warrior Daunia
does not feed in her broad oak-woods,
nor does the land of Juba, dry nurse of lions,
        bring it to birth.

Set me on barren plains
where no summer breeze revives a tree,
in a zone of the earth oppressed by clouds
        and a hostile Jupiter;                          20

set me under the very chariot wheels of the sun
in a land where no man can build a home—
I shall love my Lalage sweetly laughing,
        sweetly speaking.


23

*A slight poem about a girl who avoids Horace. Her name
is Chloe, from a Greek word suggesting greenness and
immaturity.*


You avoid me, Chloe, like a fawn looking for its mother
who has run off in fright into the trackless mountains,
        and it panics for no good reason
            at the breeze in the wood.

Whether the fluttering leaves of the thorn tree
shudder in the wind or green lizards
        part the brambles, it trembles,
            heart and knees.

Yet I am no man-eating tiger or Gaetulian lion
hunting you down to crunch your bones.                   10
        It is time to stop going with your mother.
            You are ready for a man.


24

*A lament for the death of his friend, the critic Quintilius,
who was also Virgil's friend. Horace praises him again
years later in his* Art of Poetry (438–44).

Why should our grief for a man so loved
know any shame or limit? Teach us sad songs,
Melpomene. Your father gave you a clear voice
    and with it the lyre.

So a sleep that will not end bears down
upon Quintilius. Honor, incorruptible Honesty,
sister of Justice, and naked Truth—
    when will they ever see his equal?

Many good men will weep at his death,
but none weep more than you, Virgil. You ask
10    the gods
for Quintilius, but your piety counts for nothing.
    They did not give him on such terms.

What if you were to tune a sweeter lyre than Thracian
    Orpheus
and trees came to listen? Would blood come back
into the empty shade which Mercury has once herded
    into his black flock

with fearful crook? Prayers do not easily
persuade him to open the gates of death.
It is hard. But, by enduring, we can make lighter
20    what the gods forbid us to change.


25

*A reproach to Lydia, who has spurned him: one day soon
her beauty will fade and her sexual passion—unflat-
teringly compared to that of mares, who, according to
Aristotle, could go crazy with lust—will go unrequited.*

The young bloods are not so eager now
to rattle your closed shutters with volleys of pebbles
and disturb your sleep. The door that once
    moved so very easily

on its hinges, now hugs the threshold.
Less and less often do you hear the cry 'I'm yours,
and dying for your love, Lydia, night after long night,
    and you lie there sleeping.'

Your turn will come, when you are an old rag
in some lonely alley-way, weeping at the insolence of
10    lovers
as the wind from Thrace holds wilder and wilder orgies
    between the old moon and the new,

and your burning love, the lust
that drives the mothers of horses to madness,
rages round your ulcerous liver.

There will be no shortage of complaints

about cheerful youngsters who take
more pleasure in green ivy and dark myrtle,
and dedicate dry leaves to the east wind,
    winter's crony.    20


26

*A short ode celebrating the power of poetry, addressed to
Lucius Aelius Lamia, a member of a distinguished family
from the nearby town of Formiae. The troubles of empire—
on the northern border or in the East, where Tiridates was
driven from the throne of Parthia—are nothing compared
to the pleasures of the Muse from Pimpla.*

As a friend of the Muses I shall throw gloom
    and fear
to the wild winds to carry off to the Cretan sea.
    Little care I what king is causing alarm
        on some icebound northern shore

or what is terrifying Tiridates. You who delight
in pure fountains, sweet Pimpleis, weave flowers
    grown in the sun, weave
        a garland for my friend Lamia.

Without you the honors I confer are worthless.
To sanctify this Lamia with a new lyre    10
    and the plectrum of Lesbos—there is a task
        worthy of you and worthy of your sisters.

27

*A dramatic monologue, with the speaker drinking in a
rowdy company of youths, which threatens to get out
of hand since one of them has brought along a souvenir
Persian knife. The speaker will join in the revelry but only
if one of the company, the brother of Megilla (the Greek
name suggests a prostitute), lets on about his latest love
interest.*

—Cups are made for joy. Only Thracians use them
for fighting. Put a stop to this barbarous practice.
    Bacchus is a respectable god. Keep him
        well away
        from brawling and bloodshed.

Wine and lamplight don't belong in the same world
as that Persian dagger. Moderate
    your unholy noise, friends,
        and keep the weight on the elbow.

—You want me to join you in that grim Falernian?
10    —Let's hear from Megilla's brother from Opys.
            What's this wound he's lucky enough to have?
                What's this arrow he's dying from?

—You're hanging back? No more drink
for me. These are my terms. Whatever Venus
            has you in her power, there's no need to blush
                about your burning passion. Your lovers

are always well-born. Whatever it is, come, tell me
your secret. It's safe with me.—Oh you poor devil!
            What a Charybdis you've been caught in! You
            poor boy!
20                You deserve a better flame than that.

What witch can free you? What Thessalian magician
with his potions? What god? Not even Pegasus
            will find it easy to disentangle you from
                the coils
                    of that triple Chimaera.


28

*An enigmatic ode, framed as an address at the tomb of*
*Archytas, a Pythagorean philosopher and mathemati-*
*cian of the fourth century* B.C. *As consolation the speaker*
*invokes figures from Greek myth who died, though beloved*
*by the gods, and caps this with Pythagoras himself, who*
*notoriously believed that he was the reincarnation of the*
*Greek hero Euphorbus, son of Panthous. In the surpris-*
*ing conclusion of four stanzas, we learn that the speaker*
*is himself dead by shipwreck and washed up on the shore*
*near Archytas's tomb.*


Measurer of earth and ocean and numberless sand,
        Archytas, you are now confined
near the Matine shore, by a little handful of dust duly
        sprinkled,
                and it profits you nothing to have probed

the dwellings of air and traversed the round vault
        of heaven
                with a mind that was to die.
The father of Pelops also died, boon companion of
        the gods,
                and Tithonus, though carried off into
                    the winds,

and Minos, though admitted to the secrets of the gods.
10        Tartarus keeps the son of Panthous,

though he was twice sent down to Orcus and called
        the Trojan Age
                as his witness, unfastening his shield to prove

that he had given only flesh and sinew to dark death—
        and in your eye she was no mean teacher
of truth and of nature. But one night waits for
        all of us
                and all must walk the path of death, and walk it
                    only once.

The Furies give some men over to stern Mars for
        his games.
                The greedy sea is the death of sailors.
Young and old together, the funerals come thronging.
        Proserpina is merciless and runs away from
                no man.                                                20

I, too, was overwhelmed in the Illyrian waves by the
        south wind,
                wild comrade of Orion as he sets.
But you, sailor, do not grudge me a little drifting sand
        for my unburied head and bones.

So, for all the threats of the east wind on the
        western waves,
                may you be safe when the woods
of Venusia are lashed, and may great profit flow down
        upon you from whatever giver,

from favoring Jupiter and from Neptune, guardian of
        Tarentum.
                Do you not care that you are doing a wrong      30
that will hurt your innocent descendants? It may be
        that a debt of justice and a reward for
                your pride

are waiting even for you. If you abandon me, my
        curses will not go
                unheard, and no expiation will ever
                    acquit you.

You are in haste, but it would not delay you long.
        Just throw
                three handfuls of dust and go speeding on
                    your way.


29

*An ironic address to an otherwise unknown young friend*
*of Horace, who is contemplating giving up philosophy to*
*enrich himself on military campaigns.*

Iccius, are you now envying the rich treasures
of Arabia, preparing a ruthless campaign
  against kings of Sheba never before subdued,
   and weaving chains

for the fearsome Mede? What barbarian virgin will be
your slave, mourning her bridegroom killed in battle?
  What boy of the court brought up to stretch
   Chinese arrows on the bow of his fathers

will take his place by your cup with rich oils
on his hair? Who would deny that down-rushing
10 rivers
   can flow up steep mountains
    and Tiber reverse his course

when you are in such haste to exchange for Spanish
 breastplates
the Socratic school and the works of great Panaetius
   collected from all over the world—
    you promised better things.

30

*A brief invocation to Venus, asking her to come to the girl*
*Glycera, who was mentioned above in* Ode 19.

Venus, queen of Cnidos and Paphos,
abandon your beloved Cyprus and move
to the lovely shrine of Glycera, who summons you
   with clouds of incense.

Your ardent boy must hurry along with you
and Nymphs and Graces with their girdles loose
and Youth, so uncongenial without you,
   and Mercury.

31

*The scene is the new temple of Apollo on the Palatine,*
*adjacent to the home of Augustus, which was dedicated*
*on October 9, 28 B.C. In this setting the poet prays not for*
*wealth but for simple sufficiencies and a healthy old age*
*filled with poetry.*

What does the bard ask from Apollo whose temple
is now dedicated? What does he pray for
  as he pours the new wine from the bowl? Not
   the fertile crops of wealthy Sardinia,

not the lovely herds of sultry
Calabria, not Indian gold or ivory,

not land gnawed by the quiet waters
  of the silent river Liris.

Let those to whom Fortune grants it restrain the vine
with the Calenian sickle, and let the rich merchant  10
  drain from golden goblets wine
   bought with Syrian merchandise—

darling of the very gods, visiting
the Atlantic three or four times a year
  and surviving. I eat easily digestible
   olives, chicory, and mallows.

Grant, son of Latona, that I may enjoy what I have
with good health and, I pray, with sound mind,
  and that my old age may not be squalid
   and not without the lyre.  20

32

*An ode to his lyre, in the form of a hymn and invoking the*
*legacy of Alcaeus, the citizen of Lesbos who sang of war, the*
*ship of state, wine, and love.*

We pray, if ever we have relaxed with you in the shade
and played a melody that may live a year
or more, come, my Greek lyre,
   and sound a Latin song.

You were first tuned by a citizen of Lesbos,
fierce in war, who, whether he was where the steel
was flying or had tied up his battered ship
   on the spray-soaked shore,

would still sing of Bacchus and the Muses,
of Venus and the boy who is always by her side,  10
and of Lycus with his jet-black eyes
   and jet-black hair.

O glory of Phoebus, lyre welcome at the feasts
of Supreme Jupiter, O sweet easer of my labors,
grant me your blessing whenever
   I duly call upon you.

33

*Consolation for Albius Tibullus, one of the canon of four*
*great love elegists.*

Do not grieve, Albius, remembering too well
your bitter-sweet Glycera, and do not keep chanting
piteous elegies wondering why she has broken faith

and a younger man now outshines you.

Love for Cyrus scorches the beautiful,
narrow-browed Lycoris; Cyrus leans lovingly
over hard-hearted Pholoe, but sooner will roe-deer
mate with Apulian wolves

than Pholoe soil herself with a foul adulterer.
Such is the decree of Venus, who decides in cruel jest
10  to join unequal minds and bodies
under her yoke of bronze.

I myself once, when a better love was offered me,
was shackled in the delicious fetters of Myrtale,
a freedwoman wilder than the Adriatic sea
scooping out the bays of Calabria.

34

*The "crazy wisdom" that Horace recants in this ode, after
seeing a thunderbolt in a clear sky, is Epicurean philosophy,
which regarded such a phenomenon as incredible (as do
modern meteorologists).*

I used to worship the gods grudgingly,
and not often, a wanderer expert
in a crazy wisdom, but now I am forced
to sail back and once again go over

the course I had left behind. For Jupiter
who usually parts the clouds with the fire
of his lightning has driven his horses
and his flying chariot across a
cloudless sky,

shaking the dull earth and winding rivers,
the Styx and the fearsome halls of hateful
10      Taenarus,
and the Atlantean limits
of the world. God has the power

to exchange high and low, to humble the great,
and bring forward the obscure. With a shrill cry
rapacious Fortune snatches the crown from
one head
and delights to lay it on another.

35

*A hymn to the goddess Fortuna, who had a cult site at
Antium, on the coast south of Rome. The shrine was
favored by Octavian because it had lent him money during
the civil wars; now she is being invoked to accompany him
on imagined campaigns to extend Rome's world dominion
to the Massagetae, a remote Scythian tribe, and Arabia.*

Goddess, who rule over lovely Antium,
whose present power can raise mortal man
from the lowest level or turn
his proud triumphs into funerals,

the poor farmer appeals to you with anxious prayer,
the sailor vexing the Carpathian sea
on his Bithynian ship prays to you
as mistress of the ocean.

The rough Dacian and Scythian famous in retreat,
cities and peoples and fierce Latium,                10
the mothers of barbarian kings
and tyrants clad in purple,

all are afraid that your violent foot may kick over
the standing column, that the mob may gather
to whip laggards to war, to war,
and shatter all authority.

Always before you goes your slave Necessity,
beam-nails and wedges in her bronze hand,
and never without her cruel hook
and molten lead.                                        20

Hope attends you, and Loyalty, rare upon this earth,
her hand swathed in white. They do not desert
their friend
when you change your coat
and leave the homes of the great.

Then too the faithless mob and lying prostitute
fall away, and false friends, not to be trusted
to share the yoke, disappear
when all the jars are drained to the dregs.

Preserve Caesar as he prepares to go
to remotest Britain, and preserve the new swarm     30
of warriors to spread fear in the regions
of the East and the Red Sea.

Shame on our scars, our crimes,
our brothers! Our brutal age has shrunk
from nothing. We have left no impiety
untouched. Our young men have never

stayed their hand for fear of the gods,
but have polluted every altar. If only

you would reforge our blunted swords
40          to use against Massagetae and Arabs.

### 36

*A poem to celebrate the return of Numida, an otherwise
unknown young aristocrat and friend of Lamia, the dedicatee of 1.26, from campaigns in the West, Spain that is.
There will be drinking and dancing as wild as that of the
Salian priests, and Numida will be embraced again by his
lover Damalis.*

With incense and with the lyre
and with the blood of a calf to pay my vow, I delight
          to propitiate the guardian gods
of Numida, now safely home from the furthest West

          and sharing out so many kisses
to his dear friends, but to none
          more than his beloved Lamia, remembering
boyhood when none but Lamia was king,

          and the time when they both put on the toga.
We must not fail to mark this glorious day
10     with chalk,
          and the jar we bring out must know no limit
and feet no rest from dancing like the Salii,

          nor must Damalis, that great drinker,
down a deeper Thracian draught than Bassus,
          nor at this feast must there be any shortage
              of roses
or long-living celery or soon-dying lilies.

          All will fix their melting eyes
on Damalis, and Damalis will not be torn
          from the arms of her new lover,
20    but will wind more clingingly than ivy.

### 37

*A great public ode, celebrating the suicide of Cleopatra, the
"mad queen" of line 6. She had sworn an oath to dispense
justice on the Capitol, a sure sign of her drunken madness.
But although she is called a "monster sent by fate," there is
also a note of admiration in Horace's portrayal.*

Now we must drink, now we must
beat the earth with unfettered feet, now,
          my friends, is the time to load the couches
              of the gods with Salian feasts.

Before this it was a sin to take the Caecuban
down from its ancient racks, while the mad queen
          with her contaminated flock of men
              diseased by vice was preparing

the ruin of the Capitol and the destruction
of our power, crazed with hope                              10
          unlimited and drunk
              with sweet fortune. But her madness

decreased when scarce a ship escaped the flames
and her mind, deranged by Mareotic wine,
          was made to face real fears
              as she flew from Italy, and Caesar

pressed on the oars (like a hawk
after gentle doves or a swift hunter
          after a hare on the snowy plains
              of Thrace) to put in chains                   20

this monster sent by fate. But she looked
for a nobler death. She did not have a woman's fear
          of the sword, nor did she make
              for secret shores with her swift fleet.

Daring to gaze with face serene upon her ruined
     palace,
and brave enough to take deadly serpents
          in her hand, and let her body
              drink their black poison,

fiercer she was in the death she chose, as though
she did not wish to cease to be a queen, taken
          to Rome                                           30
              on the galleys of savage Liburnians,
                  to be a humble woman in a proud triumph.

### 38

*After striking a grand note in the previous ode, the book con-
cludes with a diminuendo, a short poem about wine and love.*

I hate Persian luxuries, my boy.
Garlands woven with lime tree bark give me no
     pleasure.
There's no need for you to seek out
          the last rose where it lingers.

I'm anxious you shouldn't labor
over the simple myrtle. Myrtle suits you
as my cupbearer, and me as I drink
          in the dense shade of the vine.

## AFTERWORD

Horace's position in the literary canon evolved steadily throughout antiquity. Unlike Virgil, however, who inspired a large number of epic poets in the century following his death, Horace found few successors in the genre for which he is best known now, lyric poetry. A century after his death, Quintilian calls him practically the only Latin lyric poet worth reading, and he is hard-pressed even to come up with the names of others. Quintilian praises Horace for the distinctive qualities that succeeding centuries recognized as the hallmarks of his lyric style—variation in his deployment of figures of speech and boldness in verbal innovation, but on the whole he was not enthusiastic about the utility of Horace's *Odes* in the classroom, commenting elsewhere that "there are parts of Horace that I would not want to interpret" (*The Education of the Orator* 1.8.6). We do hear of a few writers who tried their hand at lyric after Horace, but none achieved prominence, and their works do not survive. The most spectacular gesture of appreciation for Horace's *Odes* was made by Augustus when, in the wake of the publication of the first three books, he commissioned Horace to compose the *Secular Hymn* to be performed at the celebration of the Secular Games in 17 B.C. But Horace's prediction about his first book of *Epistles* did come true nonetheless, and applied equally to all his works (*Epistles* 1.20.17–18):

This fate, too, awaits you: stuttering old age will overtake you,
As you teach boys their elementary lessons on the outskirts of the city.

Two sets of ancient notes on Horace's poetry that date at least to the second or third centuries A.D. attest to the labors of schoolmasters in interpreting his works for their students. We hear of other scholars from earlier periods who made Horace an object of study, including the famous first-century philologist Valerius Probus. But, paradoxically, Horace had relatively few imitators in antiquity, and this is especially true of the *Odes*. Only in the occasional poetry of Statius in the *Silvae* did Horace's *Odes* leave their imprint in significant measure in the first generations after his death. Ovid was clearly influenced by Horace's two books of *Epistles* when he composed his own elegiac *Epistles from the Black Sea*. And Horace's *Satires* were important benchmarks for the works of Persius a generation later, as they were for Juvenal still later. His place in the literary canon was so secure that in his parodic novel, *The Satyricon*, Petronius's travesty of a poet, Eumolpus, quotes Horace's *Odes* in an offhand way and refers to his "studied but happy gift of expression" in the same breath as Homer and Virgil.

In late antiquity Horace was still a standard author in the schools, but Christian readers had reservations about the content of his poetry: as St. Jerome put it (*Letters* 22.29), " 'What harmony can there be between Christ and the devil?' What's Horace got to do with the Psalter?" And yet their familiarity with (and affection for) his works is amply attested by the many citations in Lactantius (ca. A.D. 240–320), St. Augustine, and, indeed, Jerome himself, who elsewhere calls Horace "acute and learned." The Spanish poet Prudentius (A.D. 348–ca. 405) adopted Horace's manner and meter to write poetry on Christian themes and was so successful that he was famously dubbed "the Christian Horace" by Richard Bentley, Horace's eighteenth-century editor. The consul for the year 527, a certain Vettius Agorius Basilius Mavortius, prepared a corrected edition of Horace, with the assistance of his teacher Felix, but from this point on it is difficult to find traces of Horace until the ninth century. Before that he is not cited by any authors later than Isidore of Seville (ca. 560–636). The Carolingian Renaissance marks the beginning of renewed interest in Horace's poetry. This is the period from which our oldest surviving manuscripts date, and it is when Horace becomes a model for writers again. Throughout the remainder of the Middle Ages, Horace occupied a place in the poetic canon second only to Virgil and Ovid, and his reputation grew in nonacademic circles. In his native Venosa, his alleged tomb was an object of veneration, and there was a tradition about Horace as a magician in Palestrina, a resort town about twenty-two miles from Rome praised by the poet in the *Odes* (3.4.23).

In the Middle Ages, as in antiquity, Horace was known primarily as a writer of satires and epistles—"Horace the satirist," as Dante calls him (*Inferno* 4.89). In the thirteenth century, Hugo of Trimberg composed a "Register of Many Authors," a summary of the lives and works of about a hundred authors suitable for study, and commented that Horace had written three "important" books, meaning the *Satires, Epistles,* and *Art of Poetry,* and "two less usual ones, i.e. the *Epodes* and the *Odes,* which I think are less important for our times." Among the many factors contributing to the diminished standing of the *Odes* were the complications posed for medieval readers by Horace's artful language and difficult meters. Even so, there is abundant evidence of medieval readers who took up the challenge of adapting Horatian lyrics to medieval song. What especially attracted readers to the *Satires* and *Epistles* was their ethical content; the *Odes,* with their treatment of love affairs and drinking parties, were regarded as the frivolous output of Horace's youth, while the hexameter poems presented the poet's more sober reflections on life. The *Art of Poetry* was particularly popular during this period and inspired several medieval treatises on poetic composition.

Horace's reception in the Renaissance was anticipated by Petrarch's lifelong devotion to the poet. Four manuscripts of Horace that belonged to Petrarch are known today, and quotations from his poetry are scattered throughout Petrarch's works in quantity second only to Virgil among classical authors. Petrarch wrote a letter to Horace, which he included in the last book of his collected letters (*Familiar Epistles* 24.10). The letter is composed in verse, a distinction shared only with Virgil in this collection, and it is in the meter of the first poem in the *Odes* in which Horace addresses Maecenas, the First Asclepiadean. This is altogether fitting because for Petrarch, who addresses him as "the king of lyric poetry," Horace is first and foremost the poet of the *Odes,* not the *Satires* or *Epistles* (Petrarch's favorite satirist was Juvenal). Petrarch did compose a collection of metrical epistles in Latin, drawing on the example of Horace, but he cared most for the lyric poetry. Petrarch's sonnets in Italian are replete with reminiscences of Horace's *Odes,* and his enthusiasm was shared in the Renaissance of fifteenth-century Italy. The first printed edition of Horace's works appeared in approximately 1470, and soon after, in 1482, appeared the influential commentary by Cristoforo Landino with a dedicatory ode by Angelo Poliziano on the frontispiece. One of the greatest poets of the period, Ludovico Ariosto, drew his inspiration from Horace when, late in his life, he composed his *Satires* in the Horatian manner.

In 1601 the English poet Ben Jonson introduced Horace, "the best master of virtue and wisdom," as a character into his play *The Poetaster,* to serve as a spokesperson for Jonson's own views about literature. In subsequent years Jonson produced his own translation of the *Art of Poetry,* first printed in 1640. Horace's popularity in the world of anglophone letters is reflected in the number of prominent writers who set their hands to translation or adaptation. John Milton attempted to reproduce in English Horace's Latinized version of the Greek rhythm known as the Fourth Asclepiadean in *Odes* 1.5, first printed in 1673:

> What slender youth bedewed with liquid odours
> Courts thee on roses in some pleasant cave,
>> Pyrrha? For whom bind'st thou
>> In wreaths thy golden hair,
> Plain in thy neatness? O how oft shall he
> On faith and changed gods complain: and seas
>> Rough with black winds and storms
>> Unwonted shall admire:
> Who now enjoys thee credulous, all gold,
> Who always vacant always amiable
>> Hopes thee; of flattering gales
>> Unmindful? Hapless they

> To whom thou untried seem'st fair. Me in my vowed
> Picture the sacred wall declares t'have hung
> > My dank and dropping weeds
> > To the stern god of sea.

Christopher Smart, William Cowper, and John Dryden can be counted among those whose translations of Horace attest to his popularity in the period following the Renaissance.

In the twentieth century Horace proved to be contested ground. An eyewitness recounts that, when lecturing on Horace in May 1914, the poet A. E. Housman, who was also a rather severe classical scholar, took a moment to consider 4.7 "simply as poetry," reading his own translation to the class. According to the story, Housman then ended the lecture by pronouncing this "the most beautiful poem in ancient literature" and hurriedly leaving the room. In response to such appropriations of Horace, the controversialist Ezra Pound famously characterized (or caricatured) him in an essay from 1929 as "bald-headed, pot-bellied, underbred, sycophantic, less poetic than any other great master of literature," endowed with "the clubman's poise and no stronger emotion than might move one toward a particularly luscious oyster." And yet Pound's own translations of Horace, published toward the end of his life in 1970, imply recognition of the ancient poet's status as an experimentalist in language and rhythm rather like Pound himself. Shortly before his death, the American poet Robert Lowell spent the summer of 1974 reading "Latin and French—the last 6 books of the *Aeneid* and Horace and Racine." In his last published book, Lowell evokes Horace's return to love and lyric in *Odes* 4.1. The poem is called "Departure" and takes as its motto the Latin opening of Horace's *Ode,* an allusion that is then picked up in the poem's middle:

> Not now as you were young...
> Horace in his fifties held
> a Ligurian girl
> captive in the sleep of night,
> followed her flying across the grass
> of the Campus Martius, saw her lost
> in the Tiber he could not hold.
> Can you hear my first voice,
> amused in sorrow,
> dramatic in amusement...

Horace's poetry, especially the *Odes,* remains a standard school text, as it has been now for centuries, and the average reader encounters it, if at all, in the classroom. But poets and translators still engage with Horace as a fellow artist.

# PROPERTIUS

(Sextus Propertius, ca. 50–after 16 B.C.)

"TIBULLUS WAS YOUR SUCCESSOR, GALLUS, AND PROPERTIUS FOLLOWED HIM. I MYSELF was the fourth in chronological order." This is how Ovid denotes the great quartet of Augustan love elegists, whose central theme is the poet's account of the various trials and tribulations that he suffers in his affair with one particular woman. Drawing predominantly on Hellenistic Greek poetry and on that of Catullus and his circle, Gallus "invented" this unusually short-lived genre in his four books of *Amores* ("Loves"), written probably in the late 40s and early 30s B.C. Tibullus and Propertius started their poetic careers in the late 30s, with Ovid following no earlier than 26 B.C.

All four elegists were poets of a very high order. Tibullus has been omitted from this collection only for considerations of space, but the omission of Gallus has a much more regrettable reason. Whereas the elegies of Tibullus, Propertius, and Ovid, have survived almost intact, those of Gallus have not. Only a single stray line, quoted in a fifth-century handbook on geography, was known until the publication in 1979 of a papyrus containing ten further lines (some incomplete), recovered in Egypt from a rubbish heap outside a Roman army camp. The camp is probably of the early Augustan period, and therefore quite possibly this fragment is the earliest surviving Latin papyrus. Gallus had served Octavian loyally in his campaign against Antony and Cleopatra: he had, for example, kept Cleopatra talking while another Roman officer climbed a ladder into her mausoleum and captured her alive (Plutarch, *Life of Antony* 79). He had subsequently been governor of Egypt until he was forced to commit suicide, probably in 27 B.C., when he lost the *amicitia* ("friendship, patronage") of Augustus for arrogantly boasting of his own military achievements. Although the recovered lines refer to sex, politics, and literary criticism, all standard topics in Augustan elegiac poetry, the contents of the papyrus are disappointing; nevertheless, having probably been written within the lifetime of the author, it is almost unique as contemporary material evidence for classical Latin poetry.

Given Gallus's prominence as the first elegist and the importance of imitation and variation as principles of elegiac composition, the almost total loss of his work is an incalculable disaster for our appreciation of the genre. Much of the pleasure in reading an elegy in which, for example, Ovid laments the frustration and indignity of being locked out by his mistress, or of being ousted by a wealthier rival, or of discovering her infidelity, lies with our appreciation of the way in which he closely reworks the handling of the same scenario by Tibullus and Propertius. This pleasure is always, however, tempered by our awareness that Tibullus and Propertius will themselves have been alluding to specific details in poems written by Gallus, the exact nature of which we can hardly guess.

**Figure 13:  Gallus papyrus**
This fragment of a papyrus roll containing lines of Gallus's poetry is one of the earliest examples of Latin handwriting. It was found on a garbage dump outside a Roman army camp in Egypt, and the book may well have belonged to a soldier who served under Gallus himself, who was the first governor of that province.

From about 26 B.C., for a decade or so, Propertius and Ovid were close friends, writing elegies on the same themes, each trying to outdo the other, in much the same spirit as Catullus and his friends had interacted. Since these two elegists had this particularly close association, and since Gallus's elegies are lost and Tibullus's output was so much smaller, it is hardly surprising that modern assessment of Propertius and Ovid generally involves a comparison and contrast between them.

Very few scholars see any serious intent in Ovid's handling of the themes and conventions of love elegy. His wit is obvious and sustained, often coming close to parody of the genre. Moreover, he writes with great clarity: we are never in doubt about his thought process or the dramatic situation, and his allusions to mythology are very rarely obscure. Many of Propertius's elegies are emphatically otherwise. The situation in 4.7, with Propertius being assured by the half-burned corpse of his dead mistress that an eternity of sexual intercourse with her awaits him, seems to verge on the psychologically unhinged, and the narrative of the poem is not always clear; in particular we are left to assume that Propertius's new mistress is Chloris, suddenly named for the first and only time in any of his poems in line 72, and the significance of the two locations for women in the Underworld as they apply to Cynthia is not explained. It is inevitable therefore that the stark contrast with Ovid's remorselessly witty and lucid elegies should lead to Propertius being characterized as gloomy and obscure. Such an assessment contains an element of truth but is ultimately unfair to Propertius, whose poetry has a much wider scope, in content, in emotional levels, and in style, than do Ovid's *Amores*.

It is certainly true that death is a frequent theme in Propertius. He is especially fascinated by the contemplation of his own demise, a topic to which he turns most particularly in 1.6, 1.7, 1.19, 2.1, 2.8, 2.13, and 3.16. Nevertheless, many of Propertius's elegies are written in much the same witty spirit as are Ovid's *Amores*. For example, it was a standard scenario that the lover should beg for entry at his mistress's locked door. This undignified situation gives Ovid ample opportunity to make fun of the persona of the elegiac lover in *Amores* 1.6, as he portrays himself wheedling his mistress's doorkeeper, a broken-down slave incapable of other work, and the humor is accentuated by his inevitable lack of success and ever greater frustration. Propertius's treatment of this situation in 1.16 is at least as broadly comic as Ovid's. The speaker is a house door, which longs for its lost glory, when the house was owned by a triumphant general who fought for the simple decency of the old Roman ways. By contrast:

> Now I must often groan, disfigured by nocturnal
> > Drunken brawls and thumped by vulgar fists.
> And all the time disgraceful garlands hang upon me,
> > And torches, exclusion's token, lie around. (5–8)

The door singles out one particular lover, who "never gives my doorposts any peace, singing / Over and over this whining serenade." This especially annoying lover is obviously Propertius himself, and his useless, pathetic, and shameful pleas for admission hardly invite us to take seriously his complaints about his suffering from unrequited love, given that we are shown his demeaning antics through the words of the snobbish, puritanical, and disgusted door.

Such wit at his own expense recurs throughout Propertius's poetry. It is splendidly exemplified in 4.8. Cynthia has gone off to the little town of Lanuvium. She claims that she wanted to attend the rites of Juno, the goddess of marriage, but Propertius knows better: she has gone off with a "plucked waster" in his fashionable chariot, and he aims for revenge by inviting two prostitutes to spend the night with him. Cynthia returns suddenly, throwing the doors wide open; Propertius's glass falls from his drunken fingers, the girls run off down the street in a panic, Cynthia beats Propertius up and orders him to sell Lygdamus, the slave who connived at the evening's misdemeanors. There is nothing so dramatically farcical in Ovid's *Amores*; Propertius is in fact adapting to the specific elegiac context a popular type of lowbrow entertainment, the Adultery-Mime, in which a husband returns home unexpectedly and the wife has to hide her lover, a performance that will have been accompanied by all sorts of slapstick and obscenities. The juxtaposition to 4.7 is particularly significant: in both elegies, Cynthia returns unexpectedly and chastises Propertius, but, whereas in 4.7 she is a half-burned corpse, in 4.8 he describes her as "lovely in her fury" (52). The shift in tone is breathtaking.

Propertius's wider range in both theme and treatment is apparent also in the prominent political element in his elegies. His first book ends with a pair of ten-line poems, the first about a soldier, perhaps a relative of his, who died fighting Octavian in the siege of Perugia in 41 B.C., and the second lamenting the suffering of Propertius's family in that war, a subject to which he returns in 4.1.127ff., where we hear of the confiscation of his ancestral land. Virgil had also suffered in these same land confiscations, intended to reward veteran soldiers with farms. Whereas, however, Virgil had gone on to become the supreme propagandist for Augustus, as offering the only hope for lasting peace, it is not at all clear that Propertius was ever won over. The difficulty in interpreting Propertius's political stance is well seen in the scholarly debate over the tone and intention of 4.6, the centerpiece to his last book, a long account of the crucial Battle of Actium; some critics interpret that elegy as a celebration of Octavian's great victory, while others see it as a parody of such poems. The poet's intention will probably never be known for certain, but the ambiguity, doubt, and mutually exclusive interpretations suggest that Propertius was not altogether committed to Augustanism.

Certainly, there is undeniable halfheartedness in some of his other political poems. In 2.31, for example, he devotes a whole elegy to an account of Octavian's opening of the magnificent portico in honor of Apollo on the Palatine hill. This was part of Octavian's great building project, designed to associate Rome's newfound peace and prosperity with himself and his family—the temple of Apollo, of which the portico formed part, was closely linked to his own residence. Augustus famously boasted that "he found Rome built of brick and left it built of marble" (Suetonius, *Life of Augustus* 28). Whereas, however, Propertius's description of the portico is vivid and enthusiastic, the context rather undermines the Augustan message: Augustus was keen to restore the simple god-fearing morality of earlier times, but the elegy begins with the distracting question "You ask why I have kept you waiting?" We are not told who the addressee is, but can easily infer that it is his mistress, whose affair with Propertius is quite alien to the spirit of Augustanism. Such undermining can be detected frequently in Propertius. Throughout 3.4, for example, Propertius envisages a magnificent triumph for the god Augustus over the Parthians, avenging the massacre of Crassus's legions at Carrhae in 53 B.C., but the final couplet shows that Propertius has no personal ambition for military glory: "The spoil be theirs whose hardships have deserved it; / I'll be content to applaud on the Sacred Way," that is, to watch the triumph procession pass by. Is this conclusion a mere shrug of indifference, intended to amuse, or is it a sly and deliberate attack on the regime? This is one of the great challenges of reading Propertius: evaluation of his political intention is left to the individual reader.

However active Propertius's antagonism to Augustus may or may not be, the lifestyle that he portrays himself as leading, in subjection to a mistress and making no contribution to the welfare of the state, is a clear affront to the Augustan restoration, but it is equally clear that he was not alone in this attitude. To ensure a sufficiently large officer class in the army, Augustus tried to maintain a high birth rate by passing a series of marriage laws. In 18 B.C., he promulgated legislation designed to punish adultery and encourage marriage, a law that was made even more rigorous by the passage of further legislation in A.D. 9. It had little effect: Augustus's daughter and granddaughter were both notorious adulterers, and both the consuls who gave their names to the later law, Marcus Papius Mutilus and Quintus Poppaeus Secundus, were bachelors. Many men in the upper strata of society preferred to live as bachelors rather than assume the responsibilities of marriage. Augustus once separated the married knights from the unmarried in the Forum. After briefly thanking the smaller first group for doing their civic duty, he subjected the latter to a lengthy harangue. We do not know if Propertius ever married. Perhaps he did: the poetry of a descendant, perhaps direct, is praised more than a century later by the younger Pliny. But that reality is of little consequence for the literary impact of Propertius's poetry and the personal values it espoused, which ran counter to Augustus's moral agenda: love elegy was about intense passion and had nothing to do with wives.

Propertius repeatedly acknowledges his admiration for the carefully wrought and small-scale poetry of Callimachus, the learned Greek scholar-poet who worked in the Library at Alexandria in the first half of the third century B.C. He associates himself with Callimacheanism already in 2.1, and again praises him, in conjunction with Philetas of Cos, another of the sophisticated Alexandrian poets, in 2.34, 3.1, and 3.9. Finally, in 4.1, when he announces that he will be writing poetry on the origin of Roman institutions, in imitation of Callimachus's *Aetia,* a now mostly lost four-book collection of Greek customs, Propertius claims the title "Roman Callimachus." The veneration he felt for Callimachus is shown in the opening lines of 3.1:

Shade of Callimachus and sacrifices of Coan Philetas,
        Pray grant *me* admission to your grove.
I enter first as priest of a pure fountainhead
        To offer Italian mysteries in Greek dances.

The mystical and religious atmosphere of these lines is quite different from the casually light-hearted tone of the only passage in the *Amores* where Ovid directly compares his poetry to that of Callimachus: in a long and fairly exhaustive catalog of types of girl he finds attractive, he includes one who says "compared with mine Callimachus's / Poems are rough—I like her liking me" (2.4.19–20).

One of the most significant ways in which Propertius marks himself out as a learned poet in the Callimachean manner is in his use of mythology. The modern reader may find his habit of alluding briefly to mythological figures in dense groups rather mysterious and alienating; Ariadne, Andromeda, and the Maenad in the first three couplets of 1.3 are not so very obscure, but the three couplets on the daughters of Leucippus, of Evenus, and of Oenomaus in 1.2 require rather more explanation. Even so, we should bear in mind that overt mythological references such as these would not have offered the same challenges to Propertius's educated contemporaries as they do to us.

Much more sophisticated is Propertius's hidden exploitation of mythology, an important technique that has probably not yet been fully understood. In 1.18, for example, he describes himself wandering through the countryside, pining for Cynthia, carving her name on trees, and calling it out to the woods and the rocks. The natural milieu for an elegiac lover is the city, and Propertius's audience will therefore have wondered why he portrays himself in the countryside. Those who were alert enough and sufficiently well read will have congratulated themselves when they realized that Propertius is casting himself in the role of Acontius, wandering forlornly for love of Cydippe, a myth narrated by Callimachus in the third book of his *Aetia*. As noted earlier, 4.7 and 4.8 form a pair, however ill-matched in tone, because they both narrate a sudden return by Cynthia to Propertius. As is indicated by small but particular details, they are also connected by a hidden exploitation of mythology. In 4.7 Propertius draws on Homer's *Iliad*, portraying Cynthia on the model of the ghost of Patroclus returning to Achilles, whereas in 4.8 he draws on Homer's *Odyssey*, with Cynthia returning in the role of Odysseus, to take vengeance on the prostitutes (= suitors) and also, with a witty distortion, on Propertius, as an unfaithful equivalent to Penelope. This blending of mythology and the life of the elegiac lover is sustained in the next elegy, 4.9, but in the opposite way, presenting a mythological figure as if he were an elegiac lover rather than vice versa. Propertius explains how Hercules founded the Ara Maxima (the Greatest Altar) to commemorate the recovery of his cattle from the three-headed, fire-breathing monster Cacus, noting that women are barred from the rites of Hercules there because the priestesses of a goddess worshiped by women had tried to prevent him from slaking his thirst after the fight with Cacus with water from a spring in the temple's precinct: Propertius gives the myth a richly comic and irreverent twist by portraying Hercules locked out by the tremulous virgin priestesses, just like an elegiac lover locked out by his mistress.

# ELEGIES

## Book 1: Cynthia

*The first book of elegies takes its title from the woman who is its principal inspiration. Cynthia is a pseudonym, like Catullus's Lesbia or Ovid's Corinna, for the idealized woman whose love affair with Propertius is a recurring theme in his surviving works. The formal dedicatee of the book, however, is Tullus, an associate, perhaps a patron, who is addressed in Poems 1, 6, 14, and 22 (the last of the*

*book). He was the nephew of an important public figure, L. Volcacius Tullus, a consul and governor of the province of Asia. Such a dedication may strike a modern reader as unromantic, but Propertius was interested in love, not romance.*

1

*The first poem establishes the theme of the poet's powerlessness to resist the god Love by comparing himself to*

*Milanion, who suffered long for his love of the Arcadian huntress Atalanta, wandering on Mt. Parthenius.*

Cynthia first, with her eyes, caught wretched me
    Smitten before by no desires;
Then, lowering my stare of steady arrogance,
    With feet imposed Love pressed my head,
5  Until he taught me hatred of chaste girls—
    The villain—and living aimlessly.
And now for a whole year this mania has not left me,
    Though I am forced to suffer adverse Gods.

Milanion by facing every hardship, Tullus,
10     Conquered the cruelty of Atalanta.
Sometimes, distraught, he roamed the glens of
    Parthenius
    And was gone to watch the long-haired beasts.
Stunned by that blow from Hylaeus' club he even
    Groaned in anguish to Arcadian crags.
15  So he was able to master his fleet-footed girl;
    Such power in love have prayers and
      kindnesses.
For me, though, Love is slow, can think of no devices,
    And forgets to go his legendary way.

But you who know the trick of drawing down
    the moon
20     And the task of atonement on magic altars,
Here is your chance; come, change my mistress'
    thinking
    And make her face paler than mine.
Then I could believe you have the power to move
    Rivers and stars with Colchian sorcery.

25  And you, friends, who (too late) call back the fallen
    Seek remedies for a heart diseased.
Bravely will I suffer knife and cautery,
    Given liberty to speak as anger bids.
Bear me through farthest nations, bear me over
    the waves
30     Where no woman will know my road.

Stay home, all you to whom God nods with
    easy ear,
    And be paired in love forever true.
On me our Venus levies nights of bitterness,
    And empty Love is ever present.
I warn you, shun this evil. Let each man's darling
    hold him
     Nor quit when love has grown familiar.
But if to warnings anyone should turn slow ears,

Alas, how bitterly he'll rue my words!

2

*Propertius addresses Cynthia on the virtues of her natural beauty, which is not enhanced by silks imported from Cos or eastern perfumes any more than famous beauties of myth such as Phoebe and Hilaira, who were carried off by Helen's brothers, Castor and Pollux; or Marpessa, daughter of the river god Evenus, who chose the mortal Idas over Apollo; or Hippodamia, who was won in a chariot race by the Phrygian Pelops.*

Why choose, my life, to step out with styled hair
    And move sheer curves in Coan costume?
Or why to drench your tresses in Orontes' myrrh
    And sell yourself with foreign gifts
And lose the charm of Nature for bought elegance,    5
    Not letting limbs shine with their own
      attractions?
This doctoring of your looks is pointless, believe me;
    Love, being naked, does not love beauticians.

See what colors beautiful land sends up,
    How ivies in the wild thrive better,    10
Arbutus grows more beautifully in lonely glens
    And water knows by nature where to run.
Beaches appeal, with native pebbles painted,
    And artlessly the birds sing sweeter.

Not in such gear Leucippus' Phoebe and her sister    15
    Hilaira inflamed Castor and Pollux
And on her father's shores Evenus' daughter once
    Set eager Idas and Apollo at odds;
And Hippodamia, carried off on foreign wheels,
    Used no false white to win a Phrygian husband.
But they had looks beholden to no jewels,    20
    Fresh as Apelles' use of color.
They were not out to pick up lovers wholesale;
    Chastity, for them, was beauty enough.

Now I'm not afraid you hold me cheaper than those
    others,    25
    But a girl who pleases one man is smart
      enough—
Especially as Phoebus gladly grants you his poetry
    And Calliope her Aonian lyre,
And your delightful talk discloses unique grace—
    All things that Venus and Minerva approve.    30
For these, while I'm alive, you'll always be most dear—

So long as you've no taste for wretched finery.

3

*The poet returns late at night to find Cynthia asleep, a sight that inspires in him thoughts of Ariadne of Knossos in Crete, who was abandoned by Theseus in her sleep; or Andromeda, the daughter of Cepheus, who was chained to a rock to be devoured by a monster but rescued by Perseus; or a Maenad devoted to Bacchus, resting by the river Apidanus. And as he gazes at her he thinks of Argus with the hundred eyes, who was set to keep watch on Io.*

As the girl from Knossos, while Theseus' keel receded,
    Lay limp on a deserted beach,
And as Cephéan Andromeda in first sleep rested,
    From hard rocks freed at last,
5  And as a Maenad, less tired by the ceaseless dance,
    Swoons on grassy Apídanus,
So Cynthia seemed to me to breathe soft peace,
    Leaning her head on relaxed hands,
When I was dragging footsteps drunken with much Bacchus
    And the boys shook torches in the small hours.
10  Not yet bereft of all my senses I prepared
    To approach her, gently, pressing the couch.
But, though a prey to double passion, under orders
    (From Love on this flank, Bacchus on that,
      both ruthless Gods)
15  To edge an arm beneath her, reconnoitring,
    And kiss, with hand at work, and stand to arms,
Still I dared not disturb my lady's peace,
    Fearing the fierce abuse I knew so well;
But there I stuck, staring intent, like Argus
20    At Io's unfamiliar horns.

And now I loosed the garland from my forehead
    And placed it, Cynthia, on your temples,
Or pleased myself by re-arranging your stray hair,
    Or to cupped hands gave stolen fruit;
25  But all my gifts were lavished on ungrateful sleep,
    Gifts rolled from my pocket often as I leant.

Whenever, rarely moving, you drew a sigh,
    I froze in superstitious dread
That dreams were bringing you strange fears
30    And some man forced you to be his—
Until the moon, passing the window opposite,
    The busy moon with lingering light

Opened those calm closed eyes with
    weightless beams.
      'So!' (and she dug an elbow into the couch)
'At last, humiliation brings you back to our bed,    35
    Thrown out from another woman's door!
Where have you wasted the long hours of my night,
    Limp, alas, now the stars are set?

Villain, O how I wish you could endure such nights
    As you always inflict on wretched me!    40
Sometimes I cheated sleep with crimson thread
    Or a tired tune on Orpheus' lyre;
Or I whispered complaints to my forsaken self
    At unmarried love's long absences—
Until I dropped off, stroked by Slumber's welcome
    wings,    45
    That thought, above all, made me weep.'

4

*Another poet, Bassus, who was also a friend of Ovid, has tried to turn Propertius against Cynthia by comparing her unfavorably to the mythical beauties of Hermione, the daughter of Menelaus and Helen, and Antiope, one of Jupiter's mortal lovers.*

Why press me, Bassus, by your praise of all those girls
    To change my mind and leave my mistress?
Why not let me spend whatever life is left me
    In the familiar bondage?

Praise as you may the beauty of Spartan Hermione    5
    And Nycteus' daughter Antiope
And all the women born in Time's beautiful days
    Cynthia leaves them nameless.
Much less would a harsh critic mark her down as
    inferior
    When compared with minor figures.    10

But her beauty's the smallest part of my obsession,
    Bassus.
    Greater things there are that make it sweet
    to die:
Well-bred complexion, grace of many
    accomplishments,
    And joys over which I'd rather draw a veil.
So the more you strive to destroy our love,
    the more    15
    We frustrate you with our mutual trust.

You'll suffer for it. She'll get to know of your
    wild words
        And you'll have made no inarticulate foe.
Cynthia won't trust us together after this, and won't
20        Invite you. She'll remember your offence.
In her wrath she'll slander you to all the other girls;
        No door, alas, will welcome you.

No shrine will be ignored by her lamenting,
        No sacred stone soever or wherever,
25  No loss is a more serious blow to Cynthia
        Than when her charms are robbed of love—
Specially of mine. I pray that it remain so always
        And I find nothing to reproach for her.

5

*The poet warns off another friend, whose name is revealed in the last couplet of the poem (he might be the poet Cornelius Gallus, although this is disputed), who is setting himself up as a rival for Cynthia's affections.*

Jealous, high time you disciplined that
    tiresome tongue
        And let us run our present course in double
           harness.
Is it your mad desire to suffer my obsession?
        Unhappy man, you rush towards your ruin—
5  To blunder perilously over hidden fires
        And drink all Thessaly's poisons.

She'll prove no flighty girl in the encounter;
        You'll find her anger is no joke.
Even if she's not resistant to your prayers,
        She'll still bring you troubles—by the
10        thousand.
You'll sleep no more. Her image will not leave you.
        Her moods make proud men puppets.

Ah, many's the time you'll run to my door humiliated,
        Your brave boasts sunk to sobs.
On tearful whining trembling dread will
15    supervene
        And fear leave its ugly mark on your face.
When you complain, the words you look for will
    escape you;
        Poor wretch, you won't know who or where
          you are.

Then you'll be forced to learn subservience to our
    mistress

And what it means to go home rejected.    20
You'll cease to express amazement at my pallor
        Or wonder why I'm a mere skeleton.
As lover noble birth will not assist you;
        Love recognizes no ancestral masks.

And if you give the smallest hint of misbehavior,    25
        Your great name will become an instant
           scandal.
I shall not then have power, when asked, to offer
    comfort,
        As I can find no cure for my own trouble.
But paired in misery and shared love we'll be forced
        To weep on one another's shoulder.    30

So make no question, Gallus, of my Cynthia's power;
        When invoked, she comes—with vengeance.

6

*The poet declines an invitation by Tullus to serve with him overseas. In this poem Propertius rejects public service for the life of love, just as in the following poem he rejects epic poetry for love elegy.*

It's not that I'm scared to get to know the Adriatic
        Or sail with you the salt Aegean, Tullus—
With you I'd climb Rhipaean peaks, or march
        Far south beyond the home of Memnon—
But I'm verbally estopped by a girl embracing me,    5
        Who often lends her grave pleas cogent color.

All night long she protests her passion, and when
    I leave her
        Charges the Gods with non-existence,
Alleging she's no longer mine, with menaces
        Of injured girl-friend to ungrateful man.    10
Even for an hour I can't endure this prosecution;
        Ah, perish all cold-hearted lovers!

Would it be worth my while to visit learned Athens
        And view the ancient wealth of Asia,
If Cynthia demonstrates at the ship's launching    15
        Scratching my face with her wild censorship,
And, if the wind's against, claiming a debt of kisses
        On grounds of cruelty by a faithless man?

You must strive to surpass your uncle's well-earned axes
        And bring back law to forgetful allies.    20
Never has your youth taken time off for love,
        But served the fatherland in arms.

Never on you may that Boy bring a lover's hardships
    Or the auspices my tears have taken.

25 Let me, whom Fortune wills among the fallen,
    Lay down my life in extreme misconduct.
Many the willing casualties in love's long service,
    Among whom let me too be buried.
By birth I am ill-equipped for glory or for arms;
30    Fate drafted me for this campaigning.

So, where effete Ionia extends, or where
    Pactólus waters Lydian fields,
Whether you cover land on foot or sea by oar,
    Participant in welcome discipline,
35 Should any hour then bring you memories of me,
    Know that I owe my life to a cruel star.

## 7

*The first of a pair (with 9) of poems addressed to Ponticus, a poet writing an epic on the war between the sons of Oedipus, Eteocles, who seized the throne of Thebes, and Polynices, who sought to win it back with an army led by seven heroes. Propertius contrasts his own less serious verse on the subject of love, to which, he warns, epic poets are not immune.*

Ponticus, while you are telling of Cadmus' Thebes
    And of grim warfare between brothers
And rivalling (bless me!) the primacy of Homer
    Provided Fate is tender to your verse,
5 We, as comes natural, agitate our love
    And seek ideas to move a hard mistress,
Forced rather to be slave of suffering than of wit
    And to complain of youth's hard times.

Thus I grind out my life's measure, this is my fame,
10    For this I wish my verses to be named.
Let them praise me, Ponticus, because I only pleased
    A cultured girl—and suffered her abuse.
Hereafter may neglected lovers daily read me, finding
    Help in the knowledge of our troubles.

15 Should even you be hit by the Boy's inerrant bow
    (Which may the Gods in our heaven forbid!),
Far from your epic camp, poor wretch, and the Seven
    Captains,
    You'll weep, while they lie dumb—in dust
    eternal.
You'll long in vain to write the verse of tenderness,
20    But late love will refuse you inspiration.

Then you will marvel at me as no minor poet,
    And give me first place among Roman wits,
And young men at my grave be moved to murmur
    'Great poet of our passion, down at last.'
So take care in your pride not to despise my verse:  25
    Belated love can charge high interest.

## 8a

*Propertius tries to dissuade Cynthia from her plans to go abroad with a rich lover by invoking the cold of Illyria on the Adriatic coast during a long winter before the rising of the constellation of the Pleiades in spring. He reluctantly wishes her a safe journey from Italy's Tyyrhenian shore, guided by the sea nymph Galatea past the Ceraunian mountains to the port of Oricos in Illyria, where the tribes of the Autaries and Hyllei dwell.*

Are you out of your mind? Does thought of me not
    give you pause?
    Do I mean less to you than Illyria's ice?
And do you really think so well of whoever he is
    That you'd sail without me in the worst
    weather?
Surely you can't brave the roar of the raging sea  5
    And a hard berth amidships?
Or press with those frail feet persistent frosts
    And face blizzards, Cynthia?

O that the season of winter storms were twice as long
    And lagging Pleiades kept sailors idle,  10
That your stern-rope never were loosed from the
    Tyrrhene shore
    Nor an ill wind blew away my prayers!

And yet when the wave does carry your ship
    from harbor
    Let me never see such winds subside
As leave me stranded on an empty shore  15
    Shaking my fist and calling you cruel.

But however badly you treat me, traitress,
    May Galatea smile on your voyage,
And after prosperous oarage past the Ceraunians
    Oricos greet you with level calm.  20

For never, my life, shall other women tempt me
    To end my just complaining at your door,
Nor shall I tire of interrogating busy sailors:
    'Tell me what port interns my girl?'

And I'll say 'Though she land on Autáric or Hylléan
25    coasts,
       Her future will be mine.'

8b

*The poet celebrates Cynthia's change of mind. This pair
of poems (8a and b) artfully separates the two poems
addressed to Ponticus on the power of love (and love poetry).*

It's here she'll be. She has sworn to stay. Ill-wishers can
   go hang!
       We've won. She has given in to my entreaties.
Eager envy can drop its glad illusions:
30       Our Cynthia returns to her old ways.

She calls me *dear* and Rome *most dear* because of me,
       Would find no kingdom sweet without me,
Prefers to rest with me, though in a narrow bed,
       And be mine, at whatever cost,
35 Than dowered with Hippodamia's ancient kingdom
       Or the wealth that Elis' horses won.

To all his great gifts and even greater promises,
       Not being greedy, she prefers my pocket.
I could not move her with gold or mother of pearl,
40       But only with devoted verse.

So the Muse exists and Apollo makes haste to help
   the lover;
       In that faith I love, for peerless Cynthia's mine.
Today I walk in heaven, among the stars.
       Come day, come night, she's mine.
45 No rival can rob *me* of my true love;
       That glory shall my grey hairs know.

9

*As Propertius has predicted, love has found Ponticus,
and his epic poem on Thebes, with its walls built by
Amphion, does him no good at all. Better the love poetry
of Mimnermus, an elegiac poet who wrote about a century
or so after Homer.*

Cynic, I told you love would come
       And you'd lose free speech.
Look, you've fallen—a woman's submissive
   suppliant—
       Slave of some girl bought yesterday!
5 In love Chaonia's doves can't beat me at divining

Which young men are which girl's conquest.
I've earned my expertise by tears and suffering:
       Would I were heart-whole and a layman!

Much good it does you now, poor wretch, to mouth
   your epic
       And weep Amphion's lyre-built walls.      10
In love a line of Mimnermus is more help than Homer.
       Civilized love needs soft music.
Please go and stow away those gloomy cantos
       And sing what every girl would like to hear.

It's not as if she refused to see you. Why, at present    15
       You're like a madman in midstream
           demanding water.
You're not even pale as yet. The true fire hasn't
   touched you—
       Just the first spark of future trouble.

Then you'll sooner face Armenian tigresses,
       Sooner be bound in Hell to Ixion's wheel      20
Than in your marrow feel so often the Boy's bow
       And have no power to say her anger nay.
Love never offers anyone an easy flight
       Without at other times depressing him.

Don't be deceived because she's willing, Ponticus;    25
       When a girl's yours her sting goes deeper.
Your eyes once caught, Love won't allow you to
   withdraw them
       Or lie awake for someone else's sake.
He does not show until his hand touches the bone.
       Run, whoever you are, from his temptations.      30
Stocks and stones are powerless to resist them,
       Much less your poor lightweight soul.

So for goodness' sake confess your error now. In love
       It's often a relief to name one's ruin.

10

*Gallus, who was addressed as a rival in Poem 5, is now in
love, and Propertius represents himself as delighting in his
friend's love affair, picking up a theme from Catullus 45.*

O the delicious peace, after witnessing first love
       As an accomplice of your tears!
O the delicious pleasure in remembering that night,
       To be asked for—O how often!—in my
           prayers,
When I watched you, Gallus, dying in a girl's embrace   5

And breathing intermittent words!
    Though sleep hung heavy on my drooping eyelids
        And the riding moon blushed in mid-sky,
I could not absent myself from your love-play,
10        So passionate that dialogue.

But since you had the courage to confide in me,
        Accept my tribute to shared joy.
Not only have I learnt to keep your passion secret,
        I offer something greater, friend, than loyalty:
15 I have the power to reconcile estranged lovers
        And to open a mistress' reluctant door.
I have the power to heal another's new-found troubles;
        My words contain strong medicine.
Cynthia has taught me what to seek and what to shun
20        On each occasion; Love has helped.

Shun the desire to fight with a moody girl,
        And proud speech, and long silence.
Do not, when she wants a thing, refuse ungraciously,
        Nor let her kind words fall unheeded.
She comes, when slighted, in bad temper, and when
25    wronged
        Forgets to drop her rightful threats.
But the more humble you are and deferential to love,
        The oftener you'll enjoy success.
He who forgoes freedom and the uncommitted heart
30        Can find abiding bliss with one girl.

### 11

*Cynthia is on holiday at Baiae, a fashionable resort on the
north shore of the Bay of Naples, between the promontory
of Misenum and the Lucrine Lake. Propertius evokes the
place by reference to mythology: the causeway along the
shore reputedly built by Hercules and the channel built
by Agrippa in 37 B.C. to connect the sea to Lake Avernus,
where Thesprotus once ruled.*

While you're on holiday in Baiae, Cynthia,
        Where the causeway lies along Hercules' shore,
And marvel how sea-water from near famed Misenum
        Was channeled lately to Thesprotus' realm,
Does thought of me occur—to bring night
5    memories?
        Is there room for me on love's margin?
Or has some enemy, Cynthia, play-acting passion
        Removed you from my poetry?

I had far rather a little dinghy powered by paddles
10        Detained you on the Lucrine Lake,

Or water yielding easily to alternate arms
        Imprisoned you in Teuthras' ripples,
Than you be free to hear another man's sweet
    whispers,
        Relaxed on a beach that tells no tales.

A girl without protection is apt to fall,        15
        Play false, and forget mutual vows—
Not that I doubt your proven reputation,
        But there love's threat is ever-present.
So please forgive me if my writings cause you
        Any distress. Fear must take the blame.        20

Would I protect more anxiously my own dear mother?
        Without you what would my life be worth?
You, Cynthia, only you are home to me and parents,
        You all my times of happiness.
Whether on meeting friends I am gloomy or
    delighted,        25
        In every mood I should say 'Blame Cynthia!'

But you must quickly leave degenerate Baiae;
        Those beaches bring divorce to many,
Beaches for long the enemy of decent girls.
        A curse on Baiae's waters, love's disgrace!        30

### 12

*The poet declares that he cannot leave Rome because
Cynthia is there, and yet he feels as distant from her as the
river Hypanis, which flows into the Black Sea, is from the
river Po of Italy.*

Know-all Rome, why not stop falsely accusing me
        Of idleness because she keeps me here?
As many miles divide her from my bed as Hypanis
        Is far from Venetian Eridanus.
It is not me her embraces feed with familiar love,        5
        Nor in my ear does Cynthia sound sweet.

I was favored once. In those days no one had the luck
        Of loving with like faithfulness.
We were envied. So, does God abase me? Or
    some herb
        Picked on Promethean heights divide us?        10
I am not what I was, for travel changes a girl.
        So great a love so quickly gone!
Now I must learn to know long nights alone
        And be a weariness to my own ears.

Happy the man who could weep in his girl's presence
        (Love can enjoy the sprinkling of tears)        15

Or who, when scorned, could redirect his ardor
    (There is also joy in bondage transferred).
My fate is neither to love another nor break with *her*:
20    Cynthia was first and Cynthia shall be last.

### 13

*Another poem addressed to Gallus, who is gloating over
the poet's distress because he is separated from Cynthia.
Propertius will not retaliate even as he recognizes that
Gallus is himself overcome by a love that exceeds the passion of Neptune for Tyro, whom he seduced disguised as a
river god, or Hercules, who married Hebe after his death
on Mt. Oeta when he was admitted to the company of the
gods. Indeed, as the poet puts it, Gallus's lover is second
only to Leda, the mother of Helen by Jupiter.*

As usual, Gallus, you'll take pleasure in my plight—
    That I am love-bereft, at lonely leisure.
But I refuse to imitate your treacherous tongue:
    Never may girl wish, Gallus, to trick *you*.
5  While growing famous for female deception
    And coolly looking for short-term love,
You've fallen for someone and turn pale with
    ill-timed passion—
    The first slippery step to ruin.
She'll be the punishment for those despised
    unfortunates,
10    The One to avenge the wrongs of many.
She'll put a stop to your promiscuous affairs;
    You'll cease to enjoy the search for novelty.

It was not gossip taught me this, nor augury;
    I've seen. Can you deny my evidence?
Gallus, I've seen you swooning away, with neck
15    held tight,
    And weeping long under close arrest,
Eager to lay down your life on longed-for lips—
    The rest my friendly modesty conceals.

I could not separate your mutual embrace,
20    So wild the passion between you both.
With love less easy, in the guise of river-god,
    Neptune embraced Salmoneus' daughter.
With love less ardent Hercules experienced heavenly
    Hebe, first joy after Oeta's pyre.
25  On that one day all lovers were outrun,
    So fierce the fire she kindled in you.

Nor has she let your previous arrogance return.
    There's no escape. Passion will drive you on.
No wonder, when she's worthy of Jove, second
    to Leda,
    Greater than Leda's girls, one against three,    30
More seductive than all the heroines of old Argos.
    Her words could win the love of Jove.

But as you're doomed this time to die of love, enjoy it.
    No other door was good enough for you.
You've had a strange lapse. May it bring you luck,    35
    And she be the one for all your wishes.

### 14

*In an address to his patron, Tullus, Propertius celebrates
the joys of love, which he would not trade for riches, both
real, such as gold from the Lydian river Pactolus and eastern pearls, and mythical, such as the opulent gifts given by
Alcinous to Odysseus in the* Odyssey.

Though you lounge luxuriously by the waves of Tiber
    Drinking Lesbian wine from Mentor's work
And gazing, now at swift lighters running past,
    Now at slow barges hauled by ropes,
And though each landscaped grove stretches
    up as tall    5
    As the trees that crowd on Caucasus,
Still such things can't be matched against my love:
    Love has no respect for money.

Whenever she prolongs with me the
    wished-for night
    Or spends all day in easy love,    10
Then beneath my roof Pactólus' freshets flow
    And Red Sea pearls are gathered;
Then my joys guarantee me king of kings—
    And may they last until I die.
Who can enjoy his wealth with Love against him?    15
    No prizes for me if Venus frowns.

She can break the staying-power of heroes,
    Bring pain to the hardest heart.
She's not afraid to trespass on the onyx threshold
    And mount the crimson couch, Tullus,    20
And keep a wretched young man tossing on his bed;
    No comfort then in colored silken covers.
But granted her gracious presence, I'll not hesitate
    To scorn a kingdom or Alcinous' gifts.

15

*Propertius is sick, and Cynthia visits him only late and obviously dressed to catch another man's eye: she is not like the famous women of mythology who are wracked with distress over their lovers—Calypso, who was devastated by the departure of Odysseus; Hypsipyle, who was abandoned by Jason of Haemonia; Evadne, who committed suicide on the funeral pyre of her husband; or Alphesiboea, who killed her own brothers because they had murdered her husband, Alcmaeon.*

Many the hurts I've often feared from your light
  conduct,
   But never, Cynthia, this betrayal.
Look at me, Fortune's victim, in grave danger,
   But you're not frightened, though you've come
    at last.
And you can use your hands to re-do yesterday's
5  hairstyle,
   And spend an hour on your make-up,
Can even flash a string of Eastern pearls
   As if in honor of a new lover.

Unlike Calypso, who on the Ithacan's departure
10   Wept beside the lonely sea;
For many days in mourning, hair unkempt,
   She sat complaining to the cruel salt waves,
And though she'd never see him more, felt sorry for him,
14   Remembering their long happiness:
17 Nor like Hypsiyle—when winds swept Jason off,
18   Distraught, immobile in her empty bower,

19 Hypsipyle thereafter felt no other love,
20   Pining only for her Haemonian guest.
21 Evadne, proud to burn on her poor husband's pyre
22   Died a paragon of Argive purity.
15 Alphesiboea to avenge a husband killed her brothers,
16   Breaking blood's precious bond for love.
Could none of these inspire you to amend
23  your ways
24   That you too might become a legend?

25 Say nothing, Cynthia, now to recall your perjury;
   Beware of arousing forgetful Gods.
Alas, too reckless you would suffer at my peril,
   Should any harm befall you.
Rivers will cease to flow into the sea,
30   Seasons of the year run in reverse,
Before my heart's concern for you could alter.
   Be what you will, I should never leave you.

You must not hold so cheap those eyes of yours
   Which pass off treason as my truth.
You swore by them that if you told a lie   35
   They'd drop out into your hands,
And can you raise them now to the great Sun-God
   Without one tremor of guilt?
Who forced you to turn pale so variously
   And those reluctant eyes to weep?  40
For them I'm dying now, and warning fellow lovers
   'O it's unsafe to trust sweet words!'

16

*A soliloquy delivered by the door of a house once venerable and tracing its ancestry to Tarpeia, one of the original Vestal Virgins, but now the residence of a woman of questionable character.*

'Long ago I've stood wide open for great Triumphs,
   A door famed for Tarpeian chastity,
Whose threshold, wet with prisoners' suppliant tears,
   Gilded chariots celebrated.
Now I must often groan, disfigured by nocturnal  5
   Drunken brawls and thumped by vulgar fists.
And all the time disgraceful garlands hang upon me,
   And torches, exclusion's token, lie around.

I cannot guard my mistress from unsavory nights,
   My noble self being subject to graffiti.  10
Nor does she stop to think of reputation, living
   More loosely than even our time's
    permissiveness.
What's more, I'm forced to weep and wail in sympathy
   With a suppliant's long nights of watching.
He never gives my doorposts any peace, singing  15
   Over and over this whining serenade:

"Door, crueller by far than even your mistress' self,
   Why with hard panels closed to me and silent?
Why are you never unbarred to admit my love
   Or moved to deliver clandestine pleas?  20
Will never an end be vouchsafed to my pain,
  and must
   I sleep in disgrace on this lukewarm threshold?
Midnights and full moons and breezes that dawn
  frost chills
   Feel sorry for me lying here.
You only, never pitying human pain,  25
   Answer me back with silent hinges.

If only my feeble voice could enter through that crack
   And find a way to strike my mistress' ear!

Be she more cursed than Sicanian rock,
30      Harder be she than iron and steel,
Yet surely she could not remain dry-eyed
      And would heave a sigh in reluctant tears.
But now she lies in the lucky arms of another man,
      While I waste words on the midnight wind.

35  You, door, my only, you my greatest cause of pain,
      Are never taken with my gifts.
My tongue has never shocked you with
      immodest words
      Uttered when drunk in angry jest,
That you should let me whine on here until I'm
      hoarse,
40      Keeping tormented vigil in the street.
No, I have often spun you a song in modern verse
      And, kneeling, pressed kisses on your steps.
You traitor, many a time I've turned in homage
      toward you
      And secretly paid the vows I owed."

45  With this and much else typical of wretched lovers
      He tries to drown the birds' dawn chorus.
So now, for a lady's faults and a lover's endless weeping,
      I'm the lasting butt of malicious gossip.'

### 17

*A soliloquy by the poet during a storm at sea crossing the
Adriatic from Italy to the port of Cassiope on the Greek
island of Corfu. He laments that, like other voyagers, he
must pray to the sons of Tyndareus, Castor and Pollux,
who protect sailors, and ends with an appeal to the sea
nymphs' mother, the goddess Doris.*

And serve me right for having run away from her
      That I'm now haranguing lonely halcyons,
Nor will Cassiópe see my keel safe harbored
      And all my vows are wasted on thankless sand!

Why, Cynthia, in your absence the waves take
5      your part!
      Look how the gale howls cruel threats!
Is there no chance of the storm abating?
      Will that patch of sand cover my corpse?
Change cruel reproaches for the better, and take night
10      And treacherous shoals as punishment enough.
Will you, dry-eyed, be able to ask about my fate
      And never hold my bones to your breast?

Ah perish whoever first constructed hull and sail
      And voyaged the unwilling deep!

Was it not lighter work to weather a mistress' moods    15
      (However heartless, she was peerless still)
Than thus to gaze on a shoreline flanked by
      unknown forest
      And pray hard for the Tyndarids?

There, if some fate had entombed my sorrow
      And the last stone stood over buried love,    20
She would have offered her dear hair at my funeral
      And laid the bones gently on rose petals.
She would have cried my name over the final dust
      That earth might be weightless upon me.

But you, the deep-sea daughters of shapely Doris,    25
      In happy dance unfurl white sails:
If ever Love, in transit, touched your waves,
      Grant a fellow-sufferer safe landing.

### 18

*A soliloquy, set in a lonely countryside, home of Zephyrus,
the west wind, where he carves her name on the trees, and
the hillsides echo her name.*

Yes, this lonely place will hush up my complaining;
      The grove is Zephyrus' empty property.
Here one can safely voice unspoken sorrows,
      If solitary rocks can keep a secret.

To what shall I first trace, my Cynthia, your disdain?    5
      Where, Cynthia, do I begin to weep?
I who was lately numbered among the lucky lovers
      Must now incur a black mark in your love.
Where is my guilt? What slander changes you
      toward me?
      That I've taken a new girl to make you jealous?    10
So come you back to me, light as you are: no other
      Woman's pretty feet have crossed my
         threshold.
This suffering of mine may owe you many a hurt,
      Yet I could never feel such savage anger
As justified your being mad at me and made    15
      Your bright eyes dull with flooding tears.

Or do you count my change of color a paltry
      symptom?
      Does no devotion cry out from my face?
If trees can know love, they shall be witnesses—
      Beech and pine that's friend to Arcadia's God.    20
Ah, in their tender shade how often my words echo
      And written on their bark is *Cynthia*.

Or is it that your cruelty breeds in me resentment,

Only divulged to your silent door?
25 I am used to bear timidly all your decrees,
        Not to lamenting shrilly at what you do,
And in return am given sacred springs, cold cliffs,
        Hard resting on rough paths;
And every tale of woe I have to utter
30        Must be told in solitude to shrill birds.

Yet, be as you will, the woods for me shall echo
        Cynthia
        And the lonely rocks repeat your name.

### 19

*In an address to his lover, the poet declares that he does not
fear death so much as he dreads that she should forget him
once he is gone. That did not happen to the first casualty
of the Trojan War, Protesilaus, the grandson of Phylacus,
who was allowed to visit his wife as a ghost after his death.
And so the poet ends with an exhortation, familiar from
Catullus 5, to live and love while they may.*

It's not that I'm scared, my Cynthia, of the
        Underworld
        Or mind fate's debt to the final pyre,
But the fear that when dead I may lose your love
        Is worse than the funeral itself.
5 Not so lightly has the Boy clung to our eyes
        That with love forgotten my dust could rest.

There, in the unseen world, Phylácides the hero
        Could not forget his lovely wife,
But eager to clutch delight with disappointed hands
10        Came as a ghost to his old home Thessaly.
There, wherever I am, I shall ever be called your shadow;
        Great love can cross even the shores of fate.

There let them come in troops, the beautiful heroines
        Picked by Argives from the spoils of Troy,
No beauty of theirs for me could match yours,
15        Cynthia—
        Indeed (may Mother Earth in justice grant it)
Though fate remand you to a long old age,
        Yet to my tears will your bones be dear.

If only the living you could feel this for my ashes,
        Then death, wherever, for me would have no
20        sting.
Ah Cynthia, how I fear that love's iniquity
        Scorning the tomb may drag you from my dust
And force you, though loth, to dry the falling tears;

A faithful girl can be bent by constant threats.
So while we may let us delight in loving;     25
        No love is ever long enough.

### 20

*A narrative, set in cameo-like miniature, of how Hylas, a boy
beloved by Hercules, was carried off by nymphs of the river
Ascanius, while the two were journeying with Jason and the
Argonauts, who were also known as the Minyae. It is cast as
a warning to Gallus to be careful when he makes the rounds
of resorts like Tibur, set on the river Anio, or Baiae, where
the Giants once fought. Propertius evokes the epic sweep of
the Argonautic myth by listing places visited in the voyage
of the Argo—Pagasa in Thessaly, whence they set off, their
destination in Colchis at the mouth of the river Phasis, and
the Hellespont, where Helle the daughter of Athamas perished. He describes how the winged sons of Boreas, Zetes and
Calais, descendants of Pandion and Orithyia, tried to molest
Hylas but departed, only to leave him prey to the nymphs
at the spring of Pege beneath Mt. Arganthus. Hercules, the
grandson of Alceus, never recovered Hylas, which should
serve as a warning to Gallus as he takes his lover to the spas.*

For lasting love's sake, Gallus, we give you this advice
        (Let it not slip a heedless mind):
'Often bad luck befalls the lover unaware'—
        Cruel Ascanius could have told the Minyae.

You have a flame most like Theiódamas' son Hylas,     5
        No less in looks, no different in name.
Whether you pass by Anio's shady-wooded stream
        Or dip your feet in its ripples
Or promenade the beach along the Giants' Coast
        Or anywhere a stream gives wayward welcome,
Protect him always from Nymphs' greedy ravages     10
        (Ausonian Dryads are no less amorous)
Lest you be haunting rugged mountains, Gallus,
        And icy rocks and untried pools—
What Hercules' wretched wandering suffered on for-
        eign shores
        And wept by wild Ascanius.     15

For long ago, they say, from docks at Pagasa
        Argo set sail for distant Phasis,
And gliding on, Athamantis' waves already passed,
        Found mooring at the Mysian rocks.     20
Here the band of heroes, halting on calm shore,
        Cover soft sand with gathered leaves.
Meanwhile the unconquered youth's attendant
        went ahead

To fetch rare water from a special spring.

25  Pursuing him two brothers, breed of Aquilo,
          Above him Zetes and above him Cálaïs
Hovered with dangling hands to steal kisses and
          give
          Upward kisses in alternate flight.
He, bending down, protects himself beneath their
          wing-tips
          And with a branch drives off the airborne
30           ambush.
So Pandionian Orithyia's brood departed:
          Ah grief ! Hylas was going, going to the
          Hamadryads.

Here, beneath Arganthus' peak, was the spring Pege,
          A damp home dear to Thynian Nymphs,
35  Above which hung, indebted to no tending,
          Dewy fruit on forsaken trees,
And round them, in a water-meadow, lilies grew
          Tall and white among crimson poppies,
Which now he nips off childishly with tender nail
40           Preferring flowers to the task before him,
And now leans over the pretty waves unwarily,
          Prolonging truancy with flattering reflexions.

At last he dips his hands, ready to draw from the stream,
          Leaning on right shoulder as he filled up,
When, fired by its whiteness, the Dryad maids in
45           admiration
          Left their customary dances
And lightly drew him down headfirst in
          yielding water;
          At his body's rape then Hylas gave a cry.
Far off repeatedly Alcides answers, but
          From the distant spring the breeze returns
50           the name.
By this advised, O Gallus, you will guard your love,

For I've seen you trust fair Hylas to the
          Nymphs.

21

*An address by a soldier called Gallus, who was at Perusia
in 41–40 B.C. when Mark Antony's brother was besieged
there by Octavian.*

'You who hurry to avoid a kindred fate,
          Wounded soldier from the Etruscan lines,
Why at my groan do you roll those bulging eyes?
          I am your closest fellow-campaigner.
So may your parents celebrate your safe return;      5
          Let your sister learn what happened from
          your tears:
That I, Gallus, rescued from the midst of Caesar's
          swords,
          Failed to escape from hands unknown;
And of all the scattered bones she finds on
          Etruscan hills,
          Let her know that these are mine.'      10

22

*A sphragis, or seal poem, to conclude the book, addressing
his patron Tullus and identifying the poet's birthplace in
Umbria, near Perusia, the unhappy setting for the death of
Gallus related in the previous poem.*

You ask my rank and birth and my penates, Tullus,
          In the name of our enduring friendship.
If the Perusine graves of our fatherland are known to you,
          The dead of Italy's troubled times
When Rome's dissension drove her citizens to ruin,      5
          (But specially to me, Etruscan dust, the grief:
It was you allowed my kinsman's limbs to lie outcast,
          It was you refused his poor bones burial)
Umbria, next adjoining on the plain below,
          A fertile land, deep-breasted, bore me.      10

## AFTERWORD

Propertius's poetry enjoyed great success and continued to be appreciated for at least four centuries after his death, a fact that is somewhat obscured by its tenuous survival to our times. During the Middle Ages his works were largely unknown, and it was only with the discovery of a manuscript in the Sorbonne by Petrarch that we can begin to trace his influence again. Even in his hometown of Assisi, his fame was eclipsed by St. Francis (whose early life as a poet and partygoer seems disconcertingly Propertian). But Propertius had not always suffered such neglect; beneath the church of Santa Maria Maggiore, once the cathedral of Assisi but long since overshadowed by the Duomo di San Rufino and the Basilica di San Francesco d'Assisi, are the ruins of a substantial Roman house. Most of the site is still not excavated, but one of the numerous graffiti found there is dated February 22, A.D. 367, and reads (in not very classical Latin) *domum oscilavi Musae,* "I have kissed the house of the Muse"; the natural inference is that this was the family home of the Propertii, and that admirers of his poetry were still making pilgrimages there in the fourth century.

The canon of love elegists was defined by Ovid, who professed himself to be not only an admirer but a friend of Propertius and often heard him recite his love poetry (*Sorrows of an Exile* 4.10.45–46). Ovid's verdict had staying power, so a century later when Quintilian was ranking the most important elegiac poets in Latin (*Education of the Orator* 10.1.95), he names the same quartet—Gallus, Tibullus, Propertius, and Ovid—and adds the observation that while Tibullus was generally considered particularly elegant, "some people prefer Propertius" on that score. Indeed, Propertius's modern reputation for obscurity seems to have been entirely unknown in antiquity. At about the same time Martial penned a dedicatory epigram (14.189) as a gift card for a present of Propertius's *Cynthia* volume, a sign that the work was in common circulation. Another contemporary, the younger Pliny, was a friend of a descendant of Propertius, Passennus Paulus, who was himself an elegiac poet emulating the style of his ancestor, which Pliny (*Letters* 9.22.2) describes as "refined, tender, and attractive." Ovid's enthusiasm for Propertius's elegies is manifest not only in his programmatic references to his predecessor but, more important, in his rehandling of Propertian themes and frequent allusion to his words throughout his own elegiac works. We know of some poets in addition to Passennus Paulus who wrote elegy after Ovid, but their works have not survived, so our perspective on the influence of the genre is skewed, and yet it is certain that Propertius was much read throughout this period.

On the walls of Pompeii some lines from his poetry were scrawled as graffiti (*Corpus of Latin Inscriptions* 4.1894, 1950), and his influence is felt in many other scribblings by would-be love poets. One couplet of two hexameters composed by an anonymous poet was found in six different locations (*Corpus of Latin Inscriptions* 4.1520, 1523, 1526, 1528, 3040, 9847). It combines an imitation of a line by Propertius (1.1.5) with another attributed to Ovid (*Amores* 3.11.35) to make a humorous point: "A

**Figure 14: Roman woman**
A woman in a silk dress in a Pompeian wall-painting. Silk dresses, described by the mime-writer Publilius Syrus as "woven wind", were extremely expensive, for silk had to be imported along the trade-route from China, which guarded its monopoly very closely.

fair-skinned woman taught me to spurn dark complexions; I'll spurn them if I can, if not, I'll love them against my will." The love poetry represented for us by the works of the three surviving elegists penetrated deeply into the daily imaginations of Romans, not only those like Quintilian and Pliny who could appreciate their sophistication and elegance from a rhetorical point of view. This appreciation was later lost, however, and love elegy was not to the taste of readers from the fifth century on.

We do not know who owned the last complete copy of Cornelius Gallus's elegies, but he (or she) probably lived at about the time one of the last tourists visited the house of Propertius in Assisi. Ovid's love elegies benefited from the fact that their author also wrote the enormously popular and influential *Metamorphoses*; Tibullus and Propertius were little read and little known throughout the Middle Ages. The earliest surviving manuscript of Propertius dates from around the year 1200, and the sources from which it derived were heavily disfigured by copying errors. The restoration of the text, which began in earnest in the Renaissance, went a long way toward winning new admirers for Propertian love poetry, but these readers were far removed from the fans of antiquity who expressed their feelings in his words on the walls of Pompeii. Petrarch made a copy of the text, but there are only a few echoes of Propertius in his *Sonnets*. Aeneas Silvius (the Latinized name of Enea Silvio de' Piccolomini) wrote a collection of erotic poems entitled *Cinthia*, remarkable mostly because their author later became Pope Pius II. Ronsard alludes to Propertius in both his *Amours* and his *Amours Diverses*, and Goethe makes some use of him in his *Römische Elegien*. Much in Propertius's poetry that seems obscure is probably due to the damage done to the text over centuries of neglect, but this accident of transmission has also been productive of new interpretations.

Nowadays many students of literature first encounter Propertius through Ezra Pound's *Homage to Sextus Propertius,* published in 1919. Pound's creative translation provoked much negative reaction from the community of classical scholars, in large measure because of what were perceived to be errors in his understanding of Propertius's difficult Latin, but not least because of Pound's willingness to read Propertius within the context of his own views about World War I and the British Empire. Propertius was, as T. S. Eliot once noted, "more civilized than most of his interpreters have admitted," but in his case the challenge of interpretation is more than usually complicated. Published in the same year as Pound's *Homage,* W. B. Yeats's "A Thought from Propertius" catches the oppositions inherent in the elegist's portrayal of his mistress—in the opening lines a chaste priestess of Athena, but in the last two lines a target of rape for lusty centaurs:

> she might, so noble from head
> To great shapely knees
> The long flowing line,
> Have walked to the altar
> Through the holy images
> At Pallas Athene's side,
> Or been fit spoil for a centaur
> Drunk with the unmixed wine.

Yeats's attention was surely drawn to Propertius by Pound, and for later poets, it required an effort to get past Pound's ventriloquizing. Robert Lowell notes, in an interview in 1961, that "I got Propertius through Pound. When I read him in Latin I found a kind of Propertius you don't get in Pound at all. Pound's Propertius is a rather Ovidian figure with a great deal of fluency and humor and irony. The actual Propertius is a very excited, tense poet, rather desperate." This reading of the poet informs Lowell's own darkly colored translation of Propertius 4.7, "The Ghost," which appeared in his breakthrough collection *Lord Weary's Castle* (1946). It is present also in his version of Propertius 4.3, "Arethusa to Lycotas," the last poem in Lowell's last book (1977). Consciously or not, Lowell is echoing a famous pronouncement by one of Propertius's modern editors: "for every editor, a different Propertius" (*quot editores, tot Propertii*). And for every reader, as well.

# OVID

### (Publius Ovidius Naso, 43 B.C.–after A.D. 17)

OVID WAS THE LAST OF THE FOUR GREAT ELEGISTS OF THE AUGUSTAN ERA, FOLLOWING on Gallus, Tibullus, and Propertius, and in many ways setting a seal upon the genre. His date of birth has particular resonance, in 43 B.C., the last year of the Republic. He was born in Sulmo, about ninety miles east of Rome, a young man from the country, but he belonged to the city of Rome perhaps more than any other of her great poets. He celebrated its people, their lives and loves, their stories and their places in a dazzling array of works that took him far beyond the confines of the genre of elegy as his predecessors had defined it. In the *Heroides* (Letters of the Heroines), imaginary letters by women from myth, he explored the female characters of epic and tragedy. In the *Ars Amatoria* (The Art of Love) and the *Remedia Amoris* (Remedies for Love), he explored the vagaries of courtship and the exquisite pains of falling in and out of love. In the *Fasti* (Calendars), he used the Roman calendar as the framework for a collection of strange tales that attached themselves to religious practice. His *Metamorphoses* is one of the great masterpieces of storytelling in Western literature. For reasons that we will never know, he was sent into exile by the emperor Augustus in A.D. 8 to the farthest, most desolate, region of the empire, the outpost of Tomi on the shores of the Black Sea, a fitting punishment, it would seem, for the elegant poet of love. Banishment did not silence him, however, as he returned to the elegiac meter of his earliest works, producing first five books of "Sorrows" (*Tristia*) and then, returning to the epistolary form, four more books of "Letters from the Black Sea" (*Epistulae ex Ponto*). The rich legacy of the elegiac tradition reverberated through his verses until the end.

## THE AMORES

Roman love poets wrote about their mistresses under elegant Greek pseudonyms. It was no secret that Catullus's Lesbia was really Clodia, one or other of the three sisters of Clodius Pulcher, Cicero's arch political enemy, and that Gallus's Lycoris was really Cytheris, a mime-actress whom Cicero once met at a dinner, much to his thrilled and fussy embarrassment. Cynthia and Delia, the mistresses, respectively, of Propertius and of Tibullus in his first book, are much more obscure. Discussing the use of synonyms in erotic literature in his *Apology* (a defense against using witchcraft to induce a rich widow to marry him), Apuleius informs us that Delia's real name was Plania, and that Cynthia's was Hostia. There is no reason to disbelieve him. Like Lesbia and Lycoris, both Delia and (with slight qualification) Cynthia have the same prosody as the ladies' real names, so a copy of the poems in their honor could be given to them privately without the anonymity. All these pseud-onyms are flattering. Lesbia associates Clodia with Lesbos, the home of the great poetess Sappho, while all the others evoke Apollo, the god of poetry: Apollo had a cult title Lycius (the wolf god), he was born on the island of Delos, and Mt. Cynthus is on Delos. The identity of Delia as Plania is particularly persuasive, for it involves a clever bilingual pun, the Greek adjective δῆλος (*delos*) and the Latin adjective *planus* both meaning "clear."

In the fifth century, Sidonius Apollinaris asserted that Ovid's mistress, Corinna, was actually no less a personage than Augustus's daughter Julia. Leaving aside that wildly improbable speculation, it is significant that neither Apuleius nor anyone else suggests a real name for her. If we look for a Roman equivalent to Corinna, which is cognate with the Greek word for "girl," κόρη (*kore*), the obvious word, having the same prosody, is *puella,* meaning simply and quite uninformatively "girl." If the pseudonym Corinna does not disguise the identity of a particular real woman, it seems reasonable to conclude that Ovid's *Amores* are not based on an affair with an actual woman. It follows that Ovid's purpose in writing his personal love poetry is simply to play with the conventions of the genre, and that we should not expect the passionate revelation of deep feelings. If Gallus, Tibullus, and Propertius had written cookbooks, the *Amores* would be full of rather eccentric recipes.

Ovid's playful attitude to elegiac conventions is evident even in the way he points out the illogical-ity in hiding the mistress's identity under a pseudonym. In 2.17, he argues that Corinna should accept him as her lover because, although he may not be rich, he can offer her his poetry. (The love elegists conventionally portray themselves as poor, even though all four of them were knights, and a substan-tial property qualification was required for membership of the equestrian order.) He goes right on, however, to sabotage his argument by saying that he knows another girl who is going about claiming that she is Corinna, and warning his mistress that the other girl would do anything for that honor. He is drawing attention to the absurdity of the use of synonyms: if a pseudonym hides the mistress's identity so efficiently that another girl can lay claim to being the poet's mistress, then the immortal fame to be gained by being praised in his poetry is a very limited measure of immortal fame.

The absence of sincere emotion from the *Amores* is made clear immediately. The first poem is hardly about love at all. Ovid tells us that he was writing a war epic in the conventional meter of hex-ameters, but that Cupid stole a foot from the second line, turning it into a pentameter, so he was left with elegiac couplets, the meter for love poetry. He protests at length that Cupid should mind his own business and not interfere in poetry, which is in Apollo's sphere of influence. He ends by saying that he cannot write love poetry because he is not in love. This is a tactical error, for Cupid invalidates this objection very simply, by shooting him and thus making him fall in love. Ovid's useless and indignant protests to Cupid set the tone for the *Amores.* Very little goes right for him as he recounts his amatory adventures. A successful and happy love affair would have offered little sustained dramatic interest; obstacles to love provide more fertile themes for a poet wishing to draw out the comic possibilities of the genre. Hence, Ovid is constantly plagued by his mistress's absence or reluctance, by rivals, by husbands, by chaperones, by procuresses, by doorkeepers, by rivers in flood. Whatever happens to him, he presents himself as losing out. In 1.4, he lectures his mistress on how she is to behave at a banquet she will be attending with her husband: she must take every opportunity to flirt with Ovid and not show any affection to his rival. The reader can easily see that Ovid's urgent pleas are forlorn and helpless, and we laugh at his woebegone predicament. The same scenario recurs in 2.5; this time the girl attends the banquet with Ovid, but he still suffers, for when they think he has fallen drunkenly asleep, he spies on her as she kisses his rival. In 2.19, he urges his mistress's husband to keep a closer watch over her, for there is no spice in having an affair with a woman if it presents no challenges and difficulties. In 3.4, Ovid addresses her husband again: he has become so vigilant that Ovid now has no access to the girl at all.

By the Augustan period, boys completed their education in the schools of rhetoric, where they were prepared for a public career in politics and law. We know, particularly from the elder Seneca's memoirs of his own days in these schools, that Ovid was a star pupil. The *Amores* are very heavily influenced by his rhetorical training. Delivering a speech was much like reciting a poem, and Ovid transferred both the subject matter and the techniques of rhetoric to the *Amores*. There were two basic types of speech, the *controversia,* advocating one side or the other in a fictional court case, and the *suasoria,* the "speech of persuasion," urging a particular course of action in a historical or mythological situation. Seneca gives as examples of *controversiae,* which trained boys for the courts, such problems as "The law states that a woman who is raped can choose between marrying the rapist without providing a dowry and having him put to death. What is to be done when a man rapes two women on the same night and one woman chooses marriage and the other demands his death?" As examples of *suasoriae,* which trained boys for political life, Seneca cites situations such as "Antony agrees to spare Cicero's life on condition that he burn his speeches written against him: should Cicero do so or not?" Seneca tells us that Ovid much preferred *suasoriae,* and many *Amores*-elegies are *suasoriae* in amatory contexts. For example, 1.3, 2.17, and 3.2 are attempts to persuade a girl to accept him as her lover, 1.6, 1.13, 2.2 and 2.3, 3.6, and 3.10 are attempts to persuade, respectively, a doorkeeper, Aurora, a eunuch-chaperone, a mountain torrent, and Ceres not to obstruct his love affair. In 1.10, Ovid attempts to persuade his mistress not to demand gifts; in 2.19, to persuade his mistress's husband to be more vigilant; in 3.4, to be less vigilant; and in 3.14, he urges his mistress to dissemble her infidelities to him. In 1.8, he reports a speech in which the procuress Dipsas attempts to persuade his mistress to abandon him in favor of general prostitution, as being more lucrative. In 3.1, the personifications of Tragedy and Elegy urge Ovid to write in their own genre.

Sometimes Ovid derived the substance of his poetry, not just its techniques, from the schools of declamation. At *Education of the Orator* 2.4, Quintilian gives some examples of particular school exercises. One is the *comparatio,* in which the pupil has to argue whether the life of the lawyer or the life of a soldier is preferable. Ovid subverts that exercise in 1.9, where he argues that the life of a lover is every bit as rigorous as that of a soldier, a humorously paradoxical contention given that the elegiac poet more conventionally portrays himself as a drone, making no useful contribution to society.

The *Amores* were written for recitation, not just for personal reading. In 1.5, Ovid describes Corinna standing naked in his bedroom:

> What arms and shoulders did I touch and see,
> How apt her bosom to be pressed by me!
> Belly so smooth beneath the breasts so high,
> And waist so long, and what a fine young thigh.
> Why detail more? All perfect in my sight;
> And naked as she was, I hugged her tight.

Ovid is apparently in a fever of sexual anticipation. (We are unlikely to notice that his description of Corinna is in fact coolly objective, progressing down the body in accordance with the rhetorical rules for physical description.) When we read the poem, we can see that there is only one couplet left, so we do not expect the scene to be further developed; Ovid's original audience, however, could not have realized this as they listened to him reciting the poem, and the sudden ending "And next—all know! We rested, with a kiss; / Jove send me more such afternoons as this!" will have abruptly and wittily disappointed their expectation of more salacious details.

Just as Propertius portrays Hercules as a locked-out lover in 4.9 (see p. 244), so Ovid represents Ceres as an elegiac beloved in *Amores* 3.10: she fell in love at first sight with the Cretan prince Iasius and neglected her duties as goddess of crops while she passed her time with him. Ovid uses this technique, of adapting elegiac conventions to the mythological world, on a much larger scale in the *Heroides,* letters written by figures such as Penelope, Medea, and Dido to their absent lovers. Similarly, his account of the rites in honor of Juno in *Amores* 3.13 is a prototype for the accounts of religious festivals and other such institutions in the *Fasti.* We may perhaps even see a foreshadowing of the

*Metamorphoses* in *Amores* 2.15, a charming erotic fantasy in which Ovid imagines himself transformed into a ring that he is sending as a gift to his mistress. He alludes to his activity as a tragedian in *Amores* 2.18 and 3.1, and he is known to have written at least one tragedy, a *Medea*. Quintilian, who is generally rather disapproving of Ovid, says with surprising generosity that his *Medea* "showed what he might have produced, had he preferred to restrain his genius rather than indulge it" (*Education of the Orator* 10.1.98); unfortunately, only two very brief quotations from it survive.

## THE METAMORPHOSES

In the *Amores*, Cupid prevented Ovid writing an epic, limiting him to the much more modest genre of love elegy. Now, however, Ovid has transcended all such restrictions, calling on the gods in the opening lines of the first book to grant him inspiration and bring his poem from the origin of the world all the way down to his own times. The gods heeded his prayer, for the *Metamorphoses* is one of the greatest literary achievements of classical antiquity.

The chronological progression from the earliest times to the present gives the *Metamorphoses* a general overall structure, focused (at times rather hazily), as the title suggests, on the theme of metamorphosis, traced from the primeval shapeless chaos at the first creation of the universe through to the transformation of Julius Caesar into a god. Almost the whole of the poem is devoted to the narration of Greek mythological stories. Such a choice of subject matter is rather remarkable and may indeed have come as a surprise to Ovid's contemporaries. In the opening lines of the third book of the *Georgics*, Virgil had lamented that a poet could no longer look to Greek mythology for material for his poetry, since all such themes were now exhausted. A century later, Juvenal was to repeat this complaint in the opening lines of his first satire, declaring that, since mythological themes were overworked and hackneyed, he would write satire. And yet, despite the apparently unpromising aridity of mythology as a theme, Ovid has managed to create from it an unmatched masterpiece that sparkles with originality and wit. In the vast sweep of his poem, he ranges from legends that are largely or completely unknown to us from other sources through to the most familiar stories (including a synopsis of both Homeric epics, of Apollonius's *Argonautica*, and of Virgil's *Aeneid*, as well as reworking the subject matter of several Attic tragedies).

Just as our knowledge about classical sculpture depends predominantly on Roman copies of Greek originals that are themselves now lost, so also much of Greek literary culture was known in the West during the long centuries after the fall of the Roman Empire only through Latin translations and epitomes. The *Metamorphoses* does not fit this pattern: it is the greatest surviving repertoire of Greek mythology, with many of its stories superseding their source to be the canonical version. Ovid will be indebted to earlier collections of tales of metamorphosis, such as those of the Hellenistic poets Nicander and Boeos (so obscure that even his name is uncertain), but the loss of such works is not unduly regrettable. Ovid drew his inspiration from a much wider literary spectrum, from the grandeur of epic and tragedy, through didactic poetry, to philosophical treatises (most remarkably in the disquisition by Pythagoras, on vegetarianism and other topics, that dominates the first half of the final book), and humble handbooks of myths and legends such as the *Erotic Adventures* collected by the Callimachean scholar Parthenius and dedicated to Cornelius Gallus, the inventor of Augustan erotic elegy, and intended as raw material for his epic or elegiac poetry.

Scholars debate the validity of describing the *Metamorphoses* as an epic. Ovid would relish this controversy, for he has deliberately blurred the standard generic distinctions. We might, a priori, suppose that such a label is appropriate for a poem with legendary subject matter composed in fifteen books of hexameters. Epic convention, however, leads us to expect that the poem will be centered on the exploits of a single hero; hence Virgil's opening words in the *Aeneid*, "I sing of arms and the man." The *Metamorphoses* therefore defies such categorization. If the poem's structure, a loose concatenation of stories with a recurrent theme, may be said to have any particular single source of inspiration, that model would be the *Aetia* of Callimachus, his four-book poem in elegiac couplets on the general theme of "reasons" or "causes" for customs and traditions observed in various parts of the Greek world. Like Ovid, Callimachus points out the paradox of his writing a long poem, for he declares in the prologue to the *Aetia* that his critics gibber against him for not writing one continuous poem in many thousands of verses about kings and heroes, whereas he aspires rather to small-scale and carefully wrought poetry. The *Aetia* survives only in fragments, but these remnants are sufficient to show that Callimachus gave coherence to his highly diverse subject matter with complex and intricate patterns of arrangement of episodes, rather as Ovid has arranged his material not just by chronology but also by geographical region (e.g., the Theban cycle of legends in Books 3 and 4) and by similarity of theme (e.g., the homosexual tales in Book 10).

Callimachus's *Aetia,* the masterwork of the Hellenistic poet who shaped and influenced the literary principles of the Augustan poets, will have been more than generally significant for Ovid when he was engaged in the composition of the *Metamorphoses.* It is not known when Ovid began work on the *Metamorphoses,* but it was nearly complete when Augustus relegated him to the Black Sea in A.D. 8. By then, he had also composed the first six of a projected total of twelve books of the *Fasti,* which, being focused on the origins of various customs, is more directly and specifically modeled on the *Aetia.* It is quite probable that Ovid was at times working concurrently on both the *Metamorphoses* and the *Fasti.*

The *Metamorphoses* is Ovid's only work in hexameters and is by far the longest of all his poems. In many respects, however, it continues to display Ovid's wonderfully deft and inimitable style, being redolent throughout with ebullient wit and boundless enthusiasm for poetic composition, features of his approach to poetry that were only partially eclipsed when Augustus, with calculated sadism, imposed on him the tragic fate of exile at the farthest fringe of the empire. Just as Ovid exploits his training in the schools of declamation in framing *Amores*-elegies, so he continues to present his stories of metamorphosis in a rhetorically dramatized way. The *suasoria* is very frequently exploited in the *Metamorphoses,* and perhaps most predominantly in love stories, which abound throughout most of the poem. For example, in the early books, Apollo attempts to persuade Daphne to accept his advances, Echo attempts to seduce Narcissus, and Narcissus wheedles his own reflection. In these episodes, Ovid is reworking the conventions of amatory elegy in a mythological context, with the love-struck protagonists cast in situations typically associated with the frustrating vicissitudes of the elegiac lover. Ovid had already experimented with this combination in the *Amores,* when he portrayed the river god Anio wooing Ilia, the mother of Romulus and Remus (3.6), and in his transformation of the normally staid mother goddess Ceres as a typical elegiac woman, neglecting her traditional duties when she falls in love with the handsome Cretan prince Iasius (3.10). Ovid continues this process in the *Heroides,* with many of the heroines expressing opinions such as we might expect to hear from elegiac mistresses, and it remains prominent in the *Metamorphoses.* The Narcissus episode in Book 3 displays a particularly witty adaptation of not only a rhetorical structure but also an amatory theme. In attempting to persuade his reflection to accept him as his lover, Narcissus is cast in the role of the locked-out lover, the role par excellence of the frustrated elegiac love poet. Narcissus's arguments and complaints are presented in just the same way as Ovid's own arguments and complaints, in *Amores* 1.6 to his mistress's doorkeeper, in 3.6 to a river in flood. This scenario recurs in the next book, when Pyramus and Thisbe are kept apart by the wall between their houses, and again in Book 13, when the Cyclops Polyphemus woos the sea nymph Galatea.

If the *Metamorphoses* has a higher purpose than that of providing entertainment, that purpose is not universally agreed upon among scholars. Given that Ovid was closely enough involved with the higher echelons of Roman society to draw Augustus's unwelcome attention to him, it is inevitable that we should look for a political message in the poem. As so often, we are faced with the imponderable difficulty of determining whether Ovid's flattery of the regime is a sincere expression of his political

**Figure 15:  The Death of Pentheus**
Pentheus being torn to pieces by his frenzied mother and aunt in a Pompeian fresco. Scenes from Ovid's
*Metamorphoses* were among the most popular motifs in Pompeian home décor.

opinion. In a sense, the whole poem leads up to the praise of the imperial family in the account of
the apotheosis of Julius Caesar. But, how seriously are we to take this? In the third book of the *Fasti*,
Ovid devotes almost two hundred lines to the raucous rustic rites of the minor deity Anna Perenna
held every year on the Ides of March, before adding a mere fourteen lines on the assassination and
apotheosis of Julius Caesar, a passage he introduces with the apparently casual words "I was just about
to pass over the swords that stabbed our leader." The pantheon that Caesar is joining is not portrayed
in the *Metamorphoses* as being so very august and awesome. In Book 1, for example, when Apollo
pursues Daphne, he is not the all-powerful deity who ensured Octavian's victory at Actium; he seems
rather out of condition, for he has to appeal to her to run away from him more slowly, promising
that he will run after her more slowly. Likewise, in Book Three, Jupiter and Juno do not debate the
destinies of the Greeks and Trojans (as in the *Iliad*), or of Aeneas and Turnus (as in the *Aeneid*); they
are speculating whether sexual intercourse is more pleasurable for men or for women, a question
they resolve by consulting Tiresias, who happened to have been metamorphosed from a man into a
woman, a transformation that was subsequently reversed.

## AMORES

### Book 1

*Ovid gave this collection of his earliest elegies definitive shape after he had become a celebrity. Uniquely among the collections published by Augustan poets, it opens with a preface, in which Ovid ironically explains that he has trimmed his original five papyrus rolls of* Amores *down to three. We have no knowledge of any of the poems that he omitted from this edition, which he published perhaps around the year* A.D. 1.

### Preface

We who before were Ovid's five slim volumes
Are three: he thought it better to compress.
Though reading us may still give you no pleasure,
With two removed at least the pain is less.

#### 1

*The poet humorously claims to have intended to write epic poetry in the hexameter rhythm, in which case each line would have had an equal measure of six metrical feet. But Ovid alleges that Cupid, the god of love, stole one foot from his second line and thus converted the meter to elegiac couplets and the subject from war to love.*

I'd meant in solemn meter to rehearse
A tale of arms and war and violence,
Matching the weighty matter with my verse,
All lines alike in length—no difference;
    But Cupid laughed (they say)
    And filched one foot away.

Cruel boy, who made you judge of poetry?
We're not your rabble, we're the Muses' choir.
Shall Venus snatch blonde Pallas' weaponry,
10 Blonde Pallas fan the flames of passion's fire?
    And who'd approve if Ceres stood
    Queen of every upland wood?

Or shall the warrior Virgin rule the byre,
Long-haired Apollo learn to use the lance,
While Mars on Helicon strikes up the lyre?
Great is your reign, too strong your dominance.
    Why, greedy child, should you
    Go for this work that's new?

Is all the world then yours? The Muses' shrine
Yours too? Even Phoebus' lyre not now secure?     20
On the new page arose my proud first line,
Then came the next, unstringing me for sure;
    And there's no theme of mine
    Can suit that slighter line,

No boy, no girl with long and lovely hair—
I'd made my protest. He drew instantly
An arrow from his quiver, chosen with care
To lay me low, and braced against his knee
    His crescent bow. 'Here, poet, take
    This for the verses you next make.'     30

Poor me! That boy's sure arrows never stray.
I'm burning. In my vacant breast love reigns.
So in six beats my verse must rise today,
And settle back in five. Farewell, you strains
    Of steely war! Farewell to you,
    And to your epic meter too!

    Muse, wreathe your golden tresses
    With myrtle of the sea,
    And in eleven stresses
    Compose our poetry.     40

#### 2

*The poet cannot sleep and wonders why: it must be love. Resistance is futile and only makes the suffering worse. So he surrenders to Cupid, who is to parade him like a captive in a Roman triumphal procession.*

What can it be that I should find my bed
So hard, the blankets slipping, sleep quite fled,
And through the night, so long, I lie awake,
Tossing about until my tired bones ache?
I think I'd know if love were teasing me,
Or does his damage steal on secretly?
That's what it is. He's shot his subtle dart;
Love's in possession, tossing my poor heart.
So shall I yield, or feed the flame and fight?
I'll yield: a load borne readily lies light.     10
From torches waved I've seen the flame
    leap high;
When no one brandishes, I've seen it die.
Oxen that fight first yokes are beaten more
Than those who've learnt the plough's a
    pleasant chore.
A proud horse finds a hard bit brings distress;

One that's submissive feels the bridle less.
Love strikes the stubborn far more savagely
Than those who will confess their slavery.
Look, Cupid, I confess—your latest prize—
20 I hold out abject hands, my heart complies.
No need of war. Favor and peace are all;
No praise for you—unarmed to arms I'll fall.
 Harness your mother's doves and wreathe
  your hair
With myrtle. Your stepfather, I declare,
Will give a fitting chariot, where you'll stand
As crowds triumphant shout on either hand.
Deftly you'll drive your birds and, following,
A train of captive youths and girls shall bring
A triumph that shall make the welkin ring.
Myself, new prize, my wound just made
 shall wear,
30
And in my captive heart fresh fetters bear.
In the triumphal train Good Sense you'll see,
Hands bound behind her back, and Modesty—
Whatever stands against Love's armory.
All things fear you. In welcome loud and long
The cheering crowd will chant the triumph song.
Endearments, Madness, Wanderings of the
 brain,
Shall be your escort in the happy train,
Constant supporters, following your cause.
With these fine troops you vanquish in your
 wars
40
Both men and gods: their service lost, you'd be
All undefended in your nudity.
Your mother from Olympus' peak in joy,
Delighting in the triumph of her boy,
Her plaudits and her praises shall bestow,
And scatter roses to adorn your brow.
With jewelled wings and jewelled locks, behold,
You'll ride in golden state on wheels of gold.
And, if I know you, you'll ignite then too
50 Your furnace in the hearts of not a few.
Then many a wound you'll deal as you pass by:
Even should you wish, at rest your bow can't lie;
Your fierce flame scorches when its heat is nigh.
So Bacchus marked his Indian victory—
Though you are drawn by doves, by tigers he.
Therefore, since in your triumph I form part,
Don't waste your victor's wealth on my
 poor heart.
See how your kinsman Caesar's victories go:
The conqueror protects the conquered foe.

### 3

*The poet attempts to persuade an as yet unnamed girl to accept him as her lover. He promises to be her devoted slave, and although he has no inherited riches to offer, he is a poet and will be in her service all his life. Jupiter's lovers, such as Io, Leda, and Europa, have achieved their own measure of fame. This, the poet concludes ironically, is what awaits his love.*

I ask for justice; she who's caught me now
Must either love me or ensure that I
Love her for ever. No, I aim too high.
Just to be loved—let her but that allow
And Venus will have met my dearest vow.

Take one who through long years would slave for you;
Take one who'd love with purest loyalty.
I've no proud names of ancient ancestry,
My line stems only from a knight, it's true.

No ploughs unnumbered work rich land of mine, 10
Both parents keep good watch on what they spend—
Little enough your lover to commend.
But on my side are Phoebus and his nine
Companions and the inventor of the vine,

And love who gives you me, and loyalty
That yields to none, and frank sincerity,
A blameless life and blushing modesty.
A thousand charmers give no joy to me;

I'm not love's acrobat to leap from bed
To bed. Believe me, you'll be mine always: 20
With you may heaven let me pass my days
Through the span granted by the Sisters' thread,

And die with you there weeping. Offer me
Yourself, a happy subject for my verse:
My verse will issue worthy of its source.
So many owe their fame to poetry—

Poor Io whom her cow's horns terrified,
Leda duped by the swan's adultery,
Europa whom the false bull bore to sea,
Horns held in virgin hands on either side. 30

We too shall live in verse the whole world through,
And my name shall be ever linked with you.

### 4

*The poet sends instructions to his lover before attending a dinner where she will be with her husband. They are very*

*specific: arrive first; send secret messages; decline his offers*
*of food and wine; reject his amorous advances; let the poet*
*sneak a peek; watch for an opportunity if the husband*
*drinks too much. And finally, do not make love to him, but*
*if you do, deny it in the morning.*

Your husband will be there at the same dinner—
I wish your husband his last meal tonight.
I'm just a guest then, gazing at my darling
While at your touch another takes delight?
And you to warm another's breast will snuggle,
While round your neck his arm at will he throws?
No wonder that for fair Hippodamia,
When wine went round, the Centaurs came to blows.
I'm no half-horse, my home's not in the forest,
10   Yet I can hardly keep my hands from you.
Now, don't just give the winds my words of wisdom;
Listen, and understand what you must do.

Arrive before your husband. Not that I can
See quite what good arriving first will do;
But still arrive before him. When he's taken
His place upon the couch and you go too
To sit beside him, on your best behavior,
Stealthily touch my foot, and look at me,
Watching my nods, my eyes, my face's language;
20   Catch and return my signals secretly.
I'll send a wordless message with my eyebrows;
You'll read my fingers' words, words traced in wine.
When you recall our games of love together,
Your finger on rosy cheeks must trace a line.
If in your silent thoughts you wish to chide me,
Let your hand hold the lobe of your soft ear;
When, darling, what I do or say gives pleasure,
Keep turning to and fro the ring you wear.
When you wish well-earned curses on your husband,
30   Lay your hand on the table, as in prayer.
If he pours you wine, watch out, tell *him* to drink it;
Ask for what *you* want from the waiter there.
I shall take next the glass you hand the waiter,
And I'll drink from the place you took your sips;
If he should offer anything he's tasted,
Refuse whatever food has touched his lips.
Don't let him plant his arms around your shoulder,
Don't rest your gentle head on his hard chest,
Don't let your dress, your breasts, admit his fingers,
40   And—most of all—no kisses to be pressed!
You kiss—and I'll reveal myself your lover;
I'll say 'they're mine'; my legal claim I'll stake.

All this, of course, I'll see, but what's well hidden
Under your dress—blind terror makes me quake.
No squeezing thigh to thigh, no playing footsie!
Don't link your tender foot with his hard one.
I fear so much because I've been so naughty—
I'm tortured by the dread of what I've done.
Often my girl and I in sudden passion
Beneath her cloak have had our happy fling;          50
You won't do that, but, still, to kill suspicion
Just take it off—remove the knowing thing.
And urge your man to drink—but, mind, no kisses!
When he's not looking try to lace the brew.
If wine and sleep have got him nicely settled,
The time and place will tell us what to do.
And when you rise to leave and all rise
with you,
Make sure you're in the middle of the crush;
You'll find me in the crush, or I'll find you there;
If you can touch me, give me a soft push.          60

Alas, a few short hours for words of wisdom!
I'm forced to leave my girl at night's command.
At night he'll lock her in; in tears I'll follow
To his cruel door—where I'm allowed to stand.
Now he'll take kisses, now not only kisses.
You'll give him as his right, because you must,
What you give me in secret. Make it grudging
(You can do that) like any girl who must.

Let love be sullen—no sweet words—just silence.
If prayers of mine have power, I pray he too          70
May get no sort of pleasure; if he likes it,
I pray at least no pleasure comes to you.

But yet, whatever lot the night may send,
Next day maintain you didn't—to the end!

5

*Ovid's most celebrated erotic poem, describing a noontime*
*rendezvous with his lover, is presented in a slightly modern-*
*ized version of Christopher Marlowe's famous adaptation.*

In summer's heat and mid-time of the day
To rest my limbs upon a bed I lay.
One shutter closed, the other open stood,
Which gave such light as lies within a wood,
Like twilight shade at setting of the sun,
Or when night's gone and yet day not begun.
Such light for bashful girls one should provide,

In which their shyness may have hope to hide.
In came Corinna in a long loose gown,
10   Her white neck hid with tresses hanging down;
So to her many lovers came Lais,
Or in her bedroom fair Semiramis.
I snatched her gown; being thin the harm was small,
Yet strove she to be covered therewithal,
And striving thus as one who wished to fail,
Was simply beaten by her self-betrayal.
Stark naked as she stood before mine eye,
No blemish on her body could I spy.
What arms and shoulders did I touch and see,
20   How apt her bosom to be pressed by me!
Belly so smooth below the breasts so high,
And waist so long, and what a fine young thigh.
Why detail more? All perfect in my sight;
And naked as she was, I hugged her tight.
And next—all know! We rested, with a kiss;
Jove send me more such afternoons as this!

6

*An address to the doorkeeper at his lover's house. In ancient*
*Rome a woman from a respectable home was not able to*
*come and go as she pleased, so laments by locked-out lovers*
*were a common theme in love poetry.*

Porter!—too bad you're chained by your hard
      shackle—
            Open this tiresome door, undo the bar.
I don't ask much—a little gap to take me
            Squeezing through sideways when it's just ajar.
Long love has shrunk me for this sort of business,
            Slimmed me and shaped my body the
                  right way.
Love shows one how to slip past watching sentries
            And guides one's footsteps not to trip or stray.
Yet once I feared the night and empty phantoms,
10          Amazed when people in the dark would go:
Cupid laughed in my ear with his sweet mother,
            And whispered 'Ovid, you'll be brave, you too.'
And in a trice love came. Now I'm not frightened
            By flitting ghosts or hands unsheathed to kill;
It's you I fear, so stubborn, you I flatter;
            You wield the bolt to ruin me at will.
Look (and draw back the ruthless bars to see it),
            Look how the door my flowing tears bedew.
You know that once when you stood stripped for
      flogging,

I begged your mistress, I spoke up for you.          20
So does that favor then that did you service—
            So much for gratitude!—serve me no more?
Give me my due: you've got the chance to give it.
            The night is slipping by; unbolt the door.

Unbolt! May you not always drink slaves' water,
            But shed the chain you've worn so long at last.
Useless! You hear me but you're stony-hearted;
            The door is solid oak and still stuck fast.
Locked gates are good to guard beleaguered cities:
            Why are you scared of force? We're
                  not at war!          30
What hope for foes, if you lock out a lover?
            The night is slipping by; unbolt the door.
I'm not escorted by a force of soldiers:
            Were cruel Love not here, I'd be alone,
Nor, if I wanted, could I make him leave me,
            I'd need leave first this body of my own.
So here is Love with me, a little fuddled,
            Hair oiled and garland slipping more and more.
Who'd fear that force? Who would not go to meet it?
            The night is slipping by; unbolt the door.          40

Still stubborn? Or asleep, your ears—confound
      you!—
            Rejecting words of love for winds to take?
Yet I recall when I first wished to elude you,
            Until the midnight stars you stayed awake.
Perhaps you've got a girl-friend sleeping with you:
            Alas! more luck for you than me in store.
If I'd that luck, I'd love to wear those shackles!
            The night is slipping by; unbolt the door.

Am I deceived or are the hinges creaking,
            Was the door pushed to give that tell-tale
                  groan?          50
No, I'm deceived: the lively wind beat on it.
            Ay me! how far the breeze my hope has blown.
Boreas, if you recall raped Orithyia,
            Strike these deaf portals with your
                  whirlwind's roar.
The whole town's silent now, and damp and dewy
            The night is slipping by; unbolt the door

Or I'm all set to raid your haughty mansion
            Myself with my strong sword and torch's flame.
The night and love and wine urge no restraint now,
            Wine and love free from fear and night from
                  shame.          60
I've tried—tried everything—but I can't move you

With prayers or threats; the door's less hard
    than you.
You are not fit to guard a lovely lady,
    To be a prison warder is your due.

And now the Morning Star on frosty axles
    Rises; the cock calls men to toil anew.
Here from my mournful locks I'll take my garland;
    Let it lie all night long on the hard sill;
My girl will see it thrown there in the morning,
70    Witness of all the time I've spent so ill.
Goodbye, for what you're worth. I pay you tribute:
    Stubborn—lover locked out—a nasty knave.
Goodbye too, granite step and cruel door-posts
    And hard oak door, yourself, like him, a slave.

7

*Ovid treats the seamier side of love in this poem in which
he represents himself as having beaten his mistress. He
attributes it to a kind of madness, like that which afflicted
Ajax at Troy or Orestes, who killed his mother.*

Put handcuffs on me, friend, if any friend's here,
    (My hands deserve it) till my frenzy clears.
My frenzy roused rash hands against my mistress,
    My mad hands hurt her and my girl's in tears;
So mad, I could have outraged my dear parents,
    Or at the holy gods hurled savage spears.

Well, Ajax, master of the sevenfold buckler,
    Seized herds and over wide fields laid
        them low;
Orestes, evil champion of his father,
10    For battle with the Furies sought a bow.
So could I really tear those elegant tresses?
    Yet ruffled hair became my mistress' brow:

Quite beautiful—she looked like Atalanta
    Out hunting on the hills of Arcady,
Or Ariadne weeping when gales wafted
    False Theseus with his promises to sea,
Or (save her sacred priestess-band) Cassandra
    In chaste Minerva's shrine on bended knee.

Everyone calls me brute, they call me madman.
    She said no word: her tongue was stopped in
20        fear.
But silent looks conveyed her sad reproaches;
    Speechless, she held me guilty with a tear.
I wish my arms had fallen from my shoulders;

That part of me I usefully could spare.
To my own loss I've used my might in madness,
    My valor only punishment has won.
Hands, you're not mine, you means of crime and
    slaughter;
    You're sacrilegious: have those handcuffs on.
I'd suffer if I struck Rome's humblest citizen:
    Shall I have greater rights over my loved one?    30

Diomede's crime bequeathed the worst example:
    He first to strike a goddess, second me.
His guilt was less; I hurt the girl I worshipped;
    Diomede raged against his enemy.

Come, conqueror, get your fine triumph moving;
    Set laurels on your locks, fulfill your vow,
With crowds beside your chariot all shouting
    'Brave hero, hail—a girl's his conquest now.'

Put her in front, sad captive, tresses tumbled,
    All white but for the bruises on her face.    40
It should have been my lips that did the bruising;
    It should have been my love bites left that trace.

Why, if I stormed on like a swollen torrent,
    And rage, so blind, had got me for its prey,
Surely a scaring shout had been sufficient
    With thundered threats not over-strong
        that day.
I could have ripped her dress from top to middle
    To shame her—with her belt to bar the way.

Instead, brute that I was, I mauled her forehead,
    I used my nails to scratch her delicate face.    50
She stood distraught, her features pale and bloodless,
    Like marble quarried from the hills of Greece.

I saw her numb and faint, her body quivering,
    Like aspens trembling when soft breezes blow,
Or slim reeds rustling in a gentle zephyr,
    Or wrinkling waves when warm winds slide
        and go.
Her tears, long-hanging, down her cheeks came
    flowing,
    As water trickles from a bank of snow.

Then the first guilty feelings welled within me;
    It was my blood that flowed in every tear.    60
Three times I tried to kneel and beg for pardon;
    Three times she thrust my hands away in fear.

My darling, sweet revenge will soften anguish:

Don't wait, just use your nails and scratch
    my face;
My eyes, my hair, don't spare them, show no mercy;
    Rage helps the weakest hands in such a case;
Or—so my crime's sad signs may last no longer—
    Set your hair straight and put it back in place.

8

*The poet overhears a conversation between an old woman,*
*Dipsas, a procuress who also practices magic, and his mis-*
*tress, whom she seeks to corrupt. Her advice to the young*
*lady is crass: go for the money and forget about poets,*
*because they are poor. From his vantage point, the poet can*
*barely restrain himself from throttling Dipsas.*

There's an old hag, an old hag, name of Dipsas,
    A bawd, so listen if you'd like to know.
Her name speaks for itself—she's never sober
    Enough to see Aurora's rosy glow.
She knows the magic arts, the spells of Circe,
    Her skill turns back broad rivers to their source;
The flux of mating mares, the herbal mixtures,
    The whirling wheel, she knows their
        baleful force.
At her behest clouds mass across the heavens,
10    At her behest day shines clear in the sky.
I've seen the stars drip blood, if you'd believe me,
    And on the moon's fair face a bloody dye.
At night she changes shape; with her old body
    Thick-feathered through the dark I think
        she flies;
I think, and so it's said; and double pupils
    Flash lightning and gleams dart from dual eyes.
From ancient tombs she calls past generations
    And splits the solid earth with sorceries.
This hag proposed to desecrate a marriage;
20    Of baleful eloquence she had rich store.
Chance let me overhear her long instructions
    (I was concealed behind the double door).
'Yesterday, my dear, a rich young fellow found you
    Pleasing; he stopped and gave you a long stare.
And why not please? You're lovely—no girl lovelier;
    It's sad you're let down by the things you wear.
I'd like your luck to match your peerless beauty;
    When you are wealthy, I shall not be poor.
Your hopes were hurt with Mars in opposition;
30    Now Mars is gone and Venus' place secure.
See how her coming helps. A wealthy lover

Wants you; he's keen to fund whatever's short.
His good looks too with yours will bear comparison,
    And should he not buy you, he should be
        bought.
She's blushing! Shyness suits a pale complexion,
    A boon, if faked, a barrier if true.
You'll keep your eyes fixed on your lap demurely,
    Suit your regard to what each brings to you.
Maybe in Tatius' reign the frumpish Sabines
    Rejected more than one man with disdain;    40
Today in foreign wars Mars shows his mettle;
    In her son's city now it's Venus' reign.
Pretty girls play. She's chaste? Well, no one asked her.
    She asks herself, unless she's too ill bred.
A matron too whose brows are wrinkled—shake
    them:
    From wrinkles many a mischief may be shed.
Penelope used a bow to test her suitors,
    To prove their prowess that great horny bow.
Winged time slips by in secret and deceives us,
    And galloping away the seasons go.    50
Coins shine with use, a fine dress asks for wearing,
    Abandoned buildings moulder in neglect.
Beauty needs use and fades without a lover,
    And one or two don't have enough effect.
With plenty plunder's surer—less ill-feeling;
    Full flocks give wolves a fine prey to select.
Look, what except new verses does that poet
    Give you? You'll get a lover's thousand things.
The poet's god himself in golden mantle
    On gilded lyre plucks his melodious strings.    60
Value a giver higher than great Homer;
    Believe me, giving too's a subtle art.
And don't despise a slave who's bought his freedom;
    A whitened foot won't mean a blackened heart.
And don't let busts in stately homes deceive you;
    He's poor; off with him and his blue blood too.
He'll ask a night for nothing, he's so handsome;
    His man-friend should pay him, then he'll
        pay you.
Keep your price down till the trap's set, in case they
    Escape; once captured roast them as you
        please.    70
No harm if love's a lie; let him think you love him
    And take good care your love's not lacking fees.
Often refuse a night: pretend a headache,
    Or your excuse will be it's Isis' day.
Then take him back before he's used to patience
    And love, repulsed too often, ebbs away.

See your door's deaf to pleas but oiled to presents;
    The voice outside your man inside
        should hear.
He's hurt? Be angry, seem hurt first: his charges
80    Before your counter-charge will disappear.
But never give a lot of time to anger;
    Anger that lingers makes for enmity.
What's more, you ought to learn to weep to order,
    And wet your cheeks with tears of jealousy.
You'd cheat? Swear falsely, never fear. For love-games
    Venus adopts a deaf divinity.

Procure a well-trained lady's maid and servant
    To teach him what's the best to buy for you,
And ask small tips themselves; small tips from many
    Are straws to make a huge pile soon
90       come true.
Get sister, mother, nurse to fleece your lover;
    The plunder's swift with many hands to take.
When you've run out of reasons for a present,
    Say it's your birthday and produce the cake.
Don't let his love feel safe, without a rival;
    Take care; if love's to last it must compete;
So let him see your neck all bruised with love-marks
    And traces of a man across the sheet.
Above all show him someone else's presents,
100    And if you've got none, ask the Sacred Way.
When you've got lots, but there's still some remaining,
    Ask for a loan—which you will not repay.
Make your tongue mask your meaning; charm him,
    harm him:
    Sweet honey hides the poison down below.
If you'll do what I've learnt by long experience
    And my words aren't all lost to winds that blow,
Time and again while I'm alive you'll bless me,
    And pray my bones lie easy when I'm dead...'
Her words flowed on, when my shadow betrayed me;
    I could hardly keep my hands from her
110      white head,
That wispy straggling hair, those cheeks all wrinkled,
    Those red wine-bleary eyes. May you be cursed
With want in your old age and long hard winters,
    No roof above your head and endless thirst!

### 9

*Ovid compares lovers to soldiers in this famous elegy
addressed to his friend Atticus, for both must be young and
in good physical condition. Famous fighters like Achilles,
Hector, and Agamemnon were also lovers, but Ovid only
enlists in love's warfare.*

Lovers are soldiers, Atticus. Believe me,
    Lovers are soldiers, Cupid has his corps.
The age that's fit for fighting's fine for Venus;
    Old men are shamed in loving, shamed in war.

The spirit captains look for in a soldier
    A pretty girl will look for in her man.
Both keep night watches, on the hard ground resting,
    Each for his girl, or captain, guardian.

Long marches are a soldier's job: a lover
    After his girl to the world's end will go.    10
High mountain barriers, rain-doubled rivers
    He'll cross and trudge his way through drifts
        of snow.
At sailing time he'll not plead dirty weather,
    Or wait for stars to tell him when to row.

Soldier or lover, who but they'd put up with
    The rain, the sleet, the snow, the cold of night?
One's sent to spy upon a dangerous enemy,
    One keeps his rival, like a foe, in sight.
Besieging cities, or a hard girl's threshold,
    On barbicans—or doors—they spend their
        might.    20

It often pays to catch the enemy sleeping,
    And rank and file unarmed with arms to slay.
Thus fell the fierce brigade of Thracian Rhesus;
    The captured horses left their lord that day.

And likewise lovers use a husband's slumber
    And launch their weapons on a sleeping foe.
Soldier and wretched lover, it's their business
    To foil the watch and past the sentries go.
Venus is chancy, Mars unsure; the vanquished
    Rise, those you thought could never fall, lie low.

So chuck it, anyone who thinks love's lazy!    30
    Love's for a dashing soul who dares the most.
Achilles was aflame for lost Briseis—
    Take your chance, Trojans, smash the great
        Greek host!

When Hector left Andromache's embraces
    To fight, his wife gave him his casque to tie;
When Agamemnon saw wild-haired Cassandra
    They say that great commander's heart
        leapt high.

Mars too was caught and felt the blacksmith's meshes;
40        No tale in heaven had more publicity.

I was born idle, for unbuttoned leisure,
        Just lying languid with the shade above.
A pretty girl spurred me from my slack habits
        And bade me in her camp my service prove.
So now you see me brisk, a brave night-fighter:
        Yes, if you'd not be lazy, you should love.

10

*The disillusioned poet, who used to think his mistress as
beautiful as the heroines of mythology, now has no interest in her because she asks him for gifts. This, he says at
length, reduces love to a financial transaction like prostitution. But, he ironically concludes, if she stops asking, he will
keep giving.*

You were like Helen on the Trojan galleon,
        Stolen from Troy to make two husbands fight,
And you were Leda whom the crafty lover
        Inveigled as a swan with wings of white;
You were Amymone lost in parched meadows,
        With on her head her pitcher poised above,
And for your sake I feared the bull, the eagle,
        And everything that love has made of Jove.
Now I've no fear; I'm cured of those delusions,
        Those looks of yours attract my eyes
10                no more.
Why am I changed? Because you ask for presents—
        That's why you cannot please me as before.
While you were straight, I loved you, soul and body,
        But now your beauty's marred by
                your offence.
Love is a naked boy; his years unblemished
        And lack of clothes attest his innocence.
Why bid him price himself, the child of Venus?
        He's got no purse to stow the pelf away.
Fierce war he's just not fit for, nor his mother;
        Such gentle gods should not draw
20                soldiers' pay.
A whore stands at her price for all to purchase,
        And, body under orders, seeks her fee.
Yet on the grasping pimp she piles her curses:
        She's forced to do what you do willingly.

Take the unreasoning animals' example:
        Shame if brute beasts have softer hearts
                than you!

Cows don't claim gifts from bulls, nor mares from
        stallions,
        A ram won't bring a gift to charm his ewe.
Only a woman's proud her man to plunder,
        Auctions her body, offers nights for hire,        30
And sells what pleases both, what both were seeking,
        And sets a price that's gauged by her desire.
The love that gives the pair an equal pleasure,
        Why should the woman sell it, the man buy?
Why should that joy be my loss, be your profit,
        That man and woman share in unity?
It's not right to be bought and bear false witness,
        Nor for a judge to give his palm to grease;
It's shame when paid tongues plead for poor
        defendants;
        When courts make fortunes, that's a foul dis-
                grace.        40
It's shame to swell a heritage by a bed's income,
        With beauty prostituted for a fee.
Thanks are deserved for things one doesn't pay for;
        No thanks when beds are hired so shabbily.
The hirer pays for everything; that settled,
        In debt for service done he'll not remain.
So cease, you beauties, pricing a night's favors;
        No good can ever come from sordid gain.
Tarpeia priced too high the Sabine armlets,
        When she was crushed beneath the pile of
                arms.        50
Alcmaeon's sword transfixed the womb that bore him,
        In vengeance for the fatal necklace' charms.
Yet it's no shame to ask rewards from rich men;
        You ask—they have the wherewithal to pay.
When vines are brimming pick the hanging bunches;
        Alcinous can give his fruit away.
A poor man's coin is zeal and trust and service—
        To give his all to her who holds his heart.
It's my dower too to hymn girls who deserve it;
        The chosen one's made famous by my art.        60
Dresses get torn and gold and jewels broken;
        The fame that verses bring will always live.
Asking a price—not giving—'s vile and hateful;
        No—if you ask. Stop wanting—and I'll give.

11

*This elegy is addressed to his mistress's hairdresser,
whom the poet asks to take a letter to Corinna. In
ancient society, since there were limited opportunities
for contacting the opposite sex, the love letter took on*

*particular importance. The poem forms a diptych with
the following elegy.*

Nape, you're not just any lady's maid;
You're skilled at dressing hair that's disarrayed,
You're known for stealthy services at night,
And shrewd at giving signs kept out of sight;
And often when Corinna was in doubt
Whether to come to me and venture out,
You urged her to be bold, and often too,
When things went wrong, I found you tried and true.
I wrote these lines this morning. Take them now
10  And give them to your mistress. Don't allow
Yourself to be delayed and take good pains.
You have no steely heart or flinty veins;
As maids go, you're no bumpkin; you've got brains.
I can believe that Cupid's wounded you;
Defend, by helping me, *your* standards too.

If she should ask you how I am, just say
In hope of nights with her I live all day.
The rest incised by my fond hand she'll see.
Time flies. Give her the tablets when she's free,
20  But yet make sure she reads them urgently;
And as she reads, observe her brow and eyes:
Mute looks can tell you how the future lies.
And when she's finished reading, instantly
Tell her to write me back a long reply.
Fine wax that's mostly blank's a hateful sight,
So let her squeeze the lines of writing tight;
Right to the margin let the letters go
To hold my eyes and make my reading slow—
But why tire fingers writing a long screed,
30  When just the one word 'come' is all I need?
Triumph! With bay those tablets I'll entwine
And set them in the midst of Venus' shrine,
And underneath I'll write: 'These servants true,
Kind Venus, Ovid dedicates to you'—
Though just now they were worthless squares of yew.

12

*The tablets on which the poet wrote his letter have come
back with a "no": it must be Nape's fault somehow. The
poet curses his failure.*

Weep for my failure. Tablets back to say—
All gloom and doom—'Not possible today.'
Omens are something. When she meant to go,

Against the doorstep Nape stubbed her toe.
Next time you're sent, cross it more carefully;
Be wary, see your foot's raised properly.
Out of my sight, you tiresome coffin-wood,
And wax packed tight with words that say 'No good'!
From the tall hemlock's flower I'm sure you come,
With Corsica's notorious honeycomb,                    10
Deep-dyed with cinnabar to make you ruddy,
A color that in truth was simply bloody.
You useless wood, at crossroads you should lie,
Shattered by wheels of wagons passing by.
Yes, and the man who shaped you from a tree
Had hands, I'm certain, steeped in devilry.
That tree made gallows for some wretch to die,
It made a ghastly cross to crucify.
It gave screech-owls its shameful shade for rest,
To hawks and vultures lent its boughs to nest.         20
Did I—so mad—entrust my love to this,
To bring my darling words that meant a kiss?
That wax was fitter for a bailbond's screed,
For some hard-faced practitioner to read.
With ledgers and accounts it ought to lie,
Where misers mourn lost wealth in misery.
So, like your name, I've found your dealings double;
Duplicity's a recipe for trouble.
What curses shall I call to match my rage?
Mould, rot, and worm to crumble your old age!          30
And may that wax of yours all waste away,
And whiten filthily in foul decay!

13

*Dawn approaches, and the poet asks her to linger, for he
is in bed with his mistress. The coming of the day brings
hardships of all kinds, but especially to lovers. He appeals
to her, for she too has been in love, but daybreak comes all
the same.*

Across the ocean from her ancient husband
        Golden, on frosty wheels she brings the day.
'Dawn, why the hurry? Wait—so may your Memnon's
        Birds act their blood-rite in the ancient way.

Now in my darling's arms I love to linger
        And now, if ever, feel her close to me.
Now sleep is rich, the air is cool, and birdsong
        Pours from slim throats a liquid melody.

Why such a hurry when you're so unwelcome?            10
        Hold in with rosy hands your dewy rein.

Before your rising sailors watch stars better
    And do not wander lost across the main.

When you come, wayfarers, however weary,
    Must rise and soldiers gird fierce arms again.
It's you who are the first to see the farmhands
    Burdened with heavy hoes to till the plain.

And you're the first to summon the slow oxen
    Beneath their curving yoke to plough the rows.
You cheat schoolboys of sleep and hand them over
    To masters for their palms to take hard
20         blows.

You send men into court to give their pledges,
    Huge losses suffered from a single word;
You bring no joy to counsel or attorney,
    Both forced to rise to have fresh cases heard;
And you when women's labors might have respite
    Call back the spinners' hands to tasks deferred.

All this I could endure; but who could ever
    Endure that pretty girls should rise at dawn,
Except some fellow who had never had one,
30     And spent his long nights lonely and forlorn?

Often I've wished night would not yield before you,
    The stars not take to flight when you arrive;
Often I've wished the wind would break your chariot
    Or massed clouds trip your steeds and make
        them dive.

Why hurry, jealous creature? Your son Memnon
    Was black; his mother's heart is dyed the same.
I'd like to hear Tithonus tell your story:
    There'd be no tale in heaven of greater shame.

You fly from him because he's ages older,
    Your hateful wheels rise from him at
40         first light.
But if your arms were round your darling Cephalus,
    You'd cry: "Run slow, run slow, you steeds of
        night."

Shall my love suffer because your husband's senile?
    Your old man's match, was that a plan of mine?
See what long sleep the Moon gave her Endymion,
    And yet her beauty's not a whit less fine.

Jove—for his joy—to see you not so often,
    Made one night into two without a day—'
My last rebuke; she blushed; no doubt she'd heard me.
50     But day dawned promptly in the usual way.

14

*The poet's mistress has lost all her hair, the effect of dyeing
it so often in spite of his remonstrances to the contrary. Her
hair was beautiful, but now she will have to buy a German
wig to wear until it grows back.*

'Stop dyeing your hair.' How many times I told you.
    And now you've none to dye and you're
        disgraced.
But if you'd let it be, none more abundant,
    It reached so far, right down below your waist.

It was like silk, so fine you feared to dress it,
    Fine as the gauzes yellow Chinese wear,
Or gossamer spun by a subtle spider,
    His web hung from a beam high in the air.

Its color wasn't black, it wasn't golden;
    Though it was neither, gold was shot
        with dark,         10
Like, in the watered dales of hilly Ida,
    A lofty cedar when one peels the bark.

Obedient it was and fit for countless
    Fashions and never gave you cause to chafe.
It wasn't frayed or torn by combs or hairpins;
    The maid who managed it was always safe.

I've often watched her dress it, but my darling
    Never once snatched a pin to do her harm.
You often lay, hair loose still, in the morning
    On purple pillows, propped upon your arm;   20

Lovely then too, all ruffled, like a Bacchante
    Lying relaxed and weary on the sward.
But though your locks were downy—soft and delicate,
    What trials they bore, their sufferings
        how hard!

The iron and fire, how patiently they faced them
    To coil the ringlets spiraling so far!
'A crime', I cried, 'a crime to burn those tresses!
    Spare them, iron girl, they're lovely as they are.
No force, no violence! They're not for burning;
    Those tongs can learn a lesson from
        your hair.'         30

Those lovely locks are ruined, locks Apollo
    And Bacchus would have wished to call their own;
To those of naked Venus I'd compare them
    Held dripping, in the famous picture shown.

Why complain hair so badly treated's ruined?
    Why, silly, put the mirror down so sad?
It's no good gazing with the eyes you used to;
    You must forget yourself if you'd be glad.

You've not been hurt by magic of a rival,
    No treacherous witch has washed you in her
40         brew;
No illness—heaven forbid!—has hit and harmed you;
    No jealous tongue made those thick tresses few.
*You* made the loss you feel, *your* hand was guilty;
    The poison on your head was put by you.

Now Germany will send you captured tresses;
    A conquered nation's gift will save your day.
You'll blush—how often!—when a man admires them;
    'It's what I've purchased makes me please',
        you'll say;

'Instead of me he's praising some Sygambrian,
50    Yet once I know that glory was my own.'
Dear me. Her hand is raised to hide her blushes—
    Those dainty cheeks—tears almost
        tumbling down.

Her lost hair's in her lap, she's gazing at it,
    A gift, alas, unworthy to be there.
Make up your face, your mind; all can be mended.
    You'll soon be turning heads with
        home-grown hair.

15

*The final poem in the second, reordered version of the first book, is a defense of poetry against the claims of more traditional Roman pursuits such as the military and the law. The works of the great poets achieve immortality. Many of them are Greeks, such as Homer, Hesiod, Callimachus, Sophocles, Aratus, and Menander, but Ovid incorporates them into the Latin tradition that is represented by poets from Ennius to Virgil in his own time. The list is rounded out by Tibullus, who came after Gallus in the genre of elegy, and now by Ovid himself.*

Devouring Envy, why find fault with me
For years of sloth and call my poetry
Work of an idle wit, and grudge that I,
Unlike my forebears, while youth holds me high,
Will not pursue a soldier's dusty life,
Or study wordy statutes and the strife
Of courts of law or make my thankless choice

In politics to prostitute my voice?
Your aims are mortal, mine's eternal fame,
That the whole world may ever hymn my name.    10
Homer will live while Tenedos still stands
And Ida, and across the Trojan sands
The torrent of swift Simois is borne;
And Hesiod will live as long as corn
Falls to a scythe and grapes swell on a vine.
Callimachus throughout the world will shine,
In art supreme, in genius less fine;
Sophocles' plays from harm will be secure,
Aratus long as sun and moon endure;
Menander lives while fathers rage, slaves cheat,    20
Pimps have no shame and whores charm in the street.
Ennius' rough art and Accius' ardent strain
For evermore a name unfailing gain;
Of Varro too what age shall not be told,
And Jason's Argo and the fleece of gold?
Sublime Lucretius' verses shall not die
Till one day ends the world in tragedy;
*Aeneid, Eclogues, Georgics* shall be read
As long as Rome's the conquered globe's great head;
While Cupid's weapons still are torch and bow,    30
Your polished lines, Tibullus, men will know;
The lands of east and west know Gallus' fame,
And linked with Gallus his Lycoris' name.

And so, though rocks and ploughshares wear away,
Yet over poetry death has no sway.
To poetry let pomp of kings yield place
And all the gold that Tagus' banks embrace.
Let boors like dross; to me may Phoebus bring
His goblets filled from the Castalian spring.
I'll wear frost-fearing myrtle round my head    40
And much by anxious lovers I'll be read.
Envy feeds on the living. When men die,
It rests—each has his honor due; so I,
When the last flame devouring me has gone,
Shall still survive and all that's best live on.

## METAMORPHOSES

### Book 3

*In the opening book of the poem, Ovid told of the first great transformation of chaos to form the cosmos, the succession of the ages, and the first generation of men who were*

*destroyed in the Great Flood. The first erotic narrative of the*
*poem forms the centerpiece of the book, the story of Apollo*
*and Daphne. At the end of the book Ovid introduces the*
*story of Phaethon, which carries over to Book 2. The princi-*
*pal stories of that book, in addition to the tale of Phaethon's*
*fiery ride in the chariot of the sun, are Callisto's transforma-*
*tion into a bear and a group of warning tales about mortals*
*who are punished with metamorphosis. The second book*
*ends with Jupiter, disguised as a beautiful bull, abducting*
*Europa, the daughter of the Phoenician king Agenor. This*
*draws the reader into the third book, where her story, along*
*with that of her brother, Cadmus, continues.*

Now, safe in Crete, Jove shed the bull's disguise
And stood revealed before Europa's eyes.
Meanwhile her father, baffled, bade his son
Cadmus, set out to find the stolen girl
And threatened exile should he fail—in one
Same act such warmth of love, such wickedness!

*After the abrupt end to the story of Europa, Ovid makes a*
*swift transition to tell of her brother Cadmus. He was sent*
*to search for Europa, but upon failing to find her looked for*
*a place to settle and founded the city of Thebes in Greece.*

He roamed the whole wide world, for who could trace
Jove's secret tricks? Shunning his father's wrath
And fatherland, an exiled fugitive,
10 He knelt before Apollo's oracle
And asked what country he should make his home.
'A cow will meet you in a lonely land',
The god replied, 'A cow that never wore
A yoke nor toiled to haul a curving plough.
With her to guide you make your way, and where
She rests upon the grass, there you must found
Your city's battlements, and name the place
Boeotia.' If Cadmus left the holy cave
And saw, almost at once, as he went down,
20 A heifer ambling loose that bore no sign
Of service on her neck. He followed her
With slow and wary steps and silently
Worshipped Apollo, guardian and guide.
Now past Cephisus' shallows and the meads
Of Panope they wandered on, and there
The heifer stopped and raised towards the sky
Her graceful high-horned head and filled the air
With lowings; then, her big eyes looking back
Upon her followers, she bent her knees
30 And settled on her side on the soft grass.

Cadmus gave thanks and kissed the foreign soil,
Hailing the unknown hills and countryside.
Then meaning to make sacrifice to Jove,
He sent his henchmen forth to find a spring
Of living water for the ritual.
       There stood an ancient forest undefiled
By axe or saw, and in its heart a cave
Close-veiled in boughs and creepers, with its rocks
Joined in a shallow arch, and gushing out
A wealth of water. Hidden in the cave                    40
There dwelt a snake, a snake of Mars. Its crest
Shone gleaming gold; its eyes flashed fire; its whole
Body was big with venom, and between
Its triple rows of teeth its three-forked tongue
Flickered. The Tyrians reached the forest glade
On their ill-fated quest and dipped their pails
Into the water. At the sound the snake
Thrust from the cave its dark head and hissed
—A frightful hiss! Their blood ran cold. The pails
Fell from their hands and, horror-struck,
       they quaked                                        50
In shock and terror. Coil by scaly coil
The serpent wound its way, and, rearing up,
Curved in a giant arching bow, erect
For more than half its length, high in the air.
It glared down on the whole wide wood, as huge,
If all its size were seen, as in the sky
The Snake that separates the two bright Bears.
Then in a trice it seized them, some in flight,
Some set to fight, some fixed too fast in fear
For either. Every man of them it slew,                   60
With fang that struck or coil that crushed or breath
That dealt a putrid blast of poisoned death.
       The noonday sun had drawn the
              shadows small,
And Cadmus, wondering at his men's delay,
Followed their tracks, his mail a lion's skin,
His arms a javelin and lance that gleamed
Iron-tipped, his heart worth more than any arms.
He reached the glade and saw his murdered men,
And high in triumph that enormous foe,
Its blood-red tongue licking their sorry wounds.         70
'My faithful fallen friends!' he cried, 'Your deaths
I'll now avenge or share!' and lifting high
A rock above his head with all his might
He hurled the mighty missile, such a blow
As shatters towers and soaring battlements.
The snake, its scales like armor shielding it,
Stood fast unscathed; its hard black carapace

Bounced the blow back; but that hard armor failed
To foil the javelin that pierced its spine
80  Deep in the midmost coil, with the full length
Of iron buried in the serpent's side.
In agony it twisted back its head
To see the wound, and bit the deep-sunk shaft,
And straining it from side to side at last
Wrenched it away—but still the iron stuck fast.
        Now to its natural rage new source of rage
Was added. In its throat the arteries
Swelled huge; its poison fangs were flecked with foam;
Its scales scraped rasping on the rocks; its breath
90  Like the black blast that stinks from holes of Hell,
Befouled the fetid air. And now it coils
In giant spirals, now it towers up
Tall as a tree, now like a stream in spate
After a storm it rushes surging on,
And breasts aside the woods that bar its way.
Cadmus steps back; his lion's spoil withstands
The onslaught; his long lance's point,
Thrust forward, keeps the darting fangs at bay.
The snake is frenzied; on the unyielding iron
100  It wastes its wounds and bites the metal point.
Then from its venom-laden lips an ooze
Of blood began and spattered the green grass.
The wound was slight, for, shrinking from the thrust,
It turned its injured neck away and kept
The blow from piercing deep and striking home.
Cadmus pressed on and drove the firm-lodged lance
Deep in the creature's gullet, till an oak
Blocked its retreat and snake and oak were nailed
Together. Burdened by the serpent's weight
The tree bent curving down; its strong trunk
110      groaned
Beneath the lashings of that writhing tail.
        Then as the victor contemplates his foe,
His vanquished foe so vast, a sudden voice
Is heard, its source not readily discerned,
But heard for very sure: 'Why, Cadmus, why
Stare at the snake you've slain? You too shall be
A snake and stared at.' For an age he stood
Rigid, frozen in fear, his hair on end,
His color and his courage drained away.
120  But look, a guardian goddess! Gliding down
Out of the sky Pallas appears and bids
Him plough the soil and plant the serpent's teeth,
From which a future people should arise.
Cadmus obeys, and with his plough's deep share
Opens wide furrows, then across the soil

Scatters the teeth, the seed of humankind.
The tilth (beyond belief!) began to stir:
First from the furrows points of spears were seen,
Next helmets, bright with nodding painted plumes,
Then shoulders, chests and weapon-laden arms      130
Arose, a growing crop of men in mail.
So, when the curtain at a theater
Is raised, figures rise up, their faces first,
Then gradually the rest, until at last,
Drawn slowly, smoothly up, they stand revealed
Complete, their feet placed on the fringe below.

In fear of these new foemen Cadmus sprang
To arms. 'Lay down your arms!' a warrior cried,
One of the earth-born regiment, 'Take no part
In civil strife.' So saying, with his sword        140
He felled a soil-sprung brother by his side,
Then fell himself, struck by a far-flung lance.
He too who dealt him death was dead as soon,
And of that new-given life breath breathed his last.
In the same mould of madness all that host,
That sudden brotherhood, in battle joined,
With wound for wound fell dead. That prime of youth,
Whose lot was life so short, lay writhing on
Their mother's bloodstained bosom—all save five,
Five who survived. Among them was Echion,         150
Who at Minerva's bidding dropped his arms
And joined his brothers in a pact of peace.
These were his comrades when the Prince of Tyre,
Obedient to the oracle's command,
Founded his city in that foreign land.


*Ovid treats the story of Cadmus as a frame upon which to
hang the tales of his descendants. The first is his grandson
Actaeon's punishment by the goddess Diana for accidentally seeing her bathing. Ovid found a version of this story
in the Fifth Hymn of Callimachus.*


Now Thebes stood strong; now Cadmus might
    have seemed
Blessed in his exile. He had won for bride
The child of Mars and Venus. Add besides
From such a glorious wife a dynasty,
So many sons and daughters, grandsons too,        160
Dear links of love, by now indeed young men.
But yet in truth one ever must await
A man's last day, nor count him fortunate
Before he dies and the last rites are paid.
In his prosperity a grandson first

Was source of Cadmus' sorrow, whose young brow
Sprouted outlandish antlers and the hounds,
His hounds, were sated with their master's blood.
Though, if you ponder wisely, you will find
170 The fault was fortune's and no guilt that day,
For what guilt can it be to lose one's way?
        Upon a mountainside, whose woodland coverts
Were stained with many a kill of varied game,
The shining noon had narrowed all the shade
And midway at his zenith stood the sun.
Then young Actaeon was content; he called
His comrades as they roamed the lonely woods:
'Come, friends, our nets are wet, our javelins
Drip with our quarries' blood; today has brought
180 Success enough; tomorrow, when the dawn
On saffron wheels leads on another day,
We'll start our work again; now the sun shines
Half-way upon his journey and his rays
Crack the parched countryside. Take up your nets;
Here let us end the work in hand.' The men
Obeyed his words and rested from their toil.
        There was a valley clothed in hanging woods
Of pine and cypress, named Gargaphie,
Sacred to chaste Diana, huntress queen.
190 Deep in its farthest combe, framed by the woods,
A cave lay hid, not fashioned by man's art,
But nature's talent copied artistry,
For in the living limestone she had carved
A natural arch; and there a limpid spring
Flowed lightly babbling into a wide pool,
Its waters girdled with a grassy sward.
Here, tired after the hunt, the goddess loved
Her nymphs to bathe her with the water's balm.
        Reaching the cave, she gave her spear and quiver
200 And bow unstrung to an attendant nymph;
Others received her robes over their arms;
Two loosed her sandals; more expert than these
Crocale tied the hair loose on her shoulders
Into a knot, her own hair falling free.
Then Nephele and Hyale and Rhanis
And Phiale and Psecas brought the water
In brimming jars and poured it over her.
And while Titania bathed there in the pool,
Her loved familiar pool, it chanced Actaeon,
210 The day's hunt finished, idly wandering
Through unknown clearings of the forest, found
The sacred grove—so the Fates guided him—
And came upon the cool damp cave. At once,
Seeing a man, all naked as they were,

The nymphs, beating their breasts, filled the
    whole grove
With sudden screams and clustered round Diana
To clothe her body with their own. But she
Stood taller, a head taller than them all;
And as the clouds are colored when the sun
Glows late and low or like the crimson dawn,    220
So deeply blushed Diana, caught unclothed.
Her troop pressed close about her, but she turned
Aside and looking backwards (would she had
Her arrows ready!) all she had, the water,
She seized and flung it in the young man's face,
And as the avenging downpour drenched his hair
She added words that warned of doom: 'Now tell
You saw me here naked without my clothes,
If you can tell at all!' With that one threat
Antlers she raised upon his dripping head,    230
lengthened his neck, pointed his ears, transformed
His hands to hooves, arms to long legs, and draped
His body with a dappled hide; and last
Set terror in his heart. Actaeon fled,
Royal Actaeon, and marveled in his flight
At his new leaping speed, but, when he saw
His head and antlers mirrored in a stream,
He tried to say 'Alas!'—but no words came;
He groaned—that was his voice; the tears
    rolled down
On cheeks not his—all changed except his mind.    240
What should he do? Go home, back to the palace,
Or stay in hiding in the forest? Shame
Forbade the first decision, fear the other.
        While thus he stood in doubt his hounds had
            seen him.
Blackfoot and Tracker first gave tongue, wise Tracker,
A Cretan hound, Blackfoot of Spartan breed;
Swift as the wind the rest came rushing on:
Glance, Glutton, Ranger (all from Arcady),
Fierce Rover, sturdy Stalker, moody Storm,
Flight unsurpassed for speed, Hunter for scent,    250
Bold Woodman lately wounded by a boar,
Dingle a slender bitch sired by a wolf,
Snatch with two pups, gaunt Catch from Sicyon,
And Shepherd, once a guardian of her flock;
Spot, Gnasher, Tigress, Courser, Lightfoot, Strong,
Black-coated Sooty, Blanche with snowy hair,
Wolf and her nimble brother Cyprian,
Huge stalwart Spartan, Tempest never tired;
Clinch, his dark forehead crowned with a white star,
Blackie; rough-coated Shag; a couple of hounds    260

Born of a Cretan sire and Spartan dam,
Fury and Whitetooth; Barker, noisy bitch;
And many more too long to tell. The pack,
Hot in pursuit, sped on over fells and crags,
By walls of rock, on daunting trails or none.
He fled where often he'd followed in pursuit,
Fled his own folk, for shame! He longed to shout
'I am Actaeon, look, I am your master!'
Words failed his will; their baying filled the sky.
270  Blackhair bit first, a wound deep in his haunch;
Next Killer; Climber fastened on his shoulder.
These started late but cut across the hills
And gained a lead. They held their master down
Till the whole pack, united, sank their teeth
Into his flesh. He gave a wailing scream,
Not human, yet a sound no stag could voice,
And filled with anguished cries the mountainside
He knew so well; then, suppliant on his knees,
Turned his head silently from side to side,
Like arms that turned and pleaded. But his
280     friends
With their glad usual shouts cheered on the pack,
Not knowing what they did, and looked around
To find Actaeon; each louder than the rest
Calling Actaeon, as though he were not there;
And blamed his absence and his sloth that missed
The excitement of the kill. Hearing his name,
He turned his head. Would that he were indeed
Absent! But he was there. Would that he watched,
Not felt, the hounds' (his hounds') fierce savagery!
290  Now they are all around him, tearing deep
Their master's flesh, the stag that is no stag;
And not until so many countless wounds
Had drained away his lifeblood, was the wrath,
It's said, of chaste Diana satisfied.

         As the tale spread views varied; some believed
Diana's violence unjust; some praised it,
As proper to her chaste virginity.
Both sides found reason for their point of view.

*The theme of Juno's hatred for the house of Cadmus as*
*relatives of Europa continues with the story of Cadmus's*
*daughter Semele, who was impregnated by Jupiter. Juno*
*tricks her into destroying herself, but Jupiter rescues the*
*child Bacchus.*

Jove's wife alone said not a word of blame
300  Or praise; simply her heart rejoiced in that
Disaster fallen on Agenor's house.

Her hatred of that Tyrian concubine
She turned against her kin. Yes, now a new
Offence followed the last, the grievous news
That Semele was pregnant by great Jove.
Harsh words rose to her lips, 'But what have words
Ever achieved?' she said. That girl herself
Must now be dealt with. Her, if I'm well named
Almighty Juno, if I'm fit to wield
My jewelled sceptre, if I'm queen of heaven,          310
Jove's wife and sister—sister certainly—
Her I'll destroy. Yet secret stolen love
May well be all she wants. My marriage bonds
Suffer brief harm. No! she's conceived—that
      crowns it!
Her bulging womb carries her glaring guilt.
She means to be a mother by great Jove—
Luck hardly ever mine! Such confidence
In her good looks! I'll see it lets her down.
I'm never Saturn's child if she's not swallowed
In Styx's waves, sunk by her Jove himself!'          320
         Then rising from her throne she wrapped
            herself
In a bright golden cloud and visited
The home of Semele, and kept the cloud
Till she'd disguised herself as an old woman,
With white hair on her forehead, wrinkled skin,
Bowed back and shaky steps, and speaking too
Like an old woman. She was Beroe,
The Epidaurian nurse of Semele.
They talked of many things and then the name
Of Jove came up. 'I pray it may be Jove',          330
She sighed, 'All these things frighten me. So often
Men, claiming to be gods, have gained the beds
Of simple girls. But even to be Jove
Is not enough; he ought to prove his love,
If he is Jove. In all the power and glory
That's his when heavenly Juno welcomes him,
Beg him to don his godhead and take you
In the same power and glory in his arms.'
         So Juno moulded Cadmus' daughter's mind.
The girl, unwitting, asked of Jove a boon          340
Unnamed. 'Choose what you will', the god replied,
'There's nothing I'll refuse; and should you doubt,
The Power of rushing Styx shall be my witness,
The deity whom all gods hold in awe.'
She, too successful, happy in her ruin,
Doomed by her lover's generosity,
Answered 'Give me yourself in the same grace
As when your Juno holds you to her breast

In love's embrace.' He would have locked her lips;
350 Too late: her words had hastened on their way.
He groaned: her wish could never be unwished,
His oath never unsworn. In bitterest grief
He soared ascending to the ethereal sky,
And by his nod called up the trailing clouds
And massed a storm, with lightnings in the squalls,
And thunder and the bolts that never miss.
Even so he tried, as far as he had power,
To curb his might, and would not wield the fire
With which he'd felled the hundred-handed giant.
360 That was too fierce. There is another bolt,
A lighter one, in which the Cyclops forged
A flame less savage and a lesser wrath,
Called by the gods his second armament.
With this in hand he went to Semele
In Cadmus' palace. Then her mortal frame
Could not endure the tumult of the heavens;
That gift of love consumed her. From her womb
Her baby, still not fully formed, was snatched,
And sewn (could one believe the tale) inside
370 His father's thigh, and so completed there
His mother's time. Ino, his mother's sister,
In secret from the cradle nursed the child
And brought him up, and then the nymphs of Nysa
Were given his charge and kept him hidden away
Within their caves, and nourished him on milk.

*The story of how Tiresias, the blind seer of Thebes, acquired*
*the gift of prophecy is a diversion from the sequence of nar-*
*ratives about the descendants of Cadmus, seemingly intro-*
*duced only to set up the following episode about Narcissus.*

While down on earth as destiny ordained
These things took place, and Bacchus, babe
     twice born,
Was cradled safe and sound, it chanced that Jove,
Well warmed with nectar, laid his weighty cares
380 Aside and, Juno too in idle mood,
The pair were gaily joking, and Jove said
'You women get more pleasure out of love
Than we men do, I'm sure.' She disagreed.
So they resolved to get the views of wise
Tiresias. He knew both sides of love.
For once in a green copse when two huge snakes
Were mating, he attacked them with his stick,
And was transformed (a miracle!) from man
To woman; and spent seven autumns so;
390 Till in the eighth he saw the snakes once more

And said 'If striking you has magic power
To change the striker to the other sex,
I'll strike you now again.' He struck the snakes
And so regained the shape he had at birth.
Asked then to give his judgement on the joke,
He found for Jove; and Juno (so it's said)
Took umbrage beyond reason, out of all
Proportion, and condemned her judge to live
In the black night of blindness evermore.
But the Almighty Father (since no god                    400
Has right to undo what any god has done)
For his lost sight gave him the gift to see
What things should come, the power of prophecy,
An honor to relieve that penalty.

*The story of Narcissus was known before Ovid, although*
*his source has been lost, but it was Ovid who made it*
*famous and introduced into it the story of Echo. The*
*moment described by Ovid of Narcissus gazing at his own*
*reflection is one of the most popular scenes in the frescoes*
*that decorated the homes of Pompeii.*

So blind Tiresias gave to all who came
Faultless and sure reply and far and wide
Through all Boeotia's cities spread his fame.
To test his truth and trust the first who tried
Was wave-blue water-nymph Liriope,
Whom once Cephisus in his sinuous flow                    410
Embracing held and ravished. In due time
The lovely sprite bore a fine infant boy,
From birth adorable, and named her son
Narcissus; and of him she asked the seer,
Would he long years and ripe old age enjoy,
Who answered 'If he shall himself not know'.
For long his words seemed vain; what they concealed
The lad's strange death and stranger love revealed.
      Narcissus now had reached his sixteenth year
And seemed both man and boy; and many a youth           420
And many a girl desired him, but hard pride
Ruled in that delicate frame, and never a youth
And never a girl could touch his haughty heart.
Once as he drove to nets the frightened deer
A strange-voiced nymph observed him, who
     must speak
If any other speak and cannot speak
Unless another speak, resounding Echo.
Echo was still a body, not a voice,
But talkative as now, and with the same
Power of speaking, only to repeat,                       430

As best she could, the last of many words.
Juno had made her so; for many a time,
When the great goddess might have caught
  the nymphs
Lying with Jove upon the mountainside,
Echo discreetly kept her talking till
The nymphs had fled away; and when at last
The goddess saw the truth, 'Your tongue', she said,
'With which you tricked me, now its power shall lose,
Your voice avail but for the briefest use.'
The event confirmed the threat: when
  speaking ends,
440     All she can do is double each last word,
And echo back again the voice she's heard.
Now when she saw Narcissus wandering
In the green byways, Echo's heart was fired;
And stealthily she followed, and the more
She followed him, the nearer flamed her love,
As when a torch is lit and from the tip
The leaping sulphur grasps the offered flame.
She longed to come to him with winning words,
450     To urge soft pleas, but nature now opposed;
She might not speak the first but—what she might—
Waited for words her voice could say again.
        It chanced Narcissus, searching for his friends,
Called 'Anyone here?' and Echo answered 'Here!'
Amazed he looked all round and, raising his voice,
Called 'Come this way!' and Echo called 'This way!'
He looked behind and, no one coming, shouted
'Why run away?' and heard his words again.
He stopped and, cheated by the answering voice,
460     Called 'Join me here!' and she, never more glad
To give her answer, answered 'Join me here!'
And graced her words and ran out from the wood
To throw her longing arms around his neck.
He bolted, shouting 'Keep your arms from me!
Be off! I'll die before I yield to you.'
And all she answered was 'I yield to you'.
Shamed and rejected in the woods she hides
And has her dwelling in the lonely caves;
Yet still her love endures and grows on grief,
470     And weeping vigils waste her frame away;
Her body shrivels, all its moisture dries;
Only her voice and bones are left; at last
Only her voice, her bones are turned to stone.
So in the woods she hides and hills around,
For all to hear, alive, but just a sound.
        Thus had Narcissus mocked her; others too,
Hill-nymphs and water-nymphs and many a man

He mocked; till one scorned youth, with raised
  hands, prayed,
'So may he love—and never win his love!'
And Nemesis approved the righteous prayer.          480
        There was a pool, limpid and silvery,
Whither no shepherd came nor any herd,
Nor mountain goat; and never bird nor beast
Nor falling branch disturbed its shining peace;
Grass grew around it, by the water fed,
And trees to shield it from the warming sun.
Here—for the chase and heat had wearied him—
The boy lay down, charmed by the quiet pool,
And, while he slaked his thirst, another thirst
Grew; as he drank he saw before his eyes              490
A form, a face, and loved with leaping heart
A hope unreal and thought the shape was real.
Spellbound he saw himself, and motionless
Lay like a marble statue staring down.
He gazes at his eyes, twin constellation,
His hair worthy of Bacchus or Apollo,
His face so fine, his ivory neck, his cheeks
Smooth, and the snowy pallor and the blush;
All he admires that all admire in him,
Himself he longs for, longs unwittingly,               500
Praising is praised, desiring is desired,
And love he kindles while with love he burns.
How often in vain he kissed the cheating pool
And in the water sank his arms to clasp
The neck he saw, but could not clasp himself!
Not knowing what he sees, he adores the sight;
That false face fools and fuels his delight.
You simple boy, why strive in vain to catch
A fleeting image? What you see is nowhere;
And what you love—but turn away—you lose!             510
You see a phantom of a mirrored shape;
Nothing itself; with you it came and stays;
With you it too will go, if you can go!
        No thought of food or rest draws him away;
Stretched on the grassy shade he gazes down
On the false phantom, staring endlessly,
His eyes his own undoing. Raising himself
He holds his arms towards the encircling trees
And cries 'You woods, was ever love more cruel!
You know! For you are lovers' secret haunts.          520
Can you in your long living centuries
Recall a lad who pined so piteously?
My joy! I see it; but the joy I see
I cannot find' (so fondly love is failed!)
'And—to my greater grief—between us lies

No mighty sea, no long and dusty road,
Nor mountain range nor bolted barbican.
A little water sunders us. He longs
For my embrace. Why, every time I reach
530 My lips towards the gleaming pool, he strains
His upturned face to mine. I surely could
Touch him, so slight the thing that thwarts our love.
Come forth, whoever you are! Why, peerless boy,
Elude me? Where retreat beyond my reach?
My looks, my age—indeed it cannot be
That you should shun—the nymphs have loved
        me too!
Some hope, some nameless hope, your
        friendly face
Pledges; and when I stretch my arms to you
You stretch your arms to me, and when I smile
540 You smile, and when I weep, I've often seen
Your tears, and to my nod your nod replies,
And your sweet lips appear to move in speech,
Though to my ears your answer cannot reach.
Oh, I am he! Oh, now I know for sure
The image is my own; it's for myself
I burn with love; I fan the flames I feel.
What now? Woo or be wooed? Why woo at all?
My love's myself—my riches beggar me.
Would I might leave my body! I could wish
550 (Strange lover's wish!) my love were not so near!
Now sorrow saps my strength; of my life's span
Not long is left; I die before my prime.
Nor is death sad for death will end my sorrow;
Would he I love might live a long tomorrow!
But now we two—one soul—one death will die.'
        Distraught he turned towards the face again;
His tears rippled the pool, and darkly then
The troubled water veiled the fading form,
And, as it vanished, 'Stay', he shouted, 'stay!
560 Oh, cruelty to leave your lover so!
Let me but gaze on what I may not touch
And feed the aching fever in my heart.'
Then in his grief he tore his robe and beat
His pale cold fists upon his naked breast,
And on his breast a blushing redness spread
Like apples, white in part and partly red,
Or summer grapes whose varying skins assume
Upon the ripening vine a blushing bloom.
And this he saw reflected in the pool,
570 Now still again, and could endure no more.
But as wax melts before a gentle fire,
Or morning frosts beneath the rising sun,

So, by love wasted, slowly he dissolves
By hidden fire consumed. No color now,
Blending the white with red, nor strength remains
Nor will, nor aught that lately seemed so fair,
Nor longer lasts the body Echo loved.
But she, though angry still and unforgetting,
Grieved for the hapless boy, and when he moaned
'Alas', with answering sob she moaned 'alas',    580
And when he beat his hands upon his breast,
She gave again the same sad sounds of woe.
His latest words, gazing and gazing still,
He sighed 'alas! the boy I loved in vain!'
And these the place repeats, and then 'farewell',
And Echo said 'farewell'. On the green grass
He drooped his weary head, and those bright eyes
That loved their master's beauty closed in death.
Then still, received into the Underworld,
He gazed upon himself in Styx's pool.    590
His Naiad sisters wailed and sheared their locks
In mourning for their brother; the Dryads too
Wailed and sad Echo wailed in answering woe.
And then the brandished torches, bier and pyre
Were ready—but no body anywhere;
And in its stead they found a flower—behold,
White petals clustered round a cup of gold!

*The story of Pentheus, another grandson of Cadmus, who
was punished by Bacchus for not recognizing his divinity, was made famous in Euripides's play* The Bacchae.
*It serves as a frame for the less familiar tale of Bacchus's
abduction by pirates, which is told by Acoetes, one of the
survivors of the god's wrath.*

News of this story brought the prophet fame,
Well-merited, in all the towns of Greece.
His name was great. Even so, one man alone,    600
Echion's son Pentheus, who scorned the gods,
Spurned him and mocked the old man's prophecies,
Taunting him with his blindness and the doom
Of his lost sight. Then, shaking his white head,
'How lucky you would be', the prophet warned,
'If you too lost this light, and never saw
The rites of Bacchus. For the day shall dawn,
Not distant I foresee, when here shall come
A new god, Liber, son of Semele.
Unless you honor him with holy shrines,    610
You shall be torn to pieces; far and wide
You shall be strewn, and with your blood defile
The forests and your mother and her sisters.

So it shall come to pass. You will refuse
The god his honor due and mourn that I
In this my darkness saw too certainly.'
Even as he spoke, Pentheus thrust him away.
His words proved true; his forecast was fulfilled.
        Bacchus is there. The revelers' wild shrieks
Ring through the fields. The crowds come rushing
620     out;
Men, women, nobles, commons, old and young
Stream to the unknown rites. 'What lunacy
Has stolen your wits away, you race of Mars,
You children of the serpent?' Pentheus cried.
'Can clashing bronze, can pipes of curving horn,
Can conjuror's magic have such power that men
Who, undismayed, have faced the swords of war,
The trumpet and the ranks of naked steel,
Quail before women's wailing, frenzy fired
630     By wine, a bestial rabble, futile drums?
You elders, you who sailed the distant seas
And founded here a second Tyre, made here
Your home in exile—shame on you, if you
Surrender them without a fight! You too,
Young men of sharper years, nearer my own,
Graced by your martial arms, not Bacchic wands,
With helmets on your heads, not loops of leaves!
Recall your lineage, brace your courage with
The spirit of that snake who killed, alone,
640     So many. For his pool and spring he died.
You, for your honor, you must fight and win!
He did brave men to death. Now you must rout
Weaklings—and save your country's name! If fate
Refuses Thebes long life, I'd wish her walls
Might fall to brave men and their batteries,
And fire and sword resound. Our misery
Would have no guilt; our lot we'd need to mourn,
Not hide; our tears would never bring us shame.
But now an unarmed boy will capture Thebes,
650     And in his service not the arts of war,
Weapons and cavalry, but tender garlands,
Myrrh-scented tresses and embroidered robes
Of gold and purple. Only stand aside,
And here and now I'll force him to confess
His father's name is false, his rites a lie.
Why, if Acrisius was man enough
To spurn his sham divinity and shut
The gates of Argos in his face, shall Pentheus
And all Thebes shudder at this newcomer?
Quick, now' (he bade his servants), 'bring
660     him here,

Their ringleader, in chains, and waste no time.'
His grandfather and Athamas and all
His courtiers upbraided him and tried
Their best to stop him, but in vain. Their words
Of warning whetted him and his wild rage,
Stung by restraint, increased; endeavours to
Control him made things worse. So I have seen
A stream, where nothing blocks its course, run down
Smoothly with no great noise, but where it's checked
By trees or boulders in its way it foams     670
And boils and flows the fiercer for the block.
        Look now, the men come back spattered
            with blood,
And when he asks where Bacchus is, they say
Bacchus they did not see, 'But this man here,
His comrade and his acolyte, we seized';
And hand over a Maeonian, his arms bound
Behind his back, a follower of the god.
Pentheus, with terrible anger in his eyes,
Glared at the man and hardly could delay
His punishment. 'Before you die', he cried,     680
'And, dying, give a lesson to the rest,
Tell me your name, your family, your country,
And why you practice this new cult of yours.'
He answered undismayed, 'My name's Acoetes,
Maeonia's my country and my parents
Were humble folk. My father left me no
Acres for sturdy steers to turn and till,
No woolly sheep, no flocks, no herds at all.
He was poor too. He used to lure and catch
Fish with his lines and hooks, and with his rod     690
Drew them, leaping, to land: that skill of his
Was all his fortune. When he passed it on,
"You are my heir, successor to my craft",
He said; "receive my wealth and my estate."
And when he died he left me nothing but
The waters; that is all that I can call
My heritage. Soon after, to escape
Being stuck for ever on the self-same rocks,
I learnt as well the art of helmsmanship.
My eyes studied the stars, the rainy Goat,     700
Taygete, the Hyads and the Bear;
Harbors and havens too and the winds' homes.
One day, making for Delos, I put in
To Chios; we rowed shrewdly to the shore;
A light leap, and I stood on the wet sand.
We spent the night there; in the first red glow
Of dawn I rose and sent my men for water,
Along a track that led them to a spring.

I, myself, climbed a knoll and gazed around
710 To judge the promise of the wind, then called
My shipmates, and so back to board the ship.
Opheltes, in the lead, crying "Here we are!"
Brought to the beach a prize (or so he thought),
Discovered in this lonely spot, a boy,
As pretty as a girl. He seemed to reel,
Half-dazed with wine and sleep, and almost failed
To follow along. I gazed at his attire,
His face, his bearing; everything I saw
Seemed more than mortal. I felt sure of it,
720 And said to my shipmates "What deity
Is in that frame, I'm doubtful, but for sure
Some deity is there. Whoever you are,
Be gracious, bless our labors, and forgive
These fellows!" "Spare your prayers for us",
Said Dictys (no man nimbler to swarm up
Right to the highest yard and slide back down
The stays) and Libys backed him, and Melanthus,
Our fair-haired prow-man, and Alcimedon,
Epopeus too, who called the rowers' time,
To pull or pause, and kept their spirits up,
730 And all the others to a man: so blind
Is greed for booty. "No!" I cried, "That freight
Is holy! Never shall I let my ship
Commit such sacrilege! I'm master here!"
I stood to block the gangway. Lycabas,
Of all the crew the boldest, was incensed.
(He had been banished from a Tuscan town,
Exiled for a foul murder.) As I stood,
He seized me by the throat and would have thrown
Me overboard, had I not, half-concussed,
740 Clung to a rescuing rope. That godless group
Applauded him and cheered him. Then at last
Bacchus (for it was he), aroused, no doubt,
From slumber by the shouting, and his wits
Regathered from the wine, cried "What's this noise?
What are you doing? How did I come here?
Where do you mean to take me?" "Have no fear",
Said Proreus; "Name the port you wish to reach;
You shall be landed at the place you choose."
"Naxos", said Bacchus, "set your course to Naxos.
750 That is my home, that land will welcome you."
Then by the sea and every god they swore,
Those swindling rogues, it should be so, and bade
Me get the painted vessel under sail.
Naxos lay on the right, and for the right
I set my canvas. "Fool, what are you doing?"
Opheltes said; "What lunacy is this?
Steer to the left!" and every man of them

Supported him. They made their meaning clear
By nods and winks and some by whispers. I
Was staggered. "Someone else shall take the
    helm",                                                  760
I said—I'd not let my skill serve their crime!
All the crew cursed me. "So you think our whole
Safety", Aethalion cried, "depends on you!"
He strode and took my duty at the helm,
And, turning course from Naxos, steered away.
        Then the god, making sport of them, as if
He'd only just perceived their treachery,
Gazed from the curving poop across the sea
And seemed in tears and said "That's not the shore
You promised me! That's not the shore I want!        770
What glory can you gain, if you strong men
Cheat a small boy, so many against one?"
I had been long in tears. The godless gang
Laughed at my tears, and rowed on hastily.
Now, by that god himself (for there's no god
Closer than he) I swear I tell what's true,
As true as past belief: the ship stood still
Upon the sea as fixed as in dry dock.
The crew, bewildered, rowed with dogged strokes
And spread the sails, twin means to make
    her move.                                              780
But ivy creeping, winding, clinging, bound
The oars and decked the sails in heavy clusters.
Bacchus himself, grape-bunches garlanding
His brow, brandished a spear that vine-leaves twined,
And at his feet fierce spotted panthers lay,
Tigers and lynxes too, in phantom forms.
The men leapt overboard, all driven mad
Or panic-stricken. Medon's body first
Began to blacken and his spine was arched
Into a curve. "What magic shape is this?"              790
Cried Lycabas, but, even as he spoke,
His mouth widened, his nose curved out, his skin
Turned hard and scaly. Libys, trying to pull
The thwarting oars, saw his hands suddenly
Shrink—hands no longer—fins they might be called.
Another, when he meant to clasp his arms
Around a hawser, had no arms and jumped
Limbless and bending backwards into the waves.
His tail forked to a sickle-shape and curved
Like a half moon. All round the ship they leapt        800
In showers of splashing spray. Time after time
They surfaced and fell back into the sea,
Playing like dancers, frolicking about
In fun, wide nostrils taking in the sea
To blow it out again. Of the whole twenty

(That was the crew she carried) I alone
Remained. As I stood trembling, cold with fear,
Almost out of my wits, the god spoke words
Of comfort: "Cast your fear aside. Sail on
810  To Naxos." Landing there, I joined his cult
And now am Bacchus' faithful follower.'
      'We've listened to this rigmarole', said Pentheus,
'To give our anger time to lose its force.
Away with him, you slaves! Rush him away!
Rack him with fiendish tortures till he dies
And send him down to the black night of Styx.'
So there and then Acoetes was hauled off
And locked in a strong cell; but while the fire,
The steel, the instruments of cruel death,
820  Were being prepared, all of their own accord
The doors flew open, all of their own accord
The chains fell, freed by no one, from his arms.
      Pentheus stood firm. This time he sent no scout,
But sallied forth himself to where Cithaeron,
The mountain chosen for the mysteries,
Resounded with the Bacchants' shouts and songs.
Like a high-mettled charger whinnying
When brazen-throated trumpets sound for war,
And fired with lust for battle, so the noise
830  Of long-drawn howls that echoed through the air
Excited Pentheus, and his anger flared.
      In the encircling forest, half-way up,
There lies a level clearing, bare of trees,
Open and in full view from every side.

Here, as his impious gaze was fixed upon
The mysteries, the first to see him, first
To rush in frenzy, first to hurl her staff,
Her Bacchic staff, and wound her Pentheus was
His mother. 'Here!' she called her sisters, 'Here!
That giant boar that prowls about our fields.    840
I'm going to kill that boar!' The whole mad throng
Rush at him, all united, and pursue
Their frightened quarry, frightened now for sure,
Now using less fierce language, blaming now
Himself, admitting now that he's done wrong.
Wounded, he cries, 'Help, Aunt Autonoe!
Mercy! Actaeon's ghost should move your mercy!'
Actaeon's name's unknown. She tore away
His outstretched hand, and Ino seized and wrenched
The other off. With no hands left to stretch    850
Out to his mother, 'Look, mother!' he cried,
And showed the severed stumps. And at the sight
Agave howled and tossed her head and hair,
Her streaming hair, and tore his head right off,
And, as her bloody fingers clutched it, cried
'Hurrah for victory! The triumph's mine!'
As swiftly as the winds of autumn strip
From some tall tree its lightly-hanging leaves
That frosts have fingered, so those wicked hands
Tore Pentheus limb from limb. That lesson learnt    860
By his example, the Theban women throng
The novel rites, honoring the god divine,
And offering incense in his holy shrine.

## AFTERWORD

Ovid has always been appreciated by readers, while artists and writers have taken inspiration from his works since their earliest appearance; only by scholars has he been undervalued, although that trend has from time to time been broken, most recently in the last decades of the twentieth century. Although none of Ovid's works was read in the ancient Roman curriculum, themes from his writings, especially the *Metamorphoses,* supplied the subject matter even for interior decorators, as we can see in the surviving frescoes from homes in Pompeii. His verbal dexterity and moral ambiguity made his works less suitable for schoolchildren and earned the disapprobation of Roman rhetoricians. The elder Seneca recounts an anecdote that Ovid's friends asked him to cancel three lines of his poetry, to which the poet agreed, provided that he could exempt three lines before they identified the offending verses: of course, they turned out to be the same three lines (*Controversies* 2.2.12). Quintilian considered Ovid too much in love with his own talent (*Education of the Orator* 10.1.88) and among his works appreciated only his tragedy *Medea,* which has not survived for us to evaluate.

    Later poets took to Ovid because his manner could be more easily imitated (though never replicated) than that of Virgil or the other elegists. Imaginary responses to his *Heroides* were composed by his friend, a poet named Sabinus, in Ovid's own lifetime. And other poets composed works such as a consolation to Livia on the death of her son Drusus that later generations mistook for the real thing. Amateur poets scribbled lines in imitation of Ovid on the walls of Pompeii, and somewhere between the towns of Formiae and Fundi was found a fragment of the tombstone of a man who described himself as an "Ovidian poet." His influence on Seneca's tragedies and Lucan is imprinted on every column of writing, and later poets such as Statius, who proclaimed their admiration for Virgil, were also clearly influenced by Ovid, particularly in their treatment of the metrical line and their manner of expression. Another sure sign of Ovid's enduring popularity was the composition in late antiquity of a prose summary of the *Metamorphoses* by an author known as "Lactantius Placidus." Poets in the fourth and fifth centuries A.D. were still reading Ovid closely, and in the works of Ausonius (A.D. 310–94) and Claudian (ca. A.D. 370–400) his influence is still clear. But Ovid was not much read by the Fathers of the Christian church—or at least they did not advertise their reading—and he does not emerge as a major influence again until the Carolingian period.

Ovid continued to be read after the collapse of the Roman political structure in western Europe, and some manuscripts survive from the time of Charlemagne to corroborate the impression that echoes of his work in Carolingian authors such as Theodulf of Orleans (ca. 750–821) and Modoin (ca. 770–840) reflect firsthand knowledge of Ovid's poetry. But Ovid was only gradually accepted

**Figure 16: Bernini, *Apollo and Daphne***
Perhaps the most famous sculpture by Gian Lorenzo Bernini (1598–1680), this piece was completed in 1625 for Cardinal Scipione Borghesi and is now housed in the Galleria Borghesi in Rome. It captures the moment, recounted by Ovid in Book One of the *Metamorphoses*, when the god Apollo is just about to reach Daphne and she is rescued from his attempted rape by being transformed into a laurel tree.

into the canon of authors accessible to medieval readers, until the twelfth century, when familiarity with his works spread widely. The study of classical authors in this period served the practical purpose of instructing students in proper Latin usage, but moral instruction went hand in hand with language acquisition, and for this purpose much of Ovid's work was considered less suitable. For that reason, his works had to be sanitized, a process that we can see beginning as early as the ninth century, when an annotated text of the *Art of Love,* known as "St. Dunstan's Classbook," was produced with interlinear notes in Welsh and Latin. Throughout the Middle Ages, Ovid's most popular work was the *Metamorphoses*: altogether more than four hundred manuscripts survive. But all his works were being read during this period, with the *Fasti, Heroides,* and *Letters from the Black Sea* enjoying a wide readership as well.

The interpretative history of the *Metamorphoses* during the Middle Ages illustrates how the poet could be accommodated to the aims of a medieval readership. Allegory was the vehicle for ascribing to the poem a high moral and Christian purpose. An early example is a work by Arnulf of Orleans (ca. 1175), *Allegories of Ovid's Metamorphoses,* in which the poet's intention is described as "to tell about change, so that we may not understand only the external change that takes place in corporeal matter both good and bad but also change that takes place internally, for example in the soul, to lead us from error to knowledge of the true Creator." In the anonymous French allegory of the fourteenth-century *Ovide Moralisé,* the story of Myrrha's incestuous love for her father from the tenth book of the *Metamorphoses* begins with a condemnation of her sinful passion but ends by making of her a trope for virgin purity. And the treatment of the story of Apollo's pursuit of Daphne by Giovanni del Virgilio in his *Allegories* (ca. 1323) is typical:

> I understand Phoebus to be the modest and chaste person; Daphne the very modesty that the chaste person pursues. I take Daphne's transformation into a tree to mean that modesty is rooted in the heart of the one who pursues it. By the laurel virginity is signified, because it is always fresh and fragrant.

Not every medieval reader of Ovid required a sanitized text. The love poets of Provence and northern Italy, for example, read and appreciated Ovid's erotic poetry for what it was. But for most readers during this period, Ovid was, at least superficially, transformed into a safe and serious author.

This manner of interpreting Ovid persisted well past the Middle Ages, but even before the Renaissance, we can see Ovid beginning to exert an influence that was relatively free from Christian incrustation. Chaucer was a careful reader not only of the *Metamorphoses* but of the *Heroides* and the *Fasti* as well. His recollection of Ovid in the *House of Fame* as "Venus' clerke, Ovide" shows that he knew the love poetry too. The Wife of Bath's Prologue could only have been written by someone who knew Ovid's *Art of Love* well. And in Italy the love poems of Petrarch (1304–74) to Laura are infused with an Ovidian aesthetic derived from the *Amores.* His contemporary Giovanni Boccaccio wrote a prose romance, *Il Filocolo,* in which Florio, a prince of Spain, and an orphan girl Biancifiore grow up together and fall in love over "Ovid's holy book," the *Art of Love.*

Ovid proved extraordinarily popular in the Renaissance. First editions of his works appeared in print in 1471, and translations soon proliferated. His works were frequently lectured on by humanist scholars, and artists drew inspiration for painting and sculpture. The famous *Primavera* (ca. 1482) by Sandro Botticelli, now on display in the Uffizi Gallery in Florence, is an interpretation of Ovid's story of the goddess Flora in the fourth book of his *Fasti.* Other artists who depicted themes from Ovid include Titian, Rubens, and Poussin. Perhaps no sculpture of the Baroque period is as celebrated as Gian Lorenzo Bernini's rendition of Apollo just on the point of capturing Daphne, who is beginning her miraculous transformation into a laurel tree (1622–25). But it was not only Ovid's works that captured the imagination of artists; the figure of the poet himself drew their attention, especially as a representative of the artist persecuted by an oppressive regime. Eugène Delacroix (1798–1863), the French Romantic artist, captured the essence of the misunderstood artist in exile with his panel *Ovid among the Scythians,* first executed in 1859.

Ovid's works were translated into English early and often—the *Heroides* in 1567 by George Turberville, the *Amores* in 1597 by Christopher Marlowe. Shakespeare read Ovid not only in the original Latin but in the much admired translation by Arthur Golding, which was published in 1565–67. His many imitations of Ovid included the *Venus and Adonis,* the Pyramus and Thisbe episode in *A Midsummer's Night Dream,* and the great monologue of Prospero in *The Tempest* (5.1.33–57), which echoes Ovid's depiction of Medea in the seventh book of the *Metamorphoses*:

> Ye elves of hills, brooks, standing lakes and groves,
> And ye that on the sands with printless foot
> Do chase the ebbing Neptune, and do fly him
> When he comes back; you demi-puppets that
> By moonshine do the green sour ringlets make
> Whereof the ewe not bites; and you whose pastime
> Is to make midnight mushrumps, that rejoice
> To hear the solemn curfew; by whose aid,
> Weak masters though ye be, I have bedimmed
> The noontide sun, called for the mutinous winds,
> And 'twixt the green sea and the azured vault
> set roaring war . . .

Shakespeare echoes not only Ovid but Golding's translation, which includes in Medea's incantation the line "Ye Ayres and windes: ye Elves of Hilles, of Brookes, of Woods alone." Centuries later the virtues of Golding's translation would be extolled by Ezra Pound, but in its own time it was eventually superseded by others. The translation by George Sandys (1621–26) may be claimed as the earliest work of American literature in English, since it was composed while the author was serving in the colony of Virginia. Another influential translation, compiled by Samuel Garth in 1717, included translations by several hands, not the least that of John Dryden.

Ovid's love poetry ranked high among the sources of inspiration for English poets in this period as well. Michael Drayton recreated the genre of the imaginary verse epistle in *England's Heroicall Epistles* (1597), in which he substituted noble English women for the role that in Ovid's *Heroides* had been played by women of myth. Christopher Marlowe's *Hero and Leander* (1598) takes its story from the seventeenth and eighteenth poems in the collection of *Heroides,* while the spirit of Ovid's collection is emulated by Alexander Pope in his verse epistle *Eloisa to Abelard* (1717). Imitations of poems from the *Amores* abound in the literature of the sixteenth and seventeenth centuries. One of Ovid's more amusing takes on the unhappy lover enjoyed an especially productive afterlife. In the seventh poem of the third book, the poet describes his dismay at not being able to perform sexually for his mistress, a theme that was transformed into a minor masterpiece in the Restoration by John Wilmot, Second Earl of Rochester (1647–80), the brilliant but short-lived master of satirical verse, who describes the lover's disappointment in "The Imperfect Enjoyment" (19–27):

> Smileing she chides in a kind, murmring noise
> And from her body wipes the clamy Joyes,
> When with a Thousand kisses wandring o're
> My panting bossome, Is there then no more?
> She cries; All this to Love, and Raptures due—
> Must we not pay a Debt to pleasure too?
> But I the most forlorn lost man alive
> To shew my wish'd obedience vainly strive:
> I sigh alas! and Kiss, but cannott swive.

Many poems treated the same theme, including "The Disappointment" by the female poet Aphra Behn (1640–89), and the influence of Ovid's love elegies is apparent in poems by John Donne (1572–1631), Ben Jonson (1572–1637), and Andrew Marvell (1621–78), to mention only a few.

The Romantics had less use for Ovid, even though he was Goethe's favorite Latin poet: his brand of wit and mythic imagination held less appeal for that age. With the advent of modernism, however, Ovid was being read again and found advocates as diverse as Kafka and Pound. Pound provocatively described the *Metamorphoses* as a "holy book" and called Golding's translation the "most beautiful book" in the English language (*ABC of Reading*), but more significantly he included extensive allusion to Ovid in his early *Cantos*. Although the *Metamorphoses* remained the prime source of inspiration for artists in the twentieth century, many other poets drew on Ovid in dealing with the themes of exile and the displaced artist, most notably the Russian exile Joseph Brodsky (1940–96). The American poet Hayden Carruth (1921–2008) manages to draw those themes together with the idea of metamorphosis in "Ovid, Old Buddy, I Would Discourse with You a While":

> upon mutability—if it were possible. But you don't
> know me. Already you cannot conceive my making the second line
> of a poem so much longer than the first.
> No matter, mutability is the topic, and I see you there exiled on the
> Thracian shore
> among those hairy mariners speaking an improbable tongue,
> a location of you damnably similar to Syracuse, N.Y., and I see
> you addressing your first letter to the new emperor, Tiberius,
> looking blankly out to the rocks and the gray ocean
> as you search for rhythms and awesome words to make this
> the greatest verse-epistle ever written and obtain your pardon, your
> freedom to return
> to Rome, so long denied by Augustus.

The exiled artist has proved an attractive theme not only for modern poets but for novelists who have developed imaginative reconstructions of Ovid's life on the Roman frontier. Two notable entries in that category are David Malouf's *An Imaginary Life* (1978) and Christoph Ransmayr's *The Last World* (1988). In Malouf's novel the exiled poet forms a bond in Tomi with a boy who has been raised by wolves and disappears into the wilderness. Ransmayr's novel tells the story of a young man named Cotta who journeys to the Black Sea in search of Ovid and finds himself in a strange world that resembles Ovid's *Metamorphoses*.

The disconnected narrative structure of the *Metamorphoses* and the *Fasti* scarcely attracted the attention of dramatists, but individual episodes proved an inspiration to the writers of librettos. The first work that could be classified as an opera in the modern sense was Jacopo Peri's *Dafne*, with a libretto by Ottavio Rinuccini, which was performed before a private audience in Florence in approximately 1597. Daphne's story was often set to music thereafter, most notably by George Frideric Handel in his cantata "La terra è liberata: Apollo e Dafne" in 1710 and by Richard Strauss in his one-act opera *Daphne*, which debuted in Dresden in 1938. Most recently Ovid was brought to the Broadway stage in the imaginative production *Metamorphoses* by Mary Zimmerman, which premiered in 1996, consisting of a series of vignettes taken from Ovid's poem, all of them focusing on the theme of change.

# LIVY

### (Titus Livius, 59 B.C.–A.D. 17)

LIVY WAS BORN INTO A WEALTHY FAMILY IN PADUA, NEAR VENICE, NORTH OF THE river Po, in 59 B.C., when Padua was the most prosperous city in northern Italy. He probably died there, in A.D. 17; a tombstone found near Padua commemorates Titus Livius, his two sons, and his wife, Cassia Prima, and may well refer to him. We know very little about Livy personally. On the one hand, we are told that his readings from his work were not well attended; on the other hand, the younger Pliny asks (*Letters* 2.3.8), with a clear hint of envy, "Have you never read about the man from Cadiz [in southern Spain] who was so impressed by the name and fame of the historian Livy that he came from the farthest region of the world just to look at him, and went straight back home as soon as he had done so?"

Livy's fame rests entirely on his massive history *From the Foundation of the City* (*Ab Urbe Condita*, abbreviated *AUC*), tracing the history of Rome from its beginnings to 9 B.C. Starting within a year or so of the decisive Battle of Actium, fought on September 2, 31 B.C., which gave Octavian sole control of the Roman Empire, Livy devoted almost his whole career to the work, producing a total of 142 books, at an average rate of rather more than 3 books per year. If it was Livy himself who arranged the work in groups of 5 or 10 books, he presumably intended to write several more. Only a quarter of the *AUC* has survived, Books 1 through 10 and 21 through 45 (with major gaps in 41 and 43–45), a total of just over half a million words. The rest is lost beyond reasonable hope of recovery, though tantalizing finds are very occasionally made. In 1772, about 1,000 words of Book 91 were identified in a manuscript in the Vatican Library and, throughout the last century, scholars' hopes have continued to be fed with scraps of Egyptian papyri containing previously unknown texts of Livy, most notably about forty words from Book 11, published in 1986, and fragmentary epitomes of Books 37 through 40 and 48 through 55. These epitomes were part of an abridgment of the whole work made soon after Livy's death. That abridged version has also been mostly lost, but it was itself abridged, and this second abridgment does survive, almost intact, as the *Periochae* (Summaries), which give at least a bare outline of the contents of each book. They vary in length from several hundred words to a mere eighteen words for Books 135 and 138 (while those for the two intervening books are entirely lost).

The *mos maiorum* (ways of the ancestors) was a guiding principle in Roman life. By the Augustan Age, however, there was a widespread conviction that a return to the old ways was no longer attainable, for all that it was a prerequisite to stopping the decay in society. Livy expresses this pessimistic view very forcefully in his *Preface,* and it can be matched in other writers of the time. Horace, for example, says with admirable brevity: "Our parents were not the men their fathers were, and they bore children worse than themselves, whose children will be baser still" (*Odes* 3.6.46–48).

Ovid, true to form, has a different perspective: "The good old days indeed! I am, thanks be, this age's child: it's just the age for me (lit. 'for my *mores*')." He says this in the *Art of Love,* the poem that contributed to his being exiled by Augustus, who was determined to put a halt to modern decadence.

The *AUC* is full of moral tales. The story of Lucretia, at the end of Book 1, is a particularly famous example. Lucretia was the model for Roman women to aspire to follow. Epitaphs typically praise the virtues she displayed. For example, on her sarcophagus a well-to-do woman in the early second century A.D. is praised for her woolwork, much like Livy's Lucretia (*Corpus of Latin Inscriptions* 6.11602): "Here lies Amymone, the excellent and very beautiful wife [daughter?] of Marcius; she was devoted, decent, thrifty, chaste, a woman who sat at home and worked her wool." Augustus had the women of his household taught how to spin and weave (Suetonius, *Life of Augustus* 64), a rather forlorn attempt to instill in them the traditional virtues of Roman womanhood. He could not reverse modern ways even within his own family, and eventually he had both his daughter and his granddaughter exiled to lonely islands for breaking the laws against adultery that he himself had introduced. Ovid is again cheerfully out of step with official policy on morality: "I'm put off by a woman who offers herself to me because she has to, and thinks impassively about her wool" (*Art of Love* 2.685–86).

Since Livy was occupied through so much of Augustus's reign with teaching Romans the lessons of history, and since Augustus himself was a masterly manipulator of propaganda to bolster his power, it is inevitable that we should consider the relationship between the emperor and the leading

**Figure 17:   Titian,** *Lucretia and Tarquinius*
Titian's canvas, which was probably completed for Philip II of Spain (ca. 1571), emphasizes the violence of Tarquin's assault on Lucretia, as she vainly attempts to hold him off.

historian of the age. Tacitus observes that "Titus Livius, who enjoys an outstanding reputation for his style and reliability, gave such high praise to Gnaeus Pompey that Augustus called him 'the Pompeian', and that had no effect on their friendship" (*Annals* 4.34). He is contrasting the sinister period of treason trials under Tiberius; in A.D. 25, a historian was condemned for praising Brutus and Cassius, the assassins of Julius Caesar. Augustus, by contrast, was prepared to allow open discussion of the political events that led to the overthrow of the Republic. This tolerant attitude may be compared to Caesar's: when Pompey's statues were thrown down by the victorious Caesarian faction, Caesar ordered them to be restored, a generous act that Cicero said did more for his reputation than the erection of statues of himself (Plutarch, *Life of Cicero* 40). (The poignancy of Caesar's assassination in the shadow of one of these statues was not lost on contemporaries.) It is further indicative of Augustus's open-mindedness that he entrusted to Livy the education of the future emperor Claudius; since, however, he had no plans to allow Claudius a political career, this may not be so very significant. Since the surviving books deal with earlier periods, they do not give much scope for Livy to show his "Pompeianism" and his divergence from the version of history promulgated by Augustus. Such sentiments will have featured most prominently in the last fifty books or so, which recount the last generation of the Republic and the rise of Augustus himself, but we know very little about the views he expressed in those books, for they are almost totally lost.

Other than in Book 1, which covers such a long period, Livy generally arranges his material on a simple and convenient year-by-year basis, the annalistic method (from the Latin *annus*, "year"). First, he records the consuls who gave their names to the year; by this system, the assassination of Caesar on March 15, 44 B.C., would be described as taking place in the year of the consulship of Gaius Julius Caesar for the fifth time and Marcus Antonius. Then he recounts external events of that year; in the surviving books, this is mostly about war. Then he discusses political events in Rome itself. Finally, he lists, usually very briefly, other significant events in that year, such as omens, plagues, and famine. This last section was very significant to the Romans, for they believed that extraordinary occurrences might indicate divine wrath and require expiation. Accordingly, public records were kept of all such prodigies as occurred in a particular year. In the fourth or fifth century A.D., Julius Obsequens compiled a list of these phenomena for the years 249–11 B.C., drawing for the most part on the lost books of Livy. For example (*Book of Prodigies* 43): "In the consulship of Gaius Marius and Gaius Flavius [104 B.C.]. A cow talked.... In Lucania it rained milk, at Luna blood.... Two lambs were born with the hooves of a horse, another with the head of a monkey. Near Tarquinii streams of milk gushed up from the ground."

It is reasonable to assume that Livy's account of the first century B.C. will have been dominated by political events of each year, no less than by military campaigns, as he narrated the struggles for power in the various civil wars that blighted that century. As it is, however, we have only the earlier books, in many of which war is almost his only theme. At the start of Book 6, he frets that his readers will be tired of his accounts of the constant wars (6.12), but he is rather more assertive when he asks in Book 10 (10.31), "What sort of person could be irritated with writing or reading about all these long wars, when they did not exhaust those who actually fought them?"

That warfare should dominate Roman history is inevitable, for Rome was a very militaristic state, fighting for centuries for its survival, whether against neighboring states or, in a wider context, against Carthage. The Latin phrase *domi militiaeque,* "at home and on military service," reflects the limits of Rome's engagement with the outside world in the early centuries: the only place for Romans to meet foreigners was on the battlefield. All that Livy can find to say about 429 B.C., when there were no wars, is "The next consuls were Lucius Sergius Fidenas for the second time and Hostus Lucretius Triciputinus. Nothing of note occurred under these men" (4.30). The Romans boasted that they never fought an unjust war, but the reality was that they might even seek out reasons to fight so as to keep their military skills finely tuned. In reporting that both consuls waged war against them in 187

B.C., Livy describes the Ligurians in northern Italy as an enemy whose role was to maintain Roman military discipline in the intervals between more significant wars (39.1).

Livy states in the *Preface*: "I do not doubt that Rome's foundation and early years will bring less pleasure to the majority of my readers, who will want to press on to recent times." This assumption, that Rome's more recent history is more interesting, will surprise some modern readers. Even some historians who specialize in the study of Livy have been known to regret that Books 31 through 45 have survived, rather than almost any other later books, for the content of these books, dealing largely with the conquest of Greece in the second century B.C., is often not particularly interesting or inspiring. Nor is greater interest in the later books reflected in the survival of the text. There are nearly two hundred manuscripts of the first decade (i.e., Books 1–10), whereas there is only one manuscript containing what survives of Books 41 through 45, written in Italy in the early fifth century and left unnoticed and uncopied in a German monastery from the ninth century until 1527.

The *AUC* is remarkably imbalanced. Aeneas was generally thought to antedate Romulus by some seventeen generations, and the seven kings ruled Rome for almost two and a half further centuries. Livy deals with this whole vast period in just one book. At the beginning of Book 31, he notes that he has devoted as much space to the sixty-three years from the outbreak of the First Punic War to the end of the Second as he had to all Rome's earlier years, from the earliest times to the beginning of the First Punic War (i.e., fifteen books to each period). He compares himself to someone tempted by the shallows at the sea's edge to wade out into ever deeper waters. The remaining 193 years of the *AUC* were to occupy a further 112 books, and the period covered by each book diminishes yet further as Livy comes closer to his own time: the last forty years, from the outbreak of the civil war in 49 B.C., were treated in 33 books.

It is not, of course, only the presumed greater interest of more recent times that accounts for the imbalance in the arrangement of the *AUC*. As Livy frequently complains, lack of reliable evidence makes it difficult or impossible to give a full and authoritative account of events in Rome's early days. The Fight of the Triplets (1.24–25) is a good example. For all that this story was so famous, Livy comments: "Tradition agrees on their names, the Horatii and the Curiatii, and there is scarcely a better known episode from antiquity. Still, in an episode so famous there is uncertainty as to which nation the Horatii belonged and to which the Curiatii. There are authorities in support of both beliefs, but I find that the majority identify the Horatii as Roman, and I am inclined to follow them." Especially since, in stark contrast to Greece, Rome has almost no mythology and very few semihistorical legends, Livy's admission of ignorance about the names of the protagonists in such a cherished story may seem startling to the modern reader. It accords, however, with his general attitude to Rome's early history, as briskly stated in the *Preface*.

Since Livy is a moralist, intent on instilling in his readers a pride in their past, it is understandable that he should present the stories he tells in a favorable light for Rome. His is the best-known account of the heroic exploit of Horatius Cocles and his two comrades, Spurius Larcius and Titus Herminius, who kept a vast army at bay when the Etruscan king Lars Porsenna attacked Rome in the late sixth century. They guarded the narrow approach to the only bridge across the Tiber while the rest of the population broke it down (2.10). At the last moment, the other two ran back across the bridge. Horatius, after praying to the Tiber, jumped into the river in full armor and swam back safely to his family and friends. That is Livy's story, but the earliest surviving version forgoes the happy ending by having Horatius drown in the Tiber (Polybius, *Histories* 6.55). Even when telling a story to the Romans' discredit, Livy still manages to give it a patriotic twist. For example, in concluding his account of the execution of Mettius Fufetius, the king of Alba Longa, for disloyalty to Rome, he observes, "This was the first and last time the Romans meted out such uncivilized punishment; in all other cases they are entitled to boast that no other people have punished wrongdoing in a more humane way" (1.28). We are not to recall that, for example, just a few years before Livy's birth, six thousand slaves captured in the suppression of Spartacus's revolt were crucified along the road between Capua and Rome.

# FROM THE FOUNDATION OF THE CITY

## The Preface

*It was an established practice, going back to Herodotus and Thucydides, for the historian to begin with a preface to his work, setting out its scope and purpose and explaining his own approach to writing history. Livy is here engaging in a dialogue with his predecessor Sallust and offers a different view of the course of Roman history, one in which the corrupting influences of greed and ambition are not an entirely recent phenomenon. Much of what he says here about the escapist appeal of early history is strictly relevant only to the beginning of his work, and presumably he had more to say on recent history in later books that are now lost.*

Whether in writing the history of the Roman people from the foundation of the city the result will be worth the effort invested, I do not really know (nor, if I did, would I presume to say so), for I realize that this is a time-honored task that many have undertaken, each succeeding writer thinking he will either bring greater accuracy to the facts or surpass his unpolished predecessors in artistry and style. However that may be, it will still be a source of satisfaction to celebrate to the best of my ability the history of the greatest nation on earth; and if in this throng of writers my own fame should be eclipsed, I will console myself with the thought of the nobility and greatness of those who overshadow my own.

What is more, the task is immense, since Rome's history stretches back over seven hundred years and since the state has now grown so large from small beginnings that it struggles under the incubus of its own great size. Moreover, I do not doubt that Rome's foundation and early years will bring less pleasure to the majority of my readers, who will want to press on to recent times, in the course of which the strength of a mighty people has long been bent on its own undoing. I on the other hand shall regard as an additional reward of my labor the opportunity to turn away from the sight of the evils that our age has witnessed for so many years and, for the bit of time my full attention is fixed on those early days, to be wholly free from the anxiety that may assail a writer's mind, although it cannot deflect it from the truth.

Events before the city was founded or planned, which have been handed down more as pleasing poetic fictions than as reliable records of historical events, I intend neither to affirm nor to refute. To antiquity we grant the indulgence of making the origins of cities more impressive by commingling the human with the divine, and if any people should be permitted to sanctify its inception and reckon the gods as its founders, surely the glory of the Roman people in war is such that, when it boasts Mars in particular as its parent and the parent of its founder, the nations of the world would as easily acquiesce in this claim as they do in our rule.

Yet I attach no great importance to how these and similar traditions will be criticized or valued. My wish is that each reader will pay the closest attention to the following; how men lived, what their moral principles were, under what leaders and by what measures at home and abroad our empire was won and extended; then let him follow in his mind how, as discipline broke down bit by bit, morality at first foundered; how it next subsided in ever greater collapse and then began to topple headlong in ruin—until the advent of our own age, in which we can endure neither our vices nor the remedies needed to cure them.

The special and salutary benefit of the study of history is to behold evidence of every sort of behavior set forth as on a splendid memorial; from it you may select for yourself and for your country what to emulate, from it what to avoid, whether basely begun or basely concluded. Yet either the love of the task I have set myself deceives me or there has never been any state grander, purer, or richer in good examples, or one into which greed and luxury gained entrance so late, or where great respect was accorded for so long to small means and frugality—so much so that the less men possessed, the less they coveted. Recently wealth has brought greed in its train, manifold amusements have led to people's obsession with ruining themselves and with consuming all else through excess and self-indulgence.

But complaints, which will not be pleasing even at a later time when they will perhaps be necessary, should at least be banished from the commencement of such a great undertaking. Rather, if we were to adopt the practice of poets, we would more gladly begin with good omens, and with vows and prayers to the gods and goddesses that they may grant us success as we embark upon this vast enterprise.

## Book 1

### The Foundation of Rome (1–16)

*In the first part of the book Livy relates events from the fall of Troy to the foundation of Rome and the death and deification of Romulus as the god Quirinus. Livy is here negotiating the conflicting traditions that identified both the Trojan exile Aeneas and Romulus as founding figures, a problem that was solved by the invention of a list of kings of Alba Longa, descended from Aeneas, whose reigns spanned the four hundred years separating the fall of Troy from the traditional date of Rome's founding in 753 B.C.*

[1] There is general agreement, first of all, that when Troy fell the Greeks punished the other Trojans mercilessly but refrained from exercising any right of conquest in the cases of two men, Aeneas and Antenor, who were connected to them by long-standing ties of guest-friendship and had always advocated the return of Helen. Thereafter Antenor, having experienced various twists of fortune, penetrated to the furthest reaches of the Adriatic Sea with a large group of Eneti who had been driven by civil strife from Paphlagonia and had been seeking both a place to settle and a new leader after the death of their king Pylaemenes before Troy. The combined Eneti and Trojans expelled the Euganei, who inhabited the district between the Adriatic and the Alps, and occupied their territory. The spot where they first disembarked is now called Troy, the district thereabouts Trojan; the people as a whole were called Veneti.

Aeneas by a similar misfortune had been driven as a refugee from his homeland, although in his case the fates had destined him for the initiation of far greater things. He first went to Macedonia and then to Sicily in search of a place to settle; from Sicily he steered his ships to Laurentine territory, which today also bears the name of Troy. There the Trojans disembarked and began to plunder the area, since after nearly limitless wanderings they possessed nothing but their arms and ships. King Latinus and the Aborigines, who inhabited the territory in those days, rushed together in arms from the city and surrounding countryside to repel the attack of the strangers.

There are two versions of what happened next. Some say that Latinus was defeated in an actual battle and made peace with Aeneas, offering him a marriage alliance as well. Others say that, when the battle lines had been drawn up but before the trumpets sounded the attack, Latinus stepped from the front ranks and invited the leader of these strangers to talk matters over. He asked what manner of men they were, where they had come from, by what misfortune they had left their homeland, and what their intentions were in entering Laurentine territory. When he learned that

they were Trojans and that their leader was Aeneas, son of Anchises and Venus, and that, since their native land had been put to the torch, they were now exiles seeking a place to found a city, he was much impressed by the fame of both people and leader and by their spirit, prepared as they were for war or peace. He extended his right hand and pledged future friendship. Thereupon the two leaders struck a treaty, while the two armies saluted one another. Aeneas, the story continues, became a guest of Latinus in his home, where the king before his household gods added a personal alliance to the public one by giving Aeneas his daughter in marriage. This act in particular bolstered the Trojans' hope that at long last they had reached a permanent and secure end of their wanderings. They founded a town which Aeneas named Lavinium after Lavinia, his wife. The new union quickly produced a male child, to whom his parents gave the name Ascanius.

[2] War was what the Aborigines and Trojans jointly faced next. Because Turnus, king of the Rutuli, to whom Lavinia had been betrothed prior to Aeneas' arrival, was angry that an outsider had been preferred to himself, he took up arms against Aeneas and Latinus together. Neither side emerged from the fight unscathed. The Rutuli were defeated; the Aborigines and Trojans, although victorious, lost their leader Latinus. At this point Turnus and the rest of the Rutuli, no longer trusting to their own resources, appealed to the flourishing Etruscan nation and to Mezentius their king, who ruled the then prosperous city of Caere. From the very beginning Mezentius had been unhappy with the founding of the new city; he was now convinced that the power of the Trojans was growing far too fast for the safety of the neighboring peoples. He therefore had no hesitation in forming a joint alliance with the Rutuli.

In face of the fear generated by the prospect of such a war, Aeneas wished to win the loyalty of the Aborigines by letting them enjoy the same rights as the Trojans and, what is more, by uniting the two peoples under a common name. So it was that he called them both Latins, thereby making the Aborigines henceforth as dedicated and loyal to Aeneas as were the Trojans. It was on this new spirit of the two peoples, who he could see were becoming more united day by day, that Aeneas was relying when he decided to lead them into the field to do battle, although he could have defended himself from behind the city walls; and he did this despite the fact that Etruria was then so powerful that its fame had filled both land and sea throughout the entire length of Italy, from the Alps to the Sicilian strait. The battle that ensued went well for the Latins, but for Aeneas it was his last mortal act. He is buried, whether he should be called man or god, on the banks of the Numicus River. Men call him Jupiter Indiges.

[3] Aeneas' son Ascanius was not yet old enough to take over as ruler. Nevertheless the kingdom survived intact for him until he grew to maturity because of Lavinia's guardianship, for she was an able woman; in the interval before he came of age she preserved for her son the Latin community and the throne that his grandfather and father had held. I will not debate—for who could establish the truth of a matter so ancient?—whether the boy in question was this Ascanius or an older brother, born to Creusa before the fall of Troy and a companion of his father in his flight, the same one that the Julian family calls Iulus and claims as its founder. This Ascanius, wherever born and from whatever mother (certainly it is agreed that Aeneas was his father), handed over to his mother—or stepmother—Lavinium, which now had a surplus population and was prosperous and wealthy, as things were reckoned in that age, while he himself founded a new city at the base of Mount Alba, which, because it stretched out along a ridge, he called Alba Longa.

About thirty years intervened between the founding of Lavinium and of its colony Alba Longa. Even so, their resources had grown so great—especially after the defeat of the Etruscans—that not even the death of Aeneas or the succeeding regency of Lavinia or the apprenticeship of the young king sufficed to provoke Mezentius and the Etruscans or other neighboring peoples into making any hostile moves. Peace terms had fixed the Albula River, which is now known as the Tiber, as the boundary between Etruscans and Latins.

Silvius, son of Ascanius, was the next ruler, born by some accident in a silvan setting. He begot Aeneas Silvius, he in turn Latinus Silvius, who was the one who sent out a number of colonies called the Ancient Latins. Henceforth Silvius was the last name of all kings at Alba. To Latinus Alba was born, to Alba Atys, to Atys Capys, to Capys Capetus, to Capetus Tiberinus, who drowned in crossing the Albula River and gave to the river what was to become a famous name among posterity. Next came Agrippa, son of Tiberinus. After Agrippa, Romulus Silvius succeeded to his father's throne. He was killed by a lightning bolt and left the kingdom to his successor Aventinus, who in turn was buried on that hill which is now part of the city of Rome and bears his name. Proca was the next king. He begot Numitor and Amulius and left the ancient kingdom of the Silvian family to Numitor, the elder son. But violence had a greater effect than the wish of the father or respect for seniority. Amulius expelled his brother and seized the throne. He added a second crime to the first: he killed his brother's male issue and, under the pretext of honoring the daughter Rhea Silvia, made her a Vestal, thus depriving her of hope of children by the constraint of perpetual virginity.

[4] But in my view the fates ordained the founding of this great city and the beginning of the world's mightiest empire, second only to the power of the gods. For when the Vestal, having been ravished, became the mother of twin sons, she named Mars as the father of her dubious progeny, either because she thought he really was the father or because naming a god as the one responsible for her transgression made a more respectable story. Yet no divine or human power saved her or her offspring from the king's cruelty. He ordered that the priestess be taken into custody and put in chains, and the twins to be set out on the river where the current flowed strongly. By some providential accident the Tiber had overflowed its banks, forming quiet shallows that made approach to the river's regular channel impossible. Those who were ordered to expose the babies hoped that they would be drowned no matter how weak the current. And so, as if they were carrying out the king's command, they exposed the twins at the edge of the floodland where the Ruminalis fig tree now stands (tradition says it was formerly called the Romularis).

In those days the area was wild and desolate. Legend has it that when the receding water left the basket in which the boys had been placed on a dry patch of ground, a thirsty she-wolf from the surrounding mountains headed toward the sound of their crying; so gently did she lower her teats for them to nurse that the king's chief herdsman came upon her licking the babes with her tongue (Faustulus is said to have been his name). He carried the babies back to the sheepfold for his wife Larentia to rear. There are people who fancy that the shepherds used to call Larentia "She-wolf" because of her sexual promiscuity and that this was how the miraculous tale originated.

So were the boys born and so were they brought up. As soon as they had matured, they proved to be energetic young men, who, after finishing their chores around the sheepfold and out in the pastures, used to roam the forests for game. These activities so strengthened them in body and spirit that they would not only confront wild beasts but attack robbers laden with loot, which they would seize and share among the shepherds. With them the lads enjoyed their days together at work and at play, while the number of young men joining them increased day by day.

[5] In those days, according to legend, the present festive rite of the Lupercal was already in existence on the Palatine hill, which received its name from Pallanteum, an Arcadian city, later altered to Palatium. Once upon a time Evander had dwelt there, who was a native Arcadian and had brought from there the custom in which naked young men would cavort about in antic fashion in worship of Lycaean Pan, whom the Romans later called Inuus. The robbers, who knew when the festival was set to occur and who were angry at having lost their loot, ambushed the young men as they were caught up in the festivities. Romulus defended himself by fighting back, but Remus was captured. They took their captive to King Amulius, even going so far as to bring charges against him. The accusation they stressed the most was that the brothers had begun by poaching on Numitor's lands and had ended by plundering them with an organized band of youths like an invading enemy. Remus was therefore bound over to Numitor for punishment.

Now Faustulus from the very beginning had expected that the twins he was raising would prove to be of royal blood, since he knew that infants had been exposed by command of the king and that the date he had found them coincided with that command. But he had not wanted to reveal the situation prematurely unless a favorable opportunity arose or necessity intervened. Necessity came first. Under the stimulus of fear he revealed the situation to Romulus. It chanced that Numitor, too, when he heard from Remus, whom he was holding in custody, that he had a twin brother, and when he compared their ages with the time of exposure and their noble characters with that of the low-born, was set to thinking of his grandsons. By dint of close questioning he in the end was coming quite close to recognizing who Remus really was. And so on all sides a trap was laid for the king. Romulus ordered the shepherds not to approach the palace in a single group—for he was not equal to such an open display of force—but to split up and come by separate routes at a time agreed upon. This was how he attacked Amulius, while from

Numitor's dwelling Remus also helped with another party he had gathered. So it was that Romulus slew the king.

[6] When the uproar was in its early stages Numitor repeatedly insisted that a foreign enemy had invaded the city and had attacked the palace, thereby drawing off the soldiers of Alba to the citadel on the pretext of securing it with an armed guard; but after the murder, when he saw the young men hastening to him to offer their congratulations, he at once called an assembly in which he revealed his brother's crimes against himself, the origin of his grandsons—how they were born, raised, and recognized—and, finally, the murder of the tyrant king, a deed for which he assumed responsibility. The twins with their fighters then marched in through the middle of the assembly and saluted their grandfather as king. The multitude shouted its unanimous assent, thereby confirming Numitor's title and authority.

Now that Alba had passed into Numitor's hands, Romulus and Remus conceived the desire of founding a city in the place where they had been exposed and raised. In fact, the population of Alba and the Latins had greatly increased; in addition, there were the shepherds who had flocked to them, all of whom taken together readily raised the expectation that both Alba and Lavinium would be small in comparison to the city they intended to found. But at this point the family curse—the desire for kingly supremacy—came between them as they were making their plans, and from an innocent beginning developed an ugly fight. Because they were twins no distinction could be made between them on the basis of age. In order that the deities who presided over the area might choose by augury who should give his name to the new city and rule it once it was founded, Romulus occupied the Palatine and Remus the Aventine to mark out the sacred areas where they would look for the signs of heaven's will. [7] To Remus augury came first, legend says: six vultures. After this had been reported to the people, double the number appeared for Romulus. Accordingly, the supporters of each man hailed their candidate as king, one side claiming the sovereignty because of the priority of time, the other because of the number of birds. From a war of words anger turned them to bloodshed. In the heat of the melee Remus met his death. The more common story is that in mockery of his brother's claim Remus jumped over the half-built walls, whereupon the enraged Romulus struck him down, crying "So be it for any other who overleaps my walls!" Romulus thus became sole sovereign and gave his name to the city so founded.

He first fortified the Palatine, where he had spent his boyhood. To the other gods he instituted religious rites in accordance with Alban ritual, but in the Greek manner to Hercules, as Evander had ordained. The tale goes that Hercules, after slaying Geryon, drove the monster's magnificent cattle to this spot, and after swimming across Tiber's stream, driving the kine before him, he lay down on a grassy bank so that this serene setting with its lush pasturage might refresh his cattle and himself, exhausted as he was from his journey. As slumber stole over him, heavy with food and drink, a native shepherd named Cacus, a creature of ferocious strength, was much taken by the beauty of the beasts: he wanted them for himself. But if he drove off the herd and forced it to enter his cave, the hoofmarks would point their inquiring owner in his direction. What to do? So it was that he selected the handsomest bulls, turned them around and dragged them into the cave by their tails. When the first flush of dawn roused Hercules from sleep and his gaze swept over the herd, he realized that some of them were missing. He headed for the nearest cave to see if perchance their tracks might direct him there. But when he saw that all hoof prints pointed away from the cave and nowhere else, befuddled and uneasy, he began to drive the herd away from the alien spot. At this point certain of the heifers, as they were moving off, mooed because they missed, as is natural, the males left behind. The bulls shut up in the cave lowed in response, and Hercules turned back. When Cacus saw him striding toward his cave he tried to resist by force, but, smitten by the hero's club and calling in vain for help from his fellow shepherds, he expired.

In those days Evander, a refugee from the Peloponnesus, ruled this area more by personal influence than real power. He was revered for his ability to write, a new and miraculous skill among ignorant men, and revered even more because of his mother Carmenta, whom the natives believed to be divine and whom they held in awe for her prophetic power in the period before the Sibyl arrived in Italy. At this point in the fracas, then, Evander was summoned by the agitated shepherds as they crowded about the stranger, whom they had caught in the very act of murder. After listening to what had happened and the reason for it, and after gazing at the stranger, Evander realized that he possessed a figure and bearing rather greater and more august than those of ordinary mortals. He asked what manner of man he was. When he heard his name, father, and birthplace, he exclaimed, "Son of Jupiter— Hercules—welcome! My mother, a true prolocutor of the gods, once foretold to me that you would be added to the number of the deities in heaven and that on this site an altar to you would be dedicated which one day the most flourishing people on earth would call the Greatest Altar and would revere in the conduct of your cult." Hercules, extending his right hand, said he accepted the omen: he would fulfill destiny's decree by building and dedicating the altar.

There a fine heifer from the herd was for the first time sacrificed to Hercules, with two of the most prominent families of the area, the Potitii and Pinarii, being called in to conduct it and to provide a feast. It chanced that since the Potitii were present at the start, the entrails were apportioned to them, while the Pinarii who arrived after the entrails had been eaten received what remained. The custom of not offering the Pinarii the entrails of the sacrifice survived thereafter as long as the family did. The Potitii, whom Evander had instructed in the proper ritual, were for many generations the priests of the sacrifice, but when the family's sacred duties were handed over to public slaves to perform, the clan of the Potitii perished root and branch. This was the only foreign cult that Romulus adopted, who even then honored immortality achieved by virtuous deeds, an honor toward which his own destiny was urging him as well.

[8] After duly carrying out religious observances, Romulus summoned the populace to a meeting to promulgate laws that were essential for the formation of a unified community. He thought that the rustics would feel bound to observe the laws if he made his own person more august and imposing by adopting various insignia of power, both in his dress and particularly by the addition of twelve lictors to accompany him in public. Some think he took this number from the number of augural birds that portended his kingship. I myself incline to the opinion of those who believe that, just as the attendants and other paraphernalia of office were borrowed from the neighboring Etruscans, who gave us the curule chair and the *toga praetexta,* so also the number twelve was borrowed from the lictors the Etruscans furnished to the man they elected king of their league, each of the twelve Etruscan peoples contributing one lictor apiece.

Meanwhile the city's protective walls were continually extended as one area after another was annexed, more in the expectation of a large future population than to defend the inhabitants. In order that the enlarged city might not be empty and weak, he resorted to the time-honored fiction of city founders that the lowly and ignoble folk they attract are children "sprung from the earth." He therefore selected a site for an asylum, which is the enclosed area on the left between the two groves as one descends the Capitol. A motley mob from the neighboring peoples flocked to the spot, with no distinction made as to whether they were free or slave, and all eager for a new start in life. These men were the beginning of the real strength of the city. Satisfied now with the physical power of the citizen body, he next provided it with counsel and guidance. He created one hundred senators, either because this number seemed sufficient or because there were only one hundred suitable to be designated *patres,* or "Fathers." At all events, they were styled *patres* because of their rank; their descendants were called patricians.

[9] Rome by this time was equal to any of the surrounding cities in her prowess in war, but because of the lack of women her greatness would not last beyond a generation: there was no hope of having children at home, and there existed no right of intermarriage with their neighbors. On the advice of the senators Romulus therefore dispatched ambassadors to the surrounding peoples to seek alliance and marriage rights for the young community. The envoys were instructed to argue that cities, like everything else, had humble beginnings, and those that achieved great prosperity were the ones who enjoyed a great name by their own valor and the help of the gods: Rome's neighbors should realize that the gods had been present to bless Rome's foundation and that the valor of the Romans themselves would never fail in the years ahead. In short, let one group of humans not disdain to unite in blood and kinship with another. Nowhere did the envoys receive a sympathetic hearing. The neighboring peoples scorned them, while simultaneously fearing for themselves and their descendants the growing giant in their midst. The envoys were dismissed with the repeated question why they had not also opened up an asylum for women: only this would have provided the sort of brides they deserved! The Roman youth were stung by the insult: it looked as if the situation could be resolved only by the use of force. With this aim in mind (but disguising his resentment) Romulus

purposely instituted games (called the Consualia) in honor of Neptune, patron of horses, which would provide an opportunity and a site to implement his plan. He ordered that announcement of the spectacle be made to the neighboring peoples, while the men at Rome prepared to celebrate the games with as much pageantry as they knew or were capable of in those days, their object being to make the festival widely known and anticipated.

Many a man came to see it, with the additional motive of touring the new city. In particular, Rome's closest neighbors came, the people of Caenina, Crustumerium, and Antemnae; the whole nation of the Sabines arrived as well, accompanied by wives and children. They were hospitably lodged in private homes, and when they viewed the site of the city, with its walls and many houses, they were amazed that it had grown so rapidly in so short a time. The day for the spectacle arrived and, while their eyes and minds were intent on it, a prearranged free-for-all began, with the Roman men scattering at an agreed signal to seize the unmarried girls. Most maidens were carried off as each man chanced upon her, but certain beauties, marked out for the leading senators, were hustled off to their homes by hirelings from the plebeian class. They say that as one lass, who excelled all others in bearing and beauty, was being carried off by a gang belonging to a certain Thalassius, many asked to whom they were bringing her. To prevent any interference the gang kept crying out, "To Thalassius! To Thalassius!" This was the origin of the traditional cry we hear at weddings today.

As the games broke up in confusion and fear, the grieving parents of the maidens ran off, accusing the Romans of violating their sacred obligations as hosts and invoking the god to whose festival and games they had been deceitfully invited contrary to religion and good faith. The abducted maidens had no better hope for their plight than had their parents, nor was their indignation less. But Romulus repeatedly went about in person to visit them, arguing that what had occurred was due to the arrogance of their parents, who had refused intermarriage with their neighbors. Despite this, he promised that they would enjoy the full rights of a proper marriage, becoming partners in all the fortunes the couple might share, in Rome's citizenship, and in the begetting of children, the object dearest to every person's heart. So let them now abate their anger, let them give their hearts to those to whom chance had given their bodies. Often, he said, thankfulness replaces a sense of wrong over the course of time. In fact, their husbands would be even more solicitous than they might expect, because each one would do his utmost both to be a good husband and to fill the void created by the loss of parents and country. To Romulus' entreaties the husbands added their own honeyed words, claiming that they had acted out of desire and love, an avowal calculated to appeal most to a woman's nature.

[10] The abducted maidens were by now much mollified, but not so their parents who, garbed in mourning attire, were at that moment unsettling their fellow citizens with tears and protestations. They did not restrict their expression of outrage to their own cities, but flocked from all sides to the king of the Sabines, Titus Tatius. Official delegations came as well, since his reputation was the greatest in the region. Now some of the daughters of the peoples of Caenina, Crustumerium, and Antemnae had also been abducted, but to the men of these cities Tatius and his Sabines seemed too slow in retaliating. The three communities therefore prepared to wage a joint war on their own. Yet not even Crustumerium and Antemnae acted fast enough to suit the ardor and anger of the people of Caenina, who invaded Roman territory on their own. Romulus came upon them with his army as they were widely scattered in their plundering and in a quick fight demonstrated that anger without strength goes for nothing. He routed their army, put it to flight, and pursued it as it scattered. He slew their king in battle and stripped the corpse of its armor; when their king had been lost, the city fell to Romulus at the first assault.

Romulus returned in triumph with his army, and, being an extraordinary man in his ability to publicize his achievements no less than in his execution of them, mounted the Capitol bearing the spoils of the slain enemy hung on a frame built for the purpose, and there, after he had propped it against an oak tree sacred to the shepherds, he marked out the boundaries of a temple to Jupiter, invoking him with a new title: "Jupiter Feretrius! I, Romulus, victor and king, bring to you these armaments of a king, and on this site I vow to build a temple that I have just now marked out in my mind, a place for dedicating the spoils of honor, which later leaders, following my example, will offer you after slaying kings and leaders of our enemies." This was the origin of the first temple that was consecrated at Rome. In the years that followed the gods saw to it that these words of the temple's founder concerning future

dedications of the spoils did not go unfulfilled, and at the same time that the honor would not be cheapened by many earning it. Only twice since have the spoils of honor been won, despite so many wars over so many years. The good fortune of attaining such distinction has been rare indeed.

[11] While the Romans were engaged at Caenina, the army of Antemnae took advantage of their absence by invading Roman territory. A legion hastily marched out from Rome against them as well and defeated them as they roamed the countryside. The battle-cry raised at the first charge was enough to put them to flight; subsequently the town itself fell. Romulus' wife Hersilia, yielding to the importunate entreaties of the abducted maidens, begged him as he returned flushed with his double victory to pardon their parents and to grant them citizenship: the state, she argued, could thereby grow in strength and concord. Romulus gave his ready consent.

The people of Crustumerium then began hostilities. When he marched out against them he encountered even less resistance: their own resolution had collapsed in face of the defeat of the others. Colonies were sent to both places, although more volunteers for Crustumerium were found because of the fertile soil. On the other hand many migrated from there to Rome, especially the parents and relatives of the abducted girls.

The war with the Sabines came last in the series, and it proved the greatest by far, for they did not act out of anger or greed, nor even give a hint of their intention before commencing hostilities. They also made subterfuge a part of their strategy. Spurius Tarpeius was in command of the citadel at Rome. Tatius induced Spurius' virgin daughter by a bribe of gold to admit his armed men into the citadel; at that time she used to go beyond the fortifications to seek water for performance of her religious duties. Once admitted they crushed her under the weight of their weapons either so that the citadel might appear to have been captured by force or to set an example for the future that no one should ever keep faith with a traitor. Another legend has it that because the Sabines regularly wore heavy gold bracelets on their left arms and had splendid jeweled rings, she bargained for what they wore "on their left arms"; accordingly they heaped upon her not gifts of gold but the very shields they were carrying. A third variant is that according to the agreement of surrender she asked for the actual weapons they had in their left hands and, because she seemed to be trying to disarm them by trickery, was killed by the very reward she had asked for.

[12] However it came about, the Sabines had gained control of the citadel. On the next day the Roman army was drawn up, filling the area between the Palatine and Capitoline hills, but before the Sabines descended to level ground, anger and a desire to retake the citadel emboldened the Romans to mount an uphill attack. The commanders of each side led the fray, Mettius Curtius for the Sabines, Hostius Hostilius for the Romans. With *élan* and daring Hostilius placed himself in the front rank and pressed the Roman charge up the steep slope, but when he fell, the Roman line immediately broke and fell back to the ancient gate of the Palatine. Even Romulus was carried along in the crush of those fleeing. Lifting his weapons to the heavens he cried, "Jupiter, the augural birds you sent commanded me to lay the first foundations of our city here on the Palatine. The Sabines have now bribed their way into control of the citadel; from there in battle array they have won the valley between the two hills and are now upon us. I beg you, father of gods and men, prevent the foe at least from seizing *this* spot. Banish Roman fear, stay their shameful flight! Here I vow a temple to you, Jupiter the Stayer, which shall be a reminder to posterity that the city was saved by your very present help." And then, as if he had an intimation that his prayer had been heard, he cried, "On this spot, Romans, Jupiter Optimus Maximus bids us make our stand and renew the fight!" The Romans obeyed as if directed by a voice from heaven. Romulus himself rushed to the front line.

Meanwhile Mettius Curtius, the Sabine leader, had plunged down from the citadel, driving the Romans in confusion before him over the entire area of the present forum. Not far from the gate to the Palatine he cried, "We have vanquished treacherous hosts and a faint-hearted host: they now realize it is one thing to abduct young girls and another to fight with men!" Romulus with a band of the most mettlesome of the Roman youth attacked him in the very act of making this boast. Mettius happened at that moment to be fighting from horseback; it was therefore all the easier to put him to flight. The Romans pursued him as he fled, while the rest of their force, inspired by their intrepid king, routed the Sabines. When his horse took fright from the clamor of those in pursuit Mettius was plunged into a swampy area. The plight of their great leader caused the fleeing Sabines to wheel about and to fight back. The shouts and gestures of his many supporters gave Mettius added heart; he succeeded in extricating himself, but when the two sides renewed the general fight in the valley between the two hills the Roman forces gradually began to get the upper hand.

[13] It was at this moment that the Sabine women, whose abduction had caused the war, boldly interposed themselves amid the flying spears. Their misfortunes overcame womanish fear: with hair streaming and garments rent, they made a mad rush from the sidelines, parting the battling armies and checking their angry strife. Appealing to fathers on one side and husbands on the other, they declared that kin by marriage should not defile themselves with impious carnage, nor leave the stain of blood upon descendants of their blood, grandfathers upon grandsons, fathers upon children. "If you cannot abide the ties between you that our marriage has created, turn your anger against us. We are the cause of this war, we the cause of husbands and fathers lying wounded and slain. Only one side can win this fight. As for us, it is better to die than to live, for we must do so either as widows or as orphans." Their appeal moved both leaders and the rank and file: silence and a sudden hush fell upon the field.

The commanders then came forward to strike a treaty by which they not only made peace but united the two peoples in a single community. They elected to share the sovereignty, while fixing the seat of government at Rome. As a concession to the Sabines, they styled the doubled population Quirites from the Sabine town of Cures. They called the spot where Curtius' horse had struggled out of the swamp to shallow water the Lacus Curtius, as memorial to the battle.

The sudden shift from the distress of war to the blessings of peace endeared the Sabine women all the more to husbands and parents, and most especially to Romulus. For in dividing the population into thirty wards or *curiae,* he named them after the women. Tradition does not say—since the women were undoubtedly more than thirty in number—whether the names were chosen by lot, age, or according to their own or their husbands' rank. At the same time three centuries of knights were also created, one called Ramnenses from Romulus, and a second Titienses from Titus Tatius; the reason for the name of the third century, Luceres, is uncertain. Henceforth the two kings ruled jointly and in harmony.

[14] Some years later relatives of King Tatius did violence to ambassadors from the Laurentian territory. The injured party protested this violation of international law, but the influence and entreaties of Tatius' own people had greater weight with him. The consequence was that what should have been their punishment became his. For when attending an annual sacrifice at Lavinium, his presence caused an uproar, and he was killed. They say that Romulus was less upset by this than he should have been, either because of the untrustworthy nature of shared sovereignty or because he thought Tatius had been killed for just cause. He did not make a military response, therefore, but renewed the covenant between Rome and Lavinium in order to expiate the violence done to the ambassadors and the king's murder.

On this front, then, an unexpected peace prevailed, but on another—much closer to home and, in fact, at Rome's very gates—war broke out. The men of Fidenae, believing that the growing strength of such a close neighbor was dangerous to themselves, decided to make a pre-emptive strike before Rome should become as powerful as they believed she soon would be. An armed band of young men was dispatched and ravaged the land between Fidenae and Rome; then, because the Tiber barred their way on the right, to the west, they turned left, where they caused a great panic among the country dwellers, whose disorderly flight from the countryside to Rome was the first indication that war was upon them. Since a conflict on his doorstep naturally permitted no delay, Romulus reacted at once by leading out his army and fixing his camp a mile from Fidenae. After leaving a small garrison there, he set out with his entire force, ordering en route a contingent to conceal themselves in ambush in a spot densely overgrown with brushwood; advancing further with the greater part of his army and the whole cavalry, he executed a plan to draw out the astonished enemy by riding up virtually to the city gates in an undisciplined and threatening maneuver. The enemy was less surprised when the horsemen wheeled and retreated, although the retreat was feigned. And, while the cavalry appeared to be hesitating between combat and flight, the foot soldiers too began to fall back. Suddenly the enemy gates were filled with soldiers, who poured out pell-mell and, as the Roman line gave way, were drawn in their eagerness to harry and pursue to the ambuscade. From there the Romans suddenly rose up and attacked the enemy line on its flanks. And when the enemy saw standards advancing toward them, carried by the garrison contingent from the camp, their alarm increased. Terror-stricken by the threat from so many quarters, the army of Fidenae panicked and ran almost before Romulus and his men could rein in their horses and wheel about. Those who had lately been pursuing men pretending flight now found themselves fleeing back to the town, but in a far more chaotic stampede: their panic was genuine. Yet they did not escape. The Romans followed the enemy so closely that both pursuers and pursued burst into the town in a single thrust before the gates could be shut.

[15] War fever then spread from Fidenae to the people of Veii, who were provoked because Fidenae was of the same Etruscan stock as themselves and because their very proximity would, they were sure, be a stimulus to Roman aggression should Rome begin to view all neighbors indiscriminately as enemies. They overran Roman territory as if conducting a raid rather than standard warfare, since they pitched no camp and did not wait for an enemy response. They returned to Veii carrying booty taken from the countryside. The Romans, failing to find the enemy in their territory, crossed the Tiber prepared and eager for a decisive confrontation. When the men of Veii heard that the Romans were pitching camp and would soon be approaching, they sallied forth to decide the issue on the battlefield rather than defend homes and city from within. By brute force and without strategy the Roman king prevailed, using the might of his veteran army alone. He pursued the fleeing enemy to their walls, but did not attack the city itself, protected as it was by great fortifications and a naturally defensive site. On his return he plundered their farmland more to take revenge than for booty. And so it was that Veii, overcome as much by this misfortune as by their defeat on the battlefield, sent envoys to Rome to seek peace. Deprived of part of their territory, they were granted a hundred years' truce.

These were Romulus' chief accomplishments at home and abroad during his reign, none of which was at variance with belief in his divine origin and in the divinity they came to accept after his death—not his valor in recovering his grandfather's kingdom, nor his plan to found the city and to put it on a firm footing in war and peace. He so strengthened the city, in fact, that Rome enjoyed peace and security for the next forty years. Nevertheless, the common people favored him more than did the senators, while the soldiery showed him by far the greatest affection; from them he selected both in war and in peace three hundred armed body-guards whom he called Celeres, or "the Swift."

[16] Such were the earthly deeds of Romulus. One day during a meeting to review his troops on the Campus Martius at the Goat Swamp a sudden storm with mighty thunder-claps enveloped the king in such a dense cloud that the crowd lost sight of him. Nor was Romulus seen again on earth. The fear of the young soldiers at last subsided when the turbulence passed and the light of a calm and sunny day returned. Although they readily believed the senators who had been standing closest that he had been snatched up in the air by a whirlwind, still, as they gazed at the empty throne, they were stricken with the fear of having been orphaned, so to speak, and for quite a time stood in mournful silence. Then, after a few pro-claimed Romulus' divinity, the rest joined in, hailing him with one accord as a god born to a god, king and parent of the city of Rome. They asked in prayer for his favor: that willing and propitious he might safeguard his children evermore.

I believe that even then there were some people who maintained privately that the king had been torn apart by the hands of the senators—for this version, though little known, has also been handed down. Still, admiration for the man and the alarm felt at the time gave the other version wider currency, and it was fur-ther strengthened by the testimony of a single individ-ual. This man was Proculus Iulius, a highly respected citizen according to tradition. To assuage the distress of his fellow citizens at the loss of their king and to combat their hostility to the senators, he stepped forth in a public meeting to affirm the truth of a most extraordinary event. "My fellow citizens," he declared, "today at dawn's first light Romulus, father of our country, descended from heaven without warning and appeared before me. I was drenched in the sweat of fear and I stood rooted to the spot in veneration, praying that it might be lawful for me to be looking upon him. 'Go', he said, 'announce to the Romans that the gods in heaven will my Rome to be the capital of the world. Accordingly, let them cultivate the art of war; let them realize, and let them teach their descendants, that no human power can withstand Roman supremacy'. With these words he rose aloft and disappeared." It is aston-ishing how absolute was the conviction that Proculus Iulius' words carried and how, once belief in Romulus' immortality had been confirmed, the grief felt by the army and people was mitigated.

*In the next five sections Livy tells of the accession of Rome's second king, Numa, and the events of his reign. Under the Republic, Rome found itself from time to time without con-suls, a period that was called "interregnum" when provi-sional authority was exercised by an "interrex." According to tradition, the first interregnum occurred after the death of Romulus and was then followed by the election of Numa Pompilius, a Sabine from the town of Cures. It was symp-tomatic of Roman respect for the ways of the ancestors (mos maiorum) to find precedents for their institutions in the earliest phases of their history. Numerous religious institutions were attributed to the reign of Numa, who may be considered the priest-king who was a natural succes-sor to Romulus, the warrior-king. According to tradition, Rome's next king, Tullus Hostilius, was another warrior, distinguished for his ferocity, as suggested by his name, Hostilius. He is the subject of the next part of our selec-tion (22–28). The signal event of his reign was the capture of Alba, with which were associated the traditional stories of the battle of the champions, the Horatii and Curiatii, and the punishment of Mettius Fufetius, the Alban dictator who betrayed the Romans in battle.*

[22] At Numa's death Rome reverted to an interreg-num. The people then elected Tullus Hostilius king, grandson of that Hostilius who had fought the Sabines so brilliantly in the battle at the foot of the citadel, a choice that the senators then ratified. He was not only unlike his predecessor but even more combative than Romulus: his mettlesome nature was the product of youth, strength, and awareness of his grandfather's prowess. And so, believing the state was becoming weak from inaction, he looked about for opportunities to stir up conflict. It so happened that the country peo-ple from both Rome and Alba were making cattle raids on each other's territory (Gaius Cluilius was then ruler at Alba). Envoys were sent from each city almost simul-taneously to demand restitution. Tullus had told his men to carry out their instructions with dispatch: he well knew the Albans would refuse and that in this way war could in good conscience be declared. The Albans, on the other hand, conducted their business at a leisurely pace: hospitably received by Tullus in ease and good fellowship, they were thoroughly enjoying the king's convivial banquet during the time in which the Roman envoys in quick order demanded satisfac-tion and, when refused, declared war upon the Albans, to begin at the end of a thirty-day period. After they reported back to Tullus, he gave the Albans' envoys permission to state the purpose of their mission, who,

ignorant of what had transpired, hemmed and hawed in apology: they were, they said, reluctant to say anything that might upset such an excellent host, but they were under orders; they had come to seek satisfaction and, if it was not given, they had been commanded to declare war. Tullus replied as follows: "Tell your king that the king of Rome has the gods on his side: they have witnessed which people first rejected envoys seeking restitution and dismissed them. Utter defeat in this war will befall the guilty party."

[23] When the envoys of Alba reported what Tullus had said, each side began to make an all-out effort for a war that would be much like a civil conflict, virtually between parents and children, since both communities were of Trojan descent, Lavinium having been founded by Trojan stock, Alba by Lavinium, and Rome from the line of the Alban kings. The war was nevertheless destined to end with little loss of life, since it was not decided by the opposing armies in a pitched battle: the peoples would be merged into one, with the demolition of only the buildings of one of them.

The Albans were the first to attack, invading Roman territory with a large force. They pitched their camp not more than five miles from the city and surrounded it with a trench, which was long known as the Cluilian trench from the name of Alba's general; but in the course of time both the trench and its name disappeared. It was in this encampment that Cluilius, the Alban king, died; the Albans then elected Mettius Fufetius dictator.

In the meantime Tullus, made particularly combative by the king's death, declared that the power of the gods, which had manifested itself by first striking down the king himself, would soon exact punishment from the entire Alban people for this godless war. Slipping past the enemy's camp by night, he invaded Alban territory. Mettius was thus forced to abandon his position. While taking the most direct route toward the enemy, he sent an envoy on ahead to propose to Tullus that they confer before joining battle; if they did so, he was sure that his proposal would be as much in Rome's interest as in that of Alba. Tullus accepted and drew up his forces in preparation for the parley, even though Mettius' proposal was unlikely to convince. The Albans took up a position facing the Romans.

Accompanied by a few nobles the two leaders met in the area between the two armies. The Alban spoke thus: "Our King Cluilius said, I recollect, that the causes of this war were the wrongs committed and the failure to make restitution according to our treaty, and I do not doubt, Tullus, that this is your officially stated position. But if we are to be frank with one another and not indulge in fair sounding pretexts, we will concede that the desire to dominate one another is provoking our kindred and neighboring cities to go to war. Whether rightly or wrongly is not the issue. That would be a concern for the one who began hostilities: as for myself, the people of Alba have chosen me general simply to prosecute the war. Let me remind you, Tullus, that the Etruscans surround both of us—and you in particular, for you know full well which of the two of us is closer to them, who are even more powerful on the sea than they are on land. Please remember that the moment you give the signal to begin hostilities, they will be looking on as our two sides clash, ready to attack simultaneously the victors and vanquished in their exhaustion and affliction. In heaven's name, let us not risk losing the liberty we now possess by a throw of the dice that will bring enslavement to one of us and supremacy to the other; let us rather find a way that will allow one people to rule the other without both of them suffering crippling losses and much bloodshed." Tullus was not displeased by these words, although he was more combative by nature and confident of victory.

As each side was seeking an answer to this dilemma a solution presented itself for which Fortune herself provided the means of fulfillment. [24] For it chanced that in each army there were three brothers who were triplets, one set very like the other in age and strength. Tradition agrees on their names, the Horatii and the Curiatii, and there is scarcely a better known episode from antiquity. Still, in an episode so famous there is uncertainty as to which nation the Horatii belonged and to which the Curiatii. There are authorities in support of both beliefs, but I find that the majority identify the Horatii as Roman, and I am inclined to follow them.

Their respective kings encouraged the triplets to take up their swords on behalf of their country: to the victorious side would go dominion. They agreed, and a time and place were fixed. But before the fight, a treaty was struck between the Romans and the Albans upon condition that whosesoever champions should prevail, their country would win sovereignty with full consent of the other.

Now treaties differ, as do their terms, but they are all made in the same way. Tradition has it that this treaty, which is the oldest we know of, was made as follows. The fetial priest asked King Tullus, "Do you bid me, O king, to strike a treaty with the *pater patratus* of the Alban people?" When the king so commanded, he said, "I require of you a piece of sacred turf, O king." The king replied, "Take it, free from impurity." The fetial then took up from Rome's citadel a clump of green grass free from impurity. He then asked the king, "Do you, O king, grant me, along with my sacred utensils and attendants, royal sanction to represent the Roman people of the Quirites?" The king replied, "So far as may be done without prejudice to myself and the Roman people of the Quirites, I do." At that time Marcus Valerius was the fetial priest; he made Spurius Fusius *pater patratus* by touching his head and hair with a ceremonial branch.

The *pater patratus* is appointed to pronounce the oath—that is, to solemnize the treaty; he did this in many words that are not worth repeating, since the formula is a long one. After the provisions had been recited, he said, "Hear me, Jupiter; hear me, *pater patratus* of the Alban people; hear me, people of Alba. The Roman people shall not be the first to transgress these stipulations which, inscribed on wood or wax, have been read out without malice aforethought from first to last, and whose meaning is clearly apprehended here and now. If by public decision they should be the first to transgress with malice aforethought, then on that day, Jupiter, may you strike the Roman people as I here and now strike this pig; and may you strike with greater force, just as you are greater in potency and power." When he had said this, he struck the pig with a flint knife. In response the dictator and the *pater patratus* of Alba pronounced a similar formula and oath of their own.

[25] On completion of the treaty the triplets, as had been agreed, took up their arms. Each side cheered on its champions, reminding them that ancestral gods, homeland, and parents, together with all their countrymen at home and in the army, were at that moment looking to the weapons they held in their hands for salvation. The fighters, emboldened by the cries of their supporters and by inborn courage, advanced to the open area between the two lines. The armies had settled down before their respective camps and, though exempt from the immediate danger, were filled with apprehension: supremacy was at stake, and it depended on the courage and luck of a handful of men. As they turned their attention upon the discomfiting scene, rapt and keyed up, the signal to begin was sounded.

The three champions from each side fell upon their opponents with swords drawn and filled with the fighting spirit of their mighty armies. They were not concerned about the danger to themselves but by the thought that the future of their countries lay in their hands: supremacy or enslavement. As for the spectators, at the first onslaught they shivered in dread at the clash of arms and flashing swords, and, when neither side appeared to be winning the advantage, voice and breath strangled in their throats. In the hand-to-hand combat that followed they beheld struggling bodies and weapon thrusts that were unable to bring the fight to a decision; then wounds and blood appeared; in the end two of the Romans fell lifeless, one upon the other, but not before they had wounded all three Albans.

At the death of the Romans the army of Alba roared with delight; the Romans, hopes dashed, were now frozen in fear at the plight of the single man whom the three Curiatii had now surrounded. By good luck he was as yet unharmed, and although unequal to the three taken together he knew he was a match for them individually. He therefore took to flight to separate his opponents, expecting that each would give pursuit as his wounds would permit. After spurting ahead some distance from the scene of the fighting, he looked back to see two of them far off and widely separated, and one closing in on him. He wheeled and attacked in a ferocious rush; and even as the Alban army was calling out for the Curiatii to come to their brother's rescue, Horatius was toppling his enemy and looking about for his second victory. A mighty hurrah from his astonished supporters spurred him to finish off the fight. He felled his second foe before the last brother, who was closing in fast, could reach him.

Now only two were left to fight it out on equal terms, but their hopes and strength were not the same. The Roman, as yet unwounded, was eager for the final encounter because of his double victory; confronting him was an opponent weak from wounds and hard running, sick at heart from the slaughter of his brothers. What followed was not a real fight. The exultant Roman cried, "I have slain two foes to appease the shades of my brothers; I shall slay the third to win dominion of Rome over Alba, the prize of this war." Looming over his foe who was struggling under the weight of his arms, Horatius buried his sword in his throat. He then stripped the spoils from the corpse as it lay.

The Romans welcomed him to their ranks with rejoicing and congratulations, their joy all the greater because they had been so close to defeat. The two sides then buried their dead, but with very different feelings: one had gained supremacy, the other was now the subject of the victor. The tombs stand today on the spot where each fell, the two Roman ones together toward the site of Alba, the three Alban nearer Rome but at intervals, exactly as the battle had been fought. [26] Before they parted Mettius asked Tullus what orders he had to give in accordance with the treaty; Tullus' command was to keep his soldiers under arms, for he would need them should a war break out with Veii.

The two armies then marched back to their respective cities, with Horatius at the head of the Roman forces and bearing before him the triple spoils. He was met at the Capena gate by his unwed sister, who had been betrothed to one of the Curiatii. When she saw the military cloak over her brother's shoulders that she herself had made for her fiancé, she let down her hair in mourning and tearfully called out his name. His sister's weeping enraged the hot-tempered young man, coming as it did at the moment of his personal victory and of great public rejoicing. Unsheathing his sword, he stabbed her to the heart, crying out in his vehemence, "Go to your betrothed, along with your ill-timed love—you who have no thought for your dead brothers, for me, or for your country. So may it be for any Roman woman who mourns an enemy."

The senators and plebeians were shocked at what he had done, but in their minds it was counterbalanced by his splendid action on the battlefield. Nevertheless, they laid hands on him and hurried him off to the king for justice. Tullus, however, did not want to be responsible for convicting and punishing such a man, which would be repugnant in its own right and displeasing to the people. He therefore called the populace together and announced, "In accordance with the law I hereby appoint a two-man board to convict Horatius of high treason." The grim formula of the law was as follows: "Let a two-man board judge the accused guilty of high treason; if he appeals this verdict, let the appeal be heard; if the verdict stands, let the lictor put a hood over the guilty man's head, let him tie him up and suspend him from a barren tree; let him scourge him to death either within the sacred boundary of the city or without." These being the terms of their appointment, the two men felt that they were not empowered to acquit even an innocent man. They accordingly condemned him, one of them saying, "Publius Horatius, I find you guilty of high treason. Lictor, go bind his

hands." When the lictor had approached and was preparing to throw the ropes about him, Horatius, at the prompting of Tullus, whose sympathies were with the defendant, said, "I appeal."

The appeal was taken before the people. In this proceeding men were influenced more than anything else by the assertion of the father, Publius Horatius, that his daughter had been killed for cause: if that were not the case, he would have exercised his legal powers as a father against his son. A short time before, he said, they had looked upon him as the proud father of a splendid family. He now implored them not to take away his only remaining child. With these words the aged father embraced the young man, while pointing to the spoils of the Curiatii fastened up at that spot now called the Horatian Spears. "Fellow citizens," he asked, "can you endure to look upon this man you have just honored as he entered the city, triumphant in victory, tied up spread-eagled on a rack, tortured, and scourged? The eyes of our Alban enemy could scarcely endure the sight of such an appalling sight! Lictor, go bind those hands that with spear and shield have just won for the Roman people dominion over Alba. Go, put a hood over the head of the liberator of our city, suspend him from that barren tree. Scourge him to death within the city's sacred boundary—amid these spears and spoils he has won. Or do so outside the boundary—amid the very tombs of the Curiatii he slew! Is there any place you can take him where evidence of the glory he has won would not exempt him from suffering such a hideous punishment?"

The people could not bear to see the tears of the father or the resolute spirit of the son, ready to face every peril. They acquitted him more out of respect for his noble spirit than for the justness of his cause. But then, in order to atone for an act of outright murder by some rite of purification, they bade the father make expiation and to do so at public expense. Accordingly, after conducting certain sacrifices of atonement that became traditional in the Horatian clan thereafter, he had a wooden beam built over the roadway, beneath which he required the young man to pass with covered head, as if passing under a yoke of submission. The beam remains today, periodically restored with public moneys, and is known as the Sister's Beam. A tomb for Horatia was constructed of hewn stone on the spot where she fell.

[27] Yet peace with Alba did not last long. When the people turned against him for having placed the fate of

the entire city in the hands of three soldiers, Mettius' unstable nature led him to abandon straightforward schemes that had not succeeded in favor of devious ones that he hoped would reinstate him in his countrymen's eyes: earlier he had proposed peace in the midst of war, now he looked to war in peacetime. And because his city's will to fight was greater than its real strength, he incited other states openly to declare war on Rome, while reserving for his own people the role of Roman allies bent on treachery. Fidenae, which enjoyed the privileges of a Roman colony, was induced to go to war with Rome by the promise of Alba's defection to her side. The people of Veii were also taken into the plan as allies.

And so, when the Fidenates broke into open revolt, Tullus summoned Mettius and his army from Alba and marched out against them. He crossed the Anio River and pitched his camp where it meets the Tiber. The army of Veii had crossed the Tiber at a point between the camp and Fidenae, and had now formed up immediately next to the river as the right wing of the battle line. On the left toward the rising hills the men of Fidenae took up their position. Tullus stationed his forces opposite the Veientes, and set the Albans facing Fidenae's legion.

But Mettius proved as cowardly as he was untrustworthy. Daring neither to stay put nor to desert openly, he withdrew bit by bit toward the hills, and, when he thought he had put sufficient distance between himself and the others, deployed his whole force on the high ground, and, still hesitating, spun out the time by marshalling each line of men one after the other. His plan was to go over to whichever side fortune should give the victory.

At first the Romans closest to Mettius were surprised to find their flank left undefended by the withdrawal of their allies; then a cavalry captain swiftly galloped off to inform the king that the Albans were retiring. At this critical moment Tullus vowed to consecrate twelve Salian priests, as well as shrines to Pallor and Panic. Shouting in a voice loud enough for the enemy to hear, he ordered the captain to return to the fight: there was no reason for alarm—the Alban army at his command was shifting around to attack the unprotected rear of Fidenae. He also commanded the cavalry captain on rejoining his men to order them to raise their spears aloft. This had the effect of preventing a good many of the Roman infantrymen from seeing the withdrawal of the Albans. Even those who had seen what was happening thought it was part of Tullus' plan, and so fought all the harder.

Now it was the enemy's turn to be alarmed: they had heard what Tullus had meant them to hear, for many in Fidenae understood Latin, enjoying as they did the rights of colonists. And so, to avoid being cut off from their town by a sudden descent of the Albans from the hills, they turned and fled. Tullus gave pursuit and, after routing the men of Fidenae, turned even more fiercely upon the Veientes, who had been panicked by the panic of the others. They did not withstand his attack, but the river at their back kept them from headlong flight. At the river bank some in cowardice threw down their weapons and plunged pell-mell into the water, while others were overwhelmed as they hesitated between resistance and flight. Never before had Rome fought a bloodier battle. [28] At that point the army of Alba, which had been watching from the sidelines, descended to the plain. When Mettius ventured to congratulate Tullus on his victory, the latter made a courteous response. After praying that heaven would grant its blessing, he ordered the Alban camp to be joined with the Roman and that preparations be made for a sacrifice of purification the next day. When the morrow came and everything needful stood in readiness, he ordered each of the two armies to a meeting. Heralds, beginning on the outskirts of the camp, summoned the Albans first. To them such a gathering was a novelty: curiosity aroused, they crowded round the Roman king to hear what he had to say. By prearranged plan armed Romans stood about them, their centurions having been instructed to execute their orders promptly.

Tullus began as follows: "Romans, if ever there was a war in which you had reason to be thankful above all to the gods and then to your own courage, it was in the battle we fought yesterday. For we were contending not so much with the enemy, but—what is even more difficult and dangerous—with the treachery and betrayal of our allies. Please do not suppose that I gave the order for the Albans to withdraw toward the hills. That was not my doing: I pretended it was because I did not want your fighting spirit to desert you as your allies were doing; at the same time, by making our foe think they were being attacked from the rear, I hoped they would turn tail and flee. And yet responsibility for this treachery does not fall upon all men of Alba. No, they were following their leader, just as you would have followed me had I decided to pull my troops away from the position we were in at the time. Mettius over there led the retreat, Mettius instigated the war, Mettius broke the treaty between Rome and Alba. I intend to single out this man for an exemplary punishment that will be a lesson to anyone in the future who contemplates such treachery."

Armed centurions closed in on Mettius. The king continued: "May what I am about to do prove favorable, fortunate, and happy for the Roman people, for myself, and for the men of Alba. It is my intention to move all the people of Alba to Rome, to give the plebeians citizenship and to enroll your leaders in the senate: in short, to create a single city, a single state. Just as Alba once was split into two peoples, so now let it return to one." The reaction of the Alban youth to these words was silence: unarmed, they were surrounded by those in arms and, though feelings among them differed, they shared a common fear.

Then Tullus said, "Mettius Fufetius, if you were able to learn to keep your word and abide by agreements you have made, I would so school you and spare your life. But as it is, you are beyond saving. Your punishment nevertheless will teach mankind to hold sacred the things you have profaned. Just as yesterday your loyalties were divided between Fidenae and Rome, so today shall your body be divided." At once two four-horse teams were brought forward. Mettius was tied spread-eagled to the chariots and the teams driven off in opposite directions. His body was rent, parts of his limbs still tied to each of the ever-widening chariots. Everyone averted his eyes from the ghastly spectacle. This was the first and last time the Romans meted out such uncivilized punishment; in all other cases they are entitled to boast that no other people have punished wrongdoing in a more humane way.

*The reign of Rome's last king, Tarquin the Proud, reflects the final period of Etruscan supremacy, which ended in the violent overthrow of the monarchy. Tarquin's character is distinguished by his arrogance (the more common meaning of his name, Superbus, in Latin), but much of the narrative, treating conflicts with the Latin League and the siege of the city of Gabii is unremarkable (49–56). The story of Lucretia and her rape by the younger Tarquin provides the moral context in which revolt is justified, setting an example for subsequent generations to resist tyranny. Our selection resumes with the return of Tarquin's sons from a mission to Delphi to find Rome preparing again for war.*

Upon returning to Rome they found that preparations for war against the Rutuli were in full swing. [57] These people inhabited the city of Ardea and were very wealthy for that time and place. Their wealth was the cause of the war: Tarquin wanted to enrich himself, now that his resources were exhausted from his many public works, and to mollify the plebeians with Ardea's plunder, for they disliked his rule both because of his general arrogance and because of their resentment at having been kept so long at work fit for ordinary workmen and slaves. Tarquin tried to take Ardea in an initial

assault, but when this did not succeed, he fell back on blockading the city from behind siege works.

A permanent camp grew up and, as happens in a war that is long but not hard-fought, furloughs were freely granted, but more for the officers than for the rank and file. Now the young princes of the royal house were in the habit of spending their free time feasting and carousing among themselves. It so happened that when they were drinking in the quarters of Sextus Tarquinius, where Tarquinius Collatinus, the son of Egerius, was one of the guests, they fell to discussing their wives. Each man praised his own extravagantly. When the dispute heated up, Collatinus said there was no need of talk. Why, in a few hours they could see for themselves that his Lucretia was the best of the lot. "We're young and red-blooded. Why don't we ride off and see with our own eyes just what sort of wives we've got? The surest proof will be what each man finds when he shows up unexpectedly." By this time they were quite drunk. "Well then, let's go!" Spurring their horses they flew off to Rome.

The evening shadows were lengthening when they came upon the royal princesses feasting and frolicking with their friends. Then they sped off to Collatia: though the evening was late, they found Lucretia still in the main hall of her home, bent over her spinning and surrounded by her maids as they worked by lamplight. Lucretia was the clear winner of the contest. She graciously welcomed her husband and the Tarquins as they approached; Collatinus, happy in his victory, issued a comradely invitation for the royal young men to come in. When Sextus Tarquin set eyes upon her he was seized by the evil desire to debauch her, spurred on as he was by her beauty and redoubtable chastity. In the meantime, with the youthful lark now at an end, they returned to camp.

[58] After a few days Sextus Tarquin, without Collatinus' knowledge, came to Collatia with a single companion. He was graciously welcomed, for no one suspected what he was up to, and after dinner was shown to a guest room. When the household was safely asleep, in the heat of passion he came to the sleeping Lucretia sword in hand and, pressing his left hand on her breast, whispered, "Say no word, Lucretia. I am Sextus Tarquin. There is a sword in my hand. You die if you make a sound." She awoke in fright, and when she realized she could not call for help with the threat of death hanging over her, Tarquin confessed his passion, pleaded with her, intermingling threats with entreaties and working in every way upon her feelings as a woman. When he saw she was resolute and would

not yield even out of fear for her life, he threatened to disgrace her even in death by placing the naked body of a murdered slave next to her corpse, evidence that she had been killed in the act of committing adultery of the basest sort. When by this threat his lust vanquished her resolute chastity, he left the house exulting in his seeming conquest of the woman's honor.

Lucretia, stricken to the heart at the disgrace, sent the same messenger to her father in Rome and husband in Ardea: each was to come with one trustworthy friend; it must be done this way and done quickly: a terrible thing had happened. Spurius Lucretius arrived with Publius Valerius, son of Volesus, Collatinus with Lucius Iunius Brutus, in whose company he was traveling en route to Rome when his wife's messenger chanced to meet him. They found Lucretia seated downcast in her bedchamber. At the arrival of her father and husband tears welled up, and when her husband asked, "Are you all right?", she replied, "Indeed, no. What can be right when a woman's virtue has been taken from her? The impress of another man is in your bed, Collatinus; yet only my body was defiled; my soul is not guilty. Death will be my witness to this. But pledge with your right hands and swear that the adulterer will not go unpunished. Sextus Tarquin did this, a guest who betrayed his host, an enemy in arms who last night took his pleasure, fatal, alas, to me—and, if you act as you should, to him." Each pledged his word in turn and tried to comfort the heartsick woman by fixing the guilt not upon the victim but the transgressor: the mind sins, they said, not the body, and there is no guilt when intent is absent. "It is up to you", she said, "to punish the man as he deserves. As for me, I absolve myself of wrong, but not from punishment. Let no unchaste woman hereafter continue to live because of the precedent of Lucretia." She took a knife she was hiding in her garments and drove it into her breast. Doubling over, she collapsed in death.

Husband and father raised a ritual cry of mourning for the dead. [59] While they were taken up with lamentation, Brutus pulled the knife dripping with blood from Lucretia's body. Holding it before him he cried, "By this blood, so pure before defilement by prince Tarquin, I hereby swear—and you, O deities, I make my witnesses—that I will drive out Lucius Tarquinius Superbus together with his criminal wife and all his progeny with sword, fire, and whatever force I can muster, nor will I allow them or anyone else to be king at Rome." He then handed the dagger to Collatinus, and next to Lucretius and Valerius, who stood amazed at the miraculous change that had come over him. They

repeated the oath after him; from that moment on, anger overmastering grief, they followed Brutus' lead in bringing the monarchy to an end.

They bore Lucretia's body from the house to the forum, where they drew a large crowd that was scandalized by the extraordinary turn of events, as anyone would be. Each man expressed his personal sense of outrage at the rape the prince had committed. And not just the father's grief moved them, but Brutus also, when he rebuked them for tears and useless complaints when what they should be doing as men and Romans was to take up arms against those who had dared such violence. The most spirited young men were quick to seize weapons and join the cause; the rest followed their lead. Then, leaving a garrison at Collatia's gates to prevent anyone from getting out and reporting the uprising to the royal family, Brutus led the rest of the warriors to Rome.

The arrival of a large group of armed men caused fear and commotion wherever it went; on the other hand, the sight of the nation's leaders at the forefront made people think that whatever was afoot there must be a good reason for it. Moreover, men were as appalled by Sextus' heinous deed at Rome as they had been at Collatia. From all quarters of the city people crowded into the forum, where a herald summoned them to assemble before the tribune of the Celeres, or king's bodyguard, a post that Brutus chanced to be holding at that moment. He then delivered a speech that was wholly at odds with the spirit and character he had pretended to have up to that day. He spoke of the violence and lust of Sextus Tarquin, of the unspeakable rape of Lucretia and her wretched death, of the bereavement of Lucretius Tricipitinus and the cause of his daughter's death, which for him was more unworthy and more pitiable than the death itself. He mentioned also the arrogance of the king himself and how the plebs had been forced underground to dig out trenches and sewers: the men of Rome, victorious over all their neighbors, had been turned into drudges and quarry slaves, warriors no longer. He recalled the appalling murder of King Servius Tullius and how his daughter had driven over her father's body in that accursed wagon, and he invoked her ancestral gods as avengers. After saying these things and, I am sure, even more shocking ones prompted by his outrage of the moment, which are not easy for writers to capture on paper, he brought his listeners to such a pitch of fury that they revoked the king's power and ordered the exile of Lucius Tarquinius, together with wife and children.

Brutus armed a group of select young volunteers and with them set out for Ardea to rouse the army against the king. He left Lucretius in control of Rome, whom Tarquin had appointed prefect of the city some time before. In the midst of the tumult Tullia fled from her home. Wherever she went men and women reviled her, calling down on her head the vengeance that the spirits of kindred inflict upon those who have wronged them. [60] When the news of these events reached the camp, the king in fear at the sudden crisis hastened to Rome to suppress the disturbance. Brutus anticipated that he would be on his way and, not wanting to meet up with him, took a different route: at almost the same moment Brutus arrived at Ardea and Tarquin in Rome. The gates were closed to Tarquin and his exile proclaimed. The liberator of the city received a delighted welcome in the camp, and the king's sons were expelled from it. Two of them accompanied their father into exile at Caere among the Etruscans. Sextus Tarquin went to Gabii, apparently regarding it as his personal fiefdom; but there he was killed by those who had witnessed his murders and depredations and were bent on settling old scores.

Lucius Tarquinius Superbus reigned for twenty-five years. The monarchy at Rome from her foundation to her liberation lasted two hundred and forty-four years. Two consuls were then elected, in accordance with the precepts laid down by Servius Tullius, by the Comitia Centuriata under the presidency of the prefect of the city. They were Lucius Iunius Brutus and Lucius Tarquinius Collatinus.

## AFTERWORD

Livy's history met with instant acclaim. His books were released to the public in sets of ten, although when completed, his whole work was available for sale in its entirety. His literary approach to historiography was considered highly entertaining, and his writings remained constantly popular from his own day through the end of antiquity. On August 24, A.D. 79, Pliny the Elder, commander of the Roman fleet at Misenum and author of the *Natural History,* invited his teenage nephew to accompany him across the Bay of Naples to see the eruption of Vesuvius at closer range. The younger Pliny preferred to continue with his reading of Livy's *From the Foundation of the City,* a wise choice, as the journey to the volcano proved perilous and his uncle did not survive. Livy's accomplishment dwarfed his predecessors', and it is perhaps largely due to it that only Sallust survives from among earlier historians. Quintilian rates the two of them as the equals of the Greek historians Herodotus and Thucydides, and Livy becomes the principal source for the history of the Republic, influencing not only Roman historians such as Tacitus and Florus but also Greek ones including Plutarch and Cassius Dio. His work also provided stores of material on the period for a wide range of writers and probably influenced the portrayal of Pompey and Caesar in Lucan's historical epic about the civil war. A somewhat paradoxical confirmation of the high esteem in which Livy was held throughout this period is the verdict of the mad emperor Caligula, who judged him to be "long-winded and sloppy" and very nearly had his writings removed from all the libraries, along with Virgil's.

As episodes from his history appear to have been used for writing topics in Roman schools, it is more than likely that his works, or sections, were used as textbooks. The two ten-book sets that remained popular throughout the millennia are the first ten books, describing the founding of Rome and its conquest of Italy, and the third set of ten books (21 to 30) recounting the war with Hannibal, which he himself indicates is his greatest theme. But the great bulk of his *From the Foundation of the City* was daunting, and not only to students. The epigrammatist Martial writes during the reign of Domitian about owning an abridged version or epitome, perhaps the ancestor of the later summaries known as the *Periochae* (see p. 289). At about the same time a former consul named Mettius Pompusianus compiled a volume of extracts from the speeches of Livy's kings and generals. The availability of such summaries surely had the effect of diminishing the distribution of Livy's complete work, even though we can trace its survival into the fifth century A.D. At that time two powerful aristocratic families, the Nicomachi and the Symmachi, among the last great representatives of Rome's pagan traditions, arranged for a corrected copy of *From the Foundation of the City* to be transcribed in parchment codices. All the later manuscripts of the first ten books derive from this source.

**Figure 18:  Cincinnatus in Cincinnati**
The axe wrapped in a bundle of rods symbolizes his absolute dictatorial power. Cincinnati is named in honor of the Society of the Cincinnati, formed in 1783 by officers of the Continental army and their French allies. Its nineteenth-century nickname, "Porkopolis", reflecting its importance as a meat-packing center, has rather less dignity.

Livy was not much read in the Middle Ages, which got its Roman history, if at all, from later—and shorter—works, such as Florus (second century A.D.), much of whose epitome of Roman military history is based on Livy himself. But Livy still found some readers, including the tenth-century Archbishop Rather of Verona, who made notes in the margins of his copy of Livy's first decade. Upon reaching the account of the traitor Mettius Fufetius's dismemberment in Book 1, Rather jotted in the margin, "This should happen to the Bishop of Milan." Dante praises Livy in the *Inferno* (28.12), and he is an important source for Dante's treatise *On Monarchy*.

The reconstitution of a complete text of Livy became something of an obsession for scholars of the Renaissance, in particular Petrarch. He had used Livy as a source for his epic poem *Africa* (in Latin), and he took advantage of his presence at the papal court in Avignon to acquire manuscripts of the first, third, and fourth decades and assemble them for the first time since antiquity. From this point on, Livy was an essential text in the development of Renaissance humanism, an object of study by all the great names of the period, including Poggio Bracciolini (1380–1459), Lorenzo Valla (1406–57), and Leonardo Bruni (1369–1444). A contemporary poet, Antonio Beccadelli (1394–1471), also known as "Il Panormita," sold off his property in order to purchase a copy. But it was the first decade that particularly engaged readers. In expounding his views on how a republican government might best be structured, Niccolò Machiavelli framed the discussion as an inquiry into Livy; his *Discourses on the First Decade of Titus Livius* (ca. 1513) were written with the expectation of a reading public that would be intimately familiar with Livy's history of the Roman Republic. That familiarity has diminished in the centuries since, and Livy's readership suffered from the distinctly negative view of his work promulgated by nineteenth-century German historians such as Barthold Niebuhr. But as our principal source for Roman narratives of the Republic, Livy's *From the Foundation of the City* is drawing renewed interest as a witness to the Romans' own view of their origins and cultural legacy.

# THE EARLY EMPIRE

BY THE TIME TIBERIUS ACCEDED TO THE THRONE, ALL THE GREAT LITERARY FIGURES
of the Augustan era were dead, except one—Ovid, who continued to languish in exile on the shores
of the Black Sea. The new emperor's greatest contribution to literature was its suppression, as documented in the columns of Tacitus's *Annals*. The chief entry in Tacitus's catalog of oppression under
Tiberius is the suicide in A.D. 25 of the historian Cremutius Cordus, who celebrated Cicero, Brutus,
and Cassius in his works. But this bleak picture, as seen through the prism of Tacitus, is not the
whole story. It is true that we cannot identify any great figures in this period until the reign of Nero,
but it is too simplistic to attribute this to any direct effect of the new imperial system, since talented
writers soon flourished in the same system under future emperors who were just as oppressive. In
the first decades of the early empire, imitators of the great masters multiplied, people who recycled
the successful works of their predecessors. This was the period when many of the works that have
been falsely ascribed to Cicero, Sallust, Virgil, Ovid, and Tibullus were composed not by forgers
but by aspiring authors whose best efforts were to emulate their betters. In the fluid conditions of
the ancient book trade, with no system of copyright, the authorship of a work could very easily be
mistaken. For example, the second-century physician Galen once observed some people arguing
over the authenticity of one of his own works in a bookshop in the Vicus Sandaliarius. Authors who
composed in the manner of Ovid, for instance, might well have their works taken for Ovidian originals. The most substantial evidence for this kind of activity is a collection of poems known as the
*Appendix Vergiliana,* containing several works mistakenly attributed to Virgil. The ever-increasing
role of rhetoric in education and the growing predominance of show oratory in cultural life also had
the effect of setting a premium upon imitation.

In this climate there were still authors who found ways to adapt the aesthetics of the age to creative uses. From the early years of Tiberius's reign comes the *Astronomica* by Manilius, a technical
tour de force in five books rendering the discipline of astrology into Latin hexameter verse. Tiberius's
adopted son Germanicus also tried his hand at didactic poetry with a Latin adaptation of the Greek
poet Aratus's *Phaenomena.* Works like these perhaps coincided with the obscure literary tastes
of Tiberius and his interest in the occult. The career of Phaedrus spanned the reigns of Tiberius,
Caligula, and Claudius. He was born a slave but had been freed by Augustus and left us one of the

most original works of Latin literature, a collection of fables in verse, composed in the tradition of Aesop. The fate of Cremutius Cordus, whose history of the civil wars is lost, illustrates one aspect of the precariousness of historiography in this period; the surviving work of Velleius Paterculus, who served as an officer under Tiberius, illustrates the other. Of his two-book history of Rome beginning with mythological origins and culminating in A.D. 29 in the reign of Tiberius, almost half is devoted to Caesar, Augustus, and Tiberius. It is perhaps not deserving of all the contempt that scholars have heaped on it, but it does serve as a depressing counterpoint to all that we have lost.

Greek authors were increasingly prominent in Rome during this period, becoming an important presence also at the imperial court. The poetry of some of them is preserved in a collection of epigrams compiled in the first century A.D. known as *The Garland of Philip*. One particularly interesting figure in the group was Crinagoras, a poet from Lesbos who moved in the highest circles in the court of Augustus and lived to a great old age into the early years of Tiberius's reign. He wrote poems celebrating members of the imperial family on trivial themes such as the coming of age of the emperor's nephew Marcellus, when he cut his first beard. Many such authors, like Crinagoras himself, first came to Rome on embassies from their home cities. Among them was Philo, a philosopher and writer from Alexandria, whose family was active in the Roman administration in the eastern Mediterranean. In A.D. 39 he headed an embassy from the Jewish community of Alexandria to the emperor Caligula, which is colorfully described in a surviving treatise.

The emperor Claudius was himself a man of letters. As a young man he wrote histories of Carthage and of the Etruscans and was a friend of Livy. But it cannot be said that literature flourished in his reign. It is possible that the elegant agricultural treatise of Lucius Iunius Moderatus Columella dates from this period. He hailed from Cadiz in Spain, in the vanguard of Spanish writers, such as Seneca, Lucan, Martial, and Quintilian who dominated the coming era. Its twelve books—a canonical number in epic poetry, but not hitherto in farmers' manuals—include one in hexameter verse. The next burst of literary activity came in the reign of Nero (A.D. 54–68), who notoriously considered himself its greatest representative. The rise of new talents in the minor genres of pastoral, represented by the Virgilianizing eclogues of Calpurnius Siculus, and satire, represented by the rather severe Stoic Persius, was a distinguishing feature of the period. Roman authors, in whatever language they wrote, were now managing to navigate successfully the treacherous waters of writing under the emperors, with outstanding examples of every genre beginning in the age of Nero.

The reign of Vespasian, which ended with his death in June 79, only months before the eruption of Vesuvius, was followed by that of his son Titus, best known for sacking the Temple in Jerusalem and completing the building of the Colosseum. Titus was considered a good emperor by Suetonius, but this may only be in contrast to his brother Domitian, who succeeded to the purple after Titus's premature death in A.D. 81. Like Nero, Domitian actively cultivated the image of a patron of the arts and letters. The great temple of Jupiter on the Capitoline, the heart of Roman tradition and ritual, had burned down in a terrible fire during the brief reign of Titus. Domitian not only rebuilt the temple on a grander and more sumptuous scale but also celebrated its renewal with the institution of a public festival on the model of the great Greek games at venues such as Olympia. Known as the Capitoline Contest, this festival was celebrated every four years for the next three centuries and included contests in poetry in both Greek and Latin. The competition was stiff: the poet Statius writes of his dismay at failing to win in the games of the year A.D. 90. Another competitor was the boy prodigy Q. Sulpicius Maximus, who competed in the Greek category in the games of A.D. 94 at the age of eleven. He died in the following year, but his proud parents set up a tombstone with his likeness and had the forty-three Greek hexameters that he had improvised in the games inscribed to commemorate his talent. The episode illustrates one aspect of the increasingly cosmopolitan world of Roman letters. Greek literature flourished within the secure borders of the empire, and writers not only flocked to Rome but plied their trade across the Roman world, paving the way for the efflorescence of Greek rhetoric and literature in the next generation.

# SENECA

### (Lucius Annaeus Seneca, ca. 5 B.C.–A.D. 65)

ONE OF THE WEALTHIEST MEN IN THE HISTORY OF EARLY IMPERIAL ROME—APART FROM the emperors themselves—was also one of its most famous and controversial men of letters. Seneca the Younger, as he is called to distinguish him from his father of the same name who was also a writer and a scholar, was one of the more prominent representatives of a rising class of citizens from the provinces, who increasingly played important roles in Roman political life and culture. His father, Seneca the Elder (ca. 55 B.C.–A.D. 39), came from a wealthy family of equestrian status, which owned estates in the region of Corduba (modern Córdoba), the capital of the Roman province of Baetica. There Seneca the Younger was born, probably between 5 and 1 B.C. Born Lucius Annaeus Seneca, he was the middle of three brothers. The eldest, Novatus, is best known to posterity as Junius Gallio, the name he took after he was adopted by a close friend of his father's (a common practice among the Roman elite). As governor of the province of Achaea in the early 50s A.D. Gallio presided over the proceedings against St. Paul at Corinth and dismissed the charges against him. Seneca seems not to have been particularly close to his younger brother, Mela, but he was fond of his son, Lucan, who grew up to become the most celebrated epic poet of the age. Together, the family put Corduba on the literary map. As another Spanish poet, Martial, remarked: "Eloquent Corduba boasts of the two Senecas and the one and only Lucan" (*Epigrams* 1.61.7–8).

Although the family's roots in Spain went deep, Seneca's public life and literary career were played out almost exclusively in the city of Rome. It was there that he was educated, although it seems rather curious that it was his aunt, his mother's stepsister (whose name he does not mention), who seems to have played the most important role in his formative years, as he himself describes them: "In her arms I was carried to Rome, hers was the devoted and maternal nursing that enabled me to recover my health after a lengthy period of illness; she it was who furnished kindly support when I stood for the quaestorship" (*Consolation to Helvia* 19.2). The details of his public career before Nero's reign are murky. His tenure of public office appears to have begun late in the reign of Tiberius, and certainly by the time of the accession of Caligula he was a major public, and perhaps literary, figure. If Cassius Dio is to be believed, Seneca came very close to running afoul of the emperor even then (*Roman History* 59.19.7–8): "Lucius Annaeus Seneca, who was superior in wisdom to all the Romans of his day and to many others as well, nearly came to ruin, though he had neither done any wrong nor had the appearance of doing so, but merely because he pleaded a case well in the Senate while the emperor was present. Caligula ordered him to be put to death, but afterwards let him off because he believed the statement of one of his female associates, to the effect that Seneca had consumption in an advanced stage and would soon die anyway." Suetonius also records that Caligula was not a fan of Seneca's ostentatious style, and in the case of this particular emperor that might have been enough

313

to set off hostilities, although it often happened that personal enmities could also serve as a screen for political motives.

That appears to have been the case when Seneca was sent into exile on the island of Corsica by the next emperor, Caligula's uncle Claudius. The charge was adultery with Julia Livilla, the emperor's niece and the sister of the deceased Caligula, but this was almost certainly a pretext for some other matter. Ancient sources identify Claudius's current wife, Messalina, as the moving force behind the charges against Julia Livilla, which resulted in her exile and eventual execution, and it is likely that Seneca was caught up in these dynastic machinations. It must have been a wretched time for him: his only son had died shortly before he was relegated, and conditions on Corsica were far from easy. But just as the politics of the imperial household had led to his downfall, so they were the cause of his restoration, for Claudius's fourth (and final) wife, Agrippina, prevailed upon her husband to bring Seneca back to Rome no later than A.D. 49 to become tutor to her son and his heir, the future emperor Nero. Sometime, too, during these final years of Claudius's reign, Seneca formed an association with the new prefect of the Praetorian Guard, Afranius Burrus. When Nero then acceded to the throne in A.D. 54, the two of them were well placed to try to steer the policies of the newly minted, teenage emperor.

The first years of Nero's rule were heady days for Seneca, a time when he was uniquely positioned to influence public policy. The surviving portions of his treatise *On Clemency*, which he composed and dedicated to Nero within the first few years after his accession, provide at least a glimpse of how Seneca conceived of the ruler's task. In the first book (the only one of the original three to survive intact), he argues that clemency is not only necessary in and of itself but also useful for the monarch. Seneca's position was reflected in his holding the consulship for six months in A.D. 56, but he also attracted a great deal of ill will during this period, as he used his position to acquire vast personal wealth. The later historian Cassius Dio reports that he was even willing to put his personal finances above the public interest, as when he allegedly triggered a revolt in the province of Britain by calling in a loan of 40 million sestertii (*Roman History* 62.52). But while he and Burrus might have exercised a generally positive influence on Nero's conduct of affairs of state, they were unable to restrain his personal excesses, which included the murder of his own mother, Agrippina, in 59.

By 62, when Burrus died, a victim of poisoning by Nero according to some hostile sources, the emperor was increasingly unwilling to tolerate a partner in governing, and Seneca tried to forestall the inevitable break by withdrawing from public life. The failed conspiracy against Nero led by Calpurnius Piso in 65 gave the emperor all the pretext he needed to move against Seneca, and he now ordered his death. Seneca opened his veins, but Nero allegedly prevented his wife from following him in death, although his older brother was apparently also swept up in the aftermath.

During his eventful life, Seneca also produced a vast number of philosophical and literary works, many of which survived his personal disaster. It is impossible to date most of his works with any precision, which makes it difficult to plot the role that literature played in his life in relation to his public activities. But it seems that, like Cicero before him, he was inclined to turn to writing philosophy during times of personal travail. Much of his work could then be dated to the period of his exile on Corsica in the 40s and his final years when he had withdrawn from public life. It was not a foregone conclusion that philosophy would become one of his life's passions. It was not an interest that he acquired as a boy at home; he had to pick it up on the streets, from his teachers, that is. His father was unwilling "to relax his devotion to the practice of his forefathers" and would not consent to his wife's "being given a thorough grounding in the teachings of philosophy" (*Consolation to Helvia* 17.3). Indeed, Seneca tells us, his father "despised philosophy" (*Epistles* 108.22). But after a youthful flirtation with Pythagoreanism, Seneca himself devoted much of his energies to Stoicism, leaving behind a body of work that exercised vast influence in disseminating the Stoic views on ethics to which he subscribed. Ten essays on a variety of topics such as anger, the happy life, and the role of providence were put together in a collection known as the *Dialogues*, probably by a later editor. In

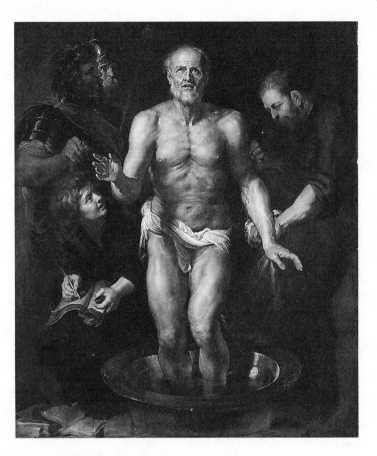

**Figure 19:  Peter Paul Rubens, *Death of Seneca***
The composition of this scene by the Flemish master Peter Paul Rubens (1577–1640) was influenced by his studies of ancient Roman sculpture. Although suicide was considered a mortal sin by many Christians, Seneca could still be depicted in poses that evoke Christian martyrs, because his suicide was forced and thus tantamount to execution.

addition to the work *On Clemency,* dedicated to Nero, there survive *On Benefits,* a work in seven books on the relationships among humans and between humans and the gods; *Natural Questions,* Seneca's only surviving work on natural philosophy, of which seven out of an original eight books remain; and the *Moral Epistles,* 124 essays on all manner of topics presented in the form of letters addressed to his friend Lucilius.

Seneca has attracted much criticism through the ages for hypocrisy. Many readers have sympathized with the negative verdict laid down in antiquity by Cassius Dio (*Roman History* 61.10.2–3):

> While denouncing tyranny , he was himself a tyrant's tutor; while running down those who associate with the powerful, he did not hold himself aloof from the palace; and though he had nothing good to say about flatterers, he himself had constantly fawned upon Messalina and the freedmen of Claudius...Though he criticized the rich, he himself acquired a fortune of 300,000,000 sestertii; and though he inveighed against the extravagances of others, he had five hundred tripods of citrus wood with legs of ivory, all identically alike, and he served banquets on them.

But Seneca had long since sworn off asceticism, and his father had known from an early age that his two older sons were bound for life in the glare of the political arena, "in which our very hopes are what we have to fear" (*Controversies* 2, *Preface* 4). Seneca was not a philosopher but a public figure with a deep interest in philosophy, a sphere with which he maintained a sometimes awkward relationship, as he did with literature.

The most startling entry in the register of literary works by this complicated man must surely be the satire known as the *Apocolocyntosis*, or "Pumpkinification of Claudius," a medley of prose and verse that describes the abortive translation to heaven of the emperor Claudius after his death. Deification was becoming something that might be expected for a deceased Roman emperor, so this satire, in which Claudius is treated as a buffoon, was not without risks for its author. Some have maintained that this was not Seneca, and indeed it is very unlike any of his other works: it is extremely funny. We know of other prose works by Seneca that have been lost, but he also wrote poetry. Unless some of the surviving epigrams that are attributed to him are genuine, then the only examples of the Senecan muse are his tragedies, which are the only complete examples of the genre in Latin to have survived from classical antiquity.

Seneca has nothing to say in his extant works about these plays, and we know nothing from any other sources about the date or circumstances of their composition. Ten plays have been transmitted under his name, but one certainly and another almost certainly are not from his stylus. The *Octavia* is a historical drama on the enforced death of the daughter of Claudius who was betrothed to Nero, set in A.D. 62. Not only does Seneca appear as a character in the play, but the script shows some awareness of events after his death in 65. But it is an interesting play in its own right, not least because it is the sole surviving example of the genre of the *fabula praetexta*, a tragedy based on events in Roman history. The authorship of another play, *Hercules on Mount Oeta*, has also struck many scholars as more likely to be an imitation of Seneca rather than by the man himself. The remaining eight plays in the corpus are certainly Senecan, and they constitute a rich testimony to the enduring place of drama in Roman literary life under the empire, for which there is so little other evidence.

For the most part we can identify the models used by Seneca in drafting these scripts. For instance, his *Oedipus* follows the action of Sophocles's *Oedipus the King* quite closely. In other cases, such as his *Phaedra*, we can also see how he has developed his source in Euripides's *Hippolytus* by introducing motifs from other literary sources such as Ovid's *Heroides* or Virgil's portrayal of Dido. In the case of the *Thyestes*, however, no earlier play survives, although we know of several productions that might well have influenced him, in particular a version that was composed on commission from Augustus by the highly regarded poet Varius Rufus. We may also guess that Seneca's *Medea*, which is obviously based on Euripides's celebrated original, might also owe a debt to the version (long since lost) by one of his favorite Roman poets, Ovid. We know nothing about the first performances of these plays; indeed, some scholars contend that they were composed for recitation, not performance, and this remains a hotly contested question. What is not disputed is that at the core of Seneca's dramatic art is a highly wrought and emotionally charged rhetoric. This, combined with the deeply pessimistic worldview reflected in his plays, accounts for the profound impact that they make on an audience, or a reader, whether the response is pleasure or its opposite.

# MEDEA

The background to this play is formed by the heroic exploits of Jason in bringing back the Golden Fleece to Greece from the barbarian land of Colchis. He was only able to do this with the aid of Medea, who put her magical powers at his service and thus enabled him to complete the tasks required of him by her father, Aeetes, the king of Colchis. Jason yoked the team of fire-breathing oxen, sowed the field with dragon's teeth, and finally, again with

*her aid, lulled to sleep the dragon that guarded the Fleece.*
*Jason and Medea made their escape, but to deflect the*
*pursuit by the Colchians, Medea murdered her brother*
*Apsyrtus. The play opens years later, after Jason and*
*Medea have been married in Greece and had children.*
*Jason is now planning to divorce Medea and marry a new*
*wife in Corinth.*

DRAMATIS PERSONAE
MEDEA
NURSE
CREON
JASON
MESSENGER
CHORUS

## Act One

MEDEA O gods of marriage! Juno, childbirth goddess,
and you, Athena, who taught Tiphys how
to harness the first ship that would subdue the waves,
and Neptune, cruel master of the ocean deep,
and Titan, portioning the world's bright day,
and you, whose moonlight sees all secret rites,
Hecate triple-formed—all gods Jason invoked
when he swore to me; and gods who better suit
Medea's prayers: Chaos of endless night,
kingdoms that hate the gods of heaven, blaspheming
10    powers,
master of the melancholy realm, and queen abducted,
but he kept his word to you. Now let me curse:
Come to me now, O vengeful Furies, punishers of
    sinners,
wild in your hair with serpents running free,
holding black torches in your bloody hands,
come to me, scowling as you did of old
when you stood round my marriage bed. Kill his
    new wife,
kill her father, and all the royal family.
What is worse than death? What can I ask for Jason?
20  That he may live!—in poverty and fear.
Let him wander through strange towns, in exile,
hated and homeless, an infamous guest, begging a bed.
Let him want me as wife, and want—the worst I could
    pray for—
children who resemble both their parents.
Now it is born, my vengeance is delivered:
I mothered it.—But why this weaving of words,
this pointless whining? Will I not attack my enemies?

I will hurl the torches from their hands, the light from
    heaven.
O Sun, my grandfather, do you see this? Are you
    still there?
Do you still ride your chariot, as usual, through
    the sky,      30
and not turn back towards the east, trace back the day?
Give me the power to ride my father's horses through
    the air,
Grandfather, give me the reins, and let me guide
with flaming harnesses the fiery team.
Let Corinth, whose twin shores now block the gulf,
burn up in flames and join two seas in one.
Just one more thing: I have to take the torch
to the marriage room myself; after the prayers,
I will be the one to kill the victims on the altar.
Find out a path to vengeance even in the
    entrails,      40
my soul, if you are still alive, if you retain
any of your old strength. Away with feminine fears,
dress up your mind like your own cruel home.
All the horrors witnessed back at home by the
    Black Sea,
Corinth will see now. Evils to make
heaven and earth both shudder equally
are what my mind revolves: wounding, murder, death
creeping through the limbs. But all this is too slight;
I did those as a girl. Let weightier rage swell up:
now I have given birth, my crimes ought to increase.    50
Take on the armor of anger, prepare for destruction
possessed by fury. The tale of your divorce
must match your marriage. How should you leave
    your man?
The same way that you married him. Enough delay.
A family formed by crime must be broken by
    more crime.
CHORUS Come to the royal wedding, all you gods,
lords of the sky, lords of the sea, and bless them,
while the people stand in respectful silence.
First a white bull must hold high his neck
for sacrifice to the royal Thunderer.    60
Then a snowy cow that never felt the yoke
should satisfy Juno with her death; and give
the goddess who restrains the bloody hands of Mars,
who brings to warring peoples peace
and holds rich plenty in her horn,
give her a soft lamb and melt her heart.
And you, who bless all legal weddings,
dispel the night and bring them luck,

come here with slow and drunken steps
70  a wreath of roses on your head.
And you the messenger of double times,
star whose return seems always slow to lovers:
mothers long for you, as do their daughters,
wanting your shining rays to shine for them right away.
This girl's beauty far surpasses
all the brides of Athens,
and the women who exercise
like boys, by the mountains of Taygetus,
by the city without a wall,
80  and Boeotian women, and those washed
by holy Alpheus.
If he wants to be judged by looks,
the commander, Aeson's Son,
would win against the child of thunder,
whose chariot tigers draw,
and the shaker of the tripods,
the fearsome virgin's brother.
Castor will yield to him,
with Pollux, better boxer.
        Just so, just so, ah gods, who live in heaven,
90          I pray,
his woman may outshine all other wives,
and he by far surpass all other men.
When this girl takes up her place in the
        women's dance,
her beauty, hers alone outshines them all:
just as the beauty of the stars is lost at sunrise,
and the thick flocks of the Pleiades lie hid
when Phoebe binds with borrowed light
her solid orb with circling horns;
as snow-white color blushes, dyed
100  with scarlet; like the shining light
the dew-wet shepherd sees at dawn.
Jason, you used to tremble as you held an
        untamed wife,
reluctant as you held her body close;
now torn away from your barbarian marriage,
lucky man, take hold of this Corinthian girl.
Your in-laws—unlike last time—give consent.
Young men, now play around, and slander whomever
        you like;
sing your songs in choruses and rounds.
Abusing masters is, for once, allowed.
Hymen, noble and bright, son of Bacchus with his
110      thyrsus,
the time is at hand to set light to the torch made of
        finely split pinewood.

Shake out with your languorous fingers prescribed
        ceremonial fire.
Pour forth festive abuse in sharp-tongued verses;
let the crowd be free with their jokes. But a woman
        who marries a stranger,
running away from her homeland—let her go to the
        silent shadows.

## Act Two

MEDEA I am done for. Wedding music struck my ears.
Such cruelty! Even I can scarce believe it.
Could Jason do this, with my father gone,
my land and kingdom lost? Abandon me, alone in a
        foreign land,
unfeeling man! Did he scorn my
        achievements,                                                  120
when he has seen how sin can conquer flames and sea?
Does he believe my evil powers so lost?
What should I do? Madness is driving me
in all directions. How can I be avenged?
If only he, too, had a brother! But—he has a wife.
Stab her in the heart. But can this answer my pain?
If any cities, Greek or barbarous,
know of a crime your hands have not
        yet done,
now is the time for it. Your past crimes urge you,
and let them all return.—The golden glory of the
        kingdom                                                         130
stolen, and the wicked girl's young playmate
ripped by the sword, his murder forced upon his
        father's sight,
his body scattered on the sea, and old Pelias'
limbs cooked up in a bronze pot. How
        much blood
I have shed by murder! When I did this
I was not even angry; I was driven by painful love.
But what could Jason do? Another's rule and power
forces him to this.—He should have bared his breast
to meet his sword.—Ah, no, find better words,
my raging grief! If he can, let him live, still
        mine,                                                          140
just as he used to be. If not—still let him live,
remember me, and spare the life which once
        I gave him.
Creon is to blame. His untamed lust for power
is breaking up my marriage, tearing a mother
away from her children, ripping a close-knit trust.

Let him be hunted down, may he alone
pay as he deserves. I will heap deep ashes on
   his house.
The dangerous curving coast of Malea
will see the black crest driven by the flames.

150 NURSE Silence, I beg you! Hide your grievances
in a secret bitterness. If one can bear deep wounds
with patient, quiet endurance and a mellow heart,
one can get payback: hidden anger hurts;
the hate you speak of will not be revenged.
MEDEA Light is the grief which can accept advice,
and mask itself; great troubles do not hide.
I want confrontation.
NURSE Stop this crazy passion!
Mistress, even silence scarcely saves you.
MEDEA Fortune fears the brave and crushes cowards.
NURSE Try valor at a time when valor has its
160    place.
MEDEA It is never inappropriate to be brave.
NURSE No hope reveals a way out from our troubles.
MEDEA The one who knows no hope knows no
   despair.
NURSE Your friends from Colchis, and your
   husband's faith
Are gone; nothing survives of all your wealth.
MEDEA Medea still survives. Here you behold
the sea, the earth, sword, flame, the gods, and thunder.
NURSE But fear the king!
MEDEA      My father was a king.
NURSE You fear no arms?
MEDEA      Not even earth-born soldiers.
NURSE You will die.
MEDEA      I want to.
NURSE      Run away!
170 MEDEA      Enough of running.
NURSE Medea—
MEDEA      I will be.
NURSE      You are a mother!
MEDEA      By you-know-who.
NURSE Hurry, escape!
MEDEA      I will, but first, revenge.
NURSE Vengeance will follow.
MEDEA      I may slow it down.
NURSE Hold back your words, madwoman, stop your
   threats,
bridle your heart; it is best to suit the times.
MEDEA Fortune can take my wealth away, but not my
   spirit.

But who is this, making the doorway creak?
It is Creon himself, puffed up with his power in
   Greece.
CREON Medea, poisonous child of Colchian Aeetes,
have you not yet got yourself away from my kingdom?—                         180
She is up to something; I know her cunning, her
   history.
Whom will she pity, whom will she leave safe?
I had intended to eliminate this infection once and
   for all,
to put her to the sword; my son-in-law begged mercy.
Life is granted her, now let her free from fear
my country. Go in safety.—Wild thing! She wants to
   attack me;
she threatens me, comes nearer, wants to talk.
Stop her, you guards, keep her away, no touching;
tell her to be quiet. Time she learnt to submit
to royal power. Go quickly on your way!      190
This monster has been here too long; take it away!
MEDEA What charge is there against me, punished
   by exile?
CREON An innocent woman asks why she is expelled!
MEDEA If you are judging, seek the truth. If ruling,
   give your orders.
CREON You must submit to power, just or unjust.
MEDEA Kingdoms which act unjustly never last.
CREON Go complain in Colchis.
MEDEA      I am going. But the man
who brought me here should take me home.
CREON      Too late; my decision is made.
MEDEA A man who makes a decision without listen-
   ing to both sides
is unjust, even if his ruling is a fair one.      200
CREON Did you hear Pelias before you punished him?
But speak, let your great case be given a chance.
MEDEA How difficult it is to turn a mind from wrath
when once it is aroused! When arrogant hands once seize
power, the ruler thinks authority resides
in stubbornness. All this I learnt in my own
   royal home.
Though pitiless disaster overwhelms me,
though exiled, abandoned, abject, and alone,
troubled on every side, once I shone bright,
born from a glorious father, descended from the Sun.
Lands made wet by Phasis, gently winding through,    210
places seen by Scythian Pontus behind its back,
and where the seas grow sweet with marshland water,

and where the riverbanks of Thermodon enclose
the ranks of women warriors, terrifying,
with their crescent shields—all this my father ruled.
I had high birth, good luck, and royal power;
I shone in glory; suitors sought my hand
who now are sought by me. Fortune is swift and fickle,
headlong, she snatched me from my kingdom and
220     gave me to exile.
Put trust in royal power, when fickle chance
carries your treasure to the winds! The greatest wealth
    of kings,
a joy forever, is to help the weak,
and shelter suppliants, give them a home.
This is the only thing I brought from all my
    kingdom:
that it was I who saved the glorious flower of Greece,
the guardians of Achaea, sons of gods:
I am their savior. Orpheus is my gift,
who softens stones with song and leads the woods;
230 Castor and Pollux, double gift, are mine,
mine are the sons of Boreas, and he whose
    darting eyes
can see across the Pontus, Lynceus,
and all the Argonauts. Their leader—I pass by.
No thanks are due for him, no debt is owed;
I brought back all the rest for you, just him for me.
    Go on, heap all my misdeeds on my head:
I will confess, but this is my one crime:
the Argo's safe return. Should that girl stay a virgin,
obey her father? Then the whole Greek land
is lost, as are its leaders, and he first—your
240     son-in-law—
will die, in the flaming jaws of the savage bull.
Let Fortune press what charge she will upon me,
to have saved such heroes needs no saying sorry.
Whatever prize I won from all my crimes
is in your hands; condemn me if you wish,
but give back my sin. I am guilty, I confess it;
Creon, you knew it when I knelt and begged
for safety and protection at your hands.
I ask some little corner, a poor hovel, home for pain,
250 but in this land; if you drive me from the city,
grant me some distant place within your kingdom.
CREON I have provided quite sufficient proof
that I am obviously not a tyrant,
the kind to trample wretchedness with lordly foot.
I chose an exile as my son-in-law:
he was in trouble, shaking, terrified:
Acastus, heir of Thessaly, said he should die.

His grudge was that his trembling weak
    old father
was murdered, and his old limbs torn apart:
his sisters were deceived by you to dare                260
this treachery to the father that they loved.
Jason has a case, if you remove yourself;
no innocent blood pollutes him, and his hands
kept clear of the sword. He is clean,
as long as he is not tainted by your company.
You! You scheming source of every criminal act,
you have a woman's wickedness; your daring
shows masculine strength, ignoring what men say.
Go, wash clean the kingdom, and take with you
your deadly drugs. Free citizens from fear;                270
stay in some other country to bother the gods.
MEDEA You force me to leave? Then give back my ship
or give me back my friend. Why tell me to go alone?
I did not come alone. If you fear war,
then drive us both from your kingdom. Why do you
    separate us?
Both are guilty. Pelias died for him, not me.
Charge him with theft, desertion, my abandoned
    father,
my brother torn apart, all the new crimes
which even now he teaches his new brides—I did not
    do them.
I have done so much harm, but never for
    myself.                280
CREON You should have left by now. Why spin things
    out with talk?
MEDEA I am on my way, but please, one final favor:
    do not make my innocent children suffer for their
        mother's guilt.
CREON Go! I will hold and cherish them like a father.
MEDEA By the happy royal marriage bed,
its future hopes, and by the state of kings,
which fickle Fortune shakes this way and that,
I beg you grant brief respite for my exile;
I am a mother; let me kiss my children one last time.
I may be close to death.
CREON     You want the time to plot.                290
MEDEA What fear of plots in such brief span of time?
CREON No time is too short for criminals to do wrong.
MEDEA You will not grant a poor, unhappy woman
    time to weep?
CREON Although my deep-set fear fights back against
    your prayers,
yes, have a single day, to ready yourself for exile.
MEDEA It is too much, you can cut back the time;

I too am in a hurry.
CREON            On pain of death
you must leave the Isthmus before the light of dawn.
Now I am summoned by the marriage rites
300    and Hymen's holy day calls me to prayer.
CHORUS That man was too bold who first in a boat—
so fragile a boat—on the treacherous waves,
went watching his homeland receding behind him
as he trusted his life to the changeable winds;
his direction uncertain, he cut through the waters,
putting his faith in the delicate wood,
though too slender a boundary made the division
between the alternatives, life and death.
          The constellations were still unknown,
and the bright stars with which heaven is
310      painted
remained unused. No boat could yet
avoid the rainy Hyades.
The shining she-goat, Capella,
and the Plough, which the slow old man
both follows and controls, and Boreas,
and Zephyr—none of these yet
had names.
Tiphys had the courage to spread out his canvas sails
to the vast ocean
320    and to prescribe new laws for the winds;
now to stretch out the ropes with the round sails full,
now to take hold of the crosswinds with foot set
      forward,
now safely to set out the yards
in the mist of the mast,
now to fasten them tight at the top
at the time when the sailor too eagerly yearns
for the full gusts of wind and above the high sail
the scarlet topsails quiver.
          Glorious were the ages our forefathers saw
330    when deception was far distant.
Each person lived an unambitious life, at home,
then growing old on ancestral farmland,
rich with a little, they knew no wealth
except what their native soil brought forth.
The world was once divided into strict partitions,
but those were broken by the pinewood ship,
which ordered the ocean to suffer a beating
and the sea, once inviolate, to turn into
one of our reasons to fear.
340    That wicked boat was given rough treatment,
sailing on and on through endless terrors,
when the two mountains, gates of the deep,

driven this way and that by impetuous force
groaned with a noise which sounded like thunder
and the sea was struck and it sprinkled the stars, right
      up to the clouds.
Brave Tiphys grew pale and his slackening hand
relinquished all hold of the tiller.
Orpheus was silent, his lyre lying idle,
and even the Argo lost her voice.
Remember Scylla, the Sicilian monster,                350
bound at her belly with ravening dogs,
opening together all her wide-gaping mouths?
Who did not shudder and tremble all over
at the multiple howlings of this single threat?
What of the time when those dangerous females
brought peace to the sea, with melodious voices,
when, singing to his own Pierian lyre,
Thracian Orpheus
almost compelled the Siren to follow him
      although
her habit was to trap ships with her voice?        360
What was the prize for this journey?
The Golden Fleece,
and Medea, greater evil than the sea,
a worthy cargo for the world's first boat.
Now at last the sea has yielded and obeys all laws.
Now there is no need of a ship made by Pallas' hand,
rowed back by kings, a well-renowned
      vessel—an *Argo*.
Any old skiff can wander the deep.
All boundaries are gone and the cities
have set up their walls in new lands:                370
the world is a thoroughfare, nothing remains
where it was.
The Indian drinks from the chilly Araxes,
the Persians can drink from the Elbe and the Rhine.
The ages will come, in faraway years
when Ocean will set free the links of Nature
and the great earth lie open, and Tethys will open,
new worlds, and Thule will be no longer
      the end of the earth.

## Act Three

NURSE Mistress, why are you rushing away
      from the house?                                380
Stop, suppress your anger, control yourself.
As a Maenad staggers on uncertain feet,
mad with the inspiration of the god,
on the peak of snowy Pindus or Mount Nysa,

so she runs to and fro, her movements wild,
her face displays her crazy passion's marks.
Her cheeks are flaming and she draws deep breaths,
she shouts, her eyes are wet with tears, she smiles;
she shows the signs of every kind of passion.
390 Hesitant, aggressive, raging, bitter, full of grief.
Where will the weight of her angry heart
    tip down?
Where will this wave break? Her madness froths over.
The crime she contemplates is complex and extreme:
she will outdo herself; I recognize this passion.
She intends some terrible deed, wild and unnatural.
I see the face of Passion. Gods, prove my fear false!
MEDEA Poor woman, do you want to know where
    hatred ends?
Look to love. Should I endure this royal wedding,
and fail to take revenge? Will I waste the day
400 I tried so hard to get, got at such cost?
No, while earth lies in the center and supports the sky,
while shining heaven in fixed circles turns,
while sands are numberless, while night brings forth
the stars, and day the sun, while the North Pole
revolves the unsinking Bears, while rivers flow to
    the sea—
never will my bitter rage fall short of total vengeance;
no, it will always grow. What vast wild beast,
what Scylla or Charybdis, who drained deep
the seas, or Etna, crushing the panting Titan,
410 will boil up with threats as vast as mine?
No rushing river, gusty sea, or ocean wild
whipped up with wind, or force of fire helped on
by hurricanes, could stop my fixed intention,
or my rage. I will destroy and ruin everything.
    Was he afraid of Creon, and of war with Lord
      Acastus?
True love is afraid of nobody.
But grant that he was forced to yield and to surrender;
he surely could have come to talk for the last time
    with his wife. That was exactly what this mighty
    hero feared…
Surely as son-in-law he could have put off the
420     time
of cruel exile: I got just one day
for two children.—I do not mind that the time is brief.
It will go far. This very day I will do
a deed of which all days will speak. I will attack
    the gods.
I will shake the world.
NURSE         Lady, you are upset;

yes, things are bad, but calm down!
MEDEA     Peace can only be mine
if I see everything ruined along with me.
Let fall the world with me. How sweet to destroy
    when you die.
NURSE See all the dangers you face if you persist.
Attacking those in power is never safe.     430
JASON My luck is always bad, and fate is always cruel:
just as bad to me, in kindness or in anger.
How often god finds for us antidotes
worse than the threatened pain. If I wanted to be
    faithful
to my wife—she had earned it—I had to forfeit
    my life.
If I did not want to die, I had to give up—poor
    me!—fidelity.
It was not fear that conquered faith
but quaking duty; she killed her parents; it was likely
the children would be next. O Holy Power, if you,
Justice, inhabit heaven, I call to you as witness:     440
love for my children defeated me. Though she is
    fierce,
spirited, she will not bear the yoke,
she still, I think, cares more for her children than her
    marriage.
I have made up my mind to beseech her, though she
    is angry.
and look, now she sees me, she jumps, in a towering
    rage. She shows
how much she hates me: all her bitterness is in
    her face.
MEDEA Jason, I have fled before, and now I flee again.
Exile is nothing new to me; only the cause has
    changed.
Once I fled for your sake. Now I leave, I go away,
because you force me to abandon your home, your
    hearth, your gods.     450
You are sending me back, but to whom? Should I go to
    the people of Colchis,
my father's kingdom, and the fields which we soaked
    with the blood
of my brother? Tell me, what country should I go
    and seek?
What seas do you point me towards? The mouth of
    the Pontic strait,
through which I led back home that glorious band
    of kings,
when I followed you—adulterer!—through the
    Clashing Rocks?

Or should I go to your uncle's lands—to Iolchos,
  or Tempe?
All the paths I opened up for you, I closed for me.
Where are you sending me back to? You impose exile
  on an exile,
but grant me no place to go.—I must go. The king's
460  son-in-law says so.
I do not resist. Pile up horrible punishments on me;
I have earned them. Let the king in his anger crush
  this concubine,
torture me, make me bleed, weigh down my hands
  with chains,
shut me up in a stony jail for an unending night.
My guilt will still outweigh my
  punishment.—Ungrateful!
wind back your mind to the bull, and its fiery gusts of
  breath,
and to all the barbarian terrors of a
  never-conquered race,
the flaming herd of Aeetes in the field of
  armored men,
and the weapons of the enemy which suddenly
  sprang up,
when at my command the earthborn soldiers fell, in a
470  mutual slaughter.
Remember the prize of your whole long quest, the
  Phrixean ram,
and the sleepless monster, whom I ordered to close
  his eyes
in mysterious sleep, and my brother, betrayed
  to death,
a crime not achieved in a single criminal act,
  but many;
and the daughters deceived by my trickery, who dared
to chop up the limbs of that old man who never would
  live again.
[I left my realm behind to come to someone else's.]
By your hopes for your children, by your nice
  safe home,
by the monsters I defeated, by my hands,
which I wore out for you, by all our dangers
480  past,
by sky and sea, witnesses of my marriage,
have pity. In your good fortune, reward me, please,
  I beg you.
From all that wealth the Colchian pirates win
from distant lands, the sunburnt Indians,
treasure that crams our house full up to bursting,

and we deck our trees with gold—from this wealth in
  my exile I took nothing,
except my brother's body; and I spent even that
  for you.
For you I gave up my kingdom, my father, my brother,
  my shame—
this was my dowry when I married you. I am leaving;
  give me back what is mine.
JASON When Creon was against you and wanted to
  destroy you,                                              490
my tears persuaded him to grant you exile.
MEDEA Exile, it seems, is a gift. I thought it was
  punishment.
JASON Go while you still can, run, take yourself far
  from here:
the anger of kings is always dangerous.
MEDEA              Your advice
is given to be loyal to Creusa. You banish her
  hated rival.
JASON Medea blames me for love?
MEDEA And murder, and betrayal.
JASON What crime, in the end, can you charge
  me with?
MEDEA All I have done.
JASON        Ah, that was all I needed;
that your crimes would be treated as my fault.
MEDEA They are yours, yours! If you gain from a
  crime,                                                    500
you did it. If your wife is disgraced, everyone is
  against her,
you alone must protect her, you shout out her
  innocence.
One who sinned for your sake should look clean
  to you.
JASON A life of which one feels ashamed is an
  unwelcome gift.
MEDEA One who feels ashamed of life need not
  cling to it.
JASON I disagree. You need to tame your heart, too
  quick to anger:
make peace with our sons.
MEDEA              They are no sons of mine!
Will Creusa give my children brothers?
JASON Yes, though she is a queen, to the wretched
  children of exiles.
MEDEA May such an evil day never come to my poor
  boys,                                                     510
for that filthy bloodline to taint my glorious stock,

the children of Phoebus joined to the sons of
   Sisyphus.
JASON Why, poor woman, are you dragging us both
   into ruin?
Leave, I beg you.
MEDEA          Creon heard my supplication.
JASON Tell me what I can do.
MEDEA          A crime for me; my turn.
JASON Hemmed in by two kings…
MEDEA          And by worse danger:
Medea. It is time for a face-off: let us fight,
and let the prize be Jason.
JASON          I am tired; I give in.
You, too, should be afraid: you have seen so many
   dangers.
MEDEA I have always stood above each turn of
520    Fortune.
JASON Acastus is pursuing us.
MEDEA          Creon is the nearer enemy:
flee both. Do not take up arms against your
   father-in-law
nor stain yourself with your own kinsman's blood.
Medea does not force you to. Be guiltless, run
   with me.
JASON But what defense is there, against a
   double war,
if Creon and Acastus join their arms together?
MEDEA Add the Colchians, and Lord Aeetes too,
with Scythians and Greeks: I will destroy
   them all.
JASON I shudder at great power.
MEDEA          Be careful not to want it.
JASON Talking too long looks suspicious; time to
530    break off.
MEDEA Now, King Jupiter, thunder your loudest
   across the sky,
stretch out your arm, prepare the flames of vengeance,
let the clouds be split, make tremble all the world.
Weigh your weapons in both hands, do not
   distinguish
between me and him: whichever of us falls
will die guilty. Your thunderbolt against us
cannot strike wrong.
JASON          Now make your thoughts more
   wholesome,
and act more calmly. If anything from my
   in-laws' home
can comfort you in exile, now is the time to ask.

MEDEA My heart, as you know, can despise the wealth
   of kings;                                        540
and it does. But let me have the children in my exile,
for company, so when my tears fall fast,
I may hold them in my arms. You will have new
   children.
JASON Certainly, I would like to say yes to your
   prayers,
but fatherly devotion must say no. To endure such a
   thing!—
not even the king, my father-in-law, himself could
   make me do it.
They are my reason for living; my scorched heart finds
   in them
my comfort for my pain. I would rather lose my
   breath,
my body, or the light.
MEDEA          Does he love his children so much?
Good! I have him trapped: there is a place to hurt him.
But of course you will allow me, as I take my leave,   550
to give the children my final words, and hug them for
   the last time?
Thank you. And this, now, is my very last request:
that if, in my distress, I have spoken out of turn,
forget about it: let your memory of me
be of my better self: let what I said in anger
be totally erased.
JASON          I have driven those words from
   my mind.
I too have a request: control the fire in your heart,
and take things easy: peace makes sorrows soft.
MEDEA He has gone. Is that it? You go off and forget
   about me                                         560
and all that I achieved? Do you see me as finished?
I will never be finished. Come on now,
   summon all
your strength and skill. The reward you have won
   from your crimes
is to think nothing a crime. There is little chance of
   deceit:
people suspect me. So choose a point to attack
which nobody could suspect. Go on, be daring, begin
to do whatever Medea can do, and even more
   than that.
   You, faithful nurse, companion of my sorrow
and of my changing fortune, help with my grim plan.
I have a cloak, a gift from the house in the sky,       570
the kingdom's glory, given to Aeetes as proof
that he was the child of the Sun. I also have a necklace

shining with plaited gold, and I tie up my hair
   with a band
of solid gold set off by brilliant gems.
Let my children carry these things as gifts from me to
   the bride,
but first, let them be smeared and daubed with deadly
   poison.
Let Hecate be summoned, prepare the rites of death:
let the altars be set up, let the flames ring through
   the halls.
CHORUS Force of flame, wind's turbulent buffet, javelins,
none of these come down with a force so
580   mighty,
none as fearful as when an ex-wife, rejected,
hates with hot passion.
Nor the wintry storms of the cloudy South Wind
nor when Hister floods in a rush, torrential,
forcing bridges down, letting none be mended,
vagabond river.
Nor the Rhone's crash into the deep of ocean,
nor when snows have melted and turned to small
   streams,
under hot sun, when in the midst of springtime
590 Haemus is melting.
Anger goaded on is a fire in darkness,
will not be controlled, will not suffer harness,
fears not death, desires to encounter danger,
runs to the drawn sword.
Mercy, gods, I pray your forgiveness for him,
let the man live safe, though he touched the ocean.
But the deep sea's master is angry his realm
now has been conquered.
Boldly that boy drove the eternal chariots,
600 never paying heed to his father's limits.
Wild, he scattered fires from the pole; the same fires
took him and hold him.
No one ever suffered from taking safe paths.
Take the same way many have trod before you.
Do not wildly break up the holy, sacred
bonds of the cosmos.
Each of those who entered that daring vessel,
seizing well-born oars from the sacred woodland—
Pelion's mountain glades were deprived of
   thick shade—
each of those who pushed through the wandering cliff
610   tops,
measured all that period of seaborne suffering,
reached at last barbarian shores, took anchor,
stole the gold from foreigners, sure of return,

paid with awful death, having boldly broken
laws of the deep sea.
Ocean punished forcefully those who wronged it.
Tiphys first, the man who had tamed the waters,
left his helm's control to a clueless captain,
far from home he died, in a foreign country,
lying on a foreign shore, in a pauper's tomb,     620
he lies among dead souls unknown to him.
Aulis keeps in mind its lost king, and therefore
makes the ships stop, keeps in harbor, stagnant,
though they resent it.
Born the child of the tuneful Muse, Orpheus
at whose plectrum, plucking the strings in rhythm,
waterfalls stood still and the winds were silent,
at whose song birds ceased their own sweet
   singing, flying
swift to him; the woods were his true companions;
he lay scattered over the Thracian farmlands,     630
while his head bobbed, rolled by the scowling Hebrus.
Styx he knew of old, and again he crossed it,
never to come back.
Hercules laid low the two sons of North Wind,
killed the sea-god's offspring, who always altered
how he looked, changing to shapes unnumbered.
After Hercules had brought peace to the land
   and ocean,
opened up the kingdoms of savage Hades,
living he lay down upon burning Oeta,
gave his body up to the cruel furnace.     640
Two destructive poisons consumed the hero,
gifts of his own bride.
Death brought low Ancaeus: the bristly wild boar
gored him. Then, bad man, Meleager slaughtered
his uncle. His angry mother kills him
with her own hands. All, all were guilty—
no: the young boy, snatched from the hero,
Hercules, who searched but never found him.
He died without guilt, seized in the quiet
   waters.     650
Come now, heroes, pray to the sea, beseech its
dangerous fountains.
Idmon also, though wise in the ways of fortune
lies beneath the Libyan sands: the serpent
killed him. Mopsus, truthful to all but himself,
fell, and Thebes has lost her most faithful prophet.
Thetis' husband, if he can tell the future,
knows he must go wandering, an exile, homeless.
Ajax, killed by thunder and ocean, paid back
father's transgression.

660 Nauplius had planned an attack on Argos;
fire betrayed him, headlong he falls to deep sea.
You reversed fate, wife, for your Pherean husband,
paid with your own life for the life of your man.
Even he who ordered the quest and booty,
'Bring me back the gold in the first of vessels!'
Pelias, boiled up in the heated cauldron,
burned, his limbs dispersed in the narrow waters.
Now enough, O Gods, of your vengeance. Jason
acted on orders.

### Act Four

NURSE My soul is terrified; it shudders. Evil is
670    near.
How great her bitterness is growing! Now it fires
itself, and it restores the force that it had lost.
I have often seen her in her rages, attacking the gods
bringing down the sky. But horrors, greater horrors,
Medea plans. She goes with feet of thunder
out from the house to the sanctuary of death;
there she spreads out all her treasures. Things that
    even she
has feared for years, she now takes out, unpacks
her whole array of evil, secrets long concealed.
With her left hand she makes ready the uncanny rites:
680 she summons the powers of destruction: scorching
        heat from the sands
of the Libyan desert, and the force of cold, which the
        mountains
of Taurus freeze with Arctic ice, perpetual snow.
She calls up every horror. Drawn by her magic spells
the scaly ones slip from their holes. They are here.
Here a savage serpent slithers its massive bulk,
its forked tongue darting to and fro; it looks for
        victims
whom it may kill. But hearing her voice, it stops,
plaits its swollen body into a heap of knots,
and piles them up in coils. Now she says: 'From the
690    earth
come only minor evils, weaker weapons.
I shall search the sky for poison. Now, now the time
    has come
to start something grander than ordinary deceit.
Let the Dragon descend, which lies like a rushing
        stream,
here let him come, whose massive coils touch
    the Bears,

those two wild beasts, the Great Bear and the Small,
(Greek sailors use the Great Bear, Tyrians use
    the Small)
and let the Serpent Holder at last release his grip,
and pour out venom. Let Python come at my call,
who dared provoke Diana and Apollo, the twin gods.
And let the Hydra come; let every snake, mown down    700
by Hercules, return, and heal its own death wound.
And you, abandon Colchis, my always-wakeful
    Dragon,
come to me; you were the first serpent I charmed to
    sleep.'
After she had summoned every kind of snake,
she heaped together all her poison plants.
Whatever grows on trackless Eryx's rocks,
and the mountain ridges clothed with eternal snow
of Caucasus, which is drenched in Prometheus' blood,
and the herbs which the wealthy Arabs use to anoint
    their arrows,    710
and the Medes, those fearsome archers, or the light-
    armed Parthians,
or the juices which the high-born German
    women gather
under a frozen sky, in their barbarian groves.
Whatever the earth produces while birds are
    building nests,
or when the frozen winter has already thrown
    aside
the beauty of the woodland, heaping up the
    freezing snow,
every plant whose blooming flowers bring death,
and deadly sap which lurks in twisted roots,
to bring us harm—she took them in her hands.
Some of the poisons came from Thessalian
    Athos;    720
Others from great Mount Pindus; on Pangaeus'
    ridges,
this plant's delicate leaves were lopped with a bloody
    sickle.
Some the Tigris fed, restraining his deep current;
others the Danube; some, bejewelled Hydaspes,
  running with warm waters through the desert lands,
and these by the river Baetis, which gave its own name
    to its country,
which hits the Western Sea with a quiet plash.
Some of the plants were cut by iron, while Apollo got
    ready the day,
the stem of others is cut at the dead of night,
others cropped with a fingernail, while a charm is said.

She gathers the poisonous plants and squeezes
730     the venom
of the snakes, and mixes it with birds of ill omen,
the heart of a melancholy eagle-owl, and the innards
cut from a living screech-owl. These, the great criminal
    mastermind
laid out separately. Some contain the devouring power
of fire; others hold the icy cold of bitter frost.
She added to the poisons certain words—themselves
equally dangerous. Listen! You can hear her
    crazy feet.
She is chanting and the world is shaking at her spell.
740  MEDEA I pray you, silent hordes, and ghostly gods,
Chaos obscure, dark home of shady Dis,
caverns of ugly Death, bound by Tartarus,
Spirits, be free from your torments, hurry to this new
    wedding.
Let stop the wheel which wrenches his body, may
    Ixion touch the ground,
may Tantalus freely drink the waters of Pirene.
Only for his in-laws should punishment increase:
let the slippery stone send Sisyphus tumbling down
    the rocks.
You too, who vainly work to fill the leaky urns,
Danaids, gather here: this day requires your hands.
Now, summoned by my rituals, come to me, moon of
750    the night,
put on your fiercest faces, scowling with all three.
    For you I have loosened my hair and bared my foot
to sway as my people do through the secret parts of
    the wood.
I have called down gushing water from dry clouds,
driven the ocean to its bed; the swelling tides,
defeated, have withdrawn inside the sea.
I have confounded the law of the sky: the world
    has seen
both sun and stars together, and you, Bears, have
    touched
the forbidden sea. I have bent the course of the
    seasons,
760  the summery earth has shuddered at my spell,
Ceres has been compelled to see harvest in winter.
Phasis' wild waters turn to their source again,
and Hister, with its many mouths, restrains
its waters, sullen in all their separate banks.
The waves have roared, the frenzied sea rose high
without the sound of wind. The home of the
    ancient wood
has lost its shadows when it heard my voice.

Phoebus, abandoning day, has stopped in the
    middle sky,
the Hyades are shaken by my spells and totter.
Now, Diana, is the time to come to your own rites.    770
    For you I weave these wreaths with bloody hand,
wreaths bound up with serpents nine,
    To you I give these limbs which rebel
        Typhon bore,
who shook the realms of Jove.
    Here is the blood of that treacherous ferryman,
which dying Nessus gave.
    Here is the ash from the fading pyre of Oeta,
which drank the poison of Hercules.
    Here you see the torch of a good sister, a wicked
        mother,
Althaea the avenger.    780
    These are the feathers left in a far remote cave
by the Harpy, fleeing Zetes.
    Add to these the wings of a wounded
        Stymphalian bird,
struck by Lernaean arrows.
    Altars, you crackle: I see my tripods tremble
as the goddess gives consent.
I can see Hecate's swift chariot in the sky,
not that which she drives when her face shines full,
all through the night,
but the one that she rides with a mournful
    expression,    790
troubled by threats from Thessalian witches,
picking her way through the sky with a tighter rein.
With just that pallid face, pour grim light out through
    the air,
frighten the people with a new source of terror,
and let the precious cymbals of bronze ring out,
to help you, Diana.
For you we offer the holy rite
on the bloody turf,
for you the torch is seized from the midst of a pyre,
to burn for you with fires in the night-time,    800
for you I toss my head and twist my neck
and chant my spells,
for you I have tied up my flowing hair
in a headband like corpses wear,
for you I shake the gloomy branch from the waters
    of Styx.
For you, bare-breasted, like a Maenad,
I slash my arms with a holy knife.
My own blood drips on the altar:
hands, get used to unsheathing the blade,

810 and submit to shed your own dear blood.
I have struck myself! The sacred fluid flows.
But if you do not like the frequent summons
of my prayers, please forgive me.
Hecate, I call so many times
for your arrows
for just one reason, always the same. Jason.
Now anoint Creusa's clothes,
and as soon as she puts them on, let a snaky flame
burn up very marrow of her bones.
820 Let the fire lie hid in yellow gold,
in darkness. He who robbed heaven for fire,
and paid with ever-growing liver for his theft,
gave me this flame, and taught me how to hide
power by art: Prometheus. Mulciber gave
flames hidden in delicate sulphur,
and I got from my cousin Phaethon
the thunder of living flame.
I have the gifts of the middle of Chimaera,
I have the flames stolen from the scorched throats
830 of the bulls,
which mixed with the gall of Medusa,
I have ordered to create a secret venom.
     Hecate, whip up my poisons,
and keep secret the seeds of flame in my gifts:
may they deceive the eyes, submit to touch,
but may the heat swim to the heart and veins,
make melt the limbs and smoke the bones
and may that newly wedded bride outdo her
     marriage torch
with her own smoking hair.
840      My prayers succeed: she barks three times,
bold Hecate, and shoots
sacred flames from her melancholy torch.
     The whole power of my rites has been achieved.
     Call here the children,
who will take my precious gift to the newly wed bride.
     Go, go my children! Though the mother who
          bore you is unlucky,
make peace with your mistress, your stepmother: give
     her these presents
and pray to her all you can. Go, and come quickly back
to your home, and let me enjoy a last embrace with you.
CHORUS Where is this blood-stained Maenad rushing,
850 headlong, seized by barbarian lust?
What crime does she plot
in her violent fury?
Her face roused up in anger
is glazed, she shakes her head

proudly, wildly;
she sets out to threaten the king.
     Who would believe her an exile?
Her cheeks flame red,
her pallor puts her blush to flight.
She keeps no color long,                                     860
her shape is ever-changing.
Here and there she moves her feet
as a tigress, her cubs lost,
scans the groves of the Ganges
on thunderous paws.
Medea cannot understand restraint
for anger, or for love.
Now anger and love have joined
to give her a cause: what will happen?
When will this Colchian monster                              870
leave the lands of Greece
and release from fear
the kingdom and royal family?
Now, Phoebus, speed your chariot,
let your reins lie loose,
may gentle night bury the light,
may Hesperus, night's leader,
drown this fearful day.


## Act Five

MESSENGER Now all is lost, the whole state of the
     kingdom is fallen:
daughter and father together lie mixed
     with ash.                                               880
CHORUS What trickery deceived them?
MESSENGER      The usual one for kings:
gifts.
CHORUS What fraud could there be in those?
MESSENGER I am astounded too, and though I know
     it happened,
I find I can scarcely believe it.
CHORUS          What was the cause of death?
MESSENGER Devouring flame is raging through the
     palace,
obeying some command. Now the whole house has
     fallen,
people fear for the city.
CHORUS          Get water, put out the flames!
MESSENGER In this disaster, something magical:
water feeds the flames, the more they fight the fire,
the higher still it burns. It robs our defenses.            890

NURSE Carry yourself away, fast as you can, from the
  land of Pelops,
Medea, run away: find anywhere else to live.
MEDEA I? Would I run? Would I yield? If I had
  fled before
I would return for this, to watch a new type of wedding.
Why hesitate, my soul? Follow your lucky strike.
This is a tiny fraction of your triumph.
You are still in love, mad heart, if this is enough:
to see Jason unmarried. Look for new punishment,
unprecedented, and prepare yourself:
900   let all morality be gone, and exile shame;
  that vengeance is too light which clean hands can
    perform.
  Spur on your anger, rouse your weary self,
  from the depths of your heart draw up your former
    passions
  with even greater violence. Whatever I did before,
  name it dutiful love. Come now! I will reveal
  how trivial and ordinary they were,
  those crimes I did before. With them, my bitterness
  was only practicing: how could my childish hands
  do something truly great? Could the rage of a girl
    do this?
  Now, I am Medea. My nature has grown with my
910   suffering.
  I am happy that I ripped my brother's head away,
  I am glad I sliced his limbs, and glad I stripped
    my father
  of his ancestral treasure, I am glad I set on the
    daughters
  to murder the old man. Now, pain, find your new chance.
  You bring to every action a hand that knows its way.
  Where then, my anger, shall I point you? Fire what
    weapons
  at that traitor? My savage heart has made a plan,
  a secret one, stored deep inside, and does not dare
  reveal it yet, even to itself. Fool! I went too fast.
920   I wish my enemy had had some children
  by that concubine of his.—Whatever was yours
    by him,
  Creusa was its mother. That kind of punishment
  is what I want; yes, good. My great heart must do
  the final wickedness. Children—once my children—
  you must give yourselves as payback for your father's
    crimes.
    Awful! It hits my heart, my body turns to ice,
  my chest is heaving. Anger has departed,

the wife in me is gone, I am all mother again.
Is this me? Could I spill my own children's blood,
flesh of my flesh? No, no, what terrible madness!   930
Let that horrible deed, that dreadful crime, be
    unthought of,
even by me. Poor things! What crime have they
    ever done?
Jason is their father: that is their crime. And worse:
Medea is their mother. Let them die; they are
    not mine.
Let them die; they are mine. They did nothing wrong,
    they are blameless,
they are innocent: I admit it. So was my brother.
Why, my soul, do you waver? Why are my cheeks
    blotched with tears,
why am I led in two directions, now by anger,
now by love? My double inclination tears me apart.
As when the wild winds make their brutal
    wars   940
and on both sides the seas lift up discordant waves,
and the unstable water boils: even so my heart
tosses and churns: love is chased out by rage
and rage by love. Resentment, yield to love.
    Here to me, darling children, only comfort
for this troubled house, bring yourselves here,
    embrace me,
fold yourselves in my arms. Let your father have
    you safe,
as long as your mother has you too.—But I must go
    in exile.
Any minute, they will be ripped from my arms,
weeping and wailing. Let their father lose their
    kisses,   950
their mother has already lost them. Again, my
    anger grows,
my hatred boils. My ancient Fury seeks
my reluctant hands again—anger, I follow your lead.
I wish as many children as proud Niobe bore
had come from my womb, I wish I had
twice-seven sons! I was infertile for revenge:
but my two are just enough to pay for brother and
    father.
Look! What are they doing, this violent crowd of
    Furies?
Whom are they seeking, at whom are they aiming
    those flaming blows,
at whom does the hellish army aim its bloody
    torches?   960

The great snake hisses and twists as the whip
    comes down.
Whom is the head of the Furies seeking, with her
    menacing brand,
Megaera? Whose shade comes half-invisible, his limbs
scattered apart? It is my brother, he wants
    revenge.
We will pay it: we will all pay. Fix deep your torch in
    my eyes,
ravage me, burn me up, see, my whole breast is open
    for the Furies.
   Leave me, my brother, and you avenging goddesses,
and order your ghosts to go back safe to the depths
    of Hell
Leave me to myself and use this hand, my brother,
which has drawn the sword: we appease your spirit
970    now,
with this sacrificial victim.—What was that
    sudden noise?
They are taking up weapons against me, they want to
    kill me.
I will climb up to the topmost roof of our house
though the killing is unfinished. All of you, come
    with me.
And I myself will carry away with me your body.
Now do it, heart: you must not waste your courage
in secret: prove to the people the things you can do.
JASON If any man is loyal, and mourns the
    princes' death,
run, gather here, let us arrest that wicked woman
who did the dreadful crime. Come, my brave band of
980    warriors,
bring here your weapons, push her from the top of
    the house.
MEDEA Now, now I have regained my throne, my
    brother, and my father.
The Colchians keep the treasure of the Golden Ram.
My kingdom comes back to me, my stolen virginity
    returns.
O gods, you favor me at last, a happy day,
O wedding day! Now leave, the crime is complete:
I am not yet revenged. Go on, while you are at it:
Why do you hesitate now, my soul? Why are you
    doubtful?
Does your powerful anger now subside? I am sorry for
    what I have done,
I am ashamed. What, wretch, have you done? Wretch?
990    Even if I regret it,

I have done it. Great pleasure steals over me against
    my will,
and see! now it grows. This was all I was missing,
that Jason should be watching. I think I have so far
    done nothing:
crimes committed without him were wasted.
JASON Look, she is hovering on the outermost part of
    the roof.
Somebody, bring fire, and burn her up, let her fall
consumed by her own flames.
MEDEA Heap up a funeral pyre
for your own sons, Jason, and strew the burial mound.
your wife and father-in-law now have their
    proper rites:
I have buried them. This son has already met his fate;
this one will die the same, but you will watch.    1000
JASON By all the gods, by the exile we shared,
and by our marriage bed, which I did not betray,
now spare this child. If wrong was done, I did it.
I give myself to death: slaughter this guilty man.
MEDEA I will drive my sword into that very spot
    which hurts you most.
Now, proud man, go off and marry virgins.
Leave mothers alone.
JASON       One boy is enough for revenge.
MEDEA If my hand had been able to find satisfaction
    in just one murder,
I should have done none. Although I shall kill
    two,    1010
the number is too small to satisfy my pain.
If my womb even now contains any pledge of our love,
    I, the mother,
will scrape my insides with my sword, I will bring it
    out with the blade.
JASON So go on with the crime you began, I will beg
    you no longer.
    But at least grant respite for my sufferings.
MEDEA Ah, bitter heart, enjoy slow crime, do not hurry:
    this is my day: I am using the time I was given.
JASON Hell-cat, kill me too!
MEDEA        You ask me for pity?—
Good, it is done. Rage, I had no more
to sacrifice for you. Now wipe your swollen
    eyes,    1020
ungrateful Jason. Do you not know your wife?
This is the way I always leave a country. The way in the
    sky lies clear.
Twin serpents lower their head, their scaly necks

accept the yoke. Now, Daddy, take your children back.
But I will fly amid the winds on my chariot
   with wings.

JASON Go, travel on up high through the deep expanse
   of the heavens, prove that there are no gods
   wherever you go.

## AFTERWORD

Seneca's literary legacy in antiquity was largely confined to his prose works, and attention focused not on the content but on the style of his writing. In contrast, the tragedies do not seem to have had a lasting impact among his contemporaries, with perhaps one exception. Very soon after the death of Nero, someone composed *Octavia,* a play very much in Seneca's own manner (some people even think it is *by* him). It is the only surviving example of a tragedy on a Roman subject (known as a *praetexta,* a play in serious Roman attire), recounting the story of Nero's first wife, whom he had murdered. The play not only exhibits a decided predilection for Senecan pyrotechnics but also features Seneca himself as a protagonist, which is just one of many factors militating against attributing it to him as author. If, as some scholars think, *Hercules on Mt. Oeta* is also not an authentic Senecan play, then it too would be evidence of Seneca's influence on dramatic productions in the Flavian period. But after this, there is little or no reason to believe that the plays were being widely read, with only rare citations found in authors of late antiquity or the Middle Ages.

As a prose stylist, Seneca was much admired and much imitated both in his own lifetime and after, especially by aspiring young orators. His pungent, epigrammatic manner was for many a welcome change from the rotund periods of Ciceronian Latin. Even among his contemporaries, however, this was contested territory: the emperor Caligula, for example, derided his style as "pure ostentation, sand without lime." The gist of this criticism was that Seneca strove for temporary effect at the expense of developing a cohesive argument. Supporters would counter that, while Seneca's sentences might be disconnected, his ideas were coherent. This dispute would be played out repeatedly in antiquity, for just as Cicero had come to represent one ideal of eloquence in Latin, Seneca would henceforth represent the principal alternative. The chief criticism came from Quintilian in the following generation. His strong preference for Ciceronian style obliged him to make a detailed critique of Seneca's influence (*Education of the Orator* 10.1.126–31). Even so, Quintilian concedes that Seneca's style possesses "alluring defects" (*dulcia vitia*) that repay study, so long as one is careful to exercise discretion in choosing what might be worth imitating. Again, the emphasis is entirely on style, since he judged Seneca to be rather a lightweight as a philosopher (a view shared by most philosophers), although Quintilian grants that in his writings at least, if not in his life, Seneca vigorously denounced vice.

Quintilian's view did not immediately carry the day, at least to judge from the favorable references to Seneca's eloquence by Tacitus, whose own style owes much to Seneca's legacy. But during the second-century craze for early Latin writers, championed by the likes of Aulus Gellius, Fronto, and Marcus Aurelius, Seneca became a target of criticism. Gellius calls Seneca's diction "commonplace and trite" (*vulgaria et protrita*) and does not consider him learned, "since he doesn't draw on the writings of the ancients." Gellius concedes that there are those who think Seneca valuable because of his censure of moral turpitude, but for him, Seneca is disqualified as a stylistic model by his recorded opinions about Ennius, Virgil, and Cicero. Criticisms of this sort seem to have had an effect, because Seneca is largely ignored by grammarians and pagan authors of late antiquity.

At the same time as he fell out of favor with Latin stylists, Seneca was adopted by Christian authors who were largely in sympathy with his brand of Stoicism. His influence can be detected in many of the Latin fathers, but he was a special favorite of Lactantius in the late third and early fourth centuries A.D. Lactantius calls Seneca the "fiercest Stoic among the Romans" (*Divine Institutes* 1.5.26) and praises him for recognizing the divinity in nature. "If you want to know all about this," he says, "pick up the books of Seneca, because when it comes to public morals and vices he produced the most accurate descriptions and the fiercest censure" (*Divine Institutes* 5.9.19). This was the climate in which, sometime in the fourth century, a Christian admirer of Seneca composed a collection of imaginary letters between Seneca and St. Paul. The *Correspondence between Seneca and St. Paul* was soon taken to be authentic, and on the strength of this collection, St. Jerome included Seneca in his Catalog of the Saints.

This was probably an important factor in the survival of Seneca's works, with the result that there were enough copies available throughout the Middle Ages to fuel the great boom in his popularity that took place in the twelfth and thirteenth centuries. In the following years, Dante and Chaucer both refer to Seneca, but Petrarch was a particularly great admirer: Seneca is one of the nine ancient authors to whom he addressed letters in his book of correspondence, and Petrarch's works are full of quotations from Seneca's *Moral Epistles*. In 1398, the University of Piacenza actually established a chair for the study of Seneca. For most of the Middle Ages interest in Seneca had been limited to the philosophical works, but during the fourteenth century the tragedies began to emerge from the obscurity that had enveloped them since antiquity.

In 1927, T. S. Eliot summed up the state of Senecan reception since the Middle Ages: "In the Renaissance, no Latin author was more highly esteemed than Seneca; in modern times, few Latin authors have been more consistently damned." By 1475, most of his prose works had appeared in print, with the exception of the *Natural Questions* and the *Apocolocyntosis*, which were published within the next generation. The great Dutch humanist Desiderius Erasmus (1466–1536) produced an edition of Seneca's works, the second edition of which in 1529 was enormously influential. Erasmus also made liberal use of Seneca's philosophical prose in his own work, especially the *Adagia* (first ed. 1500), a collection of sayings gathered from his wide reading in Greek and Latin literature. The French humanist Michel de Montaigne (1533–92) acquired a taste for Seneca during his school days and quotes extensively from him in his *Essays*. As he says, "I have not had commerce with any excellent book except Plutarch or Seneca, from whom, as the Danaids, I draw my water incessantly filling and as fast emptying." But although interest in Seneca as a moralist and a philosopher did not evaporate entirely, it is the tragedies now that for the first time defined Seneca's reception.

The first edition of the tragedies was printed in 1484. Performances of the plays in Latin were common in the following century, and translations into modern languages appeared across Europe. Seneca's influence was greatest in Italy, but it was also felt in England, where there was little knowledge of Greek tragedy. In Seneca Elizabethan playwrights found rich inspiration for their brand of drama—ghosts and witches, tyrants and heroes, bloody treachery and horrible revenge. Translations of all but one of the individual plays had appeared in print in the decade of the 1560s by Jasper Heywood, Alexander Neville, Thomas Nuce, and John Studley. These were then collected by Thomas Newton, who added his own version of *The Phoenician Women*; he published them in 1581 as *Seneca His Tenne Tragedies*. This was the only English translation available to the Elizabethans, and it helped to mediate Seneca not only to Shakespeare but to the likes of Jonson and Marlowe as well. The *Medea* was translated by John Studley (while still an undergraduate!), who employed the fourteen-syllable line that was characteristic of the time to exuberant alliterative effect, for example, in rendering Medea's invocation of the forces of darkness in Act 4:

O Flittring Flockes of grisly ghostes that sit in silent seat
O ougsome Bugges, O Gobblins grym of Hell I you intreat:
O lowryng *Chaos* dungeon blynde, and dreadfull darkened pit,
Where *Ditis* muffled up in Clowdes of blackest shades doth sit,

O wretched wofull wawling soules your ayde I doe implore,
That linked lye with gingling Chaynes on wayling *Limbo* shore,
O mossy Den where death doth couche his gastly carrayne Face:
Relesse your pangues, O spryghts, and to this wedding hye apace.

On the Continent, Corneille's *Médée* is a fairly close imitation of Seneca's version of the story, and Senecan influence can also be detected in the plays of Racine and Voltaire. But as tastes changed, assisted in part by greater familiarity with classical Greek tragedy, the salient characteristics of Senecan drama with its emphasis on rhetorical flourishes and graphic violence proved less popular.

In the present day interest in Seneca is on the upswing in academic circles, but there is no sign yet of a revival among nonspecialists, even in his home country of Spain. But in 1965 one famous son of Córdoba paid tribute to another, when Manuel Benítez Pérez, also known as El Cordobés (The Cordovan), the greatest bullfighter of his day, commissioned a statue of Seneca to be placed beside the lone surviving Moorish gate to the city, the Puerta de Almodóvar.

# JOSEPHUS

(Titus Flavius Iosephus, ca. A.D. 37–ca. 100)

JOSEPHUS WAS BORN INTO A WEALTHY JEWISH FAMILY IN JERUSALEM IN A.D. 37 OR 38, a few months after Caligula replaced Tiberius as emperor of Rome. Along with Philo of Alexandria, who was some sixty years his senior, he is the leading representative of Judeo-Hellenic literature, and we are indebted to them for most of what we know about Jewish perspectives on, and dealings with, the early Roman Empire. Whereas Philo is particularly significant for his voluminous writings within the Greek philosophical tradition, Josephus is an extraordinarily informative chronicler of political and military history, particularly the contemporary Jewish resistance to the Romans. This is hardly surprising, for he experienced the conflict from both sides. He served as a high-ranking officer in the Jewish forces when they revolted against Rome in A.D. 66. The following year, in the storming of the almost impregnable fortress of Jotapata, he was taken prisoner after notoriously escaping from a suicide pact made with his surviving comrades, of which he himself gives a naively candid account (*Jewish War* 3.8.7). After being captured, he returned to Jerusalem in the entourage of Titus, the son of the newly established emperor, Vespasian, and was an eyewitness to the bloody sack of the city and the, perhaps unintentional, burning of the temple in A.D. 70.

Josephus stands rather apart from the other authors whose works are represented in this anthology in that he is firmly rooted in a culture that is neither Roman nor Greek. Almost all genres of Roman literature would have been inconceivable without their Greek models. By contrast, the only literary work brought to Rome from the destruction of Carthage was Mago's treatise on agriculture, which was translated into Latin by order of the Senate, and which, ironically, retained its influence on Roman agricultural writers for many centuries alongside the *On Agriculture* of Marcus Porcius Cato, the politician who insisted so doggedly that Carthage must be destroyed. Josephus's Judaism is a prominent feature of all his writings, and this gives us a valuable insight into what it was like to live in the Roman Empire without belonging either to the politically dominant race (i.e., the Romans) or to the intellectually dominant culture (i.e., the Greeks).

Vespasian settled Josephus in Italy, where he devoted himself to writing, with no further political or military activity. His first work, dedicated to Titus in the mid-70s, was the *Jewish War,* which begins with the Maccabean period in the 160s B.C. but focuses particularly on the uprising against Rome that began in A.D. 66. Like all Josephus's works, it is written in Greek, but it was originally written in Aramaic, his native language. His other works were all published in the 90s: *Jewish Antiquities,* his most substantial work, an account of Jewish history, laws, and customs; *Against Apion,* a defense of Judaism's significance as a religion, established long before the philosophical schools of the Greeks; and finally, his *Autobiography,* published probably in A.D. 99.

Josephus claims that the *Jewish Antiquities* was compiled at the insistence of various "interested parties." It is easily credible that there should have been a need for such an account. With some remarkable exceptions, neither the Greeks nor the Romans were greatly interested in other cultures (hence the dismissive and all-embracing term "barbarian"). By the first century A.D., there may have been more than 40,000 Jews living in the city of Rome (population figures are always problematic), but neither the Romans nor the Greeks knew much about their culture. Alexander of Miletus, a Greek polymath who lived in Rome in the first half of the first century B.C., claimed that Hebrew law had been composed by a woman with the splendid name Moso (*Fragments of the Greek Historians* 270.70). Josephus's younger contemporary Tacitus at least knew that Moses was a man, but he supposed, contrary to Jewish tradition, that the wandering in the desert lasted rather less than forty years, and that Moses himself *did* reach the promised land: "After an unbroken journey of six days, on the seventh they expelled the inhabitants and took control of the land, in which they set up their city and their temple" (*Histories* 5.2). With a strong hint of intolerance, Tacitus goes straight on to add that "to confirm the people for the future, Moses established new rites quite contrary to those of the rest of mankind. Everything that we hold sacred they regard as profane, while what we consider unholy is permissible among them." But actively antagonistic anti-Semitic feeling in Rome should not be exaggerated. One of the benefits of the Romans' lack of interest in other cultures was their willingness to allow the various peoples of the empire to continue with their own traditions, so long as they contributed the taxes and tribute imposed on them. Although the Jews suffered appallingly at the hands of the Romans in various uprisings over the centuries, this was attributable more to political unrest than to Roman anti-Semitism. The Jewish community in Rome was greatly saddened by the assassination of Julius Caesar and kept a vigil over his pyre for many nights in succession (Suetonius, *Life of Julius Caesar* 84). In a long catalog of kindnesses done to Jews by Augustus, Philo notes that, if the dole of grain or money fell on their sabbath, he allowed them to collect it on the following day (*On the Embassy to Gaius* 158).

Although he had suffered personally in the uprising that he recounts in the *Jewish War*, Josephus attributes the blame for the war to Jewish factions, rather than to the conquering Romans (1.10):

> It was internal conflict that destroyed our fatherland, and the tyrants among the Jews dragged the Romans' hands and their fire unwillingly against our temple. Titus Caesar, who himself destroyed Jerusalem, is witness to this. Throughout the war, he pitied the Jewish people, who were kept under surveillance by the factions, and many times he deliberately held back from taking the city, so that the protraction of the siege might give those responsible time to repent.

But, of course, we should not forget that, as is clear from his Romanized name, Titus Flavius Josephus was writing in the comfort and security of the patronage of the Flavians, Vespasian and Titus, the very commanders of the Roman armies. He can hardly be expected to write without bias.

Josephus's personal cultural background has little or no particular bearing on the episode selected for inclusion here, his lengthy and at times thrilling account of the assassination of Caligula in A.D. 41. There are other versions of this event in Suetonius's *Life of Caligula* and in Cassius Dio's *History of Rome,* but they are both briefer and without the same wealth of detail and dramatic tension. Especially when dealing with the less meritorious emperors, Suetonius draws a clear line of demarcation separating his subject's virtues and achievements from his vices and misdeeds. For Nero, it comes at the end of Chapter 19: "These deeds, some of them meriting no reproach, others even deserving some praise, I have gathered together to separate them from the shameful deeds and crimes with which I shall henceforth be concerned." He is even more explicit in announcing his focus on Caligula's vicious character: "So far, I have taken account of Caligula as emperor; the rest of what I have to say is about him as a monster" (*Life of Caligula* 22). In Chapter 27, Suetonius collects incidents and practices which he regards as particularly indicative of Caligula's sadistic cast of mind, and that catalog serves eloquently to set Josephus's account of the assassination in its context. For example:

**Figure 20:   Coin of Caligula**
The Romans famously favored verism in their representations of themselves. It is therefore difficult to reconcile this rather handsome depiction of Caligula with Suetonius's unattractive catalog of his physical characteristics, describing him as, e.g., scrawny-necked, prematurely balding, with sunken eyes and temples, and an ugly and savage facial expression, which he accentuated by practising in front of a mirror (*Life of Caligula* 50).

When the cost of cattle to feed wild beasts which he had collected for a show became too high, he selected criminals to be torn to pieces by them. Running his eye along a row of prisoners, but paying no attention to the charges against them, he stood in the middle of the portico and ordered victims to be taken away "from that bald one to that bald one".

He had many people from the upper orders of society disfigured by branding, and then condemned either to the mines, or to road-working, or to wild beast shows, or else he confined them in cages, on all fours like animals, and had them sawn in two. And not always for serious offences; some had merely criticized his shows, or had never sworn by his Genius.

He had the manager of his gladiatorial and animal shows chained up and flogged for several days in a row, while he himself looked on. He did not have him killed until he was offended by the smell of his putrefied brain.

It is most unfortunate that the books dealing with Caligula in Tacitus's *Annals* have not survived. We may be confident that Tacitus will have drawn heavily on his own experience of the tyranny of Domitian in portraying the life and rule of the at least equally vicious Caligula. Just such personal animus informs the final comment in the succinct description of Caligula's death given by Cassius Dio, who knew all about imperial instability and mayhem, having lived through the reigns of the equally unsavory Commodus, Caracalla, and Elagabalus:

The assassins intercepted Caligula in a narrow passage and killed him. When he had fallen, none of them held back; they all inflicted savage wounds on his corpse, with some even tasting his flesh. His wife and daughter were quickly killed also. So it was that Caligula, after doing so many dreadful things for three years, nine months, and twenty-eight days, found through actual experience that he was not a god. (*Roman History* 59.29)

Even Tacitus, however, would have been hard-pressed to match the excitement generated by Josephus in his account of the plot against this most dastardly of emperors.

# JEWISH ANTIQUITIES

## Book 19.1–29

*The work falls into two clearly definable halves. In the first ten books, Josephus relates the history of the Jewish people from the creation of the world to the Persian Empire, while Books 11 through 20 take the narrative from Alexander the Great's conquests to the Jewish-Roman War of A.D. 66–70. In Book 18 Josephus deals with events during the reign of the emperor Gaius, more familiarly known as Caligula, who ruled from A.D. 37 to 41. Gaius's policies toward the Jews in Palestine were disastrous and included a plan to have his statue placed in the Jerusalem Temple. This perhaps supplied a motivation for Josephus to devote a long excursus at the beginning of Book 19 to the conspiracy against Gaius and the accession of Claudius. In the first section, Josephus provides a long list of examples of the emperor's insanity.*

[1] Gaius not only exhibited the madness of his insolence in relation to the Jews who dwelt in Jerusalem and throughout Judaea, but he also sent it forth to spread over every land and sea which was subject to the Romans, and infected the empire with countless ills, such as had never before been chronicled in history. Rome above all felt the horror of his actions, since he gave it no more privilege than other cities, but harried the citizens, especially the senators and those who were of the patrician class or had special honors because of distinguished ancestors. He also devised countless attacks upon the equites, as they were called. The standing and financial influence of this group gave them equal status with the senators in the eyes of the city because it was from their ranks that the Senate was recruited. He deprived the equites of their privileges and expelled them from Rome or put them to death and robbed them of their wealth; for it was usually as a pretext for confiscating their property that he had them slain. He would also have deified himself and demanded from his subjects honors that were no longer such as may be rendered to a man. When he visited the Temple of Jupiter which they call the Capitol and which is first in honor among their temples, he had the audacity to address Jupiter as brother. His other actions too did not fall short of madness. For instance, it was insufferable, he thought, to cross the bay from the city of Dicaearchia in Campania to Misenum, another maritime city, in a trireme. Then, too, he considered

it his privilege as lord of the sea to require the same service from the sea as he received from the land. So the thirty furlongs of sea from headland to headland were connected by pontoons, which cut off the whole bay, and over this bridge he drove in his chariot. That way of traveling, said he, befitted his godhead. Of the Greek temples he left none unpillaged, giving orders that paintings and sculptures and all other statues and dedicatory offerings with which they were furnished should be brought to him; for it was not right, he said, that beautiful objects should stand anywhere but in the most beautiful place, and that was the city of Rome. With the spoils which he brought from Greece, he adorned his palace and gardens and all his residences throughout the land of Italy. He even dared to give orders to transport to Rome the "Zeus" that was worshipped by the Greeks at Olympia and was therefore called Olympian, a work of the artist Phidias of Athens. He did not, however, carry out this intention, for the chief technicians reported to Memmius Regulus, who had the assignment of moving the Zeus, that the work would be ruined if it were moved. It is said that Memmius postponed removing the statue not only for this reason but because of certain portents *a* that were too serious to be discredited. *b* He sent Gaius a letter reporting these matters and explaining his failure to carry out his orders. In consequence, he risked being executed, but he was saved by the death of Gaius which intervened.

*In the following sections Josephus explains his reasons for turning from the main line of his narrative to recount the circumstances surrounding Gaius's death. He then sets the background with a brief description of three conspiracies that had formed against Gaius, and describes an incident at the chariot races that spurred Chaerea to action.*

[2] So far did Gaius' frenzy go, that when a daughter was born to him he actually carried her to the Capitol and deposited her on the knees of the statue, remarking that the child belonged to both him and Zeus and that he had appointed two fathers for her, but left open the question which of the two was the greater. Such was the behavior that the world had to put up with. He also permitted servants to bring accusations against their masters on whatever charges they pleased. Anything that was reported was bound to have serious consequences, because most of the charges were brought for his gratification or at his suggestion. Thus Polydeuces,

the slave of Claudius, dared to bring an accusation against Claudius, and Gaius was tolerant enough to attend court when a capital charge was brought against his own uncle, expecting to receive authority to put him to death. He was, however, disappointed. As he had made all of the inhabited world over which he ruled a prey to informers and their evil work and had raised high the power of slaves over their masters, conspiracies were now commonly formed against him. Some of the conspirators were angry and sought vengeance for the wrongs they had endured, others counted on doing away with the creature before they fell foul of him and suffered disaster. Therefore, since his death not only was of great importance in the interest of all men's laws and the safeguarding of them, but our own nation was brought to the very verge of ruin and would have been destroyed but for his sudden death, I am resolved to give an exact account of everything that happened. I have another particular motive in that the story provides good evidence of God's power. It will comfort those who are in unhappy circumstances, and will teach a lesson in sobriety to those who think that good fortune is eternal and do not know that it ends in catastrophe unless it goes hand in hand with virtue.

[3] There were three schemes in preparation for his death, and each of them had good men as leaders. Aemilius Regulus of Cordova in Iberia was the center of one ring and heartily hoped to dispose of Gaius either by the hands of his colleagues or by his own. A second ring was in process of organization to aid them, of which Cassius Chaerea the military tribune was leader. Finally, Annius Vinicianus was no slight addition to those who were enlisted against the tyranny. The reasons for their hatred of Gaius were as follows: Regulus was moved by general indignation and a detestation of unjust proceedings. For he had in him a free man's independent spirit, so much so that he even threw his weight against keeping any of the plots a close secret. At any rate he informed many friends of them as well as others who won his approval as men of action. Vinicianus joined the plot partly to avenge Lepidus, a special friend of his and one of the best citizens, who had been put to death by Gaius, and partly from fear for himself, because when Gaius gave vent to his anger, it was a death-dealing fury that made no exceptions. Chaerea joined because he felt disgraced by the slurs cast on his manliness by Gaius; moreover, there was daily peril in his intimate attendance on Gaius, and he considered it the part of a free man to put an end to

him. These three men thought that the matter should be laid for general consideration before everyone who had been spectators of the emperor's insolence and who desired, by removing Gaius, to avoid the sharp sword that was raging against others. Perhaps they would succeed; and a high thing it would be to achieve such good ends by their efforts, when they were ready in any case to strike for the preservation of city and empire even if it meant their own destruction. Chaerea was especially bent on action, both because he desired to win a better reputation, and because, by his freer access to Gaius as tribune, he would more easily find an opportunity to kill him.

[4] At this time occurred chariot races. This is a kind of spectator sport to which the Romans are fanatically devoted. They gather enthusiastically in the circus and there the assembled throngs make requests of the emperors according to their own pleasure. Emperors who rule that there can be no question about granting such petitions are by no means unpopular. So in this case they desperately entreated Gaius to cut down imposts and grant some relief from the burden of taxes. But he had no patience with them. and when they shouted louder and louder, he dispatched agents among them in all directions with orders to arrest any who shouted, to bring them forward at once and to put them to death. The order was given and those whose duty it was carried it out. The number of those executed in such summary fashion was very large. The people, when they saw what happened, stopped their shouting and controlled themselves, for they could see with their own eyes that the request for fiscal concessions resulted quickly in their own death. This strengthened still further Chaerea's determination to embark on the plot and to put an end to Gaius and his brutal fury against mankind. Often at entertainments he had been on the point of acting, yet nevertheless refrained when he calculated his chances. He no longer had any hesitation in his resolve to kill the man, but his search for the best moment continued, since he wished not to resort to violence fruitlessly, but to ensure the success of his plans.

*Gaius appoints Chaerea as tax collector but insults him in the process. In the meantime, Chaerea plots with Clemens, the father-in-law of the future emperor Titus, and another noble, Papinius. They are joined by Cornelius Sabinus, a military tribune, Vinicianus, and, finally, Callistus, one of the emperor's freedmen.*

[5] Progress had been blocked now for some time and Chaerea was disgusted with the conduct of Gaius. But when Gaius appointed him to the duty of enforcing payment of any taxes or other sums that were payable to the imperial treasury and that were overdue because the rate had been doubled, he took his time about these exactions and followed his own bent rather than the instructions of Gaius. Because he was merciful out of pity for the misfortunes which the people suffered under the exactions, he incensed Gaius, who called it womanly weakness to be so slow in collecting the money. Moreover, he not only insulted Chaerea in other ways, but whenever Chaerea as officer of the day asked for the password, Gaius would give him women's words and such as had quite obscene connotations. And yet, Gaius himself was not free from the same taint in the rites of certain mysteries which he had himself contrived. He would put on women's robes and devise wigs or other means of counterfeiting a feminine appearance. Yet now he actually had the effrontery to invite mockery of Chaerea on the same score. Whenever Chaerea received the password he was furious, and still more when he passed it on and was derided by those who received it from him. As a result, even his fellow tribunes made fun of him; whenever he was due to go to bring them the password from Caesar, they would mention beforehand one of the words that lent themselves to jests. As a consequence, he gained courage to seek partners in his plot, for he had good reason to be angry. Now there was one Pompedius, of senatorial rank, who had held nearly all the offices of state, but except for that was an Epicurean and consequently lived a life of ease. This Pompedius was accused by his enemy Timidius of applying opprobrious epithets to Gaius. Timidius called as a witness Quintilia, an actress who enjoyed the devotion of Pompedius and many others because of her striking beauty. This poor woman, since the charge was false, was indignant at the thought of bearing witness that would be fatal to her lover. Timidius then called for torture. Gaius in a passion ordered Chaerea not to waste a moment, but to put Quintilia to torture at once. He employed Chaerea in cases of murder and any others that called for torture, because he calculated that Chaerea's performance would be more cruel since he would not want to be abused as a weakling. Quintilia, when brought in for torture, trod on the foot of one of those privy to the conspiracy as a sign that he should keep cool and have no fear of her

yielding to torture, for she would hold out bravely. Chaerea, reluctantly, but forced by superior authority, tortured her cruelly, but when she showed no weakness, he brought her—she was now in a state that brought no delight to the eyes of onlookers—into the presence of Gaius. Even Gaius was affected by the sight of Quintilia, who was in a sorry state as a result of her suffering. He acquitted both her and Pompedius of the charge and conferred a gift of money on her as consolation for the maltreatment that marred her beauty and for the intolerable agonies that she had undergone.

[6] These things grievously distressed Chaerea, for he had been, so far as it was in his power, a source of misery to persons who were considered even by Gaius to be deserving of consolation. He thus declared himself to Clemens and Papinius, of whom the former was praetorian prefect and the latter was a military tribune like himself: "Well, Clemens, we have not failed to go to any length at least in guarding the emperor. Through our forethought and toil we have slain some of the conspirators against his rule and tortured others to the point where even he took pity. How great is the virtue with which we exercise our military commands!" Clemens was silent, but by his look and blush showed how ashamed he was of the emperor's orders; out of regard for his own safety, however, he did not think it right to refer openly to the emperor's madness. Chaerea, now plucking up courage, began to speak to him in language unchecked by fear of consequences, recounting the horrors to which the city and the realm were a prey. Though nominally, said he, Gaius bore the responsibility for such proceedings, "to those who try to investigate the facts it is I, O Clemens, and Papinius here and you, more than the two of us, who are applying these tortures to Romans and to humanity at large. We are not discharging Gaius' orders, but following our own policy if, when it is possible for us to stop him from treating his fellow citizens and subjects as outrageously as he is now doing, we act as his agents, occupying a post as his bodyguard and public executioners instead of doing our duty as soldiers—bearing these arms not to preserve the liberty and government of the Romans, but to save the life of one who makes them slaves in body and mind. And we pollute ourselves with shedding their blood and torturing them daily, up to the moment, mark you, when someone as Gaius' agent will do the same to us. For he will not favor us in his policy on account of these services, but will rather

be governed by suspicion, especially when the number of the slain has increased. For surely Gaius will never halt in his furious course since the end he pursues is not justice but pleasure. There we shall be, set up before him as targets, when we ought to be upholding the security and independence of all the people at the same time that we cast a ballot for our own rescue from a dangerous position."

[7] Clemens, it was evident, approved the resolve of Chaerea, but bade him keep silent, lest as the story spread more widely and reports got abroad of what should properly be concealed, the plot might be discovered before they succeeded in its execution, and so they would be punished. It was rather, he said, to the future and to the hope that it inspired that he preferred to entrust everything, in the belief that some stroke of luck would come to their aid. "I myself," he said, "am debarred by age from such a venture, but while I might perhaps advise a course safer than that which you, Chaerea, have designed and told me of, how could anyone propose a more honorable one?" And so Clemens returned home turning over in his thoughts the proposal that he had heard and his own response to it. Chaerea, for his part, hastened in trepidation to Cornelius Sabinus, who was a military tribune like himself, knowing him well as a noteworthy citizen whose devotion to independence ensured his hostility to the present government. He desired to take in hand with all speed what he had decided upon; and though he thought it good to add new names, yet he had misgivings that their plans might be brought to the ears of others by Clemens. Besides that, in his accounting, delays and postponements of the event favored the ruling party.

[8] But Sabinus rejoiced to hear the whole story. He had not failed to come to the same conclusion himself; and it was only for lack of one to whom he might safely speak that he had committed to silence what he was ready to join them in doing. Now he had found a man who would not only join him by keeping to himself what he was told but who even declared his own mind. Sabinus was so much the more encouraged and begged Chaerea to waste no time. So they betook themselves to Vinicianus, who was akin to them in honest habits and in devotion to high ideals but was viewed with misgiving by Gaius on account of the death of Lepidus. For Vinicianus and Lepidus had been very great friends, and Vinicianus was in fear of dangers arising therefrom. Indeed, Gaius was a source of terror to all

in authority, as one who would not desist from venting his madness upon each and all alike. They were mutually aware of their vexation at the state of affairs; yet, from fear of danger, they refrained from a full and frank statement to one another of their thoughts and their hatred of Gaius. Yet in other ways they were aware of one another's loathing for Gaius and had therefore not ceased to enjoy mutually friendly relations.

[9] At their meeting there was an exchange of courtesies. When they had previously come together, they had been accustomed to give precedence to Vinicianus, both for his higher rank, since he was the noblest of Roman citizens, and because of his high repute in all respects, but particularly when he took part in a debate. Vinicianus, getting the matter started, asked Chaerea what password he had received for that day; for the city buzzed with the insults of which Chaerea was made the victim by the passwords given him. Chaerea was delighted at his words and without further delay returned the trust that Vinicianus had put in him when he took part in a conference under such conditions and said: "Your password for me is 'Liberty', and I thank you for rousing me to greater energy than I am accustomed to display by myself; nor do I need any further words to encourage me if you too approve this course, so that we have arrived at one joint decision even before our conference. I have one sword in my belt but one will suffice for both of us. So up, let us get on with the work. Do you be leader and order me to go where you choose; and I will betake myself there, relying on your support and cooperation. Nor is there any shortage of weapons when men throw their hearts into a task, for it is the heart that is wont to make a sword effective. I have thrown myself into this enterprise unmoved by any thought of what may happen to me personally. I have no leisure to scrutinize the threats to my own life. I am tormented when I see my country reduced from unequalled freedom to slavery and robbed of its excellent laws. Because Gaius lives, the human race is overtaken by disaster. It must be that I am worthy to be trusted with such a cause in your judgment, since we are of one mind and you have not renounced me."

[10] Vinicianus, noting the urgency of his words, responded warmly and further encouraged his boldness. After he had commended and embraced him, he dismissed him with prayers and supplication. And some have maintained that there was a confirmation of their words; for as Chaerea was entering the Senate house there came from the crowd a voice of someone

bidding him, in order to spur him on: "Proceed therefore to carry out thy task and accept the support of heaven." They say that Chaerea at first suspected that one of the conspirators had turned traitor and that he was trapped; but in the end he understood that the cry was in the first place meant to encourage him, whether it was a signal of warning from one of the conspirators or whether it was actually the voice of God, who watches over men and their lives, speaking to inspire courage in him. For the secret of the plot had reached many persons and everybody who was there had arms—members of the Senate and of the equestrian order and all soldiers who were privy to the plot; for there was no one who would not have reckoned the removal of Gaius as a blessing. For this reason all were eager, in whatever manner was possible, not, so far as they were concerned, to show less courage than the situation required. With the utmost zeal, with all their strength, whether by words or by action, all were intent on the execution of the tyrant. Take the case of Callistus. He, as a freedman of Gaius, had, of all men, reached the highest summit of power both by the fear which he inspired in all and through the great wealth that he had amassed. His power was no less than a tyrant's. For he was a great taker of bribes, and most contemptuous of rights, with none to match him. His authority had been exercised beyond all reason. Above all, he knew that Gaius by temperament was implacable, that he never allowed for any counter-influence in a case that he had once decided; and that he was himself in danger not only for many other reasons but particularly because of his great wealth. In consequence, he even paid court to Claudius, secretly going over to his side because he expected that in the event of Gaius' death the empire would pass to him and that by laying up beforehand a store of favor and credit for his kindness he would have a basis for preferment and strength similar to that which he now enjoyed. At any rate, he went so far as to say that though he had been ordered to dispose of Claudius by giving him poison, he had invented countless devices for putting it off. My view is that Callistus invented this story to ingratiate himself with Claudius, since Gaius, if he had been bent on killing Claudius, would not have tolerated Callistus' excuses, nor would Callistus, if he had ever been ordered to do the deed, have regarded it as anything to deplore, nor, if he had sinned against his master's injunctions, would he have failed instantly to receive the wages of disobedience. Rather, I think that

it was through some divine intervention that Claudius enjoyed exemption from the mad fits of Gaius; and Callistus merely pretended to have put Claudius in his debt when he had done nothing at all.

*The attempt on Gaius is postponed until the occasion of the Palatine Games, a celebration established by Augustus's widow, Livia, after his death in A.D. 14. The games took place on January 21–23, and in the year of his death, Gaius had added extra days to the festival, which Josephus describes in some detail.*

[11] The party of Chaerea postponed action from day to day because many of them were cautious. For Chaerea would not of his own free will have let a moment slip; in his eyes any opportunity for action was good enough. Indeed he had frequent opportunities when he went up to the Capitol on occasions when Gaius offered sacrifice for his daughter's benefit. For as Gaius stood above the palace and scattered gold and silver money among the people, Chaerea might with a push have sent him falling headlong, for the roof overlooking the forum is high; or again he might have killed him at the performances of the mysteries that Gaius had instituted. For he was indifferent to everything else, in his concern to acquit himself honorably in what he did and in his conviction that no one would move to act. But if no divinity prevented Gaius from meeting his death, he himself, though he should have no sword, would summon up the strength to dispose of Gaius. So angry was Chaerea with his fellow conspirators, fearing that the opportunities to act would slip by. They saw that he desired only a reign of law and that his urgency was for their benefit; nevertheless they begged him to postpone action at least for a while, lest, if the plot was frustrated, they should create a commotion in the city while search was made for any who had been informed of the plot, and lest in the future any who might have intended to act should find no way open for brave deeds because Gaius would have taken greater precautions against them. It was therefore best, they thought, to undertake the business on an occasion when shows were exhibited on the Palatine. These are held in honor of that Caesar who was first to transfer authority from the people to himself; during their celebration a stage is set up a little in front of the palace, and the Roman patricians look on with their children and wives, together with Caesar himself. They would then have the opportunity, when many tens of thousands of

people would be wedged into a small space, to make the attack on him as he entered, and his bodyguards would have no chance, even if any of them should desire it, of rendering him assistance.

[12] Chaerea bore with them, and it was decided to take the business in hand when the first day of the spectacles arrived. Their plan, however, was over-ruled by Fortune, who granted one reprieve after another; and having let pass the three days prescribed for the spectacles, they barely accomplished the deed on the last. Chaerea then called together the conspirators and said; "The days that have gone by put us to shame for our tardy execution of so noble a resolve. It is an appalling thought that if someone informs on us, our enterprise will fall through and Gaius will be more insolent than ever. Or do we not see that every additional day that we grant to Gaius' tyranny is subtracted from the days of liberty? It behooves us henceforth to be fearless and, when we have laid a foundation for the eternal happiness of future generations, to establish ourselves for posterity as objects of great admiration and honor." They could neither deny that his words were wholly right nor yet undertake to act forthwith, but stood silent in dismay. "Why," he continued, "good sirs, do we still hesitate? Are you not aware that today is the last day of the spectacles and that Gaius' ship will soon depart?" (For he had made preparations to set sail for Alexandria to inspect Egypt.) "Is it honorable to let slip from our hands this blot on the proud record of the Romans that he may parade in triumph over land and sea? Should we not be justified in passing sentence against ourselves for the disgrace that would befall us if some Egyptian, finding the insolence of Gaius intolerable to freeborn men, were to slay him? I for one will no longer put up with your pretexts, but will face the risks this very day, accepting with a glad heart whatever outcome may ensue, nor would I postpone the issue even if it were possible. For what could be more galling to a man of spirit than that some other should slay Gaius while I live on and am robbed of the high valor of the deed?"

[13] With these words he himself set out to do the deed and had also put heart into the rest, so that they were all consumed by desire to take the enterprise in hand without delay. In the morning Chaerea made his way towards the Palatine girt with the sword of an equestrian; for it was the custom for the tribunes to be so equipped when they asked the emperor for the password, and it was his day to receive it. A crowd was already collecting on the Palatine in anticipation of the spectacle, and there was much noise and jostling. Gaius was delighted to see the general enthusiasm for the proceedings, and for that reason no seats had been set apart either for the Senate or for the equites, so that the seating was a jumble, women mixed with men and free men with slaves. Gaius, when his procession entered, sacrificed to Augustus Caesar, in whose honor the spectacle was presented. It happened that, as one of the victims fell, the robe of Asprenas, a man of senatorial rank, was spattered with blood. At this Gaius burst out laughing, but to Asprenas it turned out to be a manifest omen, for he was struck down over Gaius' dead body. It is reported that on that day Gaius was, contrary to his wont, most affable; and that he overwhelmed all and sundry whom he met with his adroit sociability. After the sacrifice he turned to the spectacle and took his seat surrounded by the most prominent of his companions. The construction of the theater, which was set up every year, was as follows. It had two doors, one leading to the open air, the other into a portico with exits and entrances, in order that those who were separately assembled in the portico might not be troubled by anyone passing through. Entrances had been made from the stage building itself, which had an inner partition to provide a retreat for actors and all kinds of musical performers. The crowd being seated, Chaerea had his place among the tribunes not far from Gaius, who occupied the right wing of the theater. Now a certain Bathybius, a man of senatorial rank who had been praetor, asked Cluvius, another man of consular rank who was sitting beside him, whether any news had reached him of a revolution, taking care that this remark should not be overheard. When Cluvius replied that he had perceived no indication of this, Bathybius said, "Well then, Cluvius, the programme for today will include assassination of a tyrant." Cluvius answered, "Be silent, good sir, lest some other of the Achaeans hear the word." A considerable quantity of fruit was scattered among the spectators with a number of such birds as are prized by their possessors for their rarity; and Gaius watched with amusement as the spectators fought over them and snatched them from one another. Here there were two new portents. In the first place a mime was presented in the course of which a chieftain is caught and crucified. Moreover, the play presented by the dancer was *Cinyras,* in which the hero and his daughter Myrrha are killed. Thus a great quantity of artificial blood was shed, what with the crucified man and

Cinyras. It is also agreed that the day of the year was the same as that on which Philip, the son of Amyntas and king of the Macedonians, was slain by Pausanias, one of his "Companions," as he entered the theater. Gaius hesitated whether to wait until the end of the spectacle, since it was the last day, or to bathe and dine and then come back again as he had done previously. Vinicianus, who was sitting above Gaius, fearing that the opportunity might be dissipated fruitlessly, rose to leave. When he saw that Chaerea had preceded him to the exit, he quickened his step to reach him first and bid him be bold. Gaius, with an air of friendly interest, plucked his robe and said, "Where are you going, bless you?" Vinicianus resumed his seat, apparently as a courtesy to Caesar, though fear was a stronger motive. Shortly after, however, he rose to leave again. This time Gaius did not interfere, supposing that he was leaving his seat for a necessary purpose. Asprenas, who was also in the plot, then urged Gaius to withdraw, as had been his custom, for a bath and lunch, and then to come back. His object was to see the conspirators' plans carried to fulfilment.

*Gaius is assassinated, with the first blow being struck by Chaerea. The emperor's German bodyguard, upon learning of his death, exact vengeance, killing three members of the conspiracy.*

[14] Chaerea's party had posted one another as the occasion required. There each man was bound to stick to his assigned duty without deserting in spite of weariness. They were now impatient with the passage of time and with the postponement of the matter in hand, for it was about the ninth hour of the day. Chaerea himself, since Gaius lingered on, was ready to re-enter the theater and to attack him where he sat. He foresaw, to be sure, that this would be attended by a great carnage of the senators and of such of the equites as were present. Yet, even with that fear in mind, he was still eager to act, for he thought it a sound principle, when purchasing security and liberty for all, to allow little weight to the cost in lives. They had actually turned to enter the theater, when the signal was given that Gaius had risen to leave. There was a din raised, and the conspirators returned to their positions and began to thrust back the crowd, saying that Gaius would take offence, though their real object was to render themselves secure, before they proceeded with the assassination, by removing any would-be defenders from his side. Claudius, his uncle,

and Marcus Vinicius, his sister's husband, and Valerius Asiaticus had preceded Gaius' exit. No one could have blocked their egress even if he had wanted to, such was the respect due to their dignity. The emperor himself followed with Paulus Arruntius. But when he was inside the palace, he quitted the direct route along both sides of which were lined those of the slaves who were in attendance, and which Claudius and his party had earlier taken. Instead, he turned down a deserted alley that was a short cut to the baths, where he was going. He also wished to inspect the boys who had come from Asia. A troop of them had been dispatched as a choir to sing in the mysteries which he was celebrating, and some came to take part in Pyrrhic dances that were to be performed in the theater. Here Chaerea waylaid him and: asked for the watchword. Gaius gave him one of his words of mockery, whereupon without wavering Chaerea showered abuse on Gaius and drawing his sword dealt him a severe, though not a mortal, blow. There are some, to be sure, who assert that Chaerea intentionally avoided dispatching Gaius with a single stroke, to have a greater revenge by inflicting a number of wounds. This account, however, I cannot believe; for in such actions fear leaves no room for deliberation. If Chaerea did entertain such a thought, I consider that he would have been foolish beyond the ordinary, a man who indulged his anger instead of granting himself and his conspirators a speedy deliverance from dangers. For Gaius might have been rescued in many different ways, had he not at once expired, and in that case Chaerea would have had to reckon not on the punishment of Gaius but on his own and that of his friends. Surely, even in case of success, it would be better to say nothing and to elude the anger of any who would retaliate; how much more foolish, then, when success was problematical, to choose irrationally to risk his life and miss the opportunity. The field is open, however, for such guesses as those who choose desire to make. Gaius, dazed by the pain of the blow, for the sword struck him between the shoulder and the neck, where the collar-bone held it from going farther, neither cried out in alarm nor called upon any of his friends. Either he could not believe what had happened or else he lacked the presence of mind. Instead he groaned in extreme agony and dashed ahead to escape. He was confronted by Cornelius Sabinus, who had his course of action already worked out. He pushed Gaius to the ground and brought him down on one knee. Here a number of assailants encircled Gaius and at a single word of encouragement struck at him with their swords, cheering one another on and competing too. Finally Aquila, and there is no dissent about this, delivered a blow that unquestionably dispatched him. But the credit for the feat must still go to Chaerea. To be sure, he had many to help him accomplish it, but at any rate he was the first to think of the means by which to achieve it, and he planned it long before anyone else. Again he was the first who had the courage to speak openly of a plot to the rest. Moreover, when scattered individuals accepted the proposal of the murder, he brought them together and prudently organized the whole scheme. Thus, where initiative was called for, he proved far superior to the rest. In addition, by his noble eloquence he won them over when their courage failed them and compelled them all to act. Finally, when the time came for action, there too he was clearly the first to move and to initiate the glorious assassination, thus making Gaius, who was as good as dead already, an easy mark for the rest. The conclusion is that whatever the others may have done, all will rightly be credited to the decision and valor of Chaerea and to the labor of his hands.

[15] Such was the manner in which Gaius came to his end; deprived of life by his numerous wounds, there he lay. Chaerea and his companions, once they had settled their business with Gaius, saw that there was no chance of escape if they followed the route by which they had come. For one thing they had cause for alarm in what they had done, and it was no small danger that menaced the emperor's assassins. For he was held in honor and affection by the foolish mob; and the soldiers, in their search for him, would not refrain from bloodshed. Moreover, the passage-ways along which they had done the deed were narrow and blocked by a great crowd of his attendants and of such soldiers as were present for duty that day as the emperor's bodyguard. So they took another route, and came to the house of Germanicus, the father of the Gaius whom they had just now killed, which was contiguous to the palace of Gaius. For the palace, although a single edifice, had been enlarged part by part, and this occasioned the naming of the additions for members of the ruling family who completed or else started some part of the structure. Having escaped the mob without an assault, they were now free from danger, since the disaster which had overtaken the emperor was still undetected. The Germans were the first to discover the death of Gaius. They were the emperor's bodyguard and bore the name of the nation from which they had been enlisted; and it was they who made up the Celtic band. It is a national trait of theirs to act furiously to a degree such as is rarely if ever met with among other barbarians, for the Germans pause less for calculation of the consequences. They are also physically powerful and win great success in the first onset whenever they engage any whom they consider enemies. These men, then, when they learned of the murder of Gaius, were full of resentment, for they did not decide issues on their merits according to the general interest, but according to their own advantage. Gaius was especially popular with them because of the gifts of money by which he acquired their goodwill. With swords drawn, they burst out from the palace in search of Caesar's murderers. They were led by Sabinus, a military tribune who owed his command over such men not to the services and nobility of his ancestors, for he was a gladiator, but to his physical strength. Asprenas was the first whom they came upon, and that was good reason to carve him limb from limb; it was he whose robe had been soiled by the blood of the victims, as I have mentioned above, an omen which boded no good. The second to fall in their way was Norbanus, one of the noblest of the citizens, who could boast of many generals among his ancestors. When the Germans showed no respect for his rank, his superior strength enabled him, on grappling with the first of his assailants, to snatch away his sword. He let it be seen that he would not let them kill him at their ease, but at last he was enclosed in a circle of assailants and succumbed to their many blows. The third victim was Anteius, one of the most distinguished senators. He did not, like his predecessors, fall foul of the Germans accidentally, but was attracted by the love of a spectacle and by the pleasure of seeing the prostrate Gaius with his own eyes in order to gratify his hatred for him. For Gaius had driven Anteius' father, who bore the same name, into exile; and, not content with that, he had sent a body of soldiers after him to put him to death. Such cause Anteius had to rejoice as he stood there looking on. But when the uproar began in the palace, and the need to conceal himself became urgent, he did not escape the vigilant search of the Germans nor the savage fury with which they slew both the guilty and the innocent alike. And so these three men died thus.

*As news of the emperor's death spreads, the city begins to panic, a situation that is exacerbated by the arrival of a contingent of Gaius's German troops at the theater, where the assembled crowd anticipates a massacre, until a man named Euarestus Arruntius manages to calm the situation. Meanwhile, the Senate is reconciled to the deed.*

[16] When the news of the death of Gaius reached the theater, there was consternation and incredulity. Some, who heartily welcomed his assassination and would have regarded it long since as a blessing to themselves, were incredulous from fear. There were others to whom the news was quite contrary to their hopes because they had no desire that any such thing should befall Gaius; and they did not credit it, because it seemed to them impossible for any human being to have the courage to kill Gaius. Among them were silly women, children, all the slaves, and some of the army. The last named were of this mind because they were mercenaries, and no less than partners in his tyranny; by playing the lackey to his insolence, they gained both honor and profit, for the noblest citizens were in terror of them. The womenfolk and the youth, after the fashion of the mob, were captivated by his shows and by the gladiatorial combats that he presented, as well as by the enjoyment of portions of meat that he distributed. The reason given for such provision was to cater to the crowd, but the truth was that Gaius' own savage madness fed on such things. The slaves supported him because they were now on familiar terms with, and contemptuous of, their masters, and found in his intervention a refuge from their masters' rough treatment, for it was easy for them to gain credence when they informed falsely against their lords. They also found it easy, by giving information about their masters' possessions, to gain both freedom and wealth as a reward for such denunciations, since the informer's fee was one-eighth of the property. As to the patricians, if there were any who credited the report, some from their foreknowledge of the plot and others because of wishful thinking, they not only consigned to silence their joy at the announcement but even pretended not to have heard of it. They were afraid lest, if they were disappointed in their expectation, they would be brought to punishment because they had started too soon to show what they thought. Those who had knowledge of the plot, because they were partners in it, were still more secretive, since they did not know who the others were in the plot and feared that if they spoke of it to anyone who stood to gain by the continuance of the tyranny, they would be denounced and punished if Gaius still lived. For another story had got about to the effect that though wounded, Gaius was not dead, but alive and being attended by physicians. There was no one who had sufficient confidence in anyone else to pluck up courage and tell him what he thought. For if the other were a friend of Gaius, he was suspected because of the goodwill that he bore to the tyranny, or else, if he hated Gaius, confidence was undermined in what he said by his unwillingness to tolerate anything favorable about Gaius from any source. It was reported by some and it was they who most of all banished all optimism from the patricians' minds—that Gaius, in disregard of danger and quite unconcerned to get his wounds treated, had escaped, bloodstained as he was, to the Forum and was haranguing the people. Such were the pictures drawn by the unreasoning desire of those who took it upon themselves to wag their tongues; the effect on the hearers depended on their attitude one way or the other. None, however, left their seats, because they feared the charge which might be brought against any who were the first to go out; for they would be judged guilty or innocent not because of the intention with which they might claim to have acted but because of whatever construction would-be prosecutors and jury might chose to put upon the act.

[17] But when in fact a troop of Germans with drawn swords surrounded the theater, all the spectators expected a massacre; they cringed when anyone entered, no matter who, convinced that they would be cut to pieces that very instant. They were thus at a loss what to do, for on the one hand they were unable to pluck up courage to depart, and on the other hand they had no confidence that it was safe to stay in the theater. When the troops now streamed in, the people in the theater burst into cries, turning in supplication to the soldiers and pleading that they had had no knowledge of anything, neither of the designs of the rebels, supposing that a rebellion had occurred, nor of actual events. They therefore entreated the soldiers to spare them and not to make innocent men pay the penalty for the rashness of others, and to abandon the idea of instituting a search for those who had done whatever it was that had actually been done. Such were their words and more, as they wept and beat their faces, conjuring them to listen with agonized appeals such as the danger that hovered near schooled them to repeat. Each man spoke as a man must speak when life hangs on his eloquence. The anger of the soldiers gave way under the impact of these words, and they repented of

their intended attack on the spectators, which would have been cruel and appeared so even to them, furious though they were. But first they fixed the heads of Asprenas and their other victims upon the altar. At this sight, the spectators were still more deeply moved both by consideration of the rank of the deceased men and by pity for their fate. As a result, they themselves were almost equally daunted by close contact with the threatened fate, since it was still uncertain whether in the end they would be able to make good their escape. And so even those who hated Gaius heartily and with justice were left with no chance to rejoice at his death, because they were on tenterhooks for fear of perishing with him and they had not yet even then had any trustworthy assurance that they would survive.

[18] Now Euarestus Arruntius was a professional auctioneer and therefore possessed of a powerful voice; he had accumulated money till he had as much as the wealthiest of the Romans, and was able both then and later to do just as he liked throughout the city. This man arrayed himself in the deepest possible mourning; for though he hated Gaius as much as anyone, yet the discipline of fear and the strategy required to secure his survival outweighed any pleasure of the moment. He therefore dressed himself with all the detail that would have been employed in mourning the most honored dead, and passed into the theater, where he announced the death of Gaius, thus putting an end to any further activity on the part of the people that was due to misinformation as to what had happened. By now Arruntius had got control and accompanied the tribunes recalling the Germans, bidding them sheathe their swords and giving a full account of the death of Gaius. This was certainly the thing that saved those who were assembled in the theater and all who in any way came in contact with the Germans; for, had the Germans been given any hope that Gaius still lay breathing, there is no crime from which they would have refrained. So great was their loyalty to him that they would even have risked their own lives to secure for him immunity from plots and avoidance of so great a disaster. But an end was put to their furious quest for vengeance, once they had been fully informed about the death of Gaius; for it was of no use to display their ardent devotion, now that the one who would have rewarded them had perished. They feared, moreover, that, if they proceeded further in their lawless mood, they might attract attention from the Senate, supposing that it should succeed to

power, or from the imperial ruler who won control. So the Germans did, at any rate, though it was a narrow escape, desist from the frenzy that took possession of them at the death of Gaius.

[19] Chaerea was much alarmed for Vinicianus lest he should meet with and be killed by the frenzied Germans. He went among the soldiers one by one, begging them to take precautions for Vinicianus' safety, and satisfying himself by much questioning that he had not lost his life. Meanwhile, Vinicianus was brought up before Clemens, who released him; for Clemens, together with many others of senatorial rank, bore witness to the justice of the deed and to the valor of those who had made the plans and shown no weakness in the execution of them. "For," he said, "tyranny, which is motivated by lust for unrestrained violence, lasts but a short time. As we see, there is no happy ending for the life of a tyrant, since the virtuous hate him. No, he is visited with such disaster as has come to Gaius, who had plotted against himself before there was any uprising or any organization of the attack. It was by the lessons that he gave to those who could not endure his violations, and by his abolition of legal protection, that he taught his dearest friends to make war on him. And now, though they are said to be the slayers of Gaius, he has fallen, in fact, a victim to his own design."

*Meetings of the Senate and the Assembly are held in the aftermath of the killing, but the soldiers pre-empt any other action by kidnapping Claudius, the uncle of the murdered emperor, and proclaiming him emperor. This is resisted by the Senate, but the people generally favor his elevation to the throne. Josephus next describes the role of Herodes Julius Agrippa, who acts as an intermediary between the Senate and Claudius. After having been raised in Rome and developing a close relationship with members of the imperial family, Agrippa had been given authority over much of Judaea by Gaius, along with a royal title. After a meeting of the Senate in the Temple of Jupiter Victor, it becomes clear that opposition to Claudius is hopeless because he has the support of the soldiers. Agrippa persuades Claudius to pursue a policy of leniency toward the Senate but insists on the execution of Chaerea, who had led the conspiracy, and Lupus, the military tribune who had killed Gaius's wife and daughter. In the remainder of the book Josephus resumes his narrative of events in Alexandria, where there is strife between Greek and Jewish residents. The book ends with the death of Agrippa from natural causes in A.D. 44, when his kingdom was forfeited to Rome.*

## AFTERWORD

Josephus's works, which were intended for a Greek-speaking elite, seem to have found few readers at first. One might have expected that Tacitus, for example, would have used his *Jewish War* as a source in his own account in Book 5 of his *Histories,* but there is no trace that he did. It was among the Christian Fathers that Josephus was most eagerly read in succeeding generations. Lactantius and Origen quote from Josephus's treatise *Against Apion,* and there is a Latin paraphrase of the *Jewish War* that incorporates parts of the *Jewish Antiquities* attributed to an author named Hegesippus and dated to the fourth century A.D. Eusebius, the fourth-century bishop of Caesarea, also uses Josephus as a source for the famine in Jerusalem. Josephus was also well regarded for a long time in Christian circles as the earliest non-Christian witness to the coming of Christ.

In a section of the *Jewish Antiquities* dealing with the reign of Tiberius and the governorship of Pontius Pilate in Judaea (18.63–64), there is a passage referring to Jesus:

> About this time there lived Jesus, a wise man, if indeed one ought to call him a man. For he was one who wrought surprising feats and was a teacher of such people as accept the truth gladly. He won over many Jews and many of the Greeks. He was the Messiah. When Pilate, upon hearing him accused by men of the highest standing amongst us, had condemned him to be crucified, those who had in the first place come to love him did not give up their affection for him. On the third day he appeared to them restored to life, for the prophets of God had prophesied these and countless other marvelous things about him. And the tribe of the Christians, so called after him, has still to this day not disappeared.

The authenticity of this passage, which is known as the "Flavian testimony," has been disputed since the sixteenth century. In at least its general outlines it is likely to derive from Josephus himself, although it has probably been altered somewhat in the course of transmission by Christian readers, the earliest of whom to cite it is Eusebius. And so the works of Josephus were common reading in the households of Christian Europe, especially as they became available in translation. "His books are like a storied Bible, couched in popular language, and written to be understood by all," wrote Arnauld d'Andilly in the preface to his 1667 French translation of the *Jewish Antiquities.* The English translation of Josephus's works by Thomas Lodge (1558–1625), first published in 1602, was reprinted nine times in the seventeenth century. It was succeeded by the translation of William Whiston (1737), which remained in print into the twentieth century. An edition of Josephus's works was among the forty books contributed to the library of the Collegiate School of Connecticut (now known as Yale University) upon its foundation in 1701.

# LUCAN

(Marcus Annaeus Lucanus, A.D. 39–65)

NOT ONLY WAS LUCAN THE NEPHEW OF THE YOUNGER SENECA, BUT ANOTHER UNCLE, Junius Gallio, held the consulship and was the governor of Achaea (see p. 313). A more distant, but equally celebrated, family connection, Annaeus Cornutus, probably instructed him in Stoic philosophy. It was therefore all but inevitable that he should achieve prominence in public life, whether in politics or in intellectual pursuits. Unfortunately, however, like his uncle Seneca and so many others, he fell foul of the emperor Nero and was forced to commit suicide in A.D. 65, at the tragically young age of twenty-five, because of his involvement in a failed conspiracy to oust the emperor. Even so, he had by then already produced a poem of unquestioned greatness, his ten-book epic on the civil wars in which Pompey and the Senate tried and failed to protect the Republic from Julius Caesar.

It was presumably under the influence of Seneca, who was then one of Nero's closest advisers, that Lucan was recalled from his philosophical studies in Athens to become a member of the emperor's inner circle and to take up public offices for which his youth hardly qualified him. The emperor was two years older than Lucan, and there is no reason to suppose that their regard for each other was not, initially, sincere and enthusiastic. In A.D. 60, at the Neronian Games, Lucan won a prize for a now lost poem in praise of Nero. Titles and fragments of other works survive, from poems on Troy and on Orpheus, a Descent to the Underworld, a tragedy entitled *Medea,* and a few epigrams. The chronology of *The Civil War* is quite uncertain, but it is reasonable to suppose that, by 62 or 63, his attention was focused on that poem, and that by then he had already given readings of at least three books of the poem. Two works are known to have been composed later, *On the Burning of the City,* written after the disaster of July 64, and his *Address to Polla* (his wife), but it is not known whether these were in prose or in verse. In his poem commemorating Lucan's birthday many years later, Statius refers to *On the Burning of the City*: "you will sing of the unspeakable fires of the guilty tyrant roaming the house-tops of Remus" (*Silvae* 2.7.60f.). Such openly hostile treatment of Nero is not surprising, for by A.D. 64 poet and prince had fallen out, and Nero had barred Lucan from giving further recitations and from making speeches in the law courts.

Suetonius's very brief *Life of Lucan* records that "Lucan felt insulted when Nero suddenly called a meeting of the Senate and walked out while he was reciting, his sole purpose being to spoil the recital. After that he started an unrestrained campaign against the emperor in words and deeds." Tacitus accepts this motive for opposition: "Lucan had his own particular reasons for being inflamed—Nero tried to suppress his poetry" (*Annals* 15.49). Certainly, Nero was very sensitive about his own intellectual brilliance and had little tolerance for rivals. Annaeus Cornutus (see above) almost got himself killed, and was in fact exiled to an island, because, when some people thought Nero should write an epic poem about Rome in four hundred books, he said that that was too many and no one would read them (Cassius Dio, *Roman History* 62.29), and when a rival in the tragic competition at the Isthmian Games could be neither intimidated nor bribed, Nero had his men crush his throat with the straight edges of their ivory writing tablets (Philostratus, *Nero* 9). Suetonius's *Life of Nero* (see pp. 498–513), provides ample further testimony to such imperial foibles.

In his *Life of Lucan,* Suetonius describes Lucan as the "standard-bearer" of the conspiracy against Nero but claims that "he broke down easily when the plot was discovered, groveling shamefully and even implicating his innocent mother, in the hope that such lack of filial piety would do him some good with the emperor who had killed his own mother." Who would wish to believe this of the author of a poem so aggressively assertive of the claims of freedom against the domination of willful tyranny? Is it not better to assume that Lucan had some higher motive, political and not simply personal, about which we can only speculate? Maybe so, but we should not look for too much idealism in the conspiracy. There is no indication that the conspirators were aiming for the restoration of the Senate-controlled Republic, rather than merely the supplanting of an unsatisfactory emperor with a better one.

We tend to associate epic poetry with mythological themes. The genius of Homer and Virgil makes this all but inevitable. Especially in Rome, however, there was a flourishing tradition of epics composed on historical subjects, involving real people and actual events. This tradition is obscured to us by, above all, the vagaries of transmission. Only fragments, at best, survive of most such works. The earliest original Latin poem is Naevius's *Punic War,* on the First Punic War, in which he himself actually participated, and Ennius lived through the Second Punic War, the main subject of his *Annals,* which earned him a reputation as the greatest Roman epic poet before Virgil. Cicero's poem on his own consulship is a historical epic. The *Aeneid* itself, especially with its constant foreshadowing of recent Roman history, can properly be considered an intertwining of mythological and historical epic. The civil wars and contemporary history were the theme of many early imperial epics, whose authors are little more than names to us. Eumolpus's poem on the civil war in Petronius's *Satyricon* is a parody of such historical epics and perhaps should not be regarded as being targeted directly at Lucan. At the end of the first century A.D., Silius Italicus published his *Punica,* seventeen books on the Second Punic War; with more than twelve thousand lines, it is the longest surviving poem in Latin. The *Punica,* however, is not highly regarded—many leading Latinists blithely admit to never having read even a single book of it. If it were a better poem, or at least had a better reputation, perhaps the tradition of historical epic in which Lucan was writing would be more familiar to us nowadays.

Lucan drew on several prose histories, most notably Caesar's commentaries on the civil wars, and on Livy's books covering these events, only brief synopses of which survive. He presumably also owes something to the historical writings of Asinius Pollio, who combined staunch support for Caesar with a strong belief in republican values; like all his other works, however, Pollio's histories, though known to have been extensively mined by later historians of the period, are almost totally lost. Regrettable as the loss of such sources may be, we should not imagine that precise factual accuracy was aspired to by Lucan, or expected of him. Again and again throughout the poem, he subverts reality for literary convenience. For example, Cicero's lack of military flair, which ensured that Cassius and Brutus kept him out of the later conspiracy against Caesar, was already well known; at the beginning of Book 7, however, Lucan represents him lecturing Pompey on the eve of the Battle of Pharsalus about his obligations. Likewise, we may doubt if there is much actual substance to the awesomely memorable account of Sextus Pompey's consultation with the ghastly witch Erichtho that dominates Book 6.

There are many such gruesome passages throughout *The Civil War,* which pullulates with bloody, dismembered, and decaying corpses, but nowhere else in the poem is the horror

**Figure 21: Bust of Pompey**
Pompey was said to have been remarkably handsome as a young man. Here, it is perhaps difficult to envisage him as a great leader, but he still wears his hair in a style intended to invite comparison with Alexander the Great.

sustained as long and intensively as in the Erichtho episode. With only a few exceptions, Virgil's battle scenes and other portrayals of death are not particularly graphic; Lucan's indulgence in such descriptions probably reflects a taste for sadism that he shares with the citizenry who attended the shows in the amphitheater. It may be worth noting in this context that the brief *Life of Lucan* by Vacca, a grammarian of uncertain date but not without a certain claim to authority, records that Lucan himself, when he held the public office of quaestor, organized a gladiatorial show. His uncle Seneca's tragedies are also replete with such grisly and gory details, such as are not taken over by him from fifth-century Greek tragedies, and which might be surprising in the works of a philosopher who fulminated so famously (*Moral Letters* 7) against the dehumanizing display of violence for public entertainment.

The Olympian gods conventionally play an important role in epic poetry, motivating and interfering with the actions of the human characters. Their absence from *The Civil War* is therefore very conspicuous. The closest Lucan comes to a traditional epiphany by a deity is in the appearance to Caesar of Rome in the guise of a woman at the Rubicon early in Book 1, and there are only three more such visions in the poem, the others being that of the dead Julia appearing as a Fury to Pompey at the beginning of Book 3 and the balancing dreams at the beginning and end of Book 7, to Pompey and Caesar, respectively, before and after the Battle of Pharsalus. Lucan gives considerable prominence to the vaguely defined figures of Fate and Fortune, but the absence of the anthropomorphic Olympians, with all their strengths and weaknesses, gives the poem a starkness that suits his theme and his treatment of it. It might seem reasonable to suppose that the Olympian gods are out of place in a historical epic narrating such recent events. This was not, however, felt to be so. The gods participate in the full Homeric manner in Ennius's *Annals* (and subsequently in Silius Italicus's reworking of the same theme). It is true that Cicero was criticized for portraying himself as summoned to the Council of the Gods in his epic account of his consulship, but the criticism seems to have been politically, rather than aesthetically, motivated: his opponents objected to this attempt to validate his execution of the Catilinarian conspirators as being divinely sanctioned.

The absence of a cast of divine characters draws our attention the more closely to the human protagonists. Here again, Lucan differs from the norm. He gives us no great heroes to compare with the Homeric Achilles and Hector, or the Virgilian Aeneas and Turnus, or (presumably) the Ennian Scipio and Hannibal, or even (again, presumably) the Ciceronian Cicero and Catiline. Lucan's Caesar is undoubtedly strong, but his most prominent characteristics are his cruelty and vindictiveness, while his Pompey may have an appealingly human and sympathetic personality, but he is ineffective and uninspiring, rather lost in the maelstrom of events. Epic heroes need not, of course, be supremely heroic: when Apollonius's Jason organized the expedition to fetch the Golden Fleece, the Argonauts voted for Hercules to be their leader, but that strong and decisive hero wandered off before the end of the first book of the *Argonautica*. But whereas Apollonius might experiment with the concept of heroism in a mythological epic, Lucan is portraying the destiny of Rome. It seems part of the poem's pessimism and darkness that neither Pompey nor Caesar is a convincing power for good. The major figure who is most favorably portrayed is Cato, but, though Lucan shares his Stoic ideals, he is presented as a rather too austere icon of the old republican ways to engage our sympathy. In any case, until after Pharsalus and its aftermath, that is, until Book 9, when the poem has almost run its course, he inevitably stands in the shadow of Pompey, the military leader on the republican side.

There is confusion and uncertainty about the title of the poem. Some scholars advocate the title *Pharsalia*, focusing on the decisive battle between Caesar and Pompey described in Book 7. But this title would privilege only one specific episode, albeit a crucial one. Most manuscripts record that the poem is "about the Civil War," and this more general title, *The Civil War*, seems preferable, and more in keeping with the poem's chilling first sentence, which, for all that it particularizes Pharsalus in the epithet "Emathian," is more comprehensive and wide-ranging:

> Of wars across Emathian plains, worse than civil wars,
> and of legality conferred on crime we sing, and of a mighty people
> attacking its own guts with victorious sword-hand,
> of kin facing kin, and, once the pact of tyranny was broken,
> of conflict waged with all the forces of the shaken world
> for universal guilt, and of standards ranged in enmity against
> standards, of eagles matched and javelins threatening javelins.

Fronto, the tutor to Marcus Aurelius, is sharply critical of these opening lines as being little more than repetitive verbiage (*On Speeches* 6). This interpretation is quite wrong. Lucan's subject is a dreadful one: civil war that was remorseless and inescapable, with no hope of untainted glory. It is probably not coincidental that the *Aeneid* had also started with a sweeping sentence of seven lines:

> I sing of arms and the man who first came from the shores of Troy,
> to Italy and the Lavinian shores, as an exile driven by fate,
> who was much tossed both by land and by sea
> through the violence of the gods above and the rankling anger of cruel Juno,
> and who suffered much in war also, until he could found his city,
> and bring his gods to Latium, the origin of the Latin race,
> and the Alban fathers, and the walls of lofty Rome.

Whereas, however, Virgil points to the eventually successful conclusion to the struggles and sufferings that Aeneas was to endure, Lucan holds out no such hope. In the words of Cassius Dio: "In the struggle for power between Caesar and Pompey, Rome was forced to fight both in her own defense and against herself; even if victorious, she would still be defeated" (*Roman History* 41.57).

This pessimistic interpretation perhaps needs some qualification, for it is contradicted by the fulsome flattery of Nero just a few lines later, where Lucan declares the civil war to be a price worth paying to ensure that Rome would eventually have an emperor as wonderful as Nero (1.33–45):

> But if the Fates could find no other way
> For Nero's coming, if eternal kingdoms are purchased
> by the gods at great cost, if heaven could serve its Thunderer
> only after wars with the ferocious Giants,
> then we have no complaint, O gods; for this reward we accept
> even these crimes and guilt; though Pharsalia fill its dreadful
> plains, though the Carthaginian's shade with blood be sated;
> though the final battle be joined at fatal Munda;
> though added to these horrors, Caesar, be the famine of Perusia
> and the struggles of Mutina, the fleets overwhelmed
> near rugged Leucas, and the slave wars under burning Etna,
> yet Rome owes much to citizens' weapons, because it was
> for you that all was done.

This praise of Nero, which continues in the same high-flown manner for a further twenty lines, must be interpreted either as ironic or as an indication that the poem is incomplete. A prominent reference to Nero, however ironic, seems out of place at this juncture. While it is true that Nero's ancestor Domitius is cast in a favorable light in several passages in Books 2 and 7, he himself has no integral role to play in the poem, equivalent to that of Augustus in the *Aeneid*, as the glorious leader and savior that Rome is expecting and praying for. It seems better to assume that Lucan would have removed these lines if he had lived longer. It is clear that *The Civil War* was not complete when Lucan died. The unusual length of Books 9 (1,108 lines) and 10 (546 lines), as compared with an average length of 806 lines, suggests that work was still needed at the end, and the narrative breaks off rather abruptly in any case, during the unrest that Caesar faced in Alexandria. It is at least possible that, in the early stages of transmission, the text was damaged, and the conclusion of the poem was lost. Most scholars, however, assume that Lucan died leaving it incomplete. There is a certain attraction to speculating that he planned to write twelve books, continuing until the aftermath of the Battle of Thapsus in 45, with the suicide of Cato as the climax to the poem. It would suit Lucan's Stoicism to give Cato more prominence than he enjoys in the poem as it is now. Moreover, for Book 6 to be dominated by Erichtho and the Underworld at the halfway point of the poem would enhance the affinity with the *Aeneid,* since Virgil has Aeneas guided to the Underworld by the Sibyl at that juncture in his poem. Other hypotheses have been proposed, extending the narrative to the Ides of March, or to the revenge at Philippi, or even to Actium. But, whether complete or not, and however Lucan might have chosen to end it, *The Civil War* is, in its own way, magnificent. It is relentlessly bleak, and its all but unremittingly pessimistic account of the collapse of the Republic debars it from being a national epic. Even so, we are left to wonder what Lucan might have achieved if he had not been forced to commit suicide as such an early age.

# THE CIVIL WAR

## Book 7

*The first six books have taken us to the eve of the climactic Battle of Pharsalus. In Book 1, Lucan narrates the causes of the war and Caesar's crossing of the Rubicon. In Book 2, he depicts deliberations between Brutus and Cato, with the latter persuading Brutus to join Pompey and flee Italy. The following book opens with Pompey's dream vision of his first wife, Julia, Caesar's daughter, warning him of disaster. Caesar occupies Rome, while Pompey gathers his forces in the East. At the book's end the narrative shifts to the city of Massilia (mod. Marseilles), allied with Pompey and besieged by Caesar. Caesar's campaigns against Pompey's allies in Spain are the subject of Book 4, which ends with the stage now set for the great confrontation between the two men. The next two books describe Caesar's movement of his troops to confront Pompey in Greece and the maneuverings that bring them to Thessaly, where the battle will take place. The sixth book ends with Pompey's son, Sextus, going to consult with the witch Erichtho, who summons back to life a soldier who had died in battle to reveal the ruin that awaits Sextus, his family, and Rome. Book 7 opens with Pompey, who is called "Magnus" (the Great) throughout, dreaming of his past triumphs.*

Rising from the Ocean more slowly than eternal law
    summoned him,
grief-bringing Titan never drove his horses harder
    against the ether
and reversed his course, though the sky hurried him
    onwards;
he preferred to undergo eclipses and the toils of stolen
light, and he drew the clouds towards him, not as fod-
    der for his flames
but to stop him shining clear on a Thessalian world.
But the night—the final part of happy life for
    Magnus—deceived
his troubled sleep with an empty apparition:
he dreamt that, as he sat in his own theater, he saw
the innumerable likeness of the Roman
10    plebs,
and his name was raised to the stars by joyful
voices and the resounding tiers competed in applause;
such was the appearance and applause of the
    admiring people

long ago, when as a young man, at the time of his first
    triumph,
after conquering the tribes encircled by torrential
    Hiberus
and all the troops driven onwards by elusive Sertorius,
with the West pacified, revered in his plain toga
    as much
as in the one that adorns the chariot, with the Senate
    clapping
he sat, still a Roman knight. Perhaps at the end of
    success
his mind, distressed by troubles, fled back to happy
    times;    20
perhaps, through its usual obscurity, his repose
    foretold
the opposite of what he saw, bringing omens of great
    lamentation;
perhaps, when you were forbidden any more to see
    your ancestral abodes,
Fortune gave you Rome like this. Do not break
    his sleep,
watchmen of the camp, let no bugle strike his ears
    at all.
Tomorrow's repose, hideous and gloomy with the
    image of the day,
from every side will bring him deadly battles, war from
    every side.
How will the people have such sleep and such a
    joyous night?
O blessed would your Rome be, if she could see you
    even like this!
If only the gods above had granted to your fatherland
    and you,    30
Magnus, a single day when both of you, certain of
    your fate,
could have snatched the final pleasure of your love
    so great.
You proceed as if destined to die in Ausonia's city;
she, fully knowing that her prayers for you were always
    realized,
never thought this crime was part of destiny for
her thus to lose even the grave of her beloved
    Magnus.
Joined in grief, young man and old and boy unbidden
would have wept for you, with loosened hair
    the crowd
of women would have torn their breasts, as at
    Brutus' death.

Now too, though they fear the unjust victor's
40      weapons,
though Caesar personally announce your death, they
        will weep,
even while bringing incense, bringing laurel garlands
        to the Thunderer.
O how unhappy—their groans concealed their
        anguish;
they could not bewail you together in full theater.

*Pompey is reluctant to begin battle, but his counsel is over-*
*come by the eagerness of the partisans in his camp, includ-*
*ing Cicero, here called by his family name, Tullius, and his*
*army takes the field.*

Day's first light had overcome the stars when the
        camp's throng
buzzed with mingled muttering and, while the Fates
        were dragging
the world to ruin, demand the battle-signal. Of the
        unlucky crowd most,
doomed not to see the day out, are grumbling around
their leader's tent itself and, fired by the mighty
        uproar,
50  bring on the hastening hours of imminent death.
A hideous frenzy comes upon them: each desires to
        precipitate
his own fate and the state's; slow and timorous
        is Pompey
called, too tolerant of his father-in-law, addicted
to world-rule in his desire to have beneath
        his sway
at once so many races from everywhere, in his dread
        of peace.
And more, the kings and peoples of the East protest
        that the war
is long drawn out, that they are detained far from their
        native lands.
Does it give you pleasure, O gods above, when
        universal ruin
is your plan, to add this guilt to our mistakes?
We charge to disaster, demanding warfare which will
60      injure us;
in Pompey's camp, Pharsalia is their prayer.
The utterances of all were conveyed by the
        greatest master
of Roman eloquence, Tullius—under his civilian
        authority
fierce Cataline had trembled at the peace-making Axes.

He was enraged at warfare, because he longed for
        Rostrum
and for Forum, after enduring silence so long as a
        soldier.
His eloquence gave strength to their feeble cause:

'This alone Fortune asks of you, Magnus, in return for
        all her many
favors—that you be willing to make full use of her; we
        leaders
of your camp and your kings together with the
        suppliant world                                              70
prostrate ourselves and beg you to allow
        the conquest
of your father-in-law. Shall Caesar mean war for
        humankind
for so long a time? Rightly do the nations who
        were tamed
by Pompey racing past resent that he is slow to
        conquer.
Where has your enthusiasm gone? or where your con-
        fidence in Fate?
Ungrateful man, are you alarmed about the gods? do
        you hesitate to trust
to them the Senate's cause? Of their own accord, the
        ranks will tear
your standards up and spring forward: you should feel
        shame to have won under compulsion.
If you are our bidden leader, if the war is waged for us,
give the men the right to fight on whichever field they
        wish.                                                         80
Why do you keep from Caesar's blood the swords of
        all the world?
Hands brandish weapons; hardly anyone can wait for
        the signal
slow to sound: hurry, or your trumpets may leave you
        behind.
The Senate longs to know: does it follow you, Magnus,
        as soldier or as retinue?'
The leader groaned and felt that this was trickery
of the gods and that the Fates were hostile to his own
        intention.
He said: 'If you all wish it so, if the moment
        needs
Magnus the soldier, not Magnus the general, no more
        shall I detain
the Fates: let Fortune engulf the peoples in a single
        downfall,
let this day be the last for a large part of mankind.              90

But I call on you to witness, Rome, that the day of
    universal doom
was imposed on Magnus. The toil of war could
    have cost
you no wound; I could have handed over to the peace
    which he defiled
their leader, a prisoner, tamed without slaughter.
What frenzy for wickedness is this, O blind ones? Are
    men who are
intent on waging civil war afraid to conquer
    without blood?
We have taken from him the lands, we have
    barred him
from the entire sea, we have compelled his hungry
    troops to plunder
corn too early, we have made the enemy pray
rather to be overthrown by swords, to blend the
100    deaths
of his men and mine. The war is more than
    half won
by the measures I have taken to prevent recruits from
    dreading battle,
if only they demand the signal, spurred by valor
and in fire of wrath. Simple fear of future evil
has sent many into utmost danger, but bravest is
    the man
who, quick to undergo ordeals if they loom close
    at hand,
can also postpone them. They wish to hand to
    Fortune
this our situation so successful, to surrender to the
    sword the crisis
of the world; they wish their leader to fight, rather
    than to win.
You, Fortune, gave to me the Roman state to
    govern: now
take it back enlarged and keep it safe in blind
110    warfare.
The battle shall be neither the reproach nor glory of
    Pompey.
In the gods' presence, Caesar, you prevail over me,
    with your unjust prayers:
the fight is on. How much crime and how much
    hardship
this day will bring upon the peoples! How many king-
    doms will be overthrown!
How dark will Enipeus flow with Roman blood!
I wish that the first lance of deadly war may strike
this head, if it can fall without influence upon events

or the ruin of our party, since victory is no more
    welcome
to Magnus. Today, when the carnage is
    complete,        120
Pompey will be a name either hated by the people or
    pitied:
the conquered will have every hardship brought by
    final destiny,
the conqueror will have every crime.' So he speaks
    and grants
the people warfare and, as they rage with anger, he
    lets go
their reins; like this the sailor, conquered by
    violent Corus,
concedes control to the winds and, abandoning his
    skill, is swept along,
a useless cargo on his ship. The camp roars in a tumult
of agitated haste, and fierce spirits hammer
against their breasts with irregular blows.
    The paleness
of coming death is on many faces, a look like their
    fate.        130
It is clear that the day has come which will establish
    the destiny
of human life for ever, that the battle will decide
what Rome will be. Each man is unaware of his own
    dangers,
stunned by a greater dread. Who would fear for
    himself
if he saw the shore inundated by the deep or sea-water
on the mountain-tops and ether falling towards
    the earth
and the sun hurled down—widespread destruction?
    There is no time
to feel terror for themselves: they fear for Rome and
    Magnus.
Nor did they trust in their swords unless the
    sharpened point
sparked against the stone; then every lance is
    straightened        140
on the rock, they string their bows with better cords
and carefully filled their quivers with selected arrows;
the horseman extends his spurs and tightens his
    bridle-reins.
If I may compare men's labors with the gods,
not otherwise when Phlegra reared the raging Giants
did the sword of Mars grow hot upon Sicilian anvils
and Neptune's trident redden in the flames a
    second time

and Paean forge again his arrows after stretching out in
    death the Python,
did Pallas spread the Gorgon's locks across her Aegis,
did Cyclops make Pallenaean thunderbolts anew for
150    Jupiter.
Yet Fortune did not refrain from the revelation
    of disasters to come through various signs. As they
    made for
the fields of Thessaly, the entire ether blocked their
153    approach:
it hurled down meteors in their faces and columns of
155    immeasurable
flame and water-greedy cyclones mixed with fireballs
and with a rain of lightning made them close
    their eyes;
it knocked the crests from helmets, flooded hilts
with melted swords, dissolved the javelins it snatched,
and guilty blade smoked with the ether's sulphur; and
160    hardly could
the standards be torn up from the ground, but with
162    increased weight
they pushed down and overwhelmed the
    standard-bearer's head; adrip with tears,
only as far as Thessaly did they belong to Rome and to
    the state.
The bull brought forward to the gods smashed
    the altar,
ran away and headlong hurled himself into the fields
    of Emathia,
so no sacrifice was found for the ill-omened
    rites.
—But you, Caesar, what gods of wickedness, what
    Eumenides
did you invoke with ritual? What powers of the
    Stygian realm,
170  what horror of hell and Furies steeped in night
did you propitiate when soon to wage a wicked war so
    savagely? Now—
who knows if it was by portents of the gods or if
    excessive fear
convinced them—to many people Pindus seemed to
    collide
with Olympus, and Haemus to sink into sheer valleys,
Pharsalia to emit nocturnal sounds of war,
a torrent of blood to permeate Ossaean Boebeïs;
they are amazed at one another's faces shrouded in
    darkness,
at the dimness of the daylight, at night brooding over
    helmets,

at departed parents and at ghosts of kindred blood
flitting before their very eyes. The frenzied people
    had                    180
this one comfort, that the multitude is conscious of
    its wicked
prayer—it hoped for fathers' throats, for brothers'
    breasts
and it rejoices in the portents, and thinks its mental
    turmoil
and its sudden madness is an omen of their
    wickedness.
What wonder is it, if mankind has been given a mind
foreboding ill, that people whose last day was waiting
trembled with distracted fear? The Roman visitor
    who lies
by Tyrian Gades, who drinks Armenian Araxes,
beneath whatever sky, whatever stars of universe,
he mourns, knows not the reason and rebukes his
    aching                 190
mind, unaware of what he is losing on the fields of
    Emathia.
If those who tell can truly be believed, the augur
    sitting
on the Euganean hill, where Aponus emerges
    steaming
from the earth and wave of Antenor's Timavus is split,
said: 'The final day has come, the greatest issue is
    fought,
the wicked armies of Pompey and of Caesar clash';
perhaps he noted thunder and the ominous weapons
    of Jupiter,
perhaps he saw all ether and the poles resisting
the discordant sky, perhaps the gloomy deity in
    the ether
indicated battle in the sun's dark dimness.        200
Without a doubt the day of Thessaly was quite unlike
all the days that Nature unfolds: if through an
    expert augur
every human mind had noted the sky's strange signs,
Pharsalia could have been observed in all the world.
O mightiest of men—your Fortune gave displays
throughout the world, on your destiny the entire sky
    was intent!
Even among later races and the people of posterity,
    these events whether
they come down to future ages by their own
    fame alone
or whether my devotion also and my toil can do
    anything

for mighty names—will stir both hopes and fears
210     together
and useless prayers when the battle is read;
all will be stunned as they read the destinies, as if
to come, not past and, Magnus, still they will side
    with you.
The troops, as they descended, radiant from
    Phoebus' beams
facing them, flooded all the hills with light
and not randomly were launched upon the plains: the
    doomed ranks
stood in set array. Charge of the left wing was given
to you, Lentulus, with the fourth legion and the first,
then the best for war. To you, Domitius, keen to fight
    though the deity
is hostile, is granted the front of battle on the
220     right.
But the central fighting strength was packed with
    bravest
troops brought from Cilician lands by their general
Scipio, in this region a soldier, but in Libya chief
    commander.
But next to the streams and pools of surging Enipeus
went the Cappadocians' mountain cohort and Pontic
horsemen, generous with the rein. But most of the
    dry ground
is held by tetrarchs and by kings and mighty tyrants
and by all the purple subject to the Latian sword.
There Libya sent Numidians and Crete
Cydonians, from there Ituraean arrows took their
230     course,
there you, fierce Gauls, advanced against your
    usual enemy,
there Iberia moved its aggressive shields.
Snatch the nations from the victor, Magnus, and, by
    shedding
the world's blood all at once, put an end to all his
    triumphs.

*Seeing that battle is about to be joined, Caesar addresses his
troops, invoking the fortune that has followed them in war.
In his turn, when Pompey perceives that Caesar is readying
for combat, he delivers a speech to incite his men to courage
in the last defense of Rome's republican traditions.*

It happened on that day that Caesar left his station,
on the point of moving troops to plunder crops, when
    suddenly
he sees the enemy descending to the level plains;

the moment he had prayed for a thousand times is
    presented,
when he can throw everything into the final hazard.
For he, sick of delay and blazing with desire for
    power,     240
had begun to condemn a civil war of brief extent
as a crime prolonged. When he saw the final battle
and the test between the leaders drawing near
and felt the destined downfall start to totter,
even his frenzy, so ready for the sword, for a
    short time
flagged and his mind so bold to guarantee
success stopped in doubt: his own destiny does not
    permit him fear;
Magnus' destiny does not permit him hope. He sup-
    pressed his dread,
and confidence springs forth, better for encouraging
    the host:
    'O soldiers, conquerors of the world, essence of
        my fortune,     250
the chance to fight so often longed for is here.
There is no need of prayers—now summon fate
    with sword.
How great will Caesar be?—in your hands it lies.
This is the day which I remember you promised me
by the waters of the Rubicon, the day we hoped for
    when we went to war,
the day for which we have postponed our return in
    triumph,     256
the day which must prove on the evidence of destiny
    which of us more justly     259
took up weapons: this is a battle bound to make the
    loser guilty.     260
If it was for me that you attacked your land with
    weapon and with flames,
fight fiercely now and with the sword put an end
    to blame:
once the judge of war is changed, no hand is clean.
Not for my sake is conflict waged, but so that you,
    I pray, may be
a free people and may hold power over all nations.
Personally I desire to return to ordinary life
and in plebeian garb to act the undistinguished
    citizen,
but provided that your power is universal, there is
    nothing I refuse to be.
Rule, and let me take the blame. And with no great
    bloodshed
do you realize your hope of the world: you will meet
    an army chosen     270

from Greek gymnasia, sluggish from devotion to the
    wrestling-floor
and with difficulty carrying their weapons, or
    barbaric babble
of a jumbled mob which cannot stand the trumpets,
    cannot stand
its own shout when the troops advance. Few hands
    of yours
will wage war against fellow Romans; most of the fight
    will rid
the world of these peoples and will crush the enemy
    of Rome.
Advance through cowardly races and infamous
    tyrannies
and with your sword's first stroke lay low the world;
let it be known that all the races led by Pompey's
    chariot
280  into Rome do not make up a single triumph.
Does it affect the Armenians which general
    holds sway
at Rome? Is there any barbarian who wants to put
Hesperia into Magnus' hands if it costs him
    any blood?
They hate all Romans and resent their masters,
those they know the more. By contrast, Fortune has
    entrusted
me to my own men's hands—witnessed by me
in so many wars in Gaul. Which soldier's sword
    shall I not
recognize? And when the quivering lance flies through
    the sky,
without mistake I shall declare whose arm
    propelled it.
290  But if I see the signs which never mislead
your leader—fierce looks and threatening eyes—
then you have won. I seem to look at streams of blood
and kings trampled on together and the Senate's
mangled body and nations swimming in an endless
    slaughter.
But I delay my destiny by detaining you with
    these words
when you are raging for the fight. Forgive me for put-
    ting off the battle;
I tremble with hope; never have I seen the gods so
    close to me,
about to give so much; only the plains' narrow strip
    of land
divides us from our prayers. I am the man, once war
    is over,

who will have the power to bestow the property of
    peoples and of kings.    300
By what movement in the sky, by what star of heaven
    changing course
do you, gods above, allow so much to the land of
    Thessaly?
Today provides either the reward or the penalty
    of war.
Picture the crosses, picture the chains for
    Caesar's side,
this head of mine placed upon the Rostra, my limbs
    flung far and wide,
crime committed in the Saepta, and battles in the
    closed-in Campus:
we are waging civil war with a general of Sulla.
My anxiety is all for you—for me, a destiny will
    be ready
free from care and self-inflicted: the man who
    looks behind
before the enemy is conquered will see me stabbing
    my own guts.    310
Gods—your cares have been distracted from the ether
    by the earth
and throes of Rome—give victory to the man who
    does not
think it necessary to draw the savage sword against the
    conquered,
who does not believe that fellow-citizens
    committed crime
because they bore opposing standards. When
    Pompey kept
your troops in a narrow place and denied your valor
room to move, with how much blood did he glut
    his sword!
Yet this I pray of you, soldiers: do not be keen to strike
an enemy's back; treat the man who flees as a citizen.
But, while their weapons glitter, let no image of
    affection    320
or glimpse of parents in opposing rank shake you:
disfigure with your sword the faces which demand
    respect.
If any man attacks his kinsman's breast with hostile
blade or if he violates no bond when he wounds,
let him count his unknown enemy's slaughter as a
    credit.
Level now the rampart and with fallen debris fill the
    ditches,
so the army can march out not straggling but in full
    companies.

Do not spare your camp: you will bivouac inside that
    rampart
from where the doomed army comes.' Hardly had
    Caesar finished
speaking, when each is drawn to his own task and
330    hurriedly the men
took up their weapons and ate their bread. They seize
    upon war's portents;
rush on, trampling under foot the camp; take their
    stand in no formation,
without their leader's tactics; everything they leave
    to Fate.
If in the deadly warfare you had placed so many
    fathers-in-law
of Magnus, so many seeking power over their
    own Rome,
they would not be rushing into battle with such
    headlong speed.
When Pompey saw the enemy's squadrons
    march out
straight ahead, allowing battle no delay—
the day appointed by the gods—he stood still with
    frozen heart,
stunned; and for a general so great to dread the fight
340    like that
was ominous. Then he stifles his fears and, riding
on a lofty horse all along the line, he says:
    'The day
your valor clamors for, the end of civil warfare
you demanded—it is here. Pour forth all your
    strength;
the final task of the sword remains and a single hour
drags down the nations. Whoever desires his land and
    house-gods dear,
his children, marriage-chamber, the ties he has left
    behind, must win them
by the sword: the god has set all prizes in the field in
    between us.
The better cause tells us to hope for favoring gods:
they themselves will steer the weapons through
350    Caesar's guts,
they themselves will want to sanction Roman statutes
    with his blood.
If they planned to give my father-in-law world rule,
they could have hurried my old age to an end:
to preserve Pompey as leader is not the act of gods
angered with the people and with Rome. We have
    assembled

every capability of victory. Willingly have
    famous heroes
submitted to dangers; our soldiery is that of old, in its
    sacred image.
If to these times the Fates restored the Curii,
Camilli and the Decii vowing their lives to fate,
on our side they would stand. The races and innumer-
    able cities    360
of the furthest east have assembled and stirred to
    battle hordes
in number never seen before: at a single moment all
    the world is ours to use.
All we races enclosed by the boundary of the
    zodiac,
as far as Notos and Boreas—we wield weapons.
Shall we not surround the dense-packed enemy
by pouring round our wings? Few are the sword-hands
    victory
requires, and of our squadrons most will wage war
with shouting only: for our army Caesar is not
    enough.
Imagine that your mothers, leaning from Rome's
    highest
city-walls with hair streaming, are urging you to
    battle;    370
imagine that the aged senators, prevented by
    their years
from joining the army, are laying at your feet their
    white and hallowed hair;
that Rome herself, in fear of a master, is coming to
    meet you;
imagine that the people now and the people of
    the future
bring their prayers combined: to be born in freedom is
    one throng's wish;
to die in freedom the other's. If after appeals so great,
there is a place for Pompey, a suppliant, with child
    and wife,
I would throw myself before your feet if I could do so
    with the dignity
of high office intact. Unless you conquer, Magnus will
    be an exile,
his father-in-law's laughing-stock and your dis-
    grace: I pray that I escape    380
the worst destiny and degrading years at life's
    final pivot—
may I not in old age learn to be a slave.' At their
    general's words
so gloomy, their spirits blaze and Roman valor

is excited and they resolved to die in case his fears
    were true.

*The battle is joined, and Caesar is victorious. His triumph*
*is encapsulated in his gloating over the heroic death of*
*Domitius Ahenobarbus, an ancestor of the emperor Nero*
*and a fierce adherent of Pompey.*

So from both sides the troops run forward with equal
    impetus
of anger: fear of tyranny arouses these, those the hope.
These sword-hands will achieve things that no
    future age
can make good nor humankind repair in all the years,
though it be free from warfare. That fight will crush
the future races, and it will rob of birth and sweep
390    away
the people of the generation entering the world.
    Then all
the Latin name will be a fable: Gabii, Veii, Cora
hardly will be indicated by their dust-covered ruins,
the hearths of Alba and the house-gods of Laurentum,
an empty country which no senator inhabits except
    unwillingly
on night ordained, complaining of the decree
    of Numa.
It is not devouring time which has eroded and aban-
    doned in decay
these memorials of the past: it is the crime of civil war
    we see,
so many empty cities. To what has the multitude of
    humankind
400  been reduced! We peoples born in all the world
are not enough to fill with men the town-walls and
    fields;
a single city holds us all. The cornlands of Hesperia
    are worked
by chained laborer, the house with its ancestral roof
    decaying
stands, about to fall on no one; and Rome, crowded
by no citizen of her own but filled with the dregs of
    the world,
we have consigned to such a depth of ruin that in a
    body so immense
civil war cannot now be waged. The cause of such a
    great catastrophe
is Pharsalia. The fatal names of Cannae and of Allia,
long cursed in the Roman calendar, must yield
    their place.

The dates of lighter disasters Rome has marked;    410
this day she wanted to ignore. O bitter Fates!
Air noxious to inhale, putrefying diseases,
maddening famine, cities given up to fires,
quakes which bring the walls of crowded cities
    tumbling—all
could be made good by these men who are
    dragged from
everywhere to a pitiable death by Fortune: as she
    deploys
and takes away the offerings of long ages, she stations
    on the plains
the peoples and the generals through whom to show
    you in your fall,
Rome, how mighty was your fall. What city held a
    wider sway
over the world or advanced more swiftly through
    prosperity?    420
Every war gave you nations, every year
Titan saw you advance towards twin poles
so that—because not much space of the eastern land
    remained for
you the night, for you entire day, for you the
    ether sped,
and everything the wandering stars saw was Roman.
But the fatal day of Emathia, equivalent to all
    the years,
carried backwards your destiny. Thanks to that
    bloody day
India does not tremble at the Rods of Latium,
the girded consul does not lead the Dahae, forbidden
    to wander,
inside city-walls or lean on a Sarmatian plough,    430
and Parthia owes you savage retribution still and
    for ever,
and Liberty, in Right from the crime of civil
    warfare, has withdrawn
beyond Tigris and Rhine, never to return,
and wanders on, after our so many murderous attacks,
a blessing on Germany and Scythia, no longer mindful
of Ausonia—how I wish our people had never
    known her!
When Romulus first founded the city with the vul-
    ture's left-hand
Right and filled its walls from the notorious grove
until the ruins of Thessaly, you should have stayed in
    slavery, Rome.
Fortune, I complain about the Bruti. Why did we
    have    440

times of legality or years which took their names from
   consuls?
Fortunate are the Arabs and the Medes and
   eastern earth,
kept by the Fates beneath continuous despots.
Of all the peoples who endure tyranny, our situation
   is the worst:
we are slaves, and ashamed. Without a doubt, we
   have no
deities: since human life is swept along by blind
   chance,
we lie that Jupiter is king. Will he watch Thessalian
bloodshed from the lofty ether even though he holds
   his thunderbolts?
Will Jupiter, then, aim his fires at Pholoe, at Oeta,
at the grove of innocent Rhodope, at the pines of
450    Mimas,
and let Cassius strike this head? He brought the stars
upon Thyestes, he doomed Argos to a sudden night:
for wielding swords which are alike, so many swords
   of brothers
and of fathers, will Thessaly be granted daylight by
   him? Human
affairs are cared for by no deity. Yet we have revenge
for this disaster, as much as gods may give to mortals:
the civil wars will create divinities equal to
   those above;
with thunderbolts and rays and stars Rome will adorn
the dead and in the temples of the gods will swear by
   ghosts.
With rapid charge they had reduced the space
460    delaying
the fateful crisis and now, divided by a little strip
   of land,
they look to see where their javelins will fall or what
463    hands
threaten death to them. That they might profoundly
462    know
what horrors they would commit, they saw their
464    parents
with opposing faces, their brothers' weapons close at
   hand and
did not choose to change position. Yet numbness froze
every breast and icy blood congeals in their guts,
their piety is smitten, and entire companies
long held their javelins poised with arms outstretched.
May the gods give to you, Crastinus, not death—a
470    penalty

awaiting everyone—but feeling in your corpse
   after death:
your hand hurled the lance which started fighting
and was the first to stain Thessaly with Roman blood.
O impetuous frenzy! When Caesar wielded weapons,
was there found a hand to act before his? Then air
   resounded,
shattered by the trumpets, the call to war declared
   by horns,
then bugles dared to give the signal, then the clamor
   reaches
the ether and bursts into the dome of furthermost
   Olympus
—from there the clouds keep far away, no thunders
   reach so far.
Haemus in re-echoing valleys took up the noise    480
and gave it back to caves of Pelion to reduplicate,
Pindus drives the roar, Pangaean rocks reverberate,
the crags of Oeta groan: men took fright at the utterances
of their own madness repeated by the entire earth.
Innumerable missiles are discharged with conflicting
   prayers:
some long to wound, some long to stick their weapons
   in the ground
and keep their hands undefiled. Chance swirls
   everything along
and Fortune, unpredictable, makes anyone she wishes
   guilty.    488
Then Ituraeans, Medes, and loose-clothed Arabs,    514
with their bows a threatening throng, steered their
   arrows at no target
but only at the air which hung poised above the plain;
from there falls death. But they stain their foreign steel
with no charge of wickedness; all the wrong stood
   condensed
around the Roman spears. The ether is screened
   by steel
and a night of weapons joined together hung above
   the plain.    520
But how little of the destruction was performed by
   javelins    489
and flying steel! For civil hatred the sword alone    490
suffices and leads sword-hands into Roman guts.
Pompey's army, massed in dense-packed squadrons,
had joined their shields in a chain with shield-bosses
   side by side
and had taken up position with hardly space to
   wield hands

and weapons: crushed together, it feared its own
    swords.
With headlong onrush Caesar's frenzied army
attacks the dense formations; through weapons,
    through the enemy
it seeks a path. Where twisted coat of mail presents
its heavy chains, and breast lies safely hidden under
    covering,
even here they reach the guts: it is the furthest
500    object
through so much armor that each blow reaches.
    Civil war
one line endures, the other wages; here chilled
the sword stands still, but every guilty blade on
    Caesar's side is hot.
And Fortune, not for long swaying the balance of so
    many issues,
swept away the wide-scale wreckage as Fate was
    racing on.

As soon as Pompey's cavalry deployed its wings
over all the plain and extended them along the
    battle's edge,
his light-armed troops, spread among the outer
    companies,
follow close and launch their savage bands against
    the enemy:
there every nation joins the battle with its distinctive
510    weapon,
but all are seeking Roman blood; from here fly arrows,
firebrands, and rocks and slingstones melted by their
    passage
through the air, turned to liquid with their heated
513    mass;
521    then Caesar, fearing his front line might waver
under this attack, keeps his cohorts sideways on
    behind the standards
and into the battle's flank where the enemy haphaz-
    ardly was ranging
suddenly launches a column, his wings unmoved.
Forgetful of the battle, not embarrassed by their fear,
with headlong flight they made it clear that civil war
is never happily entrusted to barbarian hordes.
When first the charger, pierced by steel in his breast,
threw his rider on his head and trampled on his limbs,
all the cavalry left the plain and, with their bridles
530    turned about,
they headlong charged at their own troops, a
    concentrated cloud.

Then the slaughter passed all limit and what followed
    was no combat
but war on one side waged with throats, with weapons
    on the other;
the one battle-line is not strong enough to slaughter
    all those
who can perish on the other side. I wish, Pharsalia,
that that gore which barbarian breasts shed may satisfy
your plains, that your springs may be dyed by no
    others' blood,
that this mass may cover all your fields with
    their bones.
Or if you prefer to be glutted with Roman blood,
then, I pray, spare these men: let the Galatians live,
    Syrians,                                                          540
Cappadocians, Gauls, Iberians from the world's edge,
Armenians, Cilicians, for after civil war
these will be the Roman people. Once arisen, panic
spreads to everyone and destiny was granted speed for
    Caesar.
They came to Magnus' strength, his central squadrons.
The fighting which had flooded in random
    course across
all the fields halted here and Caesar's fortune came to
    a standstill.
Here the soldiers waging war were not assembled
    from the royal
auxiliaries but wielded weapons in their hands
    unasked:
that place contained their brothers and their
    fathers.                                                          550
Here is your madness, your frenzy, your wickedness,
    Caesar.
Mind of mine, shun this part of battle and leave it to
    darkness
and from my words let no age learn of horrors
so immense, of how much is licensed in civil war.
Better that these tears and protests go unheard:
whatever you did in this battle, Rome, I shall not tell.
Here Caesar, maddening the people and goading them
    to frenzy,
goes ranging round the troops, adding fires to spirits
    already blazing:
wickedness must not be missing in any section of
    his army.
He inspects their swords too, to see which wholly drip
    with blood,                                                       560
which glitter, stained only at the very point,

which hand trembles as it grasps the sword, who
    wields his weapons
slack or taut, who supplies fighting at command,
who loves to fight, and whose expression alters when
    a fellow citizen
is killed. He visits bodies stretched upon the wide
    fields;
with the pressure of his hand he personally staunches
    many a wound,
which would have poured out all the blood. Wherever
    he goes round—
like Bellona brandishing her blood-stained lash
or like Mars, rousing the Bistonians, if with
    savage whips
he goads his steeds maddened by Pallas'
570     Aegis—
there is a vast night of wickedness; slaughter follows
and the groans as of a voice immeasurable, and armor
    clatters
with the weight of falling breast, and swords on
    swords are shattered.
In person he supplies fresh swords, hands them
    weapons,
and orders them to mangle with their steel the faces of
    the enemy,
in person he advances the line, onward drives his army
    from behind,
with blow of inverted spear he rouses the reluctant,
forbids them to strike the masses and indicates the
    Senate;
well he knows which is the empire's blood, which are
    the guts of the state,
he knows the starting-point of his course to Rome. the
580     spot to strike
as the Liberty of the world makes her final stand.
    Nobility mingled
with the Second Order and venerable persons are
    overwhelmed
by the sword; they slaughter Lepidi, Metelli,
Corvini along with famed Torquati, often leaders
of the state and greatest of men, with you excepted,
    Magnus.

There, covering your face with a plebeian helmet
and unknown to the enemy, what a weapon, Brutus,
    did you hold!
O glory of the state, O final hope of the Senate,
the last name of a family so great throughout the ages,
do not race too reckless through the
590     enemy's midst,

do not hasten deadly Philippi upon yourself before
    its time,
doomed to die in a Thessaly of your own. Nothing do
    you achieve here,
intent on Caesar's throat: he has not yet reached the
    citadel
or gone beyond the peak of human law controlling
    everything;
he has not yet earned from Fate a death so
    distinguished.
Let him live and let him rule, so he may tumble,
    Brutus' victim.
Here perished all the glory of the fatherland: on
    the plains
in an enormous heap patrician corpses lie, with no
    plebeians among them.
Yet in the slaughter of famous men stood out
    the death
of battling Domitius, a man led by Fate through
    every                                                   600
calamity: nowhere did Magnus' fortune collapse
without him. So often defeated by Caesar, he died
with his liberty intact: now happily he falls beneath
a thousand wounds, rejoicing not to have a second
    pardon.
Caesar saw him thrashing around in thick
blood and, taunting, said: 'Now, Domitius, my
    successor,
you abandon Magnus' army; the war is waged
without you now.' But the breath hammering at
    Domitius' breast
was strong enough for speech and he unlocked his
    dying lips:
'Caesar, because I see you not the master of the
    deadly                                                 610
wage of wickedness but uncertain of your fate
    and lesser
than your son-in-law, I go free and peaceful to the
    Stygian shades
with Pompey still my leader: though I die, I can hope
that you will be subdued in savage war and pay
a heavy penalty to Pompey and to me.' No more
    said he;
life left him and thick darkness closed his eyes.
When the world is dying I feel shame to spend
    my tears
on the innumerable deaths and to follow individuals'
    destinies,
questioning, whose guts did the fatal wound

pass through? who trampled on his vitals spilling on
620     the ground?
who faced the enemy and, dying, forced out with
     his breath
the sword thrust into throat? who collapsed when
     struck?
who stood firm while his limbs fell about him? who
     lets the weapons pass
right through the breast? or who was pinned by spear
     to the plain?
whose veins were drained of blood which split the air
and falls upon the armor of his enemy? who strikes his
     brother's
breast, cuts off the head and throws it far away
so he can plunder the familiar corpse? who
     mangles
his father's face and proves to those who watch by his
     excessive wrath
that the man he slaughters is not his father? No death
630     deserves
its own lament; we have no space to grieve for
     individuals.
Pharsalia did not have those elements of battle
which other calamities had: there, Rome was ruined
     by the destinies
of warriors, here by entire peoples; a soldier's
     death there
was here a nation's death; here streamed
     Achaean blood,
Pontic and Assyrian—all that gore is stopped from
     sticking
and congealing on the plain by a torrent of
     Roman gore.
From this battle the peoples receive a mightier wound
than their own time could bear; more was lost
     than life
and safety: for all the world's eternity we are pros-
640     trated.
Every age which will suffer slavery is conquered by
     these swords.
How did the next generation and the next deserve
to be born into tyranny? Did we wield weapons
     or shield
our throats in fear and trembling? The punishment of
     others' fear
sits heavy on our necks. If, Fortune, you intended to
     give a master
     to those born after battle, you should have also
     given us a chance to fight.

*The battle over, Pompey flees, leaving the field to Caesar,
who orders his men to take the enemy's camp. In an
uncharacteristically ungracious gesture, Caesar refuses
to grant burial to the enemy dead, and during the
ensuing night he is tormented by disturbing visions in
his sleep.*

Now Magnus had realized that the gods and Roman
     destiny had changed
allegiance, unlucky man, reluctantly compelled by the
     whole calamity
to condemn his own fortune. He stood upon a mound
     in the plain
from a distance to gaze at all the destruction
     scattered                                                    650
through the fields of Thessaly, otherwise hidden from
     view by warfare.
He saw so many weapons aimed at his own death,
     so many
bodies laid low and himself dying in so
     much blood.
But he does not choose—as is the custom of the
     doomed—to drag down everything
with him and plunge it into ruin and embroil the
     nations in his full:
even now he persisted in believing the
     heaven-dwellers worthy
of his prayers that most of Latium's multitude would
     live on
after him and cherished this as consolation for his
     defeat.
'Refrain, gods,' he says, 'from overthrowing all the
     peoples.
With the world still standing and with Rome
     surviving, Magnus can                                         660
be ruined. If you choose to wound me more, I have
a wife and sons: so many hostages have I given to
     the Fates.
Is it not enough for civil war to crush both me
and mine? Are we a trivial disaster without the inclu-
     sion of the world?
Why mangle everything? Why work for
     universal ruin?
Now, Fortune, is nothing mine?' So he speaks and
     visits all
his troops, his standards, and his squadrons
     shattered now
in every part, and calls them back from racing into
     early death,

saying he is not worth so much. The general did not lack resolve

670 to go to face the swords and suffer death in throat or breast;

but he feared that, if Magnus' body lay prostrate, his soldiers

would not flee and that the world would crash down on its leader;

or else he wished to take away his death from Caesar's eyes,

uselessly, unlucky man! When your father-in-law wants to look at it,

your head must be presented, wherever in the world it is. But you too, wife,

were a reason for his flight, your face and the Fates' refusal

that he should die with part of himself missing. Then a steed is spurred

to carry Magnus from the battle, not fearing weapons from the rear

but going to meet his final destiny with enormous courage.

No sorrowing, no tears were there; his grief deserves respect,

680 with dignity maintained, a grief exactly fitting for you

to show in Roman hardships, Magnus. With unchanged face

you gaze upon Emathia: success in war never saw you proud, adversity will never see you broken;

as far beneath him as faithless Fortune was in his happy days of three triumphs,

so is she in his days of misery. Now you have put aside the weight

of destiny, and you depart, free from care; now you have leisure to look back

on happy times; hope has vanished, never to be fulfilled;

now you may understand what you were. Escape the hideous battles,

call the gods to witness that none who stays to fight

690 now dies for your sake, Magnus. Like Africa, lamentable for her losses,

like guilty Munda and the calamity by Pharian flood,

so too, most of the Thessalian battle, after you, will be inspired

no longer now by Pompey's name so popular throughout the world

or eagerness for war, but by that pair of rivals always with us—

Liberty and Caesar; and once you had left the battle, the Senate showed by dying that it was fighting for itself.

Does it not delight you to retire defeated from battle and not watch

this horror to the end? Look back at the squadrons covered

in foaming gore, at rivers muddied by the influx of blood,                                    700

and take pity on your father-in-law. With what heart will he enter

Rome, his luck the richer by those battlefields?

Whatever you suffer in unknown lands, an exile alone, whatever you suffer subject to the Pharian tyrant,

trust the gods, trust the Fates' long-lasting favor: to win was worse. Ban the sound of lamentation,

stop the people weeping, dispense with tears and grief.

Let the world do homage to Magnus' hardships as much as his successes.

Free from care, with no suppliant look, gaze upon the kings,

gaze upon the cities you possessed and the kingdoms you bestowed,                                    710

Egypt and Libya, and choose a land for your death.

Larisa first was witness of your fall, first to see

your noble head, not subdued by destiny. With all her citizens

she poured forth her entire strength through her walls,

to meet you as in victory: with tears they promise gifts,

open up their homes and temples, long to be your partners in defeat.

It is clear that much endures of your mighty name,

that you, inferior only to yourself, could again impel to war

all the nations and again return to your former fortune.

But 'What need of peoples or of cities has a conquered man?' he says;                                    720

'Show your loyalty to the conqueror.' Caesar, you are walking still

in a lofty heap of slaughter through the guts of your fatherland,

but to you your son-in-law already grants the nations. His steed bears

Pompey off from there: tears and lamentation follow him

and the people's numerous reproaches against the
     cruel gods.
Now, Magnus, you have genuine proof and enjoyment
     of the popularity
you sought: the successful man knows not that he
     is loved.
When Caesar saw the fields drenched sufficiently with
     Hesperian
blood, thinking now that he should rein in his soldiers'
swords and hands, he granted life to worthless souls,
730     to columns
whose death would have had no point. But to stop the
     camp inviting back
the routed men, to stop night-time rest
     dispelling panic,
he decides to move at once into the enemy's rampart
while Fortune glows, while terror is all-accomplishing,
without a fear that this order would be difficult for
     men weary
or by war exhausted. With no great encouragement
the troops were ready to be led to plunder: 'Victory
     complete is ours,
my warriors' he said; 'there remains the payment for
     our blood,
which it is my task to show; I will not speak of
     bestowing
what each of you will give himself. Look: their camp is
740     open wide,
full of every precious metal; here lies gold seized from
the western races; their tents confine the treasures of
     the East.
The massed wealth of many kings and Magnus
awaits its masters; hurry, soldiers, to precede the men
that you are chasing; all the riches which Pharsalia has
     made yours
are being stolen by the conquered.' What trench, what
746/749     rampart
could withstand them as they sought reward of war
750     and wickedness?
They race to know how large their wage of guilt is.
And for sure they found an enormous mass of bullion
heaped up from a plundered world to pay the costs
     of war;
but not enough for minds which wanted everything
was all the gold mined by the Iberian, disgorged
     by Tagus,
or gathered from the surface of the sands by wealthy
     Arimaspian;

though they seize it, they will think their wickedness
     sold cheaply.
Since they have pledged themselves in victory the
     Tarpeian
citadel and promised everything in their expectation
     of looting Rome,
the plunder of a camp is a cheat.
          The wicked plebs takes          760
slumber on patrician turf and inhuman soldiers
lie on couches spread for kings, and on the beds of
     fathers,
beds of brothers, the guilty men laid down their limbs.
A maddened sleep harasses them and frantic dreams
revolve the battle of Thessaly in their tortured breasts.
Their savage crime is wide awake in everyone and in
     all their thoughts
they brandish weapons and they jerk their hands
     though no hilt is there.
I could think that the battlefield moaned, that
     the earth
breathed forth guilty spirits, that all the air
     was tainted
by the shades and the night of upper world by
     Stygian terror.          770
Victory exacts a hideous punishment deservedly, and
     slumber
brings on flames and hissing. The ghost of a murdered
     citizen
stands there; each man is tormented by a terrifying
     vision all his own:
*he* sees faces of old men, *he* the forms of younger men,
*he* in all his dreams is harried by his brother's corpse,
in *this* breast is his father—all these shades are in
     Caesar.
Just such were the faces of the Eumenides which
     Pelopean Orestes
saw when not yet purified upon the Scythian altar;
and he felt a mental turmoil no more thunderstruck
     than that
of Pentheus in his frenzy or Agave when she had
     ceased to rave.          780
On that night he is tormented by all the swords
which Pharsalia saw or which the day of retribution
     would see,
unsheathed by the Senate; he is lashed by the hellish
     monsters.
Yet his guilty mind forgives the unhappy man part of
     his punishment

because he sees the Styx, the shades and
  Tartarus thrust
into his dreams while Pompey is alive!
    Though he suffered all of this,
when shining daylight revealed the losses of Pharsalia,
the appearance of the place in no way checks his eyes
  from fastening
upon the deathly fields. He sees rivers driven on
790 by gore and mounds of corpses high as lofty
hills, he watches heaps sinking into putrefaction
and counts the peoples of Magnus; a place for feasting
is prepared from where he can discern the faces and
  the features
of the dead. He is delighted that he cannot see the
  Emathian land
and that his eyes scan fields hidden underneath the
  carnage.
In the blood he sees his fortune and his gods.
And not to lose the joyful sight of his wickedness, in
  a frenzy
he refuses those unfortunates the pyre's flame and
  forces on to guilty
heaven the sight of Emathia. The Carthaginian
  who buried
the consul and Cannae lit by Libyan torches do not
800  compel him
to observe the customs of humanity towards
  an enemy,
but, with his anger not yet glutted by the slaughter, he
  remembers
that they were his fellow citizens. We do not ask for
  individual
graves or for separate funeral-pyres: grant the nations
a single fire, let the bodies be burnt in a holocaust;
or if you enjoy punishing your son-in-law, heap up
  Pindus'
forest, raise up the woods packed with Oeta's oak,
let Pompey see the flame of Thessaly from his ship.
You achieve nothing by this anger. It matters not
  whether corpses disintegrate
by putrefaction or on the pyre; Nature takes back
810  everything
in her kindly bosom, and bodies owe their own end to
  themselves.
These people, Caesar, if not consumed by fire now,
  will be consumed
together with the earth, together with the waters of
  the sea.

A shared funeral-pyre which will mingle scars with
  dead men's bones
awaits the universe. Wherever Fortune calls your
  spirit,
there will be these spirits too: into the breezes you will
  go no higher
than they, in no better place beneath the Stygian night
  will you lie.
Death is free from Fortune; Earth has room for all
  that she
has borne; the man who has no funeral urn is covered
  by the sky.
You—exacting punishment from the nations in
  corpses without burial—                                    820
why do you flee this carnage? Why do you desert
  these stinking fields?
Drink these waters, Caesar, breathe this air, if you can.
But the rotting hordes rob you of Pharsalian
fields, they rout the conqueror and possess the plains.

To the grisly fodder of Haemonian war
  came not only
Bistonian wolves but lions too, who left Pholoe
when they scented out decay of bloody slaughter.
Then she-bears left their lairs and loathsome dogs
their homes and houses: every keen-nosed creature
which senses air impure and tainted by carrion.        830
The birds which for a long time now had followed
  the camp
of civil war flock together. You birds, accustomed to
  exchange
Thracian winters for Nile, went later
to the mild south. Never was the heaven clothed with
such a cloud of vultures, never did more wings crush
  the air.
Every forest sent its birds and every tree
dripped with bloody dew from gore-stained wing.
Often on the victor's face and unnatural standards
fell gore or rotting flesh from the lofty ether,
as a bird let drop the limbs from its talons now
  exhausted.                                                840
Even so the entire horde is not reduced to bones and
  does not disappear
inside wild beasts, torn to shreds; they care not for
  the inmost
guts nor are they hungry to suck up all the marrow:
they barely taste the limbs. Most of the Latian
  multitude
lies there rejected; but sun and rains and lapse

of time dissolved and blended them with Emathian
  fields.
Thessaly, unfortunate land! With what crime
  did you so
hurt the gods that they inflicted on you alone so many
  deaths,
so many dooms of wickedness? What length of time
  will be enough
for distant ages to forget and to forgive you for the
850    losses of the war?
Every crop will rise discolored with tainted growth.
With every ploughshare you will desecrate the Roman
  shades.
First, new battle-lines will meet and for a second crime
you will offer your plains not yet dry from this blood.
Though we empty all our ancestors' graves—
the tombs still standing and those which have
  poured out
their funeral-urns, their framework overcome by
  ancient tree-root—
more are the ashes ploughed in the furrows
of Haemonian land, more the bones which rustic har-
  row strikes.
No sailor would have tied his rope to the
860    Emathian
shore, no ploughman would have disturbed the land,
the grave of the Roman people, and the farmers would
  run away
from the haunted plains, no flocks would shelter

in the thickets, no herdsman would dare allow
  his herd
to pluck the grass which rises from our bones,
and you would lie unknown and bare, as if not
  supporting
human life because of ice or zone of excessive heat,
if you alone, instead of first, had borne the blasphemy
  of war.
O gods above, permit us to hate the guilty lands.
Why do you burden the entire world and
  so acquit it?                                                 870
The carnage of the West, Pachynus' lamentable wave,
  and Mutina and Leucas have made Philippi
  innocent.

*In the next book, following the defeat, Pompey's suggestion
that they enlist the Parthians in the struggle against Caesar
is rejected by his men. He then flees to Egypt, where he is
killed on arrival by the king, Ptolemy, who hopes thereby to
ingratiate himself with Caesar. His headless body is given
an anonymous burial on the seashore. In Book 9, Lucan
narrates the continuing resistance to Caesar, which is now
led by Cato, who leads the remnants of the republican
army in North Africa. Caesar arrives in Egypt, where he
is presented with the head of Pompey. In the last book of
the poem, we see Caesar in Alexandria first at the tomb of
Alexander the Great and then hosting a banquet attended
by Cleopatra. The people of the city revolt against Caesar,
at which point the poem ends abruptly.*

## AFTERWORD

In a characteristic burst of hyperbole, which actually proved true, Lucan proclaimed that "my poem
about Pharsalia shall live on and no age will ever doom us to oblivion" (9.985). In the years following
the poet's death and the poem's dissemination, admiration mingled with criticism. In *The Satyricon*
of his contemporary Petronius, one of the characters, the buffoonish poet Eumolpus, declaims his
own poem on the civil war that comically encapsulates some of the criticisms of Lucan's epic. Before
Eumolpus launches into his theme, he notes (*Satyricon* 118) that "the person who tries his hand at the
lofty theme of the civil war must be steeped in literature, or he will sink under the burden of the subject.
Historical events are not to be treated in verses, for historians handle such material far better. The free
spirit of genius should plunge headlong into oracular utterances, the succor lent by the gods, and the
Procrustean control of lapidary phrases; the result should appear as prophetic frenzy rather than as a
trustworthy, scrupulous account attested by witnesses." The quality of Lucan as a poet was immediately a subject of dispute. Quintilian judged him to be "fiery and passionate and famous for his pointed
epigrams" (*Education of the Orator* 10.1.90), but in the end he recommended him more to orators than

to poets. This assessment persisted throughout antiquity, and indeed beyond. In the second century, Fronto, who was not a fan of the moderns, found him verbose. An extreme position was staked out by Servius, the late fourth-century commentator on Virgil, who considered him a historian and not a poet at all (*On the Aeneid* 1.382). The appropriate response to these critics was first made by Martial (14.194), who commented wryly in the person of Lucan, "There are some who say I am no poet; but the bookseller who markets me thinks I am."

As a writer of hexameter narrative Lucan's popularity in antiquity was exceeded only by Virgil and Ovid. Surviving notes from two ancient commentaries on *The Civil War* attest to the fact that the poem was studied in schools, and later grammarians, including the severely critical Servius, quote it frequently. Lucan's widow, Argentaria Polla, who must have been very young when he died, continued to celebrate his birthday throughout her life, an occasion to which Martial (7.21–23) and Statius (*Silvae* 2.70) dedicated poems in her lifetime. Martial rated him second only to Virgil, and a similar opinion is to be found in Tacitus, when he rates Lucan together with Virgil and Horace as one of the three poets especially worthy to be employed by orators wishing to add a bit of poetic polish to their declamations.

For the Middle Ages, Lucan was an important source for Roman history, and his enduring popularity is attested by the survival of more than four hundred complete or partial manuscripts, including five complete copies from the ninth century. Not every medieval reader approved: an eleventh-century Benedictine, Otloh of St. Emmeram, objected to Boethius's liking of Lucan and attributed his own conversion to an illness he had suffered while reading *The Civil War*. But there were more who would have agreed with Dante, who placed Lucan fourth—after Homer, Horace, and Ovid—among the "spiriti sancti" (*Inferno* 4.90). Lucan's poem was translated into Italian as early as 1310 and was an influential presence in the resurgence of epic narrative, both in Latin, in Petrarch's *Africa,* and in Italian, in Tasso's *Jerusalem Delivered.* His was among the earliest Latin texts printed, with the first edition appearing in Rome in 1469 from the press of Sweynheym and Pannartz.

Editions and translations proliferated in the following centuries, when Lucan's popularity continued unabated, not least in England, where Christopher Marlowe produced a version of Book 1. During a politically sensitive moment in British history, the poet Thomas May published a translation of all ten books (1627). This was so successful that a few years later he published his own continuation of Lucan's unfinished epic in English (1630), in which he now toned down his earlier anti-imperial tone. He followed this in 1640 with a Latin version of his continuation, which was sometimes included in Continental editions of Lucan. His English translation, however, was eventually superseded by the version of Nicholas Rowe (1674–1718), on which Rowe labored for twenty years and which was published posthumously in 1719. Samuel Johnson called it "one of the greatest productions of English poetry." Rowe's rather free version does capture some of Lucan's rhetorical flashes, as in this passage from the first book, where Caesar is characterized in a memorable comparison to a lightning bolt (*The Civil War* 1.143–57):

> But Caesar's greatness, and his strength, was more
> Than past renown, and antiquated pow'r;
> 'Twas not the fame of what he once had been
> Or tales in old Records and Annals seen;
> But 'twas a valor, restless, unconfin'd,
> Which no success could sate, nor limits bind;
> 'Twas shame, a Soldier's shame, untaught to yield,
> That blush'd for nothing but an ill-fought field:
> Fierce in his hopes he was, nor knew to stay,
> Where vengeance or Ambition led the way;
> Still prodigal of war whene'er withstood,

Nor spar'd to stain the guilty sword with blood:
Urging advantage he improv'd all odds,
And made the most of Fortune and the Gods;
Pleas'd to o'erturn whate'er withheld his prize,
And saw the ruin with rejoicing eyes.
Such while Earth trembles, & Heav'n thunders loud,
Darts the swift Lightning from the rending cloud;
Fierce thro' the day it breaks, and in its flight
The dreadful blast confounds the Gazer's sight;
Resistless in its course delights to rove,
And cleaves the Temples of its Master Jove:
Alike where-e'er it passes or returns,
With equal rage the fell destroyer burns;
Then with a whirl full in its strength retires,
And recollects the force of all its scatter'd fires.

Johnson felt that Rowe had captured Lucan's "ambitious morality and pointed sentences, comprised in vigorous and animated lines," and it is perhaps the case that Rowe composed in an age more sympathetic to such qualities.

Sympathy for Lucan has occasionally resurfaced in subsequent periods, but for the most part *The Civil War* has remained largely the preserve of classical scholars rather than readers at large. For some, like Shelley, with a revolutionary bent, he has been an admired author, but for the most part he has been mined, if at all, for his memorable epigrams (*sententiae*). During the First Republic in the French Revolution, members of the National Guard carried swords inscribed with a line from Book 4 (579): *ignorantque datos, ne quisquam serviat, enses,* "and men are ignorant that the purpose of the sword is to save every man from slavery." And what is probably Lucan's most famous line is inscribed on the base of the Confederate Memorial at Arlington National Cemetery, a dedication by the United Daughters of the Confederacy: *Victrix Causa Diis Placuit Sed Victa Catoni,* from Book 1 (128), which means "The Victorious Cause Was Pleasing to the Gods, But the Lost Cause to Cato." Cato, alas, would probably have approved.

# PETRONIUS

(? Petronius Arbiter, ?–A.D. 66)

IN A.D. 65, AFTER TEN YEARS OF RULE, THE EMPEROR NERO WAS RIPE FOR ASSASSINATION.
A conspiracy was hatched to replace him with the charming and popular Gaius Calpurnius Piso, but
he proved not up to the task, and when the conspiracy was detected, Piso complacently committed
suicide. Seneca and his nephew Lucan were implicated in the plot and duly followed suit. Also
compromised was a senator, Flavius Scaevinus, who died an otherwise unmemorable death, but his
association with one of Nero's favorite courtiers, Titus Petronius, opened the door for the jealous
new prefect of the Praetorian Guard, Gaius Ofonius Tigellinus, to cast suspicion upon him too.
Before describing Petronius's end, Tacitus paints a vivid portrait of his character (*Annals* 16.18.1–4):

> His days were spent sleeping, his nights on the duties and delights of life. While others
> had been brought fame by industry, in his instance it was by idleness; and yet he was not
> considered a glutton and a spendthrift, like most who squander their fortunes, but a man
> of educated extravagance. The more outrageous his words and actions, which had a distinc-
> tive sort of nonchalance about them, the more acceptable they became as a demonstration
> of his sincerity. As proconsul of Bithynia, however, and subsequently as consul, he showed
> himself to be a man of energy who was competent in business. Then, sliding back into his
> vices, or through imitating vices, he was taken into Nero's small band of cronies as his 'arbi-
> ter of good taste'; in his jaded state, Nero considered nothing delightful or agreeable unless
> it had Petronius's approval.

After he was denounced by Tigellinus, Petronius set off to appeal to the emperor directly, who was
in Campania at the time. But by the time Petronius reached Cumae, where he had a villa, he learned
that there was no appeasing Nero. And so he set the stage for his own suicide, to which we are witnesses, again, thanks to Tacitus (*Annals* 16.19):

> He did not let fear or hope further delay him. He was, however, in no rush to end his life.
> Having cut his veins, he bandaged them and opened them again, as he felt inclined, in the
> meantime chatting with his friends, but not on serious matters or topics that would win him
> glory for his resolve. He listened in turn to their words—nothing on the immortality of the
> soul or the tenets of philosophers, but light poetry and playful verses. To some of his slaves
> he presented gifts, to others a whipping. He started dinner and let himself drop off to sleep so
> that his death, though imposed, might look natural. Even in his will he did not, like most who

perished, flatter Nero, Tigellinus, or any other of the powerful. Instead, he itemized in writing the emperor's depravities, naming the male prostitutes and women involved, and describing all their novel sexual acts, and sent it to Nero under seal. He then broke his signet ring to prevent its later use for manufacturing danger.

Tacitus clearly relished the contrast with the deaths of those who had actually been involved in the conspiracy, which were far from glorious. Before he died Lucan turned informer on his own mother, and as he died Piso heaped flattery on Nero. Seneca's suicide was a showy, Stoic affair, but, as Tacitus depicts it, botched in the execution. Instead, it was the hedonistic Petronius who died heroically.

In the medieval manuscripts that transmit the surviving fragments of the novel *The Satyricon,* the author's name is given as "Petronius Arbiter." Is this person identical with the attractive reprobate described by Tacitus? Most people would like to think that the Petronius who made his death a satire of Seneca's suicide was also the author of this great satirical novel, and most scholars do think so, although the grounds for making the association still leave some room for doubt. There is no direct evidence linking Nero's arbiter of good taste to the novel, but the probable setting of the plot in the mid-first century, the language and style in which it is composed, and the worldview it represents all coincide quite nicely with that attribution.

*The Satyricon* is a unique specimen of realistic comic fiction from antiquity. Whether it had any antecedents in Greek is impossible to say, but we know of none for certain, and the surest conclusion is that Petronius's novel is a highly original fusion of many literary forms. The title of the work offers a clue to its contents. It is a Greek word in the genitive plural, so the work would have been known to its first readers as *The Books of the Satyrica* (*Satyricon Libri*) or simply *Satyrica*. The form of the title translates into "Stories about Satyrs," but it is still conventional to refer to the work by the traditional title, *The Satyricon.* The title would also have reminded Petronius's first readers of other fictional narratives in Greek, with titles like *Ephesiaca,* "Stories from Ephesus," or *Phoenicica,* "Stories from Phoenicia." They would thus have understood this to be a work about the world of the Satyrs, the goatlike creatures of Greek mythology known for their unrestrained appetite for sex and wine. In this respect, as far as we can tell, Petronius's title is evocative only, for he does not tell stories about actual Satyrs but about three young Romans with Greek names and their adventures in the streets and taverns, brothels and baths of everyday Roman life.

The earliest surviving Greek novels all seem to postdate the probable composition of *The Satyricon* around A.D. 65, a circumstance that complicates discussions of Petronius's sources. Increasingly, scholars have interpreted the new evidence from papyri to mean that in fact the history of the novel extends back into at least the first century B.C., and consequently the view that one important aspect of Petronius's work is parody of that form has taken hold. Greek novels, with the notable exception of Longus's *Daphnis and Chloe,* have a number of distinctive traits. The plots typically revolve around a pair of young lovers, a handsome young man and a beautiful girl, whose romance is complicated by a series of misadventures. The stories involve abduction by pirates, shipwrecks, conniving rivals, and long journeys to distant lands. It is not difficult to see Petronius's portrayal of a homosexual love triangle moving about Italy as playing off the expectations created by this popular literary form. But *The Satyricon* is not simply a parody of the Greek romance novel; it incorporates a much broader range of literary models.

A distinctive feature of *The Satyricon* is the alternation of prose and verse, something that is not found in the surviving Greek novels or in Apuleius's *Metamorphoses.* Petronius is drawing on the style of Menippean satire, a genre that was associated with the Cynic philosopher Menippus of Gadara (third century B.C.). From the little that we know about his lost works, they consisted of humorous moralizing on a broad array of topics in a form that combined prose and verse. In first-century B.C. Rome, Varro produced a work that acknowledged this tradition in its title, *Menippean Satires,* and the fragments that survive suggest that he expanded its range. The only surviving such work in Latin is

Seneca's *Apocolocyntosis,* but the idea of interjecting bits of poetry into a prose narrative about topics from everyday life was adapted by his contemporary Petronius for the very different purposes of his comic novel.

Another form of popular literature exploited by Petronius is the short story. One of the best examples is the tale of the "Widow of Ephesus," included in our selection. This story, too, had a history in the Greek and Latin literary tradition that we can reconstruct as background for *The Satyricon*. It began with a work by a Greek author named Aristides of the late second century B.C., whose *Milesian Tales* was a collection of short, erotic stories set in the city of Miletus in Asia Minor. This collection was very popular in Rome. It was translated into Latin early in the first century B.C. by Sisenna, and a Roman officer brought a copy with him on Crassus's ill-fated campaign against the Parthians in 53 B.C. (Plutarch, *Life of Crassus* 32). Another example in Petronius is the story of the "Pergamene Boy," and Apuleius adapts such tales as well. But there is no limit to the range of literary genres at play in *The Satyricon,* and examples would probably be multiplied if more of the work had survived. One possibility is the interplay with Homeric models in the theme of divine anger working against the hero. Many critics suspect that, just as Odysseus must cope with the anger of Poseidon, Encolpius, the narrator of *The Satyricon,* is plagued by the wrath of Priapus—the rustic deity whose identifying trait is his oversized phallus.

**Figure 22:  Skeletons on an embossed silver cup**
A magnificently tangible illustration of the Horatian motto *carpe diem* (seize the day).

We have only extracts from the novel, ranging in length from a phrase or two to the extended scene of the *Dinner with Trimalchio*. That long episode probably occupied all of Book 15 of *The Satyricon*, and the other surviving fragments come from the books that immediately precede and follow it. The length of the complete novel is unknown, but twenty-four books is a good guess: that would evoke comparisons with Homer, and we know of at least one other ancient novel of this length, by Antonius Diogenes. The story of *The Satyricon* is narrated by Encolpius, a young man of good education and questionable character. Where it began is impossible to say, but there are some indications that Massilia (mod. Marseilles) was the starting point and that it was there that Encolpius hooked up with Giton, a good-looking boy who is the object of his affections. Their wanderings took them east and south to Italy, which is where we find them in the first fragments. The place is identified only as a "Greek city," but a number of clues point to Puteoli (mod. Pozzuoli) on the Bay of Naples. Somewhere in their wanderings up to this point they had taken up with another adventurer of dubious character named Ascyltus. Although the names of the protagonists are Greek, the settings in which their adventures take place are those of Romanized Italy and would have been enjoyed for just that reason by Petronius's readers, whether back in their townhouses in the capital or at leisure in their Campanian villas.

## THE SATYRICON

*In the first extensive fragment, Encolpius has encountered a teacher of rhetoric named Agamemnon and is found criticizing contemporary trends in oratory. One of his traveling companions, the somewhat unsavory Ascyltus, had slipped away from the school of rhetoric, and when Encolpius goes in search of him, he ends up running into him at a brothel entirely by chance. Subsequently they rejoin the third member of the company, Giton, who is the object of the amorous attentions of both Encolpius and Ascyltus. A quarrel erupts between Encolpius and Ascyltus, which ends in laughter, but tension lingers between the two. In the next fragment we find the two of them in the marketplace attempting to sell a cloak that they have stolen and at the same time recover a tunic, stuffed with cash, which they managed to lose in an earlier episode. The following fragment finds them back at their lodgings, where Giton has prepared a meal. One of their adventures in the lost portion of the novel is about to come back to haunt them.*

[16] No sooner had we filled our bellies with the dinner which Giton had kindly prepared for us than there was a peremptory hammering on the door ... We blanched, and asked who was there. "Open up," a voice said, "and you will soon find out." In the course of this exchange, the bolt gave way of its own accord, and fell off; the door suddenly yawned open and admitted our visitor. It was a woman, heavily veiled. "Did you imagine," she asked, "that you had fooled me? I am the maid of Quartilla, the lady whose ritual you interrupted in front of her chapel. She is coming in person to your lodging, and begs leave to have words with you. Don't get agitated; she is not here to condemn or to punish your sin; on the contrary, she wonders what god has led such elegant young men into her neighborhood."

[17] We were still reduced to silence, saying neither yea nor nay, when the lady herself entered, escorted by a young girl. She seated herself on my bed in a bout of weeping. Even then we did not offer a word, but waited in bewilderment for this tearful demonstration of grief to end. Once the impressive shower of tears had subsided, she unveiled her proud head, pressing her hands hard together until the joints cracked. "Why have you behaved so recklessly?" she asked. "Where did you learn to outdo the storybooks in your thieving? I swear to heaven I'm sorry for you; no one goes unpunished for having gazed on things forbidden. This locality of ours in particular is so crowded with the presence of divinities that it's easier to find a god here than a man.

Please don't think that I have come here bent on revenge. I'm more concerned for your tender years than for the harm you've done me. I still think that it was thoughtlessness that made you commit that irreparable crime. That night I myself was on edge. I got the shivers from so dangerous a chill that I even feared an attack of tertian fever. So I sought a remedy from my dreams. In them I was bidden to seek you out, and to relieve the onset of my illness by a clever device that was revealed to me. But that cure is not what bothers me most. A greater affliction seethes deep within me, dragging me down willy-nilly to death's door: it is the fear that youthful excess may induce you to noise abroad what you witnessed in Priapus' shrine, and to make the gods' designs known to the world at large. This is why I stretch out suppliant hands to your knees, begging and imploring you not to decide to betray the secrets of countless years which are known to barely a thousand mortals."

[18] She followed this entreaty with a further outburst of tears. Her body shook with protracted moaning, and she sank her entire face and breast into my bed. Shaken simultaneously by pity and fear, I urged her to be of good heart, and to be reassured on both counts: none of us would divulge the rites, and if the god had revealed to her some further cure for the fever, we would carry through the design of divine Providence even if it put us in danger. This promise cheered the lady, and she rained kisses on me. Her tears were transformed into laughter, and with lingering fingers she stroked the hair tumbling over my ears. "I declare a truce with you", she said, "and discharge you from the indictment laid against you. But if you had not consented to the remedy I seek, I had already mustered a mob to avenge the affront to my honor.

If patronized by others, I lose face;
It's arrogance to put me in my place.
I like the chance to go my own sweet way.
Why, even wise philosophers of the day,
If treated with contempt, weave words to harm.
The merciful combatant oft wins the palm."

Then she clapped her hands, and dissolved into such paroxysms of laughter that we were alarmed. For her part, the maid who had entered before her behaved likewise; so did the young girl who had come in with her.

[19] The entire place resounded with the laughter of the low stage: We were wholly at a loss about the meaning of this sudden change. We stared blankly now at each other, and now at the women . . .

"So I have given instructions that no mortal be allowed into this lodging today, so that I can obtain the cure for my tertian fever from you without interruption." When Quartilla said this, Ascyltus was momentarily struck dumb; I felt colder than a Gallic winter, and could not utter a word. However, the nature of

the company reassured me against anticipating anything unpleasant. They were three mere women, their strength puny if they tried anything on; whatever else was said about us, at least we were male, and our clothes were certainly hitched higher than theirs. Indeed, I had already mentally matched up the pairs in case we had to fight it out; I would face up to Quartilla, Ascyltus to the maid, and Giton to the young girl.

At that moment of bewilderment: our entire resolve melted away. Certain death began to shroud our unhappy eyes.

[20] "Madam, I beg you," I said, "whatever sinister plan you have in mind, get it over and done with. The crime we committed was not so monstrous that we must die by torture." . . . The maid, whose name was Psyche, carefully spread a blanket over the stone floor . . . She addressed herself to my parts, already cold through suffering a thousand deaths. Ascyltus had buried his head in his cloak; he doubtless remembered the warning that it was dangerous to witness the secret rites of others.

The maid produced two straps from her dress; she tied our feet together with one, and our hands with the other . . .

Our flow of chatter was now flagging, so Ascyltus piped up: "Don't I merit a drink, then?" The maid, prompted by my laughter, clapped her hands and said: "But I did put one by you . . . Young Encolpius, have you drunk the entire potion yourself?"

"Good heavens!" said Quartilla. "Has Encolpius downed all the aphrodisiac?" Her sides shook rather fetchingly. Finally even Giton failed to restrain his giggles, especially when the young girl hung on his neck and deluged the unresisting lad with countless kisses . . .

[21] We would have cried out in our wretched state, but there was no one at hand to lend help. On the one side Psyche was gouging my cheeks with a hairpin as I sought to raise a hue and cry, and on the other the young girl was dousing Ascyltus with a sponge which she had soaked in the aphrodisiac . . .

Eventually a catamite appeared on the scene, dressed in a cloak of myrtle green hitched up with a belt. First he wrenched our buttocks apart and forced his way in, and then besmirched us with the foulest of stinking kisses, until Quartilla, wielding a whalebone ferula and hitching her skirts high, gave the order for our release from our unhappy service . . .

We both swore an oath in the most solemn terms that so grim a secret would never be divulged by either of us . . .

Several attendants from the gym came in, and revived us by rubbing us down with the usual oil. So we were able to dispel our weariness, and to resume our dress for dining. We were escorted into the next room, in which three couches had been laid and every other elegant preparation had been made on a lavish scale. So when the word was given we reclined on the couches. There was a splendid hors d'oeuvre to start with, and we were also abundantly plied with Falernian wine. Then we were served with several main courses as well. But when we began to doze off, Quartilla said: "What's this? Are you even contemplating sleep, when you are aware that a night's vigil is owed to the guiding spirit of Priapus?"

[22] Ascyltus was wearied by the many indignities he had suffered, and he fell asleep. The maid whose approaches had been so rudely rejected coated his entire face with masses of soot, and painted his torso and shoulders vermilion. He did not feel a thing. By now I too was exhausted by all these grisly experiences, and had savored a quick snatch of sleep. So had the whole retinue of servants, both in the room and outside. Some were lying scattered round the feet of the reclining guests, others were propped against the walls, and others still waited at the threshold, heads supporting each other. The lamps too were running out of oil and giving off a dim and dying light. At that moment two Syrians came into the dining-room intending to strip the place. Their greed got the better of them as they squabbled over the silver, and they pulled a decanter apart and broke it. The table with the silver on it went flying, and a drinking cup was accidentally dislodged from a high shelf, and gave the maid a bleeding head as she lay drooping over a couch. The impact made her cry out; this both exposed the thieves and roused some of the revelers. When the Syrians realized that they had been caught in the act, they simultaneously collapsed by a couch as if by a prearranged ploy, and began to snore as though they had been asleep for some time.

By now the steward had been roused, and had poured some oil into the flagging lamps. The slave-boys rubbed their eyes for a moment or two, and returned to duty. A female cymbal-player entered and roused everyone with the clash of brass.

[23] So the party recommenced. Quartilla recalled us to our cups, and the cymbal-player sang to add to the jollity. Then in came a catamite; the most repulsive character imaginable, surely a worthy representative of that household. He wheezed as he snapped his fingers, and spouted some lines like this:

Assemble here, you wanton sodomites,
Drive yourselves forward, let your feet take wing.
Full speed ahead. Come now with pliant thighs,
And mincing buttocks, fingers gesturing!
Come, tender youths, and you in later life,
And lads castrated by the Delian's knife.

Having delivered his lines, he slobbered over me with the filthiest of kisses. He then mounted the couch as well, and stripped me with all his strength in spite of my resistance. He labored long and hard over my parts, but all in vain. Streams of brilliantine poured over his forehead as he sweated away, and so much chalk appeared in the wrinkles of his cheeks that you would have thought that a wall was flaking after being damaged by rain.

[24] I could not restrain my tears any longer, for I was reduced to extreme distress. "Please, madam," I said, "surely what you prescribed for me was a tumbler to have in bed?" She clapped her hands gently, and replied: "What a clever fellow you are, a positive fount of native wit! Did you not realize that a catamite is also called a tumbler?" Then, so that things would turn out better for my comrade, I remarked: "For goodness' sake, is Ascyltus the only one in the dining-room enjoying a holiday?"

"So it seems," said Quartilla. "Ascyltus must get a tumbler as well." At these words the catamite changed mounts and crossed over to my companion, smothering him with his buttocks and his kisses.

Giton stood there watching this and splitting his sides with laughter. So Quartilla cast an eye on him, and with great interest enquired whose boy he was. I replied that he was my friend. "So why hasn't he given me a kiss?" she demanded. She called him over to her, and kissed him. Then she slipped her hand inside his clothes, and fondled his virgin tackle. "These will make a good starter to rouse my appetite in tomorrow's encounter," she said. "As I've already had the fish course today, I don't want dry bread!"

[25] As she was saying this, Psyche came close to her ear wearing a grin, and whispered some suggestion. "Quite right," said Quartilla. "You did well to remind me. This is a most auspicious moment, so why shouldn't our Pannychis lose her maidenhead?" At

once the girl was ushered forward. She was extremely pretty, and seemed to be no more than seven years old. One and all applauded, and demanded a wedding. I was astounded and protested that Giton was an extremely modest lad, not up to such wanton behavior, and the girl was not old enough to undertake the woman's role. "What?" said Quartilla. "Is she any younger than I was when I first submitted to a man? I don't recall ever being a virgin—Juno strike me down if I lie! Even as a baby I played dirty games with boys of my own age, and as I grew up I associated with bigger lads till I reached womanhood. In fact I think that's how the proverb, 'Carry a calf, and carry a bull', originated."

[26] I was afraid that the boy would come to greater harm if he were unaccompanied, so I got up to play my part in the ceremony. By now Psyche had draped a marriage veil over the girl's head, and the Tumbler was leading the way with a marriage torch. The drunken females formed a long line, clapping their hands; they had adorned the bridal chamber with lewd coverlets. Quartilla was roused by the lecherous behavior of the sportive crowd. She sprang up, grabbed Giton, and dragged him into the bedroom. The boy had clearly offered no resistance, and the girl had not blanched fearfully at the mention of marriage. So they were tucked in, and they lay down; we seated ourselves at the threshold of the chamber. Quartilla took the lead in gluing an inquisitive eye to a chink she had shamelessly opened, and she viewed their youthful sport with prurient attention. Then with caressing hand she drew me to watch the spectacle as well. Our faces as we eyed the scene were close together, and whenever she took a rest from the show she would move her lips over, and press kisses on me from time to time on the sly . . .

We threw ourselves on our beds, and spent the rest of the night without apprehension.

*This was probably the last sentence of Book 14, and what follows is just as likely to be the beginning of Book 15. Apparently the threesome of Encolpius, Ascyltus, and Giton are considering how to break away from Quartilla when a slave of Agamemnon, the teacher of rhetoric, arrives to inform them that they are to dine with Trimalchio. They head off to the baths with him, and since the invitation is for Encolpius and Ascyltus, Giton will pretend to be their slave.*

Two days had now elapsed, and the free dinner was in prospect. But we were transfixed by so many wounds that we were bent on flight rather than relaxation. So

in our dejection we were discussing how to avoid the storm-clouds ahead, but then one of Agamemnon's servants broke in on our anxieties, and asked: "What's the matter with you? Don't you know your host for today? He is Trimalchio; a man of supreme refinement. He keeps a water-clock in his dining room, and a trumpeter at the ready, so that from time to time he can keep count of the lost hours." So we forgot all our misfortunes, and dressed with some care. Giton was playing the role of servant with great *élan*, and we bade him follow us to the baths.

[27] To pass the time we strolled about in our dinner dress. Indeed, we were laughing and joking as we approached the groups of those who were taking exercise. Suddenly we caught sight of a bald old man wearing a red shirt and playing ball with some long-haired young slaves. The boys were worth a good look, but they were not so much the attraction as was their master. He was wearing slippers, and throwing a green ball around. Any ball which came in contact with the ground he did not bother to retrieve; there was a bagful supervised by a slave, containing enough for the players. We noticed some other unusual features: two eunuchs stood in the circle facing Trimalchio. One was holding a silver chamber-pot; the other was counting the balls, not as they sped from hand to hand as they were thrown in the course of the game, but as they dropped to the ground. As we were admiring these refinements, Menelaus came bustling up. "This is the host at whose table you will rest your elbows. This in fact is the prelude to the dinner." As Menelaus was still speaking, Trimalchio clicked his fingers, and at this signal the eunuch supplied him with the chamber-pot as he continued playing. The host voided his bladder, demanded water for his hands, and after perfunctorily washing his fingers, wiped them on the slave's hair.

[28] Reporting all the details would be tedious. So we entered the baths, and as soon as we had raised a sweat we passed through to the cold plunge: By now Trimalchio was doused with fragrant oil, and was being rubbed down—not with linen cloths, but with bath-towels of softest wool. Meanwhile his three masseurs were drinking Falernian before his eyes. They spilt a lot of it while sparring with each other; Trimalchio claimed that they were commemorating him!

He was then installed in a litter, wrapped in a scarlet dressing-gown. In front were four bemedalled runners; and a go-cart in which his boy-favorite was riding, a wizened youth with watery eyes, uglier than Trimalchio his master. As the host was borne off, a musician with miniature pipes came close to his head, and played in his ear the whole way, as if he were imparting confidential information to him.

Quite wonderstruck we walked behind, and in company with Agamemnon drew near the door. On the doorpost a notice had been fastened, bearing the inscription: "Any slave leaving the house without his master's bidding will receive a hundred stripes." At the very entrance stood a janitor in a green outfit hitched up with a cherry-colored belt; he was shelling peas in a silver dish. Over the threshold hung a golden cage, in which a dappled magpie greeted the incomers.

[29] As I stood lost in amazement at all this, I nearly fell flat on my back and broke my legs. On our left as we entered, close to the janitor's office, a massive dog fastened by a chain was painted on the wall, with an inscription above it in block letters: BEWARE OF THE DOG. My companions burst out laughing at me; I gathered my wits, and proceeded to examine the entire wall. There was the representation of a slave market, with placards bearing the names and prices of the slaves. Trimalchio himself was there, sporting long hair and holding a herald's wand; Minerva was escorting him on his entry into Rome. Next the painter had carefully and scrupulously depicted, with commentary below, the detail of how Trimalchio had learnt accountancy, and had then become a steward. At the end of the colonnade, Mercury had raised him by the chin, and was bearing him up on to a lofty dais. Fortune with her horn of plenty was in attendance, and the three Fates were there spinning their golden threads. I observed also in the colonnade a team of runners practising under their trainer. In a corner I noted a large sideboard enclosing a tiny shrine. In it were set the household gods in silver, a marble statue of Venus, and a golden container of some size, in which they said Trimalchio's beard was stored . . .

So I began to question the porter about the subjects of other pictures on display. "There is the *Iliad*," he replied, "and the *Odyssey*, and Laenas' *Gladiatorial Games.*"

[30] But we were unable to examine the numerous exhibits . . . We had now reached the dining-room. A steward was posted at the entrance, approving the accounts. I was particularly surprised to see a bundle of rods and axes attached to the doorposts, supported below by what seemed to be the bronze beak of a ship, containing the inscription: "To Gaius Pompeius

Trimalchio, member of the sextet of the College of Augustus. Presented by his steward Cinnamus." A two-branched lamp with the same inscription hung from the ceiling. There were also two panels set in the two doorposts. If my memory serves me right, one of them had this inscription: "Our Gaius dines out on 30th and 31st December." The other depicted the course of the moon, with representations of the seven planets: days of good and evil omen were marked with distinctive counters.

Sated with these delights, we attempted to make our way into the dining-room. As we did so, one of the slaves allotted to this duty cried out: "Right feet first!" For a moment we were in utter panic, in case one of us disobeyed the injunction in crossing the threshold. As we all as one put our right feet forward, a slave stripped for flogging groveled at our feet, and proceeded to implore us to rescue him from punishment. The cause of his predicament, he said, was a mere peccadillo: the steward's clothes which were in his charge at the baths had been stolen from him, but they would have fetched no more than ten thousand sesterces: So we withdrew our right feet, and implored the steward, as he counted out gold pieces in his office, to grant the slave a remission. That arrogant official raised his nose in the air. "It is not so much the loss that annoys me", he said, "as that good-for-nothing slave's dereliction of duty. He lost my dining-out clothes given to me by one of my dependants for my birthday. They were Tyrian, of course, but they had been laundered once; so the loss is of no account. I make you a present of him."

[31] This lordly concession put us in his debt. As we entered the dining-room, we were confronted by the same slave for whom we had pleaded. As we stood there open-mouthed, he thanked us for our kindness by showering us with kisses. "I won't labor it," he said, "but you will soon be aware who the recipient of your kindness was. 'The master's wine is in the butler's gift.'"

At last we were able to settle on the couches. Some Alexandrian slave-boys poured iced water on our hands, while others behind them bent over our feet, and with great dexterity cut our toenails. Even this degrading duty did not silence them, for they sang as they worked. I wanted to find out if the whole entourage was composed of songbirds, so I asked for a glass of wine. A slave was immediately at hand, and took my order while singing in a shrill voice; so did all the others when complying with a request. You would have thought it was a dancer's supporting group, and not the service in the dining-room of a wealthy householder!

By now a most elegant hors d' oeuvre had been brought in, for all the guests had taken their places on the couches, with the sole exception of Trimalchio, for whom contrary to custom a top place was being reserved. In the entree dish stood a donkey made of Corinthian bronze, bearing a double pannier which contained white olives on one side, and black on the other. Covering the donkey were two dishes, on the rims of which were engraved Trimalchio's name and their weight in silver. Little bridges which had been soldered on spanned the dishes; they contained dormice dipped in honey and sprinkled with poppy-seed. There were also hot sausages lying on a silver grill, and underneath were plums and pomegranate-seeds.

[32] We were enjoying this refined fare, when to the sound of music Trimalchio himself was carried in. He was deposited between cushions piled high, and the sight of him evoked laughter from the unwary, for his shaven head protruded from a scarlet dressing-gown, and round his neck draped with a muffler he had thrust a napkin with a broad purple stripe and fringes dangling from it all round. On the little finger of his left hand he sported a huge gilt ring, and the top joint of the next finger held a smaller one, which seemed to me to be solid gold, though it was clearly studded with iron stars. Not content with demonstrating these marks of wealth, he bared his right arm to show that it was adorned with a golden bracelet and an ivory bangle fastened with a shining plate of metal.

[33] As he hacked at his teeth with a silver toothpick, he said: "My friends, I did not relish coming to the dining-room so soon, but I did not wish to detain you any longer, so I have foregone all my own pleasure. Allow me, however, to finish the game." A slave followed behind him bearing a board of terebinth wood and crystal dice; what struck me as the height of refinement was that in place of white and black counters, he was using gold and silver *denarii:* In the course of the game he exhausted every hackneyed expletive.

While we were still on our starters, a large platter bearing a basket was brought in. It contained a wooden hen, sitting as hens do when hatching eggs with wings outspread. At once two slaves drew near, and to the blaring sound of music began to rummage in the straw. They promptly unearthed peahens' eggs, and distributed them among the guests. Trimalchio surveyed this tableau and said: "My friends, I gave

instructions for these peahens' eggs to be hatched under the hen. Good Lord, I'm afraid the chickens are on their way out! However, let's see if they are still soft enough to eat." We picked up our spoons weighing not less than half a pound, and assaulted the eggs which were made of flour baked in oil. I nearly discarded my helping, as it seemed already to have hardened into a chicken, but then I heard an experienced guest say: "There is sure to be something good in this." So I poked my finger through the shell, and found inside a plump little fig-pecker, coated in peppered yolk of egg.

[34] By now Trimalchio had abandoned the game, and had demanded a helping of everything. He had just loudly authorized a second glass of the sweetened wine for anyone requesting it, when at a sudden musical signal the hors d' oeuvre dishes were all whisked away simultaneously by the singing troupe. In the mêlée, however, a dish happened to fall. As it lay there, a slave picked it up. Trimalchio noticed this, ordered the boy to have his ears boxed, and made him throw it down again. A servant whose job was to keep things tidy followed behind him, and with his broom began to sweep out the silver dish with the rest of the debris. Then two long-haired Ethiopians moved in carrying diminutive wineskins, like the men who sprinkle water on the sand in the amphitheater, and poured wine on our hands. No one in fact offered water. When our host was praised for the refined arrangements, he remarked: "Mars loves an equal contest, so I gave instructions for each guest to have his own table. So that way those stinking slaves will not make us sweat by crowding on top of us."

At that moment glass wine jars, carefully sealed with gypsum, were brought in. On their necks were fastened labels, with the inscription: "Falernian wine of Opimian vintage: One hundred years old." As we scrutinized the labels, Trimalchio clapped his hands and exclaimed: "So wine, sad to say, enjoys longer life than poor humans! So let us drink and be merry: wine is life-enhancing. This is genuine Opimian that I'm serving. Yesterday the wine I provided was not so good, though the company at dinner was much more respectable." So we got started on the wine, taking the greatest pains to express our wonder at all the elegance. A slave now brought in a skeleton of silver, constructed in such a way that its joints and spine were loose, and could be twisted in every direction. Trimalchio threw it down on the table several times, to allow its supple joints to fall into various postures. He added in commentary:

'Sad creatures we! In sum, poor man is naught.
We'll all end up like this, in Orcus' hands, so let's
    enjoy life while we can.'

[35] After our praise of these lines, there followed a dish clearly not so lavish as we anticipated, but unusual enough to rivet the eyes of all of us. The circular plate had the twelve signs of the Zodiac in sequence round it, and on each of them the chef had placed foodstuffs appropriately matching the subjects. On the Ram, he had placed chickpeas shaped like a ram's head; on the Bull, a portion of beef; on the Twins, testicles and kidneys; on the Crab, a crown; on the Lion, an African fig; on the Virgin, a barren sow's womb; on the Scales, a balance with different cakes on each side; on the Scorpion, a small sea-fish; on the Archer, a crow; on the Goat, a lobster; on the Water-bearer, a goose; on the Fishes, two mullets. In the middle of the dish was a square of turf still sporting its grass, with a honeycomb on it. An Egyptian slave was carrying bread round in a silver dish...and the host himself joined in, with a most scurrilous and tortured version of a mime-song from *The Silphium Gatherer*. As we rather gloomily contemplated this plebeian fare, Trimalchio said: "Come on, let's tuck in; this is the dinner menu."

[36] As he spoke, four servants bounded forward rhythmically in time to the music, and removed the covering of the dish. Inside we saw fowls, sows' udders, and in the center a hare equipped with wings, a veritable Pegasus. We also noticed four representations of Marsyas at the corners of the dish; from their wine-skins a peppered gravy was pouring over fish which were swimming, so to say, in the channel. The slaves applauded, and we all joined in, smiling appreciatively as we attacked the choice fare. Trimalchio too was tickled by the success of such a trick. He called out "Carver!" At once the carver came forward, and with extravagant motions in time to the music, cut up the meat in such a way that you would have thought he was a charioteer engaging to the music of a water-organist. Trimalchio still continued repeating in the most droning voice: "Carve 'er, Carver!'" I suspected that such frequent repetition of the word spelt a sophisticated joke, so I boldly questioned the man reclining next to me. He had witnessed such sportive diversions quite often, and replied: "You see the fellow carving the meat? His name is Carver, so whenever Trimalchio cries "Carver", he is at once calling on him and giving him his instructions."

[37] In my desire to learn as much as possible, I could not swallow another mouthful, so I turned to my neighbor and began at some length to elicit all the gossip: I enquired about the woman scurrying to and fro. "That's Trimalchio's wife," he answered. "Her name is Fortunata. She measures her money by the bushel. Yet what was she only a short time ago? You will pardon my saying this, but you wouldn't have taken a bread-roll from her hand. But now—there's no rhyme or reason in it—she's on top of the world, and Trimalchio thinks the world of her. To put it bluntly, if she tells him at high noon that it's pitch dark, he'll believe her. As for Trimalchio, he's so wealthy he doesn't know how much he's got. But that lynx sees to everything. She turns up in the most unlikely places. She keeps off the booze, and she's a steady influence, offering sound advice. But what a forked tongue! She's a real magpie of the couch: if she likes you, she likes you; if she doesn't, she doesn't.

As for the boss himself, his estates are so extensive that kites fly over them. He has oodles of money. There's more silver coin lying in that janitor's office than the entire fortune of any of us. As for his household—good God, I don't think a tenth of them could recognize their master. In a word, he can box and bury any of these smart Alecs.

[38] Don't imagine for a moment that there is any produce that he buys; it's all grown on his property. Wool, citrus fruit, pepper—look for cock's milk, and you'll find it. For example, the wool he was getting wasn't too good, so he bought rams from Tarentum, and got them to have a go at his ewes. He ordered bees brought from Athens to get home-produced Attic honey; the wee Greeks incidentally will improve the native strain a bit as well. And listen to this: only a few days ago he wrote for mushroom-spawn to be dispatched from India. As for his mules, he hasn't one which isn't sired by a wild ass. You see all these cushions; every one of them is stuffed with purple or scarlet. That's how well-endowed he is.

As for the other freedmen sharing his table, don't write them off; they're loaded. You see the one reclining at the end of the bottom couch? Today he's worth 800,000. He's risen from nothing; only the other day he was carting logs on his back. The story goes—I'm talking only from hearsay—that he grabbed a gnome's cap and found a treasure. I don't begrudge anyone getting what God gives him, but he's a bit of a braggart and not slow in putting himself forward. For example, he published this advertisement the other day: "Gaius Pompeius Diogenes is letting his upper room from July 1st, and is buying a house."

Take a look at the one reclining in the freedman's place: He used to be well off. I'm not blaming him. He had a million of his own to feast his eye on. But he's had a bad time; I don't think he can count his hair his own. But I swear it's not his fault. There's not a better man living. But his freedmen are real villains; they've done everything to suit themselves. You know how it is; a shared pot goes off the boil, and once things begin to slide, your friends melt away. You see him in this parlous state, yet he ran a really decent business; he was an undertaker. He used to dine like a king; boars served whole in their skins, fancy cakes, game-birds...cooks and confectioners. There was more wine poured under his table than any of us has in his cellar. He wasn't a man, he was a walking circus. Even when he was down on his uppers, he was anxious that his creditors shouldn't think that he was bankrupt, so he advertised an auction with this announcement "Gaius Iulius Proculus will auction his surplus stock."

[39] Trimalchio broke into this congenial gossip. By now the first course had been cleared away. The guests were in high spirits, and had begun to concentrate on the wine and general conversation. So the host leaned back on his elbow. "Your company," he said, "must help us savor the wine; the fishes must swim. Did you really think that I was happy to offer you just the food which you saw on the lid of the dish? 'Is this the Ulysses you know so well?' So what was the point of it? Well, even when we're dining we must advance our learning. My patron—God rest his bones—wanted me to take my place as a man among men; what the dish showed was that there's nothing that I didn't know already.

The sky above is the home of twelve gods, and is transformed into as many shapes. First it becomes the Ram. So whoever is born under that sign has many flocks, and huge stocks of wool—yes, and a hard head, a shameless front, and a sharp horn. Most of those who frequent the schools, and the muttonheads, are born under this sign." We praised our astrologer's wit, so he continued. "Next the whole sky turns into a young bull, so at that time recalcitrant people are born, and ploughmen, and those who provide their own dinners. Under the Twins are born chariot pairs, teams of oxen, big-bollocked lechers, and those who like to

have it both ways. I myself was born under the Crab, so I have several feet to support me, and a lot of possessions on both land and sea, for the Crab is equally at home on both. That's why I placed nothing over this sign earlier, to avoid putting pressure on my own natal star. Under the Lion are born those who feast gluttonously, and who boss you around; under the Virgin, woman-chasers, runaways, and slaves in chains. Under the Scales come butchers, perfume sellers, and those whose job it is to weigh things; under the Scorpion, poisoners and assassins; under the Archer, cross-eyed people, lifting the bacon while looking at the vegetables; under the Goat, those who have a hard time, whose worries make them sprout horns; under the Water-bearer, innkeepers and those with water on the brain; under the Fishes, chefs and teachers of rhetoric; so the world turns on its course like a mill-stone, always bringing harm in its train, so that people are born or die. As for the turf you see in the center, and the honeycomb on the turf, none of my arrangements is without a purpose. Mother earth is set in the middle, rounded like an egg, and containing within her like a honeycomb all that is good."

[40] As one we all cried "How clever!" We raised our hands to the ceiling, and swore that Hipparchus and Aratus were not in the same league as Trimalchio. Then servants came in, and placed coverlets over the couches. On them were depicted nets, and hunters lying in wait with hunting spears, and all the paraphernalia of the chase. Our suspicions were roused, but we had not yet divined why, when a great din resounded outside the dining-room. Would you believe it, Spartan dogs joined in, and began to bound round the table. Behind them followed a tray with a massive boar on it, wearing the cap of freedom; From its teeth hung two small baskets woven from palm-leaves, one filled with fresh dates, and the other with the dried Egyptian variety. The boar was surrounded by tiny piglets of pastry, seemingly crowding over the teats, which indicated that the beast was a sow. The piglets were in fact gifts to take away. The slave who came in to cut up the boar was not the carver who had mangled the poultry, but a huge bearded figure. His legs were encased in puttees, and he wore a multi-colored hunting coat. He drew his hunting knife, and plunged it enthusiastically into the boar's flank. This incision prompted thrushes to fly out; fowlers stood at the ready with limed reeds, and speedily trapped the birds as they circled round the dining-room. Trimalchio ordered each guest

to be served with his helping of pork, and then he added: "Do also notice what refined acorns this woodland pig has devoured." Slaves at once approached the baskets dangling from the boar's teeth, and in time to the music shared out the fresh and dried dates among the diners.

[41] Meanwhile I withdrew into myself, and pondered the various possibilities for the boar's having entered wearing the cap of freedom. After exhausting every fatuous explanation, I steeled myself to seek the solution to my nagging problem from that informant of mine. He replied: "Why, even I your humble servant can answer that. It's no riddle, but quite straightforward. Yesterday the main course claimed him, but the diners set him scot-free; so today he returns to the feast as a freedman." I cursed my stupidity, and did not ask a single question thereafter, in case I should give the impression of never having dined in respectable company.

During this conversation of ours, a handsome slave wearing a wreath of vine-leaves and ivy (he was performing successively the roles of Bacchus the Thunderer, Bacchus the Deliverer, and Bacchus God of Devotees) carried grapes round in a basket, reciting his master's poems in a high-pitched voice. On hearing this, Trimalchio said: "Dionysus, now be Liber." The slave snatched the cap from the boar and put it on his head. Then Trimalchio further added: "You won't deny that my father is Liber." We applauded this *bon mot*, and kissed the boy enthusiastically as he made his way round.

Following this course, Trimalchio rose to go to the lavatory. Now that the tyrant was deposed and we had gained our freedom, we began to entice the rest of the company to speak. So Dama spoke up first. After demanding larger wine cups, he said: "Daylight's just non-existent. Turn round, and it's nightfall. So there's no better order of the day than to get out of bed and to make straight for the dining-room. What a sharp spell of frosty weather we've had! Even after my bath I've hardly warmed up. But a hot drink's as good as a topcoat. I've had a basinful, and I'm absolutely pissed. The wine's gone to my head."

[42] Seleucus chipped in with his bit of gossip. "Myself, I don't take a bath every day. Taking a bath is as bad as being sent to the cleaner's; the water's got teeth. My blood gets thinner every day. But once I get a jug of mead inside me, I can tell the cold to bugger off. Actually I couldn't have a bath today because I attended a funeral. Good old Chrysanthus, handsome fellow that he was, has given up the ghost. He said hallo to me only the other day; I could be talking with him at this very moment. Dammit, we're nothing but walking bags of wind. Flies rank higher; they do have a bit of spark, whereas we're no more than bubbles. If only he hadn't gone on a diet! He didn't take a drop of water or a crumb of bread for five days. And yet he's away to join the majority. The doctors killed him off—or the truth is it was his bad luck, because a doctor does nothing but set your mind at rest. Still, he had a decent cortege. He was laid out on a bier, covered with good quality drapes. The mourning party was great, for he'd freed several slaves, though his widow was grudging with her tears—and him the best of husbands! But women as women are nothing but a bunch of kites. None of us should treat them decently; it's like dropping all you've got down a well. But a love-liaison of long standing is a festering sore."

[43] He was getting us down, and Phileros burst out: "Forget the dead, and think about the living! He had his money's worth, a good life and a good death. What's he got to grumble about? He started out with only a penny in his pocket; at that time he'd have picked up a farthing with his teeth out of the shit. Then he grew and grew just like a honeycomb. My God, I think he left a cool hundred thousand, all in ready cash. I'm a Cynic with a dog's tongue inside me, so I'll tell it straight. He had a rough tongue, and he opened his mouth too often; he was a living argument, not a man. His brother was a decent guy who would do a friend a good turn; he was open-handed, and kept a tidy table.

"Chrysanthus caught a cold when he first set up in business, but his first vintage set him up again, for he sold his wine at the high price he asked. But what really brought him up in the world was the estate he inherited, and he made off with more of it than had been left to him. And now, just because he fell out with his brother, the loony has left his property to some nobody. The man who runs from his family runs many a mile. But his confidential slaves were his undoing. You'll never prosper if you give credit on impulse, especially if you're in business. But it's true that he enjoyed himself all his life; it's a matter of who lays his hands on it, not who should have got it. He was a real child of Fortune; put lead in his hand, and it turned to gold. It's easy to make your way when everything goes hunky-dory. And how many years do you think he totted up? More than seventy. He was a horny old bird, carried his age well, hair black as a crow. I knew him years and years ago, and even then he was one for the girls. Heavens, I don't think he left the dog in his house unmolested. He was fond of boys as well, a real all-rounder. Not that I blame him; it was the only thing he took with him."

[44] After Phileros had his say, Ganymede spoke up. "You're all nattering on about things of no concern in heaven or on earth, and all the time no one gives a damn about the crippling price of corn. I swear I couldn't afford a mouthful of bread today. The drought still continues—there's been a shortage for a year now. To hell with the aediles, I say, for they're in league with the bakers. It's a case of "You look after me, and I'll look after you." So those at the bottom of the heap suffer, because the ones on top grind them down, and enjoy a perpetual holiday. If only we had the lionhearts whom I found living here when first I arrived from Asia! Life was good in those days. If the best Sicilian flour wasn't as it should have been, they would give those devils such a hiding that they knew heaven was frowning on them. Safinius is one I remember. When I was a boy he lived down by the old arch. He was a firebrand, not a man; wherever he put his feet, he scorched the ground. But he was straight as a die, utterly reliable, never let a friend down—you could happily play *morra* with him in the dark. How he used to dress 'em down one by one in the council chamber! He didn't use fancy language but spoke straight out. And again, when he pleaded in court, his voice would swell like a trumpet. He never sweated or spat; I think the gods had blessed him with a dry inside. He would return your greeting as friendly as you like, and address everyone by name; he was just like one of the boys.

"So at that time corn was as cheap as dirt. The bread you bought for a penny was more than enough for two of you to swallow. But today I've seen bull's eyes that are bigger. Sad to say, every day things get worse. The colony's like a calf's tail, growing backwards. Why do we put up with an aedile not worth three figs, who would rather make a penny profit for himself than keep us alive? He sits at home, laughing all over his face, raking in more money by the day than the next man's entire fortune. I know quite well where he got his thousand gold pieces. If we were men with real balls he wouldn't be so pleased with himself. But as it is, people are lions at home but foxes outside. In my own case, the rags on my back are already spoken for; if this corn shortage continues, I shall have to sell my little shack. If neither gods nor men take pity on this colony, heaven

knows what will happen to it. As I hope to have the joy of my children, I really do think that the gods are visiting all these things on us. It's because no one believes in heaven, no one observes the fasts, no one gives a toss for Jupiter; they all sit with their eyes closed, but they're reckoning what they're worth. At one time the women wore long dresses, and walked barefoot up the hill with their hair unbound and their clothes washed dazzling white, praying to Jupiter for rain. At once it came down in buckets; otherwise it never rained. They would all go home looking like drowned rats. So this is why the gods wrap their feet in wool: it's because we don't keep the faith. The fields lie fallow—".

[45] The clothes dealer Echion interrupted: "Do look on the bright side. As the countryman said when he lost his dappled pig, it's not the same all over. What we don't have today we'll get tomorrow. That's what life's all about. You couldn't name a better town than this to live in, I'll swear, if only we had real men about. But like other places, it's depressed at the moment. Let's not be too hard to please; it's the same weather for all of us. If you were living somewhere else, you would be saying that the streets here were alive with roast pork.

And remember we're due to have a marvelous show on the holiday three days from now. There'll be a lot of freedmen in the arena, not just the gang of gladiators from the training school. Our friend Titus the showman is ambitious and hot-blooded. It won't be wishy-washy; there'll be something worth watching. I'm on good terms with him; he doesn't shilly-shally. He'll offer us some bonny fighting. There'll be no chickening out; it'll be a butcher's shop for the whole amphitheater to see. And he has the wherewithal to mount the show; he came into thirty million on the sad death of his father. He can spend four hundred thousand without his estate's feeling it, and he'll be a byword for ever. He's already lined up several freaks, and a woman who fights from a chariot, and a steward of Glyco's caught in the act of pleasuring his mistress. You'll witness brawls breaking out in the crowd, jealous husbands against lover-boys. Fancy that twopenny-ha'penny Glyco throwing his steward to the beasts! He might as well expose himself to them. What sin did the steward commit, when he was forced to push it in? That piss-pot of a wife deserved to be tossed by a bull. But if you can't beat the donkey, beat the saddle. However could Glyco have imagined that Hermogenes' daughter, a chip off the old block, would turn out decent? That guy could cut the claws of a kite in flight; vipers like him don't hatch lengths of rope. It's Glyco, poor Glyco, who has paid the price. As long as he lives, he'll be branded, and only death will clear the slate. But our sins make sticks for our own backs.

My nose tells me that Mammea is going to lay on a banquet worth two *denarii* for me and my colleagues. If it comes off, he'll put Norbanus right out of the running; I'm sure you'll realize that he'll win hands down. And let's be honest, what pleasure did Norbanus ever give us? He put on some cut-price gladiators on their last legs, who would have fallen over if you blew on them. I've seen better specimens matched with the wild beasts. As for the mounted gladiators that he disposed of, they came off table-lamps; the horses pranced about like farmyard cocks. One was thin as a rake, another had club feet, and the reserve was a corpse standing in for a corpse—it was hamstrung. There was one Thracian with a bit of spunk, but even he observed the rulebook. In short, they all got a flogging later, for they were at the receiving end of shouts of 'Get stuck in!' from the crowded amphitheater; it was a total shambles. 'Well, I did put on a show for you!' claims Norbanus. Yes, and I gave you a good hand. If you work it out, I did you a bigger favor than you did me. One good turn deserves another.

[46] Agamemnon, am I right that you are saying 'Why is this boring man prattling on?' I'm doing it because, though you're the expert with words, you're saying nothing. You don't belong to our patch, so you sniff at the way we poor buggers talk. We know you're off your head with all that education. I tell you what: can I persuade you to come out to our country place one day, and take a look at our little house? We'll get a bite to eat there—some chicken, and eggs. It'll be a pleasant outing, even if the weather this year has turned everything upside down. We'll certainly get enough to fill our bellies.

My little feller is growing fast, ready to sit at your feet; he can divide by four already. If God spares him, you'll have a young devotee beside you soon. Whenever he has a spare moment he never lifts his head from the slate. He's a smart lad, made of the right stuff, though he's crazy about birds; I've already killed three goldfinches of his and told him that the weasel ate them: But now he's found another hobby; he's very fond of painting. He's begun to make a decent start on Latin literature now that he's giving the Greek boys the boot. Mind you, that teacher of his is cocky, always shifting his pitch. He knows his stuff, but he doesn't like hard work. There is another teacher; he doesn't know much, but he's got an enquiring mind, and he imparts more than he knows. He often visits us on holidays, and is happy with whatever food you put before him.

I've now bought the lad some law-books; I want him to get a smattering of the law to cope with our property. Law is where the bread is; he's had enough literature to mark him for life. If he shies at law, I've decided that he must learn a trade as a barber, or an auctioneer, or if the worst comes to the worst an advocate—some career that only death can rob him of. So every day I rail at him: 'Primigenius, believe me, education's for your own benefit. Take a look at Phileros the advocate. If he hadn't applied himself, today he wouldn't be able to keep the wolf from the door. It's no time since he was lugging goods for sale round on his shoulders, and now he's challenging even Norbanus. Education's a real treasure; a profession's something for life.'"

[47] Gossip of this sort was being bandied about when Trimalchio came in. He mopped his brow, and washed his hands with perfume. He waited only a second or two before remarking: "Excuse me, my friends, but for some days now my stomach has not responded to nature's call. The doctors are at a loss. But in my case pomegranate-rind and pinewood dipped in vinegar have done the trick. I now have hopes that my stomach will be regular as before. Anyhow, my inside is rumbling like a roaring bull, so if any of you want to relieve yourselves, there's no need to be ashamed. None of us was born rock-solid. I can't imagine any torture worse than having to hold it in: This is the one thing that even Jupiter can't forbid. I see you're grinning, Fortunata, but that's how you keep me awake at night. But even in the dining-room I don't forbid anyone to ease himself, and the doctors forbid us to keep the wind inside. If anything heavier is imminent, everything's ready outside—water, chamber pots, the other bits and pieces. Believe me, the vapors attack the brain, and flood through your whole body. I know quite a few who've died that way through refusing to face the facts." We thanked him for his generosity and consideration, and hastened to choke our laughter by taking frequent swigs of the wine.

We were blissfully unaware that we were still toiling halfway up the hill, as the saying goes. When the tables had been cleared to the sound of music, three white pigs wearing halters and bells were led into the dining-room. The spokesman said that one was two years old, the second three, and the third as old as six. I thought that some circus performers had arrived, and that the pigs were going to perform some tricks, as they commonly do in sideshows. But my anticipation was dispelled when Trimalchio asked: "Which of these would you like to have served this moment for dinner? Only country bumpkins offer a farmyard cock, or a goulash, or miserable dishes of that kind; my cooks often put on pot-roasted calves."

There and then he ordered the cook to be summoned. Without waiting for us to make our choice, he ordered the slaughter of the oldest pig. He then questioned the cook loudly: "Which company do you belong to?" The cook told him the fortieth. "Were you purchased," asked the host, "or are you home-born?" "Neither," said the cook. "I was bequeathed to you in the will of Pansa."

"Be sure, then," said Trimalchio, "to make a good job of serving this course, or I'll order you to be demoted to the company of messengers." On being reminded of the master's power over his destiny, the cook was led into the kitchen by our next course.

*After Trimalchio's return, the dinner continues with more conversation on a variety of themes, including death, which preoccupies Trimalchio. One of the freedmen, Niceros, tells the story of his encounter with a werewolf (61–62), which Trimalchio tops with a tale of witches from his youth (63). At the climax of the dinner Trimalchio tells the story of his life and reveals that an astrologer has informed him about how long he has to live. He proceeds to stage a mock funeral and asks his guests to imagine that they are commemorating his death. Finally, the horn players strike a note so loud that it brings in the fire brigade (78). In the resulting confusion, the trio of Encolpius, Ascyltus, and Giton slip away and return to their inn. There Encolpius and Ascyltus finally have it out and agree to split up, but they leave it to Giton to choose which one he will go with (79–82). To Encolpius's shock and dismay, he leaves with Ascyltus. We next find Encolpius at a picture gallery in a temple, where he meets an elderly poet, Eumolpus.*

[83] I walked into an art gallery, which had an astonishing range of pictures. What I saw there included the handiwork of Zeuxis, not as yet overcome by the ravages of time, and with a kind of awe I scrutinized rough drawings by Protogenes which vied in authenticity with Nature herself. As for the painting by Apelles which the Greeks call "The Crippled Goddess," I even bent the

knee before it; for the outlines of his figures were so skilfully clear-cut that you could imagine that he had painted their souls as well. There was one picture in which an eagle aloft was bearing away the lad from Mt. Ida; in another, the fair-skinned Hylas was trying to fend off a persistent Naiad; a third depicted Apollo cursing his guilty hands and adorning his unstrung lyre with a newly sprung blossom. As I stood surrounded by these portrayals of lovers' expressions, in a spirit of desolation I cried out: "So even the gods are pricked by love. Jupiter found no object for his affection in heaven, and though he visited earth to sin, he did violence to no one. The Nymph who took Hylas as her prize would have repressed her feelings had she believed that Hercules would appear to forbid the deed. Apollo summoned back the departed shade of his boy to turn him into a flower. All these stories, and not just the pictures, have described embraces enjoyed without a rival; but the person I hospitably befriended has turned out to be more cruel than Lycurgus."

As I shared my disputation with the winds, a striking thing occurred: a grizzled veteran entered the gallery with a look of concentration on his face which offered a hint of greatness. But his dress did not match his handsome appearance, which made it perfectly clear that he was a man of letters, such as the rich love to hate. This was the fellow, then, that stood alongside me . . .

"I am a poet," he said, "a poet of not inconsiderable genius—that is, if one can lend any credence to those awards often bestowed by influence on men without talent. You will be asking: 'So why this shabby outfit of yours?' The reason is simply this: devotion to the intellect never made anyone rich.

Put trust in sea-trade, and your profits soar;
Soldiers don arms of gold to go to war;
Cheap crawlers loll on purple, crazed with gin;
Seducers of young brides are paid for sin.
Lone eloquence shivers in rags bone-stiff with frost;
Impoverished tongue invoking arts now lost.

[84] The situation is undoubtedly this: if you confront all the vices, and start to tread an upright path in life, you first encounter hatred because your mode of life is different; for who has a good word for the man who tries to follow a different road? Secondly, those whose sole aim in life is piling up money don't like the world at large to regard any philosophy as superior to their

own. So they use every possible means to denigrate lovers of literature, trying to show that such people too are slaves to money…In some sense, poverty is sister to integrity of mind…

I could only wish that the man who assails my honesty was sufficiently guilt-free for me to soften his attitude. But as things stand, he is an inveterate robber, more worldly wise than those very pimps…."

[85] "When I was taken to Asia as a paid assistant to the quaestor there, I was given accommodation at Pergamum. I was pleased with the residence there, not just because the lodging was elegant, but also because my host had a most handsome son; and I devised a way of lulling his father's suspicions. Whenever the table-talk turned to the subject of sex with good-looking boys, I would seethe with such fury, and show such austere displeasure in refusing to have my ears outraged by foul gossip, that the boy's mother in particular regarded me as a real Stoic. So in no time I had started escorting the young fellow to the exercise ground, organizing his studies, acting as his tutor and moral adviser, and ensuring that no one set foot in the house on the hunt for sex.

It so happened that a feast-day had allowed us to relax, and because our celebration went on quite late, we were dozing down in the dining-room. It must have been about midnight when I realized that the boy was awake. So very shyly I murmured a prayer: "Lady Venus," I said, "if I can kiss this boy without his realizing it, I'll present him with a pair of doves tomorrow." When the boy heard the payment on offer for the pleasure, he began to snore. So as he feigned sleep, I planted a few fond kisses on him. I was satisfied with this modest beginning; I got up early next morning and discharged my vow by putting a pair of choice doves in his expectant hands.

[86] Next night opportunity again offered, and I stepped up my prayer. 'If I can run my roguish hands over him without his feeling a thing, I'll repay him for his trouble with a pair of really lively fighting-cocks.' On hearing this the young lad snuggled up to me without prompting; I suppose he was beginning to fear that I had fallen off to sleep. So I relieved his anxiety, and immersed myself in the exploration of his whole body, but without indulging in the final pleasure. When daylight came, he was delighted with the gift of what I had promised.

When a third night offered me the opportunity, I got up and spoke in his ear as he pretended to sleep.

'Immortal gods,' I said, 'if I can gain the full pleasure I long for from this boy, in return for the joy, tomorrow I shall give him the finest Macedonian stallion, so long as he doesn't feel a thing.' Never did that young fellow enjoy deeper repose. So first I curled my hands round his milk-white breasts, then I gave him a lingering kiss, and finally all my longings were concentrated in the single act. Next morning he seated himself on his bed, awaiting the customary routine. But you know how much easier it is to purchase doves and cocks than a stallion! And besides, I was afraid that a gift on that scale would make people eye my geniality with suspicion. So I took a stroll for a few hours, and on returning to the lodging all I gave the boy was a kiss. As he put his arms around my neck, his eyes wandered round, and he said: "Tell me, sir, where is the stallion?"

[87] By alienating him in this way, I had cut off the access which I had gained. But then I resumed my wanton behavior, for after a few days' interval I began to press the youth for a reconciliation. I begged him to allow me to satisfy his needs, and used all the other arguments which oppressive lust dictates. He was quite incensed. All he said was: 'Go to sleep or I'll tell my father.' But unscrupulousness can climb every mountain. Even as he was saying 'I'll wake my father,' I crept in close, and took my pleasure against his feeble resistance. He was not displeased by my wanton behavior. After a long rigmarole about his having been deceived and made a figure of fun and scorn among his schoolmates, to whom he had boasted of my wealth, he said: 'But you'll see I'm not one of your kind. Have another go if you want.' So all animosity laid aside, I was back in the boy's good books; and after exploiting his good will, I fell fast asleep. But he was now fully grown up, and at an age itching to play the partner; he was not content with a single repeat performance. So he roused me from my sleep, and asked: 'Anything you want?' At this stage doing him a service was not tiresome, so with much panting and sweating I somehow wore him down, gave him what he wanted, and again fell asleep in contented exhaustion. Less than an hour elapsed when he began to poke me with his finger, saying: 'Why don't we go at it?' Then I got really worked up at being wakened so often, and I answered him in his own words: 'Go to sleep, or I'll tell your father.' "

[88] I was stimulated by this conversation, and began to tap his superior knowledge about the dating of the pictures and the themes of some of them which I found mysterious. At the same time, I was trying to

elicit the reason for our present decadence in which the noblest arts had died off, painting among them having left not the slightest trace.

His response was: "It was lust for money that induced this change. In the old days, when virtue unadorned was accepted, the noble arts flourished, and there was the fiercest competition between individuals to ensure that no benefit to posterity should lie undiscovered for long. So it was that Democritus squeezed out the juices of every plant, and devoted his life to experiments to ensure that the properties of stones and shrubs became known. Eudoxus grew old on the peak of the highest mountain, seeking to understand the movements of stars and firmament. Chrysippus cleansed his mind three times with hellebore to prevent his ideas drying up. Lysippus died through poverty as he concentrated on the lines of a single statue; and Myron, who almost caught in bronze the souls of men and wild beasts, has found no heir.

But our generation is obsessed with wine and the women of the street. We don't presume to acquaint ourselves even with the most accessible arts. We censure the old ways, but teach and learn nothing but vices. What has happened to dialectic? And astronomy? What is the most secure path to wisdom? Whoever sets foot in a temple, and solemnly vows thanksgiving if he attains eloquence, or gets to grips with the sources of philosophy? No one aspires even to mental or bodily health; even before stepping on the sacred threshold, one promises a gift if he can bury his rich neighbor, another if he uncovers buried treasure, a third if he can make thirty million unscathed. Why, even the Senate, our mentor as regards good and right conduct, often promises a thousand pounds of gold for the Capitoline temple; so just in case anyone should hesitate to lust after money, the Senate adorns Jupiter with his little pile. So you shouldn't wonder that painting is on the way out, when all gods and men alike regard a gold nugget as more beautiful than anything those crazy little Greeks Apelles and Phidias have created.

[89] But I can see that you are wholly captivated by the picture which depicts the capture of Troy: so I'll try to expound the subject in verses:

Ten harvests now the Trojans had endured
In melancholy, poised 'midst anxious fears.
Black fear engulfed them; should they trust
In the seer Calchas' doubtful prophecy?
5  Now at Apollo's prompting, Ida's peaks

Are shorn of forests. Trunks are dragged below,
And the sawn logs assembled in a mass
To fashion a menacing horse. And deep within,
A spacious hollow, a cavern lies concealed
To house an army. Valor lies cloaked therein,    10
Its anger sharpened by ten warring years;
Crowding the corners, the oppressing Greeks
Lurk in the beast that they have vowed. Poor land!
We thought the thousand ships had been repelled,
That we had freed our native soil from war.    15
The inscription on the beast, and Sinon's role
In harmony with fate, and our own state of mind
With its capacity to seal our doom,
Strengthened our illusions.

The crowd feels free; now unoppressed by war,    20
They hasten from the gates to pay their vows,
Cheeks wet with weeping; these are tears of joy,
Banished before by fear from troubled minds.
Neptune's Laocoon with hair unbound
Incites the mob to uproar. Then, spear poised,    25
He gashes the beast's belly. But the fates
Debilitate his hands; the spear strikes home,
But then recoils. Greek guile thus wins our trust.
Again the priest essays with feeble hand,
As with an axe he strikes that lofty flank.    30
The enclosed warriors growl angrily;
The wooden monster snorts with alien fears.
The youths who lay within our hands emerge;
And Troy falls under theirs. This is a war
Conducted with unprecedented guile.    35

Fresh portents follow. Swollen waves rear high
Where Tenedos' high ridges span the sea.
The placid waters prised apart give place.
Over the silent night the plash of oars
Proclaims their distant message, as the ships    40
Pound the deep waters. The still surface groans
Under the burden of their wooden keels.
Our eyes are riveted. Twin coiling snakes
Are borne on ocean swell towards the rocks.
Their swollen breasts resemble lofty ships    45
Parting the sea-foam with their flanks; the deep
Echoes the impact of their tails; their crests
Range o'er the waters, conspiring with their eyes
Whose flashing gleam ignites the sea. The waves
Seethe with their hissing.
                    All are stupefied.    50
The priests adorned with headbands, and the twins,
Laocoon's pledges, in their Phrygian garb,

Stand in attendance. Then, quite suddenly,
The glistening snakes enfold them with their coils.
55  They raise their tiny hands up to their face,
Striving to free each other, not themselves,
In compact of devotion. Death itself
Destroys the wretches as they share their fear.
The father, feeble helper, spreads his frame
60  Over his children's corpses. But the snakes,
Now gorged with death, attack the full-grown man,
Dragging his limbs down to the ground. The priest,
A sacrificial victim, strikes the earth,
Prostrate between the altars. Troy, its rites
65  First desecrated, doomed to imminent fall,
Surrenders the protection of its gods.

Now the full moon has raised her radiant light,
Guiding the lesser stars with glowing torch.
While Priam's sons are buried in sleep and wine,
70  The Greeks unbar the door, disgorge their men.
Their leaders, fully armed, rehearse; just so
A steed, released from its Thessalian yoke,
Charges with tossing head and lofty mane.
They draw their swords, brandish their shields
        in front,
75  Inaugurating battle. While one slays
The Trojans heavy-eyed with wine,
Their sleep extended into ultimate death,
Another ignites torches from the altars,
Thus summoning the sacred Trojan rites
80  Against the very Trojans."

[90] As he declaimed, some of the strollers in the colonnades threw stones at Eumolpus. Acknowledging this hearty reception of his genius, he covered his head and bolted from the temple. I feared that they would pin the label of poet on myself as well, so I followed him in his flight down to the sea-shore. As soon as we were out of the firing-line and could relax, I said: "Tell me, what will you do about this disease of yours? You've been in my company for less than two hours, and in that time you've spouted poetry more often than talked like a human being. It doesn't surprise me that people chase after you with bricks; I'll do the same myself—stuff my pockets with stones, and give your head a blood-letting whenever you threaten a take-off." He nodded his acknowledgement, and said: "Young man, today is not my first experience of this kind. In fact, whenever I step into a theater to deliver a recitation, the crowd treats me to this kind of

reception. However, to save brawling with you as well, I'll go on a diet all day today."

"Good enough," I replied. "If you forswear your madness for the day, we'll dine together."

*Encolpius and Eumolpus go to the baths before dinner, where Encolpius spots Giton pretending to be a slave. They dash off together through a back door and make their way back to the inn. Ascyltus comes in search of Giton, but Encolpius manages to hide him, and Ascyltus now disappears from the novel. However, Encolpius cannot give Eumolpus the slip, and a new love triangle is formed as the old poet shows increasing interest in Giton. This trio now leaves Puteoli on board a merchant ship, but while at sea they discover that the captain is Encolpius's old enemy Lichas and that with him is another person from Encolpius's past, a woman of dubious character, Tryphaena. The text resumes with Eumolpus recounting a story.*

Eumolpus, however, who was both the spokesman on our behalf when we were on trial and the architect of our present harmony, refused to allow the happy atmosphere to dissolve without some story-telling. So he launched a lengthy attack on women's fickleness, remarking on the readiness with which they fall in love, and the speed with which they cease to think even of their offspring, and claiming that no lady is so chaste that she cannot be driven even to distraction by lust for some outsider. He said that he was not thinking of those tragedies of old, nor of names familiar to earlier generations, but of an incident which occurred within his own recollection. He would recount it to us if we wished to hear it, so we all turned our eyes and ears towards him, and this is how he began:

[111] "A married lady from Ephesus had such a celebrated reputation for chastity that women even from neighboring communities were drawn to gaze on her. This lady, then, had just buried her husband. But she was not satisfied merely to escort the body to burial, as most mourners do, with hair flowing free, beating her naked breast before the eyes of the assembled crowd: she also followed the dead man into his tomb, and when the body was laid in a subterranean vault after the Greek fashion, she proceeded to mount guard, weeping over it day and night. She remained there, abusing her body and courting death by self-starvation. Neither her parents nor her other relatives could induce her to leave; finally the magistrates after making

the attempt were rejected and turned away. This lady, as she afforded so unique an example, was the cause of grief to everyone as she dragged out five days without taking a bite to eat.

As she pined away, her most trusted maid sat with her, and lent her tears to the grieving widow. She relit the lamp in the tomb whenever it went out. The whole city talked of nothing else; people of every social rank claimed that there shone out of her an authentic example of chastity and love.

At about this time the governor of the province ordered some thieves to be crucified close to the cell in which the married lady was weeping over her late husband's corpse. The following night, a soldier guarding the crosses—he was to ensure that no one removed any of the bodies for burial—happened to notice a light gleaming quite brightly among the tombs, and he heard the groans of the grieving widow. The frailty endemic in the human race made him desirous of ascertaining who it was, and what the person was up to.

So he went down into the tomb, where his eyes fell on this supremely beautiful woman. At first he was rocked on his heels, for in his confusion he imagined that she was some prodigy, some ghostly apparition from the world below. But then he noticed the corpse lying there, and spotted the woman's tears and scratch-marks of her nails on her face; the truth dawned on him that she could not bear the loss of her dead husband. So he brought his meager supper into the tomb. He began to encourage her in her grief not to prolong her pointless sorrow, not to tear herself apart in unavailing lamentation. All of us, he told her, have to come to the same end, to the same final abode; and he added the other words of consolation by which inflamed minds are restored to normality.

But the woman in her affliction had no thought for consolation. She tore at her breast more fiercely than before; she pulled out her hair, and laid it on the prostrate corpse. But the soldier did not withdraw. With the same words of encouragement, he tried to press some food on the wretched woman. Eventually the maid was seduced by the fragrance of the wine. She first extended her own defeated hand to receive the kind offer, and once she was restored by the food and drink, she began to lay successful siege to the obstinacy of her mistress. 'What benefit will you gain,' she asked, 'if you faint away from hunger, if you bury yourself alive, if you breathe forth your innocent life before you are summoned by the Fates? Do you think the ashes or shades of the buried dead have a mind for such things. Why not return to the land of the living? Why not shake off this perverse way that women have, and enjoy life's blessings while you can? The very sight of your dead husband lying there should incite you to live.' No one is reluctant to listen when pressed to take food or to remain alive. So it was that the woman, her mouth dry from several days' fasting, allowed her obstinacy to be broken down, and she stuffed herself with food no less greedily than the maid whose resistance had been overcome earlier.

[112] Now you know the temptation which often assails a person on a full stomach. The soldier mounted an attack on her virtue, exploiting that same coaxing which had succeeded in instilling in the lady a desire to live. The young fellow seemed quite presentable to look at, and articulate as well, in the eyes of the chaste widow, and the maid conspired to win her over by this constant refrain: 'Will you strive to resist even a love that pleases?'

Need I labor the point? The woman did not hold back even from this invitation, and the soldier's persuasion was doubly successful. So they bedded down together not merely on that night's celebration of their union, but also, on the next two days. The door of the tomb, we may imagine, was closed, so that any acquaintance or stranger visiting it would assume that this most chaste of wives had breathed her last over her husband's body.

In his delight at both the lady's beauty and their hidden hideaway, the soldier would purchase such delicacies as he could afford, and as soon as darkness fell, he would take them into the tomb. So when the parents of one of the crucified thieves noticed that no watch was being kept, they hauled down the hanging corpse of their son during the night, and gave him the last rites. In this way they escaped the soldier's notice, while he was neglecting his duties, and next day he saw that the corpse was missing from one of the crosses. In his fear of execution, he told the woman what had happened. He said that he would not await the judge's verdict, but would impose sentence on himself with his own sword for neglect of duty. He asked only that she prepare a place for him before his death, and make the tomb the final resting-place for both her lover and her husband.

But the woman's sense of pity matched her chastity. 'The gods must not allow me', she said, 'to gaze on the two corpses of the men I hold most dear. I would rather surrender the dead than put paid to the living.'

She followed up this declaration with an instruction to remove her husband's corpse from the coffin, and to have it fastened to the vacant cross. The soldier took advantage of the brainwave of this most thoughtful of women, and next day the locals speculated on how a dead man had managed to mount the cross."

[113] The sailors roared with laughter at this story. Tryphaena blushed to the roots of her hair, and leant her cheek affectionately on Giton's neck. But Lichas, far from laughing, shook his head angrily, and said: "If the governor had done the right thing, he would have replaced the husband's body in the tomb, and strung the woman up on the cross." Undoubtedly Hedyle was back in his mind, together with the plundering of the ship when she set out on her sexual adventure. But the terms of the treaty did not allow him to harp on these matters, and the general mood of gaiety allowed for no angry response.

Tryphaena by now was sitting in Giton's lap, alternately showering kisses on his breast and trying to improve his shorn appearance. I was depressed and upset at this new alliance. I took no food or drink, but watched them and gave them sideways piercing looks. Every kiss, every gesture of endearment which that randy woman conjured up was a dagger in my heart. I could not at that moment decide whether I was more angry with the boy for robbing me of my girlfriend, or with the girlfriend for seducing the boy. Both aspects were equally offensive to my eyes, and more painful than the arrest which I had just endured. What added to my depression was the fact that Tryphaena was not addressing me as the friend who had earlier been her favorite lover, while Giton did not think it worth his while even to raise his glass casually in my direction, or at the very least to draw me into the general conversation. I suppose he was afraid of reopening the newly healed wound, just when his relations with Tryphaena were beginning to be patched up. Tears born of resentment welled up over my heart, and the groans of anguish lurking beneath my sighs almost caused me to faint away.

*A storm blows up, and Lichas is swept overboard, the ship sinks, Tryphaena escapes in a boat, and the three protagonists find themselves on shore not far from the city of Croton (mod. Crotone). They decide to head there to try out a confidence scheme dreamed up by Eumolpus, who will pretend to be a wealthy, childless old man. As they head to the city, Eumolpus recites a long poem on the civil war between Caesar and Pompey. For a while their scheme works and they live off the largesse of legacy-hunters who believe that Eumolpus is truly rich. We do not know how the events turned out at Croton, and the end of the novel is a complete mystery.*

## AFTERWORD

We hear very little about Petronius's novel in antiquity: such works of popular literature did not attract much attention from scholars of rhetoric, like Quintilian, and in the second century, enthusiasts (some might call them snobs) like Aulus Gellius were more interested in earlier Roman literature. We know that there were at least some copies of his work available because Petronius is mentioned by grammarians in the fourth century. Even after that the novel appears to have been known to the likes of Macrobius and Sidonius Apollinaris in the fifth century and Boethius in the sixth. But then, silence, and there is no reason to believe that anyone later had access to a complete text. Such readers of *The Satyricon* as there were during the Middle Ages knew him only in extracts, but when the selections were made and by whom we can only guess. Two sets of excerpts circulated in the Middle Ages, and it was the more abbreviated of them that surfaced first, to provide the basis for the first printed edition in 1482. For the better part of a century that was all the public knew of Petronius, until a new edition incorporating the longer set of extracts was published in Lyon in 1575. The longest episode of the novel, *Dinner with Trimalchio*, remained lost until 1650, when Marino Statileo found a manuscript containing the entire episode at Trogir, Croatia. The manuscript had been copied for Poggio Bracciolini in 1423, from an original that he had discovered in Cologne, but his copy had somehow disappeared across the Adriatic and the original left no other trace. It was not until 1669 that an edition of Petronius containing all the fragments now known to us appeared.

It is perhaps surprising that the appearance of *The Satyricon* in the late seventeenth century had comparatively little influence on the development of the modern novel. Henry Fielding, author of the great comic novel *Tom Jones* (1749), from whom one might have expected to find a sympathetic reception for *The Satyricon,* thought Petronius "unjustly celebrated." But the difficulties of Petronius's Latin, which found no great contemporary translators, were bound to limit familiarity with the work, and the licentious nature of the plot ensured that no one would read *The Satyricon* in school. And classical scholars, who generally busied themselves with the higher forms of literature, did not do much to advance understanding of the work. Indeed, as late as the mid-nineteenth century, when Franz Buecheler, who produced the first major scholarly edition of *The Satyricon,* was teaching at the University of Freiburg, he was attacked in a local newspaper for lecturing on such an obscene author. Petronius had admirers during this period and after—Gustave Flaubert, Oscar Wilde, T. S. Eliot, and James Joyce, among others. But the reputation of the work as a tale of sexual adventurism inhibited widespread familiarity, as did the absence of a definitive translation. Possibly the most successful reception was of the author, not the novel, since Petronius figures prominently in the novel *Quo Vadis* (1896) by the Nobel-winning Polish author Henryk Sienkiewicz. The novel was carefully researched, and Sienkiewicz makes Petronius its most intriguing character, taking the opportunity, for instance, to supply us with the text of the deathbed letter to Nero that Tacitus only summarizes. In the contemporary translation of Jeremiah Curtin it concludes:

> Life is a great treasure. I have taken the most precious jewels from that treasure, but in life there are many things which I cannot endure any longer. Do not suppose, I pray, that I am offended because thou didst kill thy mother, thy wife, and thy brother; that thou didst burn Rome and send to Erebus all the honest men in thy dominions. No, grandson of Chronos. Death is the inheritance of man; from thee other deeds could not have been expected. But to destroy one's ear for whole years with thy poetry, to see thy belly of a Domitius on slim legs whirled about in Pyrrhic dance; to hear thy music, thy declamation, thy doggerel verses, wretched poet of the suburbs,—is a thing surpassing my power, and it has roused in me the wish to die. Rome stuffs its ears when it hears thee; the world reviles thee. I can blush for thee no longer, and I have no wish to do so. The howls of Cerberus, though resembling thy music, will be less offensive to me, for I have never been the friend of Cerberus, and I need not be ashamed of his howling. Farewell, but make no music; commit murder, but write no verses; poison people, but dance not; be an incendiary, but play not on a cithara. This is the wish and the last friendly counsel sent thee by the—Arbiter Elegantiae.

The best-selling novel was translated into more than fifty languages and formed the basis for several screen adaptations, the most notable the Hollywood blockbuster of 1951 that ushered in the great era of sword and sandal epics of the following decade.

The fragmentary state of *The Satyricon* is perhaps less disconcerting to readers of twentieth- and twenty-first-century fiction, and the proliferation of readable translations has brought wider familiarity with the work. It is in the medium of film, however, that its most successful reception is to be found. The Italian director Federico Fellini turned the fragmentary state of the novel to his advantage in constructing a film that deliberately eschews narrative continuity and presents a series of vignettes based on Petronius. As Fellini put it, the film, "through the fragmentary recurrence of its episodes, should restore the image of a vanished world without completing it, as if those characters, those habits, those milieux were summoned for us in a trance, recalled from their silence by the mystic ritual of a séance." *Fellini - Satyricon* is not the comic romp through the Roman world that we encounter in the novel but rather a dark meditation on our alienation from the Roman past.

# PLINY THE ELDER

## (Gaius Plinius Secundus, ca. A.D. 23–79)

PLINY THE ELDER, SO CALLED TO DISTINGUISH HIM FROM HIS NEPHEW AND ADOPTED
son, was born in A.D. 23 or 24 in the Italian Alps. He had a very active public career, in the armed
forces, in the administration of the empire, in law, and in politics. As a young man, he served as a
cavalry officer in Lower Germany; the chance discovery there of a horse ornament stamped with the
words PLINIO PRAEFEC[… (*Corpus of Latin Inscriptions* 12.10026.22) testifies to this command.
During the reign of Nero, he devoted his time in public service mainly to his legal career. Vespasian
appointed him to several important administrative posts in the provinces and subsequently admitted him to his council of advisers, a position he maintained under Titus, with whom he had served
in Germany. He died in an intrepid and heroic manner in August 79, when he crossed the Bay of
Naples to get a closer look at Vesuvius and to rescue people caught by the eruption. At the time of
his death, he was commander of the fleet at Misenum, one of the main imperial naval bases.

Pliny was an efficient and successful public figure. Lower Germany, barely a generation
after the massacre of Varus's three legions in the Teutoburg Forest, was one of the wildest frontiers of the empire, and the army there needed officers who knew their business. Pliny must
have known his: while in charge of a squadron of cavalry in Germany, he wrote his first book,
a monograph on throwing a javelin while on horseback (Pliny the Younger, *Letters* 3.5.3). To
have survived in public prominence during the turbulent last years of Nero's Principate and on
through the Year of Four Emperors in A.D. 69 suggests he was not lacking in political subtlety.
This assumption is corroborated by the preface dedicating the *Natural History* to Titus, which
shows Pliny to have been perfectly capable of writing elegant and polished court flattery. No
doubt he displayed much the same political suavity in his biography of his patron, Pomponius
Secundus, consul in A.D. 41 (though almost all we have from this work is the curious detail that
Pomponius never belched). He was a prolific writer throughout his career, his other known
works being twenty books on the German wars, thirty-one books on the history of the later
Julio-Claudian period, and various studies of oratory and grammar. To have written so much
on such a wide range of subjects, as well as the *Natural History*, his last, longest, and only
surviving work, while active in high-level public service, will have required an uncommonly
disciplined and focused mind.

This view of Pliny is quite at odds with the image that has been foisted on him nowadays. He has
acquired a reputation as a naive and credulous workaholic, an unworldly figure too absorbed in his
endless studies to see life as it really is. This distorted reputation is based largely on the anachronistic way modern readers assess the contents of the *Natural History*. We tend to judge a scientific work

**Figure 23:  Statue of the elder Pliny in Como**
Both the elder and the younger Pliny are commemorated by statues in the cathedral in Como, their home town in the far north of Italy.

by rather more rigid and informed criteria than those that prevailed in Pliny's time. Many details in the *Natural History* may seem absurd to us, but often they are simply the product of their time, not a reflection on Pliny as a particularly gullible and uncritical writer. That said, however, as we shall see, he does very often display a rather endearing reluctance to ignore interesting material, no matter how far-fetched it may seem to him.

Pliny's reputation suffers also from the sheer size of the *Natural History,* thirty-six books preceded by a detailed index intended to ensure, as he says in the preface, that neither the emperor nor anyone else need waste time reading more than necessary. Because of its vast scale, not many scholars have actually read right through the whole work. Moreover, partly as an inevitable consequence of the technical nature of much of his subject matter, Pliny's Latin is often difficult, and, partly because of the evident speed of composition, he is not a very stylish writer. His nephew and adopted son, Pliny the Younger, however, had no doubt about his uncle's greatness. In one of his letters addressed to the historian Tacitus (*Letters* 6.16), he says of him that he was one of those "who by the gods' gift have been granted the ability . . . to perform deeds worth chronicling and to compose accounts which deserve to be read."

Pliny's discussion of ailments that afflict infants (30.135ff.) is fairly typical. He expresses no doubt that infantile hernia can be cured if the child is bitten by a green lizard while asleep, and the lizard is then hung over a fire: when the lizard dies, the child recovers. Likewise, snail slime smeared on a child's eyes makes its eyelashes grow straight. Pliny presents several other such remedies without qualification or hesitation about their efficacy. Then, however, he adds that there are other treatments for various childhood complaints that are hardly to be taken seriously, but that he should not omit, since he has found authority for them in his sources: for example, giving babies boiled mice in their food will prevent incontinence, and teething troubles are relieved if a baby wears as an amulet a little stone found in the brain of a snake that has had its head cut off unawares.

It is hard to distinguish the credibility of the remedies for which Pliny here vouches from those for which he does not. We are often left to wonder at his reasons for belief or skepticism. He relates without further comment the well-known story that, when charged with sexual misconduct, a Vestal Virgin named Tuccia established her innocence by carrying water in a sieve to the temple of Vesta from the Tiber. He is skeptical, however, about the Vestals' supposed power to fix runaway slaves to the spot by prayer, provided they have not yet left the city (28.12–13).

Similarly, he reports that "Cornelius Valerianus records that a phoenix flew to Egypt in the consulship of Quintus Plautius and Sextus Papinius [A.D. 36]. It was brought to Rome during the censorship of the emperor Claudius in the eight hundredth year after the foundation of the city [A.D. 47] and displayed in the Assembly. This is attested in the Senatorial Record, even though everyone is certain this phoenix is a hoax" (10.5). On the other hand, he states unequivocally, "I personally have seen a hippocentaur [part horse, part human] preserved in honey, brought from Egypt to the emperor Claudius" (7.35).

Pliny goes on in Book 7 to record that "among other examples [of ominous births] is the case of an infant from Saguntum who went straight back into the womb in the year the city was destroyed by Hannibal." This portent—the sacking of Saguntum precipitated the Second Punic War—may seem well beyond the limits of modern credibility, but it is just the sort of thing recorded in the lists of prodigies maintained by the state. Compare, for example, the following items Julius Obsequens's *Book of Prodigies* (see p. 391): a pig was born with human hands and feet; a married woman gave birth to a snake; a slave-girl's child said "Hello" as soon as it was born.

Pliny relates with evident conviction the following incident from only a decade before the publication of the *Natural History*:

> Something happened in our lifetime more ominous than anything ever heard of from earlier times: when the emperor Nero was overthrown, a whole olive-grove belonging to Vettius Marcellus, a distinguished knight, crossed the public road and the crops that had been growing over there moved to where the olive-grove had been. (17.245)

Few people nowadays could fail to find this absurd, but it is as well to remember that the Romans had an ancient law forbidding the transference of growing crops from one place to another by magic. That law, as we know from Pliny himself (18.41), had actually been invoked in the second century B.C. against a freedman who was obtaining better returns from his land than were his jealous neighbors. When he produced in court his carefully maintained implements, his sturdy slaves, and his well-fed oxen, and argued that hard work was his only magic spell, he was unanimously acquitted.

A particularly vivid illustration of the lack of a truly scientific perspective in the *Natural History* is given by Pliny's improbable opinions about seafaring. For example, "I have it on the authority of some distinguished members of the equestrian order that they saw a merman exactly like a human being in the sea near Cadiz. He climbs on board ships in the night time, they say, and the part of the deck where he sits is immediately weighed down, and ships are actually sunk if he stays on board too long" (9.10). When he published the *Natural History*, Pliny was commander of the important naval station at Misenum; we can only wonder what measures he was taking to protect the fleet from such creatures.

Having concluded his geographical survey of the world that occupies Books 3 through 6, Pliny discusses animal life in the next five books, devoting the whole of Book 7 to mankind. "The first place will rightly be assigned to man, for whose benefit great nature seems to have created everything else" (7.1). In setting humanity apart as the most elevated of all creatures, Pliny gives himself scope for moralizing against the weaknesses and failings of the human race: "Lions do not vent their ferocity against each other; snakes do not try to bite other snakes. Even the sea-monsters and fishes fight only against other species. But in man's case, by heaven, most dangers emanate from other men!" (7.5). Such criticism of human behavior is a strongly recurrent theme throughout the *Natural History*.

Almost a quarter of Book 9 is devoted to shellfish, but only brief sections describe the creatures themselves. The rest is given over to denouncing the misuse of shellfish by humans. After a brief and rather vague account of the various shapes and sizes in which they occur, Pliny asks, "But why do I catalog such trivialities, when decadence and the devastation of our morals have no other source as great as shellfish?" (9.104). He goes on to rage against the exorbitant price of luxury seafood and the wearing of pearls and of purple clothing (derived from the murex shell). He lingers especially over the scandalous stories of Lollia Paulina, Caligula's third wife, who, as he reports from personal observation, would bedeck herself with emeralds and pearls whenever she attended even the most modest gathering, taking the receipts with her to show to anyone who doubted that her jewelry had cost 40 million sestertii (9.117), and of Cleopatra, who bet Mark Antony that she could spend 10 million sestertii on a single banquet, and won the bet by drinking a pearl of that value dissolved in wine (9.120).

Pliny likewise begins his account of flax growing in Book 19 with a diatribe against sailing: flax is used for ships' sails, and overseas travel leads to greed in the exchange of merchandise. The discussion of metals in Book 33 begins with a denouncement of mining as a violation of Nature, which has given us all we actually need on the earth's surface, and with a curse on the person who instituted the practice of wearing gold rings. He devotes Book 14 to vines and wines, but only one very short section to beer, which was regarded as a drink for barbarians: "The peoples in the West have their own sort of alcoholic drink [as opposed to wine], made of grain soaked in water. How marvelously devious vice can be: a means has been found by which even water can make people drunk!" (14.149). This is a particularly fatuous piece of sanctimoniously moralizing rhetoric—ancient wine may have been rather syrup-like, but even it was made with water.

In the preface to the *Natural History,* Pliny famously boasts that he has culled 20,000 facts from some 2,000 books and from 100 select authors. These figures are understated. No one could count the "facts," but there are more than four hundred authorities cited. Greek authors outnumber Roman by well over two to one. This point is interesting, for several reasons. For more than a millennium, after the separation of the Latin-speaking West from the more cultured Greek-speaking East, the *Natural History* did more than any other single work to preserve in western Europe the tradition of ancient knowledge, in particular, the works of Greek scholarship in science and medicine that could no longer be read and ceased to be available. It is also worth noting Pliny's dependence on Greek sources despite his marked pro-Roman prejudices, which inevitably entailed a corresponding lack of enthusiasm for the Greeks.

Xenophobia directed at particular nationalities is not uncommon in ancient writers—Juvenal's hatred of Greeks is a startlingly vivid example. Greeks are proud of their superiority to the rest of the world, the barbarians, and the Romans tended to include themselves with the Greeks on the non-barbarian side. But we rarely encounter such pride in being Roman as Pliny displays. For example: "[Italy is] both the foster-child and the parent of all countries, chosen by the will of the gods to make even heaven itself more splendid, to gather the scattered empires, to civilize their customs, to draw together into dialogue through a shared language the discordant and uncouth tongues of so many peoples, to bestow humanity on mankind, in short to become the single fatherland of all the nations in the whole world" (3.39); "the gods seem to have given the Romans as a second sun to benefit humanity" (27.3).

But Pliny is too zealous. It is hard not to object that Greek is not a "discordant and uncouth tongue." On the contrary, Greeks could live without feeling any need to acquire a knowledge of Latin, the language of their conquerors whom they regarded as intellectually inferior. Even so, Pliny does his best to boost Roman achievements at the expense of the Greeks. Whereas Roman writers give straightforward titles to their works, Greeks prefer fancy eye-catching titles that the contents of their books do not then live up to (*Preface* 24). He quotes an account of a werewolf by the Greek author Euanthes, and then adds: "It is really amazing to what lengths the credulity of the Greeks will go! No lie is so barefaced that none of them will vouch for it" (8.82). This criticism might have more validity if Pliny himself did not endorse, at least implicitly, so many hundreds of far-fetched notions. Theophrastus was a natural scientist hardly less important than Aristotle, his predecessor as head of the Peripatetic school. Pliny accepts that he is generally a reliable authority, but he takes him to task for indulging in fantasy in his discussion of the aphrodisiac qualities of certain plants. He is perhaps particularly disgruntled when he specifies Theophrastus's failure to give the name and species of a plant that enables a man to have sexual intercourse seventy times in a row (26.99).

About a third of the *Natural History* is concerned with medicine, a profession dominated by Greeks. The Romans had a particularly virulent prejudice against Greek doctors. Pliny quotes with approval the negative opinion of Greek doctors expressed by Cato the Elder more than two hundred years earlier:

> The Greeks are a quite worthless and unteachable race. When they bestow their literature on us, they will destroy our whole existence. They will do this all the sooner if they send us their doctors. They have conspired to murder all non-Greeks with their medicine. They make us pay for treatment, so we will have the more confidence in them and they can ruin us the more easily. (29.14)

In the preface, Pliny laments with becoming, but conventional, modesty that it is difficult for him to make his often sterile subject matter interesting, giving novelty to what is old, authority to what is new, putting a gloss on what is tarnished, and casting light on what is obscure (15). For the modern reader, however, the *Natural History* is replete with incidental details that give it an unending fascination perhaps not always felt quite so acutely by Pliny's contemporaries. For example:

> Bear grease prevents hair loss (8.127), as do onions (20.41);
> Drinking water in which cabbage has been boiled relieves a hangover (20.34);
> They say that if a message is written on a person's body with the juice of the spurge plant and allowed to dry, the letters will appear when they are sprinkled with ash. Some men have preferred to send messages to their mistresses this way rather than on writing-tablets (26.62);
> Documents can be protected from mice by mixing the ink with wormwood (27.52);
> Urine cures gout, as is demonstrated by the fact that laundrymen, who use urine to bleach clothes, do not suffer from that ailment (28.66).

Different incidents, facts, and opinions will be memorable to different readers. Very few works on such a scale have survived through the vulnerable centuries of manuscript transmission; it is a privilege for us to be able to discover the fascinating details that await us on every page of the *Natural History*.

# NATURAL HISTORY

## Book 7

*The* Natural History *is the longest work of classical Latin prose to survive complete. Although Pliny's discursive style is marked by frequent digressions, the plan of the work as a whole is clear and rigorous; it is described in the first book, which outlines the content of each book, lists the principal sources consulted, and provides a miscellany of statistics about the material covered. This innovation made the consultation of the work a far easier task, so the reader would know which of the remaining thirty-six papyrus rolls to locate by their identifying tags. The work per se was organized in two sections, with the first half (Books 2–19) dealing with the natural world on its own terms, and the second (Books 20–37) treating nature in its relationship to humankind. In the first half, discrete sections deal with cosmology and astronomy (Book 2), geography (3–6), anthropology (7), zoology (8–11), botany (12–19). The second half of the* Natural History *covers medicine, including pharmacology (20–32), and mineralogy and metallurgy (33–37), with an enormously important digression on the history of art. This book, on the human animal, opens with a brief introduction (sections 1–5) on the paradox that man represents the summit of nature's creation but is among its weakest creatures.*

[1] The world and its component lands, peoples, seas…islands and cities are as I have described above. The nature of its animals is as worthy of study as almost any other part thereof, if in fact the human mind is capable of exploring everything. The first place will rightly be assigned to man, for whose benefit great nature seems to have created everything else. However, for her considerable gifts she exacts a cruel fee; so that it is difficult to decide whether she is more of a kind parent or a harsh stepmother to man. [2] First and foremost, man alone of all her creatures nature dresses in borrowed clothes. To the others she assigns a variety of coverings: shells, bark, hides, spines, fur, bristles, hair, down, feathers, scales, fleeces. Even the tree trunks she protects from cold and heat by bark, sometimes in two layers. Man alone on his natal day she flings forth naked on the naked ground to erupt instantaneously into weeping and wailing. No other among so many animals is given to tears and these at the very beginning of life! In marked contrast, the well-known smile of infancy is, even in

its earliest manifestation, given to no child before the fortieth day. [3] Chains of a kind experienced not even by domestic animals follow this introduction to the light of day and fetter all his limbs. Thus auspiciously delivered, the animal destined to rule all others lies bound hand and foot, weeping, and his life is initiated by punishment for one fault alone—the crime of being born. How misguided are those who believe that from these beginnings they were born to a position of pride!

[4] His initial promise of strength, his first taste of the gift of life, renders him similar to a four-footed beast. When can man walk? When can he speak? When is his mouth strong enough to chew food? For how long does his skull throb, marking him out as the weakest of all animals? Then there are diseases and all the cures contrived to counter illness, only to be themselves defeated in due course by new maladies. All other animals are instinctively aware of their own natures, one exercising fleetness of foot, another swiftness of flight, others their ability to swim. Man, however, can do nothing unless he is taught, neither speaking nor walking nor eating. In short, he can do nothing by natural instinct except weep! As a result, there have been many who have thought it best not to be born at all, or else to die as soon as possible.

[5] To man alone in the animal kingdom is granted the capacity for sorrow, for self-indulgence of every kind and in every part of his body, for ambition, avarice, unbounded appetite for life and superstition; for anxiety over burial and even over what will happen after he is dead. To no animal is assigned a more precarious life, more all-consuming passions, more disruptive fear, or more violent anger. Finally, the other animals coexist in a proper manner with their own kind. We see them flock together to make a common stand against animals different from themselves. Lions do not vent their ferocity against each other; snakes do not try to bite other snakes. Even the sea-monsters and fishes fight only against other species. But in man's case, by heaven, most dangers emanate from other men!

*In the first major section of the book (6–32), Pliny discusses the diversity of the human race (6–8) and proceeds to describe the strange peoples of the north beyond the borders of the Roman world (9–12). The geographical survey of humans is interrupted by a survey of peoples who possess magical powers (13–20), including one group, the Marsi, from Italy. This section concludes with a selection*

*(21–32) of oddities from the eastern and southern regions of the world.*

[6] The human race in general has for the most part been discussed in my account of the peoples of the world. Nor will I be dealing here with habits and customs, which are countless and almost on a par with the number of human communities. There is material, however, especially concerning those peoples furthest from the sea, which I do not think should be left out. It includes facts which will, I am sure, seem extraordinary and unbelievable to many readers. Who, after all, believed in the Ethiopians before actually seeing them? And what is not regarded as wondrous when it first gains public attention? How many things are judged impossible before they actually happen? [7] Indeed, the power and might of nature lacks credibility at every point unless we comprehend her as a whole rather than piecemeal. To say nothing of peacocks, the stippled coats of tigers and panthers, and the markings of so many animals, it is a small task to mention, but a boundless one to estimate, the great number of human languages, dialects, and modes of speech; so great, indeed, that to a man of another race a foreigner barely passes for a human being! [8] And again, although we possess few more than ten facial features, no two identical faces exist among so many thousands of human beings. This is something which no art could have succeeded in copying when using such a small number of components. Nonetheless, I shall not pledge my word as to the reliability of most of these facts, but shall ascribe them instead to the sources, who will be referred back to on all doubtful issues. We should certainly not disdain to follow the Greek writers whose commitment goes further back in time and whose scholarship is correspondingly greater.

[9] I have mentioned that there are Scythian tribes, a good number in fact, which eat human flesh. This might well seem unbelievable were we not to bear in mind that in the center of the world and in Sicily there once existed peoples equally bizarre, the Cyclopes and the Laestrygones; and that very recently, it was the custom of tribes beyond the Alps to practice human sacrifice, which is only one step removed from cannibalism.

[10] Next to those Scythians who face northwards and not far from the actual rising of the North Wind and the cave bearing his name, the place called the Entrance to Earth's Windpipe, are found the Arimaspi whom I spoke of earlier and who are distinguished by a single eye in the middle of their foreheads. Many writers, of whom the most distinguished are Herodotus and Aristeas of Proconnesus, tell us that these people are engaged in an ongoing battle over gold mines with the griffins, a type of winged animal according to popular tradition, which dig out the gold from their burrows. The beasts try to protect the gold while the Arimaspi try to steal it, both parties displaying amazing rapacity.

[11] Beyond other man-eating Scythian tribes, in a certain large valley on Mt. Imavus, is a region called Abarimon. Here live wild men of the woods whose feet are turned back to front. They run very fast and roam abroad with the wild beasts. These people cannot breathe in a foreign climate and for that reason cannot be brought to the neighboring kings and had not been brought to Alexander the Great according to his route-surveyor, Baeton.

[12] According to Isigonus of Nicaea, the first-mentioned man-eating Scythians, who I said lived to the north ten days' journey beyond the river Borysthenes, drink out of human skulls, using the scalps, hair and all, like napkins to cover their chests. The same author says that in Albania there are born people with grey eyes who are white-haired from childhood and see better by night than by day. He also states that thirteen days' journey beyond the Borysthenes are the Sauromatae who eat every other day.

[13] According to Crates of Pergamum, there was a tribe near Parium in the Hellespont whom he calls the Ophiogenes. They used to cure snakebite by touch, drawing the poison out of the body by laying their hands on it. Varro says that there are still a few people there whose saliva is effective in the treatment of snakebites.

[14] There was a similar race in Africa called the Psylli, according to Agatharchides, named after king Psyllus who lies buried in the region of the Greater Syrtes. Their bodies contained a poison lethal to snakes and its smell was enough to render the creatures unconscious. It was this tribe's custom to expose their infants immediately after birth to the most savage snakes and by this method test the fidelity of their wives, since the snakes do not flee from those who are impure of blood. This people has itself been almost exterminated by the Nasamones who now occupy that area. But there are persons descended from those who had died or were absent at the time of the fighting who live on in a few places even today. [15] A similar race, the Marsi, survives in Italy. They are allegedly descended from Circe's

son and consequently born naturally with this power. There is, however, a substance poisonous to snakes innate in every human being. For it is said that when snakes are touched with human saliva they flee as if scalded with boiling water; and if the saliva gets into their throat, they actually die, especially if it comes from the mouth of a fasting man.

Beyond the Nasamones are the Machlyae, their neighbors, who, according to Calliphanes, are hermaphrodites who possess the features of both sexes and cohabit with each in turn. Aristotle adds that their right breast is male and their left female. [16] According to Isigonus and Nymphodorus, there are in the same part of Africa certain families of sorcerers whose eulogies cause sheep to perish, trees to wither and babies to die. Isigonus adds that there are persons of the same sort among the Triballes [and the Illyrians] who bewitch with a mere glance and actually kill those whom they stare at for any length of time, especially if the stare is an angry one. Adults are more susceptible to their spell. A particularly remarkable feature is their double pupil in each eye.

[17] Apollonides says that there are women of this type in Scythia, called Bitiae. Phylarchus also reports the Thibii and many other tribes of the same kind in Pontus who he says are distinguished by a double pupil in one eye and the image of a horse in the other. He also claims that they cannot be drowned, even when weighted down with clothing. Damon records a similar tribe in Ethiopia, called the Pharmaces, whose sweat causes the bodies that it touches to waste away.

[18] In addition, among our own Roman writers, Cicero tells us that all women everywhere with double pupils possess the Evil Eye. To such an extent did nature see fit, when she had planted in man the bestial habit of eating human flesh, to plant additional poisons in his whole body and even in the eyes of some people, so that no evil should exist which was not also present in man.

[19] In the territory of the Falisci, not far from Rome, are a few families called the Hirpi who walk across a heap of glowing charcoal at the annual festival of Apollo on Mt. Soracte without getting burnt. On account of this, they have been granted permanent exemption from military service and all other public duties by senatorial decree.

[20] Certain persons are born with bodily features exhibiting remarkable qualities in specific circumstances: the right toe of king Pyrrhus, for example, used to cure splenetic diseases at a touch. It is reported that this toe could not be cremated with the rest of his body and was stored in a casket inside a temple.

[21] India and the territory of the Ethiopians are particularly abundant in marvels. The largest animals are produced in India; her dogs, for example, are bigger than those found elsewhere. The trees, they say, grow so tall that it is impossible to shoot an arrow over them. So great is the fertility of the soil, the mildness of the climate and the supply of water that squadrons of cavalry are sheltered by a single fig tree, if you can believe it. The reeds are so tall that a section taken from between two nodules makes a boat for up to three people.

[22] It is well known that many of the natives are over five cubits (2.2 m.) tall, do not spit, and do not suffer any pains in the head, teeth or eyes and rarely in any other part of the body, so toughened are they by the moderate heat of the sun. Their philosophers, whom they call Gymnosophists, stare steadfastly at the sun from dawn to dusk· with unflinching eyes, standing for the whole day first on one foot then on the other in the burning sand.

On a mountain called Nulus, according to Megasthenes, there are people with feet turned backwards and eight toes on each; [23] while on many mountains there is a race of dog-headed men who dress in animal skins, bark rather than talk and live on animals and birds which they hunt armed only with their nails. He says there were more than 150,000 of them at the time he was writing.

Ctesias also writes that in a certain Indian tribe the women give birth once in a lifetime and the hair of their children starts turning grey from the moment of birth. He also says that there is a race of men called the Monocoli ("One-legged men") by virtue of their single leg which enables them to jump with amazing agility. They are also called Sciapodae ("Shady-feet") because when it gets too hot they lie down on their backs on the ground and protect themselves with the shadow of their foot. Ctesias says they live not far away from the Trogodytae ("Cavemen") and that to the west of the latter live men without necks who have eyes in their shoulders.

[24] There are also satyrs in the east Indian mountains (the region of the Catarcludi); the satyr is an exceptionally fleet-footed creature with a human appearance which runs sometimes on all four legs and sometimes upright. Because of its swiftness only old or sick specimens are captured. Tauron mentions a

forest tribe called the Choromandae who do not talk but emit harsh shrieks. They have hairy bodies, grey eyes, and the fangs of a dog. According to Eudoxus, there are men in southern India with feet a cubit (.444 m.) long, and women with feet so small they are called Struthopodes ("Sparrowfeet").

[25] Megasthenes describes a tribe of nomadic Indians called the Sciratae who only have holes where their nostrils should be and snake-like strap feet. At the easternmost borders of India near the source of the Ganges he places the Astomi, a people with no mouths. They have hair all over their bodies and dress in cotton wool. They live only on the air they breathe and the odors they inhale through their nostrils. They have no food or drink but only the smells from the roots, flowers, and crab-apples which they take with them on long journeys so as never to lack a scent supply. A slightly stronger smell than usual can easily kill them.

[26] Beyond them, in the remotest region of the mountains are reputed to live the Trispithami ("Three-span men") and the Pygmies. They are never more than three spans in height, that is, twenty-seven inches (.666 m.). Protected by the mountains from the North Wind, the climate is healthy and perpetually spring-like. Homer has also recorded that this tribe is plagued by cranes. The story goes that in springtime the whole company goes down to the sea, mounted on the backs of rams and nanny-goats and armed with arrows, to eat the cranes' eggs and chicks. The expedition is over in three months and without it the Pygmies would be overcome by the growing flocks of cranes. Their houses are made of mud, feathers, and eggshell. [27] Aristotle, however, says they live in caves, although in other respects his account accords with the rest. Isigonus says that the Indian tribe called the Cyrni live for 140 years, as do the long-lived Ethiopians, the Seres, and the inhabitants of Mount Athos, the latter because they live on snake-meat and their hair and clothes are therefore not infested with parasites. [28] Onesicritus says that in the parts of India where no shadows fall, men grow to be five cubits and two spans tall, live for 130 years, and do not grow old but die middle-aged. Crates of Pergamum mentions Indians who live more than a hundred years. He calls them Gymnetae, though many people call them the Macrobii or Long-livers. Ctesias says that one of their tribes in the mountain valleys, the Pandae, live for two hundred years and are white haired in youth but grow black-haired in old

age. [29] Others, however, neighbors of the Macrobii, live no longer than forty years. Their women give birth just once in a lifetime. The same story is told by Agatharchides, who adds that they live on locusts and are fleet-footed. Clitarchus calls them the Mandi and Megasthenes attributes three hundred villages to them. He also says that the women bear children at 7 and that old age starts at 40. [30] Artemidorus says that on the island of Sri Lanka, the people live very long lives without the onset of bodily infirmity. Duris claims that some Indians copulate with animals and the off-spring are human-animal hybrids; and that among the Calingae who live in the same part of India, the women conceive at 5 years old and do not live longer than 8 years, and in another part of India he says that men with hairy tails are born who can run very fast; others are entirely enveloped by their ears.

The Oritae are separated from the Indians by the river Arabis. The only food they know is fish, which they tear apart with their nails and roast in the sun. In this way they make bread from them, according to Clitarchus. [31] Crates of Pergamum says that beyond the Ethiopians are Trogodytae who are swifter than horses. He also says there are Ethiopians more than twelve cubits high: they are called Syrbotae. The tribe of nomad Indians called the Menismini along the river Astragus to the north is twenty days' journey from the sea. It lives on the milk of the animals we call Cynocephali, herds of which it pastures, killing the male animals except when needed for breeding purposes.

[32] In the African deserts human phantoms suddenly appear before your eyes and then vanish away in a moment.

Nature has cleverly contrived these and similar species of the human race to amuse herself and to amaze us. As for the individual creations she produces every day, and almost every hour, who could possibly reckon them up? Let it be a sufficient revelation of her power to have placed entire races among her miracles. From these, we turn to acknowledged facts concerning the individual man.

*The remainder of the book deals with observed facts about human beings considered as individuals, treating first birth, pregnancy, and infancy (33–72). When our selection resumes (73–129), Pliny is discussing the years of maturity, including such topics as physiology, sight, and memory. He also adds two excursuses on the achievements of Caesar and Pompey (91–99) and describes outstanding examples of the human intellect (107–27).*

[73] It is an established fact that a person has grown to half of his future stature by the age of three years. But it is noticeable that, in general, the human race as a whole is getting smaller as time goes by, and that few individuals grow taller than their fathers. This is because the fertility of the semen is being dried up by the conflagration into whose era the cycle of ages is now declining. In Crete, after an earthquake split open a mountain, a body was found measuring forty-six cubits (approx. 20.5 m.). Some said it was Orion, others Otus.

[74] The body of Orestes, exhumed on the orders of an oracle, was seven cubits (approx. 3.1 m.) tall if the records are to be believed. And indeed, nearly a thousand years ago, the great poet Homer never ceased to bemoan the small stature of his contemporaries compared to the men of old. The records do not tell us how tall Naevius Pollio was, but he was clearly thought to be a prodigy since he was almost crushed to death by crowds of sightseers. The tallest man of our era was brought from Arabia in the reign of the deified Claudius. He was called Gabbara and he measured nine feet and nine inches (2.88 m.) in height. [75] In the reign of the deified Augustus, there was a couple called Pusio and Secundilla who were half a foot taller (approx. 3 m.) and their bodies were preserved as curiosities in the Sallustian gardens.

In the reign of the same emperor, the smallest man was a dwarf called Conopas, who was two feet and a palm (.666 m.) in height. He was the pet of the emperor's granddaughter Julia and he had a wife called Andromeda, a freedwoman of Julia Augusta. Marcus Varro tells us that the Roman knights Manius Maximus and Marcus Tullius were just two cubits (.888 m.) tall and I have actually seen their bodies preserved in coffins. Everyone knows that there are infants born measuring eighteen inches or more (.444 m.), whose life's span is complete by the age of 3.

[76] We find in our sources that in Salamis the son of Euthymenes grew to be three cubits tall (1.33 m.) in three years. His gait was slow and his senses dull. He had actually reached puberty and his voice had broken before he died suddenly of a seizure at the age of three. Not long ago, I myself saw almost all of these characteristics except puberty in the son of Cornelius Tacitus, a

Roman knight who was financial procurator in Gallia Belgica. The Greeks call such people *ektrapeloi*, deviants, but there is no corresponding term for them in Latin.

[77] It has been observed that a man's height from head to toe is the same as the distance from tip to tip of his longest fingers when his arms are fully stretched out on either side. It has also been observed that the right side of the body is the stronger, but sometimes both sides are equally strong and in some people the left hand predominates, although this is never the case with women. Men are heavier than women and the bodies of all creatures are heavier when they are dead than when they are alive and when they are asleep than when they are awake. Male corpses float on their backs but female corpses float on their faces as though nature were preserving their modesty even in death.

[78] I have read that there are people who have solid bones without any marrow in them. They can be recognized by the fact that they do not experience thirst and they do not perspire. We know, however, that thirst can actually be overcome by will-power. A Roman knight called Julius Viator from the tribe of the Vocontii, one of our allies, had developed dropsy in his youth and was forbidden liquids by his doctors. This regime became second nature to him and he progressed to old age without drinking a drop. There are many similar examples of such self-control.

[79] We are told that Crassus, whose grandson of the same name was killed fighting the Parthians, never laughed and was called Agelastus, Mirthless, as a result. There have been many examples of people who did not weep. The famous philosopher Socrates always wore the same expression on his face, never happier or sadder. However, this equability of temperament sometimes turns into a sort of rigidity of character and a hard inflexible severity lacking the normal human emotions. The Greeks call such persons *apatheis* or emotionless and offer many examples; [80] in particular, strangely enough, among their philosophers: Diogenes the Cynic, Pyrrho, Heraclitus, and Timon. The last mentioned was actually carried to the extreme of hating the whole human race.

But minor peculiarities of nature take many forms and are very common. Drusus' wife, Antonia, for example, did not spit and the poet and one-time consul, Pomponius, never belched.

"Horny"-boned is the term used to describe those whose bones are naturally solid; quite a rare phenomenon.

[81] In his account of marvelous examples of strength, Varro tells us that Tritanus who was a famous gladiatorial fighter in Samnite armor, was slightly built but possessed outstanding strength. His son, a soldier under Pompey the Great, had a network of sinews in a criss-cross pattern all over his body, even on his arms and hands. He defeated with his bare hands an enemy whom he had challenged to a duel, finally picking the man up with one finger and carrying him off to the camp.

[82] Vinnius Valens, a centurion in the emperor Augustus' Praetorian Guard used to lift up carts loaded with wineskins until they had been emptied. He would take hold of wagons with one hand and immobilize them, defeating the efforts of the draught animals trying to pull them. There were also other marvellous exploits of his which can be seen carved upon his tombstone.

[83] Varro also tells us the following story: Rusticelius, nicknamed Hercules, used to lift up his mule; Fufius Salvius used to climb steps with two one-hundred-pound (32.745 kg.) weights on his feet two more in his hands and two two-hundred-pound (65.49 kg.) weights on his shoulders. I myself have seen a man called Athanatus who could perform a marvellous exploit: he walked across a stage wearing a five-hundred-pound (163.725 kg.) leaden breastplate with boots on his feet of the same weight. When the athlete Milon of Croton stood firm, no one could dislodge him and when he held an apple no one could straighten a single one of his fingers.

[84] Philippides' 1,140-stade (approx. 211 km.) run from Athens to Sparta in two days was a great achievement, until the Spartan runner Anystis and Alexander the Great's courier Philonides ran from Sicyon to Elis in a day—a distance of 1,305 stades (approx. 241.4 km.).

Nowadays, we are well aware that there are runners who can manage 160 miles (approx. 236 km.) in the Circus and recently, when Fonteius and Vipstanus were consuls, a boy of 8 ran 75 miles (approx. 111 km.) between midday and evening. The real wonder of this achievement only sinks in when we bear in mind that the longest 24-hour journey by carriage ever recorded was made by Tiberius Nero as he hurried to his brother Drusus who had fallen ill in Germany. The distance covered then was 200 miles (approx. 296 km.).

[85] Perhaps the most incredible stories are those involving keen eyesight. According to Cicero, Homer's *Iliad* was copied on to a scrap of parchment which could fit into a nutshell. He also claims that there was a man who could see clearly from a distance of 135 Roman miles (approx. 200 km.) and Varro actually gives his name: Strabo. He says that, in the Punic war, he used actually to count, from the promontory of Lilybaeum in Sicily, the number of ships in a fleet sailing out of the harbor at Carthage. Callicrates used to carve ivory ants and other creatures so tiny that no one else could make out the details. A certain Myrmecides became famous through the same sort of artistic achievement, when he made a four-horse chariot, also from ivory, which a fly could cover with its wings, and a ship which could be hidden under the wings of a tiny bee.

[86] There is one amazing story connected with hearing: the battle which destroyed Sybaris was heard of on the same day at Olympia. However, the tidings of the victory over the Cimbri and the Castores who announced the victory over Perseus at Rome on the day it happened were visions and premonitions of divine origin.

[87] Of physical endurance, thanks to the frequency with which disaster is man's lot in life, there are countless instances. Among women, the most famous is that of the prostitute Leaena who under torture refused to reveal the names of the tyrannicides Harmodius and Aristogiton. Among men it is Anaxarchus who, when tortured for a similar reason, bit off his tongue and spat the one hope of betrayal into the tyrant's face.

[88] Of good memory, the most indispensable of life's advantages, it is difficult to name an outstanding example, since so many people have attained distinction in this field. King Cyrus knew the name of every soldier in his army. Lucius Scipio knew that of every Roman citizen and Cineas, King Pyrrhus' ambassador, knew that of every member of the senatorial and equestrian orders at Rome the day after his arrival. Mithridates, who ruled over twenty-two peoples, dispensed justice in as many languages, making speeches to each race without the aid of an interpreter. [89] A certain Charmades of Greece would recite by heart on demand any book in a library, as though he were reading it. Memory finally became an art form, invented by Simonides the lyric poet and perfected by Metrodorus of Scepsis. It facilitated word-perfect repetition of anything heard. [90] No other human

faculty is so fragile; it is adversely affected by damage from illness and accident and even fear, sometimes in specific areas and sometimes completely. After being hit by a stone, a man forgot only letters. A man who fell from a very high roof forgot his mother and all his friends and relations, another also forgot his slaves, and the orator Messala Corvinus actually forgot his own name. Indeed, memory is often on the brink of slipping away even from a calm and healthy person. It is cut off so effectively by the insidious onset of sleep that the bereft mind wonders where it is.

[91] In my opinion, the most outstanding example of mental vigor was the dictator Caesar. By vigor I do not mean moral excellence or resolution, nor the intellectual capacity which embraces everything under the sun. I mean an innate mental agility, with the penetrating speed and rapidity of fire. We are told that Caesar used to read or write, while at the same time dictating and listening. Indeed, he used to dictate his letters, which were on matters of the highest importance, four at a time to his secretaries; and if he was not doing anything else, seven at a time.

[92] He also fought 50 pitched battles and was alone in breaking the record of M. Marcellus, who fought 39. The number of those killed in his battles, if we exclude the civil wars, amounted to 1,192,000, but such a crime against humanity cannot, in my opinion, add anything to his glorious reputation, even if we allow that it was forced upon him. Indeed, he himself implicitly admitted as much by not publicizing the extent of the civil war carnage at all.

[93] There would be more justice in assigning to the credit of Pompey the Great the 846 ships which he captured from the pirates. To Caesar there may be credited, in addition to those qualities already mentioned, the peculiar distinction of his clemency in which he surpassed all others, ultimately to his own detriment. He provides an example of magnanimity to which no other can compare. [94] If I were to list in this context all the shows that he gave, the largesse he distributed and the splendor of his public buildings, I would be condoning luxury. But he displayed the genuine, unrivalled loftiness of an invincible spirit when the private papers of Pompey the Great at Pharsalus and later those of Scipio at Thapsus fell into his hands and he made it a point of honor to burn them without reading them.

[95] But to enumerate at this point all the records of Pompey the Great's victories and all his triumphs redounds not just to the glory of one man but to that of the Roman empire itself, rivaling in splendor as they do not only the deeds of Alexander the Great but almost even of Hercules and Bacchus.

[96] After he had recovered Sicily, which heralded his debut as his country's champion in the service of Sulla, and had subjected and brought under Roman domination all Africa, carrying away as a trophy the title of "the Great," he rode back in a triumphal chariot though only of equestrian rank, which was unprecedented. Immediately afterwards, he departed for the west, set up trophies in the Pyrenees and added to the tally of his glorious career a total of 876 towns brought under Roman rule, from the Alps to the frontiers of Further Spain, refraining, with considerable magnanimity, from mentioning Sertorius' name. After crushing the civil war which was throwing our foreign affairs into confusion, he brought into the city his triumphal chariot for the second time as a Roman knight who had also been a general twice, without ever having served in the ranks.

[97] Afterwards he was sent out to all the seas, and then to the east, returning with countless titles for his country, like the winners of the sacred contests who are not themselves crowned but crown their country. These honors, then, he bestowed upon the city in the temple of Minerva which he was dedicating from the spoils of war: "General Gnaeus Pompeius Magnus having ended a thirty years' war and having routed, scattered, killed, or received the surrender of 12,183,000 people; having sunk or captured 846 ships; having received the submission of 1,538 towns and fortresses; and having subjugated the lands stretching from the Maiotians to the Red Sea, makes his offering duly vowed to Minerva."

[98] This is a summary of his eastern exploits. As for his triumphal procession on 28 September in the consulship of M. Piso and M. Messala, the official announcement was as follows: "After ridding the sea-coast of pirates and restoring domination of the seas to the Roman people, he triumphed over Asia, Pontus, Armenia, Paphlagonia, Cappadocia, Cilicia, Syria, the Scythians, Jews, and Albanians, Iberia, the island of Crete, the Basternae and, in addition to these, King Mithridates and Tigranes."

[99] The crowning glory of his renown was, as he himself claimed when recounting his achievements in a public meeting, to have found the province of Asia lying on the fringes and to have restored it to his country at

the heart of the empire. If on the other hand anyone wishes to review in a similar way the achievements of Caesar, who proved himself greater than Pompey, then he must surely reckon up the whole world; which, it will be agreed, is a boundless endeavor.

[100] Passing on to other types of virtue, there are many individuals who have been outstanding in a variety of ways. The first of the Porcian family to bear the name Cato was considered to be outstanding in three of the most prestigious fields of human endeavor, since he was a brilliant orator, general, and senator. In all of these fields, however, I am of the opinion that Scipio Aemilianus played a more distinguished, if later, role than Cato, and without the unpopularity which plagued the latter. Thus we may more appropriately assign to Cato the distinction of forty-four lawsuits; no one has been accused so often and acquitted on each occasion.

[101] The most outstanding example of bravery is a matter of endless speculation, especially if the legends of the poets are taken into consideration. Q. Ennius particularly admired T. Caecilius Teucer and his brother, adding a sixteenth book to his *Annals* in their honor. L. Siccius Dentatus, who was tribune of the plebs in the consulship of Spurius Tarpeius and A. Aternius, not long after the expulsion of the kings, receives possibly the greatest number of votes as a result of his 120 battles, his 8 victories won in single combat and the distinction of having 45 scars all on the front of his body and none on his back.

[102] He captured 34 trophies, was awarded 18 ceremonial spears, 25 bosses, 83 necklets, 160 bracelets, 26 crowns (of which 14 were civic, 8 were gold, 3 were mural, and one the siege-hero's crown), a chest of bronze and 10 prisoners of war together with 20 oxen. He escorted 9 generals in triumphs of which he was the main architect and furthermore—his greatest achievement in my opinion—he secured the conviction of one of his commanders, T. Romilius, on the termination of the latter's consulship: he was tried before the people on a charge of military misconduct.

[103] The military glory of Capitolinus would be equally great had he not erased it by the manner of his career's conclusion. Before he was 17, he had already taken spoils from the enemy on two occasions. He was the first knight to receive the mural crown, as well as 6 civic crowns and 37 decorations. He received 23 wounds on the front of his body and saved the life of P. Servilius, the Master of Horse, although he himself

was wounded in the shoulder and thigh. Above all, he alone saved the Capitol and thereby a critical situation from the Gauls; if only he had not saved it to make himself king.

[104] In these cases it is clear that courage played a great part, but fortune played one greater still. In my opinion at least, no one could justly rate any man higher than Marcus Sergius, even though his great-grandson Catiline detracts from the honor of his name. In his second campaign he lost his right hand; in the course of two campaigns he was wounded twenty-three times with the result that he was partially disabled in both hands and both feet, his spirit alone remaining undiminished. Though a disabled soldier, he fought on through many subsequent campaigns. Twice he was captured by Hannibal (for it was with no ordinary enemy that he was engaged), twice he escaped from captivity, although he was kept shackled hand or foot every day for twenty months. He fought four times with his left hand alone, and two horses he was riding were killed under him. [105] He had a right hand made for himself out of iron and, fighting with it tied on, he raised the siege of Cremona, defended Placentia, and captured twenty enemy camps in Gaul. All these incidents appear in the speech he made during his praetorship when his colleagues were trying to debar him from the sacrifices because of his infirmity. What piles of decorations would he have accumulated with a different enemy? [106] For it makes the greatest of differences in what historical circumstances each man's heroism occurs. What civic crowns did Trebia, Ticinus, or Trasimenus bestow? What crown was won at Cannae where flight was the summit of courage? Others certainly have conquered men but Sergius conquered fortune also. [107] Who could possibly compile a list of outstanding geniuses, when the field comprises so many different areas of study and such a variety of subjects and writings—unless, perhaps, it can be agreed that there was none more inspired than the Greek poet Homer, whether he is judged by the success or by the content of his work. [108] A comment of Alexander the Great's is relevant here (for it is most appropriate and least invidious if such presumptuous assessments are made by the most distinguished of judges). After a golden casket of perfumes richly encrusted with pearls and precious stones had been captured in the booty won from Darius king of Persia, Alexander's friends were pointing out various uses for it, but the king, a battle-soiled soldier who had no time

for perfumes, replied "No! Let it be used instead to hold texts of Homer, so that the most precious product of the human mind might be preserved in the richest possible product of human craftmanship."

[109] Alexander also ordered that the home and household of the poet Pindar be spared during the sack of Thebes. He restored the birthplace of Aristotle, combining with his outstandingly famous exploits equally outstanding evidence of his kindness.

Apollo exposed the killers of the poet Archilochus at Delphi. When the leading tragic poet Sophocles died during the Spartan siege of Athens, Father Liber ordered his burial, frequently warning the Spartan king Lysander in dreams to permit the burial of the god's favorite. Lysander asked who had died in Athens. He had no difficulty working out which of those named the god meant and duly ordered a truce for the funeral.

[110] The tyrant Dionysius, who was normally cruel and proud, sent a ship bedecked with garlands to meet Plato, the high priest of wisdom; and, riding in a chariot drawn by four white horses, met him in person when he disembarked. Isocrates sold a single speech for twenty talents. The leading Athenian orator Aeschines read the speech he had made as prosecutor to the Rhodians but then went on to read them Demosthenes' defense speech which had driven him into exile. When they admired it, he told them that they would have admired it even more had they heard it from the orator himself. As a result of his own misfortune he had thus become a weighty witness to his enemy's case.

[111] As a general, Thucydides was exiled by the Athenians, but as an historian he was recalled, his compatriots admiring the eloquence of the man whose military skills they had condemned. Weighty evidence was also offered of Menander's standing as a comic poet when the kings of Egypt and Macedon sent a fleet and ambassadors to bring him to them; but even weightier evidence was offered by his own preference of literary merit to royal fortune.

[112] Leading citizens of Rome, too, have borne witness even to foreigners. When Gnaeus Pompeius, at the end of the Mithridatic war, was about to enter the house of the eminent professor of philosophy, Posidonius, he forbade his lictor to knock in the usual manner and he to whom East and West bowed in submission, bowed the fasces to the door of learning. When the distinguished embassy of three leading Athenian philosophers visited Rome, Cato the Censor, after listening to Carneades, advised that the ambassadors be sent on their way as quickly as possible because, when Carneades was expounding an argument, it was difficult to tell where truth lay. [113] How customs change! Whereas this Cato had on other occasions recommended the wholesale expulsion of Greeks from Italy, his great-grandson, Cato of Utica, brought one philosopher home with him after a spell abroad as military tribune, and another after he had been on an embassy to Cyprus. Thus of the two Catos, the elder is remembered for having driven out and the younger for having introduced the same language.

[114] But let us also review the renown of our fellow-Romans. The elder Scipio Africanus ordered that a statue of Ennius be placed in his own tomb and that the famous surname or rather, trophy, which he derived from a third of the world, be read together with the poet's epitaph over his mortal remains. The deified Augustus overrode the modesty of Virgil's will and forbade the burning of his works, thus providing a more convincing testimonial to his poetic genius than would have been achieved by authorial commendation.

[115] In the library established by Asinius Pollio, the first in the world to be endowed from the spoils of war, the only statue of a living person to be set up was that of Marcus Varro. This crowning honor, awarded by a leading orator and citizen to Varro alone out of the numerous distinguished intellectuals living at the time was no less glorious in my opinion than the actual naval crown awarded to him by Pompey for his part in the war against the pirates.

[116] In fact, for those interested in following them up, there are countless examples of Roman preeminence, since that race alone has produced more outstanding individuals in every field of excellence than all other countries put together. But how could I justify not singling you out for mention, Marcus Tullius? By which outstanding characteristic can I most aptly highlight your preeminence? What could be more appropriate than the unanimous decree of the most illustrious people in the world, selecting out of your entire life the achievements of your consulship alone? [117] As a result of your speech, the tribes rejected the agrarian law, that is, their very livelihood. As a result of your advice, they forgave Roscius, the proposer of the theater law, and accepted with good grace the inferiority implied by the allocation of seating. As a result of your eloquence, the sons of the proscribed were ashamed to seek public office. It was your brilliance which put Catiline to flight; it was you who

proscribed Mark Antony. Hail, first citizen to receive the title father of his country, first civilian to win a triumph and a laurel wreath for eloquence, father of oratory and Latin literature; winner indeed, in the words of your former enemy the dictator Caesar, of laurels greater than those of any triumph, inasmuch as it is greater to have advanced so far the frontiers of Rome's genius than those of her empire.

[118] Moving on to the remaining qualities of mind, there are those who have distinguished themselves above all others by their wisdom; among the Romans, those who have acquired surnames such as Catus and Corculus, [119] and among the Greeks, Socrates, who was placed before all men in this respect by the oracle of Pythian Apollo. It was men, on the other hand, who placed Chilon of Sparta on a footing with the oracles, by consecrating in letters of gold at Delphi his three famous precepts. These are as follows: "Know thyself"; "Nothing in excess"; and "The companion of debt and litigation is misery." The whole of Greece, moreover, followed in his funeral procession, after he died of joy on the occasion of his son's Olympic victory.

The most renowned instances of the gift of divination and a sort of communion with the celestial gods were the Sibyl among women and among men the Greek Melampus and the Roman Marcius.

[120] Only once since the foundation of Rome has the title "most excellent of men" been awarded by the Senate on oath—to Scipio Nasica, who was nonetheless stigmatized by the populace who rejected him on two occasions when he stood for election. At the end of his life, he was not allowed to die in his native land; no more, indeed, than Socrates, although judged the wisest of men by Apollo, was allowed to die unfettered by chains. Sulpicia, daughter of Paterculus and wife of Fulvius Flaccus, was on one occasion declared "purest of women" by a consensus of the Roman matrons. She was elected from a short-list of one hundred women to dedicate the statue of Venus in accordance with the Sibylline books. On another occasion, Claudia was so designated by means of a religious test, when the Mother of the Gods was brought to Rome.

[121] There have been countless examples of conspicuous devotion throughout the world but Rome offers one which stands out from all the others. A plebeian woman, whose name is not recorded because she was of humble origin, had recently given birth. She obtained permission to visit her mother, who was in prison as a punishment. She was always searched beforehand by the jailer to prevent her bringing in food, but she was caught feeding her parent with her own breast milk. As a result of this marvel, the daughter's devotion was rewarded with the mother's freedom and both were given maintenance for life. The place where the marvel occurred was consecrated to Pietas (Duty) and a temple to that goddess was built on the very site of the prison in the consulship of C. Quinctius and M'. Acilius, where the theater of Marcellus now stands.

[122] When two snakes were caught in his house, the father of the Gracchi was told by the oracle that he himself would live, provided "that he killed the snake of the opposite sex." He, however, replied, "No: kill my snake instead. Cornelia is young and still able to bear children." This effectively saved his wife's life and served the interests of his country. He died soon afterwards. M. Lepidus died for love of his wife Appuleia after divorcing her. P. Rutilius, while suffering from a mild illness, heard that his brother had been defeated in the election for the consulship and died on the spot. P. Catienus Philotimus was so attached to his patron that he threw himself on the dead man's funeral pyre, even though he had been made heir to the whole of his property.

[123] The individuals who have excelled in the various arts and sciences are beyond counting; yet they must be touched on in our anthology of human achievement. Outstanding in astrology, then, was Berosus, to whom, on account of his inspired predictions, the Athenians at public expense erected a statue with a gilded tongue in the gymnasium. Outstanding in philology was Apollodorus, whom the Amphictyons of Greece honored. In medicine, Hippocrates excelled. He predicted a plague that was coming from Illyria and sent his pupils out to the various cities to give assistance; for which service the Greeks voted him the same honors which they had given Hercules. The same profession, in the person of Cleombrotus of Ceos, received a reward of one hundred talents at the Megalensian festival from King Ptolemy for saving the life of King Antiochus.

[124] Critobulus, too, won great renown for removing an arrow from King Philip's eye and treating his loss of the eye without disfiguring his face. But the greatest renown of all goes to Asclepiades of Prusa. He founded a new sect, spurned the envoys and promises of Mithridates, devised a method of treating the sick with wine, and retrieved a man from his funeral pyre and restored him to life. Above all, he made a pact with fortune that he would lose his credibility as a doctor should he himself ever fall ill in any way. And he

actually won his bet, because he died as a result of falling down stairs when a very old man.

[125] Outstanding tribute was paid by M. Marcellus to Archimedes' genius in geometry and technology when, at the capture of Syracuse, he ordered that he alone should be spared; an order that was, however, to no avail, owing to a soldier's ignorance. Honor was also accorded to Chersiphron of Cnossos for building the wonderful temple of Diana at Ephesus; to Philo for constructing a dockyard for four hundred ships at Athens; to Ctesibius who discovered the principle of the pneumatic pump and hydraulic engines; and to Dinochares who was surveyor to Alexander when he founded Alexandria in Egypt. It was Alexander who decreed that Apelles alone should paint his portrait, Pyrgoteles alone sculpt his statue, and Lysippos alone cast his effigy in bronze. There are many outstanding examples of all these arts.

[126] King Attalus bid one hundred talents for a single picture by the Theban artist Aristides. The dictator Caesar paid eighty talents for a pair of paintings by Timomachus, a *Medea* and an *Ajax,* to dedicate in his temple of Venus Genetrix. King Candaules paid its weight in gold for a painting of considerable size by Bularchus which depicted the destruction of the Magnesians. King Demetrius, nicknamed the Besieger, did not fire Rhodes in case he burnt a picture by Protogenes which was stored in that part of the fortifications. [127] Praxiteles was renowned for his marble statues, especially that of Venus at Cnidos which was notorious for the insane passion it inspired in a certain young man and for the value set on it by King Nicomedes, who tried to take it in payment for a large debt owed him by the Cnideans. Jupiter at Olympus bears daily testimony to the genius of Phidias as do Capitoline Jupiter and Ephesian Diana to that of Mentor who engraved the vessels consecrated to them.

[128] The highest price to date for a man born into slavery has been, to the best of my knowledge, the sum paid for Daphnis, a skilled grammarian, who was sold at auction by Attius of Pisaurum to Marcus Scaurus, the leading statesman, for 700,000 sesterces.

This sum has been exceeded quite considerably in our own day by actors, but these men were purchasing their own freedom: [129] the actor Roscius, it should be recalled, was already in the time of our ancestors reputed to be earning 500,000 sesterces a year. At this point, someone might perhaps expect me to mention the paymaster of the recent Armenian war fought on account of Tiridates: Nero manumitted him for

the sum of 13,000,000 sesterces. This price, however, reflected the value of the war rather than that of the slave himself; as surely as it was the lust of the buyer rather than the inherent beauty of the slave which caused Clutorius Priscus to buy Paezon, one of Sejanus' eunuchs, for 50,000,000 sesterces. He was able to pull off this scandalous deal at a time of national mourning, when nobody had the chance to expose him.

*The next section (130–52) deals with the quality of life and the nature of happiness. Only the opening is included here, which sets the tone for the following discussion and asks the question, "What is happiness?"*

[130] Of all the peoples in the whole world it is the Roman race which is outstanding in terms of virtue. As far as happiness is concerned, no one can say who has excelled, since each person defines happiness in his own way in accordance with his own disposition. In fact, if we want to reach an accurate verdict and exclude all the flatteries of fortune when making our decision, no human being is happy. When fortune deals generously and kindly with him, a man can justly be called not unhappy. Even supposing that other misfortunes are lacking, there is always the fear that fortune might grow weary and once that fear is entertained, happiness has no firm foundation. [131] What of the saying that no man is wise all the time? If only as many people as possible would regard it as untrue and not as an oracular utterance! Delusory and ingenious in their self-deception, mortal men make their calculations in the manner of the Thracian tribe which puts into a pot stone counters of different colors, corresponding to each day's experience, and on the last day counts out the separate colors and thus makes its judgment on each individual. [132] But supposing that this man traced the seeds of his misfortune to the very day praised as happy by a gleaming white stone? How many people have been prostrated by the acquisition of power? How many have been destroyed and plunged into direst suffering by their goods; if "goods" they can be called for yielding for the time being a fleeting hour's pleasure? And so it goes on: one day passes judgment on another, but only the last day passes judgment on them all and for that reason we should not put our trust in any one day. What of the fact that good things are not equal to bad, even when they are of equal number, and that no joy can compensate for the smallest grief? Alas, what pointless and ignorant precision! We are counting the days when it is their weight that we are seeking!

## AFTERWORD

Pliny's *Natural History* must still be considered the most successful work of its kind in the Western world: it held the field as the most authoritative encyclopedia of scientific knowledge for almost fifteen hundred years. The large size of the *Natural History* led to its being excerpted and epitomized, but even so, it did not suffer the fate of so much of Livy's history, and it continued to be read and copied throughout antiquity. Sometime in the third century A.D., Julius Solinus compiled a compendium that he called *A Collection of Memorable Things* (*Collectanea Memorabilium Rerum*), which takes most of its information about curiosities of the world from Pliny. This short work was extremely popular during the Middle Ages—around 150 manuscripts survive—and was sometimes known by the title *Polyhistor* because of the wide range of topics covered. But it never replaced the *Natural History,* which is one of those few works for which we have fragments of manuscripts that date back to Roman antiquity. Another work like Solinus's from roughly the same period is the *Book of Medicine* (*Liber Medicinalis*) of Quintus Serenus, a medical textbook in verse that draws heavily on the *Natural History*. It experienced a surge in popularity in the ninth and tenth centuries. Another late antique compilation of his medical books by an unknown author, known as *Pliny's Medicine* (*Medicina Plinii*), was also popular among medieval readers. But Pliny himself remained the ultimate authority and continued to be read in whole or in part. Indeed, it is likely that the enormous popularity of Pliny's work contributed to the eventual disappearance of earlier, less successful Roman encyclopedias, such as those by Varro and Verrius Flaccus. A number of authors from the early Middle Ages appear to have had firsthand access to Pliny, including Bede. There was a copy of the *Natural History* in the court library of Charlemagne, reflecting the interests of his resident scholars, Alcuin and Dungal, both of whom probably had encountered Pliny in Northumbria or Ireland. Abridgments remained popular, the most successful of them being produced in Oxford in the twelfth century when Robert of Cricklade compressed the thirty-seven books of Pliny into nine, entitled, without irony, *The Defloration of Pliny's Natural History*.

Not surprisingly, Pliny was a popular author with Renaissance scholars, who appreciated the *Natural History* as an entry into the world of Roman science and cultural life. Petrarch's copy, which he bought in Mantua in 1350, is filled with marginalia, especially in the first fifteen books and the last four, reflecting his particular interests in Roman life and art. But for the most part the humanists were interested in correcting the text that they found in their late medieval manuscripts, for the obscure and difficult subject matter of much of the *Natural History* had rendered it particularly prone to disruption in the process of copying. The first printed edition appeared in Venice in 1469 from the press of Johannes de Spira, which stimulated further interest in the text. The great fifteenth-century scholar Angelo Poliziano carefully investigated five different manuscripts, collated their variant readings, and commented copiously on the work. Later in the century, over the course of twenty months in 1491–92, the Roman scholar Ermolao Barbaro produced his influential *Castigationes Plinianae,* with a claim to have corrected 5,000 errors in the text. But men of culture and learning were still reading the *Natural History* for its content. Barbaro's contemporary Lippo Brandolini memorized all the chapter headings and the most important facts from all of its thirty-seven books.

Translations into the vernacular made the work accessible to cultured gentlemen who were less able to cope with Pliny's difficult Latin. While there were early translations into Italian and French, the English-speaking world had to wait until 1601 for the first complete translation by the indefatigable Philemon Holland. Since the seventeenth century the demand for translations slowed as the progress of science rendered Pliny's Roman knowledge less relevant to the general reader. But even as the practical utility of Pliny's work receded, interest among classical scholars also dimmed, thanks in no small part to unflattering judgments like that of the influential Latinist Eduard Norden, who pronounced, "His work, from a stylistic point of view, is among the worst we have." Nowadays there is renewed interest in the *Natural History* as a document of Roman culture, written in the style of a busy man of affairs, much of whose life outside the public arena was consumed with books.

# STATIUS

(Publius Papinius Statius, ca. A.D. 47–ca. 96)

WE KNOW VERY LITTLE ABOUT STATIUS OTHER THAN WHAT HE TELLS US IN HIS poetry, and what little we do know is derived mostly from just two poems in the *Silvae*, 3.5, urging his wife to return with him to Naples, and 5.3, a lament on the death of his father. He was born sometime between A.D. 45 and 50, when Claudius was emperor, in Naples, which, despite being not much more than a hundred miles from Rome, was more Greek than Roman. Settled by colonists from Greece before the traditional date for the founding of Rome, Naples in the first century A.D. was one of the leading centers of Greek culture anywhere in the Mediterranean.

Greek models had always been of fundamental importance to Roman poets, but Statius felt their influence particularly strongly. Although all of his surviving poetry is in Latin, he probably regarded himself as Greek, intellectually, if not politically. His personal circumstances will have intensified this cultural influence still further, for his father, with whom he seems to have had an affectionate relationship, was one of the leading professional Greek poets of the time, winning competitions at the Augustalia in Naples, and at the Pythian, Nemean, and Isthmian festivals in mainland Greece (poetry contests were not held at Olympia). The Athenians even set up a statue of him, the base of which still survives. It would be interesting to know whether Statius *père* ever competed against Nero (for whose vicious way of eliminating artistic rivals, see p. 349). In his lament for him, Statius emphasizes his father's ability to elucidate to his pupils even the most abstruse and difficult Greek poets (*Silvae* 5.3.156–58):

> You were learned in explaining the poems of the son of Battus,
> the hidden depths of dark Lycophron, contorted Sophron,
> and the secrets of subtle Corinna.

The son of Battus is Callimachus, the doyen of learned Hellenistic poetry; Lycophron's *Alexandra* is an endearingly puzzling poem on the Trojan War, with the prophetess Cassandra foretelling the familiar story in sometimes impenetrably enigmatic circumlocutions; though his mimes were admired by Plato and Theocritus, Sophron is perhaps rather a surprise in this catalog of obscure poets; most of what little of Corinna's poetry survives is not remarkably sophisticated, but she once defeated even Pindar himself in a poetry contest (a result said to have moved Pindar to call her a "Boeotian sow"). Statius's own poetry rarely if ever plumbs the depths of elaborate obscurity to be found in the more arcane Hellenistic poetry, but he certainly inherited from them a commitment to the virtues of painstaking and careful composition.

This elaborate care is evident in all his surviving poetry, not only in his *Thebaid,* his twelve-book epic on the legendary siege of Thebes, published around A.D. 92, but also in his other works that followed, his *Silvae,* five books of occasional poems on a wide variety of topics, and his *Achilleid,* a second epic, telling the life of Achilles, but breaking off after 167 lines of Book 2, presumably because of Statius's death. In bidding farewell to the *Thebaid* at the end of Book 12, Statius declares that he "labored long into the night on it for twice six years" (811–12), that is, the poem was written at the admirably slow rate of hardly more than two lines per day. He repeats this claim to meticulous composition in the *Silvae,* when he describes the *Thebaid* as "tortured with much filing" (4.7.25–26). In the prose preface to Book 1 of the *Silvae,* Statius explicitly denies that those poems were carefully written, professing that most were composed in a single day, with none requiring more than two days: "these little books just flowed from my pen, with a sudden passionate inspiration and a kind of pleasurable haste." Lurking behind this self-deprecation is not only the conventional modesty with which a poet sent off his work to a patron but also an implicit contrast with the recently published *Thebaid.* Even so, it is reasonable to suppose that the *Silvae* were, in fact, composed relatively expeditiously. Scholarly opinion nowadays is radically divided on the literary merits of Statius's poetry, and perhaps of the *Silvae* most of all. Those eager to damn the *Silvae* as trite compositions on conventional themes naturally welcome Statius's admission of hasty production. Whatever the truth may be, composition will have been greatly facilitated by the highly rhetorical nature of the poetry. Seven poems in the *Silvae,* almost a quarter of the total, are funeral laments, and Statius adopted the rhetorical prescription established in the schools of declamation for the composing of speeches on this topic. These poems all contain the same basic elements: an introduction, stating the cause of sorrow and summoning the mourners; praise of the dead person; lamentation; an account of the final illness, death and burial; consolation for the mourners. To readers nowadays, out of sympathy with rhetoric as a pervasive force in poetry, it may seem to detract from the sincerity of Statius's lament for his father (5.3) that it is couched in the same terms as that for his patron's dead parrot (2.4). But that would be to judge the *Silvae* by anachronistic criteria. Ovid had similarly included in the *Amores* laments for his mistress's parrot (2.6) and for Tibullus (3.9); the whimsical tone of the former elegy does not diminish the genuine regret Ovid expresses for the premature demise of his fellow love elegist.

The modern reader may likewise find difficulty in coming to terms with the uncritical praise lavished by Statius on the oppressive and tyrannical emperor Domitian, addressed in six of the *Silvae.* It is hard to suppose that Tacitus, who played a prominent role in public life during Domitian's reign, would have found much to commend in such poems, but it is only fair to observe that, whereas Tacitus wrote his condemnations of the imperial system from the safety of the post-Domitian period, Statius had no such haven, for he probably died not long before Domitian's richly deserved assassination.

The plot of the *Thebaid* is fairly simple. Polynices and Eteocles, the sons of Oedipus, rule Thebes by turns, each being king for a year at a time, while the other stays away from the city. In exile at Argos, Polynices musters an army to take permanent control of Thebes. The fighting at Thebes does not begin until Book 7, and continues until Book 11, in which the two brothers kill each other in a duel and Creon, Oedipus's brother, becomes king of Thebes. In Book 12, the Argive widows appeal to the Athenian king, Theseus, to force Creon to allow them to recover their husbands' bodies for burial. Theseus marches on Thebes and kills Creon, thus bringing to an end the curse that has haunted the Theban royal house for three generations.

Despite the essential simplicity of the plot, it can be difficult at times to follow the narrative, since the poem is very episodic, with the adventures and exploits of so many characters vying for our attention. There is no well-defined primary hero, to match Homer's Achilles or Odysseus, or Apollonius of Rhodes's Jason, or Virgil's Aeneas. The recurrence of similar scene types involving different heroes, however carefully crafted in themselves, seems to many readers to dissipate the overall artistic tension, diminishing the dramatic impetus as the poem builds to the showdown between Polynices and Eteocles.

With its legendary heroes watched over by the Olympian gods, the *Thebaid* is set firmly in the tradition of epic poetry. The expedition against Thebes had been the subject of one of the poems in the early Greek epic cycle, but that work is now almost entirely lost, and little can be said about Statius's borrowings from it, whether directly or through intermediary sources. Whereas Statius owes much in a general way to the Homeric conventions for epic, his debt to Virgil is more specific. In particular, the structure of the *Thebaid* is closely parallel to that of the *Aeneid,* with a marked division halfway through, as the fighting in Italy and at Thebes gets under way in the seventh book of the respective poems and culminates in the duel between the leaders of the two armies, Aeneas and Turnus, Polynices and Eteocles. The opening words of the *Thebaid* echo the proem to Lucan's *Civil War,* and Statius shows his great admiration for Lucan in the poem he wrote for his widow, Polla Argentaria, to commemorate the anniversary of his death (*Silvae* 2.7). Lucan's influence on the *Thebaid,* however, is rarely very prominent. Perhaps most notable in this respect is Statius's fascination with gruesome battle scenes: the final lines of Book 8, in which Tydeus eats the head of his fallen enemy Melanippus, is in the same ghastly tradition fostered by Lucan and also by the tragedies of his uncle, Seneca.

One further possible epic model should also be mentioned, if only to be dismissed. In the early fourth century B.C., Antimachus of Colophon wrote a *Thebaid,* of which only a few fragments survive. Antimachus appears to have been a forerunner to the Hellenistic type of subtle and sophisticated poetry, so he might well have appealed to Statius's father (see above). Opinions of his poetry in antiquity were, however, very diverse. Plato encouraged him, and Quintilian, Statius's contemporary, ranked him as second (admittedly a distant second) only to Homer as a Greek epic poet. On the other hand, Callimachus described one of his other works as "a fat script, not well polished," and Catullus disparaged him as turgid, and appealing only to the unenlightened masses. There is no passage in Statius's poem that is demonstrably indebted to the sparse fragments of Antimachus's epic, whereas there are several where Statius diverges from the earlier version, and, in any case, since Antimachus's heroes seem to have arrived at Thebes only in his twenty-fourth and final book, there is only limited overlap in content with Statius's narrative.

The unchallenged supremacy of Virgil's *Aeneid* inevitably conditions our expectations when we read any subsequent Latin epic poem. Aeneas kills Turnus in a fit of rage in the final scene of the *Aeneid,* and hence we might expect the *Thebaid* to come to a rapid conclusion after the duel between Polynices and Eteocles, which brings the expedition against Thebes to an end. Book 12 might therefore seem somewhat anticlimactic, a prolonging of the narrative to tidy up loose ends with the burial of the heroes and the freeing of Thebes from Creon's rule. Such a diminuendo is, however, quite typical of epic: the *Iliad* concludes with the ransoming and burial of Hector, the *Odyssey* with the reuniting of Odysseus and Penelope and the reconciliation with the kinsmen of the slaughtered suitors, and we cannot even be sure that Virgil, who died with the *Aeneid* unfinished, intended his epic to end with such abrupt violence.

Book 12 therefore conforms to the epic convention of not ending with a climactic scene on the field of battle. The contrast with the *Aeneid* in this respect is very emphatic. Virgil's warring deities may be reconciled in Aeneas's favor, and Aeneas may have gained the victory over Turnus, but much is left unresolved, and the future still looks bleak. The *Thebaid* ends on a much more positive note, with every hope for peace and prosperity in Thebes. In concluding his poem in this way, Statius is heavily influenced by Euripides's *Suppliant Women,* which has much the same plot as that of Book 12. Other representations of the Theban story in Athenian tragedy on which he draws include Aeschylus's *Seven against Thebes,* Sophocles's *Antigone,* and Euripides's *Phoenician Women.* Seneca's Theban tragedies, *Oedipus* and *Phoenician Women,* as well as his *Thyestes,* with its theme of deadly fraternal discord, offered Statius a more contemporary Roman tragic model, especially in their fascination with the detailed description of the horrors of war and murder.

Statius concludes the poem by declaring his hope that the *Thebaid* will gain immortal fame, but with a crucial qualification, that it should not aspire to rival the *Aeneid* (12.814–17):

> Live! This is my prayer,
> Nor ever try to match the heavenly *Aeneid*,
> But follow from afar and evermore
> Worship its steps.

Such deference to Virgil recurs in the *Silvae*, at 4.4.51ff. and 4.7.25ff., and there can be no doubt that Statius's own modesty contributed greatly to the generally rather dismissive attitude to his poetry in the nineteenth and twentieth centuries. More recently, however, scholars have come to reassess the literary qualities of the *Thebaid* much more positively.

## THEBAID

### Book 12

*Statius's retelling of the myth of the Seven against Thebes begins in Book 1 with an aged Oedipus calling down the Furies on his two sons, Eteocles and Polynices. According to their agreement to alternate in the kingship of Thebes, Polynices is at Argos, where he is welcomed by the king Adrastus and marries his daughter Argia. There is more supernatural action in Book 2, which opens with an appearance by the ghost of Laius, Oedipus's slain father, who incites Eteocles to break his pact with Polynices. Adrastus's other son-in-law escapes an ambush set for him as he was journeying to Thebes to reclaim the throne for Polynices. Argos decides to go to war against Thebes, and the preparations are described in Books 4 and 5, when the army marches on Thebes led by seven great heroes: Adrastus, Polynices, Tydeus, Capaneus, Parthenopaeus, Hippomedon, and Amphiaraus. The army is aided along its route by Hypsipyle, who is caring for an infant, Opheltes. When Opheltes is killed by a serpent in Book 5, the Seven establish the Nemean Games, one of the four great Panhellenic festivals of classical times, and the games are celebrated in Book 6. As in the Aeneid, the actual hostilities begin with the second half of the poem, and in Book 7 the first of the Seven to perish is the seer Amphiaraus, who is swallowed up into the Underworld. Battle rages throughout the next three books, with the deaths of first Tydeus, then Hippomedon and Partheopaeus. Finally the impiety of Capaneus is punished by Jupiter, who strikes him with a thunderbolt as he attempts to breach the walls of Thebes.*

*The climax is reached in Book 11, when the two brothers, Polynices and Eteocles, kill each other in single combat. This is followed by the suicide of their mother (and Oedipus's), Jocasta, and the expulsion of Oedipus from the city. The army of the Argives is led home by Adrastus, the only one of the Seven to survive, while Creon assumes the throne of Thebes and forbids the burial of the Argive dead. The final book supplies closure. It opens on the battlefield, where the Thebans go to bury their dead, including Creon's son, Menoeceus, who is cremated on a splendid pyre.*

Not yet had wakeful dawn sloped every star
From heaven, and the moon with failing horn
Still watched the approach of day, when from the East,
Dispelling now the trembling shades of night,
Aurora rose, preparing the vast sky
To greet the sun's return. From Theban homes,
Now fewer, men roamed out complaining of
The night's delay. Though then at last they'd found
Rest after battle and first sleep, yet peace
So frail, forbade repose and victory          10
Remembered savage war. They hardly had
The heart at first to venture forth or dared
Dismantle the defences or unbar
The gates completely. Their old fears again
Stood clear before their eyes and horror of
The empty battlefield. As sailors tossed
On ocean's endless swell, when first they land,
Fancy the shore is swaying, they were dazed,
Amazed that nothing threatened and felt sure
The squadrons of the dead rose up again.          20
So doves, when they have seen a tawny snake

Climb to their sill on some high loop-holed tower,
Hustle their young inside and make a fence
Of claws to guard the nest and wave their wings,
Not meant for war, in battle; then, though he
Has soon dropped back, the snowy flock still fears
The naked air and when at last they fly
Still tremble and look back from heaven's vault.
      Forth to the lifeless multitude they went,
30 Prostrate remnants of war, wherever woe
And sorrow, blood-stained leaders, urged them on.
Weapons some saw, some corpses, some just heads
Severed beside strange bodies not their own.
Others wept over chariots, with sad words—
Since nothing else remained—for horses now
Bereft, and others printed kisses on
Huge wounds lamenting valor sacrificed.
Cold heaps are pulled apart. They light on swords
And spears clutched in shorn hands and arrows stuck
40 Standing in eyes, and many find no trace
Of their own dead and rush in brimming grief,
Grief ready everywhere. But sad disputes
Rose over mangled corpses, who should pay
Death's honors and conduct the funerals.
And often, too, over their enemies
They wept deluded—Fortune's mockery!—
With no sure means of knowing what dark blood
The poor souls should avoid or trample on.
But those whose homes escaped unharmed and hearts
50 Were free of woe roamed through the Argive camp
And fired the empty tents or searched to find
The spot—the end of war affords the chance—
Where Tydeus lay dust-grimed, or if the chasm
Of ravished Amphiaraus still gaped wide,
Or where Heaven's foe was now and if along
His limbs celestial embers were alive.
In tears the day was done; the Evening Star,
Late-rising, did not move them from the field;
They loved their weeping, relished tragedy.
60 No one went home, but all night long they sat
Beside the dead and, voicing grief in turn,
By tears and wailing drove the wolves away.
Nor did the sweetly-shining stars avail
Nor the long flow of tears to close their eyes.
Thrice had the Star of Day fought with the Dawn,
When from the ravished mountainsides there came
The glory of the groves, the mighty trunks
Of high Teumesus and Cithaeron's woods,
Good friend of funeral flames. On high-built pyres
70 Bright blazed the vitals of the ruined race.

In the last tribute Theban ghosts rejoiced,
But from the Argive troops, unburied, came
Sad protests; wailing loud they flitted round
The fires forbidden them. The wicked shade
Of Savage Eteocles was given rites
By no means royal. His brother, by decree,
Was deemed an Argive still: his shade once more
Was driven forth to exile as before.
      But for Menoeceus no plebeian pyre
Thebes and the king, his father, would permit.     80
To him they raised no customary pile
Of paltry timber, but a martial mound
Of chariots and shields and Argive arms
Of every kind. Upon his foes' huge heap
He lay, as conqueror, his locks adorned
With holy braids and bay, the branch of peace,
As once on kindled Oeta Hercules
Reclined rejoicing, summoned by the stars.
Then living victims, captured Argives, steeds
In harness, Creon sacrificed to give     90
Solace to his brave soul, and then at last
His father's grief burst forth: 'Oh, son of mine,
Had not too proud a passion fired your heart
For great-souled glory, you had shared with me
The reverence of Thebes and ruled in turn.
But now you embitter every joy that comes
And the unwelcome burden of my reign.
Though for your deathless valor's sake you dwell
In heaven's vault with heaven's company,
To me for ever you shall be a god     100
For tears. Though Thebes build altars, dedicate
High temples, let your father mourn alone.
And now, alas, what worthy obsequies,
What fitting honors, can I lavish? None,
Not though I had the power to fuse your ashes
With fatal Argos and Mycenae's ruins,
And on them throw myself whose royal state,
Whose life, is owed—Oh crime! oh wickedness!—
To my son's blood. Has the same day, the same
Immoral war, sent you to Hell's dark depths,     110
My boy, and those dire brothers? Does the doom
Of grief match me with Oedipus? The ghosts
We mourn, good Jupiter, how like they are!
Receive these tributes to your victory,
Tributes unparalleled. Receive, my son,
This scepter my hand holds, this crown that rings
My royal brow, your bitter gifts to me
Your father. So as king, yes, king, the ghost
Of Eteocles in grief may gaze at you!'

120 Thus speaking, from his hand and hair he shed
His royal emblems and in wilder rage
Continued: 'Yes, world may call me cruel,
Heartless, if I forbid the Argive dead
To burn with you. Would I could vivify
Their senses and expel their guilty souls
From the air above and Hell below, and join
The vultures and wild beasts myself and guide
Them to the corpses of those wicked kings.
Alas that time and fostering earth will rot
130 Them down as they lie there! Therefore again
And yet again I order: Let no one
Dare give the Argive fire to succor them,
Or he shall pay the price of death and fill
The count of stolen corpses with his own.
By great Menoeceus and the gods on high
I swear it!' So he spoke on that dire day,
And then his courtiers hustled him away.

*The widows of the Argives set out for Thebes to bury their
husbands, but they encounter a wounded Argive soldier,
Ornytus, who warns them of Creon's ban. The women
deflect their route to Athens, there to seek the help of
Theseus, all but Argia, Polynices's widow, who makes her
way to the battlefield before Thebes, accompanied only
by her elderly attendant, Menoetes. There she searches for
Polynices's corpse by torchlight.*

Meanwhile, drawn by the news, poor
souls, a band
Of weeping women, widowed and bereft,
140 Hastened from empty Argos like a troop
Of captives. Each had her own bleeding heart,
All were attired alike, hair hanging down
On breasts and skirts high-gathered. Down their cheeks
Blood dripped where cruel nails had torn, soft arms
Were bruised and swollen with beating. First among
Those shattered souls, queen of their sable band,
Argia, frail and helpless, sought the road
Sinking on her sad retinue and soon
Rising again. No thought of palace now
150 Or father; one sure loyalty, one name
Upon her lips, her darling Polynices.
Mycenae she disdained and wished her home
Had been at Dirce and the ill-starred walls
Of Cadmus' city. Next Deipyle,
Bold as her sister, brought from Calydon
Women who mingled with an Argive group
For Tydeus' obsequies. The poor princess

Knew of her husband's crime, his impious laws,
Yet love, ill-starred, could pardon everything.
Neacle, following, fierce yet pitiful,                    160
In fitting woe bewailed Hippomedon.
Then came the prophet's wicked wife to erect,
Alas, an empty pyre. Leading the last
Column of mourners came the votaress
Of Dian, son-less, and Evadne too,
Weighed down by woe; one protests bitterly
Over her bold lad's feats; one, mindful of
Her mighty husband, walks wild-eyed in tears
And vents her anger on the vaulted stars.
From groves of high Lycaeus Hecate                       170
Groaned as she watched them go, and when they
reached
The double shoreline Ino from the tomb
Sorrowed and Ceres, though her own grief hurt,
Wept and placed mystic fires to guide their way.
The queen of Heaven herself conducted them
Through secret byways and concealed their path
Lest their own folk should meet them and forbid
Their journey and the glorious enterprise
Should fail. And Iris too was given the charge
Of cherishing those princes' bodies there.               180
She laved decaying limbs with mystic dews,
Ambrosial essences, that they might win
Longer resistance, waiting for the pyre,
Nor decompose before the saving fire.
Pale from a yawning wound, his face befouled
Ornytus (separated from his friends
And slowed by his fresh hurt) made his weak way,
Propped on a broken spear, in timid stealth
Through pathless solitudes. He was amazed
By a strange tumult in that lonely place,                190
A flock of women, as he saw, the sole
Survivors of the Argives. Where and why
They went he did not question—it was clear—
But sadly hailed them: 'Vain, poor women, vain
Your journey! Do you hope for funeral fires
For your dead menfolk? Guards keep vigil here,
Guards of the ghosts, and give the king the count
Of bodies left unburied. Nowhere tears:
If any men approach, they're forced to flee.
Only the birds and beasts have access there.             200
Will good king Creon grant *your* grief its due?
Sooner will you find mercy from the altars
Of pitiless Busiris or the stalls
Where Thracian horses hungered or from gods
Of Sicily. Yes, if I know his mind,

He may arrest you as you plead. Then not
Upon your husbands' bodies will you lie
But far from those dear shades he'll butcher you.
Flee while the road is safe! Return to Argos
210 And carve, as still you may, your missing names
On empty sepulchres and summon back
Those absent souls to tombs untenanted.
Or else ask aid from Athens. For report
Says Theseus is at hand in triumph from
His conquest of the Amazons. By war
And weapons Creon must be forced towards
Humanity.' Then tears stood horror-struck,
The passion that impelled them stupefied,
And on each face a single pallor froze.
220 So when a tigress' famished roar is borne
To gentle heifers on the breeze and at
The sound all pastures shudder, on them all
Falls a great terror—which of them will please,
Whose shoulders will that hunger mount and seize.
        At once opinions differed, riven by
Far-varied feelings. Some would press their suit
At Thebes before proud Creon, some would see
If help may come from Athens' clemency;
Return—last in their thoughts—would be disgrace.
230 And then Argia suddenly conceived
A passion more than woman's and, her sex
Abandoned, planned a monstrous enterprise.
She chose to face and flout—heartbreaking hope
Of glorious danger—that land's wicked laws,
A land to which no bride of Rhodope,
Nor any daughter of the Colchian snows,
Ringed by her virgin escort would have gone.
Thus she contrived a ruse to rid herself
Of her companions and confront alone
240 The bloodstained monarch and the pitiless gods;
Such scorn of her own life, such rashness in
Her grief so great! True love and loyalty
And her pure passion drove. Before her eyes
In every action he was manifest,
Now guest (poor girl!), now bridegroom at the altar,
Now gentle husband, now in his grim helm
Sadly embracing her and, as he left,
Looking and looking back. But in her mind
No picture rose more often than of him
250 Returning naked from the bloody field,
Crying for burial. Such frenzies wrung
Her anxious heartstrings, and she loved a ghost
With purest ardor. Turning then to her
Companions: 'You', she said, 'call out

The arms of Attica and Marathon,
And on your loyal task may fortune smile.
Let me, who was the only cause of your
Disaster, penetrate the walls of Thebes
And bear the king's first thunder. On the gates
Of that fierce city I'll not beat unheard.          260
There dwell my husband's parents, there his sisters;
I shall not enter Thebes to be ignored.
And do not call me back. Vast urgencies
And my prophetic soul are driving me.'
Saying no more, she chose Menoetes then
Alone, the former guard and counselor
Of her youth's innocence, and, though she had
No knowledge or experience of all
That countryside, she rushed off in hot haste
Along the way that Ornytus had come.          270
Then when she saw the partners of her woe
Left well behind 'Was I to wait', she cried,
'For Theseus' slow decision while you rot—
It breaks my heart—on your foes' battleground?
Wait till his captains and her clever seer
Gave their consent to war? And all the while
Your body wastes away. I'd rather give
The vultures my own carcass! Even now,
If senses still survive among the shades,
Your faithful soul protests to Hell's dark gods          280
That I am late, am cruel. Woe, ah woe,
If you lie naked still, and woe, if you
Perhaps are buried; in either case the crime
Is mine. Is sorrow impotent? Is death
Nowhere and Creon pitiless? Good cheer
You give me, Ornytus!' Across the fields
Of Megara she hastened, striding on,
And all who met her showed the way ahead,
Shocked by her plight, revering her distress.
On her grim way she went, no thought, no sound          290
Dismaying her, but gaining confidence
From surfeit of disaster—feared indeed
Rather than fearing. So in Phrygia,
While Dindymus rebounds at night with cries,
The ecstatic leader of the Corybants
Speeds to the stream of pine-girt Simois,
Her blood claimed by the goddess, given the blade,
And on her brow the holy band displayed.
        Now in the western waves the sun concealed
His flaming chariot, to rise again          300
From other seas, but she, her weight of toil
Beguiled by grief, knew not that day had gone.
As darkness draped the fields she had no fear

But pressed ahead through rocks where no path ran,
Through secret forests, black at shining noon,
And timbers poised to fall and ploughland scarred
By hidden dykes and on, untroubled, through
Rivers, past slumbering beasts and threatening dens
Of frightful monsters. Such the power of grief
310  And passion! Poor Menoetes lagged behind
Ashamed, and marveled at the striding pace
Of his frail ward. On what abodes of men
And beasts did her harsh cries of woe not strike?
How often the track was lost and, as she strayed,
Her torch's comfort failed and icy dark
Conquered the flame! And now Cithaeron's flank
Sloped to their weary way and broadened wide,
And good Menoetes, out of breath, almost
Exhausted, spoke: 'Unless the hope that springs
320  From labor ended lulls me, Thebes, I think,
Is near, Argia, and the dead who lack
A burial. Beside us rise great waves
Of tainted air and through the void huge birds
Are flying back. This is that cruel field.
The walls are close. See how the plain projects
The battlements' huge shadow and the fires
Flicker upon the watchtowers as they die.
The walls are there. The silence of the night
A while ago was deeper and the stars
330  Alone relieved the sable pall of dark.'
Argia shuddered and stretched out her hand
Towards the walls: 'Thebes, where I longed to be,
Now city of my foes, yet even so
A soil beloved, if you restore to me
My husband's shade unharmed. See how I make
My entry—the first time—my choice attire,
The throng escorting me, me, daughter-in-law
Of mighty Oedipus! My prayer is not
Outrageous. As your guest I ask of you
340  A pyre, a body and your leave to mourn.
Give me back him, I beg, who from his realm
Was driven to exile, forced away by war,
Him whom your judgment held unworthy of
His father's throne. And you, my dearest, come
If ghosts have any form and spirits roam
Freed of their flesh, show me the way yourself,
And lead me, if I'm worthy, to your corpse.'
A shepherd's cottage standing near at hand
She entered and revived her weary torch,
350  Then rushed in frenzy to the frightful field.
So Ceres in her loss once lit her torch
From Etna's rocks and shone the shifting light

Of its huge flame upon the facing shores
Of Sicily and Italy, as through
The dust she tracked the sable ravisher
And his vast wheel-ruts. Huge Enceladus
Echoed her frantic wails and shot his fire
To light her way. The cry 'Persephone'
Went forth from forests, rivers, clouds and sea;
Only Dis' court called not Persephone.          360
   Her faithful guardian warned his frantic charge
To lower her torch and move in secret stealth.
Thus she, a princess lately held in awe
Among the Argive towns, outrageous aim
Of suitors, and her nation's proudest hope,
Through the night's terrors, with the foe
    nearby,
Went on alone without a guide through grass
Slimy with gore and arms that barred her way,
Not trembling at the dark or at the throng
Of spirits round her and the ghosts that grieved   370
For their lost bodies. Often her blind steps
Trample on swords and spears and never know,
Her labor's only purpose to avoid
Corpses, for each she thinks may be her own.
Her shrewd gaze searches bodies and she bends
To turn them on their backs and strains her sight,
Blaming the stars that shed too little light.

*Juno comes to Argia's aid, entreating the moon to cast more*
*light upon the scene. Argia finds the body before Antigone,*
*the sister of Polynices, arrives, intent upon providing the*
*last rites to her brother in spite of Creon's ban. The two*
*of them cleanse the body in the river Ismenus and then*
*attempt to burn it in a still-smoldering pyre, but this, as*
*it happens, was Eteocles's. It bursts into two competing*
*flames, attracting the attention of guards who lead the two*
*women away to Creon.*

   It chanced that Juno from her mighty lord's
Embrace had stolen and was on her way
Through the deep slumberous shadows of the sky    380
To Theseus' walls, that Pallas might be swayed
And Athens warmly greet the suppliants.
From heaven's height she saw Argia below
In undeserved exhaustion wandering
In futile search, and sorrowed at the sight.
Then, meeting the Moon's team, she fronted them
And spoke in quiet tones: 'Grant me, sweet Moon,
A small request, if you have some regard
For Juno. True it is at Jove's command

390 You brazenly contrived that triple night
When Hercules—but that old quarrel's past.
Now you can do me service. You see there
Argia, the votaress most dear to me,
Astray in the black night, too weak to find
Her husband in the darkness. Your light too
Is faint and clouded now. Extend your horns
And press your orbit nearer to the earth
Than you are wont. And Sleep, who is leaning here,
Handling your dewy reins, send him upon
400 The Theban sentinels.' She had hardly done
When through the parted clouds the Moon displayed
Her whole huge orb, the shadows fled in fear;
The lustre of the stars was shorn; the glare
Was almost more than Juno herself could bear.

     First in the flooding light she recognized
Her handiwork (poor soul!), her husband's cloak,
Though the design was hidden and the proud
Purple mourned drenched in blood, and while
    she called
Upon the gods and thought that this alone
410 Was left of him she loved, she saw the corpse
Half trampled in the dust. Then heart, voice, sight
Failed and grief locked her tears. Down to his face
She fell prostrate and with her kisses sought
His life-breath lost and from his hair and robe—
A cherished relic—chose a clot of blood.
At last her voice returned: 'Is this, my love,
How I see you, the leader who marched forth
To win your rightful realm, the son-in-law
Of powerful Adrastus? Is it thus
420 I meet your triumph? Raise your darling face,
Your sightless eyes to me. Argia comes
To your dear Thebes. Lead me within the walls,
Show me your fine ancestral seat, return
My hospitality. Alas, what words!
Your fatherland is but the naked earth
On which you lie. What quarrel now? At least
Your brother does not reign. Did you move none
Of your dear ones to tears? Where is your
    mother?
And where Antigone whose fame's so fine?
430 For me alone you lie, for me alone
You were defeated. Many a time I said,
"Why march? Why claim a scepter that's refused?
Argos is yours and in my father's palace
You shall be king. Here is long majesty,
Here power unshared." But why do I complain?
*I* gave you war, *I* begged for it from my

Sad father—to embrace you now like this!
Yet it is well, ye gods. Accept my thanks,
Fortune. My journey's far-off hope's fulfilled:
I've found his body whole. But what a wound, 440
How wide and deep! Was this a brother's work?
Where lies that plunderer? Had I the power,
I would outdo the birds and rob the beasts.
Or has that devil a pyre? But your homeland
Shall not see you unflamed. You too shall burn
And tears refused to kings shall fall for you,
And my bereft devotion shall endure
And tend your tomb for ever and our son
Shall be my sorrow's witness, in your stead
Small Polynices comforting our bed.' 450
    Now with another torch and other groans
Piteous Antigone approached the scene
Of death, her hope scarce won to leave the walls.
For hour by hour a constant guard was kept,
The king's own order given that she be held;
Watches were shortened, braziers multiplied.
So to her brother and the gods she made
Excuse for her delay, and when for one
Short moment the grim guard succumbed to sleep
She rushed out from the walls, beside herself, 460
Like a young lioness that terrifies
The pastures when, her fury free at last,
She first without her mother rages wild.
She lost no time: she knew the cruel field
And where amid the dust her brother lay.
Menoetes, briefly resting, saw her come
And hushed the moans of his dear charge. But when
Antigone's keen ears had caught the last
Low sound and by the stars and either torch
She saw a figure, robed in black with hair 470
Disheveled, face befouled with clotting blood,
'Whose body do you seek? The night is mine,'
She cried, 'Who dares come here?' No answer came
At first, but in her cloak Argia wrapped
Her face and her dead husband's, suddenly
Afraid and woe forgotten a brief while.
The more determined then Antigone
Rebuked her suspect silence, challenging
Menoetes and herself, but both stood lost,
Rooted in silence. Then Argia at last 480
Unveiled her face and spoke, yet still embraced
The body: 'If you come to search with me
In this stale blood of battle, if you too
Fear Creon's harsh command, I can for sure
With confidence reveal myself to you.

If you are wretched—tears I surely see
And signs of grief—join me in mutual trust.
I am Adrastus' daughter, his princess—
Ay me! Who overhears? I've come to tend
490 My darling Polynices' pyre despite
The royal ban.' Astounded, shuddering,
Antigone broke in: 'Do you fear *me*,
*Me*—oh, blind chance!—now partner in your woe?
Mine are the limbs you hold and mine the death
You sorrow for. I yield, take him. Ah, shame,
A sister's love so slothful! She came first!'
Then both beside him sank and both embraced him,
Their tears and tresses mingled eagerly,
Sharing his limbs, then in alternate grief
500 Back to his face, enjoying, each in turn,
His head and breast. And then as they recalled
Brother and husband, each her own, and shared
The tale of Thebes' and Argos' tragedy,
Argia spoke more fully of her woes:
'By our join sacrament of secret grief
I swear to you, and by this shade we share
And every watching star, not his lost throne,
Or native land or his dear mother's love
He longed for, wandering exile that he was,
510 But you alone, of you by day and night,
He spoke, Antigone. I counted less,
He left me easily. Yet you perhaps
Saw him from some high tower before the crime,
Giving the standards to the Argive troops,
And from the line of battle he looked back,
Saluting you with sword and nodding crest:
I far away. What god drove them to such
Extremity of anger? Did your prayers
Count nothing? Did his brother too refuse
520 Your plea?' Antigone had started to
Expound the causes and Fate's cruelty,
But loyal Menoetes warned them both: 'Come now,
Turn to your task. The stars already fade
In fear of day's approach. Finish your toil.
The time for tears will come and you shall weep
When you have lit the pyre.'
                              Not far away
A rushing roar betrayed Ismenus' banks
Where he flowed turbid still and foul with blood.
Here by united effort the frail pair
530 Carried the poor torn body and with arms
No stronger their companion joined his aid.
So once his sisters in the Po's warm stream
Laved poor charred Phaethon, Hyperion's son,

And there, as soon as he was buried, rose
the weeping poplars on the river-bank.
When they had purged the body in the river,
The grace of death restored, last kisses given,
They searched for fire, poor souls, but all around
In crumbling pits the ash was cold and dead
And every pyre at rest. But one, by chance     540
Or heaven's will, survived, the pyre ordained
To burn the body of fierce Eteocles:
Fortune perhaps was framing yet again
A scene of horror, or the Fates had kept
The fire for strife. Here both with eager eyes
Saw on the blackened logs a feeble glow
Yet living and wept tears of joy, though who
Was burnt was still to find; yet they besought
Whoever it might be to favor them
And graciously admit a partner to          550
His own last ashes and unite their ghosts.
Again the brothers! When the devouring fire
First touched the corpse, the whole pyre shook
    and cast
The newcomer aside. A flame shot up
Two-headed and each severed point shone bright.
As though the Furies' torches had been set
To battle by the death-pale lord of Hell,
Each fiery column threatened, each essayed
To outsoar the other. Even the timbers sagged
As the weight moved. Argia, terrified,        560
Screamed: 'We are ruined! We have raised
    spent wrath!
It was his brother! Who but he—so fierce—
Would refuse welcome to a homeless ghost?
That charred belt, broken shield, I recognize.
It was his brother! See, the flames retreat
Then clash again. That wicked hatred lives,
Still lives. War achieved nothing! While you fought,
Poor wretches, Creon won. Your realm is gone.
Why anger now? For whom such fury? Cease
Your threats. And you too, exiled everywhere,    570
Denied your rights for ever, yield at last.
Your wife, your sister, make this prayer, or else
To part you we shall plunge into the flames.'
        She had hardly finished when a sudden shock
Swayed the high rooftops and the countryside,
The quarreling pyre yawned wider and the guards,
Whose sleep itself had fashioned scenes of woe,
Were roughly roused. Straightway the troops
    rushed out
And spread a ring of arms on every side.

580 As they approached the old man's heart alone
Felt fear. The women, standing plain before
The pyre, confessed they'd scorned Creon's fierce
    command,
And owned their subterfuge with never a care,
Since the whole corpse, they saw, had been consumed.
They courted cruel death, the hope of doom
Sprang wide and bold, as each vied in the theft,
One of her brother's, one her husband's corpse.
They pressed their case in turn: 'I found the body',
'And I the fire', 'I came in loyalty',
590 'And I in love'. With happy hearts they asked
For savage punishment and thrust their arms
Into the chains. Gone the respect that first
Had marked their converse: anger now and hate
Are clear, so loud the shouts from each side ring;
They even dragged their captors to the king.

*Under Juno's guidance, the Argive women reach Athens*
*and its Altar of Compassion as Theseus returns in triumph*
*after his victory over the Amazons. Evadne, the widow of*
*Capaneus, tells Theseus of Creon's edict, and without hesi-*
*tation Theseus marches against Thebes to restore justice.*

    Now Juno, far away, to Athens' walls,
Assured of Pallas' grace, led the distraught
Women of Argos, no less moved herself,
And won the people's favor for their grief
600 And horror for their tears. With her own hand
She gave them olive branches and the white
Chaplets of suppliants, instructing them
To walk with faces veiled and eyes downcast,
Bearing their empty urns that held no ghost.
In that fine city crowds of every age
Streamed out and filled the housetops and the streets.
Whence came that swarm and whence so many souls
Grieving as one? Though the evil's cause was still
Unknown, groans rose already. Through both throngs
610 The goddess mingled, teaching the whole tale,
Their race, the deaths they mourned, the aim they
    sought.
And they in varying voices loud and long
Railed at Thebes' laws and Creon's savagery.
So bitterly in foreign caves the birds
Of Thrace with their maimed voices rail against
Divided love and Tereus' wickedness.
    At the town's center stands a temple raised
To no almighty god. It is the seat
Of kind Compassion, sanctified by souls

In grief and misery. She never lacks    620
New suppliants nor will reject a prayer.
Whoever asks is heard and day and night
One may approach and win the goddess' heart
By piteous tears alone. Her worship claims
Small cost: no incense-flame will she accept,
No welling blood. With tears her altar flows,
And offerings hang there, sad severed tresses,
And garments left behind when Fortune changed.
A gentle grove surrounds it, hallowed growth
Of bay, with holy braids and suppliant    630
Olive. And there no statue stands, and no
Metal is trusted with the form divine:
In hearts and minds the goddess loves to dwell.
Always the place has throngs of sufferers,
In fear or want. Only the fortunate
Know not her altars there. Its founders were,
Fame tells, the sons of Hercules, preserved
In battle after that great hero died.
Fame fails the facts: the truth one should believe
Is that the gods themselves, in Athens' land    640
Guests ever welcome, as they once gave laws
And ceremonies and the seed that came
Down to the empty earth, so in this place
For souls in travail they had sanctified
A common refuge where the wrath and threats
Of monarchs should be far removed and chance
Withdraw from sacraments of righteousness.
Already nations beyond counting knew
That shrine. Assembled there the vanquished came,
Conquered in war, and exiles driven from    650
Ancestral lands, kings who had lost their crowns,
And those whose crime was error, and they all
Sought peace. Anon this hospitable land
Tamed Oedipus' mad rage, protected dead
Olynthus, gave Orestes refuge from
His mother. Thither, guided by the crowd,
The Argive women made their anxious way.
The throng of earlier pilgrims yielded place
And in a moment troubled hearts found peace.
So, when across the deep their own north wind    660
Has chased a flock of cranes and Egypt comes
In sight, they spread their skein and fill the sky,
Choiring a happy clamor, and rejoice
Beneath a cloudless vault to scorn the snow
And thaw cold winter in the Nile below.
    And now the people's shouts of glad applause
Soaring to heaven's height, and trumpet calls,
Happy in war's discharge, announced the approach

Of Theseus in his laurelled chariot,
670 Home from harsh battles with the Amazons.
Before him spoils were borne, and chariots,
Tokens of cruel war, and sorry steeds,
And wagons piled with crests, and broken axes
Used by the Amazons to cleave the woods
And frozen Azov. Girdles too there were,
Ablaze with gems, and quivers light and slim,
And shields their owners' blood made hideous.
But they themselves, still fearless, still denied
Their sex. They made no mean lament and scorned
680 To supplicate; only their keen eyes sought
The virgin goddess', Pallas', sanctuary.
All were agog to see the conqueror,
Drawn by his four white steeds. Hippolyte
No less caught every eye, a face that charmed
And now a willing bride. The townswomen
Eyed her askance and whispered, marveling
That she had breached her country's rigid laws—
Her glossy hair, those breasts quite hidden by
Her robe—and that a foreign queen should join
690 Herself to mighty Athens and should go
To bear a child whose father was her foe.

        The sorrowing Argive women, moving from
The altar where they knelt, in wonder watched
The triumph with its train of spoils, and back
Into their thoughts their conquered husbands came.
And when the victor stayed his chariot
And from its stately height inquired the cause
That brought them and with kind attention bade
Them make their plea, Evadne dared speak first:
700 'Proud warrior son of Aegeus, king for whom
From our disaster Fortune has disclosed
Great seeds of sudden glory, we are not
An alien folk, we have no guilt of crime.
Our home was Argos and our husbands kings,
And brave men too, alas! What need was there
To rouse a sevenfold host and set to rights
Agenor's homeland? We do not complain
That they were killed. That is the law of war,
The chance of arms. But they who fell were no
710 Monsters from Etna's caverns, no two-formed
Centaurs of Ossa. I say nothing of
Their birth and noble fathers. They were men,
Illustrious Theseus, men of flesh and blood,
Born to the selfsame stars, the selfsame lot
Of human souls, with the same food and drink,
As you. Yet Creon has forbidden them
A pyre, and like the Furies' father or

The ferryman of Lethe bars them from
The gates of Hell and holds them in suspense
Between the heavens and the Underworld.      720
Alas for sovereign nature! Where is he
Who hurls the unjust back? Where are the gods?
Where Athens? Seven times the rising dawn,
Her horses terrified, has turned away
As they lie there. The starry vault of heaven
With all its radiance averts its light
In horror. Now even wolves and vultures loathe
The ghastly meal and battlefield that loads
With its foul stench the breezes and the sky.
For how much now remains? Just let him grant      730
Leave to collect bare bones and clotted gore.
Make haste, high-honored Athens! Such revenge
Becomes you well, before the folk of Thrace
And Thessaly lament and every land
In all the world that looks to burn its dead
and honor spirits with the last due rites.
What limits has his fury? True, we fought,
But hate has fallen, death has smothered rage.
You too—Fame teaches us your noble deeds—
Did not give Cercyon or Sinis to      740
Wild beasts to savage and allowed a pyre
To cruel Sciron. Tanais, I'm sure,
Scene of your triumph, smoked with funeral pyres
Of Amazons. Accept this triumph too.
Grant Earth and Heaven above and Hell below
This one exploit, if you relieved from fear
Your native Marathon and homes of Crete
And if the old crone's tears who welcomed you
Were not in vain. So may you never lack
Pallas' support in war and Hercules      750
Not grudge your matching feats, and may your mother
Ever behold you in your chariot
Victorious, and Athens never know
Defeat or come to make a prayer like mine!'
    She ceased and all of them with hands
        outstretched
Were loud in her support. Great Theseus flushed,
Moved by their tears. Then righteous anger stung:
'What fury', he cried, 'has thus transformed the course
And custom of our kings? The Greeks had no
Such hearts at my departure, when I sought      760
The Black Sea and the snows of Scythia.
Whence this new madness? Do you think,
    grim Creon,
Theseus was conquered? I am here, not tired,
Be sure, of bloodshed. This my spear still thirsts

For guilty gore. I shall not wait. Away
My trusty Phegeus! Turn your steed and ride
Forthwith to Thebes' high towers and proclaim
The Argives shall have pyres or Thebes have war.'
Forgetting warfare and the weary march,
770 With heartening words he gave his flagging men
Fresh vigor. So a bull who has regained
His wives and pastures and has ceased to fight,
If a fresh challenge bellows from the woods,
Though head and neck drip blood, he once again
Prepares for battle, stamps the ground and hides
His wounds in dust and stifles every groan.
Pallas herself, striking her shield, aroused
Medusa, Gorgon guardian of her breast,
That Libyan horror, and at once the swarm
Of serpents towered up and gazed towards
780     Thebes.
Though the Attic troops were still not set to go,
Doomed Thebes was trembling at the trump of woe.
        At once to war were fired not only those
Who had returned from Scythia and shared
The triumph: all the countryside called up
Its untrained sons to arms and, mustering,
They followed Theseus' standard unconstrained.
There were the folk whose labor vexed the fields
Of chilly Brauron and Monychia,
790 Piraeus too, for anxious mariners
Firm land, and Marathon not famous yet
For her proud Persian triumph. Men were sent
From homes of Celeus and Icarius,
Hosts to their own high gods, and green Melaeneae,
And forested Aegaleos and Parnes,
Firm friend of vines, and Lycabessos, best
For oily olives. Tillers of perfumed
Hymettus came, the fierce Alaean too,
And proud Acharnae who with ivy clad
800 Bare Bacchic wands. And Sunion they left,
Far mark for eastward ships, where Aegeus fell,
Duped by the lying sail from Crete, and gave
The roaming deep his name. From Salamis
Some came and from Eleusis, Ceres' town,
Hanging their ploughs up as they went to war,
And those Callirhoe enfolds in her
Nine wandering channels and Elissos who,
Privy to Orithyia's rape, concealed
Beneath his banks the lover from the North.
810 That hilltop too was emptied for the fight
Where gods strove mightily until a new
Tree rose from doubting rocks and by its long

Shadow dissevered the retreating sea.
To Thebes' great battlements Hippolyte
Would have gone too, leading her Amazons,
But the sure hope of her now swelling womb
Restrained her and her husband urged her to
Drop thoughts of war and hang her quiver instead,
In thanks for service done, above their bed.
        When Theseus saw them bent on war, ablaze     820
With well-loved weapons, giving their dear children
Quick kisses, brief embraces, standing high
In his proud chariot he spoke: 'Soldiers,
Who march with me to save the nations' laws
And covenants world-wide, take heed to match
Our mission. On our side stands clear the entire
Favor of gods and men and our true guide,
Nature, and all the silent Underworld;
On theirs the troops of Vengeance, busied in
Thebes' city, and the snake-haired Sisters lead     830
Their standards. March then, in the confidence
Of our great cause!' With that, he hurled his spear
And at a storming pace began the march.
So, when upon the Northern pole Jove plants
His cloudy steps and terrifies the stars
As winter comes, the Wind-god's portals burst
And storms take heart, resenting their long peace,
And all the arctic whistles in the gales;
Then seas and mountains roar, the blind clouds clash,
The thunder revels and the lightnings flash.     840
Loud groaned the pounded earth, the heavy hooves
Changed the green fields, the trampled countryside
Expired beneath the countless companies
Of horse and foot, nor did the flash of arms
Die in the murk of dust but flickered far
Into the sky and spears blazed in the clouds.
The night too and the quiet of the dark
They added to their labors. Rivalry
Was huge to force the march, to be the first
To shout from some high ground the sight of
        Thebes,     850
To plant a spear on their proud battlements.
But Theseus, in the distance, dwarfed the ranks
With his enormous shield. Around its boss
He bore, the prelude to his own renown,
The hundred cities and the hundred walls
Of Crete, and in the labyrinth himself,
Bending the struggling bull's great shaggy neck,
Throttling him with both hands and brawny arms,
His own head held away to avoid the horns.
As he goes forth to battle, shielded by     860

That gruesome blazon, fear grips every heart.
Twice they see Theseus, twice his
     blood-drenched hands;
And he remembers his fine feats of old,
Those fellow-victims and the door once feared,
And Ariadne death-pale as she found
     The guiding thread she gave him all unwound.

*The execution of Argia and Antigone is interrupted by the*
*news of the approaching Athenian army. The battle is con-*
*cluded swiftly as the exhausted Thebans are routed and*
*Creon is killed by Theseus. Order is restored, as the Thebans*
*now welcome Theseus and the Argive women bury their*
*dead. Statius concludes with a brief epilogue, predicting*
*enduring success for his poem, second only to the* Aeneid.

     Meanwhile, their hands chained fast behind
          their backs,
     Widowed Argia and Antigone
     Were led by Creon to their doom. Both proud
870  And happy in their love of death, they held
     Their throats to meet the blade and disappoint
     The cruel king, when suddenly Phegeus
     Stood there with Theseus' message. His green branch
     Of innocent olive spoke of peace, but war
     Was in his words; he threatened war,
     Storming and hectoring, too conscious of
     His orders and repeating that his king
     Was near already and the countryside
     All covered with his cohorts. Creon stood
880  Tossed in a sea of troubles, deep in doubt;
     Defiance faltered and first anger cooled.
     He braced himself and feigned a sullen smile:
     'Have we established then so poor a proof
     Of Argos' ruin? See, a second time
     Our walls are plagued. So be it! Let them come.
     But when the battle's done, let none complain:
     The law of the defeated stands the same.'
     But then he saw the daylight darkening
     In the thick dust and all the heights of Thebes
890  Losing their skylines. Even so, pale-faced,
     He bade his people arm and his own arms
     Be brought, and suddenly to his dismay
     Right in the palace's central hall he saw
     The Furies and Menoeceus there in tears
     And the Argives gloating on their burning pyres.
     That day, that day! when peace which Thebes had won
     By so much bloodshed perished! From their shrines
     They wrenched the arms so lately hung and donned
     Helmets unplumbed and fractured shields with spears

Still caked in gore; no grace, no elegance          900
Of sword or quiver now, no eye-catching
Rider and steed. No confidence remained
In ramparts, every length of wall gaped wide.
Gates cried for their defenses, taken by
The previous foe; the battlements were gone,
Thrown down by Capaneus; the soldiery,
Weak and exhausted, gave no final kiss
To wives or children; parents, in despair,
Were too distraught to utter any prayer.

     Theseus, meanwhile, seeing the gleam of day          910
Brighten through broken cloudbanks and the sun's
First glint on weapons, leapt down to the plain
Where still below the walls the bodies lay
Unburied. Breathing through his dusty helm
The grim reek of the tainted air, he groaned
And high his righteous rage for battle flared.
One honor at least the Theban ruler paid
The wretched Argives, that he placed his line
Of battle in that second war not where
The bodies themselves lay—or else, to save          920
Intact their mangled carnage, he preferred,
That criminal, a virgin soil to drink
Cruel gore again. And now the War-goddess
With very different summons calls the two
Peoples to fight. Not on both sides are heard
Trumpets, on both sides battle-cries. On one
The troops stand feeble, holding lowered swords
And slackened slings, all futile. They gave ground,
And drawing back their armor showed old wounds
Still bleeding. The Athenian captains too          930
Now lost their zeal, their fierceness ebbed away
And valor, sure of victory, relaxed.
So gales storm less when woods do not dispute
Their wrath and with no shore mad waves are mute.

     But when the Sea-god's son, Theseus, raised high
His Marathonian spear, whose cruel shade
Fell on the foe, and filling the grim field
Its bright point flashed, as if from Haemus' peak
Mars drove his chariot with Flight and Death
Riding his rushing wheels, so death-pale fear          940
Routed the fainting Thebans. But Theseus
Disdained to profit by their flight and scorned
Such easy blood. The others' valor spent
Its fury on the gore of rank and file.
So dogs and weakly wolves delight in prey
That's faint and fallen: mighty lions feed
On fury. Yet he slew Olenius
And Lamyrus, one drawing arrows from
His quiver, the other lifting a great stone,

950 And Alcetus' three sons who trusted in
　　Their triple strength. Three far-flung spears in turn
　　United them: in Phyleus' breast the steel
　　Was buried, Helops bit it in his teeth,
　　And through Iapys' shoulder passed the third.
　　And now he made for Haemon, riding high
　　Above his four-horse chariot, and hurled
　　A monstrous shaft. The horses, terrified,
　　Swerved, yet the spear's long trajectory passed
　　Through two and thirsted for a triple wound,
960 But struck the pole between and fell to ground.
　　　　Yet only Creon filled his hopes and prayers,
　　For him alone throughout the battlefield
　　His fearsome challenge called and called again.
　　On a far front he saw him, urging on
　　His squadrons, vainly shouting his last threats.
　　His bodyguard all fled, but Theseus' own
　　Left him at his command, relying on
　　The gods and his own prowess. Creon checked
　　His men and called them back, but when he saw
970 Hatred there too, with one last burst of rage,
　　Frenzy of doom, courage of looming death,
　　'You'll not fight now', he cried, 'with Amazons.
　　These are no groups of girls, be sure. Here men
　　Fight in raw battle, we, who sent to death
　　Great Tydeus, furious Hippomedon
　　and giant Capaneus. What lunacy
　　Hurls you to war, you rogue? Those you avenge,
　　Look, lie there dead!' With that he launched his spear—
　　To perish, futile, in the great shield's rim.
980 And Theseus, flaring, mocked his words and aim,
　　Poising his steel-tipped shaft for a huge throw,
　　And thundered proudly first: 'You Argive spirits,
　　To whom I give this victim, open wide
　　Hell's chaos and alert the avenging Furies!
　　See, Creon comes!' At once his quivering spear
　　Parted the air. Then, where the metal links
　　In slender sequence formed the layered mail
　　Of his cuirass it fell. His wicked blood
　　Spurted through countless chinks and, his wild eyes
990 Rolling their last, he sank. Then over him
　　Stern Theseus stood and stripped his arms and cried,
　　'Now will you wish to give dead foes the fire,
　　Their due, now give the vanquished burial?'
　　　　Standards advanced from either side with cries
　　Of mutual trust and the two armies joined.
　　So on the field of battle peace was sworn,
　　Theseus a welcome guest. They begged him to
　　Enter within their walls and deem their homes

Worthy of him. Nor did the conqueror
Despise the dwellings of his enemy.                    1000
The womenfolk of Thebes rejoiced, as once
Ganges, subdued by Bacchic wands, was glad
To give the women's revels drunken praise.
And yonder, look, from Dirce's shady peak
The shouts of Argive women shook the stars,
And down they ran like raving Bacchanals
Called to their great god's war, as if they meant
To do or had just done some monstrous crime.
Fresh tears gushed forth as now they wept
　　　　for joy.
This way and that they sped unsure whom first        1010
To seek, great-hearted Theseus or Creon
Or their own dear ones: guiding sorrow led
Those grieving widowed women to their dead.
　　　　Though Heaven should swell my voice a
　　　　　　hundredfold
To free my heart, my strains could never match
Those funerals of kings and commoners,
Those lamentations shared, the tragic tale,
How bold Evadne sprang to have her fill
Of flames she loved and sought the thunderbolt
In that huge breast; how Tydeus' ill-starred wife      1020
Made her excuse for him as she lay there
And kissed his fierce corpse; how Argia told
Her sister of the watchmen's cruelty;
Or how poor Atalanta mourned her son,
Her son who kept his grace though blood was gone,
Her son for whom two armies grieved as one.
For such high themes would hardly have sufficed
Phoebus' first presence and a fine new fire,
And now this ship of mine, so long at sea,
Deserves at last the port where she would be.          1030
　　　　My *Thebaid*, on which for twelve long years
I burnt my midnight oil, will you endure
In far-off days to come, will you survive
Your author and be read? Already now
Your present fame has surely paved for you
A kindly path and at your outset makes
Your mark for men to come. Already now
You our great-hearted Caesar deigns to know;
Already too the youth of Italy
Learn and recite you. Live! That is my prayer,         1040
Nor try to match the heavenly *Aeneid*
But follow from afar and evermore
Worship its steps. Anon, if envy still
Should cloud you, it will die and honor due,
When I have passed away, shall walk with you.

## AFTERWORD

Statius's claim to instant fame, made in the last lines of the *Thebaid,* is predictive, a familiar poetic conceit, not a reportorial account of its reception by the reading public. In fact, there is no evidence for the contemporary impact of his epics or the *Silvae,* beyond the testimony of Juvenal, who uses him as an example of the writer who must prostitute his art to survive (*Satires* 7.83ff.):

> When Statius has made the city happy by fixing a day,
> there's a rush to hear his attractive voice and the strains of his darling
> *Thebaid.* He duly holds their hearts enthralled by his sweetness;
> and the people listen in total rapture. But when, with his verses,
> he has caused them all to break the benches in their wild excitement,
> he starves—unless he can sell his virgin *Agave* to Paris.

The people will crowd in to hear Statius recite his epic, but he needs to be able to sell a script to the famous pantomime Paris in order to make ends meet. Juvenal's satiric hyperbole does not tell us much about the actual reception of the *Thebaid,* and we do not detect its influence until much later in antiquity. This is not altogether surprising, since the *Thebaid* is the last surviving narrative poem until the fourth century, and the literary tastes of the intervening period tended to favor early Roman epic over the modern works of Lucan and, presumably, Statius. In the fourth century his influence is traceable in the small-scale epics of Claudian, and we find him being quoted by Servius in his commentary on Virgil. It was probably also about this time that notes were being compiled by readers of the *Thebaid,* some of which may have been incorporated into the generally uninteresting commentary on the whole poem attributed to a certain Lactantius Placidus, probably datable to the sixth century. A revival of enthusiasm for Statius in the third century A.D. might explain the curious and improbable story that the emperor Gordian I, who ruled for a few weeks in A.D. 238, wrote a poem about the deeds of Antoninus Pius and Marcus Aurelius in thirty books, taking Statius's unfinished *Achilleid* as its model. This revived interest continued until at least the sixth century when the commentary of Lactantius was compiled and we find Sidonius Apollinaris referring to him with approval.

In the Middle Ages, Statius comes into his own. Indeed, he became an important model for poets in both Latin and the vernacular languages. There were copies of the *Thebaid* and the *Achilleid* in the court library of Charlemagne, but the *Silvae* were unknown to medieval readers, surviving in only one manuscript, which was discovered in the fifteenth century and then soon lost. Statius was thus known primarily as the poet of the Theban cycle of myth, but like that other great source of mythology for the Middle Ages, Ovid's *Metamorphoses,* his text had to be made safe for Christian readers. A twelfth-century commentary on the *Thebaid,* by an author known to us as Pseudo-Fulgentius, provides useful insights into how this might be done. The entire poem is read as an allegory of the human soul, with Polynices and Eteocles personifying greed and lust, while God, in the form of Theseus, overcomes pride, personified in Creon. Statius himself was believed to have been a Christian, and this he tells us himself, when he appears in Dante's *Purgatorio* (22.67–73) and addresses Virgil:

> You did as he who goes by night and carries
> the lamp behind him—he is of no help
> to his own self but teaches those who follow—
>     when you declared: 'The ages are renewed;

justice and man's first time on earth return;
from Heaven a new progeny descends.'
        Through you I was a poet and, through you,
a Christian.

Dante's Statius informs us that it was after a reading of Virgil's messianic *Fourth Eclogue,* which was interpreted by medieval readers as a prediction of the birth of Christ, that he converted to the new religion. Dante then portrays Statius joining him in the ascent to Paradise. Total ignorance of the *Silvae,* which would have revealed some aspects of Statius's life as a pagan Roman, certainly assisted in the evolution of such readings. Boccaccio was also a serious reader of Statius, and among English writers, it was perhaps Chaucer who knew him best.

Surely the last time there was general excitement about Statius among the public, or at least the literary public, was in the fifteenth century, when his *Silvae* were rediscovered. The collection came to the public's attention by a rather circuitous route. While attending the Council of Constance in Switzerland in 1418, the Renaissance book hunter Poggio Bracciolini came across a manuscript containing this hitherto unknown work and had a copy made by a scribe whom he later described as "the most ignorant man alive." He sent this copy back to Florence, but nobody seems to have paid much attention to it for several decades. A commentary produced by the humanist Domizio Calderini in 1475 ignited a fierce scholarly debate that included the most important figure of the period, Angelo Poliziano, who ruthlessly exposed his competitors' errors of interpretation in a series of public lectures. The *Silvae* are still a battleground for classical scholars, although they have attracted less attention than the *Thebaid* or even the *Achilleid* in the continuing revival of critical interest in Statius that began in the late twentieth century.

# QUINTILIAN

### (Marcus Fabius Quintilianus, ca. A.D. 35–ca. 95)

LIKE MANY ANOTHER TEACHER, MARCUS FABIUS QUINTILIANUS MIGHT HAVE LABORED in virtual anonymity, acquiring fame only through the accomplishments of his famous pupils, had it not been for his success as an author. He was the first public professor of rhetoric in Rome, having been appointed to the post by the emperor Vespasian sometime around A.D. 70. His students included Pliny the Younger, and late in life Domitian retained him as tutor to his two grandnephews whom he intended to succeed him. It was a heady rise for one who had come from Spain as a young man to study rhetoric at Rome, but Quintilian would hardly be known to history were it not for the stunning success of his major work, the treatise known as *The Education of the Orator.*

Today a statue of Quintilian stands in the main square of his hometown of Calahorra, known as Calagurris in antiquity, located on the river Ebro not far from Zaragosa. The town had supported the Roman rebel Sertorius in 80–72 B.C. and fiercely resisted a siege by Pompey the Great, apparently earning thereby a reputation for military toughness, since Augustus at one time chose his bodyguard from its inhabitants. By the time Quintilian was born there, in about A.D. 35, it was a Romanized municipality, and the evidence appears to suggest that his father was a teacher there. Quintilian received his advanced education in Rome, however, where he studied with two famous teachers whose reputations were eclipsed by his, Remmius Palaemon, a grammarian, and the orator Domitius Afer. His schooling completed, Quintilian returned home to Calagurris, where he attracted the attention of the governor, Servius Sulpicius Galba, who brought the talented young man back to Rome with him in A.D. 68, when for a very brief time Galba became emperor. From this point on, Quintilian's career was tied to the capital city, where he opened a school for which he drew his salary from the public exchequer. He made quite a good living at it, too, according to the later satirist Juvenal (*Satires* 7.188), who complained, "so how does Quintilian have so many estates?"

After twenty years in this post, Quintilian retired from active teaching to write. His personal life had not been happy: his young wife had died when she was only nineteen, and the two sons whom he had had with her were also taken from him at an early age. Before he set his hand to write his masterpiece, probably around the year 90, Quintilian wrote and distributed a treatise, *On the Causes of the Corruption of Eloquence,* which has not survived, although some scholars used to think that Tacitus's *Dialogue about Orators* was actually Quintilian's lost work. The title supplies hints at some of his motivation in writing *The Education of the Orator*: to provide a guide for aspiring students of rhetoric so that this perceived decline might be reversed. Quintilian spearheaded a reaction against what he considered the degenerate style of the times, whose chief representative was Seneca. Quintilian's own views were deeply influenced by Cicero, not only in matters of style but in his conviction that the decline of eloquence was fundamentally a moral question.

**Figure 24:  Statue of an Orator**
An Etruscan statue of the early first century B.C., popularly known as the *Arringatore,* the "Speaker Delivering a Harangue."

---

Quintilian's great work was probably sent into circulation before the death of Domitian in A.D. 96. He dedicated it to Victorius Marcellus, a senator in his early thirties at the time, to whom the poet Statius also dedicated the fourth book of his *Silvae.* Quintilian's stated reason for this dedication, that the work might serve as a guide to Marcellus in the education of his young son Geta, provides the guiding rationale for the entire work, which is intended as a protreptic. The training of an orator begins in childhood, and this is the starting point for Quintilian's systematic survey of his method. The first book, from which our first selection is taken, is perhaps Quintilian's most original contribution to the vast ancient literature on rhetoric, offering a practical and humane survey of elementary education. In the second book, he introduces the first principles of rhetorical education, and follows, in Book 3, with a discussion of his principal authorities. In Books 4 through 6, he provides a technical treatment of the various parts of a speech and a discussion of how to arouse the emotions. Book 7 is primarily devoted to techniques for arranging a speech. Style is the focus of Books 8 and 9, illuminated with many examples from prose and poetry on effective methods to communicate with the audience. The most accessible section of the work is probably Book 10, in which Quintilian reviews the Greek and Latin authors whom the aspiring author ought to read and imitate. Some of his judgments might strike us as a bit odd. Not everyone, for example, will agree with his dismissive assessment of Ovid as "praiseworthy in parts" or his verdict that the death of

Valerius Flaccus was a great loss. But it must be remembered that he is not assessing literary quality per se, but the utility of the reading from a rhetorical point of view. Book 11 deals with some ancillary matters essential for successful public speaking, such as details of posture and dress, before the final book, from which our last selection is taken. It is here that Quintilian sums up his ideal of the orator, one that emphasizes the ethical dimension as much as the rhetorical (12.1.1): "a good man skilled in speaking."

## THE EDUCATION OF THE ORATOR

*The complete work in twelve books was probably published before the emperor Domitian's assassination in A.D. 96. It describes the training of a public speaker from infancy to maturity. Our selection begins with the first three sections of the first book, in which Quintilian deals with the education of a child. It offers a rare and fascinating glimpse of Roman attitudes toward childhood.*

### Book 1

### Chapter 1

#### Elementary Education

As soon as his son is born, the father should form the highest expectations of him. He will then be more careful about him from the start. There is no foundation for the complaint that only a small minority of human beings have been given the power to understand what is taught them, the majority being so slow-witted that they waste time and labor. On the contrary, you will find the greater number quick to reason and prompt to learn. This is natural to man: as birds are born for flying, horses for speed, beasts of prey for ferocity, so are we for mental activity and resourcefulness. This is why the soul is believed to have its origin in heaven. Dull and unteachable persons are no more normal products of human nature than prodigious and monstrous births [but these have been very few]. The proof of this is that the promise of many accomplishments appears in children, and when it fades with age, this is plainly due to the failure not of nature but of care. "But some have more talent than others." I agree: then some will achieve more and some less, but we never find one who has not achieved something by his efforts. A parent who grasps this must devote the keenest possible care, from the moment he becomes a parent, to fostering the promise of the orator to be.

First of all, make sure the nurses speak properly. Chrysippus wished them, had it been possible, to be philosophers; failing that, he would have us choose the best that our circumstances allowed. No doubt the more important point is their character; but they should also speak correctly. These are the first people the child will hear, theirs are the words he will try to copy and pronounce. We naturally retain most tenaciously what we learned when our minds were fresh: a flavor lasts a long time when the jar that absorbs it is new, and the dyes that change wool's pristine whiteness cannot be washed out. Indeed, the worse these impressions are, the more persistent they are. Good is easily changed to worse: can you ever hope to change bad to good? So do not let the child become accustomed, even in infancy, to a type of speech which he will have to unlearn.

As to the parents, I should wish them to be as highly educated as possible. (I do not mean only the fathers. We are told that the eloquence of the Gracchi owed much to their mother Cornelia, whose highly cultivated style is known also to posterity from her letters; Laelia, Gaius Laelius' daughter, is said to have echoed her father's elegance in her own conversation; and the speech delivered before the triumvirs by Hortensia. the daughter of Quintus Hortensius, is still read—and not just because it is by a woman.) However, those who have not been lucky enough to learn themselves should not for that reason take less trouble about their sons' teaching; on the contrary, it should make them all the more careful in other matters.

As to the slave boys with whom the child born to such high hopes is to be brought up, I would repeat what I said about the nurses. Regarding his *paedagogi*, I would add that they should either be thoroughly educated (this is the first priority) or know themselves to be uneducated. Nothing can be worse than those who, having got just beyond the alphabet, delude themselves that they have acquired some knowledge. They both scorn to give up the role of instructor and, conceiving that they have a certain title to authority (a frequent source of vanity in this class of persons), become imperious and sometimes even brutal teachers of their own foolishness. Their failings have an equally bad moral effect: Alexander's *paedogogus*, Leonides, according to Diogenes of Babylon, infected him with some faults which clung to him as a result of his childhood education even when he was a grown man and had become a mighty king.

If anyone thinks I am asking too much, let him reflect that we are educating an orator, which is a hard enough business even if there is nothing lacking for his education, and that more and greater difficulties are still to come. He needs continuous application, first-class teachers, and many different branches of study. We must therefore recommend the optimum procedure: if anyone finds this too hard, the fault will lie with the individual, not with the principle. But if it is not possible to secure the sort of nurses, young companions, and *paedagogi* that I should most prefer, let there be anyway one person always at hand who knows the right ways of speaking, and who can correct on the spot any faulty expression used by the others in the pupil's presence, and so stop it becoming a habit. But it must be understood that this is only a remedy: what I said above is the ideal course.

I prefer a boy to begin by speaking Greek, because he will imbibe Latin, which more people speak, whether we will or no; and also because he will need to be taught Greek learning first, it being the source of ours too. However, I do not want a fetish to be made of this, so that he spends a long time speaking and learning nothing but Greek, as is commonly done. This gives rise to many faults both of pronunciation (owing to the distortion of the mouth produced by forming foreign sounds) and of language, because the Greek idioms stick in the mind through continual usage and persist obstinately even in speaking the other tongue. So Latin ought to follow not far behind, and soon proceed side by side with Greek. The result will be that, once we begin to pay equal attention to both languages, neither will get in the way of the other.

Some have held that children should not be taught to read under the age of seven, on the ground that this is the earliest age which can grasp the subjects taught and sustain the effort. This view is attributed to Hesiod by most writers who lived before Aristophanes the grammarian, who was the first to deny that the *Hypothecae*,

in which this can be found, was by that poet. Other authorities also, including Eratosthenes, have given the same advice. But one finds better advice in those who believe that no age should be without some interest, like Chrysippus, who gives the nurses the first three years, but holds that they too should already have a part in forming the mind on the best possible principles. But why should an age already capable of moral instruction not be capable of learning its letters? I know of course that in all this period one can hardly get the results that a single year later on can achieve; still, those who have taken this line seem to me to have spared the teachers rather than the pupils. What better thing can they be doing anyway, from the moment they are able to speak? Something at least they must be doing! Or why should we despise the gains to be made before the age of seven, however small they are? For though the knowledge contributed by the early years may be small, still the boy will be learning some more important things in the years in which he would otherwise have been learning more elementary matters. Carried forward year by year, this all adds up, and the time saved in childhood is a gain for the period of adolescence. The same advice may be taken to apply to the subsequent years: let the child not begin too late to learn what he has to learn. Let us therefore not waste the earliest years, especially as the elements of reading and writing are entirely a matter of memory, which not only already exists in little children, but is then at its most retentive.

I am not so careless of age differences as to think that the very young should be forced on prematurely, and that set tasks should be demanded of them. For one of the first things to take care of is that the child, who is not yet able to love study, should not come to hate it and retain his fear of the bitter taste he has experienced even beyond his first years. Let it be a game; let him be questioned and praised and always feel glad that he has done something; sometimes, when he refuses a lesson, it should be given to another child, of whom he can be jealous; sometimes he should compete, and more often than not think he is the winner; and finally, he should be encouraged by rewards suitable to his age.

These are trivial recommendations for one who claims to be educating an orator; but study also has its infancy, and, as the rearing of what will one day be the strongest bodies begins with breast feeding and the cradle, so the great speaker of the future once cried as a baby, tried to speak with an uncertain voice, and was puzzled by the shapes of letters. If learning something is not sufficient in itself, it does not follow that it is not necessary. If no one blames a father for thinking these things should not be neglected in his son, why should a person be criticized for bringing into public view what he would rightly do in his own home? All the more so, because little children grasp little things more easily, and, just as the body can only be trained to flex the limbs in certain ways when it is young and tender, so the acquisition of strength itself makes the mind also more resistant to many kinds of learning. Would King Philip of Macedon have chosen that his son Alexander be taught his letters by Aristotle, the greatest philosopher of the age, or would Aristotle have accepted the commission, if they had not believed that elementary instruction is best given by the most accomplished teacher and that it is important for the ultimate outcome? So let us imagine that an Alexander is entrusted to our care, that the child placed in our lap deserves as much attention (though of course every father thinks this of his son): ought I to be ashamed to point out a short way of teaching even for the first elements?

At any rate, I do not like the procedure (which I see is very common) by which children learn the names and sequence of the letters before their shapes. This is an obstacle to the recognition of the letters, since they do not when the time comes pay attention to the actual outlines, because they follow the promptings of their memory, which runs ahead of their observation. This is why teachers, even when they think they have sufficiently fixed the letters in a child's mind in the order in which they are commonly first written, next reverse this, or muddle it up in various ways, until the pupils come to recognize the letters by their shape and not by the order in which they come. It will be best therefore for them to be taught the appearance and the name side by side: it is like recognizing people.

But what is an obstacle in learning letters will do no harm when we come to syllables. Nor do I rule out the well-known practice of giving ivory letter-shapes to play with, so as to stimulate little children to learn— or indeed anything else one can think of to give them more pleasure, and which they enjoy handling, looking at, or naming.

Once the child has begun to trace the outlines, it will be useful to have these inscribed as neatly as possible on a tablet, so that the stilus is guided by the grooves. In this way, the child will not make mistakes as on wax (for he will be constrained by the edges on both sides, and will not be able to stray beyond the marks), and, by following these well-defined traces so quickly and often, he will strengthen his fingers, and not need the help of a guiding hand placed over his own. Practice in writing well and quickly, which people of standing tend to neglect, is not an irrelevance. Writing in one's own hand is important in our studies, and is the only way of ensuring real, deep-rooted progress; slow writing delays thought, ill-formed or confused writing is unintelligible, and this produces a second laborious stage of dictating what needs to be copied out. So, at all times and in all places, and especially in confidential and familiar letters, one will find pleasure in not having neglected this skill either.

With syllables, there is no short cut. They must all be learned; there is no point in the common practice of postponing the most difficult questions relating to them, to be discovered only when we come to write words. We must beware also of trusting the first memory too readily: it is better to have repeated syllable-drill over a long period. and not be in a hurry to achieve continuity or speed in reading either, unless the sequences of letters are produced without hesitation or doubt, and anyway without the child having to stop and think. Only then let him begin to construct words with the syllables themselves and form connected sentences with the words. It is unbelievable how much further delay in reading is produced by haste. The result is hesitation, interruption, and repetition, because they are venturing beyond their powers, and then, when they make mistakes, losing confidence also in what they already know. Reading must therefore first be sure, then connected, and for a long time quite slow, until practice enables correctness to be combined with speed. For to look forward to the right (as is universally taught), and so foresee what is coming, is a matter not only of theory but of practice, since we have to keep our eyes on what follows while reading out what precedes, and (most difficult of all) divide the attention of the mind, the voice doing one thing and the eyes another.

One will never regret making sure that, when the child (according to the usual practice) begins to write names, he does not waste his time on common words that occur all the time. Right from the start, he can, incidentally, learn the explanations of obscure words (what the Greeks call "glosses"), and so, at this elementary stage, acquire knowledge which would need time for itself later on. And, as we are still dealing with minor matters, I should like to suggest that the lines set for copying should not be meaningless sentences, but should convey some moral lesson. The memory of such things stays with us till we are old, and the impression thus made on the unformed mind will be good for the character also. The child may also be allowed to learn, as a game, the sayings of famous men and especially selected passages from the poets (which children particularly like to know). Memory (as I shall show in due time) is very necessary to the orator; there is nothing like practice for nourishing and strengthening it, and, since the age-group of which we are now speaking cannot as yet produce anything on its own, it is almost the only faculty which the teacher's attention can help to develop.

It would be a good idea, at this age, in order to develop the vocal organs and make the speech more distinct, to get the child to rattle off, as fast as he can, words and verses designed to be difficult formed of strings of syllables which clash with one another, and are really rocky, as it were: the Greeks call them *chalinoi* (tongue twisters). This sounds no great matter; but its omission leads to many faults of pronunciation which, unless removed in early years, persist through life as an incurable bad habit.

## Chapter 2

### *Home or School?*

But now our boy is to grow up little by little, leave the nursery, and begin his education seriously. This is therefore the best place to discuss the question whether it is better to keep him studying at home, within one's own walls, or hand him over to the general society of the schools and teachers who, as it were, are available to the public. I know this has been the favored course of those who have established the customs of the most famous cities, and of other very eminent authorities besides. But we must not conceal the fact that there are some who disagree with this publicly approved custom because of private convictions of their own. They seem to have two main reasons. First, they are making (they think) better provision for morality by avoiding the crowd of persons of an age which is particularly liable to vice; and I only wish that the view that this has often been a cause of shameful behavior were false! Secondly, the future teacher, whoever he is, seems likely to give a single pupil more of his time than if he had to divide it among several.

The first point is certainly serious. If it were agreed that schools were good for study, but bad for morals,

I should put a higher value on respectability of life than on any excellence as a speaker. In my view, however, the two are inseparably connected. I hold that no one can be an orator unless he is a good man; and even if it *is* possible, I do not want it to happen. So I take this question first.

People think that morals are corrupted in schools. Sometimes indeed they are, but so they are at home, and there are numerous instances of this, and also of course of the most scrupulous preservation of good repute in both situations. The whole difference lies in the nature of the individual and the attention he receives. Given a natural bent towards evil, and some carelessness in developing and guarding modesty in early years, privacy will give just as much opportunity for sin. The teacher employed at home may be of bad character, and the company of bad slaves is no safer than that of immodest companions of good birth. On the other hand, if the boy's natural bent is good, and the parents are not sunk in blind indifference, it is possible to choose a teacher of unexceptionable character (this is the wise parent's prime concern) and the strictest system of education conceivable, and at the same time to attach some respectable man or loyal freedman to one's son as a friend, whose regular companionship may even improve those who gave rise to our fears.

The remedy for these anxieties should be easy enough. If only we did not ourselves damage our children's characters! We ruin their infancy by spoiling them from the start. That soft upbringing which we call indulgence destroys all the sinews of mind and body. If a toddler crawls around in purple, what will he not want when he grows up? He cannot articulate a word yet, but he already understands what scarlet is, and demands the best purple. We train their palate before we teach their lips to speak. They grow up in litters; if they put a foot on the ground, they are held up by helping hands on either side. We like it if they say something outrageous; we reward with a smile and a kiss words that would be objectionable in an Alexandrian fancy boy. No wonder: it was we who taught them, they heard it all from us. They see our mistresses, our boy lovers; every dinner party echoes with obscene songs; things are to be seen which it is shameful to name. Hence comes first habit, then nature. The wretched children learn these things before they know they are wrong. This is what makes them dissolute and spineless: they do not get these vices from the schools, they import them into them.

"The teacher will be able to give more time, one to one." In the first place, there is nothing to prevent the "one" teacher being also with the boy who is being taught at school. And even if the two things were incompatible, I should still have preferred the broad daylight of honest company to darkness and solitude. All good teachers like a large class, and think they deserve a bigger stage. It is the weaker teachers, conscious of their own defects, who cling to individual pupils and seem content with something like the job of the *paedagogi*.

But let us suppose that influence or money or friendship provides a very learned and incomparable teacher at home: is he going to spend the whole day on his one pupil? Or can the learner's attention be kept up so continuously without getting tired, as the eye tires with continual looking, especially as learning requires much more private time? The teacher does not stand over the pupil when he is writing, learning by heart, or thinking something over; indeed the intervention of another person is a hindrance to any of these activities. Reading also does not always and in every case need a model rendering or an interpretation by the teacher. If it did, how could one ever get to know so many authors? Quite a short time is needed for assigning the work for the whole day, and so even teaching that needs to be given individually can be given to a number of pupils in turn. There are also many things which require to be imparted to all the pupils at once. I say nothing of the analyses and declamations of the rhetors. For them, the audience can be as large as you like, yet each individual can get the full benefit; the voice of the lecturer is not like a dinner which is insufficient for a large company, but like the sun that dispenses light and heat equally to all. Similarly, if a *grammaticus* is lecturing on correct speech, or explaining problems, or giving the historical background, or paraphrasing poems, all who hear him will profit by the lesson.

"But a large class is unsuitable for the correction of mistakes and for reading and expounding a text." It may indeed be inconvenient (what gives satisfaction in every respect?); but we shall later balance the inconvenience against the advantages.

"But I do not want my boy to be sent where he will be neglected." But, firstly, a good teacher will not burden himself with a bigger crowd of pupils than he can manage; and secondly it is very important to ensure that he becomes in every way on terms of friendship

with us, and looks at his teaching as a matter not of duty but of affection. In that way we shall never be part of a crowd. Again, any teacher who has the least tincture of literary culture will not fail to take a particular interest in any boy in whom he sees industry and talent, because this will advance his own reputation too. But even if big schools are to be avoided (though I cannot agree even with this proposition, if a teacher is deservedly popular), it does not follow that schools in general are to be avoided. It is one thing to avoid them, quite another to choose among them.

If I have succeeded in refuting these objections, let me now explain my own practice. First of all, let the future orator, who has to live in the crowd and in the full glare of public life, become accustomed from childhood not to be frightened of people or acquire the pallor that comes from that solitary life that is lived in the shade. The mind needs constant stimulus and challenge; and, in that kind of privacy, it either languishes and gathers mold, as it were, in the dark, or else swells up with vain conceit, because any person who has no one with whom to compare himself is bound to rate himself too highly. Later. when the fruits of his study have to be made public, he is dazzled by the sun and stumbles over everything new, because he has learned as a solitary something which can only be practiced among many. I say nothing of the friendships which endure firm and unbroken to old age, imbued with almost religious feelings of attachment. Initiation in the same studies is no less binding than initiation in the same mysteries. And where will he learn what we call common feeling if he shuts himself off from society, which is natural not only to humans but to the dumb animals? And again, at home he can only learn what is taught to him personally, while at school he will also learn what is taught to others. He will hear many things praised and many things corrected every day; he will profit from hearing indolence rebuked or industry commended. His emulation will be excited by praise; he will think it a disgrace to be outdone by a contemporary, and a fine thing to do better than his seniors. All these things stimulate the mind, and though ambition may be a fault in itself, it is often the cause of virtues. I remember that my own masters maintained a practice which was not without its uses. Having distributed the boys in classes, they made the order of speaking depend on ability, so that the place in which each of them declaimed was a consequence of the progress which they thought he had made. Judgments were made public; that itself was a tremendous honor, but to be top of the class was most wonderful. The decision was not permanent; the end of the month brought the defeated pupil the chance to compete again, and so success did not encourage the victor to relax, while the vexation of it goaded the unsuccessful into wiping out his disgrace. I am prepared to argue that to the best of my recollection this did more to kindle our oratorical ambitions than all the exhortations of our teachers, the watchfulness of our *paedagogi,* and the hopes of our parents.

But, while rivalry nurtures literary progress when it is more firmly established, beginners and the very young find imitation of their fellow pupils more agreeable than imitation of their masters, because it is easier. Elementary students will scarcely dare raise themselves to any hope of reproducing what they believe to be a crowning achievement of eloquence; they will prefer to embrace what is closest to them, just as vines trained on trees climb to the top by first taking hold of the lower branches. So true is this that it is the master's own duty too, if (that is) he prefers the serviceable to the showy, not to begin by overloading his pupils' limited strength when he is dealing with unformed minds, but to keep his own powers under control and come down to his hearer's intellectual level. Vessels with narrow mouths reject liquid if too much is poured in at once, but can be filled if it flows in gradually or a drop at a time; likewise, we have to consider how much the children's minds can take: what is too big for their understanding will not get into minds which have not been opened enough to accept it. It is useful to have people whom you would like first to imitate and then to surpass; this will gradually lead to hope of even higher things. I add the further point that the teachers themselves cannot develop the same intelligence and energy in speaking to an audience of one as when inspired by the more numerous gathering of which we were speaking. Why? Because eloquence is mainly a psychological matter: it is the mind which must be emotionally stirred and must conceive images and somehow be itself adapted to the subject of the speech. The nobler and more elevated the mind, the more powerful the mechanism, as it were, that it needs to stir it up. This is why it grows with praise, develops with effort, and finds joy in doing something big. There is a certain unexpressed feeling that it is unworthy to deploy a power of speech so laboriously acquired on an audience of one: the speaker is embarrassed to raise his voice above the ordinary conversational level. Just imagine the attitude of a declaimer, or the voice, gait, and delivery of an orator—the motions of mind and body, the sweat (to say nothing of anything else), and the fatigue—all for a single listener! Would it not seem a bit like madness? If we only talked to one person at a time, there would be no such thing as eloquence in human life.

## Chapter 3

### The Different Gifts of Children and How to Handle Them

As soon as a boy is entrusted to him, the skilled teacher will first spy out his ability and his nature. In children, the principal sign of talent is memory. There are two virtues of memory: quickness of grasp, and accurate retention. Next comes imitation; this also is a mark of a teachable nature, provided that it is exercised on what he is learning, not on someone's bearing or walk or some observable defect. I shall not form any expectation of good qualities, if the object of those efforts at imitation is to raise a laugh. The really gifted will also be a good boy. In any case, I cannot think it worse to be stupid than to be bad; but the good boy will be anything but a dullard or a lazybones. My ideal pupil anyway will absorb instruction without difficulty and even ask some questions; but he will follow rather than anticipate the teacher. Those precocious intellects do not readily come to fruition. They are the boys who do small things easily and then, emboldened by this, quickly show what it is that they can do—and this is just what lies nearest at hand: they string words together and bring them out with a bold face, uninhibited by any feelings of modesty. They have little to offer, but what there is comes quickly. There is no real underlying force that has any deep roots: it is like seed scattered on the surface of the soil; it comes up too quickly, the blade looks like a full ear, but it turns yellow before the harvest, and there is no substance in the crop. These things give pleasure, taking the age into account; but then progress stops, and admiration declines.

Having noticed all this, the teacher must next consider how the pupil's mind should be handled. Some are idle unless you press them; others are impatient of discipline. Fear restrains some and paralyses others. Some need continuous effort to knock them into shape; with others, the sudden attack is more effective. Give me a boy who is encouraged by praise, pleased by success, and who cries when he has lost. He is the one who will be nourished by ambition, hurt by reproof, and excited by honor. In him I shall never have to fear laziness.

However, everyone must be given some relaxation, not only because there is nothing that can stand perpetual strain—even things which are without sense or life need to be relaxed by periods of rest in order to preserve their strength—but also because study depends on the will to learn, and this cannot be forced. Thus renewed and refreshed, they will bring to their learning both more energy and that keener spirit which so often resists compulsion. I am not bothered by playfulness in the young (it too is a sign of a lively mind), nor would I ever expect a gloomy and perpetually depressed boy to show alertness in his work, lacking as he is also in the energy which is particularly natural at his age. But there must be moderation in holidays: if we refuse them, the boys will hate their work; if there are too many, they will get used to being idle. There are even some games which are useful for sharpening the wits, for example competitions in which they ask one another all sorts of little questions. Character reveals itself too more naturally in games—but bear in mind that no age is too immature to learn straight away what is right and what is wrong, and that the best age for forming character is when they do not know how to pretend, but obey their teachers most readily. It is easier to break than to straighten anything which has hardened into a bad shape. There must be no delay, then, in warning the boy that he must not behave greedily, dishonestly, or without controlling himself. Let us always keep in mind the words of Virgil (*Georgics* 2.272):

So strong is habit in the tender plant.

Flogging a pupil is something I do not at all like, though it is an accepted practice and Chrysippus approves. In the first place, it is humiliating and proper only for slaves; and certainly it is an infringement of rights (as it is agreed to be at a later age). Secondly, if a boy is so lacking in self-respect that reproof is powerless to put him right, he will even become hardened to blows, like the worst type of slave. And finally, there will be no need for this form of punishment if there is always someone there to make sure the work gets done. As it is, we try to make amends for the negligence of the *paedagogi* not by forcing boys to do the right thing but by punishing them for not having done it. Moreover,

though you may compel a child with blows, what can you do with a young man who cannot be threatened like this and who has more important lessons to learn? And again, when children are beaten, the pain and fear often have results which it is not pleasant to speak of and which will later be a source of embarrassment. This shame breaks and depresses the spirits, and leads the child to shun and loathe the light of day.

If not enough care has been taken about the character of the supervisors or teachers, I blush to mention the shameful purposes for which evil men abuse their right to flog, and what opportunities the terror felt by these poor children sometimes gives to other persons also. I will not dwell on this subject: what I am hinting at is already too much. It is enough to observe that no one ought to be allowed too much power over helpless and easily victimized young people.

I shall now proceed to name the subjects in which the boy who is being trained to be an orator should be educated, and the age at which each subject should be begun.

*In the remainder of the book Quintilian turns toward more technical subjects such as the requirements of an education in grammar. In the following books (2–11), he traces the development of the orator through the schools of rhetoric, with much discussion of topics such as the arousal of emotions and the use of humor. The best-known part of the work is Book 10, with its recommendations on appropriate readings in literature, both Greek and Latin, for the aspiring orator. Book 11 offers advice on delivery, including how to dress and appropriate gestures while delivering an oration. The following selection comes from the concluding twelfth book, in which Quintilian shows us the complete orator, whom he characterizes with a famous quotation from Cato as "the good man skilled in speaking."*

## Book 12

### Prooemium

I have now arrived at much the hardest part of the task I set myself. Indeed, if I had realized, when I first contemplated it, the weight of the load with which, now that I am carrying it, I feel crushed, I should have thought sooner about what my strength could bear. But, in the beginning, the shame of not fulfilling my promise held me to my work, and later, although the labor became more and more arduous at almost every stage, I kept myself going through all the difficulties by will power, for fear of wasting what had already been done.

And so, even now, though the burden that oppresses me is greater than ever, the end is in sight, and I am resolved to fail in the attempt sooner than despair. What deceived me was that I had started with such small matters; later, tempted as it were by a favorable wind, I sailed ahead; but so long as I was merely imparting well-known doctrine which many technical writers had handled, I still did not feel far from land, and I had many companions who had ventured, as it were, to trust themselves to the same winds. Then, when I entered upon the theory of Elocution, the last area to be discovered and the least commonly handled, those who had strayed so far from harbor proved to be few and far between. And finally, now that the orator I was educating has been dismissed by his teachers and is either proceeding under his own power or seeking greater assistance from the innermost shrine of philosophy, I begin to feel how far I have been swept out to sea. Now I have

sky all around, and all around the deep.

Only one man can I see in all the boundless waste of waters, Marcus Tullius, and even he, though he entered this sea with such a great and finely equipped ship, shortens sail and checks his stroke, content to speak merely about the type of style which his ideal orator is to use. But I, in my rashness, will seek to give him also moral principles, and assign him duties. Thus I have no predecessor to follow, but must go on and on as the subject leads. However, honorable ambition is a worthy thing, and it is (as it were) the safer sort of valor to attempt something for which people are readier to make allowances.

## Chapter 1

### *The Good Man Skilled in Speaking*

So let the orator whom we are setting up be, as Cato defines him, "a good man skilled in speaking": but—and Cato put this first, and it is intrinsically more significant and important—let him at all events be "a good man." This is not just because, if the power of eloquence proves to have put weapons into the hands of evil, there would be nothing more ruinous for public or for private life; and I myself, who have done my

utmost to make some contribution to oratory, would serve humanity very badly, if what I am doing is to provide these arms not for the soldier, but for the brigand. But why speak of myself? Nature herself, in that very respect in which she seems to have specially favored the human race and marked us off from all other animals, will have proved not a mother to us but a stepmother if she devised the faculty of speech to be the accomplice of crime, the opponent of innocence, and the enemy of truth. It would have been better for us to be born dumb and devoid of reason than to pervert the gifts of providence for our mutual destruction.

But this view of mine has further implications. I am not only saying that the orator must be a good man, but that *no one* can be an orator *unless* he is a good man. One could surely not concede intelligence to people who are offered the paths of virtue and of vice and then choose the worse nor indeed prudence either, because, owing to the uncertain outcome of events, they often become exposed by their own doing to the heaviest penalties of the law, and *always* to those of a bad conscience. If it is not only a philosophers' saying, but has always been a common belief, that "no one is bad unless he is also a fool," it will surely be true that a fool will never be an orator. Moreover, the mind is never at liberty even to study this noble art unless it is free of all vices: first, because virtue and vice cannot coexist in the same breast, and a single mind can no more harbor the best thoughts and the worst than the same man can be both good and bad; and secondly, because a mind concentrating on such a great subject needs to be free from all other distractions, even blameless ones. Only then, free and undivided, with no cause to distract it or lead it astray, will it turn its whole attention to the task for which it is girding itself. If excessive care for a landed estate, undue anxiety about family property, a passion for hunting, or days spent in the theaters take much time from study (and time spent on *anything* else is time lost to study!), what are we to think will be the effect of desire, avarice, and envy, rampant thoughts of which disturb even our slumbers and our dreams?

Nothing is so preoccupied, so many-faceted, so mauled and torn apart by so many different emotions, as an evil mind. When it is plotting something, it is tormented with hope, cares, and labor; even when it has attained its criminal ends, it is racked by anxiety, remorse, and the expectation of all kinds of punishments. What room is there amid all this for literature or any cultural activity? No more, to be sure, than there is room for a good crop where the land is given over to thorns and brambles.

And is not a frugal life essential for enduring the labors of study? So what hope is there in lust and luxury? Is not love of renown a specially strong stimulus to a passion for literature? Are we then to think that the wicked care for renown? Is it not now obvious to all that the most important element in oratory is the handling of the equitable and the good? Will a bad and unfair man speak about these things as the dignity of the subject requires?

And finally—to leave the biggest part of the question out of account—let us assume (though it can never happen) that a very bad man and a very good man both have the same amount of talent, industry, and learning: which of the two is to be called the better orator? Of course it will be the one who is also the better man. So a man can never be both a perfect orator and a bad man, because nothing is perfect if there is something else better.

However, as I do not want to seem to have been inventing answers to my own questions, like the Socratics, let us imagine a man so obstinately opposed to the truth as to dare to affirm that, given the same talent, study, and learning, a bad man will be no worse an orator than a good one: let us convince even this person's madness. No one surely will doubt that the aim of all oratory is to make its propositions appear true and honorable to the judge. Which then will find it easier to be convincing, the good man or the bad? The good man of course will also *say* true and honorable things more often; but even if some particular duty leads him (and this can happen, as I shall show later) to attempt to make some false statements, he is still bound to be believed more than the other man. Bad men, on the other hand, because they despise opinion and have no idea of what is right, sometimes even forget to keep up the pretence, and so state their case without any modesty, and make their assertions without shame. The consequence is unseemly pertinacity and vain effort spent on points which it is certain can never be made good. They cherish unethical hopes in their Causes just as much as in their lives. It often happens, too, that even when they tell the truth they are not believed, and the appearance of such an advocate is thought to show that the Cause is a bad one.

I must now deal with what seems a general conspiracy of protest against this view. "Was not Demosthenes an orator? But we understand he was a bad man. Was not Cicero? Many have found fault with *his* morals too." Well now, what am I to do? I shall have to put up with a lot of prejudice because of my answer; so I must first conciliate my audience. I do not think Demosthenes merits such grave aspersions on his character that I am bound to believe all the charges which are heaped upon him by his enemies; I read also of his noble public policies and his glorious end. Nor do I think Cicero in any way lacked the right attitudes of a good citizen. For evidence, I cite his magnificent consulship, his honorable administration of his province, his refusal of a place on the Commission of Twenty, and the fact that, in the dreadful civil wars which fell within his lifetime, neither hope nor fear deterred him from supporting the right side, that is to say the Republic. Some think him cowardly: he replied to this charge very well himself, by saying that he was "not a timid person when confronting peril, but timid in foreseeing it." He proved his point again by his death itself, which he bore with outstanding courage.

If these two lacked perfect virtue, I can still answer those who question whether they were orators by the argument the Stoics would use to answer anyone who asked them whether Zeno, Cleanthes, or Chrysippus himself was a Wise Man: they would say that they were great men, and to be venerated, but had not attained to the highest perfection of human nature. Even Pythagoras, after all, did not choose to be called a "wise man" (like his predecessors) but a "lover of wisdom." For my part, I have often said, and shall continue to say, that in the ordinary sense of the words Cicero was a perfect orator—just as we ordinarily speak of our friends as good and truly prudent men, though this is not strictly true of anyone but the perfect sage. On the other hand, if I have to speak strictly and in accordance with rigorous standards of truth, I shall go on looking for the true orator whom Cicero also was looking for. I admit of course that Cicero himself had climbed the topmost peak of eloquence, and I can scarcely find anything which could be added to his qualities—though I might perhaps find something that I think he would have gone on to prune away, because scholars have generally judged that he possessed many virtues and some faults, and he himself bears witness to having restrained much of his youthful exuberance. Nevertheless, since, though he was the last person to disparage himself, he never claimed to be "wise," and since he could certainly have spoken better if he had been granted a longer life and a more secure period in which to write, it is perhaps not ungenerous in me to believe that he failed to achieve that perfection which nobody came closer to achieving. If my feelings about him had been different, I could have argued for this position with more boldness and freedom. Marcus Antonius declared he had never seen a "competent speaker" (and this is a good deal less than an "orator"). Cicero himself is still looking for his orator, and only imagining and inventing him; so shall I not have the courage to say that, in the eternity of time to come, there may possibly be found something more perfect than anything which went before? I pass over people who do not give enough credit even for eloquence to Cicero and Demosthenes, although it is true that Cicero himself finds imperfections in Demosthenes, and says he sometimes "nods," and Cicero himself does not seem perfect either to Brutus and Calvus (who criticize his Composition to his face) or to the two Asinii, who make really hostile attacks on the faults of his style in various places.

Anyway, let us grant—though it is wholly against nature—that some bad man has been found who is supremely eloquent. I shall nevertheless deny that he is an orator. By the same token, I shall not allow everyone who is ready with his hands to be a brave man, because courage cannot be conceived apart from virtue. If a man who is called upon to defend a Cause needs (as he surely does) a loyalty which greed cannot corrupt, influence affect, or fear break down, are we to give the sacred name of orator to a traitor, a deserter, or a colluder? If the quality which is commonly called goodness is thought right even for mediocre advocates, why should not the ideal orator, who has never existed but may exist some day, be perfect in character as well as in oratory? The man I am educating is no law-court hack or hired voice, nor even (let us avoid hard words) a serviceable case advocate, what is commonly called a *causidicus,* but a man of outstanding natural talent who has acquired a profound knowledge of many valuable arts, a man vouchsafed at long last to humanity, such as history has never known, unique, perfect in every way, noble in thought and noble in speech. It will be a small fraction of this man's achievement that he will protect the innocent, repress the crimes of the wicked, and defend truth against calumny in financial disputes. Of course he will be supreme in this field too, but it is in greater things that his glory will shine more brightly, when he has to guide the counsels of the Senate or lead an erring people into better ways. It was surely some such man as this whom Virgil imagined, and whom he shows taking control when the rioting crowd hurls torches and stones:

> Then if they chance to see a man
> whose deeds and virtues have authority,
> silent they stand, and with attentive ears.

Here then we have first and foremost a good man; the poet will then go on to say that he is an able speaker:

> He rules their minds with speech, and soothes their
>     passions.

In wartime too, if the troops have to be exhorted before battle, will not the man whom I am educating draw eloquence from doctrines that are at the heart of philosophy? How can men going into battle banish from their minds all the fears of toil, pain, and ultimately death itself that they feel in that one moment, unless duty, courage, and a vivid awareness of honor step in to take their place? And surely the best man to persuade others of this will be the man who has previously persuaded himself. Insincere protestations always betray themselves, however carefully they are kept up, and there has probably never been a tongue so fluent as not to stumble or hesitate whenever the words are at odds with the speaker's real feelings. Now the bad man is bound to speak otherwise than he feels, while good men will never lack for honorable words or an Invention that provides honorable matter (for they are not only good but clever); and even if their matter lacks artificial charms, its own nature will be ornament enough, and everything that is said honorably is also said eloquently. So let our young people—or rather let all of us, of any age, for it is never too late to make good resolutions—strive for this and work towards it with all our powers; maybe we shall even have the good fortune to get there. If Nature does not prohibit the existence of a good man and the existence of a skilled speaker, why should not one person achieve both goals? And why should not everyone hope that he might be that person? And if our talents are not sufficient, we shall still better ourselves in both ways in so far as we make progress. At least let us banish from our minds the idea that the glorious thing that is eloquence can be combined with vicious attitudes of mind. If the power of speech is found in bad men, it too must be judged a bad thing; for it makes the bad men who possess it worse than they were.

I think I hear some people (there will always be those who would rather be eloquent than good) saying something like this: "So what is all this art in eloquence? Why have you told us about Colors and the defense of difficult Causes, and even about Confession of Guilt, unless force and readiness of speech sometimes triumph over truth itself? A good man only pleads good Causes, and truth itself is defense enough for them without the help of learning."

In answering these people in the first instance in relation to my own work, 1 shall be satisfying them also as regards the duty of a good man, who may sometimes have reason to undertake the defense of the guilty. It is not useless to consider how one may on occasion speak for a falsehood or even for an injustice, if only because this enables us to detect and refute such things more easily, just as the person who knows what things are harmful will be better at applying remedies for them. After all, the Academics argue both sides of a question, but live according to one side only, and the great Carneades, who is said to have spoken at Rome in the presence of the censor Cato just as vigorously against justice as he had spoken in defense of justice the day before, was a perfectly just man. In fact, what virtue is is revealed by its opposite, vice; equity is better understood by looking at its opposite; and in general most things are shown to be good by comparison with their contraries. The orator therefore must know his adversaries' plans as the general does the enemy's.

However—hard as this seems when it is first stated—rational consideration may also lead a good man, in his defense of his Cause, occasionally to want to cheat the judge of the truth. If anyone is surprised at my saying this (though it is not my own idea, but comes from persons whom antiquity regarded as authoritative philosophers), let him bear in mind that there are many actions which are made honorable or the reverse not so much because of what was done as because of the motive. If it is often a virtuous act to kill a man, if it is sometimes a very fine action to put one's own children to death, and if deeds which make an even harsher story can be excused on grounds of public interest, then neither must we concentrate on the bare question of what sort of Cause the good man is to defend, but consider also why and with what intention he does it.

First of all, everyone must grant me what even the sternest of the Stoics admit, namely that the good man will go so far as to tell a lie on occasion, and sometimes even for quite trivial reasons: with sick children, for example, we pretend many things for their good and promise to do many things which we are not going to do; even more justifiably, we lie to stop an assassin from killing a man, and deceive an enemy to save the country. Thus lying, which in some circumstances is blameworthy even in slaves, in others is praiseworthy in the Wise Man himself. If this is agreed, I can see many situations in which an orator might properly undertake a type of Cause which he would not have accepted if there had been no honorable reason for doing so. I am not talking about the defense of a father or a brother or a friend who is at risk—I am resolved to follow stricter rules—although in these cases there can be ample ground for hesitation, because justice is seen to be on one side and loyalty on the other. Let us leave no doubt about the problem. Suppose a man has conspired against a tyrant and is on trial for this. Will the orator, as defined by us, be against the man's being acquitted? Will he not, if he undertakes the defense, use falsehoods just as much as an advocate who is defending a bad Cause in court? Again, suppose a judge is set to condemn some actions which were rightly done, unless we can convince him that they never were done: will not the orator use even this means to preserve a citizen who is not only innocent but praiseworthy? Or suppose we know that certain acts, though naturally just, are against the public interest in the present circumstances: shall we not use a skill in speaking which is indeed honorable, but which looks like dishonest practice? Further, no one is going to doubt that, if the guilty parties can somehow be converted to a right way of thinking (and it is conceded that this is possible), it is more in the public interest that they should be acquitted than that they should be punished. So if it is clear to the orator that a man against whom true charges are brought will become a good man, will he not work to secure his acquittal? Next, imagine that a good general, someone without whom the state cannot defeat its enemies, is laboring under a manifestly true charge: will not the common good call our orator to his side? Fabricius anyway openly used his vote to have Cornelius Rufinus, who was a bad citizen and also his personal enemy, elected consul, because he knew he was a competent commander, and war was imminent. When people said they were surprised, Fabricius replied that he would rather be robbed by a fellow citizen than sold into slavery by the enemy. So, if he had been an orator, would he not have defended this Rufinus on a charge of peculation, however plain the facts were? Many similar instances could be given, but any one of them is enough to make the point. I am not arguing that the orator I am shaping will often have to do this, only that, if some such reason compels him to do so, the definition of an orator as "a good man skilled in speaking" still holds good.

It is necessary however to teach and to learn how to handle difficult cases also from the point of view of

Proof. Even the best Causes often look like bad ones, and an innocent defendant may be overwhelmed by many plausible charges. In that case, he has to be defended by the same line of pleading as if he was guilty. Moreover, there are countless features common to both good and bad Causes: witnesses, documents, suspicions, opinions. The probable is confirmed or refuted in the same way as the true. The speech therefore may be bent to suit the needs of the case, so long as our intentions are honorable.

## AFTERWORD

Quintilian's fame in antiquity was celebrated by his younger contemporary and fellow Spaniard, the poet Martial (*Epigrams* 2.90.1–2): "Quintilian, supreme guide of wayward youth, Quintilian glory of the Roman toga!" Even though Quintilian's advocacy of a Ciceronian purism was not in favor among many Roman intellectuals in the century following his death, his works remained in circulation and were widely known. In fact, several declamations, or practice speeches, that became popular during that period were falsely thought to have been written by him, so imprinted on the popular consciousness was his stature as the leading authority on rhetoric. St. Jerome studied Quintilian as a young man, and he adapted Quintilian's precepts on childhood education in the first book of *The Education of the Orator* to a Christian message in his epistle to Laeta on a girl's education (*Epistles* 107). He was known to Lactantius and St. Augustine as well, but his lengthy treatise was abbreviated by later rhetoricians, and most medieval readers, such as John of Salisbury and Vincent of Beauvais, encountered him in this abridged form.

Most of the manuscripts of *The Education of the Orator* that circulated in the Middle Ages derived from incomplete copies of the text, and it appears that there were only two complete manuscripts that survived from antiquity. Quintilian's reputation was so high, however, that Petrarch penned an imaginary letter to him (*Familiar Letters* 24.7) and complained about his imperfect copy. A copy of one of the lost complete manuscripts that had been made in the ninth century was eventually discovered by the humanist Poggio Bracciolini at the monastery in St. Gall, Switzerland. And from that point on Quintilian's treatise exerted an extraordinary influence on Renaissance rhetorical theory. Along with Cicero, Quintilian was an important model for the most important treatise on Latin style, *On the Elegance of the Latin Language,* by Lorenzo Valla (1406–57).

Quintilian was taken as an authority on education in Europe for as long as rhetoric was a central component in the curriculum. He was a favorite author of Martin Luther (1483–1546), who may have attempted to compose his sermons according to rhetorical principles learned from Quintilian. And in several of his works, such as *The Education of Children,* the great Dutch humanist Desiderius Erasmus (1466–1536) shows himself to be a serious student of Quintilian. In "An Essay on Criticism" (1709), Alexander Pope includes Quintilian in his survey of ancient critics, but Pope's rather lukewarm assessment shows that he was thinking primarily in terms of his usefulness to poets (669–74):

> In grave Quintilian's copious work, we find
> The justest rules, and clearest method joined:
> Thus useful arms in magazines we place,
> All ranged in order, and disposed with grace,
> But less to please the eye, than arm the hand,
> Still fit for use, and ready at command.

With the decline of rhetoric's role in the classroom upon the advent of Romanticism, the case for Quintilian's relevance became less compelling, and his work is now read primarily for the perspective it offers on ancient Roman rhetoric.

# MARTIAL

### (Marcus Valerius Martialis, ca. A.D. 40–ca. 100)

ABOUT THE LIFE OF MARTIAL, THE ROMAN POET WHO WAS MOST KEENLY INTERESTED in reflecting everyday life in his work, we know very little. He was born in Bilbilis, a small town in Roman Spain, situated on a hill near the modern town of Calatayud, between Zaragoza and Madrid. The year was approximately A.D. 40—we only know this because in a poem (10.24) published in the late 90s he tells us that he was celebrating his fifty-seventh birthday—and the date was March 1. His parents had Roman names, Valerius Fronto and Flacilla, but his background was native Hispanic, "born of Iberians and Celts, a fellow-citizen of the river Tagus," as he describes himself (10.65.3–4). We have practically no knowledge of how he passed the first forty years of his life, but we learn from his writings that he came to Rome in A.D. 64, when it must have seemed to him that the city was full of Spanish expatriates who would welcome a promising young man of twenty-four from their home province. Seneca the Younger, Lucan, and the agricultural writer Columella were among the first wave from the province to make an imprint on Roman cultural life in the first century A.D., but if Martial found a patron among them, the effects were short-lived, for the failed conspiracy of Calpurnius Piso in 65 led to the downfall of Seneca and his circle. If it is fair to extrapolate from his published work, the years that followed were not easy for him.

His first published work came some fifteen years later in A.D. 80 with the *Liber de Spectaculis* (Book on Spectacles), a collection of thirty-seven epigrams on the games presented by the emperor Titus in the Colosseum, which had recently opened to the public. The book as we have it is incomplete, but as it stands it is probably a fair reflection of the range of topics Martial touched upon. There are flattering poems about the emperor and little pieces about the exotic shows in the arena during its hundred-day opening celebration, which included gladiators, naval battles (for which the arena was flooded), and fights with wild beasts. One of the more exotic examples of these included a rhinoceros (11):

> The rhinoceros, displayed all over the arena performed for you,
> > Caesar, battles that he did not promise.
> How he lowered his head and flamed into fearful rage!
> > How mighty a bull was he, to whom a bull was as a dummy!

This book was followed five years later by two others, which are now numbered as Books 13 and 14 in modern editions. They consist of two-line tags, intended, in the first collection (*Xenia*), to accompany gifts of food and wine during the festival of the Saturnalia, and in the second (the *Apophoreta*) miscellaneous other gifts. There are tags for gifts of dates and figs, leeks and asparagus, hares and fish. And the extremely popular Roman delicacy, dormice, which were kept in jars called *gliraria* and fattened on beechnuts (13.59):

> I sleep all through the winter and am fatter in the
> Season when only sleep gives me nourishment.

Other gifts included combs, daggers, brassieres, coats, pillows, slaves, and books. For an abridged copy of Livy's 142 books in a parchment copy, the tag is (14.190):

> Vast Livy is compressed in tiny skins, for whom
> Complete my library does not have room.

And for a copy of Lucan, his fellow countryman, whose epic poem was controversial but popular (14.194):

> There are some who say I am no poet, but
> The bookseller who markets me thinks I am.

Together with the *Book on Shows* these brief, pungent epigrams are all we know of Martial's literary production prior to the publication in 86 of the first two books of the main collection.

Martial produced eleven books of epigrams during the next decade, poems composed primarily in elegiac couplets, but in other meters as well, such as hendecasyllabics, made famous by Catullus, on a dazzling array of themes from life, literature, and politics. In the political sphere, however, his legacy is less than edifying, as his obsequious epigrams flattering the villainous emperor Domitian are not his most impressive achievement. The genre of epigram had a long history before Martial, and it was practiced by many distinguished poets at Rome, including his principal source of inspiration, Catullus. Collections of epigrams in Greek had been circulating in Rome since the early first century B.C., and Martial found models of the type of epigram that he favored in the so-called *Garland of Philip*, an anthology put together by Philip of Thessalonica around the time of Martial's birth. Martial typically exploited the rhetorical resources of paradox and hyperbole to spring a surprise or joke at the end of his epigrams. His themes are not predominantly wine and love, as in many earlier writers of epigram, but the characters who populated the world around him, often portrayed in comic situations. Most of the work of his predecessors who wrote in Latin has been lost, so for posterity Martial is the prime example of the genre.

In the aftermath of Domitian's death and the accession of Nerva, Martial left behind his life in Rome, which must have been quite comfortable, in spite of his many protests of poverty and annoyance—he owned a house on the Quirinal hill and had a property in the country near Nomentum, about thirteen miles outside the city. He returned to his native town of Bilbilis in Spain, where he found a new patron in a woman called Marcella. While there he produced the final, twelfth book in the collection, which may have been assembled posthumously by an editor. In it he describes his life in Bilbilis in hendecasyllabics addressed to Juvenal, the future satirist, in which he pictures his friend roaming through the busy streets of the city (12.18):

> While you perhaps, Juvenal, wander
> restlessly in noisy Subura
> or tread Diana's hill, the Aventine,
> while your sweating toga fans you
> as you cross the thresholds of the powerful
> and the Greater and Lesser Caelian hills tire you out:

me my Bilbilis, proud of her gold and iron,
revisited after many Decembers,
has received and made a rustic.
Here in idleness I exert myself pleasantly
to visit Boterdus and Platea
(such are the uncouth names in Celtiberian lands).
I enjoy an enormous, indecent amount of sleep,
often unbroken until the third hour
and pay myself back in full now
for my wakefulness through thirty years.
The toga is unknown here, but when I ask I am handed
the nearest garment hanging from a broken chair.
When I get up, a fireplace welcomes me, stocked
with a proud pile of logs from an adjacent oak wood
and crowned by the bailiff's wife with many a pot.
The huntsman comes next but one that you
would like to have with you in a secret grove.
The smooth-skinned bailiff gives my boys their rations
and asks me to let him cut his long hair.
This is how I am pleased to live, this is how I am pleased to die.

Martial did die not long after, certainly by A.D. 104. His death was noted by Pliny the Younger in a letter that provides a suitable epitaph for the epigrammatist (3.21): "I hear that Valerius Martial has died, and I am sorry. He was a man of an acute and penetrating genius, and in his writing he displayed a great deal of wit and satire, combined with an equal amount of candor…But one might object that his poems will not be immortal. Perhaps they won't, but he wrote as if they would be." And as things turned out, perhaps surprisingly, they are.

## EPIGRAMS

*The complete collection consists of twelve books of epigrams, accompanied by a book of epigrams published in A.D. 80 in commemoration of the opening of the Colosseum, which goes by the title "On the Spectacles." In addition there are two books (now numbered 13 and 14) of "Gifts" and "Take-aways," brief examples of epigrams to be used for gift giving during the Saturnalian festivities.*

### Book 1

*1*

*The opening epigram introduces the poet and sets the tone by a metrical reference: it is composed in hendeca-syllabics, a meter closely identified with Catullus, who is a major source of inspiration for Martial throughout his career.*

You read him, you ask for him, and here he is:
Martial, known the world over
for his witty little books of epigrams.
Devoted reader, the glory you have given him
while he lives and feels                                                          5
comes to few poets in their graves.

*3*

*In an address to his still small book of poems, a motif used by Ovid, among others, Martial playfully asks if it is ready for life in the Argiletum, a street in Rome well known for its many bookshops. The poem is in elegiac couplets, the most common meter in Martial's works.*

Would you rather live in the shops of Argiletum,
        when my boxes have room for you, small book?
    Ah, little, little do you know the haughty ways of
        Lady Rome!

Believe me, Mars' children are smart to a degree.
Nowhere are sniffs more emphatic. Young men,
5    old men,
        boys—they all have noses like a rhino.
When you have heard a mighty "bravo", as you are
        throwing your kisses,
            you'll be tossed to the stars from a shaken blanket.
But rather than put up with your master's continual
        erasures,
10        rather than let his stern pen score your jests,
you are eager, you frolicker, to flit through the airs of
        heaven.
            Very well, off with you! But you might have been
            safer at home.

### 4

*Like Catullus and Ovid before him, Martial makes a dis-*
*tinction between his personal life and his bawdy literary*
*persona. He jestingly asks that Domitian, the Caesar of the*
*opening line, who also served as censor (supervisor of pub-*
*lic morals), treat his poems as he would the off-color per-*
*formances of the celebrated mimes Thymele and Latinus.*

Caesar, if you happen to light upon my little books,
        put aside the frown that rules the world.
Even the triumphs of Emperors are wont to
        tolerate jests,
            and a warlord is not ashamed to be matter
                for a quip.
Read my verses, I beg, with the expression
5    with which
        you watch Thymele and jesting Latinus.
A censor can permit harmless jollity.
        My page is wanton, but my life is virtuous.

### 10

*A common target of satirists in the imperial period is*
*the legacy hunter who woos a wealthy lady because she*
*is elderly or sick, as Gemellus, a stock figure, is wooing*
*Maronilla.*

Gemellus is a-wooing Maronilla.
He is eager and insistent, gives her presents.
Is she such a beauty? On the contrary, she couldn't be
        uglier.
So what is so desirable about her, so attractive?
        Her cough.

### 32

*This brief squib is an example of the technique known as*
*"serpentine verse," in which the opening words of the cou-*
*plet are repeated at the end for effect.*

I like you not, Sabidius, and I can't tell why.
        All I can tell is this: I like you not.

### 38

*Someone is reciting Martial's poetry as if it were his own,*
*but he does it so badly that Martial disowns his own work.*

The little book you are reciting, Fidentinus,
        belongs to me.
            But when you recite it badly, it begins to
            belong to you.

### 46

*The poet advises his sexual partner not to try to rush him,*
*for such urgings have precisely the opposite effect.*

Hedylis, when you say "I'm in a hurry, do it if you're
        going to,"
            forthwith my passion languishes; crippled, it
            subsides.
Tell me to wait, and I shall go all the faster for the check.
        Hedylis, if you are in a hurry, tell me *not* to be in
        a hurry.

### 64

*Clever advice to an arrogant young beauty.*

You are pretty: we know. You are young: true.
And rich: who can deny it?
But when you praise yourself too much, Fabulla,
you are neither rich nor pretty nor young.

### 87

*Women who drink too much are a frequent target of*
*Martial's barbs, here directed at an unknown woman*
*named Fescennia, who tries to conceal the stench of wine*
*on her breath with lozenges acquired from the pharmacist*
*Cosmus.*

Fescennia, not wishing to reek of yesterday's wine,
        you greedily devour Cosmus' pastilles.

Such breakfasts smear the teeth, but they are no
    obstacle
        when a belch comes back from the depth of
            the abyss.
Moreover, the evil element smells worse when mixed
5    with scented powder
        and the doubled odor of the breath carries further.
So away now with your too familiar tricks and
    detected frauds
        and be a simple drunk.

### 118

*A self-deprecating couplet, addressed to a certain
Caedicianus, concludes the first book.*

He for whom reading a hundred epigrams is not
    enough,
        will never have enough of a bad thing,
            Caedicianus.

## Book 2

### 9

*A man has written to a woman, who did not reply, from
which the man draws two opposite conclusions.*

I wrote. Naevia did not answer. So she won't give.
    But she read what I wrote, I suppose. So
        she'll give.

### 26

*A satirical twist on the theme of legacy hunting: Naevia is
only feigning illness to coax her lover into doing whatever
she asks.*

Naevia wheezes, she has a dry cough,
    she often sends spit into your lap.
Bithynicus, do you think you have it made?
    You're wrong. Naevia is coaxing, not dying.

### 38

*This distich plays on the theme of the annoying male friend,
who is just far enough away when the poet is at his estate at
Nomentum, about twelve miles northeast of Rome.*

Linus, you ask me what I get out of my land near
    Nomentum.

This is what I get out of the land: I don't see
    you, Linus.

### 56

*While ostensibly defending the wife of a Roman provin-
cial administrator against a charge of cheating the locals,
Martial plays on the sexual connotations of the verb "give"
to impugn her for something else.*

Among the peoples of Libya, Gallus, your wife has a
    bad reputation;
        she is charged with immoderate greed, an ugly
            charge.
But the stories are pure lies. She doesn't take at all.
    What does she do then? Give.

## Book 3

### 8

*A witty variation on the hackneyed theme "love is blind."
The name Thais was common in Rome.*

Quintus loves Thais. "Which Thais?" One-
    eyed Thais.
        Thais lacks one eye, he lacks two.

### 27

*Martial plays on the theme of the ungracious guest, who
never returns his dinner invitation.*

You never invite me back, though you often come to
    dinner at my invitation.
        I forgive you, Gallus, if only you invite nobody.
But you invite others. Both of us have a fault. "What
    fault?" say you.
        I have no sense and you, Gallus, have no sense of
           decency.

### 45

*The myth that the sun (Phoebus) hid from the sight of
the feast at which Atreus served Thyestes's children to him
humorously introduces the horrors of Ligurinus's table, at
which he recites his own poetry.*

Whether Phoebus fled Thyestes' dinner table or not,
    I don't know; but we flee yours, Ligurinus.
Elegant indeed it is, furnished with lordly repasts,

but nothing in the world gives pleasure when
    you are reciting.
I don't want you to serve me turbot or a two-pounder
5    mullet,
    nor do I want mushrooms, oysters I don't
        want: shut up.

### 49

*The poet's host serves him Veientan wine, which is
so bad that the poet would rather sniff the cup of fine
Massic wine that the host reserves for himself than drink
his own.*

You mix Veientan for me and serve Massic for
    yourself.
    I had rather smell these cups than drink.

### 55

*A woman called Gellia uses too much perfume, so much
that she smells like the shop of the well-known pharmacist
Cosmus.*

Wherever you go, we think that Cosmus is
    moving shop
    and that cinnamon oil is streaming from a
        shaken phial.
But don't let exotic trash make you complacent,
    Gellia.
    You know, I suppose, that my dog can smell good
        in the same way.

## Book 4

### 5

*Rome is no place for an honest man like Fabianus. The
road to riches such as Philomelus's is through less reputable
pursuits.*

An honest man and a poor one, true-tongued and
    true-hearted,
    you are heading for Rome: what are you thinking
        of, Fabianus?
You can't figure as a pimp or a reveler,
    nor summon trembling defendants in a voice of
        doom,
5 nor can you seduce a dear friend's wife,
    nor can you rise for chilly old hags,

nor sell empty smoke around the Palace,
    nor clap for Canus, nor clap for Glaphyrus.
What will you live on, poor soul? "A man of his word,
    a loyal friend"—
        there's nothing to that. You'll never be a
        Philomelus that way.      10

### 21

*Segius is an atheist, and the very fact of his wealth proves
that there is no god.*

Segius delcares that there are no gods, that the sky
    is empty;
and proves it, for in the course of these denials
he sees himself become a rich man.

### 38

*A distich of advice to Galla: play hard to get, but not for
too long.*

Galla, say no. Love palls, unless its joys are torture.
    But Galla, don't say no for too long.

### 70

*In an address to his friend Marcellinus, the poet wonders at
the paradox that Ammianus is now sorry that his wealthy
father is dead, seeing that he left him nothing in his will.*

Ammianus' father on his deathbed left him
nothing in his last will but a dry rope.
Who would have thought, Marcellinus,
that Ammianus could be sorry his father died?

## Book 5

### 9

*Martial was not feeling well when he was visited by his
doctor, Symmachus, who brought along his medical students: now he is seriously ill.*

I was out of sorts; but at once you visited me,
    Symmachus, accompanied by a hundred pupils.
A hundred hands chilled by the north wind
    touched me.
        I did not have a fever, Symmachus. Now I do.

34

*One of three epigrams (the others being 5.37 and 10.61) on the death of the slave Erotion, addressed to Martial's parents. She died just six days short of her sixth birthday.*

To you, father Fronto and mother Flaccilla, I commend
    this girl, my pet and darling.
Little Erotion must not be frightened by the
    dark shades
       and the monstrous mouths of Tartarus' hounds.
She was to complete the chills of a sixth midwinter,
    no more,
       if she had not lived that many days too few.
Let her now play and frolic with her old patrons
    and lispingly chatter my name.
Not hard be the turf that covers her soft bones, be
    not heavy
       upon her, earth; she was not heavy upon you.

76

*Mithridates, the king of Pontus in the first century B.C., was famous for making himself immune to poison by taking it in small doses. The poet's acquaintance Cinna has applied the same technique to bad dinners.*

By often drinking poison Mithridates achieved
    immunity from pernicious drugs.
You too, Cinna, by always dining so badly have
    taken care
       that you never die of hunger.

81

*Behind this distich lies a familiar situation: the rich always get richer.*

You will always be poor if you are poor, Aemilianus.
    Nowadays wealth is given only to the rich.

## Book 6

46

*The horses of the Blues team at the chariot races will not run; instead they "do a big job," Latin slang for defecating.*

The team of the Blues is lashed and lashed,
    but doesn't run. It's doing a big job, Catianus.

52

*An epigram on a young slave boy, Pantagathus (All-good), who used to be his master's barber.*

In this tomb lies Pantagathus, snatched away
    in his boyhood years, his master's care and grief,
skilled to cut straying locks and shave hairy cheeks
    with steel that barely touched them.
Though you be kind and light, earth, as you
    should be,               5
       you cannot be lighter than the artist's hand.

60

*The poet professes himself pleased because his books of epigrams produce what he considers the right mixture of embarrassment, anger, astonishment, boredom, and disgust.*

My Rome praises my little books, loves them,
    recites them;
       I am in every pocket, every hand.
Look, somebody turns red, turns pale, is dazed, yawns,
    is disgusted.
       This I want. Now my poems please me.

63

*Advice for the poet's elderly and wealthy friend, Marianus, who is being deceived by someone, a legacy hunter, who pretends to be his friend in order to be written into his will.*

You know you are being angled for, you know the
    angler is after money,
       and you know, Marianus, what that angler wants.
Yet you write him heir in your last testament, you fool,
    and would have him step into your shoes, you
       imbecile.
"However, he sent me valuable presents." But he sent
    them on a hook.
       And can the fish love the fisherman?
Will *he* lament your death with genuine sorrow?
    If you want him to weep, Marianus, leave him
       nothing.

## 66

*A squib directed at a slave seller, Gellianus, who is so repulsive that he drives down the price on a slave girl by kissing her at the auction.*

The other day Gellianus the auctioneer was selling
a girl of none too good a reputation,
such a one as those that sit in the middle of Subura.
Wishing to prove to all that she was clean,
since for a long time the bids were low,
he drew her close to him against her will
and kissed her twice and thrice and again.
You ask what that kissing accomplished?
Somebody who was bidding six hundred sesterces
    withdrew.

## 82

*Martial tells a potential benefactor named Rufus of his run-in with a fan, who is surprised at how shabbily the famous poet is dressed.*

The other day an individual looked me over carefully,
like a buyer or a trainer,
and after marking me down with eye and pointed
    finger,
says he, "Are you really that Martial
5  whose naughty jests everybody knows
that doesn't have the ear of a Batavian?"
I smiled a little and with a slight nod
allowed that I was the person in question.
"Then why do you wear a bad cloak?" he asked.
10  I answered: "Because I'm a bad poet."
So that this doesn't happen too often to a poet,
Rufus, please send me a good cloak.

## Book 7

## 3

*In ancient Rome as now, it was customary for authors to send each other copies of their work, but Pontilianus's poetry is so bad that Martial does not want a copy.*

Why don't I send you my little books, Pontilianus?
    For fear you might send me yours, Pontilianus.

## 30

*Martial insults Caelia, a girl with a good Roman name, by alleging that she gives herself to all the subject peoples of Rome, but not to Romans.*

You give your favors to Parthians, you give them to
    Germans, Caelia, you give them to Dacians
        nor do you despise the beds of Cilicians and
            Cappadocians;
and to you comes sailing the fornicator of Memphis
    from his Pharian city
        and the black Indian from the Red Sea.
Nor do you shun the loins of circumcised Jews          5
    nor does the Alan pass you by with his
        Sarmatian horse.
Why is it, since you are a Roman girl,
    that no Roman cock is to your liking?

## Book 8

## 12

*One of many epigrams denigrating marriage, with the off-color punch line that a man and woman are only equal when the man is on top.*

You all ask why I don't want to marry a rich wife?
    I don't want to be my wife's wife.
The matron, Priscus, should be below
    her husband.
        That's the only way man and woman
            can be equal.

## 23

*One of three epigrams (the others being 3.13 and 3.94) on the theme of beating a cook. Slave beating is a traditional comic theme.*

You think me cruel and too fond of my stomach,
    Rusticus,
        because I beat my cook on account of a
            dinner.
If that seems to you a trivial reason for lashes,
    for what reason then do you want a cook to be
        flogged?

**27**

*A wealthy old man seems oblivious to the motives of people angling for his money by giving him gifts.*

You are rich, Gaurus, and old. Who gives you pres-
    ents, says to you,
        if you have the wit to understand: "Die."

**29**

*A witty comment on the paradox of brevity as the guid-ing aesthetic principle of a book-long collection of two-line poems (distichs).*

He who writes distichs wishes, I suppose, to please by
    brevity.
        What use is brevity, tell me, if it's a book?

**35**

*Another poem critical of marriage, here of a husband and wife who are equally loathsome, but do not get along.*

Since the two of you are alike and equal in your way
    of life,
a rotten wife and a rotten husband,
I am surprised you don't suit one another.

**43**

*A satire on a man and a woman who each make a prac-tice of marrying older people for their money: they should marry each other.*

Fabius buries his wives, Chrestilla her husbands;
    each of them brandishes a funeral torch over the
        marriage bed.
Venus, match the winners; the end awaiting them
    will be one bier to carry the pair.

**69**

*Martial has no use for Vacerra and his like, who seem to admire only dead poets.*

You admire only the ancients, Vacerra,
and praise no poets except dead ones.
I crave your pardon, Vacerra;
your good opinion is not worth dying for.

**79**

*Old and unattractive women are often the targets of Martial's abuse. Here he makes fun of Fabulla, who can only be called beautiful in such company.*

All your women friends are either old hags
or frights uglier than old hags.
These are your companions whom you bring
    with you
and trail through dinner parties, colonnades, theaters.
In this way, Fabulla, you are a beauty, you are a girl.    5

## Book 9

**9**

*Ironic advice to a fictitious character named "Tankard" (Cantharus) to tone down his complaints if he wants to keep receiving dinner invitations.*

Although you like dining out, Cantharus,
you shout and curse and threaten.
I advise you to put aside your truculence.
You can't be free-spoken and greedy both.

**81**

*Martial reports to his friend Aulus that there is an unnamed poet who criticizes his work. This does not bother Martial because, like a cook, he prefers the approbation of connoisseurs rather than that of rival chefs.*

Reader and listener approve my little books, Aulus,
    but a certain poet says they lack finish.
I don't care too much; for I had rather the courses at
    my dinner
        pleased the diners than the cooks.

## Book 10

**43**

*Phileros has married for money seven times and is ironi-cally complimented by Martial.*

You have buried wife number seven on your land,
    Phileros.
Nobody, Phileros, gets a better return from his land
    than you.

## 47

*Perhaps Martial's most famous poem, offering an essentially Epicurean view of the ingredients of a happy life. The addressee is Julius Martialis, the poet's oldest and closest friend in Rome.*

Most delightful Martialis, the elements
of a happy life are as follows:
money not worked for but inherited;
land not unproductive; a fire all the year round;
5  lawsuits never, a gown rarely worn, a mind at peace;
a gentleman's strength, a healthy body;
guilelessness not naïve, friends of like degree,
easy company, a table without frills;
a night not drunken but free from cares;
10  a marriage bed not austere and yet modest;
sleep to make the dark hours short;
wish to be what you are, wish nothing better;
don't fear your last day, nor yet pray for it.

## 55

*Marulla is a fictional character who practices a humorous exactitude in her sexual activities.*

When Marulla has weighed an erect penis
with her fingers and estimated it at length,
she gives the weight in pounds, scruples, and sextules.
When the work is done and the same lies
like a limp thong after its wrestlings,
Marulla tells you how much lighter it has become.
That hand of hers isn't a hand, it's a balance.

## Book 11

## 17

*Many of the poems in this book are obscene and hence to be read at night, but in this poem Martial remarks that some of its contents are fit for a morning read.*

Not every page in my book is of the night.
    You will also find, Sabinus, matter to read in the
        morning.

## 35

*A clever play on the traditional theme of a dinner invitation, with a neat, concluding paradox that to be surrounded by people you do not know is tantamount to being alone.*

You invite hordes of people I don't know,
and you are surprised and indignant and
    quarrelsome
because I don't come to you at your invitation.
Fabullus, I don't like dining alone.

## 66

*Addressed to a man named Vacerra, the Latin word for "log," who has no money, even though all the unsavory occupations ascribed to him are potentially lucrative.*

You are an informer and a slanderer,
a swindler and a dealer,
a sucker and a trainer. I wonder
why you don't have any money, Vacerra.

## 99

*The poet describes a pair of buttocks as huge as the Clashing Rocks, known in Greek as the Symplegades or the Cyanean Rocks.*

Whenever you get up from your chair (I have noticed
    it again and again),
        your unfortunate tunic sodomizes you, Lesbia.
You try and try to pluck it with your left hand and
    your right,
        till you extract it with tears and groans.
So firmly is it constrained by the twin Symplegades of
    your arse                                                        5
        as it enters your oversized, Cyanean buttocks.
Do you want to correct this ugly fault? I'll tell
    you how.
        Lesbia, I advise you neither to get up nor sit
            down.

## Book 12

## 12

*A homoerotic squib on the theme of drinking and sexual performance.*

You promise everything when you have drunk
    all night.
        In the morning you perform nothing. Drink in
            the morning, Pollio.

### 31

*A poem of thanks addressed to his patron Marcella, who provided him with a villa in his native town of Bilbilis in Spain, more pleasant than the gardens of Alcinous described in the* Odyssey. *Martial retired there after thirty-five years (i.e., seven lusters or five-year periods) in Rome.*

This wood, these springs, this woven shade of
    overhanging vine,
        this ductile stream of flowing water,
and the meadows and the rose beds that yield nothing
    to twice-flowering Paestum,
        and the potherbs green in January and not
        frostbitten,
5  and the household eel that swims in closed water,
        and the white tower that harbors birds white as
        itself,
these are the gifts of my lady. To me, when I returned
    after seven lusters,
        Marcella gave this house, this little realm.
If Nausicaa were to offer me her father's
    gardens,
10          I could say to Alcinous: 'I prefer my own.'

### 56

*It was customary to give somebody a* soterion, *or "get-well present," upon recovering from an illness, but Polycharmus gets sick too often.*

You fall sick ten times or more in a single year,
    and this, Polycharmus, hurts us, not you.
For every time you rise from your bed, you ask your
    friends for getting-well presents.
        For shame, Polycharmus, fall sick now for good
        and all.

### 61

*A woman paradoxically hopes to become the target of Martial's invective, but he dismisses her as an unworthy target and suggests that she aspire to become the object of graffiti instead.*

You are afraid, Ligurra, of my writing verses
against you, a brief, lively poem,
and you long to seem worthy of such an apprehension.
But idle is your fear and idle your desire.
Libyan lions roar at bulls,           5
they do not trouble butterflies.
I advise you, if you are anxious to be read of,
to look for some boozy poet of the dark archway
who writes verses with rough charcoal or crumbling chalk
which folk read while they shit.         10
This brow of yours is not for marking with *my* brand.

### 97

*A humorous invective directed at a man who so exhausts himself in homoerotic affairs with boys that he cannot satisfy his rich and blameless wife.*

Your wife is a girl such as a husband would hardly
ask for in his most extravagant prayers,
rich, noble, cultivated, virtuous.
You burst your loins, Bassus, but you do it with
    long-haired boys
whom you have procured for yourself with your wife's
    dowry.         5
And your cock, which she bought for many thousands,
returns to your lady so languid that,
whether excited by coaxing words
or requested with a soft thumb, it won't rise.
Have some shame, for a change; or let us go to law.   10
It's not yours, Bassus. You sold it.

## AFTERWORD

Martial himself frequently refers to his popularity in his own time, and the testimony of contemporary writers would tend to support the proposition that he had a wide readership. As mentioned above, on hearing of Martial's death, probably about A.D. 104, Pliny writes that "he was a man of an acute and lively genius, and his writings abound with wit and bitterness, and no less candor" (*Letters* 3.21). Pliny goes on to quote, allegedly from memory, part of an epigram (10.19) that

Martial wrote about him, a fact that clearly influences his good opinion of the epigrammatist. But Pliny does not predict a long afterlife for Martial's work, adding that "his writings will not be immortal, no, perhaps they will not be, though he wrote them as if they would." Martial knew Juvenal, who borrowed several motifs from the epigrams in his satires, and Martial continued to be mined for pithy maxims throughout antiquity, even by Christian writers such as St. Jerome.

Martial was never read in the schools, but nonetheless his works never disappeared entirely during the Middle Ages, although there were few writers who demonstrated much familiarity with them. It was with the Renaissance that Martial came back into his own. Many of the humanists set their hand to attempting epigrams in Latin, most notably Angelo Poliziano (1454–94), and for the most part they took Martial as their model. In some circles, Martial's obscenity was an embarrassment, but in others it was a positive endorsement. The early humanist poet Antonio Beccadelli (1394–1471), also known as "Il Panormita," wrote a collection of eighty-one bawdy Latin epigrams in the manner of Martial known as *The Hermaphrodite* that might have brought a smile to the Roman poet's face. In contrast, the poet Andrea Navagero (1483–1529) burned a copy of Martial every year.

Most imitators of Martial focused on the moralizing themes in his works. This includes one of the earliest and best-known English translations of Martial by Henry Howard, Earl of Surrey (1517–47), a version of *Epigram* 10.47 that he called "The Means to Attain Happy Life":

> Martial, the things that do attain
>     The happy life be these, I find:
> The richesse left, not got with pain;
>     The fruitful ground, the quiet mind;
>
> The equal friend; no grudge, no strife;
>     No charge of rule, nor governance;
> Without disease, the healthful life;
>     The household of continuance;
>
> The mean diet, no delicate fare;
>     True wisdom join'd with simpleness;
> The night dischargèd of all care,
>     Where wine the wit may not oppress.
>
> The faithful wife, without debate;
>     Such sleeps as may beguile the night:
> Contented with thine own estate
>     Ne wish for death, ne fear his might.

In the following century in England, the epigrams of Martial, duly expurgated, were taught in schools, and many poets tried their hand at composing in his manner. Among the most successful was the Welsh poet John Owen, who published three volumes of epigrams in Latin (1606–12), which were so successful that he was known as the "British Martial." There was a particularly brilliant but precocious student at Christ Church in Oxford during this time, Thomas Browne (1663–1704), who was threatened with expulsion by the dean of the college, the humorless Dr. John Fell, a punishment that would be rescinded provided Browne not only apologize but produce an extempore translation of Martial's Epigram 1.32. The response that Browne produced on the spot earned him a form of immortality:

> I do not love thee, Dr. Fell.
> The reason why I cannot tell;

> But this I know and know full well,
> I do not love thee, Dr. Fell.

It was in epigrams composed in their own language that the English poets came closest to rivaling Martial, and none more so than Ben Jonson (1572–1637), the celebrated dramatist and poet. In his collection of *Epigrams* (1616), which Jonson called "the ripest of my studies," he aimed at achieving in English what Martial had done in Latin. In the range of subjects that he covers—contemporary mores, complaints against women, satires of the court—Jonson shows himself a subtle interpreter of Martial's work. In *Epigram* 36, called "To the Ghost of Martial," he displays a deft hand in doing the Roman poet one better in paying homage to his patron monarch:

> Martial, thou gav'st far nobler epigrams
> To thy Domitian, than I can to my James;
> But in my royal subject I pass thee:
> Thou flattered'st thine, mine cannot flattered be.

Martial influenced several other important English poets, Robert Herrick and John Donne among them, but none came closer than Jonson to rivaling the original. Since the eighteenth century Martial has been little read in schools or elsewhere, except by specialists, who enjoy his pungent commentary on Roman society, although a recent spate of translations and adaptations has brought him back to the attention of readers.

# THE HIGH EMPIRE

THE ASSASSINATION OF THE TYRANT DOMITIAN IN A.D. 96 USHERED IN A NEW ERA IN the governance of the empire and, with it, a new era in Roman cultural life as well. An elderly senator, already in his sixties, Marcus Cocceius Nerva acceded to the throne. Only a year into his reign, however, in response to a revolt by his Praetorian Guard, the childless Nerva adopted as his son and heir Marcus Ulpius Traianus, the powerful governor of Upper Germany. Just a few months later, in January of A.D. 98, Nerva suffered a stroke and died. With Trajan's reign began a prolonged period of political stability and relative security in foreign affairs. Trajan and the succeeding emperors followed the example of Nerva in choosing their successors by adoption, a system that ensured rule by men of character and competence until A.D. 180, when Marcus Aurelius was succeeded by his son Commodus. Wars of conquest were still fought, as is amply documented on the Column of Trajan, one of many great public monuments erected during this period to adorn the city of Rome. The empire expanded in the region of the Balkans, and new trade routes opened in the east. Nor was the border always secure and unthreatened: Marcus Aurelius spent much of his reign engaged in wars on the Rhine frontier. But for the most part, this was a period of peace, at least from the perspective of most of the inhabitants of the Roman world. The condition of the empire is described by a Greek rhetorician of the second century, Aelius Aristides, who was born to a wealthy family in the province of Mysia, in what is today western Turkey. He spent most of his life in Smyrna (modern Izmir) and died about A.D. 181. In the middle of the century he delivered this oration *To Rome*, which gives us some idea of how the elite of the provinces responded to Roman rule (70):

> Wars, even if they once occurred, no longer seem real; on the contrary, stories about them are interpreted more as myths by the many who hear them. If anywhere an actual clash occurs along the border, as is only natural in the immensity of a great empire, because of the madness of Getae or the misfortune of Libyans or the wickedness of those around the Red Sea, who are unable to enjoy the blessings they have, then simply like myths, they themselves quickly pass and the stories about them. So great is your peace, though war was traditional among you.

Aristides exaggerates, of course, but for nearly a century the Roman world was free from the internal strains that characterized the first hundred years of the empire.

The literature of this period reflects this change in conditions. In his historical writings Tacitus focuses on the first century of the empire to make a contrast with the enlightened times under Trajan. And the portrait of Roman society that can be viewed through the letters of Pliny shows us a world of cultural diversity and, at least as we see it in the upper classes, a life devoted to the pursuit of refinement. In the satires of Juvenal, too, written during the reigns of Trajan and Hadrian, we find a pointed contrast with life under the previous emperor Domitian, even as he registers his righteous indignation at contemporary mores.

This period also witnesses the flowering of literature in Greek within the empire. Surely a contributing factor was the support of emperors for cultural initiatives across the Roman world. Hadrian, in particular, was a great builder and a conspicuous philhellene, who also composed poetry. The so-called Second Sophistic was not so much a philosophical school as it was a rhetorical movement. Aelius Aristides was typical of the period, but so too were rhetoricians such as Herodes Atticus (ca. 101–77). He was the richest Athenian of his time, endowing public works there and throughout Greece, but he was also a distinguished man of letters who delivered orations in many parts of the empire. The last emperor of this period, Marcus Aurelius, himself the author of a memoir in Greek, was the friend and student of a rhetorician who in his life and works embodied the cultural ideals of the second century. Marcus Cornelius Fronto (ca. 110–76), who was born in the city of Cirta in the Latin-speaking province of Numidia and educated in Greek, served three emperors in Rome. His letters and speeches, which were lost until 1815, offer a brilliant portrait of the sophist at work in the multicultural capital of a world empire.

It is also from this period that we have the best surviving examples of the literature of entertainment, both in Greek and in Latin. The earliest surviving Greek novel is probably Chariton's tale of a heroine, Callirhoe, and her lover Chaereas, who endure long wanderings and separation before they are finally reunited. The novels of Xenophon of Ephesus, Achilles Tatius, and Heliodorus display the same outlandish blend of history and fantastic tales of kidnappings and misadventures. But arguably the most influential work of the genre is the least typical, the pastoral romance *Daphnis and Chloe* by Longus. For reasons of space, this rich vein in the literary culture of the period is not represented in this anthology as fully as could be wished. These works are an important component in the cultural background that informs the satirical set pieces of Lucian, as well as the picaresque tale of Lucius in Apuleius's *Metamorphoses*. This was not an age of great poetry—it offers nothing to compare with the masterpieces of the Augustan age, or even the poets of the early empire. But it was a period of fervent literary activity in a flourishing multicultural society in the lands that border the Mediterranean.

# TACITUS

## (Publius? Cornelius Tacitus, ca. A.D. 56–ca. 120)

HISTORY WAS CONSIDERED IN ANTIQUITY TO BE THE HIGHEST FORM OF PROSE WRITING, and Tacitus is universally regarded as by far the greatest of the Roman historians, a match for the best of the Greek exponents of the genre. He did not, however, devote himself exclusively to writing history, as Livy, for example, did. He had a very active career in politics throughout the last quarter of the first century A.D., serving as consul in 97, and then, much later, thanks to his seniority in the Senate, he was appointed to the very prestigious governorship of Asia Minor in 112/113.

His earliest surviving works, both published in 98, are the *Agricola,* a biography of his father-in-law, Gnaeus Julius Agricola, who had served as governor of Britain for seven years, and the *Germania,* an ethnographical monograph on the customs and character of the German tribes. Perhaps three years later, he published his *Dialogue about Orators,* on the state of public speaking in Rome, a work reflecting Tacitus's reputation as one of the great orators of the time, despite having a dramatic date of A.D. 75, much earlier than its publication. Thereafter, he devoted himself to the writing of a history of Rome in the first century A.D. He began with an account of the years 69 to 96, covering the reigns of Galba, Otho, Vitellius, and the three Flavian emperors, Vespasian and his two sons, Titus and Domitian. This work, the *Histories,* comprised twelve or fourteen books, but only the first four and part of the fifth survive. It is unfortunate that we have lost Tacitus's account of the years in which he himself was most closely engaged with politics at Rome and with the running of the empire. His treatment of the reign of Domitian must, however, have been relatively brief, given that the surviving books deal in such detail with 69, the "Year of the Four Emperors" ("that long year of Galba, Otho and Vitellius," as Tacitus calls it at *Dialogue* 17), and take the narrative no further than 70.

After the *Histories,* he turned to the earlier years of the century, in his masterwork, the *Annals,* which recounted the years from the death of Augustus in A.D. 14 to the death of Nero in 68. The *Annals* were planned in sixteen or eighteen books, with six devoted to Tiberius, six to Caligula and Claudius, and four or six to Nero. Rather more of the *Annals* has survived than of the *Histories*: Books 1 through 4, part of 5, 6, and the second half of 11 through to the middle of 16. It is not known whether Tacitus lived to complete the work, but it seems likely that he was still engaged on it after Hadrian succeeded Trajan in 117.

It is not coincidental that Tacitus's earliest works were published when he was about forty years old, more than a year after the assassination of Domitian in September 96. Nor is it coincidental that almost no works of history survive from the century that separates Livy from Tacitus. The exception is the two-book review of Roman history by Velleius Paterculus, probably published in A.D. 30, which devotes disproportionate space to the careers of Julius Caesar, Augustus, and especially Tiberius, who had been Velleius's commander for eight years of successful campaigning in Germany.

Throughout the first century, the political atmosphere in Rome was rarely favorable to the writing of history. The deterioration in freedom of expression is made clear in the speech that Tacitus attributes to the historian Cremutius Cordus at his trial in the Senate for treason in A.D. 25 (*Annals* 4.35):

> It is said that I praised Brutus and Cassius, whose history many have written, and of whom none has spoken unfavorably. Titus Livius, who enjoys an outstanding reputation for his style and reliability, gave such high praise to Gnaeus Pompey that Augustus called him 'the Pompeian', and that had no effect on their friendship...Antonius's letters and Brutus's speeches contain material insulting to Augustus, which, though untrue, is very caustic, and the poems of Bibaculus and Catullus, still read today, are full of abuse of the Caesars. The deified Julius and the deified Augustus themselves put up with this, and left the authors alone.

Cremutius himself was not so fortunate: he went home and starved himself to death, and the Senate voted to burn his books. Tacitus saw the same oppression in his own lifetime: when Domitian was offended by some allusions in a historical work by Hermogenes of Tarsus, he not only put Hermogenes to death but also crucified the slave-copyists who had written the work out (Suetonius, *Life of Domitian* 10).

Most of the *Annals* that is not concerned with wars on distant frontiers deals with relations between the emperor and the Senate. The idealized view of the Senate was as a distinguished and august group, rigidly adhering to the correct course of action, regardless of personal consequences. When Augustus established the Principate, he made a show of handing power back to the Senate. He was appalled when anyone addressed him as *domine*, "my lord" (Suetonius, *Life of Augustus* 53), for he was no doubt sensitive to the consequences for Julius Caesar of the suspicion that he wished to be king; a century later, however, when rule by one man was accepted by everyone as the only real possibility for government, Domitian began letters with the salutation "Our lord and god orders this to be done" (Suetonius, *Life of Domitian* 13).

But the erosion of the Senate's traditional authority was not so long in coming. Commenting on the transfer of power to Tiberius, Tacitus observes that "they all rushed into servitude—consuls, senators, and knights. The higher the rank, the greater the hypocrisy and haste" (*Annals* 1.7), and he reports that Tiberius used to say in Greek whenever he was leaving the Senate, "Ah, men ready to be slaves!" (*Annals* 3.65). Suetonius reports that Caligula was said to have considered awarding the consulship to Incitatus, his favorite horse in the Green stable (*Life of Caligula* 55). This may have been just a casual joke, but such a witticism would have been inconceivable under the Republic. To ingratiate themselves with Sejanus, Tiberius's evil minister, three senators wanted to trap a knight expressing sentiments disloyal to the emperor. They "hid themselves in a spot between the roof and the ceiling—a hiding-place whose squalor matched the vileness of the treachery—and put their ears to various chinks and cracks" (*Annals* 4.69); it is hard to imagine this sort of behavior from the senators of the early Republic who waited calmly for certain death when Rome was sacked by the Gauls.

In his brief introductory remarks to the *Annals*, Tacitus observes, "The histories of Tiberius, Gaius, Claudius, and Nero were distorted because of fear while they reigned, and, when they were gone, were composed with animosities still fresh" (1.1). He goes on to claim that he will recount the history of their reigns "without rancor and bias [*sine ira et studio*], far removed as I am from motives for these." While it is true that he was probably no more than ten years old when Nero was assassinated in A.D. 68, this claim is rather disingenuous.

In the *Histories*, Tacitus acknowledges that his political career prospered during the fifteen years of Domitian's reign, and it is reasonable to suppose that Domitian may have been responsible for his appointment to the consulship, which he held in A.D. 97, just a few months after Domitian's assassination. At the start of the *Agricola*, Tacitus bitterly denounces Domitian's cruelty in purging the Senate

**Figure 25: Tiberius**
A cameo now in Vienna, said to represent the emperor Tiberius. Suetonius describes him as big and strong, able to bore a hole in a ripe apple with his finger, with a handsome face that was often afflicted with pimples.

of its most able members, and at the end of the same work, he expresses his anger at his guilt through helpless acquiescence in such bloodshed: "*Our* hands dragged Helvidius to prison, *we* looked on as Mauricus and Rusticus died, *we* were soaked by Senecio's innocent blood" (*Agricola* 45). After administrative service for several years in the provinces, Tacitus returned to Rome in 93, during a wave of virulent treason trials that he and his fellow senators could do nothing to stop. Given this personal experience, it was not likely that Tacitus could have described "without rancor and bias" the treason trials that were the worst feature of Tiberius's reign. The earlier surviving half of the *Annals* is dominated by Tacitus's almost unremittingly negative and unsympathetic portrayal of Tiberius. He does occasionally grant that Tiberius has redeeming features, as when he acknowledges his generosity in alleviating misfortune, whether public or private (1.75, 2.37–48, 2.87, 4.64, 6.17). More typically, however, he turns even his praise of other people's noble deeds to the emperor's disadvantage, as when his account of the elder Agrippina's heroism in quelling the army's panic loses its focus and becomes vague speculation on Tiberius's dark suspicions about her ulterior motives.

Tacitus's condemnation of Tiberius is doubtless overstated. It stands in stark contrast to the adulation expressed by Velleius Paterculus, who served as a cavalry commander under Tiberius in Germany, at the culmination of his two-book history of Rome (largely ignored in antiquity and known to us from a single manuscript, now lost). Velleius's account extends to A.D. 29, but it is noticeable that even he has little to say about the preceding six years, when the treason trials raged (2.126):

> Who would recount all the achievements of Tiberius's reign, given that they are before our eyes and our minds?…Justice, equality, industry, long buried and forgotten, have been restored to the community. The magistrates have their authority again, the Senate its majesty, the courts their power. Unrest in the theaters has been suppressed. People have been either encouraged to want to act justly or forced to do so. Correct behavior is esteemed, but evil is punished. The humble respect the powerful, but without fear, while the powerful outrank the humble, but without arrogance. When has the price of grain been more reasonable? When has peace flourished more?

Tacitus writes in the same annalistic manner as Livy, grouping together events of a particular year. This method had worked well for the Republican period, when the annually elected consuls dominated and motivated political, social, and military affairs during their time in office. The establishment of the Principate meant that the consuls and the Senate as a whole lost much of their authority and were no longer the focus for Roman life. It is not of much consequence that Tacitus adheres to the annalistic method in the *Histories,* since the surviving books cover not much more than a single year, and the organization of the material is therefore inevitably focused on a very short period. In the *Annals,* Tacitus comments several times on his use of the annalistic method. Sometimes he declares that he is observing that structure:

> Were it not for my plan of assigning all events to their appropriate year, I would have liked to jump ahead and immediately record the ends that Latinius, Opsius, and the other architects of that piece of villainy experienced, not only after Gaius Caesar came to power, but even during Tiberius's lifetime.... But these and other punishments of the guilty parties I shall record at the appropriate point. (4.71)

Elsewhere, in discussing events on the frontier, he acknowledges that he is disrupting the annalistic structure:

> I have here put together the events of two summers so that the reader's mind can have some respite from domestic tragedies. (6.38)

> Although these campaigns were conducted over a number of years by two propraetors, I have put them together in case, related separately, they would not appear in my account as being as important as they were. I now return to the chronological narrative. (12.40)

One of the features of the annalistic method was the listing of portents, as recorded annually by the state for the light they might shed on Rome's destiny (see p. 394). Even as he provides one such list, Tacitus dismisses its significance:

> There were also frequent but meaningless prodigies. A woman gave birth to a serpent, and another was killed by a lightning bolt while making love with her husband. The sun was suddenly darkened, and the fourteen districts of the city were struck by lightning. But all this was far from being the result of divine intervention—Nero extended his reign and crimes for many years thereafter! (14.12)

For all that Tacitus shares Livy's annalistic method, and continues the story of Rome from roughly the time when Livy left off, nevertheless the style and spirit of his history writing owe far more to Sallust, whose *Conspiracy of Catiline, War with Jugurtha,* and *Histories* were written in the late 40s and early 30s B.C. The first two of these works, both monographs, survive complete, but the *Histories,* recounting the years from 78 B.C. onward in the annalistic style, are mostly lost. The opening sentence of Tacitus's *Annals, Urbem Romam a principio reges habuere,* "Kings first governed the city of Rome," acknowledges the influence of Sallust, for the phrases *Urbem Romam* and *a principio* are taken from the beginning of Sallust's *Catiline* and *Histories,* respectively (with *reges habuere* completing a line of rather antiquated hexameter verse, giving an elevated tone to the *Annals* right at the start). The influence of Sallust is very significant, for he preached a return to the moral rectitude of the old times (the *mos maiorum*), and Tacitus is equally or even more concerned with pointing out the degeneracy of the modern age.

# ANNALS

## Book 1

*Imperial history is inextricably entwined with imperial intrigue as the main plot line in Rome's political life under the Caesars. In the opening book of the* Annals, *which begins with the accession of Rome's second emperor, Tiberius, Augustus's adopted son, we meet also Livia, his mother and the emperor's widow; Drusus (ca. 13 B.C.–A.D. 23), Tiberius's only surviving son by his first, happy, marriage to Vipsania; Germanicus (ca. 15 B.C.–A.D. 19), Tiberius's nephew, the son of his brother Drusus by his marriage to Mark Antony's daughter; and Germanicus's wife, Agrippina (ca. 14 B.C.–A.D. 33), the daughter of Augustus's right-hand man, Marcus Agrippa, and his daughter Julia. Augustus was determined to keep power in his own family. His daughter Julia was married at various times to three of his five designated successors. Her first husband was her cousin Marcellus, son of Augustus's sister Octavia. Tiberius was devoted to his wife Vipsania Agrippina, daughter of Augustus's friend Vipsanius Agrippa, who was the second husband of Augustus's daughter Julia. When Agrippa died, Augustus forced Tiberius to divorce Vipsania and marry Julia. Tiberius thus married his own former mother-in-law and his former wife's stepmother, and Livia became Julia's mother-in-law as well as her stepmother. Chapters 1 through 4 are introductory to the main narrative of the first year and a half of Tiberius's reign, beginning with a sketch of the main periods of Roman history and Tacitus's reasons for selecting this one. He describes the increasing centralization of power under Augustus and the problems of the succession.*

[1] Kings first governed the city of Rome; liberty and the consulship were established by Lucius Brutus. Dictatorships were employed to meet crises. The rule of the decemvirs lasted no more than two years, and the consular authority of the military tribunes was also short-lived. The ascendancy of Cinna was not of long duration, nor that of Sulla; and the dominance of Pompey and Crassus swiftly passed to Caesar, the armed might of Lepidus and Antonius to Augustus. Augustus then brought a world exhausted from civil dissension under his authority, with the title of "First Citizen."

The Roman people of old had their successes and their failures related by famous authors; and there was no shortage of fine minds for recording the Augustan period, until the groundswell of obsequiousness frightened them off. The histories of Tiberius, Gaius,

Claudius, and Nero were distorted because of fear while they reigned, and, when they were gone, were composed with animosities still fresh. Hence my decision to deal only briefly with Augustus and specifically with the final days—and then to move on to the Principate of Tiberius and its aftermath, without rancor or bias, far removed as I am from motives for these.

[2] After Brutus and Cassius were killed, there was no longer a state military force; and when Pompeius had been vanquished in Sicily, Lepidus discarded, and Antonius killed, even the Julian party was left with no leader other than Caesar Octavian. Dropping the title "triumvir," Octavian presented himself as a consul, and as a man satisfied to hold tribunician authority in order to safeguard the people. Then, by seducing the military with donatives, the masses with grain allowances, and everybody with the pleasure of peace, he gradually increased his powers, drawing to himself the functions of Senate, magistrates, and laws. He met no resistance. The most dynamic men had fallen in battle or through the proscriptions; and the remaining nobles rose to wealth and offices in proportion to their appetite for servitude. Having benefited from the revolution, they preferred the security of the current regime to the dangers of the old. The provinces were not averse to this arrangement, either. Rivalries between the powerful and the greed of magistrates had raised doubts about the rule of the Senate and people, and there was little help to be had from the laws, which were constantly undermined by violence, political engineering and, most importantly, by graft.

[3] To bolster his supremacy, Augustus promoted his sister's son, Claudius Marcellus, still just a boy, to the positions of pontiff and curule aedile. He also elevated Marcus Agrippa—a man of low birth but a fine soldier, and his partner in victory—with repeated consulships, and later, when Marcellus died, took him as his son-in-law. His stepsons, Tiberius Nero and Claudius Drusus, he honored with the title *imperator*, despite his own family being still intact. For he had brought into the house of the Caesars Agrippa's sons, Gaius and Lucius, and, despite feigning opposition to the idea, had passionately wished to see them styled "Princes of the Youth" and made consuls-designate even before they had set aside the toga of boyhood. After Agrippa's demise, Lucius and Gaius Caesar were taken off by premature natural deaths, or else by the machinations of their stepmother, Livia, Lucius en route for the Spanish

armies, and Gaius as he was returning from Armenia incapacitated by a wound. Drusus was long deceased; Tiberius was the only surviving stepson; everything shifted towards him. He was adopted as son, as colleague in power, as partner in tribunician authority, and put on display throughout the armed forces, his mother not acting surreptitiously as before, but with open encouragement.

In fact, Livia had got such a hold on the ageing Augustus that he banished to the island of Planasia his only surviving grandson, Agrippa Postumus. It is true that the man was a stranger to all decent qualities and possessed of a block-headed pride in his physical strength, but he had been found guilty of no misconduct. In contrast to this treatment, Augustus put Drusus' son Germanicus at the head of eight legions on the Rhine and ordered his adoption by Tiberius, despite there already being an adolescent son in Tiberius' house. This was meant to increase the number of supports for his power.

At that time no war remained except that against the Germans, fought to erase the disgrace of the loss of the army under Quinctilius Varus rather than from a desire to advance the bounds of empire or win some worthwhile prize. At home there was tranquility, and officials bore the same titles as before. Younger people had been born after the victory at Actium and even the old, for the most part, had been born during the period of the civil wars, leaving only a minute fraction that had witnessed the Republic.

[4] Thus the nature of the state had changed, and no trace of the old integrity of character was anywhere to be found. Equality had been discarded, and everybody focused on the emperor's commands. There was no fear for the moment, as long as Augustus' age and strength could sustain the man himself, his house and the peace. When he grew weak with advanced age and attendant physical infirmity, when the end was near and hopes of change arose, a few chatted idly about the benefits of freedom; more feared war, others wanted it. The great majority disparaged their forthcoming masters with gossip of various kinds. Agrippa was a savage who had been incensed by insult, it was said; in age and experience he was unequal to such great responsibility. Tiberius Nero had maturity as far as years went, and a distinguished military record; but he also had that old, ingrained arrogance of the Claudian family and, despite all efforts to suppress them, numerous hints of his viciousness broke through to the surface. He had

also been brought up from his earliest years in a ruling house, it was noted. Consulships and triumphs had been heaped on him when he was young, and even in his years of exile on Rhodes (passed off as "retirement") resentment, hypocritical behavior and covert depravity were the focus of his life. Then there was his mother with her female capriciousness. They would be slaves to a woman and two youngsters along with her; these would tyrannize the state for the time being, and later tear it to shreds.

*The narrative begins in chapters 5 through 14 with the final illness and death of Augustus on August 19 in the year A.D. 14. Tiberius moved efficiently to consolidate his position, arranging for the murder of Augustus's grandson, Agrippa Postumus. Tacitus describes his dealings with the Senate involving the will of Augustus and arrangements for his funeral. He takes the opportunity to report favorable and unfavorable judgments of Tiberius's character, which is a frequent device for coloring his reporting of events and attributing motives to the protagonists. Tiberius appears reluctant to accept the Principate but takes offense at the observations of the senators Asinius Gallus, Lucius Arruntius, Quintus Haterius, and Mamercus Scaurus. The transfer of power is complete with the description of the honors decreed to Augustus's widow and Tiberius's mother, Livia, and Tiberius's nephew Germanicus. At the end of this section (15) almost as an afterthought comes the notice of the transfer of electoral authority from the assemblies (comitia) of the people to the Senate, which amounts to an important emblem of the reality of imperial rule.*

[5] As people made these and other such observations, Augustus' health took a turn for the worse, and some suspected foul play on his wife's part. In fact, the rumor had spread that, taking a select few into his confidence and accompanied only by Fabius Maximus, Augustus had a few months earlier sailed to Planasia to visit Agrippa. On the island there were, reportedly, floods of tears and gestures of affection from both parties, arousing expectations that the young man would be taken back into his grandfather's house. This, it was said, Maximus had divulged to his wife, Marcia, who in turn divulged it to Livia. The emperor came to know about it, and shortly afterwards, Maximus passed away—whether it was suicide or not is unclear—and Marcia was apparently heard sobbing at his funeral, blaming herself for causing her husband's death. Whatever the truth of the matter, Tiberius was summoned home by

an urgent letter from his mother when he had barely set foot in Illyricum, and it is not known for sure whether he found Augustus still breathing or already lifeless when he reached him in the town of Nola. For Livia had kept the house and surrounding streets strictly guarded, with encouraging bulletins issued periodically until all the measures that the crisis demanded were put in place. At that point notice was simultaneously given that Augustus had died and that Tiberius was in power.

[6] The first criminal act of the new principate was the murder of Postumus Agrippa. Agrippa was caught off-guard and unarmed, but a determined centurion still had trouble dispatching him. Tiberius said nothing of the matter in the Senate. He pretended that his father had left orders for the tribune in charge of guarding him not to put off killing Agrippa as soon as he himself had lived his last day.

There is no doubt that Augustus had made many bitter complaints about the young man's character and had secured ratification of Agrippa's exile by senatorial decree. But he never brought himself to murder one of his own, and that he would have killed a grandson to provide security for a stepson beggared belief. The more likely explanation is that Tiberius and Livia hurriedly effected the assassination of a young man whom they eyed with suspicion and loathing, Tiberius out of fear, and Livia from a stepmother's hatred.

When the centurion followed standard military procedure and reported that his "orders had been carried out," Tiberius replied that he had given no such orders and that what had been done had to be accounted for before the Senate. Sallustius Crispus was party to the secret—it was he who had sent the written instructions to the tribune—and when he heard of this he feared that he might be made the scapegoat, and that lying or revealing the truth would be equally dangerous. He therefore cautioned Livia not to let word get out of the inner workings of the palace, of advice given by friends or of services performed by soldiers, and to see that Tiberius did not undermine the strength of the principate by bringing everything before the Senate. The rule of governing, he said, was that accounts balanced only when set before one person.

[7] In Rome, meanwhile, they all rushed into servitude—consuls, senators, and knights. The higher the rank, the greater the hypocrisy and haste. With expressions composed to show neither pleasure at the passing of one emperor nor too much gloom at another's inauguration, they blended tears and joy, grief and sycophancy. The consuls Sextus Pompeius and Sextus Appuleius were the first to swear allegiance to Tiberius Caesar, and, in the consuls' presence, Seius Strabo and Gaius Turranius followed (Strabo was prefect of the praetorian cohorts, and Turranius prefect of the grain supply). Next came the Senate, the military, and the people.

In fact, Tiberius used the consuls to initiate every action, as though he was acting under the old republic and in two minds about taking power. Even the proclamation with which he now summoned the Senate to the Curia he made only under the title of his tribunician authority, conferred on him under Augustus. The wording of the proclamation was brief and low-key. It stated that he would raise the question of honors to be paid to his father—and meanwhile he was not leaving Augustus' body—and that this was the only official duty that he was assuming.

However, on Augustus' death he had given the password to the praetorian cohorts as *Imperator*; he had sentries, armed guards, and the other trappings of the court; he had a military escort into the Forum, a military escort into the Curia. He sent dispatches to the armies as if he had succeeded to the principate, and there was no trace of indecision—except in his addresses in the Senate. The principal reason for this was his fear of Germanicus. For Germanicus had at his disposal so many legions, innumerable allied auxiliaries, and awesome support amongst the people—and he might prefer to hold power rather than wait for it. Tiberius also made some concession to popular opinion, wishing to appear to have been summoned and chosen by the state rather than to have crept into it through a wife's scheming and a dodderer's adoption. Later on it was understood that he had feigned the indecisiveness in order to fathom out the inclinations of the leading men; he would distort their words and expressions to give them a criminal intent, and keep them in mental storage.

[8] On the first day of the Senate Tiberius permitted no business other than Augustus' obsequies. The will of the deceased was brought in by the Vestal Virgins, and it named Tiberius and Livia as heirs. Livia was adopted into the Julian family and given the Augustan name. Augustus had entered his grandsons and great-grandsons as heirs in default, and third in line the highest-ranked men of the state (most of whom he

loathed, but it was done for show, and to boost his reputation with posterity). His bequests did not exceed the norm for a private citizen, apart from the gifts of 43,500,000 sesterces to the common people, a thousand each to soldiers of the praetorian cohorts, and three hundred per man to legionaries and members of the cohorts composed of Roman citizens.

Discussion of funeral honors followed, and the most impressive proposals were those of Asinius Gallus, that the cortege be taken through the triumphal gate, and Lucius Arruntius, that it be preceded by the titles of laws Augustus had passed and the names of peoples he had conquered. A further proposal, from Messalla Valerius, was that the oath of allegiance to Tiberius be renewed each year. Asked by Tiberius if he had brought forth this suggestion on his instructions, Messalla replied that he had spoken of his own accord, and that where interests of state were involved he would rely solely on his own judgment, even at the risk of causing offence. That was the only form of obsequiousness still left to try.

The senators called out for the body to be carried to the pyre on the shoulders of members of their order. Tiberius spared them this responsibility with a condescending restraint, and issued a warning to the masses by official edict. They had once by their excess of enthusiasm disrupted the funeral of the deified Julius, he said, and they must not now try to have Augustus cremated in the Forum instead of at the resting place reserved for him in the Campus Martius.

On the day of the funeral the soldiers virtually stood on guard. There was much mirth amongst those who had personally seen—or been told of it by their parents—that day when servitude was still new, and the attempt to regain liberty came to nothing, the day when the murder of the dictator Caesar was seen by some as the worst of deeds and by others as the finest. Now, they said, an aged emperor who had long ruled, and even provided his heirs with the means to repress the state, needed military protection so that his burial could proceed peacefully!

[9] After that there was much chatter about Augustus himself. The majority expressed wonder over banalities: the day on which he once assumed power was the same date as the last day of his life, and he had ended that life at Nola in the same house and bedroom as his father Octavius. Much was said, too, about the number of his consulships—equal to those of Valerius Corvus and Gaius Marius put together—and about his

uninterrupted thirty-seven years of tribunician authority, the twenty-one occasions on which he won the title *Imperator,* and other honors, held many times or newly conferred. In discriminating circles, however, his life variously received praise or criticism. Some saw him driven to a civil conflict—one that could not be planned for or fought by honorable means—by loyalty to his father and the plight of the state, in which the laws then had no place. Many were the concessions he had made to Antonius, they said, and many to Lepidus—just as long as he could exact vengeance from his father's killers. After Lepidus lapsed into indolent senility and Antonius' debauchery proved his undoing, the only remedy for the divided country was the rule of one man. And yet the political organization had not meant monarchy or a dictatorship, but merely accepting the title "First Citizen." Now the empire's bounds were the Ocean or far-off rivers. There was an integrated complex of legions, of provinces, of fleets— of everything. There was justice amongst the citizens, restraint towards the allies. The city itself had been marvelously embellished. The use of force had been rare, and only to assure peace elsewhere.

[10] The contrary view was that Augustus' loyalty to his father and the crises faced by the state had been just a facade. In fact, these people said, it was lust for supremacy that had led Augustus to mobilize veterans with largesse, to raise an army while he was still a boy and a private citizen, to bribe a consul's legions and to feign support for the Pompeian party. Soon he appropriated the insignia and authority of a praetor by a decree of the Senate. Then Hirtius and Pansa were killed. Perhaps it was the enemy that saw them off, or perhaps it was a case of Pansa having poison applied to a wound, and Hirtius dying at the hands of his own soldiers in a plot masterminded by Octavian. In any case, Octavian then took over the troops of both, seized the consulship against the Senate's will, and turned against the state the arms he had been given to combat Antonius. The ensuing proscription of citizens and apportionment of lands did not find favor even with those who carried them out. It is true that the deaths of Cassius and the Brutuses were a concession to an inherited feud (though private animosities should be surrendered to the public good), but Pompeius was hoodwinked with a bogus peace, Lepidus with an illusory friendship. Subsequently Antonius was lured on by the treaties of Tarentum and Brundisium and by marriage to the sister, and with his death paid the

price for that treacherous connection. Certainly peace followed, but a bloody one—witness the defeats of Lollius and Varus, the killings at Rome of men like Varro, Egnatius, and Iullus.

Augustus' personal life did not escape criticism either. There was the stealing of Nero's wife and the ridiculous consulting of the pontiffs on whether she could legitimately marry if she had conceived a child but not yet given birth; there was the extravagant lifestyle of Vedius Pollio; and finally there was Livia, detrimental to the state as a mother, detrimental to the house of the Caesars as a stepmother. In wanting himself worshipped with temples and godlike effigies, and with flamens and priests, they said, Augustus had left no room for honors to be paid to the gods. Even his adoption of Tiberius as his successor was not based on affection, or on regard for the state. No, they continued, he recognized Tiberius' arrogance and ruthlessness, and had sought renown from the worst of comparisons. For it is true that a few years earlier, when requesting of the Senate a second term of tribunician authority for Tiberius, Augustus had, in an otherwise complimentary address, thrown in certain observations about the man's demeanor, lifestyle, and habits. While apparently vindicating Tiberius, these were really meant as an affront.

At all events, the obsequies were duly performed, and Augustus was officially granted his temple and heavenly honors.

[11] After that the prayers were addressed to Tiberius. He offered sundry comments on the greatness of the empire and his own lack of ambition. Only the deified Augustus had the mental qualities capable of shouldering such a burden, he observed, and when he himself had been invited by Augustus to share his responsibilities, he had learned from experience how arduous, and how subject to fortune, the task of worldwide rule actually was. In fact, their community relied on the support of many distinguished men, he said, and within it they should not make one individual responsible for everything—it would be easier for a number of people to work together to carry out the duties of state. The address was more impressive than persuasive. Even on subjects where he was not trying to obfuscate, Tiberius' language was always, whether by nature or from practice, vague and obscure, but on that occasion he was trying to cover up completely his true feelings, and so it became all the more convoluted and equivocal. The senators, whose only fear was that they might

appear to understand him, burst into tearful laments and appeals, holding out their hands to the gods, to the statue of Augustus, and to the knees of Tiberius himself. At that point he ordered a document to be brought out and read aloud. In it were catalogued the resources of the state: the number of citizens and allies under arms; all the fleets, client kingdoms, and provinces; all taxes direct and indirect; and all necessary expenditures and gifts. Augustus had listed everything in his own handwriting, and had added the recommendation, through fear, perhaps, or from jealousy, that the empire be restricted to its existing frontiers.

[12] Meanwhile, as the Senate lapsed into the most cringing entreaties, Tiberius casually remarked that, while he was not up to the task of the entire administration of the state, he would take responsibility for any part of it that he might be assigned. Then Asinius Gallus said: "Please, Caesar, which area of government would you like to be assigned?"

Flustered by the unexpected question, Tiberius fell silent for a moment. Then, gathering his thoughts, he answered that his diffidence would not let him choose or refuse any area of something that he would prefer to be excused from altogether. Gallus, who had surmised Tiberius' displeasure from his expression, added that the point of his question was not to have him compartmentalize functions that should not be divided, but to get from Tiberius himself an admission that the state was one body, and that it should be directed by one man's mind. He added a eulogy of Augustus, and reminded Tiberius of his victories and his many years of fine service as a civilian. Not even with that did he assuage the man's anger, however. For Gallus had long been hated by him because of his marriage to Marcus Agrippa's daughter, Vipsania, who had once been Tiberius' wife. This suggested that Gallus had ambitions beyond those of a private citizen, and that he retained the characteristic aggressiveness of his father, Asinius Pollio.

[13] After this Lucius Arruntius, whose remarks differed little from those of Gallus, caused just as much offence. In fact, while Tiberius had no long-standing grudge against Arruntius, he suspected him because he was wealthy and enterprising, with outstanding qualities and a correspondingly high public profile. Now Augustus, in his final conversations, had discussed possible candidates for the principate, noting those who, though suitable, would refuse it, those who were unfit but would want it, and those who were both capable

and eager to have it. He had named Marcus Lepidus as competent but uninterested, Asinius Gallus as eager but inadequate, and Lucius Arruntius as one who was not unqualified and who, given the opportunity, would venture to take it. On the identity of the first two there is agreement, but some sources have Gnaeus Piso instead of Arruntius, and with the exception of Lepidus all of them were soon unjustly convicted on various charges trumped up by Tiberius.

Quintus Haterius and Mamercus Scaurus also provoked his suspicious nature, Haterius by saying "How long, Caesar, are you going to let the republic be without a head?" and Scaurus for remarking that, since Tiberius had not vetoed the consuls' motion by using his tribunician authority, there remained hope that the Senate's prayers would not be ineffectual. Haterius received an immediate tongue-lashing, but Scaurus, for whom Tiberius felt a more deep-seated resentment, he simply passed by in silence. Then, worn down by the general outcry and individual appeals, he gradually shifted his stance, not going so far as to say he was accepting the power, but ending his refusals and their petitioning.

It is a well-known fact that Haterius went into the Palatium to apologize, threw himself down at the knees of Tiberius, who was taking a walk, and only just missed being killed by the guards because Tiberius fell over, either accidentally or because he was tripped by Haterius' grasp on him. The emperor's attitude was not softened by the danger that a man of such distinction had faced, until Haterius made an appeal to Augusta and was protected by her anxious intercession.

[14] Much senatorial adulation was focused on Augusta, too, some proposing that she be styled "Parent," and others "Mother," of the nation, and several that the words "Son of Julia" be added to the emperor's name. Tiberius insisted that honors paid to women should be circumscribed, and that he would show similar restraint with regard to those paid to himself; but he was really tormented with jealousy, and felt that the promotion of a woman was a slight to himself. So he would not permit her even to be assigned a lictor, and vetoed an "altar of adoption" and other such honors. On the other hand he requested proconsular *imperium* for Germanicus Caesar, and had a delegation sent to him to confer it, and also to console him in his sorrow over the death of Augustus. The reason for the same request not being made for Drusus was that Drusus was consul designate and

then present in the city. Tiberius nominated twelve candidates for the praetorship, the number passed on to him by Augustus, and though the Senate urged him to increase it he swore an oath never to go beyond that figure.

[15] It was at this time that elections were first transferred from the Campus to the Senate; for, up to that date, though the most important elections reflected the emperor's choice, some were still left to the partiality of the people voting in their tribes. The people, apart from some idle chatter, did not protest against the removal of this right, and the Senate, freed from having to offer bribes and from humiliating canvassing, was happy to comply. Tiberius undertook to recommend no more than four candidates whose appointment would not be rejected or contested. The plebeian tribunes meanwhile made a petition to put on games, at their own expense, which were to be added to the calendar and called the Augustal Games, after Augustus. In fact, money from the treasury was authorized for the event, and it was also decided that the tribunes should be entitled to wear triumphal garb in the Circus, but they were not allowed to ride in the chariot. Before long the celebration of the games was turned over to that praetor allotted the jurisdiction between citizens and foreigners.

*Tacitus now turns to foreign affairs, an arena in which the death of Augustus had serious repercussions. In chapters 16 through 30 he describes the mutiny of the legions in Pannonia, a vast region south and west of the Danube that covered parts of modern Hungary, Austria, Croatia, Serbia, Slovenia, Slovakia, and Bosnia and Herzegovina. The rebellious soldiers sent the son of their commander, Blaesus, to Rome to deliver their demands to the new emperor, who responded by sending a fresh force under the command of his son Drusus and Sejanus, the prefect of the Praetorian Guard in Rome. The situation continued to deteriorate until by chance a lunar eclipse gave Drusus the opportunity to take advantage of the men's superstitions and bring them back to order. Once discipline was restored, the ringleaders were punished, and Drusus was able to return to Italy.*

[16] Such was the state of civic affairs when a mutiny broke out amongst the legions in Pannonia. There were no fresh reasons for it; it was simply that the change of emperors offered the prospect of unrestricted rioting and hopes of deriving profit from civil war.

Three legions had been quartered together for the summer under the command of Junius Blaesus, and when he heard of Augustus' passing and Tiberius' accession Blaesus had suspended routine duties for mourning, or rejoicing. That was the start of the men's unruly behavior. They became fractious, lending an ear to what any good-for-nothing had to say; and eventually they were hungry for extravagant and easy living, and averse to discipline and hard work.

There was in the camp a certain Percennius who had once been a leader of a claque in the theaters and had then become a common soldier. He had a ready tongue and, from rousing support in the theater, had learned how to stir up a crowd. Percennius worked gradually on the men, who were naive and uncertain what the conditions of service would be like after Augustus. He held conversations with them at night, or when the day turned towards evening, and gathered about him all the most undesirable elements, when better men had slipped away.

[17] Eventually, after finding others who were ready to assist with the mutiny, he asked the men, as though in a public harangue, why they obeyed like slaves the few centurions they had, and the even fewer tribunes. When would they dare to demand a solution to their problems, he asked, if they would not approach a new emperor, still unsure of himself, with their appeals, or their swords. Their inertia over so many years had been a big enough mistake—enduring thirty or forty campaign seasons that turned them into old men, most of them maimed from their wounds! Even discharge did not end their service, he continued; encamped next to their standard, they endured the very same hardships under a different name! And anyone surviving all the perils was still hauled off to remote lands where he would be given some boggy marsh or hilly desert as so-called "farmland." Indeed, a soldier's life was hard and unrewarding, he said. Body and soul, he was worth ten *asses* a day, and from that his clothing, weapons, and tents were to be purchased, and bribes found to avoid the brutality of the centurions and gain exemption from chores. But the lash and wounds, the harsh winters and exhausting summers, savage war and profitless peace—there was certainly no end to those! And there would be no relief unless terms were established for entering service, with a denarius a day as their pay, and the sixteenth year marking the end of their duty—and no being kept on under the standards after that, but a cash payment of their gratuity being made

to them in the same camp. The praetorian cohorts received pay of two denarii, and were sent home after sixteen years—could it be that they faced more dangers? He was not belittling the praetorians' guard-duty in the city, he said, but in their own case it was a matter of living amongst savage tribes and having the enemy in view from their tents!

[18] There was noisy approval from the crowd as various grievances surfaced. Some indignantly pointed to stripes from the lash, others to their grey hair, and the majority to their threadbare clothing and unclad limbs. Finally they reached such a pitch of fury that they mooted the idea of merging the three legions into one. They were deterred by their rivalry, as each man wanted for his own legion the honor of providing the name; and so they changed tack, and placed together the three eagles and the standards of the cohorts. At the same time they proceeded to pile up clods of earth and build a platform, to make the spot more prominent. As they were forging ahead with this, Blaesus appeared. He began to reprimand them, and to pull them back one at a time, shouting: "Stain your hands with my blood instead! It will be a lesser crime for you to kill a legate than to revolt against the emperor. Either I shall live and keep my legions loyal, or be killed and make you regret your actions all the sooner."

[19] The turf kept rising none the less, and it was only when it had reached the men's chests that Blaesus' determination paid off and they abandoned the undertaking. Blaesus then made an eloquent address, explaining that soldiers' petitions should not be communicated to the emperor by means of mutiny and civil disorder. Those serving in the past, he said, had not made such radical proposals to their commanders, nor had they themselves to the deified Augustus— and, besides, to burden an emperor with worries at the start of his reign was very bad timing. But even if they intended to claim in peacetime what even victors in civil wars had not demanded, why were they considering violent action, abandoning their customary obedience and the discipline that was rightly expected of them? He then recommended that they choose some representatives and give them their instructions in his presence.

The men cried out that Blaesus' son, a tribune, should take charge of the delegation and request military discharge for them after sixteen years—they would give him his other instructions once that met with success. There was a measure of peace after the young man's departure. The soldiers were very self-satisfied, however: that their commander's son was presenting their common cause showed that force had extorted what they would not have gained by good behavior.

[20] Before the mutiny began, some maniples had been sent off to Nauportus to work on roads, bridges, and other projects, and on hearing about the disorder in the camp they pulled up their standards and plundered the nearest villages, including Nauportus itself, which was the size of a town. When the centurions tried to stop them, they subjected them to derision and insults, and finally to beatings. The anger was particularly directed against the camp prefect, Aufidienus Rufus. They pulled him from his wagon, loaded him with baggage, and drove him forward at the head of the column, sneeringly asking him if he was enjoying such heavy packs and such long marches. Rufus, in fact, had spent a long time as a private before becoming a centurion and, shortly afterwards, camp prefect. He had been trying to reintroduce the stringent discipline of former days and, being an old hand at hard physical labor, he was all the more exacting because he had endured it himself.

[21] The arrival of these troops revived the mutiny, and men wandered off to pillage the surrounding districts. To intimidate the others, Blaesus ordered a lashing and imprisonment for a few, particularly those loaded with plunder; for even at that stage the legate was still obeyed by his centurions and the best of the private soldiers. The men struggled with those dragging them off; they grabbed the knees of those around them; at one moment they called on individuals by name, and at the next on the century, the cohort, and the legion to which they variously belonged, crying out that they all faced the same danger. At the same time they heaped insults on their commander, appealed to the gods in heaven, and did everything possible to stir up resentment, pity, fear, and anger. All rushed to the spot. Breaking into the guardhouse, they released the prisoners and accepted into their ranks deserters and men convicted of capital crimes.

[22] The violence now flared up even more, and the mutiny acquired additional leaders. A certain Vibulenus, a common soldier, was lifted onto the shoulders of bystanders before Blaesus' dais, and he addressed his disorderly colleagues, who were eagerly waiting to see what he had in mind. "Yes, you have restored light and breath to these innocent unfortunates," he said, "but who can restore life to my brother,

who can restore my brother to me? He was sent to you from the army in Germany to discuss our collective interests, but last night *he* had him murdered by the gladiators he maintains and keeps under arms to kill his soldiers. Answer me, Blaesus—where did you dispose of the body? Even enemies do not begrudge burial! When I have satisfied my grief with kisses and tears, tell them to butcher me, too. Only let these men here bury us—killed not for any crime, but because we were acting for the good of the legions!"

[23] Vibulenus made his words all the more provocative by weeping and beating his breast and face with his hands. Then he flung aside the men on whose shoulders he was being carried, and threw himself on his face at the feet of one man after another. Such was the distress and animosity that he aroused that some of the soldiers put in irons the gladiators amongst Blaesus' slaves, and others the rest of his servants. Another group poured out to look for the corpse. They were close to killing the commander—but it quickly became known that no corpse was to be found, that the slaves denied the murder under torture, and that Vibulenus had never had a brother. Instead, they drove off the tribunes and the camp prefect, plundering their baggage when they fled, and the centurion Lucilius was murdered. (With typical soldiers' wit, the men had nicknamed this man "Give me another" because, when he broke a vine-rod on a soldier's back, he would, in a loud voice, call out for another and then a third.) The others all found places to hide, apart from Julius Clemens, who alone was held back: with his quick intelligence he was thought a good choice for relaying the soldiers' demands. The Eighth and Fifteenth legions were actually ready to fight each other, the one demanding the execution of a man named Sirpicus, and the men of the Fifteenth sheltering him; but the soldiers of the Ninth Legion intervened with appeals, and threats when they were ignored.

[24] Tiberius was a secretive man, and was especially prone to concealing bad news, but the report of these developments prompted him to dispatch his son Drusus to the scene with some leading men of the city and two praetorian cohorts. Drusus had no specific instructions, but was to take decisions as the situation required. His cohorts, too, had been brought up beyond their usual strength with some crack troops. They were further reinforced by a large contingent of the praetorian cavalry and by the strongest German troops then serving as the emperor's bodyguard.

Along with them went the prefect of the praetorian guard, Aelius Sejanus (who had been assigned to his father, Strabo, as his colleague, and who had great influence with Tiberius). Sejanus was to give the young man guidance, and keep the soldiers focused on the dangers they faced, and on their prospective rewards.

When Drusus approached, the legions, as a mark of respect, came forth to meet him. They did not, however, have their usual welcoming demeanor and glittering insignia; they were offensively squalid, and, though they tried to look downcast, their expression was closer to defiance.

[25] After Drusus entered the rampart, the men secured the gates with sentries, and ordered companies of armed men to position themselves at certain points in the camp. The others surrounded the dais in a large crowd. Drusus stood there, his hand raised calling for silence. When the men turned their eyes back on their assembled masses, there would be a burst of fractious shouts; but then they trembled at the sight of Drusus. Indistinct muttering was followed by a fierce outcry and, suddenly, silence; and their conflicting emotions made them both fearful and frightening.

Finally, when there was a break in the uproar, Drusus read out his father's letter. In it Tiberius had written that he felt a particular concern for the brave legions with which he had gone through many campaigns, and that when his mind could find respite from grief he would discuss their demands with the Senate. Meanwhile he had sent his son to grant promptly what could be given on the spot; the rest must await consideration by the Senate which, he said, they should regard as lacking neither in generosity nor in severity.

[26] The reply from the gathering was that the centurion Clemens had been given instructions to take to Rome. Clemens began to talk of discharge after sixteen years' service, of bonuses at the termination of service, of a denarius as a day's pay, and of veterans no longer being kept on duty. When, in response, Drusus pleaded that it was for the Senate and his father to decide, he was shouted down. Why had he bothered coming, they asked, if he had no intention of increasing the soldiers' pay or lightening their burdens—in fact with no power to help them whatsoever? No, but beatings and executions—everyone was allowed those! Tiberius, they continued, used to thwart the wishes of the legions by appealing to Augustus' name, and Drusus had now revived that same

tactic. Were they never to have visits from anyone apart from minors of the ruling family? Clearly the emperor referring soldiers' benefits and nothing else to the Senate was an innovation—was the Senate also going to be consulted when punishments or battles were on the agenda? Or were rewards under the control of their masters but punishments subject to no authority?

[27] Finally the men left the tribunal, shaking their fists at any members of the praetorian guard or Drusus' retinue that they came across, looking for a motive for a dispute and a way to start an armed confrontation. They were particularly incensed with Gnaeus Lentulus, for it was thought that, being older than the others and having greater military distinction, he was stiffening Drusus' resolve and was, more than anyone, scandalized at the soldiers' misbehavior. Not much later they crowded around him as he was leaving (for he started heading back to the winter quarters when he saw danger looming). Where was he going, they asked—was it to the emperor or to the senators, so that he could oppose the legion's interests before them, as well? At the same time they advanced menacingly, and hurled stones at him. Already bloodied from a blow from one of these, and sure he was facing death, he was saved only when a large contingent that had come with Drusus rushed to the spot.

[28] It was a night of foreboding that threatened to explode into villainy, but chance provided relief, for, in a suddenly clear sky, the moon seemed to become dim. The soldiers, ignorant of the cause, took it as an omen of their present circumstances. They saw the failure of the heavenly body as representing their own efforts, and assumed that their undertakings would be successful if the goddess had her radiant splendor restored. Accordingly, they raised a clamor by beating on brass instruments and by blowing trumpets and horns together, and became happy or dejected according to whether she seemed brighter or dimmer. And when some clouds arose to obstruct their view, and they believed she was buried in darkness, they lamented that unending toil was predicted for them, and that the gods were appalled at their criminal acts—when the mind is thrown off balance, so easily inclined to superstition does it become.

Feeling he should capitalize on the turn of events and make prudent use of what chance had offered him, Drusus ordered the rounds made of the tents, and the centurion Clemens was summoned, along with any others whose qualities made them favorites of the mob.

These men infiltrated the watches, the guard posts and the sentries at the gates, offering them hope and working on their fears. "How long are we going to keep the emperor's son under siege?" they would say. "How will our quarrels end? Are we going to take an oath of loyalty to Percennius and Vibulenus? Will Percennius and Vibulenus grant us pay as soldiers, land when retired? In short, will they assume authority over the Roman people in place of the Neros and Drususes? No, why should not we, the last to offend, be the first to repent? Joint demands are slowly met; you can immediately earn, and immediately receive, a private favor."

This caused excitement, and mutual suspicion, drawing new recruit away from veteran, and legion from legion. Then, gradually, their readiness to obey returned. They left the gates and replaced in their regular location the standards that they had brought together at the start of the mutiny.

[29] At daybreak Drusus convened an assembly, and although he had little experience in public speaking he criticized their past behavior and praised their present conduct with a natural dignity. He was not daunted by threats and menaces, he said, but if he perceived that they were reverting to reasonable behavior, and if he heard them pleading for forgiveness, he would urge his father in a letter to lend a forgiving ear to the legions' appeals. When they begged him to do this, the same Blaesus was once again sent to Tiberius, along with Lucius Aponius, a Roman knight on Drusus' staff, and Justus Catonius, a centurion of the first rank.

There followed a clash of opinions. Some advocated waiting for the representatives to return and in the meantime trying to pacify the soldiers with friendly overtures; others were for taking stronger measures. The crowd did not know moderation, they said—they would use terror unless they were intimidated, but once afraid they could be safely disregarded. While they were in the grip of superstition, their fear of the leader should be intensified by removing the ringleaders of the mutiny. Drusus was naturally inclined to more severe methods: he had Vibulenus and Percennius summoned and executed. Many authors relate that they were buried within the general's tent, but some that their corpses were thrown outside the earthwork for all to see.

[30] After that all the major agitators were searched out. Some wandered out of the camp and were cut down by the centurions or soldiers of the praetorian cohorts; others the companies themselves surrendered

to demonstrate their loyalty. To increase the anxieties of the rank and file, winter had arrived early, bringing relentless rainstorms that were so fierce that it was impossible for the men to leave their tents or gather together, and barely possible for them to save their standards that were being swept away by the high winds and rainwater. The fear of divine anger also persisted: it was no coincidence that stars faded and storms swooped down on them—sinners as they were! There was no other remedy for their ills but to leave that ill-starred and polluted camp, and return to their various winter quarters after purifying themselves of their guilt. First the Eighth Legion went back, then the Fifteenth. The Ninth had been clamoring for them to wait for Tiberius' letter, but soon, left alone when the others departed, they pre-empted the necessity looming before them by taking action themselves. And seeing that calm had been restored for the moment, Drusus went back to the city without awaiting the return of the soldiers' representatives.

*Events on the German frontier were equally turbulent. The legions there were under the command of Germanicus, the son of Tiberius's late brother Drusus, who was accompanied in his province by his wife Agrippina, Augustus's granddaughter, and their son Gaius, the future emperor Caligula. Germanicus's attempt to calm his rebellious soldiers met with resistance, and he found himself at considerable personal risk (33–35). His next act was to accede to some of their demands in the name of the emperor, which had the effect of instituting a temporary calm, during which the legions returned to their winter camps (36–38). The arrival of a delegation from Rome led to a fresh outbreak of disturbances at the camp in the region of the Ubii, a German tribe east of the Rhine. The situation had deteriorated to the point that Germanicus sent off his wife and son for their own protection (39–40). The shame that this inspired in the troops provided Germanicus with an opening to restore order (41–43), which was followed by the trial and execution of offenders (44). Germanicus regained control of the rebellious legions wintering nearby at a place called Vetera, near modern Xanten in Germany, by rounding up and killing the leaders of the sedition (45–49). Finally, to divert the troops' energies, Germanicus led them on an unnecessary punitive expedition against the German tribe of the Marsi.*

[31] At about the same time there was unrest amongst the legions in Germany, and for the same reasons, and

here it was all the more violent because of the greater numbers involved. They also had high hopes that Germanicus Caesar would be unable to tolerate another's rule, and would therefore put himself in the hands of his legions which, by their power, would sweep away everything before them.

There were two armies on the banks of the Rhine. The one called the "upper army" was under the legate Gaius Silius, while Aulus Caecina had charge of the "lower." Overall command lay with Germanicus, who was at that time busy conducting a census of the Gallic provinces. The troops in Silius' charge merely looked on with ambivalent feelings to see how the mutiny of the others turned out, but the men of the lower army slid into frenzy. It started with the Twenty-First and Fifth legions, and then the First and Twentieth were pulled into the troubles—they were quartered in the same summer camp in the lands of the Ubii, where they had nothing to do, or only light duties. There were present, after a recent levy in Rome, a large number of city troops used to riotous living and averse to hard work, and on hearing of the death of Augustus these proceeded to fill the simple minds of the others with ideas. The time had come, they would say, for the veterans to demand their overdue discharge, and the younger men a higher pay—and all should demand an end to the wretched conditions and seek redress for the brutality of the centurions. This came not from a single individual, as was the case with Percennius amongst the Pannonian legions, and it did not fall on the frightened ears of soldiers who saw before them other armies stronger than their own—the mutiny had many faces, and many voices. The fate of Rome lay in their hands, they said. It was by their victories that the state grew, and it was their name that commanders adopted.

[32] The legate did not stand in their way, for the madness of the mob had broken his will. In a sudden rage the men drew their swords and advanced on the centurions, the primal source of the soldiers' resentment and the starting point of their ferocity. They knocked them down and applied the lash, sixty strokes per man, to match the number of centurions, and then flung them, maimed, mangled, and in some cases lifeless, before the rampart or into the River Rhine. Septimius fled to the dais and fell prostrate at Caecina's feet, but so vehement were the demands made for him that he was surrendered for execution. The man who would gain fame with later generations for the assassination of Gaius Caesar, Cassius Chaerea, was at that time a hot-headed young man, and he opened up a path with his sword through the armed men that stood in his way. No tribune and no camp commandant had authority any longer, and the men apportioned among themselves guard-duty, patrols, and any other functions deemed necessary in the circumstances. To those with a deeper interest in the mentality of soldiers the clearest sign of a serious and uncompromising rebellion was the fact that it was not a matter of scattered pockets of unrest, or a few people inspiring it. There was uniform anger, and uniform silence, so evenly spread and so determined that one could have believed the men were acting under orders.

[33] Meanwhile, news of Augustus' demise was brought to Germanicus while he was conducting the census (which I mentioned earlier) throughout the Gallic provinces. Germanicus was married to Augustus' granddaughter, Agrippina, and had had several children by her and, being himself the son of Drusus, brother of Tiberius, he was the grandson of Augusta. He was, however, disquieted by the veiled hatred that his uncle and grandmother felt for him, a hatred all the more bitter for being unjustified. For the memory of Drusus still loomed large amongst the people of Rome, and it was believed that he would have restored their freedom had he come to power— hence their support for Germanicus, in whom they placed the same hopes. He was a young man of unassuming character and admirable courtesy, far different from Tiberius with his arrogant and inscrutable talk and looks. There were also the tiffs between the women. Livia had a stepmother's resentment to set her against Agrippina, and Agrippina herself was somewhat irascible, but by her virtue and love for her husband she could turn her indomitable spirit to good effect.

[34] In fact, the closer Germanicus came to the prospect of supreme power, the more he exerted himself on Tiberius' behalf, and he bound himself, his own circle, and the Belgic communities with an oath of allegiance to the emperor. Then, on hearing of the uprising of the legions, he left hurriedly and met them outside their camp, their eyes downcast as though from remorse. After he entered the earthwork, discordant complaints became audible. Some men took his hand and, pretending to plant kisses on it, put his fingers into their mouths so that he could feel their toothless gums; others drew his attention to their limbs bent with age.

The assembly before him seemed a total muddle, and he ordered the men to form up in companies. They would hear better as they were, came the reply. The standards should be brought forward, then—that at least would distinguish the cohorts from each other. They obeyed, slowly.

Then, after commencing with some respectful remarks on Augustus, Germanicus turned to the victories and triumphs of Tiberius, reserving his highest praise for the emperor's glorious achievements in the two Germanys with these legions now present. He went on to praise to the skies the consensus found in Italy, and the loyalty of the Gallic provinces—nowhere was unrest or discord to be found. The comments were received with silence, or low muttering.

[35] When he touched on the mutiny, Germanicus asked where their soldierly conduct had gone, and their splendid discipline of old. Where had they driven their tribunes, where their centurions? All together they bared their bodies, reproachfully exhibiting the scars their wounds had left and the marks of the lash. Next, with confused shouts, they berated him for the prices payable for exemptions, the meagerness of their pay, and the grueling nature of their tasks, mentioning specifically the construction of the earthwork and ditches, the gathering of forage, timber and firewood and all the other duties required of them from necessity or to avoid inactivity in the camp. The most ferocious cry arose from the veterans. They enumerated their thirty or more campaigns, and begged him to help them, for they were exhausted. He should not let them go to their deaths still working at the same oppressive tasks, but set a limit to their punishing service with a retirement that was not impoverished. There were even some who demanded the money left them by the deified Augustus in his will, adding words of good omen for Germanicus; and they indicated their support if he wanted supreme power.

With that, as if tainted with their crime, he leaped hastily from the dais. The men blocked his path with their weapons, threatening harm if he did not go back. Germanicus, however, crying aloud that he preferred to die rather than abandon his loyalty, grasped the sword at his side, raised it aloft and would have driven it into his breast had not those close by seized his sword hand and forcefully restrained it. The far edge of the crowd, which was also the most densely packed, urged him to carry through the stroke, and so, too—though it defies belief—did a number of individuals

who came up to him. In fact, a soldier by the name of Calusidius drew his own sword and offered it to him, adding that it was sharper. Even in their fury the crowd found this heartless and uncivilized, and there was a long enough pause for Germanicus to be hurried to his tent by his staff.

[36] In the tent there was discussion of remedying the situation. For there were reports that a delegation was being prepared to bring the upper army over to the same cause, that the chief town of the Ubii had been singled out for destruction, and that hands that had been steeped in loot would burst forth to plunder the Gallic provinces, too. Anxiety was increased because the enemy was aware of the Roman mutiny, and a pull-out from the banks of the Rhine would precipitate an invasion. On the other hand, arming auxiliary troops and allies against the defecting legions meant civil war. Severity spelled danger, bribery was unprincipled; if the soldiers were granted nothing or everything the state was likewise in jeopardy. Accordingly, when the arguments had been weighed up in their deliberations, it was decided that a letter be written in the emperor's name authorizing demobilization for all with twenty years' service, discharge for those with sixteen (these men being kept under the standard but with no duties save repelling the enemy), and payment, in double the amount, of the legacies the men had claimed.

[37] The men realized that these were measures improvised to meet the emergency and demanded instant implementation. The discharges were hurriedly put into effect by the tribunes; the financial rewards were deferred until each man reached winter quarters. However, the Fifth and Twenty-First legions would not leave until payment was made right there in the summer camp, the money being raised out of the travelling allowances of Germanicus' staff and his own personal funds. The legate Caecina led the First and Twentieth legions back to the city of the Ubii, and it was a scandalous march, since the moneybags extorted from the commander were being carried along amidst the standards and the eagles. Germanicus left to join the upper army, and found no reluctance to take the oath of allegiance among the Second, Thirteenth, and Sixteenth legions, though the Fourteenth hesitated somewhat. The cash and the discharges were delivered, even though the men did not demand them.

[38] Meanwhile, amongst the Chauci the *vexillarii* of the rebellious legions that were on garrison duty began to spread disaffection, and were momentarily

halted by the immediate execution of two soldiers. This order had been given by the camp prefect, Manius Ennius, who was setting a good example rather than acting with legitimate authority. Later, as the unrest increased, he fled, but was discovered. Concealment providing no safety, he then sought help in a stroke of boldness and declared that it was not against their prefect that their violence was being directed, but against Germanicus their commander, and Tiberius their emperor. At the same time, frightening those who stood in his way, he seized the standard and pointed it towards the river-bank. Then, crying out that anyone leaving the column would be treated as a deserter, he led the men back to their winter quarters, still fractious but not daring to take action.

[39] Meanwhile the delegates from the Senate came to Germanicus, who had now returned, at the altar of the Ubii. There were two legions wintering there, the First and the Twentieth, along with recently discharged veterans who were serving under the standard. These men were frightened and crazed with guilt, and they were overcome with fear that the men had come at the Senate's behest to annul the concessions they had extracted by the mutiny. A crowd always finds a scapegoat, no matter how groundless the charges, and the men picked on the ex-consul Munatius Plancus, the head of the delegation, as being responsible for the Senate's decree. At bedtime they began to demand their standard, which was housed in Germanicus' quarters. Swiftly converging on the entrance, they proceeded to break down the doors, forced Germanicus from his bed and with threats of death made him hand over the standard.

Shortly afterwards, as they roamed the streets of the camp, they came across the delegates who, having heard the uproar, were heading for Germanicus. They plied them with insults, and made ready to kill them, especially Plancus, whose high office had precluded flight. And, in his hour of danger, Plancus had no sanctuary apart from the encampment of the First Legion. There, grasping the standards and the eagle, he sought the protection of religion, and, but for the eagle-bearer Calpurnius, who prevented the ultimate act of violence, a delegate of the Roman people would, in a Roman camp, have stained with his own blood the altars of the gods, a rare occurrence even in a struggle between enemies.

Finally, at daybreak, general, soldiers, and what had happened between them during the night began to be recognized for what they were, Germanicus entered the camp, ordered Plancus to be brought to him, and took him onto the dais. He then berated the men for the deadly outbreak of insanity—its reappearance a result of heaven's, rather than the soldiers', anger, he said—and explained why the delegates had come. He eloquently bemoaned the violation of the rights of the delegation, and the serious and undeserved incident involving Plancus, as well as the great disgrace the legion had incurred. The crowd were awestruck rather than calmed, and Germanicus sent the delegates off with an escort of auxiliary cavalry.

[40] In this alarming situation there was general criticism of Germanicus for his failure to proceed to the upper army, where obedience and assistance against the rebels could be found. Enough, and more than enough, damage had been done, it was thought, by the granting of discharge and cash payments, and by easygoing policies. Even if Germanicus thought little of his own safety, why keep his little son and pregnant wife amid madmen who violated all the laws of humanity? Those, at least, he should send back to the boy's grandfather and the state. Germanicus vacillated a long time. His wife rejected the idea, declaring that she was a descendant of the deified Augustus and not his inferior when facing danger, but finally, with copious tears, Germanicus embraced his wife's womb, and the son they shared, and made her leave.

The wretched column of women began to move out—the commander's wife, a refugee, clasping her tiny son to her breast, and around her, uttering cries of grief, the wives of Germanicus' staff members, who were being dragged along with her. And those who stayed behind were no less dejected.

[41] It was not a picture of a Caesar at the height of success, and in his own camp, but what might be seen in a captured city; and the pitiful lamentations attracted the ears and eyes even of the soldiers. They came forth from their tents. What was this weeping, they asked. What was this sad procession? These were women of distinction, with no centurion, no common soldier to act as guard, and there was nothing appropriate to a commander's wife, no sign of her usual retinue. They were going to the Treveri, consigned to the protection of foreigners!

Then came shame and compassion, and recollections of Agrippina's father Agrippa, and Augustus her grandfather. They thought of her father-in-law Drusus, of the woman herself and her outstanding fertility and renowned chastity. They thought of the infant, born in the camp and brought up in the legions' barracks, the boy to whom they gave the soldiers' nickname "Caligula" because (in order to win the support of the ordinary soldiers) he was usually shod with this sort of footwear. But nothing affected them as greatly as the envy they felt for the Treveri. They resorted to appeals, and blocked the way, asking them to go back, and stay, some of them coming to intercept Agrippina, but most going back to Germanicus. And Germanicus, smarting with hurt and anger that was still fresh, addressed them as they milled round him:

[42] "My wife and son are not dearer to me than my father and country, but my father will be protected by his own majesty, and the Roman empire by its other armies. My wife and children I would gladly offer up to destruction for your glory, but now I am taking them far away from your frenzy. Thus whatever villainy lies ahead may receive expiation from my blood alone, and the murder of Augustus' great-grandson and the slaying of Tiberius' daughter-in-law will not add to your guilt. For what, in these past days, have you not attempted? What have you left inviolate? What name shall I give this gathering? Should I address you as 'Soldiers,' you who have laid siege to your emperor's son with your rampart and weapons? Or as 'Citizens,' you who have snubbed the Senate's authority? In addition, you have violated the rights due even to an enemy, as well as the sacrosanctity of an embassy and international convention.

The deified Julius checked a mutiny in his army with a single word, addressing as 'Quirites' men who refused the oath of allegiance to him. The deified Augustus petrified the legions at Actium with the look on his face. I am not yet in their company, but I am descended from them; if it were actually the soldiers of Spain and Syria that were flouting my authority, that would still be strange and outrageous. And is it really the First and Twentieth legions that are giving such splendid thanks to your leader—the First, which received its standards from Tiberius, and you here, who shared so many of his victories, and were enriched by him with so many prizes? Is this the message I am to take to my father, as he hears only good news from the other provinces? That his own recruits and veterans are not satisfied with discharge or money? That here alone are centurions murdered, tribunes driven out, legates kept in prison? That the camp and the rivers are sullied with blood, and that the breath that I draw remains at the mercy of men who hate me?

[43] Ah, my improvident friends! Why did you take away that sword, which I was preparing to drive into my heart, on that first day we had a meeting? His was a better and warmer gesture—that man who offered me his sword. I should at least have fallen while not yet an accessory to my army's many crimes! And you might have chosen as leader a man who could have left my own death unpunished but avenged that of Varus and the three legions. For, despite their offers of assistance, god forbid that the Belgae gain the glory and fame of having helped the Roman people and subdued the tribes of Germany! I pray rather that your spirit, deified Augustus, now taken to heaven, and the vision and memory of you, father Drusus, wash away this stain, and direct the wrath of our internecine feuding towards the destruction of the enemy. I pray that you do so through these same soldiers of yours, already starting to feel shame and entertain thoughts of glory. And, yes, I see a change in your expressions, men, and in your hearts. If you are ready to restore the delegates to the Senate, your obedience to your emperor, and my wife and children to me, then stand back from the contagion and segregate the mutinous elements. That will be sure proof of your regret, and a guarantee of loyalty."

[44] This turned the men to entreaty, and they admitted the truth of his reproaches, begging him to punish the truly guilty, pardon those who had made a mistake, and lead them against the enemy. His wife should be called back, and the legions' foster-child should return to them, and not be surrendered to the Gauls as a hostage. Agrippina could not return, Germanicus explained, because the birth of their child was imminent, and so was winter; his son would return, and all else they must see to themselves. Changed men now, they ran off in different directions, clapped the prime troublemakers in irons, and dragged them before Gaius Caetronius, legate of the First Legion. Caetronius judged and punished them individually, in the following manner. The legions stood as in an assembly, with swords drawn, and the defendant was put on show by a tribune on a raised platform. If the legions shouted out that he was guilty, he would be hurled head first into them and butchered. And the soldiers relished the bloodshed, as if they were absolving themselves of guilt. Nor did Germanicus try to check them: it was not being done at *his* bidding, and the individuals responsible for the atrocity would also suffer the opprobrium for it.

The veterans followed their example, and were shortly afterwards sent into Raetia. This was ostensibly for the defense of the province against the threat of the Suebi, but in reality so they would be pulled away from a camp that still inspired horror, as much for the severity of the remedy applied as the memory of the original crime.

Germanicus then conducted the revision of the list of centurions. When called on by the commander, each man stated his name, rank, and country of origin; and he also gave the number of campaigns he had served in, his acts of valor in battle, and his military awards, if he had any. If the tribunes and the legion vouched for his industry and good character, he retained his rank; when they were in agreement in accusing him of greed or brutality, he was discharged.

[45] The current predicament resolved, there remained a problem no less difficult—the intractability of the Fifth and Twenty-First legions, who were wintering sixty miles away, at a place called Vetera. They had been the first to start the mutiny, and had been responsible for all its most heinous crimes. They were neither deterred by the punishment of their comrades nor influenced by their remorse, and were still enraged. Germanicus therefore prepared to send armed forces, a fleet, and allied troops down the Rhine, intending to decide the matter militarily if his authority were snubbed.

[46] In Rome, what had transpired in Illyricum was not yet known, and news had arrived of the uprising of the German legions. An alarmed community criticized Tiberius for toying with the senators and commons, both bodies weak and unarmed, with his feigned reluctance, while in the meantime the troops were in revolt and could not be restrained by a couple of boys not yet possessing the authority of an adult. He should have gone himself, they said, and set his majesty as emperor before men who were bound to yield when they set eyes on a ruler of long experience, a man who had supreme power to punish or reward them. Could it be that Augustus, in the weakness of old age, had made so many visits to Germany, and yet Tiberius, in the prime of his years, was sitting in the Senate quibbling at the words of its members? Enough care had been taken to secure the servitude of Rome—now some medicine needed to be applied to the soldiers' spirits, to make them ready to accept peace.

[47] Unmoved in the face of such criticisms, Tiberius was determined not to leave the hub of the empire and put himself and the state at risk. For he had many conflicting thoughts troubling him. The army in Germany was stronger, the one in Pannonia closer. The German army could count on the resources of the Gallic provinces; the other threatened Italy. To which should he attend first? And suppose those put second were incensed by the slight! By using his sons, however, the two could be dealt with together, and without compromising his imperial stature, which enjoyed greater respect at a distance. At the same time it was pardonable for the young men to refer some items to their father, and any resistance to Germanicus or Drusus could be appeased or smashed by himself. But what was there in reserve if the mutineers spurned the emperor? Nevertheless, he selected a retinue, brought baggage together, and fitted out ships, as though about to leave at any moment. Presently, offering variously the onset of winter or the pressure of business as excuses, he fooled first the most intelligent, then the public, and finally, and for the longest time, the provinces.

[48] Although Germanicus had put together an army and stood ready to punish the rebels, he felt that they should still be given some time in case the recent lesson made them cautious about their own safety. He therefore sent a letter ahead to Caecina informing him that he was coming in force, and that unless they punished the offenders before his arrival he would resort to indiscriminate bloodshed. This letter Caecina read out in private to his eagle-and standard-bearers, and to the most reliable elements in camp, encouraging them to rescue all the men from disgrace, and themselves from death. In peace, he said, attention was paid to cases and their merits; when war broke out, innocent and guilty went down together.

These individuals approached the men they considered suitable and, observing that the legions were for the most part loyal, they fixed a time, at the legate's suggestion, for an armed assault on the most loathsome and seditious troublemakers. Then, giving a signal to one another, they burst into the tents and slaughtered the unsuspecting soldiers, with no one, apart from the accomplices, knowing how the massacre started, or where it would end.

[49] This was a scene different from all the civil conflicts that have ever occurred. It was not a battle or a fight between soldiers from different camps, but one between men from the same sleeping quarters, men whom the day had seen eating together, and the night resting together. They split into two factions and

hurled their weapons. Shouts, wounds, blood—all this was evident, but the reason unknown. Everything else was determined by chance. Some loyal soldiers were cut down, too, when the troublemakers realized against whom the savagery was directed and also took up arms. And there was no legate and no tribune present to enforce restraint; the mob was granted a free hand, and vengeance to the point of saturation. Soon Germanicus came into the camp. Weeping profusely, he cried out that this was not a cure but a disaster, and he ordered the bodies to be burned.

They were still in a bloodthirsty mood, and the desire swept over them to march on the enemy as atonement for their insanity—only if they received honorable wounds to their impious breasts could their comrades' shades be appeased. Germanicus went along with his soldiers' enthusiasm. He bridged the river and sent over twelve thousand legionaries, twenty-six allied cohorts, and eight cavalry squadrons whose discipline had not suffered in that mutiny.

[50] The Germans, who were not far off, were delighted that we were hindered first by the period of mourning for the late Augustus, and then by dissension. The Roman commander, however, marched swiftly, cutting through the Caesian Forest and the fortified boundary begun by Tiberius, and encamping on the boundary, protected by a rampart front and rear, and by a barricade on the sides. Then he made his way through dark woodlands and pondered which of the two paths to take, the usual route, which was short, or the one that was more difficult and less attempted, and for that reason not under enemy surveillance. The longer route was chosen, and the pace accelerated; for scouts had brought word that this was a festal night for the Germans and one joyously celebrated with a ceremonial feast.

Caecina was instructed to go ahead with some lightly equipped cohorts and clear away obstacles in the woods; the legions followed a short distance behind. They were helped by a starlit night. Reaching the villages of the Marsi, they surrounded the enemy with armed details, the villagers even at that point lying in their beds or hard by the tables, feeling no apprehension and with no sentinels posted. Everything was in careless disarray; and there was no fear of war—but even their peace was merely the languorous torpor of the drunken.

[51] So that the raid could cover more ground, Germanicus divided his eager legions into four divisions, and spread devastation over an area of fifty miles with fire and the sword. Neither sex nor age aroused pity. Places secular and holy alike were razed to the ground, including those tribes' most famous sanctuary, which they called the Sanctuary of Tanfana. The soldiers cut down men half-asleep, unarmed, or wandering aimlessly about, without receiving a wound.

The massacre brought forth the Bructeri, the Tubantes, and the Usipetes, and these proceeded to invest the woodlands through which lay the army's return route. The general learned of this and pressed forward, ready to march and to fight. Some cavalry and auxiliary cohorts took the lead; the First Legion followed; and, with the baggage in the center, the legionaries of the Twenty-First closed up the left flank and those of the Fifth the right, while the Twentieth Legion strengthened the rear. After these came the rest of the allies.

The enemy, however, made no move until the column was stretched out through the forest; then, with only perfunctory assaults on the flanks and vanguard, they attacked the rear with all their might. The light-armed cohorts were being thrown into disarray by the closely ordered German companies when Germanicus rode up to the legionaries of the Twentieth and kept shouting in a loud voice that *this* was their opportunity to cancel out the mutiny. They should press on, he said, and swiftly turn their guilt into glory. Their spirits flared up, and with a single charge they broke through the enemy, drove them to open ground and cut them down. At the same time, the vanguard emerged from the woods and built a fortified camp. After that it was a trouble-free march, and the men, encouraged by their recent achievements and forgetting the past, were settled in their winter quarters.

[52] The news brought joy and anxiety to Tiberius. He was pleased that the mutiny had been crushed, but what he saw as Germanicus' attempt to win the favor of his troops by doling out money and accelerating discharge—that was galling, as was the glory he had won in combat. Even so he made a report to the Senate on the man's achievements and spoke at length about his valor, but in language too ostentatiously ornate for it to be believed that it came from the heart. His praise for Drusus and the ending of the Illyrian revolt was shorter, but he was more earnest, and his language carried conviction. He confirmed for the Pannonian legions, too, all the concessions that Germanicus had made.

*Tacitus closes the narrative of the events of A.D. 14 with notices of the deaths of two of the principals in the biggest scandal of 2 B.C. Augustus's daughter Julia was exiled in that year on a charge of multiple adulteries, shipped off to the barren island of Pandateria, modern Ventotene, about twenty-five miles off the coast of southern Latium. Sempronius Gracchus was implicated in the scandal, although his relegation was delayed for almost two years, if Tacitus's chronology is accurate. It was not likely that anyone associated with this affair involving his ex-wife would long survive his accession. He follows this with the more mundane matters of the institution of a priesthood for the deified Augustus and the games instituted in his honor.*

[53] Julia saw her final day that same year. Because of her sexual misconduct she had earlier been imprisoned on the island of Pandateria by her father Augustus, and subsequently in the town of Rhegium, hard by the Sicilian strait. She had been married to Tiberius when Gaius and Lucius Caesar were still alive, and had despised him as her inferior; and this was the fundamental reason for Tiberius' withdrawal to Rhodes. After coming to power he brought about her end by letting her waste away in protracted destitution, banished, disgraced, and, after the assassination of Postumus Agrippa, devoid of all hope, for he thought that her killing would remain unnoticed because of the length of her exile.

Tiberius' vicious treatment of Sempronius Gracchus was similarly motivated. From a noble family, Gracchus had a nimble wit and a misused eloquence, and he had debauched the same Julia while she was married to Marcus Agrippa. That was not the limit of his lechery, either. When Julia was passed on to Tiberius, the determined adulterer proceeded to inspire defiance in her, and hatred towards her husband; and the letter she wrote to her father Augustus vilifying Tiberius was thought to have been composed by Gracchus. Gracchus was therefore shipped off to Cercina, an island in the African sea, where he endured an exile lasting fourteen years. Soldiers were then sent to assassinate him, and they found him on the shore, on a projecting spit of land, expecting no happy outcome. When they arrived, Gracchus asked for a few moments to relay his final instructions to his wife Alliaria in a letter, and then stretched out his neck for his killers. In the resolute manner of his death he was not unworthy of the name Sempronius; it was in his life that he had fallen short of it. Some have recorded that the soldiers

in question did not come from Rome but were sent by Lucius Asprenas, the proconsul of Africa, on Tiberius' orders, the emperor hoping—in vain—that the murder could be blamed on Asprenas when word of it got out.

[54] That same year saw a ceremonial innovation with the addition of a priesthood of Augustal brothers, modeled on the college of Titian brothers that Titus Tatius had once established to preserve Sabine ritual. Twenty-one members were drawn by lot from the foremost members of the community, and Tiberius, Drusus, Claudius, and Germanicus were added to that number. The Augustal Games were first established at that time, but they were disrupted by quarrelling that broke out because of rivalry amongst the actors. Augustus, humoring Maecenas, who was passionately in love with Bathyllus, had tolerated this form of entertainment, but he was not averse to such avocations himself, and thought participating in the pleasures of the common people a democratic gesture. Tiberius' character was rather different, but he did not as yet dare to put on a more austere course a people that had been indulged for so many years.

*The narrative of the following year, A.D. 15, begins with war on the German front (55–59). Tacitus describes Roman relations with the powerful German tribe of the Chatti, who played a major role in the revolt led by Rome's great enemy Arminius, which culminated in the destruction of an army of three legions led by Varus in the Teutoberg Forest. Germanicus attempted to pre-empt further German action by mounting a campaign across the Rhine, dividing his forces into three and taking his own troops deep into enemy territory. This operation was primarily directed against the Cherusci, whom Arminius had led against the Romans, and it brought him to the site of the celebrated massacre that was said to have haunted Augustus so much that he went unshaven and unkempt for months, beating his head and calling out "Quinctilius Varus, give me back my legions!" The narrative resumes after the Germans have been stirred to action by Arminius.*

[60] The bordering tribes were also roused to action by these words, not just the Cherusci; and Inguiomerus, Arminius' uncle, was brought on side as well, a man of long-standing influence with the Romans—hence greater fear on Germanicus' part. So that war should not descend on him in one fell swoop, he sent Caecina through the Bructeri to the

River Amisia with forty Roman cohorts to divide the enemy, while the prefect Pedo led the cavalry through the territory of the Frisians. Germanicus himself put four legions aboard some ships and sailed through the lakes, and then infantry, cavalry, and fleet rendezvoused at the river mentioned above. The Chauci promised auxiliary troops, and were accepted as brothers-in-arms. When the Bructeri proceeded to torch their own property, Lucius Stertinius, sent out by Germanicus, routed them with a light-armed unit, and during the carnage and the looting Stertinius came upon the eagle of the Nineteenth Legion that had been lost with Varus. From there, the column was marched to the furthest limits of the Bructeri, and all the land between the rivers Amisia and Lupia was devastated. This was not far from the Teutoburg Forest, in which the remains of Varus and his legions were said to be lying unburied.

[61] The desire therefore came over Germanicus to give those soldiers and their leader their last rites, and the whole army there with him was moved to pity for relatives and friends, and indeed for the vicissitudes of warfare and the human condition. Caecina was sent ahead to reconnoiter the hidden recesses of the woods, and lay down bridges and causeways over the soggy marshland and treacherous plains, and they advanced into the somber area, a ghastly sight prompting ghastly memories. Varus' first camp, with its wide circumference and with the headquarters marked out, revealed the handiwork of the three legions; then, from a half-demolished rampart and a shallow ditch, one could detect the point where an already shattered remnant of the force had taken a position. In the middle of the field were whitening bones, scattered or in piles, where men had fled or made a stand. Close by lay pieces of weapons and limbs of horses, and there were also skulls nailed to tree-trunks. In groves close by were barbarous altars where the enemy had sacrificed tribunes and first-rank centurions. And survivors of that catastrophe, who had managed to slip away from the battle or from captivity, would describe how the legates had fallen in this spot, how the eagles were taken in that; and show where Varus was dealt his first wound, and where he met his end by a blow from his own ill-starred hand. They indicated the dais from which Arminius had addressed his troops, enumerated the gibbets he used for the prisoners, and pointed out the live-burial pits, and told how he had arrogantly mocked the standards and the eagles.

[62] So it was that, in the sixth year after the catastrophe, a Roman army was present to inter the bones of the three legions, with nobody knowing whether he was covering with earth the remains of strangers or of relatives, but all doing so as though they were kith and kin. Their anger with the enemy mounted, and they were at the same time sad and wrathful. Germanicus laid the first sod for the construction of the barrow, paying a welcome tribute to the dead and sharing the grief of all present.

Tiberius did not approve. Perhaps he looked at everything that Germanicus did in a negative light, or perhaps he believed that, after the sight of soldiers dead and unburied, the army would be reluctant to do battle and more fearful of the enemy. Also, he thought, a commander invested with an augurate and its ancient ceremonial duties should have had no contact with funeral rites.

[63] Germanicus gave chase as Arminius fell back into the wilderness, and at the first opportunity he ordered the cavalry to charge ahead and seize the level ground on which the enemy had positioned himself. Arminius, who had instructed his men to form up in close order and advance towards the woods, now suddenly turned them round, and soon afterwards gave men he had concealed in the woods the signal to rush out. The Roman cavalry was thrown into disarray by this new fighting line, and reserve cohorts were sent in, but as these ran into the crowd of men fleeing the fight they only served to increase the confusion. They were being pushed into a swamp well known to the victors, and treacherous for those unaware of it, but then Germanicus brought up his legions and deployed them for battle. From that came terror for the enemy, a surge of confidence for the Roman soldiers; and they parted on equal terms.

Shortly afterwards Germanicus led his army back to the Amisia, and then ferried back the other legions by ship, as he had brought them up. Some of the cavalry he ordered to head for the Rhine along the ocean shoreline. Caecina was leading back his own troops and, although his return was along well-known paths, he was told to cross the Long Bridges with all possible speed. These constituted a narrow pathway—it had been built some time earlier by Lucius Domitius—through the bleak marshlands, and apart from that there was nothing but a bog of thick, heavy mud, intersected by streams that rendered it hazardous. Around about, on a gently rising gradient, were woods, which Arminius at that time filled with men. For, thanks to short cuts and the speed of his column, he had arrived ahead of the Roman troops that were encumbered with baggage and weapons.

Uncertain how to repair the bridges that were dilapidated with age, and at the same time ward off the enemy, Caecina decided to lay out a camp on the spot so that men could start on the work while others took on the fighting.

*In chapters 64 through 69, Tacitus describes the difficult and dangerous retreat of the detached forces led by Caecina. The Romans were constantly harassed by the enemy, who had the advantage of the terrain as well. In the final chapter of this section, he relates the actions of Germanicus's wife and in the process provides an important first sketch of her character, as she will play an increasingly prominent role in events after the death of her husband.*

[64] In an effort to break through the guard-emplacements and assault the working parties, the barbarians proceeded to harass, encircle, and charge the Romans, and the cries of the workers mingled with those of the fighters. Everything was against the Romans. The area with its deep marshes was both unstable for making a stand and too slippery for an advance; their bodies were weighed down by their breastplates; they were unable to hurl their javelins amidst the waters. It was different for the Cherusci—they were used to marshland fighting, were long-limbed, and had huge pikes for inflicting wounds even at a distance.

It was night that finally delivered the already wavering legions from the uneven fight. Their success rendered the Germans tireless. Taking no rest even at that point, they set about diverting to the lower ground all the waters that had their source in the hills rising round about, and with the ground flooded, and such work as had been completed now submerged, the labor of the soldiers was doubled.

This was Caecina's fortieth season, either under orders or in command; he had known successes and reverses, and was therefore unperturbed. As he considered the options before him, the only solution he could find was to keep the enemy shut in the woods until the wounded and the heavier-armed elements of his column went ahead—for between the mountains and the marshland stretched a piece of flat land that could accommodate a thin battle line. The Fifth Legion was then chosen to serve on the right flank, and the

Twenty-First for the left, while the men of the First were selected to lead off the column, and the Twentieth to face those who would be in pursuit.

[65] It was a restless night for various reasons. From their joyful banquets the barbarians filled the low-lying valleys and echoing woods with their happy singing and savage cries; on the Roman side there were feeble campfires and fitful murmurings, and the men lay scattered along the rampart, or wandered amidst the tents, sleepless rather than alert. Their general was terrified by a frightful dream. He thought he saw a blood-covered Quinctilius Varus arise from the marsh and heard him calling, but he did not respond and pushed away his hand when Varus stretched it out to him.

When day broke, and the legions were sent to the flanks, they abandoned their posts, either from fear or defiance, and swiftly occupied some flat terrain beyond the swamp. Arminius, however, despite having an opportunity to attack, did not charge out immediately. It was only when the Roman baggage became stuck in the mud and the ditches, when the soldiers around it were in disarray, when the standards lost their order and (as usually happens in such circumstances) every man was swift to help himself but his ears were slow to respond to commands—only then did he give the Germans the command to attack. "Look," he kept shouting, "it's Varus and his legions caught up in the same fate once more!" And with that he took a hand-picked group and cut through the column, inflicting wounds mostly on the horses. The animals, slipping in their own blood and the mud of the marshland, threw their riders, scattered those in their way, and trampled underfoot those who were down.

The greatest effort was expended around the eagles, which could not be carried forward in the face of spears raining down on them, but could not be planted in the soggy ground, either. While Caecina was attempting to hold his line together, his horse was run through beneath him, and he fell and was surrounded by the enemy—or would have been but for the intervention of the First Legion. The situation was helped by the greed of the enemy, who left the kill to chase after plunder, and as the day drew towards evening the legions clambered out on to open, solid ground.

But that was not the last of their tribulations. A rampart had to be raised and materials sought for the earthwork; and they had lost most of the implements for digging soil and cutting turf. They had no tents for the maniples, no dressings for the wounded. They shared food sullied with slime and blood, all the while bemoaning the deathly gloom and the fact that, for so many thousands of men, only a single day now remained.

[66] It so happened that a horse broke its halter and, wandering about terrified by the shouting, knocked down some of the people who got in its way. Men thought the Germans had broken in, and such was the consternation that all rushed to the gates—and the back gate was the one particularly sought since it faced away from the enemy and was safer for flight. Caecina discovered it was a false alarm, but he was unable to stop or hold back his men either by his personal authority or pleas, or even by grabbing them. He then flung himself down in the gateway and finally blocked their path by appealing to their compassion, as they would have had to proceed over the commander's body. At the same time the tribunes and centurions convinced them that their panic was groundless.

[67] Caecina then gathered the men together at his headquarters, told them to listen in silence to what he had to say and warned them of the dire situation facing them. Their only way to safety lay in their weapons, he said, but these needed to be judiciously employed; and they had to remain within the rampart until the enemy closed in on them in hopes of storming the position. After that they had to charge out from all sides, and with that charge the Rhine would be reached. If they fled, he added, they had before them more woods, deeper bogs, and a brutal enemy, whereas victory meant honor and glory. He reminded them of what was dear to them at home, what redounded to their honor in the camp; about their reverses he said nothing. After that, starting with his own, he passed on the horses of the legates and tribunes to all the bravest fighters, and without partiality, so these could charge the enemy before the infantry attack.

[68] The Germans, from anticipation, greed, and a clash of opinions amongst their leaders, were just as agitated. Arminius urged them to allow the Romans to come out and, when they came out, to surround them once more in the sodden and difficult terrain. Inguiomerus advocated a more impetuous course, which pleased the barbarians—an armed blockade of the rampart. Storming it would then be easy, he explained, there would be more prisoners and the booty would be intact.

And so, at daybreak, they filled in the ditches, threw hurdles over them, and tried to grasp the top of the rampart—there were few soldiers on it, and they were apparently rooted to the spot with fear. When the Germans had a handhold on the fortifications, the cohorts were given the signal, and horns and bugles rang out together. Then, shouting and charging, they poured around the German rear, derisively exclaiming that here there were no woods or marshes, only a fair field and fair gods. The enemy had been envisioning an easy kill, with opponents few and poorly equipped, but then the resounding bugles and flashing arms burst upon them—all the more stunning for being unexpected—and they fell, as helpless in defeat as they had been greedy in success. Arminius quit the field unhurt, Inguiomerus after a serious wound, and the slaughter of the rank and file lasted as long as Roman anger and daylight. Only at nightfall did the legions return and, though physically drained by increased wounds and the ongoing shortage of food, they found strength, health, provisions—everything, in fact—in victory.

[69] A rumor had meanwhile spread that the army had been cut off, and that a column of Germans was on the offensive and heading for Gaul; and if Agrippina had not stopped a bridge over the Rhine from being demolished, there were men ready to commit such an outrage out of fear. However, this great-hearted woman took upon herself the duties of a leader during those days, and dispensed clothing or dressings to all the needy or wounded amongst the soldiers. Gaius Plinius, the author of *The German Wars*, records that Agrippina stood at one end of the bridge praising and thanking the returning legions. This made a deep impression on Tiberius: her solicitude was no straightforward matter, and it was not against foreigners that the support of the soldiers was being sought! Commanders were left with nothing to do, he mused, when a woman inspected the maniples, appeared before the standards, tried distributing largesse—as if she were not courting popularity enough by carrying her son around dressed as a common soldier and wanting him to be called "Caesar Caligula"! And she already had greater influence with the armies than legates and generals did, and it was by her, a woman, that a mutiny had been quelled which the emperor's name could not stop. Such thoughts were inflamed and aggravated by Sejanus, who, through his acquaintance with Tiberius' character, would sow the seeds of hatreds for use much later—hatreds that Tiberius was intended to store up now and bring out when they had grown.

*The final phase of Germanicus's ill-fated incursion into German territory was the hazardous return of two legions by the coastal route to the north.*

[70] Germanicus transferred to Publius Vitellius command of two of the legions—the Second and the Fourth—that he had brought by sea. Vitellius was to march them overland so that the fleet would be lighter when it was navigating shallow seas or ran aground at ebb tide. Vitellius initially had a smooth journey on dry soil or where the tide had a gentle flow. Soon his column was seized and buffeted by the blasts of a north wind—and it was also the season of the equinox, the time at which the ocean has its greatest swell. The land was submerged, and sea, shoreline, and fields all looked the same, with treacherous areas indistinguishable from the solid, and shallow spots from the deep. They were bowled over by the waves, pulled under by the currents; pack-animals, their loads, and dead bodies floated amongst them and bumped into them. The companies became completely intermingled, standing in water sometimes up to their chests, sometimes up to their heads; and on occasion, when they lost their footing, they became separated or they sank. Shouts of mutual encouragement were of no use against the onset of the floodwaters. There was no difference between the active man and the idler, between the prudent and the incautious, between calculated and random response. Everything was swept up in the same devastating force.

Finally Vitellius struggled out onto higher ground and brought his column up to the same spot. They passed the night without provisions and without fire, most of them naked or maimed, no less wretched than men under enemy blockade. For in that situation there was the added factor of an honorable death, whereas these men faced an end without glory.

Daylight brought back the land, and they made it to the river to which Germanicus had advanced with the fleet. The legions were then put on board, while rumor was spreading that they had been drowned; and their survival was not believed before men actually saw that Germanicus and his army had returned.

[71] Stertinius had been sent ahead to accept the surrender of Segestes' brother, Segimerus, and by now he had brought Segimerus and his son to the community of the Ubii. Both were pardoned, Segimerus readily, the son with some hesitation because it was said that he had treated the corpse of Quinctilius Varus with disrespect. As for making good the losses sustained by the army, the Gallic provinces, the Spanish provinces, and Italy competed with each other with offers of weapons, horses, and gold, according to their various resources. Germanicus commended them for their enthusiastic support, but took for the campaign only the weapons and horses, assisting the men with cash of his own. To soften the memory of the disaster with an act of camaraderie, he made the rounds of the wounded and praised individuals for their exploits; and, inspecting their injuries, he used hope of victory in one case, prospects of glory in another, and encouragement and solicitude with them all, to confirm both their loyalty to himself and their spirit for battle.

*The final chapters of the book relate events at Rome during the year. For the most part this is routine business—senatorial decrees, the law courts, provincial administration, civil disturbances in the capital, and flood control—but an ominous note is sounded in the beginning with the reintroduction of the treason law as a means to suppress dissent, and in the Latin text the last word of the book is* servitium, *"slavery."*

# AFTERWORD

The younger Pliny, Tacitus's good friend and correspondent, predicted that his *Histories* would be "immortal" (*Epistles* 7.33), but, quite apart from the tenuous survival of that work (only about a third is preserved), this assessment fell wide of the mark. Even in the years following the publication of his works, there is little evidence of wide readership: schoolteachers did not assign them, grammarians did not study them, and few authors seem to have been influenced by them. To be sure, Tacitus's style cut against the grain of prevailing trends in the rhetorical schools, where, since Quintilian's time, Cicero had been established as the standard that aspiring prose writers should strive to reach. The brief, powerful turns of phrase, the variegated mixture of archaic and modern vocabulary, and the unbalanced sentence structure that are the hallmarks of Tacitus's Latin style were the antithesis of Ciceronian concinnity. An additional factor was probably the decided change of taste that took place in the mid-second century A.D., when readers' interests were focused on Rome's most ancient customs and traditions. Tacitus's narratives of recent imperial intrigue and the demise of liberty may simply not have been to the taste of many. There were of course exceptions. One of the most curious among the historian's ancient admirers was none other than an emperor himself, Marcus Claudius Tacitus (ca. 200–276), who shared his name and even claimed, rather implausibly, to be his descendant. He succeeded Aurelian late in A.D. 275, during a dark period of Roman history, and little is known about him, although one not terribly reliable source reports that he decreed that ten copies of Tacitus's works should be made each year and deposited in the public libraries (*Historia Augusta,* Life of Tacitus 10). If the story has any credibility at all, it suggests that at that time copies were hard to come by, but this attempted remedy had little effect, since the emperor was killed by his own troops in July 276, after a rule of only eight months.

The most profound evidence of Tacitus's influence comes about a century later in the work of the last great pagan historian, Ammianus Marcellinus (ca. 330–400). Ammianus was not actually a native speaker of Latin—he came from a prosperous Greek family in Antioch in Syria—and so for him, perhaps, Tacitus's noncanonical style was less of a deterrent. By the fourth century A.D., when books were no longer primarily distributed in papyrus rolls but in parchment codices, Tacitus's historical works were probably being read in inverse order of date of composition, with the *Annals* followed by

**Figure 26: Poussin, *Death of Germanicus***
The subject of this painting, which was completed in 1627, is taken from the second book of Tacitus's *Annals,* which tells how Augustus's grandson and adopted heir was assassinated by Tiberius's adherent, a Roman noble named Piso.

the *Histories* to provide a continuous narrative from Tiberius's accession to the reign of Nerva in A.D. 96. Ammianus's history began with Nerva and so is evidently set out as a continuation of Tacitus. But apart from a few stray mentions in Christian writers such as Orosius and Cassiodorus, it seems that Ammianus's enthusiasm for Tacitus was not widely shared, and in the Middle Ages his works largely disappeared from view.

The celebrated monastery of Monte Cassino in Italy played a crucial role in the transmission of many unique texts from antiquity, including Tacitus. The sole surviving manuscript of Books 11 through 16 of the *Annals* and the *Histories* was copied there in the eleventh century and eventually made its way into the possession of Giovanni Boccaccio. In 1425 his friend, the famous manuscript hunter Poggio Bracciolini, learned that there was a manuscript in the German monastery of Hersfeld containing Tacitus's three minor works, the *Germania*, the *Dialogue*, and the *Agricola*, which was subsequently brought to Rome in 1455. Copies were immediately made, but the original was soon lost, as was not uncommon in those times, except for a single quaternion of the *Agricola*, which was rediscovered in 1902. It now appears that Enoch of Ascoli, who had been charged by Pope Nicholas V with retrieving the manuscript from Hersfeld, had kept at least a portion of it for himself and sent a copy of it on to Rome. Tacitus's other works have also attracted thieves. The first six books of the *Annals* were completely unknown until a manuscript was discovered at Corvey in France in 1508, whence it was stolen and taken to Rome. It was not until 1515, then, that the works of Tacitus as we know them were published and became widely available. Even so, for most of the humanists of the fifteenth century, with their republican sentiments and the general predilection for Ciceronian style, Livy, not Tacitus was the most important Roman historian. Machiavelli, the political theorist whom one might think most sympathetic to Tacitus, wrote his *Discourses* on Livy's first decade, not on the *Annals*, even though he clearly knew its later books along with the *Histories*.

With the Counter-Reformation Tacitus came into his own, as his works supplanted Livy in popularity. Tacitus was increasingly seen as an important political theorist, both by the advocates and by the opponents of imperial rule, although increasingly under the Enlightenment "Tacitism" became an important vehicle for arguments against despotism. The French dramatists Corneille in his *Othon* (1665) and Racine in his *Britannicus* (1669) took their inspiration from his works, and Tacitus was an important author for many of the most prominent players in the French Revolution. Readers of Edward Gibbon will not miss the Tacitean tinge to the prose style of his *History of the Decline and Fall of the Roman Empire* (1776–89). The *Germania* has sometimes emerged as a contested text in the play of ideologies. During the Second World War it was required reading for students at Columbia University, presumably on the principle of "know your enemy." When German troops retreated through Italy in 1944, a detachment of the SS attempted to steal the most authoritative manuscript of the *Germania*, presumably because it portrays the German tribes as living a simple and noble life untainted by the decadence of Rome. The manuscript evaded capture by being hidden under the floor in the kitchen of its Italian owner's castle. Even so, its adventures were not over: in 1966, it was damaged in the Great Flood of Florence. It is now safely housed in the Museo Nazionale in Rome.

# PLINY THE YOUNGER

(Gaius Plinius Caecilius Secundus, A.D. 61/62–ca. 110)

THE CITY OF COMO IN NORTHERN ITALY ON THE SHORES OF THE ALPINE LAKE OF THE
same name has been celebrated by writers since antiquity. Two of them are commemorated by statues flanking the imposing rose window on the western front of its cathedral, constructed in the late
fifteenth century—Pliny the Elder, the great polymath, and his nephew, Gaius Plinius Caecilius
Secundus, better known as "Pliny the Younger." The younger Pliny was born in Como in the winter
of A.D. 61/62, the son of a wealthy landowner in the region. But his father died when Pliny was still a
boy, so his upbringing was entrusted to his maternal uncle, who eventually provided for his nephew's
adoption in his will. We know quite a bit about Pliny's life from his own writings and from occasional
references to him in other authors or inscriptions. He received the best education that money could
buy in those days, including study in Rome with the famous rhetorician Quintilian. Like his good
friend, the historian Tacitus, Pliny's political career began in the reign of the tyrant Domitian in 82 with
his appointment to a post on the "Board of Ten," a judicial committee that marked the first station in
the career of a Roman senator. Further magistracies followed, doubtless with the assistance of Pliny's
powerful connections, which included not only members of his family but influential former consuls,
such as the celebrated Verginius Rufus, whose career Pliny describes in a letter reproduced below.
Pliny reached the consulship in the year 100 and marked the occasion, as had become conventional,
with a speech of thanks to the reigning emperor, Trajan. The speech, known as his *Panegyric,* survives,
the only complete example of a speech delivered between the death of Cicero and the late third century. He later served the emperor as governor of the province of Bithynia in Asia Minor in 109 and
probably died there in his service, for we hear no more of him thereafter.

Pliny's career never acquired the luster that attended his famous uncle, but his modest contributions to literary history offer an important perspective on the life of the elite at the height of
the Roman Empire. Most of the works that we hear about—his occasional poetry and forensic
speeches—have been lost, but his major work survives, a collection of 247 letters organized into ten
books. The first nine books contain letters addressed to private friends, but unlike most of the surviving correspondence of Cicero, these letters were written with a view to publication. For the most
part, they consist of essays on a variety of topics presented in the guise of correspondence. In some
letters he comments on contemporary events in political or social life, in others he offers advice. He
discourses on law and city life, on literature and domestic life, on the treatment of slaves and the status of education. The range of subjects is as broad as Roman life, but Pliny eschews philosophy and
more serious issues to present rather a picture of his times.

**Figure 27: Villa Madama**
This villa in Rome, designed by Raphael, was partly inspired by the younger Pliny's detailed descriptions of such buildings.

The carefully crafted figure of Pliny that emerges from the letters is of a genial and benevolent patron, knowledgeable about affairs and highly literate, although not a great man of letters. In them we meet some of the most prominent names of the day. Pliny writes several letters to the imperial biographer Suetonius. In one of them he confesses his anxiety because "I am told that I read badly—verses at any rate; that I read speeches quite competently, but verses all the worse by comparison" (9.34.1). He also addresses ten letters to the historian Tacitus, including two particularly well-known ones in which he describes the eruption of Mt. Vesuvius in A.D. 79. And we hear about others who had played a role in Pliny's life and in the life of the empire, such as the statesman Verginius Rufus, who supported him early in his career (2.1). Grace and elegance are Pliny's aims in composing these letters, and for the most part he achieves them, providing a model for later epistolographers.

The tenth book contains some of Pliny's correspondence with the emperor Trajan, consisting mainly of letters sent by Pliny from his governor's post in Asia Minor. Unlike the letters in the first nine books, which are composed in a highly polished style with careful attention to formal balance, these letters appear not to have been intended for publication. Pliny addresses Trajan with specific problems that he encountered in the day-to-day management of the province, such as a proposal for new public baths in the city of Prusa, establishing a fire department at Nicomedia, or, most famously, what to do about the Christians. Each letter is accompanied by Trajan's reply with his ruling on the matter in question. The style of these letters is crisp and straightforward, offering a precious glimpse into the functioning of the empire at its zenith.

## LETTERS

### Book 3, Letter 5: To His Friend Baebius Macer

*Under the guise of answering a friend's request, for a list of titles by his uncle, Pliny describes the work habits of his more celebrated namesake. With the exception of the* Natural History, *the works listed here do not survive.*

I am pleased that you are repeatedly reading the works of my uncle with such care that you wish to possess all of them, and you ask for all their titles. I shall perform the role of an index, and I shall also inform you of the order in which the books were written, for this too is knowledge which scholars are pleased to have.

One book on throwing the javelin from horseback. He wrote this when serving as a prefect of cavalry, devoting to it ingenuity and care in equal measure.

Two books on the life of Pomponius Secundus. My uncle was held in unique affection by this man, so he wrote this work as a tribute owed to the memory of a friend.

Twenty books on the wars in Germany. In this he assembled all the wars which we have waged against the Germans. He embarked on this when he was soldiering in Germany. He was prompted by a dream, in which as he lay asleep there stood before him the ghost of Nero Drusus, who after victories over a huge area of Germany died there. He entrusted his memory to my uncle, and pleaded with him to deliver him from the injustice of oblivion.

Three books on education. He divided this work into six rolls because of its length. In it he educates the orator from the cradle, and completes his training.

Eight books on ambiguity. He wrote this in Nero's last years, when slavery had made hazardous every sort of writing which inclined to some independence or nobility of thought.

Thirty-one books continuing where Aufidius Bassus left off.

Thirty-seven books on natural history. This is a work both extensive and learned, one no less varied than nature herself.

Are you surprised that such a busy man completed so many volumes, many of them so detailed? Your surprise will be greater if you know that for a period he pleaded in the courts, that he died in his fifty-sixth year, and that his middle years were preoccupied and hindered by duties of the greatest importance, and also by

his friendships with emperors. But he had a keen intelligence, astonishing concentration, and little need for sleep. From the time of the Vulcanalia [i.e., August 23] he would begin work by lamplight, not to take the auspices, but to start studying at once while it was fully dark, in winter from the seventh or at latest the eighth hour, and often from the sixth. True, he fell asleep very readily; on occasion sleep would overcome and leave him as he worked at his books. He would make his way before dawn to Vespasian (for that emperor likewise employed the hours of darkness), and after that to the posts allotted to him. On returning home he would devote the rest of the day to his studies. After a snack (like the men of old, during the day he would eat sparingly and informally) he would often in summer spend any leisure time lying in the sun; a book would be read, and he would make notes and take excerpts; for there was no book which he read without excerpting it. He used to say that there was no book so bad that it was not useful at some point.

After sunbathing he would often bathe in cold water, then after a light lunch he slept for a very few minutes. After that, as if a new day had dawned, he worked at his books till dinner-time. Over dinner a book was read, on which he took notes at great speed. I recall that once when the reader mispronounced some words, one of my uncle's friends made him go back, and forced him to go over them again. My uncle said to him: "But surely you understood?" When his friend agreed, my uncle said: "So why did you order him back? We have lost ten lines and more through your interruption." Such economy he exercised with regard to time. In the summer he would quit the dinner-table while it was still light, and in winter during the first hour of darkness. It was as though some law had laid it down.

This was the pattern of his life when in the midst of his labors and the bustle of the city. In retirement only the time for the bath deflected him from his studies. (When I say "the bath," I mean when he was in the water, for when he was being scraped and toweled, he was either listening to or dictating something.) When on a journey, as though freed from other preoccupations he devoted himself solely to study. His secretary sat by him with a book and writing-tablets; in winter his hands were shielded with gauntlets so that not even the harsh temperature should deprive him of any time for study. For this reason even when in Rome he was conveyed in a chair. I recall his rebuke to me for walking: "You could," he said, "have avoided wasting those hours." For he believed that any time not devoted to study was wasted. It was through such concentration that he completed those numerous volumes, and also bequeathed to me one hundred and sixty notebooks of select excerpts written on both sides of the paper in the tiniest script, so that when you take this into account the number is multiplied. He himself used to say that when he was a procurator in Spain, he could have sold those notebooks to Larcius Licinus for 400,000 sesterces, and at that time they were somewhat fewer.

When you recall the volume of his reading and writing, you would surely imagine that he had never held any public offices, nor been a friend of the emperor; again, when you hear the amount of toil which he devoted to his studies, that he did not read or write enough. For what could those busy duties not have hindered, and what could such concentration not have achieved? This is why I often smile when people call me an earnest student, for by comparison with him I am the laziest creature alive. But is it just me—for I am distracted partly by official duties and partly with services to friends? Which one of those who spend their whole lives on literature, when compared with my uncle, would not blush at appearing to devote themselves to sleep and idleness?

I have prolonged my letter, though I had planned to pen only what you were seeking, namely, what books he had left. But I am sure that this additional information will please you no less than the books themselves, for this can move you not merely to read the books, but also by the goad of imitation to work away at something similar. Farewell.

### Book 3, Letter 21: To His Friend Cornelius Priscus

*A report of the death of the poet Martial, who had retired from Rome to his native city of Bilbilis in Spain in A.D. 98. He quotes ten lines from a poem (10.20) that Martial had addressed to him, in which Pliny's legal pleadings are compared to those of the famous native of Arpinum, Cicero.*

I hear that Valerius Martial has died, and I find it sad news. He was a talented and intelligent man with a keen mind, the sort of poet with abundant wit and gall, and an equal measure of openness. When he was retiring from Rome, I presented him with his traveling

expenses as a gesture of friendship and acknowledgement of the verses he composed about me. It was an ancient custom to honor poets who had written eulogies of individuals or of cities with distinctions or with money. But in our day this practice in particular, like other splendid and notable customs, has lapsed. For now that we have abandoned praiseworthy pursuits, we consider it pointless to receive accolades.

Would you like to hear the verses for which I thanked him? I would refer you to the collection, if I did not remember some of them. If you like these, you must look out the rest in his publications. He is addressing his Muse, bidding her make for my house on the Esquiline, and to approach with deference.

But be sure that you don't when drunk go knocking
At that eloquent door when you're not welcome.
He devotes all his days to stern Minerva,
While for the ears of the court of Centumviri
He works away at what men of later ages
Can compare even with Arpinum's pages.
You will go more safely when late lamps burn;
That is your hour, when Bacchus rages wildly,
When the rose is queen, when men's hair is perfumed.
Why, unbending Catos would then read me!

Surely it was right that he who penned these lines should then have been waved off in the friendliest way, and should be mourned as a close friend now he has died? For he gave me the greatest tribute that he could, and he would have given more if that had been possible. Yet what greater thing can a man bestow on a person than fame, praise, and immortality? You will respond that his writings will not be immortal. Perhaps they will not be, but he composed them believing that they would be. Farewell.

### Book 5, Letter 6: To His Friend Domitius Apollinaris

*A description of Pliny's villa in Tuscany at a site that has been identified near Città di Castello about 150 miles from Rome on the Tiber. One of two extensive descriptions of his properties—the other is Book 2, Letter 17, describing his villa at Laurentum—this letter was closely studied by students of architecture in the Renaissance.*

I was heartened by your concern and anxiety for me, for when you heard that I intended to spend the summer on my Tuscan estate, you sought to dissuade me, believing that the region is unhealthy. It is true that the Tuscan shore extending along the coast is oppressive and noxious, but my estate lies far back from the sea; indeed, it lies below the Apennines, the most salubrious of mountains. So to help you to dispense with all fear on my account, hear my recital of the climate, the geography of the region, and the pleasant situation of my villa. These details will be a pleasure for you to hear, and for me to recount.

The climate in winter is cold and frosty, so it repels and rejects myrtles, olives, and other trees which delight in continual warmth. However, it bears with laurels and yields most handsome ones, though from time to time it kills them but not more often than happens in the neighborhood of Rome. In summer it is remarkably temperate; the air is constantly stirred by currents, but more often they are light breezes rather than winds. As a result many live to old age. You can see grandfathers and great-grandfathers of men in their prime, and you can hear old stories and talk of men of the past, so that when you go there, you think that you were born in a different era.

The appearance of the area is very beautiful. Think of some massive amphitheater, one which nature alone can fashion. The broad and expansive plain is ringed with mountains, on the topmost levels of which are glades of tall and ancient trees. A good deal of varied hunting is available there, and woodland suitable for felling descends with the mountain slopes. Between these areas of woodland are hills whose soil is rich and fertile (no outcrop of rock readily meets the eye anywhere, even if you are looking for it); they do not yield in fertility to the broadest plains. The harvests that ripen there are rich; true, they arrive rather late, but they are no smaller in size. Below them, vineyards extend on every flank, presenting an identical appearance as they interweave far and wide. At the lowest level below them plantations grow, and adjoining them are meadows and fields—fields which only strapping oxen and the strongest ploughs can break through, for when the ground is first ploughed, the soil cleaves fast, and comes out in such great clods that it is only finally subdued when turned over nine times. The meadows bloom with flowers like jewels; they nurture trefoil and other delicate plants which are always soft and fresh-looking, for they are all nourished by streams all year round. Yet where much water gathers, there is no marshland because it lies on a slope, and any water

which is attracted there and fails to be absorbed pours into the Tiber.

The river cuts through the middle of the fields. It can take boats, and it conveys all the produce down to Rome, though only in winter and spring, for in summer its level lowers, and with its dry bed it abandons its reputation as a massive river until the autumn, when it claims it back. You will experience great pleasure by gazing out from the mountain over the countryside, for you will get the impression of looking not at the landscape but at some painting of a scene of extraordinary beauty. Wherever the eye settles, it will be refreshed by the variation and the pattern which is outlined.

The villa lies at the base of a hill, but the view seems to be from the top, for the hill rises so gently and gradually, and the slope is so deceptive, that you would think, not that you were mounting it, but that you had already done so. The Apennines lie in the rear, but at some distance. No matter how sunny and still the day is, the house welcomes breezes from them, but they are not piercing and excessive, but subdued, and they are played out because of the distance they travel. The house for the most part faces south, and in summer entices the sun from midday, and in winter from a little earlier, into a colonnade which is broad and correspondingly long. It contains several rooms, and also an entrance hall similar to those in days of old.

In front of the colonnade is a terrace divided into several sections of different shapes which are separated by hedges of box. From it a raised platform slopes downward, on which there are shapes of animals facing each other, fashioned from box. On the level below there is acanthus, soft and virtually transparent. There is a walkway round it enclosed by compact bushes cut into various shapes; close by there is a circular drive which encloses box in different shapes, and shrubs kept low by being cut back. The whole area is protected by a wall which is hidden from view by a tiered hedge of box. Outside the wall there is a meadow; nature has made it as much worth seeing as the garden just described, which was devised by human skill. Beyond it there are fields and many other meadows and plantations.

At the head of the colonnade a dining room juts out. Through its folding doors it surveys the end of the terrace and immediately beyond it the meadow and the expanse of countryside. From the windows on one side it looks out onto the side of the terrace and onto a projecting part of the house, and on the other the grove and its foliage, which lie within the exercise-ground for horses close by. Virtually opposite the middle of the colonnade there is a suite of rooms somewhat set back; it encircles a courtyard shaded by four plane trees. They surround a fountain in a marble basin, which gushes forth and refreshes the plane trees round it and the earth beneath them with its gentle spray. This suite of rooms contains a bedroom which shuts out the daylight, shouting, and other sounds, and adjoining it is a dining room for everyday use by me and my friends. It looks out on the courtyard which I mentioned, on one wing of the colonnade, and on the general vista which the colonnade enjoys. There is also a second bedroom which the nearest plane tree endows with greenery and shade. It is adorned with marble up to the dado, and has a mural depicting tree-branches with birds perched upon them, a scene no less charming than the marble. In this bedroom there is a small fountain enclosed by a basin, the several jets around which combine to make a most pleasing whisper.

At the corner of the colonnade, the largest bedroom faces the dining room. From one set of windows it looks down on the terrace, from the other on the meadow, in front of which there is an ornamental pool lying below the windows and enhancing the view from them, for it is pleasant both to the ear and to the eye, because the water cascades down from a height and turns white when it enters the marble basin. This room is beautifully warm in winter, for it is constantly bathed in sunshine. Adjacent to it is the hot-air room, and if the day is cloudy the steam is injected and takes over the role of the sun.

The spacious and cheerful room next to it, in which one disrobes for bathing, is adjoined by the cooling-room, in which there is a good-sized swimming-pool shaded from the sun. If you want a bigger or warmer pool to swim in, there is one in the courtyard with a well next to it, from which you can freshen up again if the warm water is cloying. The cooling-room leads into a middle room, in which the sun provides a most genial service, though this is more in evidence in the hot room, for it projects outwards. This has three plunge-baths, two in the sun and the third at some distance from it, though not from its light. Beyond the disrobing-room a ball-court has been erected, big enough to cater for several kinds of exercise and for several circles of players.

Not far from the bath is a staircase which leads up to a covered gallery by way of three suites of rooms. The first of these suites overhangs the small courtyard with the four plane trees; the second is over the meadow, and the third over the vineyard with a view of various sectors of the sky. At the end of the covered gallery there is a bedroom hollowed out of the gallery itself, which looks out on to the riding-circuit, the vineyard, and the mountains. Another room adjoining it meets the sun, especially in winter. Next comes a suite which connects the riding-circuit to the house. Such are the appearance and the perquisites of the front of the villa.

At the side there is a covered gallery for summer use, which is set on an eminence, and which seems not so much to look out on the vineyard as to touch it. At its center there is a dining room, particularly healthy since it welcomes a breeze from the Apennine valleys. It has very broad windows at the rear, from which the vineyard is visible; the folding doors also look out on the vineyard which is visible through the gallery. On the side of the dining room which has no windows there is a staircase, which by means of a more private detour allows the access of things useful for dining. At the far end there is a bedroom which is afforded a view of the gallery no less pleasant than that of the vineyard. Beneath it there is the equivalent of a subterranean gallery, which in summer remains glacial with the enclosed cold; satisfied with its own air, it neither needs nor admits breezes from outside. Behind these twin galleries, and beyond the dining room, a colonnade opens up which is cold up to midday but then heats up as evening draws near. This gives entry to two suites, in one of which there are four bedrooms, and in the other three; the sun's journey provides them successively with sunshine and shade.

Far, far more impressive than the arrangement and convenience of the buildings is the riding-ground, the center of which lies open, so that as soon as you enter, the whole complex is laid out before your eyes. It is surrounded by plane trees which are clothed in ivy and are green with their own foliage above and with that of other plants below. The ivy travels round trunks and branches, and roams across to link up with neighboring plane trees. Between these planes box-shrubs grow, and laurels circle outside the box-shrubs, associating their shade with that of the plane trees. The straight edge of the riding-circuit is broken at its end by a semicircular curve, which changes its appearance. It is encircled and shaded by cypresses, and becomes more overshadowed and darkened by the thicker shade, but in the inner circuits, of which there are several, it gets the most translucent daylight. In that area roses grow as well, and the cool in the shadows is moderated by shafts of not unwelcome sunlight.

At the far end of this curved sector, with its varied and manifold twists and turns a return is made to a straight lateral stretch, though there is not just this one, but several separated by box-hedges lying between them. At some points they are divided by lawns, and at others by box-shrubs fashioned in a thousand shapes. Here and there these form letters which spell out the names, now of the owner, and now of the specialist gardener. Miniature obelisks rise upward, alternating with fruit-trees planted there. Amidst this creative work, most characteristic of city life, you suddenly confront the imitation of an imported country scene. The central open area is adorned at both ends by plane trees of smaller height. Behind them on both sides grow acanthuses with their slippery and pliant leaves, and next come more shapes and names created from box.

At the far end of the circuit is a semicircular couch of white marble, shaded by a vine which is supported by four slender pillars of Carystian marble. From pipes within the couch jets of water stream out as if ejected by the weight of those who sit there. The water is caught by a hollowed stone and then held by a basin of delicate marble, where it is controlled by some hidden means so that it fills up without overflowing. The *hors d'oeuvre* and the more substantial courses are placed on the circumference of the basin, while the lighter ones float round on vessels shaped like tiny boats or birds. A fountain opposite sends water shooting up and recovers it, for after being ejected high in the air it falls back, and by the combination of fissures the water is both collected and expelled.

Close by the couch there is a facing bedroom which confers as much distinction on the couch as it obtains from it. Constructed in gleaming marble, it has folding doors which jut out into the greenery and lead out into it, and its upper and lower windows gaze up and down into further greenery. There is a hidden alcove, which is, as it were, part of the bedroom but also a second one. There is a bed in it, and though there are windows all round, the daylight is curtained by the shade that overhangs it, for a most luxuriant vine struggles to mount to the roof of the whole building. You could recline there as if you were resting in a glade, except that you would not experience a rain-shower as you would in the glade. Here too a fountain plays and at once retires. Marble chairs are arranged in a number of places, which please those wearied from walking as much as does the room

itself. Tiny fountains play close by the chairs. The whole riding-circuit resounds with the noise of the streams which are channeled in, and which follow the controling hand, watering now one area, now another, and from time to time all together.

Long before now I should have refrained from seeming to sing too loudly, if I had not decided to visit by letter every corner in your company. I did not fear that you would find it wearisome to read a description of what would not be wearisome to visit, especially as you could take a break should you so wish, lay down the letter, and take a seat. Moreover, I have been pandering to my affections, for I love the layout which I have for the most part arranged or which I have developed from that put in train by others. To put it briefly (why should I not reveal to you my decided view or misconception?), I think the primary task of a writer is to scrutinize his title, to ask himself repeatedly what he has embarked upon, and to be aware that if he confines himself to his topic, his treatment cannot be long-winded. If on the other hand he summons and draws in extraneous themes, it will be overlong. You know how many lines Homer takes to describe the arms of Achilles, and how many Virgil expends on those of Aeneas, yet both treat their subject economically because they achieve what they set out to do. You observe how Aratus follows up and gathers even the smallest stars, and yet he observes the due limit, because this is no digression of his, but the subject itself. In the same way, "to compare small things with great," I am attempting to present the whole house before your eyes, and as long as I do not introduce anything extraneous and irrelevant, it is the house being described and not my letter describing it which extends itself.

But to ensure that I am not justly censured in terms of my own law, if I linger longer in this digression, I shall revert to the topic with which I began. You now know the reasons why I prefer my Tuscan estate to any in Tusculum or Tibur or Praeneste. Then, too, in addition to the reasons I have given, I enjoy a leisure there more profound and more rich, and therefore more carefree. I need not wear a toga, no neighbor summons me, and all is peace and tranquility; this very fact enhances the health-giving atmosphere of the region, as if the sky were more cloudless, and the air clearer. When I am there I am supremely healthy in mind and body, for my books exercise my mind, and hunting my body. My servants too nowhere live a healthier life than here; at any rate, up to now I have never lost a single one of those which I had brought to accompany me (forgive my boasting). I only pray that in the days to come the gods may preserve this joy for me, and this fair fame for the house. Farewell.

## Book 6, Letter 16: To His Friend Tacitus

*Pliny writes to his good friend, the historian Tacitus, to describe the death of his uncle in the eruption of Mt. Vesuvius that took place over four days in August of A.D. 79. At the time Pliny the Elder was in command of the western fleet at the naval base of Misenum on the northern tip of the Bay of Naples. What began as an investigation of a natural phenomenon turned into a rescue mission when a message arrived from an acquaintance at Stabiae across the bay. Unfortunately, Tacitus's account of the event does not survive.*

You ask me to describe for you the death of my uncle, to enable you to transmit a more truthful account for the benefit of posterity. I am grateful to you, because I realize that perennial glory is in store for the manner of his death if it is extolled by you. It is true that he died in a disaster which overtook the most beautiful of regions, and in a calamity shared by communities and cities, so that his renown will seemingly live for ever, and it is true also that he wrote numerous works which will also survive. But none the less, the undying quality of your writings will greatly enhance his immortality. I myself account as blessed those who by the gods' gift have been granted the ability either to perform deeds worth chronicling or to compose accounts which deserve to be read, but I regard as most blessed those who achieve both. My uncle will be numbered among these through his books and through yours, and for this reason I more gladly undertake and even demand the task you lay on me.

My uncle was at Misenum, where he held command of the fleet in person. Just after midday on 24 August my mother pointed out to him the appearance of a cloud of unusual size and appearance. He had relaxed in the sun, had then taken a cold dip, had lunched lying down, and was at his books. He asked for his sandals, and mounted to the place from which that remarkable phenomenon could best be observed. A cloud was issuing up from some mountain which spectators from a distance could not identify; it was later established to have been Vesuvius. The pine tree, rather than any other, best describes its appearance and shape, for it rose high up into the sky on what one can describe as a very long trunk, and it then spread out into what

looked like branches. I believe that this was because the cloud was borne upward while the pressure of wind was still fresh, and then when this died down it was left unsupported, or was overcome by its own weight and so thinned out and became widespread. Its appearance varied between white on the one hand, and grimy and spotted on the other, according as it had thrust up earth or ashes. My uncle, most learned man that he was, realized that this was important, and should be investigated at closer quarters. He ordered a fast-sailing ship to be made ready, and gave me the option of accompanying him if I so wished. I replied that I preferred to work at my books, and it chanced that he had given me an exercise to write.

As he was leaving the house, he received a letter from Rectina, wife of Tascius. She was panicking at the danger looming over her, for her house lay below Vesuvius, and the only way of escape was by ship. She begged him to rescue her from that great hazard. He changed his plan, and the journey which had begun in a spirit of research he now undertook with the greatest urgency. He launched some quadriremes, and embarked in order to lend aid personally, not merely to Rectina, but to many, for the attractiveness of the coast had made it thickly populated. He headed swiftly into the area from which others were fleeing, and maintained a straight course, steering straight towards the danger. He was so fearless that he dictated and had notes taken of all the movements and shapes of that evil phenomenon as he observed them.

By now ashes were falling on the ships, whiter and thicker the nearer they approached. Then pumice stones also descended, and stones which were black, charred, and split by the fires. Suddenly they were in shallow water and the shore-line barred their way with debris from the mountain. My uncle hesitated momentarily, wondering whether to turn back, but then, as the steersman advised that course, he said to him: "Fortune favors the brave. Head for the villa of Pomponianus." This was at Stabiae, separated from the ships by the middle of the bay (for the shore gradually winds in a curve round the sea as it pours in). Though the danger had not yet drawn near, it was clearly visible, and would come very close as it spread. So Pomponianus had stowed his baggage into boats, having determined on flight if the opposing wind dropped. My uncle was then carried in by the wind, which was wholly in his favor. He embraced, consoled, and encouraged Pomponianus, who was panicking. Then in order to relieve his host's fear by a show of unconcern, he gave orders to be conveyed to the bath. After bathing, he reclined and dined in cheerful mood, or apparently cheerful, which was just as impressive.

Meanwhile from Mount Vesuvius widespread flames and fires rising high blazed forth in several places, their gleaming brightness accentuated by the darkness of the night. To calm people's apprehensions, my uncle kept saying that these were fires abandoned by peasants in their fear, and houses ablaze because they had been left untenanted. Then he retired to rest, and in fact he relaxed in sleep that was wholly genuine, for his snoring, somewhat deep and loud because of his broad physique, was audible to those patroling the threshold. But by this time the courtyard which gave access to his suite of rooms had become so full of ash intermingled with pumice stones that it was piled high. Thus if he had lingered longer in the bedroom the way out would have been barred. So he was wakened, and he emerged to join Pomponianus and the rest, who had stayed awake. Together they debated whether to stay indoors or to roam in the open, for the buildings were shaking with frequent large-scale tremors; as though dislodged from their foundations, they seemed to shift now one way and now another, and then back again. On the other hand, in the open they feared falling pumice stones, however light and hollow. But comparison of the dangers made them opt for the open. For my uncle, this was one rational choice prevailing over the other, but for the rest, fear prevailing over fear. They used strips of cloth to fasten pillows on their heads as a protection against falling stones.

By now it was daylight elsewhere, but there it was night, blacker and denser than any night, though many torches and lights of various kinds relieved it. They decided to go out onto the shore, and to investigate from close at hand whether the sea now allowed any departure, but it still remained mountainous and hostile. My uncle lay down there on a discarded sail, and repeatedly drank cold water, which he had requested. Then flames and the smell of sulphur heralding the flames impelled the rest to flight and roused him. Leaning on two of his confidential slaves, he stood up and at once collapsed. I infer that his breathing was choked by the greater density of smoke, and this blocked his gullet, which was often frail and narrow, and often unsettled. When daylight was restored, two days after his eyes had closed in death, his body was found intact and unharmed. It was covered over, still in the clothes he had worn. It was more like someone sleeping than a corpse.

Meanwhile my mother and I at Misenum—but this is irrelevant to a historical account, and you wanted to ascertain nothing other than details of my uncle's death, so I shall end here, but with a single addition. I have detailed everything at which I was present, and which I had heard at the very time when the facts were most truthfully recorded. You must select what you particularly want, for it is one thing to write a letter, and another to compose a history; one thing to write for a friend, another to write for the world. Farewell.

## Book 6, Letter 20: To His Friend Tacitus

*In this sequel to his earlier letter about the eruption of Vesuvius, Pliny describes his own experience of the eruption that destroyed Herculaneum and Pompeii.*

You say that your interest has been whetted by the letter which I wrote to you at your request about the death of my uncle, and that you are keen to know, when I was left behind at Misenum (I had embarked on this topic but then broke off), not only what fears but also what misfortunes I endured. So "though aghast in mind at recalling them, I shall begin."

Once my uncle had departed, I devoted the rest of my day to my studies, for that was the reason why I stayed behind. I then took a bath, had dinner, and then a disturbed and short-lived sleep. There had been earth-tremors for many days previously, though they were less terrifying because they were frequent in Campania. But that night they became so strong that everything around us seemed to be not merely shifting but turning upside down. My mother broke into my bedroom. I in my turn was already rising, intending to rouse her if she was sleeping. We retired to the courtyard of the house, which extended a short distance between the sea and the buildings. I am uncertain whether I should call it resolve or foolishness (I was then in my eighteenth year, you see), but I asked for a book of Titus Livy and read it, and I also copied out passages (as I had begun earlier), as though in relaxation. Suddenly a friend of my uncle appeared; he had recently come from Spain to join him. When he saw my mother and myself sitting there, and me even reading a book, he rebuked her for her forbearance, and me for my untroubled attitude. But I concentrated on the book just as eagerly.

By now the first hour of daylight had arrived, but it was still uncertain and listless. The buildings all round were shaking, and though we were in the open, it was a confined space, and our fear of falling buildings became great and definite. We then finally decided to quit the town, followed by a stupefied mob. In what passes for prudence at a time of panic, they preferred the decision of others to their own, and in an extended column they pressed close to us and drove us on as we departed. Once we were away from the buildings, we halted. There we experienced many remarkable and many fearful things, for the carriages which we had ordered to be brought out were moved in opposite directions though on wholly level ground, and did not remain stationary in the same tracks even though wedged with stones. Moreover, we watched the sea being sucked back and virtually repelled by an earth-tremor; at any rate the shoreline had advanced, and left many sea-creatures stranded on the dry sand. On the landward side there was a black and menacing cloud, split by twisted and quivering flashes of fiery breath; it opened out into extended shapes of flames, like lightning flashes, but greater.

Then that same friend from Spain spoke more urgently and pressingly: "If your brother, if your uncle is still alive, he desires your safety. If he is dead, he wanted you to survive him. So why do you postpone your escape?" Our answer was that we would not take thought for our own safety while we were not sure of his. He did not delay further, but burst out, and removed himself from the danger with all speed.

Not long afterwards that cloud descended to ground level and covered the sea. It had encircled Capri and hidden it from sight, and made the promontory of Misenum invisible. My mother then begged and encouraged and bade me flee in any way I could. She said that this was possible for a young person, but that she herself, being weighed down with years and a frail physique, would be happy to die if she were not responsible for my death. My riposte was that I would not seek safety without her. I then grasped her hand, and forced her to move faster. She reluctantly obeyed, reproaching herself for delaying me.

Ash was now descending, though slight in quantity. I looked back. Dense blackness loomed over us, pursuing us as it spread over the earth like a flood. "Let us turn aside," I said, "while we can see. Otherwise, if we stay on the road, we may be brought down and flattened in the darkness by the crowd accompanying us." We had scarcely sat down when darkness descended. It was not like a moonless or cloudy night, but like being in an enclosed place where the light has been doused. You could hear women moaning, children howling, and men shouting; they were crying out, some seeking parents, others children, and others wives, or recognizing them by the sound of their voices. Some were lamenting their own misfortune, others that of their families. A few in their fear of death were praying for death. Many were raising their hands to implore the gods, but more took the view that no gods now existed anywhere, and that this was an eternal and final darkness hanging over the world. There were some who magnified the actual dangers with invented and lying fears. Some persons present reported that one part of Misenum was in ruins, and that another was on fire; it was untrue, but their listeners believed it.

A vestige of light returned, but to us it seemed to be not daylight but an indication of advancing fire. In fact, the fire halted some distance away. But the darkness returned, and so did the ash, now abundant and heavy. We repeatedly stood up and shook it off, for otherwise we would have been buried and even crushed beneath its weight. I could boast that though encompassed by these great dangers I uttered no groan or pusillanimous word, but what deters me is that I believed that I was perishing together with the whole world, and the whole world was perishing with me—a wretched consolation for my mortal lot, yet a powerful one.

At last the darkness thinned out and vanished into smoke or cloud. True daylight came, and the sun also shone, but pallidly, as occurs at an eclipse. Our eyes, still trembling, were confronted with a scene of universal change, for everything was buried by deep ash as though by snow. We returned to Misenum, tended our bodies as best we could, and in mingled hope and fear spent the night on tenterhooks and in uncertainty. The fear was stronger, for the earth tremors continued, and many frenzied individuals made a mockery of their own misfortunes and those of others with terrifying prophecies. Even then, however, we ourselves did not plan to leave, in spite of our experience and expectation of the dangers, until the message came about my uncle.

These details are in no way worthy of your history. You will read them with no intention of recording them. If they seem to you unworthy even of a letter, you will doubtless blame yourself for requesting them. Farewell.

## Book 10, Letter 96: Gaius Pliny to the Emperor Trajan (Late 111)

*Late in the year A.D. 111, while he was serving as governor of the province of Bithynia in Asia Minor, Pliny wrote this letter to the emperor, inquiring about how to deal with what from the Roman perspective was a troublesome cult. With Trajan's brief response, we gain a rare insight into official attitudes toward the early Christians.*

It is my regular custom, my lord, to refer to you all questions which cause me doubt, for who can better guide my hesitant steps or instruct my ignorance? I have never attended hearings concerning Christians, so I am unaware what is usually punished or investigated, and to what extent. I am more than a little in doubt whether there is to be a distinction between ages, and to what extent the young should be treated no differently from the more hardened; whether pardon should be granted to repentance; whether the person who has been a Christian in some sense should not benefit by having renounced it; whether it is the name Christian, itself untainted with crimes, or the crimes which cling to the name which should be punished.

In the meantime, this is the procedure I have followed, in the cases of those brought before me as Christians. I asked them whether they were Christians. If they admitted it, I asked them a second and a third time, threatening them with execution. Those who remained obdurate I ordered to be executed, for I was in no doubt, whatever it was which they were confessing, that their obstinacy and their inflexible stubbornness should at any rate be punished. Others similarly lunatic were Roman citizens, so I registered them as due to be sent back to Rome.

Later in the course of the hearings, as usually happens, the charge rippled outwards, and more examples appeared. An anonymous document was published containing the names of many. Those who denied that they were or had been Christians and called upon the gods after me, and with incense and wine made obeisance to your statue, which I had ordered to be brought in together with images of the gods for this very purpose, and who moreover cursed Christ (those who are truly Christian cannot, it is said, be forced to do any of these things), I ordered to be acquitted.

Others who were named by an informer stated that they were Christians and then denied it. They said that in fact they had been, but had abandoned their allegiance, some three years previously, some more years earlier, and one or two as many as twenty years before. All these as well worshipped your statue and images of the gods, and blasphemed Christ. They maintained, however, that all that their guilt or error involved was that they were accustomed to assemble at dawn on a fixed day, to sing a hymn antiphonally to Christ as God, and to bind themselves by an oath, not for the commission of some crime, but to avoid acts of theft, brigandage, and adultery, not to break their word, and not to withhold money deposited with them when asked for it. When these rites were completed, it was their custom to depart, and then to assemble again to take food, which was however common and harmless. They had ceased, they said, to do this following my edict, by which in accordance with your instructions I had outlawed the existence of secret brotherhoods. So I thought it all the more necessary to ascertain the truth from two maidservants, who were called deaconesses, even by employing torture. I found nothing other than a debased and boundless superstition.

I therefore postponed the inquiry, and hastened to consult you, since this issue seemed to me to merit consultation, especially because of the number indicted, for there are many of all ages, every rank, and both sexes who are summoned and will be summoned to confront danger. The infection of this superstition has extended not merely through the cities, but also through the villages and country areas, but it seems likely that it can be halted and corrected. It is at any rate certain that temples which were almost abandoned have begun to be crowded, and the solemn rites which for long had been suspended are being restored. The flesh of the victims, for which up to now only a very occasional buyer was found, is now on sale in many places. This leads me readily to believe that if opportunity for repentance is offered, a large crowd of people can be set right.

### Book 10, Letter 97: Trajan to Pliny

You have followed the appropriate procedure, my Secundus, in examining the cases of those brought before you as Christians, for no general rule can be laid down which would establish a definite routine. Christians are not to be sought out. If brought before you and found guilty, they must be punished, but in such a way that a person who denies that he is a Christian and demonstrates this by his action, that is, by worshipping our gods, may obtain pardon for repentance, even if his previous record is suspect. Documents published anonymously must play no role in any accusation, for they give the worst example, and are foreign to our age.

# AFTERWORD

Pliny's epistles differed from the published correspondence of Cicero in that these letters, with the exception of the imperial correspondence in Book 10, were carefully composed with eventual publication in mind. In this respect Pliny had been preceded by Seneca, who had published as letters a collection of short essays on philosophy, which Pliny did not admire. Such topics, "reeking of the school of rhetoric and of the philosopher's shade, so to speak" (9.2.3), were uncongenial to his project of chronicling his experience of everyday life. At the same time he maintained that his letters should "incorporate content which is not trivial or mean or restricted to personal affairs" (3.20.11). Pliny published the first three books together, and they were evidently a success in his lifetime, for he followed with six more. He took great pride when he heard that his friend Tacitus had been mistaken for "that famous author Pliny" while spending a day at the races.

Pliny's *Panegyric* to Trajan resurfaced later in antiquity when it served as a model for orators in Gaul. Eleven orations to emperors after A.D. 289 survived in the same manuscript that preserved Pliny's speech. This manuscript was discovered in Mainz in Germany by Johannes Aurispa in 1433, and though it is now lost, enough copies were made for Pliny's oration to become a model for genteel servility in public addresses to monarchs in the Renaissance and after. In seventeenth-century England it was required reading in many schools, and it was often imitated, for example, by John Dryden in *Astraea Redux*, a full-blown panegyric that he composed in praise of King Charles II.

Pliny's influence is felt primarily through the letters, for the genre of the literary epistle proved especially popular in late antiquity. The letters of the great pagan orator Quintus Aurelius Symmachus were collected and published in nine books shortly before his death in A.D. 402, with a tenth book of official correspondence added in an obvious gesture to the precedent of Pliny. The Christian bishop Ambrose (340–97) likewise collected his correspondence in ten books on the model of Pliny. Toward the end of the fifth century, another Christian bishop, Sidonius Apollinaris of Clermont in Gaul (ca. 430–82) explicitly added a ninth book to his collected correspondence in imitation of Pliny, a sure sign that by then the tenth book was no longer known. There is little evidence that anyone was reading the letters in the Middle Ages, and it was only in the early fifteenth century that copies of Pliny's correspondence began to be widely known again.

It was not until 1494 that a complete manuscript of all ten books was discovered, but by 1419 most of the letters had become known from other copies. It was then that the humanists fastened on Pliny as a model for epistolary style, but they were particularly absorbed by Pliny's descriptions of his Tuscan and Laurentine villas. In his influential treatise *On Architecture*, published in 1452, the Renaissance polymath Leon Battista Alberti was clearly influenced by Pliny's work. Early in the following century Pope Leo X commissioned the design of a country estate in emulation of Pliny's villas from the celebrated artist Raphael. Its hilltop setting evokes Pliny's description of his Tuscan estate, while other architectural details recall the Laurentine villa. Pliny served as inspiration for country estates throughout the Renaissance, such as the Villa Giulia in Rome and the Villa Medici in Fiesole, near Florence. For American readers, the most familiar example is Thomas Jefferson's home in Monticello. But modern architects such as Léon Krier and Thomas Gordon Smith continue the fascination with reconstructing Pliny's homes.

The site of one of Pliny's villas has been identified in the northern region of Umbria at Città di Castello, which was known in antiquity as Tifernum Tiberinum. A large number of roof tiles bearing his initials C.P.C.S. have been found in the ruins of the working part of the ancient villa discovered there, although great damage was done by deep plowing of the site in the 1970s. Lamentably, excavation of the residential complex of Pliny's villa, a few hundred yards away, has been blocked by the owners of the Villa Brozzi-Capelletti, on whose grounds it is located.

# SUETONIUS

## (Gaius Suetonius Tranquillus, ca. A.D. 69–ca. 140)

NOT MUCH IS KNOWN ABOUT SUETONIUS'S LIFE. HE MAY HAVE BEEN BORN IN A.D. 69, when his father fought for Otho on the losing side against Vitellius at the Battle of Bedriacum, as a military tribune with the thirteenth legion, which then transferred its allegiance to Vespasian. His family had equestrian status and seem to have been prosperous settlers at Hippo Regius, on the coast of the North African province of Numidia. His career was greatly assisted by the patronage of the younger Pliny. Pliny agreed to try to arrange the postponement of a court case in which Suetonius was to appear as an advocate, because Suetonius dreamed of an unfavorable outcome (*Letters* 1.18); he asked a friend to urge the owner of a farm to sell it to Suetonius (1.24). Elsewhere in the *Letters* we read that Pliny agreed to transfer an administrative post from Suetonius to one of his relatives (3.8); he banteringly demanded that Suetonius publish his work or run the risk of legal action to force him to do so (5.10); and he asked Suetonius whether he should read his poems to his friends, even though he had no talent for reciting poetry (9.34). Pliny even appealed in flattering tones to the emperor Trajan to grant tax exemptions and other financial privileges to Suetonius (10.94):

> My lord, I have admitted Suetonius Tranquillus to my circle. He is utterly honest and honorable, and extremely learned. I have long admired his character and his interests, and the more I have come to see of him now, the more I have begun to love him.

In the following letter (10.95), we learn that Trajan reluctantly acceded to this request. A fragmentary inscription found at Hippo in 1952 records that Suetonius held various important administrative posts under Trajan and Hadrian. About 122, however, along with many other people, including Septicius Clarus, the praetorian prefect and dedicatee of at least some of the *Lives of the Caesars*, as also of the first collection of Pliny's *Letters*, he lost his government post, allegedly for being more familiar with Hadrian's wife, Sabina, than was appropriate in the imperial court.

Pliny may have teased Suetonius for his slowness in publishing his writings (*Letters* 5.10), but the list of his known works is long and their range is impressive. Most of them fall into distinct categories. Some are lexicographical: *On Weather-Signs, On the Names of Seas and Rivers, On the Names of Winds, On the Names and Types of Clothes and Footwear, On Physical Defects, On Insults, On Critical Signs Used in Books.* Some are about customs and institutions: *On Greek Games, On Roman Spectacles and Games, On the Roman Year, On Roman Manners and Customs, On Offices of State.* Some are biographical: *On Kings, On Famous Prostitutes, On Famous Men.* Some of these works may have been contained in a miscellany known as *The Meadows.* The only work that defies such

**Figure 28: Coin of Nero**
The Roman instinct for truth in portraiture was so strong that, even in such an official medium as coinage, no attempt is made to disguise Nero's lapse into obesity.

categorization is a study of Cicero's *Republic,* a polemical response to a critique of that work by the Greek scholar Didymus (nicknamed "Bronzeguts" from his aptitude for hard work—he is credited with thirty-five hundred or four thousand books—and also "Book-Forgetter" from his tendency to contradict himself from book to book). Apart from the *Lives of the Caesars,* little or nothing of most of Suetonius's other works survives (even the titles of some of the works listed above are uncertain). Substantial Byzantine extracts from *On Insults* and from *On Greek Games,* both of which he wrote in Greek, were discovered in a monastery on Mt. Athos in the 1860s, and it is now clear that there are further passages quoted without attribution from these and perhaps other Suetonian works in the late Greek scholarly tradition.

It is usually assumed that all of Suetonius's other biographical works predate the *Lives of the Caesars:* there is a distinct deterioration in the quality of the *Lives* of the later emperors (see below), which some scholars regard as evidence that Suetonius was losing interest in the project; if so, he was hardly likely to begin another set of biographies. *On Famous Prostitutes* is known by its title only. That might seem an eccentric choice of subject, but there were at least five treatises on *Lives of Famous Prostitutes in Athens* (Athenaeus, *Wise Men at Dinner* 13.567a), including one by Aristophanes of Byzantium, who was head of the Library at Alexandria. *On Kings* was in three books and seems, rather puzzlingly, to have included discussion of forgotten rulers of strange and exotic regions.

*On Famous Men* seems to have been a collection in five or six books of biographies of distinguished Roman intellectuals—poets, historians, orators, philosophers, and teachers. The *Lives* of a few poets survive, mainly through being absorbed into the scholarly tradition surrounding the poets themselves, notably those of Terence, Horace, Lucan, and (not quite in its entirety) Virgil. From these we learn, for example, that Virgil was born in a roadside ditch and that Horace's bedroom was lined with mirrors. The most substantial surviving portions of the work contain brief biographies of twenty teachers of grammar and sixteen teachers of rhetoric. Given the loss of the *Lives* of so many of the poets, it is often regretted that those of so many mere professors should have survived, but these texts give very valuable insights into education in Rome.

The *Lives of the Caesars* may have been published in eight volumes, perhaps appearing at separate times: one each for Julius Caesar and the five Julio-Claudian emperors (Augustus, Tiberius,

Caligula, Claudius, Nero); a single book for the brief reigns of Galba, Otho, and Vitellius; and a final book for the Flavians (Vespasian and his sons, Titus and Domitian). He would not have contemplated proceeding further, with biographies of the more recent emperors, Nerva and Trajan, and certainly not of Hadrian, the ruling emperor. Such accounts would have had to be uncritical panegyric. Tacitus, that most vitriolic historian, was able to write a glowing biography of his father-in-law, Julius Agricola; but, in doing so, he was much assisted by the opportunities it gave him for criticism of Rome and its rulers. The dullest and least successful of Suetonius's *Lives* is his account of Titus, whom he greatly admired, describing him as the "beloved darling of mankind." (If he had ruled longer, Titus might possibly have become more vicious and more interesting, like Caligula, Nero, and his own brother, Domitian, all of whom Suetonius portrays as sinking into depravity after a bright start to their reigns.)

As remarked earlier, the quality of writing deteriorates markedly in the later *Lives,* and this is sometimes taken to indicate Suetonius's loss of interest in the project. There may, however, be other factors at play. The *Lives* of Galba, Otho, and Vitellius are brief, as befits the brevity of their reigns. Moreover, so much of A.D. 68 and 69 was taken up with wars, and Suetonius is never interested in military history, which is generally remote from the biography of an individual. It is also possible that Suetonius hesitated to go into detail about incidents during the Flavian period that involved people who were still alive. At about the same time as Suetonius was writing, Juvenal announced that his *Satires* were directed at those who were safely dead. We can only speculate on how Tacitus discussed the hated Domitian's reign in the *Histories*. Suetonius is criticized for not quoting named sources in the later *Lives*. This must be at least partly because his fall from favor deprived him of access to the imperial archives, but it is also reasonable to assume that he was able to rely more on oral testimony.

Most of the sources that Suetonius read or may have read relate to the earlier *Lives*, notably Julius Caesar's *Commentaries* on his campaigns in Gaul and during the civil war, the autobiographies of Augustus, Tiberius, Claudius, and the private correspondence of Augustus. Specifically for his *Nero,* he could consult the memoirs of the younger Agrippina, Nero's mother, and Fannius's three-volume account of the deaths of Nero's victims, and Nero's own poetry. It is an easy inference that Suetonius had read Tacitus's *Histories* and probably also the *Annals* as well, and the *Lives* of Plutarch. Whereas, however, it is often clear that the same source lies behind specific passages in Suetonius and one or both of these writers, it cannot be proved that he is drawing directly on either of them.

In three cases, it is possible to compare and contrast Suetonius with Plutarch, for both of them wrote *Lives* of Julius Caesar, Galba, and Otho. The main difference is that, unlike Plutarch, Suetonius is not interested in drawing moral lessons from the events he recounts. When Plutarch tells an anecdote, he uses it to illustrate the character and personality of his subject (see p. 517). Suetonius gives more of an impression of his subjects as they actually were, not as models of good or evil. Many of his anecdotes are told with zest and panache and are to be enjoyed for their own sake, with no higher purpose. This difference is most apparent in the details that the two biographers choose to include or omit in their *Lives* of Julius Caesar. Whereas Suetonius says almost nothing about the conquest of Gaul, Plutarch devotes ten paragraphs to it (18–27). On the other hand, Plutarch has no equivalent to the wealth of anecdotes about Caesar's personal life lavished by Suetonius (chapters 45–75). It is probable that Suetonius made some statement of purpose at the beginning of his *Life* of Julius Caesar, but the introductory section to that *Life,* including the dedication to the praetorian prefect, Septicius Clarus, has not survived.

There was a clear generic distinction between biography and history. That said, however, the establishment of the imperial system, closely linking the military and political affairs of Rome with the destiny of a single man, had made biography a more than usually apposite mode for describing the history of the empire. St. Jerome says that "Tacitus wrote the *Lives of the Caesars* after Augustus till the death of Domitian in thirty volumes" (*On Zachariah* 3.14). This is rather an overstated way of describing the *Annals* and *Histories,* but it is certainly true that Tacitus does use the transitions from one reign to the next as convenient breaks between books.

It would be unfair and misleading to judge either Suetonius or Plutarch by the standards expected of a historian. One small point may, however, be taken to illustrate that Plutarch comes closer to the elevated style typical of historiography, conventionally regarded as the highest of prose genres. Tacitus, Plutarch, and Suetonius all describe the death of Galba in memorably gory detail. Tacitus and Plutarch seem to draw on the same source, focusing on the identification of the soldier who beheaded him. Plutarch adds that, since Galba was bald, the soldier had difficulty carrying his head to Otho so that he could claim a reward. Suetonius makes no attempt to identify the soldier, but his description of the carrying of the head seems particularly ghastly:

> He was slaughtered beside the *lacus Curtius* [i.e., in the Roman Forum] and left lying just as he was, until a common soldier, returning from the corn distribution, put aside his load and cut off Galba's head. Then, since he could not grasp it by the hair, he hid it under his clothing but later he stuck his thumb into the mouth and thus carried it off to Otho. (*Life of Galba* 20)

Suetonius is often regarded as the purveyor par excellence of piquant anecdotes that bring imperial society to life, rather as the discoveries at Pompeii tell us so much about life as it was lived at this same period by more ordinary Romans. Sometimes, however, his stories seem almost dull when compared with others found elsewhere that he must have known but chose not to include. Contrast these two stories about Domitian:

> His cruelty was extreme, and manifested itself in crafty and unexpected ways. The day before he had one of his officials crucified, he invited him into his bedroom, made him sit beside him on a couch, then sent him away in a carefree and happy frame of mind, even deigning to send him choice portions of his own dinner. (Suetonius, *Life of Domitian* 11)

> Domitian once invited a group of important Senators and knights to dinner in a room painted entirely black, with black furnishings. The plates were shaped like gravestones and the waiters were boys painted black. The food was black, the sort used in offerings to the dead. Domitian spoke only of death and murder. They all expected to die but, when they arrived home, he sent them expensive gifts. (Cassius Dio, *Roman History* 67.9)

This lively passage in Cassius Dio is reminiscent of the type of stories told in the *Historia Augusta* about the eccentric, cruel, and short-lived emperor Elagabalus (reigned A.D. 218–22). Much of this material about Elagabalus is drawn from the now lost works of Marius Maximus, who wrote lives of the next twelve emperors, from Nerva to Elagabalus, as a sequel to Suetonius. Even though the *Historia Augusta* drew so heavily on Maximus, it elsewhere contrasts him very unfavorably with Suetonius: "Suetonius Tranquillus was a faultless and truthful writer...It was second nature to him to cultivate brevity. But what about Marius Maximus, the most verbose of all men, who even involved himself in pseudo-historical works?" (*Lives of Firmus, Saturninus,* etc. 1). In other words, Suetonius was highly regarded as a meticulous and discriminating author, and not disparaged as a mere sensationalist. We should enjoy his *Lives* as the work of a first-rate biographer, always bearing in mind that it is not his purpose to give a comprehensive history of the reigns of the various emperors. For example, he tells us little or nothing about people and events known from other sources to have been very significant during Nero's reign: the younger Seneca, Nero's tutor and adviser, or Tigellinus, the murderous commander of the Praetorian Guard, or the military campaigns in Armenia and Britain, or the Pisonian conspiracy, or the persecution of philosophers and other intellectuals.

Whereas Plutarch tends to present the material in his *Lives* in a generally chronological sequence, Suetonius usually gives a brief summary of his subject's ancestry, early life, and career before becoming emperor, and then arranges the bulk of the work on a thematic frame: "Having stated the main themes, as it were, of his [Augustus's] life, I shall set out the individual details, not according to the order of events but by topic so that they may be more clearly perceived and assessed" (*Life of Augustus* 9). However the various topics are arranged, most *Lives* end with an account of the subject's death (that of Nero [sections 40-50] is the most sustained narrative, and perhaps the best, in the whole collection), followed by a catalog of his physical characteristics and personal idiosyncrasies.

The structure of the *Life of Nero* is particularly comparable to those of Caligula and Domitian, with a strong break rather less than halfway through each, as Suetonius turns to cataloging their depravities and acts of cruelty:

> The story so far has been of Caligula the emperor, the rest must be of Caligula the monster. (*Caligula* 22)

> These deeds, some of them meriting no reproach, others even deserving some praise, I have gathered together to separate them from the shameful deeds and crimes with which I shall henceforth be concerned. (*Nero* 19)

> His disposition towards mercy and integrity did not continue, though his decline into cruelty was more rapid than his decline into greed. (*Domitian* 10)

It is the appalling and unrelenting catalog of the emperors' various vices that attracts and impresses most readers, but it should not go unremarked that this delay in turning to the negative aspects of his subject's life, showing a willingness to give at least some prominence to his better qualities, is rather in contrast to Tacitus's much less tolerant practice. Despite his claim to be writing "without rancor or bias" (see p. 456), immediately after the account of Tiberius's accession Tacitus says, "The first criminal act of the new Principate was the murder of Postumus Agrippa" (*Annals* 1.6), and likewise, his description of the reign of Nero begins with the words "The first death under the new Principate was that of Junius Silanus, proconsul of Asia, and it was brought off by the machinations of Agrippina, without Nero's knowledge" (*Annals* 13.1).

Suetonius likewise comes out as fair-minded in a contrast with another contemporary, the satirist Juvenal. In his first poem, Juvenal seems to be announcing a balanced review of human life, for better or for worse, in all its vicissitudes: "What folks have ever done since—their hopes and fears and anger, their pleasures, joys, and toing and froing—is my volume's hotch-potch" (85–86). But the very next line shows that his real intention is to focus on attacking vice: "Was there, at any time, a richer harvest of evil?"

## LIFE OF NERO

*Following his familiar pattern, the opening section of Suetonius's biography (1–5) concerns Nero's family, the Domitii, and his recent ancestors. He begins with the legends about the branch known as the Ahenobarbi, or "Bronzebeards," ever since the appearance of the twin gods Castor and Pollux to one of them at the Battle of Lake Regillus in 496 B.C. He devotes a full paragraph (3) to Nero's great-grandfather, Gnaeus Domitius Ahenobarbus,* *who was consul in 32 B.C. and makes an appearance as a character in Shakespeare's* Antony and Cleopatra.

[1] Of the Domitian family, two branches achieved fame, the Calvini and the Ahenobarbi. The Ahenobarbi have as the founder of their branch and origin of their name Lucius Domitius. Two young men, twins of impressive bearing, are said to have appeared to him once, as he was returning from the countryside, and to have given him orders to announce to the senate and

people victory in a battle whose outcome was at that time awaited. And, as a sign of their divinity, they are said to have stroked his cheeks, turning his beard, which was black, a red color like bronze. This distinctive feature continued even among his descendants, many of whom had red beards. Between them, they achieved seven consulships, a triumph, two censorships, and promotion to the patricians, all the while continuing to use the same cognomen. And they took no other forenames than Gnaeus and Lucius. This usage they practised with remarkable variation, sometimes giving each name to three people in a row and sometimes one name alternating with the other. For we learn that the first three Ahenobarbi were all called Lucius, while the next three were all called Gnaeus, after which they alternated between Lucius and Gnaeus. I have decided to report on a number of members of the family to make clearer how Nero lapsed from the virtues of his ancestors yet reproduced each one's legacy of vice.

[2] To begin a little further back, his great-grandfather's grandfather, Gnaeus Domitius was, as tribune, furious with the pontifices, because they had co-opted someone other than himself into the place his own father had occupied, and transferred the right of selecting priests from the colleges of priests to the Roman people. When he was consul and had defeated the Allobroges and the Arverni, he travelled through the province seated on an elephant and accompanied by a crowd of soldiers, as if in a triumphal procession. The orator Licinius Crassus said against him that it was no wonder he had a beard of bronze when his face was made of iron and his heart of lead. The son of this Ahenobarbus, when he was praetor, called Julius Caesar to a senate inquiry at the end of his consulship, on the grounds that he had conducted himself in office contrary to the auspices and the laws. Not long afterwards, when he himself was consul, he dared to deprive Caesar of the command of the Gallic armies. Then, named as Caesar's successor thanks to the support of a faction, he was taken prisoner at Corfinium at the start of the civil war. Released from there, he went to the support of the people of Massilia, who were besieged and struggling, but suddenly abandoned them for no apparent reason and finally met his end fighting at Pharsalus. He was an indecisive man, though his temper was savage; having in desperation attempted suicide, he was so overcome by fear of dying that he regretted his decision, vomited up the poison he had taken, and rewarded the slave-doctor with his freedom on the grounds that, knowing his

master well, he had been prudent enough to administer an insufficiently powerful dose. When Gnaeus Pompey asked for advice on how to deal with persons who had remained neutral and taken neither side during the civil war, he was the only one who thought they should be treated as enemies.

[3] He left a son, who, without doubt, was far superior to the rest of the family. He, though he was innocent, had been condemned under the Pedian law as one of Caesar's assassins, and so joined cause with Brutus and Cassius, being closely related to them. After their deaths he kept the fleet which had been entrusted to him and increased it. Only when his side was utterly defeated everywhere did he hand the fleet over to Mark Antony—on his own initiative and as if he were conferring a great favor. And he alone, of all those who had been condemned by that same law, had his civil rights restored to him and fulfilled the highest offices. When, later, civil war broke out again and he was made a legate by that same Mark Antony, he was offered the supreme command by those of his side who were ashamed of the alliance with Cleopatra but, suffering from a sudden illness, dared neither to accept it nor to turn it down, instead going over to Augustus' side. A few days later he was dead, with his own reputation in doubt, for Antony asserted that he had changed sides through desire to be with his mistress, Servilia Nais.

[4] This Domitius was father of the man who was later well known for being named as executor in Augustus' will. He was no less famous in his youth for his skill in chariot driving than he was to be later for the triumphal ornaments he won in the war against Germany. However, he was an arrogant man, profligate and cruel, who, when he was merely an aedile, forced the censor Lucius Plancus to make way for him on the street. When serving as praetor and as consul, he organized farces performed in the theater by Roman knights and matrons. He provided animal shows in the Circus and in all parts of the city, as well as a gladiatorial show of such cruelty that Augustus, having offered him a discreet warning to no effect, was obliged to restrain him by edict.

[5] He and the elder Antonia were the parents of Nero's father, a man loathsome in every respect. As a young man, on a trip to the east accompanying Gaius Caesar, he killed his own freedman, on the grounds that the man would not drink as much as he was ordered, and was himself dismissed from the entourage, yet made no attempt to regulate his lifestyle.

Indeed, going through a village on the Appian Way he whipped up his team and knowingly ran over a boy, while at Rome in the middle of the Forum he gouged out the eye of a Roman knight who had been arguing with him too warmly. Moreover, his dishonesty was such that he not only cheated the banker intermediaries of the price of goods he had obtained but, when praetor, he even defrauded the chariot race winners of their prize money. When his own sister's jokes brought him into public disrepute for this and the team managers complained, he issued an edict that prizes should subsequently be handed over on the spot. Shortly before Tiberius died, Domitius was accused of treason, adultery, and incest with his sister Lepida but escaped prosecution because of the change of regime. He died at Pyrgi of dropsy, after acknowledging his son Nero, whose mother was Agrippina, Germanicus' daughter.

*Two chapters (6–7) are devoted to the childhood of Nero, beginning with his birth on December 15, A.D. 37, and a series of anecdotes about his earliest years. He concludes this section with Nero's adoption on February 25, A.D. 50, by the emperor Claudius, who had married his mother, Agrippina, the year before, and his eventual marriage to Octavia, Claudius's daughter by his earlier marriage to Messalina.*

[6] Nero was born at Antium, nine months after Tiberius died, on the eighteenth day before the Kalends of January, just as the sun was rising, so that he was touched by its rays almost before he could be laid on the ground. Many people made numerous and sinister predictions about his birth-signs. Among the warnings was even the pronouncement of his father, who responded to his friends' congratulations saying nothing could be born of himself and Agrippina that would not inspire loathing and bring disaster for the state. Another sign of his unhappy future occurred on the day of his purification. For the emperor Caligula, when his sister asked him to give whatever name he chose to the child, looking upon his uncle Claudius— by whom, when he was emperor, Nero was later to be adopted—said that they should give the child his name. However, he did not do this seriously but as a joke and Agrippina turned down the suggestion, for at that time Claudius was a figure of fun at court.

At three years old he lost his father. Heir to a mere third part of the estate, he did not even get that much, for his co-heir Caligula seized everything. When soon afterwards his mother was relegated he was left virtually penniless. His aunt Lepida brought him up, placing him in the care of two tutors, one a dancer, the other a barber. However, when Claudius succeeded to the empire, Nero not only got back his father's property but increased his wealth with an inheritance from his stepfather, Crispus Passienus. When his mother was recalled to Rome and re-established, his position was so improved by the favor and influence she exercised that, according to a popular rumor, Claudius' wife Messalina sent some men to strangle him during his siesta, on the grounds that he was a rival to her son, Britannicus. According to the same story, these men encountered a snake emerging from the couch and were so terrified they ran away. The story seems to have arisen because some snake skins were found in his bed around the pillow. However, at his mother's request, these were set in a gold bracelet and for some time he wore them on his right arm until, tired of being reminded of his mother, he threw it away—though later on he asked in vain to have it back, when his affairs reached their final crisis.

[7] When he was still only a young boy he participated most enthusiastically and successfully in the Troy game at the Circus. In his eleventh year, he was adopted by Claudius and handed over for his education to Annaeus Seneca, who was already a senator. People say that on the next night Seneca dreamed that he was teaching Caligula and soon afterwards Nero provided confirmation of the dream, revealing his monstrous nature at the earliest possible opportunity. For when, after his adoption, his brother Britannicus, through habit, continued to address him as Ahenobarbus, he tried to convince his father that Britannicus was not really his child but a substitute. When his aunt Lepida was on trial he publicly gave evidence against her in order to please his mother who was striving to undermine her position.

On the occasion of his first public appearance in the Forum, he promised gifts for the people and money for the soldiers and announced a parade of the praetorian guard, which he himself led, holding his shield before him. Then he spoke in the senate expressing his gratitude to his father. During his father's consulship, he gave speeches in Latin on behalf of the people of Bononia and in Greek on behalf of the people of Rhodes and of Ilium. For his first appearance as judge, he acted as prefect of the city during the Latin festival, when, although Claudius had forbidden it, many of the best known advocates competed to present to him not the usual short and conventional cases but a large number of highly important ones. Not long after this he took Octavia as his wife and gave circus games and animal shows as offerings for the health of Claudius.

*Suetonius's account of Nero's accession and the beginning of his Principate (8–10) shows him off to an auspicious start, acting a bit like Augustus in declining excessive honors and in assisting needy senators. This section concludes on an ominous note with his public recitals of his poetry, the kind of display that characterized his later excesses.*

[8] When the death of Claudius was publicly announced, Nero, who was then seventeen, approached the guards between the sixth and the seventh hour, for in consequence of the terrible omens which had occurred throughout the day, no earlier time had seemed suitable for embarking on his reign. In front of the steps to the Palatine, he was saluted emperor then taken by litter to the praetorian camp, where he addressed the soldiers briefly before returning to the senate house, where he remained until evening. Of all the great honors which were heaped upon him he refused just one—the title "Father of the Fatherland" which he deemed unsuitable for one of his age.

[9] Beginning with a display of filial respect, he provided Claudius with a most magnificent funeral at which he gave the official eulogy and declared him to be a god. He paid the highest honors to the memory of his father Domitius and allowed his mother the greatest influence over all matters private and public. Even on the first day of his reign, he gave as the password to the tribune of the watch "the best of mothers" and afterwards he often rode about the city with her sharing a litter. He made Antium a colony, enlisting veterans of the praetorian guard and, besides them, the richest of the chief centurions through residential transfer. He also had constructed there a port on a most lavish scale.

[10] In order to provide a more certain measure of his disposition, he declared that he would rule according to the prescriptions of Augustus and he let slip no opportunity to demonstrate his generosity, his clemency, or his affability. More onerous taxes he reduced or did away with. He cut to a quarter of their original rate the rewards paid to informers under the Papian law. He gave four hundred sesterces to each man of the people and, in the case of senators of noble family who had lost their ancestral fortunes, he provided annual salaries of as much as five thousand sesterces. He also distributed free grain every month to the praetorian cohorts. And when, following usual procedure, he was asked to sign his consent to the punishment of a man condemned to death, he replied, "How I wish I had never learned to write!" He used to greet members of all the orders accurately and without prompting. To votes of thanks, he replied, "When I've deserved them." He permitted even the common people to witness his exercises in the Campus Martius and often declaimed in public. He would recite his poems, not only in his home but also in the theater, causing such widespread delight that a public thanksgiving for his recitation was announced and passages from his composition which had been recited were inscribed in letters of gold and dedicated to Capitoline Jupiter.

*Free entertainment for the masses was an important part of an emperor's dossier, beginning with Augustus, who cataloged his public shows in the great inscription known as "The Achievements of Augustus." The spectacles staged by subsequent emperors are cataloged by Suetonius, who here devotes three chapters (11–13) to Nero's.*

[11] He provided a great many games of different kinds: Youth Games, circus games, theatrical performances and gladiatorial contests. In the Youth Games he included old men of consular rank and respectable old women as participants. In the circus games, he assigned separate seating to Roman knights and even ran chariots drawn by teams of camels. At the games which, since they were undertaken for the everlasting future of the empire, he wished to be termed "The Greatest," a significant number of men and women from both the senatorial and the equestrian orders took on the parts of actors. A very well-known Roman knight rode down a rope mounted on an elephant. When a play by Afranius called "The Fire" was put on, the actors were allowed to snatch the furnishings of the burning house and keep them for themselves. Every day gifts of all kinds were thrown to the crowds: a thousand birds each day of every kind, different sorts of food, tokens to be exchanged for grain, clothes, gold, silver, jewels, pearls, pictures, slaves, working animals and even tame wild ones and finally ships, blocks of apartments, and farmland.

[12] He would watch these games from the top of the proscenium. At the gladiatorial games, which he gave in a wooden amphitheater constructed in less than a year in the Campus Martius part of the city, he had no one put to death, not even criminals. However, he put on show as fighters four hundred senators and six hundred Roman knights, some of whom were wealthy

men of good reputation. Even those who fought the wild beasts and served as assistants in the arena were drawn from the senatorial and equestrian orders. He also gave a naval battle on sea water which had monsters swimming in it. He put on shows of young Greeks as Pyrrhic dancers and after the games he gave each of them a diploma of Roman citizenship. In one of these Pyrrhic dances, a bull mounted Pasiphae concealed within a wooden model of a heifer in such a way that many of the spectators believed it was no mere show. In another, an Icarus on his first attempt fell immediately to the ground right next to the emperor's couch, splashing him with blood. For he would rarely sit in state on these occasions, preferring to recline, at first watching through a small gap in the hangings but later with the whole of the balcony on view. He was also the first to establish at Rome a five-yearly competition, in the Greek manner, made up of three events, musical, gymnastic, and equestrian, which he termed the Neronia. He also dedicated his baths and gymnasium, distributing gifts of oil to each senator and each knight. He put in charge of the whole competition ex-consuls, chosen by lot, who occupied the seats of the praetors. Then he went down into the orchestra, where the senators sit, and accepted the crown he was offered for oratory and verse in Latin. All the most distinguished men had competed for it but all agreed it was rightly his. However, when the judges also offered him the crown for lyre-playing, he paid it reverence and gave orders that it should be taken as an offering to the statue of Augustus. At the gymnastic contest, which was held in the Saepta, while a magnificent offering of oxen was sacrificed, he placed the first shavings of his beard in a golden casket set with the most precious pearls which he dedicated on the Capitol. To the athletic contests he even invited the Vestal Virgins, on the grounds that the priestesses of Ceres were permitted to be spectators at Olympia.

[13] I am, I believe, justified in recording among Nero's spectacles the entry of Tiridates into the city. The king of Armenia had been induced to come with great promises and, though Nero had dismissed the crowd because of bad weather on the day when his edict had announced he would be showing Tiridates, he did bring him forth at the earliest opportunity. Armed cohorts stood around the temples in the Forum and he himself was seated in a curule chair on the rostra, dressed in the robes of a triumphant general and surrounded by military standards and flags. When Tiridates approached

up the sloping platform, Nero first let him fall at his feet but then raised him up with his right hand and kissed him. Next, while the king made the speech of a suppliant (which was translated and relayed to the crowd by a man of praetorian rank), Nero removed from his head the turban and replaced it with a diadem. Then the king was led from the Forum to the theater where he again made supplication and Nero placed him in a seat at his own right hand. Acclaimed "Imperator" for this Nero offered laurels on the Capitol and closed the gates of the temple of two-headed Janus, to show there were no longer any wars being waged.

*Suetonius describes Nero's consulships and catalogs the various good measures introduced by him (14–17). A brief discussion of his provincial and foreign policies (18–19) concludes the treatment of Nero's good works, which then contrast with the longer catalog of crimes and shameful behavior that follows, where our selection resumes. This list begins with Nero's obsession with music and charioteering.*

[20] Amongst the other attainments of his youth, he was also very knowledgeable about music so that, as soon as he became emperor, he summoned Terpnus, the leading lyre-player of the time and as he sat, while the latter sang after dinner day after day late into the night, he began himself to study and practice little by little, omitting none of those exercises by which artists of that kind preserve and strengthen their voices. Rather, he would lie on his back, holding a lead tablet on his chest, and cleanse his system with a syringe and with vomiting, and he would abstain from fruits and other foods harmful to the voice. Finally, pleased by his progress, although his voice was thin and indistinct, he conceived a desire to go on the stage, from time to time repeating to his companions the Greek proverb that hidden music has no admirers. Indeed, he made his first appearance in Naples and, though the theater was shaken by a sudden earthquake, he did not leave off singing until he had come to the end of the song he had begun. In the same city he sang often and over many days. And even when he had taken a short break to rest his voice, he could not bear being apart from his audience. After bathing he went to the theater, where he took his dinner in the middle of the orchestra, with a great crowd present. Speaking in Greek, he promised that once he'd had a drop to drink, he'd give them some hearty singing. The Alexandrians, who had come in large numbers to Naples with a

recent convoy, delighted him with their rhythmic applause and he summoned more from Alexandria. And with no less enthusiasm he selected some youths of the equestrian order and more than five thousand of the strongest young men of the common people from all over, who were divided into groups and taught different methods of applauding—they called them buzzers, hollow tiles and flat tiles—which they were to employ vigorously when he was singing. These men were remarkable for their sleek hair-styles and most refined appearance—and for their left hands, bare and without rings. Their leaders received four hundred thousand sesterces apiece.

[21] Since he set great store by singing even in Rome, he gave orders for a Neronian competition in advance of the regular date and, when everyone called out for his divine voice, he replied that, for those who wished to come, he would put on a good show in his gardens. However, when the entreaties of the crowd were supported by those even of a guard of soldiers, who were then on duty, he willingly promised them he would put on a performance at once. Without delay he gave orders that his name should be included in the list of those who had entered as lyre players and, along with the rest, he placed his lot in the urn. When his turn came, he made his entrance, accompanied by the prefects of the praetorian guard bearing his lyre, and following them, military tribunes, along with his close friends. When he had taken his position and the introduction was made, he announced, through the ex-consul Cluvius Rufus, that he was going to sing the role of Niobe. He then held the stage until the tenth hour, before declaring that the award of the crown and the rest of the competition was to be deferred until the following year, so that there would be more frequent opportunities for singing. And when that seemed too long a delay, he did not hesitate to put on a show in the interim. He even debated whether to take the stage with professional actors in private performances when one of the praetors offered a million sesterces. He also wore a mask and sang tragedies in the roles of heroes and gods and even of heroines and goddesses, having the masks made so that their features resembled his own or those of whatever woman he happened to be in love with. Among other parts, he sang those of Canace giving birth, Orestes the matricide, Oedipus blinded, and Hercules insane. The story goes that, when he was playing the part of Hercules, a recent recruit who was standing guard by the exit, seeing the emperor laden

and bound with chains—as the play required—rushed forward to rescue him.

[22] From his earliest youth he was passionate about horses and was always talking about the games in the circus, although he was told not to. On one occasion, when he and his fellow pupils were bemoaning the fate of the Greens' charioteer, who had been dragged around the arena, and his teacher reproved him, he pretended they had been talking about Hector. In the early part of his reign, he used to play every day with ivory chariots on a gaming board and would leave his country retreat to attend even the most insignificant of circus races, first secretly and then quite openly so that everyone knew he would be there on that day. He did not try to conceal his wish that the number of prizes be increased. In consequence of the greater number of races, the spectacle lasted late into the evening and the faction leaders disdained to bring their adherents unless it was for a whole day's racing. Soon he himself wanted to drive a chariot and even to do so frequently in front of an audience; once he had made his beginning in his own gardens watched by slaves and poor common people, he offered himself as a spectacle to the entire populace in the Circus Maximus, with some freedman giving the starting signal usually provided by magistrates. Not satisfied with giving displays of such talents in Rome, as I have reported, his principal motive for going to Greece was the following. Those city states whose custom it was to organize musical competitions decided to award all the prizes for lyre-playing to him. He received these with such pleasure that the messengers who brought them were not only given precedence but were even made welcome at his private supper parties. When some of them requested that he sing after dinner, he accepted with alacrity and declared that only Greeks knew how to listen and that only they were worthy of him and his talents. He did not delay his departure and, as soon as he had crossed to Cassiope, he at once embarked on his singing at the altar of Jupiter Cassius and then went off on his tour of all the competitions.

[23] For he had given orders that competitions normally held at quite different times should be made to take place in the space of one year, causing some to be repeated, and he instructed, against all precedent, that a musical competition was to be added to the Olympic Games. And, so that nothing should distract or detain him while he was engaged in these games, though he was warned by his freedman Helius

that affairs in Rome required his presence, he wrote in reply: "Although you now advise and wish my swift return, you ought rather to counsel and desire that I return worthy of Nero."

When he was singing, it was not permitted to leave the theater even for the most pressing of reasons. Thus, it is alleged that women gave birth during his shows and many who were tired of listening and applauding, when the entrance gates were all closed, either jumped furtively off the wall or else pretended to be dead and were carried out for burial. You could scarcely believe how nervous and anxious he was in competitions, or how he competed against his rivals, or how he feared the judges' verdict. He would pay attention to his competitors and seek their favor, as if they were his equals, then cast aspersions on them behind their backs. Some he would insult to their faces. He would even bribe those who were especially talented. Nevertheless, he would address the judges most reverently before he began, assuring them that he had done all that he could but the outcome would be determined by Fate. They, as wise and learned men, were to ignore what was fortuitous. And when they encouraged him to take heart, he would withdraw somewhat calmer but not altogether without concern, interpreting the silence and restraint of some as moroseness and ill-nature and saying he could not trust them.

[24] During his competition performance, he followed the rules most strictly, never daring to cough and wiping sweat from his brow with his arm. And once when he was performing a tragedy and he dropped his scepter and picked it up again, he was fearful and anxious that he might be disqualified for this fault and could only be reassured by the accompanist's assurance that no one had noticed it amid the rapturous cheers of the audience. However, it was he himself who proclaimed his own victory. For he was also an entrant in the competition for public heralds. And so that no memory or trace should remain anywhere of any other victor in the sacred games, he gave orders that all their statues and images should be overturned and dragged by a hook to the lavatories where they would be disposed of. He also entered the chariot races on many occasions, even driving a ten-horse team at Olympia, although in one of his songs he had criticized this very thing in King Mithridates. However, he fell from his chariot and although he resumed his post he was unable to finish, abandoning the race before the end. He received the victory crown, none the less. Then,

on his departure, he bestowed freedom on the entire province, at the same time giving the judges Roman citizenship and substantial sums of money. He himself announced these benefits, standing in the middle of the stadium on the day of the Isthmian Games.

[25] He returned from Greece to Naples and, because this was where he had made his first public appearance on stage, he entered drawn by white horses where the wall had been breached—this is the custom for victors in the sacred games. In a similar manner he made his entries into Antium, then Albanum, and then Rome. In Rome, however, he made use of the very chariot in which Augustus had once conducted his triumphs; wearing a purple robe, picked out with stars of gold, a Greek cloak, and, on his head, the Olympic crown, his right hand holding the Pythian, he was preceded by a procession displaying his other crowns, labeled to indicate whom he had defeated and with which songs or dramas. Following his chariot came the applauders shouting rhythmic praise and proclaiming that they were the Augustiani and the soldiers of his triumph. Then, through the Circus Maximus, where an arch had been pulled down, he made his way via the Velabrum and the Forum to the Palatine and the Temple of Apollo. Everywhere he went, sacrificial victims were slain, perfume was sprinkled in all the streets, and countless gifts of songbirds, victor's ribbons, and sweetmeats were made to him. He placed the sacred crowns in his bed-chambers around the couches and did the same with statues of himself in the costume of a lyre-player. He also had coins minted with the same device. And after this, far from restraining or putting aside his passion, he was so keen to preserve his singing voice that he refused ever to address the Roman army, unless by letter or with someone else speaking his words. Nor would he undertake any business, serious or frivolous, unless a voice-coach was standing by to give advice, relax his windpipe, and apply a towel to his mouth. And many were those who became his friends or enemies, according to whether they had praised him lavishly or sparingly.

*Nero's criminal traits are cataloged with anecdotes to illustrate each: insolence (26–27), lust (28–29), luxury (30–31), and greed (32), culminating with cruelty (33–38), which is further subdivided into three categories, describing his murders of family members (33–35), his executions of other citizens (36–37), and finally his destruction of Rome itself in the Great Fire (38).*

[26] At first the signs he showed of insolence, lust, luxury, greed, and cruelty were gradual and covert and could be put down to the errors of youth, but even then it was clear to all that these vices were due not to his age but to his nature. As soon as night had fallen, he would throw on a freedman's cap or a wig and would go around the cook-shops and wander about the streets looking for amusement—though putting himself at some risk, for he was in the habit of setting upon people returning home from dinner and would hurt anyone who fought back, throwing them into the drains, and he would even storm into the taverns and pillage them, setting up a market in his palace, where the spoils he had acquired were divided up for auction and he squandered the proceeds. And often in the course of these brawls, he would endanger his eyes or even his life. Indeed, he was almost killed by a man of the senatorial class whose wife he had molested. After that he would never venture forth at that hour without a secret escort of tribunes following at a distance. From time to time also he would have his sedan chair covertly transported to the theater where, from the upper part of the proscenium, he would look on and incite the pantomime actors as they quarreled. And when they came to blows and were fighting with stones and bits of the seating, he himself threw many missiles into the crowd and even cracked open a praetor's head. [27] Gradually, however, as his vices took root, he left off jokes and disguises and, taking no care to conceal his actions, moved on to greater misdeeds.

He would draw out his banquets from noon to midnight, refreshing himself with warm baths or, in the heat of summer, with ice-cold ones. Sometimes he would even dine in public, having drained the Naumachia or in the Campus Martius or in the Circus Maximus, while around him the prostitutes and singing girls of all the city were plying their trade. Whenever he sailed down the Tiber to Ostia or cruised around the Bay of Baiae, on the banks and shores taverns were set out and made ready along the way, remarkable for their feasting and their traffic in respectable ladies, who would imitate tavern women and would solicit him from this side and that to summon them. He would also invite himself as a dinner-guest to the houses of his friends, one of whom spent four million sesterces on a dinner where people wore turbans, while another spent even more on one accompanied by roses.

[28] Besides his seduction of free-born boys and his relations with married women, he also forced himself on the Vestal Virgin Rubria. He came very close to making the freedwoman Acte his lawful wife, having bribed some men of consular rank to swear falsely that she was descended from kings. He had the testicles cut off a boy named Sporus and attempted to transform him into a woman, marrying him with dowry and bridal veil and all due ceremony, then, accompanied by a great crowd, taking him to his house, where he treated him as his wife. Someone made a rather clever joke which is still told that it would have been a good thing for humanity if Nero's father had taken such a wife. This Sporus, decked out in the ornaments of an empress and carried in a litter, he took with him around the meeting places and markets of Greece and later, at Rome, around the Sigillaria, kissing him from time to time. And all were convinced that he had desired to sleep with his mother but was frightened off by her detractors, who were concerned lest this ferocious and power-hungry woman acquire greater influence through this kind of favor. This was all the more plausible when afterwards he added to his concubines a prostitute who was famous for her resemblance to Agrippina. People claim that at one time, whenever he traveled in a litter with his mother, his incestuous lusts were betrayed by the stains on his clothing.

[29] He prostituted his own body to such a degree that, when virtually every part of his person had been employed in filthy lusts, he devised a new and unprecedented practice as a kind of game, in which, disguised in the pelt of a wild animal, he would rush out of a den and attack the private parts of men and women who had been tied to stakes, and, when he had wearied of playing the beast, he would be "run through" by his freedman Doryphorus. With this man he played the role of bride, as Sporus had done with him, and he even imitated the shouts and cries of virgins being raped. From quite a few sources I have gathered that he was fully convinced that no one was truly chaste or pure in any part of their body but that many chose to conceal their vices and hid them cleverly. And so when any confessed to him their sexual misdeeds, he forgave them all other faults.

[30] He believed that the proper use for riches and wealth was extravagance and that people who kept an account of their expenses were vulgar and miserly, while those who squandered and frittered away their money were refined and truly splendid. He praised and admired his uncle Caligula, above all because, in so brief a period, he had worked his way through the vast

fortune left him by Tiberius. Accordingly there was no limit to his gift-giving or consumption. On Tiridates—which might seem scarcely credible—he lavished eight hundred thousand sesterces in one day and, when he left, made him a gift of a hundred million. On the lyre-player Menecrates and the gladiator Spiculus he bestowed fortunes and homes fit for triumphant generals. For the monkey-faced Paneros, a money-lender with extensive property holdings in Rome and in the country, he provided a funeral almost fit for a king. He never wore the same robe twice. When gambling he would lay bets of four hundred thousand sesterces for each point. He went fishing with a net of gold interwoven with purple and scarlet threads. It is said that he always traveled with at least a thousand carriages, the mules shod with silver and mule-drivers clothed in Canusian wool, and with a train of Mauretanian horsemen and couriers, decked out with bracelets and breast-plates.

[31] There was, however, nothing in which he was more prodigal than in construction, extending from the Palatine as far as the Esquiline the palace which he called first the House of Passage, then, after it had been destroyed by fire and rebuilt, the Golden House. It should suffice to relate the following concerning its extent and splendor. There was a vestibule area in which stood a colossal statue, one hundred and twenty feet tall, in the image of the emperor himself. So great was its extent that its triple colonnade was a mile in length. There was also a lake, which resembled the sea, surrounded by buildings made to look like cities. Besides this, there were grounds of all kinds, with fields and vineyards, pasture and woodland, and a multitude of all sorts of domestic and wild animals. Other areas were all covered in gold and picked out with jewels and mother-of-pearl. The banqueting halls had coffered ceilings fitted with panels of ivory which would revolve, scattering flowers, and pipes which would spray perfume on those beneath. The principal banqueting chamber had a dome which revolved continuously both day and night, like the world itself. There were baths running with sea water and spa water. When the house was brought to completion in this style and he dedicated it, he said nothing more to indicate his approval than to declare that he had at last begun to live like a human being.

In addition to this, he began work on a pool stretching from Misenum to Lake Avernus, which was roofed over and surrounded with an arcade, and into this he meant to channel all the hot springs of every part of Baiae; also a canal from Avernus all the way to Ostia, so that one could travel by ship without traversing the sea. It was to be one hundred and sixty miles in length and broad enough to accommodate ships with five banks of oars passing one another. In order to complete these works, he gave orders that prisoners everywhere should be transported to Italy and that even those who were found guilty of heinous crimes should have no other punishment than hard labor.

He was spurred on to this frenzy of extravagance, not only by his confidence in the empire's riches, but also by the expectation of vast hidden wealth to which he was suddenly prompted by information from a Roman knight, who asserted as a fact that a wealth of ancient treasure, which Queen Dido had brought with her when she fled from Tyre, was concealed in huge caverns in Africa and could be extracted with only the smallest trouble. [32] However, when this hope was dashed he was penniless and so wretched and desperate that it was necessary to defer and put off payment even of the soldiers' pay and veterans' pensions, so he put his mind to profiting from false accusations and robbery.

First of all he made it law that, instead of one-half, five-sixths of the property of a deceased ex-slave should pass to him, if the person had, without good reason, borne the name of any family to whom he himself was related. He also prescribed that the property of persons who had, in their wills, failed to recognize their obligations to the emperor, should pass to the treasury and that the lawyers who wrote or dictated such wills should not escape punishment either. Moreover, he ensured that any word or deed which fell within the scope of the treason law, so long as an informer was not lacking, should be punished. He demanded back the gifts he had made in recognition of the crowns he was awarded in competitions by different cities. Having banned the use of amethystine and Tyrian purple, he sent a man to sell a small quantity on market day, then closed down all the stalls. It is said that once, during one of his performances at the games, he noticed a woman wearing a forbidden color and pointed her out to his agents, who dragged her out and stripped her on the spot not only of her robe but also of her property. He never gave someone a task without saying: "You know what I need" or "The object of the exercise is to leave no one with anything." Finally, he looted many temples of their ornaments and melted down statues made of gold or silver, amongst them the Roman Penates, which were later restored by Galba.

[33] The murder of family members and general slaughter began with Claudius. For even if he was not responsible for his death he was certainly complicit and did not pretend otherwise, inasmuch as he was afterwards in the habit of praising the kind of mushrooms with which Claudius had ingested the poison as, in the words of a Greek proverb, the food of the gods. Certainly, after his death he attacked him with every kind of insulting word and deed, harping sometimes on his stupidity, at others on his cruelty. And he would often joke that Claudius had ceased to "be a fool" among mortals, lengthening the first syllable, and many of his decrees and pronouncements he disregarded on the grounds that they were the decisions of a raving idiot. Finally, he failed to provide anything but a low and insubstantial wall as the enclosure for the place where Claudius had been cremated.

Against Britannicus he employed poison, no less because of the competition he posed in singing (he had a much pleasanter voice), than through fear that one day he would prevail in public favor through memory of his father. He obtained the poison from a certain Lucusta, who was an expert poisoner, and, when it took longer than he expected and Britannicus had merely vomited, he summoned her and beat her with his own hand, claiming that she had given him medicine rather than poison. When she replied that she had used only a small quantity in order to prevent the crime becoming known and making him unpopular, he exclaimed, "Of course, I'm afraid of the Julian law!" and at once forced her into a chamber to concoct a dose in his presence that would have the most rapid and immediate effect. He then tried it on a young goat, whose death throes lasted five hours. And then, having concentrated it further, on a pig. When this animal died instantly, he gave orders that the substance be brought to the dining room and given to Britannicus as he dined with him. When Britannicus collapsed at the first mouthful, he pretended to his other dining companions that he was suffering from one of his usual epileptic fits. The next day, amid heavy rainstorms, Britannicus was taken out to be disposed of in a summary funeral. Nero rewarded Lucusta for the services she had rendered with immunity from prosecution and an ample estate. He even sent her pupils.

[34] His mother so irritated him by applying sharp scrutiny to his words and deeds and correcting him,

that, to begin with, he tried to make her unpopular by threatening to give up the empire and retire to Rhodes because of her. Later he stripped her of all honors and powers, depriving her of her guard of Roman and German soldiers and making her move out of the Palatine. Thereafter he let slip no opportunity for harassing her, secretly arranging that people annoy her with lawsuits when she was at Rome, and disturb her when she was resting on her country estates, making her the butt of jokes and abuse, as they traveled past by land and sea. Then, terrified by her violence and threats, he made the decision to do away with her. And when he had three times made attempts on her life with poison and realized that she had protected herself in advance with antidotes, he prepared to adapt the ceiling of her bedroom, which by a special device would collapse and fall on her at night while she slept. When this plan became known, through the indiscretion of those involved, he devised a collapsible boat, which would suffer either shipwreck or the caving-in of its cabin. Then, in a pretence of reconciliation, he invited her in a letter of great warmth to come to Baiae to celebrate the festival of Minerva in his company. He gave his captains the task, on her arrival, of wrecking the boat on which she had come, as if by accident. The banquet was then drawn out until late in the night and, when she wanted to set out for Bauli, he offered her, in place of her disabled craft, the specially devised boat, cheerfully escorting her and even kissing her breasts in farewell. The rest of that night he lay awake with great anxiety, awaiting the fulfillment of his plans. But news came that matters had turned out otherwise—she had swum to safety. Not knowing what to do, he secretly dropped a dagger next to Lucius Agermus, Agrippina's freedman, who had joyfully reported her safe and sound, and gave orders that he be arrested and bound, on the grounds that he had been engaged to attack the emperor, while his mother was to be killed to make it look as if she had taken her own life when her criminal plot was discovered. Worse is reported by quite good authorities who claim that the emperor rushed to view his mother's corpse and handled her body, criticizing some parts of it and praising others, in the mean time drinking to quench a sudden thirst. Yet, although he was reassured by the congratulations of the soldiers, the senate, and the people, neither in the immediate aftermath nor ever after could he bear his feelings of guilt, often confessing that he was haunted by his mother's ghost and by the blows and blazing torches of the Furies. Indeed, he even had rituals performed by mystics in an attempt to call up and appease her shade. When he made his journey to Greece, he did not dare to participate in the Eleusinian Mysteries, where a herald pronounces that criminals and the impious are banned.

To matricide he added the murder of his aunt: when he was visiting her, as she had taken to her bed with a stomach complaint, and she, stroking the downy cheek of her nearly grown-up nephew, as was her habit, said to him affectionately, "When I have your first beard, I can die happy," he turned to his companions and said, apparently in jest, he would shave it off at once. He then gave instructions to the doctors to give the sick woman an excessive dose of laxatives and, before she was even dead, took over her property, suppressing her will so that everything would come to him.

[35] Besides Octavia he later married two other wives, Poppaea Sabina, a quaestor's daughter who had previously been married to a Roman knight, and then Statilia Messalina, great-great-granddaughter of Taurus, who had been consul twice and celebrated a triumph. In order to get possession of her, he put to death her husband Atticus Vestinus actually during his consulship. He quickly tired of Octavia's companionship and, when his friends criticized his behavior, he replied that she should be content with the insignia of wife. Soon, having tried in vain to strangle her on a number of occasions, he divorced her on the grounds that she could not have children, but when the common people did not hesitate to express their disapproval of the divorce in public complaints, he sent her into exile. Then he had her killed on a charge of adultery which was so patently false that everyone denied it during the trial and Nero had to set up his old tutor Anicetus as the witness who was to make up a story and confess that he had raped her through trickery. He had a great passion for Poppaea, whom he married on the twelfth day after his divorce from Octavia. Yet he killed her, too, by kicking her when she was pregnant and ill, because she had scolded him when he came home late from the chariot-races. He had a daughter by her, Claudia Augusta, but she died in infancy.

His treatment of every one of his relatives was characterized by criminal abuse. When, after Poppaea's death, he wanted to marry Claudius' daughter Antonia, and she refused him, he had her executed for involvement in a plot, and a similar fate afflicted everyone who was related to him by blood or marriage. Among

them was the young Aulus Plautius whom, before he was put to death, Nero had subjected to oral rape, with the comment: "Now let my mother go and kiss my successor"—for he alleged that she loved the man and encouraged him to hope for the empire. His stepson Rufrius Crispinus, Poppaea's child, Nero had drowned on a fishing trip at sea by his own slaves, though he was just a boy, on the grounds that he was said to play at being general and emperor. He sent into exile Tuscus, the son of his nurse, because, when he was procurator of Egypt, he had washed himself in the baths built for Nero's visit. He forced his adviser Seneca to kill himself, even though, when Seneca requested that he be allowed to retire and give up his properties, he had sworn that Seneca's suspicions were unfounded and that he would sooner die than harm him. To his prefect Burrus he sent poison in place of the medicine for his mouth which he had promised. As for the imperial freedmen, now elderly and rich, who had supported and aided his adoption and his coming to power, he dispatched them with poisoned food in some cases and drink in others.

[36] He was no less cruel outside his household, and made attacks on many who were not his relatives. A comet—which is commonly supposed to portend the death of great rulers—had started appearing on successive nights. He was worried by this and when he learned from the astrologer Balbillus that it was the custom among kings to expiate such omens by means of the death of someone important and thus displace the danger from themselves to their nobles, he was bent on death for all the most illustrious—all the more so when two conspiracies were discovered which might serve as an excuse. Of these the first and more important was the Pisonian conspiracy at Rome, while the second, that of Vinicius, was hatched and discovered at Beneventum. The conspirators made their defense, bound in triple sets of chains; some confessed of their own accord, quite a few boasting that death was the only remedy for one so corrupted by every kind of crime as Nero. The children of the condemned were expelled from the city and died through poison or starvation. It is recorded that some were killed at a single meal, along with their tutors and attendants, while others were prevented from securing daily sustenance.

[37] After this he showed neither discrimination nor restraint in putting to death whoever he wished and for whatever reason. To give just a few examples: the fault of Salvidienus Orfitus was that he had let out

three apartments in his house near the Forum to serve as offices to some cities; that of Cassius Longinus, the blind jurist, that he kept the image of Gaius Cassius, the assassin of Caesar, in his old family tree; and that of Thrasea Paetus, that he had the miserable expression of a teacher. To men condemned to die he never allowed more than an hour's respite. And lest there be any delay, he provided doctors who were to "take care" at once of any laggards. For that was how he described killing them by opening their veins. It is believed that he even conceived a desire to throw men still living to be torn up and devoured by a fiend from Egypt who would consume raw meat and whatever was given him. Excited and thrilled by these enormities, which he regarded as achievements, he declared that not one of his predecessors had known what he might do. And he often gave clear indications that he would not spare the remaining senators but would dispose of the entire order, sending out Roman knights and freedmen to govern the provinces and command the armies. Certainly, when he arrived in the city or set out on a journey, he would never kiss any of the senate nor even return their greetings. And when he inaugurated the Isthmus project, in the presence of a great crowd, he clearly expressed his wishes that it might turn out well for himself and the Roman people, without mentioning the senate.

[38] Yet he spared neither the people nor the fabric of his ancestral city. When someone in general conversation quoted the Greek phrase "When I am dead, let earth go up in flames", he responded, "Rather, 'while I live,'" and acted accordingly. For, as if he were upset by the ugliness of the old buildings and the narrow and twisting streets, he set fire to the city, so openly indeed that some ex-consuls, when they came upon his servants equipped with kindling and torches on their property, did not stop them. He greatly desired some land near the Golden House, then occupied by granaries, and had them torn down and burnt using military machinery because their walls were made of stone. For six days and seven nights destruction raged and the people were forced to take shelter in monuments and tombs. During that time, besides the enormous number of apartment blocks, the houses of great generals of old, together with the spoils of battle which still adorned them, the temples of the gods, too, which had been vowed and dedicated by Rome's kings and later in the Punic and Gallic wars, and every other interesting or memorable survival from the olden days went up in flames. Nero watched the fire from the tower of

Maecenas, delighted with what he termed "the beauty of the flames" and, dressed in his stage attire, he sang of the "Fall of Troy." And lest he should lose any opportunity of securing spoils and booty even from this, he undertook to have the corpses and ruins cleared at his own expense, allowing no one to come near the remains of their own property. Not merely receiving contributions but extorting them, he bled dry both the provinces and the fortunes of private individuals.

*After a brief interlude in which Suetonius describes natural disasters and other setbacks, which were not Nero's fault (39), our selection resumes as the narrative turns to Nero's last days, death, and funeral (40–50). This is given ample space, and Suetonius dwells on the most melodramatic details of his final moments.*

[40] Having endured a ruler of this sort for a little less than fourteen years, the world at last shook him off. The process was begun when the Gauls revolted under Julius Vindex who at that time governed the province as propraetor. Astrologers had predicted for Nero that one day he would be rejected. Hence that famous saying of his, "My art keeps us going," a comment apparently intended to secure greater tolerance for his study of the art of lyre-playing, as being a diversion for him when emperor but a necessity for him when a private citizen. However, some of them promised him power in the East after his repudiation, several specifying the kingdom of Jerusalem, and a number the restitution of all his earlier powers. Inclined to this hope, when both Britain and Armenia had been lost and then won back, he imagined he had had all his share of ill fortune. Indeed, when he received an answer from Apollo's Delphic oracle (in response to his inquiries) that he should beware the seventy-third year, believing that he himself would die at that age, he made no connection with the age of Galba and anticipated with great confidence not only living to an old age but even perpetual and exceptional good fortune, so that when he lost many precious possessions in a shipwreck he did not hesitate to assure his friends that the fish would bring them back to him. He learned of the Gallic revolt at Naples on the anniversary of his mother's murder, but took the news so calmly and confidently that he gave the impression of being pleased on the grounds that he would have an opportunity, in accordance with the laws of war, to despoil these most wealthy provinces. He went at once to the gymnasium where with the

greatest enthusiasm he watched athletes in competition. And when he was interrupted by a more disturbing message while at dinner, he was angered but no more than so as to threaten vengeance on the rebels. For the next eight days he made no attempt to send a reply to anyone or to give any message or instructions and passed over the affair in silence.

[41] Finally, disturbed by the frequent and abusive pronouncements of Vindex, he sent a letter to the senate urging them to take vengeance for himself and the state, and claiming that a throat ailment prevented him from being present in person. But nothing annoyed him more than that Vindex criticized his poor lyre-playing and called him Ahenobarbus instead of Nero. He declared that he meant to put aside his adoptive name and resume the one he was born with and which had been used as a reproach against him. As for the other charges, the only argument he used to demonstrate their lack of foundation was that he was being accused of ignorance of the art which he had brought to such a peak of perfection and refinement—and he would repeatedly ask people one by one if they knew of anyone to whom he was inferior. But, as more and more urgent messages arrived, he returned to Rome in great fear—though on the journey his spirits were restored by a trivial and foolish occurrence: he observed a monument inscribed with the image of a Gallic soldier, defeated by a Roman knight and being dragged by his hair, and at this sight he jumped for joy and gave thanks to heaven. Without even then summoning any public gathering of the people or the senate, he called a few of the leading men to his palace and held a brief conference before wasting the rest of the day on some water organs, of a new and unprecedented kind, which he showed off one by one, discussing the workings and difficulty of each, and promising that he would produce them all in the theater—with Vindex's permission.

[42] After this, when he learnt that Galba and the Spanish provinces had also revolted, he was badly affected and collapsed and for a long time lay half dead, unable to speak. When he came to his senses, he tore his clothes and beat his head, proclaiming that it was all over for him. In response to his nurse who reminded him by way of consolation that other rulers had experienced the same, he replied that his sufferings were unheard of, unprecedented, and worse than all others, for he was losing power while still alive. Yet nevertheless he did not give up or curtail any of his usual luxuries or indulgences but rather, whenever he had some good news from the provinces, he would hold a most lavish dinner and sing obscene songs, mocking the leaders of the rebellion, which he would accompany with gestures (these became publicly known). He would make secret visits to the theater during the games and, when an actor's performance was a popular success, he sent a message saying the man was taking advantage of the emperor's distraction.

[43] It is thought that in the early days of the revolt he had formed many cruel plans—though nothing inconsistent with his own nature—to send agents to depose and dispatch those who were commanding the armies and provinces on the grounds that they were united in a conspiracy; to slaughter all exiles everywhere and all Gauls in Rome, the former in case they should join the rebels and the latter as supporters and co-conspirators of their countrymen; to let the armies lay waste the provinces of Gaul; to murder the entire senate at poisoned banquets; to set fire to Rome, having let wild animals loose on the people so that they could not properly defend themselves. Then, overcome with fear and not so much regret as despair of ever bringing matters to a close, he came to believe that a military expedition was required and, ousting the consuls before the end of their term, he himself entered upon a sole consulship in their place, on the grounds that fate prescribed that Gaul could be defeated only by consuls. He took up the fasces and, as he left his dining-room after a banquet, leaning on the shoulders of his friends, asserted that, as soon as he had reached his new province, he would appear to the armies without weapons and simply show them his tears, then the next day, when the rebels had been brought to recant, he would, a happy man amongst happy men, sing a victory ode—which he really ought to be composing at that moment.

[44] In preparing for the expedition, his first concern was selecting vehicles for carrying his stage machinery and having the prostitutes, whom he meant to bring with him, shorn in a mannish fashion and equipped with the axes and shields of Amazons. Then he urged the city voting tribes to join up and, when no one suitable responded, he obliged masters to provide a certain number of slaves, demanding the very best from each household and not even excepting accountants or secretaries. He gave orders that men of every census rating were to hand over a proportion of their wealth and, in addition to this, that tenants of private houses and apartments should present a year's rent to

the emperor's fund. He was most strict and exacting in his demands for newly minted coins, refined silver, and pure gold, so that many openly refused the entire levy and joined together in calling for him to take back first whatever rewards he had given to the informers.

[45] Resentment increased when he sought to take advantage of the corn-supply system. For it became widely known that at a time of general food shortage, the ship from Alexandria had brought a cargo of sand for the court wrestlers. Thus the hatred of all was aroused against him and there was no insult of which he was not the object. A lock of hair was placed on the head of his statue, with a Greek inscription: "Now finally there is real competition and you must give in at last." A sack was tied to the neck of another together with the tag "I did what I could but you deserve the sack." People wrote on columns that he had even roused the Gauls with his singing. And at night quite a few would pretend to fight with their slaves and call repeatedly for a Defender.

[46] His fears were also increased by the clear portents which he had received earlier and more recently from dreams, auspices, and omens. Though he had never before been in the habit of dreaming, after the murder of his mother he dreamt that he was steering a ship through quiet waters when the helm was snatched from him, that he was being dragged by his wife Octavia into the blackest darkness and covered with a swarm of winged ants, and then that he was surrounded and prevented from moving by the statues of nations which had been dedicated at Pompey's Theater, and that an Asturian horse, in which he took particular pleasure, had its body transformed, taking on the shape of a monkey, while its head, the only part which was unchanged, gave forth musical whinnies. The doors of the Mausoleum opened of their own accord and a voice was heard, calling him by name. On New Year's Day, when the household gods had been decorated they collapsed in the middle of preparations for the sacrifice. As he was taking the auspices, Sporus offered him the gift of a ring, whose stone bore an image of the rape of Proserpina. When a large crowd of all the orders had assembled for the ceremony of making vows, the keys to the Capitol were only found after much searching. And when a speech, in which he attacked Vindex, asserting that the criminals would pay the penalty and that they would soon meet the end they deserved, was being read to the senate, everyone shouted out, "It will be you, Emperor!" It had even been noticed that the

piece he had most recently performed in public was "Oedipus in Exile" of which the final line was: "Wife, mother, father, goad me to my death."

[47] When news came, while he was having lunch, that the other armies had also rebelled, he tore up the letters brought to him, overturned the table, and hurled to the ground two of his favorite goblets which he called his Homerics, as they were decorated with scenes from Homer's poems. Then, having acquired some poison from Lucusta and hidden it in a golden box, he went over to the Servilian Gardens where he attempted to persuade the tribunes and centurions of the praetorian guard to join him in escaping with the fleet, which his most trusted freedmen had been sent to Ostia to make ready. But when some were evasive and others openly refused, one even shouting out "Is it really so hard to die?," he debated various possibilities, whether he should present himself as a suppliant to the Parthians or Galba, or whether he should appear in public on the rostra dressed in black and beseech forgiveness for his past offences, appealing as much as he could to their pity, or, if he could not win them over, whether he should not beg them at least to give him the prefecture of Egypt. Later on, a speech addressing these matters was found in his desk. It is believed he was too frightened to carry out his plan, in case he was torn apart before he could reach the Forum.

Having then put off these deliberations till the following day, he woke up in the middle of the night and, realizing that the guard of soldiers had withdrawn, he leapt out of bed and sent for his friends. When he heard nothing back from any of them, he himself went with a handful of attendants to their sleeping-quarters. The doors were all closed and no one answered. Returning to his bedroom he found that the caretakers, too, had run away, having even dragged off the bedclothes and removed the box of poison. At once he called for Spiculus the gladiator or some other executioner, at whose hands he might obtain death, but could find no one. "Am I a man without friends or enemies?" he cried, and rushed out as if to throw himself in the Tiber.

[48] Then when he had checked this impulse and conceived a wish for some secret hiding-place where he might collect his spirits, his freedman Phaon suggested his own villa, located between the Salarian Way and the Nomentan Way about four miles outside the city. Nero, just as he was, unshod and wearing just a tunic, wrapped himself in a dark-colored cloak, covered his head, and held a handkerchief to his face,

then mounted his horse with only four attendants, one of whom was Sporus. All at once an earth tremor and a flash of lightning in his face filled him with terror and he heard the shouts of soldiers from a camp nearby prophesying doom for himself and success for Galba—and even one of those they met on the road was heard saying, "These men are after Nero," while another kept asking, "Is there any news from Rome about Nero?" But when his horse shied at the stench of a dead body someone had thrown onto the road, Nero's face was uncovered and he was recognized and saluted by a man who had served in the praetorians. When they came to the byway they let the horses loose and he made his way with great difficulty, even when a robe was laid out for him to walk on, through the thickets and brambles along an overgrown path, eventually reaching the back wall of the villa. There the same Phaon urged him to hide for a while in a hole where sand had been dug out, but he replied he would not descend into the earth still living. As he waited for a short time while preparations were made for him to enter the villa unobserved, he scooped up a handful of water to drink from a pool nearby and said, "This is Nero's essence." Then, though his cloak had been torn by thorns, he picked the twigs out of it and crawled on all fours through a narrow passage they had dug until he was inside the villa. There in the little room he came to first he lay down on a couch with an ordinary mattress and an old cloak thrown over it. Despite pangs of hunger and renewed thirst, he refused the coarse bread which was offered to him but did drink a small amount of tepid water.

[49] Then, as every one of his attendants urged him to place himself beyond the reach of the abuses which were imminent, he gave orders that a trench be made at once, of a size which would accommodate his own body, and that at the same time fragments of marble should be collected, if any could be found, and water and firewood should be brought for the disposal of the corpse-to-be, weeping as each instruction was fulfilled and repeating "What an artist dies with me!" During the delay caused by these preparations, a runner brought a message to Phaon which Nero grabbed, learning from it that he had been judged a public enemy by the senate and was the object of a search, so that he might be punished according to ancestral custom. He asked what manner of punishment this might be and when he discovered it meant that a man was stripped naked, his neck being placed in a fork,

then his body beaten until he died, he was overcome with terror and snatched up two daggers which he had brought with him, but, having tried the blade of each one, he put them away again, on the grounds that the fatal hour had not yet arrived. And he would at one moment beseech Sporus to commence weeping and lamenting, and at another beg that someone should help him to die by setting an example. At the same time he berated his own procrastination with these words: "My life is shameful—unbecoming to Nero, unbecoming—in such circumstances, one must be decisive—come, rouse yourself!" At that moment some horsemen drew near, under orders to bring him back living. Aware of this, he hesitantly said: "The thunder of swift-footed horses echoes around my ears," then drove the dagger into his throat with the help of his secretary Epaphroditus. Half-conscious, when the centurion burst in and, holding a cloak to his wound, pretended he had come to give assistance, Nero said only "Too late" and "This is loyalty." And with these words he died, his eyes staring widely to the horror and dread of those looking on. The first and most insistent request he had made of his companions was that no one should be able to get possession of his head but that he should in some way be completely consumed by fire. This was allowed by Icelus, a freedman of Galba, who had just recently been released from the chains with which he had been bound at the start of the revolt.

[50] His funeral cost two hundred thousand sesterces and his body was dressed in the white robes, embroidered with gold, which he had worn for the Kalends of January. His nurses, Egloge and Alexandria, together with his mistress, Acte, buried his remains in the ancestral monument of the Domitii, which is located on top of the Hill of Gardens and can be seen from the Campus Martius. The monument is made up of a sarcophagus of porphyry, on which is an altar of Luna marble, and with an enclosure of Thasian stone.

*In this section Suetonius offers a miscellany of information that could not have been easily accommodated in earlier sections, including Nero's physical appearance and various aspects of his personality (51–56).*

[51] He was of a good height but his body was blotchy and ill smelling. His hair was fairish, his face handsome rather than attractive, his eyes bluish-grey and

dull, his neck thick, his stomach protruding, his legs very thin, his general health good—for despite his luxurious and most excessive way of life, he was only ill three times in fourteen years, and even then not so as to have to abstain from drinking or his other habits. He was so very shameless in his concern for dress and the care of his person that he would always have his curls arranged in a pile on his head and, on his trip to Greece, even had them flowing down behind. He was often to be seen in public dressed in a dinner robe, with a handkerchief around his neck, his tunic unbelted, and his feet bare.

[52] In his youth he applied himself to almost all the liberal arts. However, his mother dissuaded him from taking up philosophy, warning that it was incompatible with imperial power. His teacher, Seneca, kept him from getting to know the orators of old, hoping thus to prolong his admiration for himself. Hence his inclination towards poetry, which he himself composed so freely and easily that many are of the opinion he passed off someone else's work as his own. I have had access to some notebooks and papers on which were written some of his best-known works in his own hand. These clearly show that his composition was not transcribed or taken from another's dictation but worked out with thought and creativity. For there are many crossings out and insertions and additions in the work. He also had a keen interest in painting and sculpture.

[53] Above all, however, he was moved by a passion for popularity and was envious of anyone who in any way inspired the enthusiasm of the common people. It was widely believed that after his victories in the theater, he would, at the next set of games, compete with the athletes at Olympia, for he was a keen wrestler and had looked on at the athletic contests all over Greece in the same way as the judges, sitting down at the level of the stadium, and if any pairs of wrestlers withdrew too far he would push them forward himself with his own hands. Since he was praised as equal to Apollo in song and the Sun in chariot-racing, it was inevitable that he would also emulate the achievements of Hercules. They say that a lion was trained for him to kill naked in the arena, with the people watching, either by means of a club or with the force of his arms. [54] Near the end of his life, indeed, he publicly made a vow that, if his regime survived, he would perform at the victory games on the water-organ, the flute, and the bagpipes and that

on the last day he would appear as an actor and dance the story of Virgil's Turnus. Some people say that he had the actor Paris put to death because he was a dangerous rival.

[55] He had a desire to secure eternal and perpetual fame but his method was ill-advised. For he abolished the old names of many things and places and gave them new ones based on his own, so that he termed the month of April "Neroneus" and he had a plan to give Rome the name of Neropolis.

[56] He had great contempt for all cults with the single exception of that of the Syrian Goddess and even her he soon so despised that he polluted her with urine, when he became an enthusiast for another superstition—to which alone he remained most faithful. For he had received as a gift from some unknown commoner a small image of a girl which was said to be a protection against plots and, since a plot was immediately uncovered, he persisted in worshipping this image as the greatest of divinities with three sacrifices a day and he wanted it to be believed that it could give signs imparting knowledge of the future. A few months before he died he was present at an examination of entrails but could not succeed in obtaining a favorable reading.

*Suetonius's biographies typically end with a very brief obituary notice. Here, he concludes with the curious episode of a "false Nero," who appeared in the East in Suetonius's youth.*

[57] He met his end in his thirty-second year on the anniversary of Octavia's death, thereby provoking such great public joy that the common people ran throughout the city dressed in liberty caps. Yet there were also some who for a long time would decorate his tomb with spring and summer flowers, and would sometimes display on the rostra statues of him dressed in a toga or post his edicts as if he were still alive and would soon return to avenge himself on his enemies. Indeed, even Vologaesus, king of the Parthians, when he sent ambassadors to the senate to renew his alliance, also made an earnest appeal that the memory of Nero should be honored. Moreover, twenty years later, when I was a young man, there was an individual of unknown origins who boasted that he was Nero, and the name was so popular with the Parthians that they gave him vigorous support and could scarcely be made to surrender him.

## AFTERWORD

Suetonius supplied a template for biographers in the Latin-speaking circles of the Roman world, in particular for those who set their hand to chronicle the lives of the emperors. But none of them surpassed him. In the next century, during the reign of Alexander Severus (A.D. 222–35), Marius Maximus, who had served with the emperor Septimius Severus and twice held the consulship, picked up where Suetonius had left off, writing biographies of the next twelve emperors down to his own time. What little we know of Maximus's lost work derives from the so-called *Historia Augusta* (Imperial History), a collection of imperial biographies that purports to collect the work of six authors but is probably due to a single person writing around the end of the fourth century. This series of biographies begins with Hadrian and continues, with gaps, to the late third century and is composed very much in the manner of Suetonius. But unlike his model, the author of the *Historia Augusta* also incorporates a great deal of made-up information into his biographies. There is no consensus among scholars about the purpose of this collection, but it is possible that its author or authors were catering to the tastes of a Roman elite that by the fourth century was more engaged by social satire and scandal than history. The more credible historian, Ammianus Marcellinus (A.D. 330–95), complains that the Roman aristocracy of his time was interested in reading only the likes of Juvenal and the biographies of Marius Maximus (28.4.14). Eventually it was a prurient, or academic, interest in the lives of the emperors that led readers to return to Suetonius when his *Lives of the Caesars* resurfaced in the Carolingian Renaissance of the ninth century, after the biographies had not been read for several hundred years.

Only a single manuscript of Suetonius survived the end of antiquity, but he was being read again in the court circles of Charlemagne. Sometime after the death of the Holy Roman Emperor in 814, his former associate Einhard, now secretary to his son Louis the Pious, wrote a biography of Charlemagne that drew heavily on Suetonius as a model. He adopted Suetonius's approach of organizing the various aspects of his subject's life into separate headings and, most notoriously, incorporated direct verbal borrowings from the text of Suetonius in his description of the physical appearance of Charlemagne. It is not clear how or where Einhard acquired his familiarity with this rare author, but once the influence was recognized, it stimulated in others an interest in Suetonius. From this point on Suetonius was much read, especially in excerpted versions, but in addition, more than two hundred surviving manuscripts attest to his revived popularity. Renaissance scholars shared in this enthusiasm. Not surprisingly, Petrarch, who had an intensely personal interest in the lives of famous Romans, owned several copies. And it is also unsurprising that Boccaccio, author of the *Decameron,* found Suetonius's brand of biography to his liking and even copied out substantial parts of the *Lives of the Caesars* in his own hand. But as professional historians developed more sophisticated approaches to antiquity, interest in Suetonius diminished, especially with the re-emergence in western Europe of Plutarch's *Parallel Lives.* For those who were inclined to view the ancient world through the lives of its great men, Plutarch's biographies supplied a more compelling blend of history and moralizing.

Suetonius has always appealed to readers curious about the excesses of tyrants and the bizarre distortions of human character that take place when there is no check on absolute power. While interest in Suetonius among historians and scholars waned in the seventeenth century, the needs of the general reader were supplied by numerous translations. In the English-speaking world, the most influential was the one published by the prolific Philemon Holland in 1606. Holland had already published the first translations into English of the complete works of Livy (1600), Pliny the Elder (1601), and Plutarch's *Moralia* (1603), so by comparison his *Historie of Twelve Caesars* was a trifling effort. Holland's translation was informed by the best scholarship available; in the case of Suetonius that meant that he made much use of the great edition by Isaac Casaubon, but the weight of his erudition was felt in his translations, to such an extent that many print editions bear this epigram by an anonymous, disgruntled reader:

> Phil: Holland with translations doth so fill us,
> will not let Suetonius be Tranquillus.

Holland commended Suetonius to his readers because "he seemeth to affect nothing so much as uncorrupt and plaine trueth," a view of Suetonius that prevailed through at least the following century, when he was read by the likes of Samuel Johnson and Edward Gibbon. Holland's translation remained in circulation into the nineteenth century, but even in his own day his archaizing Elizabethan style probably seemed a bit heavy-handed, and while 250 years would pass before anyone attempted another complete version of Pliny the Elder to compete with his, his Suetonius had competitors. One of these may have been by the metaphysical poet Andrew Marvell (1621–78), to whom was attributed an anonymous translation published in London in 1672.

The seventeenth century witnessed not only the broader dissemination of the *Lives of the Caesars* in translation but also the first major reflection of Suetonius's biographies in popular culture, for which they have ever since been a major source of titillating detail about Roman decadence. Claudio Monteverdi's last opera, *The Coronation of Poppaea,* was produced in Venice in 1643. With a libretto composed by Gian Francesco Busenello, it takes as its sources Tacitus and Cassius Dio but draws heavily on Suetonius's *Life of Nero* in depicting Nero's repudiation of his wife Octavia and subsequent marriage to Poppaea Sabina, the wife of a Roman noble. While the opera ends with an ecstatic duet of Nero and Poppaea and her coronation as empress, the beautiful music overlays an extraordinary story of lust and ambition, posing a broad moral challenge for the audience. Suetonius's reports of the Julio-Claudians' sins and foibles provide the basis for many an entertaining account of the period, including one by Thomas De Quincey (1785–1859), author of *Confessions of an English Opium Eater*. He published *The Caesars,* a witty rewriting of Suetonius, in 1832 when he was also busy dodging creditors. By far the most celebrated and commercially successful adaption of Suetonian material was *I, Claudius,* the fictionalized autobiography of the emperor Claudius published by the British novelist Robert Graves in 1934, followed a year later by the sequel, *Claudius the God and His Wife Messalina*. As he recorded in his journal in 1929, Graves had been inspired by his reading of Suetonius and Tacitus to tell the story of the early empire through the recollections of the most unlikely emperor, who survived the machinations of his grandmother Livia and the reigns of terror under Tiberius and Caligula. In 1976, the Suetonian legacy was transferred to the screen when the BBC aired its extremely popular miniseries, adapting Graves's two novels.

# PLUTARCH

(Lucius? Mestrius Plutarchus, ca. A.D. 45–after 120)

THE LITTLE TOWN OF CHAERONEA IN NORTHWESTERN BOEOTIA IN CENTRAL GREECE commands the valley of the river Cephisus, flat country suitable for the deployment of large armies. It was the site of two great battles: in 338 B.C., with his son Alexander distinguishing himself in his first major engagement, Philip II of Macedon crushed the alliance of southern Greek states; in 86 B.C., the Roman general Sulla, though outnumbered at least three to one, destroyed the army of Mithridates the Great of Pontus, slaughtering, according to some calculations, more than 100,000 of the enemy for the loss of twelve of his own soldiers. Chaeronea's only other claim to fame is as the lifelong home of Plutarch, who was born there about A.D. 45. But that distinction is a great one, for few writers did more to preserve knowledge of antiquity, both Greek and Roman. The *Natural History* of the elder Pliny is also a great repertoire of ancient culture; whereas, however, Pliny is famously eccentric, Plutarch is a careful and judicious writer. Though many of his works are now lost, what survives is still prodigious. Seventy-eight miscellaneous essays, mostly on philosophical, rhetorical, and antiquarian topics, are collected under the title *Moralia*, a name given originally in the Middle Ages to those works concerned with ethical philosophy. His magnum opus, however, is his "Parallel Lives," matching biographies of famous Greeks and Romans. There are eighteen such pairs with a brief formal comparison between the two subjects appended, four more pairs with no comparison, and four further lives unpaired. He is known to have written biographies of the Roman emperors, but only those of Galba and Otho survive.

It is surprising that a Greek living in an insignificant town should be such an important literary figure, and in particular that he should be such an authoritative source of information about events in Roman history. For one thing, the active centers of Greek literary life in Plutarch's time were far away, in Asia Minor on the western coast of modern Turkey, in great cities such as Ephesus and Pergamum, and in Egypt, at Alexandria. More significantly, many Greek intellectuals took, or affected to take, little interest in Roman culture. Gibbon gives an abrasive assessment of the Greek feeling of intellectual superiority in the Roman period: "Alone in the universe, the self-satisfied pride of the Greeks was not disturbed by the comparison of foreign merit; and it is no wonder if they fainted in the race, since they had neither competitors to urge their speed, nor judges to crown their victory" (*Decline and Fall* 3, chap. 53).

Two other Greek writers also contribute greatly to our knowledge of the late Republic in general, and of Mark Antony in particular: Appian (ca. A.D. 95–160) in the fifth book of his *Civil Wars* and Cassius Dio (ca. A.D. 164–229) in Books 45 through 50 of his *Roman History*. But both of these later historians lived for long periods in Rome and had active political careers there. At the beginning of his *Life of Demosthenes*, Plutarch declares rather mischievously that he has chosen "to live in a small town so that it should not become any smaller," but he recognizes the disadvantages in working in Chaeronea: most of the documents he needs to consult are not easily available, for some can only be found abroad, and are scattered among many different owners, so he really needs to live in a big city where books are available and he can consult people on details not actually recorded in writing. Like the imperial physician Galen, he had little time to practice his Latin when he actually lived in Rome but, quite unlike Galen, he found that, when he began to study Latin in his old age, he was surprised and gratified that he found it quite charming—the first recorded instance of the familiar and frequent expression of regret at not having started to learn Latin earlier.

Plutarch acknowledges that visitors laugh at him when they see him supervising the removal of dung from the streets of Chaeronea, but he is proud to perform such menial acts of public service for the benefit of the community (*Moralia* 811*b*). He was not, however, really quite so isolated as he might have us think. He was wealthy enough to enjoy the privilege of travel. As an important local official and for many years priest at the important religious center at Delphi, he had contact with the ruling Roman elite, as is borne out by his dedication of the *Lives* and other works to Sosius Senecio, who was consul twice, in A.D. 99 and 107. He shared mutual friends with Tacitus and the younger Pliny (though he seems not to have known them themselves). His nephew Sextus was one of the teachers of Marcus Aurelius, and the hero of Apuleius's *Metamorphoses* boasts descent from Plutarch and Sextus (1.1).

Even so, his works are written primarily for Greeks and from a Greek perspective. Hence, for example, in his *Life of Antony,* he explains such things as the Roman monetary system (4), the function of an augur (5), the role of the Master of the Horse (8), and the festival of the Lupercalia (12); he emphasizes Antony's love for Greece (23), his adoption of Athenian customs (33), and the famine in Greece after Actium (68), while the long discursus on Timon of Athens (70) is largely irrelevant, and the attention given to Antony's activities in Greece is probably somewhat disproportionate to their actual significance.

Although Plutarch is such an important source of information about events in both Greek and Roman history, he makes a clear distinction in the opening words of his *Life of Alexander* between his biographies and the writing of history:

> I am writing biographies of King Alexander and of Julius Caesar, who overthrew Pompey. Their achievements are so numerous that all I will say by way of introduction is that I beg my readers to forgive me and not complain if I merely summarize most of their many well-known deeds rather than record each one in detail. I am writing biographies, not history, and it is not always famous actions that illustrate virtue or vice. Something slight, a comment or a witticism, often gives a clearer impression of a person's character than do battles with countless corpses or vast battalions or city-sieges.

There is a strong contrast with the opening words of the first extant Greek historical work, Herodotus's account of the Persian Wars in the early fifth century B.C.:

> The enquiry (*historia*) of Herodotus of Halicarnassus is published here, so that the deeds of men may not fade with time, and the great and wondrous accomplishments of the Greeks and barbarians may not lose their fame.

This distinction is an important one. Historians make their inquiries in order to discover what happened, whereas Plutarch is interested in exploring the character of his subjects, and in proposing moral lessons. There are clear differences in generic conventions also. Biographies tend to be small in scale, whereas histories are among the longest and most ambitious literary projects. (It is not accidental that the works of very few ancient historians survive intact; Herodotus and Thucydides are the most notable exceptions.)

At the start of his biography of Aemilius Paullus (the victor at the Battle of Pydna in 168 B.C., which ended the Third Macedonian War), Plutarch declares that his *Lives* are intended to be a source of moral improvement:

> I happened to start writing biographies for the sake of other people, but now I find myself persisting with the project, lingering over it for my own benefit, using history as a mirror and trying to fashion and model my life in accordance with the virtues of the men whose lives I am recording. It is just as if I were living with them in turn, welcoming them one after the other as guests... and selecting from their deeds the most significant and finest. "Oh, what greater joy could you have than this?" [a quotation from Sophocles], and more effective for moral improvement?... By studying history and becoming familiar with it through my writing, I can foster in my soul the memory of the best and most reputable men, and thus dispel and reject anything mean, malicious, or base that daily life inevitably forces on me. I turn my attention calmly and gently away from such things to the most excellent of my role models.

This holds true of most of the *Lives,* but he emphasizes that the pair devoted to Demetrius (the "Besieger," king of Macedon, 337–283 B.C.) and Mark Antony is exceptional. They provide moral guidance in a negative way, illustrating how one should not behave (*Demetrius* 1):

> They were both much given to sex and drinking, warlike, generous, extravagant, overbearing, and their careers were similarly matched: not only did they enjoy great successes and suffer great disasters, with huge conquests and huge losses, with unforeseen setbacks and recoveries beyond hope, but they also died in the same way, Demetrius imprisoned by his enemies, Antony when just about to be captured.

Plutarch's pairing of Demetrius and Antony is largely successful. As he says, they both had spectacular but ultimately unsuccessful military careers, they were both given to luxurious living, and they both had severely flawed characters. To the modern reader, however, Demetrius may seem obscure, just one of many kings who ruled parts of the Greek world in the period after the glorious conquests of Alexander. Perhaps his strongest claim to fame nowadays is in his unwitting contribution to the construction of the Colossus of Rhodes, the giant statue of the sun god that was one of the wonders of the ancient world: he built a huge siege engine, the Helepolis (the "City-Taker"), to capture the city of Rhodes, but the defenders rendered it inoperable by bogging it down in a diverted stream; when Demetrius gave up the siege, the Rhodians used the metal in the Helepolis to build the Colossus. Demetrius's activities were largely confined to Greece, and little ultimately turned on his success or failure, but to Plutarch, whose focus was so sharply on Greece, writing as a Greek for Greeks, he will have seemed a major player on the stage of history.

Even so, Antony was obviously a much more significant figure, for he came close to winning control of the whole Roman world, as Octavian actually did by defeating him and Cleopatra at Actium. History is written by the winners, and Augustan propaganda makes a clear and simple antithesis between Octavian/Augustus, backed by all Rome, and Antony, the outlaw, the threat to civilization (Virgil, *Aeneid* 8.678–88):

> Here is Augustus, leading the Italians into battle at Actium, along with the Senate and the People, the household gods and the great gods,... while Antony, in barbarian splendor and with motley weapons, coming in triumph from the peoples of the Dawn and the Red Sea, brings Egypt and the forces of the Orient and farthest Bactria, with his Egyptian wife following him.

**Figure 29: Coin of Antony and Cleopatra**
A coin issued jointly by the couple, with portraits on the obverse and reverse.

---

In reality, in the year before Actium, both consuls and almost half the Senate left Rome to join Antony, and Octavian did not feel safe in the Senate without a bodyguard. Had Antony won at Actium, the division of the empire might have taken place centuries before Constantine moved the center of power to Constantinople (now Istanbul). It is reasonable to speculate that Antony would have administered the empire from Alexandria. Defeat at Actium may have ruined Antony, but, through his marriage to Octavian's sister Octavia, he was the grandfather of Claudius, great-grandfather of Caligula, and great-great-grandfather of Nero.

Plutarch is writing long after the fall of the Julio-Claudian dynasty with the death of Nero in A.D. 68 and is under no pressure to adopt the negative picture of Antony as decadently and treacherously un-Roman, the light in which he is cast in Augustan propaganda. Antony's irresponsible infatuation with Cleopatra, however, which was such a fundamental part of Augustan propaganda, was very well suited to the parallelism that Plutarch draws with Demetrius. To us, a story such as Antony and Cleopatra's fishing trip (*Life of Antony* 29) is comic, romantic, and rather endearing, but there were plenty of Romans who would hardly see it in that light: Antony was a military commander who wasted time, endangered Roman lives and the security of the empire, and was disloyal to his Roman wife. We can see just such a situation played out in Virgil's *Aeneid*. On one level Aeneas is cruel and heartless in leaving Dido, but on another level he is bound to do so, for the destiny of Rome depends on it. Dido faints after learning that Aeneas is intending to leave her, but Virgil is not being merely ironic in describing Aeneas as "pious" immediately after that scene. A Roman was pious if he did his duty to the Roman state. We are justified in making a direct comparison of Aeneas and Dido with Antony and Cleopatra, for Virgil's portrayal of Dido draws heavily on Cleopatra. Both are exotic African queens who lead Roman commanders astray (in Cleopatra's case, both Julius Caesar and Antony). Augustan propaganda portrays Cleopatra as being intent on destroying Rome, while Dido is the founder of Carthage, which nearly did destroy Rome.

Antony's life in Alexandria was offensive to the traditional Roman ways. The Greek inscription on a base of a statue of him, set up in 34 B.C., describes him as "Great [μέγας *megas*, perhaps 'Big' would be a better translation], inimitable in the deeds of Aphrodite, a god" (*Selected Eastern Greek Inscriptions* 195). But there were faults on both sides. When Octavian complained of Antony's liaison with Cleopatra, Antony responded with a letter cataloging women with whom Octavian had committed adultery (Suetonius, *Life of Augustus* 69, part of a long passage devoted to Augustus's extramarital affairs).

We may find Antony's open affair with Cleopatra more appealing than Octavian's hypocrisy, but that affair seems not to have been altogether idyllic. The practice of employing a *praegustator,* "food-taster," was said to have become common after Antony began to employ one in the period before Actium, when he feared that Cleopatra might try to poison him to ingratiate herself with Octavian. The elder Pliny refers to such a tension between the lovers:

> Cleopatra poisoned the tips of the flowers that Antony was to wear in a garland at a banquet. When the party was in full swing, she suggested that they should drink their garlands by strewing the flowers in their wine. When Antony was about to drink his, Cleopatra put her hand over his cup and called for a condemned prisoner, who drank the wine and died on the spot. (*Natural History* 21.12)

Plutarch acquired his knowledge of Latin late in life, and he was never familiar enough with Latin literature to quote from it as he does so often from Greek literature. (There is no evidence that he even knew the *Aeneid.*) He did, however, make direct use of Roman sources for his *Lives* of Antony and other Romans of the period. Most of these sources are lost, and we cannot therefore assess the use he made of them, works such as Augustus's autobiography and the accounts of the civil wars by Asinius Pollio and Quintus Dellius. At *Suasoriae* 1.7, the elder Seneca records that Dellius also wrote *Epistulae ad Cleopatram Lascivae,* "Sexy Letters to Cleopatra," the complete loss of which is probably not disastrous for Western culture, but they would have given a lively glimpse into the propaganda of the period.

The one important extant Latin source that Plutarch almost certainly drew on at first hand is Cicero's *Second Philippic.* That magnificent demonstration of what can be said in court in a society with practically no laws against slander is the probable source for numerous passages in the *Life.* It is instructive to contrast the mild and reasonable way in which Plutarch describes the follies of Antony's youth with the majestic intolerance of Cicero's version of the same topic (*Philippics* 2.44):

> You put on the toga of manhood, and promptly turned it into a woman's toga. You started out as a common prostitute with a fixed price but not a low one. Curio quickly came along and took you out of your whoring trade and set you up in a stable and steady marriage with him, as if he had bestowed on you the gown that respectable married women wear. No boy bought to satisfy lust was ever in his owner's power as you were in Curio's. How often his father threw you out of his house! How often he posted guards to prevent you crossing the threshold! But, with night as your ally, and with lust goading you, and with payment compelling you, you used to be let down through the roof-tiles.

Especially if our view of Antony is colored by Shakespeare's portrayal of him as "the greatest prince o' the world, / the noblest," it is hard to recall that Antony seems to have had a nasty and vindictive side to his character that is not often apparent in Plutarch's *Life,* the prime source for Shakespeare's play. To cite just one incident that need not be mere Augustan propaganda: Cicero was murdered on December 7, 43 B.C., his name having been added to the proscription lists by Antony, largely because of the vehemence of his *Philippic* orations. Popilius Laenas killed him even though Cicero had once defended him in court, and he went so far as to set up a statue of himself sitting with his victim's head beside him. Antony was so pleased that he gave him more than the reward originally offered for killing Cicero (Cassius Dio, *Roman History* 47.11).

# LIFE OF ANTONY

*In the first two chapters Plutarch deals at some length
with Antony's family background and, somewhat cursorily,
with his youth, presumably because he did not have good
sources for that period of his life. The first well-documented
episode in Antony's career is his service in the East with
the proconsul Aulus Gabinius in 57–55 B.C., which occupies
the third chapter and leads to a digression (4) on Antony's
popularity with his soldiers.*

[1] Antony's grandfather was the orator Antonius, who,
as a member of Sulla's faction, was killed by Marius,
and his father was Antonius surnamed Creticus, who
was not particularly well known or distinguished in
the public domain, but was a fair and honorable man,
and above all a generous one, as a single example of his
behavior should demonstrate. He was not well off, and
so his wife tended to stop him displaying his kindness,
but once, when one of his close friends came and asked
him for money, although he did not have any actual
money on him, he ordered a young slave to pour some
water into a silver bowl and bring it to him. When the
slave had done so, Antonius splashed water on to his
cheeks, as if he were about to shave, but then, once the
boy was out of the way on some other errand, he gave
the bowl to his friend and told him it was his to dispose
of. Later, when the house-slaves were being subjected
to a thorough search, Antonius could see that his wife
was angry and was prepared to examine each and every
one of them under torture, so he confessed and asked
her to forgive him.

[2] Antonius' wife was Julia, from the house of
the Caesars, as virtuous and modest a woman as any
of her day. Their son, Antony, was brought up by her,
and after Antonius' death she was married to Cornelius
Lentulus, who was put to death by Cicero as one of
Catiline's co-conspirators. She is generally thought
to have been the prime mover of the extreme hostility Antony felt for Cicero. At any rate, Antony claims
that Cicero refused even to hand Lentulus' corpse over
to them until his mother had begged Cicero's wife to
intercede for them. But this is generally taken to be
false, because none of the men who were put to death
by Cicero at the time in question were denied burial.

Antony had developed into a remarkable young
man, they say, when he was smitten, as if by a pesti-
lential disease, by his friendship and intimacy with
Curio, an uncultured hedonist who, in order to

increase his hold over Antony, introduced him to
drinking-sessions, women, and all kinds of extravagant
and immoderate expenses, as a result of which Antony
got heavily into debt—too heavily for his age—until
he owed 250 talents. Curio guaranteed the whole sum,
but when Antony's father realized what was going on,
he threw Antony out of the house. Next Antony briefly
associated himself with the career of Clodius, the most
defiant and vile of the popular leaders of the time, who
was then throwing the whole constitution into disarray. Before long, however, he had had his fill of Clodius'
insane ways and also became afraid of the party that
was forming in opposition to Clodius, so he left Italy
for Greece, where he spent his time training his body
for military contests and learning the art of public
speaking. He adopted the so-called Asiatic style of
speaking, which was flourishing with particular vigor
just then and which bore a considerable resemblance
to his life, in that it was a kind of showy whinnying,
filled with vain prancing and capricious ambition.

[3] When Gabinius, an ex-consul, set sail for Syria
and tried to persuade Antony to get involved in the
expedition, Antony refused to do so without a commission, but joined his campaign once he had been given
command of the cavalry. His first mission was against
Aristobulus, the leader of a Jewish revolt. Antony
drove Aristobulus out of all his strongholds, the largest of which he was the first to scale. Then he engaged
the enemy in battle, put them to flight, even though his
small force was vastly outnumbered, and killed all but
a few of them. Aristobulus and his son were among the
captives.

Next there was an attempt by Ptolemy to persuade
Gabinius, with a promise of ten thousand talents,
to join him in invading Egypt and restoring him to
the throne. Most of his officers were opposed to the
plan and, despite being completely captivated by the
ten thousand talents, Gabinius was hesitant about
the war. Antony, however, had his sights set on great
exploits. He also wanted to do Ptolemy a favor and see
him get his way, so he helped him win Gabinius over
and arouse his enthusiasm about the expedition. The
Romans were more afraid of the journey to Pelusium
than they were of the war, since their way lay through
deep sand and waterless desert, past the Ecregma
and the Serbonian marshes. The Egyptians call these
marshes the Outbreaths of Typhon, but they are apparently a remnant of the Red Sea, left behind when it
receded, and fed by water percolating through to them

at the point where a very narrow isthmus separates the marshes and the inner sea. However, when Antony was dispatched with his cavalry he not only occupied the narrow pass, but also captured Pelusium, which was a large city, and overcame the garrison there. In this way he simultaneously secured the route for the army and made its commander certain and confident of victory. The enemy too profited from his desire for recognition, in the sense that when Ptolemy reached Pelusium, he was so filled with rage and hatred that he intended to massacre the Egyptians, but Antony intervened and stopped him. And throughout the numerous major battles and fights that followed, Antony frequently displayed great daring and the kind of foresight that marks a leader, most conspicuously on the occasion when he gave victory to the front ranks by encircling the enemy and coming round to take them in the rear. All this gained him battle honors and prizes for valor, but his posthumous kindness to Archelaus was also widely appreciated. Although Archelaus was close to him, and they were guest-friends, he had no choice but to make war on him while he was alive, and then after Archelaus had fallen in battle Antony sought out his body, dressed it up, and gave it a royal burial. As a result he left the people of Alexandria with a very favorable impression, and the Romans involved in the expedition came to regard him as an outstanding soldier.

[4] On top of these qualities, his appearance was gentlemanly and dignified. His noble beard, broad forehead, and aquiline nose were reminiscent of the virility displayed by Heracles' features in portraits and on statues. There was also an ancient story that the Antonii were descendants of Heracles, originating from Heracles' son Anton, and Antony thought his physical appearance, which I have already mentioned, confirmed the tradition. He also dressed to support the tradition. When he was going to be seen by more than just a few people, he always girded his toga up to his thigh, wore a great sword hanging at his side, and wrapped himself in a rough cloak. Nevertheless, even those aspects of his behavior which struck other people as vulgar—his boasting and teasing, the habit he had of carousing in full view of everyone, and the way he sat next to someone who was eating and ate standing at the table while out on campaign—aroused an incredible amount of loyalty and longing in his soldiers. He was even somehow charming where love was concerned, and used it as one of his means for gaining popularity, since he helped people in their love-affairs

and did not mind being teased about his own affairs. Then his generosity, and the way he did both his friends and the men under his command favors with no mean or niggardly hand, were not only the cause of the outstanding beginning he made on the road to power, but also raised his power to even greater heights after he had acquired prominence, despite the countless flaws which held him back. I will give one example of his liberality. He gave orders for one of his friends to be given 250,000 drachmas (or a "decies," as the Romans call it). His steward was astonished and wanted to show Antony how large a sum it was, so he put all the money out on display. When Antony passed by he said, "What's this?," and the steward explained that it was the money he had ordered to be given away. Antony was not deceived. He understood the malice of the man's intentions and said, "I thought a decies was more. This is a paltry sum. Double it."

*There is a five-year gap in the narrative, which resumes here in 50 B.C. with an account of Antony's conduct during the civil war between Pompey and Caesar (5–8). In 54 B.C., Antony had joined Caesar in Gaul, but he returned to Rome in 53 to run for office. Two years later, he returned to Gaul, where he was then involved in several campaigns. Antony was elected tribune for the year 49 and from this point on plays an important part in the events of his time.*

[5] But this happened at a later time. When Roman political life was divided into two factions, with the aristocrats attaching themselves to Pompey, who was in Rome, and the popularists summoning Caesar from Gaul where he was on active service, Antony's friend Curio, who had changed sides and was supporting Caesar, brought Antony over to Caesar's cause. Curio, who had a great deal of influence with the common people as a result of his abilities as a public speaker, and also made unstinting use of money supplied by Caesar, got Antony elected tribune and then subsequently one of the priests responsible for divining the flights of birds, whom they call "augurs." No sooner had Antony taken up office than he was of considerable help to those who were Caesar's proxies in government. In the first place, when Marcellus the consul was trying not only to hand over to Pompey all the troops which were already mustered, but also to make it possible for him to raise further troops as well, Antony blocked the proposal by issuing an edict to the effect that the forces already assembled should sail to Syria and help

Bibulus in his war against the Parthians, and that the troops Pompey was in the process of raising should not be attached to his command. In the second place, when the senate refused to allow Caesar's letters to be introduced or read out, Antony drew on the authority vested in his office to read them out himself, and so changed a lot of people's minds, since Caesar's demands, as displayed in his letters, seemed fair and reasonable. Finally, when two questions had been raised in the senate—one asking whether it was the senators' opinion that Pompey should disband his army, the other asking the same question about Caesar—and only a few senators were in favor of Pompey laying down his arms, while almost all of them were in favor of Caesar doing so, Antony stood up and asked whether it was the view of the senate that both Pompey and Caesar should lay down their arms and disband their armies together. This proposal was unanimously and enthusiastically accepted, and with cries of congratulation they called on Antony to put the question to the vote. The consuls, however, refused to let this happen, so instead Caesar's supporters put forward a new set of apparently reasonable demands—but Cato spoke out strongly against them, and Lentulus, in his capacity as consul, had Antony expelled from the senate. As he left he fulminated against them, and then, dressed as a slave, he hired a chariot along with Quintus Cassius and set out to join Caesar. As soon as they were shown in to him they loudly declared that the government of Rome was in complete chaos, now that even the tribunes were prevented from saying what they wanted and anyone who spoke out on behalf of justice was harassed and in mortal danger.

[6] At this Caesar took his army and invaded Italy. This is why in the *Philippics* Cicero wrote that just as Helen was the cause of the Trojan War, so Antony was the cause of the civil war. But this is obviously false, because Gaius Caesar was not the kind of malleable or pliant man who would have let anger overwhelm reason; if he had not determined to do so a long time previously, he would not have taken the decision to make war on his country on the spur of the moment, just because he saw that Antony and Cassius had taken to a chariot and fled to him, dressed in poor clothes. All this did was provide him with a plausible excuse and pretext for what he had been wanting to do for a long time. What led him to take on the whole world, as it had led Alexander before him, and Cyrus many years before that, was an insatiable lust for rule and an insane

desire to be first in power and importance—for which the downfall of Pompey was a prerequisite.

So Caesar attacked Rome, conquered it, and drove Pompey out of Italy. He then decided to concentrate first on the Pompeian forces in Spain and afterwards, once he had fitted out a fleet, to make the crossing and attack Pompey. He left Lepidus as military governor of Rome and entrusted Italy and the army to Antony in his capacity as tribune. Antony immediately won the loyalty of the troops by making it his usual practice to join them in their exercises and at mealtimes, and by rewarding them as much as he could given the circumstances, but everyone else found him highly offensive. He was too lazy to pay attention to the pleas of injured parties, too bad tempered to listen to petitioners, and he had a poor reputation as regards other men's wives. In short, Caesar's rule, which turned out not even remotely to resemble a tyranny as far as he himself was concerned, was spoiled by his associates, and Antony was the one who was considered the worst offender, since he had the greatest power and so was held to have gone the furthest astray.

[7] Nevertheless, on his return from Spain Caesar ignored the charges against Antony and was perfectly right to do so, since in war he found him energetic, courageous, and a natural leader. So Caesar set sail across the Ionian Sea from Brundisium with a small force and then sent his transport ships back to Gabinius and Antony with orders to board their men and cross over to Macedonia as quickly as possible. While Gabinius shrank from making the difficult crossing in winter and took his army the long way round by land, Antony was worried about how Caesar had been cut off by large numbers of enemy troops. So he repelled Libo, who was blockading the mouth of the harbor, by surrounding his galleys with numerous light boats, embarked 800 horsemen and 20,000 legionaries, and put to sea. The enemy caught sight of him and gave chase, and although he escaped from this threat when a fresh southerly wind engulfed the enemy ships in heavy seas and a deep swell, his fleet was blown off course towards some cliffs and crags jutting out into deep water, and his situation looked hopeless. But suddenly a strong south-westerly wind blew from the direction of the bay and the waves began to run from the land towards the open sea, so that Antony could change direction away from the land. As he sailed confidently along, he saw that the shoreline was covered with disabled ships, because the wind had driven the galleys that were

after him there, and quite a few of them were wrecked. Antony took plenty of prisoners and a great deal of booty, captured Lissus, and greatly boosted Caesar's morale by arriving just in time with such a large force.

[8] Many battles took place, one after another, and Antony distinguished himself in all of them. Twice, when Caesar's men were in headlong flight, he confronted them, turned them around, made them stop and regroup, and so won the battle. There was more talk about him in the camp than anyone else except Caesar. And Caesar made no secret of his opinion of Antony: when the final battle at Pharsalus was imminent, the battle on which the whole issue depended, he kept the right wing for himself, but he put Antony in charge of the left wing, on the grounds that he was the best tactician apart from himself. After the victory Caesar was made dictator and went off after Pompey, but he chose Antony as his cavalry commander and sent him to Rome. This post is the second most important when the dictator is in Rome, but when he is away it is the most important and has more or less sole authority. The tribunate remains in place, but all the other offices are dissolved once a dictator has been elected.

*In this section (9–13), Plutarch deals with Antony's fluctuating fortunes during the years of Caesar's dictatorship. Antony's private life frequently proved a liability, but Plutarch represents his marriage to Fulvia as a steadying influence. At the festival of the Lupercalia on February 15, 44 B.C., Antony famously offered a royal crown to Caesar in the Forum, an incident that Plutarch ties directly to the conspiracy that soon led to his assassination.*

[9] However, one of the tribunes at the time, Dolabella, a young man who wanted to see constitutional changes, was trying to introduce a decree cancelling all debts, and he set about persuading Antony, who was a friend of his and who was always keen to please the masses, to join him and play a part in trying to get the measure passed. But Asinius and Trebellius advised him to have nothing to do with it, and it so happened that Antony strongly suspected that he had been cuckolded by Dolabella. He was furious about it, threw his wife out of his house (she was his cousin, since she was the daughter of Gaius Antonius, who was consul in the same year as Cicero), sided with Asinius, and took up arms against Dolabella, who had occupied the forum in an attempt to carry his bill by force. The senate voted

that the situation called for the use of arms against Dolabella, and Antony advanced on him. In the ensuing skirmish there were losses on both sides.

The upshot of this was that the masses came to loathe him, while at the same time his general way of life meant that he did not find favor with the upright and moral members of society, as Cicero says. In fact, they intensely disliked him, and were disgusted by his ill-timed bouts of drunkenness, his oppressive extravagance, his cavorting with women, and the way he spent the days asleep or wandering around in a daze with a hangover, and the nights at parties and shows, and amusing himself at the weddings of actors and clowns. At any rate, it is said that he was a guest at the wedding of the actor Hippias, where he drank all night long, and then the next morning, when the people of Rome summoned him to the forum, he presented himself while he was still suffering from over-indulgence and vomited into the cloak one of his friends held out for him. Then there were the actor Sergius, who had a very great deal of influence over him, and Cytheris, a woman from the same school, of whom he was fond; he even used to take her around with him on a litter when he visited various cities, and the litter was accompanied by a retinue as large as his mother's. They were also upset by the sight of his golden goblets being carried around on his excursions out of Rome as if they were part of a ceremonial procession, by the pavilions he set up on his journeys, the extravagant feasts spread out by groves and rivers, the lions yoked to chariots, and the way the houses of upright men and women were used to lodge whores and players of the *sambyke*. They were angered by the thought that Caesar himself was out of Italy, camping out in the open and experiencing great hardship and danger mopping up the remnants of the war, while others were taking advantage of his efforts to revel in luxury and treat their fellow citizens with disrespect.

[10] These habits of Antony's are also generally held to have increased the factional schism and encouraged the troops to turn to acts of terrible violence and rapacity. And so, on his return, Caesar pardoned Dolabella and, once he had been elected to his third consulship, chose Lepidus rather than Antony as his colleague. When Pompey's house was up for sale, Antony bought it, but then became indignant when he was asked to pay up. We have his own words for the fact that this is why he did not accompany Caesar on his African campaign, because he had not been recompensed for his earlier

successes. But it looks as though Caesar eradicated most of Antony's inane and dissolute habits, by letting it be known that his offences had not gone unnoticed.

So Antony gave up that way of life and turned to marriage. He married Fulvia, the former wife of the popular leader Clodius. Now, Fulvia was a woman who cared nothing for spinning or housework, and was not interested in having power over a husband who was just a private citizen, but wanted to rule a ruler and command a commander—and consequently Cleopatra owed Fulvia the fee for teaching Antony to submit to a woman, since she took him over after he had been tamed and trained from the outset to obey women. Not that Antony did not try to get Fulvia too to lighten up, by teasing her and fooling around. For instance, after Caesar's victory in Spain, Antony was one of the large number of people who went out to meet him. Suddenly a rumor reached Italy that Caesar was dead and that his enemies were advancing. Antony turned back to Rome, but dressed himself as a slave, and went to his house after nightfall, saying that he had a letter for Fulvia from Antony. He was shown in to her with his face all covered up. Before taking the letter from him Fulvia asked, in a state of considerable distress, whether Antony was alive. He handed the letter to her without saying a word, and then, as she began to open it, he threw his arms around her and kissed her. Anyway, I have mentioned only this brief tale, but it may serve as an example of many others.

[11] On Caesar's return from Spain all the leading men of Rome made journeys of many days' duration to meet him, but it was Antony who was conspicuously honored by him. When journeying through Italy on his chariot he kept Antony with him as his traveling companion, while Brutus Albinus and Octavian (his sister's son, who was later called Caesar and ruled Rome for a very long time) traveled behind him; and when he was made consul for the fifth time, he immediately chose Antony as his colleague. In fact, however, he planned to resign his consulship in favor of Dolabella, and he went so far as to put this proposal to the senate. Antony spoke out bitterly against the idea; he rained insults down on Dolabella's head and received as good as he gave from the other man, until Caesar was so ashamed at the disruption that he withdrew the motion. Later, when Caesar came forward and proclaimed Dolabella consul, Antony called out that the omens were unfavorable, so Caesar backed down and

abandoned Dolabella, who was mightily displeased. As a matter of fact, Caesar seems to have found Dolabella just as loathsome as Antony did, since we are told that once, when someone was criticizing both of them to him, he said that he was not afraid of these overweight, long-haired men, but of those pale, lean ones—by which he meant Brutus and Cassius, who were soon to conspire against him and assassinate him.

[12] The most plausible pretext for Brutus and Cassius to act was in fact given them accidentally by Antony. It was the time of the festival of the Lycaea at Rome, which the Romans call the Lupercalia, and Caesar, arrayed in his triumphal clothing, was seated on the rostra in the forum watching the runners. At this festival large numbers of well-born young men, and a lot of the city officials too, thoroughly anoint themselves with oil and run here and there in the forum, playfully touching people they meet with hairy pieces of goatskin. Antony was one of the runners, but he ignored tradition and instead ran over to the rostra with a laurel wreath he had woven around a diadem. He was lifted up by his fellow runners and put the diadem on Caesar's head, as if to say that he ought to be king. Caesar made a show of turning aside, which so delighted the people that they burst out into applause. Antony urged it on him again, and again Caesar brushed it off. This contest went on for some time, with a few of Antony's friends applauding his attempts to force the diadem on to Caesar, and the whole assembled populace applauding and shouting out their approval of Caesar's refusals. The surprising thing was that, although the people behaved as though they tolerated the actual condition of being a king's subjects, they found the mere title offensive, as if it meant the end of their freedom. Be that as it may, Caesar stood up angrily on the rostra, pulled his toga away from his neck, and shouted out that he was baring his throat for anyone who wanted to strike him. Some of the tribunes tore the garland off the statue of Caesar where it had been placed, and the people formed a train behind them, shouting out their approval of what they had done; but Caesar had them removed from office.

[13] This incident stiffened the resolve of Brutus and Cassius. While they were recruiting into their scheme those of their friends they could trust, Antony's name came up as a possibility. Everyone else was in favor of Antony, but Trebonius spoke out against him and said that Antony had shared his tent and been his travelling companion at the time when they were going out to

meet Caesar on his return from Spain; he said that he had broached the subject somewhat delicately and cautiously, and that while Antony had understood what he was getting at, he had not approved of the enterprise. Still, Trebonius pointed out, he had not denounced them to Caesar either, but had faithfully kept the conversation to himself. The conspirators next began to wonder whether they should murder Antony after killing Caesar, but Brutus put a stop to this plan by arguing that any deed which is undertaken for the sake of law and justice must be pure and untainted by injustice. But they were concerned about Antony's power and the dignity of his official position, so they gave some of their number the job of dealing with him by detaining him outside the senate-house in conversation on some pressing business, once Caesar had gone inside and the deed was about to be done.

*The turbulent period from the Ides of March in 44 B.C. to the defeat of Brutus and Cassius at Philippi in October of 42 occupies nine densely written chapters (14–22), packed with dramatic events: Antony's funeral speech for Caesar (14), the debut of the new Caesar, his adopted son Octavian (16), Antony's conflict with Cicero (17), the deals that attended the formation of the so-called Second Triumvirate (19), the victory at Philippi, followed by the suicide of Brutus (22). When our selection resumes (23), Antony's attentions were now focused on the East, leaving Italy to Octavian. The fateful meeting with Cleopatra took place in the following year, 41 B.C., at Tarsus in Asia Minor, a scene described by Plutarch in lavish detail (26–27). Antony then accompanied her to Alexandria and spent the winter with her in Egypt. Twins were born later in the year, but Antony was forced to return to Italy following the failure of his brother's revolt against Octavian. Antony made peace with Octavian but was now obliged to cement the renewed relationship by marrying his sister.*

[23] Caesar was so ill that he was not expected to live long, and he now returned to Rome. Antony left Macedonia at the head of a large force and crossed over into Greece in order to raise money from all the eastern provinces, The triumvirs had promised every soldier five thousand drachmas, and so they needed to tighten up the collection of tribute and their ways of raising funds. At first Antony behaved with exemplary civility towards the Greeks: he diverted the less serious side of his character by listening to discussions, attending athletic competitions, and being initiated into religious mysteries, and his decisions were fair. He enjoyed being described as a lover of Greece, though not as much as he enjoyed being called a lover of Athens, and he showered the city with gifts. When the Megarians wanted to show him that they too had fine things to rival Athens, they insisted on his seeing their council-house, After he had climbed up the hill and seen it, they asked him what he thought of it. "Small and rotten," he said. He also took the measurements of the temple of Pythian Apollo, since he intended to complete it; in fact, in a speech to the senate he undertook to do so.

[24] Leaving Lucius Censorinus in charge of Greece, Antony crossed over to Asia and took possession of the wealth there. Kings beat a path to his door, while their wives, rivals in generosity and beauty, let themselves be seduced by him. While Caesar in Rome was exhausting himself with feuds and fighting, Antony was enjoying abundant leisure and peace—so much so that he reverted to his usual way of life. Anaxenor and other players of the lyre, pipe-players like Xuthus, a certain dancer named Metrodorus, and a motley band of similar Asiatic players whose lascivious vulgarity surpassed the pests he had brought from Italy, flooded into his residence and made themselves at home, until the altogether intolerable situation was reached where these activities were all he was interested in, The whole of Asia, like Sophocles' famous city, was filled "both with the smoke of incense, and with hymns of joy and loud laments." At any rate, on his entry into Ephesus he was preceded by women arrayed as Bacchants, and men and boys as Satyrs and Pans, and the city was filled with ivy, thyrsi, harps, reed-pipes, and wind-pipes, all hailing him as Dionysus the gracious benefactor. And this is certainly what he was like in a few cases, though generally he was Dionysus the cruel, the devourer. He used to confiscate property from well-born people and give it as a favor to thugs and flatterers. People often pretended that someone was dead when he was not, asked for his property, and were given it. He gave the estate of a man from Magnesia to a cook who had earned his esteem, we are told, for a single meal. Eventually, when he was imposing a second round of tribute on the cities of Asia, Hybreas summoned up the courage to speak out for all Asia. His rhetorical style was low, and appealed to Antony's taste. "If you can take tribute twice in a single year," Hybreas said, "can you also create two summers for us and two harvests?" Then, in a bold and effective conclusion, because Asia had provided Antony with 200,000 talents, he said, "If

you haven't received this money, you should demand it from those who took it; but if you did get it and you no longer have it, we're in a lot of trouble."

These words of his affected Antony deeply because he was unaware of most of what went on, not so much because he was lazy as because he was so straightforward that he trusted the people around him. There was a side to him that was naïve and slow off the mark, although when he did come to realize his mistakes his remorse was profound and he would make a full confession to those he had wronged by his thoughtlessness. He never did things by halves in making compensation or in taking revenge, but he had the reputation of being more likely to go too far when doing a favor than when meting out punishment. Also, his disrespectful jokes and jibes did have the redeeming feature that one could return the jibe with equal disrespect: he enjoyed being laughed at just as much as he enjoyed laughing at others. But this trait of his was invariably his undoing, because he was incapable of imagining that people who were so candid when making a joke were really concerned to flatter him, and so he was easily caught by their compliments. He had no idea that there are people who, so to speak, temper the cloying taste of their flattery with the sharp seasoning of candor; these people use the outspoken remarks they pass over their cups as a means of making their pliancy and submissiveness in affairs of state suggest not sycophancy, but rational submission to superior wisdom.

[25] For a man such as Antony, then, there could be nothing worse than the onset of his love for Cleopatra. It awoke a number of feelings that had previously been lying quietly buried within him, stirred them up into a frenzy, and obliterated and destroyed the last vestiges of goodness, the final redeeming features that were still holding out in his nature. This is how he was caught. While he was preparing to make war on Parthia, he wrote to Cleopatra, ordering her to come to meet him in Cilicia, to answer the charge of having helped Cassius with substantial contributions towards his war effort. However, as soon as Dellius, Antony's messenger, saw what she looked like and observed her eloquence and argumentative cunning, he realized that the idea of harming a woman like her would never occur to Antony, and that she would come to occupy a very important place in his life. He therefore set about ingratiating himself with the Egyptian and encouraging her to come to Cilicia "dressed up in all her finery," to borrow Homer's

words; and he allayed her worries about Antony, describing him as the most agreeable and kind leader in the world. Since she believed Dellius and also drew on the evidence of her past love-affairs in her youth with Caesar and with Gnaeus the son of Pompey, she readily expected to vanquish Antony. After all, Caesar and Gnaeus Pompey had known her when she was no more than an unworldly girl, but she would be going to Antony at the age when the beauty of a woman is at its most dazzling and her intellectual powers are at their height. So she equipped herself with plenty of gifts and money, and the kind of splendid paraphernalia one would expect someone in her exalted position, from a prosperous kingdom, to take. Above all, however, she went there relying on herself and on the magical arts and charms of her person.

[26] Although she received a number of letters from both Antony and his friends demanding her presence, she treated him with such disdain and scorn that she sailed up the river Cydnus on a golden prowed barge, with sails of purple outspread and rowers pulling on silver oars to the sound of a reed-pipe blended with wind-pipes and lyres. She herself reclined beneath a gold-embroidered canopy, adorned like a painting of Aphrodite, flanked by slave-boys, each made to resemble Eros, who cooled her with their fans. Likewise her most beautiful female slaves, dressed as Nereids and Graces, were stationed at the rudders and the ropes. The wonderful smell of numerous burning spices filled the banks of the river. Some people formed an escort for her on either side all the way from the river, while others came down from the city to see the spectacle. The crowd filling the city square trickled away, until at last Antony himself was left alone, seated on a dais. The notion spread throughout the city that Aphrodite had come in revelry to Dionysus, for the good of Asia. Antony sent her an invitation to dinner, but she thought it preferable that he should come to her. Without a moment's hesitation he agreed, because he wanted to show her that he was a good-natured, friendly sort of person. On his arrival he found preparations that beggared description, but he was especially struck by the amazing number of lights. There are said to have been so many lights hanging on display all over the place, and ordered and disposed at such angles to one another and in such arrangements—some forming squares, others circles—that the sight was one of rare and remarkable beauty.

[27] The next day it was his turn to entertain her with a banquet. He desperately wanted to outdo the brilliance and thoroughness of her preparations, but it was in precisely these two respects that he failed and was defeated by her. However, he was the first to make fun of the unappetizing meagreness of what he had to offer. Cleopatra could see from Antony's jokes that there was a wide streak of the coarse soldier in him, so she adopted this same manner towards him, and now in an unrestrained and brazen fashion. For, according to my sources, in itself her beauty was not absolutely without parallel, not the kind to astonish those who saw her; but her presence exerted an inevitable fascination, and her physical attractions, combined with the persuasive charm of her conversation and the aura she somehow projected around herself in company, did have a certain ability to stimulate others. The sound of her voice was also charming and she had a facility with languages that enabled her to turn her tongue, like a many-stringed instrument, to any language she wanted, with the result that it was extremely rare for her to need a translator in her meetings with foreigners; in most cases she could answer their questions herself, whether they were Ethiopians, Trogodytae, Hebrews, Arabs, Syrians, Medes, or Parthians. In fact, she was said to have mastered a lot of other languages too, whereas the kings of Egypt before her had not even bothered to learn Egyptian, and some of them even abandoned their Macedonian dialect.

[28] She abducted Antony so successfully that while his wife Fulvia was fighting Caesar in Rome in defense of his affairs, and while there was a Parthian army hovering near Mesopotamia, with Labienus newly appointed by the Parthian king's generals as commander-in-chief for the planned invasion of Syria, he was carried off by her to Alexandria where he indulged in the pastimes and pleasures of a young man of leisure, and spent and squandered on luxuries that commodity which Antiphon called the most costly in the world—namely, time. They formed a kind of club called the Society of Inimitable Livers, and every day one of them had to entertain the rest. They spent incredible, disproportionate amounts of money. At any rate, Philotas of Amphissa, the doctor, used to tell my grandfather Lamprias that he was in Alexandria at the time, learning his professional skills, and that he became friendly with one of the royal cooks. Philotas, who was a young man then, was persuaded by his friend the cook to come and see the extravagance involved in the preparations

for a feast. So he was surreptitiously brought into the kitchen and when he saw all the food, including eight wild boars roasting on spits, he expressed his surprise at the number of guests who were going to be entertained. The cook laughed and said that there were not going to be many for dinner, only about twelve, but that every dish which was served had to be perfect and it only took a moment for something to be spoiled. He explained that Antony might call for food immediately and then a short while later might perhaps change tack and ask for a cup of wine, or get interrupted by a discussion. And so, he said, they prepared many meals, not just one, since they could never guess when the exact moment was going to be.

This was the story Philotas used to tell. Some years later, he said, he used to attend Antony's eldest son, whose mother was Fulvia, and often used to join him and his friends for dinner, when the young man was not eating with his father. On one occasion, a certain doctor was becoming rather outspoken and was putting the other guests off their meal, until Philotas shut him up with the following sophism: "Anyone with a slight fever needs the application of cold; but anyone who has a fever has at least a slight fever; it follows that anyone with a fever needs the application of cold." The man was so taken aback that he stopped talking, but their young host was delighted. He laughed and said, pointing to a table covered with numerous large goblets, "Philotas, I'd like you to have all of these." Philotas acknowledged his goodwill, but was not at all sure that a mere boy like him had the right to give such a valuable gift; a short while later, however, one of the slaves brought him the goblets sewn into a bag and asked him to put his seal on it. When Philotas refused and expressed a reluctance to take them, the man said, "Don't be so stupid. There's no need to worry. Don't you realize that this is a present from the son of Antony and that he can give away this much gold if he likes? However, I would suggest that you let us swap you the cups for their worth in money, because it's not impossible that his father might miss some of the cups, which are antiques, valued for their craftsmanship." These are the stories Philotas used to tell whenever the opportunity arose, according to my grandfather.

[29] Cleopatra did not restrict her flattery to Plato's four categories, but employed many more forms of it. She always found some fresh pleasure and delight to apply, whether he was in a serious or a frivolous mood, and so she kept up his training relentlessly, without

letting up either by night or by day. She was with him when he was playing dice, drinking, and hunting; she watched him while he exercised with his weapons; at night when he stood at the doors and windows of ordinary folk and mocked the people inside, she wandered aimlessly through the streets by his side. During these escapades she would dress as a serving-girl, because Antony used to do his best to make himself look like a slave, which would constantly earn him a volley of scorn and not infrequently blows too before he returned home, despite the fact that most people suspected who he was. However, the Alexandrians loved the way he played the fool and joined in his games, though not to a disproportionate or coarse extent. They liked him and said that he adopted the mask of tragedy for the Romans, but the mask of comedy for them.

It would be quite idiotic for me to describe most of the pranks he got up to then, but once, when he was out fishing, he got cross because he was having no luck and Cleopatra was there. So he told the fishermen to swim down and secretly attach one of the fish which had already been caught to his hook. He hauled in two or three fish like this, but the Egyptian queen knew perfectly well what was going on. She pretended to be impressed, but told her friends all about it, and invited them to come and watch the next day. So there were a lot of people on the fishing-boats, and when Antony had cast out she told one of her own slaves to swim over to his hook first and to stick on to it a preserved fish from the Euxine Sea. Antony thought he had caught something and pulled it in, to everyone's great amusement, of course. "Imperator," she said, "hand your rod over to the kings of Pharos and Canobius. It is your job to hunt cities, kingdoms, and continents."

[30] While Antony was occupied with this kind of childish nonsense, two messages reached him. The first, from Rome, told how his brother Lucius and his wife Fulvia had first fallen out with each other, but had then made war unsuccessfully on Caesar and fled into exile from Italy. The other message was just as bleak: it told how Labienus and his army of Parthians were conquering all Asia from the Euphrates and Syria up to Lydia and Ionia. Like a man struggling to wake up on the morning after a drunken night, Antony set out to resist the Parthians and had reached Phoenicia when he received a thoroughly miserable letter from Fulvia, as a result of which he headed for Italy with a fleet of two hundred ships. During the course of the voyage, however, he picked up some exiled friends and learnt

that the war had been Fulvia's fault: not only was she a headstrong woman who liked to dabble in politics, but she hoped to draw Antony away from Cleopatra by stirring up trouble in Italy. Coincidentally, however, Fulvia fell ill and died in Sicyon while she was on her way to him by sea, which created an even better opportunity for reconciliation with Caesar. When he reached Italy, and Caesar made it plain that he did not blame him for anything, while at the same time Antony himself was inclined to hold Fulvia responsible for the crimes with which he was charged, their friends refused to let them look too closely at the whys and wherefores. They arranged a truce between the two of them and divided up the areas of command, with the Ionian Sea forming a boundary such that everything to the east went to Antony and everything to the west to Caesar, while they let Lepidus have Africa and organized matters so that when neither Antony nor Caesar wanted to be consul, the post should go to their friends one by one.

[31] While this all seemed fine, it needed firmer assurances, and fortune provided them in the person of Octavia, who was Caesar's elder sister, although they did not have the same mother, since hers was Ancharia, while his was Atia. Caesar was very fond of his sister, who was, we are told, a marvel of womankind. Her husband, Gaius Marcellus, had recently died, so she was a widow; and Antony was generally held to be a widower, now that Fulvia had passed away, since, although he made no attempt to deny that he had Cleopatra, he refused to call her his wife. To this extent his rational mind was still resisting his love for the Egyptian. Everyone wanted to see this marriage take place, since they hoped that once Octavia was united with Antony and had won the place in his affections one would expect of a woman like her, with all her dignity and intelligence, as well as her great beauty, she would prove to be the saviour and moderator of all Rome's affairs. So when both men had agreed on this course of action, they went up to Rome and married Octavia to Antony, even though by Roman law a woman was not allowed to remarry within ten months of her husband's death. But in their case the senate passed a decree waiving the time limit.

*Antony returned to the East with his new wife, Octavia, but fresh tensions with her brother caused him to return to Italy in 37 B.C., where he met Octavian at Tarentum and the Triumvirate was renewed for another five years. This time when he departed he left Octavia behind and resumed his affair with Cleopatra on a firmer basis. In*

*36 B.C. the need to add to his prestige drove Antony to invade the Parthian empire, the great power in the East that represented an irresistible target for Roman ambitions. Caesar's plans to invade Parthia had been cut short by his assassination, and now Antony would make good on them. But the campaign was disastrous for Antony, even though it showcased his inspiring leadership in defeat. Plutarch describes the campaign on a lavish scale (37–52), then moves swiftly over the intervening years to the now inevitable conflict between Antony and Octavian. The decisive clash came at Actium on the western coast of Greece, where the narrative resumes at the point where Antony, having lost confidence in his ability to win on land, determined to face the enemy at sea. After his escape, Antony made his way back to Egypt, where he holed up on the island of Pharos off Alexandria and likened himself to the legendary misanthrope Timon of Athens (70). The selection resumes with the final days of Antony and Cleopatra in Alexandria, which soon became the stuff of legend. Antony's allies fell away from him one by one in the aftermath of Actium, and on August 30 of the following year he committed suicide as Octavian entered the city, dying in Cleopatra's burial chamber as she wept for him (77). The remainder of the Life belongs to her, as Plutarch describes her capture by Octavian (79) and his triumphant entry into Alexandria (80). Antony's son Antyllus is murdered, as is Cleopatra's son by Julius Caesar, but Octavian allows her to bury Antony. Cleopatra's suicide is preceded by a meeting with Octavian himself, in which she dupes him into believing that she intends to go on living (83). The narrative concludes with an anticlimactic account of the fates of Antony's surviving descendants.*

[71] Canidius brought Antony the news of the loss of his forces at Actium in person, rather than entrusting it to anyone else, and at the same time Antony heard that Herod of Judaea had gone over to Caesar, taking with him a number of legions and cohorts. Reports also began to arrive that the defection to Caesar by the client kings was becoming general, and that his forces outside Egypt were all falling apart. None of this news upset him, however: it was as if he was pleased to have relinquished his hopes, since that meant he could also relinquish his cares. He left his beach-house, which he called the Timoneum, found accommodation in Cleopatra's palace, and then set the city on a course of eating, drinking, and displays of generosity. For instance, he had the son of Cleopatra and Caesar enrolled among the young

men who had come of age and conferred the *toga virilis* on Antyllus, his son by Fulvia, and to mark the occasion Alexandria was filled for many days with symposia and revelry and celebrations. Antony and Cleopatra dissolved their club, the Society of Inimitable Livers, and formed another one instead. This new club was just as devoted to sensuality, self-indulgence, and extravagance as the other one, but they called it the Society of Partners in Death. Their friends registered themselves as those who would die together, and they all spent their time in a hedonistic round of banquets. Cleopatra was putting together a collection of various types of lethal poisons, and she tested each of them to see which of them was painless, by giving them to prisoners who had been sentenced to death. When she saw that the fast-acting ones brought a swift but painful death, whereas the gentler ones were slow to take effect, she started experimenting with wild animals, and watched as her men set various creatures on one prisoner after another. This became her daily routine, and she found that in almost every case only the bite of the asp induced a sleepy lethargy without any convulsions or groans; their faces covered with a sheen of light sweat and their senses dulled, the men painlessly lost the use of their limbs and resisted all attempts to stir them and wake them up, just like people who are fast asleep.

[72] They also sent a delegation to Caesar in Asia to ask, on Cleopatra's behalf, that her children might be allowed to inherit the rulership of Egypt, and, on Antony's behalf, that he might live as a private citizen in Athens, if Caesar did not want him to do so in Egypt. Because they had so few friends left, and were in any case mistrustful of them because so many others had defected, they sent the children's tutor, Euphronius, as their spokesman. Alexas of Laodicea, who had been introduced into Roman society by Timagenes, had formerly been the most influential Greek in Antony's entourage—and had also been the most violent of the tools Cleopatra had set to work against Antony, to eradicate any thoughts he might entertain in Octavia's favor. But after he had been sent to King Herod to curb his impulse to defect, he had stayed there and betrayed Antony. Later, he had the effrontery to seek an audience with Caesar, relying on Herod's influence to keep him safe. But Herod was no help to him at all, and he was immediately thrown into prison and taken in chains to his homeland, where he was put to death on Caesar's orders. And so Antony was repaid while he was still alive for Alexas' treachery.

[73] Caesar rejected Antony's request, and told Cleopatra that she would meet with decent treatment provided she either put Antony to death or threw him out of Egypt. He also sent, as a personal messenger from himself to Cleopatra, a freedman called Thyrsus, who was a man of considerable intelligence, with the ability to speak persuasively on a young commander's behalf to a haughty woman with an astonishingly high opinion of her own beauty. Thyrsus had longer meetings with her than any of the other delegates, and was treated with remarkable respect, which made Antony wonder what was going on. In the end he seized Thyrsus and had him flogged, before letting him return to Caesar with a letter from him, saying that Thyrsus' arrogant and supercilious ways had infuriated him at a time when his temper was short because of all his troubles. "If you find what I've done intolerable," he said, "you've got my freedman, Hipparchus. You can string him up and flog him, and then we'll be quits." Cleopatra next tried to redeem herself in Antony's eyes and allay his suspicions by paying him an excessive amount of solicitous attention. She celebrated her own birthday in an unpretentious way that suited their unfortunate circumstances, but she marked his with extremely flashy and costly festivities. In fact, a lot of the guests arrived at the banquet poor, but left rich. Meanwhile, however, Caesar was receiving a stream of letters from Agrippa in Rome urging him to return, since affairs there demanded his presence.

[74] This meant that war was postponed for the time being, but at the end of the winter Caesar again made his way through Syria while his commanders advanced through Africa. Pelusium fell, and despite a rumor that Seleucus had surrendered the city with Cleopatra's connivance, she let Antony put Seleucus' wife and children to death. By now Cleopatra had built for herself, near the temple of Isis, a wonderfully imposing and beautiful tomb and monument, and she collected there the most valuable of the royal treasures—gold, silver, emeralds, pearls, ebony, ivory, cinnamon—and also a great deal of firewood and tow. This made Caesar worried about the possibility of the woman getting desperate and burning up all the treasure, so he was constantly sending her friendly messages designed to keep her hopes up, even while he was advancing on the city with his army. Finally, he took up a position near the Hippodrome, but Antony came out against him and fought a brilliant battle, in which Caesar's cavalry was routed and had to retreat back to their camp with

Antony in pursuit. Antony felt good after this victory. He marched into the palace, went up to Cleopatra with his armor still on, kissed her, and introduced to her the man from his army who had fought with the greatest distinction. As the prize for valor, Cleopatra gave the man a golden breastplate and helmet—which he took with him when he deserted over to Caesar's camp in the night.

[75] Antony repeated to Caesar his earlier challenge to single combat, but Caesar replied that there were all sorts of routes for Antony to take to death. Antony realized that there was no better way for him to die than in battle, so he decided to launch a combined land and sea attack on Caesar. At dinner, we hear, he told his house slaves to serve him food and wine with a more lavish hand than usual, since there was no way of knowing whether they would be able to do so tomorrow, or whether they would be serving other masters, while he lay a lifeless, non-existent husk. When he saw that these words of his had brought tears to the eyes of his friends, he told them that he would not be leading them into the battle, since what he wanted from it was a glorious death rather than life and victory. Round about the middle of that night, the story goes, with fearful anticipation of the future keeping the city quiet and subdued, there were suddenly heard the harmonious sounds of all kinds of musical instruments, and the loud voices of a crowd of people making their way with Bacchic cries and prancing feet; it was as if a troop of Dionysian revellers were noisily making their way out of the city. Their course seemed to lie more or less through the center of the city and towards the outer gate which faced the enemy forces, where the noise climaxed and then died down. The general interpretation of this portent was that Antony was being deserted by the god with whom he had always felt a strong similarity and affinity.

[76] At daybreak Antony posted his land forces on the high ground in front of the city and watched as his ships put to sea and bore down on the enemy fleet. Since he expected to see his fleet win, he kept the land forces inactive. When his crews got close to the enemy, however, they raised their oars to salute Caesar's men, who returned their greeting. At this signal Antony's men changed sides, and all the ships combined to form a single fleet and sailed directly for the city. No sooner had Antony been confronted with this spectacle than his cavalry abandoned him and went over to the enemy. Following the defeat of his infantry, Antony retreated

back to the city, crying out that Cleopatra had betrayed him to his enemies, when he had made war on them in the first place only for her sake. Cleopatra was afraid of what he might do in his anger and desperation, so she took refuge in her tomb, released the portcullises, which were reinforced by bolts and bars, and sent men to Antony with instructions to tell him that she was dead. Antony believed this report and said to himself, "Antony, why wait? Fortune has robbed you of the only remaining reason for life to be dear to you." He went into his room, where he undid his breastplate and took it off. "Cleopatra!" he cried. "It is not the loss of you that hurts, because I shall be joining you very soon. What hurts is that for all my great stature as a commander I have been shown to have less courage than a woman."

Now, Antony had a faithful slave called Eros, to whom he had long ago entrusted the job of killing him in an emergency. He now asked him to keep his word. Eros drew his sword and held it out as though to strike Antony, but then averted his face and killed himself. Seeing Eros on the ground at his feet, Antony said, "You have done well, Eros. Although you were not able to do it yourself, you have taught me what I must do." He stabbed himself in his belly and fell back on the couch. But the blow was not immediately fatal, and his position on his back on the couch stopped the blood pouring from the wound. When he recovered consciousness, then, he asked the people there to finish him off, but they ran out of the room, leaving him crying out and writhing in pain, until the scribe Diomedes came from Cleopatra. She wanted him brought to her in the tomb.

[77] At the news that she was still alive, Antony eagerly ordered his slaves to lift him up, and he was carried in their arms to the door of her burial chamber. Cleopatra refused to open the door, but she appeared at a window and let down ropes and lines, with which the slaves made Antony secure. Then Cleopatra and two ladies-in-waiting, the only people she had allowed into the tomb with her, hauled him up. Witnesses say that this was the most pitiful sight imaginable. Up he went, covered with blood and in the throes of death, stretching his arms out towards her as he dangled in the air beside the wall of the tomb. It was not an easy job for a woman: clinging to the rope, with the strain showing on her face, Cleopatra struggled to bring the line up, while on the ground below people called out their encouragement and shared her anguish. At last she got him inside and laid him down. She tore her clothes in grief over him, beat her breast with her hands, and raked it with her nails. She smeared some of his blood on her face, and called him her master, husband, and imperator. For a while her pity for him almost made her forget her own troubles. But Antony asked her to calm down and give him a drink of wine: perhaps he was thirsty, or perhaps he was hoping for a speedier release. After drinking, he advised her to look to her own safety, if she could do so without disgrace, and of all Caesar's companions to trust Proculeius most; and he begged her not to mourn his recent misfortune, but to think of all the good luck he had enjoyed and count him happy. After all, supreme fame and power had been his, and now he had been honorably defeated by a fellow Roman.

[78] He had just breathed his last when Proculeius arrived on a mission from Caesar. After Antony had stabbed himself and been taken off to Cleopatra, one of his bodyguards, Dercetaeus, had picked up the sword, hidden it under his clothing, and made his way stealthily out of the building. He ran to Caesar and, with the bloody sword as evidence, was the first to bring the news of Antony's death. When Caesar heard the news, he withdrew further into his tent and wept for a man who had been his brother-in-law, his colleague in office, and his partner in numerous military and political enterprises. Then he took their correspondence, called in his friends, and read the letters out to them, to show that while he had written politely and fairly, Antony had always been rude and arrogant in his replies. After this he dispatched Proculeius on his mission, which was to take Cleopatra alive, if possible, not only because he was worried about her treasure, but also because he thought it would add significantly to the glory of his triumph if he were to bring her back with him. She refused to give herself up to Proculeius, but she did talk to him, after he had approached the burial chamber and was standing outside one of the doors at ground level, through which their voices could carry, for all that they remained securely bolted and barred. The gist of their conversation was that she asked for her children to be allowed to inherit the kingdom, and he told her that she could trust Caesar absolutely, with no need to worry about a thing.

[79] Proculeius looked the place over and returned to deliver his report to Caesar. Then Gallus was sent to engage Cleopatra in conversation again. He went up to the door and deliberately prolonged the discussion. Meanwhile, Proculeius put a ladder up against the wall and climbed in through the window which the women

had used to bring Antony in by. He lost no time in going down, accompanied by two slaves he had brought with him, to the door where Cleopatra was standing listening to Gallus. One of the two women who had been locked inside the burial chamber with Cleopatra shouted out, "Oh no, Cleopatra, they're going to get you alive!" Cleopatra turned around, saw Proculeius, and made an attempt to stab herself with the little dagger—the kind robbers use—that she happened to have tucked into her belt. But Proculeius ran up, wrapped his arms around her, and said, "No, Cleopatra, that would be wrong. It would be a crime against you, and it would be a crime against Caesar, since you would deprive him of an excellent opportunity to display his kindness, and you would be implicitly accusing the most even-tempered of leaders of dishonesty and intransigence." While saying this he took her dagger away from her and shook out her clothes to see if she had any poison hidden there. Another person Caesar sent was a freedman, Epaphroditus, with instructions to keep a very close watch on her to make sure she stayed alive, but otherwise to do everything to keep her comfortable and happy.

[80] Now Caesar himself rode into the city, conversing with the philosopher Arius, whom he had riding on his right: this was a way of immediately raising Arius' profile in Alexandria and of making people admire him, as someone who was held in such conspicuously high regard by Caesar. He entered the Gymnasium and ascended a dais that had been built for him. The people there were terrified out of their wits and were prostrating themselves before him, but he told them to get up and said that he gave the city of Alexandria an absolute pardon, for three reasons: first, in memory of its founder, Alexander; second, because he admired the beauty and grandeur of the city; and, third, as a favor to his friend Arius. In addition to receiving this signal honor from Caesar, Arius also successfully interceded for the lives of a large number of people, including Philostratus, whose skill at impromptu speaking was unrivalled by any other sophist of the time, and who illegitimately claimed affiliation with the Academy. This led Caesar to loathe the man's character and to refuse to listen to his pleas, so with his long white beard and draped in a dark cloak he used to traipse along behind Arius, constantly reciting the line, "If the wise are wise they save the wise." When Caesar found out what he was doing, he gave him his pardon, but not so much because he wanted to relieve Philostratus' fear, as because he did not want people to think badly of Arius.

[81] Among Antony's children, his son by Fulvia, Antyllus, was betrayed by his tutor, Theodorus, and beheaded. During the execution Theodorus stole a very valuable gem which the boy used to wear around his neck and sewed it into his belt; he denied the theft, but was found out and crucified. Cleopatra's children were kept under lock and key along with their servants, but otherwise had a relaxed regime. Caesarion, however, who was rumored to be Caesar's son, had been sent abroad by his mother, plentifully supplied with money, to travel to India via Ethiopia. But Rhodon—another tutor from the same mold as Theodorus—persuaded him to return, on the grounds that Caesar had invited him back to take up his kingdom. The story goes that when Caesar was wondering what to do with him, Arius remarked, "A plurality of Caesars is not a good thing." And so Caesarion was put to death by Caesar, but this happened later, after Cleopatra's death.

[82] Permission to bury Antony was sought by a number of kings and commanders, but Caesar would not deprive Cleopatra of the body, and she gave it a sumptuous, royal burial with her own hands. Caesar allowed her every facility she wanted for the occasion. But as a result of all the mental and physical suffering she had endured—her breast was inflamed and ulcerated where she had beaten it in her grief—she contracted a fever, and she welcomed this as a chance to stop eating and to release herself from life without anyone interfering. One of her close friends, Olympus, was a doctor, and she confided the truth to him. He became her confidant and helped her waste her body, as he himself has recorded in the account he published of these events. But Caesar became suspicious, and used threats and her fears for her children as a weapon against her. These threats and fears undermined her resolution as if they were siege engines, until she put her body in the hands of those who wanted to tend it and care for it.

[83] A few days later Caesar made a personal visit to talk to her and put her mind at ease. She was lying dejectedly on a straw mattress, but as soon as he came in she leapt up, despite wearing only a tunic, and prostrated herself on the ground before him. Her hair and face were unkempt and wild, her voice trembled, and her eyes were puffy and swollen; there was even plenty of visible evidence of the way she had lacerated her breast. In short, her body seemed to be in just as bad a state as her mind. Nevertheless, her famous charisma and the power of her beauty had not been completely

extinguished, but shone through her wretchedness from somewhere inside and showed in the play of her features. Caesar told her to recline on her mattress, while he sat down beside her. She began to try to justify her actions, blaming them on necessity and saying that she was afraid of Antony, but Caesar raised objections and disproved every point, so soon she adopted the pitiful, pleading tone of a woman who wanted nothing more than to go on living. In the end, however, she gave him an inventory she had taken of all her valuable possessions—but one of her stewards, a man called Seleucus, proved that she was making away with some of her things and hiding them. At this, she leapt to her feet, grabbed Seleucus by the hair, and pummeled his face with her fists, until Caesar stopped her with a smile. "But Caesar," she said, "it just isn't right, is it? You don't mind coming to talk to me even when I'm in such a terrible state, and yet my slaves denounce me for keeping aside a little of my jewelry. And I'm not even doing it for myself, of course—I'm too wretched for that. It's so that I can give a few things to Octavia and your Livia, and ask them to make you more compassionate and kind towards me." Caesar liked this speech of hers and was completely convinced that life was still dear to her. Before going away, he told her that he left it up to her to look after her valuables and that he would treat her more gloriously than she could ever have expected. He was sure he had taken her in, when actually it was she who had taken him in.

[84] One of Caesar's companions was a young man of distinction called Cornelius Dolabella. He was quite attracted to Cleopatra and so, when she asked him to let her know what was going on, as a favor to her, he got a message secretly to her with information that Caesar was planning to break camp and march by land through Syria, and had decided to send her and her children away in two days' time. As soon as she heard this news, she asked Caesar for permission to pour libations for Antony. He said she could, and so, accompanied by her ladies-in-waiting, she was carried to his tomb. She fell on his coffin and said, "Antony, my darling, just recently I buried you with hands that were still free, but now I pour libations as a prisoner of war. As a captive, I cannot disfigure this body of mine with the rites of mourning and lamentation; my body is a slave, closely watched and preserved for the triumph to be celebrated over your defeat. So expect no further honors or libations: you will receive no more from Cleopatra now that she is a slave. In life nothing could come between

us, but now in death it seems that we will change places: you, the Roman, will lie here, and I—ah, poor me, I will lie in Italian soil, and never possess more of your land than that. I do not appeal to the gods here, because they have let us down, but I implore you, by any of the gods of the underworld with the power and potency to grant my prayer, not to abandon your wife while she is alive, and not to let me be the centerpiece of a triumph celebrated over you. No, bury me here in this tomb beside you, knowing that the worst and most terrible of all the countless miseries I have borne has been this brief period of life without you."

[85] After this lament she garlanded and embraced the coffin, and then ordered her slaves to prepare a bath for her. Once she had finished bathing, she reclined on her couch and proceeded to eat a spectacular midday meal, in the middle of which a man arrived from the countryside with a basket. The guards asked what he had brought, so he opened the lid and showed that under the leaves the basket was filled with figs. He smiled when the guards expressed astonishment at the size and beauty of the fruit, and asked them to help themselves. They were not at all suspicious of him, and they told him he could go in. After her meal Cleopatra took a writing tablet which she had already written on and sealed, and sent it to Caesar. Then she ordered everyone out of the room except her two ladies-in-waiting, and shut the door behind them.

Once Caesar had unsealed the writing-tablet, he found inside a passionate and emotional plea that she should be buried with Antony. It did not take him long to guess what she had done. His first thought was to go there in person and see if he could help, but then he ordered some of his men to go as quickly as possible and investigate the situation. But the tragedy had unfolded rapidly. His men ran there and found the guards unaware that anything had happened. They opened the door, and saw Cleopatra lying dead on a golden couch, dressed like a queen, with one of her two ladies-in-waiting, Iras, dying at her feet. The other, Charmion, was so weak that she could hardly stay upright or stop her head from slumping forward, but she was trying to arrange the diadem which adorned Cleopatra's brow. One of the men hissed in anger, "A fine day's work, Charmion!," and she replied: "Yes, nothing could be finer. It is no more than this lady, the descendant of so many kings, deserves." These were her last words, and she fell where she was, beside the couch.

[86] The asp is said to have been smuggled in with the basket of figs and leaves, hidden underneath them,

exactly as Cleopatra had commanded; and the story goes that the creature struck at her body without her being aware of it. Then, after removing some of the figs, she spotted the snake and said, "Here it is, then," and made sure that the snake could bite her naked arm. However, others say that the asp was kept shut inside a water jar, and that as Cleopatra was trying to get it to come out by provoking it with a golden distaff, it lunged at her and fastened on to her arm. But no one knows the true story: after all, it was also said that she carried poison around inside a hollow hairpin, which was hidden in her hair, despite the fact that there were no marks on her body, and there were no other indications that she had taken poison either. However, there were also no sightings of the snake inside the room, although people said they saw its trail on the part of the shore overlooked by the windows of the room. Some people do in fact say that two faint puncture marks were seen, though they were barely visible, on Cleopatra's arm. This is the version Caesar seems to have believed, because he had a picture of Cleopatra carried along in his triumphal procession, with the snake clinging on to her. Anyway, these are the various versions of what happened.

Caesar was annoyed that the woman was dead, but, impressed by her nobility, he gave orders that her body was to be buried alongside Antony's with the kind of splendid ceremony suitable for a queen. He also arranged for her attendants to receive an honorable burial. Cleopatra was 39 years old when she died, and she had been queen for twenty-two of these years, with Antony as her co-ruler for fourteen of them. Some writers have Antony aged 56, others 53, at the time of his death. Antony's statues were pulled down, but Cleopatra's stayed in place, because one of her friends, a man called Archibius, paid Caesar a thousand talents to keep them from sharing the fate of Antony's statues.

[87] Antony left seven children by three wives. Only the oldest, Antyllus, was put to death by Caesar, while Octavia took in the rest and brought them up along with his children by her. She arranged for Cleopatra, his daughter by Cleopatra, to be married to Juba, one of the most cultured kings ever, and thanks to her Antonius, the son of Antony and Fulvia, became so important that while Caesar's particular favorites were Agrippa and then Livia's sons, the third place was held to be, and genuinely was, occupied by Antonius.

Now, Octavia had had two daughters by Marcellus, and one son, also called Marcellus. Caesar adopted this Marcellus as his son, and had him marry his daughter as well, while he arranged for Agrippa to marry one of the two daughters. But Marcellus died tragically soon after his marriage, and Caesar was finding it difficult to choose another trustworthy son-in-law from among his friends. Under these circumstances, Octavia proposed that Agrippa should divorce his present wife and marry Caesar's daughter instead. Caesar thought this was a good idea, and then she won Agrippa round to it too, so she took back her daughter and married her to Antonius, while Agrippa married Caesar's daughter.

Of the two surviving daughters from Antony's marriage to Octavia, one was married to Domitius Ahenobarbus, and the other—Antonia, famous for her virtue and her beauty—was married to Drusus, who was the son of Livia and therefore Caesar's stepson. The sons of Drusus and Antonia were Germanicus and Claudius: Claudius later became emperor, and of Germanicus' children, Gaius reigned for a few brief and demented years before being put to death along with his children and wife, while Agrippina had a son, Lucius Domitius, by Ahenobarbus, before marrying Claudius Caesar. Claudius adopted her son and changed his name to Nero Germanicus; and Nero Germanicus became emperor in my lifetime. He killed his mother and came very close to destroying the Roman Empire with his capricious and insane ways. He was the fifth in descent from Antony.

# AFTERWORD

Plutarch has always been a popular author, and his impact on literature in Latin was notable in the years after his death, when Roman writers were once again deeply engaged with Greek culture. It was his philosophical works that were read, however; not surprisingly, the *Lives* were of less interest to Latin readers who had access to biographies in their own language by writers such as Varro (116–27 B.C.), Nepos (ca. 110–24 B.C.), and Plutarch's contemporary Suetonius. In the next generation the

Antonine scholar Aulus Gellius (born ca. A.D. 125–30) mined Plutarch's philosophical works for tidbits to include in his miscellany, *Attic Nights*. Gellius was introduced to Plutarch's writings by his teacher, the philosopher Favorinus, who was also an associate of Fronto, the future emperor Marcus Aurelius's tutor. Such was the prestige of Plutarch during this period that Apuleius represents Lucius, the hero of his novel *Metamorphoses* (or *The Golden Ass*), as a direct descendant of "the illustrious Plutarch." In the world of Greek letters and philosophy, Plutarch's influence was immense, and he continued to be an important author for the Neoplatonists of late antiquity, even though for the most part they rejected his views on metaphysics. Early Christian authors writing in Greek, such as Clement of Alexandria (ca. A.D. 150–216) and Eusebius (ca. A.D. 260–339), made frequent allusion to Plutarch, whose morals and theology were considered as foreshadowing Christianity. Plutarch remained a classic in the Greek East, where his works were standard school texts. The Byzantine historian and poet Agathias (ca. A.D. 532–80) wrote an epigram for a statue of Plutarch, which was later translated by Dryden:

> Chaeronean Plutarch, to thy deathless praise
> Doth martial Rome this grateful statue raise,
> Because both Greece and she thy fame have shared
> (Their heroes written and their lives compared).
> But thou thyself couldst never write thy own;
> Their lives have parallels, but thine has none.

During the revival of classical scholarship at Byzantium in the thirteenth century, Plutarch found a particular admirer in the great scholar Maximus Planudes (ca. 1255–1305), who was devoted to him and in one letter writes, "I have decided to copy Plutarch's works because I greatly like the man." This was no mean feat, given the bulk of Plutarch's surviving writings, and Planudes's work figured largely in the transmission of the *Lives* and the *Moralia,* which eventually reached the West again.

During the Middle Ages, Plutarch had been little more than a name after the collapse of the western portion of the Roman Empire, but when Greek manuscripts began to be imported to Italy in increasing numbers in the fifteenth century, the *Lives* became a bestseller. Their popularity only increased later in the century when a Latin translation of the complete *Lives* made the work more accessible to the general reading public. There had also been some translations of Plutarch's works into the vernacular languages during this period, a development that accelerated in the sixteenth century. Queen Elizabeth herself translated one of the essays in the *Moralia*. But the most influential translation was the French version of Jacques Amyot, bishop of Auxerre, Grand Almoner of France, and man of letters (1513–93). He studied in Paris at the Collège de France, where he earned his living by performing menial services for his fellow students. Although he was naturally slow, his uncommon diligence enabled him to accumulate a large stock of classical and general knowledge. He took his degree of Master of Arts at the age of nineteen and was eventually appointed professor of Greek and Latin in the University of Bourges. During the ten years in which he held this position, he translated into French the Greek novel *Theagenes and Chariclea* and several of Plutarch's *Lives*. Francis I, to whom these works were dedicated, conferred upon their author the abbey of Bellozane. After the death of Francis I, Amyot accompanied the French ambassador to Venice and later went to Rome. On his return the king named him tutor to his two younger sons. He now finished the translation of Plutarch's *Lives* and afterward undertook that of Plutarch's *Moralia,* which he finished in the reign of Charles IX.

Amyot worked directly from the Greek, although he also consulted Latin and earlier French translations. Not so Thomas North, who produced the most influential English version of the *Lives*. He encountered Amyot's translation in 1574, when he visited the French court in the company of his elder brother, Roger, Lord North, and published the first edition of his translation of Amyot in 1579. The fact that North did not consult the Greek text did not alarm his contemporaries, and so it was essentially Amyot's Plutarch that Shakespeare read and turned to as a source for his three Roman plays, *Coriolanus, Julius Caesar,* and *Antony and Cleopatra.* North's rendition of Chapter 26 of Plutarch's *Life of Antony* makes for instructive comparison:

> When she was sent unto by divers letters, both from Antonius himself and also from his friends, she made so light of it, and mocked Antonius so much, that she disdained to set forward otherwise, but to take her barge in the river of Cydnus; the poop whereof was of gold, the sails of purple, and the oars of silver, which kept stroke in rowing after the sound of the music of flutes, howboys, citherns, viols, and such other instruments as they played upon in the barge. And now for the person of her self, she was laid under a pavilion of cloth of gold of tissue, appareled and attired like the goddess Venus, commonly drawn in picture: and hard by her, on either hand of her, pretty fair boys appareled as painters do set forth god Cupid, with little fans in their hands, with the which they fanned wind upon her. Her ladies and gentlewomen also, the fairest of them, were appareled like the nymphs mermaids (which are the mermaids of the waters) and like the Graces, some steering the helm, others tending the tackle and ropes of the barge, out of the which there came a wonderful passing sweet savour of perfumes, that perfumed the wharf's side.

**Figure 30:　Golden barge from the film *Cleopatra***
This blockbuster epic of 1963 was directed by Joseph Mankiewicz and starred Richard Burton and Elizabeth Taylor, a Hollywood couple almost as controversial as the ancient lovers they portrayed. The film cost a staggering $44 million to produce, with spectacular sets for scenes like this one, showing Cleopatra sailing up the river Cydnus in a golden barge to meet Mark Antony.

Shakespeare's depiction of Cleopatra coming to meet Antony in a gilded barge on the river Cydnus clearly shows the influence of North's vigorous English rendition (*Antony and Cleopatra* II.ii.195ff.):

> The barge she sat in, like a burnish'd throne,
> Burn'd on the water: the poop was beaten gold;
> Purple the sails, and so perfumed that
> The winds were love-sick with them; the oars were silver,
> Which to the tune of flutes kept stroke, and made
> The water which they beat to follow faster,
> As amorous of their strokes. For her own person,
> It beggar'd all description: she did lie
> In her pavilion—cloth-of-gold of tissue—
> O'er-picturing that Venus where we see
> The fancy outwork nature: on each side her
> Stood pretty dimpled boys, like smiling Cupids,
> With divers-color'd fans, whose wind did seem
> To glow the delicate cheeks which they did cool,
> And what they undid did . . .
> Her gentlewomen, like the Nereides,
> So many mermaids, tended her i' the eyes,
> And made their bends adornings: at the helm
> A seeming mermaid steers: the silken tackle
> Swell with the touches of those flower-soft hands,
> That yarely frame the office. From the barge
> A strange invisible perfume hits the sense
> Of the adjacent wharfs.

New translations continued to make Plutarch a widely influential author throughout the following centuries, and his *Lives* were the most important formative influence on popular perceptions of antiquity and the personalities of the men who had shaped the Roman world. Several tragedies based on Plutarch achieved great popularity during the eighteenth century, but none more than Joseph Addison's *Cato,* which opened to sold-out houses in 1713 and was soon translated and performed across Europe, the only contemporary English play admired by Voltaire. Addison's adaptation of Plutarch's narrative of the suicide of Cato as his last act of resistance to the tyranny of Caesar was also immensely popular in England's transatlantic colonies, where nine editions appeared before 1800. It was George Washington's favorite play, and in the winter of 1777–78 he ordered it performed for his troops at Valley Forge. Plutarch's *Lives* loomed large in the education of the authors of the founding documents of the United States and continued to supply paradigms for the lives of great men to schoolchildren into the nineteenth century. When the monster in Mary Shelley's *Frankenstein* finds a bag of books in the forest, it contains three works that provide him with an understanding of the world: Goethe's *The Sorrows of Young Werther,* Milton's *Paradise Lost,* and Plutarch's *Lives.*

A variety of factors contributed to Plutarch's gradual elimination from the curriculum—historians dismissed him as an unreliable source, classicists rejected his unclassical style, and general readers found his values quaint and obsolete. And yet the influence of the *Lives* in particular remains palpable. The enduring fascination of the public with the love story of Antony and Cleopatra is essentially Plutarchian in its inspiration, as trumpeted in the publicity surrounding Joseph Mankiewicz's screen epic *Cleopatra* (1963). Plutarch, one might imagine, would have particularly appreciated the famous scene on Elizabeth Taylor's barge.

# JUVENAL

## (Decimus Iunius Iuvenalis, Late First through Early Second Century A.D.)

Satire is entirely Roman. The first to win distinction in satire was Lucilius, who still has admirers who unhesitatingly prefer him not just to other satirists but to all poets regardless of genre. I disagree with them, but equally I disagree with Horace, who thinks that Lucilius "flows along like a muddy stream, with much in his poems that could well be cut out". For Lucilius is admirably learned and outspoken, and this makes him so sharp-tongued and full of wit. Horace is much more refined and polished, and unless I am misled by my affection for him, he is the best of all the satirists. Persius has also earned a considerable reputation, though he wrote just one book. And there are other distinguished satirists writing nowadays, whose lasting reputation is assured.

THIS IS QUINTILIAN'S ASSESSMENT OF SATIRE IN HIS SURVEY OF GREEK AND ROMAN literature at the beginning of the tenth book of his *Education of the Orator*. He was writing in the 90s A.D., at least a decade before the publication of Juvenal's earliest satires, so he can name only the three older members of the great quartet of Roman satirists.

Gaius Lucilius, from Suessa Aurunca, not far south of Rome, on the border between Latium and Campania, may have been born as early as 180, and he lived until 102 or 101 B.C. He was rich, a member of the equestrian order, a great-uncle of Pompey, and a friend of Scipio Aemilianus, the conqueror of Carthage. He was immensely productive, publishing thirty books of satires. Unfortunately, fewer than 1,400 lines survive. This is not an insubstantial total (Horace has 2,112 lines in his satires, Persius 665, Juvenal 3,869), but they give us a very incomplete picture of Lucilius's writings because they consist almost entirely of brief and disparate quotations of a few words or lines, with none longer than 13 lines, and a great number of them are preserved by grammarians as illustrations of linguistic peculiarities, with little or no indication of the context from which they are being drawn.

Even with such unpromising evidence, it is possible to deduce that Lucilius wrote on a wide range of topics: politics, philosophy, morals, literary criticism, language, and anecdotes about his own life and that of contemporaries. Unlike the later satirists, he did not restrict himself to writing only in hexameters: in his earlier books he employed a variety of meters, apparently in imitation of the *Saturae* of Ennius, who is much better known for his epic and tragic poetry. The loss of Lucilius's satires is very regrettable, not only because we get only tantalizing glimpses of his earthy and candid opinions on so many aspects of life, shot through with a particularly strong vein of humor, often at his own expense, but also because he was such a prominent figure in a crucial transitional period of Rome's history that is so little known to us.

Being rich and well-connected, Lucilius was able to direct stringent attacks against high-status individuals, but, for all his great reputation for outspokenness, it has been suggested that at least some of his victims were safely dead before he published his criticism of them. When Horace wrote his *Satires* in the 30s B.C., he felt that, as a son of an ex-slave, he could not risk offending rich and powerful contemporaries. He preferred "to tell the truth with a laugh," comparing himself to a teacher coaxing children to learn their alphabet by giving them little cakes (1.1.24–26). Such "joking in earnest" was a standard practice in the teachings of the Greek philosophical schools, not just the Epicureans, to whom Horace professed adherence, but also the Cynics and Stoics, and Horace derived much of his subject matter from the philosophers' diatribes against moral weaknesses.

In *Satires* 1.4, Horace criticizes Lucilius for writing two hundred lines in an hour while standing on one leg, and goes on to make the comparison of Lucilius to a muddy stream that Quintilian cites (see above). Horace himself had espoused the Callimachean view that poetry should be written slowly, on a small scale, and with great care. It will have been particularly challenging for him to adhere to these principles, given that he adopted such a loose, informal style. (Horace called his satires *Sermones,* which means "conversations," with none of the implication of lecturing inherent in the English word "sermon.") *Satires* 1.8 is a splendid example of Callimacheanism, despite its rather improbable subject matter. The speaker is a cheap fig-wood statue of Priapus, the god assigned the responsibility of keeping thieves and birds out of gardens. When he saw two witches carrying out magic rites at night, he was so terrified that he farted with such force that his buttocks split, and the witches ran off in a panic, the one losing her false teeth, the other her wig. The anecdote is highly comic, but it is also structured as an *aetion,* an "explanation," in the Callimachean manner. Several fragments of Callimachus's great poem, the *Aetia,* concern statues of various deities; we may note in particular fragment 114, where the poet is in conversation with a statue of Delian Apollo, asking why he is represented as he is. Only the opening words of his ninth *Iamb* survive, addressed to a statue of Hermes: "Long-bearded Hermes, why does your penis point to your beard and not to your feet…?" Horace's poem is set in the magnificent gardens recently laid out on the Esquiline by Maecenas. We may imagine them strolling together there and coming across a little statue of the ithyphallic god Priapus that had been split, no doubt by the summer heat. Rather than address Maecenas with fulsome praise for his generosity in tidying up the Esquiline, which had been a dangerous and run-down part of the city, Horace flatters his patron with this oblique compliment, presenting him with a fancifully humorous etiological poem purporting to relate how the statue's buttocks came to split.

Persius was born in A.D. 34 and died in 62. He came from a very rich and well-connected family in Tuscany and had close contacts with the Stoic opposition to Nero, all of whom were to suffer enforced suicide or banishment a few years after his premature death, men such as the philosophers Thrasea Paetus and Annaeus Cornutus, as well as Lucan and later on his uncle, the younger Seneca, who did not greatly impress him. According to Suetonius's brief *Life of Persius,* "when Persius was reciting his poetry, Lucan could hardly restrain himself from declaring Persius's poems to be real poetry whereas his own were mere playthings." His first satire discusses literary fashions, and the other five deal with particular topics drawn from Stoic doctrines. This ensured that his poetry retained a greater currency than that of most pagan poets after the onset of Christianity. Persius's poems are consequently preserved in an unusually large number of manuscripts, dating from as early as the seventh century. He does not, however, enjoy great popularity nowadays, partly because of his deliberately difficult style and partly because the discussions of morality in which he engages have only a limited appeal.

The other satirists draw frequently on their own lives for material for their poetry. In this respect there is a marked contrast with Juvenal, who, especially in his earlier satires, delivers diatribes against society in general, with little or no reference to himself personally. We do not know when or where he was born or died, or what his social status was. He lived through the increasingly vicious reign of Domitian, but, from the very few datable references within his poems, it is reasonable to suppose that he did not begin writing satires until about A.D. 106, that is to say, a decade after Domitian's assassination. The last book may not have been published much before A.D. 130.

Martial addresses three epigrams to Juvenal, but the latest can be dated to A.D. 101/102, and none of them hint that he was active as a poet. No other contemporary mentions Juvenal, and allusions to his poetry remain very sparse for more than two centuries after his death. Packed though they are with obscenities, his denunciations of Roman decadence and corruption appealed to the early Church Fathers, and this rather paradoxically gave him a great popularity that he seems not to have enjoyed in his lifetime, and that has not waned since. Because he is almost totally silent about himself, and had apparently been neglected for so long, there was no reliable source of information about his life to satisfy this new interest in Juvenal. As so often with literary figures, biographical details were cobbled together from his own poems to fill this vacuum. We have a broad range of information about Juvenal generated this way, but it is all probably quite unfounded. For example, there is no persuasive substance to the notion that he was exiled to a military post in the remote south of Egypt as punishment for mocking Domitian's baldness (at 4.38); this is concocted from his fifteenth satire, a curious tale of cannibalism in Egypt, and from the fragmentary sixteenth, about soldiering.

When we read the damning indictments of the imperial system by Juvenal's contemporary Tacitus, we are always aware that they were written by a leading senator whose survival had once depended on his passive acquiescence in the dreadful excesses of the last years of Domitian's reign. We can sense the passionate power of the outrage to which he could finally give expression. Rather paradoxically, the force of Juvenal's denunciations of Rome seems to be enhanced by our ignorance of his position in society. Since we can only speculate about his motivation for making them and about his personal perspective on life, his diatribes seem to have a peculiarly universal application.

Roman poets frequently remind their readers that their poems do not necessarily reflect their personality. Juvenal may, in real life, have been mild-mannered and broad-minded, with a sunny disposition and a charitable respect for all humanity, but the voice in which he speaks, especially in his earlier satires, suggests that he was an appalling xenophobe and misogynist, spiteful and intolerant, incapable of seeing anything but the worst in everyone. This odious and twisted persona, however, should not blind us to his literary greatness. Few critics would question his status as the author of some of the most magnificent poetry any Roman or, for that matter, Greek ever wrote. That Juvenal could raise satire to such heights is surprising. The genre had come a long way from Horace's assessment of it in, for example, *Satires* 1.4, where he criticizes Lucilius's lack of artistry and, with rather overstated modesty, denies himself a place among the ranks of poets because he writes "things closer to conversation." Juvenal's use of meter is in many respects more comparable to that of Virgil than to that of the other satirists, and it also contributes to his high stylistic level that he generally avoids colloquial and vulgar language. For example, he frequently refers to sex and bodily functions in an open and vigorous manner, but he rarely uses obscene terms in doing so.

This grand style suits Juvenal's sweeping excoriation of all he sees around him. Horace might quite properly adopt an informal tone when he tells the gentle fable of the town mouse and the country mouse (*Satires* 2.6.80–117) to contrast the drawbacks of a luxurious city life with the attractions of a quiet country life, but that would not suit Juvenal's attack on life in Rome in *Satire* 3, a remorseless catalog of intemperate invective against tricksters, flatterers, blackmailers, Jews, Greeks, Syrians, the rich, patrons, squalid and overcrowded living conditions, muggers, and much more besides. (Juvenal's xenophobia is spectacular, a feature of his poetry that strikes modern readers with particular immediacy. It is not, however, universal—he expresses no prejudice against Gauls, Spaniards, and Africans, but he repeatedly attacks the Jews, Egyptians, and Greeks who are taking over Rome. Does this selective discrimination make it worse?) Horace's poem focuses on the unassuming pleasures of the countryside rather than the dangerous splendors of the city, but even in praising rural life

Juvenal can turn it into a criticism of Rome: one of the good things about the countryside is that the only occasion when the cumbersome and inconvenient toga has to be worn is at one's own funeral. When Martial compares his own happy life in retirement in a quiet Spanish country town with the tiresome obligations of life in Rome, he pictures Juvenal sweating in his toga up and down the hills of Rome to pay his respects to patrons, whereas he himself wears anything that happens to come to hand (*Epigrams* 12.18; see p. 441).

Juvenal's shift from the relaxed, conversational style conventionally adopted by the other satirists is a result of the highly rhetorical nature of his poetry. Both the content of his satires and its presentation are heavily influenced by contemporary education in, and practice of, oratory. This can be seen both in small details and in the general themes and overall structure of his satires. It is often said that Juvenal is eminently quotable. His poems are full of brief and memorable phrases: "Honesty is praised and left to shiver" (1.74, on the lack of moral standards); "A rare bird in the world and very like a black swan" (6.165, a perfect woman); "Who will guard the guards themselves?" (6 Oxford fragment 31, on chaperones conniving at women's sexual escapades); "Bread and circuses" (10.81, the only things the Roman people are interested in nowadays); "A healthy mind in a healthy body" (10.356, the only thing for which we should pray). Others are more specifically dependent on their context and merit quotation in Latin to emphasize their well-crafted terseness: *ipse capi voluit,* "It itself wanted to be caught" (4.69, a court flatterer's comment on the privilege a fish enjoys in being served to Domitian); *hoc volo, sic iubeo, sit pro ratione voluntas,* "This is what I want, thus I command, let my wish stand instead of reason" (6.223, a domineering wife). Such pointed brevity is at least partly derived from the *sententiae,* the pithy and telling phrases with which rhetors packed their declamations.

Juvenal's first satire is programmatic, announcing what he is going to write and why and how he is going to write it. Having put up for so long with unending recitations of tedious poetry, he is going to try it for himself. His choice of genre is inevitable: with all the iniquities in Rome, "it's hard *not* to write satire" (30), and it is not even necessary to have any real talent, because "if nature fails, then indignation generates verse" (79). In the following lines, Juvenal seems to acknowledge that satire is not traditionally restricted to attacking moral corruption: "What folks have done ever since [the primordial Flood]—their hopes and fears and anger, / their pleasures, joys, and toing and froing—is my volume's hotch-potch" (85–86). In the very next line, however, he shows that he is not actually interested in any of the more pleasant and innocuous aspects of life: "Was there, at any time, a richer harvest of evil?"

As a model for such aggressive satire, Juvenal naturally turns to Lucilius:

> Whenever, as though with sword in hand, the hot Lucilius
> roars in wrath, the listener flushes; his mind is affrighted
> with a sense of sin, and his conscience sweats with secret guilt. (165–67)

He had already mentioned Lucilius driving the chariot of his poetry (19–20), but Horace is referred to only once, and very perfunctorily (51). Juvenal could hardly ignore entirely such a great exponent of the genre. In his first satire, however, Horace had declared that the purpose of his satires was "to tell the truth with a laugh" (24), and Juvenal, as a master of the vitriolic, the intolerant, and the unreasonable, would want to maintain his distance from a predecessor who aimed to coax and banter his readers out of their faults and foibles. Juvenal occasionally imitates Persius in detail, but he never mentions him. With his humane, positive, and constructive mission in writing his satires, Persius would have suited Juvenal's outlook and style even less than did Horace.

Unlike Lucilius, Juvenal cannot risk attacks on the living: "I'll try what I may against those/ whose ashes are buried beneath the Flaminia and the Latina" (171–72). This final statement may be simply an acknowledgment that the days of Republican freedom of speech are long gone, but it may also indicate that Juvenal is not writing with the security that a high social status could afford him. Throughout his satires we come across the names of people who will have been easily familiar to his contemporaries. To the modern reader, however, the majority are otherwise unknown. To identify them, we need to consult learned commentaries. Even then, many of the references remain obscure. This is hardly surprising, given that even the scholia to Juvenal's poetry written in late antiquity felt it necessary to devote substantial space to this problem. But, many such individuals are introduced as representative of a particular type of person: all we really need to know about, for example, Crispinus (1.27) is that he is an unlikable Egyptian; about Matho (1.32), that he is a fat lawyer; about Proculeius and Gillo (1.40), that they have, respectively, a small penis and a large one.

It is important to remember that Juvenal's first satire introduces only the first book. By convention, his sixteen satires are numbered consecutively, but it is generally accepted that he published them at intervals, in five books: 1 through 5 (Why write satire?; homosexuality; life in Rome; decadence at Domitian's court; patronage); 6 (women); 7 through 9 (the poverty of intellectuals; the shortcomings of the aristocracy; life as a bisexual gigolo); 10 through 12 (what to pray for; the simple life; friendship); 13 through 16 (consolation for loss; parental influence; cannibalism in Egypt; the army). The program announced in the first satire fits perfectly with the warped aggression of the second book just as well as it suits the first book, for Juvenal has nothing good to say about modern women. In Book 3, however, a rather disconcerting shift in tone begins to creep in. *Satire* 8 gives hints at positive advice, even if only through the use of examples not to be followed. This technique recurs more emphatically in *Satire* 10, which is dominated by its vignettes of things that seem worth praying for but lead to disaster: political power, eloquence, military glory, long life, beauty. It is perhaps ironic that, for all that he is such an expert at devastating criticism, the most famous phrase in Juvenal is strongly positive: "you ought to pray for a healthy mind in a healthy body [*mens sana in corpore sano*]" (10.356). Juvenal adopts a more Horatian persona in the later books, perhaps not surprisingly, since he turns, from *Satire* 9 on, to issues of private morality rather than the evils of society in general. The later books are more mellow, with Juvenal deploying less indignation and more irony, but they are also arguably less successful. He has only a mediocre talent for being reasonable. Many readers prefer the sweeping and detestable virulence of his earlier satires.

## SATIRE 1

### Why Write Satire?

*In the introductory lines (1–21), Juvenal situates his complaints about contemporary Rome in the context of literary society, in which frequent recitations were given by second-rate writers, like Codrus who wrote an epic on the Seven against Thebes and the authors of other mythological epics. Much of this poetry was informed by the common background of the rhetorical schools, which Juvenal had also attended, where students gave imaginary speeches of advice to famous men, such as Sulla. He ends by invoking the inventor of Roman satire, Gaius Lucilius, who was born in Suessa Aurunca in southern Italy.*

Must I be always a listener only, never hit back,
    although so often assailed by the hoarse *Theseid* of
        Codrus?
Never obtain revenge when X has read me his
        comedies,
Y his elegies? No revenge when my day has
        been wasted
by mighty Telephus or by Orestes who, having
        covered
the final margin, extends to the back, and still isn't
        finished?
No citizen's private house is more familiar to him
than the grove of Mars and Vulcan's cave near
        Aeolus' rocks
are to me; what the winds are up to, what ghosts are
        being tormented

on Aeacus' rack, from what far land another has
10    stolen
a bit of gold pelt, how huge are the ash-trunks
    Monychus hurls—
the unending cry goes up from Fronto's plane-trees,
    his marble
statues and columns, shaken and shattered by
    non-stop readings.
One gets the same from every poet, great and small.
I too have snatched my hand from under the
    cane; I too
have tendered advice to Sulla to retire from public life
and sleep the sleep of the just. No point, when you
    meet so many
bards, in sparing paper (it's already doomed to
    destruction).
But why, you may ask, should I decide to cover
    the ground
o'er which the mighty son of Aurunca drove his
20    team?
If you have time and are feeling receptive, here's my
    answer.

*The subject turns to the excesses of Roman society, includ-*
*ing women, like Mevia, taking up male pursuits; a bar-*
*ber becoming wealthy; and an Egyptian like Crispinus*
*advising the emperor. Under Domitian, Massa, Carus,*
*and Latinus were notorious informers, whose crimes*
*justify the turn to satire, now represented by Horace,*
*who was born in Venusia (51). After listing further out-*
*rages that recall the activities of a famous early imperial*
*poisoner, Lucusta, Juvenal, with false modesty, invokes*
*another, entirely unknown writer of satire, Cluvienus.*

When a soft eunuch marries, and Mevia takes to
    sticking
a Tuscan boar, with a spear beside her naked breast,
when a fellow who made my stiff young beard crunch
    with his clippers
can challenge the whole upper class with his millions,
    single-handed;
when Crispinus, a blob of Nilotic scum, bred in
    Canopus,
hitches a cloak of Tyrian purple onto his shoulder
and flutters a simple ring of gold on his sweaty finger
(in summer he cannot bear the weight of a heavy
    stone),
it's hard not to write satire. For who could be so
30    inured

to the wicked city, so dead to feeling, as to keep
    his temper
when the brand-new litter of Matho the lawyer heaves
    in sight,
filled with himself; then one who informed on a
    powerful friend
and will soon be tearing what's left of the carcass of
    Rome's aristocracy,
one who makes even Massa shiver, whom Carus
    caresses
with bribes, and Thymele too, sent by the frightened
    Latinus;
when you're shouldered aside by people who earn
    bequests at night,
people who reach the top by a form of social
    climbing
that now ensures success—through a rich old female's
    funnel?
Proculeius obtains a single twelfth, but Gillo
    eleven:    40
each heir's reward is assessed by the size of his organ.
Very well. Let each receive the price of his life-blood,
    becoming
as pale as a man who has stepped on a snake in his
    bare feet,
or is waiting to speak in the contest at the grim altar
    of Lyons.
Why need I tell how my heart shrivels in the heat of
    its anger,
when townsfolk are jostled by the flocks attending on
    one who has cheated
his ward and left him to prostitution, or on someone
    condemned
by a futile verdict? For what is disgrace if he keeps
    the money?
The exiled Marius drinks from two, happily
    braving
the wrath of heaven; the province which won is
    awarded—tears.    50
Am I not right to think this calls for Venusia's lamp?
Am I not right to attack it? Would you rather I reeled
    off epics of Heracles
or Diomedes or the labyrinth's frantic bellows,
the splash of the youngster hitting the sea, and the
    flying joiner,
when a pimp, if his wife is barred from benefit, coolly
    pockets
the gifts brought by her lover, trained to stare at the
    ceiling,

trained to snore in his cups through a nose that's
   wide awake;
when this man feels entitled to covet command of a
   cohort,
no longer possessing a family fortune, having
   presented
every cent to the stables—look at Automedon
60   junior
as he flies along the Flaminia, whipping the horses and
   holding
the reins himself, swanking in front of his girl in her
   greatcoat.
There, at the intersection, wouldn't you like to fill
a large-size notebook when a figure comes by on six
   pairs of shoulders
in a litter exposed on this side and that and almost
   indecent,
recalling in many ways the limp and sprawling
   Maecenas,
a forger of wills who has turned himself into a wealthy
   gentleman
with the simple aid of a sheet of paper and a moist-
   ened signet?
Here is a high-born lady, who just before handing her
   husband
some mellow Calenian adds a dash of shriveling
70   toad.
Surpassing Lucusta herself, she trains untutored
   neighbors
to brave the scandal and walk behind their
   blackened lords.
If you want to be anything, dare some deed that merits confinement
on Gyara's narrow shore; honesty is praised, and
   shivers.
Crime pays—look at those grounds and mansions and
   tables,
the antique silver, and the goat perched on the rim of
   the cup.
Who can sleep when a daughter-in-law is seduced
   for money,
when brides-to-be are corrupt, and schoolboys practise adultery?
If nature fails, then indignation generates verse,
80   doing the best it can, like mine or like Cluvienus'.

*Juvenal announces the subject of satire—human nature
as it has been since the recreation of the human race by
Deucalion and Pyrrha. As he portrays it, the wealth*

*acquired by former slaves such as Pallas and Licinus is
emblematic of the degradation of traditional Roman culture, which is represented by Corvinus, a Roman noble
reduced to working as a sharecropper.*

Once, when torrents of rain were raising the
   ocean's level,
Deucalion sailed to the top of a hill and sought for
   guidance.
Little by little the stones grew warm and soft with life,
and Pyrrha displayed her naked girls to the gaze
   of men.
What folks have done ever since—their hopes and
   fears and anger,
their pleasures, joys, and toing and froing—is my volume's hotch-potch.
Was there, at any time, a richer harvest of evil?
When did the pocket of greed gape wider? When was
   our dicing
ever so reckless? Your gambler leaves his wallet behind
as he goes to the table of chance; he plays with his safe
   at his elbow!                                                    90
There what battles are to be seen, with the banker
   supplying
the weaponry! Is it just simple madness to lose a
   hundred
thousand, and then refuse a shirt to a shivering slave?
Which of our grandfathers built so many villas, or
   dined off
seven courses, alone? Today a little 'basket'
waits in the porch, to be snatched away by the toga'd
   rabble.
First, however, the steward anxiously peers at
   your face
for fear you may be an impostor using another's name.
No dole until you are checked. The crier is ordered
   to call
even the Trojan families; they too besiege the
   portals                                                         100
along with us: 'See to the praetor, then to the
   tribune'.
A freedman's in front: 'I was here first,' he says, 'why
   shouldn't I
stand my ground, without any fear or uneasiness?
   Granted,
I was born beside the Euphrates (the fancy holes in
   my ear-lobes
would prove it, whatever I said); but the five bou-
   tiques that I own

bring in four hundred thousand. What use is the
broader purple,
if while Corvinus is tending the flocks which someone
has leased him
out in the Laurentine country, I have a bigger fortune
than Pallas or Licinus?' So, just let the tribunes wait;
let wealth prevail; no deference is due to their sacred
110     office
from one who recently came to the city with
whitened feet.
In our society nothing is held in such veneration
as the grandeur of riches, although as yet there stands
no temple
for accursed Money to dwell in, no altar erected
to Cash,
in the way we honor Peace, Good Faith, Victory, Valor,
and Concord, who when her nest is hailed replies with
a clatter.

*Juvenal now turns to the social ills that he attributes to the
system of patronage in Rome: even the consul, the highest magistrate, is a client of someone higher up. Clients
make the rounds, fishing for handouts and a free dinner
(the transition is somewhat obscured by the loss of a line in
the text). But greed and gluttony prevail, and the wealthy
magnate indulges himself in private.*

When the highest magistrate reckons up, at the end of
the year,
what the 'basket' is worth, how much it adds to his
assets,
what of his clients, who count on that for their clothes
and footwear,
bread and fuel for their houses? The litters are jammed
120     together
as they come for their hundred pieces. A sick or
pregnant wife
follows behind her husband, and is carted round the
circuit.
This man claims, with a well-known ruse, for an absent
spouse.
Indicating an empty chair with its curtains drawn,
'That's my Galla,' he says. 'Don't keep her too long.
Are you worried?
Galla, put out your head.'
                    'Leave her, she must be sleeping.'
The day itself is arranged in a splendid series of
highlights:

'The basket', then the city square, with Apollo
the lawyer
and the generals' statues—one, which some Egyptian
wallah
has had the nerve to set up, listing all his
achievements;                                             130
pissing (and worse) against his image is wholly
in order.
...............................................................
Weary old clients trudge away from the porches,
resigning
what they had yearned for, though nothing stays with
a man so long
as the hope of a dinner. Cabbage and kindling have to
be purchased.
Meanwhile the magnate will lounge alone among
empty couches,
chewing his way through the finest produce of sea and
woodland.
(Yes, off all those antique tables, so wide and so
stylish,
they gobble up their ancestors' wealth at a single
sitting.)
Soon there'll be no parasites left. But who could abide
that blend of luxury and meanness? What size of gullet could order                                          140
a whole boar for itself, an animal born for parties?
But a reckoning is nigh, when you strip and, within
that bloated body,
carry an undigested peacock into the bath-house.
That's why sudden death is common, and old age rare.
At once the joyful news goes dancing around the
dinners.
The funeral cortege departs to the cheers of indignant
friends.
There'll be no scope for new generations to add to
our record
of rottenness; they will be just the same in their deeds
and desires.
Every evil has reached a precipice. Up with the
sail, then;
crowd on every stitch of canvas.

*In this closing passage, Juvenal justifies his turn to satire,
responding to an imaginary interlocutor who longs for a
talented satirist as in the old days, when one could name
names. Nowadays, however, if you make fun of the likes of
Tigillinus, Nero's abusive praetorian prefect, you will end*

up burned at the stake. Better, he warns, to write mythological epics about Aeneas, or Achilles, or Hercules and
the boy Hylas. Juvenal's abrupt response is that his satires
will target only dead victims, whose ashes reside in their
family tombs along prominent Roman roads, like the Via
Flaminia or the Via Latina.

> Perhaps you may say 'But,
> where is the talent fit for the theme? Where is the
>    frankness

150

> of earlier days which allowed men to write whatever
>    they pleased
> with burning passion ("Whose name do I not dare
>    mention?
> What does it matter if Mucius forgives what I say or
>    not?")?
> Portray Tigellinus; soon you will blaze as a
>    living torch,
> standing with others, smoking and burning, pinned by
>    the throat,
> driving a vivid pathway of light across the arena.'
> So take this man who administered poison to three of
>    his uncles—
> is he to go by, looking down on us all from his aery
>    cushions?
> 'Yes, when he comes to you, seal your lips with your

160

> finger.
> Simply to utter the words "That's him!" will count as
>    informing.
> Without a qualm you can pit Aeneas against the
>    ferocious
> Rutulian; no one is placed at risk by the wounded
>    Achilles,
> or Hylas, so long sought when he'd gone the way of
>    his bucket.
> Whenever, as though with sword in hand, the hot
>    Lucilius
> roars in wrath, the listener flushes; his mind is
>    affrighted
> with a sense of sin, and his conscience sweats with
>    secret guilt.
> That's what causes anger and tears. So turn
>    it over
> in your mind before the bugle. Too late, when you've
>    donned your helmet,

170

> for second thoughts about combat.'
> 'I'll try what I may against those
> whose ashes are buried beneath the Flaminia and the
>    Latina.'

## SATIRE 10

### The Futility of Aspirations

*This poem is a systematic exposition of the things that
people pray for, both the wrong things and the right
ones, so it concludes on a more positive note than many
of Juvenal's satires. In the introductory section (1–55),
he remarks on the propensity of humans to pray for eloquence, strength, or wealth, a folly that would provoke
the philosopher Democritus to laughter (he was the
author of the book* On Cheerfulness), *while the more
melancholy Heraclitus would be moved to tears. The concluding lines mark the transition to the two major sections of the poem on the subject of what people do pray
for, and the things for which they actually should pray.*

In all the countries that stretch from Cadiz across to
    the Ganges
and the lands of dawn, how few are the people who
    manage to tell
genuine blessings from those of a very different order,
dispelling the mists of error! For when do we have
    good grounds
for our fears or desires? What idea proves so inspired
    that you do not
regret your attempt to carry it out, and its
    realization?
The gods, in response to the prayers of the owners,
    obligingly wreck
entire households. In peace and in war alike, we beg
for things that will hurt us. To many the art of speak-
    ing is fatal,
and their own torrential fluency. In a famous instance,
    an athlete                                                          10
met his end through trusting in his strength and his
    marvellous muscles.
More, however, are smothered by heaps of money,
    amassed
with excessive care, and by fortunes exceeding other
    men's wealth
by as much as the giant British whale outgrows the
    dolphin.
Hence it was, in those terrible times, that on
    Nero's orders
Longinus' house and the over-rich Seneca's
    spacious park
were closed, and the Lateran family's splendid man-
    sion besieged

by an entire company. A soldier rarely enters an attic.
When you make a journey by night, if you carry even
    a handful
of plain silver items, you will go in fear of the
20      sword
and barge-pole; you will quake at the shadow of a reed
    that sways in the moonlight.
The traveler with nothing on him sings in the
    robber's face.
As a rule, the first prayer offered, and the one that is
    most familiar
in every temple, is 'money': 'let my wealth increase,'
    'let my strong box
be the biggest of all down town.' But aconite never
    is drunk
from an earthenware mug; that is something to fear
    when you're handed
a jeweled cup, or when Serine glows in a golden
    wine-bowl.
In view of that, you may well approve of the two
    philosophers:
one of them used to laugh whenever he closed
    the door
and stepped into the street; his opposite number
30      would weep.
While harsh censorious laughter is universal and easy,
one wonders how the other's eyes were supplied with
    moisture.
Democritus' sides would shake with gales of incessant
    laughter,
although in the towns of his day there were no purple-
    or scarlet-bordered
togas to be seen; no rods or litters or platforms.
What *would* he have made of a praetor standing there
    in his car,
lifted high in the air amid the dust of the
    race-track,
dressed in the tunic of Jove himself, with a
    curtain-like toga
of Tyrian embroidery draped on his shoulders, and a
    crown so enormous
in its circumference that no neck could support its
40      weight;
in fact it is held by a public slave who sweats with
    exertion.
(He rides in the same chariot to restrain the official
    from hybris.)
And don't forget the bird that is perched on his
    ivory staff,

on this side trumpeters, on that a train of dutiful
    clients
walking in front, and the snow-white Romans beside
    his bridle
who have been transformed into friends by the dole
    thrust into their purses.
In his day too, in all the places where people gathered,
he found material for laughter. He showed by his
    excellent sense
that men of the highest quality who will set the finest
    examples
may be born in a land with a thick climate, peopled by
    boneheads.    50
He used to laugh at the masses' worries, and at their
    pleasures,
and sometimes, too, at their tears. For himself, when
    Fortune threatened,
he would tell her go hang, and make a sign with his
    middle finger.
So what in fact are the useless or dangerous things that
    are sought,
for which one must duly cover the knees of the gods
    with wax?

*In this, the longest section of the poem (56–345), Juvenal*
*catalogs the things that people pray for, in spite of their*
*disastrous consequences. He describes first (56–113) how*
*they ask the gods for power, taking as an example the*
*fate of Sejanus, prefect of the Praetorian Guard under*
*the emperor Tiberius. Sejanus schemed for power but*
*was undone when Tiberius denounced him to the Senate*
*in a letter sent from the imperial retreat on the island*
*of Capri.*

Some are sent hurtling down by the virulent envy
    to which
their power exposes them. Their long and impressive
    list of achievements
ruins them. Down come their statues, obeying the pull
    of the rope.
Thereupon, axe-blows rain on the very wheels of their
    chariots,
smashing them up; and the legs of the innocent horses
    are broken.    60
Now the flames are hissing; bellows and furnace are
    bringing
a glow to the head revered by the people. The mighty
    Sejanus

is crackling. Then, from the face regarded as number
  two
in the whole of the world, come pitchers, basins,
  saucepans, and piss-pots.
Frame your door with laurels; drag a
  magnificent bull,
whitened with chalk, to the Capitol. They're dragging
  Sejanus along
by a hook for all to see. Everyone's jubilant. 'Look,
what lips he had! What a face! You can take it from me
  that I never
cared for the fellow. But what was the charge that
  brought him down?
Who informed, who gave him away, what witnesses
70   proved it?'
  'Nothing like that. A large, long-winded letter
    arrived
      from Capri.'
          'Fine…I ask no more.'
                But what's the reaction
of Remus' mob? It supports the winner, as always, and
  turns on
whoever is condemned. If Nortia had smiled on her
  Tuscan favorite,
if the elderly prince had been caught off guard and
  sent to his death,
that same public, at this very moment, would be hailing Sejanus
as Augustus. Long ago, the people cast off its worries,
when we stopped selling our votes. A body that used
  to confer
commands, legions, rods, and everything else,
  has now
narrowed its scope, and is eager and anxious for two
80   things only:
bread and races.
          'I hear that a lot are going to die.'
'No question about it. The kitchen is sure to be hot.'
              'My friend
Bruttidius looked a bit pale when I met him beside
  Mars' altar.
I've an awful feeling that the mortified Ajax may take
  revenge
for being exposed to danger. So now, as he lies by
  the river,
let's all run and kick the man who was Caesar's
  enemy.
But check that our slaves are watching; then no one
  can say we didn't,

and drag his terrified master to court with his head in
  a noose.'

Such were the whispers and the common gossip concerning Sejanus.
Do *you* want to be greeted each morning, as Sejanus
  was;                                                    90
to possess his wealth; to bestow on one a
  magistrate's chair,
to appoint another to an army command; to be seen
  as the guardian
of Rome's chief, as he sits on the narrow Rock of the
  Roedeers
with his herd of Chaldaeans? Of course you would like
  to have spears and cohorts,
the cream of the knights, and a barracks as part of your
  house. Why shouldn't you
want them? For even people with no desire to kill
covet the power. But what is the good of prestige and
  prosperity
if, for every joy, they bring an equal sorrow?
Would you sooner wear the bordered robe of the man
  that you see there
being dragged along, or be a power in Fidenae or
  Gabii,                                                  100
adjudicating on weights and quantities, or a
  ragged aedile
smashing undersize measuring cups in empty
  Ulúbrae?
You acknowledge, then, that Sejanus never succeeded
  in grasping
what one should really pray for. By craving ever
  more honors
and seeking ever more wealth, he was building a
  lofty tower
of numerous storeys; which meant that the fall would
  be all the greater,
and that when the structure gave way, its collapse
  would wreak devastation.
What cast down the likes of Pompey and Crassus,
  and him
who tamed the people of Rome and brought them
  under the lash?
It was the pursuit of the highest place by every
  device,                                                 110
and grandiose prayers, which were duly heard by
  malevolent gods.
Few monarchs go down to Ceres' son-in-law free from
bloody wounds; few tyrants avoid a sticky death.

*Public speakers wielded great influence in Roman affairs, so it is not surprising that men might pray to the gods for eloquence such as was displayed by the fourth-century B.C. Athenian orator Demosthenes or Rome's own Cicero (114–32). And yet Cicero would have been better off if he had only been known to posterity as a mediocre poet.*

Glorious eloquence, such as Demosthenes and Cicero
    had that
is desired from the start, and through Minerva's
    vacation,
by the youngster who worships the thrifty goddess, as
    yet with a coin,
and who has a slave in attendance to mind his diminu-
    tive satchel.
Yet eloquence proved the undoing of both those
    statesmen; and both
were carried to ruin by the large and copious flood of
    their genius.
Thanks to his genius, one had his hands and head cut
120    off.
(The rostrum was never stained with a petty advo-
    cate's blood.)
'O fortunate state of Rome, which dates from my
    consulate!'
He could have scorned Mark Antony's swords, had all
    his sayings
been like that. So—better to write ridiculous poems
than that inspired Philippic (the second one in
    the set)
which is universally praised. An equally cruel death
removed the man whose fluent power excited
    the wonder
of Athens, as he used his reins to drive the crowded
    assembly.
The gods in heaven frowned on his birth, and fate was
    against him.
His father, with eyes inflamed by the soot of the glow-
130    ing metal,
sent him away from the coal and tongs, and the anvil
    that fashions
swords, and all the filth of Vulcan, to a rhetoric tutor.

*Military glory is the third of men's aspirations that leads them to ruin, as exemplified in this section (133–87) by three famous generals: Hannibal, the Carthaginian who crossed the Alps and ravaged Italy in the Second Punic War, only to be reduced to a refugee in Bithynia at the*

*war's end; Alexander the Great, born at Pella in Macedon, who fretted that the world was not big enough for him but learned within Babylon's brick walls that he would die young; and Xerxes, the king of Persia who invaded Greece in 480 B.C. with a vast army and navy, sailing through a channel cut across the Isthmus of Athos, and was ignominiously defeated by the Athenians off the island of Salamis.*

The spoils of war—a breastplate nailed to the trunk
    of a tree
shorn of its branches, a cheekpiece dangling from a
    shattered helmet,
a chariot's yoke with its pole snapped off, a
    pennant ripped
from a crippled warship, a dejected prisoner on top of
    an arch—
these, it is thought, represent superhuman blessings,
    and these
are the things that stir a general, be he Greek, Roman,
    or foreign,
to excitement; they provide a justification for all
his toil and peril. So much stronger is the thirst for
    glory    140
than for goodness. (Who, in fact, embraces Goodness
    herself,
if you take away the rewards?) Often states have
    been ruined
by a few men's greed for fame, by their passion for
    praise and for titles
inscribed in the stones protecting their ashes—stones
    which the boorish
strength of the barren fig-tree succeeds in
    splitting apart;
for even funeral monuments have their allotted life-span.
Weigh Hannibal; how many pounds will you find in
    that mighty
commander? This is the man too big for
    Africa—a land
which is pounded by the Moorish sea and extends to
    the steaming Nile,
then south to Ethiopia's tribes and their different
    elephants.    150
He annexes Spain to his empire, and dances
    lightly across
the Pyrenees; then nature bars his path with the
    snowy Alps;
by vinegar's aid he splits the rocks and shatters the
    mountains.
Italy now is within his grasp; but he still presses on.

'Nought is achieved,' he cries, 'until I have smashed
  the gates
with my Punic troops, and raised our flag in the central Subura!'
Lord, what a sight! It would surely have made an
  amazing picture:
the one-eyed general riding on his huge
  Gaetulian beast.
So how does the story end? Alas for glory! Our
  hero
is beaten. He scrambles away into exile, and there he
160  sits
in the hall of the monarch's palace, a great and conspicuous client,
until it shall please his Bithynian lord to greet the day.
That soul which once convulsed the world will meet
  its end,
not from a sword, or stones, or spears, but from
  an object
which, avenging Cannae, will take reprisal for all that
  bloodshed—
a ring. Go on, you maniac; charge through the
  Alpine wastes
to entertain a class of boys and become an oration!
A single world is not enough for the youth of Pella.
He frets and chafes at the narrow limits set by
  the globe,
as though confined on Gyara's rocks or tiny
170  Seriphos.
Yet, when he enters the city that was made secure by
  its potters,
he will rest content with a coffin. It is only death
  which reveals
the puny size of human bodies. People believe
that ships once sailed over Athos, and all the lies
  that Greece
has the nerve to tell in her histories: that the sea was
  covered with boats,
and the ocean provided a solid surface for wheels. We
  believe
deep rivers failed, that streams were all drunk dry by
  the Persians
at lunch, and whatever Sostratus sings with his soaking pinions.
Yet in what state did the king return on leaving Salamis—
the one who would vent his savage rage on Corus and
180  Eurus
with whips, an outrage never endured in Aeolus'
  cave,

the one who bound the earth-shaking god himself
  with fetters
(that, indeed, was somewhat mild; why he even
  considered
he deserved a branding! What god would be slave to a
  man like that?)—
yet in what state did he return? In a solitary
  warship, slowly
pushing its way through the bloody waves which were
  thick with corpses.
Such is the price so often claimed by our
  coveted glory.

*People pray for a long life (188–288) even though longev-
ity often brings only decay and misery. This is illustrated
by examples from mythology such as Nestor, famous for
his length of years, who lived to see his son Antilochus
killed at Troy; Peleus, the father of Achilles, who outlived
his son; and Priam, king of Troy, who was slaughtered in
the destruction of his city. These cases are supported by
famous Romans, such as Marius (157–86 B.C.), formerly
Rome's great hero who at the age of seventy was obliged
to hide in the swamps of Minturnae to escape his enemy
Sulla; or Pompey, who survived a serious illness in 50
B.C., only to die two years later after his defeat by Caesar,
when he was treacherously slain in Egypt and his head
was cut off.*

'Jupiter, grant me a lengthy life and many a year!'
Whether you are hale or wan, that is your only prayer.
Yet think of the endless and bitter afflictions that
  always attend                                         190
a long old age. First and foremost, look at the face—
misshapen and hideous beyond recognition; instead
  of skin,
you see a misshapen hide, baggy cheeks, and the kind
of wrinkles that are etched on the aged jowls of an
  African ape,
where Thabraca stretches its shady forests along
  the coast.
*Young* men vary in numerous ways—A is more
  handsome
than B and has different features; C is more sturdy
  than D.
*Old* men are all alike—trembling in body and voice,
with a pate that is now quite smooth, and the running
  nose of an infant.
The poor old fellow must mumble his bread with
  toothless gums.                                       200

He is so repellent to all (wife, children, and himself),
that he even turns the stomach of Cossus the
      legacy-hunter.
He loses his former zest for food and wine as his palate
grows numb. He has long forgotten what sex was like;
      if one tries
to remind him, his shrunken tool, with its vein
      enlarged, just lies there,
and, though caressed all night, it will continue to
      lie there.
As for the future, what can those white-haired
      ailing organs
hope for? Moreover, the lust that, in spite of impo-
      tence, struggles
to gain satisfaction, is rightly suspect. And now
      consider
the loss of another faculty. What joy does he get from
210        a singer,
however outstanding, or from the harpist Seleucus
      and others
who as harpists or pipers always shine in golden
      mantles?
What does it matter where he sits in the spacious
      theater,
when he can barely hear the sound of the horns or the
      fanfare
of trumpets? The slave announcing a caller's arrival or
      telling
the time is obliged to shout in his ear to make
      himself heard.
Again, so little blood remains in his chilly veins
that he's only warm when he has a fever. All kinds of
      ailments
band together and dance around him. If you asked
      their names
I could sooner tell you how many lovers Oppia has
220        taken,
how many patients Themison has killed in a single
      autumn,
how many partners have been swindled by Basilus,
      how many minors
by Hirrus, how many men are drained in a single day
by the tall Maura, how many schoolboys are
      debauched by Hamillus.
I could sooner count the country houses now
      possessed
by the fellow who made my stiff young beard crunch
      with his clippers.
Here it's a shoulder crippled, there a pelvis or hip;

*this* man has lost both eyes, and envies the fellow
      with one;
*that* takes food with bloodless lips from another's
      fingers.
He used to bare his teeth in greed at the sight of a
      dinner;                                                    230
now he merely gapes like a swallow's chick when
      its mother
alights with a beakful, going without herself. And yet,
worse than any physical loss is the mental decay
which cannot remember servants' names, nor the face
      of the friend
with whom he dined the previous evening, nor even
      the children,
his very own, whom he raised himself. By a cruel will
he forbids his flesh and blood to inherit, and all his
      possessions
go to Phiale. So potent the breath of that artful mouth
which stood on sale for many years in the cell of a
      brothel.
Suppose his mind retains its vigor, he still must
      walk                                                         240
in front of his children's coffins, and bear to gaze on
      the pyre
of his beloved wife or brother and on urns full of his
      sisters.
This is the price of longevity. As people age, the
      disasters
within their homes forever recur; grief follows grief;
their sorrows never cease, and their dress is the black
      of mourning.
The king of Pylos, if you place any trust in
      mighty Homer,
stood for a life which was second only to that of
      a crow;
No doubt he was happy. Postponing death for three
      generations,
he began to count his years upon his right hand's
      fingers;
he drank new wine at many a harvest. But listen a
      little,                                                        250
I urge you, to the bitter complaints which he makes at
      the laws of fate
and his own protracted thread, as he watches the
      beard of the valiant
Antilochus blazing, and appeals to all his friends who
      are there
to tell him why he should have survived to the
      present age,

and what crime he has committed to deserve so long
a life.
Peleus did the same as he mourned the death of
Achilles;
and so did the other, who rightly lamented the
Ithacan swimmer.
Troy would still have been standing when Priam went
down to join
the shades of Assaracus—Cassandra and Polyxena,
tearing their garments,
would have led the ritual cries of lament, while
260 Hector, along with
his many brothers, would have shouldered the body
and carried it out
with magnificent pomp amid the tears of Ilium's
daughters had
Priam died at an earlier time, a time when Paris
had not as yet begun to build his intrepid fleet.
Therefore what boon did his great age bring him? He
lived to see
everything wrecked, and Asia sinking in flame
and steel.
Then, removing his crown, he took arms, a doddering
soldier,
and slumped by the altar of highest Jove like a
worn-out ox,
which is scorned by the ungrateful plough after all its
years of service
and offers its scraggy pathetic neck to its master's
270 blade.
His was at least the end of a human being; the wife
who survived him became a vicious bitch, snarling
and barking.
I hasten on to our countrymen, passing over the
king
of Pontus, and Croesus too, whom the righteous
Solon exhorted
in eloquent words to watch the close of a long-run
life.
Exile, prison walls, the dreary swamps of
Minturnae,
begging for bread in the ruins of Carthage—it all
resulted
from living too long. What could nature, what
could Rome
have brought forth upon earth more blest than that
famous man
if, after leading around the city his host of captives
280

and all the parade of war, he had breathed his last at
the moment
of greatest glory, when poised to leave his
Teutonic car?
With kindly foresight, Campania gave a desirable fever
to Pompey; however, the public prayers of
numerous cities
prevailed; so Pompey's fortune and that of the
capital saved
his life—but only to cut it off in defeat. Such mangling
Lentulus missed; Cethegus avoided that fate and
was killed
without mutilation; Catiline lay with his corpse entire.

*The last entry in Juvenal's catalog of the things that peo-
ple wish for is beauty. A series of examples from Roman
tradition highlights its perils. Lucretia was the wife of
L. Tarquinius Collatinus, whose beauty attracted the last
king's son, Sextus Tarquinius, which led to her rape and
suicide. In the fifth century B.C., Verginia was killed by her
father to prevent her from being taken by Appius Claudius.
Nero tried to castrate a young man whom he fancied, so
he could be his "bride." Examples from mythology are
added to the list, such as Mars's risky escapade with Venus,
Phaedra's fatal attraction to her stepson, Hippolytus,
and Bellerophon, who was accused by his host's wife,
Sthenoboea. The capstone example is the good-looking
C. Silius, who was forced by the emperor Claudius's wife,
Messalina, to go through a wedding ceremony with her.*

When she passes Venus' temple, the anxious mother
requests
beauty—in a quiet voice for her sons, more loudly for
her daughters,                                                                    290
going to fanciful lengths in her prayers. 'So I do,'
she says.
'What's wrong with that? Latona delights in Diana's
beauty.'
But Lucretia discourages people from praying for
looks of the kind
which she had herself. Verginia would welcome
Rutila's hump
and bestow her own appearance on her. It's the same
with a son;
if he possesses physical charm, his parents are always
in a state of wretched anxiety. For it's true that beauty
and virtue
are rarely found together. Although he may come
from a home

which instils pure habits and is just as strict as the
    Sabines of old,
although generous Nature may add with a kindly
    hand
300   the gift of an innocent heart and a face that burns
    with modest
blushes (what greater boon can a boy receive from
    Nature,
who has more authority than any caring parent or
    guardian?),
he is not allowed to become a man. A wealthy
    seducer
with brazen effrontery actually dares to approach the
    parents.
Such is the confidence placed in bribes. No *ugly*
    youngster
was ever castrated by a despot within his barbarous
    castle.
Nero would never rape a stripling with
    bandy legs
or scrofula, or one with a swollen belly and a
    crooked back.
I challenge you now to rejoice in your son's good
310   looks! And greater
hazards still are ahead. He'll become a lover at large;
then he will have to fear whatever reprisals a furious
husband may take. (He can hardly hope to have
    better luck
than the ill-starred Mars; he too will be caught in the
    net.) Moreover,
such anger sometimes exacts more than is granted
    to anger
by any law. Thus one is cut down by a dagger, another
is cut up by a bloody whip; some make room for a
    mullet.
Your young Endymion will fall for a married lady
    and become
her lover. And then, once he has taken Servilia's cash,
he will do it to one for whom he cares nothing, strip-
320   ping her body
of all its jewelry. For what will any woman deny
to her clammy crotch? She may be an Oppia or a
    Catulla,
but when she's rotten, *that* is the center of all her
    conduct.
'What harm is beauty to one who is pure?' Ask rather
    what profit
was gained by Hippolytus, or by Bellerophon, from
    his stern convictions.

She blushed with shame at the rebuff, as though
    despised for her looks;
Sthenoboea, too, was just as incensed as the woman
    of Crete.
They lashed themselves, both, to fury; a woman is at
    her most savage
when goaded to hatred by an injured pride.
                    Decide what advice
you think should be offered to the man whom Caesar's
    wife is determined              330
to marry. He's a fine fellow of excellent birth, and
    extremely
handsome; but the luckless wretch is being swept to
    his death
by Messalina's eyes. She has long been sitting there, all
    prepared
in her flaming veil; a purple bed stands open to view
in the grounds. A dowry of a million will be paid in
    the old ancestral
manner; a priest will come with people to witness the
    contract.
Perhaps you thought all this was a secret known
    to a few?
Not at all; she insists on a proper ceremony. State your
    decision.
Unless you're willing to obey her commands, you
    must die before dusk.
If you go through with the crime, there will be a
    respite until                   340
what is known to all and sundry reaches the
    emperor's ear.
He'll be the last to hear of his family's shame; in the
    meantime
do what you're told, if you rate a few days' extra life
as highly as that. Whatever you judge to be the more easy
and better course, that fine white neck must bow to
    the sword.

*The much shorter conclusion points to what humans
should pray for, health of mind and body, while leaving it
to the gods to order the rest of one's life.*

Is there nothing, then, that people should pray for? If
    you want some advice,
you will let the heavenly powers themselves determine
    what blessings
are most appropriate to us and best suit our condition;
for instead of what's pleasant, the gods will always pro-
    vide what's fitting.

They care more for man than he cares for himself;
350    for we
are driven by the force of emotion, a blind overmaster-
    ing impulse,
when we yearn for marriage and a wife who will give
    us children; the gods,
however, foresee what the wife and children are going
    to be like.
Still, that you may have something to ask for—some
    reason to offer
the holy sausages and innards of a little white pig in a
    chapel you
ought to pray for a healthy mind in a healthy body.
Ask for a valiant heart which has banished the fear
    of death,
which looks upon length of days as one of the least of
    nature's

gifts; which is able to suffer every kind of hardship,
is proof against anger, craves for nothing, and reckons
    the trials                                                      360
and gruelling labors of Hercules as more desirable
    blessings
than the amorous ease and the banquets and cushions
    of Sardanapallus.
The things that I recommend you can grant to your-
    self; it is certain
that the tranquil life can only be reached by the path
    of goodness.
Lady Luck, if the truth were known, you possess
    no power;
it is we who make you a goddess and give you a place
    in heaven.

## AFTERWORD

It appears that Juvenal was not a very popular author in his own time or in the years that followed. Not until the late fourth century do we find evidence that his satires were being read and studied. The most famous teacher of that era, Servius, quotes from Juvenal more than seventy times in his commentary on Virgil, which was well known to every self-respecting Roman schoolboy. From this period dates a commentary by an unknown author on Juvenal's works, too, which suggests that they were now being read by students and that there was thus a demand for scholarly explication of his very difficult Latin and the many topical allusions to people, customs, and events that had long since faded from memory. His biting moral aphorisms were particularly well suited to adaptation by Christian moralists and were to make him a revered author in the Middle Ages, but in late antiquity his audience was largely pagan. For the fourth-century Roman historian Ammianus Marcellinus the taste for Juvenal among the aristocracy of Rome was a sign of decadence. "Some of them," he wrote, "hate learning as they do poison, and read with attentive care only Juvenal and Marius Maximus [an imperial biographer of the third century A.D.], in their boundless idleness handling no other books than these, for what reason it is not for my humble mind to judge."

With the revival of interest in classical literature in the ninth century that accompanied the reign of Charlemagne in western Europe, Juvenal was again an object of study. Remigius (ca. 841–908), a Benedictine monk who taught for many years at the Abbey of St. Germain in Auxerre, in Burgundy, compiled a commentary on Juvenal, drawing on the notes of his teacher, Heiric. This work formed the basis for a vast body of interpretive work on Juvenal beginning in the eleventh and twelfth centuries, a period when his popularity skyrocketed. Not that Juvenal escaped suspicion any more than other classical authors. When, in eleventh-century Ravenna, the grammarian Vilgardus was accused of heresy for promoting the classical poets, he claimed that he had been misled by demons who took the form not only of Virgil and Horace, but of Juvenal as well. More than five hundred manuscripts of Juvenal's works survive from the later Middle Ages, many of them with their margins filled with notes by students and scholars alike. Medieval authors such as the twelfth-century poet Joseph of Exeter imitated his forms of expression, and many others drew on his works for the pithy epigrams for which Juvenal is still famous today. He was well known to Petrarch (1304–74) and Boccaccio (1313–75), and Chaucer could assume that his readers would recognize an allusion to the opening of the Tenth Satire on the folly of human desires (*Troilus and Criseyde* IV 197–201):

> O Juvenal, lord, trewe is they sentence,
> That litel wyten folk what is to yerne,
> That they ne fynde in hire desir offence;
> For cloude of errour let hem to discerne
> What best is.

And, in the full assurance that her audience will recognize the reference, Chaucer's Wife of Bath can quote from the same satire on the subject of poverty (*Canterbury Tales* III 1192–94):

> Juvenal seith of peverte myrily:
> 'The povre man, whan he goth by the weye,
> Bifore the theves he may synge and pleye.'

The saying was one of many from Juvenal that had by then achieved the status of a commonplace.

In the Renaissance the satires proved a magnet for humanists eager to demonstrate their exegetical prowess by explaining Juvenal's difficult Latin and topical allusions to people and events in ancient Rome. Scholarly interest intensified after the appearance of the first printed edition in 1470, attracting such great names in the history of Italian humanism as Domizio Calderini (ca. 1444–78), who modestly remarked in the preface to his commentary (1474), "without arrogance," as he put it, that he had explained a great deal that his predecessors had overlooked. Such pronouncements were routine in the competition among humanists over classical authors, and Calderini attracted scalding criticism from Giorgio Merula (1430–94), whose own commentary appeared a few years later in 1478, and Angelo Poliziano (1454–94), whose commentaries on Juvenal from approximately 1485 are preserved in the notes of his students. All of this scholarly activity laid the groundwork for the dissemination of Juvenal's works among the reading public and also served to maintain their place in the curricula of the schools. In popular literature Juvenal's tenth poem on the folly of human wishes was a model for part of the German moralist Sebastian Brant's (1457–1521) allegorical satire, *The Ship of Fools* (1494). In Brant's work, written in vernacular German, 110 people board ship to search for a fool's paradise, which forms the frame for Brant's exposure of the follies of contemporary religious, social, and political life. This is the earliest instance of Juvenalian satire adapted to current conditions through literary imitation.

Juvenal had been translated into several other languages before the first English version appeared in 1644, when Sir Robert Stapylton (1607–69) published *The First Six Satyrs of Juvenal*. A complete translation followed in 1647, and from that time on, Juvenal exercised a powerful influence on the English literary imagination. Stapylton presented Juvenal as a study in the manners of men and followed the Latin very closely in his translation: "I have for my Country's sake taught him our Language, which if you allow him to speake intelligibly and profitably, you may please to naturalize him by your Votes." It was left to greater literary lights to adapt Juvenal's voice to English poetic language. In 1693, John Dryden produced a translation of Juvenal by several hands to which he contributed his own versions of five satires, including the sixth, Juvenal's virulent denunciation of female vice, which caused (and still causes) Juvenal's translators some embarrassment. As Dryden puts it, with chauvinistic gentility, in his preface to the poem:

> In his other satires, the poet has only glanced on some particular women, and generally
> scourged the men; but this he reserved wholly for the ladies. How they had offended him,

I know not; but, upon the whole matter, he is not to be excused for imputing to all the vices of some few amongst them. Neither was it generously done of him to attack the weakest, as well as the fairest part of the creation; neither do I know what moral he could reasonably draw from it.

Among the many imitations of Juvenal in this period, by the likes of Boileau (1636–1711) and Alexander Pope (1688–1744), pride of place is held by two poems by Samuel Johnson (1709–84). His initial creative success was scored with "London: A Poem in Imitation of the Third Satire of Juvenal," first published anonymously in 1738. The model is Juvenal's denunciation of life in the city of Rome, for which Johnson substitutes contemporary London:

> The cheated Nation's happy Fav'rites see!
> Mark whom the Great caress, who frown on me!
> London! the needy Villain's gen'ral Home,
> The Common Shore of Paris and of Rome;
> With eager Thirst, by Folly or by Fate,
> Sucks in the Dregs of each corrupted State.

Johnson's poem perfectly exemplifies the approach to imitation described by his predecessor Dryden in the preface to his translation of Ovid's *Heroides,* in which a later poet endeavors "to write like one who has written before him on the same Subject: that is, not to Translate his words, or to be Confined to his Sense, but only to set him as a Pattern, and to write, as he supposes, that Authour would have done, had he lived in our Age, and in our Country." Johnson had so fully absorbed the matter and manner of Juvenal's satires that he composed his other, more famous imitation, "The Vanity of Human Wishes, the Tenth Satire of Juvenal Imitated," in his head while walking the streets of London.

The earliest translation of Juvenal to appear in print in the United States was by the future president John Quincy Adams, a verse rendition of the thirteenth satire written while he was serving as minister in Berlin. It was published in the first issue of a new journal, *Port Folio,* in 1801, by a friend of the family who had acquired it from Adams's brother, and it was printed anonymously, although Adams's authorship soon became known. With Adams's permission the same journal printed in 1805 his translation of Juvenal's seventh satire on the low status of art and education, because he thought it particularly applicable to American society. In his preface he writes, "neither the remoteness of the age, nor the differences of manners and institutions, under which this manifesto of the Muses, against the treatment which they experienced, was issued, can disguise or conceal the pointed application of their complaints to these happy times, and this genial clime." Since then Juvenal has receded in the popular imagination, an unfortunate consequence of the fact that society's moralizing bent now employs other outlets than verse satire.

# APULEIUS

(ca. A.D. 125–after ca. 170)

THE AUTHOR OF *THE METAMORPHOSES* TELLS US A GOOD DEAL ABOUT HIMSELF IN HIS writings, especially in the speech known as the *Apology*, which he delivered in his own defense against a charge of having practiced sorcery. He was born sometime around A.D. 125 in the Roman province of Africa, at Madauros (modern M'Daourouch in Algeria), a center of Roman life and a prosperous community known for its schools (St. Augustine later studied there). In Apuleius's day it was, as he proclaimed, "a quite splendid Roman colony," in which his father had been a prominent public figure. It is possible that his first language was Punic, but his education was conducted in Latin and Greek. We know his name only as Apuleius, although some sources refer to him with the forename "Lucius," which is surely taken from the protagonist of the novel for which he was best known. His family was evidently prosperous enough to provide him with a first-rate education, sending him first to Carthage, the most important intellectual center in Roman Africa, and then to Athens. After that the course of his career for a time is that of a typical intellectual in the period known as the "Second Sophistic." He traveled around the Roman world, visiting the island of Samos and Phrygia in western Asia, before coming to Rome, where he practiced the art of rhetoric. In this respect he has been aptly described as a Latin sophist. At this point his career took a somewhat unusual turn. In the winter of A.D. 156, while en route to Alexandria, Apuleius stopped in the coastal city of Oea (modern Tripoli), where, at the urging of a former pupil, he stayed for a year. During this extended residence he was persuaded by this pupil to marry his mother, a wealthy widow named Pudentilla, whose family was after her fortune. Her relatives filed suit, claiming that Apuleius had used magic to induce her to marry him. The speech that he gave in his own defense when the case was heard in the nearby city of Sabratha obviously puts the best face on events. Among other signs are Apuleius's report of the accusation against him being not merely a philosopher but "a handsome philosopher" (*Apology* 4), a fault that Apuleius claims to share with Pythagoras. We can assume that this speech was effective and that Apuleius was acquitted. This case did, however, help to assure Apuleius's later reputation as a sorcerer. In the years that followed it seems that he made his living in Carthage as a rhetorician and philosopher, but we hear no more of him after about A.D. 170.

In his *Apology*, Apuleius presents himself as a philosopher, "undertaking the defense, not only of myself but of philosophy as well" (3). His philosophical works are now lightly regarded as largely derivative and popularizing, but they attracted readers seeking a shortcut to Platonism. Many of the philosophical treatises he is known to have written do not survive, but we do have three: *On Plato and His Doctrine*, *On the God of Socrates*, and *On the Universe*. This last work, with its grand title, dedicated to Apuleius's son, is derived from a work mistakenly ascribed to Aristotle. It asserts the ability of philosophy to probe the mysterious forces governing the universe. The two other treatises show Apuleius as an effective adapter of Greek originals, a talent that he clearly put to profitable uses in his display oratory. Unfortunately, none of his speeches, other than the speech in his own defense, survives, but some sense of the range of his talents as a rhetorical performer can be gleaned from the *Florida*. This work is a compilation of selections from public performances that Apuleius gave after his return to Carthage, following his acquittal in the trial at Sabratha. It contains twenty-three passages, ranging in length from a few lines to several pages, on a variety of themes, some of them on specific political occasions, others of a more general nature. One selection comes from a speech in which he thanks the people of Carthage for erecting a statue in his honor.

We do not know for certain where, in his career as an itinerant philosopher and public speaker, the novel known since St. Augustine as *The Golden Ass* belongs. It is most likely that Apuleius composed it late in life, in the years that he spent at Carthage, but this is only a guess based on the assumption that he would have mentioned it in his defense against the charge of sorcery. It is the only novel in Latin to have survived intact from antiquity, and like much of Apuleius's other work, it takes its inspiration from Greek literature, as the author announces in his preface:

> What I should like to do is to weave together different tales in this Milesian mode of story-telling and to stroke your approving ears with some elegant whispers, as long as you don't disdain to run your eye over Egyptian paper inscribed with the sharpened point of a reed from the Nile. I want you to feel wonder at the transformations of men's shapes and destinies into alien forms, and their reversion by a chain of interconnection to their own. So let me begin! Who is the narrator? Let me briefly explain: my antique stock is from Attic Hymettus, the Ephyrean Isthmus, and Spartan Taenarus, fertile territories established for ever in yet more fertile works of literature. In those regions, in the initial campaigns of boyhood, I became a veteran in Attic speech. Later in Rome, as a stranger to the literary pursuits of the citizens there, I tackled and cultivated the native language without the guidance of a teacher, and with excruciating difficulty. So at the outset I beg your indulgence for any mistakes which I make as a novice in the foreign language in use at the Roman bar. This switch of languages in fact accords with the technique of composition which I have adopted, much as a circus-rider leaps from one horse to another, for the romance on which I am embarking is adapted from the Greek. Give it your attention, dear reader, and it will delight you.

Apuleius transmits a great deal of information about the nature of the work that follows. By characterizing its mode as "Milesian," he signals an affiliation with the ribald tales of Aristides of Miletus from the second century B.C., collections of which have been lost, but whose imprint on prose narrative is clear also from Petronius's *Satyricon*. The narrator, who, we later learn, is named Lucius, is a native Greek who speaks to us in the Latin language that he learned later in life. With this pose Apuleius draws our attention to the extravagances of his Latin style, which is characterized by exuberant combinations of archaisms and neologisms, poetic language and rhetorical flourishes. He also tells us that he has adapted this story from a Greek source.

A novel about a man's transformation into an ass in several books by a certain Lucius of Patrae was known to the ninth-century Byzantine patriarch Photius, or so he claimed. It is almost certainly related to a much shorter narrative attributed to Lucian of Samosata and transmitted among his works, known as "Lucius, or the Ass." It is certainly not by Lucian, but its origin is disputed by scholars, as is its relationship to Apuleius's novel. It may be an epitome of a lost novel, but it may be something else altogether. And while the plot follows the general outlines of Apuleius's story,

**Figure 31: Canova, *Cupid and Psyche***
This sculpture by Antonio Canova (1757-1822) is a masterpiece of neoclassical style, evoking both the eroticism of the moment described by Apuleius in *The Metamorphoses* and emotional tenderness.

it lacks the digressions that distinguish *The Metamorphoses,* including the long tale of Cupid and Psyche that occupies the central portion of the novel. A consensus has emerged that Apuleius enlivened the narrative framework of his Greek source with these stories and substituted his own ending to the tale. In the version found among the works of Lucian, the story ends when the hero, Lucius, now reconverted to human form, visits a wealthy woman who had enjoyed his sexual favors while he was in asinine form. She is disappointed, however, with his diminished dimensions as a man and throws him out of her house. Apuleius brings his story to an end in an entirely different fashion, when Lucius's shame at being forced to have sex with a woman at a public festival drives him to pray to the goddess Isis. From the hand of one of her priests Lucius receives the roses that restore him to human form, and he learns of his salvation (*The Metamorphoses* 11.15):

> Lucius, the troubles which you have endured have been many and diverse. You have been driven before the heavy storms and the heaviest gales of Fortune, but you have finally reached the harbor of peace and the altar of mercy. Your high birth, and what is more, your rank and your accomplished learning have been of no avail to you whatever. In the green years of youth, you tumbled on the slippery slope into slavish pleasures, and gained the ill-omened reward of your unhappy curiosity. Yet somehow Fortune in her blind course, while torturing you with the most severe dangers, has in her random persecution guided you to this state of religious blessedness.

# THE METAMORPHOSES

## Book 2

*The novel begins with the hero, a young Greek named Lucius, traveling on business to the city of Hypata in Thessaly, a region of Greece with a reputation for magic and sorcery. Along the way he meets two other travelers and hears from one of them the story of a man who was killed by witches, which only whets his already active curiosity about magic. Upon arriving in Hypata, Lucius is to lodge in the home of Milo, a wealthy local, and his wife Pamphile, but first he meets his mother's relative, Byrrhena, who also lives in the town. From her he learns that his hostess, Pamphile, practices witchcraft, but she advises him to steer clear of Pamphile and focus his attentions on her servant girl, Photis, if he wants to gratify his curiosity. Upon arriving at the home of Milo and Pamphile, he makes advances toward Photis before dining with Milo, who has just finished a story about an astrologer named Diophanes at the point where our selection begins.*

[15] While Milo was giving us this long rigmarole, I was silently seething, hugely annoyed with myself for having precipitated needlessly one unseasonable anecdote after another, with the result that I was losing a large part of the evening, and the most welcome pleasure which it would yield. Eventually I swallowed all feelings of decency, and I said to Milo: "Well, then, let Diophanes bear with his fortune, and once again consign to sea and land alike the spoils which he has gained from my countrymen. You will have to pardon me, but I am still feeling the effects of yesterday's exhausting journey, and I should like to retire to bed early."

I made off even as I was speaking, and hastened to my bedroom. There I found that the arrangements for the celebration were quite as they should have been. The slaves had their floor-space arranged as far as possible away from the door; I imagine that this was so that they would not be near enough to overhear our chat during the night. Close to my bed stood a small table on which were laid acceptable leftovers from all the courses of the dinner. There were generous cups already half-filled with wine, awaiting only the necessary dilution, and by them was a flagon, its neck already smoothly cut so that it lay open for easy pouring. These, then, were the apposite preliminaries for our gladiatorial combat of love.

[16] I had just climbed into bed when my Photis, having tucked her mistress in, made her

smiling entrance. She wore a garland of roses, and had a rose-blossom tucked between her breasts. She kissed me hard, put garlands round my neck, and sprinkled petals over me. Then she seized a cup, poured hot water into the wine, and gave it to me to drink. Just before I downed the lot, she took gentle possession of the cup, and with her eyes fixed on me, she charmingly sipped the rest, allowing it slowly to vanish between her lips. A second and third cup was shared between us as we passed it quickly from hand to hand. By now the wine had gone to my head, and I felt restless and randy physically as well as in mind. For some little time now I had felt my wound swelling. I pushed my clothes clear of the groin, and showed Photis that I could not delay the love-encounter any longer. "Take pity," I said, "come to my aid with all speed. As you can see, the war which you declared on me without employing the services of the fetials is now imminent, and I am extended in readiness. Once I felt the impact of cruel Cupid's first arrow in the depth of my heart, I stretched my bow strongly likewise, and I am mortally afraid that the string may break through being drawn too tightly. Now indulge me a little further; let your hair run free and flow over me in waves as you offer me your love-embrace."

[17] At once she hastily removed all the food-dishes. She stripped off her clothes, and let her hair flow loose. Then with a show of genial wantonness she adopted the charming pose of Venus treading the ocean waves. She even for a moment covered her hairless parts with her rosy little hand, a deliberate gesture rather than modest concealment. "Engage," she said, "and do so bravely. I shall not yield before you, nor turn my back on you. Direct your aim frontally, if you are a man, and at close quarters. Let your onslaught be fierce; kill before you die. Our battle this day allows no respite." As she spoke she mounted the bed, and eased herself slowly down on top of me. She bounced up and down repeatedly, maneuvering her back in supple movements, and gorged me with the delight of this rhythmical intercourse. Eventually our spirits palled as our bodies lost their zest; we collapsed simultaneously in a state of exhaustion as we breathlessly embraced each other. Engaged in these and similar grapplings we remained awake almost until dawn. From time to time we refreshed our weary bodies with wine, which fired our sexual urges and renewed our pleasure. Several other nights we spent similarly, taking that first night as our model.

[18] One day it chanced that Byrrhena pressed me strongly to have dinner at her house, and though I made valiant excuses, she would have none of them. So I had to approach Photis and seek her advice—taking the auspices, so to say, to discover her will. Though she was reluctant to let me go more than a nail's breadth from her, she genially allowed me a short furlough from our love-campaign. But she added this proviso: "Be sure to come back from your dinner reasonably early, because there is a lunatic band of upper-class youths disturbing the peace of the streets. You will see the corpses of murdered people lying in various places on the public highways. The provincial governor's forces cannot rid the city of all this killing, because they are so far away; and your conspicuous status, together with their lack of respect for a stranger traveling abroad, may cause them to lie in wait for you."

"Photis, my dear," I said, "let me reassure you. In the first place I should much prefer my own pleasures here to dining with strangers. Secondly, I shall dispel this fear of yours by returning early, and I shall not be unattended, because with my short sword buckled by my side I shall be bearing the guarantee of my safety." I duly took this precaution, and made my way to the dinner.

[19] There was quite a crowd of guests. The hostess was a leading figure locally, so the elite of the town was there. The expensive tables gleamed with citrus-wood and ivory, the couches were draped with golden coverlets, the large cups though not a matching set were equally costly as each other. One was of glass skillfully inlaid, a second of unblemished crystal; others were of bright silver, gleaming gold, amber marvelously hollowed out, precious stones shaped into drinking-vessels. There were cups there which you would have said were impossible to fashion. Several waiters strikingly dressed were expertly serving heaped-up dishes, while curly-haired boys in splendid uniforms regularly circulated with jeweled cups of vintage wine. Once the lamps were brought in, conversation at table became animated. Laughter was rife, wit ran free, and repartee was exchanged.

Byrrhena then began to speak to me. "How pleasant is your stay in our region turning out?" she asked. "My information is that our temples, baths, and other public buildings are much superior to those of all other towns, and that we are also plentifully equipped with the practical requirements for living. Here at any rate the man of leisure is free to roam, the business-man

from abroad finds a population similar to that at Rome, and the guest of modest means can relax in a country house. In short, we serve as the holiday center in this entire province for the pleasure-seeker."

[20] I acknowledged this claim. "What you say is true. My belief is that nowhere in the world have I been so free as here. But I am quite apprehensive of the dark dens where magic is practiced, and which cannot be sidestepped. People say that not even the tombs of the dead are safe, and that human remains, parts of human bodies, are extracted from graves and funeral-pyres to encompass deadly disaster for the living. At the very moment when a body is being borne out to burial, there are aged sorceresses who move at high speed and reach the burial plots of strangers before anyone else."

Another guest took up the topic and carried it further. "Why," he said, "in this place they don't even spare the living. There was some fellow or other who had just such an experience, for he had his face completely disfigured and mutilated." At these words the entire table exploded into ribald laughter, and all turned their heads and eyes towards a man reclining by himself in a corner. He was embarrassed by this general attention paid to him, and made as if to rise, muttering at this unkind treatment. But Byrrhena interjected. "No, don't go, dear Thelyphron. Stay for a little while, and in your civilized fashion tell us again that tale of yours, so that my son Lucius here may enjoy your genial and elegant account." Thelyphron responded: "You, my lady, continue to show your unimpeachable good manners, but there are some people here whose arrogance is intolerable." His words reflected his annoyance, but Byrrhena swore on her own life that he must stay, and so overcame his reluctance that she finally induced him to consent to speak.

[21] So then Thelyphron piled up the couch-coverlets, and raised himself partly upwards on the couch by leaning on them with his elbow. He then stretched out his right hand, deploying an arm as orators do, with the two smaller fingers bent and the others extended, and with the thumb gently but accusingly pointed upward. This was how he began.

"As a young lad I set out from Miletus to attend the Olympic games, and as I was eager to visit this region of the celebrated province as well, I traveled the length and breadth of Thessaly, and arrived at Larissa in an evil hour. My travel-funds were now running low, so as I wandered about viewing all the sights, I was looking out for some means of relieving my poverty. I saw in the middle of the market-place a tall old man standing on a stone. He was making a public announcement that if any person was willing to guard a corpse, the fee could be negotiated. I remarked to one of the passers-by: 'Whatever is this all about? Do corpses often take to their heels in these parts?' 'Hush!' he replied. 'You are just a boy and a mere stranger, so naturally you are unaware that the Thessaly in which you are lodging contains witches who in different localities bite morsels off dead men's faces, and use them as additional materials for their practice of magic.'

[22] 'Do please tell me,' I replied, 'What does this protection of a corpse involve?' 'To begin with,' he said, 'you must keep intensive watch all night through, keeping your eyes trained unblinkingly and continuously on the body. Your gaze must not be distracted in the slightest, not even so much as by a swivelling of the eyes. Those most repellent hags change their outward appearance by transforming themselves into any creature, and they creep in so surreptitiously that they easily escape the eyes even of the sun-god himself and of the goddess Justice, for they take on the shape of birds, or again of dogs, or mice, or even flies. Then by their dread spells they shroud the watchers in sleep. No individual could properly assess the number of hidden tricks which those most wicked women devise to attain their lustful desires. Yet the payment offered for this mortally dangerous task is no more than about four or six gold pieces. Oh yes, and there is a further point which I had almost forgotten. If the watcher does not hand over the body intact in the morning, he is forced to make good any feature which has been prised off, wholly or partly, with the equivalent feature cut off from his own face.'

[23] On hearing this, I exhibited a manly spirit, and at once approached the man making the announcement. 'You can stop shouting now,' I said, 'I'm ready to stand guard. Tell me the fee.' 'A thousand sesterces will be credited to you,' he said. 'But look here, young man; you must be scrupulously careful to guard with care the son of leading citizens of this town from those wicked Harpies.' 'What you tell me is stuff and nonsense,' I rejoined. 'The person you see before you is a man of steel, whose eyes never close and whose sight is certainly keener than that of Lynceus himself, or of Argus. In fact he is eyes personified.' He barely heard me out, but at once led me to a house whose entrance

was barred. He ushered me inside through a tiny rear door, and opened up a room deep in shadow, since the windows were shuttered. He pointed out a tearful matron clothed in black, and he approached her side. 'This man has commissioned himself to guard your husband, and has arrived full of confidence.' The lady pushed her overhanging hair to each side, revealing a face which was attractive even in grief. She turned her eyes on me, and said: 'Do please ensure that you perform the task with the greatest vigilance.' 'Have no worries on that score,' I replied, 'as long as you have ready the appropriate payment.'

[24] When this was agreed, she rose and led me to another retiring-room. There in the presence of seven witnesses who were brought in, she uncovered with her own hand the body, which was shrouded by gleaming linen sheets. For some time she wept over it, and then she tremblingly pointed out each feature of the corpse, asking those present to witness them. One of them committed to tablets the formal inventory: 'Observe,' she said, 'the nose intact, the eyes undamaged, the ears unharmed, the lips untouched, the chin entire. Good citizens, solemnly witness to this.' After these words the tablets were sealed up, and she rose to withdraw. I said to her: 'Give instructions that everything I need is made available to me.' 'What is it you need?' she asked. 'An outsize lamp,' I said, 'enough oil to keep it alight till daylight, hot water with jars of wine and a cup, and a plate bearing the left-overs from your dinner.' 'Away with you, you silly man,' she said, tossing her head. 'The house is in mourning, and yet you ask for dinners and courses? In this house not a whiff of smoke has been visible for days on end. Do you think that you have come here to a drinking-party? The proper fare for you here is grief and tears.' As she said this, she looked round at a little maidservant and said: 'Myrrhine, bring a lamp and some oil quickly. Lock the guard in this room, and then leave at once.'

[25] So I was left alone to console the corpse. I massaged my eyes, and prepared them for the night-watch. As I sought to soothe my spirits by singing songs, dusk fell, and night came on. Soon it got darker, and then as bedtime came, darker still, until finally it was dead of night. I began to get more and more jittery, when suddenly a weasel crept in and halted facing me, fixing me with the sharpest gaze imaginable. It showed such extraordinary self-assurance for such a tiny animal that it quite upset me. Finally I said to it: 'Clear off, you filthy creature. Go and hide with your mates in the garden,

before you feel the force of my arm here and now. Be off!' It retreated, and scuttled out of the room at once. A minute later I was overpowered by a deep sleep which plunged me suddenly into a bottomless gulf. Even the god of Delphi could not easily have decided which of the two of us there was more dead than the other. I lay there lifeless, needing a second guard to watch over me. It was almost as if I were not present.

[26] The crowing of crested cocks was just proclaiming a truce to the invasion of night when I finally awoke. I was absolutely aghast, and I rushed over to the corpse. I held the lamp up to it, and uncovered the dead man's face, peering at each feature, but all were unharmed. The wretched wife now came bursting in, tearful and troubled, accompanied by the witnesses of the previous day. She at once descended on the corpse. After kissing it long and hard, she examined all its features under the revealing witness of the lamp. She then turned away, and called for her steward Philodespotus, instructing him to pay the faithful guard his reward at once. There and then the money was handed over. 'Young man,' she said 'we are most grateful to you. I swear that from now on we will regard you as one of our intimate friends, because of this conscientious service which you have performed.'

I was ecstatic with joy at this turn of events, and at the profit which I had obtained against all expectation. Those gleaming gold coins I jangled repeatedly in my hand, gazing in wonder at them. 'My lady,' I said, 'think of me not as a friend, but as one of your servants. Whenever you need my assistance you can call on me with assurance.' No sooner were the words out of my mouth than the whole ménage at once attacked me, grabbing any weapon to hand and cursing this outrageous suggestion of future misfortune. One battered my face with his fists, another elbowed me between the shoulder-blades, a third pummeled my ribs violently with his hands. They kicked me, pulled my hair, ripped my clothes. I was ejected from the house, lacerated and torn apart like the arrogant Aonian, or the Pipleian poet who sang his poems.

[27] Out in the street close by I recovered my breath. I realized all too late that my words had been ill-omened and thoughtless, and I ruefully acknowledged that I had deserved a worse beating than I had sustained. But by now the corpse had emerged and was being greeted with tears and the final lamentations. Since the dead man was from the upper class, he was being conducted through the forum in a public funeral-procession

according to ancestral ritual. Then an old man clad in black confronted the cortege; he showed his distress by weeping and tearing at his noble white hair. He laid hold of the coffin with both hands, and spoke in strained tones, punctuated by frequent sobbing. 'Citizens,' he said, 'I beg you by your sense of honor and devotion to the state to avenge this murdered citizen, and to punish harshly this wicked and criminal woman for her most pernicious crime. She and no other has poisoned this wretched young man, the son of my sister, to win the favor of her adulterous lover, and to lay hands on the spoil of his inheritance.' These were the tearful complaints loudly voiced by the old man to one and all. The crowd meanwhile was becoming aggressive, for the plausibility of the accusation inclined them to lend credence to the charge. They called for torches, demanded stones, encouraged urchins to finish off the woman. She confronted the attack with crocodile tears, and swore by all the gods as reverently as she could that she was guiltless of such a dread crime.

[28] In consequence the old man said: 'Then let us refer judgment of the truth to the foresight of the gods. Zatchlas, a leading Egyptian prophet, is here. Some time ago he promised on payment of a large fee to bring back for a short time this spirit from the dead, and to instil into this body the life which it enjoyed before death.' As he spoke, he introduced a young man clad in linen garments, with palm-leaf sandals on his feet. His head was wholly shaven. For some time the old man kissed the prophet's hands and clasped his knees, saying: 'Have pity, O priest, have pity! By the stars of heaven, by the powers of hell, by the elements of the universe, by the silences of the night, by the sacred shrines of Coptus, by the floods of the Nile, by the mysteries of Memphis and the rattles of Pharos, grant a momentary loan from the sun and inject some modest light into these eyes which are forever closed. We do not seek to deny fate, or to deny to the earth its possession, but we implore a brief moment of life to obtain the consolation of vengeance.' The prophet was won over by these words, and placed one small herb on the corpse's mouth, and another on the heart. Then he turned to the east, and silently prayed to the nascent rising of the venerable sun. The sight of this awesome drama roused those present to vie in eagerness to witness so great a miracle.

[29] I slipped into the midst of the crowd of the dead man's associates, and perched on a rock behind the bier. The rock was a little higher, and I surveyed the

whole scene with inquisitive eyes. The dead man's chest first began to swell, his life-giving veins began to throb, and his body filled with breath. Then the corpse sat up, and the young man spoke. 'Why, I implore you, now that I have drunk of the cups of Lethe and am swimming in the marshy waters of the Styx, why do you haul me back to life's duties for a brief moment? Cease to summon me, cease, I beg you; allow me to return to my rest.' These were the words heard from the corpse, but the prophet addressed him rather sharply: 'Why do you not recount the details and reveal to the citizens the secrets of your death? Are you not aware that the Furies can be summoned by my curses on you, and that your weary limbs can be subjected to torture?' The dead man raised himself from the bier, and uttering the hollowest of groans he addressed the people in these words: 'I was destroyed by the evil arts of my new bride. I was sentenced to drink a cup of poison, and I surrendered my bed while it was still warm to an adulterer.' Then that most worthy wife adopted a bold stratagem suited to the moment, and with sacrilegious spirit confronted her husband, and argued with him as he condemned her. The citizens were fired up, but took opposite stances. Some claimed that this was the worst woman alive, and that she should be buried with her husband's body, while others argued that no credence should be lent to the lying words of the corpse.

[30] But the next words of the young man removed this hesitation. Once again he uttered a hollow groan, and said: 'Very well, I shall offer you, yes, offer you, clear proofs of the untainted truth. I will reveal what no person whosoever other than myself will know or prophesy.' He then pointed me out with his finger. 'When this most prudent guardian of my corpse was keeping a careful watch over me, some aged sorceresses were hovering close to my remains. They transformed themselves several times to get at me, but in vain, because they failed to beguile his conscientious diligence. Finally they invested him in a cloud of sleep, and immured him in deep slumber. Then they never ceased summoning me by name until my immobile joints and cold limbs made sluggish attempts to render obedience to their magic art. This fellow here was actually alive, and merely dead to the world in sleep. He bears the same name as I, and at the calling of his name he rose up all unknowing, and stepped out of his own accord like the ghost of a dead man. Though the doors of the chamber had been barred carefully, there was a hole in them, and through it the witches cut off first his nose and then his ears. In this

way he took my place in undergoing such surgery. Then, to ensure that their deceit would pass unnoticed in what followed, they shaped wax to represent the ears which they had cut off, and gave him a perfect fit. Likewise they fashioned a nose like his own. The poor man now standing here gained a reward not for being diligent, but for being mutilated.'

At these words I was panic-stricken, and proceeded to investigate my face. I clapped my hand to my nose; it came away. I pulled at my ears, and they too fell off. The bystanders identified me by pointing me out with their fingers, and turning their heads towards me, and they broke out into shrieks of laughter. I was in a cold sweat, and I slipped away, threading my path between their feet. Because of my mutilated appearance I am a risible figure, and I have been subsequently unable to return to my ancestral home. I have concealed the loss of my ears by letting my hair grow on both sides of my face, and the unsightly appearance of my lost nose I have made respectable by covering it with this linen bandage which is tightly wrapped over it."

[31] As soon as Thelyphron had finished this story, the drinkers, who were now well into their cups, renewed their guffaws. As they demanded their customary toast to the god Laughter, Byrrhena explained to me: "Tomorrow is a feast-day which was established in the early days of this city. We are the only people who on this day seek the benevolence of the god Laughter in an amusing and joyful ritual. Your presence will make the day more pleasant for us. My wish is that you may devise some happy entertainment from your store of wit to honor the god, so that in this way our offering to the great deity may be enlarged and enhanced."

"That is a good suggestion," I replied, "and I will follow your instruction. I only hope that I can think of some material to enable the great god to deck himself out in a flowing mantle." Then, at the prompting of my slave, who warned me that darkness had fallen, I hastily rose from the table. By now I was as bloated with drink as the rest, and with an abrupt farewell to Byrrhena I started to weave my way homeward.

[32] But as soon as we reached the nearest street, the torch on which we depended was blown out by a sudden gust of wind. We could scarcely escape the grip of the blinding darkness, and as we wearily made our way back to the lodging, we bruised our toes on the cobble-stones. As we held on to each other, we were now nearing our goal when suddenly three lusty figures with massive frames pushed against our doors with all

their weight. They showed not the slightest concern at our arrival, but battered the doors with greater violence, vying with each other in their assaults. We both, and I myself in particular, reasonably assumed that they were ruffians of the most violent kind, so I at once extricated and gripped my sword which I had concealed beneath my clothing, and had carried abroad for just such an occasion as this. Without hesitation I flew into the band of robbers, and drove my sword up to the hilt into each one that I encountered in the struggle. Eventually they lay before my feet, punctured by numerous gaping wounds, and they gasped out their last breath. The din of this engagement had roused Photis, and she opened the door. I crept in, panting and bathed in sweat. I at once retired to bed and sleep, for I was wearied with this battle against three brigands, which had been a re-enactment of the slaughter of Geryon.

## Book 3

### *The Festival of Laughter: Lucius Becomes an Ass*

[1] Just as Aurora with her crimson trappings brandished her rosy arm and began to drive her chariot across the sky, I was wrenched out of untroubled sleep as the night restored to me the light of day. Anxiety assailed my mind as I recalled the incident of the previous evening. With my feet tucked beneath me and my hands clasped over my knees with fingers interlocked, I sat squatting on my bed and wept floods of tears, picturing before my mind now the forum as the scene of the trial, now the sentence, and finally the very executioner. "Will any juror," I asked myself, "show himself so merciful and well-disposed to me as to be able to declare me innocent, gore-stained as I am after that triple slaughter, and steeped in the blood of so many citizens? Was this the journeying which the Chaldaean Diophanes proclaimed with such assurance would bring me fame?" As I turned these thoughts over repeatedly in my mind, I lamented my misfortune.

[2] Meanwhile there was a banging on the door, and our portals echoed with the shouting of a crowd outside. At once the house was thrown open, and a great number burst in. The whole place was jammed with magistrates, their officials, and an assorted mob. Two attendants proceeded to lay hands on me on the instruction of the magistrates, and began to drag me off as I offered no resistance. As soon as we reached the nearest street, the whole township poured out and

followed us in astounding numbers. As I walked along dejectedly with head bowed towards the ground (or rather, towards the denizens of hell), I observed from the corner of my eye a most surprising sight. Of the thousands of people milling about, there was not a single one who was not splitting his sides with laughter. After being paraded through all the streets—for they led me round from one corner to another, as if they were expiating the threat of portents by driving round sacrificial victims in ceremonies of purification—I was dragged before the tribunal in the forum.

The magistrates now took their seats on the raised platform, and the city-herald loudly demanded silence. Suddenly from all present there was a concerted demand that since the huge crowd was in danger of being crushed because of the excessive numbers, this important case should be tried in the theater. At once from every side the people darted off and with astonishing speed packed the auditorium. They even jammed the aisles and the concourse at the top. Several wound their legs round columns, others hung from statues, a few were partly visible through the windows and ornamental trellis-work. All were indifferent to the hazards threatening their physical safety in this curious eagerness to observe the proceedings. Then the city officials escorted me like a sacrificial victim across the stage, and made me stand in the orchestra.

[3] The prosecutor, an elderly man, was then summoned by a further loud cry from the herald. As he rose, water was poured into a small vessel, which was finely perforated like a colander to allow it to run out drop by drop; this was to regulate the time allowed for speaking. The man addressed the assembly as follows:

"The case before us, august citizens, is no trivial one. It has a bearing on the peace of the whole community, and will be valuable for the stern example it sets. Hence it is all the more fitting that one and all here present, in the interests of the dignity of this our city, should carefully ensure that this impious killer may not escape punishment for the multiple butchery which he has bloodily perpetrated. Pray do not believe that I am fired by private enmity, or that I am indulging savage hatred of a personal kind. My job is as commander of the night-patrol, and I believe that my sleepless supervision can be censured by no one up to this very day.

I shall now turn to the matter in hand, and scrupulously recount the events of last night. Just after midnight I patrolled the city, scrutinizing in careful detail every area door by door. I caught sight of this most savage youth with his dagger drawn, wreaking slaughter all around, and before his feet I observed three victims slain by his savagery. They were still breathing, their bodies suffering convulsions in pools of blood. This man was justly apprehensive because he knew that he had committed this great outrage, and so he at once fled, slipping away under cover of darkness into some house where he lay hidden throughout the night. But the gods' foresight allows no respite to evildoers, and early this morning I waited for him before he could escape by unobserved paths, and I ensured that he was haled before this most austere court which exacts sacred oaths. Here, then, you have a defendant sullied by numerous murders, a defendant caught in the act, a defendant who is a stranger to our city. So cast your votes responsibly against this foreigner, who is charged with an offence for which you would heavily punish even a fellow-citizen."

[4] With these words that most incisive prosecutor ended his monstrous indictment. The herald bade me at once to embark upon whatever response I wished to make. But at that moment I could come out with nothing but tears, caused by contemplating not so much that remorseless indictment as my own afflicted conscience. But then I felt the accession of heaven-sent courage, so I made this response to the charges.

"I am well aware how difficult it is for a man accused of murder to persuade this large crowd of his innocence when the bodies of three citizens lie here before your eyes. This would be the case even if he speaks the truth and acknowledges the deed without prompting. But if with collective good-will you consent to grant me a cursory hearing, I shall readily persuade you that it is through no fault of mine that I am burdened with this capital charge. Rather, the considerable odium of the accusation is baselessly imposed on me through the chance outcome of my reasonable indignation.

[5] I was making my way back from dinner at a rather late hour. Admittedly I had taken too much to drink, and I shall not deny the truth of that. But as I turned in at the house of your fellow-citizen, the honest Milo, I saw before the very entrance to the lodging some most ruthless robbers seeking to force their way in. They were trying to wrench the house-doors off their hinges; all the bars which had been most securely installed had been violently torn away. The robbers were plotting with each other the murder of those within. Then one of them, more eager for action and of more imposing physique than the others, began to rouse them to the

same pitch with exhortations like these: 'Come on, lads, let's attack them, while they sleep, with all our manly spirit and ready vigor. Away with all feelings of hesitation and cowardice! Let slaughter stalk with drawn sword throughout the house. Let's cut down those who lie sleeping, and run through those who try to resist. We shall make good our retreat unscathed only if we leave no one in the house unscathed.'

I freely confess, citizens, that I sought to frighten off and rout these desperadoes. I was armed with a short sword which accompanied me in case of dangers of this kind, and I thought such action the duty of a good citizen. I was also extremely apprehensive for the safety of my hosts and myself. But those utterly savage and monstrous men did not take to their heels, and though they saw that I was armed, they none the less boldly confronted me.

[6] Their battle line was now assembled. The leader and standard-bearer of the gang promptly assailed me with brute force. He seized me by the hair with both hands, bent my head backward, and intended to batter me with a stone. But while he was urging that one be handed to him, my sword thrust was true, and I successfully laid him low. A second robber was hanging on to my legs with his teeth; I killed him with a well-directed blow between the shoulder-blades. A third who rushed blindly at me I finished off with a thrust to the heart. This was how I maintained the peace, and defended the house of my hosts and the safety of the townsfolk. I believed that I would not merely escape punishment, but would also win public praise. I had never been indicted before on even the most trivial charge. As one highly respected in my community, I had always placed unblemished behavior before any advantage. I can see no justification for now having to stand trial here on account of the just vengeance which impelled me to take action against these despicable criminals. No one can point to any previous enmity between them and myself, or indeed to any previous acquaintance whatsoever with these robbers. If it is believed that a desire for ill-gotten gains was the incentive for so great a crime, at least let such gains be produced."

[7] Tears again rose to my eyes at the close of this utterance. I stretched out my hands in doleful entreaty to one section of the audience after another, appealing to their common humanity and to the love which they bore for their dear ones. Once I was satisfied that the compassion of all was roused, and that my tears had stirred their pity, I called to witness the eyes of the Sun

and of Justice, and recommended my immediate plight to the gods' future care. But when I raised my gaze a little higher, I saw that the whole gathering without exception was splitting its sides with loud laughter, and that even my kind host and patron Milo was unable to contain himself, and was laughing loudest of all. At that moment I reflected: "So this is the nature of good faith and awareness of right conduct! Here am I, a killer indicted on a capital charge through ensuring the safety of my host, and he is not satisfied with refusing me his consoling support; he laughs aloud at my undoing as well!"

[8] At this moment a woman, sobbing and tear-stained, wearing mourning black and carrying a baby in her lap, came running down through the theater. Behind her came a second figure, an old hag clad in repulsive rags, and equally tearful. Both brandished olive-branches. They stationed themselves on each side of the bier on which the corpses of the slain were shrouded, and they raised a din of lamentation dismally bewailing their fate: "We entreat you by the sense of compassion which you share, and in the name of the universal rights of mankind. Show pity for these young men undeservedly slain. By taking vengeance afford some consolation to the one of us now widowed, and to the other left forlorn, or at any rate lend support to the fortunes of this little child orphaned in his infancy, and do justice to your laws and to public order with the blood of this ruffian."

Next the senior magistrate rose and addressed the people: "Not even the perpetrator himself can deny this crime which deserves stern punishment. Only one problem remains for us to deal with: we must seek out the associates in this dreadful deed, for it is unlikely that one man on his own took the lives of three such vigorous young men. So the truth must be extracted from this man by torture. The slave who supported him has escaped unnoticed. We have now reached the stage at which the defendant under interrogation must reveal his accomplices in this crime, so that we may once and for all dispel all our fear of this grim band."

[9] In accordance with Greek custom, fire and a wheel were brought in, together with every variety of whip. My consternation certainly grew; in fact it was redoubled at the prospect of my not being allowed to die unmutilated. But the old woman whose weeping had roused general indignation said: "Good citizens, before you nail to the cross this ruffian who has murdered the wretched victims who are my dear ones, allow the corpses of the slaughtered men to be uncovered. By gazing on their youthful and handsome

bodies you may be further roused to just indignation, and inflict harsh punishment which fits the crime." Applause greeted these words, and at once the magistrate ordered me to uncover with my own hands the bodies laid out on the bier. In spite of my struggles and lengthy refusal to revive the memory of my earlier crime by displaying the bodies afresh, at the command of the magistrates the attendants exerted the greatest physical pressure on me to compel me to do so. In short, they forced my hand from where it was dangling at my side to wreak its own doom by guiding it on to the corpses. I was finally compelled to yield; I drew back the pall with the greatest reluctance, and uncovered the bodies. Heavens, what a sight met my eyes! What an extraordinary thing! What a sudden reversal of my fortunes! A moment before I had been consigned as a slave to the household of Proserpina and Orcus, but now I was stopped in my tracks and dumbfounded at this transformation. I have no adequate words to explain the nature of that strange sight: those corpses of the slain turned out to be three inflated wineskins which had been slit open in various places. The gaping holes appeared where, as I cast my mind back to the battle of the previous night, I recalled having wounded those brigands.

[10] At that moment the laughter which some had guilefully repressed for a short time now burst out without restraint to engulf the entire crowd. Some cackled in paroxysms of mirth, others pressed their hands to their stomachs to relieve the pain. In one way or another the entire audience was overcome with hilarity, and as they quitted the theater, they kept looking back at me. From the moment when I seized the coverlet I myself stood rooted there, frozen into stone like one of the statues or pillars in the theater. I did not return to life until my host Milo came up. As I held back, and sobbed repeatedly with the tears again welling in my eyes, he laid his hand on me, and with gentle force drew me along with him. He took me home by a circuitous route wherever he spotted deserted streets, and he sought to console me in my despondency and my continuing apprehension by discoursing on various matters. But he could not succeed in mitigating in any way my anger at the insult which had struck me to my heart's depths.

[11] Now, however, the magistrates in person clad in their robes of office entered our residence and sought to mollify me with an explanation on these lines. "Master Lucius, we are well aware of your high

rank, and also of your family's pedigree, for the nobility of your famous house is known to the whole province. We assure your that the humiliation which you so bitterly resent was not intended as an insult, and so you must banish all the melancholy which at present fills your heart, and dispel your mental anguish. This festival, which we regularly celebrate in public as each year comes round, in honor of Laughter, the most welcome of the gods, always owes its success to some novel subterfuge. This deity will favorably and affectionately accompany everywhere the person who arouses and enacts his laughter, and he will never allow you to grieve in mind, but will implant continual joy on your countenance with his sunny elegance. The whole community has now bestowed outstanding honors on you for the pleasure you have given them; for they have enrolled you as patron, and have decreed that your statue be set up in bronze." To this address I replied: "The gratitude that I accord to this most glorious and unique city of Thessaly matches the distinctions which you offer me, but I urge you to reserve your statues and portraits for worthier and greater persons than myself."

[12] With this modest response I raised a fleeting smile, pretending as best I could to be cheerful, and as the magistrates departed I bade them a friendly farewell. Suddenly a servant came hastening in. "Your aunt Byrrhena summons you," he said. "She wishes to remind you of the dinner-party which late last night you promised to attend and which will shortly begin." But I was apprehensive, and even at a distance I shuddered at the thought of her house. So I made the following reply: "How I wish, dear aunt, that I could obey your bidding, if only I could do so in good faith. But my host Milo has made me promise to have dinner with him today, invoking the deity who is in close attendance on us. He does not leave my side, and does not permit me to leave his, so we must postpone that promise of dinner."

While I was still dictating this, Milo put his arm firmly in mine, and conducted me to the baths close by, giving instructions that the toiletries should accompany us. I sought to avoid everyone's eyes and made myself inconspicuous as I walked along at his side, avoiding the laughter of passers-by which I had myself promoted. My embarrassment was such that I do not recall how I bathed and toweled and returned to the house again, for I was distraught and paralyzed as the eyes and nods and fingers of all present marked me down.

[13] The outcome was that having enjoyed a hasty and extremely modest supper at Milo's table, I pleaded as excuse a sharp headache brought on by my continual weeping earlier, and I readily obtained leave to retire to bed. I threw myself down on my little couch, and in my depression I recalled every detail of what had happened. Eventually my Photis came in, after having seen her mistress to bed. Her demeanor was quite different from before, for she did not look cheerful, nor was her conversation spiced with wit. She wore a somber look, wrinkling her face into a frown.

At last she spoke hesitantly and timidly. "I have to confess," she said, "that I caused this discomfiture of yours." As she spoke, she produced a strap from under her dress, and handed it to me. "Take your revenge, I beg you," she said, "on a woman who has betrayed you, or exact some punishment even greater than this. But I implore you not to imagine that I deliberately planned this painful treatment for you. God forbid that you should suffer even the slightest vexation on my account. If anything untoward threatens you, I pray that my life-blood may avert it. It was because of a mischance that befell me, when ordered to perform a different task, that the damage was inflicted on you."

[14] Impelled by my habitual curiosity and eager to have the hidden cause of the incident of the previous night revealed, I then replied: "This is a wicked and most presumptuous strap, since you have allotted it the task of beating you. I shall destroy it by cutting it up or by slashing it to pieces rather than have it touch your skin, which is soft as down and white as milk. But tell me truthfully: what action of yours was attended by the perversity of savage Fortune, and resulted in my downfall? I swear by that head of yours which is so dear to me that I can believe no one, and you least of all, in the suggestion that you laid any plan for my undoing. In any case, a chance happening, or even a detrimental occurrence, cannot convert innocent intentions into guilty deeds." As I finished speaking, I thirstily applied my mouth to the moist and trembling eyes of my Photis, which were languid with uncontrolled desire, and were now half-closed as I pressed hungry kisses upon them.

[15] Her high spirits now restored, "Please wait a moment," she said, "until I carefully close the bedroom door. I don't wish to commit a grievous error by carelessly and sacrilegiously letting my tongue run free." As she spoke, she thrust home the bolts and fastened the hook securely. Then she came back to me, and took my neck in both her hands. In a low and quite

restrained voice, she said: "I am fearful and mortally terrified of revealing the secrets of this house, and of exposing the hidden mysteries wrought by my mistress. But I have considerable trust in you and your learning. In addition to the noble distinction of your birth and your outstanding intellect, you have been initiated into several sacred cults, and you are certainly aware of the need for the sacred confidentiality of silence. So all that I entrust to the sanctuary of your pious heart you must for ever enclose and guard within its confines, and thus repay the ingenuous trust of my revelations with the steadfast security of your silence. The love which holds me fast to you compels me to reveal to you things which I alone know. You are now to gain acquaintance with the entire nature of our household, with the wondrous and secret spells of my mistress. To these the spirits hearken and the elements are enslaved, and by them the stars are dislocated and the divine powers harnessed. But for no purpose does my mistress have recourse to the power of this art so much as when she eyes with pleasure some young man of elegant appearance, and indeed this is a frequent practice of hers.

[16] At the moment she is passionately obsessed with a young and extremely handsome Boeotian, and she eagerly deploys every device and every technique of her art. Only this evening I heard her with my own ears threatening the sun itself with cloud cover and unbroken darkness because it had not retired from the sky quickly enough, and had yielded to nightfall too late for her to practise the enticements of magic. Yesterday, when she was on her way back from the baths, she happened to catch sight of the young man sitting in the barber's, and she ordered me to remove secretly his hair which had been snipped off by the scissors and was lying on the floor. As I was carefully and unobtrusively gathering it, the barber caught me at it. Now we in this city have a bad name for practising the art of sorcery, so he grabbed me brusquely and rebuked me. 'You brazen hussy, is there no end to your repeatedly stealing the hair of eligible young men? If you don't finally stop this criminal practice, I'll have you up at once before the magistrates.' He followed up his words with action; he thrust his hands between my breasts, felt around, and angrily extracted some hair which I had already hidden there. I was extremely concerned at this turn of events, remembering my mistress's usual temper. She often gets quite annoyed if she is frustrated in this way, and she takes it out on me most savagely. I actually thought

of running away from her, but the thought of you at once caused me to reject the idea.

[17] I was just returning dispirited and afraid to go back empty-handed from the barber's, when I saw a man paring some goatskins with scissors. Once I watched the skins inflated, tightly tied, and hanging up, and the hair from them lying on the ground and of the same blonde color as that of the young Boeotian, I abstracted a quantity of it and passed it to my mistress, concealing its true provenance. So it was that in the first hours of darkness, before you returned from your dinner, my mistress Pamphile in a fit of ecstatic madness climbed up towards the overlapping roof. On the far side of the house there is an area which is uncovered and exposed to the elements. It commands every view on the eastern side, as well as those in other directions. So it is especially convenient for those magical arts of hers, and she practises them there in secret. First of all she fitted out her infernal laboratory with the usual supplies, including every kind of aromatic plant, metal strips inscribed with unintelligible letters, the surviving remains of ill-omened birds, and a fairly large collection of corpses' limbs, earlier mourned over by relatives and in some cases even buried. Noses and fingers were in a heap in one place, and in another, nails from the gibbet to which there still clung flesh from the men hanged there. In yet another place the blood of slaughtered men was kept, and also gnawed skulls, torn from the fangs of wild beasts.

[18] Then, after chanting spells over quivering entrails, she poured propitiating offerings of various liquids—now spring-water, now cow's milk, now mountain-honey; she also poured out mead. She twisted and entwined the locks of hair with each other, and placed them on live coals to be burnt with a variety of fragrant plants. Immediately, through this combination of the irresistible power of her magic lore and the hidden energy of the harnessed deities, the bodies from which the hair was crackling and smoking acquired human breath, and were able to feel and walk. They headed for the place to which the stench from the hair they had shed led them, and thus they took the place of the Boeotian youth in barging at the doors, in their attempt to gain entrance. At that moment you appeared on the scene, drunk with wine and deceived by the darkness of the sightless night. You drew your short sword, and armed yourself for the role of the mad Ajax. But whereas he inflicted violence on living cattle and lacerated whole herds, you much more

courageously dealt the death-blow to three inflated goatskins. Thus you laid low the enemy without shedding a drop of blood, so that I can embrace not a homicide but an utricide."

[19] This elegant remark of Photis made me smile, and I responded in the same joking spirit. "Well then," I said, "I can regard this as the first trophy won by my valor, in the tradition of Hercules' twelve labors, for I can equate the body of Geryon which was in triplicate, or the three-formed shape of Cerberus, with the like number of skins that I slew. But to obtain as you desire my forgiveness willingly for the entire error by which you involved me in such great distress, you must grant me the favor which is my dearest wish. Let me watch your mistress when she sets in train some application of her supernatural art. Let me see her when she summons the gods, or at any rate when she changes her shape. I am all agog to witness magic from close up. Mind you, you yourself do not seem to be a novice wholly innocent of such things. I have come to be quite convinced of this, for your flashing eyes and rosy cheeks, your shining hair, your kisses with parted lips, and your fragrant breasts hold me fast as your willing slave and bondsman, whereas previously I always spurned the embraces of matrons. So now I have no thought of returning home or planning my departure there; there is nothing which I count better than spending a night with you."

[20] "Lucius," she replied, "I should dearly love to grant your wish, but her surly disposition aside, Pamphile invariably seeks solitude and likes to perform such secret rites when no one else is present. However, I shall put your wish before my personal danger. I shall watch out for a favorable occasion, and carefully arrange what you seek. My only stipulation, as I said at the beginning, is that you must promise to maintain silence in this momentous matter."

As we chatted away, our desire for each other roused the minds and bodies of both of us. We threw off the clothes we wore until we were wholly naked, and enjoyed a wild love orgy. When I was wearied with her feminine generosity, Photis offered me a boy's pleasure. Finally this period of wakefulness caused our eyes to droop; sleep invaded them, and held us fast until it was broad daylight.

[21] After we had spent a few nights in such pleasurable pursuits, one day Photis came hurrying to me trembling with excitement. Her mistress, she said, was having no success in her love-affair by other means, and

so she intended on the following night to invest herself with a bird's plumage, and to join her beloved by taking wing. I should accordingly be ready to observe with due circumspection this astonishing feat. So just as darkness fell, Photis led me silently on tiptoe to that upper chamber, and instructed me to witness what was happening there through a chink in the door.

Pamphile first divested herself of all her clothing. She then opened a small casket and took from it several small boxes. She removed the lid from one of these, and extracted ointment from it. This she rubbed for some time between her hands, and then smeared it all over herself from the tips of her toes to the crown of her head. She next held a long and private conversation with the lamp, and proceeded to flap her arms and legs with a trembling motion. As she gently moved them up and down, soft feathers began to sprout on them, and sturdy wings began to grow. Her nose became curved and hard, and her nails became talons. In this way Pamphile became an owl; she uttered a plaintive squawk as she tried out her new identity by gradually forsaking the ground. Soon she rose aloft, and with the full power of her wings quitted the house.

[22] This was how Pamphile deliberately changed her shape by employing techniques of magic. I too was spellbound, but not through any incantation. I was rooted to the ground with astonishment at this event, and I seemed to have become something other than Lucius. In this state of ecstasy and riveted mindlessness, I was acting out a waking dream, and accordingly I rubbed my eyes repeatedly in an effort to discover whether I was awake. Finally I returned to awareness of my surroundings, and seizing Photis' hand I placed it on my eyes. "While the chance allows," I begged her, "do please allow me one great and unprecedented boon bestowed by your affection. Get me, my honey-sweet, a little ointment from that same box—by those dear breasts of yours I beg you. Bind me as your slave for ever by a favor which I can never repay, and in this way ensure that I shall become a winged Cupid, drawing close to my Venus."

"Is that what you're after, my foxy lover?" she asked. "Are you trying to force me to apply an axe to my own limbs? When you are in that vulnerable state, I can scarcely keep you safe from those two-legged Thessalian wolves! And where shall I seek you, when shall I see you, once you become a bird?"

[23] "The gods preserve me from perpetrating such an outrage," I replied. "Even if I were to fly through

the entire heavens on the soaring wings of an eagle, as the appointed messenger or happy squire of highest Jove, would I not sweep down from time to time from the enjoyment of such distinction on the wing to this fond nest of mine? I swear by this sweet knot that binds your hair and has enmeshed my heart, there is no other girl I prefer to my dear Photis. A second thought comes to my mind: once I have smeared myself and have become a bird like that, I shall have to keep a safe distance from all habitations. What a handsome and amusing lover I should make for matrons to enjoy when I'm an owl! If those night-birds do get inside a house, the residents, as we see, take care to catch them and nail them to their doors, to expiate by their sufferings the threatened destruction to the household occasioned by their ill-omened flight. But I almost forgot to ask: what word or action do I need to discard those feathers and to return to my being Lucius?" "You have no worries in ensuring that," she answered, "for my mistress has shown me each and every substance that can restore to human form those who have adopted such shapes. Do not imagine that she did this out of mere goodwill; it was so that I could aid her with an efficacious remedy on her return. Observe with what cheap and everyday herbs such a great transformation is achieved. You wash yourself with water in which a sprig of dill and some bay-leaves have been steeped, and drink some of it."

[24] She made this claim repeatedly, and then with great apprehension she crept into the chamber, and took a box from the casket. First I hugged and kissed it, and prayed that it would bring me happy flying hours. Then I hastily tore off all my clothes, dipped my hands eagerly into the box, drew out a good quantity of the ointment, and rubbed all my limbs with it. I then flapped my arms up and down, imitating the movements of a bird. But no down and no sign of feathers appeared. Instead, the hair on my body was becoming coarse bristles, and my tender skin was hardening into hide. There were no longer five fingers at the extremities of my hands, for each was compressed into one hoof. From the base of my spine protruded an enormous tail. My face became misshapen, my mouth widened, my nostrils flared open, my lips became pendulous, and my ears huge and bristly. The sole consolation I could see in this wretched transformation was the swelling of my penis—though now I could not embrace Photis.

[25] As I helplessly surveyed the entire length of my body, and came to the realization that I was not a bird but an ass, I tried to complain at what Photis had done to me. But I was now deprived of the human faculties of gesture and speech; all I could do by way of silent reproach was to droop my lower lip, and with tearful eyes give her a sidelong look. As soon as she saw what I had become, she beat her brow with remorseful hands and cried: "That's the end of poor me! In my panic and haste I made a mistake; those look-alike boxes deceived me. But the saving grace is that the remedy for this transformation is quite easy and available. Just chew some roses, and you will stop being an ass and at once become my Lucius again. I only wish that I had plaited some garlands this evening as I usually do, and then you would not have had the inconvenience of even one night's delay. But as soon as dawn breaks, the remedy will be set before you with all speed."

[26] She kept wailing on like this. Though I was now a perfect ass, a Lucius-turned-beast, I still preserved my human faculties, and I gave long and serious thought to whether I should end the life of that most nefarious and abominable woman by kicking her repeatedly with my hooves and by tearing her apart with my teeth. But second thoughts deterred me from that rash course, for I feared that if Photis suffered the punishment of death, I should lose all my prospects of saving help. So angrily shaking my drooping head from side to side, I swallowed the indignity for the time being, and submitted to this most bitter of misfortunes. I retired to the stable to join the horse which had served as my trusty mount. I found another ass stabled there, which belonged to Milo my former host. I imagined that if dumb animals shared a silent comradeship bestowed by nature, that horse of mine would register some acknowledgement and pity for me, and would offer me hospitality and a decent lodging. But Jupiter, god of hospitality, and Faith, who has withdrawn her divinity from men, can testify how differently things turned out. That reputable mount of mine and the ass put their heads together and at once plotted my destruction. I can only assume that their concern was for their provender. Scarcely had they spotted me approaching the stall when they laid back their ears, and with flying hooves launched a frenzied attack on me. I was forced back as far as possible from the barley which earlier in the evening I had set down with my own hands in front of that most grateful serving-animal of mine.

[27] Such treatment forced me to seek my own company, and I retired to a corner of the stable. There I reflected on the arrogance of my fellow-beasts, and

I planned revenge on my disloyal horse next day, when with the aid of roses I would return to being Lucius. These thoughts were interrupted by my catching sight of a statue of the goddess Epona seated in a small shrine centrally placed, where a pillar supported the roof-beams in the middle of the stable. The statue had been devotedly garlanded with freshly picked roses. So in an ecstasy of hope on identifying this assurance of salvation, I stretched out my forelegs and with all the strength I could muster, I rose energetically on my hind legs. I craned my neck forward, and pushed out my lips to their full extent, making every possible effort to reach the garlands. My attempt was frustrated by what seemed to be the worst of luck: my own dear servant, who always had the task of looking after my horse, suddenly saw what was going on, and jumped up in a rage. "For how long," he cried, "are we to endure this clapped-out beast? A minute ago his target was the animals' rations, and now he is attacking even the statues of deities! See if I don't maim and lame this sacrilegious brute!" At once he looked around for a weapon, and chanced upon a bundle of wood which happened to be lying there. In it he spotted a cudgel with its leaves still attached which was bigger than the rest. He did not lay off beating my wretched body until there was a loud explosion. The doors were staved in with an almighty din, and there were fearful shouts from close at hand of "Robbers!" At this my slave took to his heels in panic.

[28] At that very moment the doors were violently forced open, and a band of robbers burst into the whole house. Each area of it was ringed by an armed contingent, and as people rushed from every side to lend help, the marauders swiftly positioned themselves to block their progress. All the robbers were equipped with swords and torches which brightened the darkness, for the flames and weapons gleamed like the rising sun. They then attacked and split open with heavy axes the treasure-store, which was situated in the middle of the house, and was secured and bolted with bars of considerable strength; it was packed with Milo's precious stones. When they had forced their way in from every side, they bore off the entire store of treasures, each taking his share in hastily accumulated bundles. But these when assembled proved too many for those who were to carry them, for the extraordinary abundance of their rich haul caused them quite a headache. So they then led the two asses and my horse out of the stable, and loaded us as far as they could with the heavier bundles. They then drove us off from the plundered house with

threats from their cudgels, leaving behind one of their comrades to report on the enquiry into the outrage. With repeated beatings they drove us pell-mell over the trackless expanse of mountain.

[29] By this time I was as good as dead from the weight of all the baggage, the steep climb over the mountain-top, and the quite lengthy trek. Then— better late than never—the idea occurred to me to appeal to the civil authority, and to free myself from all these hardships by appealing to the august name of the emperor. So when we were now passing in full daylight through a crowded village with a busy market, as I made my way through knots of people I tried to call out Caesar's venerable name in my native Greek tongue. I repeatedly declaimed the "O" eloquently and loudly enough, but nothing further; the rest of the appeal, the name of Caesar, I could not articulate. The robbers took badly to my unmusical recital, and cut my wretched hide on both sides so severely that they left it useless even as a straining-cloth.

Finally, however, the Jupiter whom we all know handed me an unexpected prospect of salvation. After we had passed many farmhouses and large estates, I sighted a quite pleasing little garden, in which among other attractive plants some virgin roses were in full flower in the morning dew. I drew nearer, with my eyes glued on them. Hope of deliverance made me eager and cheerful. My lips were already working up and down as I made for them. But then a much more salutary plan occurred to me. Undoubtedly, if I shrugged off my ass-identity and returned to being Lucius, I should meet a sticky end at the hands of the robbers, whether because they might suspect me of magical arts, or allege that I would lay evidence against them. So necessity compelled me to steer clear of the roses. I continued to bear with my present plight, and I champed at the bit as though I were an ass.

*From this point the story is concerned with the events that befall Lucius while he is in the form of an ass. Before he has a chance to eat the roses that would restore him to human shape, he is stolen by another gang of robbers, which leads to a succession of different masters and unfortunate adventures. The central portion of the novel is occupied by the inset tale of Cupid and Psyche, covering parts of three books (4.28–6.24). A young woman named Charite is the prisoner of the same brigands who have taken Lucius. To console her, the old woman who is watching over the captives tells the story of Cupid's* love for Psyche, the most famous portion of the novel. Its fairy-tale opening is justly famous: "In a certain city there lived a king and queen with three notably beautiful daughters..." The most beautiful of them, the youngest, is carried away by the West Wind to a magical palace, but her mysterious husband hides himself from her, until one day her jealous sisters persuade her to unmask his identity. It is Cupid, whose angry mother, Venus, separates the lovers, to no avail, since they are united in the end: "Psyche was wed to Cupid, and at full term a daughter was born to them. We call her Pleasure." After more adventures, in which he observes the human world of pleasure and pain from his asinine perspective, Lucius escapes from the arena in Corinth, where he was forced to copulate with a condemned prisoner, and finds himself on the nearby beach at Cenchreae. There the goddess Isis appears to him and tells him how to recover his human form by taking roses from the hand of her priest. The final book describes his conversion to human form, his initiation into the cult of Isis, and his journey to Rome, where, with the blessing of the god Osiris, he becomes... an attorney.

## AFTERWORD

In antiquity Apuleius was not known primarily as a novelist. In the fourth century Lactantius refers to him as a magician, which is how St. Augustine describes him a century later. But Augustine also respects his fellow African as a philosopher, describing him in *City of God* (8.12) as "Apuleius the African, a noble Platonist." There were certainly readers of Apuleius's novel during this period, St. Augustine among them. It was Augustine's reference to the novel as *The Golden Ass* that gave the work, which was formally called *The Metamorphoses,* the title by which it has largely been known ever since. And in Rome in the year A.D. 395 a man named Sallustius produced an edition of the novel, which he subsequently re-edited in Constantinople two years later. That edition was the ancestor of the sole surviving manuscript of the work, which was written at the Italian monastery of Monte Cassino in the eleventh century. There is a story, from the not very reliable source known as the *Historia Augusta,* that the late second-century usurper Clodius Albinus grew senile reading Apuleius's "Punic Milesian tales," which must refer to *The Metamorphoses.* Another African author, Martianus Capella, writing in the fifth century, appears to have drawn on Apuleius's "Cupid and Psyche" to inform his allegory of the marriage of Philology and Mercury. Allegorizing interpretation of "Cupid and Psyche" began in earnest in this period, with a sample provided by the sixth-century grammarian Fulgentius, who summarizes this interpretation of the story's opening: "Some people have posited that the 'city' is, as it were, the World; and the 'king and queen' are God and Matter. They assign to them three daughters, that is, Flesh, Spontaneity (which we interpret as Free Will), and the Soul, for 'psyche' is the Greek word for 'soul'..." But that is the latest certain indication that anyone was reading *The Metamorphoses* until the later Middle Ages; during most of this period, Apuleius was the philosopher, not the novelist.

Giovanni Boccaccio (1313–75) is best known as author of the *Decameron,* a collection of one hundred short stories, but among his services to scholarship was the recovery of Apuleius's *Metamorphoses* from the manuscript at Monte Cassino. Two of the stories told in Boccaccio's *Decameron* are taken directly from Apuleius, and the spirit of the ancient novel animates much of the rest. Apuleius's works were among the first to be printed in Italy, appearing in 1469, and translations of *The Metamorphoses* began to proliferate in the following century. In Italy it was translated by Matteo Maria Boiardo before 1494, a popular version that was supplanted by a new translation by Agnolo Firenzuola in 1549. *The Metamorphoses* was particularly influential in Spain, where it played an important role in the development of the picaresque novel of the Golden Age. For example, the episodic narrative structure of Apuleius's work is reflected in the composition of the anonymous *Lazarillo de Tormes* (1553). The first English translation by William Adlington (1566) remained popular for centuries and was probably read by Shakespeare, serving as an inspiration for the portrayal of Bottom in *A Midsummer Night's Dream.*

But the best-known portion of the Apuleius's novel remained the story of Cupid and Psyche, which was retold many times and in many different genres. Thomas Heywood's dramatization of the story, *Love's Mistress* (1636), was performed three times within eight days at the court of James I. The story served as inspiration to countless poets, both great and dilettante, in subsequent centuries. John Keats composed "Ode to Psyche," first published in 1820, which he described in a letter as "the first and only one with which I have taken even moderate pains." In the poem he offers a dream vision of the lovers:

> Mid hush'd, cool-rooted flowers fragrant-eyed,
>     Blue, silver-white, and budded Tyrian,
> They lay calm-breathing on the bedded grass;
>     Their arms embracèd, and their pinions too;
>     Their lips touch'd not, but had not bade adieu
> As if disjoin'd by soft-handed slumber,
> And ready still past kisses to outnumber
>     At tender eye-dawn of aurorean love:
>     The wingèd boy I knew;
> But who wast thou, O happy, happy dove?
>     His Psyche true!

This stanza reads as if it were a commentary on the celebrated sculpture *Cupid and Psyche Reclining* (1793) by the Venetian Antonio Canova (1757–1822), now on display in Paris at the Louvre. Canova drew inspiration from the story for two other pieces, *Psyche with a Butterfly* (1792) and *Cupid and Psyche with a Butterfly* (1800), but many other artists did as well. As a theme for sculpture, Cupid and Psyche were a particular favorite in the Romantic era at the beginning of the nineteenth century, but the couple was still being carved later in the century as well, for example, by Auguste Rodin (1840–1917). The story appears frequently on canvas and in fresco, too. In the late fifteenth century, Raphael was at length persuaded by Agostino Chigi to paint the loggia of his villa (now known as the Villa Farnesina) when Chigi provided accommodations there for the woman with whom Raphael was then infatuated. The decorative theme, appropriately enough, was the passion of Cupid and Psyche. There are also versions by Peter Paul Rubens, Claude Lorrain, Nicholas Poussin, Pierre-Paul Prud'hon, and Gustave Courbet, among many others. The watercolor *Cupid Finding Psyche* (1866) by Edward Burne-Jones is one of the most distinctive and characteristic works of the Pre-Raphaelite movement.

# LUCIAN

(ca. A.D. 120–ca. 190)

Satire and comedy are not the hallmarks of literature in Greek of the second century, the period of the "Second Sophistic," but they are the distinctive preserve of one of its most influential authors. About seventy works by Lucian survive, representing a wide variety of forms, but all exhibiting the rhetorical traits characteristic of that period. Most of what we know about Lucian's life and career must be deduced from his literary works—always a hazardous enterprise—but in broad outlines we see a man representative of the literary life of the high empire, moving about the Roman world while practicing his trade as a rhetorician. He was born around A.D. 120 in the city of Samosata, modern Samsât in Turkey, on the west bank of the Euphrates. It commanded an important crossing of the river and had once been the capital of the kings of Commagene, but about fifty years before Lucian's birth the kingdom had been annexed by the Romans, and during his lifetime a Roman legion was stationed there. The region had important cultural and commercial contacts with Syria to the south, and easy access to the Greek cities of Asia Minor to the west. In his writings he always refers to himself as a "Syrian," and it is likely that his first language was Aramaic, but his education would have been in Greek, as was standard throughout the eastern regions of the empire. He probably also knew enough Latin at least to get by, since late in life he served in a minor administrative post in Egypt.

After studying rhetoric in Ionia, probably at Ephesus or Smyrna, Lucian had a varied career, practicing as an advocate in Antioch and traveling through the Roman world as far as Gaul to give rhetorical performances. This was the era of the "good emperors"—Hadrian, Antoninus Pius, and Marcus Aurelius—when the empire was at its greatest extent, its borders were relatively secure, and prosperity seemed general. Other references in his works place him in Macedonia and Thrace. In A.D. 165 a Cynic philosopher called Peregrinus committed suicide by immolation on a pyre at the Olympic Games, an event that Lucian witnessed. In one of his works, *The Death of Peregrinus,* he satirizes the career of this man whom he considered a charlatan who would do anything to achieve notoriety. Lucian's description of Peregrinus's short-lived conversion to Christianity is dismissive of both the philosopher and the religion:

> That was when he learnt the remarkable wisdom of the Christians, by getting to know their priests and scribes in Palestine. And—naturally—in a short time he made them look like children, being himself prophet, fraternity-leader, convener of synagogues, all in one person. Some of their books he interpreted and expounded, and many he wrote himself; they honored him as a god, employed him as a lawgiver, and entitled him a protector, though naturally coming after him whom they still worship—the man who was crucified in Palestine for introducing this new cult into the world.

Lucian spent perhaps twenty years in Athens before taking up a post in the province of Egypt. We lose track of him at this point and infer that his death came sometime around the year 190.

In *The Dream,* a short piece that probably served as an introduction to a longer rhetorical performance, Lucian describes how he came to pursue this career:

> When I was beginning to be grown-up and had just left school, my father discussed with his friends my further education. Most of them considered that an academic education involved a lot of effort, time, and expense, and required a well-endowed position in life; whereas ours was modest and actually needed some timely assistance. But if I were to learn one of your ordinary crafts, I would straightaway earn an adequate living from it and no longer be a drain on my family at such an age, and before long my father would be enjoying a share of my earnings.

The decision was then made that young Lucian should be apprenticed to his uncle, a sculptor and a stonemason, but the training did not go well. After the first day, Lucian had a dream in which he had to choose between two women who appeared to him, the one identifying herself as Sculpture, the other as Culture. Sculpture was not a very attractive figure, "masculine in appearance, like a workman, with dirty hair, calloused hands, and clothes tucked up, and covered with marble dust, just like my uncle." She makes a short speech about the fame that would result from skill in this craft. Culture, on the other hand, called in Greek *Paideia,* "had a lovely face, a fine figure, and a neatly worn cloak." She delivers a long, rhetorically crafted oration in which she promises him a life of fame and wealth. Lucian, of course, immediately chooses Culture. It is difficult to take this tale of conversion too seriously, particularly when Lucian points the moral as advice to the young to "take the better course and embrace Culture, especially if Poverty should make any of them play the coward and ruin a noble nature by inclining toward the worse path." But the light treatment only thinly disguises the significance of what Lucian is saying about his art. The dream motif has a long history in Greek literature, beginning with Hesiod and including the famous dream recounted by Callimachus, in which Apollo appeared to him and directed him on the narrow path to a different literary aesthetic. In his dream Lucian employs comedy to underscore his own literary commitment.

Very little can be done to establish dates for Lucian's works. He ranged widely across a variety of topics in as many different modes throughout his life. Many of the surviving pieces fall into the category of rhetorical showpieces most typical of the Second Sophistic. Education in the schools of rhetoric focused heavily on the principle of imitation: the choice of the right models to emulate was crucial, and the best orators were those who learned how to reformulate their classical models into a new literary experience. Oratory had been divided by Aristotle into three categories, deliberative, forensic, and display, but the political reality of the Roman Empire had effectively collapsed all three categories into the third. In works such as *The Tyrannicide,* Lucian is hewing fairly close to the traditions of fictitious rhetoric as it had developed in the latter half of the first century A.D. in the works of writers such as Aelius Aristides. In this speech an invented character claims a reward that had been offered for killing a tyrant on the grounds that by killing his son he had driven the tyrant to commit suicide. There are more flashes of the whimsy that we recognize as Lucian's trademark in the short speech *In Praise of the Fly,* a parody of encomiastic display speeches with all their trappings, including literary allusion:

> I need not speak of its courage and bravery, but leave it to that most mighty-voiced of poets, Homer. When he wants to praise the greatest hero, he doesn't liken his spirit to a lion's or a leopard's or a boar's, but to the courage of the fly and its fearless and persistent attack—and it is courage he attributes to the fly, not recklessness. For even if driven away, he says, it does not give up but persists in trying to sting.

Lucian's virtuosity is on display in using a serious form for a humorous subject; he follows the same route with other genres.

One of Lucian's most creative turns was his adaptation of the dialogue, a form that was closely associated with philosophy, especially as practiced by Plato and, most recently, Plutarch. In *Twice Accused,* Lucian represents himself at the age of about forty undergoing another conversion, in which he relinquishes rhetoric to adopt the dialogue as a vehicle for moralizing discourse. His unique contribution is the comic spin that he puts on "Dialogue, who is said to be the son of Philosophy." He calls on the full panoply of literary sources to deal with an equally dazzling array of themes. The *Dialogues of the Courtesans* draws on the stock scenes of New Comedy and Hellenistic love poetry, while the *Dialogues of the Gods* relies primarily on Homeric poetry. In the *Nigrinus,* Lucian takes on a theme familiar from Juvenal, a denunciation of modern vice as exemplified by the decadence of contemporary Rome. It is presented as Lucian's report of a visit that he made to Rome seeking medical treatment and a conversation that he had there with a Platonist philosopher, Nigrinus, who lived in the capital but had withdrawn from its turmoil. The thread that provides continuity to their conversation is the contrast between Athens, from which Lucian has just come, and Rome. The people of Athens come in for praise because "philosophy and poverty are their foster-brothers, and they don't look with favor on anyone, citizen or foreigner, who tries to force luxury into their lives." By contrast,

> Anyone who loves wealth and is beguiled by gold, who measures happiness by purple and power, who has not tasted liberty or known freedom of speech or observed truth, who has been nurtured entirely in flattery and servility, or gives up his soul completely to pleasure, determined to serve no other, who is addicted to elaborate meals and to drinking and sex, and is steeped in chicanery, deceit, and falsehood, whose ears delight in twangings and twitterings and licentious songs—all such as these, he said, should dwell in Rome. For all its streets and all its squares are full of what they like best, and they can receive pleasure by every door, through the eyes, the ears, the nose, the throat, the sex organs.

The political and social fabric of the Roman world is a constant presence in Lucian's writings, but this is one of his most direct engagements with it, and it is illuminating to find that there is so much common ground among the ancient moralists, whether writing in Latin or in Greek.

## A TRUE HISTORY

*Lucian's best-known work is his only narrative piece, a fantastical tale in two short books. It can be approached from many perspectives—novel, parody, or science fiction. Its chief target is the fantasy novel of the type represented by Antonius Diogenes's* Wonders beyond Thule. *This was a massive work of twenty-four books, the first-person narrative of an old man, called Deinas of Arcadia, telling of his travels with his son in search of Arcadia. They head north in the direction of the fabulous island of Thule and encounter a series of unbelievable adventures and strange creatures, such as humans who are blinded by daylight but can see at night. Unfortunately, we only know of Antonius's work through a summary made by a ninth-century Byzantine scholar, but it provides at least a partial context for Lucian's far shorter tale. Other forms of travel narrative were also popular in antiquity and are satirized in* A True History. *Lucian names two of them, by the historian Ctesias and the travel writer Iambulus. The latter wrote of his journey to the Island of the Sun in the southern ocean, where he lived for seven years. There he heard a great deal, for the inhabitants have double tongues and thus can carry on two conversations at once, and his work is a record of the island's people and their utopian society. We can see reflections of these and other more conventional forms of literature in Lucian's little masterpiece.*

# Book 1

[1] Those who are interested in athletics and the care of their bodies are concerned not just with keeping themselves in good condition and well exercised, but with timely relaxation: indeed, they regard this as the most important part of training. In the same way, I think it does students of literature good, after hard and serious reading, to relax their minds and invigorate them further for future efforts. [2] It would be suitable recreation for them to occupy themselves with the kind of reading which not only affords simple diversion derived from elegance and wit, but also supplies some intellectual food for thought—just the qualities I think they will find in this work of mine. For they will be attracted not only by the exotic subject matter and the charm of the enterprise, and by the fact that I have told all manner of lies persuasively and plausibly, but because all the details in my narrative are an amusing and covert allusion to certain poets, historians, and philosophers of old, who have written a lot of miraculous and fabulous stuff. I would give their names if they weren't bound to be obvious to you as you read. [3] For example, there is Ctesias, son of Ctesiochus, of Cnidos, who wrote about India and details of the Indians which he had neither seen himself nor heard from any truthful witness. Iambulus also wrote a lot about the marvels to be found in the countries of the great sea: he concocted a lie which is obvious to everyone, yet his subject matter is not unattractive. Many others with the same idea have written ostensibly about their journeys and visits abroad, giving accounts of huge creatures and brutal men and strange ways of living. Their leader and teacher in such tomfoolery is Homer's Odysseus, who tells Alcinous and his court all about captive winds and one-eyed men and cannibals and savage creatures too with many heads, and how his comrades were transformed by drugs: All this was the fantastic stuff with which he beguiled the simple-minded Phaeacians. [4] Well, when I read all these writers I didn't blame them greatly for their lying, as I'd already seen that this was habitual even to those professing philosophy. But what did surprise me was that they thought they could report untruths and get away with it. So, as I too was vain enough to want to leave something to posterity, and didn't want to be the only one denied the right to flights of fancy, and since I had nothing truthful to report (not having experienced anything worth recording), I turned to lying. But I am much more honest in this than the others: at least in one respect I shall be truthful, in admitting that I am lying. Thus I think that by freely admitting that nothing I say is true, I can avoid being accused of it by other people. So, I am writing about things I neither saw nor experienced nor heard about from others, which moreover don't exist, and in any case could not exist. My readers must therefore entirely disbelieve them.

[5] I started out once from the Pillars of Heracles, and with a favorable wind I set sail for the Western Ocean. The purpose and the occasion for my journey was intellectual curiosity, eagerness for new experiences, and a wish to learn what was the end of the ocean and who lived beyond it. With this end in view, I put on board a large supply of provisions and a sufficient stock of water, drafted fifty like-minded companions of my own age, procured a hefty supply of arms, hired the best skipper I could for a large fee, and fitted out my boat—she was a small craft—for a long and taxing voyage. [6] Well, we sailed gently before the wind for a day and a night without getting very far out to sea, and having land still in view; but at dawn on the second day the wind strengthened, the waves increased, darkness descended, and we could no longer even furl our sails. So we gave up and abandoned ourselves to the wind, and were driven before the storm for seventy-nine days. On the eightieth day the sun suddenly appeared, and we saw not far away a high, thickly wooded island, with only moderate breakers sounding around it, as by now the force of the gale was abating.

Having landed and gone ashore, we lay on the ground for a long time to recover from our long ordeal. Then at last we got up, and chose thirty of our group to stay and guard the ship and twenty to go inland with me and explore the island.

[7] We had gone about six hundred yards from the sea, passing through a wood, when we saw a bronze slab, inscribed with Greek letters, faint and worn away, which stated: "Heracles and Dionysus came as far as here." And there were also two footprints on the rock nearby, one of them a hundred feet long, the other shorter: I suppose the smaller one was that of Dionysus and the other that of Heracles. We saluted them respectfully and went on, but we hadn't got far when we arrived at a river flowing with wine, which was extremely like Chian.

It was wide and full, so that in some places it was even navigable. This made us much more inclined to believe the inscription on the slab, as we could see evidence of Dionysus' visit. I decided to find out the source of the river and went up beside its stream. I didn't find one single source, but a lot of large vines full of clusters, each having by its root a spring of clear wine, and from these the river took its rise. We could also see lots of fish in it, very like wine in color and taste. Indeed, when we had caught and eaten some of them we got tipsy, and when we cut them open we actually found them full of lees. However, we later had the idea of mixing them with other fish, which came from water, and so diluting our alcoholic intake.

[8] Then, having passed over the river where it could be forded, we found a most extraordinary kind of grapevine. In each one the trunk itself that came out of the ground was thick and well-grown, but the upper part was a woman, perfectly formed from the waist up: just like the paintings we've seen of Daphne changing into a tree when Apollo is about to catch her. Out of their finger-tips grew branches covered in grapes. Even the hair on their heads was formed of tendrils and leaves and grape-clusters. As we approached they greeted us warmly, some speaking Lydian and some Indian, but most of them Greek. They even kissed our lips, and each one who was kissed immediately became reeling drunk. But they didn't let us pick their fruit, but cried out in pain if we tried to pull it off. Some even wanted to make love to us; and when two of my companions had intercourse with them, they couldn't detach themselves, but were gripped firmly by their genitals, which took root with the woman's so that they grew together. And now branches had grown from their fingers, and they were so covered in tendrils that they too were almost ready to bear fruit. [9] We abandoned them and rushed back to the boat, and having got there we told the men we'd left behind all that had happened, including our companions' love-making with the vines. Then we took some jars and filled them with water as well as with wine from the river, and made our camp there on the beach close by. At dawn we set sail with the help of a moderate breeze.

Around noon when we were now out of sight of the island, a whirlwind suddenly appeared, and spinning the boat around lifted it up to a height of about forty miles and didn't let it down again onto the sea;

but while it was hanging up there a wind struck the sails, and filling the canvas drove us forward. [10] For seven days and nights we traveled through the air, and on the eighth day we saw in it an extensive land, seemingly an island, circular and shining bright with a great light. We put in to it, and dropping anchor we disembarked, and exploring it we found the place was inhabited and cultivated. From there we could see nothing by day, but after nightfall a lot of other islands began to appear nearby, some quite large and some smaller, and of a fiery color. There was also another land below us, with cities and rivers on it, and seas and forests and mountains. We assumed that this was our own world.

[11] We decided to venture even further inland, but then we encountered what were known locally as Vulture-Cavalry, and they captured us. These are men riding on large vultures and using the birds as horses. The vultures are large and generally have three heads. You can get some idea of their size if I tell you that each of their feathers is longer and thicker than the mast of a large merchantman. These Vulture-Cavalry have orders to fly around the country, and to bring any stranger they find before the king; so naturally they collared us and took us to him. He inspected us, and making a guess from our clothes said, "So, strangers, you are Greeks?" We admitted we were, and he said, "Well, how did you get here, having so much air to cross over?" We told him everything, and then he began and told us his story: that he too was a human being, named Endymion, and once while he was sleeping he had been snatched away from our land, and arriving there had been made king of that country. He told us that the land there was what to us below appears as the moon. But he urged us not to worry or feel we were in any danger, for all our needs would be taken care of.

[12] "And," he went on, "if I am successful in the war I am now waging against the inhabitants of the sun, you shall spend your lives as happily as you like with me." We asked who were his enemies and the reason for the dispute, and he replied: "Phaethon, the king of the sun's inhabitants—for it is inhabited, just like the moon—has been making war against us for a long time. It began like this. I once collected all the poorest people in my kingdom, wishing to establish a colony on the Morning Star, since it was empty of inhabitants. Phaethon was envious of this and prevented the colonization, confronting us halfway through the journey

with his Ant-Cavalry. We were defeated on that occasion, as we couldn't match their equipment, and retreated; but now I want to resume the contest and set up the colony. So, if you wish, join forces with me, and I will supply you each with one of the royal vultures, and the rest of your equipment. We shall set out tomorrow." "Agreed," I said, "since that is your plan."

[13] So we stayed and had dinner with him, and at dawn we got up and were allotted our stations: for the scouts reported that the enemy were near. Our army numbered a hundred thousand, not counting porters, engineers, and the infantry and foreign allies. Of this number eighty thousand were Vulture-Cavalry and twenty thousand were mounted on Cabbage-Wingers. This is a massive bird, which is covered all over thickly with cabbage instead of feathers and has wings much resembling lettuce-leaves. Stationed next to these were the Millet Shooters and the Garlic-Fighters. Allies also came to Endymion from the Great Bear: thirty thousand Flea-Archers and fifty thousand Wind-Runners. The Flea-Archers ride on huge fleas (hence the name), and each flea is as big as twelve elephants. The Wind-Runners are infantry, but they are borne through the air without wings. Their method of flight is that they girdle up their long tunics to form folds that fill with wind like sails, and so they are carried along like boats. Generally they serve as light-armed troops in warfare. There was a report too that seventy thousand Sparrow-Acorns and five thousand Crane-Cavalry were to come from the stars over Cappadocia; but as they never arrived I didn't see them, so I've not ventured to describe their appearance, as amazing and incredible things were said about them.

[14] This was the force that Endymion led. They all had the same equipment: helmets made of beans, their beans being big and tough; all their scale-armor of lupins (the lupin-husks being stitched together to make the armor, and the husk of lupin in their country is as unbreakable as horn); and their shields and swords of Greek design. [15] When it was time, they were deployed as follows: on the right wing were the Vulture-Cavalry and the king, with the crack troops around him (including ourselves); on the left, the Grass-Wingers; in the center, the allies, in whatever formation they chose. The infantry numbered around sixty million, stationed as follows. Spiders in that region are numerous and very large—each of them much bigger than the Cyclades islands. These were ordered by Endymion to cover with a web the air between the

moon and the Morning Star. As soon as they had done this and created a plain, he deployed the infantry on it, under the leadership of Batlet, son of Fairweather, and two others.

[16] Turning to the enemy, on the left were the Ant-Cavalry, and among them Phaethon. These are huge creatures with wings, resembling our ants except in size, as the largest was two hundred feet long. Not only the riders on the ants fought, but the ants themselves too, making particular use of their feelers. There were said to he about fifty thousand of these. On their right were stationed the Sky-Gnats, also numbering around fifty thousand, all of these being archers riding huge gnats. Next to them came the Sky-Dancers, light-armed infantry, but good warriors for all that; for they catapulted enormous radishes at long range, and anyone so struck collapsed immediately and died of a foul-smelling wound. Apparently they smear their missiles with mallow poison. Next to them were stationed ten thousand Stalk-Mushrooms, heavy-armed troops used for close fighting. Their name arises from the fact that they used mushrooms for shields and asparagus stalks for spears. Beside them stood the Dog-Acorns, sent to him by the inhabitants of the Dog Star: these were five thousand dog-faced men, who fight mounted on winged acorns. We were told that Phaethon too had late-arriving allies, slingers whom he had sent for from the Milky Way, and the Cloud-Centaurs. The latter did arrive just when the battle was decided—if only they hadn't; but the slingers never turned up at all, which it is said made Phaethon furious with them afterwards, so that he ravaged their country with fire.

[17] Such was the armament Phaethon brought with him. The battle began as soon as the standards were raised and the donkeys on both sides had brayed (donkeys being their trumpeters), and the fight went on. The left wing of the Heliots immediately fled, without even waiting for the charge of the Vulture-Cavalry, and we chased and slaughtered them. But their right wing was too much for our left, and the Sky-Gnats advanced in pursuit right up to our infantry. But when these too came to the rescue, they turned and fled, especially when they saw that their left wing had been beaten. The defeat was decisive, many being killed and many taken alive; and so much blood was spilt on the clouds that they seemed as if they were dyed red, as they look to us when the sun is setting. A lot of blood also dripped onto the earth so that I surmised that

something like this must have happened up there long ago, which made Homer suppose that Zeus had caused a rain of blood because of the death of Sarpedon.

[18] We returned from the pursuit and set up two trophies, one on the spider-webs celebrating the infantry battle, and the other on the clouds for the air battle. We were just in the middle of this when the scouts reported that the Cloud-Centaurs, who should have come before the battle to help Phaethon, were approaching. And there they were indeed advancing on us, an extraordinary sight, creatures compounded of men and winged horses. The men were as large as the Colossus of Rhodes measured from the waist up, and the horses as big as a large merchantman. However, I have not recorded their number, in case no one believes it, it was so enormous. They were led by the Archer from the Zodiac. When they realized that their friends had been defeated, they sent a message to Phaethon to return to the attack, and then putting themselves into formation they fell on the disorganized Selenites, who had abandoned battle-order and scattered in pursuit and to plunder. They routed them all, pursued the king himself to the city, and killed most of his birds. They then tore up his trophies and overran the whole spider-web plain, and they captured me and two of my companions. By now Phaethon too had arrived, and other trophies were being set up in turn by the enemy.

Well, that same day we were taken away to the sun, with our hands tied behind us with lengths of spider-web. [19] The enemy decided not to besiege the city, but as they made their way back they built a wall across the intervening air, to stop the sun's rays reaching the moon. It was a double wall and formed of cloud, so that a real eclipse of the moon resulted, and it was covered totally in continual darkness. Endymion was distressed by all this, and sent to beg them to pull down the wall and not to let them live their lives in darkness. He promised to pay tribute, and joining them as allies not to make war on them again, saying he was willing to offer hostages as pledges for all this. Phaethon called two assemblies: in the first their anger remained implacable; but in the second they changed their minds, and peace was agreed on these terms:

[20] On the following conditions the Heliots and their allies have made a truce with the Selenites and their allies:

That the Heliots destroy the dividing wall and do not attack the moon again, and that they return their prisoners, each for an agreed sum.

That the Selenites allow the stars to be self-governing, and do not bear arms against the Heliots.

That each comes to the aid of the other if it is attacked.

That each year the king of the Selenites pay as tribute to the king of the Heliots ten thousand jars of dew, and give ten thousand of his people as hostages.

That the colony on the Morning Star be established jointly, and anyone who wishes may join it.

That the truce be inscribed on a block of electrum and set up in mid-air on the boundaries of their territories.

Sworn to by Pyronides, Therites, and Phlogios for the Heliots; and Nyctor, Menios, and Polylampes for the Selenites.

[21] These were the terms of the peace; the wall was at once pulled down, and they handed over us prisoners. When we arrived at the moon, our companions and Endymion himself met us and gave us a tearful welcome. He was anxious that I should stay with him and join in the colony, and as there are no women there, he promised me his own son in marriage. But I refused firmly, and asked him to send me back down to the sea. When he saw that he couldn't persuade me, he sent us back after entertaining us for seven days.

[22] But in the course of my stay on the moon I noticed some strange and remarkable things, of which I want to tell you. Firstly, they are not born of women but of men: they marry men, and they don't even have a word for woman. Up to the age of 25 each acts as a wife, and after that as a husband. They carry their babies not in the belly but in the calf of the leg. After conception, the calf starts swelling, and when the time comes they cut it open and deliver the baby dead. They then bring it to life by holding it up to the wind with its mouth open. My guess is that we Greeks have got our word "belly of the leg" from there, since among them the calf acts as a belly. And I'll tell you something else even stranger. There is a race of people among them called Tree-men, who are born as follows. They cut a man's right testicle and plant it in the ground. From this grows a very large tree, made of flesh and shaped like a phallus, with branches and leaves, and fruit in the form of acorns a cubit long. When these are ripe

they pick them and shell out the men. These are given artificial genitals, some of ivory, others (in the case of poor people) of wood, and these serve them in having intercourse with their mates.

[23] When a man grows old, he doesn't die but evaporates like smoke. They all have the same food. Having lit a fire they roast frogs on the coals: they have a lot of frogs flying around in the air; and while they are roasting, they sit around as if at a table, greedily inhaling the rising steam, and so feast themselves. This is their food, and their drink is air, which is squeezed into a cup and condenses like dew. They pass neither urine nor stool, not even having orifices where we have them. And youths offer themselves to their lovers not using the rump, but behind the knee, above the calf, where there is an opening.

They think a man is handsome if he is bald and hairless, and they loathe long-haired people. It is quite the reverse on the comets, where long-haired men are admired: some visitors to the moon told us about them. Furthermore, they grow beards just above their knees; and they don't have toe-nails, and in fact have only one toe. Each man has a large cabbage growing over his bottom like a tail: it is always green, and doesn't break if he falls over backwards. [24] Their nose mucus is a very pungent sort of honey; and when they work hard or take exercise they sweat all over with milk, such that they can make cheese from it by adding a few drops of the honey. They make oil from onions, which is very rich and fragrant, like myrrh. They also have a lot of water-bearing vines, on which the grape-clusters are like hail-stones; and my theory is that our hailstorms are caused by the clusters bursting when these vines are roughly shaken by a wind. They use their belly as a pocket for putting useful things into, as it can be opened and shut again. They don't seem to have bowels there: the belly is just lined all over inside with thick hair, so that their children can shelter there when it is cold.

[25] Rich people among them have clothes of pliable glass, while the poor wear woven bronze; for the country there is rich in bronze, which they prepare like wool by soaking it in water. But when it comes to their eyes, I hesitate to tell you about them, in case you think I'm lying because my account is so incredible. Still, I will tell you this as well. They have removable eyes, and when they wish to they take them out and keep them safe until they want to see, when they put them back in so they can see. Many of them lose their own and borrow others' eyes to see with; and rich people keep a large supply of them. Their ears are formed of plane tree leaves, except for the acorn-men, who are unique in having wooden ones.

[26] And here's another strange thing I saw in the royal palace. A large mirror is placed over a well, which isn't very deep, and if you go down into the well you can hear everything that is said amongst us on earth; and if you look into the mirror you can see all the cities and all the countries, as if you were actually standing in each. I too was then able to see my own family and the whole of my country; but I can't tell you for certain whether they saw me too. If anyone doesn't believe all this, he'll know I'm telling the truth should he ever get there himself. [27] Well, anyway, we bade the king and his friends a fond farewell, embarked and set off. Endymion also gave me some gifts: two tunics of glass and five of bronze, and a suit of armor made of lupin—all of which I left behind in the whale. He also sent a thousand of the Vulture-Cavalry to escort us for about sixty miles. [28] On our journey we passed by many other countries, and landed on the Morning Star while it was still being colonized, where we disembarked to replenish our water. Putting out again, we headed for the Zodiac, keeping the sun on our left and staying close to the shore. We didn't land there, though my companions were very keen to do so, as the wind was against us. But we saw that the land was flourishing and fertile and well watered, and full of many good things. When they spotted us the Cloud-Centaurs, who were serving with Phaethon, flew on to the ship; but learning that we were allies under treaty they went away. [29] The Vulture-Cavalry had already left us.

*The narrator's adventures continue in this vein as they arrive the following evening at Lamp City and go on to encounter more outlandish creatures and other wonders like the Cloudcuckoo-city made famous by the comic poet Aristophanes.*

## AFTERWORD

One great classical scholar of the early twentieth century called Lucian "an oriental without depth or character." This perverse characterization aptly reflects the neglect into which his works had fallen among classical scholars by the nineteenth century and the cultural prejudices that explain it. It is perhaps more difficult to guess why his popularity waned so soon after his death, but that does indeed appear to be the case, for he is mentioned by no contemporaries, and there is hardly any trace of his influence in the immediately succeeding generations. He was rediscovered in ninth-century Constantinople, where he was read by the great Byzantine humanist and patriarch Photius (810–93), whose admiration for Lucian's prose style laid the groundwork for overcoming objections to him as an anti-Christian. In the following centuries Lucian was much imitated by Byzantine writers, and it was thus that his works became known in the West, when the first teachers of Greek brought with them the Byzantine curriculum.

The year 1397 was a pivotal date in the history of European culture: in the winter of that year the Byzantine scholar and diplomat Manuel Chrysoloras (1355–1415) began a course of lectures on Greek in Florence. Among his famous pupils were Leonardo Bruni and Guarino of Verona (1374–1460), and Lucian was among the first authors they studied. Latin translations of Lucian's works now began to appear in Italy, among the earliest of which were versions of Lucian's essays *The Fly* and *Slander* written by Guarino. For most of the fifteenth century in Italy, Lucian was as popular as Plato. His satirical works also inspired many imitators in Renaissance Italy, chief among them Leon Battista Alberti in his satirical novel *Momus*, which draws on Lucian's dialogues of the gods. The title character is Momus, whose name means "mockery" in Greek and is

**Figure 32:** Botticelli, *Calumny of Apelles*
Like all the other works of the fourth-century B.C. Greek painter Apelles, the original had perished long before, and Botticelli drew his inspiration from a description of the painting in Lucian's dialogue *On Calumny*.

depicted as a secretary to the gods in Lucian's *Council of the Gods*. In Alberti's narrative Jupiter sends him down to earth to find out how to repair human society.

Alberti was also responsible for introducing Lucian to contemporary painters. His treatise *On Painting* was an extraordinarily influential theoretical treatment of the subject, widely read in his own time and for generations after. In the third book of *On Painting* he describes a lost painting of Calumny by the fourth-century B.C. Greek master Apelles:

> In this painting there was a man with very large ears. Near him, on either side, stood two women, one called Ignorance, the other Suspicion. On one side came Calumny, a woman who appeared most beautiful but seemed too crafty in the face. In her right hand she held a lighted torch, with the other hand she dragged by the hair a young man who held up his arms to heaven. There was also a man, pale, ugly, all filthy and with an iniquitous aspect, who could be compared to one who has become thin and feverish with long fatigues on the fields of battle; he was the guide of Calumny and was called Hatred. And there were two other women, serving women of Calumny who arranged her ornaments and robes. They were called Envy and Fraud. Behind these was Penitence, a woman dressed in funeral robes, who stood as if completely dejected. Behind her followed a young girl, shameful and modest, called Truth. If this story pleased as it was being told, think how much pleasure and delight there must have been in seeing it painted by the hand of Apelles.

Alberti is indebted to Lucian, whose description he read in the essay *On Not Readily Crediting Slander*. It inspired Sandro Botticelli (1445–1510) to reconstruct the scene in the canvas known as the *Calumny of Apelles* (1494) now in the Uffizi Gallery in Florence. Other artists who took inspiration from Lucian's descriptions include Raphael, Mantegna, and Dürer.

The first printed edition of Lucian's work appeared in 1496, and the publication of the first edition of the Aldine Press in 1503 did even more to spread familiarity with his works across Europe. In 1505, the great Dutch humanist Desiderius Erasmus (1466–1536) visited his friend Sir Thomas More (1478–1535) at Bucklersbury in England, where together they produced Latin translations of Lucian's dialogues. Erasmus's debt to Lucian is evident in his Latin *Colloquies,* such as *Charon,* which acknowledges Lucian by borrowing a title from one of his dialogues. And in his paradoxical encomium *Praise of Folly* (1511), Erasmus also evokes the precedent of Lucian in the preface, which he addressed to More. Lucian's propensity for poking fun at philosophers was a particular source of inspiration for Erasmus. As he remarks in the preface to his translation of Lucian's *The Cock*, "Lucian treats no topic, even in passing, without branding it with a jibe. He is particularly hostile to philosophers, especially the Pythagoreans and Platonists for their trickery and the Stoics for their insufferable conceit. These he stabs and slashes, attacking them with every sort of weapon, and rightly so. What is more odious and less tolerable than dishonesty masked by a profession of virtue?" More himself took a slightly different tack, drawing on Lucian's fantastic voyage in *A True History* for his own fantasy, *Utopia*. In France, Lucian found a great admirer in François Rabelais (1494–1553), who tells the fantastic story of two giants, Gargantua and Pantagruel, in true Lucianic fashion.

Later in the sixteenth century Lucian's works were included by the Roman Catholic Church on its *Index of Prohibited Books,* but this did little to dampen readers' enthusiasm for him. Cyrano de Bergerac's *Voyage to the Moon and Sun* (1650) takes the narrator to another world, from which the philosophical, scientific, and religious certainties of Earth seem utterly trivial. Eighteenth-century readers could avail themselves of a translation prefaced with a *Life of Lucian* by John Dryden. And perhaps the greatest of the works inspired by Lucian's fantastic voyage appeared in 1726 with Jonathan Swift's *Gulliver's Travels*. Jules Verne is often credited with pioneering the genre of science fiction, but with *A Journey to the Center of the Earth* or *From Earth to the Moon*, he may be viewed as following in the footsteps of Lucian.

# MARCUS AURELIUS

## (A.D. 121–80)

MOST DISTINGUISHED LITERARY FIGURES NOWADAYS OWE THEIR DISTINCTION TO THEIR writings alone. Very few play a prominent role in any other aspect of public life. Rome was very different. Cicero, Tacitus, and Pliny the Younger held the consulship and governed provinces, Sallust also was a provincial governor, Seneca was one of Nero's chief advisers, Pliny the Elder was commander of the Roman fleet. Marcus Aurelius ruled the Roman world for two decades, and was deified after his death, a distinction he shares with Julius Caesar. Few societies can boast two gods among the writers included in an anthology of its greatest literary achievements.

Marcus Aurelius was born in Rome in A.D. 121. His family was very wealthy and was said to have claimed descent not only from Numa Pompilius, the second king of Rome, but also, rather more recently, from Julius Caesar's rival, Pompey the Great. Far more importantly, however, Marcus was distantly related to the emperor Hadrian, who groomed him for political prominence, perhaps even for the imperial succession, from a very early age. When he was six years old, he was enrolled in the equestrian order, and in the next year he became a member of the ancient and venerable priestly college of the Salii. In 138, when close to death, Hadrian appointed Antoninus Pius as his primary heir, requiring him to adopt Marcus as his son, along with the eight-year-old son of Lucius Aelius Caesar, who had been his primary heir until he died suddenly, of natural causes, on January 1 of that year. As emperor, Antoninus continued Marcus's prominence in public life. They served as consuls together in 140, and again in 145, when Marcus married Antoninus's daughter, Faustina, who was his cousin and, in legal terms, his own sister. They had at least twelve children and possibly as many as seventeen, but only six survived to adulthood. Five were girls, and the only surviving son was Commodus, one of two twin boys born just months after Marcus's accession to the throne in 161. Commodus was therefore the first Roman emperor to be "born to the purple," that is, when his father was reigning. Vespasian had been the only earlier emperor to be succeeded by his sons, Titus and Domitian, and the turbulence of the remaining centuries of the empire ensured that succession from father to son was very unusual afterward. Death by natural causes was a rarity for emperors in the third century, a remarkable number of them being deposed and killed by their own troops in favor of a rival who was prepared to treat the army more generously and hoped to establish a dynasty of his own.

On becoming emperor, Marcus appointed his adoptive brother, Lucius Verus, to rule as his co-emperor, a position he held until his death in 169. Similarly, he appointed Commodus to rule with him from 177 until his own death in 180. Marcus Aurelius is popularly known as the last of the "five good emperors" (i.e., Nerva, Trajan, Hadrian, Antoninus Pius, and Marcus Aurelius),

**Figure 33: Marcus Aurelius**
This massive bronze equestrian statue of Marcus Aurelius is the only surviving bronze statue of a pre-Christian emperor. It stood for four hundred and fifty years in the Piazza del Campidoglio in Rome, on a pedestal cut by Michelangelo from one of the columns belonging to the temple of Castor and Pollux in the Forum. In the 1980s, it was removed to the Capitoline Museum to protect it from pollution, and a replica now stands outside.

who ruled Rome for almost a century after the assassination of Domitian in A.D. 96. This was the longest period of political stability that the Roman Empire ever enjoyed, and it is remarkable for its unmatched peace and prosperity. Throughout this era Rome was mercifully free from the particular horrors of civil war, and from the arbitrary rule of such deranged and tyrannical emperors as Caligula, Nero, Domitian, Commodus, or Elagabalus.

Marcus himself, however, ruled the empire at a particularly difficult period. Very soon after his accession, the Parthians drew Rome into a lengthy conflict by invading Armenia, which was a client-state of Rome. Marcus and Verus had had little experience of actual fighting during the peaceful reign of Antoninus Pius and were unable to settle this crisis quickly. More dangerous, however, was the threat from barbarian tribes encroaching into the empire from the North and East. Marcus spent much of his reign fighting them, and not always with success. This long and unsatisfactorily protracted struggle was an early instance of the Romans' inability to deal with the pressure from migrating barbarians, an inability that eventually led to the collapse of the Western

Empire. In 175, motivated by a report that Marcus was dead, Avidius Cassius, one of his deputies in the war against the Parthians, attempted to seize power for himself and won the support of almost all the provinces in the Eastern Empire, but the revolt ended quickly when it was discovered that the report was unfounded. Large sections of Rome were destroyed in a particularly disastrous Tiber flood in 162, and there were earthquakes in the eastern provinces. All other setbacks during Marcus's reign, however, pale in comparison to the devastating plague, perhaps of measles or of smallpox, that was introduced by the army on its return from the East in 165 and raged pandemically throughout the empire all through the rest of his reign, with further outbreaks toward the end of the century. As many as two thousand people are said to have died every day in Rome alone at one period, and the total deaths for the empire have been estimated at anything from 5 to 18 million people; even on the lowest estimation this was a dreadful proportion of the population of the empire, which may have been about 60 million.

Since he was emperor, it is hardly surprising that we have a substantial amount of information about Marcus Aurelius. A remarkable feature of ancient assessments of him is their almost uniformly positive opinion. Books 70 and 71 of Cassius Dio's eighty-book *Roman History,* written in the early third century, deal with Marcus's reign. Dio, who was a senator, would have preferred the Senate, rather than an emperor, to have supreme authority, and he had unpleasant personal experience of the tyrannical and unbalanced reign of Marcus's son, Commodus. Even so, he gives a glowing assessment of Marcus as an exceptionally humane ruler (*Epitome* of Book 71):

> He was not as fortunate as he deserved to be. He was not physically very strong, and met with numerous disasters almost continuously throughout his whole reign. Even so, he not only survived them but also kept the empire safe despite these extraordinarily difficult circumstances, and I admire him all the more for this. One thing in particular marred his happiness: he gave his son the best possible upbringing and education, but he was a severe disappointment to him. The reign of Commodus will be my next topic, with Rome's affairs and my account of them descending from a kingdom of gold into one of iron and rust.

Apart from the *Meditations,* Marcus's own thoughts are also known to us from a collection of letters written by or addressed to Marcus Cornelius Fronto, the foremost Latin orator of the time and his tutor in rhetoric. Marcus wrote some eighty of the letters, with others exchanged by Fronto with Antoninus Pius and Lucius Verus, and yet more sent by him to other distinguished people. This correspondence was published between 1815 and 1823 by Cardinal Angelo Mai, the same scholar who would later discover also the palimpsest of Cicero's otherwise lost *On the Republic.* The Fronto letters are also a palimpsest, detected by Mai with rather astounding acumen and good luck, given that the manuscript had been divided and was partly in Milan and partly in the Vatican. Unfortunately, the text is often very hard to read, and it was further damaged with chemicals when Mai tried to make it more legible. Although this collection of letters is the third great corpus of Latin letters, after those of Cicero and Pliny the Younger, it is rather less informative than might have been hoped. The ancient editor seems to have arranged the letters rather haphazardly and, in particular, taken little care with preserving dates. Many letters could have been written at any time from the late 130s to the early 160s, and in any case about a quarter of the collection is devoted to nothing more interesting than reports of the various ailments that Fronto was suffering from.

There is almost universal consensus among scholars nowadays that the *Meditations* were not intended for publication, nor indeed to be read by anyone other than Marcus Aurelius himself. If this is true, their survival is all the more miraculous, given that so many books that were widely read in antiquity have now perished without a trace, but it makes it rather easier to understand their remarkably miscellaneous content and the sometimes rather allusive and cryptic form in which it is presented.

The first book, in which Marcus expresses his debts to those who have had the greatest influence on his life and attitudes, has a clear, if extremely simple, overall plan. Otherwise, however, there is no formal structure to the *Meditations*. We read the work in twelve books, but there is no evidence that either these or any other divisions were originally intended. There is no attempt to present a coherent treatise designed to argue toward a particular conclusion. Likewise, there is no arrangement of the content such as might be expected to warrant a division into books. If the *Meditations* were not intended for publication, no such ordering and division would be needed. Although the author was the most powerful man in the Roman world, there are, rather surprisingly, so few references to contemporary events that we cannot even be sure if they have come down to us in the order in which they were written. Scholars are, of course, tempted to detect references to specific events in Marcus's life hidden in particular sections. Because of, in particular, the lack of chronological certainty, such speculations are rarely persuasive and are mostly just an exercise in academic frustration. It is tantalizing that we are not told what Marcus "really thought" about Verus, who acquired from other sources a reputation for decadent living, or about the fidelity or otherwise of Faustina, or about Avidius's motives for insurrection, or about his choice of his already clearly dangerous son as his successor. Many of the specific allusions that do occur are entirely baffling to modern readers, and it is noteworthy that such cryptic details are found even in Book 1, the only book that has a formal arrangement. Nothing is known, for example, of his commendation of Antoninus Pius for "the way he treated the tax-collector at Tusculum" (1.16), and Benedicta and Theodotus, presumably imperial slaves, are known only because of Marcus's boast that he never took sexual advantage of them (1.17).

The title *Meditations* was added in the Middle Ages, but there is no evidence that the work originally had any title at all. *Meditations* is unsatisfactory because it suggests a work of more deliberate and balanced thought than was probably the case. An alternative title in some manuscripts is *To Himself*, which is at least consistent with the general idea that Marcus was not writing for a wider readership. If, however, he was writing just for himself, why should he add a title? If he did feel inclined to add one, perhaps he might more appropriately have called the work *To Myself*? Books 2 and 3 have the subtitles *Written among the Quadi on the River Gran* and *Written in Carnuntum*, indicating that he composed these books during the German campaign in the 170s. It has been argued that these are genuine, since a forger would have added such a heading consistently to every book. Whether this is true or not, it is reasonable to suppose that the *Meditations* were written at least in part on the German campaign, given that he refers to himself as an old man and was to die at age fifty-eight.

The contents vary, quite alarmingly at times, from simple aphorisms and exhortations, through brief and rudimentary dialogues in the Platonic manner, to quite substantial discussions of particular philosophical points, and sections of Books 7 and 11 consist of nothing more than quotations from earlier literature with little or no comment. In a letter written perhaps nearly twenty years before he became emperor, Marcus laments to Fronto: "Even if I wanted to study, my responsibilities in the law-courts prevent me from doing so. People who know about such things say that these cases will consume whole days. But I have sent you today's aphorism and yesterday's commonplace. Yesterday we spent the whole day traveling. Today it is difficult to get anything done except the evening aphorism" (in Fronto, *Letters* p. 85 van den Hout). There is no reason to envisage the *Meditations* as a diary to which Marcus turned every night to give himself a calm perspective on his busy life, but it is easy to imagine him as sometimes being too tired or distracted by his administrative or military duties to add more than the most perfunctory comments.

Certain topics recur frequently throughout the *Meditations*: the meaning of life; the transience of life; how to live a just life; how to cope with life's difficulties; how to face the certainty of death. The same ideas are processed over and over with no development in thought; indeed, there are internal inconsistencies in his views about them. This would be a serious blemish in a work intended for publication but is quite understandable if Marcus was writing for himself alone over a long period. If he is writing for himself alone, the repetition emphasizes his pre-occupations. These topics are not only repetitious but also very limited. Stoicism, the philosophical school to which he adheres most closely, focuses on three largely separate branches of inquiry: logic, the physical world, and ethics. The first two of these are all but absent from the *Meditations*; Marcus is really only interested in ethics, in how philosophy can help with the practicalities of life. As a practical manual of Stoicism designed to help other readers, the *Meditations* are too specifically focused. But if Marcus is writing for himself, he does not need to declare his affiliation to any philosophical school. In fact, he refers explicitly to Stoicism only once, in a rather distanced manner: "Realities are so veiled... that... even the Stoics think them difficult to comprehend" (5.10). In any case, Marcus opens Book 8 with a forceful disavowal of any authority to speak as a philosopher: "To yourself as well as to many others it is plain that you fall far short of philosophy."

There are problems of varying degrees of severity with the transmission of all ancient texts. Normally, we may assume that a text was submitted for publication more or less exactly as its author intended, and textual difficulties are caused either by the inattention or ignorance of later copyists, or by physical damage to the manuscripts. It may well be, however, that the text of the *Meditations* was never in very good shape. Marcus would not have been likely to proofread such a work, if he had written it out personally and intended it only for himself. (We know that he continued to the end of his life to write at least some of his private letters, rather than dictate them to an amanuensis.) The *Meditations* are written in a vigorous and down-to-earth Greek, but with little real style beyond that inevitable in the work of a highly educated writer. Difficulties with Marcus's Greek are probably to be attributed mostly to his focus on content rather than presentation: *he* would know what he meant to say. It is not, of course, surprising that he wrote in Greek; there were far more people literate in Greek than in Latin in the empire, the ruling class were bilingual, and Greek was the natural language for philosophy.

Plato had said that no government could be ideal "unless the philosophers become kings or those who are now called kings and rulers become philosophers in a genuine and adequate manner" (*Republic* 473c). Marcus Aurelius comes close to being a Platonic philosopher-king, but we should not exaggerate either his uniqueness or the profundity of his philosophy. Most, if not all, earlier emperors had also received some training in philosophy. Augustus wrote a now completely lost *Exhortations to Philosophy*; it would be fascinating to know how such a work harmonized with his grim and unscrupulous struggle to gain and maintain power. (It was even said that Plato himself was buying arms to go off and serve as a mercenary when Socrates persuaded him to turn to philosophy instead [Aelian, *Miscellaneous History* 3.27].) Marcus can hardly have exercised Stoic tolerance for his fellow men in his wars with the German tribes, and he acknowledges the difficulty of remaining true to his philosophical convictions while ruling the empire: "where it is possible to live, there also it is possible to live well: but it is possible to live in a palace, therefore it is also possible to live well in a palace" (5.16).

Marcus Aurelius is clearly influenced very heavily by Epictetus (ca. A.D. 55–135), who taught that Stoicism was a way of life, not just an intellectual discipline. No writings by Epictetus himself survive, but the *Handbook,* compiled from his lectures by his pupil Arrian, is perhaps the closest parallel in structure and content to the *Meditations*. (It is ironic that the all-powerful emperor should owe such a debt to an ex-slave, whose name in fact means "bought in addition.") Marcus is not a top-rank philosopher. Much of what he says is banal, and he is rarely original. The *Meditations* do nevertheless have a unique value. Even when the thought is commonplace or actually confused, it still has a special significance because it is expressed by a Roman emperor.

# MEDITATIONS

*The first book is more carefully composed than the rest of the work, which suggests that perhaps the author did have a future audience in mind. It consists of a listing in approximate chronological order of the people in Marcus's life with an account of what he owes to each. The last two entries (16 and 17) are the longest, recounting his debt to his immediate predecessor as emperor, Antoninus Pius, and the gods. Notable by his absence from this catalog is the emperor Hadrian, to whom Marcus owed his own place in the line of succession. In Book 6 Marcus describes the benefits of keeping such a list of ethical debts: "Nothing is so cheering as the images of the virtues shining in the character of contemporaries and meeting so far as possible in a group. Therefore you should keep them ready to your hand." The result a rare glimpse into the mind of a Roman emperor.*

## Book 1

1. From my grandfather Verus: the lessons of noble character and even temper.

2. From my father's reputation and my memory of him: modesty and manliness.

3. From my mother: piety and bountifulness, to keep myself not only from doing evil but even from dwelling on evil thoughts, simplicity too in diet, and to be far removed from the ways of the rich.

4. From my mother's grandfather: not to have attended public schools but enjoyed good teachers at home, and to have learned the lesson that on things like these it is a duty to spend liberally.

5. From my tutor: not to become a partisan of the Green jacket or the Blue in the races, nor of Thracian or Samnite gladiators; to bear pain and be content with little; to work with my own hands, to mind my own business, and to be slow to listen to slander.

6. From Diognetus: to avoid idle enthusiasms; to disbelieve the professions of sorcerers and impostors about incantations and exorcism of spirits and the like; not to cock-fight or to be excited about such sports; to put up with plain-speaking and to become familiar with philosophy; to hear the lectures first of Baccheius, then of Tandasis and Marcian, in boyhood to write essays and to aspire to the camp-bed and skin coverlet and the other things which are part of the Greek training.

7. From Rusticus: to get an impression of need for reform and treatment of character; not to run off into zeal for rhetoric, writing on speculative themes, discoursing on edifying texts, exhibiting in fanciful colors the ascetic or the philanthropist. To avoid oratory, poetry, and preciosity; not to parade at home in ceremonial costume or to do things of that kind; to write letters in the simple style, like his own from Sinuessa to my mother. To be easily recalled to myself and easily reconciled with those who provoke and offend, as soon as they are willing to meet me. To read books accurately and not be satisfied with superficial thinking about things or agree hurriedly with those who talk round a subject. To have made the acquaintance of the *Discourses* of Epictetus, of which he allowed me to share a copy of his own.

8. From Apollonius: moral freedom, not to expose oneself to the insecurity of fortune; to look to nothing else, even for a little while, except to reason. To be always the same, in sharp attacks of pain, in the loss of a child, in long illnesses. To see clearly in a living example that a man can be at once very much in earnest and yet able to relax.

    Not to be censorious in exposition; and to see a man who plainly considered technical knowledge and ease in communicating general truths as the least of his good gifts. The lesson how one ought to receive from friends what are esteemed favors, neither lowering oneself on their account, nor returning them tactlessly.

9. From Sextus: graciousness, and the pattern of a household governed by its head, and the notion of life according to Nature. Dignity without pretence, solicitous consideration for friends, tolerance of amateurs and of those whose opinions have no ground in science.

    A happy accommodation to every man, so that not only was his conversation more agreeable than any flattery, but he excited the greatest reverence at that very time in the very persons about him. Certainty of grasp, and method in the discovery and arrangement of the principles necessary to human life.

    Never to give the impression of anger or of any other passion, but to be at once entirely passionless and yet full of natural affection. To praise without noise, to be widely learned without display.

10. From Alexander the grammarian: to avoid fault-finding and not to censure in a carping spirit any who employ an exotic phrase, a solecism, or a harsh expression, but oneself to use, neatly and precisely, the correct phrase, by way of answer or confirmation or handling of the actual question—the thing, not its verbal expression—or by some other equally happy reminder.

11. From Fronto: to observe how vile a thing is the malice and caprice and hypocrisy of absolutism; and generally speaking that those whom we entitle "Patricians" are somehow rather wanting in the natural affections.

12. From Alexander the Platonist: seldom and only when absolutely necessary to say to anyone or write in a letter: "I am too busy"; nor by such a turn of phrase to evade continually the duties incident to our relations to those who live with us, on the plea of "present circumstances."

13. From Catulus: not to neglect a friend's remonstrance, even if he may be unreasonable in his remonstrance, but to endeavor to restore him to his usual temper. Hearty praise, too, of teachers, like what is recorded of Athenodotus and Domitius, and genuine love towards children.

14. From Severus: love of family, love of truth, and love of justice. To have got by his help to understand Thrasea, Helvidius, Cato, Dio, Brutus, and to conceive the idea of a commonwealth based on equity and freedom of speech, and of a monarchy cherishing above all the liberty of the subject. From him too consistency and uniformity in regard for philosophy; to do good, to communicate liberally, to be hopeful; to believe in the affection of friends and to use no concealment towards those who incurred his censure, and that his friends had no necessity to conjecture his wishes or the reverse, but he was open with them.

15. From Maximus: mastery of self and vacillation in nothing; cheerfulness in all circumstances and especially in illness. A happy blend of character, mildness with dignity, readiness to do without complaining what is given to be done. To see how in his case everyone believed "he really thinks what he says, and what he does, he does without evil intent"; not to be surprised or alarmed; nowhere to be in a hurry or to procrastinate, not to lack resource or to be depressed or cringing or on the other hand angered or suspicious. To be generous, forgiving, void of deceit. To give the impression of inflexible rectitude rather than of one who is corrected. The fact, too, that no one would ever have dreamt that he was looked down on by him or would have endured to conceive himself to be his superior. To be agreeable also (in social life).

16. From my father (by adoption): gentleness and unshaken resolution in judgments taken after full examination; no vainglory about external honors; love of work and perseverance; readiness to hear those who had anything to contribute to the public advantage; the desire to award to every man according to desert without partiality; the experience that knew where to tighten the rein, where to relax. Prohibition of unnatural practices, social tact, and permission to his suite not invariably to be present at his banquets nor to attend his progress from Rome, as a matter of obligation, and always to be found the same by those who had failed to attend him through engagements. Exact scrutiny in council and patience; not that he was avoiding investigation, satisfied with first impressions. An inclination to keep his friends, and nowhere fastidious or the victim of manias but his own master in everything, and his outward mien cheerful. His long foresight and ordering of the merest trifle without making scenes. The check in his reign put upon organized applause and every form of lip-service; his unceasing watch over the needs of the empire and his stewardship of its resources; his patience under criticism by individuals of such conduct. No superstitious fear of divine powers or with man any courting of the public or obsequiousness or cultivation of popular favor, but temperance in all things and firmness; nowhere want of taste or search for novelty.

In the things which contribute to life's comfort, where Fortune was lavish to him, use without display and at the same time without apology, so as to take them when they were there quite simply and not to require them when they were absent. The fact that no one would have said that he was a sophist, an impostor, or a pedant, but a ripe man, an entire man, above flattery, able to preside over his own and his subjects' business.

Besides all this the inclination to respect genuine followers of philosophy, but towards the other sort no tendency to reproach nor on the other hand to be hoodwinked by them; affability, too, and humor, but not to excess. Care of his health in moderation, not as one in love with living nor with an eye to personal appearance nor on the other hand neglecting it, but so far as by attention to self to need doctoring or medicine and external applications for very few ailments.

A very strong point, to give way without jealousy to those who had some particular gift like literary expression or knowledge of the Civil Law or customs or other matters, even sharing their enthusiasm that each might get the reputation due to his individual excellence. Acting always according to the tradition of our forefathers, yet not endeavoring that this regard for tradition should be noticed. No tendency, moreover, to chop and change, but a settled course in the same places and the same practices. After acute attacks of headache, fresh and vigorous at once for his accustomed duties; and not to have many secrets, only very few and by way of exception, and those solely because of matters of State. Discretion and moderation alike in the provision of shows, in carrying out public works, in donations to the populace, and so on; the behavior in fact of one who has an eye precisely to what it is his duty to do, not to the reputation which attends the doing.

He was not one who bathed at odd hours, not fond of building, no connoisseur of the table, of the stuff and color of his dress, of the beauty of his slaves. His costume was brought to Rome from his country house at Lorium; his manner of life at Lanuvium; the way he treated the tax-collector who apologized at Tusculum, and all his behavior of that sort. Nowhere harsh, merciless, or blustering, nor so that you might ever say "to fever heat," but everything nicely calculated and divided into its times, as by a leisured man; no bustle, complete order, strength, consistency. What is recorded of Socrates would exactly fit

him: he could equally be abstinent from or enjoy what many are too weak to abstain from and too self-indulgent in enjoying. To be strong, to endure, and in either case to be sober belong to the man of perfect and invincible spirit, like the spirit of Maximus in his illness.

17. From the gods: to have had good grandparents, good parents, a good sister, good masters, good intimates, kinsfolk, friends, almost everything; and that in regard to not one of them did I stumble into offence, although I had the kind of disposition which might in some circumstances have led me to behave thus; but it was the goodness of the gods that no conjunction of events came about which was likely to expose my weakness. That I was not brought up longer than I was with my grandfather's second wife, that I preserved the flower of my youth and did not play the man before my time, but even delayed a little longer. That my station in life was under a governor and a father who was to strip off all my pride and to lead me to see that it is possible to live in a palace and yet not to need a bodyguard or embroidered uniforms or candelabra and statues bearing lamps and the like accompaniments of pomp, but that one is able to contract very nearly to a private station and not on that account to lose dignity or to be more remiss in the duties that a prince must perform on behalf of the public. That I met with so good a brother...able by his character not only to rouse me to care of myself but at the same time to hearten me by respect and natural affection; that my children were not deficient in mind nor deformed in body; that I made no further progress in eloquence and poetry and those other pursuits wherein, had I seen myself progressing along an easy road, I should perhaps have become absorbed. That I made haste to advance my masters to the honors which they appeared to covet and did not put them off with hopes that, as they were still young, I should do it later on. To have got to know Apollonius, Rusticus, Maximus. To have pictured to myself clearly and repeatedly what life in obedience to Nature really is, so that, so far as concerns the gods and communications from the other world and aids and inspirations, nothing hinders my

living at once in obedience to Nature, though I still come somewhat short of this by my own fault and by not observing the reminders and almost the instructions of the gods. That my body has held out so well in a life like mine; that I did not touch Benedicta or Theodotus, but that even in later years when I experienced the passion of love I was cured; that though I was often angry with Rusticus I never went to extremes for which I should have been sorry; that though my mother was fated to die young, she still spent her last years with me. That whenever I wanted to help anyone in poverty or some other necessity I was never told that I could not afford it, and that I did not myself fall into the same necessity so as to take help from another; that my wife is what she is, so obedient, so affectionate, and so simple; that I was well provided with suitable tutors for my children. That I was granted assistance in dreams, especially how to avoid spitting blood and fits of giddiness, and the answer of the oracle at Caieta: "Even as thou shalt employ thyself;" and that, although in love with philosophy, I did not meet with any sophist or retire to disentangle literary works or syllogisms or busy myself with problems "in the clouds." For all these things require "the gods to help and Fortune's hand."

## Book 4

*The fourth book is more typical of the whole work than the first. It has no obvious structure; each section reads like an aphorism, which is perhaps one reason that Marcus is sometimes considered the most quotable philosopher. His thoughts on the world derive from his consistent view of the cosmos as an organic whole, of which each individual is a part. Human wickedness is a recurring theme, as is Marcus's contempt for fame, and his obsession with death.*

1. The sovereign power within, in its natural state, so confronts what comes to pass as always to adapt itself readily to what is feasible and is presented to it. This is because it puts its affection upon no material of its own choice; rather it sets itself upon its objects with a reservation, and then makes the opposition which encounters it into material for itself. It is like a fire, when it masters what falls into it, whereby a little taper would have been put out, but a bright fire very quickly appropriates and devours what is heaped upon it, and leaps up higher out of those very obstacles.

2. Nothing that is undertaken is to be undertaken without a purpose, nor otherwise than according to a principle which makes the art of living perfect.

3. Men look for retreats for themselves, the country, the seashore, the hills; and you yourself, too, are peculiarly accustomed to feel the same want. Yet all this is very unlike a philosopher, when you may at any hour you please retreat into yourself. For nowhere does a man retreat into more quiet or more privacy than into his own mind, especially one who has within such things that he has only to look into, and become at once in perfect ease; and by ease I mean nothing else but good behavior. Continually, therefore, grant yourself this retreat and repair yourself. But let them be brief and fundamental truths, which will suffice at once by their presence to wash away all sorrow, and to send you back without repugnance to the life to which you return.

   For what is it that shall move your repugnance? The wickedness of men? Recall the judgment that reasonable creatures have come into the world for the sake of one another; that patience is a part of justice; that men do wrong involuntarily; and how many at last, after enmity, suspicion, hatred, warfare, have been laid out on their death-beds and come to dust. This should make you pause. But shall what is assigned from Universal Nature be repugnant to you? Revive the alternative: "either Providence or blind atoms," and the many proofs that the Universe is a kind of Commonwealth. Shall then the things of the flesh still have hold upon you? Reflect that the understanding, when once it takes control of itself and recognizes its own power, does not mingle with the vital spirit, be its current smooth or broken, and finally reflect upon all that you have heard and consented to about pain and pleasure.

   Well, then, shall mere glory distract you? Look at the swiftness of the oblivion of all men; the gulf of endless time, behind and before; the hollowness of applause, the fickleness and folly of those who seem to speak well of you, and the narrow room in which it is confined. This should make you pause. For the entire earth is a point in space, and how small a corner thereof is this your dwelling place, and how few and how paltry those who will sing your praises here!

Finally, therefore, remember your retreat into this little domain which is yourself, and above all be not disturbed nor on the rack, but be free and look at things as a man, a human being, a citizen, a creature that must die. And among what is most ready to hand into which you will look have these two: the one, that things do not take hold upon the mind, but stand without unmoved, and that disturbances come only from the judgment within; the second, that all that your eyes behold will change in a moment and be no more; and of how many things you have already witnessed the changes, think continually of that.

The Universe is change, life is opinion.

4. If mind is common to us all, then also the reason, whereby we are reasoning beings, is common. If this be so, then also the reason which enjoins what is to be done or left undone is common. If this be so, law also is common; if this be so, we are citizens; if this be so, we are partakers in one constitution; if this be so, the Universe is a kind of Commonwealth. For in what other common government can we say that the whole race of men partakes? And thence, from this common City, is derived our mind itself, our reason, and our sense of law, or from what else? For as the earthy is in me a portion from some earth, and the watery from a second element, and the vital spirit from some source, and the hot and fiery from yet another source of its own (for nothing comes from nothing, just as nothing returns to nothing), so therefore the mind also has come from some source.

5. Death is like birth, a mystery of Nature; a coming together out of identical elements and a dissolution into the same. Looked at generally this is not a thing of which man should be ashamed, for it is contrary neither to what is conformable to a reasonable creature nor to the principle of his constitution.

6. These are natural and necessary results from creatures of this kind, and one who wants this to be otherwise wants the fig-tree not to yield its acrid juice. And in general remember this, that within a very little while both he and you will be dead, and a little after not even your name nor his will be left.

7. Get rid of the judgment; you are rid of the "I am hurt"; get rid of the "I am hurt," you are rid of the hurt itself.

8. What does not make a man worse than he was, neither makes his life worse than it was, nor hurts him without or within.

9. It was a law of necessity that what is naturally beneficial should bring this about.

10. "All that comes to pass comes to pass with justice." You will find this to be so if you watch carefully. I do not mean only in accordance with the ordered series of events, but in accordance with justice and as it were by someone who assigns what has respect to worth. Watch, therefore, as you have begun and whatever you do, do it with this, with goodness in the specific sense in which the notion of the good man is conceived. Preserve this goodness in everything you do.

11. Don't regard things in the light in which he who does the wrong judges them, nor as he wishes you to judge them: but see them as in truth they are.

12. In these two ways you must always be prepared: the one, only to act as the principle of the royal and law-giving art prescribes for the benefit of mankind; the second, to change your purpose, if someone is there to correct and to guide you away from some fancy of yours. The guidance must, however, always be from a conviction of justice or common benefit ensuing, and what you prefer must be similar, not because it looked pleasant or popular.

13. "You have reason?" "Yes, I have?" "Why not use it then? If this is doing its part, what else do you want?"

14. You came into the world as a part. You will vanish in that which gave you birth, or rather you will be taken up into its generative reason by the process of change.

15. Many grains of incense upon the same altar; one falls first, another later, but difference there is none.

16. Within ten days you will appear a god even to those to whom today you seem a beast or a

baboon, if you return to your principles and your reverence of the Word.

17. Don't live as though you were going to live a myriad years. Fate is hanging over your head; while you have life, while you may, become good.

18. How great a rest from labor he gains who does not look to what his neighbor says or does or thinks,—but only to what he himself is doing, in order that exactly this may be just and holy, or in accord with a good man's conduct. "Do not look round at a black character," but run towards the goal, balanced, not throwing your body about.

19. The man in a flutter for after-fame fails to picture to himself that each of those who remember him will himself also very shortly die, then again the man who succeeded him, until the whole remembrance is extinguished as it runs along a line of men who are kindled and then put out. And put the case that those who will remember never die, and the remembrance never dies, what is that to you! And I do not say that it is nothing to the dead; what is praise to the living, except perhaps for some practical purpose? For now you are putting off unseasonably the gift of Nature, which does not depend on the testimony of some one else...

20. Everything in any way lovely is of itself and terminates in itself, holding praise to be no part of itself. At all events, in no case does what is praised become better or worse. This I say also of what is commonly called lovely, for instance materials and work of art; and indeed what is there lacking at all to that which is really lovely? No more than to law, no more than to truth, no more than to kindness or reverence of self. Which of these is lovely because it is praised or corrupted because it is blamed? Does an emerald become worse than it was, if it be not praised? And what of gold, ivory, purple, a lute, a sword-blade, a flowerbud, and little plant?

21. You ask how, if souls continue to exist, the atmosphere has room for them from time eternal. But how does the ground have room for the bodies of those who for so long an age are buried in it? The answer is that, as on earth change and dissolution after a continuance for so long make room for other dead bodies, so in the atmosphere souls pass on and continue for so long, and then change and are poured out and are kindled being assumed into the generative principle of Universal Nature, and so provide room for those which succeed to their place. This would be the answer presuming that souls do continue. But we must consider not only the multitude of bodies that are thus buried, but also the number of animals eaten every day by ourselves and the rest of the animal creation. How large a number are devoured and in a manner of speaking buried in the bodies of those who feed upon them; and yet there is room to contain them because they are turned into blood, because they are changed into forms of air and heat. How shall we investigate the truth of this? By a distinction into the material and the causal.

22. Do not wander without a purpose, but in all your impulses render what is just, and in all your imaginations preserve what you apprehend.

23. Everything is fitting for me, my Universe, which fits thy purpose. Nothing in thy good time is too early or too late for me; everything is fruit for me which thy seasons, Nature, bear; from thee, in thee, to thee are all things. The poet sings: "Dear city of Cecrops," and will you not say: "Dear city of God"?

24. Democritus has said: "Do few things, if you would enjoy tranquility." May it not be better to do the necessary things and what the reason of a creature intended by Nature to be social prescribes, and as that reason prescribes? For this brings not only the tranquility from doing right but also from doing few things. For if one removes most of what we say and do as unnecessary, he will have more leisure and less interruption. Wherefore on each occasion he should remind himself: "Is this not one of the necessary things?" And he should remove not actions merely that are unnecessary, but imaginations also, for in this way superfluous actions too will not follow in their train.

25. Make trial for yourself how the life of the good man, too, fares well, of the man pleased with what is assigned from Universal Nature and contented by his own just action and kind disposition.

26. You have seen those things, look now at these: do not trouble yourself, make yourself simple. Does

a man do wrong? He does wrong to himself. Has some chance befallen you? It is well; from Universal Nature, from the beginning, all that befalls was determined for you and the thread was spun. The sum of the matter is this: life is short; the present must be turned to profit with reasonableness and right. Be sober without effort.

27. Either an ordered Universe or a medley heaped together mechanically but still an order; or can order subsist in you and disorder in the Whole! And that, too, when all things are so distinguished and yet intermingled and sympathetic.

28. A black heart is an unmanly heart, a stubborn heart; resembling a beast of prey, a mere brute, or a child' foolish crafty, ribald, mercenary, despotic.

29. If he is a foreigner in the Universe who does not recognize the essence of the Universe, no less is he a foreigner, who does not recognize what comes to pass in it. A fugitive is he who runs away from the reasonable law of his City; a blind man, he who shuts the eye of the mind; a beggar, he who has need of another and has not all that is necessary for life in himself; a blain on the Universe, he who rebels and separates himself from the reason of our common nature because he is displeased with what comes to pass (for Nature who bore you, brings these things also into being); a fragment cut off from the City, he who cuts off his own soul from the soul of reasonable creatures, which is one.

30. Here is a philosopher without a tunic, another without a book, another here half-naked. "I have no bread," he says, "still I stand firm by the Word." And I have nourishment from my lessons and yet do not stand firm.

31. Love the art which you were taught, set up your rest in this. Pass through what is left of life as one who has committed all that is yours, with your whole heart, to the gods, and of men making yourself neither despot nor servant to any.

32. Call to mind by way of example the time of Vespasian: you will see everything the same: men marrying, bringing up children, falling ill, dying, fighting, feasting, trading, farming, flattering, asserting themselves, suspecting, plotting, praying for another's death, murmuring at the present,

lusting, heaping up riches, setting their heart on offices and thrones. And now that life of theirs is no more and nowhere.

Again pass on to the time of Trajan; again everything the same. That life, too, is dead. In like manner contemplate and behold the rest of the records of times and whole nations; and see how many after their struggles fell in a little while and were resolved into the elements. But most of all you must run over in your mind those whom you yourself have known to be distracted in vain, neglecting to perform what was agreeable to their own constitution, to hold fast to this and to be content with this. And here you are bound to remember that the attention paid to each action has its own worth and proportion; only so you will not be dejected if in smaller matters you are occupied no farther than was appropriate.

33. Words familiar in olden times are now archaisms; so also the names of those whose praises were hymned in bygone days are now in a sense archaisms; Camillus, Caeso, Volesus, Dentatus; a little after, Scipio too and Cato; then also Augustus, then also Hadrian and Antoninus. For all things quickly fade and turn to fable, and quickly, too, utter oblivion covers them like sand. And this I say of those who shone like stars to wonder at; the rest, as soon as the breath was out of their bodies, were "unnoticed and unwept." And what after all is everlasting remembrance? Utter vanity. What then is that about which a man ought to spend his pains? This one thing; right understanding, neighborly behavior, speech which would never lie, and a disposition welcoming all which comes to pass, as necessary, as familiar, as flowing from a source and fountain like itself.

34. With your whole will surrender yourself to Clotho to spin your fate into whatever web of things she will.

35. All is ephemeral, both what remembers and what is remembered.

36. Contemplate continually all things coming to pass by change, and accustom yourself to think that Universal Nature loves nothing so much as to change what is and to create new things in their likeness. For everything that is is in a way

the seed of what will come out of it, whereas you imagine seeds to be only those which are cast into the earth or into the womb. But that is very unscientific.

37. You will presently be dead and are not yet simple, untroubled, void of suspicion that anything from outside can hurt you, not yet propitious to all men, nor counting wisdom to consist only in just action.

38. Look into their governing principles, even the wise among them, what petty things they avoid and what pursue!

39. Your evil does not consist in another's governing principle, nor indeed in any change and alteration of your environment. Where then? Where the part of you which judges about evil is. Let it not frame the judgment, and all is well. Even if what is nearest to it, your body, is cut, cauterized, suppurates, mortifies, still let the part which judges about these things be at rest; that is, let it decide that nothing is good or evil which can happen indifferently to the evil man and the good. For what happens indifferently to one whose life is contrary to Nature and to one whose life is according to Nature, this is neither according to nor contrary to Nature.

40. Constantly think of the Universe as one living creature, embracing one being and one soul; how all is absorbed into the one consciousness of this living creature; how it compasses all things with a single purpose, and how all things work together to cause all that comes to pass, and their wonderful web and texture.

41. You are a spirit bearing the weight of a dead body, as Epictetus used to say.

42. For what comes to pass in the course of change nothing is evil, as nothing is good for what exists in consequence of change.

43. There is a kind of river of things passing into being, and Time is a violent torrent. For no sooner is each seen, than it has been carried away, and another is being carried by, and that, too, will be carried away.

44. All that comes to pass is as familiar and well known as the rose in spring and the grape in summer. Of like fashion are sickness, death, calumny, intrigue, and all that gladdens or saddens the foolish.

45. What follows is always organically related to what went before; for it is not like a simple enumeration of units separately determined by necessity, but a rational combination; and as Being is arranged in a mutual co-ordination, so the phenomena of Becoming display no bare succession but a wonderful organic interrelation.

46. Always remember what Heraclitus said: "the death of earth is the birth of water, the death of water is the birth of atmosphere, the death of atmosphere is fire, and conversely." Remember, too, his image of the man who forgets the way he is going; and: "they are at variance with that with which they most continuously have converse (Reason which governs the Universe), and the things they meet with every day appear alien to them"; and again: "we must not act and speak like men who sleep, for in sleep we suppose that we act and speak"; and "we must not be like children with parents," that is, accept things simply as we have received them.

47. Just as, if one of the gods told you: "tomorrow you will be dead or in any case the day after tomorrow," you would no longer be making that day after important any more than tomorrow, unless you are an arrant coward (for the difference is a mere trifle), in the same way count it no great matter to live to a year that is an infinite distance off rather than till tomorrow.

48. Think continually how many physicians have died, after often knitting their foreheads over their patients; how many astrologers after prophesying other men's deaths, as though to die were a great matter; how many philosophers after endless debate on death or survival after death; how many paladins after slaying their thousands; how many tyrants after using their power over men's lives with monstrous arrogance, as if themselves immortal; how many entire cities have, if I may use the term, died, Helice, Pompeii, Herculaneum, and others innumerable. Run over, too, the many also you know of, one after another. One followed this man's funeral and then was himself laid on the bier; another followed him, and all in a little while. This is the whole matter: see always how ephemeral and cheap are the things of man— yesterday, a spot of albumen, tomorrow, ashes or a mummy. Therefore make your passage through

this span of time in obedience to Nature and gladly lay down your life, as an olive, when ripe, might fall, blessing her who bare it and grateful to the tree which gave it life.

49. Be like the headland on which the waves continually break, but it stands firm and about it the boiling waters sink to sleep. "Unlucky am I, because this has befallen me." Nay rather: "Lucky am I, because, though this befell me, I continue free from sorrow, neither crushed by the present, nor fearing what is to come." For such an event might have befallen any man, but not every man would have continued in it free from sorrow. On what grounds then is this ill fortune more than that good fortune? Do you, speaking generally, call what is not a deviation from man's nature a man's ill fortune, and do you suppose that what is not opposed to his natural will is a deviation from his nature? Very well, you have been taught what that will is. Can what has befallen you prevent your being just, high-minded, temperate, prudent, free from rash judgments, trustful, self-reverent, free, and whatever else by its presence with him enables a man's nature to

secure what is really his? Finally, in every event which leads you to sorrow, remember to use this principle: that this is not a misfortune, but that to bear it like a brave man is good fortune.

50. An unscientific but none the less a helpful support to disdain of death is to review those who have clung tenaciously to life. What more did they gain than those who died prematurely? In every case they are laid in some grave at last: Caedicianus, Fabius, Julianus, Lepidus, and any others like them, who after carrying many to the grave were themselves carried out. To speak generally the difference is a small one, and this difference long-drawn-out through what great toils and with what sorts of men and in how weak a body. Do not count it then as a thing…; for see the gulf of time behind and another infinite time in front: in this what difference is there between a three-days-old infant and a Nestor of three generations?

51. Run always the short road, and Nature's road is short. Therefore say and do everything in the soundest way, because a purpose like this delivers a man from troubles and warfare, from every care and superfluity.

# AFTERWORD

"Little the life each lives," writes Marcus Aurelius in *Meditations* 3.10, "little the corner of the earth he lives in, little even the longest fame hereafter, and even that dependent on a succession of poor mortals, who will very soon be dead, and have not learnt to know themselves, much less the man who was dead long years ago." Marcus Aurelius writes frequently on the fleeting nature of fame, and yet to moderns he is one of the most familiar Roman emperors. His image on ancient coinage is represented with typical Roman candor as rather unprepossessing, not to say slightly dimwitted. Many tourists visiting Rome encounter that face in an imposing equestrian statue atop the Campidoglio. Since 1981, a copy has stood in the center of the piazza designed by Michelangelo, because the original was removed to the Palazzo dei Conservatori to protect it against the ravages of atmospheric pollution (it is now on display in the Musei Capitolini). This is the only equestrian statue to have survived from antiquity, and it owes its survival to a case of mistaken identity. In the Middle Ages, the rider was thought to be Constantine the Great, the first Christian emperor, and therefore immune from the destruction that befell most ancient bronzes, which were melted down either out of piety or as a source of metal for medieval arsenals. Today shoppers strolling along the Via del Corso in Rome will take their bearings from the triumphal column commemorating his victories over the barbarian tribes that still stands on its original site in the Piazza Colonna.

Many filmgoers know Marcus Aurelius as a just and farsighted ruler from representations in movies such as *The Fall of the Roman Empire* (1964) or *Gladiator* (2000), but this idealized view of the emperor started long before Hollywood. A considerable contribution to the modern myth of the good emperor is owed to the historian Edward Gibbon's characterization of his reign as the apex of the Roman Empire. But this view of Marcus's reign is even older than Gibbon's *Decline and Fall*; indeed, it predates any familiarity with the emperor's literary works. In sixteenth-century Spain, the moralist Antonio de Guevara devoted eleven years to writing a didactic novel describing the ideal ruler, for whom he took Marcus as model. The result was *Reloj de Principes*, published in Valladolid in 1529, a work that proved very successful and was soon translated into several languages. There was a popular English version, known as *The Golden Boke of Marcus Aurelius* by John Bourchier, second Baron Berners, that appeared in 1535 and went through ten editions by the end of the century. Another popular version was published in 1557 with the title *The Dial of Princes* by Sir Thomas North, the famous translator of Plutarch. This was one of two books (the other was Machiavelli's *Art of War*) that captured the imagination of Captain John Smith (1580–1631) as a young man and inspired him to a life of action in the New World. But most of this occurred before the emperor's *Meditations* themselves were ever read in western Europe, in the first edition of 1558, which raises the question of the reception of the work in the ancient world and its transmission to the modern.

We know nothing about how the *Meditations* left the desk of its author. We may suspect that its distribution was posthumous, perhaps the work of a close friend such as Aufidius Victorinus, who outlived Marcus to serve a second term as consul three years into the reign of Commodus. Or perhaps it was someone on his staff, like Chryseros, a freedman who later wrote a history of Rome ending with the death of Marcus Aurelius. It is probable that its distribution was extremely limited, perhaps circulating only within a small circle of friends and admirers, since almost two hundred years were to pass before any other ancient author mentions the work. A fourth-century philosopher in Constantinople named Themistius (ca. A.D. 317–85) mentions the "precepts" of Marcus, whom he calls "a philosopher in a purple robe." The *Meditations* are occasionally cited by writers in the Greek East, including the great philologist Maximus Planudes (ca. 1255–1305), who quotes extensively from Books 4 through 12. It was probably as a result of interest in the philosopher-emperor during the late period of the Byzantine Empire that a manuscript of the work managed to reach western Europe, where it was found in the library at Heidelberg by the classical scholar Wilhelm Xylander, who produced the first printed edition in 1558. That manuscript was later lost, but editions of the work now began to multiply, and translations soon appeared in every major European language.

The earliest English translation, by Meric Casaubon, was published in 1634 under the title "Marcus Aurelius Antoninus, The Roman Emperor, His Meditations concerning himselfe: Treating of a Naturall Mans Happinesse; wherein it consisteth, and of the Meanes to attain unto it." Casaubon was the son of a much more famous classical scholar, Isaac Casaubon (1559–1614), and his translation of the *Meditations*, although much criticized, remained the standard until the nineteenth century and was reprinted even in the twentieth. Cecil Rhodes, the British imperialist, was an admirer of Marcus's views on public service, and it is not hard to imagine copies of the *Meditations* being included in the travel kit of many a colonial bureaucrat in the British Empire. In the world of letters, Marcus has had to be content with bit parts. His reign provides the setting for Walter Pater's (1839–94) only novel, *Marius the Epicurean*. And the French writer Marguerite Yourcenar (1903–87) frames her celebrated historical novel, *The Memoirs of Hadrian*, in the form of a letter from the aged emperor to his young adopted son Marcus.

The *Meditations* was included by former president Bill Clinton on his list of his twenty-one favorite books, but while the *Meditations* has proved extraordinarily popular with lay readers, it has not had much traction among philosophers. Bertrand Russell, the great British philosopher, wrote disparagingly of the "element of sour grapes" in Marcus's brand of Stoicism in his *History of Western Philosophy* (1945): "'We can't be happy, but we can be good; let us therefore pretend that, so long as we are good, it doesn't matter being unhappy'. This doctrine is heroic, and, in a bad world, useful; but it is neither quite true nor, in a fundamental sense, quite sincere." A not dissimilar view is expressed by Bertie Wooster, the hero of P. G. Wodehouse's *The Mating Season,* when he is lamenting his ill fortune and Jeeves attempts to console him with *Meditations* 4.26 (in our selection above):

> "…But I wonder if I might call your attention to an observation of the Emperor Marcus Aurelius. He said: 'Does aught befall you? It is good. It is part of the destiny of the Universe ordained for you from the beginning. All that befalls you is part of the great web.'"
>
> I breathed a bit stertorously.
>
> "He said that, did he?"
>
> "Yes, sir."
>
> "Well, you can tell him from me he's an ass."

# POSTSCRIPT

Marcus Aurelius died on March 17, a.d. 180, nearly three centuries before the final collapse of Roman administration in the West. The literature of the Roman world in this period is rich with great writers of enduring influence, as well as a host of minor figures, interesting as well in their own right. But it is a subject for another anthology. There is a degree of arbitrariness in setting any end date to a selection of writings such as this, but there are reasons why this one may seem particularly appropriate.

During the third century the prosperous provinces of Roman Africa continued to thrive, and in many respects the region assumed a central role in the cultural life of the Roman world. Following the disastrous reign of Marcus Aurelius's deranged son Commodus, control of the empire passed into the hands of the general Lucius Septimius Severus, a native of Lepcis Magna in what is now Libya. The dynasty that he founded would come to an end in a.d. 235 when the last of that line, Severus Alexander, was murdered in Germany together with his mother. His death ushered in a period of political turmoil that was to last two generations until the reins of power were seized by Diocletian, who rose from obscurity to impose a sweeping reform of the imperial system. Throughout this difficult age Africa suffered less than most other parts of the Roman world from the depredations of civil war and barbarian incursions. It was here that Christianity established itself as the most successful of the many Eastern cults that claimed adherents in the West.

Sometime in the third century Minucius Felix, a Christian from Cirta, now known as Constantine in modern Algeria, composed in Latin a dialogue, called *Octavius,* in the time-honored tradition of Plato. In style it evokes the austere classicism of Ciceronian prose, but its subject reflects the great changes that were now taking place in Roman culture. In the dialogue Minucius describes how he, his pagan friend Caecilius, and Octavius, a Christian friend visiting Rome, decided to take a walk to the seashore at Ostia. There, as they walked along the sands, dipping their toes in the water and watching boys skipping stones along the surface of the sea, they talked about religion. At first Caecilius defends his pagan beliefs, but finally he is converted to Christianity by the reasoned arguments of Octavius. In the end, the three friends depart, rejoicing in Caecilius's conversion. In the life of the empire the development of Christianity into the new state religion becomes a dominant theme in the evolution of Roman culture. This is reflected, too, in the literature of the age.

This is not to say that literature in the mainstream of the Roman tradition died out. It is true enough that there is little poetry worthy of notice stemming from the third and fourth centuries. From the third century we have practically nothing written in Latin, and this is not merely an

**Figure 34: A copyist**
A monk at work in a scriptorium. Before the invention of printing, unknown in the West till the fifteenth century, all books had to be produced in this laborious way, one copy at a time.

accident of transmission. It surely reflects not only the literary tastes of the time but also the strain placed on cultural life by the deteriorating social and political fabric of the empire in the West. And in the contemporary poetry composed in Greek, we may detect a turning away from engagement with the larger Roman world and a return to a Hellenic focus. The most important work from third century is the epic poem in fourteen books by Quintus of Smyrna, known as the *Posthomerica*, which relates the events of the Trojan War, beginning at the point where the *Iliad* leaves off. There is no reason to believe that Quintus had any interest in, or indeed had even read, works in Latin that dealt with the subject, such as Virgil's *Aeneid*. His preoccupation is entirely with the Greek tradition. The same may be said of the latest works of classical antiquity in the East, such as the narrative poem on the romance of Hero and Leander by Musaeus. With the rifts now opening in Rome's pan-Mediterranean world, cultural life was increasingly focused on a narrowing range of localized cultural traditions. In the East this resulted in a renewed focus on their own, Greek heritage, a development that is reflected, for example, in the rise of a new engagement with Plato's philosophy, inaugurated in the third century by Plotinus (205–70). But in tandem with the continuing activities of poets, philosophers, and sophists, the burgeoning development of a Christian literature becomes the dominant theme of the age. In many respects the most emblematic figure of the time is Nonnus, a fifth-century poet from the cultivated city of Panopolis in Upper Egypt.

His major work was an epic poem on the god Dionysus, composed in forty-eight books—the sum of the *Iliad* and the *Odyssey*—in which he displays a recondite knowledge of Greek literature of the previous thousand years, but no engagement with the Roman world or literature in Latin at all. Most tellingly, however, his only other surviving work is a verse paraphrase of the Gospel of St. John. The works of Claudian from the late fourth and early fifth centuries are a bit of an anomaly in this regard. Originally a Greek poet from Alexandria in Egypt, Claudian relocated to Rome around A.D. 393. There he found a patron in the great general Stilicho, for whom he composed panegyrics in Latin verse as well as for the young and ineffective emperor Honorius whom he served.

In other respects the literature of the Western regions of the empire increasingly reflects a less cosmopolitan world. While the engagement with Greek culture is a running theme in the development of Latin literature from its earliest stages, this interest is far less evident in the later period. The stage may have been set in part by the fashion for archaic Latin literature that took hold in the second century. The political chaos that enveloped the empire in the half-century that followed the Severan dynasty in the third century was certainly a contributing factor. The fourth century witnessed a perceptible decline in the position of the city of Rome as the cultural capital of the empire, just as its position in the political equation was also eroding. In addition to the great city of Alexandria in Egypt, which had been from its foundation by Alexander the Great a magnet for writers, thinkers, and artists, there were important centers of learning in Antioch in the East and the refounded city of Carthage in Africa. The emperor Constantine's new capital, Constantinople, founded on the site of the ancient Greek colony of Byzantium in 324, was further evidence of the degree to which the center of gravity was shifting away from Rome. Constantine's third son, Constantius II, who succeeded his father in 337, did not set foot in Rome until he was forty years old in 357. It was the only time in his life he looked upon the ancient capital.

Within the now Christian empire there arose an extensive body of literature in Latin that sustained the intellectual life of the new official religion. The ground had been thoroughly prepared already in the third century. In addition to the preparation of utilitarian texts of translations of the Bible and protreptic lives of the martyrs, a body of Christian apologetic and antipagan literature began to appear. Its earliest celebrated practitioner in Latin was a North African, Tertullian (ca. 160–240), whose doctrinal tracts exercised a great influence on Christian writings in Latin. He was a favorite of Augustine, among many others. The spread of Christian theological works was accompanied by a change in the technology of the book. From the third century on, the papyrus roll, which had been the standard format for literary works in Greek and Latin for a millennium, was gradually displaced by a new medium. Known as the "codex," from the word for a plank of wood, the material that was originally used to make a volume of leaves tied together for writing, the bound volume of parchment sheets was the predominant form for the book by the fifth century. It had a number of advantages over the papyrus roll for readers of a theological text, since its format allowed for easy reference to different sections without cumbersome rolling and unrolling. But these advantages for a Christian readership probably do not alone explain this shift in reading habits, since the new format had attractions for readers of more traditional Roman texts as well. For example, it allowed for the production of convenient volumes of works. Now a complete edition of the works of Virgil, for example, would consist of a single bound codex, rather than a box containing seventeen papyrus rolls.

The literature of the late empire is thus in many respects as dynamic a cultural phenomenon as that of the period covered in this volume. And not the least fascinating aspect of this literature is the way in which it struggles to account for the legacy of the past amid changes of dramatic proportions in the political, religious, social, and economic life of the lands surrounding the Mediterranean. The last word may be had by a minor poet of the early fifth century, who in so many ways was typical of the times: Rutilius Claudius Namatianus, an aristocrat from Roman Gaul, who rose to high office in the city of Rome. In 417, he journeyed back to his native Gaul in the aftermath of Alaric's sack of the city, an event that had shaken the entire world as he knew it. He recorded his journey home in a poem in elegiac couplets, evoking a type of poem well established in Latin literature. In the second century B.C. Lucilius had described a trip to Sicily in verse, and the theme was later taken up by Horace (*Satires* 1.5), Ovid (*Sorrows of an Exile* 1.10), and Statius (*Silvae* 3.2). Rutilius touches on many themes in the one book and fragment of a second that survive, as the stages of his journey evoke recollections about friends or the historical associations of the places that he passed. But he begins with an address on the greatness of Rome and a farewell to the city, invoking its legacy with a personal poignancy that resonates with every student of antiquity:

> You made one country out of scattered nations;
>> for the unjust it was a good thing to be defeated by you.
> In offering to the conquered a share in your own rights,
>> you made a city of what had once been the world.

# SUGGESTIONS FOR FURTHER READING

THE BEST PLACE TO BEGIN IS BY READING BEYOND THE SELECTIONS INCLUDED IN this anthology. Complete translations of most of the works excerpted here can be found in the volumes of the Oxford World's Classics series, which also includes many authors and works that had to be omitted here for reasons of space. Each of the translations includes a select bibliography with emphasis on works available in English. A good place to start looking for more specialized secondary works on the authors is the *Oxford Classical Dictionary* (Oxford University Press 4th ed., 2012), which also contains entries on other topics touched upon in this anthology. The most complete history of Latin literature available in English is G. B. Conte, *Latin Literature: A History,* trans. J. B. Solodow; rev. by D. Fowler and G. W. Most (Johns Hopkins University Press, 1994). The literature written in Greek during this period tends to be treated as an afterthought in the standard histories of Greek literature, such as A. Lesky, *A History of Greek Literature* (Hackett, 1996), but interested readers might turn with profit to works such as T. Whitmarsh, *Greek Literature and the Roman Empire* (Oxford University Press, 2001). An extremely valuable resource for anyone wishing to investigate the reception of the authors in this volume is A. Grafton, G. W. Most, and S. Settis, eds., *The Classical Tradition* (Harvard University Press, 2010). Of course, it goes without saying, but will be said anyway, that the richest rewards await the reader who takes up the challenge of studying Latin and Greek to experience the qualities of these texts in the languages in which they were first composed.

# CHRONOLOGICAL TABLE OF IMPORTANT EVENTS IN ROMAN HISTORY AND LITERATURE

Events in the history of the Roman state are listed in the left-hand column, while events in the history of Roman literature are registered on the right. Many of the dates are only approximate. For example, it is an article of faith among many scholars that every ancient author died shortly after penning his last datable reference; hence, the assignment of Propertius's death to 15 B.C.

## I. THE EARLY REPUBLIC

| | | |
|---|---|---|
| End of First Punic War. | 241 | |
| | 240 | Livius Andronicus stages first play at Rome. |
| | 239 | Birth of Ennius. |
| Second Punic War begins. | 218 | |
| Hannibal marches on Rome. | 211 | Plautus stages his first play. |
| End of the Second Punic War. | 201 | Birth of Polybius. |
| | 195 | Birth of Terence. |
| | 184 | Death of Plautus. |
| Roman army invades Macedonia. | 169 | Death of Ennius. |
| | 167 | Polybius taken to Rome as a prisoner; Terence begins writing plays. |
| | 159 | Terence dies. |
| Carthage is destroyed; sack of Corinth. | 146 | |
| | 130 | Lucilius's first satires. |
| Assassination of Gaius Gracchus. | 121 | |
| | 106 | Birth of Cicero. |

## II. THE LATE REPUBLIC

| | | |
|---|---|---|
| Assassination of the radical reformer Saturninus. | 100 | Birth of Caesar. |
| | 98 | Birth of Lucretius. |
| Sulla returns to Rome, seizes power. | 83 | Sulla brings a collection of Aristotle's works to Rome. |
| Sulla is dictator. | 81 | Cicero's first speech, *In Defense of Roscius of Ameria*. |
| Death of Sulla. | 78 | Cicero is in Greece. |
| Revolt of Sertorius. | 73 | Parthenius of Nicaea comes to Rome. |
| First Consulship of Pompey and Crassus. | 70 | Birth of Virgil; Cicero writes the *Prosecution against Verres*. |
| Catiline is acquitted of extortion. | 65 | Birth of Horace. |
| Octavian (later Augustus) is born. | 63 | Cicero's consulship; suppression of Catiline's conspiracy. |
| First Triumvirate: Pompey, Caesar, Crassus. | 60 | Catullus is writing poetry. |
| Caesar's first invasion of Britain. | 55 | Death of Lucretius. |
| Caesar's second invasion of Britain. | 54 | Death of Catullus. |
| | 51 | Caesar completes *The Gallic War*. |
| The Senate is increasingly hostile to Caesar. | 50 | Sallust expelled from the Senate. |
| Caesar crosses the Rubicon. | 49 | |
| Caesar returns to Italy. | 47 | Birth of Propertius. |
| Assassination of Caesar. | 44 | Cicero returns to political activity. |
| Second Triumvirate: Antony, Octavian, Lepidus. | 43 | Birth of Ovid; murder of Cicero; Sallust's *Catiline* completed. |
| Battle of Philippi: victory of Antony over Caesar's assassins. | 42 | Horace fights at Philippi. |
| Antony meets Cleopatra at Tarsus. | 41 | Virgil writes *Eclogue* 4. |

## III. THE AUGUSTAN AGE

| | | |
|---|---|---|
| Asinius Pollio founds first public library in Rome. | 39 | Sallust begins his *Histories*. |
| Renewal of the Second Triumvirate. | 38 | Virgil completes the *Eclogues*. |
| Death of Sallust. | 35 | Horace completes the first book of *Satires*. |
| Battle of Actium. | 31 | |
| Suicide of Antony and Cleopatra. | 30 | Horace completes the *Epodes*. |
| Triumph of Octavian. | 29 | Virgil reads the *Georgics* to Octavian; Propertius finishes his *Cynthia*. |
| Octavian is given the name Augustus. | 27 | |

| | | |
|---|---|---|
| Suicide of Cornelius Gallus. | 26 | Elegies of Tibullus and Propertius. |
| | 25 | Ovid begins writing the *Amores*; Livy is at work on his history. |
| Constitutional reform confirms Augustus's position. | 23 | Horace finishes the first three books of *Odes*. |
| Agrippa pacifies Spain. | 19 | Death of Virgil and Tibullus. |
| | 15 | Ovid's *Heroides*; death of Propertius. |
| Tiberius becomes consul. | 13 | Horace's fourth book of *Odes*. |
| | 8 | Death of Maecenas and Horace. |
| Augustus proclaimed "Father of His Country." | 2 | In this and the following years Ovid completes the *Amores* (2nd ed.), *The Art of Love*, and *Remedies for Love*. |
| Tiberius returns from exile in Rhodes. | A.D. 2 | Ovid is at work on the *Fasti* and *Metamorphoses*. |
| Augustus's granddaughter Julia is exiled for moral turpitude. | 8 | Ovid is banished to Tomi for undisclosed reasons. |
| Death of Augustus and accession of Tiberius. | 14 | Ovid is at work on his last book of poetry. |
| Triumph of Germanicus. | 17 | Death of Livy and Ovid. |

## IV. THE EARLY EMPIRE

| | | |
|---|---|---|
| Death of Tiberius's son Drusus. | 23 | Pliny the Elder is born at Como. |
| Tiberius dies and is succeeded by Gaius (Caligula). | 37 | Birth of Quintilian in Spain. |
| | 39 | Lucan and Martial are born in Spain. |
| Caligula is assassinated; Claudius succeeds him. | 41 | Seneca is exiled, begins to write tragedies. |
| | 48 | Birth of Plutarch. |
| Death of Claudius and accession of Nero. | 54 | Approximate date of Juvenal's birth. |
| Murder of Claudius's son Britannicus. | 55 | Birth of Tacitus. |
| | 61 | Birth of Pliny the Younger. |
| Nero's persecution of the Christians. | 64 | Martial arrives in Rome. |
| Pisonian conspiracy against Nero. | 65 | Suicide of Seneca and Lucan. |
| Nero proclaims freedom of Greece. | 66 | Death of Petronius. |
| Death of Nero. | 68 | Quintilian begins teaching in Rome. |
| Titus suppresses Jewish Revolt. | 70 | Birth of Suetonius. |
| | 77 | Pliny the Elder completes his *Natural History*; Josephus completes *The Jewish War*. |
| Death of Vespasian; eruption of Vesuvius. | 79 | Death of Pliny the Elder. |
| Dedication of Colosseum. | 80 | Martial's book of commemorative epigrams. |
| Inauguration of the Capitoline Games. | 86 | Martial completes Books 1 and 2 of the *Epigrams*. |

| | | |
|---|---|---|
| Domitian completes his palace on the Palatine. | 92 | Statius completes the *Thebaid*; Josephus completes his *Jewish Antiquities*. |
| Domitian's persecution of the Christians. | 95 | Quintilian completes *The Education of the Orator,* dies soon after. |
| Assassination of Domitian; accession of Nerva. | 96 | Death of Statius. |

## V. THE HIGH EMPIRE

| | | |
|---|---|---|
| Death of Nerva; accession of Trajan. | 98 | Tacitus writes the *Agricola* and *Germania*. |
| | 104 | Death of Martial. |
| Pliny is governor in Bithynia. | 109 | Tacitus completes the *Histories*; Pliny finishes the first nine books of *Epistles*. |
| Trajan leaves for war with Parthia. | 113 | Death of Pliny the Younger. |
| Death of Trajan and accession of Hadrian. | 117 | Tacitus finishes his *Annals,* dies soon after. |
| | 120 | Suetonius completes *The Lives of the Caesars*; birth of Lucian. |
| Construction of Hadrian's Wall in Britain. | 122 | Suetonius presumed dead. |
| | 126 | Death of Plutarch; birth of Apuleius. |
| Completion of reconstructed Pantheon. | 127 | Death of Juvenal. |
| | 158 | Apuleius at work on *The Metamorphoses*. |
| Death of Antoninus Pius; accession of Marcus Aurelius. | 161 | |
| | 170 | Death of Apuleius. |
| | 174 | Marcus Aurelius begins his *Meditations*. |
| Death of Marcus Aurelius. | 180 | Death of Lucian. |

# GLOSSARY

Polybius recognizes the importance of providing contextual information for his readers (*Histories* 3.36):

> To ensure that my account does not lack clarity because the territory Hannibal traversed is unfamiliar, I need to describe each place along his route, and not merely catalog the regions, rivers, and cities, as some historians do....A simple list of unfamiliar things is really no more useful than meaningless and inarticulate utterances, for the mind cannot connect what is said to anything that it already knows about, and so the account becomes incoherent and garbled.

Very soon, however, he gives a revised version of this declared modus operandi (3.57):

> Readers who insist on a detailed description of everything perhaps do not realize that they are like gluttonous dinner guests who sample every dish on the table without deriving any enjoyment from the food as they eat it or nourishment from it while they subsequently digest it. Quite the contrary. So it is with those who read that way: they miss out both on the pleasure to be gained while they read and on the long term benefit of reading.

So, the need to find a happy medium in such matters is not new. In the same spirit of compromise as that adopted by Polybius, this glossary provides basic information about most of the people, places, events, and institutions referred to in the anthology. It is not, however, exhaustive; further information is readily available in reference sources such as the *Oxford Classical Dictionary* (Oxford University Press, 4th ed., 2012). Place names marked with one or more asterisks can be found on the corresponding maps.

**A.:** the Roman *praenomen* Aulus.
**Accius:** L. Accius (170–ca. 86 B.C.), Roman dramatist.
***Achaea:** region in the northern Peloponnese.
**Acheron:** a river in the Underworld.
**Acrisius:** king of Argos, father of Danae, and grandfather of Perseus.
**Actaeon:** Theban prince, torn to pieces by his own hounds after seeing Diana bathing.
***Actium:** site in western Greece of Octavian's victory in 31 B.C. over Antony and Cleopatra.
**Adoneus = Adonis:** Venus's mortal lover.

**\*Adriatic:** sea between Italy and Greece.

**Aediles:** annually elected Roman magistrates, responsible esp. for maintenance of public amenities.

**Aeetes:** king of Colchis, father of Medea.

**\*Aegean:** sea between Greece and Asia Minor (Turkey).

**Aegis:** a shield or cloak worn by Jupiter, Minerva, and other deities.

**Aelian:** Claudius Aelianus (A.D. ca. 165–ca. 235), author of *On the Nature of Animals* and *Miscellaneous History*, a collection of anecdotes.

**Aelius Aristides** (A.D. 117–ca. 183): Greek author of works on history, rhetoric, religion.

**Aeneas:** son of Venus and Anchises, founder of the Roman race.

**Aeschylus:** with Sophocles and Euripides, the greatest of the fifth-century B.C. Athenian tragedians.

**\*Africa:** the continent, also a Roman province, mostly in modern Libya and Tunisia.

**Agamemnon:** king of Mycenae, leader of the Greeks at Troy.

**Agave:** mother of Pentheus, king of Thebes, whom she dismembered in a Bacchic frenzy.

**Agenor:** Phoenician king, father of Europa and Cadmus.

**Agrippa:** M. Vipsanius Agrippa (ca. 63–12 B.C.), Octavian's admiral at Actium; also Julius Agrippa, king of Judaea.

**Agrippina:** the elder (ca. 14 B.C.–A.D. 33), granddaughter of Augustus, mother of Gaius (Caligula); the younger (A.D. 15–59), daughter of Germanicus, mother of Nero.

**Ajax:** king of Salamis, cousin of Achilles; also the lesser Ajax, who raped Cassandra and was drowned by Neptune.

**Alans:** nomads from the steppes of Asia.

**Alaric:** king of the Goths, sacked Rome in A.D. 410.

**\*\*\*Alba Longa:** mother city of Rome, founded by Aeneas's son Ascanius.

**Albunea:** fountain and river near Tibur.

**Alcaeus of Mytilene:** seventh/sixth-century B.C. Greek lyric poet.

**Alcides** = Hercules.

**Alcinous:** king of the Phaeacians, visited by Odysseus.

**Alcmaeon:** son of Eriphyle, whom he killed for betraying his father, Amphiaraus.

**Alesia:** site of the Gauls' last stand against Caesar in 52 B.C.

**Alexander the Great** (356–323 B.C.)**:** king of Macedon, conqueror of the Persian Empire.

**\*Alexandria:** city founded by Alexander the Great on the Egyptian coast in 331 B.C.

**\*\*\*Allia:** tributary of the Tiber, site of massacre of Roman army by the Gauls in 390 B.C.

**Alpheus:** river in the northwest Peloponnese.

**Althaea:** mother of Meleager, whom she killed to avenge the death of her brothers.

**Amazons:** mythical race of female warriors.

**Ammon:** the Egyptian god Amun, equated with Jupiter.

**Amphion:** son of Jupiter and Antiope; built the walls of Thebes by charming the stones with his lyre.

**Anacreon of Teos:** sixth-century B.C. Greek lyric poet.

**Ancus Marcius:** the fourth king of Rome.

**Andromache:** wife of Hector, Troy's best warrior.

**Andromeda:** daughter of Cepheus, king of the Ethiopians, rescued by Perseus from a sea monster.

**\*\*\*Anio:** tributary of the Tiber.

**Antenor:** Trojan elder, who led a colony to the Po Valley.

**Antimachus of Colophon:** fifth/fourth-century B.C. Greek poet.

**\*Antioch:** Greek city in Syria.

**\*\*\*Antium:** town on the coast of Latium (modern Anzio).

**Aonian** = Boeotian, esp. in connection with the Muses on Mt. Helicon.

**Apelles of Colophon:** fourth-century B.C. Greek painter.

**Apheliotes:** the east wind.

**Apollonius of Rhodes:** fourth-century B.C. Greek scholar and author of the epic *Argonautica*.

**Apotheosis** = deification.

**\*\*Apulia:** region in southeast Italy.

**Aquilo:** the north wind.

**Aratus:** fourth/third-century B.C. Greek poet, author of the *Phaenomena,* a versified astronomical text.

**Araxes:** river in Armenia, not securely identified.

**\*Arcadia:** region in the central Peloponnese.

**Arcturus:** the third-brightest star, whose rising portends stormy weather.

**Argo:** the ship in which Jason and his companions sailed in quest of the Golden Fleece.

**\*Argos:** city in the northeast Peloponnese.

**Argus:** hundred-eyed monster sent by Juno to watch Io after she had been changed into a cow.

**Ariadne:** daughter of Minos, king of Crete, who helped Theseus kill the Minotaur.

**Aristophanes:** fifth/fourth-century B.C. Athenian comic poet.

**Aristotle of Stagira:** fourth-century B.C. scientist and philosopher.

**As:** low-denomination Roman bronze coin; see *sestertius.*

**Ascanius:** son of Aeneas and either Creusa (Troy) or Lavinia (Italy), also known as Iulus.

**Asclepius:** god of medicine.

**\*Asia:** the continent, also a Roman province in western Turkey.

**Asinius Pollio, C.** (76 B.C.–A.D. 4): soldier, politician, poet, and literary patron.

**Atalanta:** Arcadian huntress, won as his bride by Milanion in a race, in which he slowed her by throwing apples for her to pick up.

**Athamas:** Boeotian king, father of Helle, who fell into the Hellespont from the flying sheep.

**\*Athos:** promontory in northern Greece.

**Atreus:** father of Agamemnon and Menelaus.

**Attalus:** the name of several kings of Pergamum, esp. Attalus III (ca. 170–133 B.C.), who bequeathed his kingdom to Rome.

**Attica:** the hinterland of Athens.

**Augurs:** state-appointed official diviners.

**Augusta** = Livia.

**Augustus, formerly Octavian** (63 B.C.–A.D. 14): the first Roman emperor.

**Aulus Gellius:** second-century A.D. author of a miscellaneous collection on various literary, historical, philosophical, and other topics, the *Attic Nights.*

**Aurora:** the goddess of the dawn.

**Ausonia** = Italy.

**Auspices:** divination through the observation of the behavior of birds.

**Auster:** the south wind.

**Automedon:** Achilles's charioteer.

**\*\*\*\*Aventine:** one of the hills of Rome.

**Avernus:** a lake in a volcanic crater near Naples, giving access to the Underworld.

**Bacchus:** god of wine.

**\*Bactria:** region in and around northern Afghanistan.

**Baetis:** river in Spain (now Guadalquivir).

**\*\*Baiae:** resort town on the Bay of Naples.

**\*Balearics:** group of islands in the western Mediterranean.

**Batavi:** German people on the lower Rhine.

**Bellona:** goddess of war.

**Bibaculus, M. Furius:** first-century B.C. poet.

**Bistonians:** a Thracian tribe.

**\*Bithynia:** region in northwest Asia Minor (Turkey).

**Boebeïs:** lake in Thessaly.

**\*Boeotia:** region in central Greece.

**Boreas:** the north wind.

**Borysthenes:** city (also known as Olbia) and river (now the Dneiper) flowing south into the Black Sea.

**Briseis:** Achilles's concubine, taken as war booty.

**\*\*Brundisium:** city at the heel of Italy.

**Brutus, L. Iunius:** expelled the last king from Rome in 510 B.C.

**Brutus, M. Iunius** (ca. 85–42 B.C.): one of the assassins of Caesar.

**Busiris:** xenophobic king of Egypt, killed by Hercules.

**C.:** the Roman *praenomen* Gaius.

**Cadmus:** founder of Thebes

**Caecuban:** a quality Italian wine.

****Caelian:** one of the hills of Rome.

**Calabria:** region at the toe of Italy.

**Calchas:** seer with the Greek army at Troy.

**Calenian:** a quality Italian wine.

**Caligula:** see Gaius.

**Callimachus of Cyrene:** third-century B.C. Greek poet and scholar.

**Calliope:** one of the nine Muses.

**Calvus, C. Licinius:** Catullus's friend and fellow poet.

**Camenae:** Latin equivalent to the Greek Muses.

**Camillus, M. Furius:** fifth/fourth-century B.C. Roman military leader.

****Campania:** region in west central Italy.

*****Campus Martius:** the Plain of Mars, flat land between the Tiber and the hills of Rome, used for mustering and exercising the army.

**Canace:** daughter of Aeolus, the ruler of the winds, incestuously pregnant by her brother Macareus.

**Cannae:** site in Apulia of the massacre of two Roman armies by Hannibal in 216 B.C.

*****Capitol/Capitoline:** one of the hills of Rome.

***Cappadocia:** region in eastern Asia Minor (Turkey).

****Capua:** city in Campania.

**Caracalla:** nickname of M. Aurelius Antoninus, Roman emperor A.D. 198–217.

**Carneades of Cyrene** (214/3–129/8 B.C.): Greek Academic philosopher.

**Carpathian Sea:** the Mediterranean around the island of Carpathus, between Rhodes and Crete.

***Carthage:** colony of Tyre, in modern Tunisia.

**Cassandra:** daughter of Priam and Hecuba, whose prophecies were never believed.

**Cassius:** C. Cassius Longinus, one of the assassins of Caesar.

**Cassius Dio** (ca. A.D. 164–ca. 230): author of a history of Rome in Greek.

**Castor:** see Leda.

**Cato, M. Porcius:** the elder (234–149 B.C.), soldier, politician, writer, strict guardian of Roman morality; the younger (95–46 B.C.), great-grandson of the elder Cato, conservative politician and opponent of Julius Caesar.

**Cayster:** river flowing into the Aegean Sea at Ephesus.

**Cecrops:** mythical second king of Athens.

**Censors:** two senior magistrates elected for eighteen months every four to five years, esp. to review the list of citizens.

**Centaurs:** half-man horses and half-horse men, associated esp. with Thessaly.

**Centumviri:** a civil court, consisting of one hundred judges.

**Cephalus:** legendary Athenian hero, beloved of the goddess Aurora.

**Ceraunia:** "Place of Thunder," a stormy headland in Albania.

**Cerberus:** three-headed dog that guards the entrance to the Underworld.

**Cercyon:** bandit king of Eleusis, west of Athens, killed by Theseus.

**Ceres:** goddess of agriculture. Her son-in-law is Dis, who abducted Persephone to the Underworld.

**Chaldaeans:** Semitic people of Mesopotamia, associated esp. with astrology.

**Chaonia:** region in Epirus, in western Greece.

**Charybdis:** a whirlpool in the Straits of Messina, between Sicily and Italy.

**Chilon of Sparta:** one of the Seven Wise Men of Greece.

**Chimaera:** monster with the head of a lion, body of a goat, and tail of a snake.

**Chios:** island in the Aegean Sea.

**Chrysippus of Soli** (ca. 280–207 B.C.): head of the Stoic school at Athens.

**Cicero, M. Tullius** (106–43 B.C.): the greatest Roman orator.

***Cilicia:** region in southeast Asia Minor (Turkey).

**Cimbri:** a German tribe, massacred at Vercellae in Cisalpine Gaul in 101 B.C.

**Cincinnatus, L. Quinctius:** fifth-century B.C. Roman general.

**Cinna, C. Helvius:** fellow poet and friend of Catullus.

**Cinna, L. Cornelius:** early first-century B.C. politician and general.

\*\*\*\***Circus Maximus:** Rome's main venue for chariot racing.

\*\***Cisalpine Gaul:** Gaul on this side of the Alps, i.e., in north Italy.

**Cithaeron:** mountain range separating Boeotia from Attica.

**Claudius** (10 B.C.–A.D. 54): the fourth Roman emperor.

**Cleanthes of Assos** (331–232 B.C.): second head of the Stoic school at Athens.

**Cleopatra VII** (70/69–30 B.C.): last Ptolemaic ruler of Egypt.

**Client:** an individual owing deference and service to a patron, a social or economic superior, in return for assistance and protection.

**Clodius:** P. Clodius Pulcher (ca. 92–52 B.C.), popularist politician, sworn enemy to Cicero.

**Clotho:** one of the Fates, governing the thread of mortal destiny.

**Cnidos:** island in the Aegean Sea.

**Cohort:** the basic unit of the legionary army, usually consisting of 480 men.

\***Colchis:** region on the east coast of the Black Sea.

\*\*\*\***Colosseum:** the Flavian Amphitheater, built by Vespasian and Titus in the 70s A.D.

**Colossus of Rhodes:** statue of the sun god, Helios, on the Greek island of Rhodes.

**Columella, L. Iunius Moderatus:** first-century A.D. writer on agriculture and trees.

**Commodus, L. Aurelius:** Roman emperor A.D. 180–92.

**Conscript fathers** = senators.

**Consuls:** pair of chief magistrates elected annually.

\*\*\***Cora:** hill town in Latium.

\*\***Corfinium:** town in the Abruzzi, east of Rome.

\***Corinth:** city on the isthmus joining the Peloponnese to central Greece.

**Corn** = wheat in UK English.

**Cornelius Gallus, C.** (ca. 70–26 B.C.): soldier and love poet.

**Corus:** the northwest wind.

**Corybants:** spirits of nature, associated esp. with the goddess Cybele.

**Cos:** island in the Aegan Sea.

**Crassus, M. Licinius** (ca. 115–53 B.C.): formed the First Triumvirate with Pompey and Caesar, and was killed by the Parthians at Carrhae.

**Creon:** king of Corinth, whose daughter was to marry Medea's husband, Jason.

**Creon:** successor to Oedipus as king of Thebes.

**Croesus:** sixth-century B.C. king of Lydia.

**Croton:** Greek city in southern Italy.

**Ctesias of Cnidus:** physician to Artaxerxes II of Persia (ruled 405/4–359/8 B.C.), author of historical and geographical accounts of the Persian Empire.

\*\***Cumae:** Greek settlement north of Naples.

\*\*\*\***Curia:** the Senate house.

**Curius:** M'. Curius Dentatus, third-century B.C. Roman military leader.

**Curule:** a designation for the senior magistrates, censors, consuls, praetors, and curule aediles, who alone could sit in a special curule chair.

**Cyanean Rocks** = Symplegades, a pair of rocks at the Bosphorus that clashed together.

**Cybele:** the Great Mother, a fertility goddess from Phrygia.

**Cyclades:** a group of islands in the southern Aegean Sea.

**Cyclopes:** one-eyed monstrous shepherds, esp. Polyphemus; also the smiths who forged Jupiter's thunderbolts.

**Cydnus:** river in southeast Asia Minor (Turkey).

**Cydonia:** town in northwest Crete (now Chania).

**Cyllene:** mountain in Arcadia, sacred to Mercury.

**Cynicism:** the "dog" philosophy, devoted to living according to nature.

**Cynthus:** hill on the island of Delos.

\***Cyprus:** the island on which Venus was said to have been born; see also Cythera.

**\*Cyrene:** Greek city in Libya.

**Cyrus I:** sixth-century B.C. king of Persia.

**\*Cythera:** the island off the southern Peloponnese on which Venus was said to have been born; see also Cyprus.

**D.:** the Roman *praenomen* Decimus.

**Dacians:** people who inhabited present-day Romania, subjugated by Trajan in the early second century A.D.

**Daedalus:** escaped from Minos on Crete with wings he designed. His son Icarus drowned in the attempt.

**Dahae:** a nomadic Scythian tribe.

**Danaans** = Greeks.

**Danaids:** the daughters of Danaus, who killed their husbands on the wedding night and are spending eternity in the Underworld pouring water into a jar with holes in the bottom.

**Dardan** = Trojan.

**Daunia:** the northern part of Apulia.

**Decius:** P. Decius Mus ensured victory against the Latins in 340 B.C. by dying in the battle; his son of the same name is said to have done the same against the Celts in 295.

**\*Delos:** island in the central Aegean Sea, birthplace of Apollo and Diana.

**\*Delphi:** overlooking the Gulf of Corinth from the slope of Mt. Parnassus, the site of the shrine of Pythian Apollo, the most important Greek oracle.

**Demetrius of Phalerum** (ca. 360–280 B.C.): ruler of Athens, philosopher, Librarian at Alexandria.

**Democritus of Abdera** (ca. 460–? B.C.): atomist philosopher.

**Demosthenes** (384–322 B.C.): the greatest Athenian orator.

**Denarius:** Roman silver coin; see *sestertius*.

**Deucalion:** with his wife, Pyrrha, he reconstituted the human race after the Great Flood.

**Diana:** goddess of hunting, sister of Apollo.

**Dictator:** appointed with sole power at times of crisis, overriding the authority of the consuls.

**Dido:** Tyrian queen, founder of Carthage.

**Dindymus:** mountain in western Asia Minor (Turkey), sacred to Cybele.

**Dio Chrysostom** (ca. A.D. 45–after 110): orator and popular philosopher.

**Diocletian:** Roman emperor, ruled 284–305.

**Diogenes the Cynic** (ca. 410–ca. 324 B.C.): philosopher who questioned the conventions of life through his outrageous behavior and wit.

**Diomede(s) of Argos:** member of the Greek expedition to Troy.

**Dionysius of Halicarnassus** (ca. 60–after 7 B.C.): Greek author of a history of Rome and of various treatises on rhetoric.

**Dionysius I** (ca. 430–367 B.C.): tyrant of Syracuse.

**Dionysus** = Bacchus.

**Dis:** ruler of the Underworld.

**Dodona:** sanctuary and oracle of Zeus in the western mountains of Greece.

**Dog (star):** Sirius, in the constellation Canis Major.

**Domitian:** Roman emperor, ruled A.D. 81–96.

**Drachma:** basic unit of Greek coinage, of varying value in different *poleis*.

**Dryads:** tree nymphs.

**Dyrrachium:** see Epidamnus.

**Ebro:** river in northern Spain.

**Egeria:** a water nymph, wife or companion of Numa Pompilius.

**Elagabalus:** Roman emperor, ruled A.D. 218–22.

**Eleusinian Mysteries:** festival in honor of Demeter and Proserpina at Eleusis, west of Athens.

**\*Elis:** region in the northwest Peloponnese.

**Elissa** = Dido.

**Emathia** = southern Macedonia.

**Emmet** = ant.

**Enceladus:** a Giant, imprisoned under Sicily for attacking heaven.

**Endymion:** the moon goddess's mortal lover.

**Enipeus:** river in Thessaly.

**Ennius, Q.** (239–169 B.C.): leading early exponent of many genres of poetry, esp. celebrated for his epic, the *Annals,* an account of Roman history.

**\*Ephesus:** Greek city on the west coast of Asia Minor (Turkey).

**Epictetus:** first/second-century A.D. Stoic philosopher, a slave in his early life.

**Epicurus of Samos** (341–270 B.C.): moral and natural philosopher.

**\*Epidamnus:** Greek city facing Italy across the Adriatic (in Latin, Dyrrachium, modern Durrës in Albania).

**\*Epirus:** region in west central Greece.

**Epitome** = abridgment.

**Equestrian:** see knights.

**Erebus:** the darkness of the Underworld.

**Eridanus** = Po.

**Eryx:** promontory in western Sicily, famous for its temple of Venus.

**\*\*\*\*Esquiline:** one of the hills of Rome.

**Etna:** volcano in eastern Sicily.

**Etruria:** homeland of the Etruscans.

**Etruscans:** a non-Indo-European people living north of Rome, among Rome's most powerful neighbors in the early centuries.

**Eudoxus of Cnidus** (ca. 390–ca. 340 B.C.): Greek mathematician.

**Eudoxus of Cyzicus:** second-century B.C. Greek explorer.

**Eumenides** ("the Kindly-Minded Ones"): avenging goddesses from the Underworld.

**Euripides:** with Aeschylus and Sophocles, the greatest of the fifth-century B.C. Athenian tragedians.

**Europa:** Phoenician princess, abducted by Jupiter in the form of a bull.

**Euterpe:** one of the Muses.

**Euxine** = the Black Sea.

**Evadne:** wife of Capaneus, one of the Seven against Thebes.

**Fabricius:** C. Fabricius Luscinus, third-century B.C. Roman military leader.

**Falernian:** a quality Italian wine.

**Fasces:** bundle of wooden rods bound with red straps, symbolizing the authority of magistrates.

**Faunus:** nature god, identified with the Greek god Pan.

**Favonius:** the west wind.

**Fetial priests:** priests overseeing Rome's dealings with foreigners, esp. in declaring war and concluding peace treaties.

**\*\*\*Fidenae:** town in Latium.

**Flamen Dialis:** priest of Jupiter.

**\*\*\*via Flaminia:** main road from Rome to the north.

**Forum:** the market- and meetingplace in a Roman town.

**Fronto, M. Cornelius** (ca. A.D. 100–170): tutor to the future emperors Marcus Aurelius and Lucius Verus.

**Fulvia:** wife of Mark Antony.

**Furies:** Roman equivalent to the Greek Eumenides.

**\*\*\*Gabii:** town in Latium.

**\*Gades:** Phoenician settlement in southern Spain, now Cadiz.

**Gaetuli:** nomadic people in western North Africa.

**Gaius:** C. Iulius Caesar Augustus Germanicus, nicknamed Caligula, Roman emperor, ruled A.D. 37–41.

**Galatians:** Celtic tribe settled in Asia Minor (Turkey).

**Galba, Servius Sulpicius** (3 B.C.–A.D. 69): Roman emperor, ruled A.D. 68–69.

**Galen of Pergamum** (ca. A.D. 129–ca. 212): the most influential of ancient doctors, endearingly opinionated.

**Ganymede:** Trojan prince, abducted to Olympus by Jupiter.

**Gargarus:** a peak on Trojan Mt. Ida.

**Gauls:** the people of modern France and surrounding regions.

**Geloni:** nomadic Scythian tribe.

**Germanicus, Iulius Caesar** (16/15 B.C.–A.D. 19): nephew and adopted son of Tiberius, husband of the elder Agrippina, father of Caligula.

**Geryon:** three-headed monster whose cattle Hercules stole.

**Golden Age:** mythical era when life was perfect.

**Good Goddess:** a deity associated with fertility, from whose rites men were excluded.

**Gorgons:** snake-haired female monsters, esp. Medusa.

**Gracchi** (Tiberius and Gaius Sempronius Gracchus, 163–133 and 154–121 B.C.): social reformers who both fell foul of the Senate.

**Graces:** group of three goddesses personifying feminine charm.

**Greens, also Blues, Reds, Whites:** chariot-racing teams.

**Gymnosophists:** naked ascetic Indian philosophers.

**Hades:** Greek god of the Underworld.

**Haemonian** = Thessalian.

**Haemus:** mountain in Thrace.

**Hannibal:** the great Carthaginian commander in the Second Punic War (218–201 B.C.).

**Hebe:** Greek goddess of youth.

**Hecate:** goddess of the Underworld.

**Hector:** son of Priam and Hecuba, Troy's best warrior.

**Hecuba:** wife of Priam, the last king of Troy.

**Helen:** daughter of Jupiter and Leda, wife of Menelaus.

**Helice:** Greek city destroyed by an earthquake in 373 B.C.

**Helicon:** mountain in central Greece associated with the Muses.

**Hellebore:** name given to various plants with purgative qualities.

**\*Hellespont:** the strait dividing Europe from Asia at the entrance to the Black Sea.

**Hendecasyllabics:** an eleven-syllable metrical scheme.

**Heraclitus:** sixth/fifth-century B.C. philosopher.

**\*\*Herculaneum:** after Pompeii, the most important town destroyed by the eruption of Mt. Vesuvius in A.D. 79.

**Herodotus of Halicarnassus** (?–ca. 425 B.C.): author of the *Histories,* an account of the Persian Wars and the peoples involved.

**Hesiod:** eighth/seventh-century B.C. author of the *Works and Days* and the *Theogony,* and much other poetry, now mostly lost.

**Hesperia** = Italy.

**Hesperides:** goddesses who guarded the golden apples at the Western Ocean.

**Hesperus:** the evening star.

**Hexameter:** a six-foot metrical scheme.

**Hippocentaur** = Centaur.

**Hippodamia:** wife of Pelops, won by defeating her father, Oenomaus, in a chariot race; also the bride of Pirithous the Lapith.

**Hippolyte:** queen of the Amazons.

**Hippolytus:** son of Theseus, loved in vain by his stepmother, Phaedra.

**Hirtius, A. and C. Vibius Pansa:** consuls in 43 B.C.

**\*Hister:** the river Danube.

**Horatius Cocles:** sixth/fifth-century B.C. hero who, with two comrades, kept back the Etruscan army while the Tiber bridge was being destroyed.

**Hortensius:** Q. Hortensius Hortalus (114–49 B.C.), second only to Cicero as an orator.

**Hyades:** five daughters of Atlas, later a cluster of stars.

**Hydaspes:** river in the Punjab, now the Jhelum.

**Hylaeus:** a Centaur.

**Hylas:** Hercules's companion, abducted by nymphs.

**Hymen:** god of marriage.

**Hypanis:** river in the Ukraine, now the Bug.

**Hypsipyle:** ruler of the island of Lesbos, loved and deserted by Jason.

**Iacchus:** god of the Eleusinian Mysteries.

**Iambics:** a six-foot metrical scheme.

**Iarbas:** a Libyan king.

**\*Iberia:** modern Spain and Portugal.

**Icarus:** see Daedalus.

**Ida:** mountain on Crete, also near Troy.

**Ilium:** alternative name for Troy.

**\*Illyria:** region in the northwest Balkan Peninsula, later the Roman province of Illyricum.

**Imperator:** military leader, later emperor.

**Io:** Argive princess, transformed by Juno into a cow, watched over by Argus.

**\*Ionia:** region in western Asia Minor (Turkey), and also some of the Aegean islands.

**Iris:** goddess of the rainbow, the gods' messenger.

**Isis:** Egyptian goddess.

**Isthmian Games:** one of the Panhellenic Games, held every four years at Corinth.

**Isthmus of Corinth:** the narrow neck of land where the Peloponnese joins central Greece.

**Ithaca:** island home of Ulysses, off the west coast of Greece.

**Ituraeans:** Arab people in Jordan, Syria, and Lebanon.

**Ixion:** king of Thessaly, bound eternally to a wheel in the Underworld for attempting to rape Juno.

**Janus:** god of transitions, whether of place or of time.

**Jason:** Thessalian hero, leader of the Argonauts, husband of Medea.

**Jugurtha** (160–104 B.C.): king of Numidia.

**Kalends:** the first day of the Roman month.

**Knights**/*equites:* the second-highest stratum in Roman society after the senatorial class.

**\*Knossos:** city on the north coast of Crete, ruled by Minos.

**L.:** the Roman *praenomen* Lucius.

**Labienus, T.** (ca. 100–45 B.C.): served with Caesar in Gaul but sided with Pompey in 49.

**Lacedaemonians** = Spartans.

**Lacus Curtius:** the Curtian lake, which formed in the Forum after M. Curtius sacrificed his life to ensure a military victory.

**Laelius, C.** (ca. 190–ca. 128 B.C.): Roman statesman.

**Laertes:** father of Ulysses.

**Laestrygones:** man-eating giants, encountered by Ulysses on his wanderings.

**Lais:** name of several famous prostitutes.

**\*\*\*Lanuvium:** city in Latium, close to Rome.

**Laocoon:** Trojan priest of Apollo, strangled by sea snakes, along with his sons, for rejecting the Trojan Horse.

**Laomedon:** king of Troy, who reneged on his promise to pay Neptune and Apollo for building the city walls.

**Lapiths:** Thessalian clan, noted esp. for their drunken fight with the Centaurs.

**\*Laris(s)a:** city in Thessaly.

**\*\*\*Latium:** the region around Rome whose inhabitants, the Latins, spoke Latin.

**Latona** = Leto, mother of Apollo and Diana.

**\*\*\*Laurentum:** site of the younger Pliny's villa on the coast of Latium, south of Ostia.

**Lavinia:** daughter of Latinus, king of the Latins, and wife of Aeneas.

**\*\*\*Lavinium:** city in Latium, named by Aeneas in honor of Lavinia.

**Leda:** mother of Castor and Pollux, Helen and Clytemnestra, after being raped by Jupiter in the guise of a swan.

**Lepidus, M. Aemilius** (?–13/12 B.C.): the least significant member of the Second Triumvirate.

**\*Lesbos:** Greek island off the northwest coast of Asia Minor (Turkey).

**Lethe:** the river of forgetfulness, in the Underworld.

**Leucas:** island south of Actium.

**Liber:** Roman name for Bacchus.

**Libitina:** goddess of funerals.

**Liburnians:** people inhabiting the northeast coast of the Adriatic Sea.

**Lictors:** attendants and bodyguards for senior magistrates.

**\*\*Liguria:** region in northwest Italy.

**\*\*Lilybaeum:** city at the most westerly point in Sicily.

**Liris:** river in central Italy.

**Lollius:** M. Lollius Paulinus, defeated by German tribes in 16 B.C.

**Lucina:** goddess of childbirth.

**Lucretia:** her rape by Sextus, son of Tarquinius Superbus, led to the end of kingship in Rome.

**Lucullus, L. Licinius** (117–ca. 57 B.C.): soldier and politician, famously luxurious in his later years.

**Lupercalia:** ritual celebrated on February 15, in which naked young men ran along striking spectators with goat-skin thongs.

**Lyaeus:** "the Releaser," a Greek title for Bacchus.

**Lycaon:** king of Arcadia, whose daughter Callisto was turned into the constellation Ursa Major.

**\*Lycia:** region in southwest Asia Minor (Turkey).

**\*Lydia:** region in western Asia Minor (Turkey).

**Lynceus:** one of the Argonauts, famous for his keen eyesight.

**Lysippus:** fourth-century B.C. Greek sculptor.

**M.:** the Roman *praenomen* Marcus.

**M'.:** the Roman *praenomen* Manius.

**Macrobius:** Ambrosius Theodosius Macrobius, fourth/fifth-century A.D. grammarian and philosopher, author of esp. the *Saturnalia,* a wide-ranging dialogue, esp. on literary criticism of Virgil.

**Maecenas, C. Cilnius?** (70–8 B.C.): friend and adviser to Augustus, patron to Virgil and Horace.

**Maenads:** women inspired by Bacchic frenzy.

**Maeonia** = Lydia.

**Maeotians:** people living near Lake Maeotis, now the Sea of Azov.

**\*Malea:** stormy headland in the southeast Peloponnese.

**Maniple:** from the fourth to the second century B.C., the basic tactical unit of the legion.

**Marathon:** region in Attica, site of the unexpected victory of the Athenians and Plataeans over the Persians in 490 B.C.

**Marcellus, M. Claudius** (42–23 B.C.): Augustus's nephew and designated successor.

**Marcus Aurelius** (Marcus Aurelius Antoninus Augustus; A.D. 121–80): Stoic philosopher and Roman emperor, ruled A.D. 161–80.

**Mareotic** = Egyptian.

**Marius C.** (ca. 157–86 B.C.): a leading military and political figure.

**\*Marsi:** central Italian tribe, also an unrelated German tribe.

**Marsyas:** defeated by Apollo in a musical contest and subsequently flayed alive.

**Masinissa** (238–148 B.C.): king of Numidia.

**Massagetae:** nomadic tribe on the Russian steppes.

**\*Massalia:** Greek colony at the mouth of the Rhone, now Marseilles.

**Massic:** a fine Italian wine.

**Master of the Cavalry**/*magister equitum*: second-in-command to a dictator.

**Matine:** inhabiting Mt. Matinus in Apulia.

**\*Mauretania:** home of the Moors, in present-day Morocco and western Algeria, quite distinct from modern Mauritania, far to the south.

**Medea:** Colchian princess, wife of Jason, a beautiful witch.

**Medes:** people of modern Iran, often confused with the Persians by Greek and Roman writers.

**Medusa:** mythical monster, celebrated mainly for her decapitation by Perseus.

**\*Megara:** city near the Isthmus of Corinth.

**Melpomene:** one of the nine Muses.

**Memnon:** king of Ethiopia, son of Aurora and Tithonus, killed by Achilles at Troy.

**\*Memphis:** city in Egypt.

**Menander** (ca. 344–292/1 B.C.): Athenian writer of comedies.

**Menelaus:** king of Sparta, brother of Agamemnon, husband of Helen.

**Mentor:** fourth-century B.C. Greek silversmith.

**Mercury:** god of trading, the gods' messenger.

**Meriones:** young Cretan warrior at Troy.

**Messalina:** wife of the emperor Claudius.

**Midas:** legendary king of Phrygia, who turned everything he touched to gold.

**\*Miletus:** Greek city on the west coast of Asia Minor (Turkey).

**Milo, T. Annius:** political agitator, who murdered Clodius.

**Milon of Croton:** sixth-century B.C. athlete.

**Mime:** dramatic performance involving dialogue, either improvised or formally scripted.

**Minerva** = Athena.

**Minos:** son of Jupiter and Europa, king of Crete.

***Minturnae:** town at the mouth of the river Liris, on the border between Latium and Campania.

****Misenum:** promontory at the western end of the Bay of Naples, an important naval base.

**Mithridates VI of Pontus** (132–63 B.C., ruled 120–63): Rome's most dangerous foreign enemy in the first century B.C.

**Mulciber** = Vulcan.

***Munda:** city in southern Spain, site of Caesar's victory over the Pompeians in 45 B.C.

****Mutina:** city in north Italy, site of Mark Antony's victory over the senatorial forces in 43 B.C.

***Mycenae:** city in the Plain of Argos, ruled by Agamemnon.

**Myron:** fifth-century B.C. Greek sculptor.

**Myrtle:** tree sacred to Venus.

**Myrtoan:** the part of the Aegean Sea south of Euboea, named after Myrtilus, drowned there by Pelops after helping him defeat Oenomaus in a chariot race.

**Mysia:** region in northwest Asia Minor (Turkey).

***Mytilene:** the largest city on the island of Lesbos.

**Naevius:** third-century B.C. dramatist and epic poet.

**Naiads:** nymphs of rivers and springs.

**Narnia:** town in Umbria, originally called Nequinum, a name of ill omen, suggesting powerlessness.

**Nausicaa:** daughter of Alcinous, king of the Phaeacians.

**Nemean Games:** one of the Panhellenic Games, held every four years at Nemea, in the northeastern Peloponnese.

**Nemesis:** Greek goddess of retribution.

**Neoteric poets:** modern critical term for the group of poets that included Catullus.

**Nero, L. Domitius Ahenobarbus** (A.D. 37–68): Roman emperor, ruled 54–68.

**Nerva, M. Cocceius** (A.D. 30–98): Roman emperor, ruled 96–98.

**Nessus:** Centaur who tried to abduct Deianira and tricked her into poisoning her husband, Hercules, with his blood.

**Nestor:** wise old king of Pylos, who fought at Troy.

***New Carthage:** Carthaginian settlement in southeast Spain, now Cartagena.

**Niobe:** boasted she had more children than Leto, so Leto's two children, Apollo and Artemis, shot them all.

**Nisus:** king of Megara, betrayed to Minos by his daughter, Scylla, who cut off his magic purple lock of hair; they were both subsequently turned into birds.

**Noricum:** region in modern Austria, Slovenia, and Bavaria.

**Notos:** the south wind.

***Numantia:** Celtiberian stronghold in northern Spain.

**Numa Pompilius:** the second king of Rome.

****Numicus:** river in Latium.

***Numidia:** Roman province in northern Algeria and Tunisia.

**Nysa:** where Bacchus was reared; the location was quite uncertain already in antiquity.

***Ocean:** the river or sea that surrounds the inhabited world.

**Octavian:** see Augustus.

**Oeta:** mountain in central Greece where Hercules was cremated.

***Olympia:** site of the Olympic Games in the northwest Peloponnese.

**Olympiad:** Greek unit of time, the four years between one celebration of the Olympic Games and the next, counted from 776 B.C., the conventional date of the first Games.

**Olympus:** mountain in northern Greece, home of the gods.

**Opimian:** a quality Italian wine.

**Orcus:** the Underworld, also the ruler of the Underworld.

**Orestes:** son of Agamemnon and Clytemnestra.

**Orithyia:** Athenian princess, abducted by Boreas.

**Orpheus:** son of Apollo and a Muse, whose music could charm wild beasts and move stones.

**\*\*\*Ostia:** the port of Rome, at the mouth of the Tiber.

**Otho, M. Salvius** (A.D. 32–69): Roman emperor, ruled briefly in 69.

**Ovid:** P. Ovidius Naso (43 B.C.–after A.D. 17), poet.

**\*Oxyrhynchus:** city near the Upper Nile, source of almost three-quarters of all Greek literary papyri.

**P.:** the Roman *praenomen* Publius.

**Pachynus:** the southeastern promontory of Sicily.

**Pactolus:** gold-bearing river in western Asia Minor (Turkey).

**Paean** = Apollo.

**Paedagogus:** child's attendant and chaperone.

**\*\*Paestum:** Greek city south of Naples.

**\*\*\*\*Palatine:** one of the hills of Rome.

**Palimpsest:** a reused manuscript.

**Pallas:** a name of Athena (= Minerva).

**Pallene:** the most westerly peninsula in Macedonia.

**Pan:** Greek, esp. Arcadian, god of pastoral life.

**Panaetius of Rhodes** (ca. 185–109 B.C.): Stoic philosopher.

**\*Paphlagonia:** region on the south coast of the Black Sea.

**\*Paphos:** city in southwest Cyprus, associated esp. with Venus.

**Parasite:** literally "feeder beside," a companion to a social superior.

**Paris:** son of Priam and Hecuba, seducer of Helen.

**Paros:** island in the Aegean Sea, famous for marble.

**Parthenius of Nicaea:** Greek scholar and poet, came to Rome in 73 B.C., influenced the neoteric and later poets.

**\*Parthia:** empire extending over much of the area from the Mediterranean to India.

**Pasiphae:** wife of Minos and mother of the Minotaur.

**Pater patratus:** one of the fetial priests with ritual responsibilities in declaring war and concluding peace treaties.

**Patricians:** the Roman aristocracy.

**Patron:** see client.

**Paullus, L. Aemilius:** consul killed at Cannae.

**Pausanias of Magnesia:** second-century A.D. author of *Description of Greece,* a detailed account of most of the regions in the Roman province of Achaea.

**Pegasus:** winged horse, born from Medusa's severed neck.

**Peleus:** king of Thessaly, father of Achilles.

**Pelias:** deprived Jason of the throne of Iolcus in Thessaly, subsequently killed and cooked in a cauldron by his own daughters, in a failed attempt to rejuvenate him.

**Pelion:** mountain in Thessaly, source of the timber with which the *Argo* was built.

**\*Peloponnese:** large peninsula that constitutes the southern part of the Greek mainland.

**Pelops:** killed and served to the gods by his father, Tantalus; subsequently revived, he was the father of Atreus and Thyestes.

**\*Pelusium:** city on the eastern edge of the Nile delta.

**Penates:** the household gods.

**Penelope:** wife of Ulysses.

**Pentheus:** legendary king of Thebes.

**\*Pergamum:** Greek city near the west coast of Asia Minor (Turkey), also alternative name for Troy.

**Perseus:** slayer of Medusa and savior of Andromeda; also, the last king of Macedon, ruled 179–168 B.C., defeated in 168 by the Romans at Pydna.

**Persius:** Aulus Persius Flaccus (A.D. 34–62), satirist.

**\*\*Perugia:** Etruscan city in Umbria.

**Phaethon:** the son of Hyperion, the sun god, who fell to his death from his father's chariot.

**Pharos:** island off the north coast of Egypt, famous for its lighthouse, one of the seven wonders of the ancient world.

**\*Pharsalus:** town in Thessaly, site of the decisive battle between Caesar and Pompey in 48 B.C.

**Phasis:** river in Colchis, Medea's homeland at the southwest corner of the Black Sea.

**Phidias:** fifth-century B.C. Athenian sculptor.

**Philetas of Cos:** fourth/third-century B.C. Greek poet and scholar in Alexandria.

**Philip II:** king of Macedon (ruled 356–336 B.C.), father of Alexander the Great.

**\*Philippi:** city in Macedonia, site of the battle in 42 B.C. in which Mark Antony and Octavian defeated the assassins of Julius Caesar.

**Philippics:** series of speeches delivered by Cicero against Mark Antony.

**Philodemus:** first-century B.C. Greek philosopher and poet, influential on Virgil and other poets.

**Phlegra** = Pallene.

**Phoebus** = Apollo.

**\*Phoenicia:** region in Middle East, esp. Lebanon, including Tyre, mother city of Carthage.

**Phoenix:** legendary king of Tyre or Sidon, from whom the name Phoenicia is derived.

**\*Phrygia:** region in west central Asia Minor (Turkey).

**\*\*Picenum:** region of central Italy east of the Apennines.

**Pillars of Heracles:** the western entrance to the Mediterranean, the Straits of Gibraltar.

**Pindar of Thebes:** fifth-century B.C. Greek lyric poet.

**Pindus:** mountain range dividing Thessaly from Epirus.

**Pipleian:** having to do with the Muses who inhabit Pipla in Thessaly.

**Pirene:** fountain in Corinth.

**Pirithous:** king of the Lapiths, friend of Theseus.

**Pistoria:** city in Tuscany, now Pistoia.

**Plautian law:** measure to prevent breaches of the peace.

**Plebs:** the lower classes, hence plebeian.

**Pleiades:** seven daughters of Atlas, later a cluster of stars.

**Pluto:** king of the Underworld.

**\*\*Po:** the river bisecting the north Italian plain.

**Pollux:** see Leda.

**Polyhymnia:** one of the nine Muses.

**\*\*Pompeii:** the most important town destroyed by the eruption of Mt. Vesuvius in A.D. 79.

**Pompey:** Gnaeus Pompeius Magnus (106–48 B.C.) formed the First Triumvirate with Crassus and Caesar, killed in the aftermath of his defeat by Caesar at Pharsalus.

**Pompilius:** see Numa Pompilius.

**Pontifex Maximus:** the most important Roman priest.

**\*Pontus:** the Black Sea, also a region on the southern shore of the Black Sea.

**Porcian law:** measure to safeguard Roman citizens from corporal punishment.

**\*\*\*Praeneste:** town in Latium close to Rome, now Palestrina.

**Praenomen:** first name, used mostly by family and friends.

**Praetors:** after the consuls, the most important Roman magistrates.

**Praetorian prefect:** commander of the emperor's bodyguard.

**Priam:** the last king of Troy.

**Priapus:** fertility god, with distinctively oversized genitalia.

**Principate:** when Octavian/Augustus gained power, he adopted the title *princeps* ("leading man") as a means of understating his absolute authority.

**Proconsul:** magistrate or general serving outside Rome with the authority of a consul.

**Procurator:** magistrate overseeing financial and other affairs in a province.

**Prometheus:** Titan who created mankind but was later tortured on the Caucasus for stealing fire for mortals.

**Proserpina:** daughter of Ceres and queen of the Underworld.

**Proteus:** seal-herding sea god.

**Ptolemy:** one of Alexander's generals, founder of the dynasty that ruled Egypt for three hundred years.

**Punic Wars** (264–241, 218–201, 149–146 B.C.): the three wars fought by Rome against the Carthaginians (whose origin in Phoenicia in the eastern Mediterranean is reflected in the term "Punic").

**\*\*Puteoli:** town on the coast of Campania, north of Naples.

**\*Pydna:** town on the coast of Macedonia, site of the Roman victory over Perseus of Macedonia in 168 B.C.

**Pylos:** city in the western Peloponnese, ruled by Nestor.

**Pyrrha:** see Deucalion.

**Pyrrhic dances:** war dances performed in armor.

**Pyrrho of Elis** (ca. 365–275 B.C.): founder of the Skeptic school of philosophy.

**Pyrrhus** (319/8–272 B.C.): king of Epirus in western Greece, who invaded Italy in 280 to fight the Romans.

**Pythagoras of Samos:** sixth-century B.C. philosopher.

**Pythia:** the priestess through whom Apollo delivered his oracles at Delphi.

**Python:** monstrous snake killed by Apollo at Delphi, hence Pythia, Pythian Apollo.

**Q.:** the Roman *praenomen* Quintus.

**Quaestors:** officials with various administrative responsibilities.

**Quirites:** official term for Roman citizens.

**\*Ravenna:** city in northeast Italy.

**Regulus, M. Atilius:** Roman general in the First Punic War.

**Republic:** the period from the expulsion of the last king at the end of the sixth century B.C. until the establishment of the Principate under Augustus.

**Rhea Silvia:** see Romulus.

**\*\*Rhegium:** city at the toe of Italy, now Reggio Calabria.

**Rhesus:** Thracian king, killed by Ulysses and Diomedes before he could aid the Trojans.

**Rhipaean:** refers to a largely mythical mountain in the far north.

**\*Rhodes:** Greek island off the southwest coast of Asia Minor (Turkey).

**Rhodope:** mountain range in Bulgaria and Greece.

**Riphaean** = Rhipaean.

**Romulus:** Rome's legendary first king, the son of Mars and the vestal virgin Rhea Silvia.

**Rostra:** the speaker's platform in the Forum, literally "beaks," so named because the platform was decorated with the prows of captured ships.

**\*\*Rubicon:** river marking the border between Italy and Cisalpine Gaul.

**Rutuli:** a Latin tribe, led against Aeneas by Turnus.

**Sabines:** a people living northeast of Rome.

**\*\*\*\*Sacred Way:** street in Rome lined with shops, the route taken by triumphal processions.

**Saepta:** voting enclosure on the Campus Martius.

**Salamis:** island off the coast of Attica, site of the Greek naval victory over Xerxes in 480 B.C.

**Salian priests:** college of priests responsible for religious observances esp. in honor of Mars.

**Salmoneus:** father of Tyro, raped by Neptune in the guise of a river god.

**Samnites:** a warlike people in central Italy, all but annihilated by Sulla in the Social War.

**Sappho of Lesbos:** seventh/sixth-century B.C. Greek lyric poet.

**Sardanapallus:** semilegendary last king of Assyria, notorious for his decadent lifestyle.

**Sarmatians:** barbarian tribe living north and east of the Black Sea.

**Sarpedon:** son of Jupiter, killed by Patroclus at Troy.

**Saturn:** father of Jupiter and Juno.

**Saturnalia:** holiday in December, when slaves and owners apparently exchanged roles.

**Saturninus, L. Appuleius:** tribune of the plebs and populist politician, murdered in 100 B.C.

**Satyrs:** mythical folk, always male, with some animal characteristics, addicted to sex and wine.

**Scauri:** several members of this family were renowned for their probity and piety.

**Scholia:** explanatory notes written as commentaries to texts.

**Scipio Aemilianus:** P. Cornelius Scipio Aemilianus Africanus Numantinus (185/4–129 B.C.), destroyer of Carthage (146) and Numantia (133).

**Scipio Africanus:** P. Cornelius Scipio Africanus (236–183 B.C.), conqueror of Hannibal at Zama.

**Sciron:** monstrous brigand killed by Theseus.

**Scylla:** man-eating sea monster.

**Scylla:** see Nisus.

**Scythians:** barbarians living north and east of the Danube.

**Second Sophistic:** modern term for Greek culture, esp. literary, from the late first to the third century A.D.

**Sejanus, L. Aelius:** praetorian prefect, A.D. 14–31, killed by Tiberius for conspiring against him.

**Semele:** mother of Bacchus.

**Semiramis:** legendary queen of Assyria.

**Sempronia:** wife of D. Junius Brutus (consul in 77 B.C.), implicated in the Catilinarian conspiracy.

**Sertorius, Q.** (123–73 B.C.): controlled most of Spain for several years, in resistance to the Senate.

**Sestertius:** a coin valued at 2.5 *asses* and 0.25 of a *denarius*. In the early imperial period a legionary usually earned nine hundred *sestertii* annually.

**Seven Sisters** = the Pleiades.

**Sextus Pompey** (?–35 B.C.): younger son of Pompey the Great, opponent of the Second Trimvirate.

**Sibyl:** generic term for female seers, found widely throughout the Greek world.

**Sicanian = Sicilian.**

**\*Sidon:** Phoenician city in Lebanon.

**Silphium:** not specifically identifiable plant, now extinct, found only in Libya, much used in cookery and medicine.

**Simois:** river near Troy.

**Simonides of Ceos:** fifth-century B.C. Greek lyric poet.

**Sinis:** monstrous brigand killed by Theseus.

**Sinon:** Greek warrior who tricked the Trojans into taking the Trojan Horse into the city.

**Sisyphus:** pushes a rock up a hill, only for it to roll down again, as an eternal punishment in the Underworld.

**Social War** (91–87 B.C.): the Romans' Italian allies (*socii*) revolted when denied citizenship, which was granted to them as a result of the war.

**Sophocles:** with Aeschylus and Euripides, the greatest of the fifth-century B.C. Athenian tragedians.

**Sostratus:** a not certainly identifiable poet.

**Spartacus:** Thracian gladiator who led a slave revolt in 73–71 B.C.

**St. Augustine of Hippo** (A.D. 354–430): philosopher and theologian.

**Stade:** Greek measurement of distance, a little more than two hundred yards.

**Sthenelus:** Greek warrior at Troy.

**Strabo** (?64 B.C.–A.D. ?24): author of a voluminous treatise in Greek, the *Geography*.

**Strymon:** river between Thrace and Macedonia.

**Styx:** river in the Underworld.

**\*\*\*\*Subura:** district near the Roman Forum.

**Suffect:** term used to denote replacements for magistrates who resign or die in office.

**Sulla** (L. Cornelius Sulla Felix; ca. 138–78 B.C.): ruled Rome in the early years of the first century B.C.

**\*Sybaris:** Greek city in southern Italy.

**Sychaeus:** husband of Dido, murdered by her brother, Pygmalion.

**Sygambri:** German tribe that annihilated a Roman army in 17 B.C.

**Symplegades:** see Cyanean Rocks.

**Synesius** (ca. A.D. 370–ca. 413): Neoplatonist philosopher and Christian bishop.

**\*\*Syracuse:** Greek city on the east coast of Sicily.

**\*Syrtes:** sandy reefs off the coast of Libya and Tunisia.

**T.:** the Roman *praenomen* Titus.

**Taenarus:** promontory south of Sparta, now Cape Matapan.

**Tagus:** the longest river in the Iberian Peninsula.

**Talent:** the largest unit of Greek money, worth six thousand drachmas.

**Tanais:** river in Russia and the Ukraine, now the Don.

**Tantalus:** punished for various crimes with eternal hunger and thirst in the Underworld.

**\*\*Tarentum:** Greek city at the heel of Italy.

**Tarpeia:** betrayed the Capitol to the Sabines.

**\*\*\*\*Tarpeian Rock:** place on the Capitol from which traitors and murderers were thrown.

**Tarquinius Superbus:** the seventh and last king of Rome.

**Tartarus:** the Underworld.

**Taurus:** mountain range in southern Asia Minor (Turkey).

**Taygetus:** mountain near Sparta.

**Tempe:** valley in Thessaly frequented by Apollo and the Muses.

**Tenedos:** Greek island off the northwest coast of Asia Minor (Turkey).

**Terence:** P. Terentius Afer (ca. 195–ca. 160 B.C.), comic dramatist.

**Tereus:** king of Thrace, who married the Athenian princess Procne and raped her sister Philomela; they were all subsequently turned into birds.

**Terminus:** Roman god of boundaries.

**Teucer of Salamis:** exiled by his father for not avenging the death of his brother, Ajax; also a king of Troy.

**Teucrian** = Trojan.

**Teumesus:** mountain in Boeotia.

**Teuthras:** a pool near Cumae in Campania.

**Teutoburg Forest:** site of the massacre of three Roman legions by German tribes in A.D. 9.

**Thapsus:** city in modern Tunisia, site of Caesar's victory in 46 B.C. over the Pompeians.

**\*Thebes:** city in Boeotia.

**Theocritus of Syracuse:** third-century B.C. Greek poet.

**Theophrastus** (ca. 370–ca. 287 B.C.): successor to Aristotle as head of the Lyceum.

**Thermodon:** river in northeast Asia Minor (Turkey).

**Theseus:** Athenian hero, who slew the Minotaur and abandoned Ariadne on Naxos.

**\*Thessaly:** region of central Greece, associated esp. with magic.

**Thetis:** sea nymph, mother of Achilles.

**\*Thrace:** region in modern Greece, Bulgaria, and European Turkey.

**Thrasea Paetus, P. Clodius** (?–A.D. 66): Stoic philosopher and opponent of Nero.

**Thucydides** (ca. 455–ca. 400 B.C.): Athenian admiral and author of a history of the Peloponnesian War.

**Thyestes:** uttered the curse against the House of Atreus, his brother.

**Thyonian:** having to do with Bacchus.

**Ti.:** the Roman *praenomen* Tiberius.

**\*\*\*Tiber:** the river that flows through Rome.

**Tiberius:** Roman emperor, ruled A.D. 14–37.

**Tibullus, ? Albius** (?–ca. 18 B.C.): an elegiac poet.

**\*\*\*Tibur:** hill town near Rome, now Tivoli.

**Ticinus:** tributary of the Po, site of a Carthaginian victory in 218 B.C.

**Tigranes:** king of Armenia.

**Timavus:** river in Slovenia and northeast Italy.

**Timon of Athens:** misanthropic fifth-century B.C. Athenian.

**Tiphys:** helmsman of the *Argo,* the first ship.

**Tiresias:** legendary Theban prophet.

**Tiridates:** usurper of the Parthian throne in late first century B.C.; also king of Armenia mid-first century A.D.

**Titans:** race of older gods banished by the Olympians to the Underworld; Titan also denotes the sun.

**Tithonus:** Trojan prince, husband of Aurora, who was granted immortality but forgot to ask for everlasting youth, so he wasted away.

**Titus:** Roman emperor, ruled A.D. 79–81.

**Tityos:** Giant tortured in the Underworld for attacking Leto, mother of Apollo and Artemis.

**\*Tomi:** town on the west coast of the Black Sea.

**Tortoise:** defensive formation in which legionaries locked shields.

**Trajan:** Roman emperor, ruled A.D. 98–117.

**\*Tralles:** city in western Asia Minor (Turkey).

**Transpadane:** on the other side of the river Po in northern Italy.

**\*\*Trasimenus:** lake in Umbria, site of a Carthaginian victory in 217 B.C.

**\*\*Trebia:** tributary of the Po, site of a Carthaginian victory in 218 B.C.

**Treveri:** Celtic people in northern Gaul.

**Tribune:** magistrate responsible for safeguarding the interests of the plebeians; also military tribune, staff officer in charge of a legion or smaller army unit.

**Trireme:** warship with three banks of oars.

**Triumph:** a celebration of an important military success, in which a victorious general was permitted to parade through Rome with his army, his plunder, and his captives.

**Triumvirate** (literally "a group of three men"): in the late 60s B.C., Pompey, Crassus, and Caesar formed the First Triumvirate to run the state in their own interests; after Caesar's assassination, Antony, Octavian, and Lepidus formed the Second Triumvirate.

**Troy game:** equestrian battle game for Roman boys.

**Tullius:** see Cicero.

**Tullus Hostilius:** the third king of Rome.

**Tuscan** = Etruscan.

***Tusculum:** town in Latium.

**Tydeus:** one of the Seven against Thebes, father of Diomedes.

**Typhon:** monstrous son of Tartarus and Gaia (Earth), buried under Etna and/or Vesuvius.

*Tyre: Phoenician city in Lebanon.

**Tyrrhene** = Etruscan.

**Umbria:** region of central Italy.

**Urban praetor:** magistrate responsible for judicial administration in Rome.

**Valerius Flaccus:** first-century A.D. author of an epic, *Argonautica*.

**Valerius Maximus:** early first-century A.D. author of a collection of *Famous Deeds and Sayings*.

**Varro, C. Terentius:** consul in 216 B.C., killed at Cannae.

**Varro, M. Terentius** (116–27 B.C.): a voluminous author on many topics whose only works to survive complete or in substantial part are his *On Farming* and *On the Latin Language*.

**Varro, P. Terentius, of Atax** (82–? B.C.): author of amatory and epic poetry, now lost.

**Varus, P. Quinctilius:** general whose army was massacred in the Teutoburg Forest in A.D. 9.

***Veii:** Etruscan city north of Rome.

**Venusia:** town in Apulia, birthplace of Horace.

**Verres, C.:** prosecuted by Cicero in 70 B.C. for extortion in Sicily.

**Vespasian:** Roman emperor, ruled A.D. 69–79.

**Vestal Virgins:** a college of six priestesses responsible for safeguarding the sacred fire of the goddess Vesta.

**Vexillarii:** irregular contingents of troops or re-enlisted veterans.

***Via Appia:** main road from Rome to the south.

***Via Latina:** main road from Rome to the southeast.

**Vitellius** (Aulus Vitellius Germanicus; A.D. 15–69): Roman emperor, ruled briefly in 69.

*Zama: Scipio Africanus brought the Second Punic War to an end by defeating Hannibal at Zama (in modern Tunisia) in 202 B.C.

**Zeno of Citium** (335–263 B.C.): founder of Stoicism.

**Zephyr:** the west wind.

**Zeuxis:** fifth/fourth-century B.C. Greek painter and sculptor.

# ART CREDITS

Alinari / Art Resource, NY • 2

The Art Gallery Collection / Alamy • 21

Biblioteca Apostolica Vaticana, Vatican Museums • 11

Bodleian Library, University of Oxford • 6

Berlin Alte Pinakothek, Bayerische Staatsgemaeldesammlungen, / Art Resource, NY • 19

Berlin / Musei Capitolini, Rome/ Alfredo Dagli Orti/ Art Resource, NY • 8

Bridgeman-Giraudon / Art Resource, NY • 34

By kind permission of the Trustees of the Wallace Collection, London / Art Resource, NY • 12

Courtesy of the Classical Numismatics Group • 9, 20, 28, 29

De Agostini Picture Library / A. Dagli Orti / The Bridgeman Art Library • 5

De Agostini Picture Library / G. Nimatallah / The Bridgeman Art Library • 24

Erich Lessing / Art Resource, NY • 1, 3, 14, 25, 26

Fitzwilliam Museum, Cambridge / Art Resource, NY • 17

Galleria degli Uffizi, Florence, Italy / Alinari / The Bridgeman Art Library • 32

Louvre, Paris, France / Giraudon / The Bridgeman Art Library • 22, 31

Photofest © • 30

Photograph: C. J. Eyre, reproduced by permission of the Egypt Exploration Society • 13

Scala / Art Resource, NY • 7, 10, 15, 23, 27

Scala/Ministero per i Beni e le Attivita culturali / Art Resource, NY • 16

Shutterstock © • 33

Tate, London / Art Resource, NY • 4

The Vatican Library

The Trustees of the British Museum © / Art Resource, NY

William Manning / Alamy • 18

# SOURCES FOR SELECTIONS

Note: Publication dates of the *Oxford World's Classics* titles are of the editions used. For the most recent editions of these titles, please visit http://www.oup.com.

Plautus, *The Brothers Menaechmus*. From *Four Comedies*. Translated by Erich Segal. Oxford University Press, 2008.

Polybius, *The Histories*. Translated by Robin Waterfield. Oxford University Press, 2010.

Lucretius, *On the Nature of the Universe*. Translated by Ronald Melville, 1997.

Catullus, *The Complete Poems*. Translated by Guy Lee. Oxford University Press, 2009.

Cicero, *Against Catiline*. From *Political Speeches*. Translated by D. H. Berry. Oxford University Press, 2009.

Cicero, *In Defense of Caelius*. From *Defence Speeches*. Translated by D. H. Berry. Oxford University Press, 2009.

Julius Caesar, *The Gallic War*. Translated by Carolyn Hammond. Oxford University Press, 1996.

Sallust, *Catiline's Conspiracy*. From *Catiline's Conspiracy, The Jugurthine War, Histories*. Translated by William W. Batsone. Oxford University Press, 2010.

Virgil. *Eclogues*. Translated by the editors, 2012.

Virgil, *Georgics*. Translated by Peter Fallon. Oxford University Press, 1999.

Virgil. *Aeneid*. Translated by Frederick Ahl. Oxford University Press, 2007.

Horace, *Odes*. From *The Complete Odes and Epodes*. Translated by David West. Oxford University Press, 1997.

Propertius, *Elegies*. From *The Poems*. Translated by Guy Lee. Oxford University Press, 1996.

Ovid, *Amores*. From *The Love Poems*. Translated by A. D. Melville. Oxford University Press, 1990.

Ovid, *Metamorphoses*. Translated by A. D. Melville. Oxford University Press, 1986.

Livy, *From the Foundation of the City*. From *The Rise of Rome*. Translated by T. J. Luce. Oxford University Press, 1988.

Seneca, *Medea*. From *Six Tragedies*. Translated by Emily Wilson. Oxford University Press, 2010.

Josephus, *Jewish Antiquities*. From Volume XII. Loeb Classical Library Volume 433. Translated by Louis H. Feldman. 1965.

Lucan, *Civil War*. Translated by Susan H. Braund. Oxford University Press, 1992.

Petronius, *The Satyricon*. Translated by P. G. Walsh. Oxford University Press, 1997.

Pliny the Elder, *Natural History*. From *On the Human Animal*. Translated by Mary Beagon. Oxford University Press, 2005.

Statius, *Thebaid*. Translated by A. D. Melville. Oxford University Press, 1995.

Quintilian, *The Orator's Education*. From *Volumes I and II*. Loeb Classical Library Volumes 124 and 494. Edited and translated by Donald A. Russell, 2001.

Martial, *Epigrams*. From *Epigrams I, II, and III*. Loeb Classical Library Volumes 94, 95, and 480. Edited and translated by D. R. Shackleton Bailey. 1999.

Tacitus, *Annals*. Translated by J. C. Yardley. Oxford University Press, 2008.

Pliny the Younger, *Epistles*. From *Complete Letters*. Translated by P. G. Walsh. Oxford University Press, 2006.

Suetonius, *Life of Nero*. From *Lives of the Caesars*. Translated by Catherine Edwards. Oxford University Press, 2000.

Plutarch, *Antony*. From *Roman Lives*. Translated by Robin Waterfield. Oxford University Press, 1999.

Juvenal, *Satires*. Translated by Niall Rudd. Oxford University Press, 1991.

Apuleius, *Metamorposes*. From *The Golden Ass*. Translated by P. G. Walsh. Oxford University Press, 1994.

Lucian, *True History*. From *Selected Dialogues*. Translated by C. D. N. Costa. Oxford University Press, 2005.

Marcus Aurelius, *Meditations*. Translated by A. S. L. Farquharson. Oxford University Press, 2006.